Atlantic
BRIEF LIVES
A Biographical Companion to the Arts

Atlantic
BRIEF LIVES
A Biographical Companion to the Arts

Edited by LOUIS KRONENBERGER

Associate Editor EMILY MORISON BECK

An Atlantic Monthly Press Book

LITTLE, BROWN AND COMPANY · BOSTON · TORONTO

ATLANTIC–LITTLE, BROWN BOOKS
ARE PUBLISHED BY
LITTLE, BROWN AND COMPANY
IN ASSOCIATION WITH
THE ATLANTIC MONTHLY PRESS

Published simultaneously in Canada
by Little, Brown & Company (Canada) Limited

PRINTED IN THE UNITED STATES OF AMERICA

INTRODUCTION

By Louis Kronenberger

I AM not sure whether the idea for this book, which was William Abrahams', came to him fully formed, but the book's double-barreled function, which seems to me its very special and distinguishing merit, must in some sense have been present. And when, after the publishers had warmly responded to the idea, Mr. Abrahams and Peter Davison, the director of the Atlantic Monthly Press, approached me with it, the project — of a bookshelf work of reference combined with a bedside book for reading — appealed to me twice over: as a possible editor and as a prospective reader. The book would unite two kinds of reading matter that are essential for every educated household, but that had always gone their separate ways — for no better reason, it seems, than that no one had ever thought of bringing them together. Yet what is there to prevent the utilitarian and the aesthetic, reading for information and reading for pleasure, from happily marrying? After all, the car that drives you by day to work takes you to parties by night and to the country for weekends. Part of a garden will feed you; another part be all beautiful flowers. Just so this book will, for one thing, feed you *facts* about people in the arts — their birth and death dates, where they grew up, or went to college, or wandered off to in middle age. The book will also, in over two hundred cases, offer an essay on a poet or a painter or a composer — about his work and perhaps his wife; his personality and perhaps his crotchets; his relation to the age he lived in, his importance for the age we live in, not to speak of bringing him brilliantly to life with an anecdote, or catching the essence of him in an epigram. An incidental merit of such a book, or call it a possible danger, is that, having picked it up to look something up, you may be an hour putting it down again. The essays quite aside, reference books have for many people a charm of their own. The useful information they provide can become for incurable browsers delightful useless information to ply their friends with: did you know, they will ask, that both Shakespeare and Cervantes died on April 23,

1616? and did you know, they will ask next, that Charles Darwin and Abraham Lincoln were both *born* on the same day, February 12, 1809?

So much for the ground plan. The next thing was, as expeditiously as possible, to get it off the ground; to give it, within chosen limits, as compact a form, as wide a range, as accessible an approach — and, in the essays, as judicious and enjoyable a content — as we were capable of. The first thing for us to do, though in some ways the most tentative, was to fix the limits. At the very beginning we were inclined to treat of as many famous and distinguished dead people, in all fields of achievement, as there might be room for — Napoleon and Alexander Graham Bell, Nelson and Emily Brontë, Chopin and Vasco da Gama, Edmund Spenser and Herbert Spencer, Lord North and Benjamin West. It required only a day or two, however, for us to realize that just to include the *very* famous and distinguished dead — tossing out Lord North and Vasco da Gama — we should have need of far more space than even the most optimistic allowance would permit. Next, in a perhaps even more optimistic mood, we thought of a series of reference-and-reading books, each concerned with a single large field of human achievement — the arts, the sciences, the world of government, the world of action, with the first of them devoted to the arts. The series plan still remains a possibility, with Lord North in Volume III and Vasco da Gama in Volume IV, should Volume I, as they say, be warmly welcomed.

Having settled on the arts, we immediately started asking, which arts? Literature, certainly, and in many forms — poetry, fiction, drama, belles-lettres; and such history — Thucydides, Tacitus, Gibbon, Michelet, Parkman — and such philosophy — Plato, Hume, Nietzsche, William James, Santayana — as ranks as literature. But what of eloquence — Demosthenes, Daniel Webster, the elder Pitt? Well — no. And what of Hobbes, whose *Leviathan,* or Malthus, whose *Essay on Population,* is a classic? Well — no, again. And so on: there have been many borderline names, causing, editorially, a number of Border skirmishes; each name, in so overcrowded a book, needing unusually good credentials.

And in much the same way we traversed the world of music, and then that of the fine arts. The Border wars in music were mostly ancient — troubadours and minnesingers and plainsong — or pretty recent — show music and modernism and jazz. The fine arts were, both in variety and in volume, in very strong competition with literature. Painting, drawing and sculpture went without saying, as did architecture, on a slightly reduced scale. And just these few arts bulked extremely large: during several centuries, it seemed, every fifth inhabitant of Florence, Siena, and other Italian cities was a painter or sculptor good enough to deserve a Ph.D. thesis from a future art historian. They, or their work, had to be carefully scrutinized; and thereafter it became necessary to put all the other visual arts — etchers and engravers and lithographers, decorators and cabinetmakers, scene designers and landscape gardeners, book illustrators and poster artists, goldsmiths and silversmiths — on trial, and to let them in or shut them out by bringing to bear how important their field was along with how distinguished their work. Thus the Bibienas had the entrée, and Robert Adam, and "Capability" Brown, but not Chippendale or Wedgwood; and Cellini, but not Paul Storrs or Paul Revere.

This settled, music now brought up the matter of performers and conductors, and drama the matter of performers and directors, so that another big question was raised: should we include interpretative artists? It was difficult to think of a work on the arts that failed to include a Paganini or a Caruso, a Garrick or a Sarah Bernhardt. Well, perhaps names so exceptional had the right to be treated as exceptions. But then, could we leave out Jenny Lind, or Melba, or Toscanini, or Nijinsky, or Edwin Booth, or Rachel? And once interpretative artists — however few, however world-famous — were admitted, others would indignantly or peremptorily be called for; the few would become the many — what with movies and ballet, the more than many — and the amount of text would be hopelessly excessive. The book would not only be too heavy to be companionable, the price would be too high; there was nothing to do but say no.

One further decision needed to be made: whether or not to restrict the entries to artists of the Western world. Here, we observed, much that was greatest in Oriental art either quite lacked an artist's name or merely guessed at one. Who, for sure — and wasn't it more than one man? — designed the Taj Mahal? or the great mosque at Isfahan? Who painted much fine Mogul or Persian work, or fashioned superb Chinese porcelains? In such an atmosphere of anonymity, there was little to be done about biography; and once again we said no.

We now got down to work. For the reference half of the book we compiled long lists of names, adding new ones that we encountered in our reading or thought up in the middle of the night; and thereafter we checked our lists of names against those in published reference books — this a time-hallowed practice without which any new project might be very hard put to it. In due course Mrs. Beck, with great vigor and efficiency, took over the whole reference empire, and assembled a staff to put together the biographical sketches, these to be set forth with an easy-to-follow conciseness as well as with all possible *accuracy* — for if earlier reference books are a decided help, they can also cause damnable harm. Nothing is better known "in the trade" than the inaccurate information and erroneous facts copied, one generation after another, from one reference book after another, sometimes for hundreds of years. Nor need this be done lazily or irresponsibly: for, of many muddied reference rivers, the sources will have shifted ground, or dried up, or disappeared; and of many others, there are several sources — seven cities, let us not forget, claimed to be Homer's birthplace, and two or three cities or towns have claimed to be a great many other men's. Again, the month, the year, the decade in which a famous person was born is often unknown, or wrangled over, or based on legend or on a single reference in a book published a hundred and three years after his death. A picture may be dated by when it was painted, or by when it was first made public, or by nothing better than clues — the feather in the courtier's cap "very much resembles" the feather in a different picture known to be painted in 1682. Most tricky is the exact attribution of a picture or a structure — is this picture all Rubens, or partly Rubens, or school of Rubens? Is this country house Vanbrugh, or Hawksmoor, or both of them? Again, does a date follow the Julian calendar or the Gregorian? Moreover, concerning the greatest of all B.C. names and the greatest of all A.D. ones — Homer and Shakespeare — we are to an extraordinary extent in the region of mere guesswork and hearsay.

Much reference work is accordingly a form of detective work, or at least of a trial by jury where one must sift the evidence, itself often suspect and scant. Our biographical-sketch writers did their best to be accurate; their sketches were checked and, where accompanied by essays, submitted for approval to the essayists, and are sent forth in the hope of escaping censure. That they may be subject to criticism, there often being two sides to every statement, a doughty opponent to every hypothesis, a question mark over every deduction, not to speak of new discoveries since the book went to press, is certain. But it is to be hoped that as a reference book, *Atlantic Brief Lives* will convey such information, answer such questions, and settle such arguments as it aspires to do for the readership it most aims at: the college student, school and public libraries, not least the small ones, and — most of all — the cultivated home. If the specialist, be it in fourteenth-century English Perpendicular or sixteenth-century Italian motets, will not find here all he wants, neither, we assume, will he look here. But here, listed after each biographical sketch, are selected works to consult for additional information.

The second of the book's projects — the two-hundred-odd essays — actually, and necessarily, got started first. For it was they that would most individualize the book, most set it apart from other reference books. The essays were to be the equivalent of more than two full-length volumes, meant to give the reader intellectual stimulation and civilized pleasure; and were to be written, at the highest level of criticism and appreciation, by many of the best writers of our time. But the classic precept "First catch your hare" was not just something for us to smile at, it was something to act upon; and I consequently set forth to woo a great many distinguished people. Furthermore I chose, wherever possible, to call on them, not write to them. There was a good reason for doing this: though they may not be interested in the particular names you propose by mail, it may develop in conversation that they are very much interested in doing someone else. In particular, one may understandably seek out specialists, and it is not uncommon for them to be fed up with their specialties, yet very open to working on something that seems fresh, or that they have always meant to get round to. And this proved true at a number of places where I went calling. One great hurdle, of course, is that the more distinguished a hoped-for contributor is, the busier and more in demand he will be. But, perhaps because the project had a certain novelty, and the thousand-word length we had set for the essays had a relative brevity, the first dozen people I went to see agreed to contribute — giving us the nicest kind of mandate to proceed with the book.

As for just who should be the subjects of the two hundred essays, we had never thought of having the two hundred "most important" people in the arts. For one reason, no two persons' lists of them would ever be the same, and any final list could only be an arbitrary one. From the start, moreover, we felt that, though it made sense to approach contributors with suggestions, nothing could be better than for them to put forth choices of their own. Obviously Michelangelo, Shakespeare and Beethoven were to find a helpmate; obviously, also, we hoped that no one would seek the hand of Chaminade or Bouguereau or Paul de Kock. It was, furthermore, obvious that however we proceeded, all the distinguished names in the arts could not be rewarded with essays; a few more than two hundred names were all that we had book-room to accommodate, quite as four hundred were all that Mrs. Astor's famous ballroom could hold. Hence you will look in vain for an essay on Lucretius or Rabelais, on Cimabue or Holbein, on Donizetti or Mahler. But, though regretting the need for omissions, we feel that the inclusions have all earned their place in the book, have contributed to its flexibility and variousness, and have helped create just the right touch of unexpectedness: a fine minor figure like Matthew Prior; an important, somewhat special figure like Tocqueville; a slightly out-of-fashion figure like Ravel; an essentially wrongly pigeonholed figure like Harriet Beecher Stowe. What also resulted from the vis-à-vis method with contributors was that a fair number of them very much wanted to write outside their "fields"

— such literary figures as Mr. Steegmuller to write on Degas, Mr. Schorer on Caravaggio, Mrs. Trilling on Puccini; and a literary critic, Frank Kermode, and an art critic, John Russell, sharing the two great magicians of music, Mozart and Schubert. In other cases, contributors took on a pair of names that for one reason or another are often bracketed — Mr. Kerman, Verdi and Wagner; Mr. Stegner, Maupassant and Chekhov; Mr. Schulz, Giorgione and Titian. The rule for contributors was that there be no rule, just as their approach to the essays was full freedom of approach: they could, as seemed best to them, stress their subjects' personality, career, influence, achievement — even era or nationality. We hoped for diversity in treatment with no loss of adroitness, and with this in mind had sought out diversification as well as distinction in our essayists — poets, novelists, biographers, historians, scholars, literary critics, drama critics, art critics, music critics, art historians and museum heads, musicologists and composers; and the English, the Irish, the Scots as well as Americans. Here they are, one and all, and we would hope they have given the book, with its great range of periods and places, a cosmopolitan air.

In the course of their lucubrations, an all-too-human and faintly comic element sometimes emerged. Asked to turn in their thousand-odd words in something like four months, the hundred-odd contributors displayed no herdlike docility. One contributor, having chosen his man one morning, arrived with his essay the next. Another contributor took three years to do so; still other contributors chose almost every time length in between. The time length had a rather bothersome brother in the space length, though the numerous violators of it were virtually all on the long side. We soon came to regard twelve hundred words as the norm; fifteen hundred words as anything but a novelty; seventeen hundred words as too short for a prize-winner, and even two thousand words as not winning first prize. For, one afternoon, an exultant author told us over long distance that at last his much overdue essay was finished — nine thousand words, roughly speaking. We were for the most part gratified that so many contributors had written on the generous side, but the more mountainous their generosity became, the more the book overflowed its banks. Something Had to Be Done, and something was: however regretfully, all the really overlong essays were ordered cut. Yet the effect in each case, we would hope, suggests dieting rather than decapitation.

That, dear reader, is the *story* of these "lives"; of the substance, you alone are the judge.

EDITORS' NOTE

ATLANTIC BRIEF LIVES contains 1081 brief biographies, covering 1103 men and women, from Acton to Zurbarán, chosen for their importance in the literature, art, and music of the Western world. No living figures are included. From the total, 211 have been selected by contemporary authors and scholars for special treatment at greater length in essays of evaluation and appreciation.

The brief biographies include salient vital statistics and a list of the subject's major works with their dates (for a literary work, date of publication; for music, date of first performance; and for paintings, sculpture, buildings, and the like, date of execution). Wherever possible, each brief biography is followed by a selective bibliography of critical and biographical studies.

The arrangement of the *Lives,* including the essays, is alphabetical (and therefore self-indexing).

Alphabetical lists of the essayists and of the subjects of the essays appear on pages xv–xxii.

The brief biographies were written by the associate editor Emily Morison Beck, by Hollister Nash, and by other researchers whose names appear in the Acknowledgments.

ACKNOWLEDGMENTS

For scholarly scrutiny, literary and editorial discernment, *Atlantic Brief Lives* is immeasurably indebted to Mrs. Mary Rackliffe, Editor of Special Projects at Little, Brown and Company. Special thanks are also owed the following, who scanned the final list in specific fields: Howard Mumford Jones (literature), Mrs. Juan Marichal (Spanish and Latin-American literature), Robert Evett (music), and Gerald S. Bernstein (art).

In the research and writing of the brief biographies, *Atlantic Brief Lives* is grateful to the following for thoroughness and efficiency: Stephen Brook, Jane Davison, Eleanor Gates, Natalie Greenberg, Justina Gregory, Patrick Gregory, Robert Jerrett III, Joseph Kanon, Barbara Hanson Pierce, Amy Plumer, Mordeca Jane Pollock, Judith Rascoe, Evalyn Welling. Other researchers were Eloise Bender, Thomas Bestul, Dorann Bouchiatt, Jeremiah Brady, Upton B. Brady, Paul A. Cantor, Anne E. Chard, Camilla Conley, Thomas M. Curley, Dalene Henshaw, Marta Osterstrom, Alison E. Shepherd, Elizabeth M. Spingarn, Phillida Spingarn, Nancy Stockwell, and Clifford Truesdell.

The Essayists and Their Subjects

ESSAYISTS

SUBJECTS OF ESSAYS

Atlantic
BRIEF LIVES
A Biographical Companion to the Arts

ACTON, John Emerich Edward Dalberg-Acton, first baron (Jan. 10, 1834 – June 19, 1902). English historian. Born Naples, grandson of statesmen Sir J. F. E. Acton and the Duc de Dalberg. Educated at Oscott College under Cardinal Wiseman and Munich under historian and theologian Johann von Döllinger (1850–55). A liberal Roman Catholic, Acton expressed his views as editor (1859–65) of the *Rambler* (in 1862 renamed *Home and Foreign Review*) and in *Letters from Rome on the Council* (1870); he opposed the dogma of papal infallibility. Married Marie, daughter of Bavarian Count von Arco-Vallery (1865). Liberal member of Parliament (1859–65); close friend of Gladstone, who nominated him to peerage (1869). Professor of modern history at Cambridge from 1895; delivered a remarkable inaugural lecture on the study of history. Died at Tegernsee, Bavaria. Though Acton never published a·book, his literary activity was prodigious; collections are *Lectures on Modern History* (1906), *History of Freedom* (1907), *Historical Essays and Studies* (1907), and *Lectures on the French Revolution* (1910). Politically influential through lectures and association with leading statesmen and theorists, he exposed the evils of power when concentrated in the modern state. Most famous of his many aphorisms is "Power tends to corrupt; absolute power corrupts absolutely."

REFERENCES: George E. Fasnacht *Acton's Political Philosophy* (London 1952 and New York 1953). Gertrude Himmelfarb *Lord Acton: A Study in Conscience and Politics* (London and Chicago 1952, also PB). Lionel Kochan *Acton on History* (London 1954 and New York 1955). David Mathew *Acton: The Formative Years* (London 1946).

ADAM DE LA HALLE (or **LE HALE**), also called Adam le Bossu or Adam d'Arras (c.1250–c.1306). French comic playwright, musician and trouvère. Born of bourgeois family in Arras, a center of literary and dramatic production in the thirteenth century. Probably destined for the clergy, but apparently left studies to marry. His first play, *Le Jeu de la feuillée* (1276 or 1277), is the oldest known nonliturgical drama in French. Written in honor of the spring season, it combines themes of Celtic mythology with autobiographical, political and anticlerical satire and burlesque. Followed Prince Charles d'Anjou to Naples (1282) and produced for French-speaking court *Le Jeu de Robin et Marion* (c.1285), the first French pastoral drama. His rich musical and poetic production combined the best of both bourgeois and courtly traditions.

EDITIONS: *Oeuvres complètes* ed. E. de Coussemaker (Paris 1872). *Le Jeu du pèlerin* (with music) ed. Kenneth Varty (London 1960). *Canchons et partures* ed. Rudolph Berger (Halle 1900). *Rondeaux à trois voix égales*, transcribed by Jacques Chailly (Paris 1942).

REFERENCE: Henry Guy *Essai sur la vie et les oeuvres littéraires du trouvère Adam de le Hale* (Paris 1898).

ADAM, Robert (July 3, 1728 – Mar. 3, 1792). Scottish architect, most important of four sons of architect William Adam, and with brothers John, James, and William responsible for creating "Adam style." Born Kirkcaldy; studied at Edinburgh University and in Italy (1754–58). Research expedition to Dalmatia (1757) resulted in book which established his reputation, *The Ruins of the Palace of the Emperor Diocletian at Spalato* (1764). Settled in London (1758), where he and James introduced idea of designing as unified whole the exteriors and interiors of houses, including furniture. Robert served as architect to George III (1762–68). Died in London; buried in Westminster Abbey. By the time the first volume of *Works in Architecture of Robert and James Adam* (1773–1822) was published, the Adam style, an elegant, sophisticated interpretation of neoclassicism with delicate, graceful decorative devices, had superseded the more austere Palladianism in England. Famous country houses in Adam style include Luton Hoo, Croome Court, Kedleston, Kenwood, and Nostell Priory; in London, the Adelphi buildings (1768–72; almost entirely destroyed 1936), number 20 St. James Square, and Home House on Portman Square.

REFERENCES: John Fleming *Robert Adam and His Circle, in Edinburgh and Rome* (London and Cambridge, Mass. 1962). James Lees-Milne *The Age of Adam* (London and New York 1947).

ADAMS, Henry (Brooks) (Feb. 16, 1838 – Mar. 27, 1918). American historian and writer. Born Boston, son of Charles Francis Adams, grandson of John Adams, great-grandson of John Quincy Adams. Graduated from Harvard (1858), postgraduate study at University of Berlin. First publication (1860), letters to Boston *Courier* on Garibaldi. Secretary (1861–68) to his father, who was then minister to England. Taught history at Harvard and edited *North American Review* (1870–77). Married Marian Hooper (1872), settled in Washington (1877), frequently traveled abroad. Published (not under own name) two novels: *Democracy* (1879) and *Esther* (1884). After wife's death (by suicide), made long trips to Orient, returning to Washington to finish *The History of the United States During the Administrations of Thomas Jefferson and James Madison* (9 vols. 1884–89), which established

him as a major American historian. *Mont-St.-Michel and Chartres* (1904) reconstructs the medieval unity he admired. Chiefly known for *The Education of Henry Adams* (privately printed 1907), which with *The Degradation of the Democratic Dogma* (1919) formulates his "dynamic theory of history." Other important works: *Essays on Anglo-Saxon Law* (1876), *The Life of Albert Gallatin* (1879), *John Randolph* (1882). Died in Washington, D.C.

REFERENCES: George Hochfield *Henry Adams: An Introduction and Interpretation* (New York 1962, also PB). Robert A. Hume *Runaway Star: An Appreciation of Henry Adams* (Ithaca, N.Y. and London 1951). Jacob C. Levenson *The Mind and Art of Henry Adams* (Boston 1957, also PB). Ernest Samuels *Henry Adams* (3 vols. Cambridge, Mass. 1948–64).

✑

HENRY ADAMS
BY ALFRED KAZIN

Henry Adams was the grandson of one President of the United States, John Quincy Adams, and the great-grandson of another, John Adams; his father, Charles Francis Adams, was a founder of the Free-Soil party and minister to England during the Civil War; his brother Charles Francis Jr. was a distinguished Union officer, a historian, memoirist, and a principal organizer of the American railway system; his brother Brooks was an eccentric but brilliant theorist of history. John Adams, first of the many notable Adamses, was of course a founder of the American Republic, a distinguished lawyer and diplomat, a profound political theorist. John Quincy Adams, who kept what is probably the fullest diary of political life in recorded history, was a high-strung idealist, poet and scientist. In diplomatic service before he had finished his schooling, he became a distinguished secretary of state who wrote a classic report on weights and measures, a professor of rhetoric at Harvard who translated German romantic poetry, a President of the United States who after being defeated by Jackson and his popular revolution became a congressman and died on the floor of the House after defeating in turn a Southern attempt to bar all discussion of slavery.

The Adams family was certified by one English student of hereditary genius to be positively the most gifted family in American history. With such a grandfather and great-grandfather, such a father, such brothers — not all of whom made history but all of whom wrote history as if Adamses had made the best history — it is not strange that Henry Adams celebrated his family, was silently intimidated by it, and had no passion in his life equal to what he felt for "tradition," the past, the burden and beauty of historical memory.

What memory was to Proust the novelist — the mother of his every literary instinct — memory was to Henry Adams the observer of history and the historian. As he showed in the very first lines of the book that made him posthumously famous, *The Education of Henry Adams* (privately printed for a hundred friends in 1907; published by the Massachusetts Historical Society in 1918 after Adams's death), Adams could not report the birth and christening of Henry Brooks Adams on Beacon Hill without likening this auspicious historical moment to one in the Temple of Jerusalem. And in fact young Henry Adams was so habitually surrounded by power, wealth and influence (his grandfather Brooks had left the largest estate in New England, one uncle [Edward Everett] was president of Harvard, another [Nathaniel Frothingham] a pillar of the Unitarian Church) that in his *Education* Adams described school and Harvard as if conventional

education must always lack something: that sense of the great world that as a boy he had absorbed from the family's experiences in Washington, London, Paris, St. Petersburg. These had all been copiously described in the diaries all Adamses kept in obligation to the Puritan conscience, which would not permit them to be less than always righteous, and in the letters they wrote best to each other but also as a courtesy to history, which would always want to know what an Adams had been doing.

But besides his gift for writing history — besides the political bitterness which he shared with his family, all of whom had a deep sense of political failure, Henry Adams suffered, as did Proust, from an artist's openness to impressions and an artist's self-doubt. These were particularly hard for an Adams to bear, especially one who usually moved among politicians too coarse and academics too unimaginative to understand that this fearfully elegant little man, just over five feet tall, was as "sensitive" as any poet but lacked the language as well as the indulgent tradition in which to lay his heart bare.

As private secretary to his father in London during the Civil War, Adams anonymously published brilliant articles on the English political scene; on the family's return to America in 1868, he did a classic exposure of Wall Street buccaneers during the Gilded Age. Soon he became a professor of medieval history at Harvard, a subject in which he became as expert as he was in stocks and bonds (he helped save the family fortune during the panic of 1893), and in the decisive period of American history when the foundations were laid of America as a great continental power, on which Adams wrote his great Gibbonesque history in nine volumes, *The History of the United States During the Administrations of Thomas Jefferson and James Madison* (1884–89). At Harvard, Adams virtually founded the "scientific" study of history in this country, and he could have become the most dominating of American historians as well as the most intelligent. But he and his perky, brilliant wife, Marian Hooper Adams, were bored and moved to Washington.

In Washington the Adamses lived in a beautiful house just across Lafayette Square from the White House (built for them by Adams's college classmate H. H. Richardson) and were the leaders of "intellectual" society. Their closest friends were John Hay, who had been Lincoln's secretary and was to be secretary of state to McKinley and Theodore Roosevelt, and the brilliant geologist Clarence King. One day in 1885 Marian, whose father had recently died, swallowed the cyanide that as a photographer she always kept in her darkroom. Adams, for whom the past had always been the best part of life, now spent the rest of his life madly roaming the world, and writing unconventionally and profoundly on history as an irresistible force. He finished his great *History*. But the deep instinct for exclusion — one of his two novels (*Democracy*, 1879) was published anonymously and the other (*Esther*, 1884) under a feminine pseudonym — was now joined to a ferocious historical pessimism.

Adams tried hard to show that history was susceptible of "scientific" analysis; this was in the positivist tradition of his times. But he was too much of a literary artist to work his thesis out convincingly, and his greatest writing was free and, to Henry James's astonishment, "personal" — the first half of *Education; Mont-St.-Michel and Chartres;* his irresistibly witty and acerb letters. His theorizing, however, weighs down the last part of *Education* and the various essays, like *The Rule of Phase*, which with his dazzling literary gifts he turned into shows of intellectual argument. History was running down, the second law of thermodynamics, entropy, was the ruler of the universe, and the fate of the Adams line, of the only American aristocracy — intellect — could be seen in the universal cataclysm to which humanity seemed to be heading.

Yet in our rueful age Adams's historical instinct can hardly be dismissed. He prophesied exactly the groupings of power in the twentieth century, and he described the inevitability of American power in objective fashion. Power had always been his subject, for the Adamses above all saw power as an opportunity for rational intellect in office. Henry Adams, who never held a public office, was no less interested in power, and no less despairing of its unwise use, than were the other Adamses who stood over his life.

───────────

ADDISON, Joseph (May 1, 1672 – June 17, 1719). English essayist. Born Milston, Wiltshire, son of royalist clergyman Lancelot Addison. Educated at Charterhouse with Richard Steele and Queen's College, Oxford (1687–89), until his verses in honor of King William (1689) won him a scholarship at Magdalen College, of which he became a fellow (1698). Began publishing Latin and English verse (1683), winning quick repute. Granted government pension for travel and toured Continent (1699–1703). Heroic poem *The Campaign* (1704), celebrating battle of Blenheim, gained him favor with Whig party. Appointed undersecretary of state (1706), elected to Parliament (1708), made chief secretary to lord lieutenant of Ireland (1709), lost office on fall of Whigs (1711). Contributed to Steele's periodical the *Tatler* (1709–11) and joined him in producing the *Spectator* (1711–12, 1714), for which he created the celebrated character Sir Roger de Coverley. At height of his fame, Addison produced successful tragedy *Cato* (1713). Member of Kit-Cat Club with other leading Whigs. On return of Whigs to power appointed chief secretary for Ireland (1715). Became lord commissioner of trade (1716) and the same year married Charlotte, dowager countess of Warwick. Appointed secretary of state (1717), he retired from office a year later. Died in London; buried in Westminster Abbey.

EDITIONS: *Works* ed. Richard Hurd and Henry G. Bohn (6 vols. London 1854–56). *The Miscellaneous Works* ed. A. C. Guthkeld (2 vols. London 1914). *Letters* ed. Walter Graham (London and New York 1941). *The Tatler* ed. George A. Aitken (4 vols. London 1898–99). *The Spectator* ed. Donald F. Bond (5 vols. London and New York 1965).

REFERENCES: William John Courthope *Addison* (London and New York 1884). Samuel Johnson *Lives of the Poets* (London 1779–81). Peter Smithers *Life of Joseph Addison* (London and New York 1954).

AE (real name **George William Russell**) (Apr. 10, 1867 – July 17, 1935). Irish writer and painter. Born Lurgan, County Armagh. Resident of Dublin (1878–1933). Attended Metropolitan School of Art (1880–82), where he met W. B. Yeats; Rathmines School (1882–84); and the Royal Hibernian Academy School (1885–87). Entered accountant's office (1890); left (1897) to organize agricultural cooperatives. Published (1894) *Homeward: Songs by the Way*, first of many books of verse, of which the most important, *Selected Poems* (1935), contains his own choices. Yeats wrote that his poems are "the most delicate and subtle that any Irishman of our time has written." Married Violet North (1898). Edited the *Irish Homestead*, organ of the cooperative movement (1905–23) and *Irish Statesman* (1923–30). Member of Irish Home Rule Convention (1917–18) and adviser to U.S. government on rural reconstruction (1924). Died at Bournemouth, England. AE often exhibited paintings in Dublin; wrote on

politics and economics (*Cooperation and Nationality,* 1912; *The National Being: Some Thoughts on an Irish Polity,* 1916) and on religious mysticism (*The Candle of Vision,* 1918), but is chiefly remembered as a mystical poet and, with Yeats, as a leading figure in the Irish literary revival.

EDITIONS: *Collected Poems* (2nd ed. London 1926). *Selected Poems* (London and New York 1935). *Letters from AE* ed. Alan Denson (London and New York 1962).

REFERENCES: John Eglinton (pseudonym of William K. Magee) *A Memoir of AE* (London and New York 1937). Francis Merchant *AE, An Irish Promethean: A Study of the Contribution of George William Russell to World Culture* (Columbia, S.C. 1954).

AESCHYLUS (525–456 B.C.). Athenian tragedian. Born at Eleusis of noble parents; son of Euphorion, a tragic poet. Won first prize many times in Athenian contests, first time in 484 B.C. and last in 458 for the *Oresteia* trilogy. Died at Gela in Sicily, supposedly from the impact of a tortoise dropped on his head by an eagle. His epitaph records that he fought at Marathon. Seven plays survive of more than ninety written: *The Persians, Prometheus Bound, Seven Against Thebes,* as well as the *Oresteia* (*Agamemnon, Choephori,* and *Eumenides*) and the *Suppliants* of uncertain date. Aeschylus draws largely on mythic material, uses simple, direct dramatic plots, forceful characters, and a grandeur of style to express his lofty themes of moral retribution.

TRANSLATION: *Complete Works* tr. and ed. David Grene and Richmond Lattimore (2 vols. Chicago 1953, Cambridge, England, 1954 and Chicago 1956, also PB).

REFERENCES: John H. Finley, Jr. *Pindar and Aeschylus* (Cambridge, Mass. 1955 and London 1956). Gilbert Murray *Aeschylus: The Creator of Tragedy* (New York and Oxford 1940). Herbert W. Smyth *Aeschylean Tragedy* (Berkeley, Calif. 1924).

AESCHYLUS
BY MARTIN HALPERN

The Aeschylus we know is a much diminished Aeschylus. Even if we had all of his ninety-odd plays, rather than just seven plus some scattered fragments, his art would still reach us in only one of its multiple dimensions. For besides being the author of the "texts," he was almost certainly his own producer, director, designer, choreographer, composer, and either first or second leading actor. He was also — perhaps more than any other major literary or theatrical artist — the virtual creator of the medium in which he flourished. Though tragic plays of some kind had been produced in Athens for as much as two generations before him, he earns the epithet "father of tragedy" not just because his are the earliest surviving specimens of the art but also because his innovations permanently altered the essentials of that art. In staging technique alone he must have been one of the boldest experimenters ever — as witness what even today are the very demanding production requirements of a play like *Prometheus Bound*. More importantly, being the first to put two speaking actors onstage together, where formerly there had been at most one plus the chorus, he was the first to establish dialogue and the interaction of individual characters, rather than choral lyric and narration, as the prime stuff of drama. Most importantly, he liberated his art from substantive triviality, the "small fables and ridiculous diction" which Aristotle tells us had characterized it before him. Whatever else of Aeschylus is irretrievably lost, this greatest of his glories — the depth and universality of thought and feeling and grandeur of language which he first made inseparable from the idea of true tragedy — still resides in the bare texts alone.

And what we have of these, even when further diminished by translation, is bond enough between us and those contemporaries who awarded first prize at the annual competitions to at least fifty-two of his plays.

Judging from Aristophanes' rueful reflections in *The Frogs,* this audience appeal had waned somewhat by the end of the fifth century; and it is Aeschylus' successors Sophocles and Euripides, with their fuller and faster-moving plots and easier styles, who appear to have been the real popular favorites through the rest of antiquity. They rather than he, moreover, became the chief exemplars of classic excellence for seventeenth- and eighteenth-century neoclassic critics. It took the romantic revolution to create a climate of value in which he could again emerge as at least their equal. Indeed, as far as language is concerned, the qualities for which Aeschylus has been most admired since then are the ones which would naturally render him less than ideally "Greek" to anyone in whom the term evokes tidy notions of golden means. Though capable, when he needed to be, of restraint and simplicity, he preferred that kind of unfettered inspirational exuberance which expands the imagination beyond normal limits. If we accept Aristotle's dictum that of all literary virtues the one least capable of being taught or acquired is a "command of metaphor," then of all dramatists only Shakespeare rivals Aeschylus as a "natural genius." His choral writing in particular is often distinguished by brilliant profusions of imagery — visual, auditory, tactile, by turns or all at once; and the thematic development of several plays (notably the *Oresteia* trilogy) is grounded as much in elaborate patterns of recurring metaphors as in literal action and statement. Even his exposition tends to take the form not of clear, consecutive narrative, as in Sophocles and Euripides, but of the cryptic juxtaposition of images — verging, in such plays as *The Suppliant Maidens* and *Agamemnon*, on downright stream-of-consciousness. It was practices like these, together with his cultivation of the exotic in syntax and vocabulary, which gave rise in the next generation to such half-serious allegations as the one attributed to Sophocles — that his elder rival must have composed while under some form of Dionysiac intoxication.

For all this, however, each of the extant plays has at its thematic center a quite simple and lucid moral antithesis, reflective of the great historical event of the time: the long struggle to repel the Persian invaders, in which Aeschylus participated at the battle of Marathon (the one fact his epitaph mentions) and probably at the two later battles, Salamis and Plataea, commemorated in his tragedy *The Persians*. Despite the extraordinary compassion shown the then defeated enemy in that play, its main point is clearly to celebrate the triumph of Athenian rational enlightenment over Asian barbarism. Earlier, in *The Suppliant Maidens*, and later, in *The Seven Against Thebes*, the same opposition appears in mythic rather than contemporary historical terms: the idealized Greek kings Pelasgus and Eteocles pitted against the brutish aggressors led by the fifty sons of Egyptus and the renegade Polyneices. It finally assumes explicitly cosmic dimensions in *Prometheus Bound* and the *Oresteia*, where the conflicts of Prometheus versus Zeus and Apollo versus the Furies symbolize the universal struggle of the civilizing intellect against primitive instinct and the tyranny of terror.

Yet it would be wrong to take as Aeschylus' philosophical last word the mere dualistic (or propagandistic) identification of the former with good and the latter with evil. Both *The Suppliant Maidens* and *Prometheus Bound*, for example, were the opening members of trilogies; and fragments from the other plays of those trilogies suggest that the final resolutions at which he was aiming involved some fusion of the antagonistic moral and natural forces represented in one by Artemis and Aphrodite and in the other by Prometheus and Zeus. Such is certainly the case in the one complete trilogy we have — which, being both Aeschylus' last known work and his undoubted masterpiece, can be taken as the fullest expression of his thought. At the end of the *Oresteia*, the generations-old chain reaction of crime and retribution in the House of Atreus is finally arrested when the patron goddess of Athens persuades the vindictive Furies to accept conversion into the beneficent Eumenides. But, as Athena herself takes pains to remind them, that conversion means not the loss but the sanctification of the essential roles they have always played in life: inspirers of fear as a deterrent to crime, and defenders of the womb, the claims of blood relationship, and all in the human psyche that is inherited, instinctual, prerational. Hence Aeschylus pays his homage to the principle of darkness as necessary counterpart to the principle of light — the postnatal world of evolving consciousness, education, social responsibility, and free rational choice dominated by the Furies' former antagonist Apollo. In this he perhaps shows his closest affinities to those romantics — Blake, Coleridge, Hegel, Hugo, Nietzsche, Yeats — who have repeatedly insisted on the idea of the highest truth as a synthesis of contraries. For his thought, like his style and staging, embodies that sometimes undervalued strain of the Greek sensibility which sought not so much some golden mean as the vision large enough to encompass and reconcile the most diverse extremes.

AESOP (c.620–c.560 B.C.). Reputed author of Greek fables. Of unknown origin, he is thought to have spent most of his life as a slave on the island of Samos and been eventually freed, to have traveled extensively and died by mishap at Delphi. Hundreds of fables have been attributed to this semilegendary figure, and some writers link the events of his life with famous people of his supposed time — King Croesus of Lydia, the courtesan Rhodopis, Solon the Athenian lawgiver, and the Seven Wise Men. The collections in Greek prose known as *Aesop's Fables* were assembled in the second or third century A.D., but the bulk of the material, from diverse sources, must have evolved several centuries earlier.

TRANSLATION: *Aesop's Fables* tr. V. S. Vernon Jones (London and New York 1912).

REFERENCES: Joseph Jacobs *The Fables of Aesop* (New York 1889). Ben Edwin Perry *Aesopica* (Urbana, Ill. 1952).

AKHMATOVA, ANNA (real name Anna Andreyevna Gorenko) (June 23, 1888 – Mar. 5, 1966). Russian poet. Born Bolshoi Fontan, near Odessa. Educated at Smolny Institute, St. Petersburg (Leningrad), where she also attended college and spent most of her life. Married four times, first to poet Nikolai Gumilyov (1910–18), founder of Acmeist literary movement, which supported romanticism. Published (1912–23) six volumes of personal lyrics in Acmeist tradition, including *Evening* (1912), *The Rosary* (1914), *Anno Domini MCMXXI* (1922). After almost twenty years of silence, published *The Willow Tree* (1940), but her devotion to religious, mystical and tragic love themes and abstention from political themes led to denunciation of her work by Communist party (1946). Ten years later, during Soviet literary "thaw," her poetry again appeared and she gained reputation of being greatest living woman poet in Russia. Died in Moscow.

TRANSLATION of Akhmatova's poetry in preparation by Stanley Kunitz and Max Hayward.

REFERENCE: Leonid I. Strakhovsky, *Craftsmen of the Word: Three Poets of Modern Russia: Gumilyov, Akhmatova, Mandelstam* (Cambridge, Mass. 1949).

ALAIN-FOURNIER real name **Henri Alban Fournier**) (Oct. 3, 1886 – Sept. 22, 1914). French novelist. Born La Chapelle-d'Angillon, Cher. Spent childhood and youth in village of Épineuil, where his parents were schoolteachers. Educated at Lycée Lakanal in Paris (1903–1907), where after two years' military service (1907–1909) he became a journalist, then private secretary to a businessman. Killed early in World War I, in the Bois de St. Rémy. Alain-Fournier's reputation rests on his one completed novel, *Le Grand Meaulnes* (1913, tr. *The Wanderer* 1928), concerning a youth's search for the philosophical and emotional truth of his life with an exquisitely described setting of the countryside of the author's childhood. Other writings, published posthumously, include symbolist poems and prose sketches as well as a fragment of a novel, *Colombe Blanchet* (all collected in *Miracles*, 1924), also his correspondence with Jacques Rivière.

TRANSLATIONS [of *Le Grand Meaulnes*]: *The Wanderer* tr. Françoise Delisle (Boston 1928, New York PB 1958). *The Lost Domain* tr. Frank Davison (New York PB 1959).

REFERENCES: Robert Gibson *The Quest of Alain-Fournier* (London 1953). Isabelle Fournier Rivière *Vie et passion d'Alain-Fournier* (Monaco 1963).

ALBÉNIZ, Isaac Manuel Francisco (May 29, 1860 – May 18, 1909). Spanish pianist and composer. Born Camprodón, Catalonia. At four performed as piano prodigy in Barcelona, and at seven in Paris. Entered Madrid Conservatory (1868), but at thirteen ran away, and after playing in various Spanish towns embarked for Costa

Rica. Played throughout U.S. and returned via England to study at Leipzig Conservatory (1874), then with Liszt at Budapest (1878). From 1880, toured widely as virtuoso, his repertoire including many of his own piano pieces, of which he wrote some 250 between 1880 and 1892, including the popular *Córdoba, Seguidillas,* and *Tango in D.* Married Rosina Jordana (1883). Settled in Paris (1893), where he came under influence of d'Indy, Dukas, Debussy and Fauré, and wrote his best music. Major works: rhapsody *Catalonia* (1899) for piano and orchestra, and *Iberia* (1906–1909), a set of twelve piano pieces. Most successful of several works for the stage: *Pepita Jiménez* (produced in Barcelona, 1896). Developed Bright's disease and after 1900 lived mostly in Spain. Died at Cambo-les-Bains, Pyrenees. A leader of Spanish nationalist school, Albéniz evoked atmosphere of Spain, suggesting colors and rhythms of native music while employing impressionistic technique of Debussy.

REFERENCES: Henri Collet *Albéniz et Granados* (Paris 1926). Gabriel Laplane *Albéniz: sa vie, son oeuvre* (Geneva 1956). Miguel RauxDeledicque *Albéniz: su vida inquieta y ardorosa* (Buenos Aires 1950).

ALBERTI, Leon Battista (Feb. 14, 1404 – Apr. 25, 1472). Italian architect, scientist, scholar. Born Genoa; formal training in humanities at Padua, in law at Bologna. Became aide (1428) to the papal legates to Burgundy and Germany. As papal secretary lived in Rome (1431–34) and Florence (1434–52). Spent later years chiefly in Rome, where he died. Alberti published *Della Pittura* (1436), the first literary formulation of the aesthetic and scientific theories of Renaissance painting. Architectural career began with redesigning exterior of the church of S. Francesco in Rimini (1450); next important work was façade of S. Maria Novella in Florence (1456). Most famous buildings are churches of S. Sebastiano (1460) and S. Andrea (1472) in Mantua, and Rucellai palace in Florence (c.1447–1451). They embody the principles of harmonic proportion evolved through Alberti's study of ancient sculpture and architecture and expounded in his most influential treatise, *De Re Aedificatoria* (written 1452, published 1485). Besides establishing Renaissance aesthetics, Alberti wrote on all aspects of science and the arts, religion and ethics, linguistics, politics and jurisprudence, and himself was the embodiment of the Renaissance — the "universal man."

TRANSLATIONS: *On Painting* tr. J. R. Spencer (New Haven and London 1956, also PB). *Ten Books on Architecture* tr. James Leoni (New York and London 1955).

REFERENCES: Sir Kenneth Clark *Leon Battista Alberti on Painting* (London and New York 1945). Joan Gadol *Leon Battista Alberti: Universal Man of the Early Renaissance* (Chicago, Ill. 1969). Paul Henri Michel *La Pensée de L. B. Alberti* (Paris 1930). Adrian D. Stokes *Art and Science: A Study of Alberti, Piero della Francesca and Giorgione* (London 1949).

ALCAEUS (born c.620 B.C.). Greek poet. Born Mytilene, Lesbos, of noble family; contemporary of Sappho. Political activity in group of nobles contending for supremacy of kingdom of Mytilene led to exile to Egypt soon after 600 B.C.; later he returned home. His poems, surviving only in fragments and including love lyrics, drinking songs, martial hymns, political epigrams and other verses, are the best examples of the Aeolian lyric. He invented also the Alcaic strophe, used by classical poets, especially Horace, and later by Tennyson.

REFERENCE: Cecil M. Bowra *Greek Lyric Poetry* (2nd ed. rev. London and New York 1961).

ALCOTT, Louisa May (Nov. 29, 1832 – Mar. 6, 1888). American writer of children's books. Born Germantown, Pa., daughter of transcendentalist philosopher Amos Bronson Alcott (1799–1888). Lived most of her life in Concord, Mass., and Boston. Educated by father and also by members of his intellectual circle, which included Thoreau, Emerson, and Theodore Parker. Much concerned with financial support of her family, she taught for a time, turning finally to writing, producing *Flower Fables* (1854). Also contributed stories to *Atlantic Monthly*. Contracted typhoid while serving as army nurse during Civil War and was never again in good health. Achieved recognition with *Hospital Sketches* (1863). Published first novel, *Moods* (1865), also toured Europe that year. Her immensely popular children's novel, the autobiographical *Little Women*, appeared 1868–69. *An Old-Fashioned Girl* followed (1870), *Little Men* (1871), *Work* (1873). Also wrote many other children's books. Died in Concord.

REFERENCES: Ednah D. Cheney ed. *Louisa May Alcott, Life, Letters, and Journals* (Boston 1889). Madeleine Stern *Louisa May Alcott* (Norman, Okla. 1950 and London 1952). Marjorie Worthington *Miss Alcott of Concord: A Biography* (Garden City, N.Y. 1958).

ALEICHEM. *See* SHOLOM ALEICHEM.

ALFIERI, Count Vittorio (Jan. 16, 1749 – Oct. 8, 1803). Italian dramatist and poet. Born Asti, of wealthy aristocratic parents. Spent eight years at Academy of Turin, then almost seven adventuring in the capitals of Europe (1766–72). Returned to Turin; wrote plays in French, the language he had grown up speaking. Political convictions led him to study Plutarch and Italian with a view to creating Italian national drama. By the age of thirty-two Alfieri had written fourteen tragedies. In Florence (1777), fell in love with countess of Albany (1753–1824), wife of Charles Edward Stuart, the Young Pretender; they lived together from 1784 to the end of his life. In Paris (1786–92), then returned to Florence, where he died. Alfieri's greatest tragedies (published 1783–85) include *Filippo, Antigone, Oreste, Mirra,* and *Saul.* Denunciations of tyranny, they were of enormous importance in launching the movement for Italian unity and independence.

TRANSLATIONS: *The Life of Vittorio Alfieri Written by Himself* tr. Sir Henry McAnally (Lawrence, Kan. 1953). *Memoirs: The Anonymous Translation of 1810* rev. Eric R. Vincent (London and New York 1961). *The Tragedies of Vittorio Alfieri* tr. Charles Lloyd and Edgar Bowring, ed. Edgar Bowring (2 vols. London 1876).

REFERENCE: Charles R. D. Miller *Alfieri: A Biography* (Williamsport, Pa. 1936).

ALTDORFER, Albrecht (? – Feb. 12, 1538). German painter, printmaker, and architect. Little known of his life until 1506, earliest known date of his signed copper engravings and drawings. Held city offices in Regensburg (1519–35), including post of city architect. Participated in production of graphic works commissioned by Emperor Maximilian I. Died in Regensburg. An important master of the German Renaissance, he was a leading member of the Danube school of landscape artists and helped make landscape an independent subject for painting. His works, which often show figures integrated in a vast landscape or architectural setting, demonstrate his concentration on a total effect. Among his paintings are *Rest on the Flight into Egypt* (1510), *The Birth of Mary, Legend of St. Florian,* and *The Battle of Alexander* (1529).

ANACREON (born c.570 B.C.). Greek poet. Born Teos, in Ionia. He evidently accompanied the Teians to Abdera in Thrace on evacuation of Teos during Persian invasion (c.545 B.C.). From Abdera, went to court of Polycrates of Samos and, after assassination of Polycrates (c.522 B.C.), to court of tyrant Hipparchus at Athens, which is probably where he died. Anacreon was the author of graceful, elegant poems, in Ionian dialect and in a variety of lyric meters, dealing with love and wine; only a few fragments survive.

REFERENCE: Cecil M. Bowra *Greek Lyric Poetry* (2nd ed. rev. London and New York 1961).

ANDERSEN, Hans Christian (Apr. 2, 1805 – Aug. 4, 1875). Danish writer. Born Odense, son of a poor shoemaker who died when Hans was eleven. Apprenticed to various trades, then set out for Copenhagen (1819). Joined

Royal Theatre as actor and singer until 1822, when musician friends and King Frederick VI enabled him to attend school at Slagelse and Elsinore, later Copenhagen University (1828). King Frederick also provided a traveling pension. A visit to Germany (1831) inspired the first of his many travel sketches, an Italian journey (1833) his first and most successful novel, *The Improvisatore* (1835). That year published first series of fairy tales, then second series (1838) and third (1845), all of which brought him international fame. Last of several more series appeared in 1872. The 168 stories include *The Tinder Box, The Princess and the Pea, The Little Match Girl, The Snow Queen, The Red Shoes, The Ugly Duckling.* The intensely autobiographical quality of all Andersen's fiction is present even in these children's stories. He wrote and rewrote his memoirs; standard edition is *The Fairy Tale of My Life* (1855; annotated edition 1951, tr. 1951). He died in Copenhagen.

REFERENCES: Rumer Godden *Hans Christian Andersen* (London and New York 1955). Monica Stirling *The Wild Swan: The Life and Times of Hans Christian Andersen* (London and New York 1965).

ANDERSON, Sherwood (Sept. 13, 1876 – Mar. 8, 1941). American novelist and short story writer. Born Camden, Ohio, son of itinerant saddle and harness maker. As youth in Clyde, Ohio, attended school intermittently and worked at odd jobs. After serving in Spanish-American War, became successful at advertising in Chicago, later manager of paint factory in Elyria, Ohio. Abruptly abandoned job and family (1912) to go to Chicago; joined literary set that included Floyd Dell, Carl Sandburg, Theodore Dreiser, and Ben Hecht. First novel, *Windy McPherson's Son* (1916), was, like his subsequent work, autobiographical. *Marching Men* (1917) established dominant theme: conflict between instinctive forces in human nature and inhibiting effects of organized industrial society. *Winesburg, Ohio* (1919), a series of interrelated short stories, won wide critical acclaim and is his best-known work. Followed by *Poor White* (1920). In Europe (1921–22); from 1925 lived on farm in Grayson County, Va.; editor of both newspapers, one Democratic, one Republican, in nearby town of Marion. Anderson married four times. Died at Colón, Panama. His best later works are the short story collections *The Triumph of the Egg* (1921), *Horses and Men* (1923), and *Death in the Woods* (1933). His autobiographical works include *A Story Teller's Story* (1924), *Tar: A Midwest Childhood* (1926), and *Memoirs* (1942), also his *Letters* (1953).

REFERENCES: Irving Howe *Sherwood Anderson* (New York 1951 and London 1952). James Erwin Schevill, *Sherwood Anderson: His Life and Work* (Denver 1951).

ANDREA DEL SARTO. *See* **SARTO.**

ANGELICO, Fra (Giovanni da Fiesole) (c.1400 – Mar. 18, 1455). Italian painter. Born Vicchio, near Florence. Entered Dominican order at San Domenico in Fiesole (c.1418–20), ordained (c.1423–25). Earliest surviving work certainly attributable to him is the Linaiuoli triptych (commissioned 1433). It demonstrates his mature style, combining the traditional pure or unmixed colors with strong, simple figures in careful composition that reflect the newer ideas of his time. Paintings of the later 1430's and early 1440's include *The Coronation of the Virgin* (Louvre, Paris), *The Annunciation, The Flight into Egypt,* and *The Madonna Annalena* (all in Museo di San Marco). Decorated newly rebuilt Dominican monastery of San Marco, Florence (c.1438–c.1447), then moved to Rome to work in Vatican, chiefly decoration of chapel of Pope Nicholas V (*Scenes from the Lives of St. Stephen and St. Lawrence,* c.1447–c.1449). After serving three years (1449–52) as prior of San Domenico at Fiesole, returned to Rome, where he died.

REFERENCES: Giulio C. Argan *Fra Angelico: A Biographical and Critical Study* (London and Cleveland 1955). Germain Bazin *Fra Angelico* (New York and London 1949).

ANTONELLO DA MESSINA (c. 1430 – Feb. 15, 1479). Italian painter. Born Messina, Sicily; father a sculptor. In Calabria (1461–65), then at Messina again; arrived in Venice (1475), where he was briefly (1476–77) in service of duke of Milan. Returned to Messina, where he died. Antonello may have visited the Netherlands; in any case he was the first Italian painter to master oil technique already perfected by the Flemings, and is credited with teaching oil painting to the Venetians. Style combines meticulousness of the van Eycks with Italian breadth. Major works: *St. Jerome* (National Gallery, London), *St. Sebastian* (c.1475, Gemäldegalerie, Dresden), *Condottiere* (1475, Louvre, Paris), portraits of men (1470–74, Rome, London, Berlin), *Crucifixion* (1475, Antwerp Museum), *Salvator Mundi* (1465, National Gallery, London), *Dead Christ* (c.1475, Venice).

REFERENCE: Giorgio Vigni *All the Paintings of Antonello da Messina* (tr. London and New York 1963).

APOLLINAIRE, Guillaume (originally Guglielmo (or Wilhelm) Apollinaris de Kostrowitzky) (Aug. 26, 1880 – Nov. 10, 1918). French writer. Born Rome, illegitimate child of Italian officer and Polish émigrée. Spent childhood on French Riviera. After extensive travels in Germany and eastern Europe, settled in Paris (1902), where for several years he worked as a clerk. Published novel *L'Enchanteur pourrissant* (1909). Gradually publication of his poems and his friendship with avant-garde writers and painters brought recognition. Aside from collections of his best verse, *Alcools* (1913) and *Calligrammes* (1918), his major achievement was championing and explaining new artistic movements, especially cubism — his book *Les Peintres cubistes* (1913) remains an important document — and surrealism (a term he coined in 1917). Seriously wounded in action in World War I (1916), he never fully recovered from subsequent trepanning operation; died in Paris shortly after marriage to Jacqueline Kolb. Apollinaire's verse, lyrical, bizarre, and technically innovative, represents the link between symbolism and surrealism. Other works include *L'Hérésiarque et Cie.*, a collection of stories (1910), and *Les Mamelles de Tirésias* (1918), a play.

TRANSLATION: *Selected Writings* tr. Roger Shattuck (New York and London 1950).

REFERENCES: Marcel Adéma *Apollinaire* (tr. London 1954 and New York 1955). Margaret Davies *Apollinaire* (Edinburgh and New York 1964). Francis Steegmuller *Apollinaire: Poet Among the Painters* (New York 1963 and London 1964, also PB). See also Roger Shattuck *The Banquet Years: The Arts in France 1885–1918* (New York 1958 and London 1959, also PB).

APULEIUS, Lucius (born c. A.D. 123). Roman writer, orator, and mystic. Born Madauros in Numidia (near modern Mdaourouch, Algeria) of wealthy parents. Educated at Carthage and Athens; later traveled in east for initiation into religious mysteries and to Rome, achieving renown as pleader and orator; then again in Africa, at Oea (modern Tripoli). Married wealthy widow Aemilia Pudentilla (c.155). *Apologia* or *De Magia*, his defense in suit brought by her relatives for gaining her affections by magic, is chief source for his biography. Apuleius lived afterwards in Carthage, esteemed as a priest, poet, philosopher, and rhetorician. Major work, *Metamorphoses* or *The Golden Ass*, is the sole Latin novel that survives entire. A picaresque tale full of comic, exciting adventures, it became immensely popular; its influence on development of modern fiction is most clearly seen in Boccaccio and Cervantes. Among his other writings are *Florida*, excerpts from declamations on varied themes; and two philosophical treatises — *De Dogmate Platonis* and *De Deo Socratis* — which reveal the superficiality of his learning.

TRANSLATION: *The Golden Ass* tr. Robert Graves (Harmondsworth, Eng. 1950 PB and New York 1951).

REFERENCE: Elizabeth H. Haight *Apuleius and His Influence* (New York 1927).

ARCADELT, Jakob (c.1505 – before 1572). Flemish composer. Probable birthplace Liège. First composition dates from 1532 (Lyons). Went to Italy about 1538; became singer and later choirmaster at Sistine Chapel in Rome (1539–45). Returned (1547) after year's absence in France, leaving again before 1552. Entered (1555) service of Charles cardinal de Lorraine and duc de Guise, whom he followed to Paris; member of French royal chapel by 1557. Vanishes from records c.1567. Arcadelt's fame rests on some 120 chansons and over 200 Italian madrigals. With Costanzo Festa and Philippe Verdelot, determined the pure style of the four-part madrigal; exerted strong influence on Palestrina. Also published about twenty motets and three Masses.

_____

ARETINO, Pietro (Apr. 20, 1492 – Oct. 21, 1556). Italian writer. Born Arezzo (whence he took his name), son of a shoemaker. Studied painting at Perugia; then went to Rome. Published pasquinades (satirical poems). Won favor of Pope Leo X and Giovanni dalle Bande Nere, the condottiero. Lived in Venice from 1527 until his death. Aretino was noted for satiric attacks and libelous pasquinades on the wealthy and powerful; Ariosto styled him "the scourge of princes." Works include the satirical *I Ragionamenti* in dialogue form (1534–36), the tragedy *Orazia* (1546), five comedies (1525–42), and six volumes of letters. Aretino's cynical outlook and exuberant, spontaneous style had considerable effect on sixteenth-century literature.

TRANSLATION: *The Works of Aretino* tr. Samuel Putnam (2 vols. New York 1933).
REFERENCES: Thomas C. Chubb *Aretino, Scourge of Princes* (New York 1940). James Cleugh *The Divine Aretino: Pietro of Arezzo 1492–1556* (London 1965 and New York 1966). Edward Hutton *Pietro Aretino: The Scourge of Princes* (Boston 1922).

_____

ARIOSTO, Ludovico (Sept. 8, 1474 – July 6, 1533). Italian poet. Born Reggio Emilia, son of nobleman. Studied law at Ferrara (1489–94). Became diplomatic attaché in service of Cardinal Ippolito d'Este (1503); about this time began his lifework *Orlando Furioso*, an epic based on medieval legends of Charlemagne and Roland (first edition 1516). Entered service of Alfonso I, duke of Ferrara (1518), who made him governor of Garfagnana region in the Apennines (1522–25). Married Alessandra Benucci (1527) and spent rest of life revising and enlarging *Orlando Furioso* (final version 1532). Died in Ferrara. Chiefly remembered for *Orlando Furioso*, the finest example of the Renaissance romantic epic, which exerted wide influence on European literature. Minor works include five comedies (1508–29) and seven *Satires* (1517–25, tr. 1608 and 1759).

TRANSLATIONS: *Orlando Furioso* tr. Sir John Harrington (1591), ed. Rudolph Gottfried (Bloomington, Ind. 1963, also PB); ed. Graham Hough (London 1962).
REFERENCES: Benedetto Croce *Ariosto, Shakespeare and Corneille* (tr. London and New York 1920); Edmund G. Gardner *The King of Court Poets* (London and New York 1906).

_____

ARISTOPHANES (c.450 B.C. – c.385 B.C.). Greek poet and playwright. Little is known about the life of this only writer of Old Comedy whose work has survived (in eleven plays, mostly intact). He was of Athenian parentage, with property on Aegina, and the extant plays are *The Acharnians* (425), an attack on the Peloponnesian War; *The Knights* (424), an attack on the radical demagogue Cleon; *The Clouds* (423), a satire on Socrates and his disciples; *The Wasps* (422), a satire on the popular courts; *The Peace* (421), a defense of the Peace of Nicias; *The Birds* (414), a political satire set in Cloud-Cuckoo-Land; *Lysistrata* (411), another protest for peace; *The Thesmophoriazusae* (411), an assault on Euripides for his misogyny; *The Frogs* (405), a satire on Euripides and Aeschylus containing the celebrated chorus "Brekekekex ko-ax ko-ax"; *The Ecclesiazusae* (c.392), a burlesque of contemporary political theories; and *The Plutus* (388), an ironic allegory of the effects of a fair distribution of the wealth.

TRANSLATIONS (among the many): *Four Comedies: Lysistrata, The Frogs,*

The Birds, Ladies' Day (*Thesmophori-azusae*) ed. and tr. Dudley Fitts (New York 1954, 1955, 1957, 1959, also one-volume PB). *The Birds* and *The Clouds* tr. William Arrowsmith (Ann Arbor, Mich. 1961, 1962). *The Frogs* tr. Richmond Lattimore (Ann Arbor 1962). *The Acharnians, The Congresswomen (Thesmophoriazusae), Lysistrata,* and *The Wasps* tr. Douglass Parker (Ann Arbor 1961, 1967, 1963 and 1962, also PB 1969). *Complete Plays* tr. Robert H. Webb, Jack Lindsay, Benjamin Rogers, ed. Moses Hadas (New York PB 1962).

REFERENCES: Victor Ehrenberg *The People of Aristophanes: A Sociology of Old Attic Comedy* (2nd ed. Cambridge, Mass. and London 1951, also PB). Gilbert Murray *Aristophanes: A Study* (New York and London 1933). Cedric H. Whitman *Aristophanes and the Comic Hero* (Cambridge, Mass. 1964).

✍

ARISTOPHANES
BY DUDLEY FITTS

Aristophanes is the master comic poet of the ancient world. At his death (c.385 B.C.) he left some forty plays, of which eleven have survived more or less as he wrote them. Nine of these pieces are our only intact evidence for the literary genre known as Old Comedy and are consequently precious as documents; but they are also works of extraordinary power and beauty in their own right. The other two, *The Ecclesiazusae* and *The Plutus*, written towards the end of the poet's career, foreshadow the so-called New Comedy, which was to culminate seventy years later in the plays of Menander. This transition is marked by a certain lessening of comic force. Taste changes from one generation to another, and it may well be that sons will learn to blush at the excesses of their fathers. At any rate, the movement from Old Comedy to New is from the uninhibited, brilliant, lyric laughter of Aristophanes to a relatively domesticated and much less disturbing kind

of discourse, the representation of the ordinary citizen in his daily life. In Menander poetry becomes metered conversation. The huge imaginative roar is silenced.

Aristophanes was born in one of the world's great centuries. The Athens of Pericles was his Athens; the intellectual and artistic activity of the fifth century before Christ was in the air that he breathed. A man born in the lifetime of Aeschylus, a man to whom Sophocles and Euripides, Socrates and Agathon, Alcibiades, Nicias, Critias, and the like were not historical figurines in a classroom but living contemporaries in a compact little city: such a man, if he is articulate, has almost too much to talk about. And few men have been more handsomely articulate than Aristophanes. Nevertheless it is not easy to decide what his real convictions were. The tradition of Old Comedy was to be personally and abusively satirical. The poet had great license. He was expected to poke fun at the leaders of the Establishment, to violate social and religious taboos, to name names, and to pull no punches. Aristophanes, a master of disguises, would seem on the evidence of his plays to be an archconservative, a praiser of time past, a deplorer of innovation in politics, in the arts, in philosophy and physical science. Two of his enemies, if we are to take his word for it, are Socrates the thinker and Euripides the dramatist. Both are guilty of the crime of modernism. Socrates is hilariously and brutally pilloried in *The Clouds*, which is, among other things, the earliest and best parody of Life Among the Professors; and Euripides and his plays are subjected to burlesque and travesty of the most cruel kind in scene after scene. Yet the attack upon both men is so outrageous in its distortion of the truth, the caricature so absurd, that no audience could have taken it for anything but fantasy. Fantasy, however, of an ominous kind: Euripides and Socrates in these plays, like Cleon and Lamachus and other named or identifiable great men of the period, are used in distortion as symbols of social corruption. Aristophanes' theme is the downfall of the Athenian state — the threat, first evident in the vicissitudes of the long and senseless war with Sparta, which was realized at the close of the century in the destruction of the empire, the vaunted democracy, and in the eclipse of right thinking and good art. His method of attack is absurdity piled upon absurdity. Anything goes, and the actual personalities of the poet and his victims are submerged in the great rush of his satiric invention. Is Socrates traduced? If we can trust the records, the real Socrates does not seem to have thought so. So with Euripides, and so, in a sense, with Aristophanes himself. The critical fantasist hyperbolizes himself out of existence.

Of the eleven plays that have come down to us, four or five have kept their freshness undimmed. Topical satire, brilliant in one age, may be quite dead for the next; to endure, to keep fresh, satire must somehow strike through the local, the topical, and touch a general truth. And in plays in which local satire itself is subordinated to a widely and wildly ranging poetic fancy, as it is in *The Birds* and *The Peace;* or to the development of a gustily ribald metaphor, the women's sex strike against war, in *Lysistrata;* or even to literary criticism, which plays so large a part in *The Frogs* and in *The Thesmophoriazusae* — in these dramas it is the general truth to which we respond, untroubled by the scholiasts' footnotes and the cough of the professors. In the more restricted plays — *The Achar-*

nians, for example, dealing with the politics of war, or *The Wasps,* which treats the Athenian passion for going to law — there is still much to engage our uninstructed imagination. In all the plays except *The Plutus,* the last in time, it is the warm, sane humanity of Aristophanes that informs his extravagance and wins our hearts. He comes through to us somehow even in translation: the poetry is dimmed, the situations blunted; but enough remains to reveal the great comic poet whose like was not to be seen again in the western world until the emergence of Rabelais and Shakespeare. Swift and Sterne are in his train; as are Joyce and Céline, to come to our own time.

ARISTOTLE (384–322 B.C.). Greek philosopher. Born Stagira, in Chalcidice, son of Nicomachus, a physician. Member of Plato's Academy at Athens from 367 until latter's death (347); then spent three years at court of Hermias, ruler of Atarneus and Assos in Mysia. Married Hermias's niece Pythias. After living for two years on Lesbos, returned to Macedon (343 or 342) to become tutor of Alexander. Went to Athens (335) and opened famous school in the Lyceum where he lectured, organized research projects, and collected a library of manuscripts and maps and a museum of natural history. During anti-Macedonian agitation (323), Aristotle fled to Chalcis, where he died. Of his popular works and collections of scholarly data, nothing survives except the *Constitution of Athens,* an account of Athenian government (discovered in Egypt 1890). Chief among his extant works, which in their present form represent perhaps notes made by Aristotle himself, perhaps lectures recorded by pupils, are the *Organon* (consisting of six treatises on logic), *Physics, Metaphysics, De Anima, Nicomachean Ethics, Eudemian Ethics, Politics, Rhetoric,* and *Poetics.* Aristotle's empirical methods of philosophical and scientific procedure and of literary criticism are fundamental to Western thought.

TRANSLATIONS: *The Works of Aristotle* tr. J. I. Beare, ed. John A. Smith and Sir William D. Ross (London and New York, 12 vols. 1908–52). *The Basic Works of Aristotle* ed. Richard McKeon (New York 1941), a one-volume selection from the above. There are many others.

REFERENCES: Werner W. Jaeger *Aristotle: Fundamentals of the History of His Development* (tr. 2nd ed. New York and London 1948, also PB). William D. Ross *Aristotle* (5th ed. rev. London and New York 1949, also PB). John H. Randall *Aristotle* (New York and London 1960, also PB).

———

ARNE, Thomas Augustine (Mar. 12, 1710 – Mar. 5, 1778). English composer. Born London, son of an upholsterer and coffin maker. Educated at Eton; intended for the law, but studied music clandestinely. After successful production of *Rosamund* (1733) and other stage works, became attached (1734) to Drury Lane Theatre, with which he was associated during most of his life. Married famous soprano Cecilia Young (1737). Composed (1738–40) three great masques, *Comus, The Judgment of Paris,* and *Alfred,* which includes *Rule, Britannia.* Important later works: oratorio *Judith* (1761); opera *Artaxerxes* (1762), in which occur "The Soldier Tired" and "Water Parted from the Sea"; and masque *The Fairy Prince* (1771). Arne also wrote light operas, popular songs, Catholic church music, and instrumental pieces; best known for settings of songs in Shakespeare's comedies such as *Under the greenwood tree, Blow, blow thou winter wind, When daisies pied* (all from *As You Like It,* 1740), and *Where the bee sucks* (*The Tempest,* 1746). Made doctor of music at Oxford (1759). Died in London. Handel's leading rival in England, Arne produced melodies distinctively English in their natural ease and grace.

———

ARNOLD, Matthew (Dec. 24, 1822 – Apr. 15, 1888). English poet and critic. Born Laleham, son of Thomas Arnold (1795–1842), famous headmaster of Rugby. Educated at Winchester, Rugby, and Balliol College, Oxford (graduated 1844); won Newdigate Prize (1843) and fellowship at Oriel College (1845). Achieved recognition with first volume, *The Strayed Reveller, and Other Poems* (1849). Married Frances Lucy Wightman (1851) and became an inspector of schools under national Education Department (1851–1886); also made intensive study of and reports on Continental educational systems. The title poem in *Empedocles on Etna and Other Poems* (1852) was his chief work and remains a central utterance of the age. *Poems* (1853) included an important preface, *Sohrab and Rustum,* and *The Scholar-Gipsy.* In *New Poems* (1867) were *Dover Beach* (written 1851?) and *Thyrsis,* an elegy on his old friend Arthur Hugh Clough (1819–1861). Professor of poetry at Oxford (1857–67). Major works in prose: *On Translating Homer* (1861–62), a group of Oxford lectures; *Essays in Criticism* (two series, 1865, 1888); *Culture and Anarchy* (1869); *Literature and Dogma* (1873); and *Discourses in America* (1885), from an American tour (1883–84). Died suddenly in Liverpool.

EDITIONS: *Complete Prose Works* ed. Robert H. Super (in progress, Ann Arbor, Mich. and London 1960–). *Poems* ed. Kenneth Allott (London and New York 1965).

REFERENCES: D. Bush *Matthew Arnold* (New York 1971). A. Dwight Culler *Imaginative Reason: The Poetry of Matthew Arnold* (New Haven 1966). Fraser Neiman *Matthew Arnold* (New York 1968). George R. Stange *Matthew Arnold: The Poet as Humanist* (Princeton, N.J. 1967). Lionel Trilling *Matthew Arnold* (2nd ed. New York 1965, also PB).

✍

MATTHEW ARNOLD
BY DOUGLAS BUSH

Among the Victorian interpreters of their age of progress and anxiety Matthew Arnold had probably the most comprehensive range, and he has probably retained a fuller significance for our time than contemporary poets and sages. His first five books (1849–1858) were poetry; with some exceptions, such as *Rugby Chapel* and *Thyr-*

sis, the important poems were written in the decade 1843–53, in Arnold's twenties and just beyond. As a poet he lacked the prodigal and versatile creativity of Tennyson and Browning, and seldom rivaled their craftsmanship, but he ranks as a major voice because in substance and to some degree in manner he speaks to our condition; he has not lost much through time and changes in taste. His many volumes of prose (1859–88) embrace literature, social and political problems, religion, and education. Arnold's large body of writing — and the assiduous selective reading that went along with it — is something of a miracle in view of his wearing occupation as an inspector of schools (1851–86), an occupation that kept him dashing about the country in trains, lodging in provincial inns, confronting the intellectual mediocrity of pupils and teachers — while men sitting at ease pronounced the apostle of culture "an elegant Jeremiah" unacquainted with the facts of life.

The young Arnold, reacting against the burden of being the son of Dr. Arnold of Rugby, had adopted the pose of a dandy, a flippant worldling, and he surprised his relatives and close friends by the revelation, in his first volume (1849), of a lonely, troubled, questioning soul. The best introduction to these and later poems is provided by his often grim letters, chiefly of 1845–53, to his poet friend Arthur Hugh Clough. In poem after poem Arnold diagnosed, from within, the malaise of sensitive spirits in an age of rapid, confident material progress: the feeling of alienation from an acquisitive, unthinking society combined with the loss of traditional religious faith, and the resultant groping, in what seemed a bleak and meaningless universe, for a modus vivendi; the necessity of striving for an integrated self that could surmount both the distractions of the bustling outer world and the passions and confusions of the inner one. Arnold's sense of darkness and desolation received its finest expression in *Dover Beach*. In his fullest analysis of the modern "dialogue of the mind with itself," Empedocles, the physician and philosopher, is driven to suicide because he can no longer (like Arnold's Sophocles) see life steadily and see it whole: his restless, skeptical intellect has withered his capacity for simple feeling, faith, and joy — a capacity embodied in the young singer Callicles. *Empedocles on Etna* dramatizes one of the tensions that run through Arnold's poetry. Simple, strong, spontaneous feeling — represented variously and nostalgically by response to nature, by Wordsworth, by the biblical or classical infancy of the race, by the poet's own lost youth and his love for the mysterious "Marguerite" of a number of lyrics — has been dried up by the Stoic discipline he had imposed upon himself in his quest for unity and totality of character and purpose; yet the poet is not sure whether feeling is indeed a treacherous siren or the truest of all guides.

Arnold did not emulate Empedocles, but was able to move from the poetry of despair into prose which diagnosed and prescribed for the ills of the age with incisive clarity and wit — and with the fundamental seriousness of a high-minded crusader. In his writings on literature — the preface to his *Poems* of 1853, *On Translating Homer* (1861–62), *Essays in Criticism* (1865, 1888), and others — Arnold applied, with varying emphases, his definition of criticism as "a disinterested endeavor to learn and propagate the best that is known and thought in the world, and thus to establish a current of fresh and true ideas." He stood for detached disinterestedness against partisan action, for European cosmopolitanism against English insularity, for classicism (centrality and totality of moral vision, "imaginative reason," severity of style) against romantic subjectivity, emotionalism, and decorative excess (the English romantic poets, with all their creative energy, "did not know enough"), for a critical traditionalism and disciplined taste against shallow contemporaneity and vulgarity. Arnold was fully in the old humanistic tradition in believing that literature should fortify and ennoble its readers — and proved his sincerity by withdrawing *Empedocles* because, he felt, it did not achieve a genuinely tragic catharsis.

Arnold's central work of social criticism, *Culture and Anarchy* (1869), dealt with a main problem of modern industrial democracy: how was the new multitude of voters created by the second Reform Act (1867) to gain the knowledge and critical enlightenment needed for its new and immense responsibility? Much of the book is valid for our day as well as Arnold's. His conception of culture — so often unjustly assailed by contemporaries as literary dilettantism for the few — was only a broader name for his conception of criticism: it was "a pursuit of our total perfection," "the true goal of all of us." His capacity for phrasemaking appears in his chapter headings: "Sweetness and Light" (taken over from Swift to describe a finely tempered nature ordered by beauty and intelligence); "Barbarians, Philistines, Populace" (aristocracy, middle and lower class); "Hebraism and Hellenism" (the English — and Americans — have a Puritan passion for material profit and for righteousness but lack disinterested play of mind). The inadequacy of Mill's doctrine of liberty as freedom

from restraint is exposed by the mere title "Doing As One Likes." Here and in the lighter sequel, *Friendship's Garland* (1871), indeed everywhere, Arnold punctures popular gospels and slogans. Believers in external progress exult in trains that run every fifteen minutes — trains that carry a man "from an illiberal, dismal life at Islington to an illiberal, dismal life at Camberwell." Arnold's wit is urbane and lethal; he kept, as Chesterton said, "a smile of heartbroken forbearance, as of the teacher in an idiot school."

Culture and Anarchy was in some sense the first of Arnold's religious books, since he sought "to make reason and the will of God prevail," and since he appealed continually to the standard of "right reason," the old Stoic-Christian conception of what Richard Hooker had called "the general and perpetual voice of men" which "is as the sentence of God himself": in Arnoldian terms, "our best self" must purge and elevate "our ordinary self," a process that can be aided by a right understanding and functioning of the State. In *Literature and Dogma* (1873) and later books — going on, as he felt, from his father's religious liberalism — Arnold labored to free the spirit of Christ, the precious "fire within," from an untenable theology. These books were much attacked in their own time and have commonly been dismissed by modern critics; but they helped many troubled minds, and their essence is not altogether obsolete. In such works and in *Discourses in America* (1885) — Arnold's American tour gave birth to countless diverting anecdotes — his view of the times inclined him to reverse the relative values he had formerly given to Hebraism and Hellenism and to maintain that "conduct" is "three fourths of life."

Thus Arnold evolved, in accordance

with a consistent ideal, from a poet of loss and anxiety to a positive prophet of inward and general rebirth, a "Physician of the iron age" (his old label for Goethe) and "a Liberal of the future" (his label for himself). No doubt modern readers are drawn much more to the poet than to the prophet; but he is, or ought to be, alive in both roles.

ARP, Hans (or Jean) (Sept. 16, 1887 – June 17, 1966). Alsatian sculptor and painter. Born Strasbourg. Studied art there, in Weimar (1905–1907), and at Académie Julian in Paris (1908). Began experimenting with abstract design (1909); with Tzara and others was a founder of Dada movement (Zurich, 1916); and in 1920's joined the surrealists, participating in first exhibition (Paris, 1925). A pioneer in abstract art, Arp produced his finest works in the form of sculpture in stone and bronze, beginning in the early 1920's. Termed "concretions" by the artist, these objects suggest rather than represent organic forms; an example is *Human Concretion* (1935, Museum of Modern Art, New York). Married (1921) abstractionist Sophie Taeuber (she died in 1943). Arp also published monograph *On My Way* (1948) and collection of poems *Dreams and Projects* (1952), and others in French and German. Died in Basel.

REFERENCE: Herbert E. Read *Arp* (London 1968 and, as *The Art of Jean Arp,* New York 1968; also PB).

ASCHAM, Roger (1515 – Dec. 30, 1568). English writer and scholar. Born Kirby Wiske, Yorkshire. Entered St. John's College, Cambridge (1530); received B.A. and elected fellow (1534). As reader in Greek at Cambridge (c.1538) developed reputation as eminent classical scholar. Received annuity from Henry VIII for first book, *Toxophilus,* a discussion of archery (1545). Public Orator to the university (1546); tutor in Greek and Latin to Princess (later Queen) Elizabeth (1548–49). Secretary (1550–53) to English ambassador to Charles V, Holy Roman Emperor. Latin Secretary (1553) to Queen Mary; later to Queen Elizabeth until his death, in London. Married Margaret Howe (1554), who bore him three sons. His famous work, *The Schoolmaster,* a treatise on education (begun 1563, published 1570), together with his *Letters* established him as a master of prose style who exerted far-reaching influence on development of written English.

EDITIONS: *The Whole Works of Roger Ascham* ed. John A. Giles (3 vols. London 1864–65). *The Schoolmaster* ed. Lawrence V. Ryan (Ithaca, N.Y. 1967).
REFERENCE: Lawrence V. Ryan *Roger Ascham* (Stanford, Calif. and London 1963).

ASSIS. *See* MACHADO DE ASSIS.

AUBER, Daniel François Esprit (Jan. 29, 1782 – May 13, 1871). French composer. Born Caen; son of a violinist and art dealer in Paris who sent him to London to learn the trade. But music prevailed and Auber returned to Paris (1804), where he eventually studied composition under Cherubini. First publicly performed work: opera *Le Séjour militaire* (1813). Comic opera *La Bergère châtelaine* (1820) secured his fame, and he produced successful comic operas thereafter, among them *Le Maçon* (1825) and *Les Diamants de la couronne* (1841). His librettist, Augustin Eugène Scribe (1791–1861), was the best of the period. Auber's greatest work, *La Muette de Portici* (1828) is serious grand opera, and because of it he is considered the founder of French grand opera. Another still produced today is *Fra Diavolo* (1830). Auber became a member of the Académie des Beaux Arts (1829), director of the Paris Conservatoire (from 1842), and *maître de chapelle* to Napoleon III (1857 until fall of Napoleon). Died in Paris.

REFERENCES: Charles T. Malherbe *Auber* (Paris 1911).

AUBREY, John (Mar. 12, 1626 – June 1697). English biographer and antiquary. Born Easton Pierse, Wiltshire; father a wealthy landowner. Spent some years as undergraduate at Trinity College, then as law student in London. Developing interest in English antiquities, he pursued his studies throughout the countryside. Elected fellow of the Royal Society (1663). Met Anthony à Wood (1667), for whose *Athenae Oxonienses* he wrote brief lives of contemporaries, later collected as *Lives of Eminent Men* (1813). He is remembered for these vivid, intimate portraits. Aubrey spent much of his time avoiding creditors and enjoying the hospitality of friends in the country. Published (1696) the only work appearing in his lifetime, *Miscellanies*, a collection of supernatural curiosities. Died in Oxford. Two works on Surrey and Wiltshire appeared posthumously.

EDITION: *Aubrey's Brief Lives* ed. Olive L. Dick (Ann Arbor, Mich. 1968, also PB).
REFERENCE: Anthony Powell *John Aubrey and His Friends* (2nd ed. London 1963 and New York 1964).

AUDUBON, John James (Apr. 26, 1785 – Jan. 27, 1851). American artist, naturalist and ornithologist. Born Les Cayes, Santo Domingo; natural son of French parents; legally adopted by father and stepmother. Taken to Nantes, France (1791); educated there until 1800. Came to America (1803) and began ornithological study and sketches. Made first American bird-banding experiment (1804). Merchant in Kentucky (1807); married Lucy Bakewell (1808); became American citizen (1812). After business reverses (1819), he turned to taxidermy and teaching art. Traveled to England and Scotland (1826) to seek publication of bird drawings. First exhibition, Liverpool (1826). The elephant folio *Birds of America* (1827, serialized and expanded 1827–38) brought immediate fame. Fellow Royal Society, Edinburgh (1827), Royal Society, London (1830), and American Philosophical Society (1831). Bought (1842) estate in New York City, where he lived until his death. Other works: *Ornithological Biography* (with William MacGillivray.

5 vols. 1831–39); *Synopsis of the Birds of North America* (1839). Collaborated with Rev. John Bachman on *Viviparous Quadrupeds of North America* (5 vols. 1842–54). His nearly life-size paintings combine microscopic detail and natural setting with action and masterful decorative design. Audubon Society founded in his honor. His *Journal* appeared in 1929.

EDITIONS: *Audubon and His Journals* ed. Maria Audubon (2 vols. New York 1897, also PB). *Journal* ed. Howard Corning (Boston 1929). *Letters 1826–1840* ed. Howard Corning (2 vols. Boston 1930). *Birds of America* (7 vols. Philadelphia 1840–44, also PB).
REFERENCES: Alexander Adams *John James Audubon* (New York 1966). Francis H. Herrick *Audubon the Naturalist: A History of His Life and Times* (2nd ed. 2 vols. New York 1938, also PB).

AUGUSTINE, Saint (Aurelius Augustinus) (354–430). Christian theologian. Born Tagaste in North Africa, son of pagan father and Christian mother, St. Monica. Studied at Madauros and Carthage, where he lived with a woman who bore him a son Adeodatus (371). Teacher of rhetoric in Carthage, then Rome (383) and Milan (384). Influenced by St. Ambrose, bishop of Milan, was converted to Christianity (386); baptized (387) in Milan. Shortly thereafter returned to Tagaste; there founded monastic community where he lived quietly until ordained priest at nearby Hippo (391). Became bishop of Hippo (after 395); remained there until his death during the siege by the Vandals. In his three great works, *Confessions* (written 397–401), *On the Trinity* (written 400–416), and *The City of God* (written 413–426), and in his many polemical writings against pagans and various heretical Christian sects, Augustine established the foundations both of medieval catholicism and of protestantism. After St. Paul he has exerted strongest influence on Christianity.

TRANSLATIONS: *Basic Writings* ed. Whitney J. Oates (2 vols. New York 1948). *Selected Letters* ed. James H. Baxter (Loeb Library, Cambridge, Mass. 1930).

REFERENCES: Roy W. Battenhouse *A Companion to the Study of St. Augustine* (London and New York 1955). Jacques Chabannes *St. Augustine* (tr. New York 1962). Etienne Gilson *The Christian Philosophy of St. Augustine* (tr. New York 1960, also PB).

AUSTEN, Jane (Dec. 16, 1775 – July 18, 1817). English novelist. Born Steventon, Hampshire, youngest of seven children of Rev. George Austen. Lived all her life with her family; they later moved to Bath (1801), Southampton (1805), and Chawton (1809). Wrote *Love and Freindship* (*sic*) at fourteen (not published until 1922). *First Impressions* (written 1797) was turned down by publisher, later appeared as *Pride and Prejudice* (1813). *Elinor and Marianne* (begun 1797) was altered and published as *Sense and Sensibility* (1811). Death ended a romance (1801), and later Jane broke off a brief betrothal to an old friend. Other novels were published: *Mansfield Park* (1814); *Emma* (1815), and Jane had won a following. Her health began to fail (1816), and she moved to Winchester, where she died; she is buried in the cathedral. *Persuasion* and *Northanger Abbey* were published posthumously (1818); the latter was written in 1797, sold to a London publisher (1803), but never issued. Other fragments were published later: *Lady Susan* and *The Watsons* in J. E. Austen-Leigh's *Memoir of Jane Austen* (1871), and *Sanditon* (begun 1817, published 1925).

EDITIONS: *The Novels of Jane Austen* ed. Robert W. Chapman (5 vols. 3rd ed. London 1934 and New York 1935). *Minor Works* ed. Robert W. Chapman (London and New York 1954). *Letters to Her Sister Cassandra and Others* coll. and ed. Robert W. Chapman (New York and London 1952).
REFERENCES: J. E. Austen-Leigh *A Memoir of Jane Austen* (London 1870, reissue London 1951 and New York 1962). William and Richard A. Austen-Leigh *Jane Austen: Her Life and Letters: A Family Record* (London and New York 1913). Robert W. Chapman *Jane Austen: Facts and Problems* (London and New York 1949). Marvin Mudrick *Jane Austen: Irony as Defense and Discovery* (Princeton, N.J. and London 1952, also PB).

≈

JANE AUSTEN
BY EUDORA WELTY

Jane Austen will soon be closer in calendar time to Shakespeare than to us. Yet how could these novels ever seem remote? For one thing, the noise! What a commotion comes out of their pages! The exuberance of her youthful characters is one of the unaging delights of her work. Through all the mufflings of time we can hear their clamorous joys and griefs, all giving voice to a tireless relish of life. The gaiety is unextinguished today, the irony has kept its bite, the reasoning is still sweet, the sparkle undiminished. Their high spirits, their wit, their celerity and harmony of motion, their symmetry of design are still unrivaled in the English novel. As comedies they are irresistible and as nearly flawless as any fiction could be.

The felicity they have for us must partly lie in the confidence they take for granted between the author and her readers. We remember that the young Jane read her chapters aloud to her own lively, vocative family, upon whose shrewd intuition, practiced and eager estimation of conduct, and general rejoicing in character she relied almost as strongly as upon her own. The novels still have a bloom of shared pleasure. At any rate, Jane Austen enjoyed from the first a warm confidence in an understanding reception. As all her work testifies, her time, her place, her location in society are no more to be taken in question than the fact that she was a woman. She wrote from a perfectly solid and firm foundation, and her work is wholly affirmative.

There is probably some good connection between this confidence and the flow of comedy. Comedy is sociable and positive, and exacting; its methods, its boundaries, its *point*, all belong to the familiar.

Jane Austen required no more than the familiar. Given: one household in the country; add its valuable neighbor — and there, under her quickening hands, is the full presence of the world. Life, as if coming in response to a call for good sense, is instantaneously at hand and astir and in strong vocal power. Convenient and constant communication goes on between those two households; the day, the week, the season fill to the brim with news, arrivals, tumult and crises, and the succeeding invitations. Everybody doing everything together — what mastery she has over the scene, the family scene! The dinner parties, the walking parties, the dances, picnics, concerts, excursions to Lyme Regis and sojourns at Bath, all give their testimony to Jane Austen's ardent belief that the unit of everything worth knowing in life is in the family, that family relationships are the natural basis of every other relationship.

Perennial objectors like to ask how Jane Austen, a spinster who lived all her life in her father's rectory and in later family homes in Bath, Southampton, and Chawton, whose notion of going elsewhere was an excursion to Lyme Regis, could have had any way of knowing very much about life. But who among novelists ever more instantly recognized the absurd when she saw it in human behavior, then polished it off to more devastating effect, than this young daughter of a Hampshire rectory? Jane Austen was born knowing a great deal — for one thing, that the interesting situations of life can, and notably do, take place at home. In country parsonages the dangerous confrontations and the de-

cisive skirmishes can very conveniently be arranged.

Her world, small in size but drawn exactly to scale, may of course be regarded as a larger world seen at a judicious distance — it would be the exact distance at which all haze evaporates, full clarity prevails, and true perspective appears. But it is more to the point to suppose that her stage was small because such were her circumstances and that, in fact, she was perfectly equipped to recognize in its very dimensions the first virtue and principle of her art. The focus she uses is for the same end: it is central. A clear ray of light strikes full upon the scene, and the result is the prism of comedy.

And of her given world she sees and defines both sides — sensibility as well as sense, for instance — and presents them in their turns, in a continuous attainment of balance: moral, aesthetic, and dramatic balance. This angelic ingenuity in the way of narrative and this generous dispensation of the understanding could be seen in their own brilliant way as still other manifestations of her comic genius. The action of her novels is in itself a form of wit, a kind of repartee; some of it is the argument of souls.

It cannot be allowed that there is any the less strength of feeling in the novels of Jane Austen because they are not tragedies. Great comic masterpieces that they are, their roots are nourished at the primary sources. Far from denying the emotions their power, she employs them to excellent advantage. Nothing of human feeling has been diminished; its intensity is at her command. But the effect of the whole is still that of proportions kept, symmetry maintained, and the classical form honored — indeed celebrated. And we are still within the balustrades of comedy.

If the life Jane Austen wrote about was different from ours, how more different still was the frame through which she saw it. Her frame was that of *belonging to her world*. She could step through it, in and out of it as easily and unselfconsciously as she stepped through the doorway of the rectory and into the garden to pick strawberries. She was perfectly at home in what she knew, and what she knew has remained what all of us want to know.

Pride and Prejudice, Sense and Sensibility, Persuasion, looked at not only as titles but as the themes they are, are lustrous with long and uninterrupted use. Though at first glance they might not be recognized, it is possible to see most of them today in their own incarnations. They withstand time, and Jane Austen's comedies withstand time, for the same reason: they pertain not to the ever-changing outside world but to what goes on perpetually in the mind and heart.

We have our own fiction about the mind and heart today, but these are still the same dangerous territories that Jane Austen knew as well as the shrubbery walks at Steventon. Their unchangeableness strikes us forcibly when we read her novels. Man's accomplishments have reached a higher figure in our day, he may fly to the moon at any moment, but this is in contrast to the very small range of the feelings that drive him. All his motives can still be counted on his fingers.

For the best reason of all, the six masterpieces of Jane Austen cannot seem remote: they have a life of their own. The brightness of Jane Austen's eye simply does not grow dim, as have grown the outlines and colors of the scene she herself saw and lived in while she wrote — its actualities, like its customs and clothes, have receded from us forever. But her page is dazzlingly alive. Her world that is so far seems near when in her charge all its animation is disclosure. But though radiant, it is of course not near. It has to remain fixed in its own time and place, whole and intact, inviolable as a diamond. It abides in its original element, and this is of course the mind. It is not her world or her time, but her art, that is and ever was approachable. The reader is the only traveler. The novels are a destination.

BABEL, Isaac Emmanuilovich (1894–1941). Russian short story writer. Born Odessa, son of a Jewish shopkeeper. Studied Hebrew, Yiddish, the Bible and the Talmud at home; attended schools in Odessa and Kiev; graduated from University of Saratov. In St. Petersburg met Maxim Gorki, who published his first short stories in magazine *Annals* (1916), then sent him out to gain experience of the world. Served (1917–1924) in Russian Imperial Army, the revolutionary forces, and the secret police. Also worked as reporter and printer's copy editor. Experiences as a soldier inspired his savage stories in *Odessa Tales* (1923–24), which made him famous overnight, and *Red Cavalry* (1926). A brilliant stylist, he also wrote, in Russian-Yiddish dialect, stories about Jewish life in his native town; two dramas, *Sunset* (1928) and *Maria* (1935); and a screenplay, *Benia Krik* (1927). Officially criticized for defaming the heroes of the Russian Revolution in his war stories, Babel fell victim to the Stalinist purges of the 1930's and was sent (1938) to a concentration camp in Siberia, where he died.

TRANSLATIONS: *Collected Stories* ed. and tr. Walter Morison (New York 1955, also PB). *Lyubka, the Cossack, and Other Stories* tr. Andrew MacAndrew (New York PB 1963). *Isaac Babel: The Lonely Years, 1925–1939* (unpublished stories and private correspondence) tr. Andrew MacAndrew and Max Hayward, ed. Nathalie Babel (New York PB 1964). *You Must Know Everything: Stories 1915–1937* tr. Max Hayward and ed. Nathalie Babel (New York 1969).

BACH, Carl Philipp Emanuel (Mar. 8, 1714 – Dec. 15, 1788). German composer. Born Weimar, second surviving son of Johann Sebastian Bach. Studied at St. Thomas School, Leipzig, then at University of Frankfurt. Became court cembalist to Frederick the Great (1740). Married Johanna Maria Dannemann (1744). Secured release from his post under the autocratic Frederick (1767) and succeeded Georg Philipp Telemann (1681–1767) as musical director of the principal church in Hamburg. Published *An Investigation into the True Way to Play the Clavier* (two parts, 1753, 1762), the first systematic study of the art, which influenced Haydn and Mozart. C. P. E. Bach is an important figure in transition between baroque and classical eras, especially in shift of interest from counterpoint to harmony. Helped develop the sonata-allegro form. His symphonies, reflecting *Sturm und Drang* movement, often embody great dramatic power, particularly because of their unusual and abrupt modulations. Best-known works are his 210 solo clavier pieces. Died in Hamburg.

REFERENCE: Karl and Irene Geiringer *The Bach Family* (London and New York 1954). Percy Young *The Bachs, 1500–1850* (New York 1970).

BACH, Johann Christian (Sept. 5, 1735 – Jan. 1, 1782). German composer. Born Leipzig, youngest son of Johann Sebastian Bach. After father's death, traveled to Italy, where he studied with Padre Martini, was converted to Catholicism, and wrote much church music. Organist of Milan Cathedral (1760–1762). Shifting his interest to opera, he produced *Artaserse* in Turin (1761).

To London (1762) as composer for King's Theatre, where his operas *Orione, ossia Diana vendicata* and *Zanaida* were successfully produced (1763). Appointed music master to Queen Charlotte and her children (1763), he enjoyed social prominence. Married Cecilia Grassi, a singer (1773). Remained musically active in England for the rest of his life, giving a full season of concerts each year; died in London. J. C. Bach wrote songs, symphonies, overtures, clavier concerti, and chamber music in a style that was entertaining, finely wrought, thematically varied. His use of instrumental color and the resources of Italian melody strongly influenced the development of the classical symphony

REFERENCES: Karl and Irene Geiringer *The Bach Family* (London and New York 1954). Charles Sanford Terry *John Christian Bach* (2nd ed. London and New York 1967). Percy Young *The Bachs, 1500–1850* (New York 1970).

BACH, Johann Sebastian (Mar. 21, 1685 – July 28, 1750). German composer. Born Eisenach, Thuringia, of family of professional musicians. Orphaned (1695), he went to Ohrdruf to live with eldest brother, then to the Particularschule of St. Michael's Church, Lüneburg (1700–1702). Organist of St. Boniface Church, Arnstadt (1703–1707). Married (1707) his cousin Maria Barbara Bach; she died (1720) after bearing him seven children. In 1721 he married Anna Magdalena Wilcken (1701–1760) by whom he had thirteen more children. Court organist at Weimar (1708–17); then for six years kapellmeister for duke of Cöthen. Settled at Leipzig (1723), where he was director of music and cantor of St. Thomas School, responsible to town council for music in the main churches. Made kapellmeister to prince of Saxe-Weissenfels (1729) and Royal Polish and Electoral Saxon court composer (1736). Died at Leipzig. In his lifetime, Bach was more famous as organist than as composer. Among his major works: *Brandenburg Concerti* (1721), *The Well-Tempered Clavier* (Part I, 1722; Part II, 1744), *St. Matthew Passion* (1729), *Mass in B Minor*

(begun 1733), *The Musical Offering* (1747), *The Art of Fugue* (1748–50).

REFERENCES: Karl and Irene Geiringer *Johann Sebastian Bach: The Culmination of an Era* (New York 1966 and London 1967). Albert Schweitzer *J. S. Bach* (tr. 2 vols. London 1947 and New York 1950, also PB). Philipp Spitta *Johann Sebastian Bach* (tr. 2 vols. London and New York 1951). Charles Sanford Terry *Bach: A Biography* (2nd ed. London and New York 1933) and *The Music of Bach: An Introduction* (London and New York 1933, also PB). Percy Young *The Bachs, 1500–1850* (New York 1970).

✍

JOHANN SEBASTIAN BACH
BY MICHAEL STEINBERG

Johann Sebastian Bach was born into a family whose members had been professional musicians since early in the seventeenth century and were to be so almost halfway into the nineteenth. His parents were the Eisenach town musician, Johann Ambrosius Bach, and Elisabeth Lämmerhirt, and the ancestors of both had come to Thuringia as refugees from anti-Lutheran persecution.

Sebastian attended Latin school at Eisenach, lost his mother at nine, his father not quite a year later, and was sent to live with his fourteen-years-older brother Johann Christoph, organist at Ohrdruf. At fifteen, he became a choirboy at Lüneburg. By eighteen, his apprentice years were over. He went as organist to Arnstadt, having, while negotiations were in progress, filled in as "violinist and lackey" at Weimar. From Arnstadt, he moved to Mühlhausen for a year, and in 1708, taking a big step up this time, he became court organist at Weimar. From 1717 to 1723, he was music director at the court of Anhalt-Cöthen, a Calvinist enclave where unaccompanied hymns were the only music permitted in the austere church services, and where

Bach's function was to provide the instrumental chamber music of which his ·prince was a connoisseur. After Cöthen came Leipzig, where Bach moved in 1723 to become cantor at St. Thomas School and director of music at the churches of St. Thomas and St. Nicholas. He remained there until his death. He was married twice: to his cousin Maria Barbara, among whose seven children were the composers Wilhelm Friedemann and Carl Philipp Emanuel, and to Anna Magdalena Wilcken, twenty at the time of her marriage, an excellent soprano, the mother of thirteen, including Johann Christian, and who went to an almswoman's grave.

Eisenach, Ohrdruf, Arnstadt, Mühlhausen, Weimar, Cöthen, and Leipzig are in a circle of fifty miles' radius. Lüneburg is perhaps a hundred miles from the center of that circle to the north and west, and there were, for Bach, occasional journeys to Lübeck, Hamburg, Dresden, and Berlin, to hear a great performer like Buxtehude, to play a concert or audition for a job, to collect a newly built harpsichord for his patron, to see a new grandchild. But the real stations of Bach's life were within that circle, and it was a life in complete contrast to that of his globe-trotting, infinitely more famous contemporary Handel, whom he never met, though he once traveled to Halle to try. Bach had an enviable reputation as a keyboard virtuoso (he was also a first-rate string player), and he had been known since before he was twenty as a much feared expert on organ building. At eighteen, he dismayed the Arnstadt congregation with his adventurous hymn accompaniments. In his sixties, he was considered a composer of formidable learning, one whose music was old-fashioned in its "difficulty" and unconcern for charm. In

the decades following his death, he was the great underground composer, his reputation guarded by a devoted inner circle whose chief figure was his second surviving son, Carl Philipp Emanuel. He read theology for instruction and recreation, and he enjoyed intellectual complexities, including half-playful outposts like numerology. Like many Bachs, Sebastian was a scratchy man, proud to the point of touchiness, an impatient colleague, and anything other than a subservient, unproblematic employee. His Arnstadt and Mühlhausen engagements ended with relief on both sides; he spent his last twenty-six days at Weimar in jail because, with his way of doing things not quite tactfully, he had accepted the Cöthen appointment without first securing release from his current contract; at Leipzig the town council, which had begun ostentatiously exploring potential successors months before his death, took posthumous revenge by deducting from Anna Magdalena's tiny pension the two months' salary Bach had been paid twenty-seven years earlier between the signing of the contract and his actually going to work.

Like any eighteenth-century composer, Bach began by disciplining his inspiration so as to compose whatever his position required. At Arnstadt, Mühlhausen, and Weimar, he was an organist, and those were years primarily of writing organ music. The big virtuoso pieces like the *D Minor Toccata* and the *Passacaglia* come from that period, and so do most of the chorale-preludes. In Cöthen, Bach wrote concerti, sonatas, solo suites for harpsichord, violin, and cello, the *Inventions*, and the first book of the *Well-Tempered Clavier*. Leipzig, too, began that way, with the *St. John Passion*, the *Magnificat*, and an enormous number of church cantatas appearing in the first four years. By 1730 or so, Bach's attitudes and professional habits had begun to change, and, rather like a modern university professor, he had begun to think of distinctions between his obligations and his "real work." After the *St. Matthew Passion* of 1729, he produced vocal music mainly by arranging and adapting his own earlier works, and for many years he composed relatively little, at least by the standards of his previous extraordinary industry.

Bach had gone to Leipzig half reluctantly. He had first thought of settling at Cöthen for life, but the death of Maria Barbara, and then the marriage of his *Serenissimus,* whose "musical interests [became] somewhat lukewarm, especially as the new Princess seemed to be an *amusa,*" had after all made him restless and unhappy. There was prestige to the position at St. Thomas, and Bach was aware of the advantages the excellent school and the university at Leipzig offered his growing family. On the other hand, a change from kapellmeister to cantor was not really a step up, and Bach was reluctant to embroil himself in an educational and civic bureaucracy with which, in fact, he never ceased to quarrel. He had hesitated, therefore, and the town councillors, for their part, elected Bach as their third choice after George Philipp Telemann, who had used Leipzig merely as a means of getting a huge raise in Hamburg, and Christoph Graupner, who would have been delighted to leave Darmstadt but who could not get out of his contract there. Bach's difficulties with the school and town authorities are well documented. We know, too, that at least into the early 1730's he considered moving again. Later, school and church were still the centers of his professional life, though as a per-

former he became more and more involved with the university's Collegium Musicum, while as a composer he became increasingly introspective and inclined to pursue purely musical inclinations.

When Bach selected six of his Cöthen concerti to send to the margrave of Brandenburg, he made sure that each was for a different combination of instruments. He wanted to delight, of course, but he also wanted to offer a demonstration of the variety he could achieve with no more than eighteen players. So, all his life, Bach assembled cycles and systematic collections, designed to explore an idea as exhaustively and with as much variety as possible: a whole liturgical calendar of organ chorales, preludes and fugues in all major and minor keys (twice), and so forth. Then, all his life, Bach was a teacher: the *Inventions* and the *Well-Tempered Clavier* grew out of notebooks he used in instructing Wilhelm Friedemann. Later, there were still more children, the gifted Anna Magdalena, visiting cousins, sons-in-law, and other pupils. The two currents in Bach's life, the systematic and the didactic, meet gloriously in the works of the last years; following years of meditation, of studying his home-copied library of music from Palestrina to Pergolesi that he had begun as a small boy by moonlight, of seeming to lie fallow, he produced the *Goldberg Variations,* the *Musical Offering* on the theme Frederick the Great gave him for extemporization in Berlin in 1747, and the unfinished *Art of Fugue.* Bach turned his isolation from public musical life to his advantage, using the years to set his spiritual and intellectual house in order, to complete long-begun projects, to consider, revise, refine, and collect, to attempt to codify his skills because he knew what they were worth. By no means a revolutionary, Bach was the great synthesizer of traditions and ideas, who enriched whatever he inherited, and who, in the words of Webern, "composed and grasped everything conceivable."

BACON, Sir Francis (Jan. 22, 1561 – Apr. 9, 1626). English philosopher, essayist, historian and statesman. Born London, son of Sir Nicholas (1509–1579), lord keeper of the great seal under Queen Elizabeth I. Entered Trinity College, Cambridge (1573); admitted to Gray's Inn (1576). Soon went abroad with English ambassador to France; after wide travel returned to England (1579). Admitted to the bar (1582); entered Parliament two years later, quickly attaining distinction. Had published political pamphlets before appearance of first book of *Essays* (1597). Participated in prosecution of former patron Essex for treason (1601). A zealous courtier under James I, he became knight (1603), attorney general (1613), lord keeper (1617), lord chancellor (1618), Baron Verulam (1618), Viscount St. Albans (1621). Married Alice Barnham (1606). Expelled from court after proceedings on charges of bribery (1621), to which he confessed; spent rest of his life in retirement. Died at Highgate. Bacon projected a large philosophical work, *Instauratio Magna*, but completed only two parts, *The Advancement of Learning* (1605), later expanded in Latin as *De Augmentis Scientiarum* (1623), and *Novum Organum* (1620). His contribution to philosophy was his application of the inductive method of modern science; he urged full investigation in all cases, avoiding theories based on insufficient data. Other major writings: *Essays* (1597, 1612, 1625), his most popular work, aphoristic and full of practical wisdom; *History of Henry VII* (1622); *The New Atlantis* (1627).

EDITION: *The Complete Works of Francis Bacon* ed. James Spedding, R. L. Ellis, and D. D. Heath (14 vols. London 1857–74); last 7 volumes, *The Letters and Life* by Spedding, also published separately.

REFERENCES: Catherine Drinker Bowen *Francis Bacon: The Temper of a Man* (Boston 1963, PB 1965). Adwin W. Green *Sir Francis Bacon* (New York 1966).

BAGEHOT, Walter (Feb. 3, 1826 – Mar. 24, 1877). English economist and journalist. Born Langport, Somerset. Educated at Bristol College and University College, London; graduated in mathematics (1846), then studied law before entering father's banking business (1852). Married (1858) daughter of James Wilson, founder and editor of the *Economist*, which Bagehot edited from 1860 until his death, at Langport. Major works: *The English Constitution* (1867), analysis of British constitutional system as a two- instead of three-part entity, distinguishing between its effective and its merely formal institutions; *Physics and Politics* (1872), which applies Darwin's natural selection theory to development of societies; *Lombard Street* (1873), on the money market; *Literary Studies* (1879); and *Economic Studies* (unfinished; published 1880). Bagehot was an acute and independent thinker on many subjects, and had a great gift for lucid statement.

EDITION: *Collected Works* ed. Norman St. John-Stevas (4 vols. Cambridge, Mass. and London 1965).

REFERENCES: Alastair Buchan *The Spare Chancellor: The Life of Walter Bagehot* (London 1959 and East Lansing, Mich. 1960). William Irvine *Walter Bagehot* (London and New York 1939).

BALZAC, Honoré de (May 20, 1799 – Aug. 18, 1850). French novelist. Born Tours, son of a civil servant. Neglected in childhood, he was sent to boarding schools at Vendôme (1807–13) and in Paris (1814–16). Worked in lawyers' offices (1816–19), where he acquired his extensive knowledge of criminal and bankruptcy law. In pursuit of fame and wealth he produced, rapidly and pseudonymously, sensational novels (1821–28). In 1829 he published his first serious work under own name, *Les Chouans*, and scored considerable success with *La Physiologie du mariage*. In the next twenty years he produced an enormous body of novels and stories, linked by the reappearance of individual characters and known collectively as *La Comédie humaine*. Among the best known: *La Peau de Chagrin* (1831), *Eugénie Grandet* (1833), *Le Père Goriot* (1834). Despite literary success, he was throughout his life harassed by debts, which were increased by his numerous business ventures. In 1833 met Polish countess Evelina Hanska, who became his mistress and whom he married five months before his death in Paris.

REFERENCES: Maurice Bardèche *Balzac romancier* (2nd ed. Paris 1947). Albert Béguin *Balzac visionnaire* (Paris 1946). Philippe Bertault *Balzac, l'homme et l'oeuvre* (Paris 1946, tr. *Balzac and the Human Comedy,* New York 1963). André Maurois *Prometheus: The Life of Balzac* (tr. London and New York 1965). E. J. Oliver *Honoré de Balzac* (London and New York 1964). See also Martin Turnell *The Novel in France* (London 1950, New York 1951).

HONORÉ DE BALZAC
BY MARTIN TURNELL

One day in the spring of 1833 Balzac burst breathlessly into the home of his sister with the words: "Salute me. I am well on the way to becoming a genius!" It was one of the great moments in the history of nineteenth-century literature. The most celebrated novelist of the age had discovered his vocation.

Balzac, as we know, began his professional career as the anonymous author of thrillers. The formative influences were Walter Scott, Fenimore Cooper and Mrs. Radcliffe. The first of his books that "counts" was published in 1829, but it was not until the appearance of *Le Médecin de campagne* four years later that he hit on the device of the "reappearing character." He owed it to the sudden realization that there were no connecting links between the different volumes of the Waverley Novels. The discovery was vital. It gave the *Comédie humaine* a wholly original form of unity which was later adopted by Zola, Proust, and a host of other novelists.

He had already published eighteen novels or stories. They were revised in the light of the new principle and incorporated into the *Comédie humaine*. From that time onward everything he wrote was planned to fit into the grand design.

The *Comédie humaine* is divided into three groups: "Studies of Manners," "Philosophical Studies," "Analytical Studies." The "Analytical Studies" contain only his two treatises on marriage; the "Philosophical Studies" consist mainly of occult works of fiction which though not among his greatest achievements do provide the *Comédie humaine* with a kind of philosophical basis. "Studies of Manners" is by far the largest and most important of the three groups. It is subdivided into five sections: "Scenes from Private Life," "Scenes from Provincial Life," "Scenes from Parisian Life," "Scenes from Political Life," and "Scenes from Country Life." A sixth section, "Scenes from Military Life," was planned but never written.

In the celebrated foreword to the first collected edition of his work in 1842 Balzac drew a parallel between "zoological species" and the "social species" which were the subject of his novels. In the course of his survey he deals with life in every class from the aristocracy to the peasantry. He also deals with all the professions and all the principal interests of society: banking, commerce, medicine, the priesthood, journalism, the civil service. More important still, he shows the profound effect on public and private life of the new forces which developed during the nineteenth century: the press, the bureaucracy, and high finance.

Balzac's boast was no idle one. He possessed genius and possessed it abundantly. His magnificent intelligence was superior to that of almost any of his predecessors among French novelists or any of his successors until we come to Proust. Yet there is something unsatisfactory and unsatisfying about his work. He has been called a Renaissance man born out of due time. There is the same enormous vitality, the same breadth of interests, the same untidiness. But the vitality is somehow a sick vitality; the interests are unorganized; the untidiness more damaging than it should have been, and the splendid mind was clouded by the intensive study of fifth-rate theosophical systems which hampered its natural power. For at the Renaissance there was still a tradition which provided the writer with a discipline that enabled him to use his talent to the full instead of wasting it in an attempt to create the conditions in which art becomes possible.

For many critics he is the greatest novelist who ever lived. For me he is a captive and a mutilated genius. He was the captive of his age, his environment, his extravagance, his creditors, his women, and his work. His genius is mutilated in the sense that far too much that was alien and corrupt found its way into the novels. The truth is that the great man never managed to break away from the influences of his first masters or his early environment. A curious streak of immaturity runs through his entire work. His characters are divided into "good" and "bad," "heroes" and "villains" in the manner of the adventure story. *Le Père Goriot,* the most famous of all the novels, illustrates his chief weaknesses: his rhetoric, his melodrama, his sentimentality.

Baudelaire once expressed surprise that Balzac's reputation depended on passing for an "observer." "It has always seemed to me," he said, "that his great virtue lies in the fact that he was a visionary, and a passionate visionary." These few words are the foundation of all the best modern Balzac criticism. *La Cousine Bette, Eugénie Grandet, Les Illusions perdues* and *Le Curé de Tours* are undoubted masterpieces, but none of them is perfect. What he has left us is an extraordinary hallucinatory vision of French life from the Revolution to the July Monarchy. "Monstrous or prodigious?" asks one critic. It is surely both. The hallucinatory quality came from the close connection between life and literature. For Balzac's own life was sometimes more Balzacian than the novels. We remember his brutally brushing aside the story of a friend's bereavement with the words: "Let's get back to reality. Whom will Eugénie Grandet marry?" We also remember the novelist on his deathbed pathetically crying out: "Send for Bianchon [the famous doctor of the *Comédie humaine*]. He'll save me."

Yet whatever its shortcomings the influence of his great work has been immense and immensely beneficial. His technical innovations extended the scope of the novel to an astonishing degree. His prose style is not exactly elegant, but he did for the language of fiction what Victor Hugo did for the language of poetry: he forged a new instrument which was infinitely more varied than Stendhal's eighteenth-century prose. Proust spoke acidly of his "vulgarity." He was a greater novelist than Balzac, but his debt to Balzac is incalculable. Without Balzac's liberating influence, could Proust have invented a language capable of expressing his own vision or his marvelous psychological insights? Without Vautrin would there have been a Charlus? Without Balzac, indeed, would there have been a Marcel Proust at all?

BARBEY D'AUREVILLY, Jules Amédée (Nov. 2, 1808 – Apr. 23, 1889). French writer. Born St.-Sauveur-le-Vicomte, Manche, into a family among the minor nobility. Attended Collège Stanislas in Paris (1827–29), studied law at Caen (1829–33). From 1833 lived in Paris; served as literary and drama critic on several newspapers. Was successful, despite poverty, in establishing himself as a dandy. Appointed to alternate with Sainte-Beuve as literary critic for *Le Constitutionnel* (1868), and on latter's death (1869) took over the position. One of the first to appreciate Balzac, Stendhal and Baudelaire, Barbey d'Aurevilly was called High Constable of Letters for his ability as critic, though his judgment was often affected by vehement royalist and Catholic bias. Died in Paris. Critical articles collected in *Les Prophètes du passé* (1851), *Les Oeuvres et les hommes du XIXe siècle* (26 vols. 1861–1909), and *Le Théâtre contemporain* (5 vols. 1888–96). Fiction includes novels *L'Ensorcelée* (1854), *Le Chevalier des Touches* (1864), *Un Prêtre marié* (1865), and a collection of short stories, *Les Diaboliques* (1874, tr. *The She-Devils* 1964), often considered his masterpiece.

REFERENCES: Roger Bésus *Barbey d'Aurevilly* (Paris 1958). Brian G. Rogers *The Novels and Stories of Barbey d'Aurevilly* (Geneva, Switzerland, 1967).

BARCLAY, Alexander (c.1475 – June 10, 1552). English poet. Birthplace unknown. Studied at universities in England, France, and Italy. Took holy orders, and became in succession chaplain of college of Ottery St. Mary, Devonshire; Benedictine monk at Ely; Franciscan monk at Canterbury; vicar of Great Baddow, Essex, and Wokey, Somerset. Died at Croydon, before he could assume duties of rector of All Hallows, London. Fame rests on *The Ship of Fools* (*The Ship of Folys of the Worlde,* 1509), rhyme royal adaptation of *Das Narrenschiff* (1494), a popular satire in German by Sebastian Brant. Barclay's *Eclogues* (1515–21), adaptations from Aeneas Sylvius (Pope Pius II) and Mantuan, were the first in English. Also wrote prose translation of Sallust's *Bellum Jugurthinum* (1520).

EDITIONS: *The Eclogues of Alexander Barclay* ed. Beatrice White (London and New York 1928). *Life of St. George* ed. William Nelson (London and New York 1955). *The Ship of Fools* ed. T. H. Jamieson (Edinburgh and London 1874).

BARRIE, Sir James Matthew (May 9, 1860 – June 19, 1937). Scottish novelist and playwright. Born Kirriemuir, Angus, son of a weaver. Studied at Edinburgh University (M.A. 1882) and spent two years on *Nottingham Journal* before settling in London as free-lance writer (1885). *Auld Licht Idylls* (1888) and *A Window in Thrums* (1889), collections of Scottish sketches, caught public attention. His novel *The Little Minister* (1891) was successfully dramatized (1897), and from that time Barrie produced a stream of popular plays, among them *Quality Street* (1901), *The Admirable Crichton* (1902), *Peter Pan* (1904; the story appeared as *Peter and Wendy,* 1911), *Dear Brutus* (1917), *Mary Rose* (1920). Marriage (1894) to actress Mary Ansell ended in divorce (1910). Received baronetcy (1913) and Order of Merit (1922); was rector of St. Andrews University (1919–22) and chancellor of Edinburgh University (from 1930). Died in London. Whimsy, sentimentality, and a longing for the magical world of childhood characterized Barrie's plays, at a time when the theater was dominated by social realism.

REFERENCES: *Letters* ed. Viola Meynell (London 1942 and New York 1947). Lady Cynthia Asquith *Portrait of Barrie* (London 1954 and New York 1955). Denis G. Mackail *Barrie: The Story of J.M.B.* (London and New York 1941).

BARTÓK, Béla (Mar. 25, 1881 – Sept. 26, 1945). Hungarian composer. Born Nagyszentimiklos. Mother taught him piano at age of five. In 1894 he began to study music seriously, first with Laszlo Erkel, then at Budapest Academy of Music. First major orchestral work: the *Kossuth Symphony,* performed in Budapest (1904). Appointed professor of piano at Budapest Academy (1907–34). Married one of his pupils (1909). His opera *Bluebeard's Castle* performed in Budapest (1927). Divorced his wife and married Ditta Pasztory (1923), with whom he gave duo piano recitals. Moved to United States (1940), where five years later he died in poverty, in New York. Bartók combined folk material with what were during his lifetime advanced tendencies in modern music. Later major works: three piano concerti; six string quartets; *Music for Strings, Percussion, and Celesta* (1936); *Concerto for Orchestra* (1943).

REFERENCES: Agatha Fassett *Naked Face of Genius: Béla Bartók's American Years* (Boston 1958). Gyorgy Kepes ed. *Module, Proportion, Symmetry, Rhythm* (New York 1960 and, as *Module, Symmetry, Proportion,* London 1966). Halsey Stevens *The Life and Music of Béla Bartók* (rev. ed. New York and London 1964).

✍

BÉLA BARTÓK
BY ROBERT PARRIS

That a cheerful piece of music can be written in adversity continues to strike ingenuous critics and program-note mongers as astonishing and not quite cricket. "How remarkable," it generally goes, "that in 1939, Bartók, far from the Hungary he loved, and in anguish over the political and artistic upheaval in Central Europe, should have written his delightful *Divertimento for String Orchestra.*" The fact is that an artist of stature can write, at any time, any sort of music that takes his fancy. This is what style and technique are all about, after all. But if music does not lend itself to portraying outward events, a composer's work does reveal the general cast of his mind and something of the quality of his spirit. It is clear from the *Divertimento,* for example, that the composer was a man of gentle suavity and refinement who was having a marvelous time reworking the unrefined stuff of Balkan folksong. Aristocratic and folk virtues meet in Bartók; bare bones and elegant complexities continually confront each other, and one of the wonders of his music is how often he succeeds in making peace between them.

Bartók's intense involvement in ethnomusicological research dates from 1904, when he first heard an authentic Magyar peasant song and wrote it down on staff paper. He eventually made several trips into the Hungarian hinterland, often with Zoltán Kodály; they recorded thousands of indigenous melodies on wax cylinders. His fascination with music never before notated carried him to Rumania, Turkey, and North Africa; like a lepidopterist he brought back rare species, but not *sous cloche:* his original work breathes their spirit if seldom their substance, while his transcriptions, analyses, codifications and interpretations take up something like a dozen books and forty articles.

Before he was seventeen, Bartók had written a good deal of music in the German tradition that was the going model in Hungary; a bit later he discovered Strauss's *Heldenleben,* which impelled him on his own hero's life. By his early twenties he discovered that the Hungarian Rhapsodies of Liszt and the Hungarian Dances of Brahms were gypsified dilutions of the real article; then he discovered the real article. He studied the keyboard music of the baroque; he admired Debussy; Oriental, pentatonic and modal scales attracted him; finally, he took from Schoenberg and Stravinsky what he could assimilate, which wasn't much. Out of these disparities he built a style that by the time of his *Third Quartet* (1927) was exclusive and integrated.

A singularly touching piece from Bartók's young manhood is his *First Portrait for Orchestra* (1907–1908). One of its themes sounds like a quotation from Rachmaninoff's *Second Symphony*. It isn't, although both pieces were composed during precisely the same months. But no one had property rights on musical subject matter as far as Bartók was concerned: true originality lay in the transmutations of the material and in the expressivity conveyed by its formal setting. This baroque attitude was complemented by his appropriation of several constructive techniques of the early eighteenth century: monothematic movements, elaborate contrapuntal devices, phrase lengths calculated to achieve a precise measure of asymmetry, and large structures of symmetrical grandeur.

Bartók showed an infinity of musical faces to the world, but as a man he seems to have been colorless and surely all introvert. He pleaded his cause badly, relying on his music to do all the talking, which it indeed did do, but in an arcane tongue that did not endear the composer to the ticket-buying public. Luckily, Bartók was a virtuoso pianist. Like Prokofieff and Rachmaninoff, he toured for money and to show off his music, which, God knows, needed showing off; unlike that of the Russians', it was caviar to the general. Onstage he became something of a propagandist, a role that was repugnant to him in private. His recitals in the larger cities of the United States in 1927 did little to enhance his reputation as a composer, which is a shame but no surprise. The piano, for nineteenth-century composers, was a stringed instrument with hammers; Bartók, in much of his work before the 1930's, treated it as a percussion instrument with strings attached. Lovers of Chopin and Liszt were not beguiled by the savage, clanging, clustered dissonances of the *Allegro barbaro* and the *Sonata;* many of them still aren't. With the *Second Piano Concerto* (1931) and the *Sonata for Two Pianos and Percussion* (1937), his writing in general took a mellower turn, and by 1943, when he wrote the *Concerto for Orchestra,* his fire was burning cooler and prettier.

Bartók's last five years were spent in the United States. His health was bad and funds were low. As desperate as he was for money in 1940, he nevertheless refused a teaching post at the Curtis Institute in Philadelphia — all his life he had declined to teach composition for fear of its impinging detrimentally on his creative work. (At home, he had supported himself and his family by giving piano lessons; from 1907 to 1934 he was on the faculty of the Academy of Music in Budapest.) During 1941 and 1942, he made $3000 a year as visiting assistant at Columbia University; in 1943, Koussevitzky visited him in his New York hospital room to deliver a check for $500 — half the commission money for the *Concerto for Orchestra.* At about the same time, Yehudi Menuhin asked him for a solo violin sonata. In 1944 Ralph Hawkes, the publisher, commissioned a seventh string quartet (which never got written), William Primrose a viola concerto, and Bartlett and Robertson a two-piano concerto. In the same year he made something like $3000 from royalties on performances and a publisher's advance.

In 1942 he wrote to a former pupil (in English): "Our situation is getting daily worse and worse. All I can say is that never in my life since I earn my livelihood . . . have I been in such a dreadful situation as I will be probably very soon. . . . I am rather pessimistic, I lost all confidence in people, in countries, in everything. . . . Until know [sic] we had . . . two free pianos. . . . Just today I got news the upright will be taken from us. Of course we have no money to hire a second piano. . . . And each month brings a similar blow."

It is still open to question how much of this misery could have been averted, and to what extent the inhospitality he complained of was real or imagined. The facts are by no means all in. That he was penniless at the time of his death in New York from leukemia, there is no doubt at all: his doctor bills and funeral expenses were paid by the American Society of Composers, Authors and Publishers.

BARTOLOMMEO, Fra (real name **Bartolommeo di Pagolo del Fatorino;** also called **Baccio della Porta**) (Mar. 28, 1475 – Oct. 31, 1517). Italian painter. Studied with Piero di Cosimo and Cosimo Rosselli. A follower of Savonarola, he joined the Dominican order at the monastery of San Marco (1500) and gave up painting for four years. Important to his development was a visit from Raphael (1506), who taught him perspective and was in turn influenced by Bartolommeo. After visiting Venice (1508) he took Albertinelli as partner, producing the famous *St. Mark* (1517) and *St. Sebastian, Marriage of St. Catherine* (1511, Louvre, Paris), *Madonna and Saints* (1512, Uffizi, Florence). During visit to Rome (c.1514) studied later work of Raphael, Michelangelo, and Leonardo. He died in Florence. In his mature works, Bartolommeo introduced innovations in sixteenth-century painting, notably plain settings excluding picturesque detail, and for religious figures masterful treatment of drapery instead of contemporary dress. Graceful figures and brilliant pure coloring also mark his style.

REFERENCES: Lucy F. Baxter (pseudonym Leader Scott) *Fra Bartolommeo* (New York 1881 and London 1892). Gustave Gruyer *Fra Bartolommeo della Porta et Mariotto Albertinelli* (Paris 1886). See also John Addington Symonds *The Renaissance in Italy* (3rd ed. London 1927) and *The Age of Despots* (London 1930); and Giorgio Vasari *Lives of the . . . Painters, Sculptors and Architects* (1550) tr. Gaston de Vere (10 vols. London 1912–15).

BAUDELAIRE, Charles-Pierre (Apr. 9, 1821 – Aug. 31, 1867). French poet, essayist, art critic. Born Paris. Mother widowed when he was six, and married (1828) General Aupick, later ambassador to Spain and Turkey, with whom the young poet was to quarrel repeatedly. Expelled from the Collège Louis-le-Grand (1839) for disciplinary reasons (though he later obtained his *baccalauréat* with ease). In 1841, Aupick sent him on a voyage to India, which ended at Bourbon Island. Returned to Paris (1842) and lived with his mistress, the mulatto Jeanne Duval (*la Vénus noire*). Indulged in dandyism and extravagance until the Aupicks (1844) turned his inheritance into a trust, yielding small income; he was to be plagued by creditors until his death. In 1845 first published a poem, *À une Dame créole;* also *Le Salon de 1845,* first of his art criticism. A short novel, *La Fanfarlo,* was published the year (1847) he first met Marie Daubrun, who became his mistress (1852). While working on his translations of Edgar Allan Poe (which were to occupy him until 1865), continued writing poems, many inspired by the adored Madame Sabatier. Eighteen were published in *La Revue des Deux Mondes* (1855), provoking strong attacks which culminated, with publication of *Les Fleurs du mal* (1857), in a conviction for immorality and a 300-franc fine. Shattered by the action, Baudelaire nevertheless continued working on the Poe translations, his *Petits Poèmes en prose* (collected posthumously in 1868), *Les Paradis artificiels* (1860), and new poems for the augmented, final 1861 edition of *Les Fleurs du mal*. Turned down by the Academy and still plagued by creditors and bad health, Baudelaire went to Belgium (1864) in unsuccessful effort to support himself by giving lectures. Stricken with paralysis, he returned (1866) to Paris, where he died.

EDITIONS: *Oeuvres Complètes* ed. Jacques Crepet (Paris 1922–53). *Oeuvres* ed. La Pléiade: Y. G. Le Dantec (Paris 1932). Many translations.

REFERENCES: Emil Starkie *Baudelaire* (rev. ed. London 1957 and Norfolk, Conn. 1958). Martin Turnell *Baudelaire* (London 1953 and Norfolk, Conn. 1954).

✍

BAUDELAIRE

BY STEPHEN SPENDER

Rimbaud called Baudelaire *le premier voyant, roi des poètes,* UN VRAI *dieu.* There is something even more apt about this description today than when that prodigious delinquent schoolboy wrote it. Baudelaire is the Fisher King of the modern Waste Land, lord of somber realms, looking out over the future with eyes that prophesy the downfall of the age of progress, and also looking back to the past when men and women were gods and goddesses, their bodies noble machines. Inventor of the term modernism, he is the first of those great moderns who look both forward and back, who passionately contrast the dark satanic mills of the present age with the Renaissance and antiquity; Proust, Joyce, Yeats, Pound and Eliot being perhaps the last princes of his royal line.

As with these later moderns, Baudelaire's writing proceeds from an intense and dramatic awareness of the poet as an exile from the traditionalist past thrust into the modern world, where to be an artist means to be a hero and perhaps also a saint. Baudelaire interpreted this drama into all the circumstances of his personal life, which were those of the *poète maudit* living in a bourgeois society. In the famous photographs of him, his face is that of a tragicomedian acting up the roles of rejected lover of his mother, hater of his stepfather, idolater of his mulatto mistress (who could not possibly do other than behave outrageously towards the lover she could never understand), spendthrift (when he had the money), debtor hounded by his creditors, misunderstood genius execrated by bourgeois journalists and persecuted by the law, syphilitic, satanist, saint, *âme damnée* and dandy.

Much of this gets into his poems as well as into his journals and aphorisms. The poetry is enclosed within the machinery of heaven and hell and purgatory. Here, bourgeois civilization with its creed of progress is judged to be so lacking in spiritual values, good or evil, that it is difficult for a man living in it even to be damned. Baudelaire's Divine Comedy is a melodrama into whch Satan and sin have been introduced to redeem it from being about nothing but boredom. Without damnation, it is, indeed, nothing but boredom:

> *C'est l'Ennui! — l'oeil chargé d'un
>   pleur involontaire,
> Il rêve d'échafauds en fumant son
>   houka.
> Tu le connais, lecteur, ce monstre
>   délicat,
> — Hypocrite lecteur — mon sem-
>   blable — mon frère!*

The vision of ugliness, of sin, of evil, produces some of Baudelaire's greatest successes, notably *Une Charogne*, that merciless comparison of the body of the poet's mistress with the pestiferous carcass of an animal the two encounter on a beautiful morning walk. However, the satanic machinery of *Les Fleurs du Mal* is a bit creaky and the theology *simpliste*. What gives Baudelaire his *terribilità* is something much more precise than this — his clinical, analytic, instrumental eye. His ability to see institutions, epochs, cities, human flesh and feelings as functions imagized remains true today. Baudelaire stands above his material of the modern city and can lay bare the passions that make it both sublime and corrupt. The imagery which arises from a process — a soul — thus revealed is as immediate and inseparable from the process itself as the color red from blood.

Despite Baudelaire's attempts to schematize his insights and visions, the central metaphor of this poetry, so full of ships and sea and sky, is the voyage. The poet is the traveler on the earth. Although he carries a theological compass and maps of tradition, he is fundamentally a discoverer of a modern world different from the past. In his vision of man free — in the sense of his being an unconditioned being and yet trapped in circumstances which distort his nature — Baudelaire is curiously close to Shelley, though of course his theology is the opposite of Shelley's egalitarian philosophy. Shelley looks forward to a world where the unconditioned human being will cast off his chains, the world of Prometheus liberated from the tyrant God where

> *None frowned, none trembled,*
> *none with eager fear*
> *Gazed on another's eye of cold*
> *command,*
> *Until the subject of a tyrant's will*
> *Became, worse fate, the abject of*
> *his own,*
> *Which spurred him, like an out-*
> *spent horse, to death.*

Baudelaire sees the spectacle of human nature enslaved not by God but by original sin, in images not unlike those of Shelley's vision of man before his liberation.

> *La femme, esclave vile, orgueil-*
> *leuse et stupide,*
> *Sans rire s'adorant et s'aimant*
> *sans dégoût;*
> *L'homme, tyran goulu, paillard,*
> *dur et cupide,*
> *Esclave de l'esclave et ruisseau*
> *dans l'égout;*
>
> *Le bourreau qui jouit, le martyr*
> *qui sanglote;*
> *La fête qu'assaisonne et parfume*
> *le sang;*
> *Le poison de pouvoir énervant le*
> *despote,*
> *Et le peuple amoureux du fouet*
> *abrutissant . . .*

If this vision of *Le Voyage* were not set in a theological frame, it would seem simply the romantic vision of the unconditioned imprisoned within the cramping circumstances of society and under the dead hand of the past.

The romantic side of Baudelaire becomes particularly evident whenever he writes about painting, either in his poetry or his criticism. Painting was for him the depiction of the ideal, the earthly paradise. Rubens, Leonardo da Vinci, Rembrandt, Michelangelo, Watteau, Goya, Delacroix are the tutelary deities of this paradise. In his poem called, significantly, *Les Phares* they become beacons across the river of the centuries. When Baudelaire writes about painting he does not seem to feel under the obligation to relate art to theology, and he sees the problem of modern art as that of the artist being able in his own imagination to adapt the vision of the past to the heroism, boredom, and squalor of modern life. "When one says romanticism one says modern art, intimacy, spirituality, color, aspiration towards the infinite, realized by all the means available to the arts." It is in his art criticism and his writings on Poe and on Wagner that one sees the fluid, plastic imagination which Baudelaire expresses in his poetry, in the phrase borrowed from Delacroix, "imagination, queen of the faculties," without recourse to dogma. Here he clarifies what he means by beauty, an "immortal instinct that makes us consider the earth and its shows as a glimpse, a *correspondance*, of heaven." And "it is by means of and *through* poetry, by means of and *through* music, that the soul gets an inkling of the glories that lie beyond the grave."

One is tempted sometimes by the grayness and insistence on ugliness of his splenetic poems about Paris to think of Baudelaire as a realist. This mistake is corrected by his remarks about Ingres and Courbet, painters whose great power he recognizes but whom, because of the coldness of the one, the naturalism of the other, he regards as "enemies of the imagination." The hero of the imagination is the painter like Delacroix or (at an opposite extreme) Constantin Guys, who has gathered all the forms of nature into his mind like the words in a dictionary, and whose creativity Baudelaire regards as an act of pure imagination. Delacroix is the supreme genius of poetry in painting, the romantic artist who has absorbed the visions of the Renaissance into his soul and who hurls them against his contemporaries in an unending stream of dazzling visions. Constantin Guys represents Baudelaire's idea of the dandy completely contemporary, but with gaiety, courage, and style which enable him to convert the modern scene into an aristocratic art.

The insistence in *Les Fleurs du Mal*

on sin, evil, satanism, damnation, boredom, gives us a true but rather biased view of Baudelaire's own work. It was his intention to be satanic, but the performance cannot be judged entirely by the intention. There were two sides of Baudelaire. One is dark, dogmatic, malicious, almost authoritarian, but also a bit of a charlatan. The other is idealistic, elated, aesthetic, the poet who more than any other guides his bark by the star of beauty. Both are brought together in the idea of the voyager, who, however much he knows and judges, remains the discoverer, for whom even the most hideous things are rocks and islands to be passed, and for whom even the final end, whatever it may be, remains the unknown:

> O Mort, vieux capitaine, il est
> temps! levons l'ancre!
> Ce pays nous ennuie, ô Mort!
> Appareillons!
> Si le ciel et la mer sont noirs
> comme de l'encre,
> Nos coeurs que tu connais sont
> remplis de rayons!
>
> Verse-nous ton poison pour qu'il
> nous réconforte!
> Nous voulons, tant ce feu nous
> brûle le cerveau,
> Plonger au fond du gouffre, Enfer
> ou Ciel, qu'importe?
> Au fond de l'Inconnu pour trouver
> du nouveau!

BEACONSFIELD, Benjamin Disraeli, first earl of. *See* **DISRAELI.**

BEARDSLEY, Aubrey Vincent (Aug. 21, 1872 – Mar. 16, 1898). English artist. Born Brighton; attended Brighton Grammar School. Became (1888) clerk in a surveyor's office, then in an insurance company. Encouraged by Burne-Jones, he studied at Westminster

School of Art (1891). Success of illustrations for Dent's edition of *Le Morte d'Arthur* (1893–94) led to appointment as art director of the *Yellow Book* (1894) and later the *Savoy* (1896), leading literary magazines of the period. Aware that he was dying of tuberculosis, he worked with tremendous energy; notable examples among his large production are illustrations for Wilde's *Salomé* (1894), Pope's *The Rape of the Lock* (1896), Aristophanes' *Lysistrata* (1896), and Jonson's *Volpone* (1898). Beardsley was a major exponent of art nouveau. Influenced by art forms ranging from Japanese prints to French rococo, he contrasted large areas of black or white with intricate detail and fine line. Sensual, morbid, often grotesque, Beardsley's art evokes the aesthetic and decadent movement of the Yellow Nineties. Died at Menton, France, after conversion to Roman Catholicism.

EDITIONS: *Aubrey Beardsley* (collected drawings) ed. Brian E. Reade (New York 1967). *The Collected Drawings of Aubrey Beardsley* (New York 1967), *The Early Work of Aubrey Beardsley* (New York PB 1967) and *The Later Work of Aubrey Beardsley* (New York PB 1967), all edited by Bruce S. Harris.

REFERENCE: Stanley Weintraub *Beardsley: A Biography* (New York and London 1967).

BEAUMARCHAIS, Pierre Augustin Caron de (Jan. 24, 1732 – May 18, 1799). French dramatist. Born Paris; entered father's watchmaking trade. Musically talented, he taught the harp to daughters of Louix XV. Married wealthy widow (1756), who died (1757). Obtained patent of nobility (1760). Early plays, *Eugénie* (1767) and *Les Deux Amis* (1770), attracted little notice. Remarried (1768); wife died (1770). Financial speculation embroiled him in a series of lawsuits, discussion of which in his eloquent and witty *Mémoires* (1773–74) won him instant literary fame, increased by performance of his gay, satirical comedy *Le Barbier de Seville* (1775). Served as secret agent to king, became interested in American Revolution; acted for French and Spanish governments in dealings with Amer-

ica, which he aided through organizing funds, arms, supplies and ships. Wrote *Le Mariage de Figaro* (1778), sequel to first comedy, but royal opposition delayed performance until 1784. Its mordant attack on the privileged classes and ridicule of the establishment made it a great success and contributed to the advance of the French Revolution. Married again (1786). Political embroilment led to his fleeing the country as an émigré (1792), and his property was confiscated. Returned to Paris (1796), where he died. Beaumarchais also wrote other, now forgotten plays, and published the first complete edition of Voltaire's works (1785–90). Last work was the autobiographical *Mes Six Époques*.

REFERENCES: René Dalsème *Beaumarchais, 1732–1799* (tr. New York and London 1929). Georges Édouard Lemaître *Beaumarchais* (New York 1949). John Rivers *Figaro: The Life of Beaumarchais* (London 1922).

BEAUMONT. *See* **FLETCHER, John.**

BECKFORD, William (Sept. 29, 1759 – May 2, 1844). English writer. Born Fonthill, Wiltshire, where he was educated by private tutors. At five, received piano lessons from the eight-year-old Mozart. Inherited (1770) enormous fortune from his father, who had been lord mayor of London. Began (1777) the European journeys later recorded in *Italy, with Sketches of Spain and Portugal* (1834; originally *Dreams, Waking Thoughts, and Incidents,* 1783), *Recollections of an Excursion to the Monasteries of Alcobaça and Batalha* (1835), and other travel books. Married Lady Margaret Gordon (1783); she died three years later. From 1796 was occupied with construction of a magnificent Gothic residence, Fonthill Abbey, where he lived as a recluse and notorious eccentric (1807–22). Having largely depleted his fortune, sold Fonthill and settled at Bath, where he died. The wildly imaginative Oriental romance *Vathek,* for which Beckford is chiefly known, was written in French (1782); translation by Samuel Henley published anonymously (1786). Other works include two burlesques of the novel of sensibility, *Modern Novel Writing, or The Elegant Enthusiast* (1796) and *Azemia* (1797).

REFERENCES: Boyd Alexander *England's Wealthiest Son: A Study of William Beckford* (London 1962). Harold Brockman *The Caliph of Fonthill* (London 1956). Guy Chapman *Beckford* (new ed. London and New York 1952). Lewis Melville (pseudonym of Lewis S. Benjamin) *Life and Letters of William Beckford of Fonthill* (London and New York 1910).

BECKMANN, Max (Feb. 12, 1884 – Dec. 27, 1950). German painter. Born Leipzig, son of wealthy flour merchant. Studied Weimar Academy (1900–1903). After travels to Paris and Florence, settled in Berlin and married (1906). Won first prize with painting *Young Men by the Sea* (1906) at annual exhibition of German Artists' League, Weimar. Traumatic experiences in World War I resulted in illness and treatment in Frankfort, where he stayed until Nazi persecution drove him to Amsterdam (1937). To America (1947) to teach at Washington University in St. Louis. Moved to New York (1949), where he died. Under the effect of his war experiences he had painted terrifying visions of monstrous human figures, which later gave way to landscapes, still lifes, and portraits, haunting, sometimes brutal, but developing greater simplicity of expression. In last period (from 1932) he produced seven great triptychs marked by intense personal symbolism and power. They include *Departure* (1932–35) and *The Argonauts* (1949–50).

REFERENCES: Max Beckmann *On My Painting* (New York 1941). Stephen Lackner *Max Beckmann: Memories of a Friendship* (Coral Gables, Fla. 1969). Peter Selz, Harold Joachim, and Perry T. Rathbone *Max Beckmann* (New York 1964).

BÉCQUER, Gustavo Adolfo (Feb. 17, 1836 – Dec. 22, 1870). Spanish poet and writer. Born Seville, son of well-known painter. Orphaned at ten; lived with succession of relatives and re-ceived haphazard education. Arrived (1854) in Madrid, where for the rest of his life he supported himself by journalism and literary hackwork, and where he died. Signs of tuberculosis appeared (1858); he married (1861) Casta Esteban y Navarro, daughter of physician who attended him. Newspaper *El Contemporaneo* published most of the poems and tales that appeared in Bécquer's lifetime as well as series of letters *Desde mi celda* (1864). His complete works were published posthumously: *Obras de Gustavo Adolfo Bécquer* (1871) and *Páginas desconocidas de Gustavo Adolfo Bécquer* (1923). His most famous work, *Rimas*, is a suite of seventy-six poems expressing the melancholy and bitter frustration of the romantics, but in a terse, understated manner; its influence was profound on, among others, Rubén Darío, Miguel de Unamuno, and Juan Ramón Jiménez. His prose tales, *Leyendas* (1860–64), evoke an atmosphere of haunting mystery.

REFERENCE: Edmund L. King *Gustavo Adolfo Bécquer: From Painter to Poet* (Mexico City 1953).

BEDE (or **BEDA** or **BAEDA**, known as the Venerable Bede) (672/73–735). English historian and theologian. Born in what was later territory of twin monasteries Wearmouth (founded 674) and Jarrow (founded 681/82) in Northumbria. At seven placed in care of Benedict Biscop, abbot of Wearmouth, who with Ceolfrith, abbot of Jarrow, educated him. Spent rest of life at the two monasteries, which were a few miles apart. Ordained deacon at eighteen and priest at twenty-nine; died at Jarrow. Canonized and made doctor of the church (1899). Probably the most erudite Western European of his day, Bede was much sought after as a teacher and helped make Northumbria one of the great centers of scholarship in Europe. His writings, in Latin, include scientific, historical, and theological treatises, and virtually sum up Western learning of his time. His masterpiece, *The Ecclesiastical History of the English Nation*, remains an indispensable source for early history of Anglo-Saxons. Adopting methods then unusual, Bede consulted many documents, discussed their relative reliability, and duly cited them as sources.

EDITIONS: *A History of the English Church and People* tr. Leo Sherley-Price (Harmondsworth, England, and Baltimore PB 1955, Penguin Classics). *The Ecclesiastical History of the English Nation, with the Life and Miracles of St. Cuthbert and the Lives of the Abbots of Wearmouth and Jarrow* tr. John Stevens rev. L. C. Jane (London and New York 1951, Everyman's Library).

REFERENCE: Alexander Hamilton Thompson ed. *Bede: His Life, Times, and Writings* (London 1935 and New York 1966).

BEERBOHM, Sir Max (Aug. 24, 1872 – May 20, 1956). English essayist, caricaturist, critic, and novelist. Born London, of Lithuanian parentage. Educated at Charterhouse and Merton College, Oxford. As undergraduate began contributing essays to periodicals, including *A Defense of Cosmetics* to the *Yellow Book* (1894). After trip to America as secretary to actor Beerbohm Tree (1895), published first book, *The Works of Max Beerbohm* (1896) and first collection of drawings, *Caricatures of Twenty-five Gentlemen* (1896). Succeeded George Bernard Shaw (who dubbed him "the incomparable Max") as drama critic of *Saturday Review* (1898); continued producing essays, collected as *More* (1899) and *Yet Again* (1909), as well as his devastating caricatures, collected as *The Poets' Corner* (1904) and *A Book of Caricatures* (1907). Married American actress Florence Kahn (1910), and shortly after publication of his satirical novel on Oxford, *Zuleika Dobson* (1911), they retired to Rapallo on the Italian Riviera. Among his other well-known writings are *A Christmas Garland* (1912), containing brilliant parodies of Beerbohm's contemporaries Hardy, Conrad and others, *Seven Men* (1919), and *And Even Now* (1920). Caricature books include *Rossetti and His Circle* (1922), *Things New and Old* (1923) and *Observations* (1925). Beerbohm was knighted in 1939. Except for his return to England in World War II, he lived quietly in Rapallo until his death.

REFERENCES: Samuel N. Behrman *Portrait of Max* (New York and, as *Conversations with Max*, London 1960). Lord David Cecil *Max: A Biography* (London 1964 and Boston 1965).

BEETHOVEN, Ludwig van (Dec. 16, 1770 – Mar. 26, 1827). German composer. Born Bonn; musical education began early with father and C. G. Neefe. Held various musical positions in Bonn (1783–92). Visited Vienna (1787) and met Mozart; returned to settle permanently and began brief study with Haydn (1792). Supported by various patrons, including Prince Lichnowsky and Prince Lobkowitz. Public debut as pianist in his own concerto (1795). Continued to develop reputation as virtuoso pianist, traveling in Austria, Bohemia, Germany, Hungary. *First Symphony* (C Major) performed 1800. Never married, though frequently enamored. Died in Vienna; funeral a great public event, with Schubert among the torchbearers. His works divide into three periods: the first as heir to Haydn and Mozart; the second (1800–15) yielding the major popular works; the third including the *Ninth Symphony*, the five last string quartets, and the *Missa Solemnis* (1824). His only opera, *Fidelio*, at first a failure (1805), was revised several times and finally succeeded (1814). His works include nine symphonies, five piano concerti, one violin concerto (1806), thirty-two piano sonatas, sixteen string quartets, and other chamber music. Beethoven expanded the size of the orchestra and helped establish the piano as an outstanding musical instrument.

REFERENCES: John N. Burk *Life and Works of Beethoven* (New York 1946). Joseph Kerman *The Beethoven Quartets* (New York 1966). George R. Marek *Beethoven: Biography of a Genius* (New York 1969). Paul Nettl *Beethoven Encyclopedia* (New York 1956) and *Beethoven Handbook* (New York 1967). Ernest Newman *The Unconscious Beethoven* (New York 1970). Alan Pryce-Jones *Beethoven* (New York 1933, also PB). Romain Rolland *Beethoven the*

Creator (tr. London and New York 1929, also PB). John W. N. Sullivan *Beethoven: His Spiritual Development* (New York 1958, also PB). Alexander W. Thayer *Life of Beethoven* rev. and ed. Elliot Forbes (2 vols. Princeton 1964). Donald Tovey *Beethoven* (London 1943, London and New York 1945, also PB). Percy M. Young *Beethoven* (London 1966, also PB).

☞

LUDWIG VAN BEETHOVEN
BY HAROLD SHAPERO

The works of Ludwig van Beethoven constitute one of the greatest individual achievements in the history of art. Beethoven has been universally celebrated for the grandeur of his conceptions, his remarkable personal intensity, and the vast range of expressive qualities which are found in his music. His logical and structural powers have hardly been surpassed by any other composer. His influence in matters of both technique and content was immense throughout the seventy-five years following his death: Schubert, Weber, Schumann, Mendelssohn, Wagner, Brahms, Bruckner were all especially indebted to him. In the twentieth century, following the discoveries of French impressionism, Beethoven's influence can still be traced in Mahler, Schoenberg, Bartók, and certain works of Stravinsky. In our time Beethoven is still our most widely performed serious composer, and his general popularity is so extraordinary that not one of his many major works has disappeared from the repertory nearly one hundred and fifty years after his death.

Beethoven's life history is almost as remarkable as the music he has left us. Familiar to us is the epic struggle of the great composer with deafness, chronic ill health, money problems, loneliness, endless household disorder; a life of tragic suffering redeemed by a succession of heroic masterpieces: triumphs of work, will, order, inspiration, innovation, and prodigious energy.

Historians concerned with Beethoven's biography have managed to assemble an enormous mass of documentary material which includes important recent discoveries. For many areas of his life we now have available an almost complete accounting. A detailed examination of Beethoven's life in no way causes us to detract from his legend. We are reminded, rather, of the difficulties lesser men encounter in adjusting their vanities to a very great genius. The famous difficulty in establishing the identity of *Die Unsterbliche Geliebte* seems to have been resolved in favor of Josephine von Brunsvik. Strong evidence indicates that she bore Beethoven's illegitimate child, a daughter, Minona, in 1813. Beethoven's bizarre later relationship with his nephew Karl may then be understood as "displaced fatherhood." This network of relationships must be considered a chapter in the composer's life which approaches the fantastic.

Though his education was predominantly musical, Beethoven acquired a considerable knowledge of literature. He constantly read and quoted Plato and Aristotle, his "ancients," testing them against his own experience. Shakespeare inspired him directly; a reading of *Romeo and Juliet* accompanied the creation of the tragic slow movement of his *String Quartet* op. 18 no. 1. Beethoven, however, considered music a greater revelation than literature and philosophy. He had hopes that at least Goethe, among his contemporaries, might understand him. Though Goethe saw clearly that Beethoven was a man of singular genius, possessed by a daemon, he failed to comprehend Beethoven's musical structures: the classic failure of a strongly verbal mind to respond fully to the tonal world.

A great deal has been written about Beethoven's creative process. He believed in what he himself called "the *law* of association of ideas," and trusted in the specific character of the different tonalities, each with an appropriate expressive usefulness. Because of his lifelong habit of jotting down his ideas in their initial form and reworking them through many stages, we often observe the startling metamorphosis of inchoate material into patterns of remarkable originality. We can witness the emergence of a marvelous inspiration such as the finale theme of the *A Minor Quartet* op. 132, from a repetitive, primitive, waltzlike start. In his numerous sketchbooks this process is repeated continuously, some themes reaching their final form twenty-five years after their inception. Unlike Mozart and Schubert, he found it necessary to mold his themes and structural materials until they reached a required salience. No composer has given us such a variety and richness of thematic invention, or offered us such contrasts in conception from work to work.

Some mention must be made of Beethoven's technical innovations. He extended harmony greatly by an elaborate, systematic exploitation of the secondary dominants, for both phrase endings and key destinations in large structures. In his later works he re-employed the older church modes, incorporating them into his major-minor harmonic vocabulary. His modulations, though often highly idiosyncratic, are marvels of logic, surprise, and dramatic placement. Certain passages in his music contain a curious chordal overlapping (such as the preparation for the return in the *Eroica* first movement) which suggests the pandiatonic

materials of twentieth-century neoclassicism. The final sections of the "alla danza tedesca" (movement four of the Quartet op. 130) suggest vividly Webern's registral dissociation, which has been so influential in the formation of contemporary musical textures. In his sonata-form movements, Beethoven enlarged his codas until they almost balanced his development sections in complexity and dramatic significance. Similar extensions of other conventional forms, coupled with a powerful variation technique, led him to musical structures as massive as the *Ninth Symphony, Hammerklavier Sonata*, and *C-sharp Minor Quartet*. When we consider the expressive intentions of these monumental works, it seems astonishing that their continuity is still achieved with the aid of clear periodic form, traditional episodic procedure, and fugal conventions.

It is customary to divide Beethoven's work into three period's — early, middle, late — with the implication of a steady progression toward technical complexity and increasing emotional profundity. This division is useful, though the categories are, of course, blurred. In the early trio op. 1 no. 3, Beethoven's temperament is already clearly revealed. The tragic D minor *Largo* from the piano sonata op. 10 no. 3, though much less elaborate than the later slow movements, seems profound enough. It is simplest to say that he was successful throughout his career in all three periods, in forms large and small. In Beethoven's lifetime many works from the early and middle periods quickly became classics, yet it was only the music of the first two periods which exerted a strong influence on nineteenth-century composers. The last five quartets and last five piano sonatas were probably not well performed or fully comprehended until the twentieth century. The special qualities of these late works have elicited a great deal of metaphysical speculation. Do they represent power and submission? Destiny and resignation? Suffering and transcendence? Peace? Salvation? However we answer, it is significant that generations of musicians have responded to these works with reverence, an indication that Beethoven has here succeeded in creating a language and logic of the ineffable. Most composers accord the last quartets a place at the summit of all instrumental music.

The choral finale of the *Ninth Symphony*, with its setting of Schiller's *Ode to Joy*, has often been taken as a "Hymn to Democracy," when it should be more truly considered a "Hymn of Universal Destiny." Though Beethoven lived through a period in which European society had been severely disturbed by Napoleonic conquests, he had the benefit throughout most of his life of an enlightened, cultivated aristocracy. He was fully aware of the conflict between democratic social aspiration and the aristocratic principle necessary for great art. When he heard someone say, "Vox populi, vox dei," Beethoven responded roughly, "I don't believe it."

In the peculiar matter of evaluating his own music, he proved to be an excellent judge, preferring the *Third Symphony* to the more popular *Fifth*, the *C-sharp Minor Quartet* to all the others. He felt that the *Missa Solemnis* was perhaps his greatest work. This demanding, intricate, totally unconventional Mass still creates difficulties for many contemporary listeners, since most of us are incapable of bringing to it the background and concentration it requires. The daring introduction of war motives in the *Agnus Dei* and the final resolution of this movement are among the subtlest effects Beethoven ever attempted. Referring to this strange, towering masterpiece, he was able to say, simply, "Coming from the heart, may it return to the heart."

On his desk, framed under glass, Beethoven kept three religious mottoes: "I am all that is, was, and will be." "No mortal has lifted My veil." "He is only by Himself, and to Him alone do all things owe their existence." Was this the nature of his faith? By innate character and temperament he was compelled to strain at all boundaries — "No mortal has lifted My veil." His mind had the capacity to generate and sustain a maximum of intellectual tension. The maximal tensions of the *Grosse Fuge* pushed music to extreme limits, stopped just short of shattering the tonal system. His will proved equal to the task of controlling both his creative daemon and the violent intensity of his passion; he stopped just short of shattering the great moral system which had given him his spiritual conditions. We feel he knew what can be known. No previous music had originated from such agitated, remote, solitary, and elevated states of mind.

Beethoven has survived mightily; yet there are indications that even *his* universal genius may soon be overwhelmed by our specters of mass civilization, mechanization, and overkill. When we are no longer willing to hear Beethoven's noble voice, we will have succeeded in replacing the sublime with chaos.

BEHN, Aphra (c.1640 – Apr. 16, 1689). English playwright and novelist. Date and place of birth unknown. As a child, traveled to Surinam (Dutch Guiana), setting of her novel *Oroonoko* (1688). Returned c.1658 and married a London merchant named Behn. After his death (1666), Mrs. Behn was sent to the Netherlands as an English spy; unrewarded for her services, she spent a term in debtors' prison before turning to writing as means of support. A series of popular, ribald comedies followed her first play, *The Forced Marriage* (1670), the best known being *The Rover* (two parts, 1677/81). The first Englishwoman to maintain herself by writing, Mrs. Behn denied woman's subservience to man and led a bohemian existence. *Oroonoko* introduced the figure of the noble savage, and with her other novels had considerable influence on development of the English novel. Died in London; buried in Westminster Abbey.

EDITION: *The Works of Aphra Behn* ed. Montague Summers (6 vols. London 1915).

REFERENCES: Frederick M. Link *Aphra Behn* (New York 1968). Victoria M. Sackville-West *Aphra Behn* (London 1927 and New York 1928).

BELLAY, Joachim Du (c.1522–1560). French poet and critic. Born near Liré, in Anjou, of noble family. Studied law until 1547, then entered Collège de Coqueret, Paris, center of Greek studies under direction of Jean Dorat. Became member of group of poets with Ronsard, La Pléiade, and published its manifesto, *La Défense et illustration de la langue française* (1549). Its aim was to re-create the French poetic idiom by intelligent imitation of ancient Greek and Latin writers, and Italians. Du Bellay published collection of love sonnets, *Olive* (1550), followed by two editions of *Recueil de poésies* (1552–53), then abandoned Petrarchan style and imitation of Greek odes for intensely personal forms of expression. While in Rome as secretary to cousin Cardinal Jean du Bellay (1553–57) wrote *Les Antiquités de Rome* and his masterpiece, the sonnets *Les Regrets*, steeped in melancholy and homesickness. Published the Latin *Poemata* (1558) and *Jeux rustiques* shortly before his death in Paris. His poetry won him the titles of the French Ovid and Prince of Sonnets.

TRANSLATION: *Ruins of Rome* (*Les Regrets* and *Les Antiquités*) tr. Edmund Spenser (London 1591).

REFERENCES: Henri Chamard *Joachim du Bellay* (Lille 1900). G. Dickinson *Du Bellay in Rome* (Leyden 1960). Alfred W. Satterthwaite *Spenser, Ronsard and Du Bellay: A Renaissance Comparison* (Princeton, N.J. and London 1960). Verdun L. Saulnier *Du Bellay: L'Homme et l'oeuvre* (Paris 1951).

BELLINI, Gentile (c.1429 – Feb. 23, 1507). Italian painter. Born and died in Venice. Elder son of Jacopo Bellini (c.1400–c.1470), an important transitional figure between Gothic and Renaissance styles whose two sketchbooks (one in the British Museum, London, the other in the Louvre, Paris) reveal a growing attention to such Renaissance subjects as perspective, landscape, and classical antiquity. Gentile studied under his father and Andrea Mantegna, working in Padua, then Venice. Among his earliest signed works is the portrait of Lorenzo Guistiniani (1465). Its severity and dryness are Paduan traits, later mitigated under influence of his brother Giovanni. Commissioned (1474) to restore paintings and decorations in doge's palace at Venice; reputation as portraitist grew, and he was chosen to paint at court of Sultan Mohammed II in Constantinople (1479–80). Subsequently collaborated with Giovanni on frescoes in doge's palace. Finest works are his portraits and the canvases commissioned by Scuola di San Giovanni Evangelista (1490–1500: *Procession of the Relic of the Cross in the Piazza of San Marco, The Miracle of the True Cross*, Accademia, Venice) and by Scuola di S. Marco (1505, *St. Mark Preaching in Alexandria;* completed by Giovanni, 1507, Brera Museum, Milan). In these scenes of ceremonial pomp, he skillfully arranges crowds of people before minutely detailed architectural perspectives.

REFERENCES: Émile Cammaerts *Les Bellini: Étude critique* (Paris 1912). Giorgio Vasari *Lives of the . . . Painters, Sculptors, and Architects* (1550) tr. Gaston de Vere (10 vols. London 1912–15).

BELLINI, Giovanni (c.1430 – Nov. 29, 1516). Italian painter. Born and died in Venice. Trained and active in family studio of father Jacopo and elder brother Gentile until 1459 or shortly after. Early work, masterpieces of which are *The Agony in the Garden* (National Gallery, London), and *Man of Sorrows* (Milan), much influenced by the harsh, linear manner of his brother-in-law Andrea Mantegna of Padua. In the 1480's, having learned the new technique of oil painting, he developed a style founded on light and color rather than line. Best-known works of this period are series of altarpieces in Pesaro and Venice (Academy and S. Maria dei Frari), and *Stigmatization of St. Francis* in New York (Frick Collection). With Gentile's departure for Constantinople (1479), Giovanni succeeded him as chief painter of the Venetian republic and began to execute a cycle of large historical paintings for the Doge's palace (destroyed). During this time he trained the most famous of his many pupils, Giorgione and Titian. He also painted numerous portraits, including *Doge Loredano* (National Gallery, London). In the new century, he developed an abstract, evocative style that is represented by altarpieces in Venice (S. Zaccaria) and Vicenza (S. Corona), the mythological scenes *The Feast of the Gods* and *Myth of Orpheus* (National Gallery, Washington, D.C.), and *The Madonna of the Meadow* and *Portrait of Fra Teodoro* (both in National Gallery, London). Bellini is known as the founder of the Venetian school.

REFERENCES: Philip Hendy and Ludwig Goldscheider *Giovanni Bellini* (London 1946). Rudolfo Palluchini *Giovanni Bellini* (tr. London 1963). Giles Robertson *Giovanni Bellini* (Oxford 1968). Giorgio Vasari *Lives of the . . . Painters, Sculptors and Architects* (1550) tr. Gaston de Vere (10 vols. London 1912–15).

☞

GIOVANNI BELLINI
BY JUERGEN SCHULZ

Giovanni Bellini, youngest of the Venetian dynasty of painters by that name, was more responsible than any other artist for giving Venetian Renaissance painting a European significance. He lived to an extraordinary old age, and during the more than five decades of his working life he developed from an early Renaissance painter, working in a provincial idiom, to the exponent of a High Renaissance style that was the basis of the achievements of the great colorists of the Venetian sixteenth century. No other artist of the Italian Renaissance encompassed such a range.

He was the son of Jacopo Bellini, an early fifteenth-century artist known in his own right for numerous courtly paintings of *The Virgin and Child* and two volumes of compositional drawings that show late Gothic and early Renaissance styles warring for preeminence. We can guess that Giovanni was born in the early 1430's, for he was younger than his artist brother Gentile, born c.1430, but by 1459 was already living away from home. Local success was not long in coming, thanks to his abilities as well as his family connections. By the 1460's he was working for one of the six major lay confraternities, or *scuole*, of the city, the Confraternity of the Virgin of Mercy. In 1470 he received commissions from another one, the Confraternity of St. Mark. In 1480 he was appointed official painter to the Venetian Republic at an annual salary. His chief duties in this capacity were the execution of official portraits of the Doge and a cycle of historical paintings for the Hall of the Great Council in the ducal palace. But by this time his fame had spread to the Venetian mainland and beyond. Provincial cities of the Republic such as Vicenza and Zara ordered altarpieces from him, students from throughout the mainland were drawn to his studio, and princes from the houses of Mantua and Ferrara were instructing their ambassadors to obtain for them works from Giovanni's hand. Albrecht Dürer sought out the aged artist on his second visit to Venice, in 1506, and reported home with pride the notice that Bellini had taken of him. "Old as he is, he is still the best in painting," the young German said.

Bellini himself is not known to have traveled, but through his teaching his influence spread very far. His apprentices, returning to their home towns in Dalmatia, Venetia, Emilia and the Marches, established his style for almost half a century along the upper Adriatic coast. In Venice itself, all the major painters of the High Renaissance passed through his studio: Giorgione, Lorenzo Lotto and Palma Vecchio, among the generation of the 1470's, Titian, Sebastiano and Bonifazio among that of the 1480's.

From his father, Bellini had learned a late Gothic style built on fluent outlines and rich colors, naturalistic in details but unreal and hieratic in its general effect. The earliest works of the artist show him striving to introduce into this style a naturalistic representation of light, mass, and recession, together with an austere expression of the sentiment appropriate to the depicted scenes. His model was his contemporary Andrea Mantegna, the leading painter of nearby Padua and a brother-in-law. In paintings of the 1460's, such as *The Virgin and Child* (Metropolitan Museum, New York) and *The Agony in the Garden* (National Gallery, London), one recognizes not only motives drawn from the latter, but also Mantegna's realistic drawing style, in which line is subservient to the definition of form, invariably lapidarily and sharply drawn. Objects are scaled correctly to one another, importance is emphasized by accentuated corporeality or light, and feeling is conveyed by facial expres-

sions, bodily movement, and dramatization of the event portrayed. As in Mantegna's paintings, line not only defines the three-dimensional character of forms, but also serves to impart a consistent texture to the picture surface. However, Bellini uses light in a novel fashion as another unifying factor. The *Agony* takes place in the soft half-light of dawn, relieved here and there by objects supernaturally aglow. Their high tints associate them in the color scheme, although they are far apart within the represented space, and thus what notionally is separate, decoratively is drawn together. A unifying atmosphere is suggested as well. The painting contrasts most forcibly with an almost contemporary representation of the same subject by Mantegna, in the same gallery. The latter shows the *Agony* taking place in an unrelievedly bright light which separates out each object with the insistent clarity of a desert atmosphere.

By the following decade, Bellini was moving away from the rigid drawing style of Mantegna. Outlines are less clear in his paintings of the 1470's, modeling is more painterly, producing a soft atmospheric veil over the forms. The *St. Justine* of 1475, painted for an altar of the Borromeo family in Milan and still in a private collection in that city, shows a figure modeled less by a network of lines than by light and shade. Its soft plasticity is like that of the forms in the slightly later *Stigmatization of St. Francis* (Frick Collection, New York). Gradually, Bellini arrived at a style built entirely on volume rather than line, in which the forms are reduced into simple solids, the three-dimensionality of which is emphasized by a strong chiaroscuro and a compact, equally simple spatial setting. The masterpiece of this style of his middle years is the large altarpiece with *The Virgin and Child and Six Saints,* painted c.1483 for the Venetian church of St. Job and now in the Gallery of the Academy of that city. A vaulted room is represented in foreshortening, as if seen from the nave of the church, in direct communication with it and illuminated from the right as through the rose window of the church's entrance wall. The sharp light fixes every jut and cranny of the room and gives the figures an astonishing, tactile presence. But a decorative harmony is preserved nonetheless. The carefully lit and foreshortened space registers as a cubic unit. The muted values of the palette suggest a common denominator that binds all color patches together in the pictorial plane.

Geometric regularity of forms and lucidity of spatial composition were the earmarks of the style of Antonello da Messina, who had formed himself on early Netherlandish models and adopted even their technique of oil painting, then still uncommon in Italy. Antonello had worked at Venice in 1475–76, and there can be no doubt that Bellini's altarpiece reflects his influence, for there are correspondences not only of style but also of technique. The painting is one of Bellini's first to make use of oil paint and glazes. Yet the Venetian artist adapted both, forms and medium, to his own ends, for in them he found the means to realize still more fully that combination of maximum three-dimensionality of form and space with maximum decorative patterning that had informed his painting since the beginning of his career.

In the works of the 1490's and the early sixteenth century we can watch him pursue his goal ever more closely. A painting like the *Madonna of the Meadow* (c.1504, National Gallery, London) shows the solid geometry of the St. Job altarpiece turning into plane geometry — figures and other forms have little cubic volume, and the forms of different zones in depth are linked into a common geometric pattern. Contours vibrate and are uncertain. And yet an impression of depth remains, created by diminution in scale, overlappings, and atmosphere — atmosphere suggested more powerfully than ever in the blurred forms and pale translucent colors possible in the new medium. Still another change has taken place; the predominance of the Virgin over the composition as a whole gives the scene a simplicity and grandeur that are new.

At an age of seventy or more, Bellini had developed, out of his own quest and resources, a style that was in step with contemporary developments in Italian painting. The change is nowhere clearer than in the altarpiece *The Virgin and Child with Four Saints* (1505, church of St. Zacharias, Venice). It is similar in composition to the St. Job altar of twenty years before. However, the scale of the figures is larger, in proportion to the panel as a whole. All the illusionistic depth and force of the earlier painting are gone. The setting is similar, but it is now seen arbitrarily from above, not subjectively, as if from the nave of the church. The saints, now standing parallel to the picture plane and broadened in silhouette by spreading draperies, have become elements of one continuous surface pattern. Withdrawn in their own thoughts, they seem to belong to a reality beyond our own. The colors are muted by an earthen tone that runs through all and gives the scene an elegiac mood. A perfect calm and motionless silence pervades the painting, comparable to the self-contained completeness and stillness of the High Renaissance religious paintings of central Italy, of Fra Bartolommeo and the young Raphael. But the means by which this impression is achieved are typically Venetian.

The very last works of Bellini's life show him moving still one step closer to the ideal of an image constructed entirely in terms of color rather than line. The *Portrait of Fra Teodoro* (National Gallery, London), which is dated 1515 and thus was painted one year before the artist's death, when he was over eighty, is conceived entirely in terms of silhouettes — the forms have been reduced to flat patches of color, arranged in an abstract pattern. They are all of equal intensity, whether in the fore- or background, in the manner of medieval mosaics. Undiluted black and white for the first time fill separate areas, alongside hues like yellow, green and vermilion. Titian understood and imitated this use of intense color, beginning in the 1530's. But the radical simplification of a representational image into an abstract color pattern was not attempted again until Gauguin.

When he died in 1516, his powers were undiminished. "Old as he was," notes a chronicler in reporting his death, "he painted superbly." Still a year later, when Venice wished to make an impression on the politically powerful French viceroy of Milan, no finer gift could be found than a painting by Bellini, a *Pietà* owned by a private nobleman, which the Republic purchased for the purpose.

BELLINI, Vincenzo (Nov. 3, 1801 – Sept. 24, 1835). Italian composer. Born Catania, Sicily, into family of musicians. Opera *Adelson e Silvani* (1825), written while a student at Naples Conservatory, won for Bellini the notice of impresario Domenico Barbaja and through him commissions at major Italian opera houses. *Il Pirata* (1827), an immediate success throughout Europe, gave first glimpses of his mature style. Major works: *La Sonnambula* (1831), *Norma* (1831), and *I Puritani* (1835). Died at Puteaux, near Paris. With Donizetti, Bellini is the chief representative of the bel canto school. His operas are known for their melodic sweetness and for vocal embellishments which demand great virtuosity of singers.

REFERENCE: Dyneley Hussey *Some Composers of Opera* (London and New York 1952).

BELLO, Andrés (Nov. 29, 1781 – Oct. 15, 1865). South American poet and scholar. Born Caracas, Venezuela, where he received classical education and tutored the young Simón Bolívar before serving in London as diplomatic representative for Venezuela, Colombia, and Chile successively (1810–29). Settled (1829) at Santiago as secretary of Chilean ministry of foreign affairs. Served in Chilean congress (1830's) and founded (1842) University of Chile, of which he was rector until his death at Santiago. Bello was mainly responsible for Chilean civil code (1855), also adopted by Colombia and Ecuador. Prose works deal with such varied subjects as international law, philosophy, geography, sociology, literary criticism, and philology. His *Gramática de la lengua castellana* (1847) is the leading authority in its field. His poem *Silva a la agricultura de la zona tórridd* (first published in London, 1826, as part of projected series of poems to be called *Silvas americanas*), inspired by Bello's contacts with German naturalist Alexander Humboldt, describes products and geography of Spanish America and extols country life in a manner reminiscent of Virgil. It is a classic of Spanish literature.

EDITION: *Obras completas* (Santiago, Chile 1881–93).

REFERENCES: Renél Durand *La Poésie d'Andrés Bello* (Dakar 1960). Miguel L. Amanátegui *Vida de Don Andrés Bello* (Santiago, Chile 1882).

BELLOC, (Joseph) Hilaire (Pierre) (July 27, 1870 – July 16, 1953).

Anglo-French poet, essayist, satirist, historian, novelist. Born St.-Cloud, near Paris, son of French barrister and his English wife. Educated at Oratory School, Birmingham, and after a year in French army entered Balliol College, Oxford (1894), where he won many honors. Married an American, Elodie Hogan (1896). Became British subject (1902) and served as Liberal member of Parliament (1906–10). Belloc wrote from Roman Catholic point of view, and together with his friend G. K. Chesterton expressed medieval nostalgia, opposed socialism and materialism, and worked to restore the sense of Europe to English literature. Among works of this versatile and prolific writer are the celebrated books of nonsense verse *The Bad Child's Book of Beasts* (1896) and *Cautionary Tales* (1907), historical biographies including *Danton* (1899), *Robespierre* (1901), *Marie Antoinette* (1910), and *Napoleon* (1932), the travel book *The Path to Rome* (1902), light verse, satirical novels, books on the history of religion, and a four-volume *History of England* (1925–32) in which he tried to correct what he considered the overly Protestant view of history. His *Letters* appeared posthumously (1958). He died at Guildford, Surrey.

REFERENCES: Robert Speaight *The Life of Hilaire Belloc* (London and New York 1957). Frederick Wilhelmsen *Hilaire Belloc: No Alienated Man* (London and New York 1953).

BELLOTTO, Bernardo (Jan. 30, 1720 – Oct. 17, 1780). Italian painter. Born Venice; studied painting with uncle Canaletto (Antonio Canale), using same pseudonym. Joined Venetian painters' guild (1738); first signed work dated 1740. Became court painter at Dresden (1747), then at Warsaw (1767) for king of Poland, painting expert views of cities, notably of Warsaw. His work is often confused with his uncle's, but Bellotto is recognized as a brilliant realist in his own right.

REFERENCE: Mieczyslaw Wallis *Canaletto the Painter of Warsaw* (tr. Warsaw 1954).

BELLOWS, George Wesley (Aug. 12, 1882 – Jan. 8, 1925). American painter, lithographer and illustrator. Born Columbus, Ohio. Attended Ohio State University (1901–1904) and New York School of Art under Robert Henri (1904); familiar with latter's group of artists, the Eight. Opened studio (1906). Won recognition at National Academy with *Forty-two Kids* (1908, Corcoran Gallery, Washington) and was elected to Academy (1909). Married Emma Story (1910). Taught Art Students' League (1910–11). Helped organize famous Armory Show (1913), where he exhibited *Circus* (1912, Addison Gallery, Andover, Mass.). Best remembered for crude strength and realism of fight pictures: *Stag at Sharkey's* (1907, Cleveland Museum of Art), *Both Members of the Club* (1909), *Dempsey and Firpo* (1924, Whitney Museum of Art, New York). Landscapes, city-scapes, and sports pictures, often muddy in color, reveal spontaneity, simple massing, and power which balance the pensive charm of portraits like *Lady Jean* (1924). His lithographs, begun in 1916, show a draftsmanship and originality which have ranked him with Daumier. Died in New York.

REFERENCES: Charles H. Morgan *George Bellows: Painter of America* (New York 1966). Frances R. Nugent *George Bellows: American Painter* (Chicago 1963).

BENNETT, (Enoch) Arnold (May 27, 1867 – Mar. 27, 1931). English novelist. Born near Hanley, Staffordshire. Attended Newcastle Middle School. After working as solicitor's clerk in London, became editor of periodical *Woman* and (from 1900) made writing his career. *A Man from the North* (1898) was the first of over thirty novels and volumes of short stories portraying lower middle-class life in the industrial Midlands (the Five Towns in his books), of which the masterpiece is *The Old Wives' Tale* (1908). Moved to Paris (1900); married French actress Marguerite Hebrand (1907). After trip to America (1911), settled again in England and continued to produce successful books. Separated from his wife (1921), he met another actress, Dorothy Cheston

(1923), who later bore him his only child. Died of typhoid fever in London. Other notable works: *The Grand Babylon, Hotel* (1902), *Anna of the Five Towns* (1902), *Tales of the Five Towns* (1905), *Buried Alive* (1908), *Clayhanger* (1910), the series reprinted as *The Clayhanger Family* (1925), *The Matador of the Five Towns* (1912), *Riceyman's Steps* (1923), and the *Journal* of his life from 1896 on.

REFERENCES: Dudley Barker *Writer by Trade: A Portrait of Arnold Bennett* (London and New York 1966). John D. Gordan *Arnold Bennett: The Centenary of His Birth* (New York 1968). Reginald Pound *Arnold Bennett* (London 1950 and New York 1953). John Wain *Arnold Bennett* (New York PB 1967).

BENTHAM, Jeremy (Feb. 15, 1748 – June 6, 1832). English economist and philosopher. Born London, son of an attorney. A precocious child, he entered Queen's College, Oxford, at twelve. On graduating (1763), studied law for a time, but soon abandoned it to devote full time to radical critique of English law, politics, morals, and other institutions. Bentham conceived a utopian welfare state; he designed model cities and model prisons, educational and job training systems, codifications of law, improvements in political machinery. He left numerous unfinished manuscripts with John Stuart Mill and other disciples, who edited and published them. Only his first two books, *A Fragment on Government* (1776) and *An Introduction to the Principles of Morals and Legislation* (1789), are commonly known and available. Utilitarianism, the philosophy Bentham originated, equates happiness with pleasure, and postulates that the greatest happiness of the greatest number is the fundamental principle of morality and the goal of the state. Traveled via Italy, Smyrna, and Constantinople to visit his brother in Russia (1785–88). Helped found *Westminster Review* (1823), first utilitarian journal, and University College, London (1826). He never married. Died in London.

EDITIONS: *Jeremy Bentham's Economic Writings* ed. W. Stark (3 vols. London and New York 1952–54). *Collected Works of Jeremy Bentham* ed. Timothy L. S. Sprigge (in progress London and New York 1968 ff).

REFERENCES: Élie Halévy *The Growth of Philosophic Radicalism* (Boston PB 1955). Mary P. Mack *Jeremy Bentham: An Odyssey of Ideas* (London and New York 1963). John Stuart Mill *Utilitarianism; On Liberty; Essay on Bentham*, ed. Mary Warnock (Cleveland PB 1962).

BERG, Alban (Maria Johannes) (Feb. 9, 1885 – Dec. 24, 1935). Austrian composer. Born in Vienna. Met Schoenberg (1904), who became his only teacher. Composed *Seven Early Songs* (1905–1908) and *Piano Sonata*, op. 1 (1908). Married Helene Nahowski (1911). Wrote first opera, *Wozzeck* (1917–21), based on Georg Büchner's play *Woyzeck*), three fragments of which were performed as a symphonic work (1924). It was an enormous success and Berg became famous. Died in Vienna, where he had lived almost all his life. His complete oeuvre of thirteen works: *Seven Early Songs* (1905–1908), *Piano Sonata*, op. 1 (1908), *Four Songs*, op. 2 (1908), *String Quartet*, op. 3 (1910), *Five Orchestral Songs*, op. 4 (1912), *Four Pieces for Clarinet and Piano*, op. 5 (1913), *Three Orchestral Pieces*, op. 6 (1914), *Wozzeck* (1917–21), *Chamber Concerto* (1925), *Lyric Suite* (1926), *Der Wein*, for soprano and orchestra (1929), *Lulu* (1928–34), and *Violin Concerto* (1935).

REFERENCES: Willi Reich *Alban Berg* (tr. New York and, as *The Life and Work of Alban Berg*, London 1965). Hans F. Redlich *Alban Berg: The Man and His Music* (New York 1957).

☞

ALBAN BERG

BY ROBERT PARRIS

Alban Berg wrote — excluding excerpts, arrangements and a little juvenilia — only thirteen pieces of music. The shades of Vivaldi, Mozart, and Haydn may scoff, but perhaps prolificity is not after all one of the indications of true vocation. For the men who had enough feeling for the *Zeitgeist* (the *Zeit* being the first decade of this century) to realize that the common practice was not about to remain common, each new piece seemed to have to solve, or at least to confront, a new problem. The mature styles of Debussy, Hindemith, Stravinsky, Schoenberg, and Webern all reveal separate ways of coming to terms with nineteenth-century modes of musical sound and thought.

Unlike his colleague Anton Webern and his teacher Arnold Schoenberg, Berg felt no need to push music around a historical corner; he spent his life extending and enriching the romantic tradition. His small oeuvre, then, would seem to reflect the enormous difficulty of constructing a personal means of expression by amplifying rather than rejecting an aesthetic and technical apparatus that many at the time felt was quite exhausted. (There are those who still think so, and find Berg's music decadent in the historical if not the pejorative sense.) Berg had the temerity to build on Wagner and Mahler; later on he was enticed by Debussy's way of dealing with successions of whole tones. (In his *Violin Concerto* he quotes the Bach chorale *Es ist genug,* which begins with the first four tones of a whole-tone scale. Debussy's influence is clear enough, even though technical considerations were also involved in the choice of chorale tune.)

Berg, Schoenberg, and Webern are generally thought of as the leading lights of the twentieth-century Viennese atonal school. Lumping them together as a set of Three Teutonic Musketeers does each a disservice; Berg and Webern went off in entirely different directions, and between Schoenberg and Berg lies a vast difference in both method and tempera-

ment. Ignorant of Gertrude Stein's admonition on century killing ("It's hard to kill a century almost impossible"), Schoenberg tried very hard indeed; Berg not at all. He did not use Schoenberg's twelve-tone device in any orthodox or consistent way, and those who think they don't like twelve-tone music will not be put off by Berg, or at least not for that reason.

In the historical context, therefore, Berg was an eclectic conservative, which does not mean that all his music is easily accessible. A lot of it is, though, and if his music is not heard today as often as it might be, consider the solo cellist or violist, for whom he wrote not one note; the pianist, for whom there is only a faintly putrescent sonata dating from 1908 (excepting a solo part in the *Chamber Concerto*); the violinist, for whom there is one concerto but nothing else (with the same exception as above.) If you play the clarinet, there are four tiny pieces with piano; if you play any other wind or brass instrument, there's nothing for you. If you are a string quartet, however, there are two extended works: the *Quartet,* op. 3, and the *Lyric Suite.* If you are a conductor, you might play the *Three Orchestral Pieces,* op. 6, but there's no other complete work originally written for orchestra alone.

It is up to singers, mostly, to keep Berg's flag flying, and few do. Even the *Seven Early Songs* are rarely heard today, attractive as they are; nor, by contemporary standards, are they difficult either to sing or to listen to. But Berg suffers from incomprehensibility by association — implied in Berg is Schoenberg. And although there is some indication that times are changing, the older man's music has been shied away from owing largely to his use of sounds which once may have been called ultramodern, but which at this date we have a right to call ugly if we feel so inclined.

Berg wrote no such sounds; his music may occasionally jar the most delicate sensibilities, but it is never, from a purely aural point of view, unpleasant. His orchestral technique far exceeded that of his teacher. What might easily put one off is his use of overrich textures, which is to say that there often is so much going on that the ear has some trouble sorting out significant shapes and patterns, distinguishing principal from subordinate ideas.

Berg's handling of musical form can be troublesome. While he never altogether forsook eighteenth- and nineteenth-century means of organization (indeed, in *Wozzeck* he contrived ingenious ways of dealing with the passacaglia, the dance suite, the symphonic allegro and the theme and variations), the manner in which he extended these principles is highly elusive. On the other hand, he seldom used Schoenberg's twelve-tone row technique as a *prima materia* from which every tone, and consequently a form, could be derived. Lacking a consistent approach to formal organization, torn between the old and new structural principles, Berg's music is apt to sound like an intuitively arranged flight of ideas, a musical stream of consciousness. Some incohesiveness, even occasional incoherence, is bound to result.

Berg's music is invariably warm, at times to the point of gaudy purple. His lyric gift was immense, and the ease and conviction with which he wrote for the voice carries over to his instrumental work. His sense of theatre is still a matter of some discussion. In both *Wozzeck* and *Lulu*, dramatic tension lies in psychological rather than external reality, which makes for

some longueurs unless — or even if — you have the text at hand. Yet the final scene from *Wozzeck* is as pathetically wrenching as anything you're likely to encounter on the operatic stage.

Some composers are remembered chiefly for their influence on other composers; they helped shape fashion and style (Stamitz, and possibly Schoenberg). Others are called great for the intrinsic value of their work and had little or no effect on later music (Gesualdo, Mozart). Some (Bach, Beethoven) fit easily into both niches. Alban Maria Johannes Berg, coming at the tail end of a very long line of Austrian and German romanticists — Weber, Wagner, Mahler, Strauss — original in a private way but no technical or stylistic innovator or iconoclast, cannot possibly have a historical force. He lives or dies with his thirteen pieces.

BERGSON, Henri Louis (Oct. 18, 1859 – Jan. 4, 1941). French philosopher. Born Paris, of Polish Jewish father and Irish mother. After graduating from École Normale Supérieure (1881), taught at various schools, notably Lycée Henri IV in Paris (1889–98). Became professor of philosophy at Collège de France (1900). Elected to Académie Française (1914). Served on diplomatic missions in Spain and U.S. during World War I; afterward president of League of Nations committee on intellectual cooperation. Awarded Nobel prize for literature (1927). Died in Paris. Bergson's principal works are *Essai sur les données immédiates de la conscience* (1889, tr. *Time and Free Will* 1910); *Matière et mémoire* (1896, tr. *Matter and Memory* 1911); *Le Rire* (1900, tr. *Laughter* 1911); *Introduction à la métaphysique* (1903, tr. *Introduction to Metaphysics* 1912); *L'Évolution créatrice* (1907, tr. *Creative Evolution* 1911); *L'Énergie spirituelle* (1919, tr. *Mind Energy* 1920); *Les deux Sources de la morale et de la religion* (1932, tr. *Two Sources of Morality* *and Religion* 1935); *La Pensée et le mouvant* (1934, tr. *Creative Mind* 1946). Bergson conceived of reality as a continuing stream of change and movement whose essence, the vital impulse (*élan vital*) is apprehended only by intuition as opposed to the intellect, which isolates things from the flow of events, measures and characterizes them by fixed concepts. Bergson influenced Proust (whose cousin Mademoiselle Neuberger he married) and through him many twentieth-century writers.

REFERENCES: Ian W. Alexander *Bergson, Philosopher of Reflection* (London and New York 1957). Thomas Hanna, ed. *The Bergsonian Heritage* (New York 1962). Ben-Ami Scharfstein *Roots of Bergson's Philosophy* (New York and London 1943).

BERLIOZ, (Louis) Hector (Dec. 11, 1803 – Mar. 8, 1869). French composer. Born La Côte-St.-André, Isère. His father, a physician, indulged his early love of music but sent him to Paris (1821) to study medicine. Berlioz rebelled, became student of the composer Lesueur (1823) and entered the Conservatoire (1826). Won Prix de Rome (1830) after four attempts. First major work, *Symphonie fantastique* (1830); others include symphony *Harold en Italie* (1834), *Requiem Mass* (1837), opera *Benvenuto Cellini* (1838), dramatic symphony *Roméo et Juliette* (1839), *Grande Symphonie funèbre et triomphale* (1840), dramatic legend *La Damnation de Faust* (1846), *Te Deum* (1849), Christmas oratorio *L'Enfance du Christ* (1854), music drama *Les Troyens* (two parts, 1856/58), opera *Béatrice et Bénédict* (1862). Married Irish actress Henriette (Harriet) Smithson (1833). Soon after her death (1854) married Marie Recio, a singer (died 1862). After 1840, made frequent conducting tours across Europe. Berlioz was active as music critic, and published the influential *Traité d'instrumentation* (Treatise on Orchestration) (1844). Died in Paris.

TRANSLATIONS: *Memoirs* tr. D. Cairns (London and New York 1969). *Evenings with the Orchestra* tr. Jacques Barzun (New York 1956).

REFERENCES: Jacques Barzun *Berlioz and the Romantic Century* (3rd ed. New York 1969). W. J. Turner *Berlioz, His Life and Work* (London 1934). Tom S. Wotton *Hector Berlioz* (New York and London 1935).

HECTOR BERLIOZ
BY JACQUES BARZUN

The son of the country doctor had dutifully gone to Paris to study medicine, but although he liked the lectures on science, he hated dissection — and besides, his heart was already pledged to music. He spent his nights at the Opéra and much of his days reading scores in the library of the Conservatoire, then the leading music school in Europe.

He soon found teachers ready to help him, for he had scores of his own to show. Lesueur, who had been Napoleon's court composer, found the young Berlioz an apt pupil and soon got him accepted by his colleagues at the Conservatoire, Reicha and Cherubini. Following the tradition of that school, Berlioz competed for the Rome prize, to which he was eligible in 1827. But his musical ways were too unconventional, and he did not succeed until 1830, after four tries. Some of the music he composed for these competitions — notably *Cléopâtre* — now amazes our concert audiences: it is as if Keats's odes had been rejected as exam papers.

But by 1830 much else had happened to mold the mind and spirit of young Berlioz. First, he had discovered Beethoven, then a foreign bogeyman, and come to know not only the symphonies but the late quartets. Next, he had seen Shakespeare — another crude foreigner — and fallen in love at a distance with the leading lady who acted him in Paris, Harriet Smithson. Third, he had read Nerval's translation

of Goethe's *Faust* and out of his enthusiasm, with incredible rapidity, composed eight scenes from the First
Part of the poem. Finally and most important for the history of music, Berlioz had completed his first great work,
the *Symphonie fantastique*, performed
on December 5, 1830. Franz Liszt was
in the audience.

In counterpoint with these decisive
events, Berlioz's quarrels with his family and with Cherubini, his temporary
starvation and hackwork, his mad and
unsuccessful courting of the distant
"Ophelia," and his engagement — on
the rebound — with Camille Moke
(the rising and seductive pianist)
appear less important and ultimately
less interesting, though writers of program notes seize upon them as spice
they badly need. The development of
Berlioz's mind is thus obscured by the
vicissitudes of his early life.

In Rome, where the prize required
that he spend two years, Berlioz was at
loose ends, his friendships with Mendelssohn and Glinka being ostensibly
the chief gains of the sixteen months
that he actually lived in Italy. But he
wandered much over the countryside,
took endless notes of melodies and
projects — and dashed home on hearing that Camille Moke had broken her
engagement and pledged herself to a
prosperous piano manufacturer. A by-
product of the latter release was the
pair of superb overtures to *King Lear*
and *The Corsair*.

Back in Paris, Berlioz gave as a concert of re-entry the hodgepodge he
called *Lélio, or The Return to Life*, a
supposed sequel to the *Symphonie
fantastique*. It contained lovely music,
but none of it new, and the work
does not form a whole, especially
when one knows Berlioz's exacting
sense of unity and coherence. Amid
the usual troubles of Parisian artistic

life, Berlioz married his Ophelia in
1833. What the young composer then
faced, until nearly the end of his life,
was the question: how to live and
compose music? Nineteenth-century
Paris expected everyone to write operas — and thousands did who were
not even musicians. Awaiting his
chance, Berlioz became a music critic.
Out of his Italian memories he composed his *Harold in Italy;* then, after
political entanglements, the stupendous *Requiem.* At last in 1838 came
the opera: *Benvenuto Cellini,* based on
the memoirs of the Florentine artist.
The music was, once again, too advanced, and a cabal opposed to
Berlioz's backers helped to scuttle the
work.

Though Berlioz could not suspect it,
the pattern of his life was set by this,
his thirty-fourth year: he was to create
one musical model after another, meeting both fervid response and set hostility. To promote his music and his aesthetics, he would crisscross Europe
from London to Moscow again and
again, until the orchestras of Europe
had learned under his baton what the
modern style and technique were.
Wagner acknowledged that they were
revealed to him in that way, hearing
Berlioz's *Romeo and Juliet* in Paris in
1839. The later scores — *Grande Symphonie funèbre, Nuits d'Été, La Damnation de Faust, L'Enfance du Christ,
Te Deum, Les Troyens* and *Béatrice et
Bénédict* — were nearly all imposed
upon Europe in that fashion, while in
articles and books the assumptions of
these *dramme per musica* were expounded by the composer.

Understanding such riches of sound
was undoubtedly difficult, especially
since performances were infrequent
and — under other conductors than
Berlioz — often inadequate. The fact
that he was probably the greatest mel-

odist since Mozart did not help, for the nineteenth-century ear expected tunes to be *like* Mozart's — or Rossini's. A different melodic line, in turn, required a different harmony, and so did the new element of structure that Berlioz introduced: timbre. It is only now, with the aid of recordings that permit us to rehear, and after the education we have received at the hands of Wagner, Strauss, Debussy, and Stravinsky, that we have begun to hear Berlioz properly, that is, as a creator who — to quote his own words — "took up music where Beethoven left it" and fashioned a medium for his own dramatic and psychological conceptions.

Fame and influence came to him at last — official honors, adulation from young hopefuls, and (ultimate test) invitations to tour the United States. Berlioz preferred Russia, where "The Five" were his ardent disciples. Toward the end the story of his achievement was complicated, as in a Shakespearean tragedy, by the philosophical and musical pachyderm that Wagner called "the music of the future." As a result, Liszt's head was turned and the critics crystallized confusion by taking Wagnerism, program music, Liszt's symphonic poem, and the works of Berlioz as interchangeable parts. Only now is the tangle being teased out, with the consequent emergence of Berlioz for what he was — a lyric and dramatic composer of the first rank, who needed no programs to buttress his work, and who influenced all those who came after, without being imitated by any.

BERNART DE VENTADOUR (also known as **BERNART DE VENTADORN**) (fl. 1150–1180). Provençal troubadour. Born probably in Limousin district and of humble origins. Served viscount of Ventadour (Eble II or Eble III); according to legend was viscount-ess's lover and had to leave viscount's service on discovery of secret *amour.* Entered service of Eleanor of Aquitaine at Norman court (before 1154), then service of Raymond V, count of Toulouse. Ceased writing (c.1180) and is said to have become a monk. Bernart's language is an evolved form of expression to which his subtle and always surprising versification adds considerable color. In the forty-one songs we know to be his, he sings sincerely and lucidly of his own loves and of their allegorical reflection in nature.

TRANSLATION: *The Songs of Bernart de Ventadorn* ed. Stephen G. Nichols, Jr. (Chapel Hill, N.C. 1962).

BERNINI, Gian (or Giovanni) Lorenzo (Dec. 7, 1598 – Nov. 28, 1680). Italian sculptor, architect, and painter. Born Naples; artistically gifted from early childhood. Called to Rome to design the Barberini palace for Maffeo Barberini, later Pope Urban VIII. Succeeded Maderno as architect for St. Peter's (1629). Designed throne of St. Peter, the baldachin for the high altar, the colonnade of the piazza before the church, also the Scala Regia in the Vatican. Sculpture includes early *Apollo and Daphne* and *David* in the Borghese Museum, and *Ecstasy of St. Theresa* in the chapel of S. Maria della Vittoria, which he designed and which epitomizes his style by combining sculpture, architecture, and painting into an illusionistic whole. Also famous for his Roman fountains, including those of piazzas di Spagna and Navona. Invited by Louis XIV to Paris (1665) to complete the Louvre, but Claude Perrault's designs were adopted. Returned to Rome (1667) to continue his career under papal patronage. Also produced expressive portrait busts and more than two hundred paintings. Died in Rome; buried in S. Maria Maggiore. Bernini exerted the dominant influence on European sculpture and architecture for almost two centuries.

REFERENCES: Filippo Baldinucci *Life of Bernini* (tr. University Park, Pa. 1966). Howard Hibbard *Bernini* (Baltimore PB 1966). Rudolf Wittkower *Gian Lorenzo Bernini: The Sculptor of the Roman Baroque* (2nd ed. London and New York 1966).

〜

GIAN LORENZO BERNINI
BY SVETLANA ALPERS

The seventeenth century marked the end of the great Renaissance tradition in art, and Bernini, primarily a sculptor and architect but also painter, stage designer, and playwright, was the last of the great universal geniuses working in that tradition. His art exemplifies much of what is best and most characteristic in baroque art (for once this stylistic term provides an appropriate and all-inclusive description, rather than a simplification, of an artist's merits). His technically brilliant works, bearing public witness to the ideals of the Roman Catholic Church and absolute monarchy, are often conceived in terms of brilliant conceits, and are always informed with the most direct representation of the human passions. Like Rubens, the other seminal baroque artist, Bernini entertained none of the neurotic doubts about himself or his art that had tormented earlier geniuses like Leonardo and Michelangelo. He was an intimate friend of Urban VIII, the last great Maecenas among the popes, and his work for him, for succeeding popes, and for the wealthy of Rome through the century — starting as a prodigy in his teens, he was active for almost seventy years — helped once more to refashion Rome, this time into a baroque city.

Since Bernini's art lacks the concern with self that has been the hallmark of art for the past century, modern viewers have been perhaps most responsive to its naturalistic aspects: the daring rendering in hard marble, in *Apollo and Daphne*, of the transformation of a woman into a tree; the graphic description of the erotic ecstasy of St. Theresa, "the sweetness caused by this intense pain" (to quote her own account) as the arrow of the Lord pierces her; the last breath of the Blessed Ludovica Albertoni, lying on a marble bed behind the altar and clutching at her breast in her final agony.

In striving to make these scenes immediately real for the viewer, Bernini rejected many of the working assumptions about sculpture common in the Renaissance. First of all, he thought of his work less as something carved out of a single block of marble than as something built up, modeled as it were. He sacrificed the integrity of the block of marble for new representational ends. Second, he rejected the strict separation of the arts insisted upon in Renaissance theory. He embraced sculpture, architecture, and painting in single works in a way which was not only unprecedented but was also the basis for the great illusionistic displays so popular among artists and architects all over Europe at the turn of the eighteenth century. Bernini's aim, like that of many artists in the seventeenth century, was to go beyond a convincing imitation of nature to create an illusion compelling the viewer to believe that he was actually present at the scene depicted before his eyes. Thus the marble group of Theresa and the angel, set in an aedicula over the altar, seems to float on a cloud (made of stucco), and is lit by rays of light (gilded pieces of metal) illuminated from above by a hidden window, as if by a light from heaven, which is itself, in the original scheme, represented on the ceiling of the chapel in painted stucco figures and frescoes.

Bernini escaped the danger of the vulgar sensationalism always potential in such daringly illusionistic art by at all times maintaining a control over the relationship of work to viewer and by an essentially ideal notion of art. St. Theresa and the Blessed Ludovica Albertoni, for example, are set off from our world by the very architecture which presents and reveals them to us. Bernini's figures are consistently based on classical figural formulas and display ideal facial types (dazzling though Daphne's transformation is, no real girl ever forced her face into such an ideal scream). Perhaps the clearest example of the ideal aspect of Bernini's art is found in the account of his working procedure in making the great portrait bust of Louis XIV. Bernini's informal drawings, which caught the king at work and at play, and his clay models, which captured the look and virtues proper to an ideal monarch by echoing the features of Alexander the Great, were finally joined together into an image at once real and ideal. The entire bust, mounted on a base made of a gilded globe representing the world and inscribed *Picciola base*, was to have been presented in terms of a conceit implying what a small world this was to support so great a king.

Part and parcel of the modern admiration for the marvelous realism of Bernini's works and the wit involved in his conceptions has been a tendency to ignore the essentially public nature of the address and the frequent extravagance of his art. For Bernini was called upon to propagandize masses of men, specifically to woo all Roman Catholic Christendom. His angels bearing the instruments of the Passion lined the worshipers' way across the Tiber to the Vatican precincts; the great arms of the colonnades (surmounted by statues of saints and martyrs also conceived by Bernini) embraced them as they entered the forecourt of St.

Peter's; entering the narthex of St. Peter's, worshipers were greeted by the monumental statue of Constantine at the moment of his conversion; finally, the central experience within the church itself was produced by Bernini, as the faithful looked down the nave, through his baldachin over the grave of St. Peter, to the holy chair supported by four church fathers beneath the great golden glass with which Bernini, most audaciously of all, represented the Holy Dove come down to earth in a great glory of gilt rays and stucco cherubim and angels. (This account, one should add, hardly exhausts the many monuments conceived by Bernini for St. Peter's alone.) And yet for all their huge proportions (the baldachin is almost ninety feet high) and the public nature of their address, these works are informed with the detailed and intimate description of life common to all Bernini's works and to baroque art in general. Delicate branches and leaves wind their way up the columns of the baldachin and putti play with the papal emblems above, while the four church fathers bearing the chair of Peter bend and weave in expressions of tormented joy.

Since we are far removed from the beliefs and commitments of Bernini and his art, it is perhaps his fountains, which combine human forms, animal life and moving water into meaningful secular decorations celebrating the ruling papal families, that remain most accessible to us. Today, when sculptors are moving their works off tables and pedestals and into the great outdoors, and are striving once again to make monumental images which organize the space and relate to the architecture around them, we can only envy the opportunity given to Bernini and the artistic forms and meanings available to him for decorating a great city square like the piazza Navona, in this last and most confident flowering of the great age of Italian art.

BEYLE, Henri. *See* **STENDHAL.**

BIBIENA (or **BIBBIENA**). Italian family of artists and architects. GIOVANNI MARIA GALLI (1625–65), born at Bibiena, a skillful, imaginative painter, founded the family. Son FERDINANDO GALLI DA BIBIENA (1657–1743) had three sons who carried on the artistic tradition: ALESSANDRO (1687–1769), GIUSEPPE (1696–1756), and ANTONIO (1700–44) GALLI DA BIBIENA. They distinguished themselves in scenic design, especially in complex perspectives, for opera, theatre, and court occasions, as indicated by extant drawings and some two hundred engravings in several European museums.

REFERENCE: A. H. Mayor *The Bibiena Family* (New York 1945).

BIERCE, Ambrose (Gwinett) (June 24, 1842 – c.1914). American journalist and short story writer. Born Meigs county, Ohio; briefly attended Kentucky Military Institute. After distinguished Civil War service with Union army (1861–65), moved to San Francisco and began writing for periodicals, becoming editor of *News Letter* (1868). Married Mary Ellen Day (1871); left her (1872) for four years to go to London, where he wrote for magazine *Fun*. Also published three volumes of sketches, *Nuggets and Dust* (1872) on mining camps, in Bret Harte tradition, *The Fiend's Delight* (1872), and *Cobwebs from an Empty Skull* (1873), satirical fables. Back in San Francisco (1876), edited the *Wasp* and contributed to Hearst's *Sunday Examiner* (1887–96). Left for Mexico (1913); he presumably joined Pancho Villa's army, and all trace of him was lost. Bierce's major works are the famous collection of short stories first issued as *Tales of Soldiers and Civilians* (1891), then as *In the Midst of Life* (1898), which includes *An Occurrence at Owl Creek Bridge; Can Such Things Be* (1893); *The Devil's Dictionary* (1906). Savage irony, a Poe-like horror, and a severe, unembel-

lished style characterize this master of the short story.

EDITIONS: *The Collected Works of Ambrose Bierce* (12 vols. Staten Island, N.Y. 1909–12). *The Collected Writings of Ambrose Bierce* (New York 1946, PB 1960).

REFERENCES: Carey McWilliams *Ambrose Bierce: A Biography* (Hamden, Conn. 1929). Walter Neale *The Life of Ambrose Bierce* (New York 1929). Richard O'Connor *Ambrose Bierce: A Biography* (Boston 1967 and London 1968).

BINGHAM, George Caleb (Mar. 20, 1811 – July 7, 1879). American genre painter. Born Augusta county, Va. In Missouri, where family lived after 1819, met painter Chester Harding, who encouraged his interest in art. First formal training at Pennsylvania Academy of Fine Arts in Philadelphia (1838). After working as portraitist, Washington, D.C. (1840–44), returned to Missouri and took up genre painting. Famous among his scenes of river life are *Fur Traders Descending the Missouri* (c.1845, Metropolitan Museum, New York), *The Jolly Flatboatman* (1846, City Art Museum, St. Louis), *Raftsmen Playing Cards* (1847), *The Squatters* (1850, Museum of Fine Arts, Boston) and *The Trapper's Return* (1851, Institute of Arts, Detroit). Bingham entered Missouri politics with election to legislature (1848). After a year in Union army, served as state treasurer (1862–65). Became state adjutant general (1875). Such pictures as *Stump Speaking* and *Verdict of the People* (both 1854, Mercantile Library Association, St. Louis) reflect his enjoyment of political life. Traveled in Europe (1856–59), studied briefly in Düsseldorf. Died in Kansas City, Mo. Bingham's paintings, very popular in his day, are noted for their sophisticated and striking composition as well as their humor and authentic depiction of period and locale.

REFERENCES: E. Maurice Bloch *George Caleb Bingham* (Berkeley, Calif. 1967 and Cambridge, England 1968). Albert William Christ-Janer *George Caleb Bingham of Missouri* (New York 1940). John F. McDermott *George*

Caleb Bingham: River Portraitist (Norman, Okla. 1959).

BIZET, Georges (Alexandre César Léopold) (Oct. 25, 1838 – June 3, 1875). French composer. Born Paris, only child of professional musicians, who zealously nurtured his precocious talent. Entered Paris Conservatoire (1848); much influenced by music of Gounod. Won many prizes, culminating Prix de Rome (1857). One-act opera buffa, *Le Docteur Miracle,* produced (1857). After nearly three years in Rome, returned to Paris (1860), where he wrote the operas *Les Pêcheurs de perles* (1863) and *La Jolie Fille de Perth* (1867), as well as piano pieces and songs. Married Geneviève Halévy (1869). When Franco-Prussian War broke out (1870) enlisted in National Guard. His last and finest work, the opera *Carmen* (1875), was at first received with indifference by the public and with hostility by most of the press. Bizet died at Bougival three months later. *Carmen* was withdrawn after forty-eight performances in Paris, yet within the year was produced in Vienna to a triumphant reception. Henceforth its world success was assured, though it was not until 1883 that Paris saw the work revived and received it with acclaim. Other major works: *Symphony in C Major* (written 1855, discovered and first performed 1935), *Jeux d'enfants* (1871), and *L'Arlésienne* (1872).

REFERENCES: Mina Curtiss *Bizet and His World* (London and New York 1958). Winton Dean *Georges Bizet: His Life and Work* (London 1965). See also *Pages from the Goncourt Journals* (tr. London and New York 1962), James Harding *Saint-Saëns and His Circle* (London 1965), and Camille Saint-Saëns *Musical Memories* (Boston 1919).

✒

GEORGES BIZET
BY PAUL HORGAN

The short life of Georges Bizet falls into three periods. The first sets him forth as the small lord of an extraordinary talent — at four he mastered musical notation along with the alphabet, and displayed a Mozartian aptitude for musical memory which delighted his parents. They were both musicians; his father, who taught singing, was a hopeful but ineffectual composer; his mother a charming amateur pianist. Admitted to the formidable Paris Conservatoire at ten, winner of prize upon prize for composition and performance, Bizet was early granted the friendship of Gounod, who was rising in the musical world. Traces of Gounod's style and influence can be found throughout Bizet's work, even to the end.

At seventeen Bizet composed his *Symphony in C,* supposedly upon the model of Gounod's *First Symphony.* Perhaps Bizet saw it simply as an exercise, for he tucked it away among other youthful manuscripts, and it was never played until eighty years later. The one important work of his youth, it belatedly entered the repertory as a light-spirited masterpiece of the order, say, of Mendelssohn's *Italian Symphony.*

It was inevitable that Bizet should compete for the Prix de Rome, which he won on the second try. He set out for Rome in blithe certainty, based on his remarkable record of achievement as a student. Highly intelligent, well-read, witty, passionately honest in friendship and art, he seemed destined to continue his swift rise.

But the years — just under three — which he spent as a pensioner at the Villa Medici marked the beginning of the second major period of his life, which was characterized by almost unrelieved failure and disappointment. To begin with, though Rome was beautiful, its history and monuments splendid, and Italian skies and mountains ravishing, the Italians were impossible, their music inferior, and even Palestrina "deadly boring." He competed for an important prize, and lost to a nonentity. His health was intermittently poor, with recurrences of the throat infections which finally caused his death. He conceived many large, even grandiloquent works, began several, completed few, and nothing came of any of them. Despite optimistic letters home, he seemed to suffer a general crisis of confidence; and there is a sense that as he matured intellectually, his rational principles — for like most latter-day Frenchmen he was an heir of Voltaire — wore away the spontaneous lyricism of his earlier work.

His sense of frustration must have been great and may help to explain his lifelong tendency to violent outbreaks of emotion, which ended always by making him physically ill. One such attack broke out in Venice when on his way home from the Rome Academy residency he heard that his mother was dangerously ill. She survived almost another year, while Bizet lived at home with his family in Montmartre, comforted by Marie Reiter, the family servant, who bore him a son. She remained faithful even to the end, attending Bizet at his death.

A fastidious rationalist who was a learned amateur of classical and modern literature, Bizet had none of the romantic appearance of a Liszt, a Musset, a Wagner (whom he admired artistically but declared to be a "poseur," a "bore"). Even in maturity, with his curly hair, plump cheeks, full moustache and beard, pince-nez, and stocky figure, Bizet kept something of the student about his looks.

Success, in the Second Empire, had its usual false glow and urgent appeal. As Bizet strove for it, he saw Offenbach, Gounod, Saint-Saëns, Meyerbeer, Auber, Délibes, and others rewarded while he struggled in vain. He undertook many new projects between 1860 and 1870, some of which came to the stage, but none of which caught on. He seemed to struggle to express his own sort of eclecticism, with a leaning toward exotic dramatic subjects. *The Pearl Fishers* (1863), which contained charming predictions of what must come with the fulfillment of his genius, ran for only eighteen performances and was dismissed by all critics except Berlioz, who praised it in the last article he ever wrote.

For the rest, Bizet was forced to hurry about Paris at hack jobs, giving lessons, arranging other peoples' scores for popular performance, serving briefly as a chorus master at the Opéra, earning a bit occasionally as an audition pianist for newly submitted operas by hopeful composers whose full manuscript scores he was able with marvelous facility to transform at sight into rich piano reductions.

Pressed by ambition and responsibility (in 1869 he married Geneviève Halévy, who bore him a son, Jacques; their marriage was troubled with her recurrent nervous attacks), he was the hard-worked musical mole, grubbing away at obscure underground tasks. "It is maddening," he cried, "to interrupt work I love for two days in order to write cornet solos." And "Music! what a splendid art, but a dreary profession!"

Now and then Gounod took him to the musical Sundays of the Princesse Mathilde, where he was persuaded to exhibit his prodigious pianism — Liszt once said Bizet was one of the three greatest pianists in Europe. But he disliked the shoddy bustle of the new-rich society of Paris, where the tone was set by adventurers, from the emperor on down: a world, as the Goncourts said, "of shady deals, selling something of everything." When the Franco-Prussian War ended with the defeat of France, Bizet, though he had volunteered for service, was glad to see the end of a regime which, as he said, had smothered his country in a "thick coat of shame and ordure." In the commune of 1871 he saw France in further trials; but at about the same time an inner resolution of his own uncertain powers seemed to crystallize them in harmony, and the brief third, and final, period of his life at last fulfilled his gifts if not his sense of reward.

By now Bizet had created a voluminous literature — some seventy works for the voice in solo or chorus, a number of keyboard pieces, and over a dozen orchestral or other instrumental compositions, along with countless pieces of hackwork. In addition — and it is here that his most significant impulses are to be found — he undertook twenty-eight dramatic works, some of which were never completed. Of the remainder, only seven reached the stage during his lifetime, and he never saw any of them achieve success. But he was right when he said to Saint-Saëns, "I need the theatre."

The Fair Maid of Perth (1867) received a friendly press, though it too ran for only eighteen performances. His penultimate opera, *Djamileh* (1872), a piece in one act, failed immediately. In this, as in all his other operas but the final one, he was disadvantaged by a wretched libretto. But his creative courage never faltered, and when the librettists Henri Meilhac and Ludovic Halévy (the latter his cousin-in-law) asked him for an *opéra comique,* he agreed, declaring that his piece would be "gay, but with a gaiety that permits style," and he proposed to his collaborators the novel *Carmen* by Prosper Mérimée, which had been published in 1845. He took satisfaction

from "the absolute certainty," he wrote, "of having found my path. I know what I am doing."

And now everything of the past seemed somehow to be justified as preparation for his great work — all his disappointments and his one late success, which was the incidental music for Alphonse Daudet's play *L'Arlésienne.* The play was a failure, but Bizet's music for it (1872) soon became a favorite in the concert hall in the form of excerpts. Here at last emerged the mastery learned in a drudging lifetime. Long ago he had told a pupil, "In the orchestra you must have air," and to another he wrote, "Let each part have around it sufficient room to move." So the "exquisite spareness," as Winton Dean calls it, of *L'Arlésienne* released both melody and texture in a way that reached its highest expression in the work that followed.

Bizet began to compose *Carmen* in the late spring of 1873, was interrupted by other work, resumed it at Bougival, and finished it late in 1874. "This time I have written a work," he said, "that is all clarity and vivacity, full of color and melody. It will be amusing." He saw the first performance (March 3, 1875) with Célestine Galli-Marié in the title role — evidently an ideal artist, for whom he corrected the score at rehearsals, the better to suit her style. (There were those who said the prima donna and the composer were lovers.) The first night was not a scandalous failure, but it fell so far short of success that later Bizet was found, as Mary Garden describes it (*My Story,* 1951) — herself a great Carmen, she heard the anecdote long after — "all alone in his room, sitting in front of a table with his head in his hands, crying bitter tears . . . in the depths of despair." A typical criticism in the press said, *"Quelle vérité, mais quel scandale!"*

The opera played to thin houses further into the season while Bizet retired to Bougival. On the night of June 3, 1875, onstage during the third-act card scene, Galli-Marié felt a sudden heavy pang of dread, and coming offstage at the end of her scene burst into a passion of grief. She was barely persuaded to finish the performance. The next day they learned that Bizet had died in the country, of his old throat affliction, during the hour of the third act at the Opéra Comique, on that night.

Soon thereafter, *Carmen* was played in Brussels, London, and also in Vienna, where Brahms went twenty times to hear it, and it was not long until the world adopted it as one of the handful of ever-fresh repertory works of the opera theatre.

Like many a masterpiece, it has too often been allowed to lapse into stereotype. We see Carmen herself presented as a cheap baggage, full of stock beguilements and meaningless furies — the unimaginative way out for most singers who undertake the role. Actually, restudied, the score reveals not only Carmen but also her factory mates, and Don José, and the smugglers, and the rest as true human beings with their own dignity, pathos, and even grace. The crowd scenes are depicted musically in a populism as elegant as it is original; and the key to Carmen's temperament — the orchestra is full of this — is a melancholy fatalism through which she knows herself and her appetites for what they are, and accepts her subjection to them with courageous realism. Bizet was able to comprehend Carmen the better because of a certain strain in his own nature — "For many reasons," he once said, "I need absolute moral independence." With another breath he gave a

pupil a clue to his own mystery as an artist and an epitome of what lies behind *Carmen* as a whole: "Without form, no style; without style, no art." The lessons he executed so thoughtlessly as a boy of seventeen came finally under his conscious control as a mature man of thirty-six, until at last we could know the genius who for a lifetime was concealed within the craftsman.

Some years after Bizet's death, his widow Geneviève married into circumstances which he had not been able to provide. Her new husband, Émile Straus, was a wealthy lawyer, and after the grubby years on the edges of Bohemia with Bizet, she was now able to establish herself as an important hostess, with a salon which attracted Marcel Proust, who used her as a model for the Duchesse de Guermantes, "smart, and still quite young." Perhaps — though she remained a congenital victim of "nerves" — her new life was happier than the old. What remains, despite all, when we hear the name and the work of Georges Bizet is our sense of his lovely vivacity, with its undertones of civilized melancholy.

BJØRNSON, Bjørnstjerne (Martinius) (Dec. 8, 1832 – Apr. 26, 1910). Norwegian writer and political leader. Born Kvikne; a clergyman's son. To Christiania (now Oslo) (1850); enrolled at University of Christiania (1852), but abandoned studies to become journalist and critic. Succeeded Ibsen as artistic director at national theatre in Bergen (1857–59); married Karoline Reimers, an actress (1858). Bjørnson's peasant tales, notably *Synnøve Solbakken* (1857, tr. 1881), *Arne* (1859, tr. 1890), and *En Glad Gut* (1860, tr. *A Happy Boy* 1896). Following period of European travel, 1860–63, during which he produced first mature drama, the trilogy *Sigurd Slembe* (1862, tr. 1888), worked in Christiania as theatre director, journalist and editor, and political activist. Spent much of his time from 1873 abroad, mainly in France, the Alps, and Italy, though continuing his vigorous promotion of liberal social and political reforms in Norway. He died in Paris. Among Bjørnson's late dramas, dealing with contemporary problems, are *En Fallit* (1875, tr. *The Bankrupt* 1914), *En Hanske* (1883, tr. *A Gauntlet* 1912), and the two-part *Over Aevne* (1883/ 1895, tr. *Beyond Our Power* 1913–14). Most of his lyric poems, including *Ja, vi elsker dette landet,* which became Norway's national anthem, were collected in *Digte og Sange* (1870, tr. *Poems and Songs,* 1915). Bjørnson's didactic later novels include *Magnhild* (1877, tr. 1883), *Kaptejn Mansana* (1879, tr. *Captain Mansana* 1882), *Det flager i byen og på havnen* (1884, tr. *The Heritage of the Kurts* 1892), and *På Guds veje* (1889, tr. *In God's Way,* 1890). Received Nobel Prize for literature (1903).

TRANSLATIONS: *Three Comedies* (London and New York 1912) and *Three Dramas* (London and New York 1914) tr. Robert F. Sharp.

REFERENCES: Harold Larson *Bjørnstjerne Bjørnson: A Study in Norwegian Nationalism* (New York 1944). William Lyon Phelps *Essays on Modern Novelists* (New York 1910).

BLACKSTONE, Sir William (July 10, 1723 – Feb. 14, 1780). English jurist. Born and died in London; posthumous son of a tradesman. Educated at Charterhouse and Pembroke College, Oxford; became fellow of All Souls College (1744); called to the bar (1746). Unsuccessful as lawyer, Blackstone returned to Oxford (1753) and delivered lectures on English law. British universities had hitherto considered only Roman law, and recognizing importance of Blackstone's lectures Oxford appointed him first Vinerian professor (1758). In 1761, made a king's counsel, elected to Parliament, named principal of New Hall Inn at Oxford, and married to Sarah Clitherow. Made solicitor to the queen (1763). Blackstone's fame rests on his *Commentaries on the Laws of England* (4 vols. 1765–69). Written in a clear and gracefully ornate style, they reduced to a rational order the formless and unclassified bulk of law. Often criticized, notably by Jeremy Bentham, for inconsistency in basic terms and concepts, for complacent view that English law was in general beyond improvement, for glossing over ambiguities in the sources, and for lapses in historical discernment, this work nevertheless has great value as explication of Anglo-American legal system and remains the cornerstone of English and American legal practice.

EDITION: *Commentaries on the Laws of England* (facsimile reprint 4 vols. London and Dobbs Ferry, N.Y. 1966).
REFERENCE: Daniel J. Boorstin *The Mysterious Science of the Law: An essay on Blackstone's Commentaries* (Cambridge, Mass. and London 1941, PB 1958).

BLAKE, William (Nov. 28, 1757 – Aug. 12, 1827). English poet and artist. Born London, son of a hosier. No formal education; began to study drawing at ten, then served apprenticeship to James Basire, an engraver, and attended Royal Academy. By 1779 began to make his living by illustrating and engraving others' works. Began writing verse in early teens; read extensively in philosophy and poetry. Marriage to Catherine Boucher (1782) was happy though childless. Painting first exhibited at Royal Academy (1780); poems first published in *Poetical Sketches* (1783). Began to engrave, illustrate, and print his own works with *Songs of Innocence* (1789), *The Book of Thel* (1789), the prose work *The Marriage of Heaven and Hell* (c.1790), and *Songs of Experience* ("Tyger! Tyger! burning bright") (1794). Created his political and cosmological myth in *The French Revolution* (1791), *Visions of the Daughters of Albion* (1793), *America: A Prophecy* (1793), *Europe: A Prophecy* (1794), *The First Book of Urizen* (1794), *The Book of Ahania* (1795), *The Book of Los* (1795), *The Song of Los* (1795), and *Vala, or The Four Zoas* (1795–1804). Wrote long symbolic poems *Milton* (1804–1808) and *Jerusalem* (1804–20). Works little read in his lifetime; achieved some recognition as artist and engraver, but died (in London) as he had lived, in poverty. Illustrated Edward Young's *Night Thoughts* (1796–97), *The Book of Job* (1823–25), Dante's *Divine Comedy* (1825–27), and other works.

EDITIONS: *Complete Writings* ed. Geoffrey Keynes (new ed. London and New York 1966). *The Poetry and Prose of William Blake* ed. David V. Erdman and Harold Bloom (New York 1965). *Paintings* ed. Darrell Figgis (London 1925). *Drawings* ed. Geoffrey Keynes (London 1927, second series London 1956). *Engravings* ed. Geoffrey Keynes (London 1950).

REFERENCES: Sir Anthony Blunt *The Art of William Blake* (New York 1959 and London 1960). S. Foster Damon *William Blake: His Philosophy and Symbols* (Boston 1924 and New York 1947). David V. Erdman *Blake: Prophet Against Empire* (Princeton, N.J. and London 1954). Northrop Frye *Fearful Symmetry: A Study of William Blake* (Princeton and London 1947, also PB). Alexander Gilchrist *The Life of William Blake: Pictor Ignotus* (2 vols. London 1863, London and New York 1942, Everyman's Library). Kathleen Raine *Blake and Tradition* (2 vols. Princeton 1968). Mark Schorer *William Blake: The Politics of Vision* (New York 1946, also PB).

✒

WILLIAM BLAKE
BY AILEEN WARD

No other great poet has been so undervalued for so long as William Blake. In his lifetime he was regarded chiefly as an engraver of other men's designs; his own work as a painter was almost totally neglected, and the few who admired his art did not read his poems. Indeed, for the last two decades of his life he was derided as a madman, then forgotten for a third of a century. Not until the 1860's, with Gilchrist's pioneering biography of Blake — significantly subtitled *Pictor Ignotus* — and Swinburne's appreciative critical essay, was his reputation as a great

painter and lyric poet achieved. His prophetic writings were finally reprinted in 1893, in the first collected edition of his poetry, by E. J. Ellis and W. B. Yeats, whose fascination with the Celtic and cabalistic elements in his work fixed the image of Blake as an incomprehensible mystic. Modern criticism, however, insists on his "total intelligibility," and has established his place within a universal poetic and intellectual tradition and the political struggle of his own times.

In an age of revolution, Blake's revolutionary outlook was shaped by his birth and upbringing. As the son of a nonconformist London hosier who indulged his precocious talent for drawing, he escaped the stultifying education of most middle-class boys as well as the empty formalism of the established religion. His training as an engraver gave him not only a steady if modest livelihood but also complete independence of public reaction to his poetry and his ideas; in fact his poems were not written for publication in the usual sense of the word. As a young man Blake responded exuberantly to the vision of freedom proclaimed in the American Revolution, and at the outbreak of the French Revolution he was a fellow radical of Thomas Paine and Mary Wollstonecraft. But in his middle years, as the revolution betrayed its own ideals, Blake gave up his hope for a regenerated society to return — on his own unorthodox terms — to a Christian faith in spiritual regeneration. At the same time he was increasingly driven in upon himself by the weight of official repression — in 1804 he was tried for sedition because of a rash remark to an insolent soldier — and public indifference to his painting. After the failure of his exhibition in 1809, Blake disappeared into poverty and obscurity for nearly ten years. But when he emerged around 1818, the mentor of a band of devoted young disciples, it was as one who had "kept the Divine Vision in time of trouble." The work of his last decade — the Job and Dante designs especially — are of an unparalleled strength and sublimity; and he died in Job-like serenity, singing (as his wife reported) extemporaneous hymns of praise.

The dilemmas of his age made a profound impression on his thought. All the tangled ramifications of Blake's "system" spring from his basic political belief — Rousseau's paradox that man, born free, is everywhere in chains. But this is only one aspect of Blake's multidimensioned view of human experience — of mankind once whole and happy, now rent by discord and tyranny from which it must be saved by some revolutionary or apocalyptic upheaval. In theological terms, this is the familiar story of man's fall from Eden into a world of sin — which Blake, as a dissenting Protestant, saw also in ecclesiastical terms, as the negation of Christ's "Everlasting Gospel" by the dogmas of the Church. In philosophy, it is the decline from the wisdom of the ancients to the dead science of Newton, the barren logic of Locke; in art, from the sublime example of the Bible to the "stolen and perverted" tradition of the classics. In social organization, it is the change from universal brotherhood to the inequities of monarchy, the oppositions of rich and poor; in technology, from the self-reliant craftsmanship of the guild system to the oppressive mechanization of factory labor. Fundamentally, it is an inner or psychological fall, from the unselfconscious integrity of "Infant Joy" with its spontaneous love to the self-tormenting self-divisions of adulthood and the battle of the sexes. From this divided state man can be restored to his original unity, as Blake came to believe, only by a continual death to the isolated self and the material world, in re-enactment of Christ's death for mankind.

This is the master theme of Blake's painting and poetry — a unified achievement unmatched by any other artist. The symbiotic relationship between the two is best exemplified in his special technique of illuminated printing. The text of his poems, surrounded by symbolic illustrations, was first etched in relief, then after printing the pictures were finished in watercolor. Pictorial and poetic ideas, born together in his imagination, elucidate and extend each other in the completed work. For over a century most painters have scorned narrative or "historical" painting as a needless limitation on their exploration of the medium; to Blake it was the mode that set the imagination free, unhampered by the claims of *vraisemblance* as in landscape or portraiture. Virtually all his work is illustrative — whether illustrations for his own or other men's poetry or independent designs based on scenes from the Bible. The "giant forms" of his painting express the humanism central to his thought — the belief that "All deities reside in the human breast," that humanity rather than nature or the supernatural is the ground of all value and meaning.

As a painter, Blake developed slowly, moving steadily toward the final realization of certain subjects that had preoccupied him from the beginning. But in poetry he was a master of the lyric even in his teens, and his later writing represents a difficult modulation away from the limpid grace of his early songs toward a harsh "prophetic" style rather like the later Beethoven's, constantly incorporating new and intractable material in increasingly complex structures. The *Songs of Innocence and of Experience* dramatize his conviction that "Without Contraries is no progression," the theme of his cryptic prose satire *The Marriage of Heaven and Hell*. In 1790 passive conformity to the established religious and political order seemed not good but evil: revolutionary energy is called for to "stamp the stony law to dust." The earlier prophetic books, from *The French Revolution* to *The Song of Los,* develop the theme of man's political and psychological enslavement in a receding series from the present moment back to the day of Creation. In *The Four Zoas* Blake reworked these fragments in a single epic with a new cast of mythological figures, headed by the four embodiments of man's divided being — reason, sense, emotion, and imagination — and a new ending of humanistic regeneration achieved through the workings of the poetic or prophetic spirit. In *Milton* this cosmic drama is recast as the fall and redemption of a single individual, John Milton returned to earth to undo the errors that have sprung from his work. In *Jerusalem,* Blake's culminating statement of the apocalyptic theme and his masterpiece as painter-poet, the epic expands to a synoptic view of all human thought and history in which Christ's sacrifice becomes the condition and assurance of man's spiritual rebirth.

In Blake's view, the true Christian is the true artist; the Spirit of Prophecy is identical with the Poetic Genius, and man's redemptive labor is building the City of Art, the new Golgotha. Few other poets in English have created such art out of religious vision; no other poet has expressed such a religious commitment to art.

BLOCH, Ernest (July 24, 1880 – July 15, 1959). Swiss-American composer. Born Geneva. Jacques Delacroze in Geneva, Eugène Ysaÿe in Brussels (1897–99), and Iwan Knorr in Frankfurt (1900) were his principal teachers. After further study in Munich and Paris, returned to Geneva, where he taught at Conservatory (1904–15). First compositions date from 1895; principal early work is the opera *Macbeth* (1909). Came to America (1916) as conductor; became professor at Mannes School of Music, New York (1917); director of Cleveland Institute of Music (1920–25) and of San Francisco Conservatory (1925–1930). Taught many American composers, including Roger Sessions. In Europe (1930–38); returned to U.S. because of rising anti-Semitism. Died in Portland, Oregon. Bloch is noted for the Jewish identity of his work, seen especially in his use of Hebrew liturgical music. Well-known compositions include *Schelomo*, Hebrew rhapsody for cello and orchestra (1916); *Israel Symphony* (1917); two concerti grossi (1925 and 1953); *America*, symphonic poem (1926); *Sacred Service* (1933); *Violin Concerto* (1938); five string quartets.

BLOEMAERT, Abraham (1564 – Jan. 27, 1651). Dutch painter and engraver. Born Gorinchem, son of architect Cornelis Bloemaert. Studied in Utrecht and Paris. After living for a time in Amsterdam, where he married Judith Schonenburgh (1592; she died shortly afterward), he settled in Utrecht. Second marriage, to Geertruyd de Roy (1601), produced six children, four of whom became eminent painters. In early 1620's came under influence of Caravaggio; through Bloemaert and his many students, who included (besides his sons) Jacob Cuyp and Gerard and Willem van Honthorst, the Caravaggio manner spread and became the distinguishing mark of the Utrecht school. Bloemaert's brilliantly colored mannerist paintings depict historical, allegorical and genre subjects, landscapes and still life. Died at Utrecht.

BLOK, Alexander Alexandrovich (Nov. 28, 1880 – Aug. 7, 1921). Russian poet and dramatist. Born St. Petersburg into intellectual family. Educated St. Petersburg University. Married Liubov Mendeleyeva, daughter of eminent Russian chemist (1903). Traveled in Europe. Assigned to engineering corps World War I. Favored October Revolution. Achieved recognition with first publication of poetry, *Verses About the Beautiful Lady* (2 vols. 1904–1908). During this period also wrote lyrical dramas, including *The Puppet Show*. More brilliant and successful was his poetry, which brought something new to Russian literature — imaginative figures of speech, unusual visions, original use of language, marking him as both a symbolist and a master of lyric verse. His last, most famous work, *The Twelve* (written 1918, tr. 1920), in which he welcomes the revolution, won his reputation as Bard of the Revolution. He died in Petrograd (St. Petersburg).

TRANSLATION: *The Twelve* tr. Babette Deutsch and Abraham Yarmolinsky (New York 1920).

REFERENCES: Robin Kemball *Alexander Blok: A Study in Rhythm and Meter* (New York 1965). Cecil Kisch *Alexander Blok: Prophet of Revolution* (New York 1960). Franklin D. Reeve *Alexander Blok: Between Image and Idea* (New York 1962).

BLONDEL DE NESLE (fl. c.1175–1200). French trouvère. Probably born 1155–60 in district of Nesle, Picardy. Nothing known of his life, but from thirteenth century on legend has invested him with being the great favorite of Richard Coeur de Lion, whom he found in prison in Austria by means of singing a song they had jointly composed, and thus helped to escape. This tale has been treated in both Grétry's opera *Richard Coeur de Lion* (1784) and Sir Walter Scott's *Ivanhoe* (1819), and accounts more for Blondel's fame than his own prowess as author of courtly songs.

EDITION: *Die Lieder des Blondel de Nesle* ed. Leo Wiese (Dresden 1904).

BLOW, John (c.Feb. 23, 1649 – Oct. 1, 1708). English composer. Born Newark, Nottinghamshire; probably attended Magnus Song School there. At Restoration, became chorister in Chapel Royal; wrote first anthems while thus employed. Appointed organist of Westminster Abbey (1668); rejoined king's service as "musician for the virginals" (1669), and was sworn a gentleman of the Chapel Royal (1674). In same year became master of the children of the Chapel Royal, a position held all his life. Married Elizabeth Braddock, by whom he had five children. Received title doctor of music (1677). The years 1680–1700 were his most productive and prosperous: appointed organist of Chapel Royal (1676–89), master of the children of St. Paul's Cathedral (1687–1703), and composer for the Chapel Royal (1699–1708). Died at Westminster; buried in the Abbey. Blow is remembered for his church music, for *Venus and Adonis* (1680–85), the first true English opera, and as Henry Purcell's teacher.

REFERENCE: H. Watkins Shaw *John Blow, Doctor of Music: A Biography* (London 1937).

BOCCACCIO, Giovanni (1313 – Dec. 31, 1375). Italian writer and humanist. Birthplace unknown; natural son of Florentine merchant. Sent (c.1333) to Naples; studied commerce, then canon law, and took part in cultivated life of court of Robert of Anjou, King of Naples. First works, novels *Filicolo* and *Fiammetta*, inspired by intense and lifelong passion for a lady of the court. About time of his return to Florence (c.1340), wrote *Filostrato* (story of Troilus and Cressida, on which both Chaucer and Shakespeare drew) and *Teseida* (basis of Chaucer's *Knight's Tale*), both in *ottava rima*. In 1350, as diplomat in service of Florentine republic, Boccaccio entertained Petrarch, whose friend he became and under whose guidance he studied Latin classics. His masterpiece is *The Decameron* (written after 1348), a series of prose tales which gives a broad picture of the human comedy and which has influenced all of Western literature. Didactic works in Latin, including *De Casibus Virorum Illustrium* (1355–60), *De Claris Mulieribus* (1360–74), and *De Genealogiis Deorum Gentilium*

(1350 ff.), and first translation of Homer into Latin placed him beside Petrarch as a leading humanist. Delivered public lectures on Dante's *Divine Comedy*, 1374. Died at Certaldo.

TRANSLATIONS: *Amorous Fiametta* tr. Bartholomew Young (1587) ed. Edward Hutton (London 1926). *Concerning Famous Women* tr. Guido Guarino (New Brunswick, N.J. 1963 and London 1964). *Chamber of Love: A Selection of the Complete Works* tr. Gertrude Flor ed. Wolfgang Kraus (New York 1958). *Decameron* Anonymous translation (1620, London 1934–35, New York 1940); tr. James M. Rigg (London and New York 1905); tr. Richard Aldington (2 vols. New York 1930, London 1951). *The Fates of Illustrious Men* tr. Louis B. Hall (New York 1965, also PB). *Nymph of Fiesole* tr. Daniel J. Donrio (New York and London 1960).

REFERENCES: Thomas C. Chubb *Life of Giovanni Boccaccio* (New York and London 1930). Edward Hutton *Giovanni Boccaccio: A Biographical Study* (London and New York 1910). John A. Symonds *Giovanni Boccaccio as Man and Author* (London 1895, New York 1968).

BOCCHERINI, Luigi (Feb. 19, 1743 – May 28, 1805). Italian composer and cellist. Born Lucca; studied under father, a contrabass player, and in Rome. After establishing local reputation as player and composer, won international fame with performance at Concert Spirituel in Paris (1768). Invited by Spanish court to Madrid and became composer to Infante Don Luis until latter's death (1785). Then served as kapellmeister to King Frederick William II of Prussia until his death (1797), when Boccherini returned to Madrid. Here, despite influential friends, he died in poverty. A prolific composer of chamber music, his fluent style, full of melody, is likened to Haydn's. The well-known popular minuet is from his string quintet op. 13, no. 4.

REFERENCE: Germaine de Rothschild *Luigi Boccherini: His Life and Work* tr. London and New York 1965).

BÖCKLIN, Arnold (Oct. 16, 1827 – Jan. 16, 1901). Swiss painter. Born Basel, son of a merchant. Studied in Düsseldorf, Antwerp, Brussels, Paris, and from 1850 was often in Italy. Married Angela Pascucci (1853). Taught at Academy of Art at Weimar (1860–62). Made his reputation in 1860's with idealized allegorical figures in classical landscapes; in 1870's introduced into his paintings fantastic creatures from his own imagination and from German legends. Lived in Florence (1876–85) and Zurich (1886–92); settled at San Domenico, near Fiesole (1892), where he died. Böcklin's best-known work is *Island of the Dead* (1880; two versions, one in Metropolitan Museum, New York, and one in Basel Museum); others include *Pan in the Bulrushes* (1857, Neue Pinakothek, Munich), *The Hunt of Diana* (1862, Basel Museum), *Villa on the Seashore* (1864), *The Battle of the Centaurs* (1878, Staatsmuseum, Berlin), *The Play of the Waves* (1885, Neue Pinakothek, Munich), and many portraits. A major influence on nineteenth-century German romanticism, Böcklin also anticipated elements of expressionism, with his use of strong outline and bold color, and surrealism, with his use of fantastic subject matter.

BOETHIUS, Ancius Manlius Severinus (c.470–524). Roman philosopher. Born Rome, son of a consul. Made consul himself (510) by Ostrogothic ruler Theodoric the Great, but, accused of conspiracy, was arrested and imprisoned at Pavia, where he was later executed. He had already translated Aristotle, and is credited with introducing him to the Western world; also had written treatises on theological and other subjects. While in prison he wrote *De Consolatione Philosophiae*, called "the last work of Roman literature," which was very popular in the Middle Ages, and was translated by King Alfred, Chaucer, and others. In five books, in the form of prose dialogue interspersed with verses, it discusses the fickleness of fortune, the frailty of earthly power, and the value of philosophy, the nature of which is discussed in rational rather than Christian terms.

TRANSLATION: *The Theological Trac-tates and The Consolation of Philosophy* tr. Hugh F. Stewart and E. K. Rand (New York and London 1918).

REFERENCES: Helen M. Barrett *Boethius: Some Aspects of His Times and Work* (New York 1966). Howard R. Patch *The Tradition of Boethius: A Study of His Importance in Medieval Culture* (New York 1935 and London 1936). E. K. Rand *Founder of the Middle Ages* (Cambridge, Mass. and London 1929, also PB).

BOILEAU-DESPRÉAUX, Nicolas (Nov. 1, 1636 – Mar. 13, 1711). French poet and critic. Born and died in Paris. Father a clerk in Paris Parlement. After attending *collèges* of Harcourt and Beauvais (1643–52), he studied law and theology, but a small inheritance (1657) allowed him to take up literature. His nine *Satires* (1660–67) won fame and the enmity of the bad writers he called by name. The milder *Epîtres* followed (1668–77); both series were modeled on Roman poets, particularly Juvenal and Horace. Published (1674) a volume containing translation of the Greek treatise *On the Sublime;* a mock epic, *Le Lutrin*, which popularized that genre; and *L'Art poétique*. The last, his most famous work, a treatise in verse expounding classical standards for poetry, intensified the current ancients-versus-moderns controversy and established Boileau as the most influential of the neoclassical critics. Appointed, jointly with his friend Racine, royal historiographer to Louis XIV (1677). Elected to French Academy (1684).

TRANSLATION: *Selected Criticism* tr. Ernest Dilworth (Indianapolis PB 1965).

REFERENCE: Alexander F. B. Clark, *Boileau and the French Classical Critics in England, 1660–1830* (new ed. New York 1966).

BOITO, Arrigo (Feb. 24, 1842 – June 10, 1918). Italian composer, librettist, and poet. Born Padua, son of Italian painter and Polish countess. Attended Milan Conservatory (1853–61), where his first compositions were performed. After some years of European travel and musical journalism, in which he championed Wagner, he composed opera *Mefistofele*, based on Goethe's *Faust*. Its first production (1868) failed due to its length (over six hours) and Wagnerian style, but a drastically revised version met success in 1875 and has remained in Italian repertory. Of subsequent unfinished operas, most important is *Nerone* (orchestration completed by Tommasini and Toscanini; first performed 1924). Boito's masterworks are the libretti for Verdi's *Otello* (1887) and *Falstaff* (1893); also noteworthy are the libretto for Ponchielli's *La Gioconda* (1876) and translations for Eleonora Duse of Shakespeare's *Antony and Cleopatra* and *Romeo and Juliet*. Elected senator (1912). Died in Milan.

BOL, Ferdinand (June 24, 1616 – July 24, 1680). Dutch painter. Born in Dordrecht. Moved as a child to Amsterdam, where he became a student of Rembrandt. Married Lisbeth Dell (1653), who bore him two sons; after her death took a second wife, Anna van Erckel (1669). Died in Amsterdam. Bol is best known for his portraits, especially *The Four Regents of the Leper Hospital* (1649, Amsterdam town hall). His early work, closely resembling that of his master, is notable for its warm, rich coloring, skillful treatment of light and shade, and psychological penetration. The quality declined in later years as Bol grew more mannered. He also painted religious works, of which good examples are *The Rest on the Flight into Egypt* (1644) and *The Three Marys at the Tomb of Christ* (1644, Museum of Art, Copenhagen).

BONINGTON, Richard Parkes (Oct. 25, 1802 – Sept. 23, 1828). English painter. Born Arnold, near Nottingham. Father, a drawing master, moved family to Calais (1817), where Bonington studied watercolor under Louis Francia. In Paris (c.1818) became closely associated with Delacroix; entered École des Beaux Arts (1819), and Baron Gros's studio (1820). The fresh, brilliantly colored watercolor landscapes of his early career are his most famous works. Exhibited first at Salon of 1822; won a gold medal and widespread recognition at Salon of 1824, at which Constable and other English painters made a great stir. After trip to Venice (1826) which impressed him deeply, he painted in oil, depicting romantic historical subjects, and thereby strongly influenced Delacroix. Visited England (1825 with Delacroix, 1827, 1828). Died in London of tuberculosis. Bonington is an important link between English artists and the French Barbizon school.

REFERENCES: Albert Dubuisson *Richard Parkes Bonington: His Life and Works* (tr. London 1924). Andrew Shirley *Bonington* (London 1940).

BONNARD, Pierre (Oct. 30, 1867 – Jan. 23, 1947). French painter. Born Fontenay-aux-Roses near Paris. In Paris (1889) studied at École des Beaux Arts and Académie Julian, where he met Édouard Vuillard, Maurice Denis, Paul Sérusier and Paul Ranson, who became lifelong friends. Worked first in decorative arts, designing posters and stage settings. During 1890's painted in postimpressionist style, influenced by Gauguin and Japanese prints; with the group, the Nabis, exhibited at Salon des Indépendants and other galleries, and made illustrations for *La Revue Blanche*. Met Maria Boursin (1895), who became his faithful model and companion. They married (1925) and moved to the house at Le Cannet (north of Cannes) where he spent much of his old age and where he died. Between 1900 and 1920 Bonnard developed the style, akin to impressionism, for which he is known: intimate domestic scenes — the breakfast table, the open window, the bath, women and children in natural poses, still lifes, landscapes, all suffused with brilliant colors and an acute sense of light and texture. Among his illustrations are those for Verlaine's *Parallèlement* (1902), the Greek pastoral *Daphnis et Chloé* (1902), Jules Renard's *Histoires Naturelles* (1904), André Gide's *Le Prométhée mal enchaîné* (1899).

REFERENCES: John Rewald ed. for Museum of Modern Art *Pierre Bonnard* (New York 1948). Antoine Terrasse *Bonnard: A Biographical and Critical Study* (tr. New York 1964).

BORODIN, Alexander Porfirevich (Nov. 12, 1833 – Feb. 27, 1887). Russian composer and scientist. Born and died in St. Petersburg. Illegitimate son of Georgian nobleman; educated early at home, showing marked gift for languages and music. Specialized in chemistry at Academy of Medicine and Surgery (1850–58), studied abroad (1859–62), returning to teach at Academy until his death. Met Mili Balakirev (1862), who encouraged his interest in music, and Borodin became one of The Five — the five Russian composers devoted to developing Russian national music. Married (1863) Catharine Protopopova, a young pianist. Completed *First Symphony in E-flat Major* (1867), and after its successful performance (1869) began work on a second in B minor. At same time started lifelong composition of opera *Prince Igor,* completed posthumously by Glazunov and Rimski-Korsakov, and wrote two string quartets and a dozen songs. Performance of the first symphony at Baden-Baden (1880) established his worldwide reputation. The tone picture *In the Steppes of Central Asia* (1880) contributed further to his fame. His *Third Symphony in A Minor* was completed posthumously by Glazunov. A remarkable musician, Borodin excelled in both the lyric and epic-heroic style, and was important in the development of Russian national music.

REFERENCE: S. A. Dianin *Borodin* (tr. London and New York 1963).

BORROMINI, Francesco (real name Francesco Castelli) (Sept. 25, 1599 – Aug. 3, 1667). Italian architect. Born Bissone, Lombardy; son of a stonemason. Trained in Milan as stonecutter, he arrived in Rome (1621) and worked under his relatives Leone Garogo and Carlo Maderno, mainly as stonecutter at St. Peter's. After Maderno's death (1629) worked for several years under Bernini at Barberini palace and St. Peter's. An early independent commission, and one of his masterpieces, is the church of S. Carlo alle

Quattro Fontane (1634–44), whose façade he added (1662–67). Other principal works, all in Rome: churches of S. Ivo della Sapienza (1642–60), S. Agnese in Piazza Navona (1652–1657), S. Andrea delle Fratte (1653–65), S. Maria delle Sette Dolori (c.1655–1666); remodeling of St. John Lateran (1646–49); additions to Spada, Falconieri, and Pamphili palaces; oratory of San Filippo Neri (1637–50); Collegio di Propaganda Fide (1646–66). Died in Rome, a suicide.

REFERENCES: Paolo Portoghesi *The Rome of Borromini: Architecture as Language* (tr. New York 1968). Rudolf Wittkower *The Art and Architecture of Italy, 1600–1750* (Harmondsworth, Middlesex, England and Baltimore 1958, PB).

✍

FRANCESCO BORROMINI
BY JUERGEN SCHULZ

Borromini, more than any other single person, can be credited with the invention of baroque architecture. His background was that of an artisan, his temperament was melancholic, his methods of design were reactionary, and his ideal of form was molded by a highly personal taste for the involved and difficult, grandiose and massive, rhythmically animated and organically fused. Out of these elements he forged a style that represented a total break with the traditional architecture of his time and remained an inspiration for architects throughout Europe and Latin America to the end of the eighteenth century.

He was born the child of a stonemason, in a country town near Lake Lugano. The Alpine lake country abounded in quarries and masons and exported its excess population of stonemasons to cities throughout Italy and as far abroad as Poland and Russia. Trained as a mason himself, Borromini followed the normal pattern of an Alpine mason's career — he emigrated to a center of building activity where family members had already found work. In his case it was early seventeenth-century Rome, where a maternal relative, Carlo Maderno, was architect of the new St. Peter's and another relative was working on it as a mason.

He quickly established himself in the St. Peter's workshop as a carver of decorative details and assistant to Maderno. As the latter aged and became increasingly burdened with commissions from Pope Urban VIII and his wealthy family, Borromini became something like a head draftsman in Maderno's office. At Maderno's death in 1629, the pope selected Bernini to take charge of his and his family's many architectural undertakings. Borromini by then had become an experienced designing architect, through his work for and under Maderno and through his own intensive and meticulous study of the architectural details of ancient and modern buildings in Rome. He was invaluable to the inexperienced Bernini, and therefore was retained by the latter in the ill-defined position he had occupied before: chief executant of the architect's ideas, with considerable latitude over the design of individual projects, but with no authority to see them executed faithfully and no honor for his work. To this day it remains difficult to unravel the respective shares of Maderno, Bernini, and the young Borromini in the enterprises of Urban VIII and the Barberini family, such as the façade of St. Peter's, the great baldachin over the high altar of St. Peter's, and the Barberini palace.

In 1633 Bernini and Borromini broke their relationship, but to Bernini's credit it was he who obtained for Borromini the latter's first appointment as a supervising architect. He was given charge (1632) of the completion of the buildings of the University of Rome. The appointment led in time to the creation of one of his most remarkable buildings, the university church, S. Ivo della Sapienza. Meanwhile Borromini had begun another structure, the first designed and executed entirely by him, S. Carlo alle Quattro Fontane (1634–67).

S. Carlo shows fully developed the principles of his original style. The plan is based on an elongated diamond, the sides of which are bowed, and the four points of which harbor the entrance and the three altars of the church. It is true of Borromini's buildings generally that the basis of the design is a geometric form, the divisions and subdivisions of which dictate the placing and dimensions of the structure's constituent parts. The technique is the reverse of Renaissance planning, in which dimensions of the plan and lesser parts were established through multiplication or division of a basic arithmetical unit (usually the diameter of a column), based in some way on a standard that was regarded as "natural" (the height and width of a column and its parts, for instance, were made to relate to one another proportionally as does the human body to its members). Borromini's geometric, rather than modular, planning reverted to the practice of medieval architects. Very likely Borromini had learned the technique in the backward world of provincial stonemasons in which he was trained, but it helped him to conceive unorthodox plans that were unitary wholes — not divisible into self-sufficient components — and that lent themselves to the impression of continuous movement and organic fusion that was a consistent aim of his architecture throughout his life.

In S. Carlo, the membering of the walls and succession of stories abundantly fulfills this aim. Four columns stand at each point of the diamond plan. They can be read either as a quartet framing the point, or as two distinct pairs, the inner two framing the point, the outer two marking the sides of the diamond. The second story of the interior consists of four elliptical arches that can be read either as terminating the apsidal vaults over entrance and altars or as terminating the pendentives between them that carry the dome. The dome, finally, is oval in plan, but is decorated with a puzzle pattern of variously shaped, deeply recessed compartments that prevents the observer from registering which is its long and which its short axis. The observer's eye never fixes upon a motive as a separable and self-sufficient part; instead, undulating walls introduce an element of movement and the rhythms repeat and interpenetrate one another as in a richly structured fugue.

S. Ivo, the church Borromini eventually built for the University of Rome (1642–60), is a larger building, more monumental in its forms and more ingenious in plan. The basic geometrical figure of the plan is a star of David, the points of which have been blunted by alternate convex and concave walls. The dome follows the same modified star plan as the hall beneath, narrowing progressively toward the top and thereby reducing progressively the undulating movement of the walls, until it is extinguished in the pure circle of the lantern.

Borromini's architectural orders and details are as novel as his planning. The colossal pilasters of the hall are unorthodoxly and rhythmically fluted with three great and four small channels. The dome is ornamented with vertical files of stars that diminish in size as the dome narrows. Even more extraordinary is the ornamentation of the exterior of the dome. The drum, which is given a cloverleaf plan, is articulated by orders, but the dome proper is stepped, and the lantern is topped by a corkscrew spiral of stone, the edges of which are serrated and the point of which carries a crownlike shape surmounted by an orb and cross on an open, wrought-iron base. The quickening upward movement, which then melts into the sky through the fretted outlines of the uppermost elements, is similar to the soaring movement of the interior members and moldings that meet in the perfect circle of the lantern.

The style of S. Ivo is more grandiose than that of S. Carlo: there are fewer subdivisons vertically, the movement of the walls is more decisive and sculptural, orders are colossal. The forms of the exterior are equally plastic and large. The difference is characteristic of the direction of Borromini's general development. His later works are more massive, play bleak surfaces of heavy masonry against the ornament of window frames and decorative sculpture, and wring an expressive value from the ponderous movement of curving courses of stone.

Borromini's liberties with the vocabulary and syntax of classical architecture tended toward the exact opposite direction from the movement in mid-seventeenth century Rome toward a reserved and classical style. He enjoyed his last successes during the pontificate of Pope Innocent X of the Pamfili family (1644–55). At the instance of the latter he was given charge of the completion of S. Agnese, a church adjoining the Pamfili family palace on a central square in Rome, and the remodeling of the palace itself. The church had been begun by a more conservative architect, and Borromini revised the plan to the best of his ability, producing a design with all his

characteristic freedom, and the mass and drama typical of his late work. But before the completion of the church, Borromini's patron Innocent died. The new pope, Alexander VII, replaced him with a committee of architects who developed a more conventional design for the still unfinished parts, chiefly the bell towers and lantern. The incident represented a victory of classical over baroque tastes.

A solitary, suspicious personality, Borromini had suffered with bitterness the early years of anonymity and met with much misunderstanding even in the years when he had admiring patrons. He had always insisted on personally supervising his buildings, fearing subversion of his designs if any but himself guided their execution. Late in life he burned the drawings he had collected to have engraved and published, fearing to leave the charge to others. As tastes changed and his patrons died, and his own closest disciple too, he felt himself increasingly isolated and threatened. During a period of profound depression, in the summer of 1668, he finally took his life.

BORROW, George (Henry) July 5, 1803 – July 26, 1881). English linguist, writer, and traveler. Born East Dereham, Norfolk, son of a professional soldier, he led a wandering childhood as his father's regiment moved around the British Isles. At Royal Grammar School, Norwich (1816–18), began to study languages, eventually becoming proficient in twenty. After brief periods of law apprenticeship in Norwich and literary hackwork in London, he embarked on his wanderings (1825–32) through rural England, often with gypsies. During this period published *Romantic Ballads* (1826), a translation from Danish. As agent of British and Foreign Bible Society (1833–40) he traveled in Russia, Portugal, and Spain. Back in England, he married Mary Clarke, a widow eight years his senior (1840), and settled at Oulton Broad in

Norfolk. *The Zincali, or An Account of the Gypsies in Spain* (2 vols. 1841) was coolly received, but *The Bible in Spain* (3 vols. 1843), an immensely popular travel book, made him famous; it was followed by the quasi-autobiographical novels *Lavengro* (1851) and *The Romany Rye* (1857). He also translated the New Testament into Manchu, the Gospel of St. Luke into gypsy language (Romany), and wrote a dictionary of gypsy language. Scornful of "humbug and philistinism" in Victorian fiction, Borrow stands out as an eccentric, vigorous rebel whose life was as colorful and unusual as his works. After living in London and on the Continent (1860–74) he returned to Oulton Broad, where he died.

EDITION: *The Works of George Borrow* ed. Clement K. Shorter (16 vols. London and New York 1923–24).

REFERENCES: Martin D. Armstrong *George Borrow* (London 1950 and New York 1952). William I. Knapp *The Life, Writings and Correspondence of George Borrow* (2 vols. London and New York 1899). Robert Myers *George Borrow* (New York 1966). Clement K. Shorter *George Borrow and His Circle* (London and Boston 1913) and *Life of George Borrow* (London 1920). T. J. Wise *A Bibliography of the Writings in Prose and Verse of George Henry Borrow* (London 1914).

BOSCH, Hieronymus (real name Hieronymus van Aeken) (c.1450–1516). Dutch painter. Surname derived from birthplace, 's Hertogenbosch, Brabant, Netherlands, where he spent his whole life. Member of religious brotherhood, Confraternity of Our Lady, whose records provide the only known biographical data. Designed several altarpieces and stained-glass windows for the town cathedral and was commissioned (1504) by archduke of Austria to paint a Last Judgment. Fame spread throughout Europe in lifetime; after his death his paintings were particularly sought after in Spain, and Philip II acquired many of them. Bosch's work centers around themes of sin and divine retribution. Peopling his bizarre visions of temptation and hell are hybrid monsters, part animal, part vegetable, part man-made object, part human. Best-

known paintings are *Temptation of St. Anthony* (National Museum, Lisbon), *Last Judgment* (Academy, Vienna), and his great triptychs *The Hay Wain*, *The Garden of Delights*, and *The Adoration of the Magi* (all in the Prado, Madrid). Other works include painted table top of *The Seven Deadly Sins* (Prado, Madrid) and panels in the doge's palace, Venice (*The Ascension of the Just, The Descent into Hell, Paradise, Hell*). Considered by surrealists of the twentieth century as a forerunner.

REFERENCES: Ludwig von Baldass *Hieronymus Bosch* (tr. New York 1960). Jacques Combe *Hieronimus Bosch* (tr. London and New York 1947). Howard Daniel *Jheronimus Bosch* (New York 1947 and London 1948). Robert L. Delevoy *Bosch: Biographical and Critical Study* (tr. Cleveland 1960). Charles de Tolnay *Hieronymus Bosch* (tr. London and New York 1966).

BOSSUET, Jacques Bénigne (Sept. 27, 1627 – Apr. 12, 1704). French bishop, historian and orator. Born Dijon, into deeply religious middle-class lawyer's family. Educated by Jesuits at Dijon, he entered Jesuit Collège de Navarre, Paris (1642). Ordained (1652), received doctorate in theology, appointed archdeacon of Metz, where for seven years he developed as preacher and polemicist. Again in Paris (from 1659), became famous as court orator; appointed bishop of Condom (1670), but resigned to become (1670–81) tutor to the dauphin. Elected to French Academy (1671): made bishop of Meaux (1681). In late years, involved in religious controversies: the issue of Gallicanism, which occasioned famous speech *On the Unity of the Church;* campaign against Protestants; quietism controversy. Died in Paris. Bossuet is chiefly remembered for his *Discourse on Universal History* (1681) and for his inspired *Funeral Orations*, especially those on Henrietta Maria of England (1669), her daughter Henrietta Anne (1670), Queen Marie Thérèse (1683), the princess palatine Anne de Gonzague (1685), Chancellor Le Tellier (1686), and Condé (1687).

TRANSLATIONS: *Bossuet: A Prose Anthology* ed. J. Standring (London 1962). *Selections from Meditations on the Gospel* tr. Lucille C. Franchère (Chicago 1962).
REFERENCES: Ernest E. Reynolds *Bossuet* (Garden City, N.Y. 1963). Ella K. Sanders *Jacques Bénigne Bossuet: A Study* (London and New York 1921). William J. S. Simpson *A Study of Bossuet* (London 1937).

BOSWELL, James (Oct. 29, 1740 – May 19, 1795). Scottish diarist, lawyer, and biographer of Samuel Johnson. Born Edinburgh, son of Lord Auchinleck, Scottish judge. Educated at universities of Edinburgh, Glasgow, later Utrecht. Visited London (1760–61), recorded experiences in his *London Journal* (1762–63). Met Dr. Samuel Johnson (1763) and from the first made notes of his conversation. Forced by father to resume law studies, went abroad (1763–66). In Utrecht knew Isabella de Zuylen, the writer "Zélide" (later Madame de Charrière). Visited Germany, Italy, and Switzerland, where he met Voltaire and Jean Jacques Rousseau. Toured Corsica (1765). *An Account of Corsica: The Journal of a Tour to That Island and Memoirs of Pascal Paoli* (1768) resulted. Admitted to Scottish bar (1766). Married Margaret Montgomerie (1769); enjoyed active law practice in Scotland, with frequent visits to London, where Johnson helped him get elected to the Literary Club (1773). That year Boswell (known as Bozzy) accompanied Johnson on journey recorded in *The Journal of a Tour to the Hebrides with Samuel Johnson, LLD* (1785). Called to English bar (1786); settled in London (1789). His masterpiece, *The Life of Samuel Johnson* (1791), with its combination of meticulously recorded conversations and events and comment reflecting his own character and insight, established him as one of the world's great biographers.

EDITIONS: Frederick A. Pottle editor for projected fifty volumes (London and New York); published: *Boswell's London Journal 1762–1763* (1950, also PB). *Boswell in Holland 1763–1764* (1952, also PB). *Boswell on the Grand Tour 1764–1766* (2 vols. 1953/55).

Boswell in Search of a Wife 1766–1769 (1956). *Boswell for the Defence 1769–1774* (1963). *Boswell: The Ominous Years 1774–1776* (1963).
REFERENCES: Frank L. Lucas *Search for Good Sense: Four Eighteenth-century Characters: Johnson, Chesterfield, Boswell and Goldsmith* (London and New York 1958, also PB). Hesketh Pearson *Johnson and Boswell: The Story of their Lives* (London and New York 1958). Frederick A. Pottle *James Boswell: The Earlier Years 1740–1769* (New York and London 1966) and *The Literary Career of James Boswell, Esq.* (Oxford and New York 1929). Chauncy B. Tinker *Young Boswell* (Boston 1922). D. B. Wyndham Lewis *James Boswell: A Short Life* (2nd ed. London 1952).

BOTTICELLI, Sandro (real name Alessandro di Mariano di Vanni Filipepi) (1445 – May 17, 1510). Italian painter. Born and died in Florence. Son of a tanner, apprenticed to Fra Filippo Lippi (c.1465–67), later worked with Pollaiuolo and Verrocchio. His indebtedness to these three is evident in such early works as the *Chigi Madonna* (early 1470's, Gardner Museum, Boston), *Fortitude* (1470, Uffizi, Florence, first documented work), *Judith and Holofernes* diptych (c.1471, Uffizi), and *St. Sebastian* (1474, Staatlichemuseum, Berlin). A protégé of the Medici, Botticelli found in the neo-Platonist theories much discussed in the Medici circle inspiration for the great paintings of his mid-career, including *Pallas and the Centaur* (early 1480's, Uffizi), *Mars and Venus* (early 1480's, National Gallery, London), and his two best-known works, the allegories *Primavera* (1477–78, Uffizi) and *Birth of Venus* (mid-1480's, Uffizi). In Rome (1481–82) on invitation of Sixtus IV, painted three frescoes and several papal portraits in the Sistine Chapel. The works of his last years, such as the *Mystic Nativity* (1500/1, National Gallery, London) and *Stories of St. Zenobius* (c.1505, panels in Metropolitan, New York; National Gallery, London; and Gemäldegalerie, Dresden), have a visionary quality which may reflect the painter's enthusiasm for Savonarola. Throughout his life Botticelli was active as a portraitist. Also executed (1490's) a famous series of illustrations for Dante's *Divine Comedy*.

REFERENCES: Giulio Carlo Argan *Botticelli* (tr. New York and London 1957). Herbert Horne *Alessandro Filipepi Commonly Called Sandro Botticelli* (London 1908). Adolfo Venturi *Botticelli* (Rome 1925). Wilhelm Von Bode *Sandro Botticelli* (London 1925). Yukio Yashiro, *Sandro Botticelli and the Florentine Renaissance* (Boston and London 1925).

SANDRO BOTTICELLI

ANNE MARKHAM

The art of Sandro Botticelli represents the culmination of the linear, decorative trend of Florentine painting whose earliest proponent was the late trecento, early quattrocento painter Lorenzo Monaco. The source of Lorenzo's art was the international Gothic style which permeated Europe at the end of the fourteenth century, and certain aspects of that style are still evident in the works of Botticelli. In Botticelli's early *Adoration of the Magi* (National Gallery, London) the vast numbers of supernumerary figures represented in a great variety of pose and view, gesticulating with animation, disregarding the focus of the story, reflect the anecdotal or episodic narrative of the international style. The emphasis on line transmitted primarily through long and sinuous silhouettes, like the preoccupation with tiny patterns of gold brocade, betray a late Gothic origin.

Botticelli's teacher was Fra Filippo Lippi, an artist whose imitation of the robust and plastically modeled forms of Masaccio did not affect his basic allegiance to line. From Filippo Lippi, Botticelli derived his cursive, calligraphic line conveyed through sheer and fluttering draperies, densely gathered, tied in many places. The lines make a deep and rapid curve or meander nervously along the distance of a hem. Three-dimensional folds become linear through the line of light reflected from their edges.

From Antonio Pollaiuolo, Botticelli took the modulation of internal anatomical forms. A constant, subtle, gradual alternation of light and shade creates the sensation of a form which gives way to minute wavelike motions of the surface. Yet this modulation of the surface is not expressive of the underlying anatomical framework. Deformations of the anatomy are frequent: considerations of anatomical correctness yield invariably to a sense of abstract beauty. The contour line, moreover, denies what the chiaroscuro affirms; the smooth, gently curving, unbroken outline, painted by a firm brush dipped in black, suggests a body whose surface is absolutely smooth and uniform and flat.

Proportions, like anatomy, are subservient to a decorative effect, and through the elongation of the figure, the narrow sloping shoulders, the swanlike neck, excessively long arms and legs, the painter produces beings of ineffable grace. This grace informs the figures' movements. Venus standing on her shell (Uffizi) or Judith fleeing the camp of Holofernes (Uffizi) sway languidly: movement seems imposed from without, not a product of the individual's will. It causes no muscular effort and needs to overcome no force of gravity. Heads are tilted, torsos turned, the weight of the body is invariably distributed unequally; thus the pose is made to conform to a single continuous curve.

The lack of willpower and energy apparent in the movements of Botticelli's figures also characterizes their expressions. The face of St. Sebastian from the painting in Berlin belies the torture of his martyrdom. The twist and inclination of the head, the lethargically lowered upper lids, the trance-like unfocused stare, the partially opened but unmoving mouth, suggest a being given over to a dream.

Botticelli's figure style seems reflective of the same current of thought and feeling that accounts for the ascendancy of Marsilio Ficino and his neo-Platonic doctrines at the end of the fifteenth century. Central to Ficino's doctrines was the ideal of contemplation in which the soul withdraws from the external world and even from the body, into itself. Through this withdrawal the soul gains knowledge of ultimate truths, of its own divinity, of the nature of God. Contemplation has a moral as well as an epistemological value: it is the only source of a truly moral life, for there we escape from vices, and there actions are dictated by a purified conscience. As important to neo-Platonism as contemplation was the belief in the immortality of the soul (officially promulgated by the Roman Catholic Church only in 1513). If the ideal of the contemplative life is to be recognized as valid for all men, yet can be achieved on earth by very few, there must exist a future life in which the vision of God will constitute the perpetual occupation of all those who merit it. Indeed, it is only when the soul has left the body that it will attain the state of happiness and perfection for which it is destined.

Botticelli must have been cognizant of neo-Platonic doctrine. The Medici, for whom he often worked, were the patrons of the Platonic Academy. Several of Botticelli's paintings, among them *Pallas and the Centaur* (Uffizi), find their explanation in the writings of Ficino. According to the philosopher, man partakes of three levels of being. The senses of his body belong to the brute world; the exalted regions of his soul are divine. Mediating between these two is the sole prerogative of man — his reason. In the painting of Pallas, the goddess dominates the half-human, half-animal centaur as the highest region of the soul is meant to dominate man's senses and reason.

What both neo-Platonism and the art of Botticelli thus reflect is a repudiation of the real world, an escape into the inner recesses of the human consciousness where the will no longer functions. This in turn may be understood in terms of the political and economic disintegration of Florentine society in the last part of the fifteenth century. The decline of the Medici bank dates from the 1470's. The accession of Sixtus IV to the papacy in 1471 introduced friction between Florence and the Vatican which culminated in the Pazzi conspiracy of 1478, the partially successful attempt on the lives of the Medici leaders. In 1494 Medici rule was overthrown by the French invasion, and at the end of the century a theocracy was established under the friar Girolamo Savanarola, who, with the fiery passion of a fanatic, preached reform through penitence and prophesied imminent catastrophe.

How different this is from the early part of the century, when Leonardo Bruni exalted above the contemplative life an active life in the service of the state. The monumental scale and powerful musculature of painted and sculptured figures, their decisive movement — clearly the result of personal choice — imply a high estimation of the capability and worth of the whole man. The painters' progressive conquest of the means of portraying the natural world reflects their confidence of solving all visual problems through the exercise of intellect. In more aspects than just figure style, the art of Botticelli represents a repudiation of the rationalistic achievements of the earlier part of the century. In the *Primavera* (Uffizi), figures are located in the foreground, but rather than being disposed in a circle so that they occupy, and therefore become a measure of the depth of, space, they are distributed in a single plane parallel to the picture plane. There is almost no overlapping, and the recession of space is impeded by the barrier of trees. Where architectural settings are used to construct an illusion of depth, the space lacks that homogeneity and consistency that was the raison d'être of the theory of linear perspective invented in the early fifteenth century. In the *Chastisement of the Company of Korah* (1481–82, Sistine Chapel, Rome) the buildings are viewed from constantly changing points of sight, and their scale is unrelated to their distance from the vantage point of an ideal observer. In a medieval fashion, heads of figures in serried rows are piled one above the other. The *Birth of Venus* reveals no application of the device of atmospheric perspective.

Like space, light no longer has an independent existence, no longer illuminates each figure consistently, according to laws rationally deduced. In the *Primavera* light illuminates the figures but does not affect the background. Figures do not cast shadows. The composition of the picture recalls a Gothic tapestry. The dark foliage which fills the entire surface of the picture forms a uniform and unreceding ground against which a multitude of tiny accents of fruit and blossoms, of sharply etched leaves, create a *horror vacui*.

In the irrationality of his final works Botticelli presages the style of the early sixteenth-century Florentine mannerists Pontormo and Il Rosso. In the *Pietà* in Milan, figures precariously placed on top of one another are pressed into a single plane with no consideration of the normal volume of the human body; they intertwine with one another and correct relationships of scale are disregarded. The dense wall of figures fills almost the entire surface of the field, leaving space only for the vastly simplified and abstracted opening of the tomb of Christ. The artist must have felt so strongly the emotion which animates his figures that, in order to give expression to it, he ignored every rational device invented by the artists of the Renaissance.

BOUCHER, François (Sept. 29, 1703 – May 30, 1770). French painter. Born and died in Paris. Son of embroidery designer, his first teacher, he studied with François Lemoyne, a prominent decorator, and Jean François Cars, an engraver. Won first prize in painting at Royal Academy (1723). To Rome (1727), where he was influenced by Tiepolo and Castiglione. On return to Paris (1731), rapidly became most fashionable painter of his day and a favorite of Madame de Pompadour, subject of many portraits. Married Marie Anne Buseau (1733). Admitted to Academy (1734). Appointed director of the Gobelin tapestry works (1755), for which his most famous designs were for the series *The Loves of the Gods*. Received title Premier Peintre du Roi (1763); director of Academy (1765). Boucher is today best known as decorator of boudoirs and as teacher of Fragonard. His work, considered most perfect expression of French rococo period, includes paintings *Le Déjeuner* (1739, Louvre, Paris), *La Marchande de Modes* (1746, National Museum, Stockholm), *La Toilette de Vénus* (1751, Louvre), *Peace and War* (Museum of Fine Arts, Boston).

REFERENCES: Maurice Block *François Boucher and the Beauvais Tapestries* (Boston 1933). Ian McInnes *Painter, King and Pompadour: Fran-*

çois Boucher at The Court of Louis XV (London 1965).

BOUDIN, Eugène Louis (July 12, 1824 – Aug. 8, 1898). French painter. Born Honfleur, son of sea pilot who later settled down in stationer's shop in Le Havre. Here Boudin's painting won admiration of Gustave Courbet, Constant Troyon and Jean François Millet, who urged him to go to Paris (1847), where he studied with Eugène Isabey. Exhibited at Salon, winning gold medal (1889). The arresting quality of Boudin's seascapes, with foreground figures, of the coasts of northern France, Holland and Belgium and their vast expanses of sky is light — in all its mutations. He strongly influenced the impressionists and was admired equally by such critics as Baudelaire and by such painters as Corot, who called him *le roi des cieux*. Died at Deauville.

REFERENCE: Gustave Cahen *Eugène Boudin: Sa Vie et Son Oeuvre* (Paris 1900).

BOUTS, Dierik (or Dirk or Thierry) (c.1410 – May 6, 1475). Dutch painter. Born in Haarlem. Spent most of his life in Louvain, where he married (c.1447). Member of painters' guild (1457); appointed official painter to the city (1468). Died in Louvain. Though influenced by Roger van der Weyden, the van Eycks, and Petrus Christus, Bouts was one of the most original painters of the time. Responding with intense emotion to religious subjects, he created elongated figures in tense, awkward poses, their faces strangely troubled. Famous for richness of detail and color, also for his spacious landscapes, which show unusual mastery of luminous atmospheric distance. Major works: *The Martyrdom of St. Erasmus* and *The Last Supper* (both in St. Peter's, Louvain), *The Martyrdom of St. Hippolytus* (Bruges Cathedral), and *The Justice of Otho III* panels (Royal Museum, Brussels).

REFERENCES: Valentin Denis *Thierry Bouts* (Brussels 1957). Erwin Panofsky *Early Netherlandish Painting: Its Origins and Character* (2 vols. London and Cambridge, Mass. 1954).

BRAHMS, Johannes (May 7, 1833 – Apr. 3, 1897). German composer. Born Hamburg, son of a musician. Showing early talent, he studied piano under Otto Cossel and the eminent teacher Eduard Marxsen. Through Joseph Joachim met Schumann, who wrote famous article on him in *Neue Zeitschrift für Musik* (Oct. 28, 1853) and helped him find publisher for his works. Clara Schumann remained Brahms's lifelong friend after her husband's death (1856). After unrewarding period as pianist and choral conductor at court of Detmold and in Hamburg, settled in Vienna (1863), where his reputation grew steadily. Brahms's music is distinguished by its combination of romantic feeling and classical form. His adherence to the latter subjected him to criticism by Wagnerians and other contemporaries as a conservative. Directed Society of the Friends of Music (1872–75). Died in Vienna. His oeuvre contains solo piano compositions, chamber music, large orchestral works, choral works, and lieder. Among his best known works are *A German Requiem* (1868), four symphonies (1876–85), *Violin Concerto in D* (1878), *Piano Concerto in B-flat* (1881), *Piano Quintet in F minor* (1864), *Academic* (1880) and *Tragic* overtures (1880–81); *Variations on a Theme by Haydn* (1873).

TRANSLATION: *Johannes Brahms and Theodor Billroth: Letters from a Musical Friendship* tr. and ed. Hans Barkan (Norman, Okla. 1957).

REFERENCES: Hans Gal *Johannes Brahms: His Work and Personality* (tr. New York 1963). Karl Geiringer *Brahms: His Life and Work* (2nd ed. New York 1947, also PB).

⟨⟩

BRAHMS
BY ARTHUR BERGER

When Brahms made the now proverbial remark, referring to the ever so mild similarity between a theme of the finale of his *First Symphony* and Beethoven's *Ode to Joy*, that it was something "any ass could see," he provided a warning that has been ignored by the arbiters of taste who make him out as a kind of pasticheur. One chronicler has found the remark to indicate nothing so much as "crudeness masking a bad conscience," though it is grossly unjust to imply that Brahms, through any inadequacy, was obliged to borrow, or that in doing so he had to feel guilty. True, we do not think of him as a melodist, either because his mastery of instrumental forms overshadows his other contributions or because a melodist supposedly invents tunes spontaneously, which Brahms is not reputed to have done. His ability to shape the finest tunes was, nonetheless, equal to anyone else's, and would have earned him a reputation had he, terrifying thought, left us nothing more than the lieder, some two hundred of them.

Brahms could be confident that a reminiscent detail would not jeopardize his theme's uniqueness, for he was unusually aware that an artist may draw ideas and inspiration from traditional masterpieces as well as from nature or direct human experience. When elements combine and develop in art they acquire new character from the relationships in which they are placed, and this is particularly apparent in the variation form which Brahms appropriately held in favor. The theme of the *Haydn Variations* does not impose its classicism upon its transformations, and an aura of romanticism — insofar as such terms have meaning at all — may be said to prevail as soon as Haydn's *St. Anthony Chorale* has been stated. In the passacaglia of the *Fourth Symphony* it becomes still more evident that neither style nor anything else on the theme's surface need have bearing on the transformations, for here the variations are generated, in a sense, not by a theme at all but simply by something more like the foundation of one. Brahms's rich invention is set in motion by a series of peremptory chords that carry us, as it were, beyond music's concrete manifestations to its essence. A profound sense of the past brought Brahms into touch with timeless principles, inferred from many styles and periods, and from the classical masterpieces in particular. This rendered him master of the past rather than its slave, and even to end his *Fourth Symphony* with a passacaglia bespoke an independence that puzzled some of his contemporaries.

If such a context for a passacaglia was new, the passacaglia form itself, of course, was not. On the other hand, a lively interest in older forms *was,* paradoxically, quite new in Brahms's time. The revival of Bach, instigated by Mendelssohn and Schumann during Brahms's youth, was but a preliminary to the scholarship that was to flourish later in the nineteenth century. As editor of composers ranging from Couperin to Schumann, Brahms himself engaged in activities that were to afford unprecedented access to treasures of the past. Traditional art music was now in the public domain hitherto occupied almost exclusively by folk music, and Brahms's attitude toward folk music consequently suggests some parallels that may be helpful to an understanding of the effect this new status of art music had on his creative approach.

We need not assume that in drawing upon the past he must end up by evoking it, since his concern when he drew upon folk sources seems not to have been the evocation of local color. He did not share the nationalist aims of his devoted Bohemian follower Dvořák, but instead he distilled from these sources whatever served his needs. Folk sources functioned as a medium through which to convey subtleties of his own even when the folk vein was outspoken, as in the *Hungarian Dances, Liebeslieder Waltzes,* or *Zigeunerlieder.* More often the folk element is disguised, so that at the piano's entrance in the *Concerto in D minor,* for example, where I hear a touch of tzigane, Donald Francis Tovey has quite understandably heard a quality "worthy of Bach's ariosos."

An orchestral tutti, typical of the visceral early Brahms, introduces this concerto. But the piano enters gently and informally, and it is in this vein that his later sonata allegros often start right out. The result is as far from the so-called "masculine" first theme of classicism as it is from the terse motto used by Brahms's Wagnerian contemporary Bruckner, for whom the notion of beginning a sonata allegro with a tune would be frivolous. There is nothing frivolous about the way Brahms eases us into works like the clarinet quintet or the *Second Symphony,* with lovely phrases that distantly echo the Viennese waltz — even, as in the *Fourth Symphony,* when there is a two-beat measure.

A devotion to art music of the past naturally imposed a responsibility that a consciousness of folk music did not. The example of the masters made Brahms highly self-critical. He not only was given to revising his own works, but he also regarded the great symphonies as a challenge that must be met with maturity. At the age of forty-five he finally ventured out with his *First Symphony,* and only after a gestation period of some fifteen years. Such self-criticism was rewarded by a glorious fulfillment that is evident in his extraordinary grasp of structure. Brahms shared the contemporary interest in texture and local effect; however, his music reflects this interest in an original way, governed by principles of structural relationship

separated out of classical contexts. The soaring line in which Brahms found these principles, as he was imaginative enough to realize, was inappropriate to his own music's complexity at the local level — the peculiar density, the rhythmic layers that account for the unmistakable Brahms sound. In place of the soaring line, there is, in his music, remarkable meaning crowded into the given moment and checking the flow.

Brahms's grasp of structure rests to no small degree on his ingenious expansion of classical tonality. Wagner, by contrast, expanded chromaticism, thereby contributing to the dissolution of tonality. A simplistic view of progress represents Schoenberg's "atonality" as a consequence of Wagner's efforts, but it is significant that Schoenberg was more fascinated by Brahms than by Wagner. Brahms's harmonies fit into the standard classifications only if we ignore the unique heard quality that derives from such devices as the omission of a chord tone here or the reinforcement of a chord tone there. Or consider his tendency to understate the tonic. In classical music the tonic is heard — to speak loosely — as a prominent stabilizing influence. In Brahms's music we have the special experience of encountering the control of classical tonality exerting itself over the rhapsodic harmonies of romanticism.

To insist that Brahms is great because he is original would be to convict myself of the historicism that discredits him because of his putative slavery to the past. Brahms's originality concerns us simply for what emerges from the music when we *listen,* rather than for how it helps put him back into proper perspective. We do well to approach the music of Brahms in the light of its consummate balance between novelty and tradition — not for making an "assessment" that can be taken for granted, but to fortify the ear against any distraction from superficial and often legendary resemblances to the classical masters, the better to appreciate that which renders Brahms their equal.

BRAMANTE (real name Donato d'Agnolo or d'Angelo) (c.1444 – Apr. 14, 1514). Italian architect. Born at Monte Asdrualdo, near Urbino. Originally a fresco painter, he turned to architecture; first important commission, church of S. Maria presso S. Satiro, Milan (begun 1482). He painted the shallow choir in false perspective, giving illusion of great depth. In Rome (from 1499), he was employed by popes Alexander VI and Julius II. Died in Rome. Bramante's most famous Roman building, the Tempietto at S. Pietro in Montorio (1502), was intended to be set in a "molded" exterior space, a concept as novel as the design of the chapel itself, sculpture-like in its dramatic interplay of convex and concave elements. Also important is the Belvedere courtyard at the Vatican. His greatest project, altered by his successors, was the plan for the rebuilding of St. Peter's (1506) as a huge Greek cross with central dome. Bramante is known as the creator of High Renaissance architecture.

REFERENCE: Gino Chierici *Donato Bramante 1444–1514* (tr. New York PB 1960).

BRANCUSI, Constantin (Feb. 21, 1876 – Mar. 16, 1957). Rumanian sculptor. Born Pestisani-Gorj, Rumania. Studied at Bucharest Art Academy (1894–99). In Paris (1904), studied at École des Beaux Arts; left after two years to work independently. From then on seldom emerged from his Paris studio. Earliest work (1905–1907) in manner of Rodin. The Fauves' rediscovery of primitive sculpture led to his evolving a "primeval" style of wood and stone carving, exemplified by *The Kiss* (stone, 1908). About 1910 developed marble and metal abstract pieces of two types:

variations of the egg shape such as *The Newborn* (marble, 1915) and "bird" motifs, the best known being *Bird in Space* (bronze, 1919, Museum of Modern Art, New York), which conveys not an abstract image of a bird but rather the essence of flight itself. Died in Paris.

REFERENCES: Sidney Geist *Brancusi: A Study of the Sculpture* (London and New York 1968). Ionel Jianou *Brancusi* (London and New York 1963).

BRAQUE, Georges (May 13, 1882 – Aug. 31, 1963). French painter. Born Argenteuil; family moved to Le Havre in his childhood. To Paris (1900), where he studied at Académie Humbert (1902) and École des Beaux Arts (1903). Joined Fauvist movement, became deeply influenced by Cézanne. With his painting in "little cubes" for Salon of 1908, inaugurated with Picasso the cubist movement. Introduced lettering into his compositions (1911) which cubists took up, also trompe l'oeil effects, and in 1912 originated collage. Married (1912). Served in World War I; wounded (1915). After return to painting (1917) his cubistic style became freer, more flexible, more personal, and less austerely geometric. In 1920's and 1930's he evolved his best style, represented by his still lifes. Won Carnegie prize (1937) and grand prize at Venice Biennial Exhibition (1948). Commissioned to decorate ceiling at Louvre (1952). Died in Paris.

REFERENCES: Jean Cassou *Braque* (New York 1957 PB). Jean Leymarie *Braque* (tr. New York 1961). Edwin Mullins *Braque* (London 1968, also PB).

BRECHT, Bertolt (born Eugen Berthold Friedrich Brecht) (Feb. 10, 1898 – Aug. 14, 1956). German playwright and poet. Born Augsburg, into well-to-do family. Began publishing poems and reviews at sixteen. Entered University of Munich medical school (1917); was soon drafted and made an orderly in Augsburg military hospital. Returned to Munich (1920). First success as dramatist *Drums in the Night,* which won national Kleist prize (1922). Married (1922) Marianne Zoff (divorced 1927). Moved to Berlin (1924); collaborated with Kurt Weill on *The Threepenny Opera* (1928) and *The Rise and Fall of the City of Mahagonny* (1929). Also in this period: *A Manual of Piety* (1927), a collection of poems, *St. Joan of the Stockyards* (written 1929–30), *The Measures Taken* (1930) and *The Mother* (1932). Married actress Helene Weigel (1928). A Marxist, he left Hitler Germany (1933). Lived in Denmark (1933–39), Sweden and Finland (1939–41), went to U.S. (1941); then back to Europe (1947) after appearing before House Committee on Un-American Activities. Lived in East Berlin, where he and Helene Weigel founded a theatre company, the Berliner Ensemble, and where he died. Received Stalin prize (1954). Major plays include *Galileo* (1938), *Mother Courage and Her Children* (1941), *The Good Woman of Setzuan* (1943), *The Caucasian Chalk Circle* (1945).

TRANSLATIONS: *Seven Plays* (New York 1961), *Baal; A Man's a Man; and The Elephant Calf* (New York PB 1964), *Galileo* (New York PB 1966), *The Good Woman of Setzuan* (New York PB 1965), *A Manual of Piety* (New York 1966), *Mother Courage and Her Children* (New York 1963, also PB), and *Parables for the Theatre* (Minneapolis 1965) all translated by Eric Bentley. *The Threepenny Opera* tr. Eric Bentley and Desmond Vesey (New York PB 1964). *In the Jungle of Cities* tr. A. Hollo (New York PB 1965). *Bertolt Brecht: Collected Plays* ed. and tr. Ralph Manheim and John Willett (vol. I, New York 1971).

REFERENCES: Robert Brustein *The Theatre of Revolt* (Boston 1964). Martin Esslin *Brecht: A Choice of Evils. A Critical Study of the Man, His Work and His Opinions* (London 1959 and, as *Brecht: The Man and His Work*, New York 1960, also PB). Frederick Ewen *Bertolt Brecht: His Life, His Art, and His Times* (New York 1967). John Willett *The Theater of Bertolt Brecht* (Norfolk, Conn. and London 1959).

✌

BERTOLT BRECHT
BY HAROLD CLURMAN

Very few writers in the first half of the twentieth century registered its disquiet more significantly than Bertolt Brecht. It was personal, physical, moral, social, and political. It is remarkable that he believed in the benefit of these anxieties; what is moving is that to a large degree he overcame them.

Brecht often expressed himself in mottoes. He wrote a most revealing one when he had his Galileo reply to the accusation (in reference to his recantation) that his hands were dirty, "Better dirty than void." And then Galileo adds, "You have two rival spirits lodged in you. You have got to have two. Stay disputed, undecided. Stay a unit, stay divided! Hold to the crude one, hold to the cleaner one. Hold to the obscene one! Hold them united."

Brecht is all "division." He is poet, playwright, theatrical leader. Of those three the best known are the playwright and man of the theatre. The core of the man is the poet, the "minstrel." This cannot be fully appreciated by those ignorant of German. Brecht was a master of language combining a vein of folk simplicity with sophistication, mingling loftiness of thought with earthiness of vocabulary. He is never obscure, since his directness is that of living speech. Yet he is often subtle. No single term encompasses him, no single category places him.

He begins as a romantic anarchist, very nearly a nihilist. His earliest verses are filled with a pity which bursts forth in the plays of the same period in bitterness and rage. One poem of mute agony tells of a child who for no apparent reason has killed his father and mother. It is a strange elegy to the innocent and senseless savagery of the world.

The heartbroken first poems speak for the inner Brecht; the plays of his youth — chaotic, obscene, very nearly inarticulate with fury — mirror the social disarray and human degradation which followed the First World War. ("I came to the city in a time of disorder when hunger ruled . . . I ate my food between massacres.") He is immersed in that world, loathing it and also fascinated by it. For it is *existence*, and it is only through actual contact with the data of the commonplace, Brecht implies, that a man attains understanding and salvation.

Underneath the turmoil and turbulence dwelt Brecht the admirer of Goethe with dictates of moderation. Brecht wished to learn. His political study never led him to the abstract but always to the concrete and specific. He became aware of the social need to release men from the bondage of economic pressure. He had always been compassionate toward the dispossessed, the rejected, the outcast. Brecht's Marxism was a humanism which remained rather suspect to the organizationally conformist adherents of the cause.

He became a "fighter," yet his creative voice was subdued. ("You, who shall emerge from the flood in which we are sinking, think, when you speak of our weaknesses, also of the dark time that brought them forth.") He proclaimed a didactic aim, yet he espoused pleasure and sport. He advanced through irony: "A man lives by his head; his head will not suffice" are the opening lines of one of his most famous songs. His cautionary tragedy *The Measures Taken* may be construed either as a celebration of heroic party discipline or as a condemnatory dirge. He accepted contradiction: the constant and conflicting movement of life in opposite directions; they combine to shape a synthesis which awaits further change.

His work describes the unsteady arc of his experience. During the period of inflation in Germany his early hysteria dissolves to a kind of teasing raillery, an acerbic pathos, a beguiling tone of admonition. In the years of struggle against Nazism he becomes grim but his gravity is relieved by songs: calm, brave, quietly exalted, sometimes witty, stirring without clamor.

In the sixteen years of his exile ("For we went changing our country more often than our shoes") he does his most mature work. *Mother Courage* is his dramatic masterpiece — a comedy verging on tragedy, its central character an "antiheroine" who, whether Brecht willed it or not, arouses our fellow feeling. It is an unsentimental antiwar play which makes its solemn point without stress. It is couched in humor, untearful in the depiction of havoc. The rebellious quasi-expressionist of former times has become sane.

On his return to Germany, Brecht establishes one of the great theatres of our time, the Berliner Ensemble, a theatre which has survived him. To give his theatre a firm foundation he writes essays and treatises the interest of which extends beyond theatrical matters. ("Today every invention is received with a cry of triumph which soon turns into a cry of fear.") But Brecht's theories, required in his battle against ancient usage, are not as forbidding or opaque as he made them sound. "To hell with my writing," he exclaims when people are put off by the difficulty of his explications. His practice leads to simplicity. It was a reaction to the stentorian emptiness of the German court theatres and the hectic emotionalism of the postwar dramatists. The terms Brecht popularized or invented — "epic theatre," "alienation effect" etc. — were tools to discipline emotion by cool observation and objective form. Despite the frequent grubbiness of his narrative material, Brecht's productions are marked by humor, elegance and (unexpectedly) nobility, even grandeur.

Brecht speaks of himself as being "at home on pavements." But there is something peasantlike in the grossness of his imagery and in his rough common sense. Even his anti-individualism (in part a sign of his classicism as well as of his Marxist indoctrination) is expressed with a quizzical canniness. "Young Alexander," he tells us in his poem *A Worker Reads History,* "conquered India. He alone? Caesar beat the Gauls. Was there not even a cook in his company? Philip of Spain wept as his fleet was sunk and destroyed. Were there no other tears?"

Brecht considered skepticism an instrument of knowledge, a step toward independent affirmation. His verse and dialogue are marked by a sly terseness in which tenderness hovers. From the plea in his early poem *Concerning the Infanticide Marie Farrar* — "but you, I beg you, check your wrath and scorn, for man needs help from every creature born" — to the lines in the manner of a haiku: "On my walls hangs a Japanese carving, the mask of an evil demon . . . Sympathetically I observe the swollen veins of the forehead, indicating what a strain it is to be evil," we may infer a long stride in prosody; viewed together they represent the unifying note which identifies Brecht's genius in all its diversity.

In a poem entitled *To Posterity* the concluding lines read: "Even the hatred of squalor, even anger against injustice makes the voice grow harsh. Alas, we who wished to lay the foundation of kindness could not ourselves be kind. But you, when at last it comes to pass that man can help his fellow man, do not judge us too harshly."

Through suffering, thoughtfulness, and scrupulous artistry, Brecht attained wisdom.

BRETON, André (Feb. 19, 1896 – Sept. 28, 1966). French writer. Born Tinchebray, Orne. Studied medicine (1913–15) with special interest in mental disease; in World War I served in psychiatric wards. Freudian theory, as well as the ideas of symbolists and Dadaists, contributed to evolution of his theory on the kinship of madness, dreams, and art. With Louis Aragon and Philippe Soupault founded magazine *Littérature* (1919), wherein appeared *Les Champs magnétiques* (1921), an experiment in automatic writing by Breton and Soupault. The founder and theorist of the surrealist movement, in his three surrealist manifestos (1924, 1930, 1942) he urged and defined an art of "psychic automatism," free from control by reason, morals, or aesthetics. Other major works: *Le Surréalisme et la peinture* (1928), a novel *Nadja* (1928), a volume of poetry *Le Révolver à cheveux blancs* (1932), *Les Vases communicants* (1932), *L'Amour fou* (1937), *Arcane 17* (1945). Served in medical corps of French army (1939–40). In America (1941–45) founded and edited, with Marcel Duchamp, Max Ernst, and David Hare magazine *VVV* (1942–44), and studied occultism in rites of Southwestern and Caribbean Indians. Returning to Paris, resumed activity as author, editor, and inspirer of surrealist painters and writers. Breton was married three times. Died in Paris.

TRANSLATION: *Manifestoes of Surrealism* tr. Richard Seaver and Helen R. Lane (Ann Arbor, Mich. 1969).

REFERENCES: Clifford Browder *André Breton: Arbiter of Surrealism* (Geneva 1967). Mary Ann Caws *Surrealism and the Literary Imagination: A Study of Breton and Bachelar* (The Hague 1966). J. H. Matthews *André Breton* (New York 1967 PB).

BRIDGES, Robert (Seymour) (Oct. 23, 1844 – Apr. 21, 1930). English poet. Born Walmer, Kent. Educated at Eton and Corpus Christi College, Oxford, where he became a friend of Gerard Manley Hopkins, whose poems he edited (1918). Bridges studied medicine and practiced in London until 1881. First volume, *Poems* (1873), was followed by sonnet series (1876), two more volumes of lyrics (1879, 1880), and two dramatic poems, *Prometheus the Firegiver* (1883) and *Eros and Psyche* (1885). Married Mary Waterhouse (1884), and spent rest of life in rural seclusion at Boar's Hill, Oxford, composing poetry and experimenting with new verse forms and meters. Appointed poet laureate (1913). Chiefly remembered for his serene, technically flawless lyrics (collected in *Shorter Poems*, 1890/1894) and for the long philosophical poem of his last years, *The Testament of Beauty* (1929). Also produced essays, including *Milton's Prosody* (1893) and *John Keats* (1895), and edited a wartime anthology *The Spirit of Man* (1916).

EDITIONS: *Collected Essays, Papers, etc.* (3 vols. London 1927–33). *Poetical Works with The Testament of Beauty but Excluding the Eight Dramas* (2nd ed. London 1953).

REFERENCES: George S. Gordon *Robert Bridges* (New York 1947). Albert J. Guerard *Robert Bridges: A Study of Traditionalism in Poetry* (Cambridge, Mass. 1942). Edward G. Thompson *Robert Bridges 1844–1930* (London 1944).

BRILLAT-SAVARIN, (Jean) Anthelme (Apr. 1, 1755 – Feb. 2, 1826). French jurist, writer, and gastronome. Born Belley, Ain. Following family tradition became a lawyer and later a member of estates general (1789) and mayor of Belley (1792). Forced to flee during the Terror, went first to Switzerland, then to U.S., where he spent two years in New York (1794–96), supporting himself by giving French lessons and playing the violin in a theatre orchestra. Returning to France (1796), received several government appointments under Directory and Consulate. He never married. Died in Paris. Brillat-Savarin was the author of several treatises on political economy and the law, but is remembered for his *Physiologie du goût*, a work on gastronomy published at his own expense (1825).

Witty and informal, it contains aphorisms, anecdotes, and philosophical musings as well as recipes and discussions of health and the scientific properties of food.

TRANSLATION: *The Physiology of Taste* with introduction by Arthur Machen (London 1925, also PB New York 1960).

REFERENCE: Maurice des Ombiaux *La physiologie du goût de Brillat-Savarin* (Paris 1937).

BRONTË, Charlotte (Apr. 21, 1816 – Mar. 31, 1855). English novelist. Born Thornton, Yorkshire, daughter of Rev. Patrick Brontë (1777–1861). Family moved to Haworth (1820); mother died (1821). Two older sisters fell mortally ill at Cowan Bridge boarding school (1824), leaving Charlotte, Branwell (b.1817), Emily (b.1818), and Anne (b.1820). Charlotte and Emily were brought home from the same school, and Charlotte went to Miss Wooler's at Roe Head, returning as a teacher (1834), bringing Emily. She became a governess for several years; then with Emily, hoping to start a boarding school, spent eight months (1842) at school in Brussels, studying languages. For the projected school they received not one application, and Charlotte returned briefly to Brussels (1843) as an English teacher. At home, the three sisters published (1846) *Poems by Currer, Ellis, and Acton Bell* (their assumed names). Each then began a novel. Although Charlotte's *The Professor* remained unpublished until 1857, she was sufficiently encouraged to produce *Jane Eyre* (1847), an immediate success. The following two years saw the deaths (within a nine-month period) of Branwell, Emily, and Anne. Charlotte continued publication with *Shirley* (1849) and *Villette* (1853). Married (1854) her father's curate Arthur Bell Nicholls (1817–1906), but died at Haworth the next March.

EDITION: *Letters of the Brontës* ed. Muriel Spark (London and Norman, Okla. 1954).

REFERENCES: Mrs. Elizabeth C. Gaskell *The Life of Charlotte Brontë* (2 vols. London and New York 1857).

Winifred Gerin *Charlotte Brontë: The Evolution of Genius* (London and New York 1967). Margaret Lane *The Brontë Story: A Reconsideration of Mrs. Gaskell's Life of Charlotte Brontë* (London and New York 1953). Fannie E. Ratchford *The Brontës' Web of Childhood* (London and New York 1941). Clement K. Shorter *Charlotte Brontë and Her Circle* (London 1896 and New York 1899). See also references for EMILY BRONTË.

CHARLOTTE BRONTË
BY MARK SCHORER

Charlotte Brontë was the third of six children, five girls and one boy, all born within as many years. When Charlotte was five the mother of this brood died, calling out repeatedly, "Oh God, my poor children!" When the Reverend Patrick Brontë could persuade no other woman to become her successor, her sister, a cold but not unkind woman, came to Yorkshire from Penzance as housekeeper. At eleven and twelve, the two oldest girls died. That left four to amuse and instruct themselves as best they could in the lonely Haworth parsonage, among the tombstones of the graveyard beside it, on the empty moors that stretched away from it. Charlotte, in effect, was the mother.

They played games, of course; but what extraordinary games! Beginning almost accidentally in 1826 when the boy, Branwell, acquired some wooden soldiers and each girl appropriated one as her own and gave it a hero's name, a whole set of extravagant legends unfolded in their group collaboration. These stories are chiefly remarkable for having been written down: this was above all a *literary* effort. As with most literary work, there were "influences," and notably two: Lord Byron in his overreaching narrative poems, and John Martin, the painter possessed of a kind of architectural megalomania, whose favorite subjects were the great ruined cities of the past like Babylon and Nineveh, nearly inconceivable splendor and mammoth catastrophe. Such influences, entering their solitude, inevitably gave their kingdom of Angria its shape and color and emotional tone.

For the kingdom of Angria they invented an entire fabulous society and then recorded it all in little handmade pamphlets which equal, in words, their entire combined publications. Emily and Anne broke off from the saga of Angria to begin their own legends of Gondal; but Angria flourished as Branwell occupied himself chiefly with its military affairs while Charlotte chose for herself the hardly less spectacular and aggressive area of the passions.

"Never shall I, Charlotte Brontë, forget what a voice of wild and wailing music now came thrillingly to my mind's, almost my body's ear, nor how distinctly I, sitting in the schoolroom at Roe Head, saw the Duke of Zamorna leaning against that obelisk. . . . I was quite gone. I had really, utterly, forgot where I was and all the gloom and cheerlessness of my situation. I felt myself breathing quick and short as I beheld the Duke lifting up his sable crest, which undulated as the plume of a hearse waves to the wind, and knew that music which sprang as mournfully triumphant as the scriptural verse, 'O Grave, where is thy sting? O Death, where is thy Victory?' was exciting him and quickening his ever-rapid pulse."

The Duke of Zamorna is a stereotype out of the Byronic tradition, and indeed, under Byron's influence, the swooning young Charlotte wrote not only streams of verse in his meters but all that prose as well. Under an influence so facilely satanic, the young woman's imagination slipped readily not only into the worn Gothic moods but also beyond them, sometimes into the quite grotesque. At the same time, in this fevered Angrian world, she was establishing the prototypes of some of her most famous later characters; not only, for example, Rochester in the magnificently imperious Zamorna, but even plain Jane Eyre herself in a character called Elizabeth Hastings, a girl who, under the commonplace exterior, possesses a noble, sensitive, high-spirited soul, and to whom, like Rochester after him, one Sir William Percy proposes that she become his mistress. Small wonder that Charlotte and Branwell habitually referred to Angria as "the infernal world," or better yet, "the world below."

But Charlotte Brontë herself was no longer a girl. She was a young woman in the England of Queen Victoria, a parson's daughter, and by no means entirely comfortable with the untamed flights of her own fancy. Another strain, that of conscience, protested, and explicitly in 1839: "I long to quit for a while that burning clime where we have sojourned so long — its skies aflame — the glow of sunset is always upon it — the mind would cease from excitement and turn now to a cooler region where the dawn breaks grey and sober, and the coming day for a time at least is subdued by clouds."

This is the mundane voice of common sense and rationality, wishing for the repose of the orderly commonplace; but at the same time, a very opposite habit of the imagination had been formed, with a preference for unchecked flights into the irrational and even the outrageous. Her mature efforts would demonstrate an uncertain swinging back and forth between these extremes.

Her first novel, *The Professor,* written in 1846 but not published until after her death, attempts to stay within the limits of the commonplace and the commonsensical. This effort is perhaps surprising, since the novel manipulates material out of her recent experience in Brussels, where, teaching English in a school kept by the wife of a Latin professor named Constantin Heger, she had developed a hopeless attachment for the autocratic M. Heger. Remembering that experience, she might well have been led into the strain of "something more imaginative and poetical — something more consonant with a highly wrought fancy, with a taste for pathos, with sentiments more tender, elevated, unworldly," which, in a preface she later wrote for this novel, she had avowedly eschewed. The result was a lifeless, unpublishable work.

Shirley, her third novel, was written during the brief time in which Branwell, her by then hopelessly depraved brother, and her two frail sisters, Emily and Anne, died. Such sorrows may account for its longueurs. In this work she reverts, although in a wider framework, to the workaday world. Her only historical novel, it is set early in the century, among mill workers, during the time of the Luddite riots. It is almost as though she thought to write a kind of *Middlemarch,* twenty years before that novel was written. But her talent did not lie in the dramatization of social and political tensions, and such vitality as this novel has exists in moments that realize the intensities of personal relationship. In spite of one extraordinary passage, however, in which, using phrases later employed by D. H. Lawrence, she writes of men as "the lords of creation . . . the sons of God," and asserts that "a great, good, handsome man is the first of created things," there is not enough of this to animate the heavy bulk of the whole.

In her final novel, *Villette,* turning again to the Brussels experience, she yields to that other strain of the "elevated, unworldly," the strain of dark romance where the everyday is all the time threatened by Gothic terrors, by hysteria and hallucination, by the grotesque extravagances of melodrama. But the novel is not of the first rank. Her most ambitious work, it is also, because of her clumsy mismanagement of her materials, her most disappointing.

Only once did she truly succeed — in her second novel, *Jane Eyre: An Autobiography* of 1847, a triumphant translation of Angrian characters, intensities, anxieties and sufferings, excesses of feeling, into the recognizable terms of English life. In this novel, which every reader knows, everything comes beautifully together — all the bits and pieces of her provincial intelligence, all the wispy, gaudy dreams of her yearning virginity, all the hopeful fragments of her deprived experience, all the depressed hopes for an embrace at last in the stout arms of a lord of creation: a work of art, astonishing.

BRONTË, Emily (Jane) (July 30, 1818 – Dec. 19, 1848). English novelist and poet. Born Thornton, Yorkshire, fourth in family of six. Family moved to Haworth (1820). When the two eldest sisters fell ill at boarding school and died soon after, Emily left the school with Charlotte (q.v.) (1824). Attended briefly Miss Wooler's school at Roe Head, where Charlotte was teacher (1835). Accompanied Charlotte to Brussels (1842) to study languages, but soon returned home, where she continued the writing begun as a child with her sisters and brother. *Poems by Currer, Ellis, and Acton Bell* (1846; pseudonyms of Charlotte, Emily, and Anne Brontë) resulted from Charlotte's discovery of a manuscript of Emily's

poetry, called "Gondal Poems" after the imaginary kingdom she and Anne created as children. Her only novel, *Wuthering Heights,* appeared (1847) after her sister's more popular *Jane Eyre.* A year later she died of tuberculosis, having caught cold at Branwell's funeral.

EDITION: *Letters of the Brontës* ed. Muriel Spark (London and Norman, Okla. 1954).

REFERENCES: Phyllis Bentley *The Brontës and Their World* (New York and London 1947, new ed. 1969). Mrs. Elizabeth C. Gaskell *The Life of Charlotte Brontë* (2 vols. London and New York 1857). Laura Hinkley *The Brontës: Charlotte and Emily* (New York 1945 and London 1948). Margaret Lane *The Brontë Story: A Reconsideration of Mrs. Gaskell's Life of Charlotte Brontë* (London and New York 1953). Fannie E. Ratchford *The Brontës' Web of Childhood* (London and New York 1941). Clement K. Shorter *Charlotte Brontë and Her Circle* (London 1896 and New York 1899). Muriel Spark and Derek Stanford *Emily Brontë: Her Life and Work* (London 1953 and New York 1960).

✍

EMILY BRONTË
BY ELIZABETH HARDWICK

The Brontës! One can hardly say the name of the family or of its single, extraordinary members without feeling crushed by the romantic, even cinematic moors, the "bewitched parsonage," as one critic called it, the neurasthenia, seclusion, alcoholism, early death — and the inexplicable talents in all, the genius in two. They are indeed a drama, full of pathos and grand gestures. Only an exaggerated inclination for the prosaic would wish to deny this. Emily Brontë's life was of such extreme quiet that the absence of event, the presence of so much reticence and isolation, are themselves striking and memorable.

The dramatic sufferings of the Brontës tend to overshadow the great deal that was practical, dedicated, and above all ambitious in the family. That the father and the brother, Branwell, were seriously affected by their failures in literature and painting there can be no doubt. Charlotte and Emily thought of their futures in terms of work, work necessary to make a living, and work prompted by great creative ambition. They trained in Brussels as schoolteachers. When Emily cut short that work to return home, she was acting under the commands of her shyness (and a small legacy left by her aunt), but also under the compelling desire to devote herself seriously to writing. The failure of her poems and the disappointing reception of *Wuthering Heights* were blows to her spirit of the most distressing kind. Her novel was not understood and was, in addition, overwhelmed by the popularity of *Jane Eyre.*

Emily Brontë's poems came out, with those of her sisters, in the famous volume of 1846: *Poems by Currer, Ellis, and Acton Bell.* This volume contained twenty-one poems by Emily. Her collected poems, gathered definitively much later, came to around two hundred poems. Of these perhaps a dozen or so survive in anthologies — a judgment and criterion of some seriousness, if not infallible. Matthew Arnold's lovely poem about the Brontës, *Haworth Churchyard,* speaks of Emily as having no equal since Byron for "might, passion, vehemence, grief, daring." He saw her as "self-consumed," and "too bold." These are strong words for the reclusive spinster, and yet they do not, when applied to her, violate our sense of fitness. Emily Brontë, in her poetry, came at the end of the Byronic tradition, when it was in decay, and much of her effort in the long sequence laid in the imaginary kingdom of Gondal is engulfed in Byronic mannerisms and exaggerations. However,

her best poems, such as "Cold in the Earth," "Fall, Leaves, Fall," and "No Coward Soul Is Mine," have an enduring vigor of rhythm and thought.

Emily Brontë wrote only one novel, *Wuthering Heights,* a singular, literally *unique* work, one of the oddest and most interesting in English fiction. Swinburne thought it best to think of it as a kind of poem; Virginia Woolf saw it as an immense, ambitious effort to create "a world cleft into gigantic disorder." The book is a profoundly moving mixture of Gothic elements — family doom, windswept landscape, ghosts from the past — and a love story that seems to come directly, innocently if you will, from the unconscious.

In structure the novel is as complicated and hard to follow as any elaborate Victorian plot. The interminglings of the generations of Lintons and Earnshaws, the narration by old servants and outsiders: these elements make the perplexing love story all the more dramatic. Catherine and Heathcliff are mutations, instinctual figures, trapped in an isolated but in some ways a realistic social structure. Thrushcross Grange and Wuthering Heights are the names of the two estates; one stands for orderly life and civilized manners and the other for chaos and destruction.

The love of Catherine and Heathcliff does not have any social destiny or purpose: it is a fate. We cannot even imagine the proper consummation of this love; it is, as Muriel Spark has written, essentially celibate. Neither Catherine nor Heathcliff has any inclination for marriage or domesticity, even though Catherine marries Edgar Linton and Heathcliff marries Isabella Linton. Edgar and Isabella experience fully the suffering and frustration that comes to those who unite with unmarriageable, driven natures. Catherine and Heathcliff do not themselves know how to describe their feelings. It is a sense of a consuming identity. "I *am* Heathcliff," Catherine insists. Their love represents the freedom and intensity of childhood, and in that way there is something incestuous about it.

Heathcliff is a brutal man, unredeemably brutal. He has been an orphan, mistreated, unprotected, and in that he connects with the older literature of the scorned, revengeful man. He leaves and makes a fortune, thereby freeing himself from the pathetic and making it possible for him to become the romantic, demonic hero. The power he has over our imagination and feeling perhaps comes from our acceptance of the roots of his demonic, obsessive love, roots planted in his suffering childhood. Catherine says of him, "He's not a rough diamond, a pearl-containing oyster of a rustic; he's a fierce, pitiless, wolfish man."

Catherine too is a heroine of a perplexing sort. She is selfish and self-indulgent and frightening in the emptiness and idleness that drown her when she is away from Heathcliff. Both the hero and the heroine have a schizophrenic indifference to the claims of others. They are lost natures, but genuinely impressive in their strange completeness, the way they carry through to the end the torment of their feelings. They truly represent the anarchic, destructive Id.

In the novel, Catherine is only twenty-three when she dies and Heathcliff is forty-two. It is usual for critics to point out that while Emily Brontë was writing the book she was watching at home the tragic disintegration of her brother Branwell. But Emily's own nature was itself under the control of a strangely exaggerated will. In Mrs. Gaskell's superb *Life of Charlotte Brontë* we have a picture of Emily's death. She had refused doctors and would not cooperate with any attempt to slow down the pace of her tuberculosis. Charlotte said of her sister, "Never in all her life had she lingered over any task that lay before her, and she did not linger now. She sank rapidly. She made haste to leave us. I have seen nothing like it; but indeed, I have never seen her parallel in anything. Stronger than a man, simpler than a child, her nature stood alone."

BRONZINO, Il (Agnolo di Cosimo di Mariano) (Nov. 17, 1503 – Nov. 23, 1572). Italian painter. Born Montecelli, near Florence. His principal teacher and lifelong friend, Jacopo da Pontormo, exerted strong influence on early works. After two years at Pesaro (1530–32), where he assisted in decorative projects at Villa Imperiale, settled in Florence for rest of his life. Increasingly devoted himself to portraiture and within a decade had established his supremacy as one of the foremost mannerists. After 1539 he was court painter to Cosimo I de' Medici, duke of Florence. The proportions of Bronzino's figures are artificially elongated, their modeling smooth and hard. Emphasis is on elegance and on decorative surface patterns of clothing and jewels. He painted religious and allegorical works such as *Venus, Cupid, Folly, and Time* (c.1542–45, National Gallery, London), as well as the portraits for which he is especially renowned. Of these the best known is *Eleanora of Toledo and Her Son* (c.1545–50 Uffizi, Florence), in which, characteristically, the sitter's ornate costume encases her like armor, and her stylized face reveals nothing of her character save an aristocratic hauteur.

REFERENCE: Arthur McComb *Agnolo Bronzino: His Life and Works* (Cambridge, Mass. 1928).

BROOKE, Rupert (Aug. 3, 1887 – Apr. 23, 1915). English poet. Born Rugby, where his father was housemaster. Educated there and took degree at King's College, Cambridge (1909). Lived near there at Granchester (1909–12). First book of verse: *Poems* (1911). Awarded fellowship at King's for thesis on John Webster (published 1916). After visits to Europe, returned to England to work on Edward Marsh's anthology *Georgian Poetry: 1911–1912*. Left soon again for long trip through United States, Canada, South Seas; travel letters to *Westminster Gazette* published as *Letters from America* (1916). On outbreak of World War I received commission in Royal Navy. Ordered to Dardanelles (1915), but en route suffered sunstroke and blood poisoning and died on island of Skyros, Greece. Brooke's reputation is founded chiefly on posthumous volume *1914 and Other Poems* (1915), which expresses the romantic patriotism of the early days of the war. *Collected Poems* appeared (1918) with Edward Marsh's memoir.

EDITIONS: *Prose of Rupert Brooke* ed. Christopher Hassall (London and New York 1956). *Poetical Works of Rupert Brooke* ed. Geoffrey Keynes (London 1946). *Collected Poems* ed. Edward Marsh (London and New York 1915).

REFERENCES: Walter de la Mare *Rupert Brooke and the Intellectual Imagination: A Lecture* (London 1919 and New York 1920). Christopher Hassall *Rupert Brooke* (London and New York 1964). Geoffrey Keynes *Bibliography of Rupert Brooke* (2nd ed. London and New York 1959). Arthur J. A. Stringer *Red Wine of Youth: A Life of Rupert Brooke* (Indianapolis 1948).

BROOKS, Van Wyck (Feb. 16, 1886 – May 2, 1963). American critic, biographer, and cultural historian. Born Plainfield, N.J. Graduated from Harvard (1907), then worked as journalist in England. The theme of his first book, *The Wine of the Puritans* (1909) — that American culture is influenced by the materialistic strain of its Puritan tradition to the neglect of aesthetic values — was further developed in *America's Coming-of-Age* (1915), *Letters and Leadership* (1918), *The Ordeal of Mark Twain* (1920, revised 1933), and *The Pilgrimage of Henry James* (1925). In New York (1908–20) as critic, editor, and translator of French books, then moved to

Connecticut. Died in Bridgewater. Brooks's literary history of the U.S., *Makers and Finders,* comprises five volumes: *The Flowering of New England* (1936, Pulitzer prize (1937), *New England: Indian Summer* (1940), *The World of Washington Irving* (1944), *The Times of Melville and Whitman* (1947), and *The Confident Years: 1885–1915* (1952). Among his other works: *On Literature Today* (1941), *A Chilmark Miscellany* (1948), *The Writer in America* (1953), *The Dream of Arcadia* (1958), and the autobiographical *Scenes and Portraits: Memories of Childhood and Youth* (1954), *Days of the Phoenix: The Nineteen-Twenties I Remember* (1957), and *From the Shadow of the Mountain: My Post-Meridian Years* (1961).

EDITION: *Van Wyck Brooks: The Early Years. A Selection from His Works 1908–1921* ed. Claire Sprague (New York PB 1968).

REFERENCES: Gladys Brooks *If Strangers Meet: A Memory* (New York 1967). William Wasserstrom *Van Wyck Brooks* (Minneapolis PB 1968).

BROUWER (or BRAUWER), Adriaen (c.1606 – Jan. 1638). Flemish painter. Born Oudenaarde, where his father, a tapestry designer, probably gave him his first training. Left home at sixteen; in Amsterdam (1625). In Haarlem (1627–c.1631), joined circle of Frans Hals, and was probably Hals's pupil and assistant. Spent remainder of his short life in Antwerp; imprisoned there (1633) for several months by Spanish rulers on charges of spying. Brouwer's scenes of tavern life such as *Smokers* (Metropolitan Museum, New York) and country merrymaking enjoyed great popularity; one admirer was Rubens, who acquired seventeen of his paintings. Vigorous and dramatically constructed, his work at first tended heavily toward caricature; but in later years, under the influence of such artists as van de Velde and Rubens, he displayed warmer sympathies with humanity and a splendid gift for landscape. Well-known paintings include *The Sleeping Peasant* (Wallace collection, London), *Quarreling Players,* and *Spanish Soldiers at Dice* (both at Munich Gallery).

REFERENCE: Gerhardus Knuttel *Adriaen Brouwer: The Master and His Work* (tr. New York 1962).

BROWN, Charles Brockden (Jan. 17, 1771 – Feb. 22, 1810). American novelist and editor. Born and died in Philadelphia. Of Quaker parentage, received good education, then studied and practiced law, which he abandoned for writing. Settled in New York, where he became the first professional writer in America. Strongly influenced by radical ideas of William Godwin, he produced the profeminist *Alcuin: A Dialogue on the Rights of Women* (1798). Reputation as sensational Gothic novelist established by *Wieland, or The Transformation* (1798). His romance *Ormond, or The Secret Witness* (1799) was admired by Shelley; *Arthur Mervyn* (2 vols. 1799/1800) involved the yellow fever epidemic in Philadelphia; *Edgar Huntley* (1799) introduced the Indian into American fiction. A man of prodigious industry, Brown also wrote other novels and pamphlets, edited literary magazines, and developed the *American Register, or General Repository of History, Politics and Science*. Married Elizabeth Linn (1804); they had four children.

EDITION: *Novels* (6 vols. Philadelphia 1857; Port Washington, N.Y. 1967).
REFERENCES: William Dunlap *Life of Charles Brockden Brown* (2 vols. Philadelphia 1815). David L. Clark *Charles Brockden Brown, Pioneer Voice of America* (Durham, N.C. 1952).

BROWN, Lancelot (1715 – Feb. 6, 1783). English landscape gardener and architect. Nicknamed Capability Brown from his habit of estimating the "capabilities" of a landscape. Born Harle-Kirk, Northumberland, where he worked as gardener until 1739. Became (1740) Lord Cobham's gardener at Stowe, Buckinghamshire, and met William Kent, under whose inspiration he developed the gardening style characteristic of the English country estate from his time to the present. Rejecting the formal, geometric French gardening style, Brown emphasized the natural, undulating lines of the English countryside; main elements in his landscapes are isolated clumps of trees, rolling greensward, and a surrounding belt of woodland. Married Bridget Wayet (1744). Established himself (1751) as gardener and architect at Hammersmith; met with immediate and lasting success. Designed grounds of over 140 estates, including Kew, Blenheim, Harewood, and Bowood. Among his houses, in the Palladian manner, are Croome, Redgrave, and Claremont. Appointed (1764) royal gardener to George III, whose close friend he became. Died in London.

REFERENCE: Dorothy Stroud *Capability Brown* (London 1950 and New York 1951).

BROWNE, Sir Thomas (Oct. 19, 1605 – Oct. 19, 1682). English physician and writer. Born London, son of a mercer. Educated at Winchester and Broadgates Hall (now Pembroke College), Oxford (1623–29). Studied medicine at Montpellier, Padua, and Leiden, taking M.D. at Leiden (1633). Established himself as physician in Norwich (1637), where he spent rest of his life. Married Dorothy Mileham (1641). Knighted by Charles II (1671). The self-revelatory *Religio Medici* (written c.1635, published 1642, first authorized edition 1643) in which Browne expressed both religiousness and skepticism, was immediately popular; it circulated widely in Europe in Latin translation. *Pseudodoxia Epidemica* (also called Vulgar Errors) (1646) attempted to correct many popular beliefs and superstitions. *Hydriotaphia: Urn Burial*, published with *The Garden of Cyrus* (1658), begins as a treatise on archaeology and develops into a magnificent prose poem on death and immortality. Mystical and reflective, it is the finest example of Browne's baroque style, studded with such splendid lines as "The iniquity of oblivion blindly scattereth her poppy." Other works include *A Letter to a Friend* (1690) and *Christian Morals* (1716).

EDITION: *The Works of Sir Thomas Browne* ed. Geoffrey Keynes (new ed. 4 vols. Chicago and London 1964).
REFERENCES: Joan Bennett *Sir Thomas Browne: A Man of Achieve-*

ment in Literature (Cambridge, England 1962). William P. Dunn *Sir Thomas Browne: A Study in Religious Philosophy* (2nd ed. Minneapolis 1950 and Oxford 1951). Jeremiah S. Finch *Sir Thomas Browne: A Doctor's Life of Science and Faith* (New York 1950, also PB). Frank L. Huntley *Sir Thomas Browne* (Ann Arbor, Mich. 1962, also PB). Leonard Nathanson *The Strategy of Truth: A Study of Sir Thomas Brown* (Chicago 1967).

BROWNING, Elizabeth Barrett (Mar. 6, 1806 – June 29, 1861). English poet. Born Coxhoe Hall, near Durham. Educated at home, she displayed great precocity. Published *An Essay on Mind and Other Poems* (1826) and *Prometheus Bound* [translation of Aeschylus] *and Miscellaneous Poems* (1833). In 1835, after series of financial reverses, the Barretts moved to London, where Elizabeth published verses in many periodicals before achieving recognition with *The Seraphim and Other Poems* (1838). Series of illnesses from 1821 and death of her brother (1840) caused her to live in seclusion as invalid. Her popular volume *Poems* (1844) brought about correspondence with Robert Browning (1845). After courtship kept secret because of Mr. Barrett's disapproval, they were married (1846) and left for Italy, settling in Florence. Son, Robert Wiedemann Barrett Browning, born (1849). Second volume entitled *Poems* (1850) included the love poems *Sonnets from the Portuguese*, her finest work because of the discipline the form imposed on her lyric expression. *Casa Guidi Windows* (1851) proclaimed hopes for Italian independence and unity. *Aurora Leigh* (1856), a sentimental verse-novel, enjoyed immense popularity. Other volumes: *Poems Before Congress* (1860) and posthumous *Last Poems* (1862). She died in Florence. Mrs. Browning's sincerity and passionate enthusiasm account for both the virtues and the faults — diffuseness and lack of discipline — of her poetry.

REFERENCES: Alethea Hayter *Mrs. Browning: A Poet's Work and Its Setting* (London 1962 and New York 1963). Dorothy Hewlett *Elizabeth Barrett Browning: A Life* (New York 1952 and London 1953). Gardner B. Taplin *The Life of Elizabeth Barrett Browning* (New Haven 1957).

BROWNING, Robert (May 7, 1812 – December 12, 1889). English poet. Born Camberwell; educated largely at home by intellectual parents. First published poem *Pauline* (1833) poorly received, but *Paracelsus* (1835) brought critical appreciation and acquaintance with Wordsworth, Landor, and other writers. Wrote series of unsuccessful plays (1837–46). After poor reception of *Sordello* (1840) because of its obscurity, Browning turned to producing a little series (1841–46) collectively entitled *Bells and Pomegranates*, which included *Pippa Passes* (1841), *Dramatic Lyrics* (1842), and *Dramatic Romances and Lyrics* (1845), containing some of his best-known poems — *My Last Duchess, The Pied Piper of Hamelin,* and *The Lost Leader.* Married Elizabeth Barrett (1846); they lived in Florence, where their son was born (1849). After wife's death (1861) returned to London, where he became a leading literary figure and produced his finest works. His major contribution is the dramatic monologue, the technique of which he perfected in *Men and Women* (1855), *Dramatis Personae* (1864), and *The Ring and the Book* (1868–69), considered his masterpiece. Continued to write until his death in Venice. Later works include *Dramatic Idyls* (1879–80) and *Asolando* (1889).

EDITION: *The Complete Poetical Works of Robert Browning* ed. Augustine Birrell (London and New York 1915).

REFERENCES: William H. Griffin and Harry C. Minchin *The Life of Robert Browning* (rev. ed. London 1938). Betty B. Miller *Robert Browning: A Portrait* (London 1952 and New York 1953). Maisie Ward *Robert Browning and His World* (2 vols. New York 1967/68).

BRUCKNER, (Josef) Anton (Sept. 4, 1824 – Oct. 11, 1896). Austrian composer. Born Ansfelden, son of a poor schoolteacher. Became chorister at monastery of village of St. Florian (1837), where he learned music; at same time attended teachers' training college at Linz, and in 1840's worked as schoolmaster. Became organist of Linz cathedral (1856). Settled in Vienna (1868) for rest of his life, taught at conservatory (1868–91) and university (1875–94), and became ardent disciple of Wagner. Bruckner's nine symphonies (1866–96) are remarkable for their imposing grandeur, length, and loose organization; other major works are his three Masses (1864–71) and *Te Deum* (1881, revised 1884). Not appreciated even in Austria until the 1880's, Bruckner's work did not achieve worldwide recognition until well into twentieth century. His chief follower was Gustav Mahler.

REFERENCES: Erwin Doernberg *The Life and Symphonies of Anton Bruckner* (London 1960 and New York 1961, also PB). Robert W. L. Simpson *The Essence of Bruckner: An Essay Towards the Understanding of His Music* (London 1967).

BRUEGEL, Pieter (the Elder) (c.1525 – Sept. 5, 1569). Flemish painter. Place of birth unknown. He first appears in Antwerp, where he was apprenticed to Pieter Coecke van Aelst and was accepted (1551) into painters' guild. Traveled in Italy (1552–53); painted numerous mountain views on return trip through Alps. Worked in Antwerp until marriage to Coecke's daughter Mayken (1563); they moved to Brussels, where he died. Best-known of his works of genre, landscape, and allegory are *Fall of Icarus* (Musées Royaux des Beaux Arts, Brussels), *Netherlandish Proverbs* (1559, Berlin-Dahlem), *Tower of Babel* (1563, Kunsthistorisches Museum, Vienna), the series of *Months* (1565, among them *Hunters in the Snow*, Kunsthistorisches Museum), *Wedding Dance* (1566, Art Museum, Detroit), and *Parable of the Blind* (1568, Museo Nazionale, Naples). Executed designs for numerous prints published by Hieronymus Cock. Bruegel founded a family of prolific painters. His son Pieter Bruegel the Younger (c.1564–1637/8), a close imitator, painted genre and rural subjects as well as the fantastic scenes of hell which earned him the nickname Hell Bruegel.

REFERENCES: R. Delevoy *Bruegel: Historical and Critical Study* (tr. Geneva, Switzerland (1959). Max J. Friedlaender *Pieter Bruegel* (Berlin 1921). Fritz Grossmann ed. *Bruegel: The Paintings* (2nd ed. London and Greenwich, Conn. 1966). H. Arthur Klein ed. *Graphic Works of Pieter Bruegel The Elder* (New York PB 1963). Ludwig Münz *Bruegel: The Drawings* (London and Greenwich, Conn. 1961). Carl G. Stridbeck *Bruegelstudien* (Stockholm 1956). Charles de Tolnay *Pierre Bruegel L'Ancien* (2 vols. Brussels 1935).

✍

PIETER BRUEGEL THE ELDER
BY ANNE MARKHAM

At a time when art had become a mere criticism of art Pieter Bruegel's painting signified a criticism of life. While Bruegel's Flemish contemporaries, such as Maerten van Heemskerck and Frans Floris, were elaborating elegant contorted nudes and incorporating into their involuted compositions quotations from Michelangelo's *Last Judgment* and antique monuments recently exhumed at Rome, Bruegel, as Karel van Mander tells us in *Het Schilderboeck,* "went out into the country to see the peasants at their fairs and weddings . . . Here Bruegel delighted in observing the droll behavior of the peasants, how they ate, drank, danced, capered, or made love, all of which he was well able to reproduce cleverly and pleasantly in water colors or oils." Yet Bruegel had little sympathy for those he observed. He viewed humanity as ignorant and foolish, acquiescing without reflection to the promptings of base instinct. For Bruegel, the individual was of no significance: no man was specially endowed and all were doomed without exception.

In the *Peasant Dance* in Vienna,

Bruegel comments on the sins of lust, anger, gluttony. Peasants boisterously dance, kiss, quarrel, drink. The occasion of this excessive jubilation is a kermess in honor of a saint. But the church stands empty and a picture of the Madonna is ignored. The *Wedding Banquet,* also at Vienna, is an allegory of the abuse of generosity. In the *Tower of Babel* (two versions in Vienna and Rotterdam) the precariously tilted tower, symbol of man's most ambitious fabrications, is modeled on the ruins of the Roman Colosseum. Thus the destructive effect of time on the greatest structure of classical antiquity becomes a metaphor for the destruction of the tower of Babel by the wrath of God. The *Way to Calvary* of 1564 in Vienna takes place in a Flemish landscape and is peopled by Bruegel's own contemporaries. Not only are the actors indifferent to the fate of Christ but they enjoy the event as though it were a public outing. In the middle ground on the left Simon of Cyrene is being forced by soldiers to assist Christ in carrying the cross. In his struggle with the soldiers Simon is aided by his wife, who wears a rosary with a cross. This sign of her outward piety stands as a condemnation of the hypocrisy of Christians.

Several of Bruegel's paintings refer to precise contemporary political events. Invariably the references are disguised: Bruegel dared not arouse the Spanish persecutors, and when on his deathbed he had his wife burn some drawings "from remorse or for fear that she might get into trouble and might have to answer for them" (van Mander). Already in 1550 Hapsburg attempts to extirpate Protestant heresy in the Netherlands had sent great numbers of religious martyrs to the stake. The apogee of terror was reached, however, when, following the

Calvinist iconoclasm and armed rebellion against the rule of Philip II, the Netherlands were invaded in 1567 by Spanish troops led by the Duke of Alva. Under the Inquisition, which he instituted, large-scale arrest, torture, and wholesale executions were frequent occurrences. The contemporary chronicle of Gascoigne tells us: "They neither spared age nor sex . . . strong nor feeble: but without mercy did tyrannously triumph, when there was neither man nor mean to resist them. They slew great numbers of young children. The rich was spoil because he had, and the poor were hanged because they had nothing." With these events we may connect Bruegel's *Massacre of the Innocents* (two versions in Vienna and Hampton Court), into which the artist has introduced an inconspicuous figure of the Duke of Alva. The *Triumph of Death* in the Prado has also been interpreted as a veiled reference to the depredations of the Spanish troops. For the first time in art the *Triumph of Death* is represented as an actual assault upon the living by an army of the dead. Death occurs invariably by violent means, and the personification of Death does not gently summon the pilgrim to his inevitable end but slits his throat.

Yet all of Bruegel's paintings were not as macabre or pessimistic as these. Some paintings, such as the *Peasant and the Birdnester* of 1568 (Vienna) or *Netherlandish Proverbs,* 1559 (Berlin-Dahlem), illustrate with a sardonic wit common Flemish proverbs. A series of five paintings executed for Niclaes Jonghelinck of Antwerp (originally there may have been six) are dedicated to the depiction of the months. Months, characterized by the different activities of peasants, had been a frequent theme in medieval manuscript illumination. In Bruegel's paintings, however, nature has become protagonist.

Just as Bruegel represents not men but humanity, so his view of nature is panoramic in extent. Impressions of Alpine landscapes received during his Italian journey of 1552–53 are recalled throughout his life and combined with domestic villages and plains and occasional motifs drawn from the paintings of Joachim Patinir. The artist almost invariably looks down upon his landscape from mountain heights so that the horizon is high and the major portion of the field is filled with the components of his landscape. From his great distance, even objects on the foremost planes are small in scale, diminution in scale is gradual, and objects many miles distant from each other appear within one painting. Through such devices as a *repoussoir* of trees or houses perched on a hill on one side of the foremost plane, the overlapping of mountains along a diagonal path, and aerial perspective obliterating details, blurring contours, fading colors, Bruegel's landscapes seem to recede to almost infinite distances. Invariably the state of the vegetation indicates a particular time of year, and such natural effects as snowstorms or the approach of dusk, rarely portrayed before in painting, are here explored with the attention that artists normally focused on the human figure.

Drawings as well as paintings record Bruegel's views and visions of landscape. The drawings in pen and brown ink over a preliminary design in black chalk have the appearance of finished works of art. Landscapes are constructed out of small delicate strokes and points, widely spaced. Forms are neither outlined nor depicted in detail, and only the slightest increase in the density and length of strokes serves to suggest an area of shadow. The constant interpenetration of the substance by the blank ground of white paper produces the impression of a landscape bathed in shimmering light reflected from the smooth surfaces of rocks or the mirror-like surface of a river or refracted by the droplets of a dense atmosphere.

Bruegel never painted a portrait, and indeed, in many of his paintings, faces are hidden beneath broad-brimmed hats or wrapped in scarves, or the figure is depicted from the rear. Faces, when they do appear, are caricatured: two huge round eyes, a crescent lipless mouth, emerge from a moonlike face. The type is varied only in the direction of the grotesque. The bodies of Bruegel's figures are reduced to abstract geometric forms: shapeless peasant garments, far more than anatomical structure, control the form his figures assume. The varieties of movement are endless, yet invariably clumsy. Figures are bowlegged, flat-footed, incipiently hunchbacked. The lack of detail or internal modeling, the absence of the characterization of texture, divert attention to the contours, which, with the economical force of the cartoonist's art, are immediately expressive.

A change in Bruegel's style toward the end of his career seems to have been precipitated by his move to Brussels in 1563, where he came in contact with the works of Romanist painters and their Italian prototypes. For Hieronymous Bosch's inspiration in subject matter, facial types, monsters, and compositions constructed of innumerable small figures dispersed throughout the surface of the painting, Bruegel substituted motifs drawn from Italian High Renaissance and mannerist art. Compositions now are sometimes so filled with figures that a setting is excluded. When landscapes reappear, the view is far more intimate than before — the artist's vantage point is lower and the landscape flatter. This, together with a closer viewpoint, limits radically the extent of the vista. Figures now are large in scale and there are fewer of them. Yet Bruegel's view of human nature has undergone no transformation. In the *Parable of the Blind* of 1568 (Naples) six blind old men, so grotesquely deformed as to seem insane, lead one another into the abyss: the inevitable fate, so Bruegel seems to say, of those who are blind to Christian truth.

BRUNELLESCHI, Filippo (1377 – Apr. 15/16, 1446). Italian architect. Born Florence, initially trained as craftsman in gold and silver. Four silver statuettes made for cathedral of Pistoia during his early years survive. Entered competition (1401) for bronze doors of baptistery of Florence (his trial relief survives), but lost commission to Ghiberti under circumstances that remain obscure. From c.1418 concentrated on architecture. His masterpiece is the ribbed brick dome of S. Maria del Fiore, the cathedral of Florence (begun 1420); other important works are churches of S. Lorenzo (1421–28), S. Maria degli Angeli (begun 1434), and S. Spirito (begun 1434), foundling hospital called Ospedale degli Innocenti (begun 1419), Pazzi chapel (begun 1429), Pitti palace (begun c.1440). Died in Florence.

REFERENCES: Eugenio Luporini *Brunelleschi: Forma e ragione* (Milan 1964). Peter Murray *The Architecture of the Italian Renaissance* (New York 1964). Piero Sanpaolesi *Brunelleschi* (Milan 1962).

✍

FILIPPO BRUNELLESCHI
BY JUERGEN SCHULZ

In the history of architecture Filippo di ser Brunellesco is credited with the revival of the antique orders of architecture. He stands beside the early fifteenth-century sculptor Donatello and painter Masaccio as one of the three pivotal figures of Florentine Renaissance art who introduced new norms in the fine arts and launched the artistic movement that is called the Renaissance.

This estimate dates back to the Renaissance itself and is true as far as it goes. Brunelleschi is celebrated as the reviver of "good" (that is, ancient) architecture by the unknown author of a biography written sometime after 1482 — the first independent biography of an artist of modern times. The same claim is made in a collection of famous lives by the humanist Antonio Manetti, of 1494–97, and in *Lives of the Painters* by Giorgio Vasari, published in 1550. However, in the crowded half-century of Florentine art that lies between 1400 and 1450 Brunelleschi played a far larger and more fertile role than that of the classicizing architect.

The son of a notary and destined first for a professional life like his father's, then trained as a goldsmith and active as a sculptor, it is indeed as an architect that he made his career. It is correct furthermore that he revived the ancient orders and ancient construction techniques, although he did so only by degrees and never entirely abandoned formal patterns and construction techniques of the thirteenth and fourteenth centuries.

The loggia of the Foundling Hospital, Florence (begun 1419), marks the first appearance of his vocabulary of round arches outlined by dark stone archivolts, classicizing columns, capitals, and entablatures, domical vaults, and gabled openings in the walls. The actual details of the orders and other members, however, are derived not from Roman buildings but from Gothic and Romanesque edifices of Florence and provincial Tuscany.

In later buildings, such as the church of S. Lorenzo (begun 1421) and the Pazzi chapel at S. Croce (under way in 1433), Florence, Brunelleschi's membering approached more and more closely the appearance of ancient building details. In the former, capitals are based on capitals of Tuscan Romanesque structures that in Brunelleschi's day were believed to be antique in origin (for example, SS. Apostoli, S. Miniato and the Baptistery at Florence). In the latter they are very close to Roman imperial capitals. Moldings are progressively heavier and richer than in the Foundling Hospital.

The discovery of authentic Roman architecture, an experience that probably took place during Brunelleschi's visit to Rome in the company of Donatello in 1432–33, led him to modify not only the detailing of architectural members but also his handling of such basic elements as space and wall. In a late building such as the church of S. Spirito, Florence (designed in 1434, but built chiefly after Brunelleschi's death in 1446), walls are curved, the spectator perceives not only the enclosing surfaces but also volumes of enclosed space that induce him to move through the building rather than to behold it as a static whole, and the membering itself is plastically heavy and sculptural.

Brunelleschi observed not only details but also engineering techniques from the ancients. Thus in the dome of Florence Cathedral (1420–36) he achieved what by contemporaries was believed to be the impossible; namely, to vault an area fully 138.5 feet across without the use of centering. To a traditional Gothic dome, ogival and built on vertical ribs, he wedded the Roman device of horizontal tie ribs and Roman brick-laying techniques. He was able in this way to erect a self-sustaining brick fabric strong enough to carry even the cantilevered platforms from which the brick masons worked.

This feat of design demonstrates Brunelleschi's interest and capability in structural engineering as distinct from systems of wall articulation. His earliest recorded architectural activity is, in fact, as an expert adviser to the builders of the cathedral, who consulted him in 1404 and 1410 in matters pertaining to the structural underpinnings of the future dome, before he had acquired renown as a practicing architect.

The analytical intelligence that Brunelleschi demonstrated before such problems is precisely that further quality of the artist which the conventional estimate fails to appreciate. His life's work is animated by the most rigorous and sustained intellectualism, which in itself was as important a contribution to the new style as his revival of the ancient architectural vocabulary. In planning his buildings he sought a mathematical proportionality between every component of an edifice. Major and minor spaces were proportioned on the ground plan according to strict ratios of whole numbers ($1:2, 2:3$, etc.) and on the elevation according to fractions derived geometrically from the plan — $1:\sqrt{2}$ (the diagonal of a square unit on the plan), $1:5$ (the diagonal of two square units on the plan), etc. — in the traditional manner of Gothic architecture. The members of the orders that articulated such a building he proportioned according to ratios of whole numbers based on a module contained within the members themselves (for example, the diameter of a column) in the manner of the ancients. It was impossible to mesh perfectly geometrical and arithmetical ratios such as these, and Brunelleschi was left with discrepancies wherever the two systems came into contact, but his architectural ideal of perfect metrical coherence set a standard that remained valid for architects throughout the Renaissance and into the age of the baroque.

In connection with his search for strict proportionality in architecture, he encountered the problem of the perception of proportional relationships by the seeing eye. It led him to attempt the demonstration that the eye's image of a series of proportionate relationships is governed by the same ratios as the series itself. He did so by painting (c.1427) two views of actual edifices in Florence (one of the Baptistery and one of the Palazzo della Signoria), reduced by an accurate perspective construction to only a fraction of their actual size. He had applied principles of Euclidean geometry to the medieval diagram of the process of vision as a pyramid of rays connecting eye and object. It yielded a mathematically correct formula for calculating the reduced size of any real dimension in a small image, a computation that is the basis of artificial perspective. Florentine painters quickly possessed themselves of the technique as a tool by which to attain a perfect naturalism in the rendering of space, such as they sought in the rendering of light, mass, and expression as well.

All of Brunelleschi's innovations were built upon medieval foundations, wherefore the notion that he "revived" ancient architecture or "invented" perspective is not strictly correct. But he applied to structural engineering and problems of representation the method of rational analysis that was the lesson of antiquity and detected in the ancient vocabulary of architectural forms a rational coherence that gave an intellectual basis for a preference of taste. It is not solely as an architect but as a mind that he was one of the founders of the Renaissance in art, a fact recognized by the earliest theorist of the new art, Leon Battista Alberti, who dedicated to Brunelleschi the Italian version of his treatise *On Painting* (1435), saying: "Day in, day out, you continue to discover things by which your marvelous intelligence acquires perpetual fame and renown."

BRYANT, William Cullen (Nov. 3, 1794 – June 12, 1878). American poet and editor. Born Cummington, Mass., son of a learned physician. First publication a juvenile poetic satire, *The Embargo* (1808). Attended Williams College (1810–11); then studied law, was admitted to bar (1815), and practiced law. Poem *Thanatopsis* (1817) brought him immediate recognition. In Wordsworthian manner it expressed deep affinity with nature ("Go forth, under the open sky, and list/ To Nature's teachings"). Married Frances Fairfield (1821). Abandoned law and moved to New York (1825) as editor of *New York Review,* then joined staff of *Evening Post* (1826), serving as editor from 1829 until his death. Published *Poems* (1832), which included *To a Fringed Gentian* and many of his other best lyrics. Traveled with family to Europe and Middle East (1834, 1845, 1849), recording trips in *Letters of a Traveler* (1850, second series 1859) and *Letters from the East* (1869). Under his powerful antislavery leadership the *Post* finally abandoned support of Democrats, and after formation of Republican party (1854–56) became a strong radical Republican partisan. Though of first rank as an editor, Bryant is best known as an American romantic, a nature poet of simple nobility of style. Other publications include *The Fountain and Other Poems* (1842), *The White-Footed Deer and Other Poems* (1844), *A Forest Hymn* (1860), *The Flood of Years* (1878), translations of the *Iliad* (1870) and *Odyssey* (1871–72), and *Orations and Addresses* (1873). He died in New York.

EDITIONS: *The Poetical Works of William Cullen Bryant* ed. Parke Godwin (2 vols. New York 1883). *Prose Writings of William Cullen Bryant* (2 vols. New York 1884).

REFERENCES: Albert F. McLean, Jr. *William Cullen Bryant* (New York PB 1964). William Lyon Phelps *Howells, James, Bryant and Other Essays* (New York 1924).

BÜCHNER, Georg (Oct. 17, 1813 – Feb. 19, 1837). German dramatist. Born Goddelau, Hesse. Studied medicine at universities of Strasbourg (1831–33) and Giessen (1833–34). While at Giessen, organized revolutionary secret society and published pamphlet *Der Hessische Landbote* (1834), which resulted in warrant for his arrest. Fled to family home in Darmstadt, where he spent winter reading philosophy and history. Study of French Revolution culminated in drama *Dantons Tod* (*Danton's Death*, 1928), his first creative work and the only one published (1835) in his lifetime. Returned to Strasbourg (1835–36) and completed doctoral dissertation. Spent final months as lecturer in anatomy at University of Zurich. Died in Zurich, apparently of typhus. Other works: fragmentary tragedy *Woyzeck* (published 1879), the basis for Alban Berg's opera *Wozzeck* (1925); comedy *Leonce und Lena* (published 1850, tr. 1928); and *Lenz*, an unfinished novella (published 1838). Büchner exercised a marked influence on the naturalistic drama of the 1890's and, later, on expressionism, whose revolutionary dramatic technique and thematic interests he anticipated.

TRANSLATION: *Complete Plays and Prose* tr. Carl R. Mueller (New York 1963, also PB).
REFERENCE: Arthur H. J. Knight *Georg Büchner* (London 1951 and New York 1952).

BUCKINGHAM, George Villiers, 2nd duke of (Jan. 30, 1628 – Apr. 16, 1687). English politician and writer. Born London, son of George Villiers (first duke and intimate friend of Charles I). Brought up in royal household after father's assassination (1628). At Trinity College, Cambridge (1641–43), left to join royalists in Civil War. During Commonwealth with exiled court of Charles II in Holland. Returned secretly to England and married Mary Fairfax (1657). After Restoration constantly involved in court intrigues, alternately in and out of favor with Charles II. Stripped of all offices (1674), he thenceforth worked in opposition to the government. Characterized by Dryden as "chemist, fiddler, statesman, and buffoon" (*Absalom and Achitophel*), Buckingham is also remembered as author or part author of several comedies, notably *The Rehearsal* (1671), a satire on Dryden's heroic drama. Died at Kirby Moorside, Yorkshire.

EDITION: *Three Restoration Comedies* (*The Rehearsal* with Wycherley's *The Country Wife* and Congreve's *The Way of the World*) ed. George G. Falle (London PB 1964, New York PB 1965).
REFERENCES: Hester W. Chapman *Great Villiers: A Study of George Villiers, Second Duke of Buckingham* (London 1949). John H. Wilson *A Rake and His Times: George Villiers, Second Duke of Buckingham* (London and New York 1964).

BUFFON, Georges-Louis Leclerc, comte de (Sept. 7, 1707 – Apr. 16, 1788). French naturalist and writer. Born into middle-class family, Montbard, Burgundy; educated by Jesuits there. Studied law (1723–26) and medicine (1728–30); traveled through France, Italy, Switzerland (1730–32). Elected to Académie des Sciences (1732), translated Stephen Hales's *Vegetable Statics* (1735) and Isaac Newton's *Treatise on Fluxions* (1740). Journeyed to England (1738–39), where he was elected to Royal Society. Director of Jardin du Roi from 1739, he began (with the assistance of Louis J. M. Daubenton) preparation of the *Histoire naturelle, générale, et particulière* (36 vols. 1749–88; 8 vols. by B. G. E. de Lacépède 1788–1804), whose descriptive pages he punctuated with theories of scientific method, of knowledge and development of the earth. Married Marie-Françoise de Saint-Belin-Melain (1752); one son survived. Elected to Académie Française (1753), delivered his *Discours sur le style*, stressing primordial role of content in writing: *"Le style c'est l'homme même"* — The style is the man himself. Buffon's eloquence and tireless exploration of natural phenomena made the European reading public aware of the importance of the natural sciences and their technological applications.

TRANSLATION: *Buffon's Natural History* tr. W. Kenrick (6 vols. London 1775–76); tr. W. Smellie (9 vols. London 1791).

REFERENCES: Franck Bourdier "Principaux Aspects de la vie et de l'oeuvre de Buffon" in Roger Heim ed. *Buffon* (Paris 1952). Louis Dimier *Buffon* (Paris 1919). Agnes M. F. Duclaux *The French Ideal: Pascal, Fénelon and Other Essays* (Freeport, N.Y. 1967).

BULFINCH, Charles (Aug. 8, 1763 – Apr. 4, 1844). American architect. Son of physician; born and died in Boston. Graduated from Boston Latin School and Harvard (1781); toured Europe (1785–87). Impressed by English buildings in Georgian and Adam styles, influenced also by Thomas Jefferson, whom he met in France and who favored a classic revival for American architecture. Back in Boston, Bulfinch married Hannah Apthorp (1788) and began designing in Federal style a series of buildings, including the Beacon Hill monument (1789), the Federal Street Theatre (1794, since destroyed), and the Old State House, Hartford, Conn. (1792–95). Other important Boston buildings are the Massachusetts State House (1795–98), Harvard's University Hall (1814–15) in Cambridge, the Massachusetts General Hospital (1817–20). Member of Boston board of selectmen (1791–1818), chairman (equivalent to mayor) from 1799. Completed work of Benjamin Latrobe on National Capitol, Washington (1818–30), which with the Massachusetts State House especially provided the style for state capitols throughout the country. Bulfinch's style is characterized by such classical elements as porticoes, pilasters, arcades, and domes, and by graceful proportions. He also designed numerous private houses, including those of the Tontine Crescent in Boston (1793, now destroyed), and churches, including Christ Church, Lancaster, Mass. (1817).

REFERENCE: Harold and James Kirker *Bulfinch's Boston: 1787–1817* (New York 1964).

✍

CHARLES BULFINCH
BY ALBERT BUSH-BROWN

Charles Bulfinch (1763–1844), chairman of Boston's board of selectmen (1799–1818) and architect of public buildings, guided the growth of Boston in the manner of a modern city planner, through ordinance, financial planning, the development of new institutions, and the improvement of public services; his extensive architectural legacy is only one aspect of his public service. His talent did not show itself in any grand, geometric plan for Boston comparable with L'Enfant's plan for Washington, D.C., but evolved pragmatically within the constraints of an existing urban pattern, seizing intermittent opportunities to develop Georgian squares and to situate public buildings prominently. His patience with administrative detail (even the licensing of chimney sweeps), his reasonableness in negotiation, and his determination to find practical, tasteful, and enduring solutions enabled him to improve municipal services such as police, water, and education, and to design the buildings those services required. Although he is celebrated as an architect, Bulfinch's contributions to municipal government were equally remarkable and deserved the praise they received from Josiah Quincy: "During the many years he presided over the town government, he improved its finances, executed the laws with firmness, and was distinguished for gentleness and urbanity of manners, integrity and purity of character."

The Boston Bulfinch knew after

the revolution was a maritime town of 18,000 inhabitants who occupied wooden houses set on the narrow, curved, and unpaved streets of a hilly peninsula, deeply indented by tidal marshes and coves, that was bordered by forty wharves, a dozen shipyards, six ropewalks and several duck factories. Its prosperity in local commerce and foreign trade with China, Russia, and the Oregon Coast drew seamen from many nations and called men to manufacture soap, candles, rum, sugar, cordage, twine, and linen; its carpenters, masons, blacksmiths, and cabinetmakers built for a population, grown to 40,000 by 1840, who required new houses, markets, banks, counting-houses, and insurance companies; the old colonial buildings such as King's Chapel (1750), Christ Church (1723), and the State House no longer sufficed; and Bulfinch designed new buildings for each of those functions for religion and government.

Overall, Boston was expanding, and Bulfinch hoped, beyond any authority he held as chairman of the selectmen, to guide that expansion in the style of Georgian London, even as speculators leveled hills, filled coves, and pressed expedient building. As senior selectman and, after 1800, superintendent of police, Bulfinch administered Boston's detailed laws restricting everything from theatre and gambling to the sale of oysters and firewood; he widened and paved streets and lighted them; he built bridges, markets and wharves, a hospital, a jail, a courthouse and three schools — and he administered the town's finances. That he did all of this while enhancing Boston's architecture is a tribute to his talent in practical planning, which he executed within Georgian precedents.

Beginning with an amateur's interest in Georgian houses, Bulfinch, on an eighteen-month grand tour starting in England in 1785, was confirmed in a taste for the more conservative architecture of the brothers Adam, John Soane, and William Chambers. His plans, which departed from convention to accommodate a hillside or to afford a view, were regulated by rectilinear axes and confined within rectangles, showing little of the inventiveness of Soane or the Adamses; but still, his buildings' façades, emphasized by low relief and planar walls, have light proportions and elegance as in the Second Harrison Gray Otis House (1800). The progressive architecture of the English Soane or the French Ledoux and Clérisseau, with elevations expressing articulated plans, which intrigued Latrobe, elicited no more interest from Bulfinch than he showed for the Roman temple at Nîmes, which he visited after speaking in Paris with Jefferson, who, enamored of Roman architecture, advocated a classic revival for the United States. Bulfinch's models were late eighteenth-century English (Chambers's Somerset House in London), and this *retardataire* taste Bulfinch developed with ingenuity and restraint in his stately, often elegant buildings for Federalist Boston.

His residential architecture shows his urban ideal. In the West End, which grew rapidly after a new bridge (1793) was built to Cambridge, Bulfinch designed "noble mansions," beginning with the Palladian house (1792) for Joseph Coolidge; thereafter, other prosperous merchants quit the center of town and erected large, freestanding houses in the West End, recalled today by the headquarters of the Society for the Preservation of New England Antiquities, which was built by Bulfinch for Harrison Gray Otis in 1796. Rather than such mansions, Bulfinch hoped to see row houses surrounding large urban squares, courts, and parks, all designed as coherent ranges and associated with schools, churches, theatres, libraries, clubs, and markets. An unpromising plot of land on Franklin Street, in the South End, gave him an opportunity in 1793 to build the Tontine Crescent, consisting of sixteen connected brick houses, three stories high, all facing a common park, as in the residential squares of John Wood in Bath and the brothers Adam in London. Large rooms at the center of the crescent were given to the Boston Library and the Historical Society, while a theatre (1798) and a church (1803), both designed by Bulfinch, were erected on adjoining sites. Although the crescent was completed in 1793–95, the form of financing, a tontine, was disapproved by the General Court and a financial recession deterred subscribers, forcing Bulfinch to incur large debts and losses on sales; declaring bankruptcy in 1796, Bulfinch barely supported himself thereafter by his professional practice and salaried positions in the municipal government, which did not prevent his being jailed for debt in July 1811, even while he remained superintendent of police.

He was unsuccessful in persuading the Mount Vernon Proprietors to develop Copley's hilly upland pasture on Mount Vernon and Beacon Hill into large lots facing a great open square (460 by 190 feet), which would have avoided the subsequent shearing of some fifty feet from the hill and filling the cove below. But upon the sheared hill Bulfinch built his most generous and noble houses, notably the Second House of Harrison Gray Otis on Mount Vernon Street (1800) and also, when that fashion-setting gentleman moved to Beacon Street, his Third House (1806). Later, the pattern of mansions

on the hill gave way to the dense blocks of narrow row houses that were relieved later by Louisburg Square (1826ff), a reminder of the greater square Bulfinch had proposed. In 1804–1805 he set spacious row houses along the length of Park Street and nineteen houses of Colonnade Row on Tremont Street, thereby defining two edges of the Common and giving that approach to the hill a character befitting the new State House.

Bulfinch's most memorable building, the State House at Boston (1795–98), followed by his profile for the National Capitol, set the idiom for subsequent state legislatures, turning taste from the domestic scale of Independence Hall, the New York City Hall, and the colonial buildings of Annapolis and Williamsburg. Its plan, preserved in the New York Public Library, disposed the executive offices and bicameral legislature in three principal rooms separated by two staircases. The southern façade, recalling Somerset House in London (1775), crowns Beacon Hill, resting upon a terrace and basement (exposed since 1833), its brick arcade carrying a stately Corinthian colonnade which terminates decisively with two pairs of doubled columns; above, a pedimented attic supports a lofty dome rising buoyantly to a delicate lantern and pinecone finial. Paul Revere covered the dome, originally shingled and whitewashed, with copper in 1802; later it gained its distinctive gilding (1861) and gold-leafing (1874), and was rebuilt with steel beams (1896–1898).

Asked whether he would train any of his children in architecture, Bulfinch replied that he did not believe there would be much left for them to do: "The states and prominent towns were already supplied with their chief buildings." For Boston, that was nearly true. He had built churches for the Congregationalists, the Roman Catholics, and the Unitarians, the latter being, incongruously, his single essay in Gothic style. He had urged repeal of laws against theatre, helped to form a company, and built the Federal Street Theatre. His public buildings fulfilled Boston's needs: schools, an almshouse, wharves, markets, a prison, a courthouse, a hospital. And his reputation called him outside Boston: the courthouse in Worcester (1801), University Hall at Harvard (1814–15), the state houses for Maine and Connecticut — culminating with President Monroe's invitation to succeed Latrobe as architect of the Capitol, which took Bulfinch to Washington in 1818. There, where he designed the Unitarian church, Bulfinch rebuilt the wings of the Capitol, burned by the British in 1814, and built the central block, which he completed, with its distinguished interiors (notably, the old Library of Congress), magnificent eastern and western façades, and a low dome, in 1830. Having accomplished so much, Bulfinch could not forecast upon his return to Boston in 1830 that the growing West and South would require buildings, that railroads and industries and universities would make new demands for architecture, and that his Federalist taste, which caused him to deplore Greenough's statue of Washington in 1841, would be succeeded by a preference for reviving Gothic and Grecian styles and even a determination to invent new ones.

BULWER-LYTTON, Edward George Earle Lytton, 1st Baron Lytton (May 25, 1803 – Jan. 18, 1873). English writer and politician. Born London into scholarly family. Began writing Byronic verse early; educated at Trinity College and Trinity Hall, Cambridge; won Chancellor's Medal (1825) for his poem *Sculpture*. After tour of Scotland and Lake country and a season in Paris, returned to London and married Rosina Doyle Wheeler (1827), from whom he separated (1836) after turbulent domestic life and birth of son Edward Robert Bulwer Lytton (Owen Meredith; 1831–1891). Wrote and published novels, achieving recognition with *Pelham* (1828). Especially popular were his historical novels *The Last Days of Pompeii* (1834), *Rienzi* (1835), *The Last of the Barons* (1843), and *Harold, the Last of the Saxon Kings* (1848). Other successful novels: *Ernest Maltravers* (1837), *My Novel* (1853), *The Coming Race* (1871). Also wrote collections of verse, produced three successful historical plays, including *Richelieu* (1839), and translated Schiller and Horace. In addition to prolific literary activity, had political career, sat in Parliament first as Liberal (1831–41), then as Conservative. Made secretary to the colonies (1858), organized new colony of British Columbia. Created 1st Baron Lytton (1866). Died at Torquay.

REFERENCES: Victor A. G. R. Bulwer-Lytton *The Life of Edward Bulwer, First Lord Lytton* (2 vols. London 1913, reissued 1948). Edwin Perry Burgum *The Literary Career of Edward Bulwer, Lord Lytton* (London 1924 and Urbana, Ill. 1926). Michael Sadleir *Bulwer: A Panorama, 1803–1836* (Boston and London 1931).

BUNYAN, John (Nov. 1628 – Aug. 31, 1688). English writer and preacher. Born Elstow, Bedfordshire, son of a devout tinker whose trade he took up after brief schooling. Conscripted by Cromwell's army (1644–46), he was further exposed to Puritan movement. Religious zeal developed particularly after marriage (c.1648, name of wife not known). Joined Bedford Baptist congregation (1653), began preaching about two years later and became very popular with working people. Wife died (1658), he remarried (1659). Agents of restored monarchy, suspicious of his close rapport with laborers, arrested him for unlicensed preaching (1660). During twelve-year imprisonment he read the Bible and John Foxe's *The Book of Martyrs* (1563/70), and wrote several books, including his spiritual autobiography, *Grace Abounding to the Chief of Sinners* (1666). Released (1672), he became Baptist pastor in Bedford, also famous as traveling preacher. It was probably during his second imprisonment (of unknown length, c.1675) that he began his masterpiece *Pilgrim's Progress* (part I, 1678; part II, 1684), an allegory of the Christian's quest for salvation. Its style is influenced by the Bible, its characters for the most part drawn from his own humble class, and its simple, fervent spirituality brought immediate popularity. The story became a classic and has been translated into many languages. Other works: *The Life and Death of Mr. Badman* (1680) and *The Holy War* (1682).

EDITION: *The Pilgrim's Progress from This World to That Which Is to Come* ed. James B. Wharey (2nd rev. ed. Roger Sharrock, Oxford 1960).

REFERENCES: John Brown *John Bunyan: His Life, Times, and Work* (London 1885, rev. ed. 1928). Roger Sharrock *John Bunyan* (new ed. London and New York 1968). Henri A. Talon *John Bunyan: The Man and His Works* (tr. London and Cambridge, Mass. 1951). William Y. Tindall *John Bunyan, Mechanick Preacher* (New York 1934).

BURCKHARDT, Jacob (May 25, 1818 – Aug. 8, 1897). Swiss historian and art critic. Born and died in Basel. Son of a pastor. Studied at University of Berlin under historian Leopold von Ranke. Traveled in Italy (1846, 1847–1848). Early important works: *The Age of Constantine the Great* (1853) and *Cicerone: A Guide to the Works of Art of Italy* (1855). Appointed professor of history at Basel (1858) and became famous as founder of *Kulturgeschichte* (culture history). His major works, *The Civilization of the Renaissance in Italy* (1860) and *History of the Renaissance in Italy* (1867), examine the period as a whole, in its political, social, moral, philosophic, religious, and artistic aspects, and serve as the basis for all subsequent interpretations of the Renaissance.

TRANSLATIONS: *The Age of Constantine the Great* tr. Moses Hadas (New York 1949, also PB). *The Civilization of the Renaissance in Italy* tr. S. G. C. Middlemore (3rd ed. London and New York 1950, also PB). *Force and Freedom: Reflections on History* tr. James H. Nichols (New York 1943, also PB). *History of Greek Culture* tr. Palmer Hilty (New York 1963). *Judgments on History and Historians* tr. Harry Zohn (Boston 1958 and London 1959). *Letters* tr. Alexander Dru (London and New York 1955).

BURKE, Edmund (c. Jan. 12, 1729 – July 9, 1797). British statesman and writer. Born Dublin, son of an attorney; attended Trinity College there (1743–48, B.A. degree) before going to London (1750) to read law. Never passed the bar; turned to writing, publishing (1756) satire on Bolingbroke, *A Vindication of Natural Society*, and *A Philosophical Inquiry into the Origin of Our Ideas of the Sublime and the Beautiful*. That same year married Jane Nugent. Began thirty-odd-year editorship of *Annual Register* (1759), a journal of politics and economics. To Ireland (1761) as secretary to William Gerard Hamilton, who was secretary to the lord-lieutenant. In England elected to Parliament (1765), remaining for twenty-nine years, vigorously opposing ministries of George III. Supported such causes as abolition of the slave trade, Catholic emancipation of Ireland, and especially emancipation of the American colonies in speeches *On American Taxation* (1774) and *On Conciliation with the Colonies* (1775). Advocated reform in India, framed the East India bill, and exposed evils of government through vehemently impressive speeches on the impeachment of Warren Hastings (1783–95). Most celebrated work is *Reflections on the Revolution in France* (1790), in which he forcefully opposed the atheism and lawlessness of the new radicals while championing the stability of the old order. Retired from Parliament (1794); continued to write eloquently until his death on his estate at Beaconsfield. Other notable works: *Thoughts on the Cause of the Present Discontents* (1770), *Speech upon Mr. Fox's East India Bill* (1784), *Two Letters on the Proposals for Peace with the Regicide*

Directory of France (1796), *Letter to a Noble Lord* (1796).

EDITIONS: *The Works of the Right Honorable Edmund Burke* (6 vols. London and New York 1907–1934). *The Correspondence of Edmund Burke* ed. Thomas W. Copeland (10 vols. Cambridge, Eng. and Chicago 1958–   ). *Selected Works* ed. Walter J. Bate (New York 1960).

REFERENCES: Thomas W. Copeland *Our Eminent Friend Edmund Burke: Six Essays* (New Haven 1949) and *Edmund Burke: Six Essays* (London 1950). Harold J. Laski *Edmund Burke* (Dublin 1947). Sir Philip Magnus *Edmund Burke: A Life* (London and New York 1939). John Morley *Burke* (London and New York 1879).

✍

EDMUND BURKE
BY CONOR CRUISE O'BRIEN

Edmund Burke was born in Dublin early in 1729. His father, Richard Burke, was an attorney who appears to have conformed to the established church (Anglican) about the time he began his legal studies. His mother, born Mary Nagle, remained a Catholic. Edmund Burke was brought up a member of the established church, but his family connections with the Roman Catholics of Ireland, a people then subject to severe penal laws, was to influence his life and to be used by his enemies and critics: cartoonists habitually depicted him in the garb of a Jesuit, and the French historian Jules Michelet later erroneously described him as *élève des Jésuites de St.-Omer.*

He was in fact educated first at a "hedge school" (the open-air form of education which was all that was available to Catholics at this time) but later at a Quaker school at Ballitore, County Kildare. He entered Trinity College, Dublin, in 1743 and took his B.A. degree there in 1748. In 1750 he went to London to read for the bar.

Little is known of his life from this time to about 1757, but he was not called to the bar. In 1756 he published his first literary works: *A Vindication of Natural Society* and *A Philosophical Enquiry into the Origin of Our Ideas of the Sublime and Beautiful.* The latter work interested Lessing and Herder and influenced the development of aesthetic theory on the Continent. Almost a century and a half later in *What Is Art?* the old and antiaesthetic Tolstoi was to use it, to show that the sublime meant war and the beautiful meant sex.

At some time in the winter of 1756–57 Edmund Burke married Jane Nugent; where and how is not known. Jane's father, Dr. Nugent, a friend of Samuel Johnson's, was a Catholic. Edmund and Jane had two sons, of whom only one, Richard (b. 1758), survived into adult life.

In 1758–59 Edmund Burke undertook the production of the *Annual Register*, with which he continued to be associated for about thirty years. During 1759 he became secretary to William Gerard Hamilton (1725–96), who in 1761 became chief secretary to the lord lieutenant of Ireland. Having broken with Hamilton in 1764, Burke became in 1765 private secretary to the second marquis of Rockingham (1730–82). Burke was by this time a member of the Literary Club at the Turk's Head in Gerrard Street, and became a lifelong friend of Garrick, Reynolds and Johnson.

By the influence of the generous Whig Lord Verney (1712?–91) — who also lent him very large sums of money — Burke was elected to Parliament for the borough of Wendover and took his seat January 14, 1766. He supported the Rockingham Whigs, who were in office from August 1766 to May 1767, and he followed Rockingham into opposition. In 1768 he bought the estate of Gregories at Beaconsfield, a purchase which involved him in lifelong financial difficulties. In 1770 his pamphlet *Thoughts on the Cause of the Present Discontents* attacked the influence of the crown and urged the principle of loyalty to party. Burke figures here as something of an innovator, the kind of role which he later came to abhor.

In 1771 he was appointed New York's agent in London. By the elections of 1774 he became a member of Parliament for Bristol, and laid down the principle that a parliamentary representative betrays his constituents if he sacrifices his judgment to their opinion. He was now a friend and ally of Charles James Fox, with whom he conducted a strong opposition to Lord North's administration and especially to its American policy, the folly of which he exposed in his speeches *On American Taxation* (1774) and *On Conciliation with the Colonies* (1775). In 1776 he and his friends withdrew from Parliament on all questions relating to America: he justified this policy in his *Letter to the Sheriffs of Bristol* (1777).

It would be incorrect to describe Burke as a supporter of the American Revolution. Rather, in the case of America as in the case of Ireland, Burke was the opponent of governmental policies which he saw as driving people to revolutionary extremes.

In 1780 Burke lost his Bristol seat, having offended the Bristol merchants by advocating the commercial rights of Ireland. Rockingham provided him with a seat for the borough of Malton. When the Rockingham Whigs took office in 1782, Burke became paymaster of the forces. Rockingham's death in 1782 was a severe blow to Burke. He became paymaster again under the Portland coalition (1783), but his conduct in that office attracted controversy and censure. After the triumph of Pitt in the elections of 1784, Burke was in opposition again and was frequently interrupted contemptuously, especially by the younger Tory members of the new house.

In 1787 he began the impeachment of Warren Hastings (1732–1818), ex-governor-general of India. This impeachment attracted great public interest, but increased the number of Burke's enemies in Parliament and in the country. By the time of the outbreak of the French Revolution, Burke had become an isolated and rather unpopular figure. This isolation, however, left him free to speak in a more personal vein than would have been open to him had he remained closely involved in practical politics, and the last years, from 1790 to his death, are the years of his most splendid eloquence and eventually of regained and enhanced influence.

Burke early regarded the French Revolution with hostility. He did not share the feelings of most middle-class Englishmen who saw it at first as a liberating event. His family background made it impossible for him to share the antipopery sentiments which were natural to most Englishmen and predisposed them in favor of an anti-Catholic revolution. His *Reflections on the Revolution in France,* which appeared in November 1790, was a counterrevolutionary tract of great power. It predicted much of what subsequently happened: the Terror — specifically the use of terrorism in the country in order to supply the cities — and the emergence of a class of speculators as the economic victors and of a military despot as the political victor. The progress of the revolution in the sense predicted by Burke enormously increased Burke's stature in the eyes of "the gentlemen," as George III told him. He was correspondingly assailed from the left by Tom Paine, Mary Wollstonecraft, and others, and by some who — like Sir James Mackintosh — later recanted and sang his praises. Burke broke with most of his former Whig friends — including Charles James Fox — and criticized even the Tories for lack of counterrevolutionary consistency and zeal.

Burke retired from Parliament in 1794. His last years were clouded by grief over the death of his son Richard in August 1794. His activity was, however, undiminished, and his last writings, notably his *Letter to a Noble Lord* (1796) — later used by Karl Marx against Sir John Russell — and *Letters on a Regicide Peace* (1796–97), contain perhaps the most astonishing examples of his rhetorical powers. Towards the end Burke was greatly troubled in his mind, not only by the victories of revolutionary France but by the menacing situation in Ireland, in relation to whose people his conciliatory advice had been inadequately followed. Rebellion broke out there in the year after his death.

Burke died at Beaconsfield on July 9, 1797. "There is but one event," wrote George Canning, "but that is an event for the world — Burke is dead."

Burke brought to the discussion of politics extraordinary gifts: practical experience near — if not quite in — a great center of power, a mind capable of reflecting deeply and subtly on this experience, and a superb command over the resources of English prose. He writes as a defender of the interests — broadly and often generously conceived — of the English ruling class of his day. The reader should allow for this fact without letting it blind him to the reality of Burke's insights. It should be remembered that Burke, as distinct from some later conservative polemicists, was usually not writing as a propagandist *for* the class which he served but as an educator of that class. As he took his duties seriously, his writings have a value and importance derived from their penetration into reality and transcending the immediate preoccupations of the writer and his contemporaries.

BURNE-JONES, Sir Edward Coley (Aug. 28, 1833 – June 17, 1898). English painter and designer. Born Birmingham. At Exeter College, Oxford, met lifelong friend William Morris, with whom he shared enthusiasm for the medieval. In London (1856) joined Rossetti and Pre-Raphaelites; in Italy (1859) studied early Italian painters and sculptors, became influenced by Botticelli and Sienese School. Married Georgiana Macdonald (1860) and settled in London. Painted watercolors and series of illustrations for William Morris's *Earthly Paradise*, but made his reputation with exhibition of oil paintings at Grosvenor Gallery (1877). His dreamy, romantic, "literary" style, executed in a flat technique, was effective also in his designs for stained glass, tapestry, mosaics, and reliefs. His famous paintings include *King Cophetua and the Beggar Maid* (1884, Tate Gallery, London) and *The Star of Bethlehem* (1891, City Art Gallery, Birmingham), his best-known illustrations are those for Kelmscott Press edition of Chaucer (1897). Named associate of Royal Academy (1885), Chevalier of Légion d'Honneur (1889), and created baronet (1894). Died in London.

REFERENCES: Lady Burne-Jones *Memorials of Edward Burne-Jones* (London 1906). Lord David Cecil *Visionary and Dreamer: Two Poetic Painters, Samuel Palmer and Edward Burne-Jones* (London 1969 and New York 1970).

BURNEY, Fanny [Frances] [Madame d'Arblay] (June 13, 1752 – Jan. 6, 1840). English novelist and diarist. Born King's Lynn, Norfolk, daughter of music historian Charles Burney (1726–1814). Read prodigiously and began writing at early age. Family moved to London (1760), where Miss Burney joined Dr. Samuel Johnson's literary circle. Her first novel, *Evelina* (1778), was published anonymously, but with discovery of its authorship she enjoyed literary prominence, and repeated success with *Cecilia* (5 vols. 1782). She had created a new genre soon perfected by Jane Austen — a novel of manners the development of whose plot depends upon the experiences of a virtuous, innocent young girl entering society. While satirical humor and insight into personality gave life to her first two novels, the later *Camilla* (1796) and *The Wanderer* (1814) fail through excessive moralizing and melodrama. Presented to Queen Charlotte and King George III, Miss Burney spent five miserable, exhausting years as the queen's second keeper of the robes (1786–91). She married General Alexandre d'Arblay, a French émigré (1793). A son, Alexandre, was born (1794). From 1802 to 1812 they lived in France, where he held a government post under Napoleon. Her great contribution is her *Diary and Letters of Madame d'Arblay* (7 vols. 1842–46), which gives a lively account of English culture and society from 1768 to 1840, when she died in London.

EDITIONS: *The Early Diary of Frances Burney 1768–1778* ed. Annie R. Ellis (2 vols. London 1889). *Diary and Letters of Madame d'Arblay* ed. Charlotte F. Barrett rev. Austin Dobson (6 vols. London and New York 1904–1905). *The Diary of Fanny Burney* ed. Joseph W. Cove (London and New York 1940).

REFERENCES: Emily Hahn *A Degree of Prudery: A Biography of Fanny Burney* (New York 1950 and London 1951). Joyce Hemlow *The History of Fanny Burney* (London 1958).

BURNS, Robert (Jan. 25, 1759 – July 21, 1796). Scottish poet. Born on father's farm in Ayrshire. Largely self-educated, receiving only brief periods of schooling at parish school in Dalrymple and John Murdoch's school in Ayr (1773). Years of poverty and hard work partly ameliorated when Kilmar-nock edition of his *Poems, Chiefly in the Scottish Dialect* appeared (1786). Burns's reputation was established with the Edinburgh edition (1787), and he was lionized in Edinburgh circles. Married Jean Armour (1788) and settled on farm near Dumfries. Appointed excise officer (1789) and moved (1791) to Dumfries, where he remained for the rest of his life. Later years spent chiefly in contributing to two collections of Scottish songs, James Johnson's *The Scots Musical Museum* (1787–1803) and George Thomson's *A Select Collection of Original Scottish Airs* (1793–1805). Now considered a preromantic because of his democratic views and use of lyric forms, Burns wrote nearly all of his best work in the Scots dialect and is today considered Scotland's national poet. Burns's best-known works include *The Cotter's Saturday Night, Tam o' Shanter, To a Mouse, Auld Lang Syne, The Banks of Doon, A Man's a Man for A' That,* and *Afton Water.*

EDITIONS: *The Poems and Songs of Robert Burns* ed. James Kinsley (3 vols. London and New York 1968). *The Letters of Robert Burns* ed. De-Lancey Ferguson (2 vols. London 1931).

REFERENCES: Catherine Carswell *The Life of Robert Burns* (London 1930 and New York 1931). David Daiches *Robert Burns* (rev. ed. London 1966 and New York 1967). Robert T. Fitzhugh *Robert Burns: The Man and the Poet* (Boston 1970). Hans Hecht *The Life and Work of Burns* (tr. London 1937). Franklyn Bliss Snyder *The Life of Robert Burns* (New York 1932).

ROBERT BURNS

BY EDWARD DAVISON

Of all Scotsmen, living or dead, surely the most famous is Robert Burns. He died at the age of thirty-seven, worn-out and broken down on the treadmill of an existence that had undermined his vital being at two different though not unrelated levels. At the first of these levels his role in life was that of an indigent tenant farmer, a typical figure in the Ayrshire of that time.

Like his father before him he was in-ured to the daily demands of back-breaking manual labor, dependent on the favor of exacting landlords and the mercies of a soil and climate not alto-gether favorable to the profitable rais-ing of kale and potatoes. But he was a failure. At the other level he emerged as a local poet whose humor, skill, and personal charm won the admiring re-spect of his neighbors, especially of their sisters and daughters. "The sweet-est hours that e'er I spend/Are spent among the lasses, O." He was too often the life of the party, the kind of party so vividly described in some of his more rampageous poems, like *Halloween, The Holy Fair, Tam o' Shanter* and *The Jolly Beggars*. In the flush of his early elevation to national fame he was fre-quently the life of other parties too. In Edinburgh he found himself con-stantly in the class-conscious company of the *unco guid*, "men to whom he must not speak his mind and women whom he must not love." To him, at the time, most of this must have seemed like failure too.

Fifty years after these nightmares ended with the burial at Dumfries, Thomas Carlyle was moved to prepare an exalted place for the poet in the tiers of world renown. Wordsworth, Hazlitt, Byron, Keats, Scott, Lockhart were among those whose acclamations fed the thunders heard even to this day in *Heroes and Hero Worship*. "Once more a giant Original . . . One of those men who reach down to the per-ennial Deeps . . . The largest and most gifted British soul in all that cen-tury." But even before his work had been thus hailed at the high altar, the man who made poems as sturdy and diverse as *Scots Wha Hae*, the incom-parable *Holy Willie's Prayer, Oh Wert Thou in the Cauld Blast,* and *The Cotter's Saturday Night* had already

begun to achieve a fame that was far-borne beyond the borders of the British Isles. The Scottish emigrants, men of his own independent mettle who were driven in their thousands (as Burns himself so nearly was) to gamble their wretched conditions of life at home for whatever might have to be encoun-tered overseas, carried his book with them. It companioned the Bible in their settlements from New Zealand to Nova Scotia and New England and to the Canadian Northwest, and they could wale a portion with judicious care either from the psalms of David or from the poems of Robert Burns. Year after year the exiles from Caledo-nia forgathered, as still they do over the haggis and whiskey, to toast their man on his birthday and to join in the singing of his and their country's songs. It is a consoling thought that few po-ets have ever come so fully into their own as he has. Fresh laurels of posthu-mous recognition are still being cut for him. Although vast numbers of people who can vocalize the tune possess (like Mr. Micawber) only the haziest knowledge of all but a sediment of its key words, *Auld Lang Syne,* the secular anthem Burns provided for hogmanay, has been popularly adopted for singing old years out and new years in over widespread regions of the modern world. And at Grenoble the valedictory song chosen and heartily rendered at the Olympic Games by the international chorus of the participating countries was *Auld Lang Syne.*

First and last Burns is a poet of and for the people. Moreover, the works in-separable from his name have now for close on two hundred years maintained an unchallenged place in the vital lit-erature of the English-speaking world: and that in spite or possibly even be-cause of their vernacular character. During that same span of time the backstair exaggerations about the influence on his everyday life of bawdry and intemperance, like many of the scandals that formerly besmirched his reputation (the Highland Mary disaster, for example), have been worn down to the bedrock of established fact. Even those readers who look askance at *The Merry Muses of Caledonia* will agree with Catherine Carswell that "to lack sympathy with Burns is to lack sympathy with mankind." The essential truth about him has never been better stated than by that great and clearheaded teacher, Sir Walter Raleigh: "The only just comment on his life is the story of it, if the story could be told truly with none of the delights omitted. The faults of a man like Burns have an awkward habit of being also his virtues. His is the voice of a million inarticulate consciences who, if it were required of them, would cheerfully sign all he says and in so doing would be signing nothing that they do not understand and believe."

Burns, as a voluntary labor of pure love, relinquished only on his deathbed, took upon himself the making and preservation of the songs of his nation. Almost every song of mark made by his predecessors was filtered through him into James Johnson's *The Scots Musical Museum*, of which Burns was virtually the editor. Scores of others, salvaged out of what the country folk could render from contemporary oral tradition, were melted in the furnace of his vital genius and poured into the same collection. Moreover, during the four last years of his life he contributed almost a century of his very own finest songs to George Thomson's *A Select Collection of Original Scottish Airs*. This precious body of work comprises as a whole over three hundred lyrical pieces. They are the songs whose words, stripped as they had to be from the airs on which the poet begot them, are everywhere familiar today in the uncountable printed editions of his *Collected Poems*. They are the utterance, simple, sensuous, passionate, of an archetypal poet, a natural man speaking to natural men and women in their own habitual everyday tongue, a crying, human equivalent of wild birdsong, like:

> *And I will luve thee still, my dear,*
> *Till a' the seas gang dry.*

> *Till a' the seas gang dry, my dear,*
> *And the rocks melt wi' the sun;*
> *And I will luve thee still, my dear,*
> *While the sands o' life shall run.*

Such is the purity of this most natural and immediately human of poets.

That Burns's essential impulse derives from the most mundane encounters with Scotch religion, character, customs, manners, drink, and, above all, love does not in the least diminish the universal appeal of his poems. What has been said in praise of his songs should not divert anyone from the delights of his other work, the joyous fun of his epistolary pieces and of the satires with their interplay of humor, irony, good nature and high spirits in such things as *To a Louse, Address to the De'il, Death and Dr. Hornbook, Verses on Dining with Lord Daer,* or the compassionate and profound pathos of *To a Mouse* and the miraculous irresistibility of *Tam o'Shanter*. Any reader who may be curious to know what made the author of *The Essays of Elia* lean over to kiss a passage in the *Epistle to William Simson* may refer to the fifteenth stanza of that utterly charming poem. Posterity, at many levels below the happy reach of Charles Lamb, continues to respond wholeheartedly to Burns, not only because his poems shun hypocrisy and cant but even more for their positive truth, courage, freshness and candor, all immanent in a mere four lines like —

> The Kirk an' State may join, an'
>   tell
> To do sic things I mauna:
> The Kirk an' State may gae to hell
>   And I'll gae to my Anna.

Coleridge says somewhere that "Burns preached from the text of his own errors." "Preached" is perhaps not just the right word: it might have been better said that Burns's work, like his life, provides those who feel the need to preach with texts for all occasions. What other poet is so far from literature and yet so close to life? Burns could mock the Holy Willies out of court because he understood the extremes of human nature and was therefore consistent only in being human. His poetry never concealed or falsified the truth about himself. For these same reasons, moreover, he is one poet who could afford in the end to dispense with the apologists who try so hard to make poets look more respectable than they commonly are or need or want to be. For the best biography of Robert Burns, footnoted by his letters, is plainly set forth and best read in the book of his poems.

BURTON, Sir Richard Francis (Mar. 19, 1821 – Oct. 20, 1890). English explorer, author, translator. Born at Torquay. After two years at Trinity College, Oxford, joined Indian army (1842), proceeded to learn Iranian, Hindustani, and Arabic languages, and write of his travels. One of the first Englishmen to penetrate unexplored Arabia and reach Mecca (1853), which he describes in *Personal Narrative of a Pilgrimage to Al-Medina and Mecca*

(3 vols. 1855–56). To Somaliland with John Hanning Speke (1854, recounted in *First Footsteps in East Africa*, 1856), with whom he discovered Lake Tanganyika (1858), as described in *The Lake Regions of Central Africa* (1860). Visit to Utah in U.S. (1860) recounted in *The City of the Saints* (1861). That year secretly married Isabel Arundell. As British consul at Fernando Po, West Africa (from 1861), Santos, Brazil (from 1865), Damascus (from 1869), and Trieste (from 1871) continued to explore. Died at Trieste. Insatiably curious regarding the exotic, demonic and erotic, Burton acquired a great number of languages and dialects, and in addition to producing forty-three volumes of exploration and travel made numerous translations, including the famous *Arabian Nights* (*The Thousand Nights and a Night*, 16 vols. 1885–88), *The Lusiads* of Luís de Camões (2 vols. 1880) and other Portuguese works, two volumes of Latin poetry, and four volumes of folklore.

REFERENCES: Fawn M. Brodie *The Devil Drives: A Life of Sir Richard Burton* (New York 1967). Byron Farwell *Burton: A Biography of Sir Richard Burton* (London and New York 1963).

BURTON, Robert (Feb. 8, 1577 – Jan. 25, 1640). English scholar. Born Lindley, Leicestershire. Entered Brasenose College, Oxford (1593); elected fellow of Christ Church College, Oxford (1599), where he received the degree of bachelor of divinity (1614) and remained as librarian, tutor and scholar for the rest of his life. Appointed vicar of St. Thomas's, Oxford (1616), he also held livings in Lincolnshire (1624–(1631) and Leicestershire (1630–1640). Wrote several Latin poems and a Latin comedy, *Philosophaster* (performed at Christ Church, 1617), but his fame rests on *The Anatomy of Melancholy* (1621, under pseudonym "Democritus Junior"). Enlarged and revised several times by its author, this work, basically a treatise on various forms of emotional disturbance, covers in its extensive digressions a vast array of subjects, and is a valuable document for the study of the intellectual history of the seventeenth century.

EDITION: *The Anatomy of Melancholy* ed. Holbrook Jackson (3 vols. London and New York 1932).

REFERENCES: Lawrence Babb *Sanity in Bedlam: A Study of Robert Burton's Anatomy of Melancholy* (East Lansing, Mich. 1959). William Randolph Mueller *The Anatomy of Robert Burton's England* (Berkeley, Calif. 1952). Jean Robert Simon *Robert Burton et l'Anatomie de la Mélancolie* (Paris 1964).

BUSONI, Ferruccio Benvenuto (Apr. 1, 1866 – July 27, 1924). Italian pianist and composer. Born Empoli, Tuscany, son of Ferdinando Busoni, a clarinet player. Learned piano from German mother and made first public appearance at age of eight in Trieste. Taught piano at Conservatory of Helsingfors (1889). Married Gerda Sjöstrand (1890). Taught at Moscow Conservatory (1890), then New England Conservatory, Boston (1891–94). Returned to Europe, settling in Berlin (1894), and concentrated on composing pieces for advanced students, *Violin Concerto* (1896–97), *Comedy Overture* (1897), *Piano Concerto* (1903–1904), opera *Die Brautwahl* (1912). Also conducted orchestral works of new composers, including Bartók, Delius, Debussy, Elgar, Sibelius. Director of lyceum of Bologna (1913–15). Produced two short operas, *Turandot* and *Arlecchino*, in Zurich (1917). He was composing his masterpiece, *Dr. Faustus* (produced 1925), when he died in Berlin. Busoni was remarkable for both his extraordinary technique and his powers of interpretation.

TRANSLATION: *The Essence of Music and Other Papers* tr. Rosamond Levy (London and New York 1957).

REFERENCE: Edward J. Dent *Ferruccio Busoni* (New York 1933).

BUTLER, Samuel (c. Feb. 8, 1612 – Sept. 25, 1680). English poet. Born near Strensham, Worcestershire, son of a farmer. After attending King's School, Worcester, became secretary to countess of Kent and later to Sir Samuel Luke of Cople Hoo, a strict Presbyterian and colonel in Parliamentary army; he and cohorts provided subjects for satire in *Hudibras*. At Restoration,

Butler became secretary to Richard Vaughan, earl of Carbery, lord president of Wales, who made him steward of Ludlow Castle (1661–62); about same time, married reputedly wealthy woman who soon lost her fortune in speculation. In latter part of life probably attached to suite of George Villiers, 2nd duke of Buckingham, whom he may have helped write *The Rehearsal* (1671). Died in London. Butler is remembered for *Hudibras* (part I, 1663; part II, 1664; part III, 1678), a satirical heroic poem in octosyllabic couplets which ridicules the hypocrisy, the self-important pomposity and pedantry of the Puritans. Also wrote satires on the Royal Society, on heroic tragedies, and on the fashionable Pindaric odes.

EDITIONS: *Characters and Passages from Notebooks* ed. Alfred R. Waller (Cambridge, England, and New York 1908). *Hudibras* ed. Alfred R. Waller (Cambridge, England, and New York 1908); ed. John S. Wilders (Oxford and New York 1967). *Satires and Miscellaneous Poetry and Prose* ed. René Lamar (Cambridge, England, and New York 1928).

REFERENCES: Edward A. Richards *Hudibras in the Burlesque Tradition* (Oxford and New York 1937). Jan Veldkamp *Samuel Butler* (Amsterdam 1923; in English).

BUTLER, Samuel (Dec. 4, 1835 – June 18, 1902). English novelist and essayist. Born Langar Rectory, near Bingham, Nottinghamshire, son of clergyman and grandson of Dr. Samuel Butler, bishop of Lichfield. Educated at Shrewsbury School and St. John's College, Cambridge, he was intended for the church but determined to become a painter instead. The ensuing family quarrel resulted in his going to Canterbury Island, New Zealand, to raise sheep. Finding the venture profitable, he remained five years, began writing on Darwin's theory of evolution for local journals. Back in London (1864) he continued painting, composing music, and writing. Fame came with *Erewhon* (1872), his satire on Victorian industrialism and morality, but financial disaster two years later left him in a precarious state unrelieved until his father's death (1886). Meanwhile, turning against Darwinism, he wrote a number of controversial works, *Evolution Old and New* (1879), *Unconscious Memory* (1880), and others, then turned to classicism, advancing the theory that the *Odyssey* was written by a woman (*The Authoress of Homer,* 1897). After his death, in London, his great work, the highly autobiographical *The Way of All Flesh* (written 1873–1883), appeared (1903). A satiric portrait of Victorian life, it became important in the reaction against Victorianism. Other works: *Life and Letters of Dr. Samuel Butler* (1896), travel books, translations of the *Iliad* and *Odyssey* into vigorous plain prose (1898 and 1900), *Shakespeare's Sonnets Reconsidered* (1899), and *Erewhon Revisited* (1901).

EDITIONS: *Collected Works of Samuel Butler* ed. Henry F. Jones (20 vols. London and New York 1923–26). *The Essential Samuel Butler,* a selection ed. G. D. H. Cole (London and New York 1950). *Correspondence of Samuel Butler with His Sister May* ed. Daniel F. Howard (Berkeley, Calif. 1962).

REFERENCES: G. D. H. Cole *Samuel Butler and The Way of All Flesh* (London 1947, also PB). Henry F. Jones *Samuel Butler, Author of Erewhon* (*1835–1902*): *A Memoir* (2 vols. London and New York 1919, reprinted New York 1968). Joseph Jones *The Cradle of Erewhon* (Austin, Tex. 1959). Malcolm Muggeridge *The Earnest Atheist: A Study of Samuel Butler* (London 1936 and New York, as *A Study of Samuel Butler, the Earnest Atheist,* 1937). Clara G. Stillman *Samuel Butler: A Mid-Victorian Modern* (London and New York 1932).

✍

SAMUEL BUTLER
BY BERNARD BERGONZI

During the final decades of the nineteenth century, when Samuel Butler lived and wrote, such dominating figures as Ibsen and Nietzsche proclaimed that the past was dead, that principles of conduct must be reexamined and many hallowed assumptions overthrown. The perturbation they aroused is apparent in the vigorous counterattack in Max Nordau's *Degeneration,* a book which had a great vogue in the Nineties; Nordau claimed that all the most advanced representatives of the art and thought of his day, whether represented by Zola, Nietzsche, Wagner, Ibsen, or the French symbolists, showed clear evidence of physical and moral degeneration. But in England, whose intellectual relations with the Continent were fairly tenuous and where tradition was all too visibly enthroned in the person of Queen Victoria, the transvaluation of values had few practitioners of any stature. There was Wilde, of course, but he made the mistake of manifesting his originality in his life rather than in his art. Shaw inevitably comes to mind too; but despite the brilliance of his theatrical writing, he was a secondhand thinker who picked up most of his ideas from Ibsen and Samuel Butler. It is, in fact, to Butler, born twenty years before Shaw, that we must turn in order to find an approximate English equivalent of the intellectual revolutionaries of the Continent.

After the initial success of *Erewhon,* a satirical romance of a utopian — or antiutopian — kind, that still keeps its sharpness, Butler's reputation suffered because he persisted in attacking on several fronts at once. Thus, his satirical attitude to Christianity alienated conservative opinion, while at the same time his onslaughts on Darwin lost him the sympathy of positivist and radical opinion. But Butler's masterpiece, *The Way of All Flesh,* which he kept unpublished for twenty years until it finally exploded like a time bomb after his death, showed how far he had been a pioneer in undermining the most seemingly secure of Victorian citadels — the family. In the years that followed its publication, this novel established a pattern for a characteristically twentieth-century type of *Bildungsroman,* in which hostility between father and son is a crucial element. Lawrence's *Sons and Lovers* and Joyce's *A Portrait of the Artist as a Young Man* are two celebrated examples. Butler's family letters, published a few years ago, make it plain that the novel was rooted in autobiographical actuality. Butler's father may not have shown the odious cruelty of Theobald Pontifex in the novel, but he seems to have had a total lack of affection for his son, and when Butler was established as an author he refused to read his books. He remarked of *Erewhon:* "I shall take your advice and not read your book. It would probably pain me and not benefit you." Butler was also hostile to his mother: in chapter 25 of *The Way of All Flesh* Christina Pontifex addresses a devastatingly sanctimonious letter to her two sons when she fears she may not survive her next confinement, a document which is transcribed almost literally from one written by Butler's own mother in similar circumstances.

Yet Butler's revolt against Victorian attitudes was not confined to the family. It is in his preoccupation with money that he lays bare the foundations of his society in a virtually Marxist fashion. Certainly, Butler's own concern with money had a somewhat obsessive quality, and there are many passages in his letters which are unintelligible because of the intricacy of his financial preoccupations, often resembling those parts of Victorian novels where the plot thickens with talk of wills and entails. Even when he wants to be lighthearted he naturally resorts to the imagery of the stock market: "If Aunt Sarahs at par are a hundred, they had stood at about seventy-five when I began my visit; when I ended it they had dropped to fifteen or fourteen and a half." In *The Way of All Flesh* and his notebooks Butler constantly argued that money was the most important thing in life, far more so than health or reputation. In a vigorous entry in his notebooks he wrote:

"A man will feel loss of money more keenly than loss of bodily health, so long as he can keep his money. Take his money away and deprive him of the means of earning any more, and his health will soon break up; but leave him his money and even though his health breaks up and he dies, he does not mind it so much as we think. Money losses are the worst, loss of health is next worst, and loss of reputation comes in a bad third. All other things are amusements provided money, health and good name are untouched."

In its quiet, wholly rational exposition of a point of view that seems, at first glance, quite unacceptable, this is very typical of Butler's polemical method. He allows himself no vestige of irony or rhetorical emphasis, and there is every reason to suppose that the sentiments are Butler's own. Yet a Victorian reader — or for that matter, a modern reader — who attempted to refute them in a similarly calm and rational tone would be forced to think very hard indeed about what his real, as opposed to his conventional, convictions were about the importance of money in human life. If Butler's contemporaries found it hard to forgive him, it was beyond doubt because he made wholly explicit the assumptions by which they lived. As an analyst of his age Butler was marred by a cranky spirit, and he lacked the centrality of the major Victorian social critics. He was, though, a man of great honesty, who contrived to write a couple of books of genius, even if he lived an eccentric, embittered, and mostly trivial life. The childhood traumas so painfully recorded in *The Way of All Flesh* can explain much that was odd in Butler's makeup. It was part of his achievement both to dissect his age and to give later generations a fresh sense of its essential complexity.

BUXTEHUDE, Diderik or **Dietrich** (c.1637 – May 9, 1707). Danish organist and composer. Presumably studied with father, organist at Helsingor (Buxtehude's probable birthplace) and Helsingborg. Succeeded (1668) Franz Tunder (whose daughter Anna he married in same year) as organist at Marienkirche, Lübeck, Germany. Held this lucrative and extremely prestigious post until his death, in Lübeck. Buxtehude became the great musical influence for northern Europe; Bach and Handel were among those who came to hear him. He introduced (1763) concerts (*Abendmusiken*) held annually on the five Sundays before Christmas. Extant are organ compositions, choral works, and chamber music. Buxtehude exerted important influence on Bach, especially through his cantatas and instrumental organ work.

REFERENCE: Farley K. Hutchins *Dietrich Buxtehude: The Man, His Music, His Era* (Paterson, N.J. 1955).

BYRD, William (1543 – July 4, 1623). English composer. Born probably in Lincolnshire. Appointed organist of Lincoln Cathedral (1563); held post until he assumed (with Thomas Tallis) duties of organist at Chapel Royal in London (1572). Married Juliana Birley (1568); she died some time after 1586, and he married a second time. Published (1575) first set of *Cantiones Sacrae* for five and six voices, under exclusive royal patent granted to himself and Tallis which passed wholly into Byrd's hands on Tallis's death (1585). Settled (1593) at Stondon Massey, Essex, where he remained until his death. A Roman Catholic, Byrd was professionally engaged in the service of the Church of England throughout his life; composed much music for both the Catholic and the Anglican liturgy. Works include Masses for three, four and five voices; Latin motets; secular songs and madrigals; and instrumental music.

REFERENCE: Edmund H. Fellowes *William Byrd* (2nd ed. London and New York 1948).

~

WILLIAM BYRD
BY JOSEPH KERMAN

Nothing is known for certain about Byrd's early life. We may assume that he began his musical career in time-honored fashion as a choirboy in some major ecclesiastical establishment — very likely the Chapel Royal, which was by far the greatest of these in England. A certain Thomas Byrd of the chapel may have been his father, and William is said to have been "bred up" under Thomas Tallis, the most distinguished member of the chapel at mid-century. Byrd was born in 1543, just in time to spend his years of apprenticeship during England's last period of Roman Catholicism, under Queen Mary — that is, during England's last period of the intensive cultivation of church music. For under Edward VI and then again under Elizabeth I, the Reformation cut drastically into the ornate Catholic services with their rich musical appendages. It is no wonder that many "singing-men" (church musicians) held stubbornly to the old religion; and among those that did so, William Byrd was the most outspoken.

Even at the time of his first position, as a provincial cathedral choirmaster at Lincoln, we hear of unusual concessions and influential friends. Byrd counted on powerful patrons all through his life, even gaining entrée to the aristocratic literary circle around Sir Philip Sidney. He came to the Chapel Royal in 1572. Only three years later, he and Tallis were granted a monopoly by the crown for music printing, and published *Cantiones Sacrae,* an ambitious joint volume of motets, the first ever printed in England. To forestall Puritan attacks — for Latin motets certainly look Catholic — it is carefully explained that they can be called "sacred" only in an informal sense (*Cantiones quae ab argumento sacrae vocantur*); the book is boldly dedicated to Queen Elizabeth, and eminent authorities explain in Latin hexameters that now, at long last, the glories of English music are made manifest to the world at large. Between Byrd and the seventy-year-old Tallis, it is not hard to guess who was the guiding force behind all this. The queen must have smiled; she had a weakness for elaborate church ritual and a special fondness for music; Byrd was never persecuted for his rather open Catholic activities. As for the *Cantiones,* they were a great commercial failure.

In musical terms, however, they deserve to be called revolutionary on the English scene. Music of such expressivity, brilliance, and variety of form and style had never been written by native composers. Byrd was the first to penetrate to the heart of the great Netherlandish musical tradition that also produced Palestrina and Lasso — composers quite different from Byrd in personality, and more "modern" in spite of being older men, but hardly superior to him as masters of the Latin motet and Mass. And when around 1590 Byrd tried publishing again, his works were received eagerly. Two further books of motets display a new smoothness of technique and new developing trends of style. Very many of the texts treat subjects such as liberation, the Babylonian captivity, and the coming of God; it seems that Byrd was

speaking in this way for the Elizabethan Catholic community. Innocent texts from the psalms, and so on, may even have masked near-treasonous comments on the martyrdom of Father Edmund Campion and the Spanish Armada. Half surreptitiously, Byrd published three famous Masses, which are perhaps the most beautiful examples of Renaissance music that can still be heard with some frequency today. Then 1605 saw the *Gradualia,* a great collection of over a hundred motets and short motet sections specially ordered for Catholic services — undercover services, we must assume; included are *Ave verum, Justorum animae,* and *Non vos relinquam orphanos.* When the Gunpowder Plot late in 1605 made anything Catholic extremely dangerous, Byrd coolly withdrew the *Gradualia* and held the copies for reissue a few years later.

His secular polyphonic songs were also very famous at the time, though less so today. They adhere to an older, graver, more complex idiom than that of the madrigal, whose great vogue in England was initiated by Byrd's pupil Thomas Morley. Byrd's relation to the madrigal is very interesting. He actually wrote (or at least published) the first English madrigals — two fine pieces in praise of Eliza, "beauteous Queen of second Troy," in 1590. But he wrote no more, evidently disdaining the genre — and also the lute-ayre — as essentially frivolous and below the dignity of a learned composer. He did not even contribute to Morley's well-known madrigal anthology *The Triumphs of Oriana* in 1601.

Byrd played a leading role in the development of Elizabethan instrumental music, both chamber music for viols and music for harpsichord or virginal. Building upon next to no tradition, he wrote brilliant and imaginative sets of variations on folksongs (*Walsingham, The Carman's Whistle*); he brought the pavane and galliard to a stage of sophistication comparable to that of the allemandes and courantes of the Bach suites. Later composers scarcely added to the possibilities of virginal music that Byrd had opened up, except in the matter of keyboard technique. Finally, although Catholic, Byrd produced quantities of excellent music for the Anglican rite: verse anthems, full anthems, psalms, and services.

Serious-minded, high-principled, and — from what little we know of his personal life — as tenacious in litigation as in doctrine, Byrd presided over the golden age of English music which found its focus in the reign of Queen Elizabeth. A true Elizabethan, his musical personality developed in the 1560's, flowered in the 1570's, and matured in the 1580's and beyond. Neither old Tallis nor the younger men — Morley, John Dowland, John Wilbye, Orlando Gibbons, John Bull — approached him in range, profundity, or even in extent of output. Byrd lived to the age of eighty, the most honored Gentleman of the Chapel Royal, and he was still writing and publishing music after 1610.

BYRON, George Gordon Noel, 6th Baron Byron of Rochdale (Jan. 22, 1788 – Apr. 19, 1824). English poet. Born London, son of Captain John Byron, a notorious libertine. The child was lame (with clubfoot) from birth. Educated at Harrow (1801–1805) and Trinity College, Cambridge (1805–1808). Replied to severe reviews of his first book of verse, *Hours of Idleness* (1807) with satiric poem *English Bards and Scotch Reviewers* (1809). A Mediterranean tour occasioned first two cantos of *Childe Harold* (1812), which made him famous. The more mature cantos III and IV (1816 and 1818) followed. Married bluestocking heiress Annabella (Anne Isabella) Milbanke (1815). A daughter Augusta Ada was born (1816); she then insisted on a separation, and Byron left England because of the resultant scandal (in which hints of incestuous relations with his half-sister Augusta were circulated; and because of his political liberalism. In Switzerland carried on a liaison begun in London with Claire Clairmont, who bore him a daughter Allegra (1817). In Italy established more lasting relationship with Countess Teresa Guiccioli (1819). Poetry written 1815–24 includes *The Prisoner of Chillon and Other Poems* (1816), *Manfred* (1817), *Beppo* (1818), *Mazeppa* (1819), *Cain* (1821), *The Vision of Judgment* (1822), and his unfinished masterpiece, *Don Juan* (1819–24). Wrote political poems favoring independence of Italy, and at suggestion of Prince Alexandros Mavrokordatos joined Greek insurgents against Turkish rule (1823). Died of fever at Missolonghi.

EDITION: *The Works of Lord Byron* (13 vols. London) ed. E. H. Coleridge (*Poetry* 7 vols. 1898–1904) and R. E. Prothero (*Letters and Journals* 6 vols. 1898–1901). *Lord Byron's Correspondence, Chiefly with Lady Melbourne, Mr. Hobhouse, Douglas Kinnaird, and P. B. Shelley* ed. John Murray (2 vols. London and New York 1922).

REFERENCE: Leslie A. Marchand *Byron: A Biography* (3 vols. New York 1957 and London 1958).

✍

LORD BYRON
BY HOWARD MUMFORD JONES

Byron is an author, a personality, a legend, and an eternal point of view. As an author he matured with amazing rapidity in some of the deadest years in English poetry: at twenty-four he astonished Regency society by publishing the first two cantos of *Childe Harold* and following this with an output of verse narratives, lyrics, fragments of political satire, rhymed confessions, and outbursts of rebellion against hypocrisy. Canto III (1816) and canto IV (1818) of *Childe Harold* are superior to their predecessors, but the whole work has the strength and the weakness of being "public" poetry, whereas most poetry by Keats is private poetry. Whole stanzas read like parts of an impassioned oration; and since Byron wore the robe of the Spenserian stanza loosely, the rhetorical magnificence of particular passages rather than the evocation of a poetical universe is what one remembers. He was already the noble liberal commenting with sympathy or scorn upon men, nations, politics, and events. Since he had a stronger sense of history than any other poet since Milton, both the glory and the tragedy of the past are reviewed by the meditative Childe Harold, who also, notably in the last two cantos, has a fine eye for sweeping landscapes among the mountains or at sea.

The young man hastily scribbled, and the maturer bard composed, verse narratives, the hero of which, as Macaulay pointed out, is always Byron himself, or rather the image Byron found it emotionally satisfactory to project. He was a skillful but also a careless prosodist, a defect that helps explain why, despite occasional lovely passages, his verse tales have fallen into neglect. Though it is probably impossible to revive them, their very fragmentariness, partly a function of careless workmanship, anticipates the modern obsession with plot, narrative, and character only half indicated. In the later narrative poems irony and satire intrude upon the descriptive melancholy, the egotism, and the melodrama of the earlier tales: compare, for example, the humorless, if powerful, *The Corsair* of 1814 with the *Mazeppa* of 1819.

Between his self-imposed exile of 1816 and his death in Greece in 1824 Byron wrote most of the works the moderns have found enduring, includ-

ing his brilliant and inimitable letters. He was concerned to reform the English stage, but his dramas, too closely imitative of the Italian neoclassical Alfieri, can for the most part be neglected save for *Manfred* (1817) and *Cain* (1821). *Cain* no longer shocks, but *Manfred,* especially if it can be heard in Schumann's poignant musical setting, is one of the great and permanent romantic triumphs, a moving statement of Byron's rebellion against the Christian universe. Despite some uncertain lines, *Manfred* is not only the most finished piece of blank verse by Byron, but its superb setting in the Alps, its dignified evocation of the powers of evil, and the enigmatic figure of Astarte (part of the "Byron mystery") keep it forever fascinating. The same cannot be said of the political poems of the Italian years (or the Swiss ones), rhymed pamphlets in favor of freedom: *The Prisoner of Chillon, The Lament of Tasso,* and *The Prophecy of Dante.* Their libertarianism is honorable, but they have few passages of immortal verse.

For most readers the unique glory of Byron is in *Beppo* (1818), *The Vision of Judgment* (1822), and the incomparable unfinished masterpiece *Don Juan* (1819–24). In *The Vision of Judgment* Byron is a comic anti-Milton, playing carelessly with all the furniture of heaven, earth, and hell and doing it with the nonchalance of an enfranchised archangel. *Beppo* is a trial run for *Don Juan;* it is important that all three poems are written in *ottava rima,* a form then new in English and one that avoided the stiffness of the Spenserian stanza and gave plenty of scope for the greatest master of comic rhyme in English. Like Faust, Don Juan sweeps through the little world and then the great, for this titular hero, a spoiled brat when the work begins, ends as the ambassadorial representative of Catherine the Great of Russia at the British court. The poem is a mighty medley; and though a straight-line biographical narrative holds the cantos together, only a fool, as Dr. Johnson hinted of another masterpiece, would read it for the story. The mood of the poem runs from grave to gay, from lively to severe, the style changes with the mood, the narrative disappears for whole cantos to be replaced by wonderful passages of satiric comment on the world, which time has not dulled, and the traditional Don Juan is not the hero but the occasion of an "epic" as disorderly as anything by Sterne seems to be. No more brilliant piece of social satire has appeared since Byron's death.

Many come to Byron for the personality rather than the poetry; and the personality is one of the most enigmatic in literary history. Scores of biographers have labored to get at the truth. It should be remembered that Byron was half a Scotsman in a period when the Scots had to make their way by sheer force in London society, that he was a poor nobleman in a period of extravagant expenditure, that the nature of his sexuality is still a riddle though he lived in a world of easy conquest and yielding mistresses, that though like other members of his caste he affected to despise craftsmanship, he toiled to master the art of writing, and that, an aristocratic radical, he took the unpopular liberal side when Waterloo ensured the triumph of the Holy Alliance and the dominance of reaction in Britain and on the Conti-

nent. His trip to Greece helped the Greeks but little; his death there, and of course his poems, turned him into the hero of young Europe preparing for the revolutionary movements of 1830.

Byronism is an eternal point of view. In its crudest expression it is mere egotism, but egotism may become sublime. Like Mark Twain, Byron defied the God of the Old Testament, and like a more affirmative Schopenhauer, he believed that the will is paramount. Fundamentally antisocial, Byron refused to be confined by social norms that seemed unworthy of man's potentiality. Unlike the doctrine of nescience Byronism holds that man's very defiance may alter the nature of things. Its hero is Prometheus, not St. Francis. It believes in the possibility of a fairer society. But this altruistic vision is crossed by darker lines. In Byronism it is inevitable that the lover shall destroy the beloved, that fate shall unpredictably wreck the fairest scheme, and that the most splendid hope shall be forever haunted by mortality. Byronism has its relation with Faust (Goethe admired Byron's poetry), with the paradoxes of Baudelaire's moral values, and with the intense, crime-haunted suffering of Dostoevsky's heroes. From time to time, then, it recurs in Western art and thought. It chiefly differs from the social alienation implicit in *The Waste Land* and in many modern novels by refusing to accept apathy as a substitute for the life, however tragic, of the human will.

CABLE, George Washington (Oct. 12, 1844 – Jan. 31, 1924). American writer. Born New Orleans; his father was of old slaveholding Virginia family, his mother of Puritan stock. At fifteen began work as clerk. Served two years (1863–65) in Confederate army and started literary career writing for New Orleans *Picayune*. Married Louise S. Bartlett (1869; she died 1904). His short stories of Creole and Negro life in Louisiana began to appear in *Scribner's Monthly* (1873). Collected as *Old Creole Days* (1879), they established him as leader of local color movement in South, as did his novels, also on antebellum Creole life, *The Grandissimes* (1880), *Dr. Sevier* (1884), and others. Author also of *The Creoles of Louisiana* (1884) and *Strange True Stories of Louisiana* (1889). During 1880's lectured and wrote effectively supporting prison reform and, especially, increased rights for Negroes (*The Silent South*, 1885). Criticism of his views in South caused him to move North, and he settled permanently in Northampton, Mass. (1885). Married Eva C. Stevenson (1906). Died in St. Petersburg, Florida. Cable's books on Louisiana are important for preserving a part of American life in the South, and for launching the movement in regional literature that included Joel Chandler Harris, Lafcadio Hearn, and William Faulkner.

REFERENCES: Charles P. Butcher *George W. Cable: The Northampton Years* (New York and London 1959, also PB). Louis D. Rubin Jr. *George W. Cable: The Life and Times of a Southern Heretic* (New York 1969). Arlin Turner *George W. Cable: A Biography* (Durham, N.C. 1956).

CALDERÓN DE LA BARCA, Pedro (Jan. 17, 1600 – May 25, 1681). Spanish dramatist. Born and died in Madrid. Son of well-to-do government official. Attended Jesuit school in Madrid and studied canon law at universities of Alcalá and Salamanca. Entered poetry competition (1620); wrote (1623) his first play *Amor, Honor y Poder* (Love, Honor and Power). After military service (1625), became court playwright for Philip IV and, after death of Lope de Vega (1635), undisputed master of Spanish stage. Of his more than a hundred *comedias* (serious and comic dramas) written before 1651, the best known are *La Vida es sueño* (Life Is a Dream), a fantasy; *El Alcalde de Zalamea* (The Mayor of Zalamea), a tragedy; and *El Mágico prodigioso* (The Wonderful Magician), based on the life of St. Cyprian, which was admired by Shelley. Ordained a priest (1651), Calderón turned to producing *autos sacramentales* (religious allegorical plays) and occasional plays for the royal theatre. Of his over seventy *autos*, notable is *El Gran Teatro del Mundo* (The Great Theatre of the World). The last outstanding figure in the golden age of Spanish literature, Calderón is noted for his stylized dramatic technique, his intense spiritual sensibility, and the rich hyperbole of his poetic diction. He was greatly admired by nineteenth-century German critics like Gotthold Lessing and August Schlegel, and Shelley translated scenes from *El Mágico prodigioso* (1824).

TRANSLATIONS: *Eight Dramas* tr. Edward FitzGerald (1853, Garden City, N.Y. PB 1961). *Six Dramas* tr. Denis F. MacCarthy (New York 1961).

REFERENCES: Alexander A. Parker *The Allegorical Drama of Calderón:*

An Introduction to the Autos Sacra-mentales (London and New York 1943). Albert E. Sloman *The Dramatic Craftsmanship of Calderón: His Use of Earlier Plays* (Oxford 1958). Bruce W. Wardropper ed. *Critical Essays on the Theatre of Calderón* (New York 1965, also PB).

CALLIMACHUS (c.305–c.240 B.C.). Greek poet and scholar. Born in Cyrene in Africa; educated probably at Athens. Migrated to Alexandria, became celebrated schoolmaster in suburb of Eleusis. Acquainted with Ptolemy II, who appointed him to Alexandrian library. His major work *Pinakes*, a 120-volume catalogue raisonné of the library's contents, is now lost, like all his prose work. Of his poems, six hymns, a number of epigrams, and fragments survive, some well known, like "Great book, great evil." Most important poem, *Aetia* (Causes), in fragments, is a narrative elegy in four books. Fragments of a poem of episodes, *Hecale*, survive, while Catullus's *Lock of Berenice* and Ovid's *Ibis* are Latin adaptations of now lost works of Callimachus. Acknowledged the leading Alexandrian poet of his day, who strongly influenced Roman poetry, his own work is more distinguished for its learning than its inspiration.

TRANSLATIONS: *Aetia, Iambi, Lyric Poems, Hecale, Minor Epic and Elegiac Poems, Fragments of Epigrams, Fragments of Uncertain Location* tr. C. A. Trypanis (Cambridge, Mass. and London 1958). *Hymns and Epigrams* tr. A. W. Mair (2nd ed. Cambridge, Mass. and London 1960).
REFERENCE: Émile Cahen *Callimaque et son oeuvre poétique* (Paris 1929).

CALLOT, Jacques (c.1592 – Mar. 24, 1635). French engraver and etcher. Born in Nancy, then capital of Lorraine. Journeyed to Rome (1608), then to Florence (1611), where he worked for ten years. Learned to draw from life and perfected technique of varnishing copperplates which permitted hitherto impossible accuracy and subtlety in etching. From 1615, when he began

The Life of Ferdinand II, Callot was commissioned by the great houses of Europe to engrave important events and persons. Returned to Nancy (1621) and etched much material he had already drawn or engraved in Italy (*The Gypsies, The Beggars, The Hunchbacks, The Italian Comedians*). Traveled to Netherlands (1627), painted *The Siege of Breda* (1628). Worked in Paris (1629–31), called there by Louis XIII to engrave *The Siege of La Rochelle* (1630). Produced (1633) his most celebrated work, eighteen plates on the Thirty Years War called *Les Misères de la guerre* (The Miseries of War). He died in Nancy. The technical perfection of Callot's drawing and engraving and his expression of human sympathy and joy had great influence on the arts of drawing, engraving, and painting. Other major works are *The Fair of the Impruneta* (1620), *The Siege of the Isle of Ré* (1630), and *The Temptation of St. Anthony* (1634).

REFERENCES: Jacques Lieure *Jacques Callot* (Paris 1924–27). Edwin de Turck Bechtel ed. *Jacques Callot* (New York 1955).

CALVERLEY, Charles Stuart (Dec. 22, 1831 – Feb. 17, 1884). English poet and parodist. Born Martley, Worcestershire, son of a clergyman. Educated at Harrow and Balliol College, Oxford, where he won chancellor's prize for Latin verse (1851); left (1852) because of an escapade. Entered Christ's College, Cambridge, where he also won chancellor's prize for Latin verse. Noted for his wit and gift for parody and light verse, he came to be considered one of the most brilliant men of his time. Published *Verses and Translations* (1862). Called to the bar the same year (1865) he married his cousin Ellen Calverley. *Translations into English and Latin* (1866) appeared just before he suffered a skating accident which invalided him for life. Other works include *Theocritus Translated into English Verse* (1869) and *Fly Leaves* (1872), a collection of parodies. Died at Folkestone, Kent.

EDITION: *Complete Works* ed. Sir Walter J. Sendall (London 1901).
REFERENCE: Richard B. Ince *Calver-*

ley and Some Cambridge Wits of the Nineteenth Century (London 1929).

———

CAMERON, Charles (c.1740 – 1812). Scottish architect. Places of his birth and death unknown, as are most details of his life. A Jacobite, he lived in the house of Charles Edward Stuart, the Young Pretender, while studying classical architecture in Rome. In London (1767 and 1772) exhibited drawings of Roman baths (*Baths of the Romans,* published 1772). Went to Russia (1779) on invitation of Catherine the Great, and except for brief visit to England (c.1800) remained in Russia in service of Catherine and her successors for rest of his life. While his neoclassic style closely adhered to that of the classical Adam brothers, Cameron introduced into his decoration exotic materials such as agate and porphyry, rare woods, ormolu, and lapis lazuli, and colors like mauve, pistachio, and olive. Major works: Agate Pavilion and Cameron Gallery, with their interiors, at Tsarskoe Selo (1779–99); palace and garden buildings, Pavlovsk (1782–1800); palace at Baturin, Ukraine (1790–1800).

REFERENCES: Georges Loukomski *Charles Cameron* (London 1943 and New York 1944). George Heard Hamilton *The Art and Architecture of Russia* (Harmondsworth, England and Baltimore 1954).

———

CAMÕES (English spelling CAMOËNS), Luis Vaz de (1524 – June 10, 1580). Portuguese poet. Of poor noble family, he was born probably in Lisbon, where he died. After thorough classical education at University of Coimbra (from 1538), returned to Lisbon without degree. Entered court circles, making a name for himself with lyrics addressed to "Natercia," — Caterina de Ataide, the queen's lady in waiting — and three successful comedies, *El-Rei Seleuco, Filodemo,* and *Os Amphitriões.* Volunteered for military service in Ceuta, Morocco (1547), and lost right eye in campaign against the Moors. Back in Lisbon, wounded court official in street fight and was imprisoned (1552). Released (1553), he joined troops being sent to Goa, and was not

to return to Lisbon for seventeen years. A life of adventure ensued, including a stay in Macao, but accused of maladministration he was recalled to Goa (1558). A shipwreck during which he lost all his possessions but the first several cantos of his epic *The Lusiads* delayed his arrival until 1561. Started homeward voyage (1567), and after a period in Mozambique reached Lisbon (1570). Published his magnificent work *Os Lusiadas* (1572), an immediate success which assured Camões his reputation as Portugal's greatest poet. Modeled on Virgil's *Aeneid,* it is an epic of ten cantos which in recounting in ottava rima Vasco da Gama's discovery of the sea route to India glorifies the history and heroes of Portugal. Camões left a collection of fine lyrics published posthumously as *Rhythmas* (1595).

TRANSLATIONS: *The Lusiads* tr. Sir Richard Fanshawe (1655) ed. Jeremiah D. M. Ford (Oxford and Cambridge, Mass. 1940), ed. Geoffrey Bullough (London 1963 and Carbondale, Ill. 1964); tr. Sir Richard Burton (*Os Lusiadas* 2 vols. London 1880); tr. W. C. Atkinson (Harmondsworth, England, and Baltimore PB 1952). *The Lyricks: Sonnets, Canzons, Odes and Sextines* tr. Sir Richard Burton (2 vols. London 1884).

REFERENCES: Aubrey F. G. Bell *Luis de Camões* (London 1923). Cecil M. Bowra *From Vergil to Milton* (London 1945 and New York 1946, also PB). Sir Richard Burton *Camoëns: His Life and His Lusiads* (2 vols. London 1881). Henry H. Hart *Luis de Camoëns and the Epic of The Lusiads* (Norman, Okla. 1962).

———

CAMPBELL, Colin (d.Sept. 13, 1729). Scottish architect. Nothing is known of his birthplace, parentage, education, or activity until 1717, when he was commissioned by the earl of Burlington to remodel Burlington House in London. His best-known country houses, in the Palladian tradition, are Newby in Yorkshire (1720), Mereworth castle in Kent (1720–23), Wanstead in Essex (1720; razed 1822), Houghton Hall in Norfolk (1722). Published *Vitruvius Britannicus, or The British Architect,* a series of plates depicting English architectural works (3 vols. 1717–25). Appointed (1725) architect to Prince of Wales (George II), and (1726) surveyor of the works at Greenwich Hospital. Died in London.

CAMPIN, Robert (probably the **MASTER OF FLEMALLE**) (c.1378–1444). Flemish painter. Birthplace possibly Valenciennes. Lived (from 1406) in Tournai, where he became a free citizen (1410) and dean of painters' guild (1423). A leading citizen and celebrated teacher, he trained Jacques Daret and Roger de la Pasture, who is identified with Rogier van der Weyden. Died in Tournai. If he is the Master of Flémalle (so called from fragments of an altarpiece in the Städelsches Kunstinstitut, Frankfurt, presumably from an abbey at Flémalle), to Campin must be attributed the *Mérode Altarpiece* (c.1425–c.1428, Metropolitan Museum, New York), a beautiful representation of the Annunciation, which marks a dramatic departure from the stylized elegance of international Gothic to a robust realism reflecting in its contemporary interior the tastes of the rising middle class. Other works ascribed to him include the *Nativity* (Dijon), *Annunciation* and *Marriage of the Virgin* (Madrid), *Madonna of the Firescreen* (London), the wings of the Werl altarpiece (Madrid), and several portraits. Campin exerted an enormous influence on the succeeding generation of painters.

REFERENCE: Erwin Panofsky *Early Netherlandish Painting: Its Origins and Character* (2 vols. Cambridge, Mass. and London 1954).

CAMPION (or **CAMPIAN**), **Thomas** (Feb. 12, 1567 – Mar. 1, 1620). English poet and composer. Born and died in London. Son of prosperous court clerk, educated at Peterhouse College, Cambridge (1581–84). Entered Gray's Inn (1586) but never called to the bar. Little known of him thereafter until he became a physician (c.1602–1606). First poems published anonymously in Sir Philip Sidney's *Astrophel and Stella* (1591). His name appeared as author of *Poemata* (1595), Latin poems and epigrams. *A Book of Airs* (1601) is in two parts, one with words and music by Campion, the other by Philip Rosseter; four additional books of airs followed (1613–17). Campion also wrote masques, occasional verses, Latin epigrams and elegiacs, and two theoretical works: *Observations in the Art of English Poesie* (1602), advocating use of unrhymed "quantitative" meters derived from classical examples rather than rhymed accentual meters, and *A New Way of Making Four Parts in Counterpoint* (c.1617–18). One of the masters of the Elizabethan lyric, he is known for the freshness and delicacy of both his verses and their musical settings.

EDITIONS: *Works* ed. Percival Vivian (Oxford 1909). *The Works of Thomas Campion* ed., Walter R. Davis (Garden City, N. Y. 1967).
REFERENCE: Miles M. Kastendieck *England's Musical Poet: Thomas Campion* (London and New York 1938).

CAMUS, Albert (Nov. 7, 1913 – Jan. 4, 1960). French writer. Born Mondovi, Algeria, son of farm laborer who died in action in World War I. In 1930's, after studying at University of Algiers, became committed to politics, theatre, and writing. Briefly a Communist, he broke with the party (1937). As a journalist incurred hostility of local colonial authorities by his campaigns for economic and social reforms on behalf of Algerians. Participated in amateur theatrical group as actor and director. First books, *L'Envers et l'endroit* (1937) and *Noces* (1938), collections of essays. Visited Spain, Czechoslovakia, Italy, and France (1938–40), then taught at private school in Algiers. Returned to France (1942), where he took active part in French Resistance and wrote for various underground journals, including *Combat*, which he edited (1944–47). Major works include novels *L'Étranger* (1942, tr. *The Stranger* 1946), *La Peste* (1947, tr. *The Plague* 1948), and *La Chute* (1956, tr. *The Fall* 1957); dramas *Caligula* (1938, produced 1945), *Le Malentendu* (1944, tr. *The Misunderstanding*), *L'État de siège* (1948, tr. *The State of Siege*), and *Les Justes* (1941, tr. *The Just Assassins*); essays *Le Mythe de Sisyphe* (1943) and *L'Homme révolté*

(1951) translated in *The Myth of Sisyphus and Other Essays* (1955); and *L'Exil et le royaume* (1957, tr. *The Exile and the Kingdom,* 1958), a collection of short stories. Awarded Nobel prize for literature (1957). Married twice. Died in an automobile accident near Sens, France.

REFERENCES: Germaine Brée *Albert Camus* (New York 1959 rev. ed. 1964, also PB). Germaine Brée ed. *Camus: A Collection of Critical Essays* (Englewood Cliffs, N. J. 1962, also PB). Albert Maquet *Albert Camus: The Invincible Summer* (tr. New York 1957). Conor Cruise O'Brien *Camus (Fontana Modern Masters* ed. Frank Kermode, London PB 1970).

✍

ALBERT CAMUS
BY DAVID CAUTE

"After all, the best fashion of speaking about what one loves is to speak about it lightly." Thus Albert Camus, in *L'Été.* Both as artist and philosopher, Camus carried his profound seriousness with urbanity and charm. Athlete and invalid, sensualist and moralist, he dissected massive and intractable problems in a lucidly classical style humanized always by wit, irony, and the artist's gift of illustration. He was not humble, but arrogance glimmered only when he was stung.

This slender young French-Algerian, who rose within a few years from obscurity to fame, was perhaps a better novelist and short story writer than playwright. His superbly calculated variations of the novel form were perfectly adapted to transcend the thesis and embody the philosophy. But of the plays, only *Caligula* achieves the visual flexibility and sense of external gesture which the theatrical medium demands. *Le Malentendu* and *Les Justes* appeal more to the intellect than to the emotions; they are better read than seen.

In a world deprived of God and of the moral norms that He had sanctified, Camus offered an alternative to nihilism and despair. As with Malraux, Camus's philosophy was an activist's response to the epic social tragedies of the twentieth century. But whereas Malraux's heroes must breathe the oxygen of high historical crisis or die, Camus throve on understatement. We could all be, or believe ourselves to be, Meursault in *L'Étranger* or Jean-Baptiste Clamence in *La Chute.* And if the circumstances of pestilence which dominate *La Peste* are hardly commonplace, Camus had nevertheless composed an allegory whose mood of mundane endurance contrasts with the dramatic and clandestine life of the armed partisans whom Camus himself had known as a member of the southern Resistance organization Combat. The alternatives that Camus offered to nihilism and despair were not those associated with the Enlightenment. The events of his own time made him laugh at the myths of universal reason and dialectical materialism. He insisted that when human aspirations confront the outer world, when the rational and the irrational come face to face, a sensitive man discovers not meaning but absurdity. As his character Caligula remarks: "The world has no importance. Once he realizes that a man wins his freedom."

But Caligula drew false conclusions, taking refuge in scorn, hatred, and vindictiveness. "I've taken the wrong path," he finally conceded. "My freedom isn't the right one." According to Camus, respect for human life and love for the limitations of human endeavor, moderation, a sense of *"la mesure,"* these are the principles on which man must construct a life endowed with shape, purpose, and integrity. Compared with Christians, Hegelians, and Marxists, Camus looked like an existentialist. But his was in fact a religious spirit; he was an essentialist. To the preservation of human life he attached an absolute value, so long as that life could be preserved in terms of dignity and self-respect.

For Camus, Caligula's nihilistic rampage was only one of several disastrous human reactions to the recognition of absurdity. Camus's growing disenchantment with Stalinist Communism, reflected in the postwar years in the editorials he wrote for *Combat,* indicated a growing awareness that revolutionary fanaticism is as hostile to human dignity as the aggressive nihilism of a Hitler or a Caligula. In his play *Les Justes* the intransigent revolutionist Stefan declares: "I don't love life . . . I love something higher than mere life . . . I love justice." Stefan will stop at nothing to "rescue humanity from itself." Thus Camus traveled from the anti-Nazi position of *Lettres à un ami allemand* to the anti-Marxist propositions of *L'Homme révolté.* "In this new Jerusalem, echoing with the roar of miraculous machinery, who will still remember the cry of the victims?" As an alternative to triumphant revolution, with its police, trials, and excommunications, its worship of power, Camus offered what he called "rebellion." The rebel, skeptical of all transcendent reasons and ideologies, resorts to violence in the bitter knowledge that he is mutilating himself. Scrupulously limiting the scope of his resistance to his refusal to be treated like an object, he prefers self-sacrifice to the acquisition of power.

According to Sartre, Camus had opted out of history. There is some truth in this. Like Romain Rolland before him, he had decided to stand *"au-dessus de la mêlée."* This was the posture he strove to maintain during the Algerian revolution, when he condemned equally the brutality and torture employed by both sides. This former Communist, who as a young man had been fired by the revolt of the Asturian miners, the Spanish Civil War, the novels of Malraux and the appalling poverty of the Arabs of Kabylia, had in effect become a reformist liberal. But more was involved than political theory. Camus had been born in Algeria, and he never ceased to insist that the majority of white *colons,* far from being exploiters, had survived by dint of courage and hard work. France's commitment to them was for him a moral imperative. Consequently, he refused to contemplate independence for Algeria.

The prejudices of Camus's ancestry and upbringing appear in his imaginative writings. Only the whites emerge in full human dimensions. Where are the Arabs in the Oran of *La Peste?* Frugality, self-sacrifice, unimpeachable honor — these are the essential qualities of white Algeria embodied by the schoolmaster Daru in the short story *The Guest.* With a hint of self-pity, Camus depicts Arab nationalists as unjustly threatening to kill Daru: "In this vast landscape he loved so much, he was alone." In *L'Étranger,* the author appears to share Meursault's indifference to the brutal beating of an Arab girl and the subsequent murder of her brother. The intended irony of the novel rebounds at Camus's expense: would the Algerian court, so anxious to reprieve Meursault, have shown the same indulgence to an Arab who had murdered a *colon?*

But Algeria did not afford easy solutions, nor did Camus trade in them. If man will never achieve the summits, the ascent — the struggle — is in itself enough. One must imagine Sisyphus happy. In *La Peste,* Camus's hero,

Dr. Rieux, takes the world as he finds it, rejects superstition and escapism, and summons all his resources of courage and knowledge to the struggle against the defects of biology and creation. He concludes that there are more things in men to admire than to despise. Camus's own hard and tragically short journey was a constant celebration of human life and of the glittering sunlight and sea of the Mediterranean, where in springtime "flowers burst into bloom by thousands, above the white walls."

CANALETTO (Giovanni Antonio Canal) (Oct. 18, 1697 – Apr. 20, 1768). Italian painter. Born and died in Venice. Received early training from his father, Bernardo Canal, painter of theatrical scenery. After stay in Rome (1719–20), where he was influenced by Dutch and Flemish landscape painters, established himself as painter of Venetian views for foreign, especially English, tourists. Immensely successful, he formed (by 1730) connection with Joseph Smith, merchant, art collector, and later British consul at Venice, who acted as his agent. Canaletto went to London (1746), where, except for two short visits to Venice, he remained ten years, producing views of London and the Thames as well as popular Italian scenes. Elected to Venetian Academy (1763). As commissions increased Canaletto's style became (after c.1730) less impressionistic and atmospheric, more linear and precise, with cool, even lighting, better suited to the accurate views in demand. Canaletto also produced *capriccii* (imaginary scenes in which real buildings from different sites were combined in fanciful settings), drawings, and etchings. He was widely imitated in his lifetime in Venice and England. *See also* BERNARDO BELLOTTO.

REFERENCES: Wililam G. Constable *Canaletto: Giovanni Antonio Canal, 1697–1768* (2 vols. Oxford and New York 1962). Adrian Ecles *Canaletto* (London 1968). Jacob Kainen ed. *Etchings of Canaletto* (Washington, D. C. 1967). Vittorio Moschini ed. *Drawings by Canaletto* (New York PB 1968). Giuseppe M. Pilo *Canaletto* (New York PB 1962).

CANOVA, Antonio (Nov. 1, 1757 – Oct. 13, 1822). Italian sculptor. Born Possagno, near Venice. Orphaned at early age and brought up by grandfather, a stonecutter, who apprenticed him to a local sculptor (1768). In Venice (1774) began producing his own works in a lively and naturalistic style. Moved to Rome (1779) and became influenced by ancient Roman monuments; signs of conflict between the two styles exist to some degree in all his mature work. Success of his first major commission, tomb of Clement XIV (completed 1787), led to series of commissions for monuments, including those to Clement XIII (1787–92) and Archduchess Maria Christina (1798–1805, Vienna). An admirer of Napoleon, he executed a number of portraits of him and of other Bonapartes, the most famous of which is the reclining statue of Pauline Borghese as Venus Victrix (1805–1808). Pius VII appointed Canova director of Accademia di San Luca (1810), commissioned him (1815) to negotiate return to Italy of masterpieces taken to Paris during French occupation, and for his success in this venture made him marchese d'Ischia. Died in Venice. The leading exponent of neoclassicism, Canova was worshiped through much of his life as the supreme arbiter of taste; his reputation began its steady decline in his final years. Other works include *Perseus* (1801) and *The Pugilists* (1802), the only modern works in the Vatican's Belvedere.

REFERENCE: Countess Isabella Albrizzi *The Works of Antonio Canova* . . . with biographical memoir by Count Cicognac (tr. 2 vols. Boston 1878).

CARAVAGGIO, Michelangelo Merisi da (Sept. 28, 1573 – July 18, 1610). Italian painter. Named for birthplace, village in Lombardy. Began apprenticeship in nearby Milan, aged ten. Went to Rome (probably about 1590), where he turned against the prevalent taste for the classics to real life for his models, including himself in *Concerto* (Metropolitan Museum, New York). First commission, three St. Matthew paintings for Contarelli chapel in S. Luigi dei Francesi. A brawl resulting in a stabbing forced him to flee Rome (1606), first to Naples, then to Malta (1607), where he painted portraits of Grand Master of the Order of St. John (one in Louvre, Paris), finally to Sicily. Died at Port'Ercole while returning to Rome, having learned of pardon from pope. His realistic style exerted formative influence on emerging seventeenth-century style in Italy and in Spain, France, Flanders (upon Rubens), and Holland (upon Rembrandt).

REFERENCES: Walter F. Friedlaender *Caravaggio Studies* (Princeton, N. J. and London 1955). Roger Hinks *Michelangelo Merisi da Caravaggio: His Life, His Legend, His Works* (London 1953 and New York 1954).

CARAVAGGIO
BY MARK SCHORER

After a four-year apprenticeship in Milan, probably before 1590, in his late adolescence, Michelangelo Merisi da Caravaggio arrived in Rome. He had a hard time of it at first, going about in rags in search of employment. Dependent as he was on models for the naturalistic painting that alone interested him from the beginning, he now, when he could not afford models, developed the habit of painting mirror images of himself. It was a habit that stayed with him, and if now we have a whole series of paintings that show him as a lustful boy, later we have paintings that show him both in his ravaged maturity and in the guise of the flirtatious boy in Rome that the older man remembered.

The moods of his pictures vary from a bright mischievousness to an often anguished physicality, but in the first paintings, with their Giorgionesque lightness and purity of color, the first mood dominates, and it probably derives from this early habit of self-

portraiture. It is his face under the writhing snakes of the early *Medusa,* a face contorted into a positive parody of rage. It is his face in the early *Boy with a Basket of Fruit* and in the early portraits of Bacchus, all of them, even the *Sick Bacchus* giving out a kind of open lechery. The same mood pervades, but now quite paradoxically, in the Pamphili *St. John the Baptist,* but here the mischief is more complex: the naked figure parodies a famous *ignudo* in the Sistine Chapel; the older Michelangelo's pensive figure is made younger, softer, and again, almost lewdly invitational, and the saint appears not with the conventional *Agnus Dei* but, for the first time, with a ram, in the boy's embrace; the irony is heightened when we know that the ram is borrowed from Michelangelo's nearby *Sacrifice of Noah.* The reminiscence of Michelangelo appears even more boldly in Caravaggio's *Love Victorious,* where the older man's sculptured *Victory* (Palazzo Vecchia), heroically towering in manneristic musculature and with blank face, is pushed down into the figure of a wicked, rather chubby boy, brazenly smiling, the outspread legs rather more than merely wanton. It is Caravaggio's face in the frightened, effeminate boy bitten by a lizard, in the calm lute player who could be either boy or girl, and in each of the yearning boys in the *Concerto,* all the same but painted at different angles, only the hair varying from one to the other. Finally, we should mention the later *David with the Head of Goliath,* where the victorious David is again the young Caravaggio, in a meditative mood, and the severed head of the giant is the suffering man as he then was.

The early Roman hardships may have been briefly alleviated by a number of painters who rescued him from the streets, but it is fairly certain that presently he was employed by Giuseppe d'Arpino, for whose shop he painted fruits and flowers. Charming as these may be, he chafed to be free to paint in his own way — that is to say, to paint the human figure, exactly. This was made possible at last when he was discovered by the Cardinal del Monte, who took him into his house. In 1597, in the first recorded mention of him in these Roman years, the abbot of Pinerola referred to him as the *"celeberrimo pictore."* By now, Caravaggio was painting in that heavier, darker style for which he was becoming famous.

It was probably the Cardinal del Monte who was most instrumental in obtaining for Caravaggio his first great commission, the three St. Matthew paintings for the Contarelli chapel in S. Luigi dei Francesi. The *First St. Matthew,* intended as the altarpiece, was rejected. Here Caravaggio had followed what was something of a tradition in Lombardy, the democratization of saints: his St. Matthew is a simple, rough peasant, sitting with crossed legs, his big toe jutting out of the painting, a lovely girl-angel guiding his hand in a completely natural way. This was a conception not agreeable to current Roman clerical taste. The two lateral paintings, which he executed in the last years of the century, are different: no less natural, but brilliant and elegant in costume. The second version for the altarpiece is different, too. The composition is contained severely behind the picture plane, with the legs of the saint placed horizontally and he himself a normal patriarch with long gray beard, a balding head with, even, a small halo. The angel is placed decorously and conventionally in the sky. But the painting employs his innovative techniques of luminosity, the bare wall back-ground, shadows and darkness giving the figures plasticity, and light color tones at the front pulling the figures into the world of the observer, to put them almost literally in the real world.

Caravaggio grew into an angry man and a brawler. He affected a sword and dagger with which he swaggered through the streets, and, unlicensed, he was on one occasion arrested and jailed for the offense. From 1600 until his departure from Rome he rampages through the police records, wounding a captain, assaulting a waiter, throwing stones at police, insulting a corporal, offending women, injuring a notary. Giovanni Baglione, a lesser artist and his first biographer, sued him and his friends for libel because of their insulting verses. But then, more somberly: after a brawl in which Caravaggio was severely injured and his opponent killed, he fled Rome. Hiding at first in the Sabine Hills, he went on to Naples to await a pardon from the pope. All the time he was painting. From Naples he went on to Malta, where he painted two portraits of the grand master and where, with great honor, he was received into the Order of Malta as *cavaliere.* But presently a quarrel with one of his superiors put him in jail, from which, however, he escaped by a rope ladder and fled to Sicily. After a time he returned to Naples, and there, in a vendetta-like punishment, he was set upon by his enemies, who hideously disfigured his face. Then a pardon came from the pope in 1610 and he set out at once for Rome, but somewhere near Port'Ercole he was mistakenly arrested. When he was released, his boat, with all his belongings, including such paintings as he was taking back, had departed. In despair, he began to run up the beach in the full glare of the summer sun, and when he reached Port'Ercole, he collapsed. In a few days he was dead of a malignant fever.

His life had been as dark and colorful and violent as much of his painting. In his early paintings, the innovations, the techniques of realism that constituted his rejection of the decadent absurdities of mannerism, were accepted and appreciated when they limited themselves to exquisite fruits and flowers, lute players, cardsharps, fortunetellers. Patronage and renown came to him early, and his commissions from and sales to private collectors were steady. Even the *Amore Vittorioso,* announcing so boldly that profane love rules the world, seems to have been acceptable. But when Caravaggio turned to religious subjects and cultivated the later style and the "ignoble" manner, more genteel painters, like the clergy, objected. The great *Madonna of the Serpent* was quietly removed from the Vatican and given to Scipione Borghese for his private collection. This is the painting that, behind the lovely, solicitous Madonna and the naked little Roman boy Jesus, both treading on the serpent's head, presents St. Anne, never before in all art history put in such a context, and painted quite differently from Mary — a strong peasant figure, old and worn, seeming to say that holiness proceeds from such as me, the most humble. The clergy of S. Maria della Scala rejected the *Death of the Virgin* because it showed her as a very poor woman, swollen like an ordinary corpse, surrounded by barefooted old men, her own bare legs showing. Almost all the Roman religious paintings, even those in churches, like the great St. Paul canvases in S. Maria del Populo, were commissioned by private individuals.

The force of the paintings lies in their direct address to the observer through the medium of the real world. With his penchant for a lower-class milieu and peasants, Caravaggio was constantly humanizing the holy and the miraculous, saying, "This is of *you.*" The luminosity, heightened by the use of shadow and the heavy black paint, the color organization that thrusts the subject forward, the subtle use of completely real detail to humanize the miraculous, the close-pressing particularity as opposed to the abstract distancing of mannerism, the new presentation of space and the easy integration of figures in space, the insistent and increasingly brutal corporeality that at the same time creates an aura of mystery and magic and even madness — all this made him the threat to the established that he was and the great innovator that he became.

CARDUCCI, Giosuè (July 27, 1835 – Feb. 16, 1907). Italian poet and critic. Born at Val di Castello, Tuscany. From his father, a physician and one of the revolutionary Carbonari, he derived liberal republicanism and anti-Catholicism. Studied at University of Pisa, published first volume of poems, *Rime* (1857), became celebrated professor of Italian literature at University of Bologna (1860–1904). Married Elvira Menicucci (1859). Principal elements of Carducci's writings are opposition to the then prevailing romanticism and to Catholicism, the call for return to classical and preromantic Italian models, and enthusiasm for the Risorgimento. Chief volumes of poetry are *Giambi ed epodi* (1867–79), *Rime nuove* (1861–87), *Odi barbare* (1877–89), *Rime e ritmi* (1887–99). Carducci became a senator (1890), was revered by Italians as a national poet, and received Nobel prize for literature (1906). Died in Bologna.

TRANSLATION: *Carducci: A Selection from His Poems* tr. Geoffrey L. Bickersteth (London 1913).

REFERENCE: Benedetto Croce *Giosuè Carducci* (5th ed. Bari, Italy 1953).

CAREW, Thomas (c.1598–c.1639). English poet. Born West Wickham, Kent, son of a master in chancery. Graduated from Corpus Christi College, Oxford (1611) and entered Middle Temple (1614), but was never called to the bar. In service of ambassador Sir Dudley Carleton first in Venice (1616), then in The Hague, but quarreled with him and returned to England. Talented, witty, and licentious, he became a favorite of Charles I, who made him gentleman of the privy chamber and gave him a royal estate. A Cavalier poet with Sir John Suckling, Richard Lovelace, and others, Carew published only a court masque *Coelum Britannicum* (1634) in his lifetime. His posthumous collection, *Poems* (1640), contains the celebrated elegy on the death of Donne, *The Rapture*, and numerous lyrics in the Ben Jonson vein addressed to Celia, including the one beginning "Ask me no more where Jove bestows."

EDITION: *The Poems of Thomas Carew with His Masque Coelum Britannicum* ed. Rhodes Dunlap (London and New York 1949).

REFERENCE: Edward I. Selig *The Flourishing Wreath: A Study of Thomas Carew's Poetry* (New Haven 1958).

CARLYLE, Thomas (Dec. 4, 1795 – Feb. 4, 1881). Scottish essayist and historian. Born at Ecclefechan in Annandale, Dumfriesshire, Scotland. Entered Edinburgh University as divinity student, but rejected Calvinism and left without degree (1809). After period as schoolmaster, turned to literature, producing life of Schiller (1823–25) and translating Goethe's *Wilhelm Meister* (1824). Began (1826) his tempestuous marriage with the gifted, strong-willed, Scottish Jane Baillie Welsh (1801–1866); (collections of her brilliant letters published 1883, 1924, 1931). In financial straits, they spent six years on a lonely farm at Craigenputtock, where Carlyle wrote *Sartor Resartus* (1831; published as book in U.S. 1836, England 1838), a philosophical discourse and autobiographical account of his spiritual crisis over religious unbelief. They moved to Chelsea, London (1834), where after fire destroyed the only copy Carlyle rewrote *The French Revolution* (3 vols. published 1837), which made him famous. Gave popular lecture courses including those published as *Heroes and Hero-Worship* (1841). *Chartism* (1839) and *Past and Present* (1843) discuss current political problems and excoriate democracy and the rights of individuals. Other notable works: his edition of *Oliver Cromwell's Letters and Speeches* (1845), *History of Frederick the Great* (6 vols. 1858–65), and critical and miscellaneous essays. Elected lord rector of Edinburgh University (1865). After wife's death (1866) wrote little of importance. Carlyle is best remembered as social critic who decried evils of industrial society and propagated doctrine of work, duty, and spiritual idealism. Known for number of sayings such as "Happy are the people whose annals are blank in history books."

EDITIONS: *The Works of Thomas Carlyle* ed. Henry D. Traill (Centenary Edition 30 vols. London and New York 1896–1901). *Selected Works, Reminiscences and Letters* ed. Julian Symons (London 1955 and Cambridge, Mass. 1957).

REFERENCES: Jane Welsh Carlyle *Letters to Her Family 1839–1863* ed. Leonard Huxley (New York 1924 and Chester Springs, Pa. 1966). James Anthony Froude *Thomas Carlyle: A History of the First Forty Years of His Life, 1795–1835* (2 vols. London and New York 1882) and *Thomas Carlyle: A History of His Life in London 1834–1881* (2 vols. London and New York 1884). David Gascoyne *Thomas Carlyle* (New York PB 1952). John Holloway *The Victorian Sage: Studies in Argument* (New York PB 1965). Julian Symons *Thomas Carlyle: The Life and Ideas of a Prophet* (London and New York 1952).

CARPACCIO, Vittore (c.1465–c.1525). Italian painter. Born and died in Venice. Little known of early life. Flemish characteristics of his style indicate close association with Antonello da Messina; also influenced by Gentile Bellini. Earliest (1490–95) and most celebrated narrative cycle is series of scenes from legend of St. Ursula commissioned by Scuola di S. Orsola (now in the Accademia, Venice), which combine charming Flemish minuteness of detail with Venetian love of pageantry and rich color. Later narrative cycles, which depict splendor of Renaissance Venice, include episodes from lives of saints (Scuola di. S. Giorgio degli Schiavoni, Venice), of which *St. Augustine in His Study* (formerly called *St. Jerome*) is particularly noted. Also painted (after 1504) scenes from life of Virgin for Scuola degli Albanesi and (1511–20) from life of St. Stephen for S. Stefano. Another major work is *Presentation in the Temple* (1510), an altarpiece for S. Giobbe (now in Accademia, Venice). Modern critics have increasingly credited Carpaccio with sophisticated treatment of light and atmosphere, as well as adept composition of large groups of buildings and figures.

REFERENCES: Jan Lauts *Carpaccio: Paintings and Drawings* (tr. London 1962). Terisio Pignatti *Carpaccio* (tr. Lausanne and New York 1958).

———

CARRACCI. Family of Italian painters, born in Bologna. Enormously influential, they, along with Caravaggio, brought mannerism to an end and developed a baroque art which blended classical idealism with naturalistic representation and employed dramatic color and lighting effects. LODOVICO (Apr. 21, 1555 – Nov. 13, 1619) studied in various north Italian cities, and after returning to Bologna founded with his cousins Agostino and Annibale, the Accademia degli Incamminati, famous academy of art (c.1582). The three collaborated on many frescoes in Bolognese palaces. Lodovico's greatest achievement was fresco series in cloister of S. Michele in Bosco, outside Bologna (1592–1605, now in ruined state); he later painted many altarpieces for Bolognese churches. Died in Bologna. ANNIBALE (Nov. 3, 1560 – July 15, 1609), considered greatest of the three, studied Venetian, Florentine, and Roman Renaissance masters, and Correggio. Went to Rome (1595), where assisted by his brother Agostino he executed his masterpiece, frescoes of scenes from classical mythology in Farnese Gallery (1597–1604), first of the great baroque ceilings. His later style, quiet and melancholy, is seen in famous *Flight into Egypt* (c.1600, Gallery Doria Pamphili, Rome), whose po-

etic landscape established the type used by Poussin and Claude Lorrain. Died in Rome. AGOSTINO (Aug. 15, 1557 – Feb. 23, 1602), engraver as well as painter, was chief theoretician of Carracci school. His style followed Annibale's, but was more cold and hard. Works include *Last Communion of St. Jerome* (early 1590's, Pinacoteca, Bologna), and *Cephalus and Aurora* and *Galatea* (Farnese Gallery). Died in Parma.

REFERENCES: Giovanni P. Bellori *The Lives of Annibale and Agostino Carracci* (tr. University Park, Pa. 1968). Walter F. Friedlaender *Mannerism and Anti-Mannerism in Italian Paintings: Two Essays* (New York and London 1957, also PB). John R. Martin *The Farnese Gallery* (Princeton, N.J. 1965).

———

CARROLL, Lewis. *See* DODGSON, Charles Lutwidge.

———

CASANOVA DE SEINGALT, Giovanni Jacopo or Giacomo (Apr. 2, 1725 – June 4, 1798). Italian adventurer and writer. Born Venice, son of an actor. Attended seminary of St. Cyprian, but was expelled for immoral conduct after taking minor orders. Traveled throughout Europe, supporting himself by violin-playing, gambling, spying, writing, and especially through his charm. Arrested in Venice (1755) for practicing magic, he made a brilliant escape from the Piombi (1756), later described in *Histoire de ma fuite* (1788). In Paris, where he enjoyed favor in court circles, he instituted and directed the royal lottery. A diplomatic mission to Holland gained him title chevalier de Seingalt. Became secretary and librarian to Count Waldstein (1785) and spent rest of his life in the count's castle of Dux in Bohemia, where he wrote a fantasy novel *Isocameron* (1788) and, in French, his famous memoirs, the full text of which appeared in print for the first time in 1960 (*Histoire de ma vie*, Wiesbaden and Paris). Casanova numbered among his acquaintances Voltaire, Catherine the Great, and Frederick the Great. His memoirs, otherwise typical of the erotic literature of the time, provide a colorful picture of the eighteenth-century beau monde.

TRANSLATION: *History of My Life* tr. Willard R. Trask (10 vols. in 5, New York 1966– and London 1967–).

REFERENCES: James Rives Childs *Casanova: A Biography Based on New Documents* (London 1961). John Masters *Casanova* (New York 1969).

CASSATT, Mary (May 22, 1845 – June 14, 1926). American artist. Born Alleghany City (now part of Pittsburgh), Pa.; studied at Pennsylvania Academy of Fine Arts, Philadelphia, traveled and studied further in France, Italy, Spain, and Belgium (1866–73). Settled in Paris and exhibited at Paris Salon (1877), attracting attention of Edgar Degas, who persuaded her to join the impressionists. Thenceforth she exhibited with them, beginning with *The Cup of Tea* (1879). Her subjects are usually women and children, especially a mother and child engaged in daily home activities, like bathing or playing. Japanese prints at Paris exhibition of 1890 influenced her most original works, like *The Bath* (1891) and *The Boating Party* (1893), which emphasize flat planes and surface designs. Equally important are her color prints and etchings of this period, like *The Letter*, inspired by work of Utamaro and Yeishi. Her best-known etchings are the *Maternity* series. Blind in her last decade, she died at her Château de Beaufresne, near Paris.

REFERENCES: Adelyn D. Breeskin ed. *Graphic Art of Mary Cassatt* (New York 1968, also PB) and *Mary Cassatt: A Catalogue Raisonné* (Washington 1970). Frederick A. Sweet *Miss Mary Cassatt: Impressionist from Pennsylvania* (Norman, Okla. 1966). Forbes Watson *Mary Cassatt* (New York 1932).

CASTAGNO, Andrea del (c.1423 – Aug. 19, 1457). Italian painter. Born Castagno, Tuscany; spent most of life in Florence. Extremely poor, he received no formal education in art, but early attracted notice of Bernadetto de Medici, who provided training in Florence. He was commissioned (1440) to paint fresco (now lost) of hanged traitors on façade of Palazzo del Podesta, thereby earning nickname Andreino degl'Impiccati (Andrew of the Hanged Men).

Died in Florence of plague, eleven days after his wife. Influenced by works of Donatello, Castagno produced (c.1445) impressive life-size figures in fresco of Dante, Petrarch, Boccaccio, and other eminent Italians (in refectory of S. Apollonia), a heroic equestrian portrait of Niccolò da Tolentino (1456, Florence cathedral) and a *David* painted on a leather shield (National Gallery, Washington, D.C.).

REFERENCE: George M. Richter *Andrea del Castagno* (Chicago 1943 and Cambridge, Eng. 1944).

CASTIGLIONE, Baldassare (Dec. 6, 1478 – Feb. 2, 1529). Italian writer and diplomat. Born Casatico, near Mantua, of illustrious Lombard family. Educated in Milan. After brief attachments to courts of Milan and Mantua, entered (1504) service of Guidobaldo da Montefeltro, duke of Urbino, who employed him on diplomatic missions. After Guidobaldo's death (1508), continued to serve his successor, Francesco Maria della Rovere. Took part in various Italian wars and was successively envoy from Urbino and Mantua to the pope. Married Ippolita Torelli (1516; she died 1520). Sent to Spain (1524) as papal nuncio to Charles V, he died at Toledo. Castiglione's major work, *Il Libro del Cortegiano (The Courtier*, begun c.1507 at Urbino, published 1528), a treatise on the perfect courtier and on ideal courtly conduct, in the form of dialogues between well-known figures at the court of Urbino, helped spread Italian humanism throughout western Europe and deeply influenced the concept of the ideal gentleman, as well as of the perfect lady and of Platonic love.

TRANSLATIONS: *The Book of the Courtier* tr. Sir Thomas Hoby (1561, London 1948); tr. Charles S. Singleton (Garden City, N.Y. 1959, also PB).

REFERENCES: Julia C. Ady *Baldassare Castiglione: The Perfect Courtier, His Life and Letters 1478–1529* (2 vols. new ed. New York 1927). Ralph Roeder *Man of the Renaissance; Four Lawgivers: Savonarola, Machiavelli, Castiglione, Aretino* (New York 1933, also PB).

CATHER, Willa Sibert (Dec. 7, 1876 –
Apr. 24, 1947). American writer. Born
near Winchester, Va. Family moved to
ranch outside Red Cloud, Nebr., where
she attended high school, then University of Nebraska (1891–95). Worked
on Pittsburgh, Pa. newspaper, then
taught school (1901–1906). First book
of poems, *April Twilights* (1903), was
followed by short story collection *The
Troll Garden* (1905). Joined *McClure's
Magazine* staff in New York, became
managing editor (1908–12). After publication of first novel, *Alexander's
Bridge* (1912) devoted whole time to
writing. Sarah Orne Jewett's suggestion
that she turn to her own Nebraska experiences and interest in the pioneering
spirit of nineteenth-century immigrant
families on the Nebraska plains resulted in important novels *O Pioneers!*
(1913), *The Song of the Lark* (1915),
and *My Antonia* (1918). Published
short story collection *Youth and the
Bright Medusa* (1920), then novels
One of Ours, in part concerning World
War I (Pulitzer prize 1923), and *A
Lost Lady* (1923). Established as an
outstanding regionalist writer of deep
insight into character and a beautiful
stylist, Miss Cather turned to the early
Southwest for her superb novel *Death
Comes for the Archbishop* (1927) and
to Quebec for *Shadows on the Rock*
(1931). Other works: novels *The Professor's House* (1925), *My Mortal Enemy* (1926), *Lucy Gayheart* (1935),
Sapphira and the Slave Girl (1940);
short stories *Obscure Destinies* (1932),
The Old Beauty and Others (1948); essays *Not Under Forty* (1936), *Willa
Cather on Writing* (1949). She received
honorary degrees from numerous universities, the Prix Femina Américain
(1933) and American Academy of Arts
and Letters gold medal (1944), and is
considered one of the country's foremost writers of the first half of the
twentieth century.

REFERENCES: Mildred R. Bennett
The World of Willa Cather (Lincoln,
Neb. rev. ed. 1961, also PB). Edward
K. Brown and Leon Edel *Willa Cather:
A Critical Biography* (New York 1953).
David Daiches *Willa Cather: A Critical
Introduction* (New York 1962, also PB).
Edith Lewis *Willa Cather Living: A
Personal Record* (New York 1953).

Elizabeth S. Sergeant *Willa Cather: A
Memoir* (Philadelphia 1953, also PB).

CATLIN, George (July 26, 1796 – Dec.
23, 1872). American painter. Born
Wilkes-Barre, Pa.; educated to the law.
Practiced in Philadelphia (1817–21)
before shifting to portrait and miniature painting. Became particularly interested in Indians, and sensing that
civilization would soon destroy their
way of life, he set out from St. Louis
(1832) to visit and paint different
tribes. Traveled through wilderness,
about 5000 miles by canoe and 550 on
horseback, creating a collection of
over 500 paintings that record the
North American Indian — his costumes, dwellings, customs, and country. Exhibited 494 paintings of 48
tribes in New York (1837), and published the beautifully illustrated *Letters and Notes on the Manners, Customs, and Conditions of the North
American Indians* (2 vols. 1841). Exhibited in London (1840) and Paris
(1845), where King Louis Philippe had
collection installed in Louvre and commissioned further paintings of Indians
and series on explorer Robert de La
Salle. Revolution of 1848 ended Catlin's
Paris sojourn; he continued to paint
Indians and record their customs in
South America and on west coast of
North America. Exhibited the results at
Brussels (1869) and New York (1871).
He died in Jersey City. Catlin's extraor-
dinarily detailed paintings and portraits and his writings provide an
invaluable ethnological and anthropo-
logical record of Indian life. Major col-
lections are in Smithsonian Institution,
Washington, D.C., and American Mu-
seum of Natural History, New York
City. Other books include *Catlin's North
American Indian Portfolio* (1845), *Cat-
lin's Notes of Eight Years' Travel and
Residence in Europe* (1848), *Life
Among the Indians* (1867), *Last Rambles Amongst the Indians of the Rocky
Mountains and the Andes* (1867).

EDITION: *Episodes from Life Among
the Indians and Last Rambles* ed. Marvin C. Ross (Norman, Okla. 1959).
REFERENCES: Harold McCracken
George Catlin and the Old Frontier
(New York 1959). Robert Plate *Palette
and Tomahawk: The Story of George

Catlin (New York 1962). Marjorie C. Roehm ed. *Letters of George Catlin and His Family: A Chronicle of the American West* (Berkeley, Calif. and Cambridge, Eng. 1966).

CATULLUS, Gaius Valerius (c.84–c.54 B.C.). Roman poet. Born Verona. Most of what we know of his life derives from the 116 surviving poems, which place him as one of Rome's greatest lyric poets. Of wealthy family, he went to Rome (c.62 B.C.), joining the fashionable and literary society. Journeyed to Bithynia (57–56 B.C.) as member of governor's staff, visited brother's grave and wrote the moving elegy *Ave atque Vale* as a result. In Rome his mistress, the Lesbia of his lyrics, was Clodia, wife of consul Metellus Celer and sister of Clodius, Cicero's enemy. She inspired the great love lyrics like "Let us live and love, my Lesbia," the lines on the death of her sparrow, and later the poems of sensual passion, rage and disillusionment ("I hate and I love . . ."). Influenced by meter and form of Callimachus and other Alexandrians, Catullus evolved his own highly personal style to express forcefully his passions. Besides the lyrics, he wrote epigrams, the long poem *Attis,* the epithalamium *Thetis and Peleus,* and elegies. Strongly influenced work of Horace, Virgil, Martial, and was greatly admired as well as translated by English poets from Elizabethans on.

TRANSLATIONS: *Poems* tr. Horace Gregory (New York and London 1956; tr. Peter Whigham (Harmondsworth, England and Baltimore PB 1966). *Carmina* tr. Roger A. B. Mynors (London and New York 1958). *The Carmina of Catullus* tr. Barriss Mills (Lafayette, Ind. 1965).

REFERENCES: Eric A. Havelock *The Lyric Genius of Catullus* (rev. ed. New York 1967). Arthur L. Wheeler *Catullus and the Traditions of Ancient Poetry* (Berkeley, Calif. and Cambridge, England 1934, also PB).

CAVAFY, C(onstantine) P(eter) (Konstantinos Patrou Kabaphes). (Apr. 17, 1863 – Apr. 29, 1933). Greek poet. Born and died in Alexandria, Egypt; father's family, originally from Istanbul, became prominent in Alexandria. Spent part of childhood in England; English and French were his first languages. Returned to Alexandria (1878), spent two years in Istanbul (1881–83), then settled in Alexandria, working in government office and making visits to Paris, London, and Athens. Published little during lifetime; first introduced to English readers in E. M. Forster's *Pharos and Pharillon* (1923). John Mavrogordato's translations of some of his poems (1951) helped establish his reputation in English-speaking world. In free iambic verses he draws upon people and episodes in ancient history, especially in Hellenistic cities like Alexandria and Antioch, and upon sensual love affairs for his themes. His diction is at once an archaic and a colloquial Greek, free of any hyperbole. Truth that sometimes appears to be cynicism (as in *In a Township of Asia Minor* and the brilliant *Waiting for the Barbarians*) and unique insight into the relationship between the distant past and the immediate present mark his poetry.

TRANSLATIONS: *Poems* tr. John Mavrogordato (London 1951 and New York 1952). *The Complete Poems of Cavafy* tr. Rae Dalven (London and New York 1961, also PB). *Passions and Ancient Days* tr. Edmund Keeley and George Savidis (New York 1970).

REFERENCES: Peter Bien *Constantine Cavafy* (New York PB 1964). C. M. Bowra "Constantine Cavafy and the Greek Past" in *The Creative Experiment* (New York 1949, also PB). George Seferis *On the Greek Style: Selected Essays on Poetry and Hellenism* (tr. Boston 1966 and London 1967).

CAVALCANTI, Guido (c.1255 – Aug. 28/29, 1300). Italian poet and philosopher. Born and died in Florence. Friend of Dante, who admired his love lyrics, *Canzone d'amore,* and called his exquisite style *dolce stil novo.* The fifty surviving poems also include sonnets and ballades. Cavalcanti belonged to a distinguished Guelph family, married Beatrice, daughter of Farinata degli Uberti, leader of the Ghibellines. The Florentine citizens exiled leaders of both the Guelph and Ghibelline factions to Saranza, where Cavalcanti contracted the malaria of which he died.

TRANSLATION: *The Sonnets and Ballate of Guido Cavalcanti* tr. Ezra Pound (Boston and London 1912; in *The Translations of Ezra Pound* Norfolk, Conn. 1963, enlarged edition 1964).

REFERENCE: James E. Shaw *Guido Cavalcanti's Theory of Love: The Canzone d'Amore and Other Related Problems* (Toronto and London 1949).

CAVALLINI, Pietro (c.1250–c.1330). Italian painter and mosaicist. Born Rome, member of noble Cerroni family. The name Cavallini derives from nickname Caballinus, or Cavallinus. Much of his work has been lost, but Ghiberti's *Commentaries* give a careful account of his activities. Most of his major works were done in Rome, including decoration of S. Maria Maggiore (1273); apse mosaic in S. Maria in Trastevere (1291); fresco cycles in S. Paolo fuori le Mura (1282–97, known only through copies), S. Cecilia in Trastevere (1291–93), and S. Giorgio in Velabro (after 1295). In Naples (1308), where he later frescoed church of S. Maria Donnaregina (1316–20). Also in later years completed *Ascension* on entrance wall of upper church of S. Francesco at Assisi, and his influence dominated frescoes of upper section of nave walls. Cavallini ranks with Giotto (whom he may have assisted in mosaic of the navicella in Old St. Peter's) and Cimabue as a major innovator of the naturalism that replaced Byzantine style.

REFERENCE: Emilio Lavagnino *Pietro Cavallini* (Rome 1953).

CÉLINE, Louis Ferdinand (pseudonym of Louis Fuch Destouches) (May 27, 1894 – July 3, 1961). French novelist. Born Courbevoie, a Paris suburb; educated in public schools. Severely wounded in action in World War I, decorated for bravery. Completed medical studies at Rennes (1924) and traveled throughout world doing research for Rockefeller Foundation (1925–28). Divorced by wife Edith Follett, daughter of director of Rennes medical school (married 1919). Settled (1928) in poor district of Clichy, where he practiced medicine and wrote his two major novels, *Voyage au bout de la nuit* (1932, tr. *Journey to the End of the Night* 1934) and *Mort à credit* (1936, tr. *Death on the Installment Plan* 1938). Immediately acclaimed, these hallucinatory, autobiographical works, in seemingly crude, slangy style, expressing morbid despair and full of obscenity, crime, and the dregs of humanity, are precursors of black humor and the literature of the absurd. Married Lucette Almanzor, a dancer (1943). Suspected of Nazi affiliations because of his antiwar and anti-Semitic writings (1937–39), fled to Germany (1944) and thence to Copenhagen (1945), where French authorities imprisoned him. Released in 1947, he was permitted to return to France and spent last years as recluse and doctor for the poor in Meudon, outside Paris, where he died. Other important novels: *Guignol's Band* (1943, tr. 1954), *D'un Château à l'autre* (1957, tr. *Castle to Castle* 1969).

REFERENCES: Milton Hindus *The Crippled Giant: A Bizarre Adventure in Contemporary Letters* (New York 1950). Brika Ostrovsky *Céline and His Vision* (New York 1967, also PB).

CELLINI, Benvenuto (Nov. 3, 1500 – Feb. 13, 1571). Italian goldsmith and sculptor, author of celebrated autobiography. Born and died in Florence. Son of architect-musician, served apprenticeship to goldsmith. Exiled at sixteen for dueling, went to Siena, Bologna, Pisa, and Rome. Returned (1521) to Florence, and again fled (1523) after a fight. Back in Rome (1523–40), he received commissions from princes and popes for jewelry, medallions, and other small objects; meanwhile, his capacity for wrath, pride, and restlessness undiminished, he murdered two men (one a rival goldsmith), fought others, was imprisoned, escaped, and traveled frequently. Lived in France (1540–45) in service of Francis I; made for him famous saltcellar in gold and enamel with figures after Michelangelo, whom he greatly admired (1539–43, Kunsthistorisches Museum, Vienna), and *Nymph of Fontainebleau* (1543–44, Louvre, Paris). Returning to Florence as protégé of Cosimo de' Medici, he concentrated on full-scale sculpture; important examples are *Perseus* (cast by lost-wax method, 1554, Loggia dei Lanzi, Florence) and bust of Bindo Aldoviti (1550, Gardner Museum, Boston), both in bronze. Though Cellini developed classicism in his sculpture, his style remained essentially mannerist. Married his housekeeper, Piera di' Parigi (c.1564), mother of his two legitimate children. *The Life of Benvenuto Cellini* (written 1558–66, published 1728), full of extravagant accounts and the bragging characteristic of his age, gives vivid picture of Cellini's complex personality and of the period.

TRANSLATION: *The Life of Benvenuto Cellini* tr. John Addington Symonds (1888, rev. ed. John Pope-Hennessy, London and New York 1949, also PB).

CERVANTES SAAVEDRA, Miguel de (c.Sept. 29, 1547 – Apr. 23, 1616). Spanish novelist, playwright, poet. Born Alcalá de Henares, son of poor apothecary-surgeon. Probably educated at Valladolid (possibly by Jesuits), then Seville and university of Madrid. Became chamberlain to Cardinal Giulio Acquaviva (1569), traveling widely. Enlisted with forces of Diego de Urbina and served in fleet of Don John of Austria at battle of Lepanto (Oct. 7, 1571); permanently maimed left hand. Captured by Turks and imprisoned in Algiers (1575–80). Returned to Madrid (1581), wrote several plays and a pastoral novel *La Galatea* (1585). Married Catalina de Palacios Salazar y Vosmediano (1584). A troubled domestic life, misadventures, and poverty mark the next years, during which he served as commissary to navy and was imprisoned for fraud. Part I of *El Ingenioso Hidalgo* [*The Ingenious Gentleman*] *Don Quixote de la Mancha* (1605) brought recognition, was followed by part II (1615). Also produced *Novelas ejemplares*, twelve "cautionary tales" (1613), *Viaje del Parnaso* (*Journey from Parnassus*), long burlesque poem (1614), *Eight Comedies and Eight Interludes* (*Ocho Comedias y ocho entremeses nuevos*, 1615), and an allegory *Los Trabajos de Persiles y Sigismunda* (posthumous, 1617). Died in Madrid. In *Don Quixote*, Cervantes attacked contemporary romance forms with parody and satire, succeeded in inventing the novel.

TRANSLATIONS: *Complete Works* ed. James Fitzmaurice-Kelly (7 vols., unfinished, Glasgow 1901–1903). *Don Quixote* tr. Thomas Skelton (1612–20, London and New York 1900); tr. Peter Motteux (1700, London and New York 1909); tr. Samuel Putnam (New York 1949); tr. J. M. Cohen (Harmondsworth, England and Baltimore PB 1950).

REFERENCES: Aubrey F. G. Bell *Cervantes* (Norman, Okla. 1947, also PB). William J. Entwhistle *Cervantes* (London 1940 and New York 1941). James Fitzmaurice-Kelly *Miguel de Cervantes Saavedra* (London 1913). Richard L. Predmore *The World of Don Quixote* (Cambridge, Mass. and London 1947). Rudolph Schevill *Cervantes* (New York 1919).

MIGUEL DE CERVANTES SAAVEDRA
BY ALASTAIR REID

If ever the act of writing were heroic endeavor, surely it was never more so than in the case of Miguel de Cervantes Saavedra, who gave us the most durable work of literature we have. The astonishing truth is that his masterpiece, *El Ingenioso Hidalgo Don Quixote de la Mancha*, is as much of a best seller at this moment as it ever was, although it enjoyed great fame in his own lifetime; but even more astonishing is the fact that after more than three hundred and fifty years, it is still the most profound study ever made of the Spanish character, if not of the paradox of human nature. It is unquestionably the most *complete* book ever written, a vast tapestry of the Spain of Cervantes' day, a catalogue of human types, comic, satiric, and tragic all at once.

Don Quixote has proved so inexhaustible a study that several writers have devoted a fair part of their lives to unraveling its complexities — Miguel de Unamuno confessed himself transfixed by it, and wrote *Our Lord Don Quixote* almost as an extension of the work, while the pure paradoxes in it have preoccupied writers like Jorge Luís Borges, W. H. Auden, and Joaquín Casalduero. But even more fascinating is the fact that it is still not only read exhaustively in Spanish schools but read with intense pleasure — Spaniards are proud of it as a national possession, and I doubt whether any culture was ever so dominated and so defined by a single work of literature.

What is so fascinating about Don Quixote is that it contains, perfectly resolved, all the checkered circumstances of Cervantes' life. He was born in 1547 into a time when Spain was in the international ascendant, and he reflected his time by serving as a soldier, seeing a great deal of action, being captured by pirates, imprisoned in Algiers, and later having to scrape a living as a government tax collector in Spain, where he was eventually put in prison for fraud. It was in prison that he began to write *Don Quixote* and, when the first part was published in 1605, it received instant attention. Cervantes had all the satisfactions of being widely read in his own time, but his popularity brought him small financial yield, and he had to write furiously to keep alive. Moreover, *Don Quixote* was so popular that it was pirated, imitated, and plagiarized at once, so that, when a sequel by another writer (Alonso Fernández de Avellaneda) appeared in 1614, Cervantes was forced to work feverishly on the second part, which was published in 1615, the year before he died. His writing life was one of constant struggle, but his huge heart sustained him and he mirrored his time — both his own thought and observation, and the great sprawl of Spain — more

completely than has any writer before or since. Even without *Don Quixote* he would live through his *Exemplary Novels,* published in 1613; but of course it is his triumph to have contained so much in one single consistent work of the imagination.

Cervantes was no misunderstood genius who had to wait for the world to catch up with him — *Don Quixote* is made entirely out of contemporary characters, situations, and conventions. It was begun as a satire on the romances of the day, and might even have ended there had not the persona of Don Quixote come alive and begun to grow and exist in his own right. Even so, the Knight of the Sad Countenance was not a single incarnation of human aspirations, but was complemented by his squire Sancho Panza, the earthy peasant whose feet are as firmly fixed to the ground as is his master's head to the clouds. One does not have to know much about Spain to see that the Spanish character, so full of paradox, such a tangle of idealism and realism, is a mixture of knight and squire, and that the arguments which run on between them are precisely the arguments that each Spaniard has with himself, in his own nature. The wild adventures which befall Don Quixote on his unreal quests bring him into conflict with a slew of characters who represent almost every conceivable human attitude. But the genius of the book lies in the fact that it is never a *theory,* never a neat personification of any simplifying point of view — the wistful knight is intensely lovable beyond his insanities, even Sancho's grossness is sympathetic, and the sheer energy of the book, wildly funny in its slapstick episodes, unbearably sad in its disillusionments, is impossible to sum up or to boil down. Critics make a great deal out of the difference between the spirit of part I and part II, but even that difference is extremely hard to decipher exactly, since it is embodied in Don Quixote as a slow dawning, not an abrupt change of heart. Sufficient enough to point out that *Don Quixote* has survived more than three centuries of critical analysis; the final instance of all explanations of it is, triumphantly, the book itself.

There has never been a work so plundered and so plunderable, by painters, dramatists, choreographers, poets — it will continue to be mined by all the arts, for it is an inexhaustible source. It is a classic for which we need make no allowances of time, but rather which seems always to be coming true. It has been translated into the full span of literate languages, not once but over and over, and each age creates its own necessary version. It foreshadows the literary *jeux* of Nabokov, the existential paradoxes of Camus, the theatre of the absurd, and possibly some literary conventions yet unrealized. For any writer, it is an intimidating precedent; but equally, for any writer or reader, it is an achievement so towering as to be safely unsurpassable, nothing more nor less than the greatest book in the world.

CÉZANNE, Paul (Jan. 19, 1839 – Oct. 22, 1906). French painter. Born and died in Aix-en-Provence. Educated at Collège Bourbon, where he formed friendship with Émile Zola, who encouraged him to give up study of law and settle in Paris (1861). Here he met impressionists and (from 1862) devoted himself to painting, supported generously by wealthy father. Franco-Prussian War drove him to L'Estaque (1870), and he joined Pissarro at Pontoise (1872). Cézanne's early style, chiefly inspired by Courbet and Delacroix, was violent and naturalistic. Adopted impressionist techniques when he began working with Pissarro, then departed from these to an art which emphasized underlying geometric forms of visible objects, using color as means of modeling. His formula became the basis for cubism. Exhibited with impressionists (1874–77), but his genius did not begin to be recognized until c.1900. By time of his death, of diabetes, his fame was widespread. Cézanne is best known for his still lifes, landscapes, and groups of bathers.

REFERENCES: Kurt Badt *The Art of Cézanne* tr. Berkeley, Calif. and London 1965). Jean de Beucken *Cézanne: A Pictorial Biography* (tr. New York and London 1962). Roger Fry *Cézanne: A Study of His Development* (2nd ed. New York PB 1958). Jack Lindsay *Cézanne: His Life and Art* (London and Greenwich, Conn. 1969). Julius Meier-Graefe *Cézanne* (tr. New York 1927; London 1928). Alfred Neumayer ed. *Drawings* (New York 1958 and London 1959). John Rewald *Paul Cézanne: A Biography* (tr. New York 1948, also PB, and as *Ordeal of Paul Cézanne* London 1950). Meyer Schapiro *Paul Cézanne* (3rd ed. New York 1965). Lionello Venturi *Cézanne, son art, son oeuvre* (2 vols. Paris 1936).

✎

PAUL CÉZANNE
BY JAMES S. ACKERMAN

Nothing came easy to Cézanne. His art emerged from a constant struggle to reach an almost unattainable profundity. He would set every goal a little beyond his means and, unlike other artists, would never rest upon a facility he had gained. At first there was no facility to rest on; as an untrained beginner in the provinces and later in Paris, he had a heavy hand that blocked him from achieving the forms he wanted. The battle with every stroke produced some embarrassing failures along with some unforgettably powerful images. It took him a long time to find his real strengths. In his early paintings and drawings he tried to emulate complex and active narratives of traditional figure painting which were fundamentally alien to his nature; frequently he used his painting to work out sexual and sadistic fantasies.

Once he had found himself, Cézanne stopped painting events. The people he portrayed either do nothing in particular or they are immobilized in concentration on what they are doing, like the famous cardplayers. Perhaps the many compositions of bathers that he made throughout his career are an exception to this rule; they seem to engage actively in ordinary riverbank activities; but then, they are not meant to be seen as real people; invariably faceless, they are integers which the artist manipulates in a complex compositional equation the demands of which flatten and distort their bodies.

Cézanne's world is still to the point of being timeless. The landscapes, while they often give a vivid sense of reality, are rarely seen at a particular time of day or in particular light conditions, as Monet or Renoir would have seen them, but rather in a situation as permanent as if they had been represented by a sense of touch rather than of sight. Rarely are they committed to a season of the year.

Cézanne's penetrating to the unchanging essentials made him less radical in theme than his contemporaries who, from Courbet and Manet on, had searched for a new subject matter as a vehicle for their innovations in form and attitude. While the impressionists settled on the everyday diversions of a comfortable bourgeois society — dancing, drinking, boating — Cézanne stayed with the baroque genres: still life, idealized landscape, classic figural compositions, portraiture. He was no more concerned with commenting on the passing parade than in conveying momentary sense impressions; he sought and achieved

in painting structures as firm and as permanent as those of architecture. He liked to paint apples and oranges more than flowers and fish because they lasted longer, and he mortified his portrait subjects with interminable sittings. Cézanne revived still-life painting, which had become a minor art in the century since Chardin, and made of it a vehicle of monumental expression. That it kept this stature in cubist painting is one of the many signs of Cézanne's impact on modern art, particularly in its abstract forms.

The first impression we are likely to get from a Cézanne canvas is of the massiveness of the things in it. Every object seems solider, weightier than life. Another artist might paint a tree trunk or an orange so as to give an impression of the appearance of its surface in a particular light; Cézanne would paint it as if he were building it up, plane by plane, each brushstroke corresponding to one of the planes, like a brick in a curved wall, so that we get not only a clear impression of the surface but an extraordinary sense of the body beneath. Cézanne had a way of imparting density to everything; in his paintings of the Mediterranean at L'Estaque the water seems no less solid than the buildings alongside it.

Ultimately, the structure of individual objects — trees, oranges, ocean — was a function of the structure of the entire image, to the point that the appearance of things could be distorted grossly by the exigencies of their position within a composition. Every inch of the painted surface contributes actively to the structure; there is no neutral "back" ground because stretches of wallpaper or of sky are fashioned with as much vitality and commitment as the objects up front.

To impart a structural vitality to the whole canvas, Cézanne abandoned the perspective system of the Renaissance with its emphasis on the foreground and diagonals reaching to a point on the horizon. He found that he could convey an illusion of space by the overlapping of the planes into which he analyzed forms; often he gave the dominant planes more or less horizontal and vertical edges in response to the borders of his canvas. Diagonals, no longer required by the perspective system, he could use freely for expressive emphasis. But this could not have been done without radical innovations in color.

Cézanne learned from the impressionists — particularly Pissarro, with whom he began to paint in 1871 — to replace with brighter hues the soupy tones that deadened the backgrounds of his early pictures. But he did not follow the impressionists in fragmenting every surface into dabs of pure pigment; his color never is brilliant; the blues have a silver-gray tone, the yellows tend toward ocher (he was fond of using these two together), and the range of light-dark values is restricted. At first, Cézanne applied colors in a heavy impasto; in his maturity, in dense glazes. But in the later work, every stroke is distinct and defines a plane; gradually the pigment thins out to a watercolor-like transparency without losing its capacity to convey the impression of density. The last landscapes, constructed of an incredible variety of greens, blues, and earth hues, become increasingly geometric; they seem in retrospect to prophesy the coming of cubism.

Cézanne's pictures belong to a tradition of classic art that extends to the ancient Greeks; it shares with its great predecessors in that tradition the capacity to form a world more grave and silent than the world about us. Cézanne distilled from his sense perceptions structures more abstract than those of his antecedents, but no less real.

CHABRIER, (Alexis) Emmanuel (Jan. 18, 1841 – Sept. 13, 1894). French composer. Born Ambert, Puy-de-Dôme. Studied law in Paris (1858–62) and worked for French ministry of interior (1862–80). Meanwhile studied music with private teachers, began to compose as amateur, and was friend of leading artistic figures Manet, Verlaine, and fellow musicians Henri Duparc, d'Indy, Fauré. Married Marie Alice Dejean (1873). Among early works: operettas *L'Étoile* (1877) and *Une Éducation manquée* (1879). After hearing Wagner's *Tristan und Isolde* at Munich (1879), decided to resign from government service and devote himself to composition. Publication of *Dix Pièces pittoresques* (1881) for piano was followed by trip to Spain, whose folk music provided inspiration for much of his subsequent work. Well-known compositions include: for orchestra, *España* (1883; his first great success and still most frequently heard work) and *Joyeuse Marche* (1888); for piano, *Trois Valses romantiques* (1883, for two pianos), *Habañera* (1885), *Bourrée fantasque* (1891); comic opera *Le Roi malgré lui* (1887). Died in Paris. Chabrier's music displays wit, exuberance, often broad humor. He developed a sophisticated Parisian style, with unconventional instrumental combinations and bold harmonies; Ravel, Erik Satie, and Les Six were particularly indebted to him.

REFERENCE: G. Servières *Emmanuel Chabrier* (Paris 1912).

CHAMBERS, Sir William (1723 – Mar. 8, 1796). British architect. Born Stockholm, Sweden, son of a Scottish merchant. Educated in England; at sixteen joined Swedish East India Company. A voyage to China was the basis for his *Designs of Chinese Buildings* (1757). Left sea (1749) to study architecture in Paris and Rome, with Joseph Wilton and C. L. Clérisseau. Returned to England (1755), married, and became architectural tutor to Prince of Wales (George III). In his extremely successful career from then on he became one of the two architects of the works (the other was Robert Adam), comptroller of the works, and surveyor general. He was knighted (1771) and was a dominant figure in the Royal Academy from its founding (1768). Chief work, Somerset House in London, a block of government offices. Others are the casino at Marino, near Dublin, and the ornamental buildings, of which only the pagoda survives, at Kew Palace, Surrey (1757–62). Despite Kew, he was basically a conservative, refining the English Palladian manner with elements of French classicism. His *A Treatise on Civil Architecture* (1759) became a standard and influential work on classic design. Died in London; buried in Westminster Abbey.

REFERENCE: Arthur T. Edwards *Sir William Chambers* (London and New York 1924).

CHAMFORT, Sebastien Roch Nicolas (c.1741 – Apr. 13, 1794). French journalist, playwright, and aphorist. Parentage unknown; brought up in village near Clermont-Ferrand. Educated through the church at Collège des Grassins, but rejected priesthood. In Paris, began to achieve notice as brilliant conversationalist and man of letters. Contributed to *Journal Encyclopédique* (1761–63). Produced one-act comedy, *La Jeune Indienne* (1764). Won first prize from Académie Française for *Éloge de Moliere* (1769) and from Académie de Marseille for *Éloge de La Fontaine* (1774). Tragedy *Mustapha et Zéangir* (1776) brought him a pension from the royal family and confirmed his success in high society. Elected to Académie Française (1781). A friend of Mirabeau, he worked as a ghost writer for various moderate revolutionaries. With Jacobins who stormed Bastille (1789), and later secretary of Jacobin club. Disillusioned by the revolution, he was persecuted under the Terror for his outspoken opinions, and when about to be arrested a second time attempted suicide (1793), dying later in agony of his wounds. His major works, *Maximes et pensées, Caractères,* and *Anecdotes,* as well as his *Tableaux*

de la révolution française, appeared posthumously.

TRANSLATION: *The Maxims and Considerations of Chamfort* tr. E. P. Mathers (2 vols. Boston 1926).

REFERENCE: Julien Teppe *Chamfort, sa vie, son oeuvre, sa pensée* (Paris 1950).

✍

SEBASTIEN ROCH NICOLAS CHAMFORT
BY W. S. MERWIN

From his birth to his reputation, both the life and the writings of Chamfort present a series of enigmas many of which seem to be proof against all examination. He was aware of some of the paradoxes he embodied:

"My whole life is a fabric of apparent contrasts with my principles. I have no love for princes and I am attached to a princess and a prince. I am known for my republican maxims and several of my friends wear decorations presented by the monarchy. I love voluntary poverty and I live with the rich. I flee honors and one or two have sought me out . . ." Elsewhere in his *Maxims and Thoughts* he says: "What I admire in the ancient philosophers is the desire to make their conduct conform to their writings."

The passages are important in the complex and unresolved dialogue which the maxims and other sections of Chamfort's "Products of the Perfected Civilization" prove to be. And they bespeak something in Chamfort himself that makes even the contemplation of his suicide at last a source of further questions, instead of the triumphant proof of consistency which, at first sight, it seems.

Chamfort's literary output falls into two separate and indeed antithetical sections. The first is made up of academic eulogies of French classical authors, three plays which embrace in three different ways the theatrical conventions of the period, a theatrical dictionary, and other works which contributed to the considerable reputation that was Chamfort's in his lifetime; they (assisted, to a degree we can only guess at, by his personal charm and his celebrated wit) won him the acquaintance and patronage of some of the rich and powerful in France, including Marie Antoinette herself, and a seat in the Academy, an income, and the praise and censure of contemporary critics in print and elsewhere which provided material for a number of his reflections about human malice, the vanity of literary glory, and the inducements to retirement and silence. With the exceptions of a few literary observations in the eulogies, this first section of his writings is now virtually without interest. The second division of Chamfort's work is made up almost exclusively of writings which were neither published nor known during his lifetime — the chapters of maxims, thoughts, portraits and anecdotes, which he had begun, at least, to collect under the title "Products of the Perfected Civilization." What we have come to think of as the real Chamfort is almost all in this collection, but having recognized the fact we are faced at once with an impasse that seems to typify the study of him. These writings were found by P. L. Ginguené after Chamfort's death; they had been scribbled on separate scraps of paper and left in no particular order. Many of them had vanished before Ginguené could protect them; those that reached his hands he arranged under headings and published in the first *Collected Works* in the Year III of the revolution (1795). But the original manuscript was subsequently lost and there is no way now of being sure whether Chamfort regarded all of these entries as finished, or in what order he would

have presented them. Most serious and baffling of all, perhaps, is that there is no way of forming opinions with any hope of accuracy about when, and with reference to what circumstances, individual entries may have been written, so that when two passages seem inconsistent we cannot tell whether the disparity represents a change, a shift of emphasis in time, or a contradiction dividing Chamfort at a single given moment.

The question is especially important because one aspect or another of an essential contradiction is at the source of much of the interest, pain, and intensity of Chamfort's best writing, and the desire for consistency, or what that figment represented to him, was one of his unfulfilled but unrelinquished passions. The bitterness for which he is famous ("In studying the ills of nature one acquires a contempt for death. In studying the ills of society one acquires a contempt for life") expresses a vehement rejection of hope in general, of human aspiration and society, and in the end of experience and action themselves, since the purpose of both is said to be inadequate to the risks and deceptions they involve. But the rejection is usually couched in terms of justification; it is described as a preference based on moral superiority and as a reaction to the indignities that are all that society has to offer it. Yet the moral principles which Chamfort is invoking are never clearly nor coherently presented, and the fragmentary and uncomposed nature of the material itself is not the main reason for this incompleteness. His "philosophy," insofar as it can be inferred from the fragments that have come down to us, was in itself a largely unformed miscellany of Rousseau and other figures of the Enlightenment, and of various assumptions commonly associated with stoicism. His search for a moral finality grounded in the innermost life of the individual was essentially a private and religious one, yet his approach to it was wholly and even narrowly secular, and his expression of it (even though he made no attempt to publish it while he lived) took a form that had been shaped by and assumed the presence and values of a sophisticated public. The ultimate interest of his attitude and his writings does not lie in the principles which he invoked but in the sharpness of observation to which his mixture of disenchantment and moral unrest continually spurred him; and these in turn indicate a profound contradiction. One returns to some of the best of Chamfort as one might to the work of a poet because of the intensity and directness with which it speaks for a condition that is at once universal and unique.

CHAPMAN, George (c.1559 – May 12, 1634). English poet, dramatist, and translator of Homer. Born Hitchin, Hertfordshire. Probably studied at Oxford and Cambridge. In London published first poem, *The Shadow of the Night* (1594), followed by *Ovid's Banquet of Sense* (1595). Began career as major Elizabethan playwright with comedy *Blind Beggar of Alexandria* (1596), and started his great masterpiece, the translation of Homer (part of *Iliad* appeared 1598, completed rendition 1611, *Odyssey* 1614–15, *Hymns* 1624). Praised by Pope, the translation inspired Keats's great sonnet *On First Looking into Chapman's Homer*. Chapman's plays include tragedies *Bussy d'Ambois* (1607) and *The Conspiracy and Tragedy of Charles Duke of Byron* (1608), comedies *All Fools* (1605), *The Gentleman Usher* (1611), *Monsieur D'Olive* (1606), and, in collaboration with Ben Jonson and John Marston, *Eastward Ho!* (1605), whose mocking allusions to the Scots offended James I and incurred imprisonment of the authors. Chapman regained court favor, however, and produced royal masque

(1614). Was in financial straits all his life despite patronage of Prince Henry and earl of Somerset. Died in London.

EDITIONS: *The Plays and Poems of George Chapman* ed. Thomas M. Parrott (London and New York 1910–14). *The Poems of George Chapman* ed. Phyllis Bartlett (New York and London 1941).
REFERENCES: George de F. Lord *Homeric Renaissance: The Odyssey of George Chapman* (New Haven and, as *Odyssey of George Chapman*, London 1956). Millar McLure *George Chapman: A Critical Study* (Toronto 1966). Ennis S. Rees *The Tragedies of George Chapman: Renaissance Ethics in Action* (Cambridge, Mass. and London 1954).

CHAPMAN, John Jay (Mar. 2, 1862 – Nov. 4, 1933). American writer. Born in New York City; father president of New York Stock Exchange until money lost in panic of 1870's. Graduated from Harvard (1884) and traveled in Europe, where he met Tennyson and Henry James. Admitted to New York bar (1888), practiced law for ten years, though he disliked it. In 1887 Chapman deliberately burned his left hand after beating a youth whom he accused of trifling with his fiancée Minna Timmins. Married her (1889); they had three sons. Joined City Reform Club, published *The Political Nursery*, a review (1897–1901). Wife died (1897) and following year Chapman married Elizabeth Chanler of wealthy family, and was able to live rest of his life as something of a country squire at Tarrytown-on-the-Hudson, N.Y. Published best-known work, *Emerson and Other Essays* (1898), reinterpreting Emerson and attacking Walt Whitman. Same year published *Causes and Consequences*, a tract against business power in government. Chapman had wide-ranging interests: classics (*Greek Genius and Other Essays*, 1915), politics (*William Lloyd Garrison*, 1913), and religion (*Notes on Religion*, 1922). An intellectual maverick, Chapman cannot be simply described: a moralist, yet later accused of being a bigot; a playwright whose works seem more literary than dramatic (*Benedict Arnold*, 1909);

and a great letter writer, even in his most erratic moods. He died in Poughkeepsie, N.Y.

EDITION: *John Jay Chapman and His Letters* ed. M. A. DeW. Howe (Boston, 1937).
REFERENCES: Melvin H. Bernstein *John Jay Chapman* (New York 1964, also PB). Richard B. Hovey *John Jay Chapman: An American Mind* (New York 1959 and London 1960). Edmund Wilson "John Jay Chapman" in *The Triple Thinkers: Ten Essays on Literature* (New York and London 1938, also PB).

CHARDIN, Jean Baptiste Siméon (Nov. 2, 1699 – Dec. 6, 1779). French painter. Born and died in Paris, son of a carpenter. Studied painting under Pierre Jacques Cazes and Noël Nicolas Coypel. Began career by painting details in other artists' works and signposts for shopkeepers; gained recognition when several of his canvases appeared in exhibition of young painters in the Place Dauphine (1728). Elected to Academy that year. Chardin's individual style was fully developed in the 1730's: his subjects were still life and genre, and his technique, notable for unmixed colors and emphasis on abstract composition, introduced a new simplicity to the rococo era and looked forward to the work of Cézanne. Widespread success came with his exhibition at the Salon (1737). Elected treasurer of the Academy (1755). The pastel portraits executed in his last years are perhaps his finest achievement. Famous works include *The Skate* (1728, Louvre, Paris), *Pourvoyeuse* (Louvre), and his pastel *Self-Portrait* (1775, Louvre).

REFERENCES: *Chardin, 1699–1779* with an introduction and notes by Walter de la Mare (London PB 1948). Pierre Rosenberg *Chardin: Biographical and Critical Study* (tr. Cleveland 1963).

CHARLES, DUKE OF ORLÉANS (known as **CHARLES D'ORLÉANS**) (Nov. 24, 1394 – Jan. 4, 1465). French poet. Born Paris, nephew of Charles VI of France. Married his cousin Isabella, widow of Richard II of England (1406; she died 1409), and succeeded to duchy after father's assassination by Burgundians (1407). Cemented alliance with count of Armagnac by marrying his daughter Bonne (1410; she died 1435). Captured by English at Agincourt (1415), he remained prisoner until 1440, when he was ransomed by duke of Burgundy, whose niece, Marie de Clèves, he married. In retirement at Blois, Charles devoted rest of life to writing verse and entertaining literary men. His poems, in French, Latin, and English, include chansons, ballades, and rondeaux. Considered the last of the medieval poets, he is noted for his intense subjectivity and graceful manipulation of the meters and figures of speech traditional in court poetry. Died at Amboise, leaving two daughters and a son who was to become Louis XII of France.

REFERENCES: Jacques Charpier *Charles d'Orléans* (Paris 1958). Norma Lorre Goodrich *Charles, Duke of Orleans: A Literary Biography* (New York 1963).

CHASSÉRIAU, Théodore (Sept. 20, 1819 – Oct. 8, 1856). French painter. Born Samaná, Dominican Republic, where his father was French consul. Family moved to Paris (1822), where he studied under Ingres (1830–34). First pictures shown (Salon of 1836) won immediate admiration, confirmed (1839) by *Suzanne au bain* and *Vénus Anadyomène* (both in Louvre, Paris). *Le Christ au jardin des oliviers* (1840, church of St. Jean d'Angély) shows the dualism characteristic of his subsequent work, in which he attempted to combine the classicism of Ingres with the romanticism of Delacroix and the latter's color and vitality. From 1836, in his sketches of Bedouins at Marseilles, then after a visit to Algeria (1846), Arab themes were predominant in his work. Important commissions: frescoes in the churches of St. Merri (1843) and St. Roch (1854) and in the Cour des Comptes in the Palais d'Orsay (1844–48, mostly destroyed in burning of Palace, 1871). Other major works include portraits *Père Lacordaire* (1841, Louvre) and *Les Deux Soeurs* (1843, Louvre), *Othello* etchings (1844); *Portrait équestre d'Ali ben Hamet, calife de Constantine* (1848, Musée de Versailles) and *Le Tepidarium* (1853, Louvre). Died in Paris.

REFERENCES: Valbert Chevillard *Un Peintre romantique: Théodore Chassériau* (Paris 1893). Henry Marcel and Jean Laran *Chassériau* (Paris 1911). Léonce Bénédite *Théodore Chassériau, Sa vie et son oeuvre* (Paris 1932).

CHATEAUBRIAND, François René de (Sept. 4, 1768 – July 4, 1848). French writer and statesman. Born St. Malo into family of old Breton nobility. Received commission in army (1786); in Paris (1787–90) he witnessed outbreak of the revolution. Left for America (1791) on project for discovery of Northwest Passage, but route obscure after Niagara. On return to France married young heiress Céleste Buisson de Lavigne (1792) and joined émigré army in Rhineland. In exile and penury in London (1793–1800) published first book, *Essai historique, politique et moral sur les revolutions* (1797). Tragic family experiences as a result of the revolution turned Chateaubriand towards Christianity. Returned to France (1800) and published *Atala* (1801); like *René* (1802) it became a romantic episode in *Le Génie du christianisme* (1802), which established him as France's leading writer and helped revive religious feeling, as well as literary interest in nature. His diplomatic career began with appointment by Napoleon as secretary to legation in Rome (1803), but execution of the duc d'Enghien (1804) turned him bitterly anti-Bonapartist. Traveled in Greece, Near East, and Spain (1806–1807). Upon restoration of Bourbons and Louis XVIII, was made peer of France (1815). Served as ambassador to Prussia (1821) and Great Britain (1822), and represented France at Congress of Verona (1822). After brief appointments as minister of foreign affairs (1823) and ambassador to Rome (1828), he retired from politics (1830). Died in Paris. His great memoirs, *Mémoires d'outre-tombe* were published posthumously (1849–50). He initiated romantic movement in France, and his style influenced poetry, history, and the novel. Other works include *Les Martyrs* (1809), *Itinéraire de Paris à Jérusalem* (1811), *Les Natchez* (1826), *Les Aven-*

tures du dernier des Abencérages (short Moorish novel, 1826), *Voyage en Amérique* (1827), and *Vie de Rancé* (1844).

TRANSLATIONS: *Atala* and *René* tr. Irving Putter (Berkeley, Calif. PB 1952). *The Memoirs of Chateaubriand* tr. Robert Baldick (London and New York 1961).

REFERENCES: Joan Evans *Chateaubriand* (London and New York 1939). André Maurois *Chateaubriand: Poet, Statesman, Lover* (tr. London and New York 1938). Friedrich Sieburg *Chateaubriand* (tr. London 1961 and New York 1962). Victor L. Tapié *Chateaubriand par lui-même* (Paris 1965).

✍

FRANÇOIS RENÉ
DE CHATEAUBRIAND
BY GEORGE D. PAINTER

Chateaubriand himself divided his career into three distinct parts, a trinity which forms a unity: the traveler, the writer, the statesman. No man of action has ever been so great a writer, and no great writer such a man of action. In all three characters he pursued the romantic quest for a reality identical with the ideal.

Like other writers of innovatory genius he derived from childhood and youth the tensions that would motivate his work, the experiences that would provide its themes and symbols, and the reading of his predecessors that would fashion its revolutionary means of expression. His father's severity and mother's neglect, though both half fancied, deprived him of the love and interior peace which he would seek forever in vain. The adoration of his sister Lucile began the search for an unattainable counterpart of himself. The stormy seascapes of his birthplace, St. Malo in Brittany, the wooded solitudes of his father's castle at Combourg, gave him the romantic view of wild nature as an image of the writer's soul. He read the classics and preromantics who had pioneered his way:

Rousseau, Goethe's *Werther*, Bernardin de Saint-Pierre's *Paul et Virginie*, Macpherson's *Ossian*, Homer, Virgil, Fénelon, Bossuet, Milton, Gray.

The revolution drove him from France as an émigré aristocrat. In 1791 he sailed to America, saw President Washington and Niagara, traveled down the Ohio and back over the Alleghenies. After seven years of exile in England he returned to France in 1800, served Napoleon with love-hatred till 1804, and then boldly opposed his growing tyranny. "Chateaubriand has the sacred fire," declared Napoleon at St. Helena. The alternating explosions and repressions of his time brought historic necessity to his inner need for reconciliation between liberty and discipline, progress and tradition, future and past: eternal problems which he was among the first to explore at a profound level of creative imagination.

His first works, *Essai . . . sur les révolutions* (1797) and *Le Génie du christianisme* (1802), were attempts at vast world pictures, the first to explain the French Revolution as a historical process, the second, in revulsion after his reconversion to religion ("I wept and believed"), to present the Catholic faith as a divine instrument of human advance in art, sensibility, and true liberty. Concurrently he wrote *Les Natchez* (first published in 1826), an enormous Miltonic epic in prose, complete with mythological machinery, but intensely original in style and exotic atmosphere. The hero René, a young French exile who joins a Red Indian tribe and resembles the author not in name only, witnesses and personifies the conflict between corrupt civilization and the noble savage, the dichotomy between convention and freedom in the human psyche.

In *Le Génie* he inserted two episodes from *Les Natchez* which made him immediately and internationally famous. *Atala* (prepublished separately in 1801) is the tragic love tale of a Red Indian warrior and maiden, set in sublime dreamlike landscapes of the American wilderness; and *René*, with its celebrated invocation to the "longed-for tempests" of passion and death (*"Levez-vous, orages désirés . . ."*), is the story of his own youth at Combourg and his intimacy with Lucile. *Les Martyrs* (1809), another prose epic, on the persecution of the Christians under Diocletian (here equated with the despotism of Napoleon), resembles *Les Natchez* in its imitation of Homer and Milton, and in its significance as a double allegory of his own life and of the history of his time; but it marks a change of direction from his former extremist romanticism towards a personal neoclassicism and perfection of style, culminating in *Itinéraire de Paris à Jérusalem* (1811), a narrative of his journey to Greece and the Near East in 1806–1807 made "in quest of images" for *Les Martyrs*. His next and last major work published in his lifetime, *Vie de Rancé* (1844), a biography of the seventeenth-century Trappist monk, was written in old age with autobiographical violence of feeling and rejuvenated audacity of style, and is nowadays considered his masterpiece next to his memoirs.

During his career as statesman from 1814 to 1830, when he published little but a superb series of political pamphlets, Chateaubriand was ambassador in Berlin (1821), London (1822), Rome (1828–29), and foreign minister in 1823–24. As a one-man liberal opposition he strove to save the ungrateful Bourbon monarchy from itself, but hastened its downfall by goading its reactionary obstinacy. He has been accused of ambitious opportunism, but in fact, by his repeated resignations of office and pay in loyalty to his principles, he passes the supreme test of political sincerity, and his defeats were moral victories which ensured the survival of his cause. Meanwhile women pursued, captured, and lost him; but to two he remained faithful till death in his fashion, the star of beauty Madame Récamier, and his own clever, ill-tempered, longsuffering wife, who called his mistresses "the Madams," and Madame Récamier "the Arch-Madam."

After refusing allegiance to the usurping Louis Philippe in 1830, and supporting the Bourbon duchesse de Berry in 1833 ("Madame, your son is my king!"), Chateaubriand devoted his old age to the completion and elaboration of his posthumous memoirs, the work of forty years which he had conceived in 1803, begun in 1809, and resolved to keep unpublished till after his death. All his other works had been attempts to universalize his own life and personality in allegorical form, and their real power had lain in their autobiographical elements rather than in their fiction. Now at last, in a direct presentation through imaginative vision of the whole reality of his world, he found his true greatness as a writer. His *Mémoires d'outre-tombe* (*Memories from Beyond the Grave*) are at once, as he planned, "the explanation of my inexplicable heart" and "the epic of my time." As an autobiography they are a Quest for Time Lost with affinity to Proust's, full of moments of affective memory when past becomes identical with present; as history they treat immense human movements with unparalleled poetic grandeur and insight. This vast work (nearly a million words in its completest form) is among the supreme creations of imaginative realism, and deserves to be read not in selections but as an organic whole.

Chateaubriand holds in French romanticism a place which has no equivalent in English: that of a prose writer comparable in stature to the major romantic poets. He enlarged the scope and resources of human sensibility, and created a style of modern immediacy and daring with the harmony and rhythm of great music. He influenced Hugo, Flaubert, Baudelaire, Proust, even his enemies Sainte-Beuve and Sartre. Joubert called him the Enchanter; "There are few of us who do not owe to him all we were, are, or will be," wrote Lamartine in 1834; "We owe him almost everything," wrote Julien Gracq in 1960. His reputation, after many vicissitudes, approaches a new peak. Chateaubriand is now seen as a founder of modernism, as one of the most permanently contemporary and inexhaustible bequests from the nineteenth century to the readers, writers, and critics of the twentieth.

CHATTERTON, Thomas (Nov. 20, 1752 – Aug. 24, 1770). English poet. Born and died in Bristol. Posthumous son of a writing master who possessed fifteenth-century manuscripts which interested the precocious youth. At sixteen wrote for Bristol *Journal* a description supposedly taken from ancient manuscript of *The Friar's First Passing over the Old Bridge*. Had also written a number of poems which he attributed to ancient writers, principally to one Thomas Rowley. Attempted to interest Horace Walpole in these, and in a history of ancient painters Chatterton claimed to have discovered (1769). Discouraged by reception, went to London, where he wrote poems, political diatribes, and satires for periodicals, living in near-destitution. At length, desperate with his situation and lack of literary recognition, he poisoned himself before his eighteenth birthday. His poetry immediately began to be read and admired for its vigorous, inventive imagination and depth of feeling. Thomas Tyrwhitt first exposed "Thomas Rowley" (1777–78), but a controversy continued until Walter William Skeat proved that the poems were Chatterton's own in his edition of *The Poetical Works of Thomas Chatterton* (1871).

EDITIONS: *The Poetical Works of Thomas Chatterton* ed. Walter William Skeat (London 1871). *The Complete Poetical Works of Thomas Chatterton* ed. Henry D. Roberts (2 vols. London and New York 1906). REFERENCES: Edward H. W. Meyerstein *Life of Thomas Chatterton* (New York and London 1930). John C. Nevill *Thomas Chatterton* (London 1948).

CHAUCER, Geoffrey (c.1343–1400). English poet. Born London into family of prosperous wine merchants; probably received early education at St. Paul's Cathedral School. Served as page (1357 or earlier) in household of countess of Ulster, wife to Prince Lionel. Captured on military campaign in France (1360). Possibly later studied at one of the Inns of Court or was in service of King Edward III. Married (c.1366) Philippa Roet, one of the queen's ladies, and was listed among the esquires of the royal household (1368); his duties often entailed diplomatic missions on the Continent, including his first journey to Italy (1372–73). Appointed controller of customs of port of London (1374), he was also involved in several diplomatic missions (1376–81). Made controller of the petty customs (1382) and continued active public life, serving as justice of the peace in Kent (1385) and for one session as member of Parliament (1386). Held important position of clerk of the king's works (1389) but resigned (1391) and became deputy forester for royal forest of Petherton until his death. Buried at Westminster Abbey. Despite his active career of civil service, Chaucer's literary output was large. It is usually divided into three periods: his earliest works draw heavily on French models and include dream visions such as *The Book of the Duchess* (1369) and *The House of Fame* (c.1375–80); strong Italian influence (1380–86) marks *The Parliament of Fowls, Troilus and Criseyde* (based on Boccaccio's *Filostrato*), and *The Legend of Good Women;* England is the scene, however, of his masterpiece *The Can-*

terbury Tales (1387–1400), a great project still uncompleted at his death.

EDITION: *The Works of Geoffrey Chaucer* ed. Fred N. Robinson (2nd ed. Boston and London 1957).

REFERENCES: Marchette G. Chute *Geoffrey Chaucer of England* (New York 1946, also PB). George G. Coulton *Chaucer and His England* (8th ed. London and New York 1963, also PB). George Lyman Kittredge *Chaucer and His Poetry* (Cambridge, Mass. 1915). John Livingston Lowes *Geoffrey Chaucer and the Development of His Genius* (Boston and, as *Geoffrey Chaucer,* London 1934; also PB as *Geoffrey Chaucer*).

✍

CHAUCER

BY THEODORE MORRISON

Chaucer's identity and many of his activities are abundantly established by historical records, but the records are impersonal, occurring in royal household account books, transcripts of law cases, notices of appointments and of perquisites such as pensions and allowances of clothing or wine. Chaucer was similarly "objective" in his work. He lurks behind his characters and stories. His references to himself largely take the form of self-kidding, though he may well have been truthful, at least about his later years, in confessing that he was portly, "a fine poppet for a woman to embrace," as the Host twits him in *The Canterbury Tales,* or "hoar and round of shape," as he describes himself and his friend in his *Envoy to Scogan.* Yet his works do give certain irresistible impressions of his temperament: his love of letters and learning, of old books, old traditions, old authorities, including the sciences of his day, which he absorbed with unfailing zest and tenacious memory; his sense of humor and irony, which he could never long repress, even when dealing with essentially tragic or pathetic materials; his warm and rich appetite for people, learned and ignorant, dignified and rowdy alike.

In a turbulent half-century that saw the Black Death, the Peasants' Revolt, the schism of the papacy, and varying episodes in England's long dynastic wars with France, Chaucer's life as a man of affairs may well have been the busiest ever to compete with the needs of a poet for leisure to read, reflect, and exercise his talent. For once he must have been literally autobiographical when, in *The House of Fame,* he described himself hurrying home to his quarters over Aldgate, after a day of keeping his accounts as comptroller of the wool customs for the port of London, to go to bed at last with book and candle and read into the small hours. Yet the very range of his activities shows how it was possible for him to gain his knowledge of both letters and people. As a young man he was captured in the French wars — perhaps no very dangerous adventure in itself — and Edward III paid or contributed to his ransom. Later he was sent to Genoa on a negotiating mission of commercial importance, during which he was detached on secret royal business to Florence, and again he was sent to Italy to help negotiate a royal marriage. These Italian journeys, acquainting him with the language and at least some of the writings of Dante, Petrarch, and Boccaccio, were of crucial importance to his literary growth. One of the busy posts he held under Richard II was the clerkship of the king's Works. In this capacity he supervised the maintenance or construction of buildings, managed payrolls, and took custodianship of assorted royal valuables and junk such as a broken cable and a frying pan. He was twice the victim of what we should call payroll robberies. These and many more activities make a wistful reminder, in an age given to talk of alienation and the isolation of the artist, that Chaucer as a poet could work, write, and view himself as a full participating member of his nation and his society.

Modern readers rightly enough neglect Chaucer's edifying works, but they were extensive. Aside from such labors as his prose translation of Boethius, edification intruded even into his great *comédie humaine, The Canterbury Tales.* The Second Nun's Tale is a life of St. Cecilia. The good Parson's "little thing in prose," which was to wind up the Canterbury pilgrimage on a pious note, is a staggeringly long and dreary moralizing treatise. Chaucer did not come at once to his mature achievements, *Troilus and Criseyde* and the best of the *Tales.* He began as a composer in English of ballades and roundels on the fashionable French model. It is a sobering thought that Chaucer might not have become an English poet at all, but might have written in French or Latin. Chaucer also worked in the tradition of the French dream allegory, telling us that he translated its chief example, *The Romance of the Rose,* though how much if any of the existing Middle English version is his remains uncertain. Of Chaucer's dream-framed poems, *The Book of the Duchess* and the unfinished *The House of Fame* contain episodes no Chaucerian would want to lose, but they are written in the prolix, helter-skelter, four-stress couplets he had to outgrow. *The Parliament of Fowls* is complete and charming, and its rhyme royal stanzas show Chaucer in full command of the pentameter line, the instrument of his greatest work, and beginning to exploit his gift of dialogue counterpointed against meter that flowered to the full in the talk of Pandarus and the Canterbury pilgrims. Chaucer returned once later to the dream frame in the

Prologue, existing in two versions, of *The Legend of Good Women.* Here are some of his most ingratiating and personal notes; but his most sophisticated and amusing treatment of dreams occurs in *The Canterbury Tales,* in the famous discussion between Chanticleer, the learned cock, and Pertelote, his favorite hen.

Exposure to Italy and its poets greatly liberated Chaucer's conception of his art, but the unique gift as a comic realist that emerged in full force in *The Canterbury Tales* was his own. On the way to the *Tales,* he translated and transformed the story of Troilus and Cressida from Boccaccio's *Filostrato. Troilus and Criseyde* is Chaucer's greatest completed work, and one of the great narratives in English of any sort. If it is not in the fullest sense a tragic work, this is for no lack of tragic vision. Witness the climactic scene when Troilus stands daylong on the Trojan wall, peering toward the Greek encampment and expecting the promised return of Cressida on the tenth day. Chaucer presses the emotions of the young Troilus to their limit. Bitterly acknowledging that Cressida has not come, Troilus cries out that nonetheless he still feels at heart an unexplainable joy that must be a good omen. The conflict between illusion and fact, the intuitions of the heart and the treachery of circumstance, could not be put more sharply. If we do not feel the scene as unreservedly tragic, it is because we are conscious, standing all the while beside Troilus, of Chaucer's most sophisticated, subtle, original character, the well-enough-meaning, worldly, busybody Pandarus, who agrees with everything Troilus says but laughs quietly to himself, saying in effect that from never-never land will come all that Troilus so confidently expects. "Yea,

farewell all the snows of far-off years!" The genuine sympathy of Pandarus is tinctured with the wry amusement of experience. The reader shares it, and the tragic conception is blended with urbane irony.

The Canterbury Tales inevitably remained unfinished. If each pilgrim, according to the Host's plan, had told two stories on the way to St. Thomas à Becket's shrine and two on the way back, Chaucer would have had to compose about one hundred and twenty stories, besides carrying on the byplay of the pilgrimage itself in the General Prologue, the end links, and the tale prologues that give us such portraits in action as the rattle-tongue marital railings of the Wife of Bath or the Pardoner's pride of artistry as a hypocritical preacher on avarice. The pilgrimage itself is better than all but the best of the tales told by the pilgrims, and without it Chaucer's comic realism as a portraitist of his times would only have half flowered. Traces of intended rearrangement and revision can be discerned in the huge fragment of his original scheme that Chaucer left us, but as it is the *Tales* are a ragbag of every sort of story, ranging from apprentice work to perfection of brilliance, from rowdy *fabliaux* to dignified romance to animal fable to parody to folktale to clerical satire.

A modern reader finds it hard to believe that Chaucer wrote the "retractions" at the end of *The Canterbury Tales* in which he begs forgiveness for substantially all the work for which we value him. Yet Chaucer and all his pilgrims were good Christians and Catholics, and hell was very real to the Middle Ages. It is hard not to be touched by the words, if they are his, as they may well be, in which Chaucer craves pardon for his sinful works, thanks Christ and His blessed Mother for his pious writings, and prays to be "one of them at the day of doom that shall be saved." Granting all sincerity to the prayer, perhaps Chaucer had to suppress a twinge or two of delight in his remembered creations — Harry Bailly, the profane Host; the ingenuous Prioress with her court manners; the leprous and impotent Summoner; the Wife of Bath with her crude vitality and her lament, "Alas, alas, that ever love was sin!"

CHAUSSON, Ernest (Amédée) (Jan. 20, 1855 – June 10, 1899). French composer. Born Paris. Studied law, then entered Paris Conservatoire (1880) in Massenet's composition class, but soon left to become pupil of César Franck (1880–83). Possessed of a large fortune, Chausson worked slowly and carefully, producing comparatively little during remaining sixteen years of his life, which was cut short by a bicycle accident at Limay, Seine-et-Oise. He was active in organization of Société Nationale de Musique, and from 1889 was its secretary. Decisively influenced by Franck, and to some extent by Wagner, his music is mystical, introspective, delicate, and melancholy. His reputation is greatest for chamber music. Works include "concert" for piano, violin and string quartet (1890–91), trio in G minor, quartet in A major for piano and strings, *Poème* for violin and orchestra (1897), his most popular composition, *Symphony in B-flat Major* (completed c.1890, first performed 1898), and songs.

REFERENCE: Jean-Pierre Barricelli and Leo Weinstein *Ernest Chausson: The Composer's Life and Works* (Norman, Okla. 1955).

CHAVANNES. See PUVIS DE CHAVANNES.

CHEKHOV, Anton Pavlovich (Jan. 17, 1860 – July 2, 1904). Russian playwright and short-story writer. Born Taganrog; educated in classical gymnasium there and at Moscow University School of Medicine. At nineteen began writing humorous stories for newspapers and magazines. Published many stories while still in medical school, and his first collection, *The Fairy Tales of Melpomene,* same year he took degree (1884). The second, *Motley Tales* (1886) brought wide recognition, and with Maxim Gorki he became one of the great exponents of realism in Russian literature. His successful play *Ivanov* (1887) was followed by a third collection of stories, *In the Twilight* (1888). Traveled much in southern Russia and journeyed (1890) across Siberia to Russian penal colony on Sakhalin Island, where he studied conditions. Published his findings in *The Island of Sakhalin* (1891). Increasing tuberculosis obliged him to stay for longer and longer in southern resort Yalta, where he came under, and shortly fell out from under, the influence of Tolstoi. During last decade of life Chekhov wrote his dramatic masterpieces *The Sea Gull* (produced 1896), *Uncle Vanya* (1899), *The Three Sisters* (1901), and *The Cherry Orchard* (1904), the last three triumphantly produced by the Moscow Art Theatre. Married (1901) an actress from the same theatre, Olga Knipper. Died of tuberculosis in German resort Badenweiler; buried in Moscow. Besides the famous stories and plays, Chekhov also wrote numerous one-act plays and conducted voluminous correspondence.

TRANSLATION: *The Complete Works of Anton Chekhov* tr. Constance Garnett (13 vols. New York 1916–22).

REFERENCES: Walter H. Bruford *Chekhov and His Russia: A Sociological Study* (New York and London 1948). William Gerhardi *Anton Chekhov: A Critical Study* (New York 1923). David Magarshack *Chekhov: A Life* (London 1952 and New York 1953). Ernest J. Simmons *Chekhov: A Biography* (Boston and London 1963, also PB).

ANTON CHEKHOV
BY WALLACE STEGNER

Anton Chekhov was impatient with literary theories and theorists, and he considered critics the flies that keep the horse from plowing. If there is a theory behind the four major plays with which he revolutionized the modern theatre, and the nearly six hundred short stories which demonstrate him the most extraordinary master of that form in literary history, it is a theory so unelaborated as to be almost rudimentary.

The aim of serious literature, he wrote to M. V. Kiselev, "is truth, unconditional and honest." If one hears echoes of French naturalism in his remark, also to Kiselev, that a writer should be as objective as a chemist, one hears Chekhov himself in the letters to his editor Alexei Suvorin in which he defends his apparent indifference to good and evil: "The artist should be, not the judge of his characters and their conversations, but only an unbiased witness."

"You confuse two things: solving a problem and stating a problem correctly. It is only the second that is obligatory for the artist."

"My business is only to be talented, i.e., to be able to distinguish between important and unimportant statements, to be able to illuminate the characters and speak their language."

The objectivity that Turgenev developed to delude the censors and mask his attack on serfdom is in Chekhov not only a technique but a temperamental bias, a substratum of character. No one could accuse him of inhumanity — he is incomparably tender with the little, young, or helpless, understanding with the impassioned, forgiving of the foolish. But he stands outside. He speaks as little from within his characters as Maupassant, but unlike Maupassant he appears to have no bitterness, and he almost never breaks his own rule that an author, like a puppeteer, should keep his hands and feet concealed.

His tenderness and indulgence are rarely intrusive. They are an emanation from a compassionate Creator (see *In Exile, Dreams, On the Way, The Steppe,* any of a hundred stories). When occasionally, as in the superb story *Enemies,* he does intercede, he makes his intercession a lament for the failure of human brotherhood. "Never in their lives, even in a frenzy, had they said so much that was unjust and cruel and absurd. In both the selfishness of the unhappy is violently manifest. Unhappy men are selfish, wicked, unjust, and less able to understand each other than fools. Unhappiness does not unite people, but separates them."

His young disciple Gorki said of him that no one understood "so clearly and finely . . . the tragedy of life's trivialities." It is not the least remarkable thing about this remarkable writer that a man so fundamentally untheatrical should have had so profound an effect on the world's theatre. He suggested to Alexander Kuprin that writers should cut off the beginnings and endings of their stories, since it was there that they were most inclined to lie. Manipulation, plot, building a situation through complications toward a resolution, was a form of falsehood conditioned by the writer's own intentions and biases. Even in the plays, Chekhov is not that kind of manipulator. As often as not, the plays come out where they began, just as many of the stories do. *Uncle Vanya, The Sea Gull, The Three Sisters, The Cherry Orchard,* are as surely tragedies of life's trivialities as are *Vierochka, The Kiss,* or *The Darling.* "Going to Moscow" is a cry that goes on, thin as a cricket's chirping, long after the curtain has gone down on the provincial discontents of the three sisters.

His motive is very often the lack of motive, spiritual deadness, spiritual impotence. He concentrates on the complications and lets the resolutions go, he turns the rheostat up slowly until the light and the understanding are full on, and then he turns it off. It is dangerous to say that any character speaks for him. He does not have the habit of concealing himself in mouthpieces. His characters are merely expressions of his talent: he understands them and speaks their language. But it is clear that he is a long way from being an optimist, that for him the real problems of the world are likely to have no solution, unless one so far off that it is equivalent to heaven's.

Despite this, he keeps his serenity. He remains aloof and without self-deception, but he does not lose his humanity. In his little book on Chekhov, William Gerhardi quotes a fragment to demonstrate the difference between Chekhov's impersonal reporting and the analytical method of Henry James: "I listened to the doctor, and according to my habit, applied my usual measures to him — materialist, idealist, moneygrubber, herd instincts, and so forth — but not a single one of my measures would fit him even approximately; and curiously, while I only listened to him and looked at him, he was, as a man, perfectly clear to me, but the moment I began applying my measures to him, he became, despite all his sincerity and simplicity, an extraordinarily complex, confused, and inexplicable nature."

Measures, judgments, analyses, are foreign to Chekhov's genius, impartial observation is basic to it. If fiction is a mirror in the roadway, it may also be a mirror in hallway or drawing room, and in Chekhov often is. It reflects pompous entrances, treacherous kisses, false friendship, agonized self-examination, ridiculous self-deception — reflections of an extraordinary complex-

ity. But in Chekhov's plays, as in his stories, however bewildering the reflections may be, the reflecting surface is cool, shadowless, perfectly clear. It neither judges nor analyzes nor comments, yet the things that show in it will serve as well as anything in literature as the images of truth.

———

CHÉNIER, André Marie de (Oct. 30, 1762 – July 25, 1794). French poet and journalist. Born Constantinople, where his father was consul. His mother, of Greek descent, stimulated his interest in classical antiquity and Hellenism. Moved with family to France (1765); attended Collège de Navarre (1773–81). Settled in Paris after six months in the army (1782) and travels in Switzerland and Italy (1783–84). Secretary to French ambassador to London (1787–90); returned to France after outbreak of revolution to devote himself to political journalism. Enthusiasm for revolution turned to vigorous protest at growing extremism; he assisted in defense of Louis XVI (1792–93) and was incarcerated on Robespierre's order (1794), then four months later guillotined, in Paris. Aside from two minor poems, only his political articles were published during his lifetime, and he was virtually unknown until 1819, when the publisher of his brother Marie-Joseph's writings discovered his poems and brought out an edition, including bucolics, elegies, epistles, odes, hymns, and epic fragments. While working in classical forms, Chénier in his later poems (especially *La Jeune Captive* and *Les Iambes,* both written in prison) influenced both the romantic poets and the Parnassians with his personal emphasis and metrical innovations. He inspired Umberto Giordano's best opera, *Andrea Chénier* (1896).

REFERENCES: Vernon Loggins *André Chénier: His Life, Death and Glory* (Athens, Ohio 1965). Francis Scarfe *André Chénier: His Life and Work, 1762–1794* (New York and London 1965).

———

CHERUBINI, (Maria) Luigi (Carlo Zenobio Salvatore) (Sept. 14, 1760 – Mar.

15, 1842). Italian composer. Born Florence. Instructed by his father and other musicians, studied counterpoint under Giuseppi Sarti in Milan (1777–80). At sixteen, he had composed a quantity of church music. First opera, *Quinto Fabio* (1780), was in florid Neapolitan style, as were others for next eight years. In London (1784–86), produced four operas for King's Theatre and was composer to the king (1785–86). Settled in Paris (1788) and introduced new style, with rich harmonic and orchestral color and generally heightened dramatic effect, which revolutionized French opera. Achieved first success with *Lodoïska* (1791), followed by *Médée* (1797) and *Les deux Journées* (1800), his two masterpieces. Married Cécile Tourette (1795). In Vienna, where he produced *Faniska* (1806), Cherubini met Beethoven, who admired his work. From 1809, composed mainly church music, including *Mass in F* (1809) and requiems in C minor (1817) and D minor (1836); also wrote a symphony and chamber works. Appointed director of Paris Conservatory (1822), with which he had been connected since its foundation (1795). His *Treatise on Counterpoint and Fugue* (1835) became a classic. Died in Paris.

REFERENCES: Frederick J. Crowest *Cherubini* (London 1890). Basil Deane *Cherubini* (London and New York 1965).

CHESTERFIELD, Philip Dormer Stanhope, 4th earl of (Sept. 22, 1694 – Mar. 24, 1773). English statesman and writer. Born and died in London. Educated at Trinity Hall, Cambridge, then in Europe (1714). Whig member of Parliament (1716–26), also served as gentleman of the bedchamber to George II. Appointed ambassador to The Hague (1728), where his liaison with Elizabeth du Bouchet brought him a son, Philip Stanhope (1732–1768), later the recipient of the eloquent *Letters to His Son* (1737–68, published 1774). Dismissed from position as lord high steward by Sir Robert Walpole, Chesterfield thenceforth led opposition in House of Lords. Married Melusina von Schulemberg, countess of Walsingham (1733), illegitimate daughter of George I, which deeply offended George II. Continued campaign against king and government, writing political pieces under name of Geoffrey Broadbottom. After fall of Walpole, served again as ambassador to The Hague (1774), then as lord lieutenant of Ireland (1745–46) and as secretary of state (1746–48), after which he retired from public affairs. Noted for his polished style in essays and parliamentary speeches, Chesterfield is above all remembered for *Letters to His Son*, which instruct the youth how to become a man of the world through learning, study of fellow men, and especially through social graces. *Letters to His Godson* (1776), also named Philip Stanhope, go further in paternal counsel, advocating good sense and a knowledge of foreign countries as well as languages and grace of manners. Chesterfield is also remembered for Dr. Johnson's famous criticism of him as patron of the *Dictionary* in a letter (Feb. 7, 1754): " . . . The notice which you have been pleased to take of my labors, had it been early, had been kind; but it has been delayed till I am indifferent, and cannot enjoy it; till I am solitary, and cannot impart it; till I am known, and do not want it."

EDITIONS: *The Letters of Chesterfield* ed. Bonamy Dobree (6 vols. London and New York 1933). *Some Unpublished Letters of Lord Chesterfield* ed. Sidney L. Gulick, Jr. (Berkeley, Calif. 1937).

REFERENCES: Roger Coxon *Chesterfield and His Critics* (London 1925). William H. Craig *Life of Chesterfield* (London and New York 1907). Frank L. Lucas *The Search for Good Sense: Four Eighteenth-Century Characters, Johnson, Chesterfield, Boswell and Goldsmith* (London and New York 1958, also PB). Samuel Shellabarger *Lord Chesterfield and His World* (London 1935 and Boston 1951).

CHESTERTON, Gilbert Keith (May 29, 1874 – June 14, 1936). English essayist, novelist, poet. Born in London. Educated at St. Paul's School, London; left to study art (1891) and write book reviews. Published first book of poems *The Wild Knight* (1900) and began contributing articles to important periodicals. Married Frances Blogg (1901).

A versatile, prolific writer, Chesterton's best work was literary criticism, including *Robert Browning* (1903), *Charles Dickens* (1906), *George Bernard Shaw* (1909), and *The Victorian Age in Literature* (1913). Also wrote fiction, including *The Man Who Was Thursday* (1908) and the popular Father Brown detective stories (1911–1935), plays, and poetry — *The Ballad of the White Horse* (1911), *Collected and New Poems* (1927). After conversion to Roman Catholicism (1922), published *St. Francis of Assisi* (1923), *The Everlasting Man* (1925), *Catholic Essays* (1929), *St. Thomas Aquinas* (1933), and other works championing Catholicism. His autobiography was published 1936. Died in Beaconsfield, Buckinghamshire. A leading controversialist in his day, his approach to subjects like Victorianism was often such as to win him the title of "master of the paradox."

REFERENCES: Hilaire Belloc *On the Place of G. K. Chesterton in English Letters* (London 1940). Patrick Braybooke *Gilbert Keith Chesterton* (London and Philadelphia 1922). Maisie Ward *Gilbert Keith Chesterton* (New York 1943 and London 1944).

CHOPIN, Frédéric (François); in Polish, Fryderyk (Franciszek) (Feb. 22, 1810 – Oct. 17, 1849). Polish pianist and composer. Born Zelazowa Wola near Warsaw, son of Frenchman teaching French in Poland. Was taught music (1816–22) by Adalbert Zywny, a violinist, composer and pianist. As pianist, mainly self-taught. Studied composition under Joseph Elsner at Warsaw Conservatory (1826–29). From 1818 played as a young prodigy in Warsaw salons. Toured Germany and Italy (1829). Concert of his music in Warsaw (1830) led people to call him the rising national composer of Poland. Settled in Paris (1831) as a fashionable piano teacher. Engaged for a brief time to Maria Wodzinska. Met Aurore Dudevant (George Sand) (1836) and lived with her for nine years. Died of tuberculosis in Paris. Works include two piano concertos in F minor and E minor, scherzos, ballades, preludes, nocturnes, mazurkas, études and waltzes.

TRANSLATION: *Selected Correspondence of Fryderyk Chopin* tr. and ed. Arthur Hedley (London 1962).

REFERENCES: André Coeuroy *Chopin* (Paris 1951). Arthur Hedley *Chopin* (London 1947). Alan Walker ed. *Frédéric Chopin: Profiles of the Man and the Musician* (New York 1967).

✍

FRÉDÉRIC CHOPIN
BY SEYMOUR SHIFRIN

Two books were found in the apartment in Paris where Frédéric Chopin spent his last days: one Voltaire's *Dictionnaire Philosophique*, still open to the article on Taste; the other an anthology of Polish poetry. The two books speak volumes. A composer of extraordinary sensibilities and refinement, his life was pervaded by a longing for his homeland. Chopin had left Poland as a young man of twenty-one to settle in Paris, where he was to live and work his remaining eighteen years. It was an exile imposed by his gifts, which required an audience. Though not to the manner born, he was aristocratic in temperament, a virtuoso pianist who refused the vicissitudes of display in large concert halls in preference for the salons of his titled admirers. Chopin is a nostalgic figure, but a remarkable one. His is not simply a nostalgia in the usual sense — that is, for a rosy past. Rather, the idealization and transfiguration which are part of the nostalgic mode are directed toward the dances of his homeland.

If, within twenty years of Beethoven's death, one were to suggest making a career of writing almost nothing but pieces related to the dance, and those only for the piano, the proposition would seem extremely dubious. Chopin was clearly capable of defying plausibility.

There is almost allegorical meaning in Chopin's use of the simple surface of the dance. The subtleties and complexities of his extraordinary musical imagination are enhanced by the referential and traditional qualities of the dance. There is the steady insistent rhythm, the rigid frame, and, against it, the arching flow of melody and figuration. The contradistinctions lend an air of having encompassed, captured, the irreconcilable.

The sense of his daring is closely related to the range and scope of his melody. His melodic line suggests qualities of an acrobatic feat, culminating in that moment of intense danger when it seems to have climbed too high with no visible means of getting down, or to have plummeted too low with a suddenness that borders on loss of control, only to assure us in the ensuing moments that these dangers were clearly within the composer's artistic means to control. It is an aerial display, tailspin and all, from which the pilot pulls out at the last possible moment, but with such skill that our sense of his peril seems illusory. This is probably the element that most attracts virtuoso pianists to Chopin — this and the fact that he never failed to make the piano sound like the ultimate instrument. However, there is reason to complain that many pianists swamp the counterpoised restraint, the masterful linear and harmonic control, with their overemphasis on acrobatic daring. The performer has his own tightrope to walk and it is critical that he not lose his sense of balance.

Scholars speak of Chopin's melodic indebtedness to Italian opera, most particularly to Bellini. It is a game some scholars play. The name of the game is "precursoring," and the force of most of their argument is to attest that the composer was in fact alive at the appointed time and that he did not live a hermetic existence. Granting their premise that Chopin brought to his work an admiration for Bellini's bel canto, questions remain as to why his melodies are so uniquely suited to the piano with its relatively sharp attack and inevitable swift decay, and why the same melodies lose much in being sung or played on a sustaining instrument.

If we think of chromatic harmony as essentially a charged way of moving to the structural harmonic goals we find in the music of the seventeenth and eighteenth centuries, then, clearly, there is no one among his contemporaries of Chopin's caliber as innovator. His nearest rival perhaps was Liszt, but with him it can be argued that the chromatic intensification became an end in itself and no longer is the tonal goal as clearly evident. The potency of Chopin's harmonic innovation relates directly to his care in shaping the linear elements of his music. Though there are very few instances of the larger formal media of counterpoint (such as canon or fugue), he was a supremely gifted contrapuntalist. His voice-leading counts; that is, he engages us with a particular shape of his bass and inner voices against which the upper line soars.

He was not a prolific composer, given the standards of his day: seventy-four published listings in all — though, to be sure, some of the single opus numbers include as many as twenty-four preludes or twelve studies. Only the two piano concerti and the three piano sonatas can be said to be large-scale works in any conventional sense. Of these, all but the last two sonatas are works of his youth, and then only the earlier of the two, op. 35 in B-flat minor (with the *Marche Funèbre* that shall bury us all), is up to his standard. It is indicative of the degree of his self-knowledge that he did not try to be a symphonist. Yet the *Fourth Ballade*, the last scherzo, and the *Polonaise Fantasie* are of an order of formal and structural design that far exceed their modest clocked time. Within the bounds of the *F minor Ballade* there is the realization of a formal idea as rich and bold as any in the nineteenth century. Modesty and restraint have their own grand eloquence.

Thin, ascetic, tubercular, there was in Chopin the attitude of a fugitive, wary of familiarity. The biographer Louis Enault put it this way: "He lent himself sometimes, but gave himself never." George Sand, Chopin's mistress, wrote: "As he had charmingly polite manners, one was apt to take as a friendly courtesy what in him was only frigid disdain if not an insuperable dislike." He was said to be conventional in his taste. Though he valued his friendship with the painter Delacroix, he preferred the traditional styles of David and Ingres. Bach and Mozart were his favorite musicians. Given his predilections, it is one of history's small ironies that he was justly celebrated in his time as a man of the *"nouvelle vague"*; his dance rhythms, daring harmony, and unique brilliance in writing for his instrument offered a vital antidote to what seemed the weariness of musical tradition.

CHRÉTIEN DE TROYES (c.1130–c.1190). French poet. Born probably in Champagne, educated in Latin disciplines, his patrons were Marie de Champagne, daughter of Louis VII and Eleanor of Aquitaine, and Philip of Flanders. Earliest literary efforts were imitations of Ovid; mature works were Arthurian metrical romances (c.1160–c.1180) *Érec et Énide; Cligès; Lancelot, ou Le Chevalier de la charette; Yvain, ou Le Chevalier au lion;* and *Perceval, ou Le Conte du graal,* the first known version of the Grail legend. Chrétien wrote in the tradition of courtly love, yet brought subtle characterization, inventiveness and poetic mastery to his works, which were highly popular and translated into English and German. Author of the earliest known Arthurian romances, he was one of the single most influential writers of the Middle Ages.

TRANSLATIONS: *Arthurian Romances,* tr. William W. Comfort (London 1958). *The Story of the Grail* tr. Robert W. Linker (Chapel Hill, N.C. 1952).

REFERENCES: Jean Frappier *Chrétien de Troyes: l'homme et l'oeuvre* (Paris 1957). Roger Sherman Loomis *Arthurian Tradition and Chrétien de Troyes* (New York and London 1949).

CHRISTUS, Petrus (c.1420–1472/3). Flemish painter. Born in Baarle. Possibly a student of Jan van Eyck, he was his closest follower and seems to have completed some of his works. Christus became a free citizen of Bruges (1444), where he remained until his death. His known output, which is small, includes portraits — notably those of Edward Grymestone (1446, Earl of Verulam Collection, England), an unknown Carthusian monk (1446, Metropolitan Museum, New York), and a pale young woman (Staatliche Museen, Berlin) — and religious paintings which show, along with that of the van Eycks, the influence of Rogier van der Weyden. Examples are the *Madonna with SS. Francis and Jerome* (c.1457, Städelsches Kunstinstitut, Frankfurt), *Nativity* (National Gallery of Art, Washington, D.C.), and *Lamentation* (Musées Royaux des Beaux Arts, Brussels; another version in Metropolitan Museum, New York). Christus's chief contribution to northern painting was his completion of the development toward realistic perspective: the Frankfurt *Madonna* is the earliest Netherlandish picture with a single vanishing point.

REFERENCE: Erwin Panofsky *Early Netherlandish Painting: Its Origins and Characters* (London and Cambridge, Mass. 1954).

CICERO, Marcus Tullius (106–43 B.C.). Roman statesman, orator, writer. Born Arpinum (Latium, Italy) into middle-class family. Well educated in law, oratory, Greek literature and philosophy. Military service under Strabo, then Sulla. Quaestor in Sicily (75 B.C.); prosecuted governor Gaius Verres for maladministration (70). Curule aedile (69); praetor (66). As consul (63), crushed Catiline's conspiracy to seize government. Accused by First Triumvirate of executing Catiline without trial, went into voluntary exile (58–57). On return became spokesman for preservation of republican form of government against Caesar's idea of popularly supported dictatorship, though the oligarchic senators never fully trusted Cicero because he advocated compromise in the form of *concordia ordinum* (harmony among the classes). After Caesar's victory at Pharsalus (48) he turned from political to literary activity, producing some of his greatest works. Following Caesar's assassination (44), led republicans against Mark Antony through his speeches, the fourteen Philippics. Second Triumvirate had him proscribed and murdered. A quixotic statesman and philosopher, Cicero was the greatest master of Latin prose style. The passion, wit, and rhetorical sophistication of his speeches are no less admirable than the concise elegance and simplicity of his essays. His major works include speeches, *In Verrem* (70), *De Lege Manilia* (66), *Pro Cluentio* (66), *In Catilinem* (four speeches, 63), *Pro Archia* (c.60), *Pro Milone* (52), *Philippics* (44–43); essays, *De Oratore* (55), *De Republica* (54), *De Legibus* (52), *Brutus, De Oratore, De Senectute, De Amicitia* (in 40's); and letters, *To Atticus, To Quintus* (Cicero's brother), and *To Brutus*.

REFERENCES: Frank R. Cowell *Cicero and the Roman Republic* (London 1948; Harmondsworth, England, and Baltimore PB 1956). John Dickinson *Death of a Republic: Politics and Political Thought at Rome 59–44 B.C.* (New York 1963). Henry J. Haskell *This Was Cicero* (New York 1942, also PB). Robert N. Wilkin *Eternal Lawyer: A Legal Biography of Cicero* (New York 1947).

CICERO
BY ESTHER WAGNER

When Mark Antony and his tigress-wife Fulvia had the head and hand of murdered Cicero nailed to the rostrum in the Roman forum, they thought they were celebrating the silence of the great voice of republican Rome, the destruction of its recording pen. But at the beginning of the Christian era, St. Jerome speaks his fear that God will find him a better Ciceronian than Christian. At the dawn of the Renaissance, when Petrarch unearths and makes available to the mind of his time the wealth of Cicero's correspondence, the man as a living being, not only the orator, becomes a part of the concept of human fate known as humanism. In the seventeenth and eighteenth centuries, "Ciceronian" and "anti-Ciceronian" are fighting words among men of letters, standards by which styles of thought and speech are pugnaciously defined. In writing of the beginnings of the French Revolution, Camille Desmoulins says that "these republicans were mostly young fellows who, having been brought up on Cicero at school, had developed a passion for liberty." When George Washington receives from his countrymen the title of Father of His Country, it is the image of Cicero, rescuer of the republic from evil, embodiment of civic virtue, that is evoked.

There is a Cicero for all seasons. When the historian of style speaks the word "Ciceronian," he means a kind of official rhetoric, characterized by long elaborate sentences swelling toward some crashing climax; he speaks of symmetrical figures such as the tricolon (blood . . . sweat . . . *tears*) and a flowery display of conventional emotions with a maximum of ornament. The leaner eloquence of

Swift, the fire of Burke, are, however, as much inspired and taught by Cicero as the more ponderous periods. In all his orations, Cicero knew how to blend the most colloquial, urbane, conversational of styles with the great rolling roars of his massive indignations and exhortations.

The historian of Rome when he speaks of Cicero does so with gratitude, for the volume, inclusiveness, and candor of the correspondence. Roman social life, political undercurrents, the give-and-take of the power exchange on the high hills of Rome, the gossip of the day and the plans for the next day — the man lives and breathes, the moment comes again, the city exists and survives.

The historian of philosophy looks with impatience on Cicero as philosopher; eclectic, inquiring, unable to support the weight of systems or the hardships of originality, Cicero's "thought" can hardly be said to exist. But the essays on life in general which the grief-weary retired statesman set himself to write in order to stop mourning his beloved daughter, a short time before his own terrible death, command respect and thanks as a durable pioneering attempt at something like philosophical journalism. He wished to make the main currents of Greek thought accessible to the literate but non-Hellenist Roman public. There was hardly a vocabulary for this; he invented and found. The essays are above all lucid. They formed centuries of minds. Church Fathers, Renaissance humanists, French revolutionaries, American founding fathers found in them a humane, enlightening vision of what good feeling and good sense can make of human life.

The historian of law can see in Cicero something quite different: a concept of advocacy that made of him the greatest pleader of his day, notably in cases for the defense. His most famous speech for a prosecution, which indicted the gangster-governor Verres, was really a speech for the defense of a suffering subject people. The idea of Roman law as "the bond of all the dignities which we in this state are privileged to enjoy" was to him a lifelong excitement, a passion. Conscious as he had to be of the strange relationship existing between law and justice, he could perform and enjoy as few others in advocacy's history the curious high-wire walk of the lover of justice suspended between the poles of theory and practice, fact and truth. Defending a good man charged with a low murder, when the case itself was a danger to his own political ambitions, he could face the case squarely: the defendant is really to be prosecuted on a charge of jury-bribing, a charge full of dynamite because of recent shifts in party supremacies. The advocate knows his client guilty of the jury-bribing, because the circumstances of the earlier trial under a most corrupt administration *demanded* such action — there was no choice. Knowing also that his client is a just man and in the light of any justice not guilty, he clears him of the bribery charge (of which he was technically if not morally guilty), laughs off the murder charge, and concludes with a kind of glorious pageant dramatizing the faith of Roman citizens in Roman virtue and Roman justice. The virtuoso performance includes jokes, vaudevilles, scandalmongering, tears, roars, shouts of savage scorn. The text of the *Pro Cluentio* shows the color of the performance, even in translation. But a great passion informs and colors the performance; lies are told in the service of truth, deceptions employed in order to reveal. The philosophical questions raised by Cicero's law cases are hard, dangerous, as those raised in his philosophical essays are not. He does not discuss them, but embodies them in his performances. A rich and magnificent temperament appears in these supposedly evanescent works: wit, worldliness, idealism charged with a melancholy sophistication enchant the spectator. These orations — *Pro Cluentio, Pro Caelio, Pro Murena, Pro Roscio* — are spectacles, and as such nonpareil.

The hero of the French and American revolutionary imaginations, liberty-loving, august, all togaed with integrity, evaporates before the modern eye into a kind of antihero, suitable for the season of our contemporary imagination. He flinched, he vacillated, he could do a calculated grovel. Vanity ate at him; he writes to a contemporary historian that he hopes the man will mention him frequently and with praise, even if he has in the process to "neglect the laws of history." When Petrarch first read these letters, he writhed and suffered. But the modern rather enjoys this de-togation. The great white robe falls aside, the man stands shivering in a raw but rather reassuring humanity.

The doubling of heroism with antiheroism is apparent in Plutarch's report of Cicero's death at the hands of Antony's thugs, in retaliation for the *Philippics,* which he had not feared to pronounce, conscious of the dangers though too trusting in Octavian. There are ignominies in his conduct as the assassins approach. He can't make up his mind, go or stay, capitulate, what? But when his household prevails on him to try flight, and the pursuers intercept his litter, then he looks "steadfastly upon his murderers, his person covered with dust, hair and beard untrimmed, his face worn with his troubles. So that the greatest part of those that stood by covered their faces while Herennius slew him." The late distinguished classicist Moses Hadas says the final word on his death: "For his faltering and his compromises there is one sufficient answer: he suffered death for his views." As beneath the toga of the hero the naked skin of the antihero appears in time, so beneath that skin the bones of the great man appear again, in their time.

CIMABUE, Giovanni (Cenni di Pepo) (c.1240–after 1302). Italian painter and mosaicist. Little is known of the life of this first great master of the Florentine school. Born probably in Florence, visited Rome (1272), and is buried in the cathedral of Florence, S. Maria del Fiore. Traditionally regarded as teacher of Giotto. At first worked in Byzantine tradition, with its gold background, stylization, and sacred themes, but gradually gave it up for more natural style and expression of emotion in his figures. Thus emerged the Florentine school of painting. His most famous work, *Madonna and Child Enthroned with Angels and Prophets* (Uffizi, Florence), was probably painted in early 1280's for church of S. Trinità, Florence. Others include frescoes in upper church of S. Francesco at Assisi (c.1277–81) and two large painted crosses, one in church of S. Domenico at Arezzo, the other in church of S. Croce in Florence (badly damaged by floods in 1966). Dante sums up the relation of master and pupil: "Cimabue thought that he held the field in painting, but now Giotto is acclaimed and his fame obscured" (*Purgatorio* XI, 94–96).

REFERENCES: Eugenio Battisti *Cimabue* (tr. University Park, Pa. 1967). Alfred Nicholson *Cimabue: A Critical Study* (Princeton, N.J. and London 1932).

CIMAROSA, Domenico (Dec. 17, 1749 – Jan. 11, 1801). Italian composer. Born Aversa, near Naples; trained at Conservatorio S. Maria di Loreto at Naples

(1761–72). First operas, *Le Stravaganze del conte* (1772) and *La Finta parigina* (1773), established him as popular favorite composer of comic operas in Italy; achieved international renown with *L'Italiana in Londra* (1779). Lived in various Italian cities, producing works for opera houses, until invited to St. Petersburg as court composer to Catherine II (1787). Went to Vienna (1791) as kapellmeister to Leopold II; there produced his masterpiece *Il Matrimonio segreto* (1792). Back in Naples (1793), he enjoyed continued success until his expressions of enthusiasm at entry of French republican army (1799) resulted in imprisonment. Pardoned at public insistence, he went to Venice, where he died. Other major operas from Cimarosa's enormous output include *La Ballerina amante* (1782), *L'Impresario in angustie* (1786), *Le Vergine del sole* (1789), and *Gli Orazi e curiazi* (1796). Noted for its merriment, wit, and charming melodies, his *opera buffa* style resembles Mozart's.

CLARE, John (July 13, 1793 – May 20, 1864). English poet. Born Helpstone, Northamptonshire, son of a farm laborer. Had little schooling; began farm work in seventh year. In brief period following publication of *Poems Descriptive of Rural Life and Scenery* (1820), the "peasant poet" was a popular celebrity; later volumes, including *The Village Minstrel* (1821), *The Shepherd's Calendar* (1827), and *The Rural Muse* (1835), though admired by critics, sold poorly. Married Martha Turner (1820), daughter of neighboring farmer; they had seven children. Worked as farmer to support family. Became subject to delusions (1837), and from 1841 until his death was confined to St. Andrew's asylum, Northampton, where he continued to write, producing visionary lyrics of great purity, often compared with those of Blake. Late poems include *Love Lies Beyond the Tomb, Invite to Eternity, I Am,* and *A Vision*. Edmund Blunden edited his autobiography (1931).

EDITIONS: *The Later Poems of John Clare* ed. Eric Robinson and Geoffrey Summerfield (Manchester, Eng., and New York 1964). *Selected Poems and Prose* ed. Eric Robinson and Geoffrey Summerfield (London and New York 1966).

REFERENCES: Frederick Martin *The Life of John Clare* (2nd ed. New York and London 1964). John W. and Anne Tibble *John Clare: His Life and Poetry* (London 1956).

CLARENDON, Edward Hyde, 1st earl of (Feb. 18, 1609 – Dec. 9, 1674). English statesman and historian. Born Wiltshire of landed family. Educated at Oxford and Middle Temple, London. Married Anne Ayliffe (1631/32; she died in six months). Soon after marriage (1634) to Frances Aylesbury, daughter of master of requests, received government appointment. Entered Parliament (1640), joined royalists (1641), and became secret adviser to Charles I. Remained with king throughout Civil War and followed Prince Charles into exile (1646), when he began his *History of the Rebellion*. Appointed lord chancellor and chief minister by Charles II (1658), he was chief architect of national restoration of king and monarchy. Created earl of Clarendon (1661). Unpopular because of sale of Dunkirk to France (1662) and failure of second Dutch war (1665–67), he was dismissed from office (1667) and spent rest of his life in exile in France. He died in Rouen. His daughter Anne Hyde married the future James II. His *History of the Rebellion,* a valuable account of the Civil War, first appeared 1702–1704. Presented with the rest of his works (including an autobiography and *State Papers*) to Oxford University by his heirs, its profits were used to build a new printing house (1829) for the University Press, which bears his name.

EDITION: *The True Historical Narrative of the Rebellion and Civil Wars in England Begun in the Year 1641* ed. William Dunn Macray (6 vols. Oxford 1888).

REFERENCES: Sir Henry Craik *The Life of Edward, Earl of Clarendon, Lord High Chancellor of England* (2 vols. New York 1911). Brian H. G. Wormald *Clarendon: Politics, History and Religion, 1640–1660* (London and New York 1951).

CLAUDE LORRAIN. *See* **LORRAIN, Claude.**

CLAUDEL, Paul (Louis Charles Marie) (Aug. 6, 1868 – Feb. 23, 1955). French dramatist, poet, essayist, and diplomat. Born Villeneuve-sur-Père, Aisné. Family moved to Paris (1882), where he attended Lycée Louis le Grand and École des Sciences Politiques. After years of inner struggle became converted to devout Catholic (1890). Thereafter religion was his way of life and the most important element in his writing. Entered diplomatic service (1890), served in U.S. (1893–94) and China (1895–1909). Married Reine Sainte-Marie Perrin (1906) while briefly again in France. Held diplomatic posts in Prague, Frankfurt, Hamburg, Rio de Janeiro, and Copenhagen (1911–21); ambassador to Tokyo (1921–27), to Washington (1927–33), and to Brussels (1933–35). Elected to French Academy (1946). Died in Paris. Best-known works are plays *Partage de midi* (1906, rev. 1948, tr. *Break of Noon* 1960), *L'Annonce faite à Marie* (1912, tr. *Tidings Brought to Mary* 1922), lyrical drama *Christoph Colomb* (1928, tr. *The Book of Christopher Columbus* 1930), and *Le Soulier de satin* (1929, rev. 1944, tr. *The Satin Slipper* 1930). *Cinq Grands Odes* (1910), written in unrhymed lines and natural rhythm rather than formal meter — a form inspired by the symbolists and called *verset claudélien* — is his chief work of poetry. Prose includes *Art poétique* (1907) and his *Correspondance 1899–1926* with André Gide.

REFERENCE: Wallace Fowlie *Paul Claudel* (New York 1958).

CLEMENS, Samuel Langhorne. *See* **TWAIN, Mark.**

CLOUET, Jean (c.1485–1540) and **François** (c.1510–1572). French portrait painters. Jean, born probably in southern Netherlands, arrived in France before death of Louis XII (1515) and eventually became chief painter and valet de chambre to Francis I. Died in Paris. Extant works include about 130 preparatory drawings of members of French court, a collection of which is at Chantilly, also small group of portraits, notably two of Francis I (Louvre, Paris), *Dauphin Francis as a Child* (c.1522, Antwerp), and *Unknown Humanist with a Volume of Petrarch* (c.1535, Hampton Court). Clouet developed a technique of lively and acute characterization modified by reticence and polished stylization which determined the manner of French portraiture for centuries. His son FRANÇOIS, born at Tours, succeeded him as official painter to Francis I and continued in this capacity under the next three kings. Painted mythological and genre subjects as well as portraits, and directed large workshop at Fontainebleau. Died in Paris. His style combines Flemish meticulousness with Italian mannerist elegance: works include *Portrait of Pierre Quthe* (1562, Louvre), *Lady at Her Toilette* (National Gallery, Washington, D.C.), *Francis I on Horseback* (c.1545, Uffizi, Florence), and *Charles IX as a Boy* (1561, Kunsthistorisches Museum, Vienna).

REFERENCES: Louis Dimier *Histoire de la peinture du portrait en France au XVIe siècle* (3 vols. Paris and Brussels 1924–26). Étienne Moreau-Nelaton *Les Clouets et leurs émules* (Paris 1924).

CLOUGH, Arthur Hugh (Jan. 1, 1819 – Nov. 13, 1861). English poet. Born Liverpool, son of a cotton merchant. Educated at Rugby, where he became friend of Matthew Arnold, who commemorated him in poem *Thyrsis*. Entered Balliol College, Oxford (1837); elected fellow of Oriel College (1841). Resigned (1848) because of disagreement with Oxford movement and reaction against the establishment because of Irish famine. First and best-known poem, his pastoral *The Bothie of Toberna-Vuolich* (1848), was followed by volume of poems *Ambarvalia* (1849). Appointed head of University Hall, London (1849). Visited Cambridge, Mass., at invitation of Emerson (1852). Returned to England (1854) to become examiner in Education Office, London, and that year married Blanche Smith. Died in Florence while traveling in Italy for his health. A collection of his poems appeared posthumously (1862), containing *Say Not the Struggle Naught*

Availeth and other fine lyrics expressing concern with social problems and the religious and political skepticism characteristic of his time.

EDITIONS: *Poems* ed. Howard F. Lowry, Frederick L. Mulhauser and A. L. P. Norrington (Oxford and New York 1952). *Correspondence* ed. Frederick P. Mulhauser (Oxford and New York 1957). *Selected Prose Works* ed. Buckner B. Trawick (University, Ala. 1964).

REFERENCES: Isobel Armstrong *Arthur Hugh Clough* (London and New York PB 1962). Matthew Arnold *The Letters of Matthew Arnold to Arthur Hugh Clough* ed. Howard F. Lowry (New York 1932, 1968). Katharine C. Chorley *Arthur Hugh Clough: The Uncommitted Mind* (Oxford and New York 1962). Walter E. Houghton *The Poetry of Clough: An Essay in Revaluation* (New Haven 1963). David Williams *Too Quick Despairer: The Life and Work of Arthur Hugh Clough* (London 1969).

COBBETT, William (pseudonym Peter Porcupine) (Mar. 9, 1763 – June 18, 1835). English writer, reformer, and publisher. Born Farnham, Surrey, son of a laborer; was self-educated. After year as law clerk in London enlisted in army (1784). Served in Canada, where he met Ann Reid, whom he married (1792). Upon discharge, determined to expose corruption in higher ranks by demanding court-martial of certain officers, but met with official resistance. Threatened with arrest, fled (1792) first to France, then to America. In Philadelphia wrote political tracts, some against French Revolution, and published *Porcupine's Gazette* (1797), writing under pseudonym Peter Porcupine. Violent in his criticisms, he became involved in several libel suits and was forced to return to England (1800), where he started anti-French paper the *Porcupine* (1800–1801), succeeded by more successful *Cobbett's Weekly Political Register*. By 1804 his pro-conservative attitude was reversed. His new radical opinions again involved him in libel suits; he was convicted of sedition (1810), fined, and imprisoned for two years, continuing, however, to edit *Register* and produce polit-

ical pamphlets. Released from prison (1812), Cobbett became working-class spokesman for economic and political reforms, but on suspension of habeas corpus (1817) left for America. Spent two years on Long Island farm, continuing to publish *Register*. Returned to England (1819) to continue literary and reform activity, publishing numbers of books and pamphlets, among which the most famous today is *Rural Rides* (1830), a series of travel sketches depicting the change from an agricultural to an industrial society in England. Following Reform Act (1832), which he had supported as a beginning of parliamentary reform, he was elected to Parliament. Continued to serve, always representing strong radical viewpoint, until his death.

REFERENCES: Marjorie Bowen *Peter Porcupine: A Study of William Cobbett* (London 1935 and New York 1936). G. D. H. Cole *The Life of William Cobbett* (3rd. ed. London 1947). Morris Leonard Pearl *William Cobbett: A Bibliographical Account of His Life and Times* (London and New York 1953).

COCTEAU, Jean (July 5, 1889 – Oct. 11, 1963). French writer, artist, and film maker. Born Maisons-Laffitte, near Paris; son of a nonpracticing lawyer. Educated at Lycée Condorcet (1900–1904) and in his youth traveled about Europe with his mother. Published first volume of poetry, *La Lampe d'Aladin* (1909). Served with ambulance units in World War I. His ballet *Parade* (1917, score by Satie, scenery by Picasso) launched his career as champion and popularizer of avant-garde movements in all branches of the arts. Later spectacles include *Le Boeuf sur le toit* (1920, score by Milhaud) and *Les Mariés de la Tour Eiffel* (1921, score by five of Les Six). Cocteau's literary production includes volumes of poetry *Le Cap de Bonne-Esperance* (1919), *Plainchant* (1923), *Poésie 1916–1923* (1924), *Opéra 1925–1927* (1927), and *Clairobscur* (1954) and novels *Thomas l'Imposteur* (1923), *Le Grand Écart* (1923), and *Les Enfants terribles* (1929, Cocteau's film version 1950). He is best known for his work in the theatre, notably the plays *La Voix humaine* (1930), *La Machine infernale* (1934), and *Les Parents terribles* (1938, Cocteau's film version 1948); the opera-oratorio *Oedipus Rex* (1927), music by Stravinsky); and the films *Le Sang d'un poète* (1930–32), *L'Éternel Retour* (1943), *La Belle et la bête* (1946), and *Orphée* (1950). Elected to French Academy and Royal Belgian Academy (1955) and the American Academy and National Institute of Arts and Letters (1957). Died in his house at Milly-la-Forêt, near Fontainebleau.

TRANSLATIONS: Among many are *Five Plays* (New York 1961, also PB). *The Infernal Machine and Other Plays* (Norfolk, Conn. 1963, also PB). *Screenplays and Other Writings on the Cinema* tr. Carol Martin-Sperry (New York 1968). *The Journals of Jean Cocteau* tr. Wallace Fowlie (New York and London 1956).

REFERENCES: Jean-Jacques Kihm *Cocteau* (Paris 1960). Jean-Jacques Kihm, Elizabeth Sprigge, Henri C. Behar *Jean Cocteau, L'homme et les Miroirs* (Paris 1968). Francis Steegmuller *Cocteau* (Boston 1970).

✍

JEAN COCTEAU
BY FRANCIS STEEGMULLER

Jean Cocteau and his kaleidoscopic work constitute one of the curiosities of French literature and of the French world of art. Poet, novelist, dramatist, cineast, draftsman, portraitist, muralist, designer of posters, pottery, tapestries, mosaics, neckties, costume jewelry, and objects executed in glass and other media including pipe cleaners — the list of his activities over a period of more than half a century could be prolonged indefinitely. He was a showman, with a taste for publicity that sometimes drove antagonists to make the mistake of dismissing his work: in fact, he was a true poet, and to fall into the easy trap of saying that "his principal work was his life" is to miss a great excellence.

In his characteristically self-dramatizing way he insisted on the word "poet," classifying his great variety of work under the headings of *"poésie, poésie de roman, poésie de théâtre, poésie critique, poésie graphique,* and *poésie cinématographique."* Even his sculpture he dubbed *"poésie plastique."* One can dislike the insistence, but the validity of the term is undeniable. It is sometimes charged against him that he constantly impersonated others, modeling himself on a series of artists "greater" and "more genuine" than himself, notably Anna de Noailles, Apollinaire, Gide, Stravinsky, and Picasso. What he did was to use, very often, a touch of "somebody else" as an ingredient among other ingredients in the fabrication of works of his own; and persons who denigrate him on this count might ask themselves why a work by Cocteau, whatever its "influences" or "reminiscences," is always strongly characteristically Cocteau.

Much of all this had its root in a crucial condition of his childhood — the self-subordination of his father, Georges Cocteau, to his wife's family, a self-effacement that culminated in suicide when Jean was nine. The latter's life became a search for heroes (heroes in the arts, since he was a precocious artistic genius), a search that broadened with age into the habit of associating with himself "adopted sons" whose hero he could be. In his teens he postured as a poet of the salons; involvement with Sergei Diaghilev and the Russian Ballet gave full play to his aestheticism and his homosexuality. Stravinsky's *The Rite of Spring* provided a vitalizing shock, and he read Gertrude Stein and met the cubists.

Diaghilev, he claimed, challenged him to "astound" him, and in the midst of the 1914–18 war Cocteau persuaded Picasso and Satie, with Diaghilev as impresario and Léonide Massine as dancer-choreographer, to collaborate with him on the famous *Parade*, which revolutionized the ballet in being, as Lincoln Kirstein has said, the first balletic "metaphor of the everyday." More spectacles followed — *Le Boeuf sur le toit* to music by Milhaud, *Les Mariés de la Tour Eiffel,* with music by five members of the group called Les Six. He was also writing witty, acute essays on art and adapting Sophocles' *Antigone* for a Paris production.

During his infatuation with the sullen young genius Raymond Radiguet, Cocteau wrote poetry of a classical cast and two excellent, short, "straight" novels, *Le Grand Écart* and *Thomas l'Imposteur.* When Radiguet died at twenty in 1923 after writing *his* two novels, *Le Diable au corps* and *Le Bal du Comte d'Orgel,* Cocteau fell into a depression: he took to opium and entered a brief period of active Catholicism with Jacques Maritain, and the lifelong procession of "adopted sons" began — more or less talented youngsters, attempts to replace Radiguet.

In 1925 came the play *Orphée,* in 1930 the first film, the beautiful *Blood of a Poet,* probably the culmination of his artistic career. Success and celebrity in the Parisian and international worlds of the theatre and the arts brought with them a deterioration of an always vulnerable personality. Not through wealth, as so often happens — Cocteau was not financially minded, and never grew rich. But he was involved in too many things, knew too many people, fed his insecurity with too much publicity, and in the great whirl lost his faculty for discriminating, which had been a weak point from the beginning. The German rape and occupation of France seemed to trouble him only insofar as it interfered with his supply of opium.

In the late 1940's and the 1950's he could still produce marvels — the films *La Belle et la bête* and *Orphée* among them — but there was a deepening of the insecurity that had often led him into breakdowns when it hadn't forced him into his greatest brilliancies, and he spent most of his last decade as the guest of a wealthy friend, Madame Weisweiller, in her villa at St. Jean Cap Ferrat, where she sheltered also the last of the "adopted sons," Édouard Dermit, (who became Cocteau's heir). From that gilded refuge he frequently emerged to attend a premiere or revival of one of his plays or films, to sit on a film jury, or to unveil one of his mural decorations.

Cocteau's work provides many beauties as well as many disappointments. In much of it there is an alienating brittleness, stemming from the incomplete opening of his heart, so crippled by early circumstances. And yet there is scarcely a volume of French verse more beguiling than Cocteau's *Opéra;* his poems of desire in *Plain-chant,* inspired by Radiguet, are in the great tradition of French love poetry; his film adaptations of his own plays *Les Parents terribles* and *Orphée* are considered by cinema critics a triumphant accomplishment, the lesson in bridging the gap between theatre and cinema.

Jean Anouilh dates his theatrical career from a chance reading of *Les Mariés de la Tour Eiffel;* Cocteau's epigrams — "Victor Hugo was a madman who thought he was Victor Hugo" and its companions — find their place in any anthology of French wit; and W. H. Auden has written: "The lasting feeling that [Cocteau's] work leaves is one of happiness; not, of course, in the sense that it excludes suffering, but because, in it, nothing is rejected, resented or regretted. Happiness is a surer sign of wisdom than we are apt to think, and perhaps Cocteau has more of it to offer than some others whose claims are louder and more solemn."

COLERIDGE, Samuel Taylor (Oct. 21, 1772 – July 25, 1834). English poet and critic. Born at father's vicarage, Ottery St. Mary, Devon. Educated at Christ's Hospital school, London (with Charles Lamb), and Jesus College, Cambridge, with a brief interruption for service with the 15th Dragoons. With Robert Southey developed pantisocracy, a plan for a socialist community on the Susquehanna River in Pennsylvania. Married (1795) Sarah Fricker, sister of Southey's wife; they had four children. Play in collaboration with Southey *The Fall of Robespierre* (published 1794) followed by Coleridge's *Poems on Various Subjects* (1796). Pantisocracy having failed for lack of funds, he settled in Nether Stowey, Somerset (1797), and became close friends with William Wordsworth. Together they produced *Lyrical Ballads* (1798), considered a literary landmark in development of nineteenth-century romanticism. It includes Coleridge's *The Rime of the Ancient Mariner* and Wordsworth's *Lines Composed Above Tintern Abbey.* Traveled to Germany with the Wordsworths, having developed interest in German literature and philosophy, and produced Schiller translation *Wallenstein* (1799–1800). Haunted by ill health, he became increasingly addicted to opium. *Dejection: An Ode* written during this period (1802). Separated from family and lived with friends during remainder of life. Lectured on literature, published *Christabel* and *Kubla Khan* (1816, both begun 1797), and his great prose work *Biographia Literaria* (1817). A poet whose extraordinarily creative imagination evoked the mysterious and the supernatural, Coleridge was also a profound critic, especially on Shakespeare, Milton, and Wordsworth. Other works include *The Pains of Sleep* (1816), *Sibylline Leaves* (1817), *Aids to Reflection* (1825), *On the Constitution of the Church and State* (1830), and *Confessions of an Inquiring Spirit* (posthu-

mous, 1840). Died at home of his friend Dr. James Gillman at Highgate, London. The *Collected Poems* of Coleridge's eldest son Hartley (1796–1849) appeared in 1851.

EDITIONS: *Complete Works* ed. Henry Nelson Coleridge (7 vols. London and New York 1871). *Biographia Literaria* ed. George Watson (London and New York 1956). *Coleridge's Shakespearian Criticism* (2 vols. Cambridge, Mass. and London 1931) and *Coleridge's Miscellaneous Criticism* (Cambridge, Mass. and London 1936) ed. Thomas M. Raynor. *The Political Thought of Samuel Taylor Coleridge* ed. Reginald J. White (London 1938). *The Philosophical Lectures of Samuel Taylor Coleridge* ed. Kathleen Coburn (New York and London 1949).

REFERENCES: E. K. Chambers *Samuel Taylor Coleridge: A Biographical Study* (Oxford and New York 1938). John Colmer *Coleridge: Critic of Society* (Oxford and New York 1959). Lawrence Hanson *The Life of Samuel Taylor Coleridge: The Early Years* (New York 1962). John Livingston Lowes *The Road to Xanadu: A Study in the Ways of the Imagination* (Boston 1927, also PB). I. A. Richards *Coleridge on Imagination* (London 1934 and New York 1935, also PB).

☛

SAMUEL TAYLOR COLERIDGE
BY KENNETH BURKE

Underlying all of Coleridge's mature work there was his hankering after an idealistic metaphysics, of strongly theological cast. But though when he came to Cambridge in 1791 it was expected that he was destined to take orders, he rarely entered a church. The point is worth keeping in mind when considering such tracts as his *Aids to Reflection* (1825) and *On the Constitution of the Church and State, According to the Idea of Each* (1830). His piety had to be enacted in ways of his own; but it also had, as a notably characteristic secular counterpart, what one biographer refers to as "the instinct of reverence to superiors in worldly rank."

Yet the statement that a pronounced theological strain permeates all his writing goes as well for a masterpiece such as *Christabel*, which one anonymous reviewer, a contemporary of Coleridge, called "the most obscene Poem in the English Language."

Born in 1772, dying in 1834, he underwent in 1798–99 what is generally agreed to have been his "wonderful year." It was the time of his first close contact with Wordsworth (whom he already called "the best poet of the age"), the time when he wrote three of the most astonishing literary "deviants" in all history (*The Rime of the Ancient Mariner*, the first part of *Christabel*, and *Kubla Khan*, a "fragment" with its own peculiar kind of *perfection*), and the time when Thomas and Josiah Wedgwood, in offering him an annuity of 150 pounds for life or as long as their fortune might permit, solved some pressing financial problems in connection with his recent marriage.

Also, these three rare poems were written during the "honeymoon period" of his addiction to opium, a drug whose "withdrawal symptoms" would, at a later stage, greatly intensify whatever sense of guilt might be associated with his theological proclivities, his troubled marital situation, and his unsettled relations to the society of his day. By 1802, in *Dejection*, he was lamenting that his "genial spirits fail." Symptoms that were but inchoate at an earlier stage had by then become imperious. And though those stanzas (of a sort for which he invented the name of "conversation poem") greatly command our respect, they lack the odd magic of the three great mystery poems (or, as I'd prefer to call them, the poems of fascination).

Also, about this period in Coleridge's life there hinges a set of doctrinal transformations. A few years previously he had proclaimed himself a democrat and "necessitarian." He had been much exercised by the promises of pantisocracy, a project that he, Southey, and some others had conceived for founding a communist ("aspheterist") colony on the banks of the Susquehanna (a way of life designed to "make virtue inevitable"). Such hankerings were in response to the stirrings of revolution in France. But during the *annus mirabilis*, events like Napoleon's invasion of Switzerland and threatened invasion of Britain had radically modified such attitudes (see such poems as *France: An Ode* and *Fears in Solitude*). Also, of course, there was the influence of Wordsworth's break with his political past and its personal involvements. So, all told, Coleridge emerged with an ardent desire to dissociate himself from all suspicion of Jacobin trends. And henceforth this former "necessitarian" was to proclaim with fervor his belief in the freedom of the will, even while bemoaning the effects of what he called "this *free-agency-annihilating* Poison," on the grounds that "by the long Habit of the accursed Poison my Volition . . . was compleatly deranged."

More later on the poems. Meanwhile, we should consider another notable development in the career of this exceptionally complex, sensitive, and learned genius: the *Biographia Literaria*, published in 1817. What Aristotle's *Poetics* had done for criticism, in spinning out the implications of the term "action," Coleridge's critical masterpiece (and it is a masterpiece, despite its lapses and entanglements) does by spinning out the implications of the term "imagination."

Coleridge splits the concept of imagination two ways. First, there is the distinction between imagination and fancy, with the unifying ("shaping and modifying") principle of imagination rated much higher than the diversifying (merely "aggregative and associative") principle of fancy. (The distinction is summed up at the end of chapter 13.) Next, imagination itself gets cut in two. There is imagination in the *general* sense that all human beings translate the underpinnings of reality into the imagery of sensation. And there is a *special* sense of the term, as applied to the unique gifts of a great poet (such as Wordsworth, whose work is treated at length, though in *Biographia Literaria* and elsewhere Coleridge also discusses many other examples of this "genial" aptitude). There is also admirable method in Coleridge's judicious way of considering the integrally related virtues and shortcomings of a poem or poet.

A possible line of investigation would be to consider the dialectical devices whereby Coleridge's concept of poetic *imagination* contrives to overlap the Aristotelian concept of poetic *action.* But for present purposes we should turn, rather, to the ambiguous relationship between the concept of imagination when it is on parade in Coleridge's critical treatise and the concept as used when, in his letters, he is decrying (even in one letter written during the "wonderful year") "my body diseased and fevered by my imagination." Many other such expressions could be cited. For despite its high rating in *Biographia Literaria,* elsewhere Coleridge often uses the term imagination "problematically." (Except perhaps for one other notable "deviant," Longinus *On the Sublime,* such is traditionally the case in Western thought prior to the term's upgrading in German philosophy at about the time of Kant.)

But *poetic* imagination, he says, is never "fixed on one image." Rather, it makes for "the substitution of a sublime feeling of the unimaginable for a mere image." And in this capacity it may introduce "persons and characters supernatural, or at least romantic." This brings us back to the fascination poems, clearly part of the eighteenth-century Gothic reaction that was haunted by thoughts of the West's feudal past.

In the ballad of *The Ancient Mariner,* with its guilt-laden wanderer (a constantly recurrent theme of Coleridge's), he transcends his typical complexities by an archaizing quasi-simplicity. In essence the poem is a ritual for the symbolic transforming of evil into good. But though the peripety comes at the ideal spot (in the middle, or fourth, of the poem's seven sections), the guilt is not ultimately resolved, and the poem ends on the likelihood of relapse.

The romantic agony in *Christabel* catches the principles of good and evil at a moment of integral indecisiveness, each implicit in the other (as with the portentous vision of a snake coiled round a dove, "swelling its neck as she swelled hers").

In *Kubla Khan* the sinister possibilities are kept in the offing. And though they are present (as with references to "Ancestral voices prophesying war" and the admonition to "Beware! Beware!"), the poem is essentially euphoric (the first stanza ends on "sunny spots of greenery" and the last on "the milk of Paradise"). This poem, with its ingredient of "automatic writing" (it was conceived verbatim in a dream), is so perfectly the surrealist ideal, it greatly antedated the critical norms of its time, and the more we learn of Coleridge's notebooks the more clearly we begin to peer into the prophetic mazes of his labyrinthine mind (with his many observations built around his interest in himself as a syndrome of symptoms). See, for instance, the charming fragments in *Anima Poetae.*

Early in his life, Coleridge became interested in a possible poem, *The Brook*, tracing a stream from its beginnings. This project later developed into speculations on the sources of the Nile — and thus in time the scheme got reversed, becoming in effect an imagery of *regression*. The full complexity of such speculations attains almost rhapsodic simplification in *Kubla Khan*. Accordingly, this really miraculous poem lends itself to many interpretations.

Above all, if we would look at it as a poem about the psychology of the creative process itself, we should go a step farther and see in it a poetic equivalent of Kantian transcendentalism, with its reduction of experience to the sheer *forms* of thought (except that here the forms are presented in terms of imagery and acts rather than as metaphysical abstractions). Or the exhilarations and self-accusations of creative novelty can be seen to merge with problems of *eros* and *agape* (*amor* and *caritas*) as we proceed from the thesis (the "innocence" of the Edenic garden in the first stanza) to the antithesis of the second (the "fall" into a tangle of romantic passions), to the synthesis of the third and final stanza, with its analogue of the Madonna, plus romantic interweavings, and the poetic son at once elated and guilt-laden.

COLETTE, (Sidonie Gabrielle Claudine) (Jan. 28, 1873 – Aug. 3, 1954). French novelist. Born St. Sauveur-en-Puisaye, Burgundy, daughter of retired army officer. Precocious student and avid reader. At sixteen moved with family to Chatillon-Coliquy and met young novelist and music critic Henri Gauthier-Villars, whom later she married. They settled in Paris and under pseudonym of Willy collaborated on the four Claudine novels (1900–1903). Divorce ended collaboration (1906), and Colette took up a music hall career, later the subject of her novel *La Vaga-*

bonde (1910). Married writer Henri de Jouvenel (1910, later divorced) and resumed writing. Worked as army nurse in World War I, for which she was made chevalier of Legion of Honor. Under name Colette produced the celebrated novels *Chéri* (1920), *La Fin de Chéri* (1926), *Sido* (1929), *La Naissance de jour* (1932), *Duo* (1934), *Gigi* (1945, later a film), and others. With delicacy of perception she wrote of sensitive relationships between men and women, often over a crisis in their emotional lives, of country life, and of animals, especially cats. She also contributed a wide variety of articles to periodicals. Her role as France's foremost woman writer won her the honor of being the only woman ever elected to the Goncourt Academy. Married (1935) Maurice Goudeket (see References below). Died in Paris, and was accorded formal state funeral. Numerous translations of her books are available.

REFERENCES: Margaret Crosland *Madame Colette: A Provincial in Paris* (London 1953 and, as *Colette: A Provincial in Paris*, New York 1954). Maurice Goudeket *Close to Colette: An Intimate Portrait of a Woman of Genius* (New York 1957).

COLLINS, William (Dec. 25, 1721 – June 12, 1759). English poet. Born Chichester. His father, a wealthy hatter, was twice mayor of the town. Entered Winchester College (1733), where Joseph Warton was his friend. While at Magdalen College, Oxford (1742), published *Persian Eclogues* (2nd ed. 1757 called *Oriental Eclogues*), which alone of his works attracted attention during his lifetime. After graduating from Magdalen (1743) settled in London, where he frequented green rooms and made friends with David Garrick and Samuel Johnson. *Odes on Several Descriptive and Allegorical Subjects* (1747) contains his two best-known works, *Ode to Evening* and *Ode Written in the Beginning of the Year 1746* ("How sleep the brave"). Other important poems are his *Ode Occasioned by the Death of Mr. Thomson* (1749) and *Ode on the Popular Superstitions of the Highlands of Scotland* (1788), which anticipates themes of the romantics. Suffered from mental illness from 1751 and was confined to an asylum (1754), later removed to the care of his sister in Chichester, where he died. Little admired in his time, when Samuel Johnson, for example, wrote: "The poetry of Collins may sometimes extort praise when it gives little pleasure," Collins is now appreciated for his odes.

REFERENCES: Edward G. Ainsworth *Poor Collins: His Life, His Art, and His Influence* (Rochester, N. Y. 1937). Samuel Johnson *The Lives of the Poets* (Dublin 1779–81).

COLLINS, (William) Wilkie (Jan. 8, 1824 – Sept. 23, 1889). English novelist. Born and died in London. Educated in English private schools, with interval (1836–38) in Italy. Called to the bar (1851), became friend of Dickens, and soon turned all his attention to writing. Published biography of his father, a landscape painter (1848). Met (1854) lifelong friend Caroline Graves, whom he never married. Many of his novels were published in installments in Dickens's periodicals *Household Words* and *All the Year Round*, including (in the latter) his best and most popular works, *The Woman in White* (1860), a mystery, and *The Moonstone* (1868), forerunner of the modern detective novel. Other successful novels from this period, notable for their ingenious and highly dramatic plots, are *No Name* (1862) and *Armadale* (1866). Later works inclined heavily toward didacticism and social criticism, including *Man and Wife* (1870) and *The New Magdalen* (1873). Following a reading tour of the U.S. (1873–74), Collins's health began to fail and he became a recluse, though continuing to write.

REFERENCES: Robert Paul Ashley *Wilkie Collins* (New York and London 1952). Nuel P. Davis *The Life of Wilkie Collins* (Urbana, Ill. 1956). Kenneth Robinson *Wilkie Collins: A Biography* (London 1951 and New York 1952).

CONGREVE, William (Jan. 24, 1670 – Jan. 19, 1729). English dramatist. Born Bardsey, Yorkshire, son of an army officer who was soon transferred to Ireland. At Kilkenny school (1681–86) and at Trinity College, Dublin (1686–88), he was the friend of Jonathan Swift. In England again, he briefly studied law while launching literary career with *Incognita* (1692), a romance. First comedy, *The Old Bachelor* (1693), extremely successful, was followed by *The Double Dealer* (1693) and *Love for Love* (1695). A staunch Whig, Congreve was rewarded by his party (1695) with appointment as commissioner for licensing hackney coaches. His only tragedy, *The Mourning Bride* (1697), was followed by his masterpiece *The Way of the World* (1700), which was coolly received. Thereafter Congreve wrote little, spending much of his time as a retired gentleman with members of the Kit-Cat Club. Appointed commissioner of wines (1705) and secretary to island of Jamaica (1714). Died in London. Congreve surpassed his fellow playwrights of the Restoration in the sophisticated wit and brilliant dialogue that characterize the comedy of manners of the period.

EDITION: *The Complete Works of William Congreve* ed. Montague Summers (4 vols. London 1923).

REFERENCES: Edmund Gosse *Life of William Congreve* (London 1924). John C. Hodges *William Congreve, the Man* (New York and London 1941). D. Crane Taylor *William Congreve* (London 1931).

CONRAD, Joseph (Joez Teodor Konrad Nalecz Korzeniowski) (Dec. 3/6, 1857 – Aug. 3, 1924). Polish-born English writer. Born Berdichev, Ukraine, then under Russian rule, of nationalistic, intellectual parents, whom he accompanied into exile in Russia. Orphaned (1869), Conrad lived with uncle in Cracow, where he was educated. Traveled in Europe and at seventeen went to sea, first in French marine service, then — after personal difficulties in France — in English merchant service (1878–94). Voyaged to Mediterranean and Far East, received master mariner's certificate (1886), and became naturalized British subject. After harrowing trip up the Congo, left the sea for good and in London (1894) turned to writing. Surmounting agonizing difficulties of composition in English, produced *Almayer's Folly* (1895) and *An Outcast of the Islands* (1896). Married Jessie George (1896); they had two sons. Success came with *The Nigger of the Narcissus* (1898) and especially with *Lord Jim* (1900), which use his sea experiences, as do the notable short stories *Youth* and *Heart of Darkness* (1902), *Typhoon and Other Stories* (1903), and *The Secret Sharer* (1912). Other novels include *Nostromo* (1904), *The Secret Agent* (1907), *Under Western Eyes* (1911), *Chance* (1914), *Victory* (1915), *The Shadow-Line* (1917), *The Arrow of Gold* (1919), *The Rescue* (1920), *The Rover* (1923), and with Ford Madox Ford *The Inheritors* (1901), *Romance* (1903), and *The Nature of a Crime* (1924). Conrad also wrote essays, studies, and the autobiographical works *The Mirror of the Sea* (1906) and *Some Reminiscences* (1912). There are several collections of his letters. The structural art of his work, his extraordinary descriptive power, and his psychological realism make Conrad one of the twentieth century's great writers. Died at Bishopsbourne, England.

REFERENCES: Jocelyn Baines *Joseph Conrad* (New York and London 1960, also PB). Edward Crankshaw *Joseph Conrad: Some Aspects of the Art of the Novel* (London and New York 1936). John D. Gordan *Joseph Conrad: The Making of a Novelist* (Cambridge, Mass. and London 1940). Albert J. Guérard *Conrad the Novelist* (Cambridge, Mass. 1958, also PB). Gérard Jean-Aubry *The Sea Dreamer: A Definitive Biography of Joseph Conrad* (tr. New York and London 1957).

✍

JOSEPH CONRAD

BY FRANK KERMODE

Nearly always at the end of his tether, Conrad brought to the art of novel writing a gloomy dedication for which it would be hard to find a parallel even in Flaubert, who had his amusements. Now and again a book came easily — *The Secret Agent,* for example; and writing *Chance,* in the flush of long-delayed popular success, he described himself as "pelting along." But the writing of *Nostromo* gives a better pic-

ture of his working style: he finished it in a thirty-six-hour stint interrupted only by the necessity of having a tooth extracted ("It broke!"), and experienced only exhaustion, "no elation, no relief, even." The book cost him nearly two years, punctuated by his own illnesses, the crippling of his wife, the failure of his bank, and the constant professional attentions of Ford Madox Ford, then called Hueffer, who actually seems to have written parts of it. When he emerged from his study he observed that his children had grown considerably in the interval. "Man is a worker, or he is nothing": this was his belief, pronounced in an England that was already forgetting Carlyle.

What did he work towards? "A meticulous precision of statement," he tells us in *Lord Jim,* for that alone will "bring out the true horror behind the appalling face of things." To achieve such a precision one underwent all that sense of failure, that exhaustion, those dry periods, what Baudelaire called *les stérilités des écrivains nerveux.* He had, at least, one negative qualification for producing good art: an utter inability to repeat himself, to repeat a successful formula or solution. He felt that honesty required him always to cut against the grain. Few men have ever taken on material so recalcitrant. Polish was his first language, and French his second; but he wrote in English. His foreign notions about fiction required him to import into England structural and narrative devices of a distinctly French variety. At the same time he maintained, with very few aberrations, a reticence about sex which is neither English nor French. Verloc's beefy sexuality at the moment of his death is the more effective because of it; Heyst, in victory, is betrayed into it by a failure to keep his promise never "to be tempted into action." It is part of the horror of

Heart of Darkness. Sex for Conrad is more often an aspect of dishonor than part of a living relationship. This is against the whole tradition of the novel. But thus he worked. He told stories of the sea, in many of which he played his own part as a younger man; but they are changed, by those foreign devices, into complex artifacts, violating chronology, illustrating a bleak order.

Why did he work thus? "Above all," he said, "to make you see." The means may appear oversophisticated if one underestimates the end, or its remoteness. "Conrad *writes:* it shows," said his erstwhile friend H. G. Wells. It shows not only in the occasional lapse into rhetorical overemphasis, or the occasional fussiness of the narrative sequence in *Lord Jim*, but even in the structure and texture of *Nostromo*, which is undoubtedly a great book. *The Secret Agent* he called "a simple tale," but in it he brought off effects — the café, the cab drive of Winnie Verloc's mother — he could not hope for in the heavier work. The more serious the intention the harder the work had to be. "*C'est un art trop difficile,*" he complained.

It is when the difficulty, self-created, is fully met that the sneering stops: for example, the balancing of the whole enormous weight of *Nostromo* on one point, the reaction of Decoud to his solitude. To get this Conrad laboriously imagined a whole politics, invented a state and a topography — almost a continent — and thought his way into revolutions. This is a particular instance of what he called the art of rendering "the highest kind of truth to the visible universe, by bringing to light the truth, manifold and one, underlying its every aspect."

Conrad, said Henry James, takes a "prolonged hovering flight over the outstretched ground of the case exposed."

What are the features of this terrain? It is the world seen by one who, having loved the humanity of it, renounced action and saw in it the pattern of evil. Jim's need was *not* to jump, but also to be a convict rather than an idiot. Rasumov the betrayer, storming out of Mikulin's office in *Under Western Eyes*, has passed out of the region of idiotic gestures; if he is going he must go somewhere. "Where to?" asks Mikulin, softly. Over the crazily decorated surface of the earth men carry guilt, or bombs, stupidly acting. Conrad carried the memory of his suicide attempt, perhaps the memory of the Poland he deserted; he carried also a paybook marked D.R. (Decline to Report), which in the merchant service is a dishonorable discharge. But he remembered also a youth which might have ended not only in Rasumov or Kurtz but in the honor betrayed of Captain Whalley, at the end of his tether, or of Il Conde in the story so called. He was a convict.

So he labored on, a gentleman, the friend of Galsworthy, a visionary who despised visionaries, saved by Work and Fidelity, expiating "the curse of consciousness." To be conscious was tragic; any human design to mitigate this punishment he detested, as he detested anarchism and Communism, and the Russians who valued them. In a world full of suffering, a religion which taught that it was expiatory was "an infamous abomination." When the idiots started a war and released the horror into the streets — where no Inspector Heat could check it — he fled, suffering "exquisite tortures," from Poland to England. He was successful, no longer poor, and too old for action. He wrote *The Shadow Line*, once more remembering his own youth, out of which he could make all the patterns of the struggle of fidelity against the horror of consciousness.

Recalling that past, Conrad sometimes extolled the simple man, the sea captain calm and unaffected at the heart of the typhoon, mastering a destructive element. But he also recalled the young officer confronted with his criminal double, his *semblable*, and the old man tormented by fate and his own nobility. He knew, in his own life, these tensions; he did not kill himself, quite; he never "jumped"; in 1898, with two novels and other important writing behind him, he was still looking for a command. One of his characters carefully sees to his beautiful chronometer before jumping overboard. Conrad saw to it, then did not jump.

CONSTABLE, John (June 11, 1776 – Mar. 31, 1837). English painter. Born East Bergholt, Suffolk, son of a prosperous miller. After education in local school, worked in father's mill, studying painting on the side. Encouraged by art connoisseur Sir George Beaumont, went to London (1795) to study painting and engraving. Entered Royal Academy schools (1799) and, encouraged by Academy president Benjamin West, exhibited (1802). Influenced in variety of ways by Gainsborough, Reynolds, Hoppner, Claude Lorrain, and Dutch landscapists. Married Maria Bicknell (1816) and moved to London permanently. Elected as associate of Royal Academy (1819), but not to full membership until 1829. Meantime his reputation grew at home and in France, where *The Hay Wain* (1821, National Gallery, London) received gold medal at Paris Salon of 1824 and *The White Horse* (1819) the same honor at Lille (1825). Other famous works are *View on the Stour* (1822, Royal Holloway College, Surrey), *The Leaping Horse* (1825), and many views of Salisbury Cathedral, such as *Salisbury Cathedral from the Meadows* (1831, National Gallery, London). Died in London.

REFERENCES: Sidney J. Key *John Constable: His Life and Work* (London and New York 1948). E. V. Lucas *John Constable the Painter* (London and New York 1924). Carlos Peacock *John Constable: The Man and His Work* (Greenwich, Conn. and London 1965). Graham Reynolds *Constable: The Natural Painter* (London and New York 1965). Mark Roskill *English Painting from 1500 to 1865* (London 1959). R. H. Wilenski *English Painting* (London 1964).

JOHN CONSTABLE
BY ANDREW C. RITCHIE

As Ellis Waterhouse has noted, "the most important spiritual descendant of Gainsborough's landscape style is John Constable" (*Gainsborough,* 1958). Constable himself said in one of his lectures of landscape painting delivered in the 1830's: "The landscape of Gainsborough is soothing, tender and affecting. The stillness of noon, the depths of twilight, and the dews and pearls of the morning, are all to be found on the canvases of this most benevolent and kindhearted man." Constable like Gainsborough was country-bred and both were born and brought up in Suffolk, one of the most beautiful counties of England. Constable, son of a well-to-do miller in East Bergholt, was tolerably well educated in a country grammar school, where he acquired some knowledge of Latin and French and learned to express himself with some ease in his own tongue. He was in his beginnings self-taught as a painter and trained first of all as a miller (at his father's insistence). In other words, the father, with traditional middle-class caution, tried to turn his son from an artistic career to his own. Constable was thus early associated with nature on a professional basis, and must have learned to observe wind and weather as they directly affected the waterwheel of his father's mill.

Torn between devotion to painting and respect for his father's wishes, Constable began his career as a painter slowly and in fits and starts. He learned something in the beginning from Dunthorne, a local painter in East Bergholt, and attended the Royal Academy schools in 1799. He was encouraged by Sir George Beaumont, an amateur painter, connoisseur, and devotee of Claude. He copied landscapes by Claude, Ruisdael and Gaspard Poussin as a form of self-teaching. He greatly admired J. R. Cozen's watercolors and must have learned from him, as did so many English artists of this time, something fresh and exciting in the construction of landscape as opposed to the clichés of the picturesque tradition.

While Constable's first love was landscape, in order to acquire financial independence he painted some portraits in the early 1800's and carried out two commissions for church altar paintings. A few of these portraits are interesting. The altarpieces are best forgotten.

As Constable progressed along his true course of landscape painting his objective became comparable to Wordsworth's in poetry — to liberate art from accumulated artificialities. In his preface to *Lyrical Ballads,* published in 1798, which Constable as an admirer of the poet had undoubtedly read, Wordsworth said: "The principal object, then, proposed in these poems was to choose incidents and situations from common life, and to relate or describe them . . . in a selection of language really used by men, and at the same time to throw over them a certain coloring of imagination, whereby ordinary things should be presented to the mind in an unusual aspect . . . Humble and rustic life was generally chosen, because, in that condition, the essential passions of the heart find a better soil in which they can attain their maturity." As applied to painting, no better description of Constable's purpose can be imagined. He said himself: "The sound of water escaping from mill-

dams, etc., willows, old rotten planks, slimy posts, and brickwork, I love such things. . . . The landscape painter must walk in the field with an humble mind. No arrogant man was ever permitted to see nature in all her beauty." And further: "My limited and abstracted art is to be found under every hedge and in every land, and therefore nobody thinks it worth picking up."

This last comment may be taken as a somewhat bitter reaction to the lack of enthusiasm in public and official circles with which his work was generally received throughout his life. He tried to appease the Royal Academy authorities by "finishing" his canvases for exhibition — slicking over what appeared to the conventional eye to be the rough surface of his brushwork and the crude directness of his coloring. For example, it was the "finished" version of *The Hay Wain* which he sent to Paris for exhibition in 1824, which so impressed Delacroix and is said to have led him to repaint his *Massacre of Chios.* How much more impressed Delacroix might have been by the so-called "sketch" for *The Hay Wain,* now in the Victoria and Albert Museum!

Despite his efforts to please official taste, Constable was not made an associate of the Royal Academy until 1819, when he was forty-three; and he had to wait until he was fifty-three, eight years before his death, before he was made a full academician — in contrast to Turner, who became an A.R.A. at twenty-four and an R.A. at twenty-seven. (One recalls Cézanne's pathetic efforts to be admitted to the Salon and how less successful, because more uncompromising, he was than Constable.)

Towards the end Constable became disillusioned by the lack of recognition of his work, and he was lonely and somewhat embittered after the death of his wife, to whom he was extremely devoted. This explains the sharpness of his criticism of reactionary painters and connoisseurs and their lack of sympathy for his own experimental approach to nature. In the final years of his life we find him more in sympathy with the inquiring minds of the scientists than with the backward-looking minds of his fellow academicians.

With reference to Constable's paintings, the word "sketch" should be explained. Constable made two kinds of sketches. The first are quite small and personal in nature, like Seurat's *croquetons,* and not all were intended for exhibition. Some of these he used as studies for pictures on a larger scale; others were never taken beyond the small sketch stage. The second type is on a larger scale, free in execution, and while as pictures they were often as final as Constable would wish, they were not, he knew, acceptable as finished works according to the academic standards of his day. In this category are *Weymouth Bay* (National Gallery, London), *Sketch for a View on the Stour* (Royal Holloway College, Surrey, England) and *Salisbury Cathedral from the River* (National Gallery, London). "Sketches" such as these Constable would either exhibit as they were or translate into "finished" canvases. Towards the end of his life he became less concerned with the distinction between sketch and finished picture.

Salisbury Cathedral from the River is the most fluent and lyrical of all Constable's many studies of this, his favorite cathedral. A number of these are quite careful architectural renderings, commissioned portraits, so to speak, of the building and its surroundings (he was actually commissioned to paint the cathedral by Dr. Fisher, the bishop of Salisbury, his patron). The view from the river is painted with an uninhibited excitement and love of the scene which seem to indicate that the artist was painting for his own pleasure rather than to please a patron. So, too, *Fording the River* (Guildhall Art Gallery, London), a picture on a much grander scale, is truly pictorial rather than topographical in conception.

In *Stoke-by-Nayland* (Art Institute, Chicago), painted a year before his death, Constable sums up, in what must be considered one of his greatest masterpieces, all those qualities of "light — dews — breezes — bloom — and freshness" which he had been striving for, "not one of which," he added, "has yet been perfected on the canvas of any painter in the world."

CONSTANT, Benjamin (full name **Henri Benjamin Constant de Rebecque**) (Oct. 25, 1767 – Dec. 8, 1830). French writer and statesman. Born Lausanne, Switzerland, son of an army man of Huguenot ancestry. Educated by tutors and at universities of Erlangen (1782) and Edinburgh (1783–84). Formed (1787) close friendship with novelist Madame de Charrière (1740–1805, known also as Zélide). Became chamberlain to duke of Brunswick (1788) and married a lady of the court, Wilhelmina von Cramm (1789). Met Madame de Staël (1794), with whom he maintained a tempestuous liaison until 1811, and under whose influence he entered French politics. Having divorced his wife, he accompanied Madame de Staël to Paris (1795), where he became a tribune under Napoleon (1799–1802). In exile in Germany because of his liberal views (1802–14), he wrote *Adolphe* (1815), the novel on which his literary reputation chiefly rests and a landmark in the development of the psychological novel. Married Charlotte von Hardenberg (1808). Reconciled with Napoleon (1815), became a councillor of state. After Waterloo joined liberal opposition to the Bourbons, first as a journalist, then as a deputy (1819–22, 1824–30). Elected president of council of state (1830).

Died in Paris. His works include numerous political treatises, the journals *Le Cahier rouge* (1907) and *Journal intime* (1887–89), the novel *Cécile* (not published until 1951, after very late discovery), and *De la Réligion considérée dans sa source, ses formes et ses développements* (5 vols. 1824–31).

TRANSLATIONS: *Adolphe* tr. Carl Wildman (new ed. New York and London 1948). *Cécile* tr. Norman Cameron (London 1952). *The Red Notebook* tr. Norman Cameron (new ed. New York and London 1948).

REFERENCES: Lord David Cecil *Poets and Storytellers* (London and New York 1949). Harold G. Nicolson *Benjamin Constant* (London and New York 1949). Geoffrey Scott *Portrait of Zélide* (New York 1925).

COOPER, James Fenimore (Sept. 15, 1789 – Sept. 14, 1851). American novelist, social critic, and historian. Born Burlington, N.J., son of wealthy landholder who moved family (1790) to estate at Cooperstown, which he had founded. Expelled for a prank from Yale (1805), Cooper went to sea (1806) and was commissioned as midshipman in the navy (1808). Married Susan Augusta De Lancey (1811) and settled on country estate. After first novel, *Precaution* (1820), achieved international fame with *The Spy* (1821) and thenceforth devoted himself to writing. Moved to New York (1822), produced sea story *The Pilot* (1823), and continued the Leatherstocking Tales begun with *The Pioneers* (1823), following career of frontier hero Natty Bumppo in *The Last of the Mohicans* (1826) and *The Prairie* (1827). Traveled in Europe (1826–33), writing sea stories (among them *The Red Rover*, 1828) and a defense of America against European criticism, *Notions of the Americans* (1828). After settling in Cooperstown (1833), became disillusioned with Jacksonian democracy. Expressed his criticism and conservative ideas in *The American Democrat* (1838) and in novels *Homeward Bound* (1838) and *Home as Found* (1838), which were attacked by the press; he was generally victorious in the libel suits he thereupon brought. Produced scholarly *History of the Navy of the United States*

of America (1839), completed Leatherstocking Tales with *The Pathfinder* (1840) and *The Deerslayer* (1841). Continued social criticism in three novels of manners: *Satanstoe* (1845), *The Chainbearers* (1845), and *The Redskins* (1846). Of over thirty fictional works, Cooper is best remembered for his American frontier tales full of adventure in a vivid historical setting.

EDITIONS: *The Correspondence of James Fenimore Cooper* ed. J. F. Cooper (2 vols. New Haven 1922). *A Descriptive Bibliography of the Writings of James Fenimore Cooper* ed. R. E. Spiller and P. C. Blackburn (New York 1934).

REFERENCES: Henry W. Boynton *James Fenimore Cooper* (New York 1931). James Grossman *James Fenimore Cooper* (New York 1949 and London 1950, also PB). Robert E. Spiller *Fenimore Cooper: Critic of His Times* (New York and London 1931). Warren S. Walker *James Fenimore Cooper: An Introduction and Interpretation* (New York 1962, also PB).

✍

JAMES FENIMORE COOPER
BY ROBERT PENN WARREN

About one hundred years ago the Leatherstocking Tales fell from the hands of grown-ups into the hands of boys. About fifty years ago they fell from the hands of boys into the hands of scholars. What the scholars now find there is not what the boys found, and probably not what the great-grandfathers of the boys found, either. But what the scholars find is what Cooper put there — a thing central to his other work: a criticism of American society.

Cooper spent his boyhood in the great house of a wilderness village, Cooperstown, which his father had established in the midst of the domain he was opening up for settlement. Old William Cooper was a land speculator, a wrestler, a congressman, a judge, a friend of Aaron Burr, and a ferocious Federalist who died of a blow on the head received in a political affray. But if young James lived in the citadel of conservatism called Otsego Hall, he could still see the shadow of the forest, and in that contrast we find adumbrated the polarity of his thought and work.

At the height of the fame gained from the Leatherstocking Tales, Cooper, during his seven-year stay in Europe, wrote *Notions of the Americans* (1828) to rebut the calumnies he encountered abroad, but no sooner was he back home than he found himself violently at loggerheads with his native land and writing a series of novels very different from the frontier saga of Leatherstocking, polemical fictions addressed to the abuses of American democracy.

But if Cooper attacked the actual workings of American democracy, he could, at the same time, avow himself "as good a democrat as there is in America." By the same token, if Cooper was bred up a Federalist, he could come to support Andrew Jackson, the wild man from the coonskin West, even in his attack on the Bank of the United States, declaring that now the conservative was the "best democrat." Now, in other words, he saw the rising Whig plutocracy, not the mob, as the most dangerous enemy of democracy. The key of Cooper's criticism was the fear that a majority, swayed by popular passion manipulated by wealth, would create a tyranny equally devoid of justice and taste. The only counterweight he saw to such a tyranny lay in those rare individuals who were both thoughtful and independent, and more broadly in a class of "gentlemen," informed and public-spirited (not a hereditary aristocracy), which might stand against the irrationalities of the democratic system.

Cooper's social novels deal directly with such questions, but the Leatherstocking Tales are not polemical in this sense; they are directed, not to the corrigible abuses of society, not to the relatively simple ironies explicit in democracy, but to the incorrigible pains and complex ironies implicit in human experience and, specifically, in the history of America. The two groups of novels are, however, related. They stem from the same life view, and they afford different perspectives on the same issues.

In *The Pioneers* (1823), out of a nostalgic vision of boyhood in Cooperstown, emerges Cooper's great theme, with the conflict between Judge Templeton (an image of William Cooper) and Natty Bumppo, who in this first appearance is old and poor, a relic of the frontier, with his only companion the drunken old "Indian John" — who was once the great chief Chingachgook. Judge Templeton is the bringer of civilization — with on one hand the blessings of social order and refinement and on the other the corruption of man and the ravaging of nature, a ravaging exemplified in the famous scene of the maniacal slaughter of passenger pigeons in which even a cannon is used. Natty has saved the Judge's daughter from a panther, but this does not save him from the stocks when he, who must live by his rifle but never kills beyond his need, is haled before the Judge for taking a deer out of season. The Judge is aware of the virtues of Natty, but, as he says to his daughter, the law must be enforced, for "the law alone removes us from the condition of savages." Later, Templeton, having fulfilled his role as judge, acts as a man, and wants to take Natty under his protection, but Natty, out of his steadfast commitment to the free life of the forest, refuses, and disappears west.

So, almost by accident, Cooper stumbled on the theme he was to develop throughout the saga. As Marius Bewley suggests, here is an embodiment of the tensions of the American experience — the tension between freedom and law, natural goodness and the requirements of the social order, the individual and society, the religion of personal intuition and that of theology. In *The Pioneers,* it would be easy to take Natty as representing one set of opposites (freedom, etc.) and Judge Templeton the other; and very likely Cooper began by taking matters in this way. But as he explored his theme, its meaning must have grown deeper. When Cooper came to write the novels of the forest days of Natty's youth, we see that Natty is no simple child of nature. That is the Indian, and the "gifts" of the Indian are not those of Natty, who appreciates the Indian, much as might Levi-Strauss with his structuralist philosophy, but who knows that his own "gifts" are those of the white man.

Balzac calls Natty a "magnificent hermaphrodite born between the savage and the civilized." Natty is more than that, but Balzac does indicate his role as a mediator between opposites. In leaving the realism of *The Pioneers,* Cooper began the idealization of Natty which presents him as the mediator between nature and civilization, the "gentleman" of the wilderness defining values by which society might try to live, but himself remaining outside society, the mythic hunter who is also the embodiment of a philosophy.

The relevance of Cooper is greater now than ever. If Cooper's notion of a class of "gentlemen" sounds quaint to modern ears, we may still realize that the problems of the tyranny of the majority and of maintaining standards of excellence are yet painfully with us. Even more painfully with us is the problem of man's relation to nature

and to other men in the great modern state.

One index of the relevance of Cooper is indicated in his resemblance to Faulkner. Cooper, like Faulkner, came from a personal world that seemed retarded and stood outside his "modernity." Both saw a "doom" in history, in Cooper's case involving the crime against the Indian, in Faulkner's that against the Negro. For both, the violation of the fellow man is associated with a violation of nature, and both hold a vision of a world of "communal brotherhood" in nature. If Cooper dislikes New England Puritans (see also Ishmael Bush in *The Prairie,* the ravager of nature, who, though not a New Englander, justifies his arrogant vengeance by his "fragments" of a Bible), Faulkner equally dislikes his Southern Calvinists. Their philosophers, Ike McCaslin and Natty, are deliberately outside society; what Ike learns in the Big Woods, under the tutelage of Sam Fathers, is what Natty learns in his forest; and both stand as a rebuke to what Faulkner calls the world of "manipulators of money and politics and land" and to those who, corrupted by the "abstractions" of civilization, deny reverence before nature and compassion toward man. If neither believes in a gospel of progress, both see life as redeemed by human kindness, valor, and fidelity.

COPLEY, John Singleton (July 3, 1738 – Sept. 9, 1815). American painter. Born probably in Boston, child of Irish immigrants. Largely self-taught, he assimilated the influence of various colonial portraitists and soon surpassed them all. Copley's American portraits, his finest works, are noted for brilliant color, dramatic chiaroscuro, and particularly for their vitality and realism: his prosperous, upright New England subjects emerge as living and distinct personalities. Among them are Samuel

Adams, John Hancock, Thomas Boylston, John Quincy Adams, the Copley family, and many others in the Museum of Fine Arts, Boston. His first dated work is from 1753; he sent (1766) *The Boy with a Squirrel* (1765) to London, where it was exhibited at Society of Artists and admired by Reynolds and West. Married Susannah Clarke (1769), daughter of wealthy Boston merchant. With decline of work in political upheavals of the early 1770's, Copley emigrated to Europe (1774), settling in London (1775). Continued to paint portraits, in more idealized style suited to English tastes, but concentrated on series of historical subjects, including *Watson and the Shark* (1778, Christ's Hospital, London), which anticipated nineteenth-century romanticism, *The Death of Chatham* (1779–81, Tate Gallery, London), *The Death of Major Pierson* (1782–84, Tate), and *The Siege of Gibraltar* (1784–91). Died in London.

REFERENCES: James Thomas Flexner *John Singleton Copley* (Boston 1947). Jules D. Prown *John Singleton Copley* (2 vols. Cambridge, Mass. and London 1966).

CORBIÈRE, Tristan (real name Édouard Joachim Corbière) (July 18, 1845 – Mar. 1, 1875). French poet. Born Coat-Congar near Morlaix, Brittany, son of writer Jean Corbière (1793–1875). Attended schools in Morlaix, St.-Brieuc, and Nantes until illness forced him to withdraw (1861). Aside from brief trips to southern France, Palestine, and Italy, and sporadic periods of bohemian existence in Paris, he spent all his life on the Breton coast and died at Morlaix. Corbière's only volume of poems, *Les Amours jaunes* (1873), is original in its use of irony and sarcasm, and of a colloquial language in contrast to the lofty rhetoric of the romantics, whom he frequently parodied. Unknown until his inclusion in Verlaine's *Les Poètes maudits* (1884), he was a precursor of the symbolist and surrealist movements.

TRANSLATION: *Selection from Les Amours jaunes* tr. Carlyle F. MacIntyre (Berkeley, Calif. 1954).

REFERENCES: René Martineau *Tristan Corbière* (Paris 1925). Albert Son-nenfeld *L'Oeuvre poétique de Tristan Corbière* (Paris 1960).

CORELLI, Arcangelo (Feb. 17, 1653 – Jan. 8/9, 1713). Italian composer and violinist. Born Fusignano, near Imola. Little is known of his early years beyond his being trained by Matteo Simonelli in counterpoint and by Giovanni Battista Bassani in violin. After travels to Germany and probably France, Corelli settled in Rome (by 1685) for rest of his life, at palace of Cardinal Pietro Ottoboni, where he conducted concerts and composed most of the music for which he is known — numbers of sonatas and concerti grossi notable for rhythmic imaginativeness and for melody. In chamber music he exerted a wide influence, also contributed greatly to the development of violin technique.

REFERENCE: Marc Pincherle *Corelli: His Life, His Work* (tr. New York 1956, also PB).

CORNEILLE, Pierre (June 6, 1606 – Sept. 30, 1684). French dramatist. Born Rouen; educated in Jesuit school there. Studied law; entered Rouen parliament (1629), where he served twenty-one years. Corneille's first play, *Mélite*, a comedy, appeared successfully in Paris (c.1630). Other comedies followed in next six years, also the Senecan tragedy *Médée*, which revealed his genius. Invited by Richelieu (c.1634) to collaborate with four other poets for the cardinal's own theatre. Left this to write *Le Cid* (1636 or 1637), based on a Spanish drama, Guillén de Castro's *Las Mocedades del Cid*. This, his first masterpiece, helped to establish French classical tragedy. After leaving the theatre for three years because of controversy over *Le Cid* brought on by his enemies, Corneille produced three more of his greatest plays: *Horace* (1640), *Cinna* (c.1640), and *Polyeucte* (c.1642). Appointed to French Academy (c.1643), he produced successful comedy *Le Menteur* (c.1643), *La Mort de Pompée* (c.1643), *Rodogune* (c.1644), *Théodore* (1646), *Héraclius* (1647), and *Nicomède* (c.1650). Failure of *Pertharite* (1651) caused him to retire again (in the interval translating Thomas à Kempis's *Imitation of Christ*) until 1659. His later plays, of which the most notable are *Pulchérie* (1672) and *Suréna* (1674), met with diminishing success, and he was at last eclipsed by the triumph of Racine. Moved to Paris (1662) to live quietly with his family and close to his brother Thomas (1625–1709), also a dramatist and writer, until his death.

TRANSLATION: *The Chief Plays of Corneille* tr. Lacy Lockert (2nd ed. Princeton, N. J. and London 1957). *Pierre Corneille: Seven Plays* tr. Samuel Solomon (New York 1970).

REFERENCES: Paul Bénichou *Morales du Grand Siècle* (Paris 1948). G. Couton *Corneille, l'homme et l'oeuvre* (Paris 1958). O. Nadal *Le Sentiment de l'amour dans l'oeuvre de Pierre Corneille* (Paris 1948). Martin Turnell *The Classical Moment: Studies of Corneille, Molière, and Racine* (London 1947).

✍

PIERRE CORNEILLE
BY MARTIN TURNELL

It seems strange at first not only that "the father of French tragedy" should have begun his career with a comedy, but also that six out of his first eight plays should have been comedies. When we look into it, however, we see that the eight plays were in the nature of approach shots, that in the early comedies no less than in the first two tragedies the dramatist was working towards the creation of the Cornelian hero. It is most evident in *La Place Royale*, which reminds us that for all its fun comedy does not exclude seriousness. Alidor jilts Angélique because he feels that love is only one phase in a man's life and is not worth the sacrifice of his freedom. The play ends with Alidor a free man and the disappointed lady taking the veil. It illustrates the slogan contained in the dedication: "You must never allow love to reach the stage when you cannot help loving." Corneille never abandoned this precept. It is, indeed, an article of faith which

explains the similarities between *La Place Royale* and many later works like *Pulchérie*.

One of the main problems of the emerging hero is to discover what manner of man he is. Alidor has not made this discovery. His will triumphs over love on the flimsiest of pretexts; he has no positive goal in view; freedom is an end in itself. The change comes with *Le Cid*. In his first masterpiece the hero, unlike Alidor, is placed in a clearly defined milieu. The conflict arises between the claims of society and of personal inclination. Love must be subordinated to a higher purpose. In *Le Cid* it is honor, in *Horace* patriotism, in *Cinna* politics, in *Polyeucte* religion. These plays reveal the essence of Cornelian tragedy. The conflict ends not in death and destruction, but in moral growth. The moment of truth comes when the protagonists suddenly perceive the path they must follow and possess the moral strength to do it whatever the personal cost. In these plays, too, we see most clearly one of the fundamental differences between Corneille and Racine. In *Bérénice* Racine tried to beat Corneille on his own ground by showing Titus and Bérénice renouncing love in deference to the *raison d'état*, but far from emerging strengthened from the conflict they are both completely broken by it.

There are considerable differences of opinion about the twenty-one plays which followed *Polyeucte*. At one time they were dismissed as inferior work. More recently Corneille's admirers have claimed that his work from the first comedy to the last tragedy is a unified whole. Neither view can be accepted without qualification. Continuity is a better word than unity. In spite of the classical setting, Corneille's work reflects contemporary political trends more closely than Racine's. Continuity is best seen in the importance attributed to the part played by the ruler. Corneille combined support for absolute monarchy with a horror of tyranny. In his most celebrated plays the ruler is the arbiter whose word restores order or sets his seal on a new order. In later plays he first becomes the rival of the hero, then degenerates into the bloodthirsty tyrant who destroys him. Nearly all the plays contain splendid things. *Nicomède*, described as a tragedy, is a brilliantly ironical masterpiece in a novel genre — the heroic comedy; *Pulchérie* and *Suréna* are surely neglected masterpieces, and it is difficult to refuse the same title to *Théodore*.

At the same time it cannot be denied that there was a falling off after *Polyeucte*. It is sometimes ascribed to the influence of Corneille's younger brother Thomas, an immensely popular playwright who was adept in turning out imitations of most of the leading dramatists of the day, including his brother and Racine. There is substance in this criticism. The influence is apparent in the crudeness, the violence, and the love of declamation which in plays like *Rodogune* and *Pertharite* become almost a parody of the heroic style. The real reasons, however, lie deeper. The truth is that the heroic age was over, and that in trying to go on producing heroic plays Corneille was writing against the grain of a new age. It was demonstrated by the triumph of Racine's *Andromaque* in 1667. The play was a contribution to what Paul Bénichou calls "the demolition of the hero" — a debunking operation in which the heroes of the Trojan War are ruthlessly cut down to life size. There is much talk in Racine of *gloire*, but in his plays duty, honor, and most other moral values are swept aside. Only one thing counts: whether or not the lover will get his, or more often her, "prey." It is

significant that in the last plays of all there are marked resemblances between Corneille and Racine, particularly in the versification. Corneille's protagonists still preserve their ideals, but in *Suréna* it is clear that they no longer believe in them in the same way: they are broken men and women for whom death is the only outcome.

It has been argued that the "rivalry" of Corneille and Racine is now of only historical interest. That is true insofar as it means that two professional writers were battling against one another for public favor, but the word is misleading. Racine is the greater writer, but they are both what are known as "constants" of the French genius. They both give consummate expression to something permanent in human nature. Corneille occupies a place which Racine could never have filled. For their effect on us is entirely different. We love Racine because he speaks to us as man to man, exposes our weaknesses to our shocked and fascinated gaze. This should not prevent us from responding to the immense élan, the enormous lift that comes from a good production or a proper reading of Corneille. In some moods I prefer Racine, in others Corneille, but of one thing I am certain: they are both necessary to me.

COROT, Jean Baptiste Camille (July 16, 1796 – Feb. 22, 1875). French painter. Born and died in Paris, son of prosperous draper. Educated at boarding schools in Rouen and Poissy. Apprenticed to Paris drapery shops, he attended night classes at Académie Suisse. Received (1822) allowance from his father to devote himself to painting. Stay in Italy (1825–27) resulted in some of his best early work, like *Bridge of Narni* (Louvre, Paris), and he began to exhibit, sending paintings to Salon of 1827. *Flight into Egypt* (1840) and other historical landscapes increased his reputation, resulting in cross of the

Legion of Honor (1846, made an officer 1867) and position on Salon jury (1849). With *Morning, the Dance of the Nymphs* (1850) his style changed to the romantic landscapes which were to make him famous, particularly after Napoleon III purchased (1855) *Souvenir de Marcoussis*. The style of this, of *Souvenir de Mortefontaine* (1864, Louvre, Paris) and other landscapes marked his last years. Also executed series of figure paintings when attacks of gout made it impossible to travel. Again a jury member at Salon in 1870, he was a revered figure to a generation of French artists.

REFERENCES: Jean Leymarie *Corot: Biographical and Critical Study* (tr. New York 1966). Alfred Robaut *Corot* (4 vols. Paris 1905). *Corot: Paintings and Drawings* (Chicago 1960). Keith Roberts *Corot* (London 1966).

✍

JEAN BAPTISTE CAMILLE COROT
BY JOHN RUSSELL

No one with any judgment at all could glimpse Corot in the street, or at the theatre, or at work in the forest of Fontainebleau, and not realize that he had seen somebody quite out of the ordinary. Corot was tall, well-built and well-knit, with shoulders cut on the square and a complexion like raw beef. He had, as one observer said, "that relaxed, unhurrying manner which goes with independence of mind, a small private income, and very good health." His forehead was broad and high, his hair curly and abundant even in old age, his mouth generously drawn, his glance wide open, direct, and fearless. He had a trusting, unmercenary nature. He disapproved of painters who kept open house and aspired to go into society: as he saw it, the work, not the man, should stand out. In Paris he did not much care to go to his friends' houses, preferring to eat simply and by himself somewhere on the boulevards, take one or two puffs at a cigar, and

go on to the opera, where he would usually have been able to prompt the leading singer if she had chanced to have a lapse of memory. He was never known to read a newspaper, and after twenty years of trying to get through Corneille's tragedy *Polyeucte* he was still stuck in act IV. He would sing solo, in a small company and if pressed, and he had a hefty, persuasive line in gallantry, though he stopped some way short of the blatant approach then in favor among commercial travelers. He was what the French call *entier;* a whole man, in all that he did. Taine put it about in Corot's lifetime that the English gentleman farmer represented the human male animal in its finest form: "Corot was a man of that sort," said the painter J. F. Raffaelli, "but translated into French — not quite so correct in his dress, perhaps, but more convivial."

One can be a whole man, and a big man, and a good man in every way, and still not be much of a painter. For most of his life, Corot was not ranked in the top class, and he was resigned to seeing his pictures hung, as he said, "in the catacombs" when he sent them to mixed exhibitions. But in the last fifty years one generation after another has gone to him for what it most needed to find, and no one has come away disappointed: not a bad record for someone who once said, "I have only a little flute, but I try to play in tune."

This side of Corot did not come through strongly till quite a long time after his death. When he was alive, and tried his hand at big Salon subjects like *Homer Among the Shepherds* and *Hagar in the Wilderness*, he had the air of one competing in a league that he was not fitted for. Those pictures were conscientiously worked up from landscapes that he actually knew, but no one could seriously believe in the events portrayed: we are glad to know that Orpheus in the picture of that name derives from the memory of Pauline Viardot-García in Gluck's opera, but this does not make the picture itself any the less cardboardy. Corot could never pretend — it is part of his greatness — and in this picture the pretending falls apart from the outset.

Our grandfathers knew quite another Corot: the elegiac poet best represented by *Souvenir de Mortefontaine* in the Louvre and later travestied by variants, copies beyond number, imitations, and downright fakes. These pictures — the real ones — nurtured our grandfathers' craving for a certain elevated vagueness in landscape: they call to mind a silvery never-never land in which trees bend in unison from right to left, the light above forest pools is hooded and veiled, and a group of nymphs is forever engaged in some implausible round game. The name of Mortefontaine has a Tennysonian dying fall which our elders found irresistible; in Corot, that magic was multiplied.

Today's taste thinks very little of those paintings. Our preference goes to another Corot: the one who, long before the impressionists, backed his own "little sensation" against everyone else's idea of what a picture should be. Ten years before Cézanne had even got born, this same Corot was pioneering the attitude to landscape which Cézanne was to fight out, stroke by painful stroke, in the Carrière de Bibémus. It was in Rome in the late 1820's that Corot settled for a total candor, an entire honesty with self, in the face of subjects hallowed by long usage. Painting the famous view across the city from the road beyond S. Trinita dei Monti, he disupholstered it of all previous associations and rebuilt it, slab by slab, selecting and rejecting until he ended up with something so plain and so severe, so tender and so palpably truthful, that it teaches us once and for all how to look at a great city. Other people's eyes will never be enough for us again if we have once learned Corot's lesson.

Corot's was, then, a constructive art: all nature held its breath as he took the easygoing countryside of the Île de France and remade it — again long before Cézanne — in terms of a geometry of his own devising. He took nothing at second hand. Truth to experience, not truth to formula, was what he wanted. A still later generation went through his figure subjects — not the got-up Salon paintings, and not the reclining nudes which harked back to Giorgione, but the single figures — and found that they too had a monumentality which was all the more convincing for being so patently unstudied. Braque kept in his studio, till the last day of his life, a reproduction of Corot's portrait of the great singer Christine Nilsson; and when he and Picasso made the seated figures which are among the grandest products of cubism, they drew on the figure paintings of Corot which they had seen not long before at an exhibition in Paris. (The cubists borrowed, even, the stringed instruments which found their way quite naturally into the portraits that Corot posed in his studio). Corot in those figure paintings looks back to J. L. David, his equal in candor, and forward to Braque and Picasso.

So that Corot, who thought so much of and for others and so little of himself, was indispensable to the tradition which runs unbroken in French painting from the brothers Le Nain in the seventeenth century to the majestic achievement of Picasso and Braque just before 1914: that tradition exalts painting as our noblest way of negotiating with fact and bringing experience under close control. Corot would be the last to encourage this point of view: who can doubt that, faced with a eulogy such as this, he would reply to us as he once replied, in his late sixties, to Berthe Morisot? "Let us carry on with the work, quite steadily," he wrote, "and let's not think too much about Papa Corot. Nature is still the better guide."

CORREGGIO (real name **Antonio Allegri**) (c.1489 – Mar. 5, 1534). Italian painter. Born and died in Correggio, Emilia. Probably studied under various teachers in north Italy; was active in Correggio and Parma, and was chiefly influenced by Raphael, Michelangelo, and Leonardo. Married Girolama Merlini (c.1519). His most impressive works are series of mural decorations, all in Parma: ceiling of abbess's parlor in convent of S. Paolo (1518–19), dome of S. Giovanni Evangelista (1520–24, *Ascension of Christ*), dome of cathedral (1526–30, *Assumption of the Virgin*). The latter, his most famous painting, was a work far ahead of its time. With its swirling clouds, intertwined figures flying toward heaven, airiness and effect of immense space, severe foreshortening, exuberant movement, and play of light, it anticipated the baroque. Other important works include altarpieces *Madonna of St. George* (1530–32, Gemäldegalerie, Dresden); *Madonna of St. Jerome* (1527–28, Gallerie Nazionale, Parma), called *Il Giorno* because of its golden light; *Adoration of the Shepherds* (c.1530), Gemäldegalerie, Dresden), called *La Notte* because of its night setting; and a series of mythological subjects (c.1530) including *Danaë* (Borghese Gallery, Rome), *Ganymede, Io* (both in Kunsthistorisches Museum, Vienna), and *Leda* (Staatliche Museum, Berlin), painted at the end of his life and noted for their soft modeling and extreme sensuousness. Correggio exerted an enormous influence on the Carracci and on baroque and rococo decorators.

REFERENCES: Arthur E. Popham *Correggio's Drawings* (London and New York 1957). Corrado Ricci *Correggio* (London 1930).

CORTONA, Pietro da (real name **Pietro Berrettini**) (Nov. 1, 1596 – May 16, 1669). Italian painter and architect. Born in Cortona, Tuscany. Studied under various masters in native town and in Florence. Went (1612) to Rome, where he won renown with series of large historical and mythological frescoes for Sacchetti family (c.1620–c.1630) and with decoration of church of S. Bibiana (1624–26), commissioned by Urban VIII. Another papal commission, the ceiling of the Barberini palace (1633–39), proved his most famous and influential feat of illusionist decoration. In this gigantic fresco, full of swirling figures and clouds, Pietro perfected the baroque manner which changed the course of Italian painting. Thereafter he lived in splendor, employed by princes throughout Italy. In Florence, he decorated with frescoes a series of rooms in the Pitti palace (1637–47) for Grand Duke Ferdinand II. Early architectural designs such as SS. Martina e Luca (1635–50) in Rome were ornate, but greater simplification and massiveness characterize his later style in the façades of S. Maria della Pace (1656–57) and S. Maria in Via Lata (1658–62). He died in Rome.

REFERENCES: Rudolf Wittkower *Art and Architecture in Italy, 1600–1750* (Harmondsworth, England, and Baltimore PB 1958, 2nd rev. ed. 1965).

CORVO, Baron. *See* ROLFE, Frederick William.

COSIMO. *See* PIERO DI COSIMO.

COTMAN, John Sell (May 16, 1782 – July 24, 1842). English landscape painter and etcher. Born in Norwich. Went to London (c.1798), where through Thomas Monro he met and studied with J. M. W. Turner and Thomas Girtin. Exhibited watercolors at Royal Academy (1800–1806). Soon after return to Norwich (1806), married Ann Miles. Worked as drawing master to support family, and exhibited with Norwich Society of Artists, of which he became president (1811). Lived in Yarmouth (1811–23) and concentrated on architectural etchings. Visited Normandy (1817, 1818, 1820). Became drawing master at King's College, London (1834), where he remained until his death. Unappreciated in his own time, Cotman is now considered the leading painter of the Norwich school and is praised particularly for his early watercolors, including the famous *Greta Bridge* (1805, British Museum, London), whose broad, simplified patterns reveal a fine sense of geometrical construction and silhouette. His sons Miles Edmund (1810–58) and Joseph John (1814–78) were also landscape painters.

REFERENCES: T. S. R. Boase "English Art 1806–1870" in *Oxford History of English Art* (Oxford 1959). Sydney D. Kitson *The Life of John Sell Cotman* (London 1937). V. G. R. Rienaecker *John Sell Cotman 1782–1842* (Leigh-on-Sea, Essex, England 1953).

COUPERIN, François (called Le Grand) (Nov. 10, 1668 – Sept. 12, 1733). French composer and clavecinist. Born and died in Paris; most distinguished member of a famous musical family which flourished in the seventeenth and eighteenth centuries. Studied under his father Charles Couperin and Jacques Thomelin, succeeding former as organist at church of St. Gervais (1685) and latter as organist of the royal chapel (1693). Married Marie-Anne Ansault (1689). Highly esteemed by Louis XIV, he was made clavecinist and organist to the king (1701), composed for him the *Concerts royaux* (1714–15, published 1722), and instructed members of the royal family in music. Other major works include *Pièces de clavecin*, programmatic dance suites (4 vols. 1713–30); a group of ensemble pieces *Les Gouts réunis* (1724); four trio sonatas, *Les Nations* (1726); and, among his many sacred compositions, the *Leçons de ténèbres* (1715).

REFERENCE: Wilfrid Mellers *François Couperin and the French Classical Tradition* (London 1950 and New York 1951, also PB).

FRANÇOIS COUPERIN
BY DOUGLAS ALLANBROOK

François Couperin is known as "le grand." He came from a long line of musicians and his descendants were musicians until the middle of the nineteenth century, being employed traditionally as organists at the church of St. Gervais in Paris. His well-earned title, "the Great," does not however serve merely to distinguish him from his relatives. Nor is his "greatness" to be understood by tracing his musical inheritance and noting that the French school of clavecinists reaches its culmination in the four books of his *Pièces de clavecin*. His father Charles and his two paternal uncles Louis and François were all three pupils of Jacques Chambonnières, clavecinist to both Louis XIII and Louis XIV and the first great representative of the French harpsichord school. Many of the keyboard works of J. S. Bach bear witness to Couperin's greatness and his influence outside his native France. Both Couperin's style of writing and his way of playing the harpsichord were assimilated and transformed by the German master. Couperin himself, whose harpsichord works represent the essence of the French style, was a profound admirer of Corelli, as is evidenced in his chamber works *Les Nations* and *Les Gouts réunis*. His *Apothéose de Lully* is an homage to the Florentine master who occupied an almost legendary post in French music, and in this work Corelli as delegate of the muses welcomes Lully among the celestial spirits. The work is an elaborate contest between the French and Italian styles and shows Couperin's thorough mastery and insight into Italian music.

None of these considerations catch what is distinctive, what it is in his music and in his style which is of interest in and of itself. Cultural and historical discussions about great artists serve only as frames for a picture, and works of art which are cherished are only incidentally illustrations of trends. What is unique in Couperin must be examined. What he has in common with a host of other musicians, some mediocre, is not essential.

It is quite clear that he played the harpsichord superbly and was interested in seeing to it that it was played properly. His *L'Art de toucher le clavecin* (1716) is the most authoritative book on keyboard playing up to his day. In this work he puts finger technique into order, rationalizes it. He suggests that adults "should sit about nine inches from the keyboard, measuring from the waist, and young people proportionately less." He suggests that facial grimaces can be corrected by placing a mirror on the reading desk of the harpsichord. There are eight harpsichord *Préludes* at the end which illustrate principles outlined in the work. He laid the greatest stress on the correct realization of the ornaments, the *agréments,* and developed a consistent notation which would express his precise intentions in regard to their execution. Few composers have ever been as exacting in their notation.

The first of the four books of harpsichord pieces appeared in 1713, the second in 1716–1717, the third in 1722, and the fourth in 1730, three years before his death. They appeared under Couperin's own name as publisher and he carefully corrected the proofs of them himself. They were engraved on copper and represent perhaps the most beautiful example of printed music of the period. There are twenty-seven suites or *ordres* (as the composer called them) in the four books. The number of pieces gathered together in one *ordre* varies from very few to as many

as twenty. In general there is no particular unity among the pieces collected together in an *ordre*. They are superficially held together by a common key, though many of the *ordres* admit of the opposite mode and of the relative keys. Though he constantly employs the traditional dance forms (gavottes, sarabandes, allemandes, passacaglias, jigs, etc.), almost all of the pieces bear fanciful titles. Some of the titles refer to real people (*La Princesse Marie*); some are probably allegorical compliments (*La Visionnaire, L'Audacieuse, La Reine des coeurs, L'Amazone*); others refer to states of the soul (*Les Langueurs tendres, L'Âme en peine*); others are portraits of animals (*L'Anguille, Le Rossignol en amour*); some refer to games (*Les Tours de passe-passe*). There is one that is concerned with knitting (*Les Tricoteuses*). *Les Petits Moulins à vent,* with its quick scurrying imitations, seems to be a pointed reference to gossips at court. In addition to the titles many of the pieces are prefixed by emotive adverbs such as *gaijement, naïvement, tendrement, fièrement,* even *audacieusement.* In his book on harpsichord playing Couperin notes that measure, or what we generally call musical meter, is often confused with cadence or rhythm. He is at pains to point out that cadence or rhythm properly embodies the soul or spirit of the music, which of necessity must work together with the measure. Certain Italian music seemed to him to be merely metrical. He goes on to say that his music wishes to express this spirit or soul, and that since he has not devised symbols to express this particular idea he has tried to remedy it by indications of an affective nature which would suggest more or less what he would like to have heard. A contemporary of Couperin's, the composer Jacques Aubert, pointed out that Italian music was not generally to the tastes of the ladies, who in France at least, usually determined the pleasures of the nation. Couperin was employed at the court of Versailles; he instructed the duke of Burgundy and six other royal princes and princesses. His style is an inimitable blending of the aristocratic and the intimate.

His genius is wedded to his sense of limits. He never indulges in the long-winded sequences which make the music of many of his contemporaries the equivalent of background music. His phrases are generally short, exquisitely articulated, and ornamented with intricacy and precision. The music is wedded to the harpsichord and impossible to conceive of apart from that instrument. His ornamentation transformed even such a form as the *air tendre*, borrowed from opera, into a thoroughly instrumental conception. He is not at all interested in what in more modern times has generally been referred to as "development." The great majority of the pieces are in two parts, the first section ending on the dominant key. The longer pieces are generally rondeaux, a form in which length is gained by simple repetition of the refrain. Though he sometimes uses the full resources of the two keyboards of the double harpsichord (one of the few keyboard composers to do so), his music is not intent on dazzling the listener. A few of the pieces, notably the two noble passacaglias in B minor and A major, are deeply serious constructions, full of rich and ponderous harmonies. Occasionally he imitates and transcribes for the keyboard the weighty rhythms of the French overture. On the whole, however, his intention is to please quietly, and he is one of the few composers whose music is sometimes witty. He is the true master of the harpsichord for those who cherish the sweet precision and the crystalline clarity of its wiry concord. He may be compared only to Chopin in the perfection of his writing for his chosen instrument and in the quiet aristocracy of his spirit.

COURBET, (Jean Désiré) Gustave (June 10, 1819 – Dec. 31, 1877). French painter. Born Ornans, Doubs, son of a rural landowner. Studied at Collège Royal at nearby Besançon (1837), but spent more time at École des Beaux-Arts there. Went to Paris (1840), exhibiting for first time at Salon of 1844. By 1848 had cast off the romantic style for a new naturalism, and at Salon of 1849 attracted attention with five works, including *After Dinner at Ornans* (Musée des Beaux Arts, Lille). At Salon of 1850 the unequivocal realism of *The Stonebreakers* (destroyed at Dresden, 1945) and *Burial at Ornans* (Louvre, Paris) aroused an impassioned controversy that continued throughout his life. When his paintings for the Paris World Exposition of 1855 were rejected, he arranged an exhibition on his own in a large shed nearby, centering around his huge canvas *Interior of My Studio: A Real Allegory Summing Up Seven Years of My Life as an Artist* (Louvre). Visit to Germany (1856) inspired series of landscapes and hunting scenes, including *Fighting Stags* (Louvre). Official recognition began in 1860's; he refused (1870) cross of the Légion d'Honneur offered him by Napoleon III. An atheist and ardent democrat, Courbet held office under the Commune, and in consequence was later considered responsible for destruction of the Vendôme column. Imprisoned for six months (1871), he was sentenced (1873) to pay for its reconstruction. Fled to Switzerland, and died near Vevey.

REFERENCE: Gerstle Mack *Gustave Courbet* (New York 1951).

COWLEY, Abraham (1618 – July 28, 1667). English poet. Born in London. King's scholar at Westminster; revealed precocity with publication of verses *Poetical Blossoms* (1633). Fellow of Trinity College, Cambridge (1636–43), where he wrote *Love's Riddle* (1638) and a Latin comedy. In Civil War sided with Stuarts against Puritans, and fled to France (1646) to become secretary to exiled Queen Henrietta Maria, acting also as royalist agent. Returned to England, studied medicine at Oxford (degree 1657). After Restoration, awarded lease of land at Chertsey, Surrey, where he spent rest of his life quietly, occupied with horticulture and writing. Buried in Westminster Abbey. Principal works: *The Mistress* (1647), a collection of love poems, and *The Miscellanies* (1656), including *Pindarique Odes* and four books of religious epic *The Davideis* (unfinished). Prose includes two philosophical tracts and familiar essays (1668). Extremely popular in the Restoration period, Cowley's form of the ode in uneven stanzas was imitated by Dryden and others.

EDITION: *Poems* (New York 1905) and *Essays, Plays and Sundry Verses* (New York 1906) ed. A. R. Waller.

REFERENCES: Samuel Johnson *Lives of the Poets* (London 1779–81). A. H. Nethercot *Abraham Cowley: The Muse's Hannibal* (London and New York 1931). Geoffrey Walton *Metaphysical to Augustan: Studies in Tone and Sensibility in the Seventeenth Century* (London and New York 1955).

COWPER, William (Nov. 26, 1731 – Apr. 25, 1800). English poet. Born at father's rectory, Great Berkhampstead, Hertfordshire. Educated at Westminster School. Called to the bar (1754), but never practiced law. Afflicted with deep depression, he was confined after suicide attempt (1763) two years in an asylum. Went to live with Rev. Morley Unwin and family (1769), in Huntingdon, near Cambridge, and on Unwin's death retired with family to Olney, where Methodist preacher Rev. John Newton was a friend. About to marry Mrs. Mary Unwin, he again suffered (1773) attack of religious melancholia and suicidal obsession. Later collaborated with Newton in writing *Olney Hymns* (1779), which include *Oh! for a Closer Walk with God* and other familiar hymns. *Poems* appeared (1782), followed by long pastoral poem in blank verse *The Task*, published with *Tirocinium, or A Review of Schools* in one successful volume (1785). Moved

with Mrs. Unwin to East Dereham, where he died. A forerunner of the romantics, Cowper helped to free English verse from the style of Pope, who "made poetry a mere mechanic art," and his followers. Other notable poems: *The Diverting History of John Gilpin* (1785), *To Mary* (1803), *The Loss of the Royal George* (1803), and *Verses Supposed to be Written by Alexander Selkirk* ("I am monarch of all I survey"). His last poem, *The Castaway* (1799) was final expression of obsessive theme that he was forsaken by God. Cowper is also known as one of the best letter writers in English.

EDITIONS: *Works* ed. Robert Southey (15 vols. London 1836–37). *The Poetical Works of William Cowper* ed. Humphrey S. Milford (4th ed. London and New York 1934). *The Correspondence of William Cowper* (4 vols. London 1904) and *The Unpublished and Uncollected Letters of William Cowper* (London 1925) ed. Thomas Wright. *Selected Letters of William Cowper* ed. William Hudley (London and New York 1926).

REFERENCES: Hugh l'A. Fausset *William Cowper* (London and New York 1928). Lord David Cecil *The Stricken Deer, or The Life of William Cowper* (London 1929 and Indianapolis, Ind. 1930).

CRABBE, George (Dec. 24, 1754 – Feb. 3, 1832). English poet. Born Aldeburgh, Suffolk, son of a customs officer. Apprenticed first to a doctor, he began to practice medicine (1775) with small success. Poem *Inebriety* appeared (1775). Went to London (1780) and sought aid of Edmund Burke, who arranged for him to take holy orders (1781). That year became curate of Aldeburgh and published poem *The Library*. Recognition came with poem in heroic couplets *The Village* (1783), an antisentimental rejoinder to Goldsmith's *The Deserted Village*. Married Sarah Elmy (1783). *The Newspaper* appeared (1785), then nothing until *The Parish Register* (1807). His popularity increased with *The Borough* (1810) and *Tales in Verse* (1812). Became rector at Trowbridge, Wiltshire (1814), where he died. Remembered for his realistic portrayal of simple rural life.

EDITIONS: *The Life and Poems of the Reverend George Crabbe by His Son* (1834) ed. E. M. Forster (London and New York 1932). *New Poems* ed. Arthur Pollard (Liverpool, England 1960).

REFERENCES: Alfred C. Ainger *Crabbe* (London and New York 1903). Lilian Haddakin *The Poetry of Crabbe* (London 1955). René L. Huchon *George Crabbe and His Times 1754–1832: A Critical and Biographical Study* (tr. London 1907, London and New York 1968).

CRANACH (Kronach), Lucas the Elder (Oct. 4, 1472 – Oct. 16, 1553). German painter and engraver. Born in Kronach, Germany. Studied painting in father Hans's workshop until c.1498, then went to Vienna where his first known works were painted. Celebrated for their beautiful landscapes, they include *St. Jerome* (1502, Kunsthistorisches Museum, Vienna), *Crucifixion* (1503, Alte Pinakothek, Munich), and *Rest on the Flight into Egypt* (1504, Staatliche Museum, Berlin). Invited to Wittenberg (1505) as court painter to electors of Saxony, a position he held until his death, at Weimar. Held offices of councillor (from 1519/20) and burgomaster (1537/38–43/44). Knew Martin Luther, designed woodcuts for him, made engravings useful to the Reformation, and painted several portraits of him, including the example (1525) at Bristol City Art Gallery. To suit court tastes Cranach developed style of mannered elegance. The trained assistants who made possible his enormous output included his painter sons Hans (d. 1537) and Lucas the Younger (1515–86). His official portraits excel in details of dress and hair, emphasizing linear rhythms and calligraphic effects. He also painted Biblical and mythological scenes, featuring smooth erotic nudes as in *Venus* (1529, Louvre, Paris) and *Lucretia* (1530, Alte Pinakothek, Munich).

REFERENCES: Eberhard Ruhmer *Cranach* (London 1963).

CRANE (Harold) Hart (July 21, 1899 – Apr. 27, 1932). American poet. Born

Garrettsville, Ohio. Early childhood marked by family moves and divorce of parents, which contributed to his emotional instability. Began to write poetry at thirteen. After traveling to France and Cuba, worked in munitions plant during World War I. Moved to New York (1923), and published first book, *White Buildings* (1926). These early poems signaled Crane's special qualities, his extraordinary imagery that describes the sea as "this great wink of eternity," refers to "adagios of islands" and "siroccos harvesting the solstice thunders." Rimbaud and the French symbolists as well as Whitman inspired his experimentation with words and rhythm, especially in the great work *The Bridge*, in which Brooklyn Bridge is the symbol that links America's present to the past. While Crane wrote *The Bridge* (published 1930), financier Otto Kahn helped him (from 1925). Crane won the Levinson prize from *Poetry* (1930) and was awarded a Guggenheirn fellowship (1931). Returning from Mexico to New York, Crane leaped to his death from the ship.

EDITION: *The Collected Poems of Hart Crane* ed. Waldo Frank (New York 1933, new ed. 1946). *Letters: 1916–1932* ed. Brom Weber (New York 1952).

REFERENCES: Philip Horton *Hart Crane: The Life of an American Poet* (New York 1937). John Unterecker *Voyager: A Life of Hart Crane* (New York 1969). Brom Weber *Hart Crane: A Biographical and Critical Study* (New York 1948).

CRANE, Stephen (Nov. 1, 1871 – June 5, 1900). American writer. Born Newark, N.J., son of a Methodist minister. Attended Lafayette College (1889–90) and Syracuse University (1890–91), but on death of mother moved to New York City (1891) as reporter for New York *Herald* and *Tribune*. Under pseudonym published first novel himself, *Maggie: A Girl of the Streets* (1893), a realistic study of New York slum life that was not a commercial success but brought him to the attention of Hamlin Garland and other writers. Intensely interested in the Civil War and the experience of battle, he wrote *The Red*

Badge of Courage (published 1895). The brilliant, realistic flash scenes of the battlefield, the portraits of ordinary soldiers, and the honed-down style, using such vivid images as "The red sun was pasted in the sky like a wafer," established him as a major novelist, and the book has become an American classic. A shipwreck experience off Cuba (1896) provided material for the celebrated short story *The Open Boat.* Served as war correspondent for *New York Journal* in Greco-Turkish and Spanish-American wars (1897–98). Married Cora Taylor (1898). Spent last years in England, and became friend of Joseph Conrad and Henry James. Died of tuberculosis at Badenweiler, Germany. Other important works: two volumes of poems, *The Black Riders and Other Lines* (1895) and *War Is Kind* (1899), *Whilomville Stories* (1900), and *Men, Women and Boats* (1921).

EDITION: *The Works of Stephen Crane* (12 vols. New York 1925–27) and *The Collected Poems of Stephen Crane* (New York and London 1930) ed. Wilson Follett.

REFERENCES: Thomas Beer *Stephen Crane: A Study in American Letters* (New York 1923). John Berryman *Stephen Crane* (New York 1950 and London 1951, also PB). R. W. Stallman *Stephen Crane: A Biography* (New York 1968).

CRASHAW, Richard (c.1613 – Aug. 21, 1649). English poet. Born London, son of Puritan poet and clergyman William Crashaw. Educated at Charterhouse and at Pembroke Hall, Cambridge (B.A. 1634 and M.A. from Peterhouse 1638). Published anonymously *Epigrammatum Sacrorum Liber* (1634). Went to France during Civil War and became convert to Roman Catholicism. Major poetical work *Steps to the Temple,* expressing religious ecstasy, and secular poems *The Delights of the Muses* both published (1646) in England during his absence. Through Abraham Cowley was introduced in Paris to Queen Henrietta Maria, through whom he was appointed secretary to Cardinal Palotta in Rome. Became canon in church at Loreto (1649), where he died. The posthumous collection *Carmen Deo Nostro Te Decet Hymnus* (1652) includes the celebrated hymn to St. Teresa, *The Flaming Heart,* and twelve engravings designed by Crashaw. His baroque poetic style combines sensual imagery and religious passion, characteristic of the metaphysical school.

REFERENCES: Joan Bennett *Five Metaphysical Poets: Donne, Herbert, Vaughan, Crashaw, Marvell* (3rd ed. Cambridge, England 1964, also PB). Ruth C. Wallerstein *Richard Crashaw: A Study in Style and Poetic Development* (Madison, Wis. 1959, also PB). Austen Warren *Richard Crashaw: A Study in Baroque Sensibility* (Ann Arbor, Mich. 1957, also PB).

CRÉBILLON, Prosper Jolyot, Sieur de (Feb. 13, 1674 – June 17, 1762). French dramatist. Born Dijon, into family of magistrates. Educated for the law, he went to Paris to practice, but turned to playwriting. Beginning with *Idoménée* (1705), he produced series of successful tragedies, including *Atrée et Thyeste* (1707), *Électre* (1709), and *Rhadamiste et Zénobie* (1711), his masterpiece. Elected to Académie Française (1731). After 1729, had numerous unfriendly literary exchanges with rival Voltaire, which became more frequent after Crébillon was made royal censor (1735) and, through efforts of Madame de Pompadour, was granted pension and post in royal library (1745). A follower of Corneille and Racine, he excelled in scenes of horror and creation of complicated intrigues. Died in Paris. His son, CLAUDE PROSPER JOLYOT DE CRÉBILLON (Feb. 14, 1707 – Apr. 12, 1777), novelist, was born and died in Paris. His licentious tales portrayed depravity of Parisian high society; best known are *L'Écumoire* (1734), *Les Égarements du coeur et de l'esprit* (1736), and *Le Sopha* (1740). Exiled twice for theological allusions in his writings. Married Lady Henrietta Maria Stafford, a wealthy Englishwoman (1748), to whom he remained devoted. Known also for his cheerfulness and high moral principles. Appointed royal censor (1749).

REFERENCES: Clifton C. Cherpack *An Essay on Crébillon Fils* (Durham, N.C. and Cambridge, England 1962).

John G. Palache *Four Novelists of the Old Régime: Crébillon, Laclos, Diderot, Restif de la Bretonne* (New York 1926).

CRESPI, Giuseppe Maria (Mar. 16, 1665 – July 16, 1747). Italian painter, known as Lo Spagnuolo. Born and died in Bologna. Noted for strong contrast of light and dark in his genre paintings, thought to resemble Rembrandt, although actually derived from tradition of Caravaggio. Painted *The Seven Sacraments* for Cardinal Ottoboni (Gemäldegalerie, Dresden) and *Massacre of the Innocents*. Knighted by his patron Pope Benedict XIV.

CRÈVECOEUR, J. Hector St. John de (Michel Guillaume Jean de) (Jan. 31, 1735 – Nov. 12, 1813). French-American essayist. Born Lesches, near Caen, France; educated there by Jesuits. Migrated to Canada (1754) and served under Montcalm in French and Indian War. Explored Great Lakes and Ohio River regions, New York, Pennsylvania, and North Carolina. Married Mehitable Tippet (1769), became farmer in Orange County, N.Y., and began to write the famous *Letters from an American Farmer,* later published in London (1782) under name J. Hector St. John. After imprisonment on suspicion of espionage during American Revolution, returned to France (1780). La Rochefoucauld helped him to publish the *Letters,* which are concerned with the plight of the colonial farmer, politics and economics, and give vivid, idealistic picture of the emergent New World. They were immediately successful. Crèvecoeur returned to America (1783) as French consul to New York, found wife dead, children gone, and farm destroyed by fire, but devoted self to furthering French-American relations. Became friend of Franklin and Jefferson. Wrote widely read agricultural articles for American journals under name of Agricola, and as result a newly settled town in Vermont, St. Johnsbury, was named for him. Returned to France (1790), remaining there until his death at Sarcelles, near Paris. Published *Voyage dans la haute Pennsylvanie et dans l'état de New York* (3 vols. 1801).

In 1922 H. L. Bourdin discovered manuscript published as *Sketches of Eighteenth-Century America* (1925).

TRANSLATIONS: *Eighteenth-century Travels in Pennsylvania and New York* tr. Percy G. Adams (Lexington, Ky. 1961). *Journey into Northern Pennsylvania and the State of New York* tr. Clarissa S. Bostelmann (Ann Arbor, Mich. 1964). *Letters from an American Farmer* ed. Warren B. Blake (London and New York 1912).

REFERENCES: Julia P. Mitchell *St. Jean de Crèvecoeur* (New York 1916). Howard C. Rice *Le Cultivateur Américain: Étude sur l'oeuvre de St. John de Crèvecoeur* (Paris 1933).

CRIVELLI, Carlo (c.1430/35–c.1493/95). Italian painter. Born in Venice. His teachers are not known, but influence of Francesco Squarcione's school at Padua, especially of latter's pupil Mantegna, is evident in his work. Seems to have left Venice forever (1457) and thereafter worked in towns of the Marches. Crivelli produced exclusively religious paintings. Characteristics of his strikingly individual style are hard, severe outline and modeling, angular drapery, intense emotion, and emphasis on decorative motifs: garlands of fruit and flowers, and classical friezes and columns. In his later paintings, these decorative accessories overpower the figures, while the latter's brittleness, twisted poses, and pathos of expression become exaggerated to the point of grotesqueness. Works include altarpiece at Municipio of Massa Fermana, Ascoli (1468), Demidoff altarpiece (1476, National Gallery, London), *Pietà Panchiatichi* (1485, Museum of Fine Arts, Boston), *Annunciation* (1486, National Gallery, London), *Madonna della Candeletta* and *Coronation of the Virgin* (1493, both Brera, Milan).

REFERENCE: Bernard Berenson *The Italian Painters of the Renaissance* (rev. ed. London and New York 1953, also PB).

CROCE, Benedetto (Feb. 25, 1866 – Nov. 20, 1952). Italian philosopher, historian, and critic. Born at Pescasseroli, Aquila. Educated at Catholic school in Naples and at Rome University (1883–86). Settled in Naples (1886), where he remained until his death. Married Adele Rossi (1914). Early philosophical writings were essays (1893 and 1895) on history and on literary criticism. Founded and edited (1903–44) *La Critica*, a review of literature, history, and philosophy. Became senator (1910) and minister of education (1920–21). A staunch opponent of Fascism, he lived in retirement until 1943, when he refounded and was made president of Liberal party. Again served in government (1944–47). Croce's system of philosophy, in which the spirit constitutes the only reality, is presented in his four-volume *Philosophy of the Spirit* (1902–17, tr. 1909–21): *Aesthetics as the Science of Expression and General Linguistics, Logic as the Science of Pure Concept, Philosophy of the Practical,* and *History: Its Theory and Practice.* Other works include *History of Italy* (1927, tr. 1929), *History as the Story of Liberty* (1938, tr. 1941), and *My Philosophy* (selected essays in English translation, 1949).

TRANSLATION: *Philosophy, Poetry, History: An Anthology of Essays,* tr. C. J. S. Sprigge (London and New York 1966).

REFERENCES: Angelo A. De Gennaro *The Philosophy of Benedetto Croce* (New York 1961, also PB). C. J. S. Sprigge *Benedetto Croce: Man and Thinker* (Cambridge, England, and New Haven, Conn. 1952).

CROME, John (Dec. 22, 1768 – Apr. 22, 1821). English painter. Born and died in Norwich, son of a journeyman weaver. Began (1783) seven years' apprenticeship to coach, house and sign painter. Collector in nearby Catton allowed him (c.1790) to study paintings by Dutch and Flemish masters and by Gainsborough, and introduced him to William Beechey, who provided further instruction. After marrying Phoebe Berney (1792), supported his family as drawing master. Chief founder of Norwich School through organizing (1803) Norwich Society of Artists. Exhibited with society (from 1805) and at Royal Academy (1806–18). Visited Paris (1814) to see Napoleon's art collection. The well-known *Boulevard des Italiens* (1814–15, Gallery, Norwich) and other paintings of French scenes resulted from trip. The familiar scenery of his own country was his usual subject matter, and his chief aim, fidelity to nature. *Mousehold Heath* and *Poringland Oak* (c.1816, both National Gallery, London) are celebrated examples of his work, which had numerous imitators. His appellation Old Crome distinguishes him from his son John Berney Crome (1794–1842), also a painter.

REFERENCES: Charles H. C. Baker *Crome* (London 1921). Ralph H. Nottram *John Crome of Norwich* (London 1931).

CUMMINGS, E(dward) E(stlin) (Oct. 14, 1894 – Sept. 3, 1962). American poet and painter. Born Cambridge, Mass., son of Rev. Edward Cummings, who taught English at Harvard. Attended Harvard (B.A. 1915, M.A. 1916) and joined American Red Cross in France (1917). Through error of French military he spent three months in jail, which served as basis for novel *The Enormous Room* (1922). First volume of poetry, *Tulips and Chimneys* (1923). Publication of *&* and *XLI Poems* (1925) established him as important avant-garde poet. Other works include *Is 5* (1926), *Christmas Tree* (1928), *W: Seventy New Poems* (1931), *No Thanks* (1935), *1/20 Poems* (1936), *50 Poems* (1940), *1 x 1* (1944), *Poems 1923–1954* (1954), *95 Poems* (1958), *73 Poems* (1963). Also published three plays (*Him,* 1927; *Anthropos,* 1944; and *Santa Claus,* 1946) and a ballet (*Tom,* 1935), and exhibited paintings (1931, 1949, 1959). Was Charles Eliot Norton lecturer at Harvard (1952) and published *i: six nonlectures* (1953). Received Dial award (1925), appointed fellow of Academy of American Poets (1950), won National Book award (1955) and Bollingen poetry prize (1957). Died in North Conway, N. H. Cummings's highly individual style, in which he experimented with many techniques, even with typography, to point up his meaning, is a vehicle nonetheless for the traditional themes of love, nature, and the satirical indictment of contemporary materialism.

EDITION: *Selected Letters of E. E. Cummings* ed. F. W. Dupee and George Stade (New York 1969).

REFERENCES: R. P. Blackmur *The Double Agent: Essays in Craft and Elucidation* (New York 1935). Babette Deutsch *Poetry in Our Time: A Critical Survey of Poetry in the English-Speaking World 1900–1960* (2nd ed. New York PB 1963). Charles Norman *The Magic-Maker: E. E. Cummings* (New York 1958, also PB). Allen Tate *Reactionary Essays in Poetry and Ideas* (New York 1936). Robert E. Wegner *Poetry and Prose of E. E. Cummings* (New York 1965).

CUYP, Aelbert Jacobsz (1620 – Nov. 1691). Dutch painter. Born and died in Dordrecht. Studied under his father, portraitist Jacob Gerritsz Cuyp, from whom he also inherited a considerable fortune. Married (1658) wealthy widow Cornelia Boschman, and occasionally held public office; considered as candidate for regency of Dordrecht (1672). Cuyp first painted still lifes, interiors with figures, and animals. The later pastoral landscapes, depicting riverbanks and meadows with cows, are famous for their golden luminosity and serenity, and show marked similarity to Claude Lorrain's work, with which Cuyp is thought to have been acquainted. Well-known examples are *Piper with Cows* and *Huntsman* (both Louvre, Paris), *Night on the Banks of a River* (Grosvenor Gallery, London), *View of Dordrecht, Riders with Boy and Herdsman* (both National Gallery, London), and *Herdsmen Tending Cattle* (National Gallery, Washington, D. C.).

REFERENCE: John Walker *Albert Cuyp* (Washington, D. C. 1960).

DADDI, Bernardo (c.1290–c.1348). Italian painter. Born and died in Florence. A pupil of Giotto; also influenced by Sienese painting and Gothic sculpture. His work, scattered and much disputed, consists mainly of altarpieces of Madonna and Child, often with side panels and predellas depicting saints. Important paintings include *Virgin and Child* in Or San Michele, Florence; triptych *Virgin and Child with Saints* in Ognissanti, Florence; frescoes *Martyrdom of St. Lawrence* and *Martyrdom of St. Stephen* in S. Croce, Florence; polyptych of S. Pancrazio (Uffizi, Florence); panels of story of St. Cecilia (Museo Civico, Pisa); predella depicting legend of the Virgin's Girdle (Museo Comunale, Prato). Daddi's style closely resembles Giotto's in the fullness of its human forms and in its serenity. He is particularly noted for his subtlety of design and the dreamy tenderness of his Madonnas.

REFERENCE: Richard Offner *Bernardo Daddi* (New York 1930).

DANIEL, Arnaut (or Arnaud or Arnault) (fl. latter part of twelfth century). Provençal troubadour. Born in Ribérac, Dordogne. Became attached to court of Richard Coeur de Lion. His poetry was noted for intricacy of verse structure and rhyme scheme, and for verbal inventiveness. Only eighteen short lyrics are extant; the best known is a sestina, a form he is credited with inventing. Dante quotes him in the original Provençal ("Ara vos prec . . .") in *Purgatorio* canto XXVI and praises his work elsewhere as do Petrarch and Tasso. Ezra Pound, who wrote a master's thesis on him, and T. S. Eliot, who quotes him, revived interest in Daniel.

TRANSLATIONS: See works by Sir Maurice Bowra and Ezra Pound below.
REFERENCES: Sir Maurice Bowra *Inspiration and Poetry* (Cambridge, England 1951). Louis Cazamian *A History of French Literature* (Oxford and New York 1955, also PB). William P. Ker *Form and Style in Poetry* (London and New York 1928). Ezra Pound "Arnaut Daniel" in *Literary Essays* ed. T. S. Eliot (London and Norfolk Conn. 1954, also PB). Maurice J. Valency *In Praise of Love: An Introduction to the Love-Poetry of the Renaissance* (New York 1958, also PB).

DANIEL, Samuel (c.1562 – Oct. 14, 1619). English poet. Born near Taunton, Somerset. Studied at Oxford but received no degree. Employed by English ambassador at Paris (1586), and later traveled in Italy. Back in England (by 1592), served as tutor in various noble households. Early in reign of James I, Queen Anne made him master of the queen's revels (1603). Wrote masques, including *The Queen's Arcadia* (1605) and *Hymen's Triumph* (1615), and plays for the court. Died at his farm near Beckington, Wiltshire. First published poems were sonnets printed with Sidney's *Astrophel and Stella* (1591). Best-known work is sonnet sequence *Delia,* which appeared with the narrative poem *The Complaint of Rosamond* (1592). His sonnets are noted for their restraint and meditative tone, traits uncharacteristic of the Elizabethan era. Other writings include *Cleopatra* (1594), a Senecan tragedy; *The Civil Wars* (1595–1609), verse history of Wars of the Roses; *Musophilus* (1599), verse debate between learning and action; and the prose *Defense of*

Rhyme (1603), an answer to Campion's *Observations in the Art of English Poesy.*

EDITION: *Complete Works in Verse and Prose* ed. Alexander B. Grosart (5 vols. London 1885–96, new ed. New York 1963).

REFERENCES: Joan Rees *Samuel Daniel: A Critical and Biographical Study* (Liverpool 1964). Cecil C. Seronsy *Samuel Daniel* (New York 1967).

D'ANNUNZIO, Gabriele (Mar. 12, 1863 – Mar. 1, 1938). Italian writer and soldier. Born Pescara, Abruzzi, son of a wealthy landowner. Published first volume of verse, *Primo vere* (1879), while a student at Collegio Cicognini, Prato. From 1881 in Rome, attended university of Rome, and published numerous stories and poems, including *Canto novo* (1882), which made him famous. Plays and novels, including *Il Piacere* (1889, tr. *The Child of Pleasure,* 1898), *L'Innocente* (1892, tr. *The Intruder* 1899), and *Il Trionfo della morte* (1894, tr. *The Triumph of Death* 1896), added to his popularity. Married Maria Hardouin, duchess of Gallese (1883). Novel *Il Fuoco* (1900, tr. *The Flame* 1906) describes his love affair with actress Eleonora Duse, for whom he wrote most of his plays, including his masterpiece *La Figlia di Iorio* (1904, tr. *The Daughter of Jorio* 1907). On outbreak of World War I returned from France, where he had been living and writing since 1910, and helped persuade Italian government to join Allies. In the air force fought with spectacular bravery and became a national hero; awarded English Military Cross and medal of French Legion of Honor. With a few followers seized Fiume (1919) to prevent its cession to Yugoslavia; expelled by Italian forces (1921). Spent rest of his life at Gardone on Lake Garda. An ardent Fascist, he received from Mussolini the title Prince Monte Nevoso (1924). D'Annunzio's writings, enormously popular in his day, are characterized by dramatic power, full play of the senses, and lushness of language. He is considered one of the founders of Italian realism. In poetry his greatest lyrical power is reached in *Alcione* (1907).

REFERENCES: Federico Nardelli and Arthur Livingston *Gabriel the Archangel: Gabriele D'Annunzio* (New York and, as *D'Annunzio: A Portrait,* London 1931). Anthony Rhodes *The Poet as Superman: A Life of Gabriele D'Annunzio* (London 1959, New York 1960). Frances Winwar *Wingless Victory: A Biography of Gabriele D'Annunzio and Eleonora Duse* (New York 1956).

DANTE ALIGHIERI (May 1265 – Sept. 14, 1321). Italian poet. Born Florence, of Guelph family of minor nobility. Took part in defeat of Ghibellines at Campaldino (1289). Active in Florentine politics, serving (1295–1300) as councilman, elector, and prior (chief magistrate). Married (c.1287) Gemma Donati; they had several children. First important work, *La Vita nuova* (*The New Life,* c.1292), a collection of prose and lyrics celebrating his love for Beatrice Portinari (d.1290), the God-bearing figure in *La Divina Commedia* (*The Divine Comedy* c.1307–21), his masterpiece. As a member of the White Guelphs (Bianchi), Dante was dispossessed and banished (1302) after victory of the Black Guelphs (Neri). Wandered for rest of his life over northern and central Italy, serving various princes, but with Ghibellines supporting Emperor Henry VII as potential savior of a united Italy. Died at the court of Guido da Polenta in Ravenna, where he is buried. Latin works include *Il Convivio* (*The Banquet,* c.1304–1307), in prose and verse, a discussion of love and science; *De Monarchia* (c.1313), a treatise on the need for kingly dominance in secular affairs; and *De Vulgari eloquentia* (*Concerning Vernacular Eloquence,* c.1304–1307), an unfinished treatise on the literary use of Italian vernacular, one of the earliest philological studies of the language.

TRANSLATIONS: *The Divine Comedy* tr. Henry Francis Cary (London 1814); tr. Henry Wadsworth Longfellow (Boston 1867); tr. J. A. Carlyle and P. H. Wicksteed (New York 1900); tr. Charles Eliot Norton (Boston 1902); tr. Charles H. Grandgent (London and Boston 1909–13); tr. Laurence Binyon (London and New York 1943, in *The Portable Dante* New York 1947); tr. John D. Sinclair (with Italian text, cor. ed.

London and New York 1948, also PB); tr. Dorothy L. Sayers (London and New York 1963, also PB). *The Banquet* tr. P. H. Wicksteed (London 1903 and New York 1904). *The New Life* tr. Dante Gabriel Rossetti (1861, in *The Portable Dante* New York 1947).

REFERENCES: Michele Barbi *Life of Dante* (tr. Berkeley, Calif. 1954). Thomas Caldecot Chubb *Dante and His World* (Boston 1966). Benedetto Croce *The Poetry of Dante* (tr. New York 1922). Charles H. Grandgent *Dante* (London and New York 1916). Paget J. Toynbee *Dante Alighieri* (3rd ed. London 1905) and *Dante Studies* (London and New York 1921).

🖎

DANTE ALIGHIERI
BY GEORGE P. ELLIOTT

It would be interesting to know more about the propertied family Dante came from and his wife's propertied family; to know more about his children, at least how many there were; to know the details of his nineteen years of exile, especially whether his wife joined him and if not why not. But those accidents are trivial beside these known essentials: he had an unexceptional family and for the last third of his life he ate the bread of strangers.

From the courtly lyrics of his youth we know that this "liege of love" was a passionate man: this woman, here, now. From his essays about poetry, government, philosophy, we learn his trust that reason could help him find what is true everywhere always. Some men have spent their lives shuttling between the extremes of reason and emotion, but Dante's necessity was to incorporate both at once: a man of passionate idea and ideal passion.

Most of what little we know about him from external sources has to do with another of the principal coordinates of his life, politics and religion. It would be interesting to know more about his political activities: how he came to be elected one of the six priors (or chief magistrates) of Florence for the May-June term in 1300, and exactly what counsels he gave as a leader of the Whites during their years of power in the city. Interesting but not necessary, for we know the bald facts of two political actions that reveal the man and also the intrigue and violence circumstancing these actions.

During his brief term in office, the political disturbances in Florence were so violent that the priors, themselves Whites, took severe action in an attempt to avert civil war. In direct defiance of the Pope they banished some Black leaders (including one who was a cousin of Dante's wife and also the brother of a close friend). But they also banished some of the Whites (including Dante's "first friend" Guido Cavalcanti, the poet to whom he had dedicated *The New Life*). That is to say, given power, Dante endeavored to rule justly, even against his own self-interest.

But at the end of 1301, the brother of the king of France, in his capacity as the pope's newly appointed "peacemaker of Tuscany," betrayed the Whites, who were ruling Florence legitimately, into the power of the Blacks. In January 1302, after the great betrayal, Dante was convicted *in absentia* of a shabby, improbable graft (selling church offices) and of the proud, actual offense of refusing to recognize the pope's authority in civil matters. He was banished from his native city and his property was confiscated. Years later, when Florence offered amnesty to exiled Whites, he scornfully refused the offer because he found its conditions humiliating, though his love of his native city never faded.

We know another political essential about him. In 1310 a high-minded young emperor, Henry VII, invaded

Italy intending to restore there the long-forgotten imperial authority. Dante greeted his advent in the most exalted terms, attributing his elevation to Providence and anticipating an age of peace and justice; Henry was to extricate civil government from the machinations of the papacy and to establish one universal state separated from the one catholic (and cleansed) church, emperor equal and equivalent to pope. Fired by the supposed incarnation of his political ideal, Dante ignored, even more than Henry did, the actualities of power, and when the emperor failed, Dante's hope faltered. But the necessity was on him to find another incarnation which would endure. If not in actual politics, then where?

What makes Dante worth our knowing, and what in the nature of the case we know best about him, is the central axis of his being: dreamer and poet. Dreamer alone is not enough. The lover who hardly spoke to the Beatrice of his dreaming, the lovely lyricist, the impractical exile who hailed Henry as savior of church and state, no one of these alone nor all severally would ever have become a part of the mind of Europe. If he was to become himself, he must find a way to assemble the parts of his dreams into one whole. No life of the world's devising would allow this whole. He had to make it himself. The tale is told that not long after composing the last lines of the greatest of human fantasies, Dante died.

Just as this man of ideas, being also a man of passion, could not be content with even the most elaborate purely intellectual construction, neither could this man of faith, being also a political man, assemble the parts into some exclusively religious whole, not even into religion's intellectual construct, theology. When the nine-year-old boy saw the little Beatrice, the love that stabbed him seemed holy; but thereafter his loves were profane as well. There was nothing he wanted more than for the church to be set in order; but there was something he wanted as much, for the state to be set equally in order. Reason is so weak that it cannot go very far down or very far up without the aid of grace; yet it was pagan, rational Virgil, not a divinized Christian lady or a saint of contemplation, whom Dante chose to lead him through hell and to the top of purgatory, through most of his poem. This world is not enough, but he was of it. For him to renounce the world, as a religious does, would be to deny a great deal of himself, and this he was far too proud a poet to do. He wanted to get it all in, even his own evil. To get it all in he had to make an order that would hold it in proportion.

When we say "Homer" we mean two anonymous poems; we have a few scraps of legends about a blind bard, but from inside the poems we learn nothing about the man (men? a man for one and a woman for the other?) who made them. For the most part when we say "Dante" we do not mean the pilgrim in *The Divine Comedy* or the man in history who wrote that poem, though something of these; we mean poem and poet at once. He was a particular man and he was a greatly gifted poet; but even more than these he was a man, everyman, anyman. To conceive the true order of everyman, Dante thought it necessary to conceive the orders in which everyman also finds his being: the true social order, the one church, the real universes physical and moral. To conceive his own nature, Dante had to imitate God and conceive the nature of all things. That he did this without losing his identity and dissipating into a boundless All, that on the contrary by doing this he defined himself, is the ultimate measure of his greatness, of the poem's greatness. He did not exalt the vocation of poet over all others. The saint, the true pope, the true emperor, he believed to be above the poet. To write a great poem was not the highest thing a man could do, but it was the highest thing Dante could do. That too he got in.

We do not even know for sure what he looked like; yet you can, if you wish, know him as well as you know yourself, and perhaps better than you know yourself. On the frozen lake of traitors at the bottom of hell, we see how base he could be: the poet shows us the pilgrim hurting one of the helpless sinners and betraying another. From reading the poem itself, we both know — what he says in purgatory — that pride is his greatest sin and believe — what his vision rises to in paradise — that he is capable of transcendent exaltation. More nearly than any other writer, he became his poem.

DARÍO, Rubén (real name Félix Rubén Garcia-Sarmiento) (Jan. 18, 1867 – Feb. 6, 1916). Nicaraguan poet and short story writer. Born at Metapa. Brought up by relatives in León, where he studied at Jesuit secondary school and National Institute, and published verses while still a child. After several years as journalist in Chile, returned to Nicaragua (1889) and married Rafaela Contreras. She died (1892) and a subsequent marriage ended in separation. Darío was one of the great Latin American poets who brought to his native literature, notably in *Azul* (1888), a collection of verse and prose sketches, the techniques and esprit of French modernism. From his first visit to Spain (1892) as delegate to quadricentennial celebration of discovery of America, Darío was seldom in Nicaragua, holding diplomatic, consular, and journalistic posts in various Latin American cities, Paris, and Madrid. Became seriously ill while visiting New York (1915) and returned home, where he died at León. His two other major works are the collections of verse *Prosas profanas* (1896), a landmark in the modernista movement containing further poetical innovations, mostly inspired by symbolists, and *Cantos de vida y esperanza* (1905), his masterpiece, dealing with social issues and the writer's own anguish.

TRANSLATION: *Selected Poems of Rubén Darío* tr. Lysander Kemp (Austin, Tex. 1965).
REFERENCES: H. E. Davis *Latin American Leaders* (New York 1949). Arturo Torres-Rioseco *Rubén Darío* (Cambridge, Mass. 1931). Charles D. Watland *Poet-Errant: A Biography of Rubén Darío* (New York 1965).

DARLEY, George (1795 – Nov. 23, 1846). Irish poet, critic, and mathematician. Born Dublin; educated there at Trinity College (1815–20). Came to London, published a volume of poems, *The Errors of Ecstasy* (1822), and began contributing criticism, verse, and short stories to the *London Magazine*, where his best story, *Lilian of the Vale,* appeared (1826). A book of poems and tales, *The Labors of Idleness* (1826), and the verse drama *Sylvia* (1827), received little attention (though Coleridge admired the latter), and Darley began writing mathematical textbooks (1826–28) while working as critic for the *Athenaeum.* His unfinished poem *Nepenthe* (1839), like all his verse ignored in his own day, has become famous in the twentieth century for its intricate and effective use of meter and especially its febrile intensity and self-revelatory dream symbolism. Severely afflicted by a stammer, Darley eschewed society. Died in London.

EDITION: *Complete Poetical Works of George Darley* ed. Ramsay Colles (London and New York 1908).
REFERENCES: Claude C. Abbott *Life and Letters of George Darley: Poet and Critic* (London 1928). John Heath-Stubbs *The Darkling Plain: A Study of the Later Fortunes of Romanticism in English Poetry from George Darley to W. B. Yeats* (London 1950).

DARWIN, Charles Robert (Feb. 12, 1809 – Apr. 19, 1882). English naturalist.

Born Shrewsbury, son of noted physician Robert Waring Darwin and grandson of naturalist Erasmus Darwin. Entered Edinburgh University (1825) to study medicine; decided on the church and entered Cambridge University (1828, degree 1831). Botanist John Stevens Henslow arranged post for him as unpaid naturalist on exploration ship H.M.S. *Beagle* sailing to South America and Pacific (1831). After voyage (nearly five years) Darwin was committed to career in science and had accumulated observations which laid foundation of his theory of evolution. Back in England, published (1839) *Journal of Researches into the Geology and Natural History of Various Countries Visited During the Voyage of H.M.S. Beagle Round the World,* an immediate success which has become a classic under many titles (*A Naturalist's Voyage on the Beagle, The Voyage of the Beagle,* etc.). Also from the voyage came *Structure and Distribution of Coral Reefs* (1842) and *Geological Observations* (1844–46). Served as secretary of Geological Society (1838–44) and became closely associated with geologist Sir Charles Lyell. Married cousin Emma Wedgwood (1839); four of their sons became notable scientists. In ill health after voyage, moved (1841) to Down, Kent, where he prepared his masterwork *On the Origin of Species by Means of Natural Selection.* Its theory and similar theory which Alfred Russel Wallace (1823–1913) had sent him (1858) had already been presented to Linnaean Society (1858). On publication (1859), *The Origin of Species,* one of the most important books of all time, was a sensation, selling out in a day. *The Variation of Animals and Plants Under Domestication* followed (1868) and *The Descent of Man, and Selection in Relation to Sex* (1871). Always in ill health, Darwin seldom left home and defended his theories through others, most famous of whom were Thomas H. Huxley and Ernst Haeckel. Continued to produce works on botany, including *The Formation of Vegetable Mold Through the Action of Worms* (1881), until his death at Down. He is buried in Westminster Abbey.

REFERENCES: Charles Darwin *Autobiography, 1809–1882, with Original Omissions Restored* ed. Nora Barlow (London and New York 1952, also PB). Francis Darwin ed. *Life and Letters of Charles Darwin, Including an Autobiographical Chapter* (3 vols. London 1887, 2 vols. New York 1888) and *More Letters of Charles Darwin* (2 vols. London and New York 1903). G. A. Dorsey *The Evolution of Charles Darwin* (New York 1927). Loren C. Eiseley *Darwin's Century: Evolution and the Men Who Discovered It* (New York 1958 and London 1959, also PB). Gertrude Himmelfarb *Darwin and the Darwinian Revolution* (New York PB 1970). Sir Arthur Keith *Darwin Revalued* (London 1955). Alan Moorehead *Darwin and the Beagle* (New York 1969).

DAUBIGNY, Charles François (Feb. 15, 1817 – Feb. 19, 1878). French painter and etcher. Born in Paris. Studied under father, a successful landscape painter; in Italy (1835–36); and in studio of Paul Delaroche (1838–41). First exhibited at Salon of 1838; from 1840 showed paintings and etchings at almost every Salon, and by year of his marriage (1843) was an artist of repute. From 1857, often painted while floating on the Seine and Oise rivers on a houseboat, later the working method of several of the impressionists. Traveled (1870–71) in England and in Holland, where he met Monet. Made chevalier of Légion d'Honneur (1859). Died at Auvers-sur-Oise. Daubigny was influenced by the Barbizon school, and in depicting in his peaceful countryside views such natural phenomena as light reflected in water, he foreshadowed the methods of the impressionists, whose work he encouraged in the 1870's. Among his well-known paintings are *Écluse dans la vallée d'Optevuz* (1855, Rouen Museum), *Le Printemps* (1857, Museum of Fine Arts, Boston), and *Lever de Lune* (1877, Louvre, Paris). There are several collections of etchings dating from 1851 and *Voyage en bateau* (1862). His son Karl Pierre (1846–86) was a close imitator.

REFERENCES: Jean Laran *Daubigny* (Paris 1913). Étienne Moreau-Nélaton *Daubigny, raconté par lui-même* (Paris 1925). Robert J. Wickenden *Charles*

François Daubigny, Painter and Etcher (Boston 1914).

DAUDET, Alphonse (May 13, 1840 – Dec. 16, 1897). French novelist and short story writer. Born Nîmes, son of Provençal silk manufacturer. Attended lycée at Lyons. Financial difficulties prevented completion of schooling and he became instructor at Alès, an experience recorded in his first novel, *Le Petit Chose: Histoire d'un Enfant* (*The Little Good-for-Nothing*, 1868). Went to Paris (1857), where brother Ernest (1837–1921, later author of histories) worked on *Le Spectateur*. Produced volume of romantic verse, *Les Amoureuses* (1858), and his first published short story, *Audiberte* (1859). Their success won him post as secretary to duc de Morny, with whom he traveled to Algeria (1860). In Paris began writing plays, usually in collaboration, most notable being *L'Oeillet blanc* (1865). Married Julia Allard (1867), who wrote verse and also collaborated with him. They moved to Champrosay, where he began writing the numerous novels and stories that made him famous. Story collections *Lettres de mon moulin* (*Letters from My Mill*, 1869) and *Contes de lundi* (*Monday Tales*, 1873) and *Tartarin de Tarascon* trilogy (1872, 1885, 1890) drew on his Provençal background; he became noted for his realism and sympathetic warmth and humor regarding character. Other novels depicted the social life of the Second Empire: *Fromont jeune et Risler aîné* (1874), *Le Nabab* (1877), *Les Rois en exil* (*Kings in Exile*, 1879), *Sapho* (1884), and *L'Immortel* (1888). Daudet adapted some of his novels for the stage until failure of *L'Arlésienne* (1872, music by Bizet). Wrote memoirs *Souvenirs d'un homme de lettres* and *Trente Ans de Paris* (1888). Died at Champrosay. His son Léon (1867–1942) was a journalist in Paris and author of numerous books.

REFERENCES: Y. E. Clogenson *Alphonse Daudet peintre de la vie de son temps* (Paris 1946). Lucien A. Daudet *Vie d'Alphonse Daudet* (Paris 1941). G. Vera Dobie *Alphonse Daudet* (London 1949). Murray Sachs *The Career of Alphonse Daudet: A Critical Study* (Cambridge, Mass. 1965).

DAUMIER, Honoré (Feb. 26, 1808 – Feb. 11, 1879). French caricaturist and painter. Born in Marseilles. Moved to Paris (1816), where at twelve he went to work as office boy, then shop assistant. Studied briefly at Académie Suisse, became interested in lithography, and worked as assistant to printer Belliard (1825–30). Joined staff of Charles Philipon's weekly *La Caricature*, where his devastating political cartoons of the Louis Philippe regime made him famous and resulted in a charge of sedition and six months' imprisonment (1832). Continued producing political cartoons after his release as well as drawings satirizing bourgeois society; enjoyed enormous popularity with his *Robert Macaire* cartoon series (begun 1836). The law courts were caricatured in famous series *Parliamentary Idylls* and *The Representatives Represented*, and the plight of the poor of Paris was the subject of much of his work. Exhibited first painting *The Miller, His Son and the Ass* (Glasgow Art Gallery) at Salon of 1849, but soon returned to the more popular lithographs until 1872, when he began to go blind. Recognized more as a cartoonist than a serious artist in his lifetime, his work now hangs in the museums of Europe and the U.S. He died at Valmondois in a cottage given him by Corot.

REFERENCES: Oliver W. Larkin *Daumier: Man of His Time* (New York 1966 and London 1967, also PB). Michael Sadleir *Daumier: The Man and the Artist* (London and New York 1924).

DAVID, Gerard (or Gheerardt) (c.1450–60 – Aug. 13, 1523). Dutch painter. Born at Oudewater. Stylistic traits suggest that he studied with Albert van Ouwater in Haarlem before settling in Bruges, where he joined painters' guild (1484), became dean (1501), and was last master of Bruges School. Married (1496) Cornelia Cnoop, daughter of dean of goldsmiths' guild, and became one of town's leading citizens. Also admitted to Antwerp guild (1515), returning (by 1521) to Bruges, where he died. Among his major works are

Baptism of Christ triptych and *Judgment of Cambyses* (1498), both Communal Museum, Bruges), *Madonna with Angels and Saints* (1509, Musée des Beaux Arts, Rouen), *Virgin and Child with Saints and Donor* and *Pietà* (both National Gallery, London), *Annunciation* (Metropolitan Museum, New York), *Marriage at Cana* (Louvre, Paris), *The Rest on the Flight to Egypt* (National Gallery, Washington, D.C.). David achieved great technical finish and skill in use of color.

REFERENCE: Martin Davies *The Early Netherlandish School of Painting* (2nd ed. London 1955).

DAVID, Jacques Louis (Aug. 30, 1748 – Dec. 29, 1825). French painter. Born in Paris. Won prix de Rome (1774) while student of Joseph Marie Vien (1766–74). In Italy (1775–81) evolved classical style inspired by ancient sculpture. Admitted to Academy (1783). *The Oath of the Horatii* (1784, Louvre, Paris) and *Death of Socrates* (1787, Metropolitan Museum, New York) established neoclassic style in France, as well as David's reputation. Took active part in Revolution, was elected to National Convention, caused abolition of Academy (1793). Developed starkly realistic technique for revolutionary subjects, seen in *The Death of Marat* (1793, Brussels Museum). Imprisoned briefly after fall of Robespierre. Appointed court painter to Napoleon (1804), he produced several large works on commission, including *Coronation of Napoleon and Josephine* (1805–1807, Louvre) and *Distribution of the Eagles* (1810, Versailles). David's portraits, often considered his best works, include *Madame Sériziat and Her Daughter* (1795), *Madame Récamier* (1800), *Pope Pius VII* (all in Louvre). After Waterloo he fled (1816) to Brussels, where he died. David's neoclassicism determined new course for French painting, the theories of which were carried forward by Ingres and other pupils.

REFERENCES: David L. Dowd *Pageant-Master of the Republic: Jacques Louis David and the French Revolution* (Lincoln, Nebr. 1948). Walter Friedlaender *David to Delacroix* (tr. Cambridge, Mass. 1952, also PB). Louis Hautecoeur *Louis David* (Paris 1954). Helen Rosenau *The Painter Jacques Louis David* (London 1948).

DAVIDSON, John (Apr. 11, 1857 – Mar. 23, 1909). Scottish poet. Born Barrhead, Renfrewshire, son of a minister of the Evangelical Union. Family's poverty compelled him to interrupt schooling to work in chemical laboratory. After year at Edinburgh University (1876–77) taught at various Scottish schools, married Margaret McArthur (1885), and published plays *Bruce* (1886), *Smith* (1888), and *Scaramouch in Naxos* (1889). Settled in London (1890) to devote full time to writing, earned livelihood by hackwork. *Fleet Street Eclogues* (1893) gained him some recognition, furthered by *Ballads and Songs* (1894), *Fleet Street Eclogues: Second Series* (1896), *New Ballads* (1897), *The Last Ballad* (1899), and other volumes. Also wrote *Perfervid* (1890) and other novels, more plays, and a series of *Testaments* (1901–1908), expounding his own nonconformist philosophy. Lack of recognition, ill health, and poverty (despite small civil list pension granted 1906), brought on deep depression, and he committed suicide by drowning at Penzance. Davidson's most noted work is his lyric poetry, which though rough and uneven in quality expresses with vigor his rebelliousness and despair.

EDITION: *John Davidson: A Selection of His Poems* ed. Maurice Lindsay (London 1961).
REFERENCE: James B. Townsend *John Davidson: Poet of Armageddon* (New Haven 1961).

DAVIES, William Henry (Apr. 20, 1871 – Sept. 26, 1940). English poet. Born Newport, Monmouthshire, where he was brought up in grandfather's public house. At twenty-two, after some years of schooling and apprenticeship to picture frame maker, embarked on career as tramp in America, cattleman on Baltimore to Liverpool freighters, Klondiker (a project he abandoned after losing a foot train-jumping in Canada), London peddler and street singer, and flophouse habitué. First volume of poems, *The Soul's Destroyer* (1905), impressed G. B. Shaw, who provided encouragement and wrote preface to Davies's *Autobiography of a Super-Tramp* (1908), an immediate success and still his most popular work. Settled at Nailsworth, Gloucestershire, where he remained until his death. Granted civil list pension (1911) and received honorary Litt.D. from University of Wales (1926). Married Helen Payne, a farmer's daughter (1923). His numerous books of poetry were collected (1943) by Osbert Sitwell. Also wrote novels and *The Adventures of Johnny Walker, Tramp* (1926). Davies's poetry treats of nature and country life simply and effectively.

REFERENCE: Richard J. Stonesifer *W. H. Davies: A Critical Biography* (London 1963).

DEBUSSY, (Achille) Claude (Aug. 22, 1862 – Mar. 25, 1918). French composer. Born at St.-Germain-en-Laye. Attended Paris Conservatoire (1873–84) and won grand prix de Rome (1884) for cantata *L'Enfant prodigue*. Visits to Russia (1881, 1882) as piano teacher to children of Madame Nadezhda von Meck, Tchaikovsky's patroness, acquainted him with music of Borodin and Moussorgsky. In late 1880's became interested in Oriental music and associated with symbolist poets. Important early works: *String Quartet in G Minor* (1892), *Prélude à l'après-midi d'un faune* (1894), *Three Nocturnes* for orchestra (1900–1901). Married dressmaker Rosalie Texier (1899), but left her to marry Emma Bardac (1905). Opera *Pelléas et Mélisande,* an immediate success upon its first performance (1902), is generally considered his masterpiece. Subsequent works include *Estampes* (1903), *Suite bergamasque* (1905), *La Mer* (1905), twenty-four *Préludes* for piano (1913), vocal settings to poems by Baudelaire, Verlaine, Villon, and Charles d'Orléans. Though he became seriously ill with cancer during World War I, he continued to compose chamber music (*Three Sonatas*), *En Blanc et noir* for two pianos, and *Douze Études* for piano (all 1915). Died in Paris.

REFERENCES: Edward Lockspeiser *Debussy* (3rd ed. London 1951 and New York 1952, also PB). André Suarès *Debussy* (Paris 1949). Léon Vallas *Claude Debussy: His Life and Works* (tr. London and New York 1933).

༄

CLAUDE DEBUSSY
BY DOUGLAS ALLANBROOK

On April 30, 1902, Debussy's opera *Pelléas et Mélisande* received its first performance at the Opéra Comique in Paris. Debussy was forty years old at the time. He was little known outside of certain circles in Paris and proudly held himself aloof from considerations of career. Indeed, all of his life is characterized by a shy fierceness best expressed in the French adjective *sauvage*. Before *Pelléas* he seems to have written sporadically, as the mood dictated. He abandoned many works, envisaged many others which never came to fruition.

After *Pelléas* propelled him into fame and international importance, in the sixteen years of life that were left to him Debussy wrote the greater part of his work. To these last sixteen years belong the two towering orchestral works *La Mer* and the *Images* for orchestra; the incomparable series of piano works which include the two sets of *Images*, the two books of *Préludes*, the twelve *Études;* the ballets *Jeux* and *Khamma;* the incidental music for d'Annunzio's *Le Martyre de St. Sébastien;* the three sonatas written in the last years of his life; and the song cycles to words of Mallarmé, Villon, and Verlaine. These last sixteen years were also years of personal, physical, and national anguish. His first wife, Lily Debussy, attempted suicide in October 1904. In 1909 appeared the first signs of the rectal cancer which was to kill him in 1918; the disease obliged him to take cocaine and morphine for the remainder of his life. His last years were overshadowed by the hideous tragedy of the First World War, and his death on March 25, 1918, occurred at the moment of the greatest anxiety for France and the world as to the outcome of that war.

It is appropriate that *Pelléas et Mélisande* should have been the work that first brought renown to Debussy. It is his longest and greatest work. It is a unique work, with no predecessors and no descendants. It is a subtle and somber drama, a web of understatement and allusion. The orchestra, as large as Wagner's, is employed as a vast chamber music ensemble, intelligently and sensually reflecting what might be called the auditory vision of the keenest ear in musical history. Its libretto is not a libretto. Debussy simply took the complete play of Maeterlinck and set it to music, cutting out only four slight scenes. The singers, before the first performance, were instructed by Debussy to forget that they were singers. The words are set in a kind of recitative mingled with melisma. The essential cadence of the French language is everywhere respected. The effect of the words and the effect of each scene is like a ring dropped in a forest pool. The music surrounds and deepens the words and the actions, not in any through-going fashion full of rhetorical cadences and flourishes, but in a manner that can only be deemed symbolic and reflective. To understand how this is accomplished is to understand the uniqueness of Debussy, as all of his mature works exhibit this quality.

Debussy broke the back of classical harmony and the structure in phrases and periods that is the work of major-minor dominant-based harmony. In doing so he became the first "modern" composer. In doing so he did not found any school. There are no true followers of his style; he is by himself. He was

too much of an artist to be a pedagogue, too aristocratic in his sensibilities to be interested in either influences or influencing within the frame of any overt historical or cultural theory. The quality of a work which stands by itself, which Debussy achieved in *Pelléas*, is characteristic of nearly all of the great pieces of this century, whether such works be *Pelléas et Mélisande, The Rite of Spring* or *The Symphony of Psalms* of Stravinsky, or any of the works of Webern. Such works are in a sense dead ends, which is not to denigrate them in any fashion but merely to point out that they do not initiate any common practice or way of dealing with notes that is immediately fruitful to other composers.

In Debussy every note and chord becomes immediately important as a sonorous event. There can be no mistakes of the ear in the selection of the exact sound, of the right note for the right instrument in the right register of that instrument. Chance discoveries at the keyboard were seized upon by him and refined. Improvisation was to be cherished. The old formulas of harmonic sequences, perpetual perfect cadences, and what he called the "hateful six-four chord" were all to be abandoned as sterile and stupid. He is reported to have said to his teacher at the Conservatoire, Ernest Guiraud, that there was no theory, that one had merely to listen, and that pleasure was the law. If pleasure is the law then fastidiousness must be the rule, and this is the greatness of Debussy and the danger of Debussyism for anyone less equipped than he who tries to follow his way.

Debussy was in no sense of the word an amateur. All of his music demands skilled professional musicians. He himself entered the Conservatoire at the age of ten in 1872, and twelve years later was awarded the prix de Rome, the highest academic prize in France. He did what was expected of him during those years at the Conservatoire, whose discipline is still notorious for its rigidity. It was in the practical side of his work at the Conservatoire that he was most outstanding, in solfège, in playing, and in improvising, and his only first prize was in practical harmony. The piece he wrote for the prix de Rome competition, *L'Enfant prodigue,* is one of his least interesting works and he showed little respect for the prize, detested living in Rome, and returned to Paris as soon as was legally possible.

Paris is not a musical town; its sensibilities have always been (and still are) more deeply involved in literature and painting. The life and the music of Debussy reflect this. His first piano teacher as a little boy was Verlaine's mother-in-law. The most famous work of his earlier period, *L'Après-midi d'un faune,* is a musical commentary on the poem of the same name by Mallarmé. The first concert dedicated entirely to his works was given in the gallery of Le Libre Esthétique in Brussels in 1894. The gallery (which served temporarily as a concert hall) was hung with new works of Pissarro, Renoir, Gauguin, and Toulouse-Lautrec. There were on display illuminated books of William Morris, Aubrey Beardsley's illustrations for Wilde's *Salomé,* and objects designed by the London Guild of Handicraft. His most intimate friend at this time was Pierre Louÿs, poet, critic, and connoisseur of the arts. His songs to poems of Verlaine, Louÿs, Mallarmé, and Villon exhibit a sensitivity to the cadences and implications of verse unmatched by any other composer. Mallarmé felt that poetry should aspire to the state of music, and there is in Debussy this fusion, this dream state where the symbols of sound, color, and cadence mingle, the poetic world of Baudelaire's *Correspondances.* The fusion of the arts which Wagner aspired to in the works of his maturity (*Parsifal, Tristan and Isolde,* the *Ring*), works which deeply and ambiguously moved Debussy throughout his life, was more truly captured by the intelligence and economy and refinement of the art of the French musician.

Debussy strives for this sensuous unity not only in his vocal works; it is present in the purely instrumental works. Mallarmé bears witness to it when in writing to Debussy he speaks of "your illustration of *L'Après-midi d'un faune* which presents no dissonance with my text: rather it goes further into the nostalgia and light with subtlety, malaise, and richness." The works for piano alone aspire to this unity and in so doing realize new potentialities inherent in the most mechanical of instruments. He told several of his pupils that the piano should sound in his music as if it were an instrument without hammers. The timbres and resonances discovered on the keyboard were treated in a new way; dissonances and consonances were no longer employed in releasing tensions in the context of regular articulated phrase lengths but rather became ways of articulating color. This new way of dealing with harmony meant a rejection of classical forms and classical formulas. Sonatas and symphonies and the structures inherent in such forms were thrown aside by Debussy, and the grammar of those structures, cadential formulas, dominant harmony, development through sequences, became anathema to him. Verlaine had proclaimed, "Take hold of Eloquence and wring her neck." Debussy's music fulfills this maxim in its search for evocation, in its reticence, in its deep and pictorial reflections on the present moment of experience.

DEFOE, Daniel (1659 – Apr. 26, 1731). English journalist and novelist. Born and died in London. Son of tallow chandler James Foe, he assumed surname Defoe (c.1703). Family was Presbyterian; he received good education at Rev. Charles Morton's dissenting academy. By 1683 had begun dual career as merchant and pamphleteer. Continually in debt after first bankruptcy (1692). Married Mary Tuffley (1684). His first long work, *An Essay upon Projects* (1697), offered such suggestions as an income tax, insurance, road improvement, an insane asylum. The poem *The True-Born Englishman* (1701), a defense of William III, brought fame. His ironic pamphlet *The Shortest Way with Dissenters* (1702) outraged both Whigs and Tories and led to the pillory and imprisonment (1703). Released through intervention of Tory politician Robert Harley, Defoe started his famous periodical the *Review*, which he carried on singlehanded (1704–13) while continuing to write political tracts for both parties. To further support himself turned to the novel. *Robinson Crusoe* (1719) proved an instant success; it was followed by the popular picaresque novels for which he is also remembered: *Moll Flanders* (1722), *A Journal of the Plague Year* (1722), *Roxana* (1724), and other products of his last prolific years.

REFERENCES: John R. Moore *Daniel Defoe: Citizen of the Modern World* (Chicago 1958). James R. Sutherland *Defoe* (rev. ed. London 1950).

⟡

DANIEL DEFOE

BY V. S. PRITCHETT

Daniel Defoe has some right to be called the father of the English novel and a complete right to be called the first great English newspaperman. Shopkeeper, merchant-speculator, brickmaker, and later spy — or more politely, confidential agent — who found no difficulty in swapping his party, he was a born collector of facts and inventor of news. On the one hand he was a dogged dissenter and fighter for religious liberty, very ready with the moralizations of the newly emancipated middle class and constantly asserting his virtue; on the other a born impersonator and dedicated liar. To be fair, he was also a natural and practical moderate in times of extreme faction. His business career was, except for the brickmaking, a tale of bankruptcy, and his political career as a journalist ended in disaster. By the age of sixty his reputation was ruined; but, not a man ever to say die and having enormous energy, he suddenly turned to fiction. In five years he wrote *Robinson Crusoe*, which made him famous at once; *Moll Flanders*, the life story of a woman thief; *Roxana*, the life of a courtesan; *Colonel Jack*, a soldier of fortune, and *A Journal of the Plague Year*, which purports to be an eyewitness account of the plague in London in 1665. It is a most remarkable piece of self-projection. He was only five at the time of the plague, but his ears must have picked up a lot from the talk of the small tradesmen in his father's tallow shop in Cripplegate.

Defoe is a picaresque novelist. The genre came from Spain and was immensely popular in France and England. These novels were tales of roguery and adventure about people who took to the road to seek their fortunes; but fundamentally they represented a sort of propaganda for self-interest in a social class who were rebelling against the decaying feudal world. The picaresque novel stood for everyday realism; the extravagant sensibility and the impossible situations which were the material of the fashionable romances were rejected. Defoe's originality lay in imposing a dissenter's morality upon the picaresque subject, and in his verisimilitude. There was a vogue for tales of strange islands and peoples, which had been created by the great age of discovery and colonization. The more fantastic the tale the better. But Defoe eschewed fantasy. When he put Crusoe on his desert island he first made him an ordinary London trader like himself and then described the ordeal from the ordinary practical man's point of view. His survival depends on hard work and ingenuity in building his hut, getting food and clothes and so on, and he records his life from day to day with a Puritan's care. In his inner life, Crusoe is stoical and, again a true Puritan, he is more likely to be hysterical about the devil than afraid of visible enemies. Defoe was a superb observer and knew that in writing it is necessary to make the fact seem true by an extra detail that clinches conviction. Speaking of his lost companions he says simply, "I never saw them afterward, or any sign of them, except one of their hats, one cap, and two shoes that were not fellows." A conventional observer would have said "a pair of shoes" and would have lost the final, convincing picture of shipwreck. Defoe is a fine storyteller because he always thinks of one more thing. The brilliant idea of one (not two) footprints in the sand and the invention of Man Friday give life to the story and have put the stamp of surprise and complication on a book which might have rambled on and gone to seed. This is always the weakness of the picaresque novel.

Defoe thoroughly domesticates his stories. Extraordinary people become plain to us because he knows their daily lives and the calculations that are on their minds. *Moll Flanders* is the most complete portrait of a woman who is driven to theft and worse, but who is nevertheless watchful and never quite gives up a cheerful regard for

money and respectability. Again, she has not quite got rid of her Protestant conscience; temptation scares her. In her love affairs, her marriages, and her crimes, she is really seeking solid security which she can reckon up in terms of linen and chattels. She is very much a woman in her regard for property, domestic at heart, "bold" as she would say, and pretty confident about her physical attractions. She is very "true-born English" — to use Defoe's phrase — and like all his characters in the sense that her passions are strong but do not make her lose her head. She is not exhibitionist in her appetites. She is a close observer of others. The important thing in Defoe's writing is that he is careful to answer all our questions. Why did Moll first steal from a child? Because that seemed easiest. But why steal a child's necklace — surely that would be worthless? No! Moll is sharp. She has perceived the child's mother has lent her own, more valuable necklace. Is Moll remorseful? Only up to a point. She blames the vanity of the mother for letting a child go out dressed up like that. Criminals are masters of self-justification: the psychological examination of the theft is complete. And so close is Defoe to the London scene that you can follow Moll's steps today, yard by yard, in Bartholomew's Close.

Defoe's verisimilitude does not exhaust because he writes in a plain, almost talking style. The upper-class writers like Swift and Pope despised him as a hack and said he was writing "kitchen literature." So it may be — but it is marked by his independence of mind. He is interested — and this is where he is historically interesting — in people who, for the first time, stand on their own feet. It is also said he is hypocritical when he says he is describing low life among immoral or criminal people in order to teach a moral lesson. This is partly true, but the hypocrisy is native to the kind of people he wrote about. If they beat their bosoms piously, they amuse because they are as practical as he was. What is very striking about him is a respect for women as independent persons. This is almost Shavian. Roxana, the successful courtesan, may repent of her sins, but her greed is a protest against the marriage system of the time. Women are married off to fools and rogues who run through their own money and the money of their wives. They shame you publicly. A sensible woman goes in for economic independence. This is not a matter of morals but of good sense, and there Defoe agrees with her. Like himself, Defoe's characters are unkillable.

The higher or more intricate feelings of the human heart are unknown to Defoe; his view of life is perhaps mean though not ignoble. We are captivated by his alacrity and by his directness. His knowledge of the life of his time was immense, and he laid the foundation of realistic narrative in the English novel.

DEGAS, (Hilaire Germain) Edgar (July 19, 1834 – Sept. 27, 1917). French painter, sculptor, engraver. Born and died in Paris. Of well-to-do family, he studied law, then decided on painting. Attended École des Beaux Arts (1855), studied with Louis Lamothe, a pupil of Ingres. Visited Italy several times (1856–61); on return met Manet, which brought him into impressionist movement for a while. First exhibited at Salon of 1865, then with the impressionists (1874–86), beginning with his *Dancing Class* (1874, Louvre, Paris). In 1870's worked with pastels, studying ballet dancers and the racetrack. Spent six months in New Orleans (1872). Highly productive, he was more interested in visual phenomena than in portraiture or the narrative scene. He was

a superb draftsman and a linear master. He experimented with other media than pastel and oils — lithography and wax for sculpture, the latter especially as his eyesight failed. In later years lived as a recluse and became a notable collector. By 1909 he was almost totally blind, but persisted in working at new techniques.

REFERENCES: Jean Bouret *Degas: His Life and Work* (London 1965 and New York 1966). François Fosca *Degas: Biographical and Critical Studies* (tr. London and New York 1954). Daniel Halévy *My Friend Degas* (tr. Mina Curtiss, Middletown, Conn. 1964 and London 1966). Paul Valéry *Degas, Manet, Morisot* (tr. New York 1960).

✍

EDGAR DEGAS
BY FRANCIS STEEGMULLER

Degas is a marvelous example of the "lion in the path," to use Henry James's phrase about Maupassant — a great artist who has made a certain territory his own and whom no subsequent artist has yet been able to challenge.

Just as the French impressionist outdoor painters have enraged subsequent generations of painters in France because of the difficulty of seeing French seascape and countryside except through impressionist eyes, so Degas stands between subsequent artists and the ballet dancers and racehorses that they might have wished to paint in ways of their own. Whatever Picasso and Braque may have thought or felt they were doing when they invented cubism, their invention has been seized on and modified in a thousand ways by painters who have felt it to be the only escape from the blessedness, the state of grace, the marvelous inevitability with which the impressionists painted landscape. But Degas's two great subjects have not been made accessible by these or any other means. Few artists have dared paint ballet dancers and racehorses since Degas.

And that is to speak only of technique and subject. As to the nobility of Degas's line whatever he drew, the distinction of his color wherever he used it, it is unlikely that his rivals in coming centuries will prove to be more numerous than his precursors. One has to go to some of the Italian masters of the Renaissance to find the pride, the Stendhalian feeling of the superb, that Degas's art displays.

Although his name is French and he was born in Paris, his ancestry was mixed: he had a Genoese grandmother, a mother from New Orleans, and Neapolitan cousins. There is no record of previous artistic talent in the family. The entire clan was of the *grande bourgeoisie,* very serious, with considerable means and, in Naples, with a few titles added. The Neapolitans were not smart or elegant aristocrats: as portrayed by Degas — some of his earliest work was done in Italy, in the 1850's, copying from the old masters and painting his relatives — they seem rather dowdy, filled with a gloomy reserve. But their existence, and his visits to them, gave him an early sense of the largeness, the man-made grandeur, of the Italian background; and an Italianate largeness was thenceforth to characterize his art, whereas in his conversation and in many of his habits he was always to be the Parisian. Almost all his life he lived in the heart of Paris. He took little enjoyment in the country and had no patience with outdoor painting: his not very numerous, exquisite landscapes in pastel were done from memory in his studio, almost like the recording of dreams.

After a generation of splendor before the Franco-Prussian war, ballet in Paris fell into a decline that persisted until the arrival of Diaghilev and the Ballets Russes in 1909. It was during that lull that Degas painted his ballets and ballerinas: he conferred on ballet its greatest glorification in a place and at a time when ballet itself was at its lowest ebb. One of his latest pastels, a particularly brilliant group of Russian dancers, is thought by some to have been inspired by the great revival of his favorite art by Diaghilev's troupe, but by 1909 Degas's sight was badly impaired, and it is doubtful that he could appreciate the dancing of Pavlova and Nijinsky. *His* dancers are apt to be humbler performers — *rats d'opéra* practicing their positions or, sometimes in small compositions in the then fashionable fan shape, scurrying across the stage from between the flats. Moments of arrested movement were what Degas liked most to record. If his model was not a dancer it might be a gesticulating singer, a violinist, a jockey, a racehorse, a woman stepping in or out of her tub, or a man's or a woman's face, usually expressive of animation or with the next moment's animation implied. He has been "accused" of preferring to record a woman's gesture rather than her soul, of painting chiefly ugly women, and for those reasons he has been called a misogynist: if he is one, in painting, then so is Rembrandt, and that would be to deprive the word of much of its meaning.

With Degas less than with most artists does one ask whether a particular picture is "finished." Some pictures he failed to finish to his own satisfaction, others he left in a finished state of unfinish, recognizing that at that stage they were complete; still others he brought to the highest point of conventional finish, whether large compositions achieved with a secret pastel technique of his own, or tiny, exquisite oils on wood panels, usually racetrack scenes, painted with jewel-like colors but thinly, with the fine grain of the wood showing here and there with a ravishing effect attained by no one else. Some of his photographs are among the best early examples of that art, and his etchings and monotypes combine strength with refinement.

Among his friends were some of the most distinguished men of his time — Manet, Mallarmé, Valéry, Daniel Halévy. Both Valéry and Halévy have written splendidly of him, the former in *Degas, Danse, Dessin*, the latter in *Degas Parle* (see references page 211). Everyone tells of his biting wit, his harsh judgments that could often be softened by affection (not during the Dreyfus case, when he broke with anyone who defended the "traitor"), his sonnets that brought him the only rebuke he is said to have found unanswerable, when in reply to his saying, "I don't know why it's so hard to write them, I have so many ideas," Mallarmé pointed out, "You can't make a poem with ideas, you make it with words." He accepted that, doubtless recognizing it as the equivalent of his own quick puncturing of irresponsible talk about painting.

"Painting isn't so difficult when you don't know about it," he once said. "But when you do, it's a different matter." What he made of this "different matter" is the glory of Degas's art.

DE HOOCH, Pieter. *See* HOOCH, Pieter de.

DEKKER, THOMAS (c.1570–c.1632). English dramatist, poet, and pamphleteer. Born London; little known of his parentage or education. First mentioned as playwright working for Philip Henslowe's company (1598). Despite early successes *The Shoemaker's Holiday* (1600) and *Old Fortunatus* (1600), he was continually plagued by poverty and imprisoned for debts. A prolific playwright, he participated in the War of the Theatres, and when ridiculed with John Marston by Ben Jonson in *The*

Poetaster wrote a rejoinder, *Satiromastix* (1602). Also wrote religious poems, lyrics, and pamphlets, in which his ironic style is a forerunner of Daniel Defoe's; the most famous is *The Gull's Hornbook* (1609). Because of collaboration, there is no agreement as to which plays Dekker actually wrote, but the best in which he had a hand include *Patient Grissil* (1603), *The Honest Whore* (part I, 1604; part II, 1630), *The Whore of Babylon* (1606), and *The Witch of Edmonton* (1621). Died probably at Clerkenwell, London.

EDITIONS: *Dramatic Works* ed. R. H. Shepherd (4 vols. London 1873); ed. Fredson Bowers (4 vols. Cambridge, England 1953–60). *Non-Dramatic Works* ed. Alexander B. Grosart (5 vols. London 1884–86).

REFERENCES: E. K. Chambers *The Elizabethan Stage* (London and New York 1923), vol. III. Kate L. Gregg *Thomas Dekker: A Study in Economic and Social Backgrounds* (Seattle, Wash. 1925). George B. Harrison *Elizabethan Plays and Players* (London 1940). Marie Thérèse Jones-Davies *Un Peintre de la vie Londonienne: Thomas Dekker* (2 vols. Paris 1958). Henry W. Wells *Elizabethan and Jacobean Playwrights* (London and New York 1939).

DELACROIX (Ferdinand Victor) Eugène (Apr. 26, 1798 – Aug. 13, 1863). French painter and engraver. Born Charenton-St. Maurice, near Paris; his real father may have been Talleyrand. At seventeen entered studio of Pierre Guérin, became influenced by Théodore Géricault. Made debut at Salon of 1822 with *Dante and Virgil* (Louvre, Paris), which created a sensation by its dramatic departure from academic neoclassical style. Subsequently came under influence of English landscape artists, notably Richard Bonington, and produced *Massacre at Chios* (1824, Louvre), *Execution of the Doge Marino Falieri* (1826, Wallace collection, London), *Death of Sardanapalus* (1827, Louvre). Sympathetic with the July Revolution of 1830, he painted the famous *Liberty on the Barricades* (1830, Louvre). Travels to Algeria, Spain, and Morocco (1832) intensified his predilection for rich color, sensuous effects, and the exotic, expressed in paintings of lion hunts, Arab horses fighting, and especially in the celebrated *Algerian Women at Home* (1834, Louvre) and *Jewish Wedding in Morocco* (1841, Louvre). Though Delacroix continued to offend public taste, the patronage of Thiers secured him many state commissions, including decoration of libraries at Palais Bourbon (Chambre des Députés) and Palais du Luxembourg (1838–47), the Apollo ceiling at the Louvre (1848–50), and two murals in chapels of St. Sulpice (1857–61). After long wait finally elected to Institut (1857). Died in Paris. His famous journal has been edited by André Joubin (rev. ed. Paris 1950) and translated (abridged) by Walter Pach as *The Journal of Eugène Delacroix* (1948).

EDITION: *Correspondance générale* ed. André Joubin (5 vols. Paris 1936–38).

REFERENCES: Charles Baudelaire *Eugène Delacroix: His Life and Work* (tr. New York 1947). Raymond Escholier *Delacroix: Peintre, graveur, écrivain* (3 vols. Paris 1926–29). Walter Friedlaender *David to Delacroix* (Cambridge, Mass. 1952, also PB). George P. Mras *Eugène Delacroix's Theory of Art* (Princeton, N.J. 1966).

☙

EUGÈNE DELACROIX
BY JACQUES BARZUN

Whether or not he was the son of his ostensible father or of Talleyrand is one of those questions that must be left to those who nibble at the arts for gossip's sake. The interesting fact is that like Berlioz and Balzac and Hugo, Delacroix is a cultural product of Revolutionary and Napoleonic France. His father was at his death in 1805 an Imperial official in southern France, and the remembered tumult and glory of the years of Delacroix's childhood and youth inform his work to the very end.

An orphan at sixteen, Delacroix left the lycée a year later, to enter the studio of Guérin. His first published drawings also date from that same year of Waterloo, 1815. Precocious, taciturn,

and shy, Delacroix worked with fierce concentration, though not without the solace of friendship: he lived with his sister, and found among his fellow students three friends who remained his intimates for life. Overwork brought on a serious illness in 1820. Then comes another friendship with Géricault, soon cut short by the latter's death. In 1822 Delacroix prepares his first salon exhibition: *Dante and Virgil*. This work may seem equally remote from the French Revolution and from Delacroix's later dramatic distortions of form, but his temperament is already in evidence. Indeed, it might be said that all his life Delacroix depicted only one subject in many forms — the menace and mystery of the universe. In the *Dante and Virgil*, the glowing walls of the fortress of Dis in the background and the limbs of the damned clutching at the boat in which the poets cross the infernal waters render the characteristic Delacrucian mood.

Soon the expression of that mood was to undergo technical development, thanks to a new artistic contact, with the young English painter Bonington. Delacroix was preparing his second salon, due in 1824, with a subject taken from current events in the manner of Géricault, the Turkish massacre of Greeks at Chios. A sight of Bonington's work led Delacroix to remake his own scheme. There follow portraits of friends and historical, literary, and religious scenes, culminating in the *Marino Faliero,* exhibited with nine others at the Salon of 1827.

By then Delacroix had begun to keep his famous Journal, in which he records his technical observations, his friendships, his relations with women, and his dissertations on style and on the great masters. Delacroix firmly believed that his taste and his art were alike austere, classical, anti-Romantic.

He disliked the new literature of Hugo and Balzac and preferred Racine to Corneille. True, he let himself become friends with George Sand, but it was probably because of Chopin, whose music he relished, while abominating that of Berlioz.

The paradox here is visible, but not inexplicable. To those who did not analyze but only tasted, it might seem as if the new literature and new music of the 1830's made a point of looseness and extravagance. The truth is that the geniuses among the crowd — Hugo, Berlioz, and Balzac — were deliberate craftsmen, whose main principle was exactly Delacroix's: the expression of the highest passion in the most controlled form. Only, the form need not be set form: it was to be original form, and used only for the one unique purpose; whereat the critics complained that all was lost. Delacroix, whether he liked it or not, was (correctly) lumped in with his great contemporaries as a Romanticist. Did he not paint *Liberty on the Barricades* after 1830? The artist nevertheless suffered from what he considered a deep misunderstanding, though he vented his spleen only occasionally in the Journal. Publicly, he was stoical, enduring until nearly his sixtieth year the contumely of the newspapers and the "right-thinking" bourgeois. Indeed, it took the World's Fair of 1855 in Paris before that all-knowing city was really aware of the great creator it had harbored for a third of a century.

At the beginning of that span, in 1832, Delacroix, aged thirty-four, underwent the last of his formative experiences: invited by a cousin in the government he went to Morocco, then a new and "exotic" land. Those seven months under a burning sky were the revelation of a new world of color. Delacroix discovered that shadows are not necessarily black but can be purple — or reflect other deep colors. His mind (and some wonderful notebooks) was filled with new shapes, costumes, animals, and architecture. He returned, dazzled, to begin the works of his maturity, starting with the great decorative compositions of the Chamber of Deputies and City Hall — commissions obtained, once again, through official connections.

About this time also began his first serious liaison, with Mme de Forget. All his ladies, until the end, when he came under the ascendancy of his housekeeper, were women of taste, position, and discernment. This last they must have had, to appreciate the haughty and penetrating intellect that one finds in the letters and the Journal and again in the hypnotizing *Self-Portrait*. It is a remarkable coincidence that Delacroix and Berlioz should have been, contrary to the norm, masters of the word as well as of their respective arts, and that Victor Hugo the poet should have been an extraordinary draftsman. The synesthesia of the arts, which we hear so much of nowadays, begins earlier than we think.

Out of the Moroccan trip came, in 1834, that seminal work *Algerian Women at Home,* which pulled like a magnet at nearly every great nineteenth-century painter. Then in 1838 comes the first of the two *Medeas,* each a diagnostic work in its period. By 1839, Delacroix had three times offered himself for membership in the Institut and been rejected. Illness, casual love affairs, heavy work on the ceilings and walls of public buildings fill out the years until the consecration of 1855. Only at the ninth trial, in 1857, did the Institute catch up with public opinion and elect him a member.

In the wonderful variety of Delacroix's work, some stand out as not merely characteristic but unique in the history of art for the expression of ideas and feelings in a form no other artist could have conceived. Such are those already mentioned — the Dante, the two Medeas, the self-portrait, and the Algerian Women. To these must be added as summits of his art: The Crusaders Entering Constantinople, the Execution of Marino Faliero, the Death of Sardanapalus, the Battle of Poitiers, and — to name only one of the stupendous murals, the Apollo ceiling in the Louvre. By their titles all these suggest the historical and mythological subjects typical of the time; but Delacroix does not illustrate incidents any more than Berlioz fits sounds to programs. Each renders in his medium his vision of existence and communicates the thrill of recognition to thousands who know neither history nor literature but have some awareness of the multiform enigma of life.

By the time of his election to the Institute, Delacroix was chronically ill, worn out by a kind of warfare that the twentieth century scarcely understands: he had won innumerable battles; painted, drawn, or engraved nearly a thousand important works; lived in physical comfort and close friendships worthy of his genius — and yet the crown of recognition as it was then understood was wanting: to be an academician, even if nonacademic. By 1858, he had just enough strength and willpower left to undertake the chapels of St.-Sulpice, with which he closed his career as painter in 1861. Between that year and his death two years later, we have — a symbolic touch — a fine essay on the work of a neglected contemporary and a painting on an Arab subject.

DE LA MARE, Walter (Apr. 25, 1873 – June 22, 1956). English poet, novelist, and man of letters. Born at Charlton, Kent; educated at St. Paul's Cathedral School. Became (1890) accountant with Anglo-American Oil Company (a post he kept for eighteen years) and began writing poems and stories (first publication 1895). All his work through the first book, *Songs of Childhood* (1902), was signed Walter Ramal. A government pension and numerous magazine offers encouraged him to devote himself entirely to writing (1908). After second novel, *The Three Mulla-Mulgars* (1910), he settled in Middlesex with his wife, Constance Ingpen, and spent the rest of his quiet life writing numerous poems, stories, essays, and novels. Best-known prose work is novel *Memoirs of a Midget* (1921), for which he received James Tait Black memorial prize, but his popularity rests largely with his poetry (collected 1941, 1944, and 1969) and his most famous anthology *Come Hither* (1923). He was the recipient of many honors, including doctorates from Oxford, Cambridge, and London Universities (among others), the royal Companion of Honor (1948), and the Order of Merit (1953). He died at Twickenham.

EDITION: *The Complete Poems of Walter de la Mare* (London 1969 and New York 1970).

REFERENCES: Leonard Clark *Walter de la Mare* (London 1960 and New York 1961). Doris R. McCrosson *Walter de la Mare* (New York 1966). Forrest Reid *Walter de la Mare: A Critical Study* (London and New York 1929).

✍

WALTER DE LA MARE
BY EDWARD DAVISON

The work of Walter de la Mare almost exactly spans the first half of our century. He was an actively productive writer whose publications attracted an ever-increasing number of devotees and, at the same time, maintained the abiding admiration of his fellow craftsmen — witness the wealth of their recognition showered upon him by their symposium *Tribute to Walter de la Mare on His Seventy-fifth Birthday*. In addition to the steady mainstream of poems and the diversity of some eighty prose tales and several full-scale novels, including *The Return* and *Memoirs of a Midget,* he also produced an overflowing cornucopia of unashamedly personal criticism of life and letters. This is all the more fragrant because its flowers and fruits sprang from the soil of imaginative human experience, a vast reading, and impeccable scholarship. His Warton Lecture on *English Poetry in Prose* is the definitive scholarly work on this touchy subject. Inevitably perhaps it is a shade less impressionistic than the main run of his work: nevertheless, only a poet, in fact only de la Mare, could have written it. So marked is his individuality that the same may be said of nearly every book on the long shelf of his published work, including such unclassifiable things as *Henry Brocken, The Three Royal Monkeys, Ding Dong Bell,* and *Early One Morning.* The sensitive wisdom of his personal insights in terms of sheer perceptivity are only to be compared with the best things in Coleridge's *Anima Poetae* and *Table Talk* and some miraculous passages on poetry in the letters of Keats. If it be true that the most understanding criticism of poets and poetry has always been the product of men who were themselves poets of the proud old lineage, de la Mare's achievement is only one more exemplary illustration of that truth.

In his introduction to *Private View,* a bookful of the poet's occasional reviews, essays and lectures, Lord David Cecil remarks: "These critical essays, as much as his poems, are themselves works of art; an exquisitely wrought expression of the same odd, profoundly beautiful vision of reality." And that judgment is sustained in de la Mare's lengthier works in that kind. One of the most delightful, *Desert Islands,* began as a lecture delivered to the Royal

Society of Literature in 1920. Ten years later it blossomed into print as a book of prose, a prose lined with the shot silk of poetry. The original lecture occupies only seventy of its three hundred pages. The rest is a rich, multicolored tapestry, a creative interweaving of quotation, wise and witty commentary, and scholarly interpretation masquerading, if you please, as a mere Appendix to the lecture. But we encounter his critical powers at their fullest tide in his three great anthologies: *Come Hither,* "a collection of rhymes and poems for the young of all ages," *Behold, This Dreamer,* and *Love.* Each is a massive selection, mainly of poetry, from the trove of several hundred years. And each has its own accompaniment composed of de la Mare's roving reveries, meditations, and rememberings as his imagination pursues the thematic contents and variations of the central text. Those accompaniments, incidentally, cast oblique lights of intimate self-revelation on his own poetry, which, however, is never quoted or referred to in any of these volumes. *Dream and Imagination,* the hundred-page introduction to *Behold, This Dreamer,* for example, anatomizes the abstractions of reverie, night, sleep, dream, nightmare, divination, death, the unconscious and the imagination, all of which happen to be the most conspicuous preoccupations of his own poems and tales. In *Come Hither,* the prefatory *Story of This Book* is beyond question the most effective parable that has ever pronounced "Open Sesame!" at the portals of poetry. It is also the master key to de la Mare's personal kingdom. These three anthologies, declares Edward Wagenknecht, "are all made on the same plane where only something like genius can handle the material. Each is an incomparable piece of mosaic work, quite as expressive as his own 'creative' work." And he makes the further fine point that the various segments of de la Mare's work comprise "a singularly multiform output singularly unified in its inspiration."

Those (and they are many) who persist in thinking of de la Mare as a children's poet must be warded off by W. H. Auden's pregnant warning that there are some good poems which are only for adults, but there are no good poems which are only for children. De la Mare is indeed something better and different. He is the poet of childhood without a peer or even any close rivals. A note prefacing the *Collected Rhymes and Verses* in 1944 refers to the difference in content between them and the work reprinted in his *Collected Poems.* "Somewhere the two streams divide — and may intermingle. Both, whatever the quality of the water, and of what it holds in solution, sprang from the same source." There are many different levels of enchantment in his work. They range from the odd wonder of realizing that

> *Whatever Miss T. eats*
> *Turns into Miss T.*

to the word painting of *Arabia* and the tender sadness of his five-page prose tale *The Riddle,* but what these have most in common is that they too spring from one and the same fountainhead. The lyrics and tales, of course, hold the core of his poetic vision, for in them the climate of his imagination rises to its highest temperatures. We cope with his hottest intensity in such poems (how one longs for space to quote them here!) as *Futility, The Tryst, The Moth, The Old Angler, Cornerstone, Vain Questioning, Winged Chariot,* and, perhaps more explicitly, in a score of his

prose tales like *The Return, Miss Duveen, All Hallows, The Wharf, Out of the Depths,* and *Seton's Aunt* (or *Missing*), which has been cited as "the most appalling murder story ever written." Yet all these adventures on the borderlands of the human spirit are less of the body than of the mind and imagination. There is at the heart of his poetry a conflict between two not wholly unrelated moods, both of which appear to draw deeply upon the wellspring of his childhood impressions. The one is of the senses as they respond to the phenomena of the physical world without. But the senses cannot tell everything the spirit yearns to know about reality. The other is a psychic mood, a brooding awareness that what we see may be only a fraction of what is. It is a mood endured by the soul that has wrestled with its own prescient intimations and apprehensions of those realities that lurk half concealed beyond whatever veil creates the twilight realm between sleep and wake. There its imagination encounters strange and sinister apparitions in the mind's underworld of sleep and dream. The supernatural rides on its nightmares and memories of horror half-remembered from the edges of our sunlight hours, threatening our very identity with alienation and destruction. This second mood was potent in de la Mare's work from the beginning, but it did not come to dominate his poetic vision until middle age. As Lord David Cecil states it in the seventy-fifth birthday symposium: "De la Mare is concerned with some of the profoundest critical issues that confront the human soul, occupied with nothing less than the ultimate significance of experience." The traveler in his most widely known poem, *The Listeners,* lingering by the door of the dark house in hope of some whisper of a reply to his knocking, may perhaps be taken as an analogue of the poet's own plight as he confronts the mysteries of being.

DELATOUR, Georges. *See* LA TOUR, Georges de.

DELAUNAY, Robert (Apr. 12, 1885 – Oct. 25, 1941). French painter. Born in Paris. Apprenticed to stage designer (1902), he began to paint (1904). From the first preoccupied with pure color, he experimented with post-impressionism and Fauvism before allying himself (1909) with cubists, to whose monochromatic palette he introduced brilliant color (characteristically in form of color prisms) and light, and whose range of themes he expanded. Married Russian painter Sonia Terk (1910). Exerted (from 1912) strong influence on German Blaue Reiter group, including Franz Marc, Klee, Kandinsky, and Feininger. Same year marks his experimenting with a purely abstract art constructed of colored planes and simple geometric forms, offering further dimensions for cubism. Spent World War I years in Spain and Portugal, returned to Paris (1921). Executed decorative murals for Paris Exposition Internationale des Arts Décoratifs (1925) and Paris Exposition Universelle (1937). Died at Montpellier. Among famous paintings are the *Eiffel Tower* series (1910, Kunstmuseum, Basel), *The City of Paris* (1912, Musée d'Art Moderne, Paris), *Simultaneous Prismatic Windows* (1912), *Disks* series (begun 1912, Museum of Modern Art, New York), *Rhythms* series (begun c.1930). Inspired by Delaunay's style, called Orphism by Apollinaire, the Americans Morgan Russell and Stanton MacDonald-Wright developed similar nonrepresentational style called synchronism.

REFERENCES: Michel Seuphor *L'Art abstrait: ses origines, ses premiers maîtres* (Paris 1949). Gille de la Tourette *Robert Delaunay* (Paris 1950).

DELIBES, (Clément Philibert) Léo (Feb. 21, 1836 – Jan. 16, 1891). French composer. Born St.-Germain-du-Val, Sarthe. Studied at Paris Conservatoire (1848–53). Became (1853) accompanist at Théâtre Lyrique, later working as organist at various Paris churches. First stage work, one-act operetta *Deux Sous de charbon* (1856), was followed by series of operettas, parodies, and farces in collaboration with Offenbach and others. After appointment (1863) as accompanist at Paris Opéra, turned to writing ballets, of which the most succesful were *Coppélia* (1870) and *Sylvia* (1876). Also wrote operas, among them *Le Roi l'a dit* (1873) and *Lakmé* (1883), his masterpiece. Worked as second chorus master at Opéra (1865–72) and married (1872) daughter of Mademoiselle Denain, former actress at Comédie Française. Appointed professor at Conservatoire (1881) and member of Institut (1884). Died in Paris. Delibes's music is sprightly and melodious; he contributed greatly to the twentieth-century vogue for ballet.

REFERENCE: Henri de Curzon *Léo Delibes: sa vie et ses oeuvres* (Paris 1926).

DELIUS, Frederick (Jan. 29, 1862 – June 10, 1934). English composer. Born Bradford, Yorkshire; educated at Bradford grammar school and International College at Isleworth. His father, a German wool merchant, intended him for business career; Delius escaped to Florida (1884–85), worked there as orange planter and studied music with organist Thomas Ward. Having made money as music teacher, went to study at Leipzig Conservatory (1886–88), where he met Grieg. Orchestral suite *Florida* first performed (1888). Settled in France. Worked eight years in Paris, and after marriage to Jelka von Rosen (1897) lived at Grezsur-Loing until his death. Despite onset of illness (1922) which developed into paralysis and blindness, Delius continued to compose, with the help of Eric Fenby. In England for festival of his music presented by Sir Thomas Beecham (1929), he was made Companion of Honor by King George V. Delius's music is marked by free form and rich chromatic harmony. Among his works are opera *A Village Romeo and Juliet* (1900–1901, first performed 1907); chamber music; songs; large orchestral works *Over the Hills and Far Away*

(1895), *Paris: The Song of a Great City* (1899), *Brigg Fair* (1907), *In a Summer Garden* (1908), *Eventyr* (1917), *A Song of Summer* (1929); miniature orchestral pieces, notably *On Hearing the First Cuckoo in Spring* (1912); choral works *Appalachia* (1902), *Sea Drift* (1903), *A Mass of Life* (1904–1905), *A Song of the High Hills* (1911–12).

REFERENCES: Sir Thomas Beecham *Frederick Delius* (London 1959). Eric Fenby *Delius As I Knew Him* (London 1936). Arthur Hutchings *Delius: A Critical Biography* (London and New York 1948).

DELLA ROBBIA. *See* **ROBBIA,** Luca della.

DELONEY, Thomas (c.1543 – March, 1600). English writer. A silk weaver by trade, he wrote topical ballads (included in *Strange Histories*, 1602) until, having offended the authorities with a ballad on the scarcity of corn (1596), he turned to prose fiction. His stories *Jack of Newbury* (1597), concerning the weaver's trade, *The Gentle Craft* (two parts, 1597/98) on the shoemaker's trade, which served as basis for Dekker's *The Shoemaker's Holiday*, and *Thomas of Reading* (1600) dealing with the clothier's trade, depict London life vividly and with humor, and represent the earliest English popular fiction.

EDITIONS: *The Works of Thomas Deloney* ed. Francis O. Mann (London 1912). *The Novels of Thomas Deloney* ed. Merritt E. Lawlis (Bloomington, Ind. and London 1961). REFERENCE: Merritt E. Lawlis *Apology for the Middle Class: The Dramatic Novels of Thomas Deloney* (Bloomington, Ind. 1960, also PB).

DELORME (or **DE L'ORME**), Philibert (c.1510 – Jan. 8, 1570). French architect. Born Lyons; father a master mason. Received theological training in Lyons; studied ancient and Italian Renaissance architecture in Rome (1533–36). Built mansion at Lyons for finance minister of Brittany (1536) and Châ-

teau de St.-Maur near Paris (1541–47) before becoming royal architect under Henry II (1547–59). Chief works for the king: tomb of Francis I at St.-Denis (1547–57/58); royal arsenal, Paris (1547–56); royal stables, Paris (1554–57); parts of châteaux at Vincennes (1546–56), Fontainebleau (1548–59), Villers-Cotterets (1555), St.-Germain-en-Laye (1548–59). For Diane de Poitiers built his most celebrated work, Château d'Anet (1547–56), and gallery of Château de Chenonceau (1556–59). Delorme's ecclesiastical titles included that of canon of Notre Dame in Paris (1550). Though in disgrace after Henry II's death (1559), was called by Catherine de Médicis to design Tuileries (1564). Died in Paris. A learned humanist, he adapted spirit of classical architecture to French construction techniques and local conditions. Wrote two influential treatises, *Nouvelles Inventions pour bien bastir et à petits frais* (1561) and *Le Premier Tome d'architecture* (1567, revised 1568).

REFERENCES: Anthony Blunt *Philibert de l'Orme* (London 1958). Jean Prevost *Philibert Delorme* (Paris 1948).

DE QUINCEY, Thomas (Aug. 15, 1785 – Dec. 8, 1859). English writer. Born Manchester, son of a prosperous merchant. Intermittently attended Worcester College, Oxford (1803–1809), where he contracted opium habit. An admirer of Wordsworth and Coleridge (both of whom he met, 1807), he spent most of years 1808–21 in the Lake region. Married Margaret Simpson (1817; she died 1837). Achieved literary prominence with *The Confessions of an English Opium-Eater* (1822, enlarged edition 1856), still his most popular work. Became a prolific contributor to such journals as *London Magazine* (1821–25) and *Blackwood's* (after 1825), in which appeared the visions *Suspiria de Profundis* (1845) and *The English Mail Coach* (1849), and the famous essay on *Murder Considered as One of the Fine Arts* (1827). Died at Edinburgh, where he had lived a secluded life since 1830. Though De Quincey is best known for his exploration of the world of dream and fantasy, his writings cover many fields, including history, economics, theology, autobiography and biography, criticism (including *On the Knocking at the Gate in Macbeth*), and fiction. His prose style, while ornate and discursive, is full of arresting imagery.

EDITIONS: *The Collected Writings* ed. David Masson (14 vols. Edinburgh 1889–90 and London 1896–97). *The Uncollected Writings* ed. James Hogg (2 vols. London 1890). *The Posthumous Works* ed. Alexander H. Japp (2 vols. London 1891–93). *A Diary of Thomas De Quincey* ed. Horace A. Eaton (London 1927). *Selected Writings of Thomas De Quincey* ed. Philip Van Doren Stern (New York 1937).

REFERENCES: Horace A. Eaton *Thomas De Quincey* (New York and London 1936). John E. Jordan *Thomas De Quincey, Literary Critic: His Method and Achievement* (Berkeley, Calif. 1952). John C. Metcalf *De Quincey: A Portrait* (Cambridge, Mass. and London 1940). Edward Sackville-West *A Flame in Sunlight* (London and New Haven, Conn. 1940).

DERAIN, André (June 10, 1880 – Sept. 10, 1954). French artist. Born Chatou, near Paris. Educated at École des Mines, Paris, but decided to take up painting. Attended Académie Carrière (1898–99), and Académie Julian (1904), and shared studio with Vlaminck at Chatou. First exhibited at Salon des Indépendants and Salon d'Automne in the Fauves exhibition (1905). Married Alice Princet (1907). Friends included Apollinaire, Matisse, Vlaminck, Pablo Picasso, Braque, Kees Van Dongen, Clive Bell. Served in army in World War I. Won Carnegie prize (1928) for *Still Life: Dead Game* (painted 1918). Died at Chambourcy. Painting styles run from Fauvistic exuberance and color to neotraditionalism. Studied the old masters and impressionists intently, but refused to take up cubism. Became a realist after 1920's. Derain painted some of the best Fauvist paintings: *Westminster Bridge* (1906, private collection, Paris), *The House of Parliament* (1905–1906), the scenes of *Collioure* (1905), *The Bathers* (1907). Also designed stage decors and costumes, and illustrated works by Rabelais and Apollinaire.

REFERENCE: Denys Sutton *André Derain* (London 1959 and New York 1960).

DES PRÉS, Josquin. Also known as JOSQUIN DES PRÉS (c.1445 – Aug. 27, 1521). Flemish composer. Born probably Condé-sur-l'Escaut in province of Hainaut. Believed to have received early musical training as chorister in collegiate church of St.-Quentin and then to have studied under Jean d'Okeghem. Served at various Italian ducal courts until he entered Sistine Chapel at Rome (1486), where he worked until 1494. Lived in France (1495–1503); evidently had connections with chapel of Louis XII and cathedral of Cambrai. Became choirmaster of chapel of Ercole I, duke of Ferrara (1503); returned to France after duke's death (1505). Became provost of collegiate church of Condé (c.1516), where he died. Des Prés, whose works mark the transition from the late Middle Ages to the Renaissance and are noted for their development of antiphonal techniques and expressiveness, was the most renowned musical figure of his time. His extant works include twenty masses (of which the *Da Pacem* and *Pange lingua* masses are particularly beautiful), numerous motets, chansons, psalms, and hymns.

DICKENS, Charles (John Huffam) (Feb. 7, 1812 – June 9, 1870). English novelist. Born Portsmouth, son of a naval clerk who was imprisoned for debt, resulting in brief period of factory work for Charles as a child. Served as a law clerk at fifteen and became a shorthand reporter in the courts and Parliament. The first *Sketches by Boz* (1836) began appearing in the *Morning Chronicle* and *Evening Chronicle* (1833); the following year he joined the *Morning Chronicle*. His growing reputation led to commission to write the extraordinarily successful serial *The Posthumous Papers of the Pickwick Club (Pickwick Papers)* (1836–37). Serialized novels followed: *Oliver Twist* (1837–38), *Nicholas Nickleby* (1838–39), *The Old Curiosity Shop* (1840–41), and *Barnaby Rudge* (1841). Married Catherine Hogarth (1836) and traveled with her to America (1842), which resulted in

American Notes (1842) and *Martin Chuzzlewit* (1843–44). Poor reception of latter was compensated for by *A Christmas Carol* (1843), perhaps the most famous of all Dickens's works, whose sequels were the Christmas books *The Chimes* (1844) and *The Cricket on the Hearth* (1845). A year in Italy with growing family and a brief period at editing a newspaper were followed by *Dombey and Son* (1846–48), begun while again in Europe, a theatrical production venture, and the great work of his early years *David Copperfield* (1849–50.). Dickens's interest in public affairs resulted in his founding two weekly magazines, *Household Words* (1850) and *All the Year Round* (1859), as well as the works of his maturity: *Bleak House* (1852–53), *Hard Times* (1854), *Little Dorrit* (1855–57), *A Tale of Two Cities* (1859), *Great Expectations* (1860–61), and *Our Mutual Friend* (1864–65). Separated from his wife (1858), and attached to the actress Ellen Ternan, Dickens began a series of public readings which taxed his failing health. An enormously profitable tour of America (1867–68) so exhausted him that he collapsed during a farewell series in England. He nevertheless continued work on the novel *Edwin Drood* (1870; unfinished) until his death at Gadshill, Kent. Perhaps the most popular novelist of all time, he was buried in Westminster Abbey.

EDITIONS: *The Nonesuch Letters of Dickens* ed. Walter Dexter (3 vols. London 1937–38). *The Oxford Illustrated Dickens* (21 vols. London 1947–53). *The Pilgrim Edition of the Letters of Charles Dickens* ed. Madeline House and Graham Storey (2 vols. London 1965–   ). *Speeches* ed. Kenneth J. Fielding (New York and London 1960). REFERENCES: G. K. Chesterton *Charles Dickens: A Critical Study* (London and New York 1906; also PB). Philip Collins *Dickens and Crime* (London and New York 1962). *The Dickens Critics* ed. George Ford and Lauriat Lane, Jr. (Ithaca, N.Y. 1961). John Forster *The Life of Charles Dickens* (London 1872–74). George Gissing *Charles Dickens: A Critical Study* (London 1898, reprinted New York 1969). *Dickens and the Twentieth Century* ed. John Gross and Gabriel Pearson (London 1962). Edgar Johnson *Charles Dickens: His Tragedy and Triumph* (2 vols. New York 1952 and London 1953). Angus Wilson *The World of Charles Dickens* (London and New York 1970). Edmund Wilson *The Wound and the Bow* (New York 1941).

☙

CHARLES DICKENS
BY DAN JACOBSON

If Dickens had written the story of his own life, we would probably have accused him of displaying all his characteristic faults: melodrama, sentimentality, morbidity, excess and exaggeration of every kind. The child who is so closely acquainted with squalor, penury, loneliness, and despair, grows up into a young man who almost overnight wins for himself public acclaim of a sort that no other writer in the English-speaking world has ever enjoyed, and that hardly slackens in intensity until the day of his death. As a novelist he is applauded and revered above all for celebrating the delights of domesticity, and he zealously upholds in his work all the Victorian sexual pieties; yet he breaks up his own marriage in a blaze of largely self-inflicted publicity and conducts a secret, desperate affair with an actress many years younger than himself (who later claims to remember him only with distaste). The readings of his work in public bring him a new career, a new fortune, when he is at the height of his powers; but these readings have such a physical and emotional effect on him that his compulsive insistence on continuing with them, in spite of the pleas of his friends and medical advisers, turns the performances into a protracted method of committing suicide, carried out in front of huge, semihysterical audiences.

How crude such ironies and reversals of fortune are, we might object if they were presented to us as fiction; how implausible. But the most profound and instructive irony of all, in a way, is that the man in whose life they occurred should have been the greatest comic genius the English language has ever produced: a writer whose never-failing readiness to laugh at life was indistinguishable from his appetite for life in all its manifestations, and whose most delicate spiritual insights as often as not take the form of sheer high spirits. Nowadays our critical tastes lead us to slight Dickens as a comic writer in favor of the "darker" figure whose presence is also to be felt everywhere within his work. But we cannot begin to do him justice if we are not ready to acknowledge that the haunted, obsessed Dickens is no more the complete man, and no more the great poetic novelist, than the humorist, or the satirist, or the outright *farceur*. Moreover, our sense of the unending complexity of Dickens's character should always be qualified by the evidence we have of his directness, his frankness, his courage, the resolution and address with which he carried out the personal and professional tasks he set himself. Of these qualities his work, his letters, and his contemporaries' accounts of his life all speak unmistakably, in their different ways.

It has sometimes been said that genius, ultimately, is energy; that what distinguishes the genius in any field is not his possession of faculties that other men do not have, but simply his capacity to exert all his faculties to the very utmost in the attainment of his ends. More than any other writer I know of, with the possible exception of Tolstoy, Dickens is capable of persuading one that this partial truth is indeed the whole truth. One thinks of the wholehearted passion with which he flung himself into amateur theatricals, prison visiting, mesmerism experiments, travel, walking and horse riding,

dinner parties and convivial gatherings of every kind, letter writing, newspaper editing, house decorating, schemes of social relief . . . all these activities being carried on in the margins, as it were, of producing an oeuvre which is prodigiously large even by the bloated standards of the Victorians. However, the idea or slogan that genius is energy is endorsed most importantly for us by the essential characteristics of Dickens's prose style. For it is by virtue of that style that his work lives, and will continue to live, one must hope, as long as there are people interested in reading novels of any kind.

To many people, both among those who admire Dickens's work and those who do not, to speak of the energy of his prose is much the same thing as speaking of his copiousness of output. The distinguishing mark of his style, they would say, is its fecundity, its floridity, its way of accumulating details which to some readers remain gratuitous but to others acquire an artistic significance through their very profusion. However, I believe that the energy of his style is as strikingly shown in a manner that might seem the exact opposite of the one just described above: namely, in his conciseness, his trenchancy, his ability to strike off a sentence, or a phrase, or even a single word, that fuses together, as wit and poetry always do, the most widely disparate elements of experience. But the contradiction or opposition between these two manners is often more apparent than real. At his very greatest, Dickens achieves his effects through a brilliantly sustained *succession* of trenchancies, a lavishness not of random detail but of tightly compacted descriptions and metaphors. One can even say that many of his characters, in all their insistent vitality, strike us as a special variety of walking and talking metaphor, instances of a range of life brought together in so many single, active images. I am not thinking here, by the way, only of his grotesques, but also of some of his people who are capable of change and development.

There is no work by Dickens which is not radically flawed; not even *Great Expectations*, which is as nearly perfect a book as he ever wrote, but which he spoiled by tacking on an insignificant happy ending. Naturally one resents his errors, his misjudgments, the self-indulgences which so often are a form of pandering to his audience's prejudices. But I am not in the least tempted to belittle the wealth he has given us by yearning for the abstract, imaginary perfection that was out of his reach.

DICKINSON, Emily (Elizabeth) (Dec. 10, 1830 – May 15, 1886). American poet. Born Amherst, Mass., daughter of Edward Dickinson, a lawyer and prominent citizen. Attended Amherst Academy (1840–47) and Mount Holyoke Female Seminary (1847–48). Except for occasional visits to Boston and one trip to Washington and Philadelphia (1854–55), lived whole life quietly in Amherst at parents' home. Probably saw Emerson on his Amherst visit (1857). Began correspondence with Thomas Wentworth Higginson (1862), whom she looked to for poetic advice as her preceptor. First publication, a Valentine Day poem "Awake ye muses nine, sing me a strain divine" was in Amherst College *Indicator* (1850). Largely unpublished during her lifetime, her poetry reached the public eye after her death. Its publication, initiated by Higginson and Mabel Loomis Todd with *Poems* (1890), brought her into the front rank of American poets long before the final volume of hitherto unpublished poems (*Bolts of Melody*, 1945). Thomas H. Johnson's edition of the complete poems (listed below, 1955) is based on the manuscripts and lists variations from them in earlier editions.

EDITIONS: *The Poems of Emily Dickinson* (3 vols. Cambridge, Mass. 1955) and *The Letters of Emily Dickinson* (3 vols. Cambridge, Mass. 1958) ed. Thomas H. Johnson.

REFERENCES: Charles Anderson *Emily Dickinson's Poetry: Stairway of Surprise* (New York 1960). Richard V. Chase *Emily Dickinson* (New York 1951). Thomas H. Johnson *Emily Dickinson: An Interpretive Biography* (Cambridge, Mass. and London 1955, also PB). Albert J. Gelpi *Emily Dickinson: The Mind of The Poet* (Cambridge, Mass. 1965). Clark Griffith *The Long Shadow: Emily Dickinson's Tragic Poetry* (Princeton 1964, also PB). Jay Leyda *The Years and Hours of Emily Dickinson* (2 vols. New Haven, Conn. 1930). Klaus Lubbers *Emily Dickinson: The Critical Revolution* (Ann Arbor, Mich. 1969). Ruth Miller *The Poetry of Emily Dickinson* (Middletown, Conn. 1968). Rebecca Patterson *The Riddle of Emily Dickinson* (Boston 1951). Richard B. Sewall ed. *Emily Dickinson: A Collection of Critical Essays* (New York 1963, also PB). Genevieve Taggard *The Life and Mind of Emily Dickinson* (New York and London 1930). George F. Whicher *This Was a Poet* (New York 1938).

✍

EMILY DICKINSON
BY JEAN GARRIGUE

What has biography to do with this "life too simple and too stern to embarrass any," if we are to take the poet at her word? That she did not go from her father's grounds after the year 1865 everyone knows. The action was extreme even in an age of recluses and eccentrics. Not as extreme, but sufficiently dramatic, was her dressing in white after 1862, the white of bridal hue and death-in-life, the white "of tribulation," the white also of the sinner washed whiter than snow. What stung her to choose the circumscription? Nearly two thirds of her 1775 poems were written in seven prodigious years, stitched together in the famous "packets" — three hundred and sixty-six poems in 1862 alone — much of it coinciding with the Civil War, the trouble with her eyes that obliged her to seek a doctor in Boston, but also with the first signs of her withdrawal from society. Was it not Creation itself that drove her upstairs and forced her life to converge to its center? Biographers have looked for a lover as the inciting cause — first the tutor, then the minister and/or the *Springfield Republican* editor. Some critics would dismiss them all in favor of God; others insist that there is no literal or even spiritual protagonist in this drama of idolatry and renunciation.

Indeed, any explanation seems inadequate to her vision of a love supernatural in its "perfect — paralyzing Bliss," absolute too in its patience to wait for eternity if the other might be met. That is to say, her greatest love poems derive much of their unholy power, their depth and their enormous space to resound in, from the Puritan theology and imagery which, though she had rejected it, was also the legacy from which she drew her metaphors. Brought up on the Bible as children at a later date were brought up on fairy tales, she nevertheless refused (at the age of fifteen) to submit to the revivalists' harrowing of the mind to gain a subjected soul, and from then on remained the skeptic of the creeds and, incidentally, a critic of God. "I have a King, who does not speak —" one poem begins, and the king here is poetry; in other poems he is death. But love, death, and poetry seem members of a trinity who meet at "that junction, Eternity." Poet of the "Calvaries of Love," she is also a poet of its triumphs — "Mine — by the Right of the White Election!" and all those other dazzling marriages beyond earth; poet also of the lesser "transports" "learned by pain" who wrote, "My Worthiness is all my Doubt," "spotted," "freckled" as she

calls herself. And as one fearfully alive, poet of the many kinds of dying, those celebrated funerals, of the brain, those battles fought and lost, those drownings by sea — "Just lost, when I was saved!" Poet also of the prison — "I never hear the word 'escape'/Without a quicker blood"; of the famine that increased "The mystery of Food," and "that white Sustenance — Despair." Of all poets she seems the most alone because she visualizes so acutely the vastness of time, the length of the grave, the sphere on sphere of infinity. "Some pale Reporter from the awful doors/Before the Seal!" There her dramas are pitched.

The unattainable is her passion and her woe, her ecstatic bereavement, that loss she gets strange gain from. That restless mind, driven to an extremity and, visited by velocities of intuition, a kind of victim of its own phosphorescent gleanings from the seas of the dimensions she perished but survived in. Is she not odd, oblique, quivering, overstrung, "blue-peninsulaed"? She has the delirious eye for attars and Arabias — the paradise of the senses. Or was she so far in the north she had to figure forth the tropic east, the noon, the spices that were the opposite? Nearer at home are her erotic bees, those "Far psalteries of Summer." But there is also a plainness of speech, a terse abstractedness. No substances were common for her. She saw them all as rare. Her effort was to achieve the language that would allow their rareness to be known. And thus her astigmatic gaze, her ear for the "sunrise' yellow noise." Her verbs are magnificent; she can make you feel the full value of a word as if for the first time — eyes "soldered down" by death. Dramatic rather than lyrical, she is direct, vigorous, and so original that she suffered for it throughout her lifetime.

Not "literary," she had to create her own tune, one she borrowed from hymn meters, elect her own language in a time of smooth numbers and genteel adjustments. Her slant rhymes, a sometimes ungainly dissonance, seemed only odd in her time; her compression, too, her angularity, her gift for arguing, for the aphorism, for the definition ("Remorse — is memory — Awake —"). Like a great Examiner she notes the degrees of consciousness, the soul's "awful mate," with that genius for introspection also a part of her Puritan heritage. She had read Emerson and perhaps learned from him, but her most outright kinship is with Donne, whom she had probably not read, and other metaphysicals, including Sir Thomas Browne, for she had fed on awe, her "business was circumference." The impossibility of the possibility — the request for belief and the doubt of it — her thought runs between all the attendant dualities. Her intense emotional nature required dedication to what had become by her time a mere orthodoxy, and so she must gnaw on paradox.

Whoever the God is (or fate) that she quarrels with, it is because she has been robbed that she quarrels. She has sustained a loss, a desolating deprival. He was "swindler," "marauder," a "blond assassin" like the frost. And, close kin of Jonathan Edwards, distant kin of Emerson, she thought herself a kind of equal on some grounds at least. "The Brain is just the weight of God —" she wrote, and heaven's very site is "of the mind." Dissolve the mind and you dissolve the site. The heaven God withholds from earth is what she partly rages against. Would she not have it that earth is heaven "To Him of adequate desire"? And yet it is also the heaven of heaven she leans to: "This world is not conclusion./A species

stands beyond —" Out of conflicts like this her poetry is made.

DIDEROT, Denis (Oct. 5, 1713 – July 31, 1784). French encyclopedist and man of letters. Born Langres, Haute-Marne, of bourgeois family. Educated there by Jesuits, received M.A. from University of Paris (1732). Supported himself until 1744 as hack writer, meanwhile studying languages and science. Married Antoinette Champion (1743). Engaged (1745) to translate Ephraim Chambers's *Cyclopaedia* (1728), he gathered a team of writers including the great Enlightenment thinkers Voltaire, Montesquieu, Turgot, Buffon, and others, contributed innumerable articles himself, and with Jean d'Alembert edited the monumental *Encyclopédie* or *Dictionnaire raisonné des sciences, des arts et des métiers* (completed 1772). In it Diderot strove to record all available knowledge for man's enlightenment and thus to advance the politically dangerous cause of rationalism. Other works include *Pensées philosophiques* (1746); *Lettre sur les aveugles* (1749), which led to three-month imprisonment at Vincennes; *Pensées sur l'interprétation de la nature* (1753); *Le Rêve de d'Alembert* (written 1769, published 1830); the novels *La Réligieuse* (1760, published 1796), *Le Neveu de Rameau* (1762, published 1823), *Jacques le fataliste* (1773, published 1796). Traveled to St. Petersburg (1773–74) to thank Catherine the Great for her patronage. Died in Paris. Also wrote plays and criticism: his theories of drama exerted great influence, and his *Salons* (articles published in newspapers from 1759) laid foundations of art criticism.

TRANSLATION: *Diderot, Interpreter of Nature: Selected Writings* tr. Jean Stewart and Jonathan Kemp (London 1937, 2nd ed. New York 1963, also PB).

REFERENCES: André Billy *Vie de Diderot* (Paris 1931, rev. ed. 1941). Lester G. Crocker *The Embattled Philosopher: A Biography of Denis Diderot* (Lansing, Mich. 1954 and London 1955). Otis B. Fellows and Norman L. Torrey *Diderot Studies I and II* (Syracuse, N. Y. 1949 and 1953). Arthur M. Wilson *Diderot: The Testing Years*,

_1713–1757_ (New York and London 1957).

D'INDY, Vincent. _See_ INDY, Vincent d'.

DINESEN, Isak (Baroness Karen Blixen) (Oct. 17, 1885 – Sept. 7, 1962). Danish author, who wrote primarily in English. Born and died at Rungstedlund, near Copenhagen. Her father was a Danish officer and writer. An aspiring painter, she entered the Royal Academy of Fine Arts, Copenhagen (1902), and the Académie de Simon et Ménard, Paris (1910). After her marriage (1914) to Baron Bror Blixen, lived in Kenya, on a coffee plantation which the couple owned, until 1931. Having published two short stories in Copenhagen magazines (1907), she took up writing again after her return to Denmark. _Seven Gothic Tales_ enjoyed immediate success on American publication (1934); subsequent short story collections include _Winter's Tales_ (1942) and _Anecdotes of Destiny_ (1958). _Out of Africa_ (1937) and _Shadows on the Grass_ (1961) are reminiscences of her years in Kenya. Traveled frequently in Europe (from 1950) and visited U.S. (1959). Among her honors were the Danish Critics' prize and membership in American Academy and National Institute of Arts and Letters (both 1957). Isak Dinesen is known for her striking use of the English language and for her mastery of the storytelling art.

REFERENCE: Parmenia Migel _Titania: The Biography of Isak Dinesen_ (New York 1967).

DISRAELI, Benjamin, 1st earl of Beaconsfield (Dec. 21, 1804 – Apr. 19, 1881). English statesman and novelist. Born and died in London. His father, literary historian and critic Isaac D'Israeli (1766–1848), abandoned Judaism (1817); his children were baptized in the Anglican Church. Disraeli was largely educated at home. After apprenticeship in lawyer's office (1822–24) and disastrous ventures in stock market and publishing (1824–26), began literary career with satirical novel _Viv-_

ian Grey (1826–27), which brought celebrity. Traveled abroad. Wrote _Vindication of the English Constitution_ (1835). After four failures, he was elected to Parliament as a Conservative (1837). Married wealthy widow of parliamentary colleague Wyndham Lewis (1839). His finest novels, _Coningsby_ (1844) and _Sybil_ (1845), expressed his theory of popular Toryism as an alliance of crown, church, and people against Whig oligarchy. Became leader of Conservatives in Commons (1848–52), chancellor of exchequer (1852, 1858–59), and prime minister (1868, 1874–80). During second ministry, put through housing, factory, health acts and furthered British foreign policy by purchasing Suez Canal and adding imperialism to democracy as fundamental tenet of Tory party. He is considered the architect of the modern Conservative party. A favorite of Queen Victoria's, Dizzy crowned her empress of India (1876) and was made 1st earl of Beaconsfield (1877). Other novels include _Henrietta Temple_ (1837), _Tancred_ (1847), _Lothair_ (1870), and _Endymion_ (1880).

EDITIONS: _The Works of Benjamin Disraeli, Earl of Beaconsfield_ ed. Sir Edmund Gosse (20 vols. London and New York 1904–1905).

REFERENCES: Robert Blake _Disraeli_ (London and New York 1966, also PB). Bernard R. Jerman _The Young Disraeli_ (Princeton, N.J. 1960). André Maurois _Disraeli_ (tr. rev. ed. New York and London 1947). William F. Monypenny and George E. Buckle _The Life of Benjamin Disraeli_ (6 vols. London 1910–20, rev. ed. 2 vols. New York and London 1929). David C. Somervell _Disraeli and Gladstone_ (London and New York 1926).

DODGSON, Charles Lutwidge (pseudonym Lewis Carroll) (Jan. 27, 1832 – Jan. 14, 1898). English poet and author of children's books. Born Daresbury, Cheshire, where father was vicar, later to be archdeacon of Richmond. Educated at Rugby and Christ Church, Oxford, where he was lecturer in mathematics (1855–81). Contributed poems and stories to the _Comic Times_ (later the _Train_), using pseudonym Lewis Carroll for the first time in 1856. Achieved renown with _Alice's Adven-_

tures in Wonderland (1865), originally written to amuse his young friend, Alice Liddell, whose father was dean of Christ Church; it was followed (1872) by the equally popular *Through the Looking Glass,* both works illustrated by Sir John Tenniel. Producing mathematical treatises under his real name, nonsense verse and children's books under his pseudonym, he led a quiet bachelor's life at Oxford, interrupted only by a trip to Russia (1867), the diary for which he published as *The Russian Journal.* In last years continued to publish mathematical works and children's books, including *The Hunting of the Snark* (1876) and *Sylvie and Bruno* (1899). Died of influenza at Guilford.

EDITIONS: *The Complete Works of Lewis Carroll* ed. Alexander Woollcott (New York 1937 and London 1939). *The Annotated Alice: Alice's Adventures in Wonderland and Through the Looking Glass* ed. Martin Gardner (New York 1960, also PB). *The Annotated Snark* ed. Martin Gardner (New York 1962).

REFERENCES: Roger L. Green *Lewis Carroll* (London and New York 1960). Derek Hudson *Lewis Carroll* (London and New York 1954, also PB). Florence B. Lennon *The Life of Lewis Carroll* (rev. ed. New York PB 1962).

DOMENICHINO, Il (real name Domenico Zampieri) (Oct. 21, 1581 – Apr. 6, 1641). Italian painter. Born Bologna; trained there in Carracci academy. Went to Rome (1602), where he joined Bolognese artists at work in Farnese palace; subsequently received commissions for decoration from different Cardinals. Major paintings of this period are frescoes *The Last Communion of St. Jerome* (1614, Vatican Gallery) and *Scenes from the Life of St. Cecilia* (1615, S. Luigi dei Francesi, Rome) and canvas *Diana at the Chase* (1618–19, Borghese Gallery, Rome). On election of Pope Gregory XV (1621), Domenichino was appointed architect of the Vatican. Continued work in Rome, notably frescoes for S. Andrea della Valle (1624–28), until he went to Naples (1631) to paint *Scenes from the Life of St. Januarius* for the cathedral. Died in Naples. A painter of the eclectic school, Domenichino continued the mingled classicist and baroque manner of the Carracci, but also felt the direct influence of Raphael. His landscapes profoundly influenced those of Poussin and Lorrain.

REFERENCE: John Pope-Hennessy *The Drawings of Domenichino in the Collection of His Majesty the King at Windsor Castle* (London and New York 1948).

DOMENICO VENEZIANO. *See* VENEZIANO, Domenico.

DONATELLO (real name Donato di Niccolò di Betto Bardi) (c.1386 – Dec. 13, 1466). Italian sculptor. Born and died in Florence. Active in Ghiberti's workshop (c.1403–1407), may have been influenced by Brunelleschi and ancient sculpture, visited Rome sometime between 1408 and 1412. Earliest authenticated work a marble *David* (1408–1409, Museo Nazionale, Florence). Made second trip to Rome (1430–33); also worked in Padua (1443/44–1453/54) and Siena (1457–61). Enjoyed patronage of the Medici. Major works: *St. Mark* (1411–13) and *St. George* (c.1415–16) for exterior of Or San Michele; *St. John the Evangelist* (1408–15) for façade of Florence cathedral; gilt-bronze *St. Louis* for Or San Michele (1423, now in S. Croce, Florence); *Jeremiah* (1427–1435/6) and *Habbakuk* (1423–25, known as *Zuccone*) for campanile of Florence cathedral; *Feast of Herod* relief for baptistery of Siena (1423–27); reliefs on tabernacle of the Sacrament (c.1432) for a chapel in Vatican (now in Sagrestia dei Beneficiati in St. Peter's, Rome); "singing gallery" relief for Florence cathedral (1433–39); bronze *David* (c.1430), the first life-size, free-standing nude statue of the Renaissance; *Gattamelata* (1443/6–53, Padua); bronze crucifix in S. Antonio, Padua (1446); high altar of S. Antonio, Padua (1447–50); wooden *Magdalen* (c.1455, Baptistery, Florence); bronze *Judith and Holofernes* (1457–61, Loggia dei Lanzi, Florence); two bronze pulpits for S. Lorenzo, Florence (his last works, completed by others after his death).

REFERENCES: Giorgio Castelfranco *Donatello* (tr. New York 1965). H. W. Janson *The Sculpture of Donatello* (2nd ed. Princeton, N.J. 1963).

☞

DONATELLO

BY ANNE MARKHAM

Donatello, together with the architect Filippo Brunelleschi and the painter Masaccio, was considered from the sixteenth century on a founder of the art of the Renaissance, and hence the father of all modern sculpture. His career marks the transition from medieval sculpture — abstract in form, symbolic or overtly religious in meaning, created in the service of the church — to sculpture which glorified man, as youth, warrior and saint. The forms he used were not those transmitted through centuries of workshop practice but were based on a study of human anatomy and movement as well as on a knowledge of antique art in which a naturalistic view of man had found its most comprehensive artistic definition. Illustrative of this is Brunelleschi's famous criticism of Donatello's *Christ* in S. Croce, which looked to him more like a peasant than the perfect man "most delicate in every member." A corollary of Donatello's humanism is the new consideration he gave his audience. If works were to be seen from far away, Donatello accentuated the most important features to make them visible. If works were to be placed at extraordinary heights he introduced certain distortions to compensate for the optical illusions attendant upon unusual points of sight. His architectural settings always established for the spectator the precise place from which a relief was to be viewed. But Donatello not only accommodated his style to the aesthetic sensibilities of his audience: he wished also to affect their emotions, and to that end utilized numerous expressionistic devices such as crowded compositions, violent poses and expressions, bizarre architectual settings, an irrational treatment of space. A concomitant of Donatello's esteem of man was his own view of himself as an artist, in contrast to the medieval conception of the sculptor as a craftsman. A story is told of a Florentine merchant who objected to the price Donatello asked for a bronze head he had made for him, saying that Donatello had worked on it for only a month, which came to more than half a florin a day. Donatello, incensed that his work should be judged in terms of hours spent, replied that the merchant was accustomed to bargaining for string beans and not for statues and destroyed his work.

Donatello's oeuvre is very large, and though art historians still argue about the attribution of certain works, he is known to have executed over thirty-seven works of sculpture. In part, his prolificness may be explained by his longevity as well as by the existence of a large workshop of trained assistants, among whom were Michelozzo and Bertoldo. But even more, his fertility was the expression of a boundless energy, a decisiveness and facility, a boldness and resolution that is manifested in every work. He tackled every form of sculpture — free-standing figures, high and low relief, equestrian monuments, fountains, animals. He worked in every medium — bronze, marble, terracotta, stucco, wood — and in every scale. Each piece of sculpture that he created was an innovation so revolutionary in nature that its import was frequently not recognized until long after it was made.

In one of his earliest sculptures, the statue of *St. Mark* (Or San Michele, Florence), Donatello revived the antique *contrapposto* or hipshot pose in which the major portion of the weight of the body is supported on one leg. While the effect of the pose is akin to that of the Gothic sway — namely, the replacement of the static symmetry of the human body by a mobile balance and the creation of an impression of potential movement within an attitude of repose — the means of achieving it were wholly new. For the first time movement was conceived of, not in terms of a sinuous silhouette, but as the result of the unequal distribution of weight, as the interaction of tensed and relaxed muscles: an expression of the autonomous will of the figure rather than an imposition of movement from without. In *St. George,* also made for Or San Michele, Donatello progressed beyond a description of the organic basis of movement to the use of movement to reveal a state of mind. He suggested alertness in response to danger by raising the center of gravity of the figure into the thorax, as inevitably occurs when an athlete prepares to leap. In his prophets intended for the niches of the campanile Donatello used drapery, twisting it, excavating it, abjuring patterns of easy grace, in order to reveal that state of manic tension appropriate to inspired prophecy. The bronze *David* of c.1430 (Bargello, Florence) was the first life-size, free-standing nude executed since antiquity, and so naturalistic for its time that it was thought to have been cast from life. In the equestrian statue of the Gattamelata (Padua) Donatello again broke with medieval tradition. As in classical antiquity, this monument has triumphal rather than funerary connotations: it celebrates the victories and not the death of a great general. Moreover, it was not dedicated to a sovereign. Thus Donatello made explicit the greater appreciation of a man's capabilities than of his pedigree so

fundamental to the Renaissance. In his late *Mary Magdalene* Donatello created a haunting image of an ascetic through the emaciated face, the sunken eyes, the toothless mouth and matted hair. *Judith and Holofernes* (1457–61) shows the first integration of two figures within a single sculpture, and was preceded only by the bronze *David* in its possession of four distinct viewpoints: front, back and either side. So much was art a convincing reproduction of reality for Donatello that he cast the drapery of Judith from real cloth dipped in wax.

In relief Donatello is noted for the invention of *schiacciato* or "squashed" relief, in which the sculptured forms may project no more than half an inch from the background. It is through means appropriate to drawing, through fine linear incisions which catch the shadow, that effects of mass or distance are achieved. In his *Ascension of Christ and the Delivery of the Keys to St. Peter* (Victoria and Albert Museum, London) an infinitely distant landscape is suggested by the portrayal of a mountain range as though seen through layers of intervening atmosphere, with flattened surfaces, broken contours and loss of detail. In his last reliefs for the bronze pulpits of S. Lorenzo, Donatello eschewed a rational composition for the sake of a more urgent emotional effect. Figures are more densely crowded than the space allows, compositions are arbitrarily truncated by the edges of the field, and actors are shown in strangely foreshortened views, in attitudes and gestures of extreme hysteria.

The generation of sculptors that followed Donatello built upon his technical innovations but did not comprehend the significance of his work. They sought to refine and beautify, and the moods they chose to represent were ones of maternal intimacy expressed through graceful gestures. It was not until the work of Michelangelo in the following century that the force and monumentality and expressiveness of Donatello's sculpture found new embodiment.

DONIZETTI, (Domenico) Gaetano Maria (Nov. 29, 1797 – Apr. 8, 1848). Italian operatic composer. Born in Bergamo. Studied under Simon Mayr at Naples Conservatory, and at the Liceo Filarmonico, Bologna. While serving in Austrian army, wrote his first opera, *Enrico di Borgogna* (Vienna, 1818). Of the thirty-one operas produced during the next twelve years, *Zoraide di Granata* (1822) represents his first substantial success. Married Virginia Vasselli (1828; she died 1837). With *Anna Bolena* (1830) achieved fame throughout Europe. It was followed by *L'Elisir d'amore* (1832), *Lucrezia Borgia* (1833), and the tragic opera *Lucia di Lammermoor* (1835), his most popular work. Appointed professor at Royal College of Naples (1835), but when opera *Poliuto* (1839) was censored moved to Paris (1840). There produced the moderately successful *La Fille du régiment* (1840), *La Favorita* (1840) and, after triumph of *Linda de Chamounix* (Vienna, 1842), *Don Pasquale* (1843), his best *opera buffa*. Stricken with paralysis during his last years, he retired to Bergamo (1847), where he died. Donizetti's facility as a composer resulted in an enormous output of works that, though lacking in dramatic mastery, are notable for graceful melody and skill in composing for vocal virtuosity.

REFERENCE: Herbert Weinstock *Donizetti and the World of Opera in Italy, Paris and Vienna in the First Half of the Nineteenth Century* (New York 1963 and London 1964).

DONNE, John (1572 – Mar. 31, 1631). English poet and divine. Born in London to Roman Catholic parents; his father was a prosperous tradesman, his mother was John Heywood's daughter Elizabeth. Studied at Oxford (1584–87), entered Lincoln's Inn (1592). During 1590's, renounced Catholicism for Anglican faith. Poems of this period: the witty, cynical *Satires* and *Elegies*. Joined earl of Essex's expeditions to Cádiz (1596) and Azores (1597). Appointed secretary to lord keeper Sir Thomas Egerton (1598), he was dismissed and briefly imprisoned following clandestine marriage to Lady Egerton's sixteen-year-old niece Anne More (1601). For next few years, lived in penury, helped by friends. Most of the *Songs and Sonnets*, his best-known works, were written around the time of his marriage. At length regained aristocratic patronage and was active in anti-Catholic campaigns. Acceded to wishes of James I and took orders (1615); an eloquent preacher, he became reader in divinity at Lincoln's Inn (1616), chaplain with Lord Doncaster's mission to Germany (1619), dean of St. Paul's (1621). Later verse includes two *Anniversaries* (*The Anatomy of the World*, 1611; *The Progress of the Soul*, 1612) and *Divine Poems*. Major prose works, *Devotions* (published 1624) and sermons. Donne's poems were first published in 1633, two years after his death. He died in London.

EDITIONS: *Complete Poetry and Selected Prose of John Donne* ed. Charles M. Coffin (New York 1952). *Poems of John Donne* ed. Sir Herbert J. C. Grierson (2 vols. Oxford 1912). *Devotions Upon Emergent Occasions* ed. John Sparrow (Cambridge, England 1923). *Essays in Divinity* (London and New York 1952). *Divine Poems* ed. Helen Gardner (London and New York 1953). *Sermons* ed. George R. Potter and Evelyn M. Simpson (10 vols. Berkeley, Calif. and Cambridge, England 1953–56).

REFERENCES: R. C. Bald *John Donne: A Life* (Oxford and New York 1970). Edmund Gosse *Life and Letters of John Donne* (2 vols. London and New York 1899) is unreliable; brief life correcting Gosse's errors is in Evelyn M. Simpson *A Study of the Prose Works of John Donne* (2nd ed. Oxford 1948). J. B. Leishman *The Monarch of Wit: An Analytical and Comparative Study of the Poetry of John Donne* (London 1951; New York PB 1966).

JOHN DONNE
BY DENIS DONOGHUE

Of his *Biathanatos*, a treatise on suicide, Donne wrote: ". . . yet because I thought, that as in the poole of Bethsaida, there was no health till the water was troubled, so the best way to finde the truth in this matter, was to debate and vexe it, (for *We must as well dispute de veritate, as pro veritate*,) I abstained not for feare of mis-interpretation from this undertaking."

It is a typical gesture. Donne's mind delights in conflict, challenge, interrogation. "I would not that death should take me asleep," he wrote to Sir Henry Goodyer in September 1608. In the satire *Of Religion* he said:

> To adore, or scorne an image, or
>   protest,
> May all be bad; doubt wisely; in
>   strange way
> To stand inquiring right, is not to
>   stray;
> To sleepe, or runne wrong, is. . . .

Far from evading paradoxes and problems, he conspired with them, lest he should miss the pleasures of casuistry. He preferred the possible to the probable, because it provided more scope for energy and force. Poems like *The Apparition* and *The Flea* are begotten upon possibility; to enlarge the boundary of possibility is to enlarge the boundary of gratification when possibility is realized. All the better if the realization is, up to the final moment, improbable.

So the first mark of a poem by Donne is its dramatic note, a quality of force and speed: "For Godsake hold your tongue, and let me love." The reader is accosted, challenged to attend to a speaking voice, in the first instance; the ostensible theme may be understood as coming later. But in fact there is no distinction between the voice and its theme. The energy engaged is, to a remarkable degree, personal; it issues from one man, speaking, demanding, so that the reader who responds to the poet's voice responds to everything. The conventional gap between subject and object does not exist, because the entire experience is unitary. The voice is imperative: the reader who is not held by the voice is not held at all, he is not reading the poem. This does not mean that the reader is meant to be passive. On the contrary, Donne's poems compel the reader to participate in a personal relationship, while the poem lasts. The ideal reader responds to the poem with something of its own qualities: force, speed, continuity of power so long as power is required. These qualities are demanded by the poetic voice, but they depend upon the human will. There is no contradiction. Voice is the first manifestation of will; when we speak of dramatic power in the voice, we speak of will, the force of will directing the phrases. Donne's greatest poems are almost impudent in their demands, but their first demand is that the reader resist. A passive reader defeats the poem and humiliates himself. Sending his Paradoxes to Sir Henry Wotton, Donne wrote: "If they make you to find better reasons against them they do their office: for they are but swaggerers: quiet enough if you resist them. If perchaunce they be pretly guilt, that is their best for they are not hatcht: they are rather alarums to truth to arme her than enemies: and they have only this advantadg to scape from being caled ill things that they are nothings."

The poet's will invokes the reader's will; the experience is powerful if both wills are commensurate. In *The Relique* Donne uses words as if, left to themselves, they would conceal the truth; so they must be forced, interrogated. If the language seems extraordinarily active, the reason is that Donne refuses to allow the words to rest in conventional modes and relationships. Every relationship must be earned, as if at every moment the language had to start from nothing.

For the same reason, the conventional gap between thought and feeling does not obtrude. In Donne's greatest poems, like *A Nocturnall upon Saint Lucies Day*, there is no distinction between the dynamics of thought and the direction of feeling. If we attend to the thought, we elect to register our response in those terms, but this is merely a manner of speaking. If we attend to the feeling, we choose a different manner of speaking; but the response is the same, the dramatic action of the poem remains the same. The music of the *Nocturnall* is personal, voluntary rather than set; we read the poem by moving with the voice. Our own movement of will is assumed.

But Donne's voice, always personal, is never merely idiosyncratic; it is invariably sustained by traditional procedures, even when those procedures are questioned. Many of them are inherited from the Church Fathers, especially from Augustine, Jerome, and Aquinas, where the patristic tradition of eloquence and learning is defined. Pointing to this kinship, Donne's contemporaries called him "our English Tertullian." The same tradition offered him the kinship of wit and poetry. The evidence is clear in the continuity of feeling between Donne's poems and sermons. In the great Valediction Sermon (April 18, 1619) Donne preached upon the text: "Remember now thy Creator in the days of thy youth." His method is to press hard upon the crucial words, especially upon "remember," since memory, understanding, and will form the great triad, the faculties of the soul. Donne presents memory as the picture gallery of the soul: "And as a well made, and well plac'd picture, looks alwayes upon him that looks upon it; so shall thy God look upon thee, whose memory is thus contemplating him." These figures are the *imagines agentes* of medieval rhetoric, turned again to a devotional purpose. The same process is found in the poems, secular and religious. In *Good Friday, 1613: Riding Westward* Donne's voice exerts upon the words the same pressure which it exerts upon the text of the sermon:

> *Though these things, as I ride, be
> from mine eye,*
> *They'are present yet unto my
> memory,*
> *For that looks towards them; and
> thou look'st towards mee,*
> *O Saviour, as thou hang'st upon
> the tree.*

In the secular poems the images are pictures in an erotic gallery, "places" in a memory theatre. Hence, in these poems, the imagery of exploration. Donne is a geographer of passion, moving from one world to another; planets, stars, the sun, meteors, compass, map, and so forth.

The typical procedure is juxtaposition. Permanence invokes change, the other worlds call to earth, body challenges soul, Nothing demands the recognition of All. In the great *Nocturnall* the idiom of being, privation, and nothingness — essentially a scholastic idiom — is answered by a corresponding sense of its opposite, largely drawn from alchemical sources. The same movement of feeling in *The Extasie* incriminates physical passion with the figure of the incarnate Christ. Seeming incongruities are resolved by the personal force of feeling; in this kind of feeling, incongruities are shamed. Donne's dramatic imagination is the executive form his will takes, committing itself to the available language. The will commits itself to that form as the imagination commits itself to that language. This is the double source of Donne's power. In the poems he seems to possess his experience without any impediment in kind, and with only that impediment in degree which is the extreme limit of his imagination. His permanent significance is recognized in such terms; experience wide enough and diverse enough for any conceivable purpose, imagination capable and demanding. Speaking of death, he said: "I would not have him meerly seise me, and onely declare me to be dead, but win me, and overcome me." If there is a "mythology of self," Donne's place in it is marked by such gestures as these, defined in poems, letters, and sermons. It is unwise to turn him into a twentieth-century figure, a Hero of Our Time, but on the other hand it is hard to rebuke a generation which took particular note of the possibility he disclosed.

DOOLITTLE, Hilda (known as H.D.) (Sept. 10, 1886 – Sept. 27, 1961). American poet. Born Bethlehem, Pa.; at eight moved with family to Philadelphia, where her father, a noted astronomer, taught at University of Pennsylvania. At this time H.D. became friends with Ezra Pound, with whom she was closely associated in England, where she moved (1911) after attending Bryn Mawr College for two years. Began publishing poems (1913) and married British writer Richard Aldington (1913, divorced 1938). Became known as a leader of imagist movement. Her work includes collections *Sea Garden* (1916), *Hymen* (1921), *Heliodora* (1924), *Collected Poems* (1925), *By Avon River* (1949), *The Walls Do Not Fall* (1944), *Tribute to the Angels* (1945), *The Flowering of the Rod* (1946), *Selected Poems* (1957), *Helen in Egypt* (1961), the prose work *Tribute to Freud* (1956), and an autobiographical novel *Bid Me To Live* (1960). Her poetry is praised for its objectivity and directness without hyperbole. Pound called it "straight talk, straight as the Greek!" After World War II, she lived mainly in Switzerland, and died in Zurich.

REFERENCES: Stanley K. Coffman *Imagism: A Chapter for the History of Modern Poetry* (Norman, Okla. 1951). Horace Gregory and Marya A. Zaturenska *History of American Poetry 1900– 1940* (New York 1946). Thomas B. Swann *The Classical World of H.D.* (Lincoln, Neb. 1962).

DORÉ, (Paul) Gustave (Jan. 6, 1832 – Jan. 23, 1883). French illustrator, engraver, painter, and sculptor. Born in Strasbourg. Went to Paris (1847), where he produced weekly lithographic caricatures for *Le Journal pour rire* (1848–51). Though active throughout his life as a painter and sculptor, Doré is chiefly remembered for his wood-engraved book illustrations, especially those for the works of Rabelais (1854), Balzac's *Contes drolatiques* (1856), Dante's *Inferno* (1861), Cervantes' *Don Quixote* (1862), the Bible (1864), Milton's *Paradise Lost* (1865), the *Fables* of La Fontaine (1867) and Perrault's fairy tales (1883). Doré's theatrical, macabre style caught the public fancy and was much imitated. Best-known sculpture is statue of Alexandre Dumas *père*, Place Malesherbes, Paris. Decorated by the Légion d'Honneur (1861) and made an officer (1879). Died in Paris.

REFERENCES: Blanchard Jerrold *Life of Gustave Doré* (London 1891). Millicent Rose *Gustave Doré* (New York and London 1946).

DOS PASSOS, John (Roderigo) (Jan. 14, 1896 – Sept. 28, 1970). American writer. Born Chicago, son of well-to-do lawyer of Portuguese descent. After travel with parents, attended Choate School and graduated from Harvard (1916). During World War I drove ambulance in France and served with U.S. Army Medical Corps, experiences that provided material for his first novel *One Man's Initiation — 1917*

(1920). More successful novels followed: *Three Soldiers* (1921), a bitter indictment of war, and *Manhattan Transfer* (1925), an impressionistic portrait of New York. As free-lance writer and journalist, he traveled about Spain, Mexico, the Middle East, and in Paris associated with E. E. Cummings, Fitzgerald, Hemingway, and others of the international set. Increasingly left-wing in political views during this period, he became involved in social struggles, supported Sacco and Vanzetti, helped Kentucky miners during a strike, visited the Soviet Union, wrote articles and plays of social protest. Great literary success came with first volume of his *U.S.A.* trilogy, *The 42nd Parallel* (1930), which achieved an immediacy by using news events and sketches of contemporary figures prominent in American life. *1919* (1932) and *The Big Money* (1936) followed. The trilogy, a radical portrait of industrial America 1898–1929, won for Dos Passos his reputation as one of the finest novelists of his time. By the late 1930's, he had broken with Communism and was disillusioned by the Spanish Civil War. He wrote critically of proletarianism, and as time went on espoused conservatism. At the same time, his literary powers declined; *District of Columbia* (1949), a second trilogy *Midcentury* (1961), and other works revealed a narrowing view of his life. Married Katharine Smith, a writer (she died 1947), and Elizabeth Hamlin Holdridge (1949). Lived on his father's old farm in Westmoreland County, Va., also traveling and continuing to write books on history and travels. Died in Baltimore, Md.

DOSTOEVSKY, Fëdor Mikhailovich (Nov. 11, 1821 – Feb. 9, 1881). Russian novelist. Born Moscow, son of a physician. Went to St. Petersburg (1837) to enter army engineering college, where he spent three years. First publication, a translation of Balzac's *Eugénie Grandet* (1844). Gained critical acclaim for novel *Poor Folk* (1845). Arrested (1849) for political activities as member of Fourierist Petrashevsky circle; death sentence commuted to four years' hard labor in Siberia where he developed chronic epilepsy, followed by military service. Married Marya Dmitrievna Isaeva (1857; she died 1867). Resigned from army because of illness (1858) and returned to St. Petersburg, where he wrote for and edited several periodicals and produced his six great novels: *The Insulted and the Injured* (1861), *Crime and Punishment* (1866), *The Idiot* (1869), *The Possessed* (1872), *A Raw Youth* (1875), and *The Brothers Karamazov* (1880). Married (1867) Anna Grigoryevna Snitkina, and with her visited western Europe frequently. Died in St. Petersburg.

TRANSLATIONS: *The Novels of Fyodor Dostoevsky* tr. Constance Garnett (12 vols. London 1912–20). *The Brothers Karamazov* tr. Constance Garnett (London 1927). *The Possessed* tr. Constance Garnett (New York 1931). *A Gentle Creature and Other Stories* tr. David Magarshack (London 1950). *Crime and Punishment* tr. David Magarshack (London 1951). *The Devils* tr. David Magarshack (London 1953). *The Diary of a Writer* tr. Boris Brasol (2 vols. New York 1949). *The Letters of Fyodor Mikhailovich Dostoevsky to His Family and Friends* tr. Ethel C. Mayne (London and New York 1914). *The Letters of Dostoevsky to His Wife* tr. Elizabeth Hill and Doris Mudie (London and New York 1930).

REFERENCES: Anna Grigorevna Dostoevskaia *Dostoevsky Portrayed by His Wife: The Diary and Reminiscences of Madame Dostoevsky* (tr. New York 1926). Helen Muchnic *Dostoevsky's English Reputation 1881–1936* (New York 1969). W. W. Rowe *Dostoevsky: Child and Man in His Works* (New York 1968). Ernest J. Simmons *Dostoevsky: The Making of a Novelist* (London and New York 1940, also PB). George Steiner *Tolstoy or Dostoevsky: An Essay in Contrast* (New York 1959 and London 1960, also PB). Avrahm Yarmolinsky *Dostoevsky: His Life and Art* (2nd rev. ed. London and New York 1957).

✍

FËDOR MIKHAILOVICH DOSTOEVSKY

BY ALFRED KAZIN

When Thomas Mann defined art as the fusion of suffering and the desire for form, he summed up the life of Dostoevsky. Dostoevsky's life was so tragic, his literary instinct so powerful, that the man himself, who used every bit of his life in his fiction, understandably felt at times that he had made it all up. Dostoevsky's faith in literary imagination as the highest form of life is typical of nineteenth-century novelists brought up on romanticism. But the greatest shaper of his life and work was the authoritarianism of Russia itself, forever binding its best spirits yet calling out of oppression visions of spiritual freedom that have never been matched in the literature of the West.

Dostoevsky was born in the charity hospital of which his father was chief surgeon, and like so many of the greatest Russian writers before Chekhov belonged to the (minor) nobility. He lost his mother early; his father, an alcoholic who was the writer's first and perhaps greatest model for the violence that fascinated him in Russia and himself, was murdered by his serfs. Dostoevsky began his career as a draftsman in the Engineer Corps of the army, but he was obsessed with Schiller and other poets of romantic freedom and idealism, was drawn to radical and liberal publicists like Vissarion Belinsky and Nikolai Nekrasov, and soon astonished them with the emotional power of his first novel, *Poor People*.

Dostoevsky was thus one of the rising stars among the "Westernizers" who were attempting to lead Russian opinion toward a more "progressive," European direction. In the 1840's, a time of particular radical ferment, Dostoevsky as a free-lance writer in St. Petersburg was steadily more attracted to utopian socialism. He attached himself to the Petrashevsky circle, a group of radical intellectuals who in April 1849 were rounded up by the police and condemned to death. On December 22,

1849, Dostoevsky and his friends were led out to be shot, and only at the last possible moment were "reprieved." Nicholas I had planned a mock execution from the first. Dostoevsky, who had already spent eight months in a dungeon, was sentenced to four years of penal servitude in Siberia and then to serve in the lowest ranks of the army.

Dostoevsky was to spend exactly ten years away from his beloved St. Petersburg for the "crime" of associating with utopian socialists. Those ten years of exile, humiliation, suffering turned him from an eager young romantic writer into one of the most astute, complex, and commanding writers in the history of the world. The grisly mock execution made him an epileptic; the penal colony at Omsk gave the relatively sheltered young littérateur an awed sense of the prisoners as "an extraordinary people . . . the soul of Russia." Even in the dungeon, deprived of writing materials, he had thought out two whole novels and three tales. His ability to use and redeem the most painful and shameful experiences was to save him through his ten years' ordeal and to give him an entirely new vision as the novelist of the "insulted and the injured," of "the possessed," of "crime and punishment" — of the duality of good and evil in himself and in the Russian people. It also led him to believe in the necessity of authority in Russia, the legitimacy of the throne and the church, and above all, in the uniqueness of Christ as a religious support.

Dostoevsky's personal cult of Christ as the supreme image of goodness in the world meant the strongest possible negation of the moral conflict and "subversiveness" in his own nature of which he was to feel everlastingly guilty. But it is typical of his extreme either-or psychology, of the pressing human contradictoriness of which he was to become the most expressive novelist in history, that even about this supreme loyalty, to Christ, he could say, "If it could be shown to me that Christ is not in the truth, and the truth not in Christ, I would rather be with Christ than with the truth."

Dostoevsky the anguished convert, patriot, and defender of orthodoxy was, as a novelist, to make his greatest characters out of dissidents, rationalists, supreme heretics and atheist "supermen" like Raskolnikov in *Crime and Punishment*, Stavrogin in *The Possessed*, Ivan Karamazov, the Grand Inquisitor and the devil himself in *The Brothers Karamazov*. Even "the Russian Christ," Prince Myshkin in *The Idiot*, is always seen, like the saintly Alyosha in *The Brothers Karamazov*, in relation to the most violent lust, greed, and murderousness on the part of other characters who embody all the passion for the demonic and destructive in the human heart. Dostoevsky's greatest novels are all, ritualistically as well as symbolically, stories of murder. And the murder, as Dostoevsky well knew, is always of the Father God. But though the slain, like old Karamazov, are often enough wicked symbols of repressiveness, the slayers, like Raskolnikov in *Crime and Punishment*, are not morally hopeless but are tormented by the search for an object equal to their endless rationalistic striving, for a meaning to the world equal to their ceaseless tormented life of thought.

The classic antinomies of Dostoevsky's fiction are between the world of thought, striving, aspiration, of pure "reason" — and the world of pure experience that opposes all rational definition and expectation. "The Russian Christ," who in Dostoevsky's world finally becomes Russia itself, thus stands above every effort to make life coldly reasonable. Dostoevsky's God of pure existence is by this token the God of mystery. But as only a very great novelist can, Dostoevsky rose above all other "existentialists" who have been moralists only, to show the defeat of reason itself in the dramatic confrontation of the Grand Inquisitor with Christ, of Ivan Karamazov with the devil, of Raskolnikov with himself. The greatest drama in Dostoevsky's novels is of the human mind contending with itself to make a universe as full of action, and of *dramatis personae*, as the plays of Shakespeare.

DOU, Gerard (Dow, Douw) (Apr. 7, 1613 – Feb. 1675). Dutch painter. Born and died in Leiden. Trained in workshop of his father, a glazier, then with the engraver Bartholomeus Dolendo and the glass painter Pieter Couwenhorn. In Leiden still he also studied with Rembrandt (1628–31), whose influence is evident in his early work. Went to Amsterdam (1631) and developed his own style, first portraits in a miniature-like manner, then elaborately detailed genre paintings, some depicting candlelight effect, for which he is noted. His most characteristic device is the painted "frame within the frame," a gray stone window providing a view of a domestic scene. His meticulous, enameled style found many imitators. His best known works include the candlelit *Evening School* (Rijksmuseum, Amsterdam), *Young Man* (The Hague, Mauritshuis), *Dropsical Woman* (Louvre, Paris), and *Self-Portrait* (New York, Metropolitan Museum).

DOUGHTY, Charles Montagu (Aug. 19, 1843 – Jan. 20, 1926). English writer and traveler. Born Theberton Hall, Suffolk, son of a minister. Studied at universities of Cambridge (1861–66) and Oxford (1868–70), then traveled widely in Europe and Middle East, his chief interests being geology and archaeology. Joined a Bedouin group (1876) and journeyed through Arabia, returning to England (1878). His remarkable observations on Arab life and on the geography and geology of Arabia are recorded in an elegant, Elizabethan style in *Travels in Arabia Deserta* (1888). It received little attention at the time, and Doughty turned to writing epic poetry, also in a highly polished Elizabethan style. The best-known works are *The Dawn in Britain* (6 vols. 1906–1907), *Adam Cast Forth* (1908), and *Mansoul, or The Riddle of the World* (1920). Married Caroline Amelia McMurdo (1886). Died at Sissinghurst, Kent.

REFERENCE: David G. Hogarth *The Life of Charles M. Doughty* (London 1928).

DOUGLAS, Gawin or Gavin (c.1475 – Sept. 1522). Scottish poet and bishop. Son of Sir Archibald Douglas, 5th earl of Angus, known as Bell-the-Cat. After receiving master's degree at St. Andrews (1494), took holy orders and was made provost of St. Giles, Edinburgh (c.1501). Involved in Scottish politics (from 1513), siding with pro-English faction of which his nephew Archibald, 6th earl of Angus, was leader. Appointed bishop of Dunkeld (1515), but the triumph of pro-French party (1520) compelled his withdrawal to England (1521), where he died in London of the plague. Douglas's poetry was written in his early, peaceful years. He is chiefly remembered as the first British translator of a Latin classic, Virgil's *Aeneid,* in heroic verse (completed 1513). Earlier poems are *The Palice of Honour* and *King Hart* (the latter possibly not by Douglas), both moral allegories.

EDITIONS: *Poetical Works* ed. John Small (4 vols. Edinburgh 1874). *Selections from Gavin Douglas* ed. David F. C. Coldwell (London and New York 1964).

REFERENCE: C. S. Lewis *English Literature in the Sixteenth Century Excluding Drama* (London and New York 1954).

DOUGLAS, (George) Norman (Dec. 8, 1868 – Feb. 9, 1952). British writer. Born Tilquhillie, Aberdeenshire. Studied at gymnasium at Karlsruhe (1883–88), where he displayed scientific precocity. At eighteen began writing for British scientific publications; also published zoological treatises. Entered for-

eign service (1893), but left after three years in Russia. Married Elsa Fitzgibbon (1898, divorced 1903). First book, *Unprofessional Tales* (1901), scarcely noticed; his second, a travel book, *Siren Land* (1911), published with help of Joseph Conrad, also failed. Further travel books *Fountains in the Sand* (1912) and *Old Calabria* (1915) followed. International success came with novel *South Wind* (1917), which with witty, polished urbanity and irony depicted the effect of southern Europe upon a group of eccentrics who settled on the Mediterranean island of Nepenthe (for which Capri, which Douglas first visited in 1896, is the model). Other notable works include the autobiography *Looking Back* (1933), and *Late Harvest* (1946). He died at Capri.

REFERENCES: Richard Aldington *Pinorman: Personal Recollections of Norman Douglas, Pino Orioli and Charles Prentice* (London 1954). Lewis Leary *Norman Douglas* (New York 1968). Ralph D. Sindeman *Norman Douglas* (New York 1965).

DOVE, Arthur Garfield (Aug. 2, 1880 – Nov. 23, 1946). American painter. Born Canandaigua, N. Y.; attended Hobart College and Cornell University. Began career as a magazine illustrator, saved enough to go to France for eighteen months, and exhibited a Cézannesque still life at Salon d'Automne of 1909 in Paris. After meeting Alfred Stieglitz in New York began to paint abstractions of forms from nature. Gained American reputation upon exhibiting at Stieglitz Gallery 291 (1910). His were among the earliest abstract works painted in America. His aim was to discover the exact color and form or motif to represent the essence of the object painted. Constantly beset by financial problems, he lived aboard a boat, first in the Harlem River, then in Long Island Sound (1920–28). During this period he divorced his first wife and married the painter Helen Torr. Spent most of his remaining years on Long Island, where he died at Huntington.

REFERENCE: Frederick S. Wight *Arthur G. Dove* (Berkeley, Calif. 1958).

DOWLAND, John (1563 – Apr. 1626). English composer and lutenist. Born and died in London. Nothing is known of early life or training. In Paris (1579–84), in the service of English ambassador, he adopted the faith of the exiled Catholics whom he met there. Returned to England, married, and received B. Mus. degree from Oxford (1588). Went to Italy (1594), where he became famous as lutenist. Alarmed, however, at Italian antipathy to the English monarchy, he renounced Catholicism and returned to England (c.1597). Served as lutenist to King Christian IV of Denmark (1598–1606), then settled in London, where he was appointed one of King James's musicians for the lutes (1612) for the remainder of his life. Major works are the four volumes of *Songs* (1597, 1600, 1603, 1612) and three songs in *A Musical Banquet* (compiled by his son, 1610); *Lachrimae* (1605), a collection of instrumental pieces; *A Pilgrim's Solace*, songs (1612). Dowland's major contribution to music is the art song: he evolved a form in which a single voice carries the melody while the instrumental accompaniment develops an independent importance.

DOWSON, Ernest (Christopher) (Aug. 2, 1867 – Feb. 23, 1900). English poet. Born Lee, Kent, of well-to-do parents who traveled widely, especially in France, during his youth. Attended Oxford, without getting a degree, and when family fortune failed left for London (1888), where he managed his father's docks in Limehouse and cultivated literary associations. Through Oxford friend Lionel Johnson became member of the Rhymers' Club (1891), which included Arthur Symons, William Butler Yeats, and Johnson, who also persuaded him to become a Catholic convert. Worked at translating French poets, and collaborated with Arthur Moore on two novels. After death of both parents (1894), went to live in France, except for brief visits to London. His best work, *Verses* (1896), which includes the celebrated Cynara poem ("I have been faithful to thee, Cynara! in my fashion"), was influenced by Latin erotic poetry and the French aesthetes. It was followed by the verse play *The Pierrot of the Minute* (1897).

Soon after he returned to London (1900), he died of tuberculosis at Catford in Lewisham.

EDITIONS: *The Poems of Ernest Dowson* ed. J. Mark Longaker (Philadelphia 1963). *The Poetical Works* ed. Desmond Flower (London 3rd ed. 1967). *The Letters of Ernest Dowson* ed. Desmond Flower and Henry Maas (London 1966). *Stories* ed. J. Mark Longaker (Philadelphia 1947).

REFERENCE: J. Mark Longaker *Ernest Dowson* (Philadelphia 1944, 3rd ed. 1967).

DOYLE, Sir Arthur Conan (May 22, 1859 – July 7, 1930). British novelist and historian. Born Edinburgh; educated at Edinburgh University (medical degree 1885). First publication, *The Mystery of Sasassa Valley*, in *Chambers Journal* (1879). Practiced medicine until 1891, when he turned entirely to literary pursuits. Married Louise Hawkins (1885). Gained recognition with *A Study in Scarlet* (1887), first of the Sherlock Holmes stories. Achieved prominence as a writer and devoted much time to public affairs; knighted (1902). First wife died (1906); he married Jean Leckie (1907). Made public (1917) his belief in spiritualism, with which he was closely identified the rest of his life. Died at Crowborough, Sussex, "leaving behind him," as Howard Haycraft says, "the greatest reputation in the history of detective fiction and a detective whose name bids fair to remain a permanent part of the English language" — as well as a cult which developed such groups of Holmes devotees as the Baker Street Irregulars and the Speckled Band. Besides the Sherlock Holmes series, which includes *The Hound of the Baskervilles* (1902), he wrote many historical romances, including *Micah Clarke* (1889) and *The White Company* (1891).

REFERENCES: William S. Baring-Gould *Sherlock Holmes: A Biography of the World's First Consulting Detective* (London and New York 1962). John Dickson Carr *The Life of Sir Arthur Conan Doyle* (London and New York 1949). Christopher Morley ed. *Sherlock Holmes and Dr. Watson: A Textbook of Friendship* (New York

1944). Edgar W. Smith *Profile by Gaslight: An Irregular Reader About the Private Life of Sherlock Holmes* (New York 1944).

DRAYTON, Michael (1563 – Dec. 23, 1631). English poet. Born Hartshill, Warwickshire, son of a prosperous tradesman. At an early age received encouragement in literary pursuits from Sir Henry Goodere, to whose daughter Anne he addressed much of the sonnet sequence *Idea's Mirror* (1594), containing "Since there's no help, come let us kiss and part." First published book of verse, *The Harmony of the Church* (1591). Also wrote numerous plays in collaboration (1597–1602). Rebuffed by James I on his accession, wrote satire *The Owl* (1604), followed by *Poems Lyric and Pastoral* (c.1605), which includes the splendid *Ballad of Agincourt*, "Fair stood the wind for France." Extremely prolific, Drayton remained prominent in literary circles for the rest of his life. Died in London; buried in Westminster Abbey. His best-known works include *Polyolbion* (1598–1617), a long topographical poem of the English countryside, *Nymphidia*, a mock-heroic (published in a 1627 collection); *England's Heroical Epistles* (1597), poetic imaginary letters; and *The Muses' Elisium* (1630).

EDITIONS: *Poems* ed. J. Buxton (2 vols. Cambridge, Mass. and London 1953). *Works* ed. J. William Hebel (5 vols. London new ed. 1961).
REFERENCE: Bernard H. Newdigate *Michael Drayton and His Circle* (London and New York new ed. 1961).

DREISER, Theodore (Herman Albert) (Aug. 27, 1871 – Dec. 28, 1945). American novelist. Born Terre Haute, Ind., of poor, religious immigrant parents. Attended public school and University of Indiana (1889–90). Worked on various Midwestern newspapers before moving to New York (1894), where he had a successful career as writer and editor for magazines until he turned to writing as a full-time occupation (1911). Became deeply influenced by works of Thomas H. Huxley, Herbert Spencer, Darwin, and Balzac. First novel, *Sister Carrie*, suppressed by publisher soon after its appearance (1900). Most important of subsequent novels are *Jennie Gerhardt* (1911), the Cowperwood trilogy (*The Financier*, 1912; *The Titan*, 1914; and *The Stoic*, 1948), *The "Genius"* (1915), and *An American Tragedy* (1925), his first popular success and finest novel. A writer of the naturalist school, Dreiser's realism and skeptical view of American society involved him in continuous battle against censorship. Participated in left-wing activities (1920's and 1930's); after trip to Russia (1927) expressed socialist views in *Dreiser Looks at Russia* (1928) and *Tragic America* (1931). Also wrote essays, plays, stories, and such autobiographical works as *A Traveler at Forty* (1913), *A Hoosier Holiday* (1916), *Hey Rub-a-Dub-Dub* (1920), *A Book About Myself* (1922). Married twice: to Sarah White (1898) and to Helen Richardson (1944). Died in Hollywood, California.

REFERENCES: Robert H. Elias *Theodore Dreiser: Apostle of Nature* (New York 1949). F. O. Matthiessen *Theodore Dreiser* (New York and London 1951). William A. Swanberg *Dreiser* (New York 1965).

DRYDEN, John (Aug. 9, 1631 – May 1, 1700). English poet, dramatist, and man of letters. Born into Puritan family at Aldwinkle, Northamptonshire; educated at Westminster School and Trinity College, Cambridge. First publication, *Heroic Stanzas* (1659) on Oliver Cromwell, but after Restoration became royalist celebrating return of Charles II in *Astraea Redux* (1660). Married Lady Elizabeth Howard (1663). Appointed poet laureate (1670). Comedies and tragedies, including *Aurengzebe* (1675) and *All for Love* (1678), established his reputation. Displayed full powers in political and satirical poems *Absalom and Achitophel* (1681) and *Mac Flecknoe* (1682), both denigrating Thomas Shadwell as part of a quarrel arising from Dryden's view (inadequate in Shadwell's) of Ben Jonson's powers as a comic playwright. Defended Protestantism in ratiocinative *Religio Laici* (1682) but became Catholic (1685) and lost laureateship with accession of Protestant King William III. Afterwards, translated Virgil and wrote his greatest odes and *Fables Ancient and Modern* (1699). Died in London; buried in Westminster Abbey. A master of diverse literary genres, he combined his own kind of vigor and flexibility with the ideal of correctness, and helped greatly to establish the use of the heroic couplet which would dominate poetic practice in the eighteenth century. Other major works: the *Essay Of Dramatic Poesy* (1666), *The Hind and the Panther* (1687), and *Alexander's Feast* (1697).

EDITIONS: *Poetical Works* ed. James Kinsley (London and New York 1958). *Essays* ed. William P. Ker (2 vols. Oxford and New York 1926). *Letters* ed. Charles E. Ward (Cambridge, England, and Durham, N. C. 1942).

REFERENCES: James M. Osborn *John Dryden: Some Biographical Facts and Problems* (New York 1940, rev. ed. Gainesville, Fla. 1965). Mark Van Doren *John Dryden: A Study of His Poetry* (New York 1946, also PB).

JOHN DRYDEN
BY THEODORE MORRISON

John Dryden was born to a Northamptonshire family of Puritans in 1631, in the midst of the Civil Wars. A cousin, Sir Gilbert Pickering, acted as a judge at the trial of King Charles I. Dryden responded to the death of Oliver Cromwell with a panegyric in *Heroic Stanzas* (a form he was to use again in his *Annus Mirabilis*, a long poem on a British naval victory and the ensuing great fire of London in the "wonderful year" 1666). Then, on the restoration of Charles II to the throne, Dryden greeted the returning monarch with an extravagant poetical welcome under the title *Astraea Redux*. But if Dryden changed his allegiance, as Dr. Johnson observed, the country changed with him. Dryden moved still farther from his Puritan background. His *Religio Laici* is a defense of the Anglican church. When the Catholic James II briefly ascended the throne, Dryden too became a Catholic. This was the end of

his road of religious change. When the Glorious Revolution overthrew James and brought in William and Mary, Dryden could hardly revert to the Protestant faith of the new regime, though his position as a "nonjuror" cost him his poet laureateship and opportunities for income of which he always felt the need. Whatever part expediency played in his motives, genuine tastes and fears, lodged in his temperament, must also have had a share. Dryden's work makes it evident enough that he shared with his older contemporary Thomas Hobbes a horror of the chaos of religious wars, an antipathy to democracy, and a strong desire for stability and authority in the state.

Dryden lived through a period of change on many fronts. With the end of Puritan domination, morals and mores became anything but austere. The Royal Society, of which Dryden was an unscientific member, typified the revolt against Scholastic philosophy and the advancing prestige of science, which had been championed by Bacon and eventuated in the Newtonian world view. The revived theatre developed new fashions after the Puritan suppression. Dryden spent a large share of his literary energy writing plays for a living, despite his doubt that the stage really suited his "genius." But he was a complete man of letters; he practiced every genre for which a taste existed, and made himself the representative literary master of his time. If he was outdone in his day, it was by such contemporaries as Wycherly and Congreve in the comedy of manners. Besides his achievements in verse, he wrote some of the best prose criticism in English.

That he represented his age so expertly and comprehensively is a limitation as well as a strength. Revolutions of taste are unpredictable, but it is hard to imagine one that would bring back a vogue for the "heroic play" in rhymed couplets. To reread *The Conquest of Granada* or *Aurengzebe* is to expose the ear to torrents of rhetorical extravagance with little semblance of characters or any emotion except such excitement as rhetoric itself can generate. For Dryden's supreme dramatic effort, the tragedy *All for Love,* he turned from the rhyme he had defended to blank verse. *All for Love* is a thoroughly admirable work, a triumph in almost every respect, but it lies heavily under the shadow of Shakespeare's *Antony and Cleopatra,* and Dryden's candid remark in his preface, that "by imitating him, I have excelled myself," leaves the relative excellence unaltered.

If it is hard to imagine a renewal of taste for heroic plays, it is hard to imagine that *Alexander's Feast,* an ode celebrating the powers of music in honor of St. Cecilia's day, will again enjoy the admiration it received from Voltaire and the eighteenth century. Dryden in elegiac or lyrical vein is seldom at his best; an exception is the impressive memorial in couplets to his deceased young friend John Oldham. To understand the immense reputation Dryden attained, one must appreciate his achievement in the use of his chief instrument, the heroic couplet. Couplet writing is as old as Chaucer, and was richly enough represented in Elizabethan times, but with the changes of the Civil Wars and the Restoration, it more and more took its position as the chief verse instrument for Dryden and his successors through Pope and Johnson. Mark Van Doren estimates that in and out of drama Dryden wrote some thirty thousand heroic couplets. His developing expertness enabled him to use the couplet for satire, for narrative in translating episodes and tales from Virgil, Ovid, Boccaccio, and Chaucer, and for exposition and disputation in

such works as *Religio Laici* and *The Hind and the Panther.* To be thus adaptable, Dryden's couplet instrument had to be astonishingly flexible in structure and rhythm.

In all the variety of his work, Dryden comes nearest to transcending his age in satire. One can still laugh heartily and spontaneously at *Mac Flecknoe.* This attack on Thomas Shadwell, who succeeded to the laureateship when Dryden's Catholicism disqualified him, contains the couplet familiar to all readers of English verse:

> *The rest to some faint meaning*
> *   make pretense,*
> *But Shadwell never deviates into*
> *   sense.*

But it contains many another sharp hit as well, and its ludicrous design, the enthronement of Shadwell as legitimate heir in dullness to the poet Flecknoe, under the patronymic Mac, is still fresh and funny. In political satire also Dryden was supreme. His *Absalom and Achitophel,* in which he discovers a biblical parallel between King David and his son Absalom and King Charles and the bastard duke of Monmouth, is rich in satirical character portraits equaled only by Pope at his best. Witness his lines on Zimri (the duke of Buckingham, who with others had mocked Dryden under the name of Bayes in a play, *The Rehearsal*):

> *A man so various that he seemed*
> *   to be*
> *Not one, but all mankinds' epit-*
> *   ome:*
> *Stiff in opinions, always in the*
> *   wrong,*
> *Was everything by starts, and*
> *   nothing long;*
> *But in the course of one re-*
> *   volving moon*

Was chemist, fiddler, statesman,
and buffoon.

Yet even at the height of enjoying *Mac Flecknoe* it is possible to feel that brilliant abuse of dullness reaches a limit of interest, and really to be at home with *Absalom and Achitophel* one must be at home with the complicated intrigues of Charles and his ministers, with literary quarrels and rivalries, with such vanished concerns as the "Popish plot" and the Protestant succession.

In the last year of his life, when Dryden was in poor health and pinched circumstances, a benefit performance of one of Fletcher's plays was arranged for him. Dryden wrote, for inclusion in this performance, *The Secular Masque*, in which he reviewed the history of the century that was coming to a close. As the allegorical figures representing England from the death of Elizabeth to the year 1700, Dryden chose Diana (James I, with his passion for hunting), Mars (Oliver Cromwell), and Venus (Charles II and the amours of his court). Momus, god of mockery, points at each in turn as he sums up:

All, all of a piece throughout:
Thy chase had a beast in view;
Thy wars brought nothing about;
Thy lovers were all untrue.
'Tis well an old age is out,
And time to begin a new.

DU BELLAY, Joachim. *See* BELLAY, Joachim du.

DUCCIO DI BUONINSEGNA (c.1255–c.1318). Italian painter. Born and died in Siena. Founder of the Sienese school, painted in somber, austere Byzantine tradition. Received commission in Florence (1285) to paint altarpiece of the Madonna for S. Maria Novella, now identified as the famous *Ruccellai Ma-*

donna. Worked as illuminator in Siena (1285–95), and completed (1302) an altarpiece, now lost, in chapel of Palazzo Pubblico. His greatest and only fully authenticated work is the *Majesty* for the high altar of the Siena cathedral (1308–11). A sense of the dramatic characterizes Duccio's narrative painting, and he is noted for skillful draftsmanship, good grouping of figures, and rich, subtle color. His principal pupil was Simone Martini.

REFERENCES: Cesare Brandi *Duccio* (Florence 1951). Edward B. Garrison *Italian Romanesque Panel Painting* (Florence 1949).

DUCHAMP, Marcel (July 28, 1887 – Oct. 1, 1968). French painter. Born Blainville, son of prosperous notary and brother of painter Jacques Villon (1875–1963) and sculptor Raymond Duchamp-Villon (1876–1918). Attended lycée at Rouen and Académie Julian, Paris, then began to paint in various avantgarde idioms. Exhibited Cézannesque *The Artist's Father* at 1910 Salon d'Automne; participated in cubists' 1912 Section d'Or exhibition. His cubist-futurist *Nude Descending a Staircase* (Museum of Art, Philadelphia) was a sensation at Salon des Indépendants (1911) and at New York Armory show (1913); it is probably the most famous of all cubist paintings. With his "readymade," objects transformed into works of art through the "accidental" choice of the artist — such as *Why Not Sneeze?* (1921), a birdcage containing small squares of marble, a thermometer, a canceled postage stamp, and some parrot food — Duchamp assaulted traditional concepts of art and opened the way for new forms of artistic expression. Moved to New York (1915). After 1923, stopped painting and devoted most of his time to chess. Married Alexina Sattler (1954). Died at Neuilly, France. Duchamp was a major influence with Francis Picabia on Dadaists, also on surrealists, and is regarded as the spiritual father of pop, op, and kinetic art.

REFERENCES: Pierre Cabanne *Entretiens avec Marcel Duchamp* (Paris 1967). Robert Lebel *Marcel Duchamp* (tr. New York 1959). Calvin Tomkins

The Bride and the Bachelors: The Heretical Courtship in Modern Art (New York 1965) and *The World of Marcel Duchamp* (New York 1966).

DUFAY, Guillaume (c.1400 – Nov. 27, 1474). Burgundian composer. Born probably in Hainaut. Educated in Cambrai, where he became chorister in the cathedral (1409) and entered priesthood. Sang in papal choir in Rome (1428–37), then went to court of Savoy until he settled at Cambrai (1445), where he was canon of the cathedral. Outstanding in both religious and secular composition, producing masses, magnificats, motets, and three-part chansons, he made advances in polyphonic music and was esteemed by both church officials and musicians. Dufay is considered the most important Renaissance composer of his time in Europe. Died at Cambrai.

DUFY, Raoul (Ernest Joseph) (June 3, 1877 – Mar. 23, 1953). French painter. Born in Le Havre. Sent to Paris (1900) to study at École des Beaux Arts. Van Gogh exhibition (1901) and work of the Fauves, especially Matisse, led him to use flamboyant color and simplified forms. Exhibited with the Fauves at Salon d'Automne (1906), then joined Georges Braque and Émile Othon Friesz at L'Estaque in Provence (1908–1909), and came under influence of Cézanne. Became known for illustrations of Guillaume Apollinaire's *La Bestiaire* (1911), made wood-block designs for textiles, designed ceramics, a ballet set (1926), and painted a number of murals (late 1930's). Developed a calligraphic line for a lively variety of subjects — racetracks, esplanades, parks, casinos. Visited America (1950–51), painting numerous scenes east and west. Returned to Europe for retrospective exhibition at Geneva (1952), received grand prize at Venice Biennale, and settled at Forcalquier, where he died. His oil paintings hang in museums throughout Europe.

REFERENCE: Jacques Lassaigne *Dufy: Biographical and Critical Studies* (tr. London and Cleveland, Ohio 1954).

DU GARD, Roger Martin *See* **MARTIN DU GARD, Roger.**

DUMAS (Davy de la Pailleterie), **Alexandre** (known as Dumas père) (July 24, 1802 – Dec. 5, 1870). French novelist and playwright. Born Villers-Cotterêts, son of mulatto general in Napoleon's army. After desultory education by a priest, went to Paris (1823), where he became a copyist for the duc d'Orléans. Established supremacy of romanticism in French drama, and his own reputation, with historical plays *Henri III et sa cour* (1829), *Christine* (1830), *Antony* (1831), and *La Tour de Nesle* (1832). After marriage to actress Ida Ferrier (1840) and several unsuccessful plays, turned to full-time novel writing, often in collaboration with Auguste Maquet. Of the prodigious number he produced, the best-known are *Les Trois Mousquetaires* (1844), *Le Comte de Monte Cristo* (1844–45), *Vingt Ans après* (1845), and *Le Vicomte de Bragelonne* (1848–50), and *La Tulipe Noir* (1850). Lavish spending and Revolution of 1848 combined to deplete his resources and he fled to Belgium to escape creditors (1851). Returned to Paris (1853). Journeyed through Russia to Caucasus (1858) and joined Garibaldi in Sicily (1860). Lived in Naples for four years thereafter. Died at Puys, near Dieppe. Dumas also wrote travel books, memoirs, historical studies. His illegitimate son ALEXANDRE DUMAS (known as DUMAS FILS) (July 27, 1824 – Nov. 27, 1895), dramatist and novelist, was born in Paris and died at Marly-le-Roi. He is chiefly remembered for his dramatization (1852) of his first novel, *La Dame aux camélias* (1848). Other plays, all of which deal with social ills, include *Le Demimonde* (1885), *Le Fils naturel* (1858), *Un Père prodigue* (1859), *Denise* (1885).

REFERENCE: André Maurois *Les Trois Dumas* (tr. *Three Musketeers* London and, as *The Titans: A Three-Generation Biography of the Dumas*, New York 1957, also PB).

DUNBAR, William (c.1460–c.1520). Scottish poet. Born Salton, East Lothian. Circumstances of his early life are conjectural; presumed to have been educated at St. Andrews and member of Franciscan order. Attached to court of James IV, who granted him a life pension (1500) and employed him on diplomatic missions (on one he was wrecked off Zealand). His first great poem, *The Thrissill and the Rois* (1503), is an allegory written for marriage of James IV and Margaret Tudor of England. Other poems include *The Dance of the Sevin Deidly Synnis* (1503–1508); *The Goldyn Targe* (c.1508), a series of allegories after the manner of Chaucer; *Lament for the Makaris* (makers: poets) (c.1508), with the haunting refrain "Timor Mortis conturbat me"; *The Twa Maryit Women and the Wedo* (c.1508), a ribald satire on love, marriage, and women, also suggestive of Chaucer. Dunbar was notable for his versatility with long and brief occasional poems, and especially for his earthy humor, lively satirical vein, and imagination.

EDITIONS: *Poems* ed. James Kinsley (London and New York 1958); ed. William Mackay Mackenzie (Edinburgh and London 1932, new ed. London 1960).

REFERENCES: J. W. Baxter *William Dunbar: A Biographical Study* (Edinburgh 1952). Tom Scott *Dunbar: A Critical Exposition of the Poems* (Edinburgh 1966).

DUNSANY, Edward John Moreton Drax Plunkett, 18th baron (July 24, 1878 – Oct. 25, 1957). Irish writer. Born London; educated at Eton and Sandhurst. Served in Boer War and World War I, and spent most of life in soldiering and sport. Married Lady Beatrice Villiers (1904). Lord Dunsany's writings explore a world of fantasy. He created his own mythology for his plays and tales, frequently with an element of the macabre. First book of short stories, *The Gods of Pegana* (1905). First play, *The Glittering Gate* (1909), produced by Abbey Theatre, Dublin, made his reputation as a playwright and was followed by many others. They were collected in *Five Plays* (1914), *Plays of Gods and Men* (1917), *Plays of Near and Far* (1923), *Plays for Earth and Air* (1937), and others. He wrote several further volumes of stories, including *The Sword of Welleran* (1908)

and *A Dreamer's Tales* (1910); collections of verse; several novels, among them *The Charwoman's Shadow* (1926) and *The Curse of the Wise Woman* (1933); and three autobiographical volumes. He died in Dublin.

DUNSTABLE, John (c.1385 – Dec. 24, 1453). English composer. Few facts are known about his life. Obtained (1419) a secular canonry at Hereford cathedral, probably a gift of his patron the duke of Bedford. Wrote sacred music for the crowning of Henry VI as king of France (1431) and probably lived there during the duke of Bedford's regency (1423–35). Mathematician as well as musician, he compiled (1438) tables of latitude and longitude, now preserved in libraries at Oxford and Cambridge universities. Died in London. Dunstable exerted an important influence on French music, introducing such English characteristics as the relaxation of harmonic and rhythmic structures, and emphasis on the melodic line. Extant work is, with the exception of three songs, Latin church music.

REFERENCE: Frank L. Harrison *Music in Medieval Britain* (London 1958).

DÜRER, Albrecht (May 21, 1471 – Apr. 6, 1528). German painter, engraver, draftsman, theorist. Born in Nuremberg. Apprenticed first to his father, a goldsmith, then to painter and woodcut designer Michael Wolgemut (1486). Wandered as journeyman artist through southern Germany, Switzerland, and Alsace, working as woodcut designer in book publishing centers of Basel and Strasbourg (1490–94). Soon after return, married (1494) Agnes Frey, daughter of prosperous merchant; set up his own workshop (1495). Sojourns in Venice (1494–95 and 1505–1507) intensified Italian influence in his art. Employed by Emperor Maximilian I to execute various decorative works (1512–19). Magnificently entertained by leading artists and intellectuals during a year in Netherlands (1520–21), and found fresh inspiration in work of northern masters. Died in Nuremberg, leaving an oeuvre of nearly 100 paintings, about 250 woodcuts, 110 engravings, over 1000 drawings, and three treatises on geometry, fortification, and the theory of human proportion.

REFERENCES: Erwin Panofsky *The Life and Art of Albrecht Dürer* (London and Princeton, N.J. 1955). Wilhelm Waetzoldt *Dürer and His Times* (tr. enlarged ed. London and New York 1955).

~

ALBRECHT DÜRER
BY JOACHIM E. GAEHDE

Albrecht Dürer had been a precocious talent. At the age of thirteen he drew a remarkable self-portrait (Vienna) on which he later proudly wrote: "I drew myself while facing the mirror in the year 1484, when I was still a child." Two later drawings (Erlangen and R. Lehmann collection, Metropolitan Museum, New York) and one painting (Louvre) date into the *Wanderjahre* and show a handsome youth with a strong hooked nose, full lips, and keenly observant eyes — brooding or self-assured in the drawings and tranquil in the painting, a mood matching its confident inscription: "My affairs will go as ordained on high." This was the period of his first success as a designer of woodcuts in Basel and Strasbourg. A self-portrait of 1489 (Prado) is perhaps the first painting ever produced for the sake of self-scrutiny. It has a new and prouder air: formal pose, modish dress and hair proclaim the artist as a gentleman, a status new to Germany but tasted by Dürer during his first sojourn in Italy.

Having avidly studied Italian prints and drawings even before his journey, he was now to transform these lessons into his own graphic language, whose originality and power of expression surpassed the work of his northern predecessors and Italian contemporaries. Dürer's fame was founded on his prints, which had an easy market and allowed him a freedom of choice and

expression that his commissioned paintings could not afford. The series of woodcuts on the Apocalypse which appeared in 1498 was the first book published by an artist from his own designs, and it became a sensational success in Germany and abroad. It was a new vision of a traditional theme whose phantasmagoric mood Dürer dramatically enhanced by a faithful rendering of the visible world.

A fundamental change toward contemplative mysticism is marked by the self-portrait of 1500 (Munich). Casting himself in the idealized mold of a frontal and symmetrical Savior image, Dürer professed the doctrine of *Imitatio Christi* and his debt to the Creator's gift of his own creative power.

Search for the ultimate truth in art led Dürer again to Italy and to the ancient theories of proportion and perspective resurrected by the Italian Renaissance. Speculations on the formative laws of nature and art were to occupy him for the rest of his life. They were finally published in his treatises on *Mensuration* (1525) and *Human Proportion* (1528), written in a formidably clear language which, like Luther, he had to wrest from the unwieldy German of his time.

Dürer's theoretical concerns can be traced in many of his works, for instance in the engraving of *Adam and Eve* of 1504 (Bartsch 1), for which he used his construction drawings of classical nudes but placed them in the twilight of a northern forest populated by animals which symbolically enrich the religious theme of the fall of man, such as the cat near Eve eyeing the mouse between Adam's feet. The vivid reality of landscape and animals in this and other prints shows that Dürer never ceased to be absorbed by the spectacle of nature. His drawings from life, whether landscape, plant, animal, or portrait, are as accurate as they are reverent. Dürer studied theory not to set up rules of aesthetics but, as he wrote, with the belief that "art lies hidden in nature — he who can wrest it from her possesses art." And if he finally came to the honest conclusion that "such things I hold to be unfathomable," he did so in the conviction that the secrets of nature and the gift of genius are ultimately God's.

Neither Dürer's humanistic learning nor his technical perfection can explain the hold much of his art still has today. It is his disciplined passion, his gravity tinged by humor, and the range and depth of his vision which infuse a timeless humanity into accumulated research. When we are moved by the knight riding steadfast through a forbidding landscape of rocks and trees, heedless of death and devil, when we are touched by the intimate and peaceful mood of St. Jerome in his study or by the figure of Melancholia brooding among the instruments of science and art, we need not know that these three engravings (Bartsch 98, 60, 74) were allegories on the moral, theological, and intellectual virtues. Dürer gave life to abstract Scholastic concepts by showing the active Christian as a knight fearlessly advancing through danger and temptation and by placing the theologian's contemplation of sacred Scripture into the seclusion of a comfortable late Gothic study. These images he contrasted with the tragic futility of human striving for knowledge in the engraving of Melancholia. For all its learned symbolism, this print is perhaps the most revealing of Dürer. Far from suffering a passing mood of melancholy, the noble winged figure pondering insoluble problems is the personification of Melancholia, one of man's four temperaments in medieval thought and associated with genius by

the humanists. Dürer's Melancholia expresses an existential despair which he well knew himself as artist and man.

Dürer's last great religious painting, *The Four Apostles,* was given by him to the city of Nuremberg in 1526. It is his monument to the Reformation and his testament to Martin Luther. Nuremberg had turned Lutheran one year before, but radicals within the city endangered authority by new heresies while the peasants revolting in southern and central Germany claimed the cause of Luther for their economic grievances. The inscription attached to Dürer's painting and drawn from the writings of the four holy men depicted is a warning against these enemies in the Reformation's own camp and the papists as well, thus proclaiming the apostles as the guardians of Nuremberg's secular and ecclesiastical authority.

Dürer had never met Martin Luther, "the Christian man who has helped me out of great anxieties," as he wrote in 1520. His admiration sprang from a kinship of spirit. He found in Luther's writings not only a kindred earthy love of life but also a clarification and a liberation on which he could anchor his own restlessness in restless times. And, like Luther in the field of religion, so was he an innovator in the field of art. It was he who brought the fresh wind of the Renaissance to the late medieval north, infusing into it at the same time a spiritual tension peculiarly German. Of this he was conscious when he signed his name ALBERTUS DURER NORICUS.

DVOŘÁK, Antonín (Sept. 8, 1841 – May 1, 1904). Czech composer. Born Nelahozeves, Bohemia, son of an innkeeper. Studied at Organ School, Prague (1857–59) and played viola with Czech National Theatre Orchestra (1861–71). With performance of his *Hymnus* for chorus and orchestra (1873) he attracted attention, and won (1875) the Austrian state prize (an honor often repeated) for a symphony in E-flat (performed 1874). Married Anna Cermakova (1873). Championed by Liszt, Brahms, and Hans von Bülow, he gained international fame as composer and teacher, and received honorary degrees from universities of Cambridge and Prague (1891). While artistic director of National Conservatory of Music, New York (1892–95), wrote his most celebrated work, symphony *From the New World* (1893). He returned to Prague (1895), where he died. Dvořák's music includes nine symphonies, symphonic poems, concerti, overtures, chamber music — notably the *Piano Quintet in A*, op. 81 (1887), string quartets op. 51 (1879), 105 (1895),

and 106 (1895), *Sextet*, op. 48 (1878), and *Dumky Trio*, op. 90 (1891) — operas, songs, choral works, and piano pieces. His work is noted for rhythmic variety, abundant melodic inspiration, and use of Czech folk music elements.

REFERENCES: Viktor Fischl ed. *Antonín Dvořák: His Achievement* (London 1943). Alec Robertson *Dvořák* (London and New York 1945). Otokar Sourek *Anton Dvořák: His Life and Works* (rev. and tr. New York 1941 from German *Dvořák: Leben und Werk* Vienna 1935 tr. and abridged from original [in Czech] 4 vols. Prague 1916–33).

DYCK. *See* VAN DYCK, Sir Anthony.

EAKINS, Thomas (July 25, 1844 – June 25, 1916). American painter. Born and died in Philadelphia. Studied at Pennsylvania Academy of the Fine Arts, also anatomy at Jefferson Medical College. In Paris (1866–69) studied with J. L. Gérôme at the École des Beaux Arts, also with Léon Bonnat and the sculptor A. A. Dumont. During visit to Spain (1870) became deeply influenced by Velázquez and other realist painters. Returned to Philadelphia, taught at the Academy, became director (1879). Married former pupil Susan Macdowell (1884). Painted American sporting scenes and also *The Gross Clinic* (1875, Jefferson Medical College, Philadelphia), showing a medical operation in progress, which scandalized conventional public. His teaching methods, advocating use of nude models, encouraging anatomical dissection, emphasizing painting over drawing, also invoked criticism, resulting in his discharge as director (1886). He then concentrated on portraiture, of which he became a master, though never commercially successful. Notable examples: *Professor Benjamin Howard Rand* (1874, Jefferson Medical College, Philadelphia), *Walt Whitman* (1887, Pennsylvania Academy of the Fine Arts, Philadelphia), *The Chess Players* (1876, Metropolitan Museum, New York), *Mrs. Thomas Eakins* (1899, Hirshhorn Collection), *The Thinker* (1900, Metropolitan), *The Concert Singer* (1892, Philadelphia Museum of Art). Other major paintings: *Max Schmitt in a Single Scull* (1871, Metropolitan), *The Chess Players* (1876, Metropolitan), *The Swimming Hole* (1883, Fort Worth Art Association, Texas), and *The Agnew Clinic* (1889, University of Pennsylvania, Philadelphia).

REFERENCES: Lloyd Goodrich *Thomas Eakins: His Life and Work* (New York 1933). Sylvan Schendler *Eakins* (Boston 1967).

✑

THOMAS EAKINS
BY JAMES THOMAS FLEXNER

Thomas Eakins was the first major American artist to be alienated from American life, and his work is of such quality as to make it not unreasonable to argue that he was America's greatest painter. Naturally, at a time when alienation is so much the trend, Eakins's reputation is outdistancing that of all other American artists.

Before the Civil War, which broke out when Eakins was a youth, Americans were enchanted with their land and its inhabitants: Our native school of painting presented the local scene in lyrical and positive terms. But the fratricidal conflict, which brought dragging in its train a raw and untamed industrialism, created great disillusionment among individuals of sensibility. It became common for artists to hurry abroad while still beginners. In foreign studios — usually French — they adopted the latest aesthetic fashions, and then regarded the practice of these fashions as their life's work. They subscribed to the doctrine of art for art's sake, as promulgated by the American expatriate James McNeill Whistler, which preached that *what* an artist painted was of no importance. All that mattered was *how* it was painted. This justified seeking aesthetic effects that avoided contact with American life.

Eakins started his career much in the conventional manner of his contemporaries. He had not completed a picture when he sailed abroad, and he practiced for the rest of his life — although with personal variations — the sound, realistic technique of the French workshops in which he studied. However, Eakins never regarded technique as an end in itself. He moved in the opposite direction from the fashionable painters; he returned, with a determination almost violent, to his American roots. Living in the house to which his family had carried him when he was two and where he was to die, he began a passionate exploration of his own bit of the world. He became in the first instance the depicter of the Eakins family — their appearance and the sports they engaged in — and then of the Philadelphia that was his: intellectual; more scientific, really, than artistic.

As a boy, Eakins had built a steam engine that actually ran. During his artistic studies, he had frequented places where the more delicate artists of his time would have swooned: the dissecting rooms of medical schools. He wanted to know from the inside how the body works. And, when he wished to make a splash with a major picture, he painted a surgical operation: *The Gross Clinic*. This rendition — devoid of rhetoric or heroics — of science routinely and bloodily at work at its healing mission seemed shocking to Eakins's contemporaries. Although blood was commonplace in battle paintings, that he showed a splatter on the surgeon's hand made the picture seem unsuitable for ladies to look at. Eakins finally sold the large canvas,

today considered a masterpiece, for a pittance to a medical school.

Eakins's closest contact with the world as a doer rather than as a recorder came from his activity as a brilliant teacher of painting at art schools. Here he ran head on against the sexual mores of his time. The overt issue, which resulted in his being discharged from the directorship of the Pennsylvania Academy of the Fine Arts, was that he exhibited, in order more effectively to teach anatomy, a totally naked male model to female art students. However, there were (as has recently come to light) ugly rumors involving his female students, which members of his own family accepted, that extended even to blaming him for the suicide of his niece. Eakins carried his revolt against the prudery of the time to the extent of appearing himself in costumes that were considered indecent.

During his later years, Eakins concentrated on portraits. They were at the opposite extreme from the society concoctions of fashionable artists. Inviting friends and acquaintances — professors, scientists, writers, actresses, pretty girls — to pose, he dug for and expressed all the discouragement, frustration, and despair hidden in their natures. These are as much paintings of suffering humanity as the old martyrdoms of saints, but Eakins's subjects were inspired by no faith that justified their pain. The martyrdoms of Eakins's neighbors in nineteenth-century Philadelphia were inflicted by the flesh on itself and, in passing, by an ununderstanding, an unpitying, an indifferent world.

The technique Eakins learned abroad and refined at home aimed at utter realism: to make the human face and the human figure seem, as far as was possible for paint on a flat surface, actually to exist before the viewer in its weight, color, texture, tension, visible meaning. He achieved this end so successfully that few other painters in the history of art and no other American could rival his achievement. The emotional aura of his work is powerful, unhappy, morbid — well suited to our own time.

EDGEWORTH, Maria (Jan. 1, 1767 – May 22, 1849). Anglo-Irish novelist. Born Black Bourton, Oxfordshire, daughter of educational theorist Richard Lovell Edgeworth (1744–1817), who moved his family to Edgeworthstown, Ireland (1782). Her first publication, *Letters for Literary Ladies* (1795), was a plea for reform in women's education, presenting views largely her father's. Collections of didactic little stories for children followed, of which *The Parents' Assistant* (1796–1801) was the most notable. Recognition came with *Castle Rackrent* (1800), a lively novel of Irish life. Other novels with Irish themes followed: *The Absentee* (1812) and *Ormond* (1817). During visits to London (1813) and Paris (1820), she enjoyed considerable social success and the friendship of Sir Walter Scott, who acknowledged her influence on his own work. Despite the moralizing passages inspired by her father, her novels depict humorous characterizations and vivid scenes of Irish life. She died at Edgeworthstown. Other novels: *Belinda* (1801), *Vivian* (1812), *Harrington* (1817), and *Frank* (1822).

REFERENCES: Augustus J. C. Hare ed. *The Life and Letters of Maria Edgeworth* (2 vols. London 1894). Elizabeth Inglis-Jones *The Great Maria: A Portrait of Maria Edgeworth* (London and New York 1959). Emily Lawless *Maria Edgeworth* (London 1904).

EDWARDS, Jonathan (Oct. 5, 1703 – Mar. 22, 1758). American theologian and divine. Born East Windsor, Conn., son of a minister. Attended Yale University (1716–20), then prepared for ministry. After a year at a church in New York, returned to Yale, took M.A.

(1724), became a tutor. Ordained as his grandfather's colleague at church in Northampton, Mass. (1726), where he married Sarah Pierrepont (1727) and remained until 1750. First published sermon *God Glorified in the Work of Redemption* . . . (1731). Developed fame as preacher and theologian, and produced first revival (1734–35), which anticipated the Great Awakening that swept the colonies and was supported by Edwards in sermon *A Faithful Narrative of the Surprising Work of God* . . . (1736). More famous still was the sulphurous sermon *Sinners in the Hands of an Angry God* (1741), with the terrifying description of hell. As the revival petered out, Edwards became involved in bitter controversy with his congregation, was deposed (1750), and went to a frontier church at Stockbridge, Mass., where he also served as missionary to the Indians. Despite his reputation as a hellfire preacher, Edwards was America's most original theological mind; his major works adapt Calvinist doctrines to the philosophy of the Enlightenment as expounded by Newton and Locke. At Stockbridge he wrote the works on which rests his reputation as a theologian: *Freedom of the Will* (1754), *The Great Doctrine of Original Sin Defended* (1758), and others. Chosen (1758) president of the College of New Jersey, later Princeton University, he served only a few weeks before dying as a result of smallpox inoculation.

EDITIONS: *The Works of Jonathan Edwards* ed. Perry Miller (New Haven, Conn. and Oxford 1957–). *The Philosophy of Jonathan Edwards from His Private Notebooks* ed. Harvey G. Townsend (Eugene, Ore. 1955, also PB).

REFERENCES: Perry Miller *Jonathan Edwards* (New York 1949, also PB). Ola E. Winslow *Jonathan Edwards 1703–1758: A Biography* (New York and London 1940).

EICHENDORFF, Joseph Karl Benedikt, Freiherr von (Mar. 10, 1788 – Nov. 26, 1857). German poet. Born Schloss Lubowitz, Upper Silesia, of noble Catholic ancestry. Attended Catholic Gymnasium at Breslau and studied law at Halle (1805–1806) and at Heidelberg (1807–1808), where he associated with leaders of the romantic movement and published poems (1808). After more literary life in Berlin (1809–10) and Vienna (1810–13), served (1813–15) in Prussian army in coalition against Napoleon. Married Luise von Larisch (1815) and began long career of government service in Breslau, Danzig, Königsberg, and Berlin. After retiring (1844), devoted full time to writing and moved about frequently. Died at his daughter's home in Neisse, Upper Silesia. Eichendorff's lyric verse, in folk song style, is notable for its expressions of nostalgia, worship of nature, and deep faith in God. Many of his poems were set to music by Schumann, Brahms, Hugo Wolf, and others. His prose works, which are richly interspersed with poems, include an autobiographical novel (1815) and the novellas *Das Marmorbild* (1819, tr. *The Marble Statue* 1927) and *Aus dem Leben eines Taugenichts* (1826, tr. *Memoirs of a Good-for-Nothing* 1955).

TRANSLATION: *The Happy Wanderer and Other Poems* tr. Marjorie Rossy (Boston 1925).

EILSHEMIUS, Louis Michel (Feb. 4, 1864 – Dec. 29, 1941). American painter. Born Laurel Hill Manor near Newark, N.J., son of wealthy Dutch importer. After early education in Dresden, Germany, attended Cornell University (1882–84), then studied painting at Art Students League, New York (1884–86), and at Académie Julian, Paris (1886–87). Returned to New York, where except for travels in Europe, North Africa, and the South Seas he remained for rest of his life. Though Marcel Duchamp and other artists championed him in 1917, he had no commercial success, and in 1921 gave up painting altogether. After c.1932, demand became widespread for his work, which shows influence of Barbizon school and Albert Pinkham Ryder in romantic landscapes and mysticism. A major example of his painting is *Delaware Water Gap Village* (Metropolitan Museum, New York).

REFERENCE: William Shack *Biography of Louis M. Eilshemius: And He Sat Among the Ashes* (New York 1939).

ELGAR, Sir Edward (William) (June 2, 1857 – Feb. 23, 1934). English composer. Born Broadheath, near Worcester. Received early training from his father, a musician; played in and composed for local ensembles from childhood. Held local conducting positions and served as organist of St. George's, Worcester, until 1889, when he married Caroline Alice Roberts and settled in London to devote full time to composing. Finding London uncongenial, retired (1891) to Malvern, Worcestershire, where for next thirteen years he wrote works which established him as England's foremost composer, including *The Black Knight* (1893) for chorus and orchestra; *Enigma Variations* (1899) for orchestra; *The Dream of Gerontius* (1900), oratorio; first two of the five *Pomp and Circumstance* marches (1901–30); *The Apostles* (1903), oratorio. Knighted (1904), and received numerous honors. Later major works include symphonies, concerti, chamber music, oratorio *The Kingdom* (1906), and symphonic poem *Falstaff* (1913). As master of the king's music (1924), wrote occasional pieces. Died at Worcester. Elgar's music is in the nineteenth-century romantic tradition.

REFERENCES: Diana M. McVeagh *Edward Elgar: His Life and Music* (London 1955). Percy Young *Elgar, O.M.: A Study of a Musician* (London and New York 1955).

ELIOT, George, pen name of **Marian** (or **Mary Ann) Evans** (Nov. 22, 1819 – Dec. 22, 1880). English novelist. Born Arbury Farm, Warwickshire, where her father was an estate agent. At mother's death became his housekeeper. From early strict religious views emerged as a freethinker and joined circle of intellectuals, including Tennyson, Dickens, Huxley. Translated Friedrich Strauss's *Life of Jesus* (1846); German was her second language. Contributed to and edited *Westminster Review* (1850–53). Began (1854) relationship with George Henry Lewes that lasted until his death (1878); she called herself Mrs. Lewes, though he was married and a father. Adopted nom de plume George Eliot with publication of *Amos Barton*, first of the stories collected as *Scenes of*

Clerical Life (2 vols. 1858). *Adam Bede* (1859), which brought recognition, was followed by *The Mill on the Floss* (1860), *Silas Marner* (1861), and *Romola* (1863), inspired by visits to Florence. *Felix Holt the Radical* (1866) deals with English politics. *Middlemarch,* her finest novel (1872), and *Daniel Deronda* (1876) were her last works. She married John Walter Cross (1880), and died six months later at home in Chelsea. Her letters (6 vols. 1954) are edited by Gordon S. Haight.

REFERENCES: Gordon S. Haight *George Eliot* (New York 1968). Lawrence and Elisabeth Hanson *Marian Evans and George Eliot* (New York 1962). Walter Allen *George Eliot* (London 1965).

≈

GEORGE ELIOT
BY ROBERT GARIS

In her late teens George Eliot entered into a deeply felt and thought commitment to Evangelical Christianity; but very soon afterwards, under the influence of new friends and new books, she broke through to that attitude of rational disbelief in which she continued the rest of her life. During the post-Victorian decline in her reputation this early religious enthusiasm was often remembered to her disadvantage: when E. M. Forster spoke of her as a "preacher" (in distinction to the "prophet" Dostoevsky) he was calling attention to what he thought of as an artistic limitation. And even now George Eliot's experience with Methodism is ordinarily linked with her piety about family and country life as having provided merely subject matter for her early work. But it may well have been through Evangelical Christianity that Marian Evans all but unconsciously learned the entire aim and in particular the method of the art that George Eliot did not begin to practice until almost twenty years later. "Revival"— the dramatic re-experiencing of what was always known — is not a

bad account of what art always tries to accomplish, and this religious term will help to give the right emphasis to the dramatic element in the work of a greatly admired artist whose capacity for drama is still under question.

Nobody questions the range or the depth of George Eliot's realism, which from the beginning could register both the rich plenitude of the Poyser farm in *Adam Bede* and the stifling respectability of St. Ogg's in *The Mill on the Floss.* And everybody admires the way this natural gift for realistic observation was broadened and deepened by the new sociological interest and its new information to the point where it could achieve that sure and detailed — and still unrivaled — knowledge of an entire world that one finds in *Middlemarch.* But there is a more dramatic aspect to George Eliot's realism which she may have learned through religious experience. Christianity had always affirmed the precious uniqueness of the individual soul, and the Evangelical movement revivified this conception in its dramatic attempt to "touch" an increasingly brutalized and irreligious populace. George Eliot's loving attention to unlovely and unloved people has the Evangelical drama and stringency: stringent because hers is a discriminating love, merciful but just; dramatic because her portrayals of ordinary unlovely people had to be urgent exercises of the dramatic imagination, the only faculty whereby one can conceive of the existence of a precious soul beneath a petty or brutal exterior. In her remarkable first story, *The Sad Fortunes of the Reverend Amos Barton,* the power with which George Eliot creates respect for this raw and ungainly man is a dramatic power, and she continued to re-create and refine this dramatic realism of the inner life throughout her career.

The extraordinary intelligence and imagination at work in George Eliot's characteristic mode of extended psychological and moral analysis is everywhere recognized and admired, but one still hears murmurs that this is not the right mode of truly dramatic art. Perhaps here too the practices of Evangelical Christianity may direct attention to the dramatic intensity that so powerfully propels this analytic mode. The Evangelical exercise of soul-searching — that untiring vigilance against the ingenious disguises of egotism and self-seeking — is by its very nature dramatic; it is a matter of life or death. One hears this easily enough in the tones of Dinah Morris in *Adam Bede.* George Eliot's analyses of Lydgate in *Middlemarch,* of Tito in *Romola,* of Gwendolyn in *Daniel Deronda* are of course far subtler, more sophisticated, wiser than Dinah Morris's "preaching," but they are no less dramatic because of this ripening and refinement, as Henry James was to testify in inheriting the method.

George Eliot's attempts to secularize the conversion experience itself are less successfully dramatic, not surprisingly, since this sublime reach of art asks for miracles of tact and tone that one scarcely finds outside Shakespeare and Tolstoy. When we read those climactic scenes in George Eliot in which Pentecostal comfort and illumination are conferred by the influence of a grand but merely human spirit, we more often feel the author's yearning for this possibility than a firm belief that the conversion is really taking place. Yet the intention is heroic, and there are in addition discriminations to be made: if there are few clear successes, there are some remarkably intelligent near-misses and some almost deliberate failures. In the early work, in *Janet's Repentance* and *Adam Bede,*

the inspirational language of the Reverend Mr. Tryan, Dinah Morris, and the narrator herself is in decorum with the explicitly religious context; and the Arcadian simplicity of Hetty's offense encourages belief in her Arcadian conversion. Security of tone and continence of emotion make Silas Marner's conversion beautifully credible. Yet these successes are less interesting and important than the insecurities of tone that develop when George Eliot writes about more sophisticated people whose need for salvation is subtler. For the insecurities are not entirely inadvertent. From *Romola* onward certain doubts about the possibility of the conversion experience begin to darken the work. In Romola's inner debate about Savonarola's fanatical dedication, the validity of the inspirational influence of a large spirit is questioned very closely, and in *Middlemarch,* George Eliot remains in two minds about the ennobling effect of the single human being, though the ambivalence is not always under control. Dorothea's enlarging influence is confusingly both affirmed and denied: the language describing her effect on Lydgate and Rosamund is unconvincingly and embarrassingly inflated, as F. R. Leavis has pointed out, but Dorothea's actual effect on these two characters is minimal and the skepticism about the whole question at the end of the novel is admirably controlled. Indeed, the most affecting act of love in *Middlemarch* is Mrs. Bulstrode's perfectly life-sized, perfectly uninspirational ritual of participation in her husband's shame. But *Daniel Deronda* shows that George Eliot had not given up higher hopes, nor do we wish she had. Deronda himself, with his implausible beauty, his richly inspiring voice, his mysterious origin and grandiose destiny, represents in its most unchastened form George Eliot's yearning for the human incarnation of the Holy Spirit; but this refusal to disbelieve in the highest possibility did not in the least harm, and may in fact have energized, the extraordinary rightness of every detail in the love affair between Mary Arrowroot and Herr Klesmer, which is not only a life-sized vision of high dedication but one that isn't afraid of comedy and irony. Nor does the glorification of Deronda diminish our belief that Gwendolyn has in fact experienced conversion through his teaching. And in Gwendolyn's poignant insecurity about her new purposefulness, in her panic when Deronda deserts her for his Zionist quest, in Deronda's self-questioning about that desertion, one sees George Eliot's greatest quality as an artist, her power to continue learning and growing.

ELIOT, T(homas) **S**(tearns) (Sept. 26, 1888 – Jan. 4, 1965). American-born English poet, critic, playwright. Born St. Louis, Mo.; educated at Harvard, Sorbonne, Oxford. Settled in London (1914), where he was assistant editor of the *Egoist* (1917–19); founded and edited the *Criterion* (1922–39). First volume of poems, *Prufrock and Other Observations* (1917); others include *Gerontion* (1919), *The Waste Land* (1922), which made him famous and remains his best-known work, *Ash Wednesday* (1930), *Four Quartets* (1943), *Collected Poems, 1909–1962* (1963). Eliot's criticism, as influential as his poetry, appeared in *The Sacred Wood* (1920), *Homage to John Dryden* (1924), *Selected Essays* (1932; enlarged edition 1950), *The Use of Poetry and the Use of Criticism* (1933), *After Strange Gods* (1934), *Essays Ancient and Modern* (1936), *On Poetry and Poets* (1957), and other volumes. From 1927, when he became British subject and member of Church of England, expressed antiliberal views on sociological and cultural issues in numerous books, essays, lectures. Verse dramas include *Murder in the Cathedral* (1935), *The Family Reunion* (1939), *The Cocktail Party* (1949), *The Confidential Clerk* (1953), *The Elder Statesman* (1958). Married Vivienne Haigh-Wood (1915; she died in 1947) and Valerie Fletcher (1957). Received (1948) both Nobel prize for literature and British Order of Merit. Died in London.

REFERENCES: Helen L. Gardner *The Art of T. S. Eliot* (London 1949 and New York 1950, also PB). Hugh Kenner *The Invisible Poet: T. S. Eliot* (New York 1959 and London 1960). F. O. Matthiessen *The Achievement of T. S. Eliot: An Essay on the Nature of Poetry* (3rd ed. London and New York 1958, also PB). Leonard Unger *T. S. Eliot: Moments and Patterns* (Minneapolis and Oxford 1966, also PB). George Williamson *A Reader's Guide to T. S. Eliot* (New York 1966 and London 1967, also PB).

T. S. ELIOT

BY FREDERICK W. DUPEE

Throughout his long career as a man of letters, Thomas Stearns Eliot was many things to many men: a great critic, an interesting playwright, a far-sighted editor, an earnest Christian publicist, an exemplary literary friend. But surely it was as a lyric poet that Eliot was most original and most commanding. In that medium he produced a body of poems that continue to be urgently readable, ponderable, quotable. Indeed, they arrest our attention, stir our hearts, and chill our blood like Hamlet's "fearful summons" from his ghostly father. In that medium, too, Eliot originated a special form — the confessional monologue — which persists amid many changes in the work of more recent poets.

Is there a "place for poetry" in the modern world? Yes, Eliot seems to reply, and the place is deep within us. It is that mid-region of the mind in which the poet's memories and desires, dreams and fantasies, communicate themselves to the minds of his readers. Talking to themselves, the protagonists of Eliot's monologues likewise talk to everyone, and in everyone's language: the language of half-conscious aspiration and anguish. Eliot is the great modern poet of average human suffering.

To be sure, verses of several kinds go to make up Eliot's *Collected Poems*. His principal achievement, however, is probably the series of monologues that extends from *The Love Song of J. Alfred Prufrock* to *Gerontion* to *The Waste Land* to *Ash Wednesday* to the Ariel Poems to *Four Quartets* and includes the choruses of *Murder in the Cathedral,* his best play. Taken all together they form a kind of continuous and developing drama of the mind *in extremis.* To add that his use of monologue was influenced by the practice of earlier poets — chiefly Shakespeare, Browning and Laforgue — is not merely to acknowledge a literary debt on Eliot's part; it is also to define the tradition he worked in. And defining a tradition by reference to the novel works which that tradition is capable of engendering in really creative minds was a major preoccupation of Eliot's criticism. Indeed, he was never a better critic than when he went about relating — in what was often an indirect, even an unconscious, process — the work of some older poet to his own work.

So, in an essay on Shakespeare, Eliot glances significantly at Othello's parting lines, the speech that begins "Soft you: a word or two before you go." Othello, he writes, is "cheering himself up . . . adopting an aesthetic rather than a moral attitude, dramatizing himself against his environment." And Eliot adds: "Humility is the most difficult of the virtues to achieve;

nothing dies harder than the desire to think well of oneself." If Eliot is wrong about Othello, as I think he is, that is probably because he has in mind his own conception of the vanity of uncontrolled self-communion. His Prufrock, for example. That gentleman's wild and whirling words are always promising to lead him to an "overwhelming question," the answer to which, if it were honest, might induct him into a state of true humility. At each of these critical moments, however, his ego rebounds in one or another of several possible directions, all of them absurdly unpredictable. Recoiling from the questioning looks of strangers in a strange street, he cries:

I should have been a pair of ragged claws
Scuttling across the floors of silent seas.

Well, for a man so sensitive as Prufrock the life of a crustacean, armored, armed, predatory, and active, is doubtless tempting. But alas, Prufrock is irremediably human. Another time, seeking to strike a note of genuine resignation, he sighs, "I am not Prince Hamlet, nor was meant to be." Here he is trying to escape real judgment by raising, rather than lowering, his status — for who ever would dream that he *was* Prince Hamlet?

If poor Prufrock's confessions tend toward comedy, Gerontion's come close to being tragic, and here the Shakespearean analogue is the desperate, aging Macbeth of the "Tomorrow" speech, a true monologue, as Othello's "Soft you" speech is not. Gerontion is an old man, blind, alone, though possessed, as Prufrock is not, of an equivocal treasure: the remembrance of some great prior passion, of love or religion or both together.

*I that was near your heart was
    removed therefrom
To lose beauty in terror and ter-
    ror in inquisition.*

But although Gerontion is capable of
uttering these lines, and they are as
moving as any lines in modern poetry,
he is still talking to himself in a self-
dramatizing spirit. And so he inevitably talks himself *out* of his despair,
resigns himself to his loss as if it were
an act of blind fate, and finally seeks
consolation in a fantasy of universal
annihilation:

*De Bailhache, Fresca, Mrs. Cam-
    mel, whirled
Beyond the circuit of the shud-
    dering Bear
In fractured atoms.*

Only an incipient Christian, perhaps, could have made poetry so affecting out of such failures of humility as
afflict Prufrock and Gerontion. And
afflict everybody? It remained for Eliot to broaden the scope of his monologues by writing *The Waste Land*, a
long poem in which the voices of
the many are heard, crying, murmur-
ing, cajoling, threatening. But this composite monologue has as its principal
speaker a not easily identifiable someone for whom explicit Christian doctrine is already a reality and who
finally utters the poem's "moral":

*The awful daring of a moment's
    surrender
Which an age of prudence can
    never retract
By this, and this only, we have
    existed.*

In the act of humility, in the surrender of the ego, lies the possibility of
real existence.

Eliot's later monologues, from *Ash
Wednesday* to *Four Quartets,* are the
work of a poet who had formally
adopted the Christian faith, becoming
a communicant of the Church of England. So the poems of this period move
from stream of consciousness speech
towards the speech of disciplined meditation, and end not in dreams of ex-
tinction but in half-formed prayers for
spiritual survival. Or as Pericles says
in *Marina:*

*Living to live in a world of time
    beyond me; let me
Resign my life for this life, my
    speech for that unspoken.*

But Eliot was the rare kind of Christian convert for whom the process of
conversion is never actually completed
until death. "Humility is endless," he
wrote. His meditative monologues thus
remain distinctly poems, with a dramatic structure of their own. The
drama is provided by the many temp-
tations of daily life which the poet
calls "distractions," and not least by
"the intolerable wrestle/With words
and meanings." And when in *Four
Quartets* he writes:

*All shall be well,
All manner of things shall be well,*

he is only quoting a thirteenth-century
mystic. At the same time he is, in a
very special sense, and now quite consciously, "cheering himself up."
T. S. Eliot's achievement was to
make great poetry out of the common,
sad, ludicrous, but profoundly significant human habit of talking to oneself.

———————

ELLIS, (Henry) Havelock (Feb. 2, 1859 –
July 8, 1939). English psychologist and
writer. Born Croydon, Surrey, son of a
sea captain. Spent most of his child-

hood on the Pacific; studied medicine at St. Thomas's Hospital, London (degree 1889). Edited *The Law-Breaker and the Coming of the Law* (1884), his first publication; also the *Mermaid Series of Old Dramatists* (1887) and the *Contemporary Science* series (1889–1914). Married Edith Lees (1891). Gained recognition (1898) on publication of the first of his *Studies in the Psychology of Sex* (7 vols. 1898–1928), which became the subject of legal proceedings on an obscenity charge. The material contained in *Studies* and in *The World of Dreams* (1911) was later freely used by Sigmund Freud. Died at Hintlesham, Suffolk. Chiefly remembered for his analyses of sexual behavior, Ellis wrote fluently on a variety of subjects; other major works are *A Study of British Genius* (1904), *The Soul of Spain* (1908), and *The Dance of Life* (1923). Also wrote autobiographical *My Life* (1939).

REFERENCE: Arthur Calder-Marshall *Havelock Ellis: A Biography* (London 1959 and, as *Sage of Sex: A Life of Havelock Ellis*, New York 1960).

ELSHEIMER, Adam (Mar. 18, 1578 – Dec. 1610). German painter and etcher. Born Frankfurt-am-Main; studied there under Philipp Uffenbach. Traveled via Munich and Venice to Rome, where he settled (c.1600) for the rest of his life. Specialized in small paintings on copper, chiefly Biblical and mythological subjects, in which landscapes play a dominant part. These landscapes, minutely executed, depart from mannerist coloring and artificiality toward a new naturalism, and are particularly successful in rendering light effects and in creating a mysterious, poetic mood as in *Flight into Egypt* (1609, Alte Pinakothek, Munich). *Myrrha* (Frankfurt), *Philemon and Baucis* (Gemäldegalerie, Dresden), and *The Good Samaritan* (Louvre, Paris) are also among Elsheimer's best-known works. Through his friend Rubens, his pupil Pieter Lastman, who was in turn Rembrandt's teacher, and Claude Lorrain he exercised a decisive influence, and is considered one of the founders of modern landscape painting.

ÉLUARD, Paul (real name **Eugène Grindel**) (Dec. 14, 1895 – Nov. 18, 1952). French poet. Born St.-Denis, of humble parents. Illness interrupted his schooling at sixteen; during recuperation he began reading and writing poetry. First volumes of poems, *Le Devoir et l'inquiétude* (1917) and *Poèmes pour la paix* (1918). Badly gassed in World War I. After war joined Dadaists, then helped formulate surrealist principles based on exploration of dreams and the unconscious. Edited surrealist reviews and stated tenets of the movement in poem *Les Nécessités de la vie et les conséquences des rêves* (1921). Vanished from Paris on world tour (1924); after his return *Capitale de la douleur* (1926) established reputation. With André Breton wrote *L'Immaculée conception* (1930), an exploration of various mental disorders. The Spanish Civil War brought to his writing new social consciousness and militancy, and he broke with the surrealists. During World War II he joined the Resistance, then the Communist party (1942), remaining active as Communist for rest of his life. Married three times. Died at Charenton-le-Pont. A founder of the surrealist movement, his other works include: *Cours naturel* (1938), *Poésie et vérité* (1942), *Dignes de vivre* (1944), *Au rendez-vous allemand* (1945), *Poésie ininterrompue* (1946), *Poèmes politiques* (1948).

TRANSLATION: *Selected Writings of Paul Éluard* tr. Lloyd Alexander, introductory notes by Louis Aragon, Louis Parrot, Claude Roy (Norfolk, Conn. 1951).

REFERENCE: Louis Perche *Paul Éluard* (Paris 1963).

EMERSON, Ralph Waldo (May 25, 1803 – Apr. 27, 1882). American philosopher, essayist, and poet. Born Boston, son of Rev. William Emerson, one of a line of New England ministers. His aunt Mary Moody Emerson was formative influence on early years. Educated at Boston Latin School and Harvard (graduated 1821), spent next years school-teaching. Studied briefly at Harvard Divinity School. Already "approbated to preach" (1826) the Unitarian faith, he was appointed to Second Church in Boston (1829). That same year married Ellen Tucker (she died 1831). Resigned pastorate (1832) and went abroad, calling on Landor in Florence and on Coleridge, Wordsworth, and Carlyle in Great Britain. Returned to Concord, Mass. (1834), preached "on call," and lectured. Married Lydia (Lidian) Jackson (1835). Now launched on public career, he published *Nature* (1836), an orderly statement of transcendental philosophy. *The American Scholar* address at Harvard (1837) encouraged the younger literary generation; *The Divinity School Address* (1838) puzzled or infuriated the elder. *Essays, First Series* (1841) and *Essays, Second Series* (1844) are reductions of his lectures and notebooks. *The Conduct of Life* (1860), *Society and Solitude* (1870), and rest of his later prose are also the substance of his lectures. Published two volumes of poetry, *Poems* (1847) and *May-Day and Other Pieces* (1867). Lecture tour of Great Britain (1847–48) resulted in *English Traits* (1856). Liberal in politics and philosophy, yet skeptical of doctrinaire positions, he denounced the Fugitive Slave Law, came out for abolition. Grew in popular esteem, though later books reiterate a message already familiar. The burning of his Concord house (1872) was a severe shock; friends contributed to its rebuilding and to a trip abroad. But Emerson's mind was already weakening; his last years, though serene, were marked by increasing senility. Died in Concord; buried there near Thoreau.

EDITIONS: *Complete Works* (Centenary ed. Boston 1903–1904) and *Journals* (10 vols. Boston 1909–14) ed. E. W. Emerson and W. E. Forbes; a new edition is in preparation. *Letters* ed. Ralph Leslie Rusk (6 vols. New York and Oxford 1939).

REFERENCE: Ralph Leslie Rusk *Life of Ralph Waldo Emerson* (New York 1949).

≈

RALPH WALDO EMERSON
BY HOWARD MUMFORD JONES

Emerson was the chief figure in the American transcendental movement, a fact that complicates all accounts of him in literary or cultural history. Never systematic, the transcendental-ists owed most of their ideas to European theologians and philosophers, often, however, at second hand. A phase of the rebellion in the Western world of the generation of 1830 against conservatism, transcendentalism was also a local product of eastern Massachusetts. There Unitarianism had begun as a revolt against orthodoxy, but by 1820, influenced by Federalist culture, old-line Unitarianism had grown so arid that thirty years later Emerson could, somewhat unjustly, write in his journal that from 1790 to 1820 there was not a book, a speech, a conversation, or a thought in the state. In 1832 he resigned as minister of the Second Church in Boston and, surrounded by domestic sorrows, went to Europe to think things out. After his return he published *Nature* (1836), the best organized of his books until *English Traits* (1856), which expresses another side of Emerson. *Nature* is one of the few books by Emerson which did not begin as a sermon or a lecture. From *Nature, The Divinity School Address* (1838), and *The Over-Soul* in *Essays* (1841) it is possible to put Emersonian doctrine into coherent order.

Emerson repudiates the sensationalistic psychology of Locke, the philosophy of the Scotch common sense school, and traditional Christian orthodoxy. He grants that we get along in practical life by the use of good sense and empirical deductions. But man is more than a biological being, he is a spiritual entity having a perpetual possibility, experienced or latent, of direct contact with deity. Through common sense we judge our business affairs or discover the law of universal gravitation operating in or on matter, but man is more than the sum of his mundane experiences, and the law of universal gravitations, like other laws in science or experience, is the echo of some mightier principle still. The way by which supernatural influence pours in upon the soul is intuition, but Emerson prefers to call it the reason as against the understanding (or common sense). All principles discoverable in ordinary life are but the shadows of spiritual principles beyond space and time, that is, in eternity. Nature seen from the point of view of common sense is commodity; from the point of view of reason it is an alphabet or allegory of divinity. Since the soul in any man (therefore in all men) is a part of deity, God is immediately present in man, and in some sense (this shocked conservatives) *is* man. This mystical union Emerson defines as the Over-Soul, or:

". . . that Unity . . . within which every man's particular being is contained and made one with all other; that common heart of which all sincere conversation is the worship, to which all right action is submission; that overpowering reality which confutes our tricks and talents, and constrains every one . . . to speak from his character . . . and which evermore tends to pass into our mouth and hand and become wisdom and virtue and power and beauty."

Such is the transcendental affirmation of individualism. As all lines meet at infinity, so all individual affirmations fuse in God.

Emerson, however, was also a Yankee, a master of pithy speech, shrewd, sagacious, ironical, capable of making a little money go a long way, seldom taken in by pretense, never persuaded that slavery was a good investment or Brook Farm a practical scheme for agriculture. The Yankee in him conditions his style, which is aphoristic, as when he writes that a weed is a plant whose virtues have not been discov-

ered, notes that if we walk in the woods we must feed mosquitoes, and sardonically observes that every hero becomes a bore at last. If the Over-Soul expresses individualism raised to the highest spiritual power, Yankee confidence in self is evident in a passage like this from *Self-Reliance:*

"A sturdy lad from New Hampshire or Vermont, who in turn tries all the professions, who *teams it, farms it, peddles,* keeps a school, preaches, edits a newspaper, goes to Congress, buys a township, and so forth, in successive years, and always like a cat falls on his feet, is worth a hundred of these city dolls."

This is salty enough. Emerson the Yankee gave good advice to Young America, passed sagacious judgment on Napoleon, told off the State Street merchants, and in *English Traits* wrote one of the most penetrating analyses of another nation by a native writer in the whole nineteenth century.

Emerson is the master of sentences, a quality that is the great virtue and the chief defect of his style. Only a few of his poems — for example, *Days* — fuse into flawless beauty; in too many of them sentences or couplets tend to break away into a series of separated statements. The composition of his essays was agglutinative rather than organic. As striking thoughts occurred to him, he recorded these in his journal; and when he had a new lecture to write, he culled appropriate statements from these notebooks and arranged them, with new ones, in the loosest possible pattern. A paragraph by Macaulay and one by Emerson are at opposite poles of the rhetorical spectrum, the one fully organized with its topic sentence, its developing statements, and its concluding asseveration, the other less a piece of architecture than a pile of blocks. Even though the blocks are very good blocks, the reader comes by and by to feel that the verbal motion is circular, not forward. But it is easy to exaggerate. Emerson, when he wants to, can be thoroughly pliant and cohesive. Thus a minor essay like *Culture* in *The Conduct of Life* (1860) is structured with skill; and nobody has ever found fault with the movement of *The American Scholar* (1837), the most famous demand for intellectual independence in our history. And in everything that he wrote the accuracy and pungency of his diction are beyond praise.

When he died, Emerson was thought of as the representative American writer *par excellence,* and his point of view was still so potent that William James was honored to be asked to speak at a centenary celebration. Emerson then incarnated the moral optimism, the progress, and the energy of the American spirit. In the twentieth century he has been increasingly charged with ignoring or minimizing the force of evil in the universe; and since twentieth-century mysticism in America, so far as it exists, is more likely to find a Freudian or Jungian base than one in philosophic idealism, Emerson's appeal has weakened. Yet with greater linguistic economy than Whitman, his disciple, Emerson created for American individualism a metaphysical matrix more interesting than anything in the so-called Protestant ethic. He remains one of the great shining figures in the history of moral idealism in the United States.

ENSOR, James Sydney, Baron (Apr. 13, 1860 – Nov. 19, 1949). Belgian painter and etcher. Born Ostend to English father and Belgian mother. After attending Brussels Academy (1877–80) returned to Ostend, where he spent whole life. Although his early work was nat-

uralistic, by 1885 he had developed an art of symbolic sarcasm and macabre fantasy in tradition of Hieronymous Bosch. His paintings, full of strident color, skeletons, and caricature-like figures with grotesque masks for faces, anticipated both expressionism and surrealism. Their influence was strongest on German expressionism, particularly on Paul Klee. Famous works include the huge, tumultuous *Entry of Christ into Brussels* (1888), *Intrigue* (1890), *Maskers Quarreling Over a Hanged Man* (1891; all in Museum of Fine Arts, Antwerp), and the etching *The Cathedral* (1886). Widespread recognition came (c.1900), after Ensor had done his most important work. Made baron by Albert I of Belgium (1929).

REFERENCE: Paul Haesaerts *James Ensor* (Brussels 1957).

EPSTEIN, Sir Jacob (Nov. 10, 1880 – Aug. 19, 1959). Anglo-American sculptor. Born New York of Polish-Jewish parents. Studied at Art Students League and (from 1902) in Paris at École des Beaux Arts under Rodin and at Académie Julian. Settled in London (1905); two years later received first important commission, a frieze of eighteen large figures for new British Medical Association building. Vehement controversy greeted completed work (1908), as it did most of Epstein's subsequent sculpture. Usually massive in scale, primitivistic and harsh, it contrasted sharply with ornate, pretty, traditional art forms. Works include Oscar Wilde memorial, Père Lachaise cemetery, Paris (1909); marble *Venus* (1917, Yale Art Gallery, New Haven, Conn.); bronze *Christ Showing the Stigmata* (1919, A. Cheny-Garrard Collection, Weathanstead, England); William Henry Hudson memorial, a statue of "Rima" of *Green Mansions,* Hyde Park, London (1925); *Night* and *Day* on façade of London Transport Building (1929). Also well known are his expressive portraits in bronze, including Joseph Conrad (1924), Chaim Weizman (1933), Albert Einstein (1933), George Bernard Shaw (1934), and many other famous contemporaries. Epstein was married twice and knighted in 1954. His autobiography, *Let There Be Sculpture* (1940), was expanded and republished as *Epstein: An Autobiography* (1955). He died in London.

REFERENCE: Richard Buckle *Jacob Epstein, Sculptor* (Cleveland 1963).

———

ERASMUS, Desiderius (Latin and Greek rendering of his father's name Gerhard — "beloved") (1466/1469 – July 12, 1536). Dutch humanist. Born Rotterdam, illegitimate son of a priest and a physician's daughter. Educated at schools of Brethren of the Common Life in Deventer and 's Hertogenbosch. Entered Augustinian order (1487/88). After taking orders went to Paris (1492) as secretary to bishop of Cambrai and in order to study at University of Paris. On visit to England (1499) met John Colet and Thomas More, under whose inspiration he turned toward rescuing theology from the Scholastics and referring it to its original sources, reviving classical learning and exposing abuses of the church. From 1500 on, Erasmus moved about the Continent and England (where he taught at Cambridge University, 1509–14), publishing editions of Greek and Latin classics and the Church Fathers, as well as the original works which made him the most influential writer of his time, notably *Adagia* (*Adages* or *Proverbs*, 1500), *Enchiridion Militis Christiani* (*Handbook of the Christian Knight*, 1503), the famous satire *Moriae Encomium* (*Praise of Folly*, 1509), *Institutio Principis Christiani* (*Education of a Christian Prince*, 1515), *Colloquia* (Colloquies, 1516), and his edition of the Greek text of the New Testament, with a new Latin translation (1516). Refusal to participate in the violent religious warfare of the time (except for an exchange with Martin Luther) provoked attacks from Reformers and Catholics alike. Died in Basel, Switzerland.

TRANSLATIONS: *The Colloquies of Erasmus* tr. Craig R. Thompson (2 vols. Chicago 1965). *The Enchiridion* tr. Raymond Himelick (Bloomington, Ind. PB 1963). *The Essential Erasmus* tr. John P. Dolan (New York PB 1964).

REFERENCES: Preserved Smith *Erasmus: A Study of His Life, Ideals and Place in History* (New York 1923, also PB). Johan Huizinga *Erasmus of Rotterdam* (tr. 4th ed. London 1952 and New York 1953, PB New York 1957 as *Erasmus and the Age of the Reformation*).

———

ETHEREGE, Sir George (c.1635–1691/92). English dramatist. Birthplace unknown. He may have attended Cambridge University briefly, and seems to have lived awhile in France as a young man. In London he won fame with *The Comical Revenge, or Love in a Tub* (1664), which with *She Would If She Could* (1668) and *The Man of Mode, or Sir Fopling Flutter* (1676) set the style of the Restoration comedy of manners which Congreve was to perfect. Lived in Turkey (1668–71) as secretary to English ambassador. Knighted (c.1679) and also married a rich widow, Mary Arnold (née Sheppard). Appointed envoy to Imperial Diet of Ratisbon (1685), but his diplomatic career ended with overthrow of James II. He was ruined financially, and went to Paris, where he remained until his death.

EDITIONS: *Dramatic Works* ed. H. F. B. Brett-Smith (2 vols. Oxford, Boston, New York 1927). *Poems* ed. James Thorpe (Princeton 1963).

REFERENCES: Frances S. Tinker *Sir George Etherege: A Study in Restoration Comedy* (Cedar Rapids, Iowa 1931). Dale Underwood *Etherege and the Seventeenth-Century Comedy of Manners* (New Haven 1957 and Oxford 1958).

———

EURIPIDES (c.485 B.C.–c.406 B.C.). Greek tragedian. Born of well-to-do Athenian family, possibly at country home on Salamis, where from childhood he spent most of his life in seclusion, showing little interest in Athenian social or public life. Of the ninety-two plays he is said to have written, seventeen tragedies survive, including *Alcestis* (438 B.C.), *Medea* (431), *Hippolytus* (428), *Suppliants* (421), *The Trojan Women* (415), *Electra* (413), *Orestes* (408), *The Bacchae* (405), *Iphigenia in Aulis* (405), and one satyr play, *The Cyclops*. "Sophocles drew men as they ought to be," said Aristotle, "Euripides as they were." Besides his psychological penetration, he was noted for religious skepticism and daring innovations in dramatic technique. Highly controversial in his own day, he won only five first prizes at Dionysiac festivals. Spent last years at court of King Archelaus of Macedon, where he died. His genius at last recognized upon his death, a great tomb at Pella was built for him.

TRANSLATIONS: *Plays of Euripides* tr. Gilbert Murray (London and New York 1902–54); tr. David Grene and Richmond Lattimore in *The Complete Greek Tragedies* (Chicago 1955–59).

REFERENCES: Desmond J. Conacher *Euripidean Drama: Myth, Theme and Structure* (Toronto 1967 and Oxford 1968). L. H. G. Greenwood *Aspects of Euripidean Tragedy* (Cambridge, England, 1953). G. M. A. Grube *The Drama of Euripides* (London 1941, reprinted New York 1961). Gilbert Murray *Euripides and His Age* (2nd ed. London and New York 1955, also PB). Erich W. Segal ed. *Euripides: A Collection of Critical Essays* (Englewood Cliffs, N.J. 1968, also PB).

EURIPIDES
BY WALTER KERR

We are inclined to be wary of Euripides for the same reasons that we admire him. In the theatre, Euripides is the first realist, passing over the elevated, self-exalting gestures of the male giants who chose to defend Troy to ask — in a new voice — how it was with the women they left behind them in defeat. To ask after women at all, whether in *The Trojan Women* or *Medea* or *Electra*, was a radical, deeply domesticating departure for Greek tragedy. In the tragedies of Aeschylus and Sophocles the women are really men.

Euripides is the first rhetorician, calling attention to language as an independent power, generator of emotion as much as recorder of emotion, master as much as servant. In a single scene in *Iphigenia in Aulis* two men meet to argue the fate of a young girl. One is the girl's father, the other her uncle. The father wishes to save her, the uncle to sacrifice her. By the end of the uninterrupted sequence their positions are exactly reversed: through argument, through the sheer force of language ably exercised, each has persuaded the other.

Euripides is the first nonconformist. Again and again in the seventeen tragedies which survive (out of a possible ninety-two), the respect formerly shown to established myth and to the gods is reduced in the interests of a freshly perceptive human psychology. Were Orestes and Electra essentially pawns in an Olympian game, or did they have purposes — and feelings — of their own? A woman might be rescued because a god was a drunk. If the outright burlesque of myth is quite proper to a satyr play like *The Cyclops,* tragedy can probe it for soft spots, too. The very form of tragedy gives way under the probing — its structure is challenged because its premises are challenged — and in certain plays like the *Orestes* or the *Alcestis* we can now profess to see, or try to see, that mixing of tones which once led to tragicomedy and in the twentieth century leads to black comedy. Euripides was not afraid to ask questions to which he did not pretend to know the answers.

But haven't the same qualities which make Euripides seem eternally modern also opened the doors to some of the later theatre's least admirable habits? Realism has led to the small, rather petty play of individual psychology. Rhetoric leads to oratory, to the aria, finally to bathetic sentimentality. And iconoclasm, for all its openness of mind, makes us apprehensive. When iconoclasm comes, is disintegration far behind?

History tends to reinforce this last apprehension. We know that Greece, in the throes of the Peloponnesian

War, was working its way toward disaster at the time Euripides wrote. The social growth that Aeschylus registered and the social stability upon which Sophocles rested were now things of the past, or nearly so. Dangerous moral rot had set in. Aren't the freedoms Euripides took reflections of that rot as much as they are prophetic warnings against it? Isn't such a playwright so *involved* in the things he means to question or even to castigate that his own liberties must be taken as evidence of the social looseness that is leading to failure?

Not necessarily. Great drama rises out of a great social impulse. For convenience, that impulse may be said to move through three phases: assertion, consolidation, criticism. (Almost too patly, Aeschylus asserts, Sophocles consolidates, Euripides criticizes.) But there is criticism and criticism.

There is a criticism that despairs, and therefore simply mocks. Its natural theatrical home lies in comedy, and the amount of comedy in Euripides' work does hint at a trace of irreverence founded on hopelessness. There is also criticism founded on the belief that questioning *cannot hurt*. This sort of ruthless inquiry still rests on confidence, still draws energy from the earlier period of consolidation, still assumes that some balance, some harmony, exists somewhere in the universe and that further pressing by way of investigation can only amplify our knowledge of that complex harmony, not damage its delicate fabric. This sort of criticism simply wants to know more, wants to pry for what's been missed, wants to face up to any possibility that has hitherto been overlooked, basically in the belief that increased knowledge, increased awareness, increased exposure may help forestall the dismantling that is

threatened. There is no reason why it might not, though in the Greek experience it did not; some societies have reformed themselves by coming to understand themselves better.

Euripides' thrust — random and erratic at times — was toward maximum exploration of the possible, and not only in domestic psychology or tonal coloration. In his last play, *The Bacchae,* he seems to step to the borders of all religious and political experience and to stand there sweeping the horizon with open eyes, uncommitted, unyielding. The god Dionysus is not derided. He is dramatized, to the last reaches of his awful power. The excesses of his cult are not justified. They, too, are dramatized, in all of their enthusiasm and horror. Opposites are argued but are not artificially reconciled. The issue is left open, as the world is open — unpredictable, terrifying, *there*. The play is an act of courage, a refusal to flinch or take refuge in anything less than the whole truth, wherever that may be found. It does assume that man is capable of having such a vision, and surviving it.

EVELYN, John (Oct. 31, 1620 – Feb. 27, 1706). English diarist. Born Wotton, Surrey, son of wealthy landowner. After studying at Balliol College, Oxford (1637–40), traveled in Netherlands (1641–42), France and Italy (1643–52), studying languages, science, art, music. Married Mary Browne, daughter of English ambassador to Paris (1647). On return to England, settled at Sayes Court, Deptford. A staunch royalist, Evelyn frequented court after Restoration, was close friend of Charles II, and served on numerous government commissions. Formed friendship with Samuel Pepys (c.1665). Helped found and became secretary (1673) of Royal Society. On older brother's death (1699), inherited Wotton, where he spent rest of life. Evelyn, a man of widely ranging interests, produced treatises on such subjects as urban air pollution, horticulture, arboriculture, numismatics, architecture; translations; a biography, *The Life of Mrs. Godolphin* (first published 1847). He is remembered, however, for his *Diary* (first published 1818), a valuable record of life from 1620 to 1706 in Commonwealth and Restoration England.

EDITIONS: *Diary* ed. Esmond S. de Beer (6 vols. London and New York 1955). *Life of Mrs. Godolphin* ed. Harriet Sampson (London and New York 1939).

REFERENCES: Walter G. Hiscock *John Evelyn and Mrs. Godolphin* (London 1951 and New York 1952) and *John Evelyn and His Family Circle* (London 1955). Clara Marburg *Mr. Pepys and Mr. Evelyn* (Philadelphia and Oxford 1935). Arthur A. W. H. Ponsonby *John Evelyn: Fellow of the Royal Society: Author of Sylva* (London 1934).

EYCK, Hubert van (c.1370–1426) and Jan van (c.1385–1441). Flemish painters. Born probably Maaseik or Maastricht. Jan was court painter first to count of Holland (1422–1425), then to Philip, duke of Burgundy, for whom he also made several long journeys on missions of state. After a trip to Portugal (1428–29), during which he painted a portrait of Philip's fiancée Isabella, he settled in Bruges for rest of his life, and married (c.1433). Little is known of Hubert's life. He painted the diptych *The Crucifixion* and *The Last Judgemen* (Metropolitan Museum, New York). He also began and Jan completed (1432) the great twenty-panel polyptych, the Ghent altarpiece in St. Bavon, Ghent. The center of the work is the *Adoration of the Lamb,* the wings continuing the crowded processions of worshipers, all painted with exquisite clarity and exactness. Jan continued to perfect his oil medium in the richly colored *Madonna with Canon van der Paele* (1436, Groeninge Museum, Bruges), the *Madonna with Chancellor Rolin* (c.1436, Louvre, Paris), *Man with the Red Turban* (c.1434, National Gallery, London), portraits of Jan de Leeuw (1436, Kunsthistorisches Museum, Vienna) and his wife (1439, Groeninge Museum), and the serene, exquisitely detailed *Arnolfini Marriage Portrait* (1434, National Gallery). Hubert and Jan founded the Flemish school, are of major importance for the innovative realism of their style and astounding mastery of oil technique, which they are sometimes credited erroneously with inventing.

REFERENCES: Ludwig Baldass *Jan van Eyck* (London and New York 1952). L. J. Bol *Van Eyck* (tr. New York PB 1965). M. W. Brockwell *The Van Eyck Problem* (London 1954). Martin Conway *The Van Eycks and Their Followers* (New York 1921). Robert Hughes *Complete Paintings of Van Eyck* (New York 1969).

FABRIANO. *See* **GENTILE DA FABRIANO.**

FABRITIUS, Carel (born Carel Pietersz.) (c.1622 – Oct. 12, 1654). Dutch painter. Born Midden-Beemster, near Amsterdam; took name Fabritius from trade of carpentry, which he practiced at least until his marriage (1641). Studied painting (c.1641–43) in studio of Rembrandt. From 1650 lived in Delft, where he became member of painters' guild (1652) and established reputation for painting mural decorations with trompe-l'oeil effects. Though none of these remain, two well-known paintings, *A View of Delft* (1652, National Gallery, London) and *The Goldfinch* (1654, The Hague), demonstrate his gift for illusionism. Other important works are portrait of Abraham de Potter (1648) and two portraits of a young man, probably himself (one in Rotterdam, the other, dated 1654, in the National Gallery, London). Unlike Rembrandt, Fabritius silhouetted his figures against light backgrounds, and specialized in soft, subtle daylight effects. A major influence on Vermeer and de Hooch, he played an important role in the history of Dutch painting. The explosion of a powder magazine in Delft which took his life is believed also to have destroyed many of his paintings.

FALLA, Manuel de (Nov. 23, 1876 – Nov. 14, 1946). Spanish composer. Born Cadiz; received early musical education from mother. Later, in Madrid, studied piano with José Trago and composition with Felipe Pedrell. Won prize for piano playing and another for opera *La Vida Breve* (1905). In Paris (1907–14) became friend of Debussy, Dukas, and Ravel, and published his first piano pieces and songs (1909). *Nights in the Gardens of Spain* for piano and orchestra (Madrid, 1916) established his European reputation. Diaghilev produced his ballet *The Three-Cornered Hat* (London, 1919), which was an instant success and became part of regular repertoire. Falla then retired to Granada, where he organized (1922) a festival of traditional folk song of southern Spain. Avoided political upheaval in Spain by spending winters (1933–34) in Majorca. Went to Argentina (1939) for rest of his life, where he worked on *La Atlantida*, which expressed national spirit of Spain (completed by pupil Ernest Halffter; performed 1962). Other important works include *El Amor Brujo* (1915), *El Retablo de Maese Pedro* (1922), *Harpsichord Concerto* (1926). Falla's music is highly individualistic, adapting the themes and rhythms of Spanish folk music to traditional forms and precision of early masters like Domenico Scarlatti.

REFERENCES: Jaime Pahissa *Manuel de Falla: His Life and Work* (tr. London 1954). John B. Trend *Manuel de Falla and Spanish Music* (2nd ed. New York 1935).

FANTIN-LATOUR, (Ignace) Henri (Joseph Théodore) (Jan. 14, 1836 – Aug. 25, 1904). French painter. Born Grenoble. After training by his father, a pastel painter, he studied under Lecoq de Boisbaudran and Courbet, and (from 1854) at École des Beaux Arts. Worked as copyist at Louvre, where he met Whistler and Charlotte Dubourg, whom he later married. First exhibited at Salon of 1861. He was a friend of the impressionists, but his style derives from realist and romantic schools, with some of the muted, misty quality of Moreau and Redon; his paintings also reflect his deep interest in the music of Schumann, Berlioz, and especially Wagner. Best-known works are his group portraits of avant-garde artists, writers, and musicians, such as *Hommage à Delacroix* (1864), showing Whistler, Alphonse Legros, Manet, Baudelaire, Champfleury, and himself; *Un Atelier à Batignolles* (1870, Louvre, Paris), with Monet, Manet, Zola, Renoir; *Un Coin de Table* (1872, Louvre), with Verlaine, Rimbaud, Camille Péladan and others; portraits of Chabrier, d'Indy, and other composers. Fantin-Latour is also noted for elegant still lifes, and for lithographs and pastels. Died at Buré, Orne.

REFERENCES: F. Gibson *The Art of Henri Fantin-Latour: His Life and Work* (London 1924). Gustave Kahn *Fantin-Latour* (tr. New York 1927).

FARQUHAR, George (1678 – Apr. 29, 1707). British dramatist. Born Londonderry, Ireland, son of a clergyman. Left Trinity College, Dublin, to become an actor, then gave up stage after accidentally wounding a fellow player. Settled in London (c.1697), where his first comedy, *Love and a Bottle* (1699), was successfully produced; enjoyed continued popularity with *The Constant Couple* (1700), *Sir Harry Wildair* (1701), *The Inconstant* (1702, adapted from Beaumont and Fletcher), and *The Twin Rivals* (1702). Married Yorkshire woman he mistakenly thought wealthy (1703). Served as recruiting officer in regiment of earl of Orrery (1704–1706), but poverty forced him to sell commission. Last plays, *The Recruiting Officer* (1706, adapted by Bertolt Brecht as *Pauken und Trompeten* [*Trumpets and Drums*]) and *The Beaux' Stratagem* (1707), were his best. Farquhar helped destroy the artificial Restoration style of comedy. His wit is humane and genial rather than ironic; his characterizations, settings and plots are realistic. Died penniless in London.

EDITION: *Complete Works* ed. Charles Stonehill (2 vols. London and New York 1930).

REFERENCES: Willard Connely *Young George Farquhar: A Restoration Drama at Twilight* (London 1949). Eric Rothstein *George Farquhar* (New York 1967).

FAULKNER, William (Harrison) (Sept. 25, 1897 – July 6, 1962). American writer. Born New Albany, Miss.; in childhood moved to Oxford, Miss., where he spent most of his life. Without finishing high school, enlisted in British Royal Air Force (1918). Returned after Armistice to Oxford and became student (1919–20) and postmaster (1922–24) at University of Mississippi. First book was a collection of poems, *The Marble Faun* (1924). While working for newspaper in New Orleans met Sherwood Anderson, who persuaded him to write fiction and helped him publish first novel, *Soldier's Pay* (1926). Married Mrs. Estelle Oldham Franklin (1929). With *Sartoris* (1929), Faulkner found his best subject, the decadent old South and the grasping, materialistic new South in the town of Jefferson and the Mississippi county he called Yoknapatawpha, whose county seat it was. This was the material for several novels, including *The Sound and the Fury* (1929) and *As I Lay Dying* (1930), both of which earned him a literary reputation. *Sanctuary* (1931), dashed off as a moneymaker, made him famous. Other major works: *Light in August* (1932), *Absalom, Absalom!* (1936), *The Wild Palms* (1939), *The Hamlet* (1940), *Go Down Moses* (1942), *Intruder in the Dust* (1948), *Requiem for a Nun* (1951), *A Fable* (1954, Pulitzer prize), *The Town* (1957), *The Mansion* (1959). *Collected Short Stories of William Faulkner* (1950) comprises several volumes of short stories. Worked occasionally (1932–54) in Hollywood as scriptwriter. Won 1949 Nobel prize for literature. Died in Oxford.

REFERENCES: Warren Beck *Man in Motion: Faulkner's Trilogy* (Madison, Wis. 1961, also PB). Malcolm Cowley *Faulkner-Cowley File: Letters and Memories 1944–1962* (New York PB 1968). Irving Howe *William Faulkner* (2nd rev. ed. New York 1962, also PB). L. R. Thompson *William Faulkner:*

An Introduction and an Interpretation (2nd ed. New York PB 1967).

✍

WILLIAM FAULKNER
BY MARK SCHORER

He began in a very slow and Southern way. Indeed, he seems to have become a writer almost by accident, like the spelling of the name by which we know him, Faulkner, which was changed from Falkner through the carelessness of the printer who set up his first book, an error that, rather than troubling to correct, he decided to live with.

William Harrison Faulkner was born near and brought up in Oxford, Mississippi, the town with which we must always associate him not only because he spent almost all his life there but because it is the model of the town called Jefferson around which so much of his fiction circled, just as his Yoknapatawpha County is in fact Lafayette County. One would not know from the fiction that Oxford is the seat of the state university, of which his father, once he gave up his livery stable and hardware store, became the business manager, or that Faulkner himself, for a short time, was a student in those halls and for a brief time its postmaster.

He was an indolent student and left the local high school after two years to take a job in a bank. Free of supervision, he read widely as his own taste dictated. When he tried to enlist in the army he was rejected because he was so small, five feet, five inches tall, and underweight; but, although he was to see no active service, he was accepted by the British Royal Flying Corps in Canada, and after the war he earned his living for a time by stunt flying. Before that, however, he enrolled in the university, where he wrote a little for the student publication, but he dropped out at the end of a year to become a clerk in New York bookstores. Leaving that work, he lounged about Oxford for several years, living by odd jobs, writing occasional poems, generally thought of as a queer fellow, and finally, through the subsidy provided by a friend, privately publishing his first book, a negligible little volume of imitative verse called *The Marble Faun* (1924), to no acclaim at all.

Starting out for Europe, he got as far as New Orleans, where he mingled with artists and writers, including Sherwood Anderson, and himself wrote occasional pieces for local periodicals and his first novel, *Soldiers' Pay*, for which Anderson found him a publisher. After six months in Europe with his artist friend William Spratling, for whose book of caricatures called *Sherwood Anderson & Other Creoles* (1926) he wrote a two-page foreword that parodied Anderson's sleepy, groping style, he was again in Mississippi, at work on his next novel. Though *Soldiers' Pay* (1926) was an uneven novel, characterized by bursts of affected, self-conscious prose, it is more readable than *Mosquitoes* (1927), about the bohemian life of New Orleans, which is probably ridiculous. In this novel, Sherwood Anderson appears in the feeble if not exactly unkind portrait of Dawson Fairchild, a novelist.

Faulkner did not begin to find himself as a novelist until his next book, *Sartoris* (1929), based on his own ancestral history, and did not come wholly into his greatness until *The Sound and the Fury* (1929), about the Compsons, based less directly on his immediate family. Here he established himself as the original experimental genius that he was, exploring with poised confidence those fictional techniques which would make possible his rich pursuit of the ancestral themes that henceforth would be his large concern. In the following ten years, in a grand procession, came his most splendid work.

As I Lay Dying (1930) moves more deeply into the macabre; *Sanctuary* (1931), into the violent and the sexually deranged. *Light in August* (1932) consolidates everything that had gone before and may be his greatest novel. In *Absalom, Absalom!* (1936) finally the foundations of the whole mythohistorical legend of Yoknapatawpha County are laid down. *The Wild Palms* (1939) and *The Hamlet* (1940) build nobly on them.

But in that decade of depression, fascism, and approaching war, Faulkner's critical reception was largely patronizing and his audience small. He had to continue to earn his living from sources other than his writing, notably Hollywood. A great writer now, he himself scorned the term "writer" and called himself a farmer, which he was not. In 1946, when Malcolm Cowley published *The Portable Faulkner*, none of his books was in print, but with the appearance of this historic work, everything changed, and he became a figure of international renown. Ironically enough, none of the work of the remaining sixteen years quite came up to the achievements of the great decade, but the later work did fill out the details, extend the scope and the complexities of that legend that obsessed him with all its dark anguish and historic guilt, corruption, violence, and brutal grandeur.

The mood of his fiction, long and short, ranges from the deeply tragic to the grotesquely comic, and often most effectively in a compound of the two. He wrote apparently out of some visceral compulsion, without aesthetic calculation, and he could fall readily into the melodramatic, the overblown, the baldly allegorical. His lack of critical power is evident in his attempts to talk about his own work or the achievements of others. That he had no great power of mind is suggested by the shallow rhetoric of his acceptance speech when he was awarded the 1949 Nobel prize. Mere rhetoric, often enough, substituted for real insight and genuine feeling in some of even the best of his fiction.

Yet there has been no other such imaginative triumph in our fiction as his in the work for which he is most esteemed. It is a unique achievement in the face of which the usual categories — realism, naturalism, symbolism, surrealism, etc. — are simply of no use. With a kind of imaginative rage, he wrote of the individual groping and searching in the bewildering caverns of his history as of his heart, of the individual psyche in its interchange with its own history and tradition and its attempt to maintain itself as that history and tradition glide away from it into the dark labyrinth of an irrecoverable past. In his exploration of the mazes of that past and of the labyrinthine psyche itself, he developed an expressive style of involutions and exfoliations and protracted sinuosities that is as extraordinary as it is often baffling. Our literature has known no other such pyrotechnical display and Southern literature none at once so demonic and profound.

———

FAURÉ, Gabriel Urbain (May 12, 1845 – Nov. 4, 1924). French composer. Born Pamiers, Ariège. Studied under Saint-Saëns while at École Niedermeyer in Paris (1855–65). First published work, *Trois Romances sans paroles* for piano (1863). Began career as organist at Rennes (1866–70), then returned to Paris to become assistant organist and choirmaster at church of the Madeleine (1877), then chief organist (1896). Married Marie Fremiet (1883). Appointed professor of composition at

Paris Conservatoire (1896); director (1905–20). Elected to Académie des Beaux Arts (1909), Legion of Honor (1910). Died in Paris. Particularly famous for his exquisitely lovely songs, and for piano pieces and chamber music noted for delicate grace and clarity, taste and sensibility, as well as musical originality. Also produced large-scale compositions, including *Requiem* (1887), incidental music for Maeterlinck's *Pelléas et Mélisande* (1898), and lyric dramas *Prométhée* (1900) and *Pénélope* (1913). An illustrious teacher and important innovator, Fauré influenced development of contemporary French music. Pupils included Ravel, Georges Enesco, Roger-Ducasse, Nadia Boulanger, Charles Koechlin.

REFERENCES: Charles Koechlin *Gabriel Fauré: 1845–1924* (tr. London 1945). Claude Rostand *L'Oeuvre de Gabriel Fauré* (3rd ed. Paris 1945). Émile Veuillermoz *Gabriel Fauré* (Paris 1960).

_____

FEININGER, Lyonel (Charles Adrian) (July 17, 1871 – Jan. 13, 1956). American painter. Born and died in New York; parents both professional musicians. Went abroad (1887) to study music, but decided to paint and attended art schools in Hamburg, Berlin, and Paris. Worked (from 1893) as cartoonist and illustrator for European and American periodicals, including *Chicago Tribune,* until he began serious canvases (1907). So impressed Blaue Reiter artists Franz Marc and Kandinsky that he was invited to exhibit with them in Berlin (1913); joined Klee, Kandinsky, and Aleksey von Jawlensky (1924) to form Die Blauen Vier, a Blaue Reiter successor group which exhibited in Germany, America, and Mexico. Asked by Gropius to teach at Bauhaus (1919–33). Returned to America (1937) after Nazi accession; received two important commissions for New York World's Fair (1939–40). Feininger's style is characterized by prismatic, interpenetrating planes of color, which give a crystalline structure to his cityscapes and seashores.

REFERENCE: Hans Hess *Lyonel Feininger* (tr. New York and London 1961).

_____

FÉNELON, François de Salignac de la Mothe (Aug. 6, 1651 – Jan. 7, 1715). French writer and divine. Born Château de Fénelon, Périgord. Educated at Collège du Plessis in Paris and at seminary of St. Sulpice, where he took holy orders (1675). Appointed head of an institution in Paris for women converts (1678), then head of mission to Huguenots of Saintonge (1686). First published work, *Traité de l'éducation des filles* (1687), shows his brilliant insight into psychology. Appointed tutor to Louis XIV's grandson the duke of Burgundy (1689), for whom he wrote his most famous work, *Télémaque* (published 1699), a romance which provided models and precepts for the ideal monarch and held that a king exists to serve his subjects, not they to serve him. Elected to Académie Française (1693); created archbishop of Cambrai (1694). Fénelon's dispute with Bossuet on quietism, which the pope settled in Bossuet's favor, and the condemnation of despotism in *Télémaque* incurred anger of Louis XIV, who banished him to his diocese (1699). Spent rest of his life doing church work in Cambrai. Fénelon's mystical theology is expressed in *Explication des maximes des saints sur la vie intérieure* (1697) and other treatises; *Lettre à l'Académie* (1714) demonstrates his originality as literary critic.

TRANSLATIONS: *Christian Perfection* tr. Mildred W. Stillman (New York and London 1947). *Dialogues on Eloquence* tr. Wilbur S. Howell (Princeton, N.J. and Oxford 1951). *Letters* (London 1964) and *Letters of Love and Counsel* (New York 1964) tr. John McEwen. *Fénelon on Education: A Translation of the "Traité de l'éducation des filles" and Other Documents Illustrating Fénelon's Educational Theories and Practice* tr. Howard C. Barnard (Cambridge, England 1966).

REFERENCES: Élie Carcassonne *Fénelon: l'Homme et l'oeuvre* (Paris 1946). Jeanne L. Goré *L'Itinéraire de Fénelon: humanisme et spiritualité* (Grenoble 1957). Katherine D. Little *François de Fénelon: Study of a Personality* (New York 1951).

_____

FEYDEAU, Georges (Dec. 8, 1862 – June 6, 1921). French writer. Born in Paris.

His father, Ernest Aimé Feydeau (1821–73), was the author of *Fanny* (1858), a highly successful novel of the realist school. Georges Feydeau became an unsurpassed master of French farce (*vaudeville*) and brought new life and standing to the genre. Attained popularity with *Tailleur pour dames* (1887); other comedies include *Monsieur Chasse* (1892), *L'Hôtel du Libre-Échange* (1894, written with Maurice Desvallières; English version *Hotel Paradiso*, 1956), *La Dame de chez Maxim's* (1899), *Occupe-toi d'Amélie!* (1908; English version *Look After Lulu*, 1959), *Feu la Mère de Madame* (1910), *Mais n'te promène pas toute nue* (1912). Misunderstandings, often resulting from attempts at deception by an unfaithful husband or wife, supply the basis for his ingeniously constructed comic situations. Feydeau died at Rueil-Malmaison.

REFERENCE: *L'Esprit de Georges Feydeau* ed. Léon Treich (Paris 1927).

FIELDING, Henry (Apr. 22, 1707 – Oct. 8, 1754). English novelist and playwright. Born Sharpham Park, near Glastonbury, Somerset; cousin of Lady Mary Wortley Montagu. Attended Eton (1719–25/26), and after brief period in London, where he produced comedy *Love in Several Masques* (1728), continued studies at Leiden University (1728–29). Again in London, earned living by writing comedies, most successful of which was *The Life and Death of Tom Thumb the Great* (1730). Licensing Act (1737) ended his career as dramatist. Studied law (1737–40), and for rest of his life was a hardworking barrister and magistrate; became justice of the peace for Westminster (1749) and then for all Middlesex. Married Charlotte Cradock (1734); she died after ten happy years, and Fielding married (1747) her servant, Mary Daniel. His first novel, *Joseph Andrews* (1742), was followed by *Miscellanies* (3 vols. 1743), which includes *A Journey from This World to the Next* and *The History of the Life of the Late Mr. Jonathan Wild the Great*. *The History of Tom Jones, a Foundling* (1749), Fielding's masterpiece, had immediate success. Journeyed to Portugal (1754) for his health, but died in Lisbon within two months. Other works include the romantic novel *Amelia* (1751) and travel account *Journal of a Voyage to Lisbon* (1755).

EDITION: *Complete Works* ed. W. E. Henley and others (16 vols. New York 1903).

REFERENCES: Frederick T. Blanchard *Fielding the Novelist: A Study in Historical Criticism* (New Haven 1926). Wilbur L. Cross *The History of Henry Fielding* (3 vols. New Haven 1918). Austin Dobson *Henry Fielding* (London 1883; many subsequent editions). F. Homes Dudden *Henry Fielding: His Life, Works, and Times* (2 vols. Oxford and New York 1952). Benjamin M. Jones *Henry Fielding: Novelist and Magistrate* (London 1933 and New York 1934). Claude J. Rawson *Henry Fielding* (London and New York 1968, also PB). Mary P. Willcocks *A True-Born Englishman: Being the Life of Henry Fielding* (London 1947).

✍

HENRY FIELDING

BY DENIS DONOGHUE

It is a commonplace that the development of the English novel largely depended upon the emergence of the middle class, in the first half of the eighteenth century, as an articulate political force. Fielding was in a particularly favorable position to speak to that audience and to lead their attitudes in a certain chosen direction. He himself was a gentleman, but not an aristocrat; his ancestors were distinguished, but not great. He was connected with the army, the law, and Christian ministry. But he had to make a living, diversely, as a journalist, a playwright, eventually as a magistrate. So he saw a good deal of the middle life, and for the most part he cherished its values. He was not, in any extreme sense, a satirist. "I have endeavoured," he said of *Tom Jones* (1749), "to laugh mankind out of their favorite follies and vices." He was not concerned, like Swift, to "vex the world."

Indeed, his sense of life was remarkably genial. He thought that the vast majority of people were, as he writes in *Jonathan Wild* (1743), "of the mixt kind; neither totally good nor bad." By temper, he was a moral empiricist, content to live a reasonable life in the middle way of feeling. In one of his essays in *The Champion* he argued that there is "no better rule for the conduct of life than *Ne quid nimis.*" So in *Tom Jones* he addressed himself "to common men, and who partake of the more amiable weaknesses of human nature; not to those elevated souls whom the consummation of virtue and philosophy hath raised to a divine pitch of excellence and placed beyond the reach of human calamity." In that novel the Man of the Hill expresses contempt for "the silly business of the world," but Tom Jones speaks and acts for human value in terms which Fielding extends in *Jonathan Wild* and *Joseph Andrewes* (1742). When Tom hears a woman screaming and rushes to help her, the Man of the Hill, though he has the security of a gun, stays safely where he is, sitting down "with great patience and unconcern."

Fielding's moral values are worthy, then, but perhaps too simple. Bad people are aggressive, good people are benevolent. Actions speak louder than words. Charity begins at home, but thereafter it goes out and participates in the world. The vices and follies of mankind are the obstacles by which society thwarts the natural flow of goodwill and charity. Among these obstacles the most insidious are affectation and hypocrisy. It may be argued that this moral diagram is too simple to allow the most profound analysis of human behavior. Indeed, it has often been argued that Fielding's values are too blunt even for more conventional

purposes. Samuel Johnson took this view. "He was a blockhead," he said of Fielding; quoting Samuel Richardson, who "used to say, that had he not known who Fielding was, he should have believed he was an ostler." Johnson told Boswell that "there is more knowledge of the heart in one letter of Richardson's than in all *Tom Jones.*" Boswell labored in Fielding's defense. "The moral tendency of Fielding's writings," he said, "though it does not encourage a strained and rarely possible virtue, is ever favorable to honor and honesty, and cherishes the benevolent and generous affections. . . . He who is as good as Fielding would make him," Boswell continued, "is an amiable member of society, and may be led on by more regulated instructors to a higher state of ethical perfection."

Some of Johnson's strictures on Fielding arise from a sense of the limits beyond which the novels do not go — limits of feeling and sensibility. The most celebrated incidents in Fielding's fiction often appear little more than illustrations of a parable. The postilion's charity toward Joseph Andrewes, for instance, has ethical and social bearings, but the incident can hardly be said to do more than illustrate the parable of the Good Samaritan. At the same time it would be wrong to push this consideration too far. The morality of *Tom Jones,* for instance, may appear blunt, but in some respects the book is a remarkably cogent critique of orthodox Christianity. To mention one aspect of the critique: in the presentation of Tom, Fielding takes every opportunity of telling the reader that Tom's actions are immoral, but on the other hand the rhetoric of the book implies that Tom is a good fellow and that his actions, in a certain light, are good and true. The reader is never allowed to condemn

Tom; any move in that direction is restrained. Fielding achieves this double effect by setting the spirit of Christianity against the letter. The letter is too rigid, often too ethereal, out of this world. The spirit is deemed to be strong, earthy, manly, honest, and so forth. Many incidents in *Tom Jones* are designed to show that exactitude in the letter of Christianity often goes along with cruelty and desiccation of spirit. Blifil's Christianity, for instance, is merely theoretical, and he is totally incapable of love. Tom's sins are the follies of a good man; in Fielding's chosen light, the reader is made to feel, Tom is not a sinner at all. Fielding contrives this effect mainly by having Tom's actions judged, throughout the book, by Sophia Western and Squire Allworthy. At several stages in the novel these judgments are severe, and perhaps final, so the reader is not inclined to go beyond these saintly characters in severity. Indeed, he is bound to feel that the burden of judgment has been lifted from his shoulders. Who would think of setting up as a third judge, since these two are already on the magistrate's bench? In any event, their judgments on Tom, however severe, are never final. There is always time for another chance. In fact, once the crisis with Lady Bellaston is passed, Tom's pardon is safe. When Sophia and the Squire forgive, the reader forgives.

Fielding's moral critique is formidable. If he has no time for knowledge of the heart, he is still not as blunt as Johnson's charge implies. But it is foolish to argue that his imagination is endless in its resource, as if he were Shakespeare or Tolstoi. There are things which he cannot do. His greatest gift is energy; in this respect, too, he embodies the characteristic virtue of the early English novel. We often feel, confronting the evidences of energy and accordant talent, that with these gifts anything is possible; anything, that is to say, short of the greatest achievement of the creative imagination. Henry James expressed this feeling in the preface to *The Princess Casamassima*. "It is very true," he said, "that Fielding's hero in *Tom Jones* is but as 'finely,' that is but as intimately, bewildered as a young man of great health and spirits may be when he hasn't a grain of imagination: the point to be made is, at all events, that his sense of bewilderment obtains altogether on the comic, never on the tragic plane." Tom has, James went on, "so much 'life' that it amounts, for the effect of comedy and application of satire, almost to his having a mind, that is to his having reactions and a full consciousness." Tom's limitations and Fielding's limitations are not, of course, identical. Fielding, James says, is "handsomely possessed of a mind," so he surrounds Tom with "an amplitude of reflection." The result is that we see Tom "through the mellow air of Fielding's fine old moralism, fine old humor and fine old style, which somehow really enlarge, make everyone and every thing important." How we take this, as a critical view of Fielding, depends upon our sense of James's tribute, and of the touch of condescension in his account. The "fine old moralism" and the other fine old powers are recognized, along with their limitations. We are not to identify any of these powers with "full consciousness," James's name for the imagination of greatest latitude. But reading *Tom Jones* we feel that Fielding has so much life, so much energy, that it almost amounts to his having everything else. The feeling is hyperbole, but pardonable.

FIRBANK, (Arthur Annesley) Ronald (Jan. 17, 1886 – May 21, 1926). English novelist. Born London, to rich middle-class parents. Educated largely by private tutors before attending Trinity Hall, Cambridge (1906–1909). During this period was converted to Catholicism. First stories, *Odette d'Antrevernes* and *A Study in Temperament* (both 1905). Precious and of delicate health, Firbank lived as a leisured aesthete, traveling in Mediterranean countries. Detested women and never married. Died in Rome. His best-known novel, *Sorrow in Sunlight* (*Prancing Nigger* in the U.S.) (1925), was inspired by a trip to Haiti. Other novels include *Valmouth* (1919), *The Flower Beneath the Foot* (1922), and *Concerning the Eccentricities of Cardinal Pirelli* (1925). Short, without conventional plot, and noted for perverse, fantastic humor, brilliant dialogue, and cleverly drawn, eccentric characters, they influenced the work of Evelyn Waugh, Aldous Huxley, Ivy Compton-Burnett, and others.

REFERENCES: Miriam J. Benkovitz *Ronald Firbank* (New York 1969). Jocelyn Brooke *Ronald Firbank* (London and New York 1951, also PB).

FISCHER VON ERLACH, Johann Bernhard (July 1656 – Apr. 5, 1723). Austrian architect. Born Graz; son of a sculptor, who provided his early training. Went to Italy (1670), where he studied architecture under Philipp Schor and was influenced by the great masters of baroque, Bernini and Borromini. Returning to Austria (1686), he settled in Vienna and soon achieved great patronage. Entered royal service as architectural tutor to Joseph I of Hungary (1689), and was thereafter entrusted with all important royal building. Married Sophia Constantia Morgner (1690); she died (1704), and a year later he married a widow, Franziska Sophia Willer (née Lochner). Important buildings include Frain castle in Moravia, with the oval Hall of the Ancestors (1688–94); Kollegienkirche, Salzburg (1694–1707); palace of Prince Eugene, Vienna (1695–97, enlarged 1707–10); Clam-Gallas palace, Prague (1707–13); Trautson palace, Vienna (1709–12); Karlskirche (church

of San Carlo Borromeo), Vienna (begun 1715) and work in the Hofburg and Imperial Library (both begun 1722); these last three were completed by his son Joseph Emanuel (1693–1742). Died in Vienna. The first important native baroque architect in northern Europe, Fischer von Erlach successfully combined elements of the new Italian style with classical forms.

FITZGERALD, Edward (Mar. 31, 1809 – June 14, 1883). English poet and translator. Born Bredfield, Suffolk. Educated at Trinity College, Cambridge (1826–1830), where he became friend of Thackeray. Later, friendships with Tennyson and Carlyle developed. Spent most of his life in quiet retirement at Woodbridge, Suffolk. Marriage to Lucy Barton (1856), daughter of Quaker poet Bernard Barton (1784–1849), soon ended in amicable separation. FitzGerald's major work, *The Rubáiyát of Omar Khayyám* (1859, enlarged edition 1868), a free adaptation, first appeared as anonymous pamphlet and attracted little attention until discovered and praised by Dante Gabriel Rossetti (1860) and soon afterward by Swinburne. It quickly became widely read and quoted, and remains a classic. Other works include *Euphranor: A Dialogue on Youth* (1851), translations of *Six Dramas of Calderón* (1853), Jami's *Salámán and Absál* (1856), Aeschylus' *Agamemnon* (1865), and the two Oedipus tragedies of Sophocles (1880–81). He is also noted for his letters. Died at Merton, Norfolk.

EDITIONS: *Letters and Literary Remains* ed. William A. Wright (7 vols. London and New York 1902–1903). *Letters* ed. Francis R. Barton (London and New York 1923); ed. Charlotte Quaritch Wrentmore (London 1926); ed. N. C. Hannay (New York 1932); ed. John M. Cohen (Carbondale, Ill. and Chichester, England 1960).

REFERENCES: Arthur C. Benson *Edward FitzGerald* (London and New York 1905). Alfred M. Terhune *Life of Edward FitzGerald* (New Haven and London 1947). Thomas Wright *Life of Edward FitzGerald* (2 vols. London and New York 1904).

FITZGERALD, F(rancis) **Scott** (Key) (Sept. 24, 1896 – Dec. 21, 1940). American novelist and short story writer. Born St. Paul, Minn. Attended Princeton University (1913–17), but left without degree to join army. After the war, worked briefly for New York advertising agency before rewriting novel begun at Princeton. *This Side of Paradise* (1920), an immediate success, established him as spokesman for the "lost generation." Married Zelda Sayre (1920); they lived much of early married life in France and had one daughter. Next publications were *Flappers and Philosophers* (1920) and *Tales of the Jazz Age* (1922), brilliant short story collections, and a second novel, *The Beautiful and Damned* (1921). After appearance of his masterpiece *The Great Gatsby* (1925), and short stories *All the Sad Young Men* (1926), financial and spiritual crises dominated his life. *Tender Is the Night* (1934), though one of his best works, had indifferent reception, and he turned out stories for popular magazines and finally wrote for films in Hollywood. While there he met Sheila Graham (1937), who helped cure his alcoholism and encouraged him in writing *The Last Tycoon*, a novel about the movie industry left unfinished at his death, in Hollywood. Other works: short story collection *Taps at Reveille* (1935), which includes *Babylon Revisited*, and *The Crack-Up* (1936), his narrative of his own breakdown, later published with other uncollected pieces and letters edited by Edmund Wilson (1945).

REFERENCES: Nancy Milford *Zelda* (New York 1970). Arthur Mizener *The Far Side of Paradise* (Boston 2nd ed. 1965, also PB). Robert A. Sklar *F. Scott Fitzgerald The Last Laocoön* (London and New York 1967). Andrew Turnbull *Scott Fitzgerald* (New York and London 1962, also PB).

⚓

F. SCOTT FITZGERALD
BY JOHN CHEEVER

"One of my most vivid memories is of coming back West from prep school and later from college at Christmastime. Those who went farther than Chicago would gather in the old dim Union Station at six o'clock of a December evening, with a few Chicago friends, already caught up in their own holiday gaieties, to bid them a hasty good-by. I remember the fur coats of the girls returning from Miss This-or-That's and the chatter of frozen breath and the hands waving overhead as we caught sight of old acquaintances, and the matchings of invitations: "Are you going to the Ordways'? the Herseys'? the Schultzes'?" and the long green tickets clasped tight in our gloved hands. And last the murky yellow cars of the Chicago, Milwaukee & St. Paul railroad looking cheerful as Christmas itself on the tracks beside the gate.

"When we pulled out into the winter night and the real snow, our snow, began to stretch out beside us and twinkle against the windows, and the dim lights of small Wisconsin stations moved by, a sharp wild brace came suddenly into the air. We drew in deep breaths of it as we walked back from dinner through the cold vestibules, unutterably aware of our identity with this country for one strange hour, before we melted indistinguishably into it again.

"That's my Middle West — not the wheat or the prairies or the lost Swede towns, but the thrilling returning trains of my youth. . . ."

Most of us know this from *The Great Gatsby*. Out of context it loses the excitement of having the scene shifted from Gatsby's lonely funeral on Long Island to a Chicago railroad station; but even out of context it is characteristic of Fitzgerald at his best. *Gatsby*, published in the spring of 1925, was of course his third novel, and there were to be two more as well as one hundred and fifty short stories. In spite of their very uneven quality these were not rueful vignettes or overheard conversations but real stories with characters, invention, scenery and moral conviction. As early as *Gatsby* Fitzgerald was internationally notorious for the worst sort of drunken pranks, pratfalls and ghastly jokes, and yet in his work and in his letters to his daughter he preserved an angelic austerity of spirit. Noble might be a better word, since as a boy in what had been the frontier town of St. Paul he had considered himself to be a lost prince. How sensible of him. His mother was the ruthless and eccentric daughter of a prosperous Irish grocer. His gentle father belonged to the fringe aristocracy of the commercial traveler, moving from Syracuse to Buffalo and back again. How else could he explain his giftedness?

There are eight books in all, and here and there one finds those appalling lapses in discipline of a serious writer working to support a beautiful and capricious wife, but his singular grace is never quite lost and even the sorrows in *The Crack-up* are not maudlin. The best of the stories were lived as well as written — an irreversible process that sometimes ends in grief, but he remained astonishingly hopeful. In the posthumous *Last Tycoon* there is no trace of that darkness and fatigue that sometimes appears in a writer's last work.

Everyone knows the story by now — Zelda's madness, intelligence and beauty, the years of expatriation, booze-fighting, debt, sickness, and the bizarre badlands of Hollywood. Grown men have been known to cry over the last chapters of his biography. In the spate of criticism, commentary, gossip, and venomous recollection that followed his death, explicit periods in time — the Twenties, the Jazz Age, the Crash — are mentioned repeatedly. Great writers are profoundly immersed in

their time and he was a peerless historian. In Fitzgerald there is a thrilling sense of knowing exactly where one is — the city, the resort, the hotel, the decade and the time of day. His greatest innovation was to use social custom, clothing, overheard music, not as history but as an expression of his acute awareness of the meaning of time. All the girls in their short skirts and those German tangos and the hot nights belong to history, but their finer purpose is to evoke the excitement of being alive. He gives one vividly the sense that the Crash and the Jazz Age were without a precedent, but one sees that this is a part of his art and that while Amory, Dick, Gatsby, Anson — all of them — lived in a temporal crisis of nostalgia and change they were deeply involved in the universality of love and suffering.

FLAUBERT, Gustave (Dec. 12, 1821 – May 8, 1880). French novelist. Born Rouen, son of a surgeon. Began literary career while a schoolboy at Collège de Rouen (1832–40); first published work, *Le Colibri* (1837), appeared in a theatrical review. Studied law in Paris without enthusiasm (1841–43). Onset (1843) of nervous disease similar to epilepsy but never satisfactorily diagnosed made active life impossible, and after father's death (1846) Flaubert settled down with his mother at Croisset. He never married; his most celebrated love affair (1846–55) was with poet Louise Colet. Traveled through Mediterranean countries and often wintered in Paris, where he associated with such writers as the Goncourts, Turgenev, Taine, Sainte-Beuve, and George Sand, and was friend and teacher to younger men like Zola, Daudet, and Maupassant. He died at Croisset. Flaubert's first and greatest novel, *Madame Bovary* (1857), is a landmark in the history of the modern novel. Other works include *Salammbô* (1862), *L'Éducation sentimentale* (1869), *La Tentation de Saint Antoine* (1874), *Trois Contes: Un Coeur simple; La Légende de Saint Julien l'hospitalier;*

et Hérodias (1877), and *Bouvard et Pécuchet* (1881, unfinished).

TRANSLATIONS: *Selected Letters* (New York and London 1954) and *Intimate Notebook 1840–1841* (New York and London 1967) tr. and ed. Francis Steegmuller. *Madame Bovary* tr. Francis Steegmuller (New York 1957).

REFERENCES: Benjamin F. Bart *Flaubert* (Syracuse, N.Y. 1967). Enid Starkie *Flaubert: The Making of the Master* (London and New York 1967). Francis Steegmuller *Flaubert and Madame Bovary: A Double Portrait* (new rev. ed. New York and London 1968, also PB).

✍

GUSTAVE FLAUBERT
BY FRANCIS STEEGMULLER

Until a generation or so ago, Gustave Flaubert was usually hailed by literary critics and historians as the master of *"le mot juste."* By that they meant that he put "the right word" in the right place, that he used exactly the right verb or noun or adjective to express exactly the right shade of feeling or detail of description. It was their form of high praise, but today it sounds arrogant as well as matter-of-fact: for now we tend to feel that there are multifarious "right" ways of putting almost anything, and anyway, isn't to write "right" merely what a writer is for?

More recently, in accord with what was apparently thought to be a change in critical fashion, Flaubert was acclaimed rather for the immense richness of his symbolism, for the depth and power he attains by means of images. Critics spoke of his "patterns," formed by the repetition and recall of various motifs, and achieving tremendous effects. Essays were written on "The Theme of Slipping and Falling," for example, in his work, on "The Circular Concept in *Madame Bovary.*" But that sort of thing, belonging to the then-called New Criticism, was soon seen to be little more than a reprise of

a form of discussion that had been particularly current in the age of Wagner concerning that master's musical patterns, called leitmotifs. *"Plus ça change, plus c'est la même chose"*: for admiration of a "circular concept" that is expressed in words is praise of the words themselves, and the New Critic was but intoning *"Le mot juste!"* in his own way. No doubt the tribute will continue to be paid in one form or another down the ages, for Flaubert does indeed do as a writer should: Flaubert writes "right."

Thus praise of a great writer's finished works, even the most fashionable or analytical praise, reduces itself, in essence, to no more than that brief and banal-sounding "Well done!" But in the case of some writers, and Flaubert is the prime example, their life is so completely given to their work that biographical, and especially autobiographical, data are especially instructive and interesting. In Flaubert's case the keynote is a precocious awareness of certain special aspects of himself and others that found early expression in juvenile writings (he began to write stories, he once said, as soon as he could form letters) and eventually, with maturity, richer expression in his great books. This is sometimes put differently by critics: they say that Flaubert kept returning, for the themes of his great books, to the reflections and experiences of his early life.

His words about adultery, for example, written when he was twenty about himself at a still earlier age, show extraordinary psychological acumen, pinpointing as they do a dream common among children: "There was one word that seemed to me the most beautiful of all human words — adultery. It is vaguely enveloped with an exquisite sweetness, it is fragrant with a peculiar magic. . . ." (It was, of course, a woman's adultery that he thought so beautiful as an adolescent — and more particularly, one suspects, a mother's: a man's adultery was taken for granted.) Equally clear-seeing was his early determination to travel to the "Orient" (Egypt and the Near East) to steep himself in one of the great sources of the romanticism he saw so rampant around him in literature, in the other arts, and in human behavior. Then came the revelation of what he could do with that purging that had been achieved by the Eastern journey: he could paint a picture of a lovely provincial bourgeoise sick with the contemporary romanticism that he had come to recognize as being but an exaggerated form of an essential human mood. He could portray the atmosphere in which she grew up and married, plunge her into adultery, and, at the end, describe the results. The book turned out to be *Madame Bovary*. It took him to court on charges of immorality, and he was always displeased that the success of this, his first published work, was due in part to scandal.

He was equally clear, in his very early days, about the value of the perceptions of the Marquis de Sade, and about the immense human obsession with what has come to be called sadism, and about its literary possibilities. After the publication of *Madame Bovary*, he turned his attention to covering a great literary canvas with the colors he had seen in the "Orient," and with the colors of violence and physical suffering, and above all with the color of blood; and he called the finished picture *Salammbô*.

From his adolescence he retained all the details and implications of what, to another youth, might have been merely a briefly turbulent but inconsequential experience of calf love; and he was,

even at that same early time, fascinated and repelled by the large and the petty aspects of the revolutionary and counterrevolutionary currents in French politics. Out of the calf love and the rest came *L'Éducation sentimentale*. And this chronicle of interwoven lives under Louis Philippe — for many it is the favorite among Flaubert's novels — is also one of the great classic portrayals of disillusion, futility, the passage from youth to middle age. Like all the other books, it was meticulously documented: factual and historical exactitude Flaubert considered aesthetically essential.

The adage that "a little learning is a dangerous thing" he saw not as a cliché but as one of the great tragicomedies of the nineteenth century: he undertook *Bouvard et Pécuchet*, unfinished on his death. And it was the early clearsightedness penetrating his own life and the life around him that similarly led him at one time or another to the composition of the learned visions that make up *La Tentation de Saint Antoine* and of all three of the *Trois Contes* — *Un Coeur simple*, a tale of a servant in a bourgeois household; *Hérodias*, said to have been inspired by the sculpture of the dancing Salomé on the façade of Rouen cathedral; and the medieval *Saint Julien l'Hospitalier*.

How that all worked, in the case of this writer who wrote so "right," is to be seen, of course, primarily in the novels and tales themselves. But Flaubert has left us more than those. He left a body of other writings, of a kind that is usually considered secondary, but which in his case are of such rare richness and intensity as to be of independent value. These are his early *Intimate Notebook*, the travel notes made during his journey to the "Orient," and especially his vast correspondence. This last, fascinating in it-self, is so eloquent as to be among the prime sources for the study of all literary creation.

FLAXMAN, John (July 6, 1755 – Dec. 7, 1826). English sculptor and illustrator. Born York, son of a plaster cast maker in whose studio in London he worked. Entered Royal Academy School (1770); designed cameos for Wedgwood pottery firm (1775–87). Married Anne Denman (1782). In Rome (1787–94), studied especially ancient art. Produced sculpture groups *Fury of Athamas* (1791–92) and others, as well as line drawings for Homer's *Iliad* and *Odyssey* (1793), which brought him fame as leading exponent of neoclassicism. Returned to London (1794), began to execute numerous monuments, some groups in the round, and bas-reliefs that established his reputation as a sculptor. His most famous works include the relief *The Shield of Achilles*, and memorials to the earl of Mansfield (Westminster Abbey), Lord Nelson and Sir Joshua Reynolds (St. Paul's Cathedral), and William Collins (Chichester Cathedral). Also illustrated works of Aeschylus (1795), Dante (1802), Hesiod, Milton and Bunyan. Elected member of Royal Academy (1800) and first professor of sculpture at the Academy (1810). Died in London.

REFERENCE: William G. Constable *John Flaxman* (London 1927).

FLÉMALLE, Master of. *See* **CAMPIN, Robert.**

FLETCHER, John (Dec. 1579 – Aug. 1625) and **BEAUMONT, Francis** (1584 – Mar. 6, 1616). English dramatists. BEAUMONT was born at Grace-Dieu, Leicestershire. Studied at Broadgates Hall, Oxford (1597–99), and enrolled (1600) in the Inner Temple to study law but never became a lawyer. The dominant partner of the collaboration (1607–14) with Fletcher, he married (c.1613), and died in London. FLETCHER, born at Rye, Sussex, entered Benet (later Corpus Christi) College, Cambridge (1591), but probably did not take a de-gree. Moved (1596) to London, where he died. Both had already begun careers as dramatists when they met, and Fletcher was to continue to write plays, largely in collaboration with Philip Massinger, until his death; but it is their joint efforts, notably *Philaster*, *The Maid's Tragedy*, and *A King and No King*, for which they are famed. In these plays, which in their own day and throughout the Restoration surpassed those of Shakespeare in popularity, Beaumont and Fletcher developed the form of the tragicomic romance, achieving dramatic effect by sacrificing character development in favor of extravagantly contrived plots full of suspense and surprise.

EDITIONS: *The Works of Francis Beaumont and John Fletcher* ed. Arnold Glover and Alfred R. Waller (10 vols. Cambridge, England, 1905–12).

REFERENCES: William W. Appleton *Beaumont and Fletcher: A Critical Study* (London 1956). John F. Danby *Poets on Fortune's Hill: Studies on Sidney, Shakespeare, Beaumont and Fletcher* (London 1952). Charles M. Gayley *Beaumont, the Dramatist* (New York 1914). Lawrence B. Wallis *Fletcher, Beaumont and Company* (New York 1947).

FLETCHER, Phineas (Apr. 8, 1582 – 1650) and Giles (the Younger) (c.1588 – 1623). English poets, sons of poet and diplomat Giles Fletcher (c.1549–1611), author of *Of the Russe Common Wealth* (1591) and *Licia, or Poems of Love* (1593). PHINEAS was born at Cranbrook, Kent, and educated at Eton and King's College, Cambridge (B.A. 1604, M.A. 1608). Married Elizabeth Vincent (1615). Became chaplain to Sir Henry Willoughby at Risley, Derbyshire (1616), and from 1621 until his death was rector of Hilgay, Norfolk. Best known for *The Purple Island* (1633), an allegorical poem in style of Spenser. GILES FLETCHER was born in London and educated at Westminster School and Trinity College, Cambridge (B.A. 1606). Took orders and held a college living until becoming vicar of Alderton, Suffolk (1619), where he spent rest of his life. His masterpiece, *Christ's Victorie and Triumph in Heaven and Earth Over and After*

Death (1610), a long devotional poem, shows influence of his Greek scholarship and of Spenser, and in turn had some effect on Milton's *Paradise Regained* (1671).

EDITION: *Poetical Works of Giles and Phineas Fletcher* ed. Frederick S. Boas (2 vols. Cambridge 1908–1909).

REFERENCES: Herbert E. Cory *Spenser, the School of the Fletchers, and Milton* (Berkeley, Calif. 1912). Abram B. Langdale *Phineas Fletcher: Man of Letters, Science and Divinity* (New York 1937).

FLOTOW, Baron Friedrich von (Apr. 26, 1812 – Jan. 24, 1883). German composer. Born Teutendorf, Mecklenburg. Sent to Paris to study for diplomatic career, he instead took up music and became pupil of Antonin Reicha. Performance of complete form of opera *Alessandro Stradella* (1844) enjoyed great popularity. Reputation established with *Le Naufrage de la Méduse* (1839). Produced (1835–78) many successful light operas, including *Rob Roy* (c.1836) and *Martha* (1847). Wrote ballets for the court theatre at Schwerin, of which he was appointed intendant (1856). Returned to Paris (1863). Elected to Institut de France (1864). Settled in environs of Vienna (1868) and died at Darmstadt.

FONTENELLE, Bernard Le Bovier de (Feb. 11, 1657 – Jan. 9, 1757). French man of letters, scientist, philosopher. Born Rouen, into family of lawyers. Studied with Jesuits and at law faculty there. Nephew of Corneille brothers, he began his literary career as playwright, but gained recognition with *Dialogues des morts* (1683), the first of his attacks on authoritarianism. Published (1686) two works of scientific popularization: *Entretiens sur la pluralité des mondes*, on Cartesian cosmology, and *L'Histoire des oracles*, on credulity and superstition. About this time composed work on psychological and intellectual roots of mythology, *De l'Origine des fables* (1724). Participated in Quarrel of the Ancients and the Moderns, making a case for evolution in the arts in *Digression sur les anciens et les modernes* (1688). Moved permanently to Paris (c.1678). Elected to Académie Française (1691); became perpetual secretary of Académie des Sciences (1697), and wrote histories of the Académie and its members. Died in Paris. In his rational approach to the nature and significance of scientific progress and his refutation of popular superstition and beliefs, Fontenelle was a precursor of the *philosophes* of the Enlightenment.

TRANSLATION: *Dialogues of Fontenelle* tr. Ezra Pound (London 1917).
REFERENCES: J. R. Carré *La Philosophie de Fontenelle, ou le sourire de la raison* (Paris 1932). Louis Maigron *Fontenelle, l'homme, l'oeuvre, l'influence* (Paris 1906).

FORD, Ford Madox (real name Ford Hermann Hueffer) (Dec. 17, 1873 – June 26, 1939). English novelist and critic. Born Merton, Surrey; educated at Praetoria House, Folkestone, and University College School, London. His German father, a music critic, and his mother, daughter of pre-Raphaelite painter Ford Madox Brown, provided early cultural environment and he produced series of works at early age; a children's fairy tale, *The Brown Owl* (1892), was well received. Married Elsie Martindale (1894). In addition to writing fiction, poetry and criticism, collaborated with Joseph Conrad on novels *The Inheritors* (1901) and *Romance* (1903). Founded short-lived *English Review* (1908), whose contributors included Hardy, Henry James, H. G. Wells, Conrad, Galsworthy. An affair with artist Violet Hunt led to unsuccessful attempt to divorce his wife (1910), a situation reflected in his first important novel, *The Good Soldier* (1915). Out of his harrowing experiences in World War I came much of the material for his best work, the tetralogy *Some Do Not* (1924), *No More Parades* (1925), *A Man Could Stand Up* (1926), and *Last Post* (1928). Retired to Sussex farm after the war (changing his German name to Ford), but moved (1922) to France and became editor of *Transatlantic Review* (1924), publishing Joyce, Pound, Hemingway, and other writers. His life thereafter was divided between France and America. Died at Deauville, having produced an enormous quantity of fiction, biography, criticism, and four autobiographical volumes.

REFERENCES: Richard Aldington *Life for Life's Sake* (London and New York 1941). Douglas Goldring *The Last Pre-Raphaelite* (London 1948; American edition *Trained for Genius* New York 1949).

FORD, John (April 1586 – c.1640). English dramatist. Born Ilsington, Devonshire. Little known of his life. Entered Middle Temple (1602), remaining till 1617. Wrote *Fame's Memorial* (1606), elegy on death of earl of Devonshire, as well as several plays which were lost. Those surviving from period 1621–24 are in collaboration with Thomas Dekker and others, of which the best is *The Witch of Edmonton* (1621). Of his own the chief are *Lover's Melancholy* (1629), *'Tis Pity She's a Whore* (1633) and *The Broken Heart* (1633), tragedies full of melancholy, morbidity and despair, with intricate, bloody plots. Criticized for his exaggeratedly gloomy themes, he is also commended for his insight into human passion and for austerity of language in a time of decadence in the theatre.

EDITIONS: *Works* ed. William Gifford (2 vols. London 1827 and New York 1831; new ed. with additions by Alexander Dyce 3 vols. London 1869; enlarged by A. H. Bullen ed. London 1895); ed. Willy Bang and Henry de Vocht (2 vols. Louvain 1908/27). REFERENCES: S. Blaine Ewing *Burtonian Melancholy in the Plays of John Ford* (Princeton, N.J., also PB 1940). Clifford Leech *John Ford and the Drama of His Time* (London and New York 1957). Harold J. Oliver *The Problem of John Ford* (Melbourne and Cambridge, England 1955). George F. Sensabaugh *The Tragic Muse of John Ford* (Stanford, Calif. and London 1944).

FORSTER, E(dward) M(organ) (Jan. 1, 1879 – June 7, 1970). English writer. Born in London. Attended Tonbridge School and King's College, Cambridge, to which he retired (1946) as an honorary fellow. After Cambridge he went to Italy, the setting of his novels *Where Angels Fear to Tread* (his first, 1905) and *A Room with a View* (1908), both gentle social satires which pit honest emotion against accepted behavior. *The Longest Journey* (1907), partially autobiographical, deals with Tonbridge and Cambridge. The introductory motto, "Only connect," proclaims the theme of his fourth novel, *Howards End* (1910). Served in Egypt on civilian duty in World War I, from which grew his *Alexandria: A History and a Guide* (1922). Before and after the war he was in India, and his masterpiece and final novel, *A Passage to India* (1924), is a classic study of Anglo-Indian conflict. He also published short stories, collected in *The Celestial Omnibus* (1911) and *The Eternal Moment* (1928); essays, collected in *Abinger Harvest* (1936) and *Two Cheers for Democracy* (1951); *Aspects of the Novel* (1927); another book about India, *The Hill of Devi* (1953); *Marianne Thornton: A Domestic Biography, 1797–1887* (1956); and with Eric Crozier wrote the libretto for Benjamin Britten's opera *Billy Budd* (1951). In all his works, Forster suggests the primacy of human feeling over social convention. Awarded the Order of Merit (1969). Died in Coventry.

REFERENCES: Karl W. Gransden *E. M. Forster* (New York and Edinburgh 1962). Wilfred Stone *The Cave and the Mountain: A Study of E. M. Forster* (Stanford, Calif. and Oxford 1966, also PB). Lionel Trilling *E. M. Forster* (2nd ed. New York PB 1964 and London 1967). Alan Wilde *Art and Order: A Study of E. M. Forster* (New York 1964 and London 1965, also PB).

FOSTER, Stephen Collins (July 4, 1826 – Jan. 13, 1864). American song writer. Born near Pittsburgh, Pa.; attended Jefferson College. First published song was *Open Thy Lattice, Love* (1844) to George P. Morris's words. Went to Cincinnati, Ohio, as bookkeeper (1846), returning (1850) to Pittsburgh, where he married Jane McDowell. His song *Oh! Susanna* (1848) became so popular that he was commissioned to write similar "Southern Negro" songs for E. P. Christy's minstrel show. Of these, for most of which he also wrote the words, the most popular to this day are *Camptown Races* (1850), *Old Folks at Home* (1851), *Massa's in de Cold, Cold Ground* (1852), *My Old Kentucky Home* (1853), and *Old Black Joe* (1860). *Jeanie with the Light Brown Hair* (1854) is also a favorite. They represent his mastery of the simple, sentimental melody with widespread appeal. Moved to New York (1860), but had financial trouble, separated from wife (1861), and spent rest of his life in penury. He died in Bellevue Hospital, New York. Last popular song was *Beautiful Dreamer* (1864).

REFERENCE: John T. Howard *Stephen Foster, America's Troubadour* (New York 1954, also PB).

FOUQUET (or FOUCQUET), Jean (c.1420–c.1481). French painter and illuminator. Born and died in Tours. In Italy between 1443 and 1447, where he studied techniques of perspective developed by Masaccio, Fra Angelico, and Piero della Francesca. On his return to Tours, his work showed blending of Italian and Flemish elements, in, for example, portrait of Charles VII (Louvre). For the royal secretary and lord treasurer Étienne Chevalier, he produced (1450–60) the celebrated illuminations in the *Book of Hours* (Chantilly castle), a diptych for Notre Dame at Melun containing a portrait of Chevalier (Kaiser Friedrich Museum, Berlin) and a Madonna (Antwerp Museum). Louis XI founded (1469) order of St. Michael and commissioned Fouquet to illuminate its statutes; appointed him (1474) *peintre du roi.* Other important works are illustrations for a French translation of Boccaccio (1458) and those for Flavius Josephus's *Les Antiquités judaïques* (c.1474, Bibliothèque Nationale, Paris); also illuminations for Marie de Clèves (1472) and Philippe de Comines (1474). Fouquet is credited with introducing Renaissance ideas into French art. He exerted a dominant influence on subsequent miniature painting.

REFERENCES: Trenchard Cox *Jehan Foucquet, Native of Tours* (London 1931). Klaus G. Perls *Jean Fouquet* (London and New York 1940). Paul R.

Wescher *Jean Fouquet and His Time* (tr. London 1947).

FOURNIER, Henri Alban. *See* ALAIN-FOURNIER.

FRAGONARD, Jean Honoré (Apr. 5, 1732 – Aug. 22, 1806). French painter. Born Grasse; brought to Paris as a child, where he studied briefly with Jean Baptiste Chardin, then with François Boucher. Won prix de Rome (1752), and after studying three years at École Royale des Élèves Protégés went to Rome (1756). Here he was influenced by Tiepolo and seventeenth-century decorative art. Having returned to Paris (1761), was elected to the Academy (1765) with painting *Corésus Sacrificing Himself to Save Callirhoé* (Louvre, Paris) which established his reputation. The success of his first sentimental "boudoir" painting, *The Swing* (1765, Wallace Collection, London) led him to abandon the grand manner and continue in this vein, depicting in vivid colors the sprightly scenes of romantic dalliance amid luxury favored by courts of Louis XV and Louis XVI. *The Bathers, La Musique* (both in Louvre), *Le Billet Doux, Portrait of a Lady with a Dog* (both in Metropolitan Museum, New York) are further examples. He also decorated houses with series of panels, most notable being *The Progress of Love* painted for Madame du Barry (Frick Collection, New York). Out of favor during the Revolution, and impoverished, he fled to Grasse, later attempted to become reinstated with the new postrevolution art in Paris, but died there, forgotten and out of fashion.

REFERENCES: Louis Réau *Fragonard, sa vie et son oeuvre* (Brussels 1956). Jacques Thuillier *Fragonard* (Geneva 1967). Georges Wildenstein ed. *The Paintings of Fragonard* (tr. London 1960).

FRANCE, Anatole (real name Jacques Anatole François Thibault) (Apr. 16, 1844 – Oct. 13, 1924). French writer. Born Paris, son of a bookseller. Attended Collège Stanislas (1855–62). Joined publishing firm, wrote literary articles for periodicals, and published a volume of poems (*Les Poèmes dorés,* 1873) and the poetic drama *Les Noces corinthiennes* (1876). Married Marie-Valérie Guérin de Sauville (1877; divorced 1893). First novel *Le Crime de Sylvestre Bonnard* (1881) a success, followed by, among others, *Thaïs* (1890), which attacked conventional Christianity, and *Le Lys rouge* (1894), all in light, charming satirical vein. The Dreyfus case, in which he supported Zola, changed him into a serious, forceful writer, attacking the bigotry of church and army and the narrowness and prejudice of French society. After writing a number of violently partisan novels, his political satire became more universal, and he produced his finest books: *L'Île des Pengouins* (1908, tr. *Penguin Island* 1909), *Les Dieux ont soif* (1912, tr. *The Gods Are Athirst* 1913), and *La Révolte des Anges* (1914, tr. *Revolt of the Angels* 1914). A deep influence upon him was Madame Arman de Caillavet, with whom he had a liaison lasting until her death (1910). He was elected to Académie Française (1896), won Nobel prize (1921). Died at La Béchellerie near Tours.

REFERENCES: Jacob Axelrad *Anatole France: A Life Without Illusions, 1844–1924* (New York and London 1944). Jean Jacques Brousson *Anatole France Himself* (tr. Philadelphia and London 1925). Haakon Chevalier *The Ironic Temper: Anatole France and His Time* (Oxford and New York 1932). Edwin P. Dargan *Anatole France: 1844–1896* (London and New York 1937). David Tylden-Wright *Anatole France* (London and New York 1967).

FRANCESCA. *See* PIERO DELLA FRANCESCA.

FRANCK, César (Auguste Jean Guillaume Hubert) (Dec. 10, 1822 – Nov. 8, 1890). Belgian-French composer and organist. Born Liège; studied at Liège Conservatoire before moving with family to Paris (1835), where he attended Conservatoire (1837–42). First important works: *Trois Trios concertants* (1842); *Ruth,* an oratorio (1845). Supported family as virtuoso pianist and composer of showy concert pieces until marriage

to daughter of actress Madame Desmousseaux (1848) gave him independence. Became organist Ste. Clotilde (1858) until his death. From 1872 taught at Paris Conservatoire, exerting strong influence on such pupils as Vincent d'Indy, Ernest Chausson, Henri Duparc. Died in Paris. Major works: *Six Pièces* (1860–62), *Trois Pièces* (1878), and *Trois Chorals* (1890), all for organ; *Les Béatitudes,* an oratorio (1869–79); symphonic poems *Les Éolides* (1876) and *Le Chausseur maudit* (1882); *Les Djinns,* for piano and orchestra (1884); *Prélude, choral et fugue* (1884), *Variations symphoniques* (1885), and *Prélude, aria et finale* (1886–87), all for piano; piano quintet (1878–79); sonata for violin and piano (1886); *Symphony in D Minor* (1886–88); string quartet (1889). Although during his lifetime Franck received almost no recognition as a composer, his teaching methods and his style, characterized by rich chromaticism and by employment of the cyclic principle (use of recurrent themes), were carried on in Schola Cantorum, founded by d'Indy (1894).

REFERENCE: Vincent d'Indy *César Franck* (tr. London 1909 and New York 1910, new ed. New York PB 1965).

FRANKLIN, Benjamin (Jan. 17, 1706 – Apr. 17, 1790). American statesman, scientist, writer, philosopher. Born Boston, fifteenth child of tallow chandler's family. Briefly attended Boston Latin school. Apprenticed to elder brother as printer (1718–23), but desiring independence settled in Philadelphia as printer and journalist. Married Deborah Read (1730; she died 1774). Edited *Philadelphia Gazette* (1729–66) and became widely known through *Poor Richard's Almanack* (1733–58). Its kindly, witty, sometimes earthy simplicity and practicality are characteristic of Franklin, and many of its sayings ("Time is money"; "Snug as a bug in a rug") have come down to this day. Franklin founded a discussion club, the Junto, which became the American Philosophical Society (1743), organized the semipublic Philadelphia Library (1731), a fire department and other services, became postmaster (1737–53), helped found city hospital and

College of Philadelphia (1751), which became University of Pennsylvania. Invented Franklin stove and lightning rod, also the armonica, and made discoveries in experimental physics, particularly electricity (1746–52) that made him famous throughout Europe. His *Experiments and Observations on Electricity,* published in London (1751) was translated into French, Italian and German, and earned him honorary degrees and membership in Royal Society, London. Appointed deputy postmaster-general of North America (1753–74), member of Pennsylvania Assembly and agent of Pennsylvania and other colonies (1757–75), he spent nearly twenty years in England attempting to preserve American liberty within the British Empire. Realizing failure of mission, he returned to Philadelphia, where he was elected delegate to Continental Congress (1775), helped draft and signed Declaration of Independence, was sent to France to negotiate treaty (1776), remained as sole U.S. minister to France (1778–85), where he was enormously popular. Appointed commissioner with John Jay and John Adams in peace negotiations with Great Britain (1781); one of three to sign Treaty of Paris (1783). On return to Philadelphia (1785), made president of Pennsylvania executive council (1785–87) and member of Constitutional Convention (1787). One of last public papers was for abolition of slavery (1790). Died in Philadelphia. His *Autobiography,* covering his life through 1757 (begun 1771 and published in America posthumously, 1867), is a modest, simple yet salty account of a life and achievement that reveals Franklin as "a universal genius, more so than any other man of his day, American or European . . . the embodiment of what we like to call the American spirit — idealistic but practical, principled but expedient, optimistic for human betterment and the world's future" (S. E. Morison).

EDITION: *The Writings of Benjamin Franklin* ed. Albert H. Smyth (10 vols. New York and London 1907–10). *The Papers of Benjamin Franklin* ed. Leonard W. Labaree and others (vols. 1–11 [January 6, 1706, through December 31, 1764], New Haven, Conn. 1959–67; others in process).

REFERENCES: Alfred Owen Aldridge *Franklin and His French Contemporaries* (New York 1957). Verner W. Crane *Benjamin Franklin and a Rising People* (Boston 1954, also PB). Carl Van Doren *Benjamin Franklin* (New York 1938 and London 1939, also PB).

FRAZER, Sir James George (Jan. 1, 1854 – May 7, 1941). British classicist and anthropologist. Born Glasgow. Attended Glasgow University (1869–73); entered (1874) Trinity College, Cambridge, of which he became a fellow (1879). First published revision of George Long's edition of Sallust's *Catilina et Jugurtha* (1884). Eminence as anthropologist established with publication of *The Golden Bough* (2 vols. 1890, expanded to 12 vols. 1911–15). Married Mrs. Lilly Grove (1896). Except for a year (1907) as professor at Liverpool, remained all his life at Cambridge, where he died. Received numerous academic honors; knighted (1914). Frazer's distinction between magic and religion, and his synthesis and comparison of a broad range of primitive customs, represent an important step in the development of modern social anthropology. Other works include *Totemism and Exogamy* (1910), *Folklore in the Old Testament* (1918), and *Anthologia Antropologica* (4 vols. 1938–1939).

REFERENCE: R. A. Downie *James George Frazer: The Portrait of a Scholar* (London 1940 and New York 1941).

FRENEAU, Philip Morin (Jan. 2, 1752 – Dec. 19, 1832). American poet and editor. Born New York City, of French Huguenot family. Graduated (1771) from College of New Jersey (now Princeton), where he wrote with Hugh Henry Brackenridge *A Poem on the Rising Glory of America* (published 1772); also wrote *The American Village* (1772) and other poems. Two years in West Indies (1776–78) inspired romantic poems *The Beauties of Santa Cruz* and *The House of Night,* but harrowing experiences at hands of British captors while returning to U.S. produced trenchant satire, in particular *The British Prison Ship* (1781), which won him title Poet of the Revolution. Starting with 1786, many editions of his verse and prose appeared in his lifetime. After five years as master of a brig (1784–89), married Eleanor Forman (1789). Having expressed pro-revolution and anti-British sentiments in journals, and being known as a radical democrat, he was employed by Thomas Jefferson to edit *National Gazette* (1791–93) in which he vehemently attacked Federalists, especially Alexander Hamilton. Yellow fever epidemic closed paper down (1793). Freneau then edited first *Jersey Chronicle*, later the *New York Time-Piece*, with such lack of success that he took to the sea again (1802–1807) as master of freighters. Lived last years in poverty; died near Freehold, N.J. Freneau was the first poet to use themes from American nature, to anticipate the English romantics and Walt Whitman. Best-known poems are *The Wild Honey Suckle* and *The Indian Burying Ground* (1786).

EDITIONS: *The Poems of Freneau* ed. Harry H. Clark (New York 1929). *The Last Poems of Philip Freneau* ed. Lewis Leary (New Brunswick, N.J. 1945). *The Prose Works of Philip Freneau* ed. Philip M. Marsh (New York and London 1955).

REFERENCES: Mary S. Austin *Philip Freneau, the Poet of the Revolution* (New York 1901). Jacob Axelrad *Philip Freneau, Champion of Democracy* (Austin, Tex. 1967). Samuel E. Forman *The Political Activities of Philip Freneau* (Baltimore 1902). Lewis Leary *That Rascal Freneau* (New Brunswick, N.J. 1941). Philip M. Marsh *Philip Freneau, Poet and Journalist* (Minneapolis 1968).

FRESCOBALDI, Girolamo (Sept. 1583 – Mar. 1, 1643). Italian organist and composer. Born Ferrara, where he studied under cathedral organist Luzzasco Luzzaschi and, while still a youth, gained renown as both singer and organist. After serving briefly as organist of church of S. Maria in Trastevere, Rome, he journeyed to the Netherlands (1607), publishing his first work, a collection of five-part madrigals, in Antwerp (1608). Returned to Rome (1608) and became organist at St. Peter's, where he performed before huge audiences for rest of his life, except for

period as court organist at Florence (1628–34). Died in Rome. Frescobaldi composed *canzoni,* motets, hymns, and madrigals, but his important baroque compositions are for organ and harpsichord, which through his pupil J. J. Froberger strongly influenced the German baroque school.

REFERENCE: Armand Machabey *Girolamo Frescobaldi Ferrarensis: 1583–1643* (Paris 1952).

FREUD, Sigmund (May 6, 1856 – Sept. 23, 1939). Austrian physician, founder of psychoanalysis. Born Freiberg, Moravia, of middle-class Jewish parents, who moved to Vienna (1859), where he was a brilliant student in classics, English, and French. Became deeply interested in Shakespeare, Goethe, Leonardo da Vinci, and Dostoevsky. Received M.D. at University of Vienna (1881). Married Martha Bernays (1886). Work with Josef Breuer on treatment of hysteria through hypnosis resulted in their book *Studies of Hysteria* (1895). Freud developed free association method (1892–95), then psychoanalysis (1895–1900), both important discoveries, with which he replaced hypnotism as treatment. His self-analysis (1897) revealed significance of dreams, resulted in *The Interpretation of Dreams* (1900). *The Psychopathology of Everyday Life* (1904) and *Three Contributions to the Theory of Sex* (1905) followed, arousing widespread antagonism and misunderstanding. Recognition came only in final years with Goethe prize (1930) and membership in Royal Society (1936). Professor at University of Vienna from 1902 until Nazi invasion forced flight to London (1938), where he died. Other works: *Introductory Lectures on Psychoanalysis* (1909), *Totem and Taboo* (1913), *Beyond the Pleasure Principle* (1919), *The Ego and the Id* (1923), *The Future of an Illusion* (1927), which with *Civilization and Its Discontents* (1930) discusses modern culture, *New Introductory Lectures on Psychoanalysis* (1933), *Moses and Monotheism* (1938), *An Outline of Psychoanalysis* (1949). Freud's exploration of the effects of unconscious mental forces on conscious life has had a profound impact on twentieth-century culture, especially in arts and letters.

EDITION: *Complete Psychoanalytical Works* ed. James Strachey (24 vols. London and New York 1957).

REFERENCES: Ernest Jones *Sigmund Freud, Life and Work* (3 vols. London and New York 1953–57, also abridged PB).

___

FRIEDRICH, Kaspar David (Sept. 5, 1774 – May 7, 1840). German painter. Born Greifswald, son of a maker of candles and soap. After four years at Academy of Copenhagen, moved to Dresden (1798), where he remained until his death. Became central figure of a circle of romantic painters and writers, among them Philip Otto Runge, Ludwig Tieck, and Novalis. Received prize for two sepia drawings in competition sponsored by Goethe (1805). Important work began with *The Cross in the Mountain* (1807, Gemäldegalerie, Dresden), a characteristic romantic landscape, sharply realistic in detail yet conveying deep melancholy and a mystical sense of nature. Other major works (chiefly in Dresden) are *Cemetery of a Cloister in the Snow* (1810), *Lonesome Tree* (1823), and *Moonrise at Sea* (1823). Married Christiane Carol Bommer (1818). A member of the Dresden Academy (from 1816), he became a professor there (1824). Friedrich never gained public recognition during his lifetime, and after his death his works were almost forgotten until the early twentieth century.

___

FROISSART, Jean (c.1337–c.1404). French chronicler and poet. Born Valenciennes, Hainaut, he crossed to England to become secretary to Queen Philippa (1361). Traveled extensively, visiting Scotland and the Continent, and reaching Rome. On Philippa's death entered service of Wenceslas of Brabant (1369), then of Guy de Châtillon, count of Blois, whom he accompanied on long trips around western Europe. Nothing is known of his life after 1404. Though a courtly poet, author of Arthurian verse romance *Méliador*, he is best known for his *Chronicles* in four books (begun c.1369), an invaluable source for history of Hundred Years War, covering 1326–1400. Froissart drew on work of chronicler Jean Le Bel for period up to 1356, and used his own information, often firsthand, for succeeding years. A courtier all his life, Froissart, though often inaccurate and biased on one side or the other in his *Chronicles*, presents a vividly narrated, lively re-creation of feudal chivalry in its pageantry, tournaments, battles — such as Crécy and Poitiers — sieges of castles, and massacres. Immensely popular during fifteenth century.

TRANSLATIONS: *Chronicles* tr. John Bourchier, Lord Berners (2 vols. 1523–25), ed. W. P. Ker (6 vols. London 1901–1903); tr. and ed. John Jolliffe (London 1967 and New York 1968).

REFERENCES: G. G. Coulton *The Chronicler of European Chivalry: A Study of Jean Froissart* (London 1930). Frederick C. Shears *Froissart: Chronicler and Poet* (London 1930). Maurice Wilmotte *Jean Froissart* (Brussels 1948).

___

FROST, Robert (Lee) (Mar. 26, 1874 – Jan. 29, 1963). American poet. Born San Francisco. After death of father moved (1885) to latter's native New England with sister and mother, who took up schoolteaching. Graduated from Lawrence, Mass. High School (1892), where he met Eleanor Miriam White, whom he married (1895). Attended Dartmouth briefly and later Harvard, worked in Lawrence woolen mill, on newspaper, and at other odd jobs, but throughout these years dedicated himself to poetry. Published first poem, *My Butterfly*, in *New York Independent* (1894). Settled on farm in Derry, N.H., when poor health threatened (1901). Taught school to help provide for family of three daughters and son. Sold farm and went to England (1912), where he published his first two books of poems, *A Boy's Will* (1913) and *North of Boston* (1914). These brought recognition in England and later in America. On his return to New Hampshire (1915) he soon found himself in demand for public readings and teaching positions, "barding around" at University of Michigan, Amherst (1926–38), Harvard (1939–43), Dartmouth (1943–49); finally received permanent appointment at Amherst (1949). Resided variously in Vermont, Florida, and Boston in between lecture and teaching engagements. Awarded Pulitzer prize in 1924, 1931, 1937, and 1943. Poet for inauguration of President John F. Kennedy (1961). Visited USSR (1962). Died in Boston. First *Collected Poems* appeared 1930; reissued and enlarged 1939 and (as *Complete Poems*), 1949.

EDITION: *The Poetry of Robert Frost* ed. Edward Connery Latham (New York 1970).

REFERENCES: Reuben A. Brower *The Poetry of Robert Frost* (New York 1963, also PB). Elizabeth Shepley Sergeant *Robert Frost: The Trial by Existence* (New York 1960). Lawrance Thompson *Robert Frost: The Early Years 1874–1915* (New York 1966) and *The Years of Triumph 1915–1938* (New York 1970).

≈

ROBERT FROST
BY PETER DAVISON

From Columbus and Sir Walter Raleigh onward, America has been traveling the road west, but most American writers have faced the other way. Some, like James, Pound, Eliot, and Hemingway, expatriated themselves. Others, like Twain, Howells, Sinclair Lewis, and Robert Frost, began as westerners but pitched their tents in the East. All found sources of creative energy in this retrograde motion. The surface of Robert Frost's poetry reveals almost nothing about his first, formative eleven years in San Francisco. Left behind in the unconscious were the climatic stimuli of the balmy foggy bay and the freedom of western customs, abandoned in favor of "dry light, hard clouds, hard expressions, and hard manners," as Frost's mentor Emerson had it.

Frost's father's death forced his mother east to teach school (without marked success) in a series of Massachusetts milltowns. His young manhood was spent in unemployment and isolation on New Hampshire farms, inadequately supporting a growing family. He was not to grow into a poet without inner storms of anger, pride, and shame. He took immense pains to take on the color of the country by concealing his emotions and pretending unpretentiousness. As his poetry matured, he bent himself to clothe the most exalted themes in the plainest language. "I alone among English writers," he wrote proudly in 1913, "have consciously set myself to make music out of what I may call the sound of sense."

His was the poetry of experience, and it came hard and late. His maturing years were dogged by poverty and his mature years by disaster. His wife at first refused to marry him; she yielded to the strength of his will (see *The Subverted Flower*), and for the forty years of their marriage she continued to submit and to resent. Of their six children, two died in infancy, one by suicide, one after giving birth, and at least one was plagued (like Frost's only sister) by mental illness. From his marriage until he was over seventy, Frost was seldom at any far remove from personal disaster and sorrow (see *Home Burial* and *The Hill Wife*), yet these disasters are never directly, and only infrequently, touched on in the poetry.

At first transcendental and Emersonian, Frost's early lyric manner evolved into something at once more ambiguous, more Yankee, more sly. In *North of Boston* (1915) he had arrived at the style and manner that are his permanent contribution to the art of poetry. His younger life had been marked by repeated runnings away — from college, from home when his wife first refused him. In 1912 he embarked on the last and most fortunate escape, when he uprooted his family from New Hampshire and took them to England for three years. The move marked his having found his true voice; and the English recognized its quality before his countrymen did. It had developed between his twentieth and fortieth years; it had been accompanied by a conscious adoption of New England speech and by excursions into schoolteaching, which remained his second love.

North of Boston is a collection of dramatic eclogues set in rural New England. The speakers are the leathery, heartbroken people of the half-abandoned villages and the stony soil; the theme, explicit and implicit, is "the death of the hired man," for the energy of America had flowed westward, leaving relatively few people behind on their hillsides and lonely, barely arable, farms, nurtured by courage and silence and not much else, somehow bereft of the benefits of home. After *North of Boston*, Frost's work turned gradually toward song on the one hand and philosophy on the other. The great sonnets (*The Oven Bird, Design, The Silken Tent, A Soldier*) and lyrics (*Stopping by Woods on a Snowy Evening*) and philosophical poems (*West-Running Brook*) began, like shrubbery in a fallow field, to push out the eclogues. In his least successful later poems the abstract speculations turned into wisecracks or glosses on current affairs; in his best, they took on a gnomic resonance:

> Nature within her inmost self
>   divides
> To trouble men with having
>   to take sides.

Once America had discovered Frost in 1915, his reputation burgeoned. He became the most popular of poets, a sought-after speaker, one of the great teachers and talkers of his age. As his audience grew large, it discriminated less, paying homage to the hayseed sage rather than to the poet and craftsman. He was revered by old and young, town and gown, poets and Presidents, but he faced his public in a disguise that had been manufactured with as much artifice as the private disciplines of his verse. Just as the effortless talk of his poetry conceals difficulties and ambiguities that remain hidden from most readers, so Frost's rugged face and foxy humor concealed an uncanny awareness of his audience. The disguise also hid a jealous, wary sense of career, as his friends knew and his posthumously published letters and biography show.

The contradictions in Frost actually lie at the heart of his achievement. To have written some of America's most intricate poetry (e.g. *Directive*) in America's simplest diction; to have built out of personal tragedy a poetry that seemed to take life lightly; to have constructed north of Boston a pastoral territory that was national, artificial, and archetypical; to have developed out of the rhythms of colloquial speech a poetry that had designs on philosophy; to have utilized traditional English metrics to liberate the American language from its English fetters; to have been among the most quixotic of aspirants, the most stoic of moralists, the most canny of careerists — these contradictions bred his greatest poems. In one of them, *West-Running Brook*, he writes mysteriously:

> It is this backward motion to-
>   ward the source,
> Against the stream, that most
>   we see ourselves in,
> The tribute of the current to the
>   source.

Who knows how much the long journey east against the current had to do with his secrets and his contradictions and his greatness?

FROUDE, James Anthony (Apr. 23, 1818 – Oct. 20, 1894). English historian, biographer, essayist. Born Dartington, Devonshire, son of archdeacon. Educated at Oriel College, Oxford (1835–42); there he was influenced by Oxford movement and Cardinal Newman, with whom his brother Richard Hurrell Froude (1803–1836) was closely associated. Fellow, Exeter College (1842), and took deacon's orders (1845). Broke with Oxford movement and became a skeptic, causing a turmoil with his *Nemesis of Faith* (1849). Went to London, married Charlotte Grenfell (1849; she died 1860); married Henrietta Ware (1861). Friendship with Thomas Carlyle from 1849 greatly influenced him. Major work, *The History of England from the Fall of Wolsey to the Defeat of the Spanish Armada* (12 vols. 1856–70), aroused heated criticism for inaccuracy and subjectivity, but is appreciated today for emphasis on role of great men (an attitude derived from Carlyle). Froude edited *Fraser's Magazine* (1860–74), wrote essays, and *The English in Ireland in the Eighteenth Century* (1872–74). Elected rector of St. Andrew's University (1868). Produced the great biography of Carlyle (4 vols. 1882–84), the frankness of which aroused a storm of indignation, together with his edition of Carlyle's papers (2 vols. 1881). Traveled widely among British colonies and wrote a number of books on his observations. Appointed regius professor of modern history at Oxford (1892). Died at Kingsbridge, Devonshire.

REFERENCES: Waldo H. Dunn *James Anthony Froude: A Biography* (2 vols. London and New York 1961–63). Herbert W. Paul *The Life of Froude* (London and New York 1905).

FULLER, (Sarah) Margaret (Marchioness Ossoli) (May 23, 1810 – July 14, 1850). American journalist, critic and social reformer. Born Cambridgeport, Mass. A precocious child, intensively educated by her father, her incisive intellect was admired by Emerson, George Ripley, William Henry Channing, James Freeman Clarke, and Frederic Henry Hedge; it was criticized by Hawthorne and Thoreau. Published translation of Eckermann's *Conversations with Goethe* (1839). Edited *The Dial*, transcendentalist journal, with Emerson and Ripley (1840–42). Led discussion classes for women (1839–44), material from which appeared in her philosophical feminist work, *Woman in the Nineteenth Century* (1845). *Summer on the Lakes in 1843* (1844) prompted Horace Greeley to employ her as literary critic for *New York Tribune* (1844–46). Her articles from *Tribune* were published as *Papers on Literature and Art* (1846). She went abroad that year; married Marquis Angelo Ossoli (1848) after conceiving his son. Like Ossoli became ardent supporter of Mazzini and Roman Republic of 1849, a history of which she wrote. On return voyage she perished with her family in a shipwreck off Fire Island, N.Y. *The Memoirs of Margaret Fuller* (2 vols. 1852) were edited by Emerson, Channing and Clarke. *At Home and Abroad* (1856) and *Life Without and Life Within* (1859) appeared posthumously.

EDITION: *The Writings of Margaret Fuller* ed. Mason Wade (New York 1941).
REFERENCES: Faith Chipperfield *In Quest of Love: The Life and Death of Margaret Fuller* (New York 1957). Joseph Day Diess *The Roman Years of Margaret Fuller* (New York 1969). Julia Ward Howe *Margaret Fuller* (Boston 1883). Madeleine B. Stern *The Life of Margaret Fuller* (New York 1942). Mason Wade *Margaret Fuller, Whetstone of Genius* (New York 1940).

FULLER, Thomas (June 1608 – Aug. 16, 1661). English writer and clergyman. Born Aldwincle, Northamptonshire, where his father was rector. Entered Queens College, Cambridge, at thirteen and at twenty became university's youngest M.A. Appointed curate of St. Bene't's, Cambridge (1630), then prebendary there and rector of Broadwindsor, Dorset (1634). Married Ellen Grove (1638; she died 1641); married Mary Roper (1651). A moderate royalist, he advocated peace while preacher at Savoy Chapel, London (1641–43), but finally had to flee, spending rest of Civil War period as chaplain with king's army and household. During Commonwealth, influential friends among Puritans enabled him to preach again in London. After Restoration, became chaplain to Charles II; further preferment prevented by his sudden death, in London. A noted wit, Fuller filled his vast and varied array of writings with gems of whimsical humor as well as valuable antiquarian information. Best known works: *The Holy War* (1639), history of the Crusades; *The Holy State and the Profane State* (1642), short essays and biographies; *Church History of Britain* (1655); *History of the Worthies of England* (1662), describing the English counties and their notable men; *Good Thoughts in Bad Times* (1645), *Good Thoughts in Worse Times* (1647), and *Mixt Contemplations in Better Times* (1660), comprising short, pithy meditations.

REFERENCES: William Addison *Worthy Dr. Fuller* (London and New York 1951). John E. Bailey *The Life of Thomas Fuller* (London 1874). Dean B. Lyman *The Great Tom Fuller* (Berkeley, Calif. and Cambridge, England 1935).

FUSELI, Henry (Johann Heinrich Füssli) (Feb. 7, 1741 – Apr. 16, 1825). Anglo-Swiss painter. Born Zurich, son of a portrait painter and art critic. At first a writer, he settled in London (1764) and supported himself by translating books. Began to paint seriously (1767) on advice of Sir Joshua Reynolds. Left (1769) for Italy, where he remained eight years, studying works of Michelangelo and mannerists. On return to England, devoted himself to painting scenes from history, the Bible, mythology, literature and imagination. *The Nightmare* (1782), whose mannerist reclining figure, supernatural presences, and mood of terror effect a fusion of the classic and Gothic elements of romanticism, made him famous and remains his best-known work. From 1786, produced for John Boydell's Shakespeare Gallery a number of canvases, including *Titania and Bottom* (c.1790). Married Sophia Rawlins (1788). Exhibited (from 1774) at Royal Academy; became full member (1790) and highly influential professor there (1799–1805, 1810–25). Died in London. Fuseli's work, which includes important drawings, is most akin to that of Blake, who owed much to his friendship.

EDITION: *The Mind of Henry Fuseli: Selections from His Writings* ed. Eudo C. Mason (London 1951).

REFERENCES: Frederick Antal *Fuseli Studies* (London 1956). Paul Ganz ed. *The Drawings of Henry Fuseli* (London and New York 1949). Nicolas Powell *The Drawings of Henry Fuseli* (London 1941).

GABRIEL, Jacques Ange (or Ange Jacques) (Oct. 23, 1698 – Jan. 4, 1782). French architect. Born Paris, son of royal architect Jacques Gabriel (1667–1742) and outstanding member of architectural family active in France from the Renaissance to the Revolution. Succeeded father as first architect to Louis XV (1742). Spent life working for the king at his various residences, producing two types of design: a small pavilion on the grounds of a large château, and enormous projects involving harmonious arrangement of numerous structures within a site. His neoclassic masterpieces are the Petit Trianon at Versailles (1762–68) and Place Louis XV (now Place de la Concorde), Paris (1755–75). Other works: the Opéra at Versailles (1748–53); enlargements of Fontainebleau (1749) and the Louvre (1755–57); châteaux at Compiègne (1751) and Choisy (1752); École Militaire, Paris (begun 1752). Died in Paris. Elegance and classical purity characterize Gabriel's style.

REFERENCES: Edmond, comte de Fels *Ange-Jacques Gabriel, premier architecte du roi* (2nd ed. Paris 1924). Georges Gromort *Jacques-Ange Gabriel* (Paris 1933).

GABRIELI, Giovanni (1557 – Aug. 12, 1612). Italian organist and composer. Born and died in Venice. Nephew and chief disciple of Andrea Gabrieli (c.1520–1586), a highly versatile and original composer of sacred and secular instrumental and vocal works, who was also the teacher of Hans Leo Hassler. Giovanni probably worked under Orlando di Lasso at Munich (1575–79). Appointed permanent second organist at St. Mark's, Venice (1585). Perfected uncle's technique of using two or more choirs; further developed the three-part instrumental form which became the trio sonata, and introduced to vocal music the *concertato* style, in which instrumental parts, instead of simply doubling voice parts, were individually scored. Major works: *Sacrae Symphoniae* (part I, 1597; part II, 1615); *Canzoni e Sonate* (1615); *Reliquiae Sacrorum Concentuum* (1615). Through his numerous German pupils, notably Heinrich Schütz, Giovanni Gabrieli exerted great influence on baroque music.

REFERENCE: Manfred Bukofzer *Music in the Baroque Era* (New York 1947 and London 1948).

GADDI, family of Italian painters. GADDO DI ZANOBI (documented 1318/1319, still alive in 1327), by whom no known works survive, is thought to have been pupil of Cimabue and to have executed mosaics in Florence and Rome. His son TADDEO GADDI (c.1300–1366) was Giotto's student and assistant. Works include triptych *Madonna and Child with Saints and Scenes* (1334, Staatliche Museen, Berlin); polyptych *Madonna and Child with Angels, Saints, and the Annunciation* (1353, S. Giovanni Fuorcivitas, Pistoia); *Madonna and Child with Angels* (1355, Uffizi, Florence); frescoes illustrating life of Joachim and Anna, childhood of Mary, and infancy of Christ (probably 1330's, Baroncelli chapel, S. Croce, Florence); panels representing scenes from lives of Christ and St. Francis from sacristy of S. Croce (probably 1330's; now almost all in Galleria della Academia, Florence).

Taddeo died in Florence. His style differs from Giotto's in its emphasis on creating illusionistic settings, with use of elaborate architectural perspectives and naturalistic lighting effects, rather than on the figures. Of Taddeo's three painter sons, only AGNOLO GADDI (c.1345–1396) produced works that survive. He was born and died in Florence. His frescoes of the Holy Cross legend in S. Croce, (c.1380) and of the life of Mary and legend of the Holy Girdle in cathedral of Prato (1392–95) are known for their light colors and crowded, flat compositions.

GAINSBOROUGH, Thomas (May 14, 1727 – Aug. 2, 1788). English portrait and landscape painter. Born Sudbury, Suffolk, youngest of nine. Studied art in London (1740–42), including etching. Married Margaret Burr (1746) and settled in Ipswich as portrait and landscape painter (1752). Moved to Bath (1759), where his portraits were much in demand; exhibited with Society of Artists in London (1761). Became one of thirty-six founding members of Royal Society (1768), where he exhibited regularly until a falling out (1784). Moved to London (1774), where royal family favored him over his rival Sir Joshua Reynolds. Gainsborough painted George III three times, and painted many leading society, theatre, and state figures — William Pitt, Edmund Burke, Robert Clive, Mrs. Siddons, Mrs. Sheridan, and others. Characteristic of his aristocratic grace and freshness is the famous *Blue Boy* (1779, Huntington Gallery, San Marino, Calif.), while his style of portraiture is typified by the *Duchess of Devonshire* (1783, Metropolitan Museum, New York), and his landscape illumination and treatment by *Harvest Wagon* (Barber Institute, Birmingham, England) and *The Watering Place* (1777, Tate Gallery, London). He died in London.

REFERENCES: Hugh Stokes *Thomas Gainsborough* (New York and London 1925). Ellis K. Waterhouse *Gainsborough* (London 1958). Mary Woodall *Thomas Gainsborough: His Life and Work* (New York and London 1949).

THOMAS GAINSBOROUGH
BY ANDREW C. RITCHIE

Until the coming of Turner and Constable the history of British painting is largely concerned with portraiture. Landscapes were bought and commissioned during this time but they were essentially topographical portraits of a patron's house or estate. And so while Gainsborough's first love was landscape painting, he was forced to paint portraits for a living, leaving landscapes to his spare time and for his own pleasure.

His career as an artist can be conveniently divided into three periods: the early years in his home shire of Suffolk, fourteen years in Bath, followed by fourteen years in London, where he died in 1788. He was in the main a self-taught painter, although in his youth he did work for Gravelot (Hubert François Bourguignon, 1699–1773), a French illustrator who practiced in London, and certainly from him he acquired a knowledge of rococo draftsmanship that is a mark of his art throughout his life. Unlike Reynolds, he did not go abroad to study the Old Masters. What study he made of them was done in England. Private collections in Suffolk contained many Dutch landscapes, probably because of the close commercial connections between East Anglia and Holland and the similarity of this part of England to the flat Dutch terrain. As a consequence, no doubt, Gainsborough's first picture of note was his *Connard Wood* (National Gallery, London), a youthful work clearly inspired by Ruisdael. As a frequently delightful compromise with the demand for portraiture, Gainsborough in his Suffolk years produced a number of informal portraits of sitters in a landscape, in pose and composition deriving from Watteau and his older contemporary Francis

Hayman — a fusion, in short, of French grace and English informality. His *Mr. and Mrs. Andrews* (National Gallery, London) is his masterpiece in this genre.

In 1759 he removed to Bath, the social capital of England outside London. Meanwhile, he had married an expensive wife and had acquired two daughters whose demands upon him proved to be expensive also. At Bath he found himself quickly the most popular portrait painter of the town, and since he chose to paint without assistants — drapery painters as they were usually called — with the possible exception of some help from his nephew apprentice Dupont Gainsborough, he found himself burdened at times with more portrait commissions than he could handle or accept. The pressure of these Bath years is summed up in an excerpt taken from a letter he wrote to a musician friend, William Jackson (Gainsborough was an amateur musician himself and many of his friends were musicians):

"I'm sick of Portraits and wish very much to take my Viol da Gamba and walk off to some sweet village where I can paint Landskips and enjoy the fag End of Life in quietness and ease. But these fine Ladies and their Tea drinkings, Dancings, *Husband huntings* and such will fob me out of the last ten years, & I fear miss getting husbands too. . . ."

Despite his frustrations and his nostalgia for the "Green trees & Blue Skies" of his native Suffolk, he continued to develop his portrait style. At Wilton, near Bath, he was able to study an important collection of Van Dykes, and his admiration for this master of the elegant formal portrait soon became evident in some of the finest canvases of these Bath years. The portrait of Mrs. Philip Thicknesse (Cincinnati Art Museum) is an outstanding example.

While at Bath, he submitted pictures to exhibitions in London, first to the Society of Artists in 1761 and later to the Royal Academy in 1769, of which he was a founder member in 1768. Before settling in London in 1774 he had become well known there from these annual exhibitions of his works. He was, in fact, Reynolds's chief rival as a portraitist and in due course was patronized by the court, which found Reynolds not to its taste. Gainsborough's London popularity as a portrait painter, particularly of women, can be understood by reference to two of the most successful canvases of his last period — *Mrs. Sheridan* (National Gallery, Washington, D.C.) and *Mrs. Graham* (National Gallery of Scotland, Edinburgh).

Despite this portrait popularity, or perhaps because of it, Gainsborough never ceased to wish for recognition as a landscape painter. Removed as he was from his beloved country, he substituted for nature arrangements on his table of pebbles, moss and pieces of cork, and from these compositions produced an almost endless series of charcoal drawings. From these he drew inspiration for many of his landscapes in oil, such as *The Cottage Door* (Huntington Gallery, California) and *The Bridge* (National Gallery, London). The climax of his career in his last years is surely his fusion of figures in an ideal landscape, some commissioned as portraits such as *Squire Hallet and His Wife,* popularly known as *The Morning Walk* (Lord Rothschild's collection, London), and some as in *The Mall* (Frick Collection, New York), using an arrangement of lay or doll figures, much as for landscape ideas he used the pebbles, moss and cork mentioned above.

Together with such "elegant" and artful, in the best sense, paintings of figures in a landscape Gainsborough in his Bath and London periods produced a number of so-called "fancy pictures," such as *The Harvest Wagon* (Barber Institute, Birmingham) and *Haymaker and Sleeping Girl* (Boston Museum of Fine Arts). These are rustic fantasies of a high poetic order, foreshadowing the Wordsworth of the *Lyrical Ballads*. It was probably with pictures such as these in mind that Reynolds was able to discount any rivalry he may have felt between him and Gainsborough as portrait painters and to present in his Fourteenth Discourse a judgment of Gainsborough which is still valid today:

"If ever this nation should produce genius sufficient to acquire us the honorable distinction of an English School, the name of Gainsborough will be transmitted to posterity, in the History of the Art, among the very first of that rising name."

GALDÓS. *See* PÉREZ GALDÓS, Benito.

GALLI DA BIBIENA. *See* BIBIENA.

GALSWORTHY, John (Aug. 14, 1867 – Jan. 31, 1933). English novelist and playwright. Born Kingston, Surrey, son of wealthy lawyer and businessman. Educated at Harrow and Oxford; called to the bar (1890). Independently wealthy, he traveled extensively around the world (meeting Conrad on one voyage), but did not begin writing until encouraged by Ada Galsworthy, his cousin's wife. Beginning with story collection *From the Four Winds* (1897), he published four unsuccessful books under pseudonym John Sinjohn, meanwhile carrying on an affair with Ada, whom he married (1905). His most famous novel, *The Man of Property* (1906), opens *The Forsyte Saga* (1906–1922), which includes the novels *In Chancery* (1920) and *To Let* (1921),

and the interludes *Indian Summer of a Forsyte* (1918) and *Awakening* (1920). A portrait of the wealthy industrial middle class as represented by over forty years of the Forsyte family, it is the work on which his reputation chiefly rests. The film version of the *Saga* by the BBC in London became a worldwide hit from 1968. His first successful play, *The Silver Box* (1906), was followed by *Strife* (1909), *Justice* (1910), *The Skin Game* (1920), *Loyalties* (1922), and *Old English* (1924). The *Saga* was continued in the trilogy *A Modern Comedy* (1929), and Galsworthy produced other novels, stories and essays. He received numerous honorary degrees, the Order of Merit (1929) and the Nobel prize (1932). Died in London.

REFERENCES: Ada Galsworthy *Over the Hills and Far Away* (London 1937 and New York 1938). Harold Vincent Marrot *The Life and Letters of John Galsworthy* (London and New York 1936). M. E. Reynolds *Memories of John Galsworthy* (London and New York 1937).

GARCÍA LORCA, Federico. *See* LORCA, Federico García.

GARLAND, (Hannibal) Hamlin (Sept. 14, 1860 – Mar. 4, 1940). American writer. Born near West Salem, Wis. Family moved to farm in Iowa (1869), where Garland graduated from Cedar Valley Seminary, Osage (1881). After a time in North Dakota and Illinois, went to Boston (1884) to pursue literary career and became influenced by Henry George and new school of realism in fiction. His short stories *Main-Traveled Roads* (1891) and *Prairie Folks* (1893) savagely describe the Midwestern farmer's struggle against rising industrialism and dispel the old myth of the farm idyll. Together with the novels *A Spoil of Office* (1892) and *Rose of Dutcher's Coolly* (1895) they established him as leading exponent of realism (he called his style "veritism") and brought friendship with William Dean Howells and Stephen Crane. Married Zulime Taft (1899) and settled in Chicago; later (1915) moved to New York. After series of mediocre novels and stories (1895–1916), wrote autobiographical *A Son of the Middle Border* (1917), considered his best work. It was followed by *A Daughter of the Middle Border* (1921), which won Pulitzer prize, *Trail-Makers of the Middle Border* (1926), *Back-Trailers from the Middle Border* (1928) and other works of reminiscence. From 1930 until his death Garland lived in Los Angeles.

REFERENCES: Lars Ahnebrink *Beginnings of Naturalism in American Fiction: A Study of the Works of Hamlin Garland, Stephen Crane, and Frank Norris* (Cambridge, Mass. 1950). Jean Holloway *Hamlin Garland: A Biography* (Austin, Tex. 1960). Edward G. Wagenknecht *Cavalcade of the American Novel* (New York 1952).

GASKELL, Elizabeth Cleghorn (Stevenson) (Sept. 29, 1810 – Nov. 12, 1865). English writer. Born London, daughter of Unitarian minister. Educated privately and at boarding school at Stratford-on-Avon. Orphaned as a girl, she lived with relatives in Manchester, where she met the young Unitarian minister, William Gaskell, whom she married (1832). They had five children. After the death of a son (1844) she began to write seriously. Her first novel *Mary Barton* (1848), a realistic portrayal of Manchester factory life, was an instant success. She became one of the most popular Victorian novelists, admired by Thomas Carlyle and Maria Edgeworth, and a friend of Dickens. *Cranford* (1853), her little classic of English village life, was followed by *Ruth* (1853), a novel of sexual morality, and *North and South* (1855), another novel about workers' lives. She knew Charlotte Brontë and wrote her biography (1857), and after an interval produced four more novels before her sudden death at her country house Alton, near Holybourne, Hampshire.

EDITIONS: *The Works of Mrs. Gaskell* ed. Adolphus W. Ward (8 vols. new ed. London 1929). *Letters of Mrs. Gaskell and Charles Eliot Norton 1855–1865* ed. Jane Whitehall (Oxford 1932). *The Letters of Mrs. Gaskell* ed. J. A. V. Chapple and Arthur Pollard (Manchester, England, 1966 and Cambridge, Mass. 1967).

REFERENCES: Annette B. Hopkins *Elizabeth Gaskell: Her Life and Work* (London 1952). Arthur Pollard *Mrs. Gaskell: Novelist and Biographer* (Manchester, England, 1965 and Cambridge, Mass. 1966).

GAUDI Y CORNET, Antoni (June 26, 1852 – June 10, 1926). Spanish architect. Born Reus, Tarragona, son of a coppersmith. While still a student at Barcelona School of Architecture (graduated 1878), collaborated on projects in Barcelona and Monserrat. First independent work, Casa Vicens, Barcelona (1878–80). Commissioned (1884) to construct church of the Holy Family in Barcelona, which occupied him until his death there. Other major works, all in Barcelona: Palacio Güell (1885–89); Sta. Coloma de Cervello, church crypt (1898–c.1915); Park Güell (1900–14); two apartment buildings. Gaudi created fanciful architectural forms and sculpturesque curved shapes, which paralleled art nouveau. He combined old-fashioned materials and methods with ingenious technological innovations, is known for undulating façades, rich, variegated surface textures, and use of polychrome tile for color.

REFERENCES: George R. Collins *Antoni Gaudi* (New York and London 1960, also PB). James J. Sweeney and José L. Sert *Antoni Gaudi* (New York and London 1961).

GAUGUIN, (Eugène Henri) Paul (June 7, 1848 – May 8, 1903). French painter. Born Paris; as a child visited mother's family in Lima, Peru (1851–55). At seventeen joined merchant marine and navy and saw several countries before returning to work for Paris exchange broker (1871). Married Danish Mette Sophie Gad (1873). Took up painting in spare time and through friend Pissarro exhibited with impressionists (1880–82). Abandoned job (1883) for painting; soon separated from family and outraged wife. Briefly at Pont-Aven, Brittany (1886). Began friendship with Van Gogh in Paris. In Martinique (1887) he found the simple life and the exotic tropical country that seemed ideal, but lack of funds forced him to return to Paris, then Brittany (1888–90). Here he painted the great works *The Vision of the Sermon* or *Jacob and the Angel* (1888, National Gallery, Edinburgh) and *The Yellow Christ* (1889, Albright Knox Gallery, Buffalo, N.Y.), in a style called synthetism, of massive, simplified forms, abstraction of design, and brilliant colors, later influenced by the Japanese print. Auctioned his paintings and sailed for Tahiti (1891), where he lived (1891–93, 1895–1901) and produced numerous woodcuts and paintings, including *Whence come we, What are we, Where are we going?* (1897–98, Museum of Fine Arts, Boston). His primitiveness, achieved through his impassive figures and serene gravity, and his use of color exerted great influence on later art. Traveled (1901) to the Marquesas Islands, where he died. We have Gauguin's own account of his first years in Tahiti, *Noa Noa*, in various versions and editions, and also his posthumously published memoir *Avant et Après* (tr. *Intimate Journals* 1921).

REFERENCES: Georges Boudaille *Gauguin: His Life and Work* (tr. London 1964 and New York PB 1966). Raymond Charmet *Gauguin* (tr. London and New York 1966, also PB). Charles Estienne *Gauguin* (tr. New York and London 1953). Robert Goldwater *Gauguin* (New York 1957). René Huyghe *Gauguin* (tr. London and New York 1959). Bruno F. Schneider *Gauguin* (tr. New York PB 1966).

✒

PAUL GAUGUIN
BY MARK ROSKILL

Gauguin's quest for a setting in which he could truly live and be himself, and for a corresponding subject matter for his art, led him by successive stages to Martinique (1887), Brittany (1888–90), Tahiti (1891–93 and 1895–1901), and finally to the Marquesas. At each stage he was going one step further back, in terms of time or geographical remove, on the tracks of a true "primitivism" of existence — one might say an "Ur civilization." This search was the central driving force and ideological commitment behind his life as a whole; and on it rests the popular appeal of that life, with all of its personal anguish and, later, physical suffering.

It is a mistake, however — a form of romanticizing like that which Gauguin himself sank into when he talked of dreaming before nature and establishing a studio of the tropics — to think that this artist cut himself off completely from his European background and consciousness and from the European artistic tradition (or that he ever really intended this). It has become increasingly clear that this was absolutely not the case. On the personal side, Gauguin never succeeded in articulating for himself the positive aspects of the freedom that he was looking for. Rather, he characteristically defined that freedom purely in negative terms: as a freedom *from* the restraints and conventions of European civilized life. Correspondingly, even when he had fully adopted the Tahitian way of life, he expected, in moments of crisis, to be recognized and treated by the authorities as a European; this is the least agreeable side of an extremely complex and difficult character, which could never entirely reconcile itself to the practical consequences of its felt drives and ambitions. And on the artistic side, Gauguin took with him to Tahiti a whole archive of photographs, prints, and other mementos which he expected to use as a continuing source of motifs and suggestions for his work. More and more cases have been discovered of his doing exactly this. His Tahitian horses are paraphrases — or better, perhaps, "translations," since an imaginative transposition was involved — of the horses of the Parthenon frieze; his poses of relaxation are adapted from Javanese reliefs; his *Papa Moe* (*Mysterious Water*) is based on a photograph. And so on through all of the tropical paintings.

It is important to recognize, in this light, what exactly the Tahitian works do offer, in terms of subject matter and suggestion. They show religion, the fears and beliefs of the natives, not as they were (by that time Europeanized), but as they seemed to have been once, and might be or should be still — insofar as Gauguin could reconstruct this imaginatively from much earlier books, the memories of older people and surviving superstitions. They add up collectively to a kind of life cycle of native existence, in its exotic setting — from birth through maturity to old age. The major invented motifs in them, such as the idols, are based in some small measure on Polynesian native art (where Gauguin could find examples); but essentially they are a combination, or syncretism, of Western and Far Eastern (Buddhist) motifs and concepts. And finally (1899–1901), the paintings present a vision of an ideal, pristine world, beyond time and place, in which the figures' stature and physique recall, by association, the great classical traditions of both Western and Eastern art.

None of this was ever systematically brought together. In his writings, Gauguin was never really capable of a full, integrated formulation of his ideas and their foundations. When it came to theoretical statements, he characteristically borrowed directly from whatever was nearest to hand and amenable to his purposes. Honesty and the true expression of what he felt equally characteristically came into conflict with his desire to be recognized (another unpleasant side to his nature) — as one sees in his way of dealing with critics, even sympathetic ones. He was happiest, in fact, with a kind of loose, freewheeling assemblage of jottings, recollections and worked-up passages on a single theme, as in his memoir *Avant et Après*.

Similarly with the paintings: Gauguin never moved for long in them in any one single direction. It took him ten years (1876–86) — longer than any other of the postimpressionists — to pass through impressionism; but during this time he developed his characteristic way of drawing on the art of others — the transcription of a trait or style or motif so that it stood isolated as a quotation or paraphrase in a surrounding context that was entirely personal to himself. He also developed during those years some of the basic devices that he would later use to carry allusion, suggestion, and humor. The succeeding years, 1886–90, the period of "synthetism," gave rise to a series of brilliantly inventive ideas — real breakthroughs in terms of structure and content: for example, the juxtaposition in the famous *Jacob and the Angel* of the vision and the people experiencing it, one flattened, the other stereometric; the play with suggestive ambiguity of shape; and the inclusion of works of art in the background presented in such a way that there is a two-way play of association between them and the main image. But these innovations are not then developed or carried further in the succeeding paintings, or only rarely so; rather they are put aside to be taken up later, and then on an *ad hoc* basis. There is greater consistency in Gauguin's prints and ceramics — important sidelines to a multiple talent — but the reason here is that Gauguin worked in these media in a concentrated way at certain limited, spaced-out periods.

The same unresolved multiplicity of contrasting directions continues to be true of the Tahitian paintings, if anything more acutely. In terms of handling and organizational principles, Gauguin never fully succeeded in reconciling together the demands of three-dimensional sculptural treatment (reflecting his work as a wood sculptor) and of the flat, wall-like picture surface (which invited ornamental arabesques); or in fusing strongly bounded areas of a single, resonant color with a looser, more texturally varied type of handling (the enduring legacy of impressionism). Instead, he worked forward, often simultaneously, along all of these lines, guided most often by his immediate thematic ambitions.

It remains, nevertheless, an extraordinarily impressive achievement; most impressive, finally, in terms of the marvelous sensual harmony and immediacy of a few magnificent works, such as the 1892 *Aha oe feii* (*Why, you are jealous*) and the *Two Tahitian Women* of 1899. And it may be argued that the work proved more fertile for succeeding artists — for the Fauves, for Kandinsky, and for the German expressionists — because of this very multiplicity. Thus, when Kirchner in 1910–11 came to feel the need for a greater grandeur and sensual harmony in his figures, he was able to turn, with Gauguin's procedure for guidance, to an analogous source: reproductions of Indian wall paintings.

GAUTIER, (Pierre Jules) Théophile (Aug. 31, 1811 – Oct. 23, 1872). French poet, novelist, critic. Born Tarbes, Hautes-Pyrénées; moved early to Paris, where he attended Collège Charlemagne, studying art and literature. Joined rising young group of romantics led by Victor Hugo, in revolt against the classicists. First book *Poésies* published same year (1830), as dramatic opening of Hugo's *Hernani*. Published more poems, *Albertus* (1833), which were favorably received, then the sensational novel *Mademoiselle de Maupin* (1835),

with its famous preface espousing the doctrine of "art for art's sake" and denouncing bourgeois philistinism. From 1836, wrote brilliant critical pieces on theatre, art, and literature, first for *La Presse*, then for *Le Moniteur Universel*. In addition to further novels (*Le Roman de la Momie*, 1856; *Le Capitaine Fracasse*, 1863), he produced his finest volume of poetry, *Émaux et Camées* (1852), a forerunner of the Parnassian school, containing his most famous poem, *L'Art*. Also wrote vividly descriptive travel books resulting from his journeys to Spain, Egypt, Russia and elsewhere. From 1858 until his death he lived quietly with his family in Neuilly, continuing to write. An outstanding literary figure of his day, it was to him that Charles Baudelaire dedicated *Les Fleurs du Mal* (1857).

TRANSLATION: *Complete Works* ed. and tr. F. C. de Sumichrast (12 vols. New York 1900–1903, 24 vols. 1907).
REFERENCES: Adolphe Boschot *Théophile Gautier* (Paris 1933). Louise Bulkley Dillingham *The Creative Imagination of Théophile Gautier: A Study in Literary Psychology* (Princeton, N.J. 1927). Joanna Richardson *Théophile Gautier: His Life and Times* (London and New York 1958).

GAVARNI (pseudonym of Sulpice Guillaume Chevalier) (Jan. 13, 1804 – Nov. 24, 1866). French caricaturist, lithographer, draftsman, illustrator. Born and died in Paris. Studied mathematics and engineering, and worked for an architect and for a manufacturer of precision instruments before publishing first lithograph (1824). Gained popularity as contributor to fashion magazines, such as *La Mode* (from 1830), and to satirical journals, especially *Charivari* (1837–47), which published his series *Fourberies de femmes en matière de sentiment. Les Étudiants, Les Lorettes, La Politique des femmes, Les Enfants terribles.* Founded and directed *Le Journal des gens du monde* (1833), which soon failed, causing his imprisonment for debt (1835). Until c.1845, Gavarni's pictorial commentary on foibles of Parisians, in a style resembling Daumier's, remained numerous and elegant; his later work revealed a bitterly satirical social view. In London (1847–51), depicted scenes of slum life for *Illustrated London News;* later work for *L'Illustration* in Paris dealt with same subject matter. Illustrated several books, including works by Balzac and Eugène Sue.

REFERENCE: Paul André Lemoisne *Gavarni: peintre et lithographe* (2 vols. Paris 1924–28).

GAY, John (c. Sept. 16, 1685 – Dec. 4, 1732). English poet and dramatist. Born Barnstable, Devonshire. Educated locally, then apprenticed to silk merchant in London. Became secretary to duchess of Monmouth (1712), then to Lord Clarendon, with whom he traveled abroad. Published burlesque in blank verse, *Wine* (1708), and achieved recognition with *Rural Sports* (1713), becoming a friend of Pope and Swift. *The Shepherd's Week*, mock pastorals, followed (1714), also burlesque drama *The What D'Ye Call It?* (1715), and mock heroic poem *Trivia, or The Art of Walking the Streets of London* (1716). Brought out his *Poems* (1720), and speculated disastrously with proceeds in South Sea stock. Duke of Queensberry became his patron, and he published his satirical *Fables* (1727), the second series appearing posthumously (1738). Of his several works for the stage *The Beggar's Opera* (1728) was immediately successful, but sequel *Polly* denied production. Wrote libretto for Handel's *Acis and Galatea* (1732), and opera *Achilles* (produced 1733). He died in London. His epitaph for himself is characteristic of his spirit:

> Life is a jest; and all things
>   show it.
> I thought so once; but now I
>   know it.

EDITION: *Works* ed. Geoffrey C. Faber (London and New York 1926). *The Letters of John Gay* ed. C. F. Burgess (Oxford and New York 1966).
REFERENCES: Sven M. Armens *John Gay: Social Critic* (New York 1954 and London 1955). William Irving *John Gay: Favorite of the Wits* (Durham, N.C. and Cambridge, England, 1940). Oliver Warner *John Gay* (London and New York PB 1964).

GENTILE DA FABRIANO (real name Gentile di Niccolò di Giovanni Massi) (c.1370–1427). Italian painter. Born in Fabriano, trained in Lombardy. Important early works: *Madonna and Child* (1390–95, Staatliche Museen, Berlin) and a polyptych executed for Convento di Valle Romita in Fabriano (c.1400, Brera, Milan). In Venice by 1408, he was commissioned (1409) by government to paint frescoes (destroyed) in doges' palace. While there, he deeply influenced such painters as Pisanello and Jacopo Bellini, who became his pupil in Florence (1423). Worked in Brescia (1414–19), in Rome as papal painter to Martin V (1419), and in Siena (1420–21), then settled in Florence (1422–25), where he painted his two greatest surviving works, *Adoration of the Magi* (1423, Uffizi, Florence) and the Quaratesi altarpiece (1425), which is now broken up: its central panel, *Madonna and Child with Angels,* is in the National Gallery, London, and its wings are in the Uffizi. Died in Rome, where he had been summoned to execute frescoed decoration of interior of St. John Lateran (completed by Pisanello; now lost). The last great examples in Italy of international Gothic, Gentile's works, elegant and aristocratic, with rich color and sumptuous garments, had special impact on Florentine painting.

REFERENCE: Bernard Berenson *Italian Painters of the Renaissance* (London and New York 1953, also PB).

GEORGE, Stefan (Anton) (July 12, 1868 – Dec. 4, 1933). German poet. Born Büdesheim, Germany. From an early age interested in experimenting with and learning languages, classical as well as modern. From 1888 visited London, Paris, and Spain; from 1890 Denmark and Italy. First poems, *Hymns* (1890), influenced by symbolists; also he was first to translate into German poems of Mallarmé, Baudelaire, Rimbaud, and others of the period. The pilgrimage of the poet, solitary, exalted, towards aesthetic realization is the theme of *Pilgrimages* (1891); man and woman in nature that of *The Year of the Soul* (1897). *The Tapestry of Life and Songs of Dream and of Death*

(1899) and *The Seventh Ring* (1907), concerning the poet's sacred mission, are considered his greatest works. Other important volumes: *Algabal* (1892) and *Kingdom Come* (1928). George's dedication to his art, his linguistic inventiveness, his originality had far-reaching influence and created a following known as the George Circle. He died near Locarno, Switzerland.

TRANSLATION: *Poems by Stefan Anton George Rendered into English* tr. Carol North Valhope and Ernst Morwitz (New York 1943 and London 1944).
REFERENCES: Cecil Maurice Bowra *The Heritage of Symbolism* (London and New York 1943, also PB). G. R. Urban *Kinesis and Stasis: A Study in the Attitudes of Stefan George and His Circle to the Musical Arts* (The Hague 1962). Peter Viereck *Dream and Responsibility: Four Test Cases of the Tension Between Poetry and Society* (Washington, D.C. 1953).

GÉRARD, Baron François Pascal Simon (May 4, 1770 – Jan. 11, 1837). French painter. Born Rome; his father was French. Brought to France at the age of ten, he became pupil of Jacques Louis David (1786), through whose influence he was named member of Revolutionary Tribunal (1793). Reputation made by portrait of *Isabey and His Daughter* (1795, Louvre, Paris), *Love and Psyche* (1798, Louvre). By 1800 had become official painter to Napoleon; continued as court painter under Louis XVIII, who made him a baron (1819). Gérard painted portraits of all the great figures of the first empire and Restoration; fine examples are *Empress Josephine* (1802, Malmaison) and *Madame Récamier* (1802, Petit Palais, Paris). His success was due as much to his personal charm as to his skill in painting. Best known of his historical works are *Battle of Austerlitz* (1810, Versailles) and *Entrance of Henry IV into Paris* (1815, Versailles). His style owes much to David. Died in Paris.

GÉRICAULT, (Jean Louis André) Théodore (Sept. 26, 1791 – Jan. 26, 1824). Born Rouen. Studied in Paris under Carle Vernet, historical and animal painter, then under neoclassicist Pierre Narcisse Guérin (1810–16), and soon began to reveal the qualities that made him the first French romantic painter. *Mounted Officer of the Imperial Guard* (Salon of 1812, Louvre, Paris) established his reputation at twenty-one, and was followed by *The Wounded Cuirassier* (Salon of 1814, Louvre). In Italy (1816–19), he was profoundly influenced by works of Michelangelo. Back in Paris, his *The Raft of Medusa* (Salon of 1819, Louvre) created a sensation with its heroic nude figures, surging dramatic motion, and authentic detail of a recent shipwreck that created a furor. Géricault accompanied his masterpiece on a traveling exhibition in England (1820–22), where he made series of lithographs of horses and London slum scenes, as well as watercolors and paintings of racing subjects. In his last years also painted a famous series of portraits of the insane. He died in Paris following a riding accident. The initiator of romanticism in French painting, Géricault inspired Delacroix, the realists and early impressionists.

REFERENCES: Denise Aimé-Azam *Mazeppa: Géricault et son temps* (Paris 1956). Klaus Berger *Géricault and His Work* (tr. Lawrence, Kan. 1955).

GERSHWIN, George (Sept. 26, 1898 – July 11, 1937). American composer. Born Brooklyn, of Jewish-Russian immigrant parents. Studied harmony under Rubin Goldmark and was employed in a music publishing house in New York. At eighteen published his first popular song, and at twenty-one the hit song *Swanee* (1919). Subsequently collaborated with his brother Ira (b. 1896), and together they produced successful musical comedies on Broadway, among them *Lady Be Good* (1924), *Funny Face* (1927), *Strike Up the Band* (1929), and *Of Thee I Sing* (1931), a political satire that was awarded the Pulitzer prize. *Rhapsody in Blue* (1924) and its sequel *Concerto in F* (1925) introduced a new genre of symphonic composition which worked jazz rhythms and melodic patterns into traditional forms. Last and finest work was the opera *Porgy and Bess*, based on novel *Porgy* by DuBose Heyward (1885–1940), who wrote the libretto. After its production (1935), Gershwin left New York to write film music in Hollywood, where he died. More than any other, Gershwin is responsible for having introduced jazz as a universal and sophisticated musical idiom.

REFERENCES: Gilbert Chase *America's Music from the Pilgrims to the Present* (New York 1955). David Ewen *A Journey to Greatness: The Life and Music of George Gershwin* (New York and London 1956).

GESUALDO, Don Carlo, prince of Venosa (c.1560 – Sept. 8, 1613). Italian composer. Born and died in Naples. Son of a nobleman, he probably studied music under Pomponio Nenna, musician at his father's court. Married his cousin Maria d'Avalos (1586), whom he had murdered with her lover (1590). Second marriage was to Leonora d'Este (1594), who outlived him. Gesualdo's fame rests on his six books of five-part madrigals. While the madrigals in the first four books (1594–96) display sound craftsmanship and conform to conventions of the time, those in the last two books (1611) are strikingly novel and expressive. Noted for their short, ejaculatory phrases breaking up the musical texture, arresting chromaticisms and other unique approaches to harmony, these madrigals show complete independence from contemporary musical developments. Gesualdo had no followers.

REFERENCE: Cecil Gray and Philip Heseltine *Carlo Gesualdo, Prince of Venosa, Musician and Murderer* (London and New York 1926).

GHIBERTI, Lorenzo (real name Lorenzo di Cione di Ser Buonaccorso) (1378 – Dec. 1, 1455). Italian sculptor. Born Florence. Trained as goldsmith under stepfather Bartolo di Michele, called Bartoluccio. Won (1402) competition for the north bronze doors of the Florentine baptistery, representing the life of Christ. After completion (1424), was commissioned to execute the east doors with scenes from the Old Testament (1425–52), known, from a comment of Michelangelo, as the "Gates of Paradise." Other works: bronze over-life-size statues of St. John the Baptist (1414–16), St. Matthew (1419–22), and St. Stephen (1425–29) all three at Or San Michele, Florence; shrine of the Three Martyrs (1426–28), shrine of St. Zenobius (1432–42) and two reliefs (1417–27) for the baptismal font in the baptistery at Siena. Ghiberti's *Commentarii* (written c.1447–48) is a pioneer work in art history. Died at Florence; buried in S. Croce.

REFERENCE: Richard Krautheimer and Trude H. Krautheimer *Lorenzo Ghiberti* (Princeton and Oxford 1956, reprinted 1971). Giorgio Vasari *Lives of the . . . Painters, Sculptors and Architects* (1550) tr. Gaston de Vere (10 vols. London 1912–15).

LORENZO GHIBERTI
BY ANNE MARKHAM

Among the founding fathers of the Renaissance — Brunelleschi, Donatello, Masaccio — Ghiberti's name does not appear. And yet he is representative of the period in a way that no genius can ever be who invents what his colleagues do not understand and employs a style that only later generations appreciate. The sources of his art were those which exerted their influence throughout the Renaissance: the monuments of Roman antiquity on the one hand, and Gothic art of the Italian trecento and the international style on the other. His concern with the depiction of a detailed yet coherent narrative located within a deep yet measurable setting was also the prime concern of most of Ghiberti's contemporaries and followers. And when Leon Battista Alberti enunciated the principles of artistic theory which remained operative until the sixteenth century, Ghiberti's models for the panels of the "Gates of Paradise" must have been uppermost in his mind.

The earliest surviving work by

Ghiberti is the relief he made for the competition announced in 1401 for the bronze doors of the Florentine baptistery. In it the *Sacrifice of Isaac* is surrounded by a quatrefoil frame which imitated, in size and shape, the field employed by Andrea Pisano in the first pair of baptistery doors executed between 1330 and 1336. The finely chased and highly polished ornamental details betray Ghiberti's early training as a goldsmith in the workshop of his stepfather: the jeweler's preference for the miniature in scale was a trait which persisted throughout Ghiberti's life. Ghiberti's treatment of the narrative emerges clearly from a comparison of his relief with the only other surviving competition panel, that of the architect Filippo Brunelleschi. While Brunelleschi's depiction of the story focused on the climax and was calculated to evoke the strongest possible reaction, Ghiberti preferred to concentrate on the personal relationships of his characters and seems to have been aware of psychological subtleties of which, in fact, the Bible is devoid. While Brunelleschi disposed his figures with such diagrammatic clarity that the order of events is immediately evident, Ghiberti shifted his protagonists from center in an effort to represent the scene as it might really have looked. The setting in Brunelleschi's relief, as inessential to the meaning of the story, is woefully out of scale and has the character rather of stage properties. Ghiberti's setting, on the other hand, encompasses his figures and suggests a space that continues beyond the borders of the relief. Indeed, even in his earliest essay, Ghiberti insinuated that the relief background is not an impenetrable flat plane but rather sky that envelops a receding landscape. The devices he used to this end include the traditional one of overlapping and the novel ones of causing figures to emerge diagonally from the background and the gradual flattening of the relief as forms recede into the background. This last device he was to develop most fully in the second pair of baptistery doors.

His first pair of bronze doors, with scenes from the life of Christ, occupied Ghiberti from 1403 to 1424. The greater number of the reliefs (probably those modeled before 1415) reveal the influence of the international style, of which Ghiberti may have been the first Florentine proponent and through whom the style gained wide currency. Within the richly anecdotal scenes figures gesticulate with animation. Poses are inevitably curvilinear and great swaths of drapery are wound about the bodies in order to create a calligraphic pattern of oscillating hemlines and syncopated reverse curves. Towards the end of the series Ghiberti's compositions become simpler and more tectonic. Classical influences are visible, and his greater technical command now enables the sculptor to suggest that air and space envelop even the component members of a crowd.

Ghiberti's commission for the second pair of doors, containing stories from the Old Testament, followed fast upon the first and occupied him for as long a time, though the modeling of the panels was concentrated within a period of about eight years (c.1429–1436/7). It was here that Ghiberti succeeded in making the relief ground seem to vanish, replaced by an atmosphere that causes forms to lose their detail and rotundity as they recede into space. In this he was aided by the changed format of the doors. The relief field, rectangular now instead of quatrefoil, was enlarged (with a consequent reduction in the number of panels to ten), allowing Ghiberti to deploy far vaster landscapes. The scale of the figures was greatly reduced, thus reinforcing the illusion of the spaciousness of the setting. Objects and figures diminish rapidly in scale, indicating location in distant planes, and the relief was gradually flattened until forms were hardly more than drawn upon the background. Whereas in the earlier pair of doors gilding was applied only to those portions of the relief which had been modeled, now the entire surface, background as well as modeled forms, is gilded. By this means Ghiberti eliminated that disturbing contrast between three-dimensional and flat surfaces accentuated by the selective gilding of the relief and created the impression of a single continuum of receding space to which the background, too, belonged.

For his illusion of deep space receding behind the borders of his relief, like a scene viewed through a window frame, Ghiberti was partially indebted to the technique of linear perspective discovered by Brunelleschi. Ghiberti's relief of *Isaac and Esau* contains one of the earliest instances of its use: the form in which it occurs here was subsequently canonized by Alberti in his *De Pictura* of 1435. An interior setting with a pavement divided into square tiles provides coordinates of length, height and depth which allow the spectator to measure the distances between objects in all directions. All figures and objects diminish in scale according to a fixed ratio determined by the presumed distance of the spectator from the relief. At the same time, the spectator's position opposite the center is fixed by the tendency of the receding planes of architecture to converge in the middle of the relief. The scale of the figures is proportionate to that of the architecture: the height of a figure equals three tiles. Thus both figures and architecture belong to a single

homogeneous space, every dimension of which is commensurable.

The figures of the "Gates of Paradise" manifest the Gothic predilection for graceful swaying movements and linear folds of swinging drapery that trail upon the ground combined with elements of antique inspiration that show Ghiberti's renewed contact with the monuments of Rome just prior to 1430. The tall but broad proportions of Ghiberti's figures are related to Pliny's accounts of Lysippus' athletes. Drapery folds diagram the anatomy and movement of figures precisely as they do in classical statuary. The later panels, such as *Joshua and the Battle of Jericho,* indicate the adaptation of a style of relief typical of the Column of Trajan with its layers of mechanically repetitive figures in settings, filling the entire surface of the relief. Numerous poses, facial expressions and gestures derive from Roman sarcophagi, but Ghiberti invariably assimilate them so thoroughly, ringing changes on conventional motifs and combining the borrowed with the invented, that his antique quotations are almost indistinguishable as such.

In addition to the two pairs of bronze doors, Ghiberti also executed three over-life-size bronze statues of saints for the niches of Or San Michele. The earliest of the three, *St. John the Baptist* (1414–16), is a prime example of the Gothic international style. The proportions of the figure are slender, the movement is an effortless sway which presupposes no organic articulation of the body, the linear folds fall in a cascade of catenary curves which conceal the body underneath. *St. Matthew* (1419–22) manifests the influence of Donatello's *St. Mark* (1411–13) in its classical contrapposto in which an unequal distribution of the body's weight provides the pose with an organic basis, as well as in its classical proportions and drapery. The unnaturally elongated *St. Stephen* (1425–29), finally, evinces a return to a *retardataire* Gothic style.

In his *Commentarii,* written between 1447 and 1448, Ghiberti assumed the role of humanist critic and theoretician of the arts. Not only does Ghiberti present us here with descriptions of antiquities and the first known account of the lives of several artists of the preceding century, but his book contains, as well, the first known autobiography written by an artist. In the enumeration of his achievements Ghiberti reveals a self-consciousness in regard to his own artistic goals and an awareness of the relation he bore to art of the distant and more recent past which was altogether new and was to differentiate thenceforth the Renaissance from the Middle Ages.

GHIRLANDAJO (real name Domenico di Tommaso Bigordi) (1449 – Jan. 11, 1494). Italian painter. Born and died in Florence. Trained by his father, a goldsmith, and by painter Alessio Baldovinetti. Active as fresco painter by early 1470's; first known works include three saints in church at Cercina and *Mater Misericordiae* and *Pietà* over Vespucci altar in church of Ognissanti, Florence (c.1423). Ghirlandajo's frescoes in chapel of S. Fina in the Collegiata at San Gimignano, Pieve (c.1475), show his characteristic traits: skillfully organized composition; naturalistic detail and background; and above all serenity and objectivity. After painting frescoes of *St. Jerome* and *Last Supper* (both 1480) in Ognissanti, went to Rome (1481) to help decorate Sistine Chapel; of his two frescoes there, only *Christ Calling the First Apostles* survives. Returned to Florence (1482), where he and his assistants — of whom there were many, including Michelangelo — executed last three major frescoes: *Roman Heroes* in Sala dei Gigli, Palazzo Vecchio (1482); scenes from life of St. Francis, together with

an altar panel of *Adoration of the Shepherds* (1485), in Sassetti chapel, S. Trinità (1482–86); scenes from lives of Virgin and St. John in choir of S. Maria Novella (1485–90). Among Ghirlandajo's many portraits, the best known is *Old Man with His Grandson* (Louvre, Paris).

REFERENCE: Bernard Berenson *The Italian Painters of the Renaissance* (London and New York 1953, also PB).

GIACOMETTI, Alberto (Oct. 10, 1901 – Jan. 11, 1966). Swiss sculptor and painter. Born Stampa near St. Moritz, son of a landscape painter. After studying at École des Arts et Métiers, Geneva (1919–20), and traveling in Italy (1920–21), settled in Paris, where for three years he was a student of Antoine Bourdelle. At first associated with the surrealists, he achieved recognition in early 1930's for such works as *The Palace at 4 A.M.* (1932–33, Museum of Modern Art, New York) in wood, wire, and string. In 1940's adopted the more personal style for which he is best known, creating fragile, elongated human figures such as *Man Pointing* (1947, Tate Gallery, London) and *Man Walking* (1947, Museum of Modern Art, New York). Received first prize for sculpture at Carnegie Institute (1961) and Venice Biennale (1962) and Guggenheim international award for painting (1964). Died at Chur, Switzerland. Among other famous works are *The Nose* (1947), *City Square* (1948), and *Chariot* (1950), the last two in Museum of Modern Art, New York.

REFERENCES: Jacques Dupin *Alberto Giacometti* (Paris 1963). James Lord *A Giacometti Portrait* (Garden City, N.Y. 1965, also PB).

✍

GIACOMETTI
BY CARLTON LAKE

Few artists in this dealer-dominated age of venality have remained as uncontaminated as Alberto Giacometti. No one was ever more single-minded. His background was traditional: his father was a respected Italian-Swiss impressionist painter, and Alberto came to Paris in 1922, after travel and study in Italy, to work in Bourdelle's atelier. He abandoned figurative sculpture in 1925 because, he said, "it was absolutely impossible for me to do a human head." For ten years his sculpture was abstract, the best that surrealism produced. Then, in 1935, he returned to figuration. When he began again to work from the model, he realized that what he looked at and what he turned out were two different things. The rest of his life was spent in trying to narrow that gap.

If painting or sculpture is a voyage of discovery, Giacometti was the tireless, perpetual traveler, always en route, never arriving. For the most part he worked slowly and almost never considered a work finished. "It's impossible to finish . . . The more you try to finish, the more you find yourself beginning all over again." Someone who worked from memory might make out, but since Giacometti worked from life, and life — for him, to a unique degree — is in continuous evolution, the model never looked the same from one moment to the next. So for every one painting or sculpture he kept he destroyed ten, to set out the next day, just as tirelessly, on the same unending voyage.

For him, as for Cézanne, the visual sensation was everything. The work of art was only a means to that end. But increasingly, art and its effort to capture life came to seem "a tragic and absurd attempt," because "reality is always behind a curtain one is trying to pull aside. It is an endless search; the harder one tries to find the answer, the more elusive it becomes."

When Giacometti first moved into the ramshackle, comfortless studio in the Rue Hippolyte-Maindron in 1927,

he felt it was too small. He planned to leave it as soon as he could find something better. But the longer he stayed, the bigger it seemed to grow. In a larger atelier the space he would use wouldn't be any greater than the space he had there, he decided. He became preoccupied with the infinity and extensibility of space. He made the metaphysical rationalization that the space around a still life arranged on a stool was the same space — just as infinite — as the space in a sweeping landscape. But he would not compromise with the physical consequences of that rationalization by adjusting the scale of his subjects to allow for the distance that separated him from them. He refused to reconstruct everything to theoretical life-size proportions: they were "not what you see." Life size to him was a meaningless concept. "It's your own size and you can't see yourself." And so the size of Giacometti's figures varied according to where he saw them. First his sculptures grew smaller, then elongated and thinner, occasionally shrinking to near-nothingness. He did parts of figures — a nose, an arm — then single figures, larger than life, standing or walking, and groups of tiny, rigid figurines or walking men on a single base. Toward the end of his life he came to believe there was no point in making figures larger than life size, because "the eye can't take in such big things all at once." That same reasoning lay behind his characteristic concentration on a single human figure or an isolated object. However fanciful the interpretations some have attached to this aspect of his work, Giacometti's own basis for it is clear: "When you're painting one person, you can't paint two at the same time, unless they're very small. Close up I can't draw you and someone else too. Either I look at you or I look at someone else. The same thing with a glass on a table."

Giacometti's continuing battle with classical art and its idealized forms led him to an obsessive concern for the substructure as the basis of portraiture. "If you want to construct a head the way you see it, you have to feel the structure of the skull . . . You have to understand the function of a nose. So at one moment your sculpture *is* the bone of the nose. If you want to paint the most beautiful girl in the world, that's what you have to work from. If not, you've got nothing."

His wife Annette and his brother Diego were his favorite models. Another girl posed for him nearly every evening for three years while he probed her skull and eye cavities, the bridge of her nose, working alternately on one canvas and then another, laying on thinly diluted black and white, blending to gray, with an occasional touch of ocher or mauve, then painting her out and starting fresh the next day when she no longer resembled the girl he had seen the day before. Despite the thinness of his washes, in his preoccupation with an eye or a kneecap he would sometimes build up a near-trompe-l'oeil effect in startling contrast with the somber sketchiness of other sectors of the canvas. In the end it was always an impossible goal. "Everything is impossible. And yet . . . I have all the more desire to work."

His chronic dissatisfaction with himself was not a pose. Nor was it saccharine humility. By his own admission Giacometti was neither modest nor humble. The job he had cut out for himself — setting down just what he saw, exactly as he saw it — seemed to him such a staggering one, he felt he had "to be a little stupid and pretentious to do anything at all. Just to have the courage to start, you need a touch of idiocy." When he began a head in sculpture, he never looked beyond the first step — his attempt to understand the function of the nose. "If I thought ahead to the job of getting as far as the ears or the back of the head, that would seem so immense I'd feel there was no hope of making it."

When Giacometti gave up abstraction in 1935, he knew he was working against the current of his time. Others may have abandoned "reality" for fear of looking old-fashioned or unoriginal, but he was completely indifferent to fashions and trends. "The closer you stick to what you *really* see, the more astonishing your work will be. Reality isn't unoriginal; it's just unknown." Giacometti's refusal to leave it behind while he ran after the will-o'-the-wisp of the future has given us one of the few completely original bodies of work in our time.

———

GIBBON, Edward (May 8, 1737 – Jan. 16, 1794). English historian. Born Putney, Surrey, of wealthy landed family. A sickly child, had little formal schooling. While briefly at Oxford became Roman Catholic, whereupon his father sent him to the care of a Calvinist minister in Lausanne, Switzerland. There (1753–58) he studied Latin and French literature, met Voltaire, became engaged to Suzanne Curchod. Father promptly summoned him home and forced him to break the engagement, but the pair remained lifelong friends (she became wife of French statesman Jacques Necker and mother of Madame de Staël). Gibbon served as captain in South Hampshire regiment (1759–63); his memoirs state that "the Captain of the Hampshire grenadiers . . . has not been useless to the historian of the Roman Empire." Published *Essai sur l'étude de la littérature* (1761). Conceived idea of *The History of the Decline and Fall of the Roman Empire* while in Roman forum during grand tour (1763–65). In six volumes (1776–88), it won immediate acclaim with the first volume and has become a classic, admired for its masterly composition, accuracy of detail, brilliant, ornate style and critical view of history. The famous chapters on the history of Christianity aroused a controversy and were defended by author in the *Vindication* (1779–81). Gibbon was a member of Dr. Johnson's Literary Club and served in Parliament (1774–83). From 1783 lived in Lausanne, and died while on a visit to London. His memoirs were first published by Lord Sheffield with other writings as *The Miscellaneous Works of Edward Gibbon, Esq.* (1796, enlarged edition 1814).

EDITIONS: *The History of the Decline and Fall of the Roman Empire* ed. John B. Bury (7 vols. London and New York 1896–1900). *Miscellaneous Works* ed. John B. Holroyd (Lord Sheffield) (5 vols. London 1814–15). *Private Letters of Edward Gibbon* ed. Rowland E. Prothero (2 vols. London 1896, 1 vol. New York 1907). *Letters* ed. Jane E. Norton (3 vols. London and New York 1956). *Gibbon's Journal to January 28, 1763* ed. David M. Low (London and New York 1929). *Le Journal de Gibbon à Lausanne 1763–1764* (Lausanne 1945) and *Gibbon's Journey from Geneva to Rome 1764* (London 1961) ed. Georges A. Bonnard.

REFERENCES: Sir Gavin DeBeer *Gibbon and His World* (London and New York 1968). David M. Low *Edward Gibbon* (London and New York 1937). Joseph W. Swain *Edward Gibbon the Historian* (London and New York 1966). George M. Young *Gibbon* (London 1932 and New York 1933).

GIBBONS, Grinling (Apr. 4, 1648 – Aug. 3, 1721). English woodcarver and sculptor. Born Rotterdam; father an Englishman. Settled at Deptford, England (c.1667), where diarist John Evelyn met him (1671) and brought his work to attention of Charles II and Sir Christopher Wren. Charles appointed him master carver in wood to the crown, a post he held under five monarchs. Besides carving woodwork in royal residences at Windsor, Kensington, Whitehall, and Hampton Court, Gibbons decorated many country houses, including Petworth, Sussex; Badminton, Gloucestershire; Burghley,

Northamptonshire; Hackwood, Hampshire; Kentchurch, Herefordshire; Luton Hoo, Bedfordshire. Wren employed him to carve choir stalls and other woodwork in St. Paul's Cathedral and other London churches. Gibbons's characteristic motifs are flowers, fruit, birds, fish, and musical instruments, exquisitely carved and beautifully arranged in groups and festoons. Also executed stone ornamentation at Blenheim, Hampton Court, and St. Paul's Cathedral; marble monuments in Westminster Abbey and other churches; bronze statues of Charles II (Chelsea Hospital) and James II (Trafalgar Square). Died in London.

REFERENCES: David Green *Grinling Gibbons: His Work as Carver and Statuary* (London and New York 1964). Henry Avray Tipping *Grinling Gibbons and the Woodwork of His Age* (London and New York 1914).

GIBBS, James (Dec. 23, 1682 – Aug. 5, 1754). British architect. Born Aberdeen, son of Catholic merchant. After receiving M.A. from Marischal College, Aberdeen, went to Rome (1703–1709), where he studied architecture under Carlo Fontana. Returned to London; was appointed to commission to build fifty new churches there (1713), of which ten were completed, including two of Gibbs's finest works, St. Mary-le-Strand (1714–17), which established his reputation and St. Martin's-in-the-Fields (1722–26), which served as model for churches in England and colonial America. Other celebrated works: Senate House, Cambridge (1722–30), Radcliffe Camera, the library, Oxford (1737–49). His style, considerably indebted to Christopher Wren's, reveals an Italian baroque influence and exemplifies the best of the English Georgian period. His buildings and his books, especially *A Book of Architecture* (1728), exerted great influence in England and America. Died a bachelor in London.

REFERENCES: Bryan D. G. Little *The Life and Work of James Gibbs 1682–1754* (London 1955). Sir John Summerson *Architecture in Britain: 1530–1830* (4th rev. and enlarged ed.

Harmondsworth and Baltimore PB 1963).

GIDE, André (Paul Guillaume) (Nov. 22, 1869 – Feb. 19, 1951). French writer. Born and died in Paris. Son of a law professor and raised in strict Protestantism. His first work, the poems *The Notebooks of André Walter* (1891), brought him into symbolist group with Mallarmé and Valéry. Went (1893) with a friend to North Africa, where he discovered a freedom and sensuality that he celebrated in another book of poems, *Les Nourritures terrestres* (*Fruits of the Earth*, 1897). Returned to France (1895) to attend his dying mother. Inherited considerable fortune, married his cousin Madeleine Rondeaux, and soon returned to Algeria. When his wife later discovered his predilection for homosexuality, she fled to the estate at Cuverville and Gide began extensive travels, publishing his first novel, *The Immoralist* (1902). Founded (1909) *La Nouvelle Revue Française*, which became the most influential literary publication in France, and in same year produced his first successful novel, *La Porte étroite* (1909, tr. *Strait Is the Gate* 1924), followed by the equally popular novel *Les Caves du Vatican* (1914, tr. *The Vatican Swindle* 1925). World War I temporarily ended publication of the magazine and Gide went to work in a refugee center. Published *La Symphonie pastorale* (1919, tr. *Two Symphonies* 1952) and returned to editing the *Revue*, but *Corydon* (1924), a defense of homosexuality, caused such a scandal that he sold his property and departed for French Equatorial Africa, leaving his masterpiece *Les Faux-Monnayeurs* (1926, tr. *The Counterfeiters* 1927) to be published in his absence. Traveled widely through Africa and wrote an exposé of colonial policies, *Travels in the Congo* (1927), which began his involvement with politics. Attracted to Marxism, he made a trip to Russia, but his disillusioned report, *Return from the U.S.S.R.* (1936), drew fire from leftist critics. Subsequent controversy convinced him that an artist should stay free of current problems, and in World War II he remained quietly in Cannes. Awarded Nobel prize (1947). Died in Paris. Other important works include *The Journals of André Gide* (1939, 1944, and 1950); plays, including *Oedipus* (1931); critical studies, including *Pretexts* (1903), *Dostoevsky* (1923), *Imaginary Interviews* (1943), and *A Definition of Poetry* (1947); and *Correspondence* with Francis Jammes (1948) and with Paul Claudel (1949).

REFERENCES: Wallace Fowlie *André Gide: His Life and Art* (New York 1965, also PB). Albert J. Guerard *André Gide* (Cambridge, Mass. and London 1951, also PB). Justin O'Brien *Portrait of André Gide: A Critical Biography* (New York and London 1953). George D. Painter *André Gide: A Critical Biography* (London and New York 1968).

GILBERT, Sir William Schwenck (Nov. 18, 1836 – May 29, 1911). English humorist and dramatist. Born London, son of William Gilbert (1804–1890), surgeon and novelist. Educated at Ealing and at King's College, London (B.A. London University, 1857). Became clerk in Privy Council Office (1857–61), then used a legacy to study law; called to the bar (1863), but practiced little. Contributed (from 1861) comic verses to *Fun*, signing himself "Bab"; these verses were collected as *Bab Ballads* (1869 and 1873). First dramatic production, *Dulcamara*, a burlesque (1866), was followed by series of light pieces and Victorian melodramas of little interest today. Married Lucy Blois Turner (1867). Famous collaboration with composer Sir Arthur Sullivan began with *Thespis* (1871); among their operettas are *Trial by Jury* (1875), *H.M.S. Pinafore* (1878), *The Pirates of Penzance* (1880), *Patience* (1881), *Iolanthe* (1882), *The Mikado* (1885), *Ruddigore* (1887), *The Yeomen of the Guard* (1888), *The Gondoliers* (1889). From 1881, these works were produced at Savoy Theatre, built for them by impresario Richard D'Oyly Carte (1844–1901). Following a business disagreement (1890), Gilbert and Sullivan produced only two more operettas, *Utopia Limited* (1893) and *The Grand Duke* (1896). Gilbert continued thereafter to write plays and libretti.

Knighted (1907). Died at Harrow Weald, Middlesex.

REFERENCES: Sidney Dark and L. K. Rowland-Brown *W. S. Gilbert: His Life and Letters* (New York 1923 and London 1924). A. H. Godwin *Gilbert and Sullivan: A Critical Appreciation of the Savoy Operas* (1926, reprinted Port Washington, N.Y. 1969). Isaac Goldberg *The Story of Gilbert and Sullivan, or the Complete Savoyard* (New York 1928 and London 1929). Raymond Mander and Joe Mitchenson. *A Picture History of Gilbert and Sullivan* (London 1962 and Chester Springs, Pa. 1965). Hesketh Pearson *Gilbert and Sullivan: A Biography* (London and New York 1935). Hesketh Pearson *Gilbert: His Life and Strife* (London and New York 1957).

✎

W. S. GILBERT
BY FELICIA LAMPORT

The name William Schwenck Gilbert is not always familiar today, but its bearer made a considerable fortune and reputation as the author of such works as *The Wicked World, The Happy Land,* and a *Pygmalion and Galatea* that alone earned him £40,000. Preceded by "W. S.," Mr. Gilbert becomes more familiar; followed by "and Sullivan" he springs into universal recognition as the author of *The Mikado, The Pirates of Penzance, Iolanthe,* and the rest of the fourteen delightfully humorous operettas that have been keeping audiences in stitches and managers in riches for a century.

Gilbert would far rather have had his reputation rest on his dramas, but to his lifelong frustration he was taken seriously only as a humorist. His solemn works were laughed at: "I called it *Gretchen* and the public called it rot," he said ruefully of one of them. Perhaps this frustration accounted for the malevolence that lurked like a dark shark under the bright waters of his "innocent merriment." More probably the discrepancy was inherent in his character: he was a mass of contradictions and contrasts — his own strangest paradox.

It is hard to understand why a man born handsome, gifted and in comfortable circumstances should have been a cantankerous curmudgeon from the start. Gilbert quarreled with everyone, critics, associates, friends and neighbors, holding a grudge like an amulet, and starting lawsuits at the slightest provocation, and he provoked easily. It seems inexplicable that such a fractious man should have achieved a long, highly successful collaboration with his complete opposite, charming, popular, easygoing Arthur Sullivan.

Fate showed wry ingenuity by starting and ending Gilbert's life with dramatic paradoxes. The first came in his infancy when he was kidnapped from his nursemaid by a pair of plausible brigands and returned unharmed for a ransom of £25, endowed with a lode of plot material that was to net him hundreds of times the investment. The second came at seventy-four when Gilbert died with ironic heroism while rescuing a girl he was teaching to swim from drowning in his own pond. The years in between were relatively undramatic: a progression from small failures to large triumphs, with each failure profitably ticked off in future lyrics. As a young man he spent four wretched years as a government clerk before a small legacy enabled him to turn to the bar, where his career was brief and virtually briefless, but it was to pay handsome fees in *Trial by Jury* and such lyrics as the Lord Chancellor's memorable:

The Law is the true embodiment
Of everything that's excellent.
It has no kind of fault or flaw,
And I, my Lords, embody the
Law.

While he was still at the bar he spent his ample spare time writing and selling humorous verses with his own bizarre illustrations. These *Bab Ballads* that made his name were vastly entertaining excursions into the rational lunacy that was to make Gilbert the eponym of topsy-turvydom. They were flawless in verse technique, complex and ingenious in rhyme, satiric, sadistic, whimsical and grotesque. All of Gilbert was in them, and much of the later Gilbert came out of them as he plagiarized them unabashedly throughout his theatrical career. This began while he was still in his ballad days with a series of burlesques that he turned out with extraordinary speed and dexterity, at first quite willing to conform to the crude, vapid standards of the Victorian stage in order to succeed. But it was not long before the satiric brilliance of his comic operas began to transform the English theatre, blowing it out of its century of doldrums into a current lively enough for Wilde and Shaw.

Gilbert spent his professional life deriding Victorian ideals and adhering to them strictly. As a thorough Victorian prude, he barred all hint of sex from his work and treated even romance with coy gentility. But if his humor was never blue, it was often black. He approached physical violence with uninhibited relish and a kind of macabre gusto:

> *Now though you'd have said that*
> *head was dead*
> *(For its owner dead was he),*
> *It stood on its neck with a smile*
> *well-bred*
> *And bowed three times to me!*

His plots were compendia of incongruities, defying gravity by making steely shafts of satire rest on fluffballs of fantasy. He was equally contradictory in style. His lyrics were natural, airy, graceful, and marvelously attuned to song; his prose was stilted, forced, ponderously periphrastic — quite unspeakable. Happily there was little of it, barely enough to provide breathing space between prodigious numbers of prodigiously funny songs. He knew his strengths and combined them skillfully into a formula that mocked the stolid Victorian world by setting it on its ear, and made the Victorians love it.

Mockery, however, was not enough for Gilbert, who saw himself as a reformer, teaching with a quip and rousing with his gilded "philosophic pill." But since he attacked without passion or involvement and lacked a positive program, his criticism, however brilliant, was essentially negative, serving more to amuse than arouse:

> *When in that House M.P.'s divide*
> *If they've a brain and cerebellum,*
> *too,*
> *They've got to leave that brain out-*
> *side*
> *And vote just as their leaders tell*
> *'em to.*

Here a true reformer might have pressed on to action, but Gilbert went into reverse, continuing with:

> *But then the prospect of a lot*
> *Of dull M.P.'s in close proximity*
> *All thinking for themselves is what*
> *No man can face with equanimity.*

His arrows nicked every profession and every class from *polloi* to peer, but they seemed fired more for the sport than the target. His shafts were often aimed at pomposity, which was admirably logical, and even more often at plump middle-aged women, which was somewhat puzzling. His mother? Queen Victoria? The problem may be one for psychiatrists, but plump middle-aged Victoria must have had her own opinion, which may account for her knighting Sullivan and ignoring Gilbert at a time when the two were a single household word to the public. Perhaps she had other reasons as well: Sullivan's friends in the peerage were pressing him to dissolve the union. But Sullivan's extraordinary tact and patience with his collaborator held the team together for two decades, for which posterity may well be grateful. Individually the two men had pleasant but ephemeral talents; together they became a single comic genius far greater than the sum of their separate potentials. And it was Gilbert, whose words came first in every sense, who literally called the tune, setting the level that best suited their common abilities if not their separate aspirations. He may not have been the reformer he hoped to be or the Victorian Aristophanes his more effusive devotees have called him, but his superb satiric eye has made his happy impertinences pertinent wherever and whenever the ridiculous exists.

GIORGIONE (real name Giorgio or Zorzi or Zorzo da Castelfranco). (c.1477–1510). Italian painter. Born Castelfranco; very little known of his life. A pupil of Giovanni Bellini, and himself a master of the Venetian school, he exerted powerful influence on early sixteenth-century painting in Venice and Emilia, especially on Titian and Sebastiano del Piombo. Giorgione died of the plague in Venice. Seven paintings of certain attribution survive: *Laura* (1506, Kunsthistorisches Museum, Vienna), *Three Philosophers* (also Vienna), *The Tempest* (Accademia, Venice), fragment of fresco from façade of Fondaco dei Tedeschi (1508, Venice), *Self-Portrait as David with Head of Goliath* (Herzog Anton Ulrich Museum, Brunswick), *Venus and Cupid*, completed by Titian (Gemäldegalerie, Dresden), *Madonna with Two Saints* (S. Liberale, Castelfranco).

REFERENCES: Ludwig Baldass and Gunther Heintz *Giorgione* (tr. New York and London 1965). George M. Richter *Giorgio da Castelfranco, Called Giorgione* (Chicago and Cambridge, England, 1937).

✍

GIORGIONE
BY JUERGEN SCHULZ

Giorgione is among those artists who, in a strikingly short life, under circumstances that remain largely unknown to us, effected a fundamental revolution in the history of painting. We know that he studied with Giovanni Bellini in the 1490's, as somewhat later did Titian and Sebastiano; that he was unable to set himself up independently for many years and was probably unappreciated, except by younger artists such as the latter two; and that by the time of his death from the plague in 1510 he had produced only a very few works, most of which are lost today. Yet not a single Venetian remained unaffected by his art, his influence soon spread to other north Italian centers, and through the changes he worked in the style of Venetian painting of the early sixteenth century his impact determined the later course of European painting.

The combination of obscurity and brilliance has meant that he was soon romanticized. We hear (from Vasari) that he was a great lover, played the lute and sang divinely. Carlo Ridolfi, biographer of the Venetian painters, tells the usual tale of jealousy toward the young man on the part of his master, and paints Giorgione's beginnings as a period of struggle and poverty. His end he explains by an amorous adventure: Giorgione caught the plague from his mistress, from whom he could not part.

Also our understanding of his art has been tainted by the tendency to fabulize. Through the testimony of contemporaries and near-contemporaries, we have record of seventeen compositions that he produced, six of which survive. But Ridolfi, whose book of lives appeared in 1648, lists some ninety works by Giorgione. The Giorgione retrospective held at Venice in 1955 exhibited sixty-four paintings as works of the artist that had managed to survive into the present day. The baffling obscurity of many of his paintings, which represent unconventional religious subjects, or unsolved allegories and unfamiliar mythological scenes, led in the nineteenth century to the improbable view that he painted meaningless idylls in an anachronistic spirit of *l'art pour l'art*.

Only the six surviving compositions noted above, together with an altarpiece vouched for by a pedigree of great antiquity, can actually be regarded as authenticated works by Giorgione. In chronological order they are: an altarpiece of *The Madonna with Two Saints* (Castelfranco), the so-called *Portrait of Laura* and *Three Philosophers* (both at Vienna), *The Tempest* and remains of some façade frescoes (Venice), *David with the Head of Goliath* (Brunswick) and *Venus and Cupid* (Dresden). They are quite enough to show us what Giorgione meant for his contemporaries.

The altarpiece, unlike the altarpieces of Giorgione's master and other Venetians of the fifteenth century, makes no use of an architectural setting, but shows the holy personages grouped around a steep throne that stands inexplicably in a spacious landscape, washed by the soft, moist air of the Venetian mainland. The floor slopes upward; the figures, with swimming faces and luminously colored draperies, stand and sit in moody self-absorption, their limbs relaxed or gently demonstrating some inner movement of the mind.

The Tempest, a puzzle of a picture because it represents an undecipherable subject in two different ways — in a first version, visible in X-rays, as two nude women in a landscape, one of them suckling a child, and in the final version as a soldier and the same nude nursing mother — reverses the traditional relationship between landscape and figure. The figures are small and loosely placed into the setting, not architecturally firm and standing before the landscape, as was the norm in earlier Venetian painting. Large trees frame the scene, a meandering brook wanders from the front to the rear, the sky is heavy with clouds and streaked with lightning, which reflects a sulphur yellow on the buildings in the back. The ensemble has a remarkable softness and instability. No line is really straight, no outline firm, all the forms are in movement and the colors shift and shimmer with reflections.

The *Laura* shows the same vision brought to bear on the traditional subject of the portrait. It is a new type of composition, unlike the fifteenth-century Venetian portrait bust with its architectural base (usually a parapet) and stable, timeless forms. In this case the body provides its own base in the form of a relaxed arm, muffled in soft draperies and placed casually at the bottom edge of the picture. The bust is clothed in indistinctly outlined stuff and fur, the collar falling open negligently, a white veil moving in a serpentine from behind the neck across the chest. The whole soft body is embedded in a limpid atmosphere and set before a spray of laurel leaves.

In the other certain works and those

that can be reasonably connected with them, we see Giorgione striving to loosen the tectonic order of inherited formulae, and to translate the immutable and intellectualized order of his predecessors' art into something shifting, unstable, laden with mood and atmosphere. This is the meaning of his abandonment of architecture, his uncertain outlines, his loose and swaying figure poses, large and moving natural forms, and flaming colors.

The lesson was not lost on his contemporaries. The young Titian, after an early start with compositions aiming at the monumental order of Bellini's late work, quickly fell under the spell of Giorgione. For a short space of time he produced paintings so Giorgionesque in mood and style that, except for a certain grandiosity of forms and a distinctive, open and creamy handling of the paint, they could be easily mistaken for Giorgione's own. A case in point is the famous *Concert Champêtre* in the Louvre, which is quite unlike Giorgione in its quality of pigment, but bafflingly close in forms and mood.

Titian's style underwent many revolutions during his long life, but he never forgot Giorgione's vision of a unified nature, shimmering in a warm light, swaying in an invisible current of air, touched by feeling of a quite different complexity and profundity than the constructed world of previous generations. Through Titian, and his immense output of paintings of every class, Giorgione's painterly ideals became a part of the European tradition of painting. They animated contemporary painters of northern Italy, such as Correggio, baroque and rococo painters throughout Europe, from Rubens to Watteau in the north and Domenico Feti through the Guardi brothers in the south, and were still a potent force in the nineteenth century, at the moment of the birth of impressionism.

GIOTTO DI BONDONE (1266/7 – Jan. 8, 1337). Italian painter. Born Colle di Vespigniano, near Florence. Probably studied under both the Florentine Cimabue and the Roman Cavallini. Active in Rome, Padua, Arezzo, Rimini, Assisi, Naples, and Florence, enjoyed widespread fame, and was cited as the most important artist in Italy by Dante, Boccaccio, and Petrarch. Invited to work for King Robert of Naples (1329–32). As official architect of Florence (appointed 1334), he designed the campanile of the Florence cathedral. Died in Florence. Few of Giotto's works can be documented or clearly dated. Extant, undisputed fresco cycles: *Life of the Virgin* (1303–1306, Arena chapel, built for Enrico Scrovegni, Padua), *Life of St. Francis* (Bardi chapel), and *Lives of St. John the Baptist and St. John the Evangelist* (Peruzzi chapel), both in S. Croce, Florence. Frescoes in Upper and Lower Church of S. Francisco in Assisi probably not by Giotto. The Ognissanti *Madonna* (Uffizi, Florence) and the *Crucifix* in the Arena chapel are the only panel paintings universally accepted as Giotto's.

REFERENCES: Eugenio Battisti *Giotto: A Biographical and Critical Study* (Cleveland and London 1960). Millard Meiss *Giotto and Assisi* (New York 1960, also PB). Leonetto Tintori and Eve Borsook *Giotto: The Peruzzi Chapel* (New York 1965). John White *The Birth and Rebirth of Pictorial Space* (London and New York 1957).

GIOTTO

BY ANNE MARKHAM

For the early writers who recorded Giotto's art, the significance of his achievement lay in his capture of the appearance of reality. In the *Decameron* Boccaccio wrote: "The genius of Giotto was of such excellence that there was nothing [produced] by nature . . . which he did not depict by means of stylus, pen or brush with such truthfulness that the result seemed to be not so much similar to one of her works as a work of her own. Wherefore the human sense of sight was often deceived by his works and took for real what was only painted." Such lines reveal to what extent Boccaccio's criticism was conditioned, not by looking, but by reading Pliny's description of the development of ancient art. Artists of succeeding generations, however, such as Masaccio and Michelangelo, perceived an artist who sacrificed the appearance of the real world for the sake of the moral significance of his religious narrative. Though Giotto may no longer seem to us solely responsible for having "restored to light the art [of painting] which for many centuries had been buried," he is surely the father of that abstract and monumental style of religious painting that leads to the Brancacci chapel and the Sistine ceiling.

The earliest extant paintings of Giotto are the frescoes, dated between 1303 and 1306, which decorate the interior of the Scrovegni chapel at Padua. Small and simple in plan — a rectangle crowned at the eastern end by a polygonal apse — and free of any architectural articulation but six windows in the southern wall, the chapel was evidently intended from its foundation to be embellished with frescoes. Indeed, the entire surface of the nave is covered with thirty-nine scenes from the lives of the Virgin and Christ, while a representation of *The Last Judgment* fills completely the west wall above the entrance. The comprehensiveness of the program recalls French Gothic cathedrals which present an encyclopedic visualization of Christian doctrine, on the exterior in sculpture, and in the interior in stained glass windows.

The technique is a typically Italian one, used for decoration of palaces and churches in the thirteenth through the seventeenth centuries. In the fresco technique the painter applies water-soluble pigments to a freshly plastered surface. As the plaster dries, the pigments are absorbed and incorporated into the very substance of the wall. Since plaster dries quickly, the technique depends upon rapid execution. It also requires confident draftsmanship, for the sketch of the composition, executed on the underlying layer of rough plaster in a red paint called sinopia, is covered by the freshly laid plaster that represents the extent of the day's work.

Typical of Giotto's narrative is its concentration on the essential. The number of bystanders is reduced to the minimum necessary to the tale. Details of costumes, properties, landscape or architecture rarely intrude. The few figures out of which the narrative is constructed are large in scale and placed at the front of the illusionistic space. They stand upright, rarely move; facial expressions are restrained: figures seem to think rather than to act, and expression "becomes the projection of an abiding inner state rather than of a momentary impulse." Hence the climax of an event is avoided: for the instantaneousness of a climax is substituted the eternity of conception or effect, as in *The Last Supper,* where Christ has long ago announced that He will be betrayed. In *The Raising of Lazarus* several moments are combined: the pleading of Martha and Mary, Christ commanding Lazarus to rise, and the accomplishment of the miracle. Thus the meaning, not the drama, is accentuated. The uniformity of figure type, the simplicity of costume, and the repetitiousness of pose imply a universality of meaning that is not contradicted by the architectural and landscape backgrounds which, abstract in the extreme, do not betray a specific time or place. Meaning is elucidated through the isolation of the protagonist, hierarchic scaling, explicit gestures. Motifs within the setting draw the spectator's attention to the focus of the event.

The weight and monumental proportions of the figures become a physical corollary of their moral stature as actors in a universally valid drama. Abundant and regularly falling draperies give figures an approximately conical shape and folds invariably falling to the ground endow figures with the stability of any object whose base is broad and center of gravity is low. Beneath the drapery the body disappears: it was not until the fifteenth century that out of the uniform columnar mass of the figure, body and drapery were to differentiate themselves. Yet in a way unprecedented, Giotto has conveyed the three-dimensionality of his figures on a two-dimensional surface. In part this is accomplished through light's gradual metamorphosis into shadow as the surface of a figure curves away from the path of light. In part it is accomplished by the ascending curves of transverse folds, hems, belts or necklines which suggest a continuation of the volume of the figure beyond the visible boundary of its silhouette.

Architectural settings inhabit space as aggressively as figures. Where the solid figures displace space, the architecture creates discrete three-dimensional units enclosing space, a plasticity in reverse where the shell, rather than the contents, is depicted. Wherever possible, structures have overhangs, roofs, balconies, porticoes. Even when represented from outside, buildings are penetrated, so that their space-containing function is made explicit.

In Giotto's frescoes the architectural metaphor is omnipresent. Figures located on a plane parallel to the picture plane and standing erect span the width of the field with an almost equal density. Heads arranged isocephalically divide the picture horizontally at approximately its midpoint. Crowds of figures are confined by rectangular boundaries. The source of such tectonic compositions is surely Roman imperial reliefs such as the Aurelian reliefs from the Arch of Constantine. But Giotto borrowed motifs as well as compositions from antique art: the figure of Joachim returning to his flocks derives from the drunken Dionysus on a neo-Attic crater in the Camposanto, Pisa, while John the Evangelist in the *Pietà* comes from an antique sarcophagus with the legend of Meleager.

Towards the end of his career, Giotto frescoed two adjacent chapels in the Florentine church of S. Croce. In what is probably the later of the two, the Bardi chapel, Giotto painted six scenes from the life of St. Francis plus a scene of the *Stigmatization* over the entrance arch. The Peruzzi chapel contains three scenes from the life of John the Baptist on the left and the life of John the Evangelist on the right. Here the technique confirms what the style suggests — the widespread participation of assistants. Unlike the Scrovegni chapel, the paintings in the two chapels were largely done *a secco;* that is, after the plaster had already dried. Painting on dry plaster permitted the artist to sketch the design on the final layer — an unnecessary procedure if the master intended to execute the entire work himself. The narrative is less concise, the attention of subsidiary figures is less rigidly directed toward the central focus. Where at Padua stories are told entirely in terms of figures, and settings function like stage properties, here settings carve out a deep and homogeneous space which encompasses entire groups. The tectonic composition has been relaxed and voids predominate over solids. Figures have become smaller in scale, taller in proportion, and their movements contain the implications of a sway.

A definition of Giotto's style as derived from the frescoes of the Scrovegni chapel makes it evident that, early literary sources notwithstanding, the frescoes of the life of St. Francis in the Upper Church at Assisi painted shortly before 1307 cannot be by Giotto. Indeed, stylistic analysis reveals that the greater number of paintings attributed to Giotto by Renaissance and modern art historians, including some inscribed with Giotto's name, are in fact works of his assistants. About the attribution to the master himself of the *Crucifix* in the Scrovegni chapel and the *Madonna and Child Enthroned* in the Uffizi from the church of Ognissanti in Florence, however, there is no dispute. In the latter panel the massive Madonna, hieratically composed, sitting erect, viewed frontally, posed almost symmetrically, does not so much as reveal awareness of her Son's existence. Majestically aloof, she is no human mother who bestows intimate caresses on an infant son. Rather, she is the eternal Mother of God in her divine epiphany, already assumed to a resplendent heaven, seated upon an imaginary throne and adored by legions of saints and angels.

GIRAUDOUX, (Hippolyte) Jean (Oct. 29, 1882 – Jan. 31, 1944). French dramatist and novelist. Born Bellac, Haute-Vienne. Graduated from École Normale Supérieure in Paris, spent year in Mu-

nich (1905) and another at Harvard (1907), and traveled extensively until 1910. Having written stories, he published (1909) first book *Les Provinciales*, a collection, and entered Ministry of Foreign Affairs (1910). Served four years as soldier in World War I, continued to write. Having established himself as a novelist (*Suzanne et le Pacifique*, 1921, tr. 1923; *Juliette au pays des hommes*, 1924; and others), he turned to drama with *Siegfried* (1928). Among its highly successful followers were *Amphitryon 38* (1929, tr. 1938), *La Guerre de Troie n'aura pas lieu* (1935, tr. *Tiger at the Gates* 1955), *Ondine* (1939, tr. *Undine* 1954), and *La Folle de Chaillot* (1943, tr. *The Madwoman of Chaillot* 1947). Appointed director of information for the French Republic (1939), he continued to serve in this capacity for Vichy government after 1940. Died in Paris.

REFERENCES: Robert Cohen *Giraudoux: Three Faces of Destiny* (Chicago 1969). Donald Inskip *Jean Giraudoux: The Making of a Dramatist* (New York and London 1958). Laurent Le Sage *Jean Giraudoux: His Life and Works* (University Park, Pa. 1959).

✐

JEAN GIRAUDOUX
BY HAROLD CLURMAN

Jean Giraudoux's writing has often been described and sometimes denigrated as "precious." Closer examination proves that Giraudoux was gnawed by pessimism. He kept his eyes free of tears by the grace of his artifice. He believed in the sunniness of France and hoped that the teeming romanticism of Germany (where he received part of his education) might remain pacific. He was betrayed by France and — so it is rumored — put to death by the Germans.

He was an artist and a functionary of the foreign office. Politics was his profession, writing his pleasure, literature his realm of purity, politics his compromise. Giraudoux's work is the projection of his soul's battlefield, where the engaged forces fought each other to a standstill while Giraudoux observed the event with gently ironic assent. As he contemplated his own dilemma so he saw life itself. In several of his later plays it is not easy to determine whether Giraudoux is spinning a magic robe of glowing gossamer or a glamorous shroud.

The novels and short stories which announce the writer's entrance onto the literary scene are chiefly charming paeans to living in its most domestic or "provincial" aspects and even more to the enchantment of language. His pages are scented with the names of flowers. We find in them also a constant gamboling of animals of every breed. Similes and metaphors abound. They are sometimes used for their effect as sound as much as for their sense. The tone is flirtatiously facetious. Under his pen France becomes the land of exquisitely intimate pleasures.

Though humor and wit are always present, the intoxication with words occasionally threatens to turn the reader's elation into irritation. There are long streams of gnomic playfulness which seem to possess an existence of their own apart from any human guidance. Though one senses a persistent shrewdness in them we wonder whether these flights foreshadow the automatic writing of the surrealists or simply constitute a dilettante's mirage.

Such passages frequently render Giraudoux's novels static. We find their frothy verbiage again in his plays, but in them the phenomenon is mitigated by the fact of dialogue: different voices vary the monotony of the flow. And beside Giraudoux there stood Louis Jouvet, who knew how to lend stage action to the spate of speech.

Giraudoux was "saved" by the theatre and by something which happened to him at about the age of thirty-six. An inner tension revealed itself, present even in his blither comedies. In *Siegfried*, his first play, which gives evidence of the temperamental resistance and attraction between the French and German strains within him, he speaks of "the inward duel which is destroying him" apropos of his French protagonist who through a wound inflicted in war finds himself a German.

This duel was the struggle between his roots in a radiant and rational French hedonism and the foreboding of doom, some destructive force immanent in the universe itself — the worm in the apple! The contest becomes a recurrent theme: purity and its nemesis and sometimes purity as nemesis. "One has to fear everything — or nothing," Jupiter says in Giraudoux's *Amphitryon 38* — a play which smiles at the unaccountability of life. But Giraudoux was rarely able to free himself of fear, while several of his plays suggest fear of everything.

Intermezzo (*The Enchanted*) pictures an idealistic girl in love with the natural freedom which is life's fairest promise. Here yearning and hope are crushed by the tradesmen and functionaries of a small French town. One of the townsfolk humbles himself before the corpse of the girl's dream (represented as a Ghost) and is asked why he does so. "I apologize," the man replies, "because in this world the truth is always vulgar. I apologize because life has no spirit and death no dignity. Because the illusions of youth are illusions, and age is generous only in destruction. I apologize because the Inspector [the philistine] is always right and the Ghost is false." Yet in the last act the girl is persuaded that wisdom consists in marriage to the Ghost's "double" (a young fellow citizen) and the enjoyment of little village blessings. Sensibly, she accepts the compromise with "the facts of life."

The pure are supremely admirable, but if they insist on remaining pure they usually cause havoc and are themselves destroyed — a fate they may deserve! In Giraudoux's *Electra* we read that "life is a failure, but all the same it is a fine thing, life," and in the posthumous play *For Lucrèce* (*Duel of Angels*) Lucile dies to preserve her purity. Throughout the play she appears as a rather unsympathetic character who merits mockery; yet a procuress standing over Lucile's dead body apostrophizes: "Purity's not for this world, but every ten years we get a gleam of it . . . They [those who failed to understand Lucile] will suddenly see it for the holy thing it was, and they will feel it reproach them . . . What struck you down was being made aware of man's stupidity, and coarseness and wickedness." The water sprite in *Ondine* cannot endure in the worldly court, nor can her princely consort survive without her.

Hector in *The Trojan War Will Not Take Place* (*Tiger at the Gates*) does everything in his power to avoid war, but nature itself in the beautifully smiling and callous person of Helen brings it on, nature which here is equated with the "tiger": destiny. Judith in the play of that name slays Holofernes, the embodiment of the most enlightened paganism, because she can never again attain the ecstasy she has known during the night she has spent with him. But she finally yields to the bidding of the rabbis who demand that she declare that she killed Holofernes not, as she has said, for "love" but because he was the enemy of her people. In this way she sustains legend (history) and thus serves God's will. Legend in Girau-

doux's plays is both false and true, just as humanly appropriate compromise in life belies the absolute which is godlike.

A political conservative, Giraudoux could think of no remedy for the spoliation of his country by its own racketeers, crooked functionaries, pimps and bawds except in "fairy-tale" terms by having them all drowned in a sewer through the wiles of a mad countess with the aid of the poor and pure in heart, as we see in his enchanting *The Madwoman of Chaillot*.

The rigor of French classicism, which Giraudoux revered in Racine, was no longer possible for this troubled and cultivated heir of French clarity and light. They had darkened in the dusk of decadence between the First and Second World War at the moment Giraudoux was to meet his death. His sparkling plays had become the most honored of the period. They have been retrospectively seen as plays which furnished premonitions of the evil days to come — to which no one had given heed.

Giraudoux's language and his use of traditional patterns (Greek and Biblical) freed the French theatre from its boulevard prosiness. His plays influenced the next generation — Jean Anouilh for example — and left a heritage of his "blackness" to be cultivated by others in an entirely different vein, a blackness that is less well recognized than his effulgence, which still gladdens most of us and disconcerts a few.

GIRTIN, Thomas (Feb. 18, 1775 – Nov. 9, 1802). English painter. Born Southwark. After some instruction in drawing was apprenticed (1789–c.1791) to painter and engraver Edward Dayes. Worked as colorist in engraving shop of John Raphael Smith, where he met coworker J. M. W. Turner. The two made sketching trips and were also employed by connoisseur Thomas Monro to copy watercolors by J. R. Cozens, whose influence is clearly seen in Girtin's early work. Exhibited at Royal Academy from 1794. From 1796 date Girtin's mature watercolor landscapes, chiefly of northern England and Scotland, in which he achieved great breadth and expressiveness. Also introduced new watercolor techniques such as use of large brush and rough, absorbent paper, and the method of shading and tinting with the same colors instead of shading with black and gray. Among his finest works are *Kirkstall Abbey* (1800, British Museum, London) and *The White House at Chelsea* (1800, Tate Gallery, London). A 2000-foot panorama of London, *Eidometropolis* (1802), has been lost, but studies remain in British Museum. Died in London.

REFERENCES: Thomas Girtin and David Loshak *The Art of Thomas Girtin* (London 1954). Jonathan Mayne *Thomas Girtin* (Leigh-on-Sea 1949).

GISSING, George (Robert) (Nov. 22, 1857 – Dec. 28, 1903). English novelist. Born Wakefield, Yorkshire, into middle-class family. His brilliant academic career at Owens College, Manchester, ended with an unfortunate marriage to a Manchester girl (1875). After wretchedly failing as a journalist in America (1876–77), he returned to live in poverty in Manchester, where he made a second unhappy marriage (1890). His first novel of social realism, *Workers in the Dawn* (1880), was followed by twenty-one others, including *The Unclassed* (1884), *Demos* (1886), *The Nether World* (1889), *New Grub Street* (1891), perhaps his best-known work, based on personal experiences, and *The Private Papers of Henry Ryecroft* (1903). He also produced a travel book *By the Ionian Sea* (1901), the account of an Italian trip with his friend H. G. Wells (1897), and the perceptive *Charles Dickens: A Critical Study* (1898). He wrote of poverty and its effect upon the character with devastating bitterness, but his last years of travel and living in

southern France were relatively carefree. Died at St. Jean de Luz.

REFERENCES: Mabel C. Donnelly *George Gissing: Grave Comedian* (London and Cambridge, Mass. 1954). Jacob Korg *George Gissing: A Critical Biography* (Seattle 1963). Frank Swinnerton *George Gissing: A Critical Study* (London 1912, 3rd ed. Port Washington, N.Y. 1966).

GLACKENS, William James (Mar. 13, 1870 – May 22, 1938). American painter and illustrator. Born Philadelphia. Studied at Pennsylvania Academy of the Fine Arts there and did illustrations for local newspapers. After studying in Paris (1895), worked as illustrator for New York newspapers and magazines. Persuaded by Robert Henri to devote full time to painting and became one of The Eight, with John Sloan, George Luks, and Everett Shinn. This group, inspired by Thomas Eakins and under leadership of Henri, set out to found a school of native American style; they put on a revolutionary exhibition (1908) and later became the "ashcan school." Glackens more than the others revealed in paintings like *Chez Mouquin* (1905, Art Institute, Chicago) and *Nude with Apple* (1910, Brooklyn Museum) the influence of Renoir and impressionist use of color. Became a member of the National Academy of Design (1933). Died at Westport, Conn.

REFERENCES: Ira Glackens *William Glackens and the Ashcan Group* (New York 1957, also PB). Bennard P. Perlman *The Immortal Eight: American Painting from Eakins to the Armory Show* (New York 1962).

GLASGOW, Ellen (Anderson Gholson) (Apr. 22, 1874 – Nov. 21, 1945). American novelist. Born Richmond, Va., into aristocratic Southern family. Because of poor health, she was educated at home and spent her whole life in retirement there. First novel, *The Descendant* (1897). *The Voice of the People* (1900) gained public attention. In the series of novels that followed, including *The Battleground* (1902), *The Deliverance* (1904), *Virginia*

(1913), *Barren Ground* (1925), *Vein of Iron* (1935), and *In This Our Life* (1941, Pulitzer prize 1942), Miss Glasgow presented an unsentimental social history of Virginia from 1850. Rebelling against the romantic tradition of Southern fiction, she made her chief theme the stubborn refusal of Southerners, in the face of a changing social order, to discard such archaic concepts as the code of chivalry and masculine superiority. She died in Richmond. Her autobiography, *The Woman Within,* appeared in 1954 and her *Letters of Ellen Glasgow,* in 1958.

REFERENCES: Frederick P. W. McDowell *Ellen Glasgow and the Ironic Art of Fiction* (Madison, Wis. 1960, also PB). Blair Rouse *Ellen Glasgow* (New York 1962, also PB).

GLAZUNOV, Alexander Konstantinovich (Aug. 10, 1865 – Mar. 21, 1936). Russian composer. Born St. Petersburg. Extremely precocious, he studied with Rimski-Korsakov from 1880, producing (1882) his first symphony, which established his reputation. Met Liszt in Weimar (1884), who with Wagner influenced him. By the time he was made director of St. Petersburg Conservatory (1905) he had completed eight symphonies. Received honorary degrees from Oxford and Cambridge (1906). The last of the great composers of the Russian national school, he left Russia (1928) and conducted concerts of his works in Europe and U.S. until his death in Paris. Works include a violin concerto (1904), two piano concertos, chamber music, symphonic poems, ballets, and piano pieces.

GLINKA, Mikhail Ivanovich (June 1, 1804 – Feb. 15, 1857). Russian composer. Born Novospasskoi, Smolensk. Studied at Pedagogic Institute, St. Petersburg (1817–22), then entered government service (1824–28). Traveled in Italy (1830–33), met Donizetti and Bellini and fell under spell of Italian opera. However, after some months of studying theory with Siegfried Dehn in Berlin, Glinka returned to St. Petersburg and composed the opera which first brought him fame, *A Life for the Czar* (1836). This and the opera *Rus-*

slan and Ludmilla (1842), his finest work, established him as the acknowledged founder of the Russian national school; his symphonic techniques provided the basis for the work of Borodin, Rimski-Korsakov, Tschaikovsky, and others. Glinka married Maria Petrovna Ivanova (1835; divorced 1846). Served as choirmaster of imperial chapel (1837–39) and traveled abroad (1844–1854), returning to Russia during Crimean War, when he began to write his memoirs. Renewed his studies with Dehn in Berlin (1856) and died there. Other important works include *Spanish Overtures* (1845–51) and incidental music for *Prince Kholmsky* (1840).

REFERENCE: Mikhail Osipovich Zetlin *The Five: The Evolution of the Russian School of Music* (tr. New York and London 1959).

GLUCK, Christoph Willibald (July 2, 1714 – Nov. 15, 1787). German composer. Born Erasbach, Upper Palatinate, son of gamekeeper. Received early musical training at Prague and became member of chamber orchestra, Vienna (1736). Travel to Italy brought him under influence of Giovanni Battista Sammartini. Produced successfully first opera, *Artaserse,* Milan (1741). Having mastered Italian operatic style went to London (1745), where he met Handel. Visited Hamburg, Leipzig, Dresden with traveling opera company and wrote operas for Copenhagen, Dutch cities, Naples, Vienna, Prague. Married Marianna Pergin, daughter of rich merchant (1750). Appointed court kapellmeister by Empress Maria Theresa, Vienna (1754). *Don Juan* (1761), a landmark in development of dramatic ballet, was followed by the revolutionary *Orfeo ed Euridice* (1762), libretto by Raniero da Calzabigi (1714–1795). Their preface (1769) to *Alceste* (1767) was a manifesto for the reform of opera. After the failure of *Paride ed Elena* in Vienna (1770), Gluck moved to Paris. He revised *Orfeo* (1774) and *Alceste* (1776) for Paris Opera, and composed *Iphigénie en Aulide* (1774) after Racine, and *Iphigénie en Tauride* (1779), his masterpiece. Last opera, *Écho et Narcisse* (1779) a failure; he retired thenceforth to Vienna, where he died. The nobility and grandeur of Gluck's operatic style and the theories embodied in his credo for opera influenced the rising generation of composers like Mozart and Cherubini.

REFERENCES: Martin Cooper *Gluck* (London and New York 1935). Alfred Einstein *Gluck* (tr. London and New York 1955, also PB). Patricia Howard *Gluck and the Birth of Modern Opera* (London and New York 1964). Ernest Newman *Gluck and the Opera: A Study in Musical History* (London 1964 and Mystic, Conn. 1965).

✐

CHRISTOPH WILLIBALD GLUCK

BY DALE HARRIS

It is Gluck's particular distinction to have led a movement that changed the entire course of opera. Though there may be some uncertainty about the merits of his specific compositions, there can be none about his importance in the history of music. Gluck helped to make opera once again what it had been in the days of Monteverdi, a species of music drama. Before the appearance of Gluck's first influential score, *Orfeo ed Euridice,* opera had declined into decorativeness and formalism. The noncomic works of many of Gluck's contemporaries and immediate predecessors, like Johann Fux, Niccolò Porpora and Johann Hasse, consisted essentially of a string of elaborate arias which, having no truly dramatic function and bearing only a casual relationship to the events that made up the plot, amounted to hardly more than a concert in costume. *Orfeo,* with its new emphasis on cogent action, led to a reappraisal of the nature of opera that has never been reversed. Expressivity, not abstract beauty, became opera's avowed end. After Gluck, the success of the music could no longer be judged without reference to its dramatic and psychological propriety. Such was the case even in works that

accorded primary importance to the voice and exploited fully its capacity for virtuosity: Lucia's Mad Scene, no less than Isolde's Love-Death, traces its ancestry back to Gluck's reforms.

Metastasian *opera seria,* the preponderant mode of the first half of the eighteenth century, was ripe for reform. Although it was not to disappear completely until the last decade of the century, its rigid conventions had begun to seem unduly restrictive long before then. In the arts the influence of the Enlightenment had led to a growing desire for the natural as distinct from the ceremonial, for the rational and the reasonable, for aesthetic experiences that reflected ordinary human behavior. Hence the dissatisfaction with a form of opera so bound by courtly decorum that the plot could only be advanced by means of *recitativo secco* in between arias. The plots, in any case, though highly complex, were inconsequential, mere excuses for a set of noble-minded disquisitions on subjects like honor and the conflict between love and duty. All real conflict was dissolved in sententiousness and in remote heroic action, which, though rarely ever shown, had consequences so dire that nothing short of a monarch's (or a god's) magnanimous intervention could remedy them.

With the encouragement of Count Giacomo Durazzo, director of the imperial Austrian theatres, and the help of Raniero da Calzabigi, poet and librettist, Gluck set out to introduce good sense, genuine feeling, and meaningful action into the Viennese opera, first with *Orfeo ed Euridice* in 1762, then in 1767 with *Alceste,* the preface to which appeared two years later and constituted the manifesto of the already ascendant reform movement. In this document Gluck (or Calzabigi) set forth the old objections to *opera seria:*

the indulgence granted to virtuoso singers, the inappropriate ornateness of the musical style, the customary discrepancy between the form of the *da capo* aria and the words to which it was set, the general lack of regard for credibility — in sum, the absence of dramatic integrity. Gluck, who with *Don Juan* (1761), choreographed by Gasparo Angiolini, had already helped to propagate the dance reform ideas of his contemporary Jean Georges Noverre, remedied the situation in opera by a series of simple and effective measures. He abolished the *recitativo secco* in favor of orchestrally accompanied recitative, thus ensuring more dramatic cohesion, and he abolished the luxuriantly ornamented *da capo* style in favor of an almost austerely plain vocal line, which allowed emotional directness. Above all, he abolished the heroic intrigue from operatic plot in favor of the clear outlines of myth. We see his characters responding passionately to powerful, recognizably human situations, like the bereavement of a husband or the self-sacrifice of a wife. Though in one opera the husband is Orpheus, a god, and in another the wife is Alcestis, granddaughter of Poseidon, and though Gluck shows no interest in their psychological individuality, yet what distinguishes them from their operatic contemporaries is their ability to give memorable expression to experiences of common significance.

None of Gluck's reforms, either in matter or manner, was entirely original. What gave them their initial force, and gives them lasting historical importance, is the propitiousness of their timing. Gluck and Calzabigi turned opera from the heroic to the human at a moment when far-reaching changes were taking place in the European sensibility, when middle-class values were replacing the old aristocratic or-

der. The Gluckian reforms are part of the same historical and cultural development that came to a climax in the American and French revolutions and ushered in the modern world. It is no accident that, despite the musical glories of Monteverdi and Handel, it is *Orfeo* that remains the oldest opera in the regular repertory.

Orfeo is also the only one of Gluck's works to be seen with any frequency. There have been few staged revivals of his other reform scores. *Iphigénie en Aulide* and *Iphigénie en Tauride* are seldom mounted, even in Paris, for which city they were written. The rest of his formidable output (over forty titles) is extinct, rendered obsolete by Gluck himself. Apart from the handful of his revolutionary works, Gluck was a regular court composer, whose Italian musical training equipped him to write, in acceptable, international style, *opere serie*, ceremonial spectacles, staged cantatas and dramatic serenades. He set almost twenty of Metastasio's texts, three of them, moreover, after *Orfeo*. Even his revolutionary works are compromised by eighteenth-century conventions like arbitrary happy endings and the appearance of a *deus ex machina,* which his technical resources are insufficient to transform and justify. Gluck was not technically an especially gifted musician. When he lacked divine fire he tended to plod along uninventively, even clumsily. What remains of abiding intrinsic worth is a succession of sublime inspirations: in *Alceste* "Divinités du Styx," in *Iphigénie en Tauride* "O malheureuse Iphigénie," in *Orfeo* the *Dance of the Furies* (taken over from *Don Juan*), the *Dance of the Blessed Spirits,* "Che puro ciel," and "Che farò senza Euridice." The last three in particular have a calm perfection and purity that seems, despite one's better knowledge of the creative process, to owe nothing to skill and everything to grace.

GODWIN, William (Mar. 3, 1756 – Apr. 7, 1836) and Mary Wollstonecraft (Apr. 27, 1759 – Sept. 10, 1797). Godwin, an English philosopher and writer, was born in Wisbeach, son of a dissenting minister. Raised and educated in radical nonconformism, he entered ministry (1777), gave it up (1782), and went to London for literary career. Steeped in political and economic theories of the Enlightenment, he became a radical journalist who supported the French Revolution. Embodied his own libertarian creed and utopian ideal based on the free play of reason in his first important work, *Inquiry Concerning Political Justice* (1793), called by Crane Brinton "one of the most extreme assertions of rationalistic philosophical anarchism ever made." It caused a sensation, and Godwin was nearly prosecuted; he then published a novel illustrating the same views, *The Adventures of Caleb Williams* (1794). Began living (1796) with MARY WOLLSTONECRAFT, whom he had met in 1791. She was born near London, ran a school (1783–1785), was a governess, then worked for a publisher (from 1788). Wrote her radical feminist work *Vindication of the Rights of Women* (1792); that year went to Paris to observe the French Revolution, and wrote *Historical and Moral View of the French Revolution* (1794). In Paris she lived with the American Gilbert Imlay (1793–95) and bore him a child. They separated and she returned to London, where she married Godwin. Shortly after the birth of their daughter Mary (1797) (see SHELLEY, MARY WOLLSTONECRAFT) she died there. Godwin married Mary Jane Clairmont (1801), mother of Claire Clairmont, who became Byron's mistress. He continued to write — novels, including *St. Leon* (1799), and *Of Population* (1820), an answer to Malthus, and *History of the Commonwealth* (1824–28). In bankruptcy during his last years, he was awarded (1833) a government sinecure until his death. Died in London.

REFERENCE: Henry N. Brailsford *Shelley, Godwin, and Their Circle* (London and New York, 2nd ed., 1951.)

GOES, Hugo van der (c.1440–1482). Flemish painter. Though he is considered one of most gifted of early Netherlands painters, little is known of his life. Apparently settled early in Ghent, where he was a master of the artists' guild (1467). Chosen dean of the guild (1474), he served one year, then entered the monastery Roode Kloster near Brussels, where he continued painting. Suffered (1481) severe mental breakdown (melancholia), and died soon after. Surviving works consist of religious paintings and donors' portraits. Best known works are the early *Fall of Man* (c.1468, Vienna), the serene *Monforte Altarpiece* (c.1472, Berlin), and the Portinari *Altarpiece* (c.1475, Uffizi, Florence), triptych commissioned by a Florentine banker, with *Adoration of the Shepherds* on central panel and life-size portraits of Portinari family on the wings. Also notable is the late melancholy *Death of the Virgin* (c.1480, Bruges). Hugo's superb oil technique and realism in figures and landscape impressed Florentine painters, notably Ghirlandajo, and foreshadowed work of Pieter Bruegel the Elder.

REFERENCE: Erwin Panofsky *Early Netherlandish Painting: the Origins and Character* (2 vols. Oxford and Cambridge, Mass. 1954).

GOETHE, Johann Wolfgang von (Aug. 28, 1749 – Mar. 22, 1832). German poet, dramatist, and novelist. Born Frankfurt; father a wealthy lawyer, mother the Bürgermeister's daughter. Entered Leipzig University (1765); completed legal studies in Strasbourg (1770–71). First publication, *Die Laune des Verliebten*, a play (1769). During his *Sturm und Drang* period (1771–75) wrote historical drama *Götz von Berlichingen* (1773). His romantic novel *Die Leiden des jungen Werthers* (*The Sorrows of Werther*, 1774) created a sensation throughout Europe. Invited to Weimar by Duke Karl August (1775), he remained there for rest of his life, eventually holding important administrative posts. Visit to Italy (1786–88) fired his enthusiasm for the classic, evident in the dramas *Iphigenie auf Tauris* (1787), *Egmont* (1787), and *Torquato Tasso* (1789). On his return, he established a household with Christiane Vulpius, who bore him five children — of whom only one son, August, survived — and whom he married in 1806. From 1791, devoted himself increasingly to scientific studies. His deep influential friendship with Friedrich Schiller began in 1794 and lasted until Schiller's death (1805). Produced novel *Wilhelm Meisters Lehrjahre* (1796) and the long poem *Hermann und Dorothea* (1797). The later years he spent writing his autobiography, *Dichtung und Wahrheit* (1808–31), the second part of *Wilhelm Meister* (*Wilhelm Meisters Wanderjahre*, 1829), and completing his monumental work *Faust* (two parts, 1770 and 1831); an early draft, *Urfaust*, remained undiscovered until 1887. Died in Weimar.

TRANSLATIONS: *Autobiography: Poetry and Truth of my Life* tr. R. D. Moon (London 1932). *Elective Affinities* tr. Elizabeth Mayer and Louise Bogan (Chicago 1963, also PB). *Wisdom and Experience* tr. Hermann J. Weigand (New York and London 1949).

REFERENCES: Stewart Atkins *Age of Goethe* (Boston 1968). Ernst Cassirer *Rousseau, Kant, Goethe* (tr. New York 1961, also PB). Erich Heller *The Disinherited Mind: Essays in Modern German Literature and Thought* (New York 1957 and London 1959, also PB) and *The Artist's Journey into the Interior and Other Essays* (New York and London 1966, also PB). George H. Lewes *Life of Goethe* (reprint New York 1965). Thomas Mann *Essays of Three Decades* (New York and London 1947). Karl Viëtor *Goethe the Poet* (tr. Cambridge, Mass. and London 1949) and *Goethe the Thinker* (tr. Cambridge, Mass. and London 1950).

ᔐ

GOETHE

BY ERICH HELLER

During the last hundred years acknowledgments of Goethe's genius by American or English poets or critics have become rarer and rarer. Of course, the printing mills of Germanic scholarship in every language have continued plentifully to supply the anemic market of academe with microscopic examinations of this or that aspect of Goethe's works, but the literary public has remained unimpressed. This neglect, indifference, or even dislike is, for instance, shown by the fact that T. S. Eliot, among Anglo-Saxon poets and critics of recent decades the most "European" in taste, expressed — in asides occurring in some of his essays — nothing but irritation at the big "classical" shadow cast by that German "romantic." Goethe, he once wrote, "dabbled in both philosophy and poetry and made no great success of either"; and when years later he apologized for the indiscretion, it was in an address entitled "Goethe as the Sage," and not "Goethe the Poet." True, he did not wish to distinguish radically (as in the past he had done on several occasions) between the "poetry" of a poet's poetry and its "thought," its "philosophy," or its wisdom; and yet the very title of Eliot's address suggests that Goethe's works might survive more as the repository of his wisdom than as poetry (and it is one of the abiding paradoxes of literary judgment that this distinction cannot be quite avoided even if we are convinced that it is ultimately invalid).

Indeed, Goethe's wisdom has the kind of greatness that time and again induces in the reader the momentary happiness of unquestioning assent; and many of the sayings of the sage can be separated the more easily from his poetry as they have a separate existence in the form of *Maxims and Reflections*. Also, it would by no means be capricious to say that nowhere in his writings is Goethe as pertinent as here to the worries and anxieties of the present age. "Everything that liberates our minds without at the same time adding to our resources of self-mastery is pernicious." Does this not anticipate the embarrassment — indeed the terror — of an epoch that has allowed itself to be liberated from the prejudices and the obscurantism of the past only to be enslaved by a scientific progress that progresses tyrannically and without concern for the moral status or the moral needs of the human person? "What is there exact about mathematics except its own exactitude?" This is aimed at the theoretical hubris of men who have looked upon the mathematical definitions of the universe as if they were revelations of its "true nature," and therefore regard the world as wholly comprehensible, negotiable, and changeable through human calculation and experimentation.

"Goethe as the Sage" — the sage, as this aphorism shows, had little patience with the higher claims of mathematics, and no patience whatever with a natural science that proceeded in accordance with purely mathematical designs. Such a science struck him as profoundly unnatural, because it thrived upon abstraction; and abstraction he denounced again and again as a sin against the sensuous concreteness of nature, its "naturalness" and *Anschaulichkeit,* through which alone man could attain true understanding and the kind of knowledge that would not be inimical to the good life. Besides, a man, he wrote, "who has been brought up on the so-called exact sciences will, from the height of his analytical reason, not easily comprehend that there is also something like an exact concrete imagination." And had he ever reflected upon his own sagacity (in violation of his belief that he owed all intellectual accomplishments to the refusal to give any thought to thinking), he would have seen the highest wisdom in his campaign against Newtonian physics. For he once said — rather quixotically, no doubt — that his anti-Newtonian science was much more important than his poetry: there had lived before him greater poets than he; whereas it was, he claimed, his unique distinction that he knew "the truth in the difficult theory of colors." And the truth he knew was "concrete," light was an *Urphänomen,* an irreducible phenomenon, and Newton's doctrine was manifestly foolish in reducing the white light to a compound made up of many colors.

Sage or poet, quixotic or not, it is Goethe's "exact concrete imagination" that is the glory of his poetry. When he is at his best — and he is more often at his best than even the best among other poets — he appears to vindicate Hamann's dictum that "poetry is the mother tongue of the human race"; and not only, he could have added, of the human race but of nature too, for often in Goethe's poetry nature herself appears to open her mouth, making known what she is. Nothing, therefore, was farther from Goethe's genius than the suspicion voiced by T. S. Eliot (and not merely by him but, if we replace "words" in the following lines by "shapes" or "colors" or "sounds," by most of the artists of this epoch and by most of its arts): that

> . . . one has only learnt to get the
>   better of words
> For the things one no longer has
>   to say, or the way in which
> One is no longer disposed to say
>   it . . .

To Goethe this would hardly have made sense. Get the better of words? If anything, words got the better of him; and even this would suggest a tension between self and language, or between things and signs, which is alien to his poetry. In *Über allen Gipfeln ist Ruh* — to quote only one (and the briefest) of his lyrical masterpieces — *Gipfeln* not merely "signifies" the mountaintops, and *Ruh* not merely "means" the peace written into the fading daylight that lingers above the peaks. No, it is as if neither mountaintops nor peace had ever been truly known before that line was written; and nonetheless, they are known now as something that had been dear to the eyes and dear to the soul from time immemorial. But of course, this oneness of word and thing is untranslatable, and untranslatable is therefore the lyrical poetry of such a poet. Small wonder that "Goethe the Poet" is little appreciated and little known in the world.

"Words for the things one no longer has to say"? T. S. Eliot was not only the poet who wrote this; he was also — and one is tempted to say: because of it, and because he was a poet in an age unpropitious to poetry — the inventor of a critical theory that Goethe would have found extremely baffling, the theory that insists upon the "impersonal" character of all art, upon an essential difference between the poet's "empirical self" as it experiences "life" and the poet's "poetical activity" as it produces poetry. Goethe, on the contrary, once called all his poetry "occasional poetry" insofar as it arose from "real" occasions, real experiences: "I think nothing of poetry that is not rooted in the real." For the gift given to the poet — his Torquato Tasso calls it a divine gift — was the power to say, with the precision of truth and poetry, what and how he experienced and suffered, and to say it even when other men would be silenced by their agony:

Und wenn der Mensch in seiner Qual verstummt,

Gab mir ein Gott zu sagen, wie ich leide.

This is not only what Goethe's hero-poet comes to recognize at the climax of the drama *Torquato Tasso,* it also is the motto its author gave, a long time afterward, to the greatest poem of his old age, the *Marienbad Elegy.* This poem owes its existence to the passionate love Goethe, in his seventies, felt for a girl of eighteen, an upheaval of mind and soul that brought him to the brink of despair and — literally — death. Yet the poem is by no means the result of Wordsworthian "emotion recollected in tranquillity" or of a state of mind resembling Eliot's "depersonalization." It is, as Goethe himself said, "the outcome of a highly impassioned condition," was begun immediately upon the final farewell, and was written almost in its entirety in the horse-drawn coach that took him from the scene of his passion, the Bohemian spas, back to Weimar. No, there is for Goethe no threshold to be crossed from experience to poetry, from thing to word, from feeling to articulation, or from nature to mind. There is good reason to believe that he was the last great poet of Europe whose immediate perception of life had the quality of poetry, and whose modes of experience, the aesthetic, the ethical, the religious, and the scientific modes, were pervaded and held together by a continuum that bore the imprint of the poetic. This is why his most celebrated dramatic poem, *Faust,* is, in the history of literature, the only "optimistic" treatment of the Faust legend that poetically succeeded despite the unresolved contradictions in which it was bound to get entangled, theologically and dramatically, through the poet's determination to *save* the traditionally hellbound magician. For where there is no discontinuity between spontaneous experience and poetic language, or between nature and mind, there can be no such extreme oppositions as heaven and hell. Their common idiom is poetry, and poetry, for Goethe, is therefore beyond good and evil.

GOGH, Vincent van. *See* VAN GOGH, Vincent.

GOGOL, Nikolai Vasilievich (Mar. 31, 1809 – Feb. 21, 1852). Russian writer. Born Sorochintsy in Ukraine, son of a small landowner nobleman. Educated at Poltava and Nezhin schools (1821–1828). Left for St. Petersburg to seek career as actor and writer. Epic poem *Hans Küchelgarten* (1829) a failure; he then entered civil service. Began writing Ukrainian tales; his two-volume *Evenings on a Farm Near Dikanka* (1831–32) won him recognition and friendship of Pushkin, who helped him get a post teaching history. Two books of stories followed (1835), *Mirgorod*, (which included *The Old-World Landowners*, *Viy*, *Taras Bulba*) and *Arabesques* (which included *Nevsky Prospect*. His famous satirical comedy *Revizor* or *The Inspector General* (1836) created a storm among the petty bureaucrats it ridiculed. For twelve years thereafter Gogol lived abroad, mostly in Rome, where he wrote his satirical masterpiece, the novel *Dead Souls* (first part, 1842), and the immortal tale *The Overcoat*. Made pilgrimage to Jerusalem (1848). In later years suffered from deep depression and religious fanaticism, in course of which he destroyed second part of *Dead Souls*. He produced nothing further in the brilliant vein that inspired the Russian realists who came after him. His illness overcame him, and he died in Moscow.

TRANSLATION: *The Collected Works of Nikolai Gogol* tr. Constance Garnett (6 vols. New York and London 1922–1928).

REFERENCES: Janko Lavrin *Nikolai Gogol* (London 1951 and New York 1952, also PB). David Magarshack *Gogol: A Life* (London and New York 1957). Vladimir Nabokov *Nikolai Gogol* (Norfolk, Conn. 1944 and London 1947).

✍

NIKOLAI GOGOL
BY GERALD SYKES

Gogol had three precarious desires: to write well, to be famous, to rid himself entirely of sin. So long as he could control the third desire (which was later to disturb the lives of Tolstoy and Dostoevsky with similar Byzantine fury) he did write well, very well, and he did become famous. But when his childhood's primitive religiosity reattacked him, and when he fell under the spell of a fanatic priest who considered literature the sin against the Holy Ghost, he wrote badly, burned his manuscripts, refused to eat, and within weeks passed from "the picture of health" to death from malnutrition — and bloodsucking leeches in the nose — at forty-two.

So complete a collapse occurred because Gogol had much more substance as a talent than as a man. His talent was real, wildly comic but humane, a delicate intermingling of realism and fantasy, and both subtle and bold; but it was not matched by an equal portion of character, thought and experience. When it encountered a few of the classic tests of everyman, it retreated from them into preachy art and, when that failed, a refusal to live.

As psychology-addicted moderns we search his lonely life, a great deal of which was spent in western European hotels, for any woman except his mother. No luck; there wasn't any. His mother was a pious owner of land and serfs in the Ukraine who collected folklore for his first volume, sent him money, and from the cradle spoiled him. Perhaps it was she who helped to turn him away from other members of her sex, and then again perhaps it was the rough serf girls with whom he seems to have had his first erotic encounters. On his deathbed he confessed to his physician that he had never enjoyed intercourse with a woman. His letters suggest latent homosexuality, since they were excessively noble when they described the prostitute whom he briefly — and fashionably — pretended to love, and excessively jealous when they were sent to a man, a friend from childhood, who borrowed money from him and never wrote. "I kiss you hundreds of times."

Such inquiries throw little or no light on what seems to have been the essential question about Gogol. How, out of so little shared experience, out of a generally unimpressive personality that resembled that of his own silly Inspector General, was he able to cut so deep, so humanly? Where for example did he find the empathy — truly religious, by the way, and a literary justification of his search for God in everyone — that makes each line of *The Overcoat* so outrageously funny, so outrageously pathetic, so mysterious, so right?

Gogol appears to have been the kind of writer who, when he was able to keep the demons of the absolute at bay, could mine an inexplicable lode of insight with rare artistic cunning. (The anecdote from which he took *The Overcoat* was slight compared to the finished product.) Once his boyish sense of mischief had been ignited — and this occurs without fail in each of his best works, with Pushkin twice legendarily providing the spark — he was free to pull together a world that may have sorely perplexed him until he took his pen in hand. Writing enabled him to re-establish a solid cosmos — for a while. But when the world re-quired more than juvenile fun — and revenge — to put it in order, he had to fall back on a reasoning process that was as undeveloped in him as his storytelling was masterly. He then wrote the books that are now forgotten; he then burned the long-promised second part of *Dead Souls* — and starved himself to death. He had lost his raison d'être.

The phenomenon of a prodigious talent in a negligible person has long fascinated those who are lost in private despair. It makes some of them write. It also restores the amour propre of publishers, encourages parents to dream, and provides revenue to teachers and therapists. We all like to hope that we too may stumble, without any particular merit, upon an undiscovered archetypal deposit like the one that brought fame to Gogol. In his own day, as soon as the medical tortures had ceased and his pulse had come to rest, a quarrel broke out as to who should pay for his funeral. He had left nothing but some old clothes and two hundred and thirty-four books.

Finally the expenses were assumed by Moscow University, which in spite of his lack of a good education had elected him a fellow a few years earlier. He was taken to its chapel, where he lay in state with a laurel wreath on his head and some immortelles in his hands. Warring factions, political and literary, agreed at last that he had been a great writer. All Moscow appeared at his funeral. There was a stampede among book-loving mourners who tried to snatch the dried flowers from his grasp. The impression he made by dying was so profound, throughout all of Russia, that the Czar's government instantly forbade any mention of it in the press. Turgenev was arrested for writing an obituary. The whole ceremony was handled, in fact, in the very best style of the corpse.

GOLDONI, Carlo (Feb. 25, 1707 – Feb. 6, 1793). Italian dramatist. Born Venice. After numerous interruptions in his education, usually connected with the theatre, he (1731) took law degree at Padua, married, and settled in Venice. Unsuccessful in his first dramatic effort, the tragedy *Amalasunta* (1732), he next produced *Belisario* (1734), a tragicomedy which pleased the public. Thereafter, Goldoni concentrated on depicting real life as opposed to the artificiality of the old *commedia dell'arte*: he abolished the wearing of masks, and following the example of Molière, represented real persons, generally of the lower and middle classes, behaving naturally in lifelike situations. Discouraged by the hostility of Carlo Gozzi and his followers, he went to Paris (1762), where he directed the Comédie Italienne (1762–64); subsequently taught Italian to the French royal princesses and, for the wedding of Louis XVI, wrote in French one of his best-known works, *Le Bourru bienfaisant* (1771). Wrote his delightful *Mémoires* (tr. *Memoirs of Carlo Goldoni* 1926), also in French, at Versailles (1783–87). Deprived of his pension by the revolution, he died in poverty in Paris. Goldoni's total dramatic output, including tragedies and libretti for *opera buffa*, numbers some 250 works, in Italian, French, and Venetian dialect. His reputation as the founder of modern Italian comedy flows from such works as *La Locandiera* (1753), *I Rusteghi* (1760), and *Le Baruffe Chiozzotte* (1762).

REFERENCE: Hobart C. Chatfield-Taylor *Goldoni: A Biography* (New York 1913, 2nd ed. New York 1928).

GOLDSMITH, Oliver (Nov. 10, 1728 – Apr. 4, 1774). Irish poet, novelist, playwright. Born in Ireland, probably at Pallas, Longford; son of a clergyman. An indifferent scholar, he attended Trinity College, Dublin; received degree (1749) and spent some years attempting various projects, including medical studies, before taking famous European tour on foot (1755–56). Settled in London and struggled to support himself by various means, chiefly hack writing. First attracted notice with *Enquiry into the Present State of Polite Learning in Europe* (1759), edited the shortlived weekly *The Bee*, and soon was well known as contributor of essays to various periodicals, including the delightful *Chinese Letters* for the *Public Ledger*, later collected as *The Citizen of the World* (1762). Success came with first the long poem *The Traveler* (1764), then the novel *The Vicar of Wakefield* (1766), followed by the well-received robust comedy *The Good-Natured Man* (1768), which anticipated his crowning triumph *She Stoops to Conquer* (1773), still popular to this day. In the meantime his long poem *The Deserted Village* (1770) was enthusiastically received. Goldsmith became the friend of Samuel Johnson and members of the Literary Club, which he helped to found (1764). Though his major works, characterized by warmth, simplicity, and humor, brought success, he was always in financial difficulties, forced to undertake hackwork in the form of histories, biographies, and other writings. Never married, and died in London.

EDITIONS: *The Works of Oliver Goldsmith* ed. J. W. M. Gibbs (4 vols. London 1885–86). *The Plays of Oliver Goldsmith* (London and New York 1903) and *Complete Poetical Works of Oliver Goldsmith* (London 1906) ed. Austin Dobson

REFERENCES: Austin Dobson *The Life of Oliver Goldsmith* (London 1899). William Freeman *Oliver Goldsmith* (London and New York 1952). Ricardo Quintana *Oliver Goldsmith: A Georgian Study* (New York 1967).

GONCHAROV, Ivan Alexandrovich (June 18, 1812 – Sept. 27, 1891). Russian novelist. Born Simbirsk into well-to-do merchant family; educated privately and at Moscow University. Entered civil service as interpreter of French, and began to write. First novel, *A Common Story* (1847), was well received. Sent (1852) on government mission to Japan, an experience recorded in *The Frigate Pallas* (1858). His masterpiece was *Oblomov* (1859), a satire on Old World Russia as personified by the noble young hero who does nothing. It soon became a classic, and the word "Oblomovism," meaning the opposite of noblesse oblige, entered into the Russian language. Goncharov retired from government service (1867) to devote himself to literature. After travels in Germany and France he produced his final novel, *The Precipice* (1869), a tendentious work about a nihilist. Spent last years writing his reminiscences and an essay on the dramatist Alexander Griboyedov. He died in St. Petersburg.

TRANSLATIONS: *A Common Story* tr. Constance Garnett (New York 1894). *Oblomov* tr. C. J. Hogarth (London and New York 1915); tr. David Magarshack (Harmondsworth, England, and Baltimore 1954). *The Precipice* tr. M. Brant (London and New York 1915).

REFERENCE: Janko Lavrin *Goncharov* (New Haven 1954, new ed. 1969).

GONCOURT, Edmond (Louis Antoine Huot de) (May 26, 1822 – July 16, 1896) and **Jules** (Alfred Huot de) (Dec. 17, 1830 – June 20, 1870). French novelists, art critics, historians, and diarists. Edmond was born in Nancy, Jules in Paris. From 1848, when Jules left school, until his death in Paris, the Goncourt brothers lived and worked inseparably. They began as artists, touring France (1849) and keeping notes which soon directed them toward writing. As art critics and social historians, they specialized in the eighteenth century: *Histoire de la société française pendant la Révolution* (1854), *Histoire de la société française pendant le Directoire* (1855), *Portraits intimes du dix-huitième siècle* (1857), *L'Art du dix-huitième siècle* (1859–70, tr. *French Eighteenth-Century Painters* 1948), *La Femme au dix-huitième siècle* (1862). They also wrote novels — documentaries — describing lives of everyday characters as if social history: *Soeur Philomène* (1861), *Renée Mauperin* (1864), *Germinie Lacerteux* (1865), *Manette Salomon* (1867), *Madame Gervaisais* (1869). While the Goncourts founded the school of naturalism, it was their disciple Émile Zola who be-

came famous as leader of naturalist movement by emulating their technique. Their best-known work is the *Journal* (begun 1851, continued by Edmond after Jules's death into his own last days), a detailed, invaluable record of the period. Edmond later wrote *La Fille Élisa* (1877, tr. *Elisa* 1959), *Chérie* (1884), and other novels. He died in Chamrosay, leaving a large sum in his will to found Académie Goncourt, which annually awards the celebrated prix Goncourt.

TRANSLATIONS: *The Goncourt Journals 1851–1870* tr. Lewis Galantiere (Garden City, N.Y. and London 1937). *Pages from the Goncourt Journal* tr. Robert Baldick (London and New York 1962).

REFERENCES: Robert Baldick *The Goncourts* (London and New York 1960). André Billy *The Goncourt Brothers* (tr. New York and London 1960).

GORKI, Maxim (real name Alexei Maximovich Peshkov) (Mar. 14, 1868 – June 18, 1936). Russian writer. Born Nizhni Novgorod (renamed Gorki, 1932). Orphaned early, spent childhood in hardship and poverty, and ran away to live as vagabond. Used name Gorki, "the bitter one," when he published his first story, *Makar Chudra*, in Tiflis newspaper (1892). Second story, *Chelkash*, highly popular, and subsequent stories based on his own experiences as a tramp made him internationally famous. Novels followed, including *Foma Gordeyev* (1899, tr. 1928) and *Mother* (1907, tr. 1947), and plays, the best known being *The Lower Depths* (1902, tr. 1912). Gorki was arrested and exiled for revolutionary activities and pacifism, but fought in World War I and was wounded at Galicia. Supported Bolshevik revolution, became chief of propaganda bureau (1918). His autobiographical trilogy, *Childhood, In the World,* and *My Universities* (1915–23, tr. 1917–24), is among his finest writing. Poor health took him to Italy (1921); returned (1928). Was made first president of Soviet Writers' Union (1932), and helped found the official literary method known as socialist realism. Circumstances of death in Moscow mysterious. Gorki's art at his best reveals powerful humanitarianism and vivid detail of the lowest strata of human life. Too frequently in the plays and novels it is marred by tendentiousness and social preaching, but he is one of the first in Russian literature to express the view of the worker and the social revolutionary.

TRANSLATION: *The Autobiography of Maxim Gorki* tr. Isidor Schneider (New York 1949).

REFERENCES: Filia Holtzman *Young Maxim Gorky: 1869–1902* (New York 1948 and London 1949). Dan Levin *Stormy Petrel: The Life and Work of Maxim Gorky* (New York 1965).

GORKY, Arshile (Oct. 25, 1904 – July 3, 1948). American painter. Born Khorkom Vari Haiyotz Dzor, Armenia. Studied engineering at Polytechnic Institute of Tiflis, and after emigration to U.S. (1920) at Brown University. From 1925, lived in New York and taught at several art schools. An early representational phase led to increasingly abstract works, in which, after absorbing the influences of Pablo Picasso, André Masson, Joan Miró, and surrealism, he went beyond them: he purified form by eliminating all anthropomorphic symbolism and figurative reference, yet conveyed strong human emotion and a sense of organic growth and movement. One of the most influential of the abstract expressionists, Gorky was widely recognized by the time of his death, by his own hand, in New York. He is well represented in such American collections as the Museum of Modern Art and the Whitney Museum, New York, where there was (1950) a large retrospective exhibition. Among his paintings in the U.S. are *Dark Green Painting* (1947) and *Agony* (1947), both in Museum of Modern Art, New York, *The Plow and the Song* (1947), *The Betrothal II* (1948).

REFERENCES: Harold Rosenberg *Arshile Gorky: The Man, the Time, the Idea* (New York 1962). Ethel Schwabacher *Arshile Gorky* (New York 1957).

GOUJON, Jean (c.1510–c.1565). French sculptor. Little is known about his life.

Earliest known works are sculptures for interior and doors of church of St. Maclou at Rouen (1541). Employed by Pierre Lescot, architect of the Louvre, to carve reliefs in church of St. Germain l'Auxerrois, Paris (1544); five of these reliefs, including the *Deposition*, one of his best works, are now in the Louvre. Two other masterpieces are relief ornamentation of Fontaine des Innocents, Paris (1547–49), and that of courtyard façade of Louvre (c.1549–1553). Goujon seems to have left France about 1562. Many of his works are lost and many attributions to him are disputed. His style belongs to the school of Fontainebleau, showing influence of Il Rosso, Francesco Primaticcio, and other Italian mannerists in the elongation and contortion of the figures. Particularly characteristic of Goujon is the contrast of well-modeled muscular figures with elegant linear drapery.

REFERENCES: Anthony Blunt *Art and Architecture in France, 1500–1700* (Harmondsworth, England 1953 and Baltimore 1954). Pierre du Colombier *Jean Goujon* (Paris 1949).

GOUNOD, Charles (François) (June 17, 1818 – Oct. 18, 1893). French composer. Born Paris, son of painter François Louis Gounod. Trained at Paris Conservatoire (from 1836) and won grand prix de Rome (1839). In Rome studied old church composers, especially Palestrina, and produced first composition, a Mass (1841). Returned to Paris, and after preparing for priesthood decided on full career as composer, which meant producing opera. *Sapho* (1851) and others had little success until *Faust* (1859), which continues to be enormously popular. In 1852 Gounod conducted the choral society the Orphéon, a valuable experience for him in working with voice and choral effects. During Franco-Prussian War and aftermath lived (1870–75) in England, where his music was well received. Oratorios *La Rédemption* and *Mors et Vita* were performed at Birmingham Festival (1882 and 1885). Other major works: operas *Mireille* (1864) and *Roméo et Juliette* (1867), and *Ave Maria* (1859), a soprano solo set to J. S. Bach's first prelude in *The*

Well-Tempered Clavier, perennially popular. Gounod died in St.-Cloud, near Paris. His style, though lacking dramatic and imaginative force, influenced through its lyricism and mysticism César Franck, Debussy's early work, and the operas of Jules Massenet.

REFERENCES: Henri Busser *Charles Gounod* (Lyon 1961). Norman Demuth *Introduction to the Music of Gounod* (London 1950). Jacques G. Prod'homme and Arthur Dandelot *Gounod: sa vie et ses oeuvres* (2 vols. Paris 1911).

GOURMONT, Rémy de (Apr. 4, 1858 – Sept. 27, 1915). French novelist and critic. Born Bazouches-en-Houlme, Orne. Studied law at Caen and entered (1881) the Bibliothèque Nationale. Dismissed (1891) because of allegedly unpatriotic article published in *Mercure de France,* of which he was a founder (1889). Disfigured by mysterious facial disease at age thirty-three, he spent most of his life in semiretirement. Best known as a leading apologist for the symbolists in study *Le Livre des masques* (1896 tr. *Book of Masks* 1921) and as a critic and philosopher of enormous erudition and analytic powers. Belletristic and philosophical works include *Le Latin Mystique* (1892), *L'Esthétique de la langue française* (1899), *Le Problème de style* (1902), *Promenades littéraires* (7 vols. 1904–1928), and *Promenades philosophiques* (3 vols. 1905–1909). Among his novels are *Les Chevaux de Diomède* (1897, tr. *The Horses of Diomede* 1923), *Une Nuit au Luxembourg* (1906), and *Un Coeur virginal* (1907, tr. *A Virgin Heart* 1921). Died in Paris.

TRANSLATIONS: *Natural Philosophy of Love* tr. Ezra Pound (New York PB 1961). *Selected Writings* tr. Glenn S. Burne (Ann Arbor, Mich. 1966).

REFERENCES: Glenn S. Burne *Rémy de Gourmont: His Ideas and Influence in England and America* (Carbondale, Ill. 1963). Garnet Rees *Rémy de Gourmont* (Paris 1940).

GOYA Y LUCIENTES, Francisco José de (Mar. 30, 1746 – Apr. 16, 1828). Spanish painter and etcher. Born Fuentetodos of humble parents; apprenticed at fourteen to José Luzan in nearby Saragossa. In Madrid (1763) became pupil of Francisco Bayeu, whose sister Josefa he married (1773). Visited Italy (c.1766–71). Commissioned (1775) to paint cartoons for royal tapestry factory of Santa Barbara, which brought him to royal attention. Became member of Royal Academy (1780) and painter to King Charles IV (1789). Also painted religious frescoes in San Antonio de la Florida, Madrid (1798). Produced first series of savagely satirical etchings, *Los Caprichos* (1796–98), followed by *Los Desastres de la Guerra* (1808–14) and *Proverbios* (1808–28). His most famous paintings include *Family of Charles IV* (1799) among many notable portraits; *Nude Maya* and *Maya Clothed* (c.1800); *Charge of May 2, 1808* and *Execution of May 3, 1808* (1814 Prado, Madrid), which commemorate rebellion of people of Madrid against Napoleon's soldiers. Although he had remained in favor during changing regimes, on restoration (1824) Goya went into voluntary exile in Bordeaux, where he continued to paint portraits and still lifes and make etchings. He died in Bordeaux. Goya exerted a strong influence on Manet and nineteenth-century French painting.

REFERENCES: Enriqueta Harris *Goya* (New York 1969). Philip Hofer, introduction to *The Disasters of War* (New York PB 1968). José Lopez-Rey *Goya's Caprichos: Beauty, Reason and Caricature* (2 vols. Princeton and Oxford 1953). August L. Mayer *Francisco de Goya* (tr. London and Toronto 1924). F. J. Sánchez Cantón *Goya* (New York and, as *Goya and the Black Paintings,* London 1964).

☞

GOYA

BY FREDERICK B. DEKNATEL

Goya stands apart from the main movements in painting which replaced the rococo style of the eighteenth century, yet quite as much as the leading painters of the neoclassic style or those who were moving in the direction of romanticism, in his mature work he departed from the old conventions and, even more pronouncedly, from the old tone of serenity and decorum. Goya differs also from these artists in coming late to his new conceptions. It was not until the 1790's, when he was nearly fifty, that a turn in his style is clearly apparent.

His artistic career, therefore, seems to be made up of two separate phases. He developed within the framework of eighteenth-century tradition, and the changes which took place in his earlier work conformed in general to those occurring in the last stages of the rococo. The major undertaking of his early career, the series of painted cartoons to serve as models for tapestries, which occupied him at intervals for more than twenty years, called for pastoral subjects, and Goya carried them out in the appropriate spirit of picturesque charm. In the last paintings of the series and in paintings commissioned by aristocratic patrons in the 1780's there was more emphasis on realism and on characterization of individual figures, and here something of Goya's originality can be felt. Although hints of what he would become in his later career can be found, there is truth in the saying that if he had died at fifty we would look on him today as an interesting practitioner of the eighteenth-century manner, not as a great artist and a great innovator.

Goya's change in outlook which altered his style and also led him to new types of work followed an illness in 1793 which left him deaf and coincided with the European-wide crisis brought about by the French Revolution. From that time on, as if determined to rely only on what meaning he could see for himself in his themes, he avoided conventional approaches.

Technically his painting became more subtle and controlled. His portraits stand out in a period noted for fine portraiture by their quality as paintings and, above all, by their unusually vivid revelation of individual character. Goya was extraordinarily candid in putting down what he saw, so much so that he has been accused, mistakenly, of having had a satirical purpose in his painting of the *Family of Charles IV* of 1799. A famous instance of his departure from the traditional way of treating a subject is the *Nude Maya*, done a few years later, which established a precedent for the realistically painted nudes of the later nineteenth century. In more complex compositions Goya was ingenious in devising arrangements which brought out with a new kind of intensity the crux of a situation or the essential character of an action. The *Execution of May 3, 1808*, painted some years afterward, conveys the horror and tragedy of the scene through the contrast between the unified mass of the firing squad and the chaos of forms made up of the postures and actions of the victims. The German scholar Theodor Hetzer saw this coordination of expressive stress and pictorial structure as a new kind of composition which was to become predominant in the later nineteenth century.

The significant new undertakings were works intended for the general public in which Goya expressed his views on the condition of the world. Thanks to modern scholarship, the old notion of Goya as an uncultivated, natural genius have been corrected. We know that as he gained prominence as a painter in the 1780's he was drawn into progressive intellectual circles in Madrid where liberal ideas, derived chiefly from the French Encyclopedists, prevailed. His deep commitment to the humane and rational ideas he encountered there is most clearly revealed in three series of etchings. Done at intervals of about ten years, they show how, as Goya lived through the events of his time, his reactions and his mode of expressing them changed.

The eighty etchings of *The Caprichos*, Goya's first major project after the crisis of his illness, were published in 1799. They demonstrate in more specific ways than the later etchings the close relation of his thought to eighteenth-century rationalism. Their aim "to ridicule and condemn prejudices, impostures and hypocrisies" is typical of satire with a moral purpose, and a number of the stupidities and vices he treated were traditional objects of attack. However, the harsh, bitter tone with which he treated these themes of human frailty is far removed from the usual wit and humor of satire. The scenes of witches and demons of the second half of the series provided subjects for derisive comment on superstition or for grotesque parodies of the foibles of the real world. Though Goya's view of the nightmare world of the supernatural as representing the absence of reason conforms to eighteenth-century conceptions, the weird and sometimes brutal vitality of these scenes seems closer to the imaginings of later romantics. The expressive use of the blacks and the whites made possible by the medium of etching and aquatint has a brilliance of effect that has made *The Caprichos* a landmark in the history of printmaking.

The desperate character of the war which broke out after Napoleon's armies occupied Spain in 1808 provided Goya with subjects far more drastic for his longest series of etchings, *The Disasters of War*, begun in 1810 but not published until long after his death. In them Goya followed the didactic method of *The Caprichos*, treating each main theme in a number of scenes and adding captions to drive home the point. The result is a visual catalogue of savage cruelty, bestiality, and suffering, forming an indictment of the inhumanity of war still unequaled in modern art or literature.

Around 1820, in a mood of pessimism and disillusion which was due perhaps to illness or to the defeat of liberal hopes by the policies of the restored monarchy, he did a short series called *The Proverbs* which also was not published during his lifetime. Here he turned again to fantastic images to comment on man's condition and probably also to refer to events of the time, for Goya's precise meaning is obscure. The so-called *Black Paintings*, done at the same time as decorations for his own house, are scenes of a similar dark and savage side of existence. The strange visions of the two series are Goya's most original creations. They are, however, but one extreme of the range of his work in the last decades of his life, for the breadth of his interest was maintained as the command of his art continued to grow. The almost impressionistic lithographs of bullfighting done during his self-imposed exile in Bordeaux, when he was nearly eighty, are examples of the other limit.

The particular nature of the individualism which was the basis of Goya's work isolates him in his own time and also separates him from the painting in Europe which came immediately after him. The French romantics were the first outside Spain to recognize his genius, but true appreciation and understanding of Goya began in the period of the realists and impressionists. It is with Manet and Degas that his style has its closest formal affinities. On the other hand, the concern for human values and the breadth of human experience that his work embodies link

Goya with the greatest masters of the past.

GOYEN. *See* **VAN GOYEN,** Jan.

GOZZOLI, Benozzo (real name **Benozzo di Lese di Sandro**) (1420 – Oct. 4, 1497). Florentine painter. Born Florence. Worked as goldsmith under Ghiberti on his second pair of bronze doors for baptistery at Florence (1444). Early paintings show influence of Fra Angelico, whom he assisted in Rome and Orvieto (1447–49). Worked independently as fresco painter in Montefalco and Viterbo (1449–57), made brief trip to Rome (1458), and finally returned to Florence, where he decorated chapel in Medici palace (known as Riccardi palace) with *The Journey of the Magi* (1459–60). This fresco contains portraits of the Medici and other prominent Florentines and in style recalls international Gothic and especially Gentile da Fabriano, with emphasis on splendid costumes and abundant detail. Later frescoes, in same manner: scenes from life of St. Augustine in church of S. Agostino at San Gimignano (1463–67); Old Testament scenes in Camposanto at Pisa (1468–84). Died at Pistoia. Gozzoli also painted many panel pictures.

REFERENCES: Piero Bargellini *The Medici Palace and the Frescoes of Benozzo Gozzoli* (tr. Rome 1965). Bernard Berenson *Italian Painters of the Renaissance* (London and New York 1953, also PB). Robert Rowe *Benozzo Gozzoli: Florentine School* (rev. ed. London 1967).

GRAHAME, Kenneth (Mar. 8, 1859 – July 6, 1932). English writer. Born Edinburgh, Scotland. Orphaned early and brought up by grandmother in Berkshire. Educated at St. Edward's School, Oxford, then became clerk in Bank of England (1879). Appointed acting secretary (1893), then permanent secretary (1898) until he retired for health reasons (1908). Married Elspeth Thomson (1899). His writing was discovered by W. E. Henley, who published in *National Observer* his first essays, which appeared in book form as *Pagan Papers* (1893). Also wrote charming, nostalgic sketches of childhood for *Yellow Book,* later collected as *The Golden Age* (1895) and *Dream Days* (1898). His most popular book, *The Wind in the Willows* (1908), has become a children's classic. It began as stories about the adventures of Toad, Ratty, and Mole for Grahame's six-year-old son, nicknamed Mouse (who died in an accident, 1920), and was dramatized as *Toad of Toad Hall* by A. A. Milne (1930). Grahame died in Pangbourne, Berkshire.

REFERENCES: Patrick R. Chalmers *Kenneth Grahame: Life, Letters, and Unpublished Work* (London 1933 and New York 1935). Peter Green *Kenneth Grahame: A Study of His Life, Work, and Times* (London and, as *Kenneth Grahame: A Biography,* New York 1959).

GRAY, Thomas (Dec. 26, 1716 – July 30, 1771). English poet and scholar. Born Cornhill, London, son of a merchant. Educated at Eton, where he became friends with Horace Walpole, and at Peterhouse, Cambridge (1734–38). Accompanied Walpole on grand tour (1739–41), but quarreled with him and returned to Stoke Poges. Here in 1742 he wrote first important poems, including *Ode to Spring, Ode on a Distant Prospect of Eton College,* and *Hymn to Adversity.* Returned to Cambridge (1743) to remain as a scholar the rest of his life. Was reconciled to Walpole, for whom he wrote the charming poem *On the Death of a Favorite Cat* (1747). His *Elegy Written in a Country Churchyard* (1751) made him famous. He refused poet laureateship (1757), and was appointed professor of history and modern languages at Cambridge (1768). Published through Walpole (1757) two Pindaric odes, *Progress of Poesy* (written 1754) and *The Bard* (written 1757). His study of Old Norse poetry inspired *The Descent of Odin* and *The Fatal Sisters* (both written 1761), published with his *Collected Poems* (1768). His chief prose work, *Journal* (1775), records his impressions of travels among the English lakes, and with his letters expresses delightfully his character.

EDITION: *Correspondence of Thomas Gray* ed. Paget Toynbee and Leonard Whibley (3 vols. Oxford and New York 1935). *The Works of Thomas Gray in Prose and Verse* ed. Sir Edmund Gosse (4 vols. London 1885 and New York 1895).

REFERENCES: David Cecil *Two Quiet Lives: Dorothy Osborne, Thomas Gray* (London and New York 1948). William Powell Jones *Thomas Gray, Scholar: The True Tragedy of an Eighteenth-Century Gentleman* (Cambridge, Mass. and Oxford 1937). Robert W. Ketton-Cremer *Thomas Gray* (Cambridge, England, and New York 1955).

☙

THOMAS GRAY
BY DAVID FERRY

As Joseph Wood Krutch says, Gray's life was "a series of retirements from what is commonly called living," the withdrawn and uncompetitive life of a sequestered scholar. He was stand-offish to the many, presenting to them a side of himself which put them off by coldness, indifference, affectation, or merely distant courtesy; to the few, in his continuing friendships, he displayed quite different qualities of affection, considerateness, sympathy, which nevertheless always had their own kind of self-protective reserve. He was thought by at least one admirer to be "the most learned man in Europe," and indeed the extent of his learning was astonishing, ranging from ornithology, botany, other sorts of natural history, to current politics, diplomacy, economics, to history, to architecture, to painting, music, the theatre, to the northern literatures and mythologies, and of course to the classics. Hazlitt says of him: "He had nothing to do but to read and to think, and to tell his friends what he read and thought. His life was a luxurious, thoughtful dream." The luxuriousness of the dream needn't imply indolence; the detail and scrupulosity of his knowledge is as impressive as its range. But Hazlitt's word "dream" does imply the special relation of Gray's intellectual life to his temperament. He is an instance of a familiar eighteenth-century type, the scholar-poet-amateur, a man whose interests are all, as it were, hobbies, in Gray's own case undoubtedly pursued to fend off a persisting and essential melancholy and pursued with an alert intelligence that commands respect, but hobbies nevertheless. Even his poetry, it might be said, was a hobby for him, though of the most elevated and serious kind. At any rate he was accustomed to speak of it as if this were so. He was for a time without question the most celebrated living poet in England, yet he seems to have been more or less indifferent to his fame and there is small reason to think that his indifference was pretended. It seems rather to have been another aspect of his self-sequestration.

Of course one limitation of such a retired life is that it lacks intensity, opens itself up to few possibilities of development and change by putting itself in the way of few involvements and therefore of few dangers. In this connection Hazlitt says ironically of Gray: "What a happiness never to lose or gain anything in the game of human life, by being never anything more than a looker-on." Probably Gray's temperament and style of life did prevent him, gifted as he was, from achieving a more fully developed and adventurous greatness. But it also probably supported in him the disengagement and objectivity, the ability to look about so freely and be so interested in so many things, which characterize his career in general and which are at the source of what is most charming and impressive about his letters. Brief quotation is helpless to convey their quality, since what is chiefly remarkable is neither aphoristic brilliance nor the special force of any passionately held opinions, but the continuous ease and flexibility of the voice we hear speaking in them and our cumulative sense of the accuracy of his observations and of his attentiveness to interesting detail. His letters are among the records which tell us most clearly what it was like to live in his century, and they are always fully alive in doing so. They give us pleasure also in being almost always free of the peevishness, waspishness, which a bare recital of the facts of this withdrawn celibate life might lead us to expect and which we so often find in personalities of Gray's general type. In this way they are a victory of character. They are great letters in an age in which the writing of letters was a conscious art, and was so for some of the reasons that explain why the novel was developing very rapidly at the same time. The letters and novels have a common interest in the materials and surfaces, the things, of the world, and in the detailed behavior of ordinary men and women in that world. Here Gray is no exception but a distinguished representative. He lived withdrawn from the world, but his eyes were not averted from it.

Almost all the poems are of considerable interest to the specialist and to him alone. They display Gray's learning and his willingness to experiment, yet for the most part, with all their virtues, they read like academic exercises. (Among the minor poems I would except *On Lord Holland's Seat Near Margate*, an extraordinary tough-minded moral-satiric performance, still very much alive.) His just claim to greatness as a poet rests of course on the *Elegy Written in a Country Churchyard*. Gray's triumph in this poem is, as F. R. Leavis says, "to crystallize into distinguished expression the conventional poetizing of the meditative-melancholic line of versifiers who drew their inspiration . . . from the minor poems of Milton" and to have done so by "adapting to his ruminative sentiments and commonplaces an Augustan style." The special expressive power of this unique poem resides in the way two modes of feeling and attitude, opposed to one another almost everywhere else in the literature of the century, are subtly fused and mutually pacified. The Augustan ironic distance and impersonal strength are softened, rendered glamorous and darkly luminous, without losing their essential authority; the passive ruminative and melancholic elements, conversely, have more character and strength than they are usually capable of, without losing their own special tonality. (All this is true, I think, till nearly the end; but the falling-off that takes place there has mainly the effect of pointing up the wonderful success of what went before.) I think Gray was able to achieve this work because he was able to bring to it the best qualities of his temperament and life style, his own melancholy and passivity, to be sure, but also his own kind of disengagement and objectivity. If the other poems exemplify the limitations for Gray of being a looker-on at life, the *Elegy*, like the letters in their very different way, demonstrates the advantages as well.

GRECO, EL (real name **Domenikos Theotokopoulos**) (1541 – Apr. 6/7, 1614). Spanish painter. Born in Crete. Nothing known about his early life. Arrived (1560's) in Venice, where he probably studied with Titian. Also influenced by Jacopo Bassano, Tintoretto, and the mannerists Pontormo and Parmigianino. He is thought to have visited Rome (c.1570), then Spain, and by 1577 had settled in Toledo, where he remained for rest of his life. Here he developed his highly original style, charged with emotion and intense religious mysticism. His figures are distortedly elongated, clothed in agitated draperies, while his somber palette is dramatically illumined by livid colors and strange lighting effects. El Greco worked mainly for churches and religious orders. Commissioned to decorate on a large scale the high altar and two transept altars of S. Domingo el Antiguo (1577–79), he painted the *Trinity* (Prado, Madrid) and *Assumption* (Art Institute, Chicago). One of his most famous religious paintings is *The Burial of Count Orgaz* (1586) in S. Tomé, Toledo. Other celebrated works are his portraits: *Cardinal Fernando Niño de Guevara* (c.1600, Metropolitan Museum, New York) and *Fray Félix Hortensio Paravicino* (c.1606, Museum of Fine Arts, Boston); two views of Toledo (1600, Metropolitan Museum; 1609, Casa del Greco, Toledo); and *Laocoön* (National Gallery, Washington, D.C.).

REFERENCES: Ludwig Goldscheider *El Greco: Paintings, Drawings, and Sculptures* (3rd ed. London and New York 1954). Elizabeth du G. Trapier *El Greco's Early Years at Toledo: 1576–86* (New York 1958). Antonina Vallentin *El Greco* (Paris 1954 and New York 1955). Harold E. Wethey *El Greco and His School* (2 vols. Princeton, N.J. 1962).

GREENE, Robert (c.1560 – Sept. 3, 1592). English writer, pamphleteer and dramatist. Born Norwich, Norfolk. Educated at St. John's College, Cambridge (1575–78). Traveled in Spain and Italy, returned to receive M.A. at Cambridge (1583). Sometime during next two years he married, but soon deserted his wife and settled in London, where he lived as a bohemian among cutpurses, rogues, and prostitutes, and died of a surfeit of pickled herrings and Rhenish wine. Published (from 1580) several romances, all strongly influenced by Sir Philip Sidney and John Lyly; best known are *Pandosto* (1588), source of Shakespeare's *The Winter's Tale*, and *Menaphon* (1589). Also produced six "coney-catching" pamphlets, vivid firsthand descriptions of London lowlife, and two autobiographical pamphlets published posthumously: *A Groatsworth of Wit Bought with a Million of Repentance* and *The Repentance of Robert Greene*. His chief dramatic works, *Friar Bacon and Friar Bungay* and *James IV of Scotland* (published posthumously), provided models for Shakespeare's comedies. He is best known for the charming lyrics in his romances, like "Weep not, my wanton" from *Menaphon*.

EDITIONS: *The Life and Complete Works in Prose and Verse of Robert Greene* ed. Alexander B. Grosart (15 vols. London 1881–86, new ed. New York 1964). *The Plays and Poems of Robert Greene* ed. J. Churton Collins (2 vols. Oxford 1905).
REFERENCE: John C. Jordan *Robert Greene* (New York 1915).

GREGORY, Lady Isabella Augusta (Persse) (Mar. 15, 1852 – May 22, 1932). Irish playwright. Born Roxborough, County Galway, of Anglo-Irish family. Married (1880) Sir William Gregory, Anglo-Irish landowner, whose letters and autobiography she edited after his death (1892). Interest in Gaelic studies brought her into contact with leaders of Celtic Revival, including Douglas Hyde and W. B. Yeats. Through latter, became involved in establishing an Irish theatre devoted to works by Irish-born playwrights. As codirector of Abbey Theatre in Dublin, she championed plays of Synge, Yeats, Shaw, and O'Casey and contributed plays of her own. Best known are her one-act comedies of Irish rural life, *Spreading the News* (1904), *The Workhouse Ward* (1907), and the moving patriotic drama *The Rising of the Moon* (1907). Her work reveals a sensitive ear, sure wit, and firm sense of stagecraft. Among her other works are numerous translations of Irish folktales and legends, including *Gods and Fighting Men* (1904), and a brief history of the Abbey Theatre, *Our Irish Theatre* (1914). Her home at Coole Park, County Galway, was a rallying ground for Irish writers, and she perhaps more than any other was responsible for the continued existence of the Abbey Theatre and the high standards of its productions.

EDITIONS: *Selected Plays* ed. Elizabeth Coxhead (London 1966). *Journals 1916–1930* ed. Lennox Robinson (London and New York 1947).

REFERENCE: Elizabeth Coxhead *A Literary Portrait* (London and New York 1961, rev. ed. London 1968).

GREUZE, Jean Baptiste (Aug. 21, 1725 – Mar. 4, 1805). French painter. Born Tournus, Burgundy. After several years' study under portraitist Charles Grandon in Lyons, came to Paris (c.1750) to study at the Academy (admitted 1755). First painting exhibited (Salon of 1755), *A Father Explaining the Bible to His Children,* was a success, and Greuze left for two years' further study in Italy. Encouraged by his friend Denis Diderot he painted a series of sentimental genre scenes, such as *L'Accordée de Village* (1761, Louvre, Paris) and *The Paralytic Cared for by His Children* (1763, Hermitage, Leningrad), which brought him enormous popularity. As portraitist, Greuze counted the dauphin, Robespierre, and Napoleon among his sitters; he also specialized in seductive pictures of adolescent girls, such as *Young Girl Weeping Over Her Dead Bird* (1765), *Offering to Love* (1769), and *The Broken Pitcher* (1773). On failing to receive membership in the Academy (1769) as a painter of history rather than of genre, a lower category, Greuze resigned, and for the next thirty years exhibited his works in his own studio. The revolution ended his prosperity and public favor. Died in Paris.

GREVILLE, Sir Fulke, 1st Baron Brooke (Oct. 3, 1554 – Sept. 30, 1628). English poet and statesman. Born Beauchamps Court, Warwickshire, of aristocratic family. Entered Shrewsbury School (1564), where he began lifelong friendship with Philip Sidney, whose biography he wrote (*Life of Sir Philip Sidney,* 1652). After studies at Cambridge, went with Sidney to court (1577); was soon a favorite of Queen Elizabeth. Held series of offices, becoming chancellor of the exchequer (1614–20/21). Created Baron Brooke (1620/21) by James I. He never married. Died in London. Very few of Greville's works were published in his lifetime. A posthumous collection (1633) included sonnet sequence *Caelica,* much influenced by Sidney, and two Senecan tragedies, *Mustapha* and *Alaham,* which are vehicles for Greville's political views.

EDITIONS: *Life of Sir Philip Sidney* (1652) ed. Nowell Smith (London and New York 1907). *Poems and Dramas* ed. Geoffrey Bullough (2 vols. Edinburgh, London and New York 1938).

GRIEG, Edvard Hagerup (June 15, 1843 – Sept. 4, 1907). Norwegian composer. Born Bergen. Studied piano from age of six with his mother; attended Leipzig Conservatory (1858–62). Crucial to Grieg's musical development was meeting (1864) with Norwegian nationalist composer Rikard Nordraak, who led him to abandon early German manner by introducing him to Norwegian folk music. Married his cousin Nina Hagerup (1867), a singer who became chief interpreter of his songs. Spent winter of 1865–66 in Rome, where he met Ibsen; during second Roman visit (1869–70), was in frequent contact with Liszt, who offered him much encouragement. Settled (1866) in Christiania (Oslo), where he remained until 1874, conducting, giving concerts, and teaching. Annual stipend granted by Norwegian government (1874) enabled him to devote full time to composing. Ibsen invited him to write music for stage performance of *Peer Gynt,* a sensational success (1876) which brought Grieg world fame and honors, as well as adulation of his country. From 1885 he lived in Troldhaugen, a country home near Bergen, where he died. Drawing on Norwegian folk music, Grieg evoked the atmosphere of the northland and the spirit of its tales and legends. His 125 songs were his largest achievement. Other major works include short pieces for piano, notably ten collections of *Lyric Pieces* (1867–1901), *Piano Concerto in A Minor* (1868), scenes from unfinished opera *Olaf Trygvason* (1873), two *Peer*

Gynt suites for orchestra (1876), *String Quartet in G Minor* (1877–78).

REFERENCES: Gerald E. H. Abraham ed. *Grieg: A Symposium* (London 1948 and Norman, Okla. 1950). Henry T. Finck *Grieg and His Music* (rev. ed. New York and London 1929). David Monrad-Johansen *Edvard Grieg* (tr. Princeton, N.J. 1938).

GRILLPARZER, Franz (Jan. 15, 1791 – Jan. 21, 1872). Austrian dramatist. Born and died in Vienna. Entered University of Vienna (1807), but father's death (1809) obliged him to leave and support family, first by tutoring, then in Austrian civil service (1813–56). His first dark verse tragedy, *Die Ahnfrau* (1817), brought him fame, but he suffered spells of deep depression, and his generally gloomy outlook was increased by censorship imposed on his work by Metternich regime. His finest dramas are the tragic Hero and Leander legend *Des Meeres und der Liebe Wellen* (1831, tr. *Hero and Leander* 1962), the dream play *Der Traum, ein Leben* (1834, tr. *A Dream Is Life* 1946), and the political tragedy *Bruderzwist in Habsburg* (1827–48, tr. *Family Strife in Habsburg* 1940) expressing disillusionment with the Revolution of 1848. Other works include the Jason and Medea trilogy *Das Goldene Vliess* (1821), the historical plays *König Ottokars Glück und Ende* (1825, tr. *King Ottocar, His Rise and Fall* 1962), *Die Jüdin von Toledo* (1873, tr. *The Jewess of Toledo* 1953), and his last play *Libussa* (1873). Also wrote autobiographical novella *Der arme Spielmann* (1848) and critical studies on Spanish drama. Made occasional journeys and met Goethe (1826), but, always pessimistic, he died unhappy and embittered. Now considered the greatest Austrian dramatist, who influenced later playwrights Hauptmann and Maeterlinck, Grillparzer perpetuated the German classic and romantic traditions and brought to the theatre new qualities of searching human understanding, lyricism, and effective stage technique.

REFERENCES: Douglas Yates *Franz Grillparzer: A Critical Biography* (2 vols. Oxford 1946 and New York 1947). Gisela Stein *The Inspiration Motif in the Works of Franz Grillparzer* (The Hague 1955).

GRIMM, Jacob Ludwig Carl (Jan. 4, 1785 – Sept. 20, 1863) and Wilhelm Carl (Feb. 24, 1786 – Dec. 16, 1859). German philologists, folklorists, and lexicographers. The brothers were born at Hanau, Hesse-Cassel, and studied at Marburg. They worked as librarians at Kassel (1816–29), during which period Wilhelm married Dorothy Wild (1825). The Grimms moved to Göttingen (1829), where both became professors. Exiled because of participation in a protest of seven professors against elector of Hanover's coup d'état (1837), they spent a few years in Kassel, then settled in Berlin, where both became professors at University of Berlin (1841) and were elected to Academy of Sciences (1841). They died in Berlin. Jacob, a founder of comparative philology, formulated Grimm's Law; his independent works include *Deutsche Grammatik* (4 vols. 1819–37) and *Deutsche Mythologie* (1835). Wilhelm wrote independently numerous studies of early Germanic literature, notably *Die Deutsche Heldensage* (1829) on German heroic legends. Best known of the Grimms' works in collaboration is *Kinder- und Hausmärchen* (1812–15, tr. *Grimm's Fairy Tales*, 1823), which had major influence on German romanticism. The brothers also planned and inaugurated the great *Deutsche Wörterbuch* (16 vols. 1854–1954).

GRIS, Juan (real name José Victoriano Gonzáles) (Mar. 13, 1887 – May 11, 1927). Spanish painter. Born Madrid, where he attended engineering school for two years. Turned to painting (1904) and went to Paris (1906), settling at the Bateau-Lavoir, a group of studios in Montmartre, where he met Picasso, Braque, and other cubists. At first worked chiefly as graphic artist, drawing for various satirical journals. Began exhibiting paintings with cubists at Salon des Indépendants (1912). Evolved (1913) technique known as synthetic cubism, his major contribution to the school; based on geometrical architecture, it aims at comprehensible objectivity. At its best, in composition and palette, his art is "a logical, complex coherent system" (Jacques Lassaigne) with the pure, austere qualities of classicism. Although exempt from service because of his Spanish citizenship, he became impoverished during World War I and suffered (1920) a long illness which cost months of work. Designed several ballet sets for Diaghilev (1922–24). Produced at Sorbonne (1924) a widely influential paper, *Les Possibilités de la peinture,* and in 1925 painted his greatest, most serene and clean-cut still lifes. His health worsened steadily, however, and he died at Boulogne-sur-Seine, near Paris, two years later.

REFERENCE: Daniel-Henry Kahnweiler *Juan Gris: His Life and Work* (tr. New York 1969).

GROPIUS, Walter (Adolf) (May 18, 1883 – July 5, 1969). German-American architect. Born Berlin. Studied architecture in Munich and Berlin (1903–1907), then worked as assistant to Peter Behrens, Berlin, soon gaining reputation for revolutionary functional designs, as in his famous steel and glass Fagus factory building at Alfeld. At outbreak of World War I enlisted in German army, winning Iron Cross. Married twice: Alma Mahler (1916; divorced 1921) and Ise Franck (1923). Founded the Staatliches Bauhaus at Weimar (1919), which moved to Dessau (1925), a school combining study of architecture, art, and industrial design, its purpose: form to follow function. Gropius assembled a faculty of people outstanding in their fields, including Mies Van der Rohe, Paul Klee, Wassily Kandinsky, Marcel Breuer, Ladislau Moholy-Nagy. He set forth his principles in *Internationale Architectur* (1925, 2nd edition 1928), and resigned as director of Bauhaus (1928) in order to concentrate on own work of prefabricated houses, industrial buildings, and design. The Nazis closed the Bauhaus (1933), and Gropius went to London (1934), where he worked with Maxwell Fry and published *The New Architecture and the Bauhaus* (1935). Came to U.S. (1937) as professor of architecture at Harvard, and next year became head of department of architecture of Graduate School. Formed his own firm,

the Architects Collaborative (1945), where upon retirement (1952) he continued an extraordinarily active career, with commissions to build U.S. Embassy in Athens, University of Baghdad, and numerous academic buildings, as well as the satellite city Gropiusstadt outside Berlin. He died in Boston. Considered one of the great architects of the time, Gropius was an important inventor in modern industrial design and educator in architecture, city planning and design.

EDITION: *The New Architecture and the Bauhaus* (tr. London and New York 1937, also PB; new ed. Cambridge, Mass. 1969). *Scope of Total Architecture* (New York 1955). *Apollo in Democracy: The Cultural Obligation* ed. and tr. Ise Gropius (New York 1968).

REFERENCE: James M. Fitch *Walter Gropius* (New York 1960 and London 1961, also PB). Sigfried Giedion *Walter Gropius: Work and Teamwork* (New York 1954).

GROS, Baron Antoine Jean (Mar. 16, 1771 – June 26, 1835). French painter. Born Paris. Received early training from father, a miniaturist. Entered studio of Jacques Louis David (1785–1793), where he attracted attention of Napoleon, whom he portrayed in his first major work, *The Victor of Arcole* (1796). Gros, at Napoleon's behest, remained with French army and produced his three masterpieces, *The Pesthouse at Jaffa* (1804, Louvre, Paris), *The Battle of Aboukir* (1806, Versailles), and *The Battle of Eylau* (1808, Louvre). The authentic detail, emotional drama, color, and movement of these pictures belied Gros's professed classicism. After Napoleon's fall, he worked for the restored monarchy; designed the Pantheon dome (1811–24). Took over David's studio (1816), and in reverting to former classicism, lost esteem of younger painters. In 1835, the year he was elected professor at the Academy, he drowned himself in the Seine at Meudon. Gros's realism strongly influenced Géricault and Delacroix.

REFERENCE: J. E. Delestre *Gros, sa vie et ses ouvrages* (2nd ed. Paris 1867).

GROSZ, George (July 26, 1893 – July 6, 1959). German painter and graphic artist. Born in Berlin, raised in provincial town of Stolp. Expelled from high school at thirteen, he studied art at Royal Academy in Dresden (1909–10) and at Royal Arts and Crafts School in Berlin (1911), where he began publishing caricatures in such newspapers as *Ulk*. Influenced by the futurists, he expressed his anger and disillusionment as a soldier during World War I in scathing drawings. After the war, affected by Dada and later (c.1925) *neue Sachlichkeit* (new objectivity) movements, he produced, largely in watercolor, drawings portraying the materialism and decadence of Weimar Germany. Often fined for libel or blasphemy, he became famous as social critic with his series *The Face of the Ruling Class* (1919), *Gott mit Uns* (1920), *Ecce Homo* (1922), and *Mirror of Boobs* (1924). Married Eva Peter (1920). Moved to America (1932), became citizen 1938) to teach at Art Students League in New York. Here his work became less aggressively satirical, but the late 1940's saw return to violence, with a new element of apocalyptic vision, in famous series *The Stickman* (c.1947). Published autobiography *A Little Yes and a Big No* (1946). Received gold medal from National Institute of Arts and Letters (1959). Died little more than a month after returning to Berlin.

REFERENCES: Imre Hofbauer ed. *George Grosz* with intro. by John Dos Passos (London 1949). Herbert Bittner ed. *George Grosz* (New York 1960 and London 1965).

GRÜNEWALD, Matthias (real name Mathis Gothart Nithart) (c.1470/83 – 1528). German painter. Born Würzburg. As court painter, superintendent of works, and architect to the archbishop-elector of Mainz, Uriel of Gemmingen, and to his successor, Albrecht of Brandenburg, lived mainly at Aschaffenburg. Left post (c.1526), perhaps dismissed because of support of Martin Luther. Thereafter worked as a waterworks specialist, architect, and engineer in Frankfurt am Main, Magdeburg, and Halle, where he died. In his masterpiece, the *Isenheim Altarpiece* (1510–

15) for monastery church of Order of St. Anthony at Isenheim (now in Colmar Museum), Grünewald employed the resources of the great Flemish masters with unprecedented boldness and flexibility. Particularly impressive are his intensity of feeling and illuminating color. Other works by Grünewald, who remained in obscurity until the twentieth century, include *The Meeting of St. Erasmus and St. Maurice* (Alte Pinakothek, Munich), *Crucifixion* and *Christ Carrying the Cross* (Staatliche Kunsthalle Karlsruhe), and two panels depicting female saints Furstlich Furstenbergische Sammlung, Donaueschingen).

REFERENCES: Arthur Burkhard *Matthias Grünewald: Personality and Accomplishment* (Cambridge, Mass. and Oxford 1936). J. K. Huysmans and Ernst Ruhmer *Grünewald: Paintings* (London 1958). Nikolaus Pevsner and M. Meier *Grünewald* (London 1948). G. Schönberger ed. *The Drawings of Mathis Gothart Nithart Called Grünewald* (New York 1968).

GUARDI, Francesco (Oct. 5, 1712 – Jan. 1, 1793). Italian painter. Born and died in Venice, the son of a painter. Trained, along with his brother Nicolò (1715–1785), in workshop of their elder brother Giovanni Antonio (1699–1769). The three collaborated on religious paintings, figure subjects, genre, and still lifes. Francesco is known particularly for his views of Venice, extremely popular with foreigners, imaginary landscapes, and *capriccii* (architectural fantasies). After closely following Canaletto (1750–60), he evolved his own style, departing from the older painter's clear, photographic manner; achieved shimmering atmospheric effects painted with swift, bold brushstrokes. Married Maria Pagani (1760); their son Giacomo (1764–1835) was an imitator of his father. Francesco depicted festivities honoring visit of Archduke Paul of Russia (1712), and in same year was officially commissioned to paint scenes of Pius VI's visit. Elected to Venetian Academy (1784).

REFERENCES: Michael Levey *Painting in Eighteenth-Century Venice* (London and New York 1959). Vittorio Moschini

Francesco Guardi (2nd ed. tr. London and New York 1957). James Byam Shaw *The Drawings of Francesco Guardi* (London 1951).

GUERCINO (real name Giovanni Francesco Barbieri) (Feb. 8, 1591 – Dec. 22, 1666). Italian painter. Born Cento, where he received first training. Work early shows influence of Lodovico Carracci. Executed fresco decorations and religious paintings in Cento, Bologna, and Ferrara, and visited Venice (1618), before accepting Pope Gregory XV's invitation to Rome (1621). Here he painted his baroque masterpiece, the *Aurora* fresco in Villa Ludovisi, and a celebrated canvas, the *Burial and Reception into Heaven of St. Petronilla* (for St. Peter's, now in Pinacoteca Capitolina). Guercino returned to Cento on Gregory's death (1623), but moved to Bologna after the death (1642) of Guido Reni, who had dominated that city's artistic world. His early style, combining classical and baroque elements, and especially noted for its strong chiaroscuro and warm Venetian colors, gave way after his Roman years to a cold and derivative classicism. Died in Bologna.

REFERENCE: Denis Mahon *Studies in Seicento Art and Theory* (London 1947).

GUILLAUME D'AQUITAINE, 9th duke of Aquitaine and 7th count of Poitou. (1071–1127). Provençal lyric poet and first known troubadour. Twice married, to Ermengarde of Anjou, then to Philippa of Toulouse. Used Philippa's rights to county of Toulouse as pretext for two invasions (1097, 1113–19); both ended in disaster, as did his crusade into Holy Land (1101–1102). Met with greater success as ally of Alphonso I of Aragon against Saracens (1119). Famous for elegance of his verse and his manners, for his stormy temperament and his amorous prowess, he wrote the first known lyric verses in a modern language, Provençal. Eleven of his songs have survived. Half of them are plainly sensual and, by modern standards, coarse. The other half deal with themes which were to be exploited by Guillaume's literary heirs the troubadours of Provence, whose famous patroness, Eleanor of Aquitaine, was his granddaughter.

EDITION: Alfred Jeanroy *Les Chansons de Guillaume IX,* (Paris 1927).

REFERENCES: Henri Davenson *Les Troubadours* (Paris 1964). E. Hoepffner *Les Troubadours* (Paris 1955). Alfred Jeanroy *La Poésie lyrique des troubadours* (Paris 1934).

GUYS, (Ernest Adolphe Hyacinthe) Constantin (Dec. 3, 1805 – Mar. 13, 1892). French watercolorist and draftsman. Born Flessingue, Holland, of French parents. Spent a vagabond life, of which little is documented. After fighting in Greek struggle for liberty (1824), he became war correspondent for *Illustrated London News,* observing and sketching events in Revolution of 1848 and Crimean War, and traveling in the Orient, Italy, Spain, England, and Germany. Settled (c.1860) in Paris, where with insatiable curiosity he observed all aspects of the city's social life, which he rendered with vividness and elegance, leaving an invaluable pictorial history of Second Empire society. Nonchalant about his work, he avoided publicity, and neither signed nor dated the majority of his sketches. The enthusiasm of Baudelaire, Manet, the Goncourts and others made him famous. Died in Paris.

REFERENCES: Charles Baudelaire *Le Peintre de la Vie Moderne* (Paris 1863). Paul George Konody *The Painter of Victorian Life: A Study of Constantin Guys* (New York 1930, with a translation of Baudelaire, above).

HAKLUYT, Richard (c.1552 – Nov. 23, 1616). English geographer. Born probably in London; of prominent Herefordshire family. As a youth became passionately interested in geography and exploration. Educated at Westminster School and Christ Church, Oxford (1570–77). Ordained (1578) and enjoyed successful career in the church. First work, *Divers Voyages Touching the Discovery of America and the Islands Adjacent* (1582), led to post of chaplain to Sir Edward Stafford, English ambassador to Paris (1583–88), where Hakluyt collected information about colonization and overseas trade. His researches were recorded in *The Discourse on the Western Planting* (1584; not published until 1877, because lost), which served to support Sir Walter Raleigh's colonizing project in Virginia and brought Hakluyt a canonship in Bristol cathedral. His major work, *The Principal Navigations, Voyages and Discoveries of the English Nation* (1589), is a chronicle of the voyages of explorers to North America, including the mythical Welshman Madoc, the Cabots, Sir Humphrey Gilbert and others, of Sir John Hawkins's voyage to Guinea and the West Indies, of Frobisher's search for the Northwest Passage, Drake's voyages of 1570–72, Davy's voyages to the Arctic, and many others. Much enlarged, it was reissued in three volumes (1598–1600). The inspiring effect of Hakluyt's *Voyages* on British discovery and colonization is reflected in James Froude's recognition of it as the "prose epic of the modern English nation" and in the contemporary tribute of Michael Drayton's *Ode to the Virginian Voyage* (1605):

> *Industrious Hakluyt,*
> *Whose reading shall inflame*
> *Men to seek fame.*

Hakluyt also translated foreign works on geography and colonization and received the living of Jamestown, Virginia (1605). Married Douglas Cavendish (1590), served as rector of Wetheringsett, and rose to the archdeaconry of Westminster cathedral before his death in London.

EDITIONS: *The Principal Navigations, Voyages and Discoveries of the English Nation* ed. David B. Quinn (facsimile of London 1589 edition; Cambridge, England, and New York 1965); Hakluyt Society edition (12 vols. London and New York 1903–1905). *Divers Voyages Touching the Discovery of America and the Islands Adjacent* ed. John W. Jones, Hakluyt Society edition (London 1850). *The Original Writings and Correspondence of the Two Richard Hakluyts* ed. Eva G. R. Taylor, Hakluyt Society edition (2 vols. London 1936).

REFERENCE: George B. Parks *Richard Hakluyt and the English Voyages* (1928, new ed. New York 1961).

HALIFAX. *See* **SAVILE, Sir George.**

HALLECK, Fitz-Greene (July 8, 1790 – Nov. 19, 1867). American poet. Born and died in Guilford, Conn. Worked as bank clerk in New York (1811–19). His series of satirical verses, *Croaker Papers* (1819), written in collaboration with Joseph Rodman Drake for the New York *Evening Post*, brought instant success. *Fanny*, a Byronic satire on society, appeared the same year. In Europe (1822) he wrote the romantic-satirical poem *Alnwich Castle*, followed by the rousing poem *Marco Bozzaris* (1825) for the Greek patriot. This and his elegy *On the Death of Joseph Rodman Drake* ("Green be the turf above thee") (1821) are among his best-known poems. After publication of *Alnwich Castle, with Other Poems* (1827), he wrote little, though he brought out *Poetical Works* (1847). Became confidential secretary to John Jacob Astor (1832–49) and trustee of Astor Library. Halleck belonged to the Knickerbocker Group with Washington Irving, William Cullen Bryant, and others.

REFERENCES: Nelson F. Adkins *Fitz-Greene Halleck: An Early Knickerbocker Wit and Poet* (New Haven and London 1930). James Grant Wilson *Life and Letters of Fitz-Greene Halleck* (New York 1869).

HALS, Frans (c.1580 – Aug. 26, 1666). Dutch painter. Born Antwerp, but moved early with family to Haarlem, where he studied under Karel van Mander, joining painters' guild (1610). Talent for portraiture brought him commissions to paint large groups of guildsmen and officers, such as *Banquet of the Civic Guard of St. Adrian* (1622–27, Frans Hals Museum, Haarlem), also portraits of distinguished civic leaders, artists, merchants and other important figures, including Descartes (c.1649). His special gift was to catch a fleeting gesture or expression, and his seemingly quick, light brushstroke reinforced the effect of spontaneity. One of his most brilliant examples is *The Laughing Cavalier* (1624, Wallace Collection, London). His genre subjects, as distinct from formal group portraits, include casual gatherings — market folk, tavern characters, boys with musical instruments. His later group paintings commissioned by regents and governors of charities reflect a greater sense of humanity and feeling for character, and were executed while he himself was struggling to support wife and family. Other famous works include his first group portrait *Banquet of the Officers of the Guild of Archers of St. George* (1616, Frans Hals Museum), *The Jolly Toper* (1627, Rijksmuseum, Amsterdam), *Hille Bobbe* (c.1650, National Gallery, Berlin), *Regents of the Hospital of St. Elizabeth* (1641), *Regents of the Old Men's Almshouse* (1664) and *Regentesses of the Old Men's Almshouse*

(1664; all in the Frans Hals Museum). Besides his five sons, his pupils included Adriaen van Ostade, Philips Wouwerman, and Adriaen Brouwer. He died in Haarlem.

REFERENCES: Willem A. L. Beeren *Frans Hals* (tr. New York PB 1963). Numa S. Trivas *The Paintings of Frans Hals* (London and New York 2nd ed. 1949).

HAMSUN, Knut (real name Knut Pedersen). (Aug. 4, 1859 – Feb. 19, 1952). Born Lom, Norway. Began writing early, and worked as laborer to earn enough to attend University of Christiania. Failing to do so, he emigrated to U.S., where he worked at odd jobs on farms and in towns of Middle West. Returned to Norway (1884) for two years of lecturing on his life in U.S. Again in U.S. (1886–88) lecturing and working as farmhand and as streetcar conductor in Chicago. Returning to Norway (1889), wrote *Intellectual Life of Modern America* (1889), attacking American culture. Produced (1890) first successful novel, *Hunger*, enabling him to settle down, marry Berg Pjot Göpfert, raise a family, and continue writing. Novel *Mysteries* (1892) was followed by *Pan* (1899) and finally his realistic rural masterpiece, *Growth of the Soil* (1917). Won Nobel prize (1920). During both world wars Hamsun was a German sympathizer, collaborating with Nazis during invasion of Norway (1940), for which he was tried and fined. After confinement in a psychiatric hospital, he returned to his home near Grimstad, where he died. Other important works also in English translation: *The Women at the Pump* (1928), *Vagabonds* (1930), *August* (1931), *The Road Leads On* (1934), *The Ring Is Closed* (1937), and *Look Back on Happiness* (1940).

REFERENCE: Hanna Astrup Larsen *Knut Hamsun* (New York 1922).

HANDEL, George Frideric (Feb. 23, 1685 – Apr. 13/14, 1759). Anglo-German composer. Born in Halle, son of a barber-surgeon. Attended gymnasium and university (1702–1703) in Halle; started organ lessons (1693) and served as organist at the cathedral (1697–1703). In Hamburg (1703–1706), was a musician at the opera house and saw (1705) first performances of his own work, a *St. John Passion* and the opera *Almira*. In Italy (1706–1709), composed vocal music and acquired considerable renown, which spread to Germany and led to his appointment as kapellmeister to the elector of Hanover (1710). That year went to London, where his opera *Rinaldo* was performed (1711) with great success. Finally, took up (1712) permanent residence in London, where he was chiefly engaged in producing operas (1719–41) and in later years the English oratorios. Died in London; buried in Westminster Abbey. Major works include forty-six operas, notably *Rinaldo* (1711), *Giulio Cesare* (1724), *Serse* (1738); thirty-two oratorios, notably *Israel in Egypt* (1739), *Messiah* (1742), *Judas Maccabeus* (1746); fifteen chamber sonatas (1724); concertos for orchestra and various instruments (1739).

REFERENCES: Otto Eric Deutsch *Handel, a Documentary Biography* (New York, 1955). Paul Henry Lang *George Frideric Handel* (New York 1966 and London 1967).

✍

GEORGE FRIDERIC HANDEL
BY ROBERT EVETT

In his petition for naturalization as a British subject, he used the name George Frideric Handel, and this is the style that English-speaking persons should use in referring to him. The name rhymes with candle.

Handel — born a few weeks before J. S. Bach and a few months before Domenico Scarlatti — was very likely a precocious musical talent, but the apocryphal yarns about his accomplishments at the age of eight or ten cannot be documented. Apparently, his family did oppose his choice of music as a profession. He matriculated at the University of Halle (recently founded and already one of the shabbiest institutions of higher learning in North Germany) in 1702. His academic ca-

reer was dismally short-lived. A year later, he was sawing away in the violin section of the Hamburg Opera orchestra. Then Italy (1706-10), then a little more of Germany (he was appointed court conductor to the elector of Hanover), and finally, in the fall of 1710, London. His goal from the beginning was to take over the musical life of the city, and if he was not totally successful in this, he came close to achieving his purpose. The first few years he spent making a tactical withdrawal from the Continent. When his German patron ascended the British throne as George I, he was already on his way to being as English as Gilbert and Sullivan or steak-and-kidney pie.

To win the following he needed, Handel had to write music that was attractive and safe. During his German student days, critical opinion had it that his gift for melody was poor. To correct this, he followed Italian models until the generation of long, voluptuous melodies became second nature to him. The greatest single strength of Handel's music during his English period (which lasted until his death) is the spontaneity of his melodic invention. Paradoxically, this is also his greatest weakness. In his ruthless determination to get a good box office, Handel was willing to exploit whatever sentimentality he was able to create. This sentimentality pervades some of his most famous arias (such as "Come Unto Him" from *Messiah* and "Ombra mai fu" from *Xerxes*) and it also affects his counterpoint. Given his Teutonic heritage and his natural abilities, Handel was one of the most richly endowed contrapuntists ever born, but a close look at his scores shows that his counterpoint was generally uncomplicated to the point of being deceptive. He gives the impression of writing elaborate polyphony when what he is delivering is simple two-part counterpoint with padding. It does, of course, sound good — very good indeed — because it was Mr. Handel's intention to stir them up, and that is what he did and is still doing to this day.

In point of style, Handel made the necessary distinctions between vocal and instrumental music, but none between the sacred and the profane. He was a man of the theatre and of the world, and many of his twentieth-century critics find it inconceivable that he had any more burning interest in theology or in his risen Lord than any other British gentleman of the period. From the age of eighteen, he made it clear that he was for hire, and happy to put his talents as a church composer at the disposal of the Lutherans, the Calvinists, the Roman Catholics or the Church of England, without prejudice.

His switch, late in his career, from opera to oratorio, was dictated largely by fiscal considerations. Opera was expensive to produce, even in the eighteenth century, and the chances of losing a fortune on a new production were large. Handel found in the oratorio an opportunity to exploit his dramatic gifts without the enormous financial risk involved in staging an opera.

Handel's private life was very private indeed. If he took mistresses, nobody knows who they were, though the chances of a man in his station living to the age of seventy-four in total celibacy are not great. He did live alone until he became blind. This was not a precipitous event. On a score page of *Jephtha,* he wrote (in German): "Got so far as this on Wednesday, February 13, 1751, because of [?] weakening of the left eye."

During his last years, he was tended by a young musician, John Christopher Smith, who took dictation, conducted Handel's works in theatres and other halls, and tended to his personal needs. Blind as he was, and old, Handel played harpsichord publicly throughout the season of 1758-59. He fainted in the orchestra pit during a performance of *Messiah* on the last day of the season, April 6. On April 14, he was dead.

————

HARDY, Thomas (June 2, 1840 – Jan. 11, 1928). English novelist and poet. Born Upper Bockhampton, near Dorchester, Dorset. Father a stonemason and choir leader; both parents of rural background. After attending local schools, Hardy was apprenticed at sixteen to an architect. In London (1862–67) while working as architect, read widely in contemporary literature, science, philosophy. Returned to Dorset, began writing poetry, and published first novel, *Desperate Remedies* (1871) anonymously. *Under the Greenwood Tree* (1872) followed. Recognition came with *Far from the Madding Crowd* (1874), and Hardy gave up architecture. Married Emma Lavinia Gifford (1874; she died 1912), then Florence Emily Dugdale (1914). Best of twelve later novels: *The Return of the Native* (1878), *The Trumpet-Major* (1880), *The Mayor of Casterbridge* (1886), *The Woodlanders* (1887), *Tess of the D'Urbervilles* (1891), *Jude the Obscure* (1896). Published eight volumes of poetry, from *Wessex Poems* (1898) to *Winter Words* (posthumous, (1928); *Collected Poems* appeared (1932). Best-known collection of his short stories is *Wessex Tales* (1888); also wrote three-part epic drama of the Napoleonic Wars, *The Dynasts* (1904/1906/1908). Received Order of Merit (1910). Died at Max Gate, near Dorchester; his heart was buried in the parish churchyard, his ashes in Westminster Abbey.

REFERENCES: David Cecil *Hardy the Novelist: An Essay in Criticism* (London 1943 and Indianapolis 1946). Albert J. Guérard *Thomas Hardy: The Novels and Stories* (Cambridge, Mass.

1949 and London 1950). Evelyn Hardy *Thomas Hardy: A Critical Biography* (London and New York 1954). Florence Emily Hardy *The Early Life of Thomas Hardy, 1840–1891* (London and New York 1928) and *The Later Years of Thomas Hardy, 1892–1928* (London and New York 1930), published in one volume as *The Life of Thomas Hardy, 1840–1928; compiled largely from contemporary notes, letters, diaries, and biographical memoranda, as well as from oral information in conversations extending over many years* (London and New York 1962). Irving Howe *Thomas Hardy* (New York 1967 and London 1968). J. Millis Miller *Thomas Hardy: Distance and Desire* (Cambridge, Mass. 1970). Carl J. Weber *Hardy of Wessex: His Life and Literary Career* (New York and London 1940). Harvey C. Webster *On a Darkling Plain* (Chicago 1947 and Cambridge, England, 1948).

☞

THOMAS HARDY
BY IRVING HOWE

Like many great or near-great writers, Thomas Hardy is an elusive, almost protean figure. The more one reflects upon his work, the more it seems to grow into multiplicity. We can read him as a philosopher spinning fables of determinism, an elegist of rural simplicities, a poet of tenderness, a Christian whose faith has been hollowed by skepticism, a country pagan whose mind is covered over with Christian pieties, an imaginative historian of the revolutionary changes in nineteenth-century moral consciousness, an autodidact who keeps stumbling into sublimities of intuition.

As a boy Thomas Hardy absorbed the unspoken assumptions of the traditional Dorset culture. The Dorset of his youth (Wessex, in his novels) was still rural, traditional, fixed in old country ways, rituals and speech. The threat of change in an England already deep into the convulsive transformations of the Industrial Revolution was just

becoming visible there. For the man who would experience the turning from country faith to modernist skepticism in the most personal way, his possession of that slowly fading world of Wessex, remembered with pathos and unrivaled knowledge, would make possible a fabled reconstruction, which he would then set off against the ruthlessness of historical change.

In 1862, at the age of twenty-two, Hardy went to London, where he completed an apprenticeship to the advanced thought of his time. There is something admirable and touching in the sight of this country youth as he pores over Darwin and Spencer, Huxley and Mill, striving to provision his mind and discover the truth about God, man and nature. The youth who had for a time considered becoming a clergyman was forced, through the pain of integrity, to surrender a faith by which childhood had been warmed and moral sentiments forged, and to accept a mechanistic universe, one containing neither inherent purpose nor moral quality. The passage of time has been somewhat unkind to the agnostics and rationalists of the mid-nineteenth century, and few of us can now wholly share their confidence in the idea of progress. But one need not wholly accept their doctrines to see why a young man like Hardy should have declared himself their disciple. His feeling that pain and cruelty are built into the very structure of existence was thereby confirmed, while he kept on searching for philosophical cues by means of which ethical discipline and human solidarity might be maintained in the frigid universe postulated by the skeptics.

Having given up architecture for poetry, he returned to Dorset in 1867, and between about 1868 and 1896, Hardy proved to be an enormously productive writer, turning out fourteen novels as well as three volumes of short stories. The Wessex novels, with the major exception of *Jude the Obscure*, form a prolonged celebration, if at times dropping into a minor key, of the English countryside. In *Under the Greenwood Tree* Hardy evokes the charm of an "unspoiled" village; in *The Return of the Native* the permanence of the heath; in *Far from the Madding Crowd* the curative freshness of farm life.

In the world of Wessex there survives the experience of an "organic culture," the memory of a time in which nature and society are at peace. The past lives on, a repository of history but also something else, something not always to be grasped through the categories of history. For here in Wessex long stretches of the past can be seen as embodying the sameness and continuity, the unifying rhythms, of a human existence that extends beneath or beyond the agitation of the historical process. Generations work the soil mostly with age-old methods, and the same moral and social precepts are handed down.

The more Hardy became aware of the thrust of social change, the more he felt a need to turn back to those memories of the past which could yield him a fund of stories, legends, superstitions, folk sayings, and fragments of wisdom. Folk material brought to the threshold of the present and set off against the grimness of Hardy's fables permitted him to impute a fatalistic pessimism to the cycle of history.

Meanwhile, in all the Wessex novels but *Jude the Obscure*, the natural world figures as a vibrant and autonomous being, in effect a "character" with its own temperament and destiny. Hardy's observation of nature is expert in detail; it is often especially power-ful for the way he spontaneously transmits to the external world qualities we usually take to be confined to the human. There is a strong Wordsworthian quality in Hardy's passionate intuition that the natural world is the source and repository of all the energies that control human existence. Like Wordsworth, Hardy makes the external setting a kind of sharer in the human fate.

The Hardyan hero is usually a solitary man with an "experiencing nature." For not only does Hardy transform the Wessex landscape into a scene of timeless vastness and historical echo, he also lends it an aura of contemplativeness. And it is this aura of contemplativeness which produces the true Hardy note: plangent and deep, ruminative and awestruck, fraternal and uncensorious; patient before the monotony of change and the sameness of novelty.

The countryside in the Wessex novels comes to embody the accumulated richness of an old and stable culture, but since Hardy is realistic, also the accumulated stagnation. As long as that culture remains available for Hardy's protagonists to come back to, away from the pressures of ambition and thought, they need not feel entirely homeless in the world. Once it is no longer there or no longer felt to be vital, there follows the deracination of *Jude the Obscure*.

As a thinker, Hardy could do no more than restate in his own idiom the assumptions of the advanced circles of his time. But Hardy's power derives far less from his ideas than from his intuitive grasp of what their triumph might mean for the nerves of sensitive men. He refers to "the ache of modernism," and that striking phrase points not only to Clym Yeobright's troubles, but also to the effect of intellectual change upon exposed human beings. In *Tess of the D'Urbervilles* he speaks of "the chronic melancholy which is taking hold of the civilized races with the decline of belief in a beneficent Power," and in *Jude the Obscure* the hero remarks that a new breed of boys "unknown to the last generation" is springing up: "They seem to see all [of life's] terrors before they are old enough to resist them . . . It is the beginning of the universal wish not to live." Such insights, caught in the first of these two sentences and dramatically fleshed in the novel itself, are more striking by far than Hardy's formal ideas.

In his youth Hardy had written poetry, and he continued intermittently to do so throughout his life. In his old age he began, in effect, a second career, devoting himself entirely to verse, and it is by no means a critical indulgence to suggest that as a poet Hardy's stature is greater than as a novelist. The themes of his fiction are carried over into his verse, as are his characteristic tones of quizzical and resigned tenderness. But freed from the obligation to construct plots, Hardy is able in his poetry to concentrate and purify his vision of human pain. In his seventies he composed a series of elegies after the death of his wife which are surely the greatest of their kind in English poetry: the ultimate expression of the experience of loss, resignation and recovery.

Neither as a traditionalist alone nor a modernist alone is Hardy at his best. His writing, at its most distinguished, displays a unique convergence of the traditional and modern, in a sustaining friction one with the other. The pessimistic anxieties of a modern intellectual rub against the stoic bias of a country mind; "modern nerves," as Hardy writes in *The Woodlanders*, against "primitive feelings"; skepticism against superstition. Through this strange union, Hardy could brush past the conventional ties of moralistic optimism which had virtually asphyxiated official nineteenth-century England. The truth he had found struck him as bleak, and joined to the country fatalism, which in Dorset lay buried beneath the surface of Christianity, does much to explain the melancholy and pessimism of tone that run through his work. Hardy achieved something far more valuable than any philosophy: his own deeply considered and contemplative wisdom.

HARRIS, Joel Chandler (Dec. 8, 1848 – July 3, 1908). American journalist, short story writer, and novelist. Born Eatonton, Ga. At sixteen became printer's apprentice on literary newspaper, *The Countryman*, published on nearby plantation. After Civil War gained reputation for humorous writing as journalist in Macon, New Orleans, and Savannah. Married Esther LaRose (1876) and settled in Atlanta, where he joined staff of *Atlanta Constitution* (1876–1900). His *Uncle Remus* stories first appeared in the *Constitution* — Negro folk tales in authentic dialect, gathered from plantation slaves, and retold through the famous Negro character Uncle Remus. Books of these tales include *Uncle Remus, His Songs and His Sayings* (1881), *Nights with Uncle Remus* (1883), *Uncle Remus and His Friends* (1892), *The Tar Baby* (1904), *Uncle Remus and Br'er Rabbit* (1906). Harris was equally skilled in conveying a picture of the Georgia cracker, as seen in *Mingo and Other Sketches* (1884) and *Free Joe and Other Georgian Sketches* (1887). He died in Atlanta.

REFERENCES: Stella B. Brookes *Joel Chandler Harris, Folklorist* (Athens, Ga. 1950). Paul M. Cousins *Joel Chandler Harris: A Biography* (Baton Rouge, La. 1968). Julia C. Harris *The Life and Letters of Joel Chandler Harris* (Boston and New York 1918).

HARTE, Bret (real name Francis Brett Hart) (Aug. 25, 1836 – May 5, 1902). American writer. Born Albany, N.Y., son of a schoolteacher whose death left family in poverty (1845). Quit school for job as clerk (1849), then went to California (1854), working at odd jobs. Began to write for San Francisco *Golden Era* (1857), then for *Northern Californian*. Married Anna Griswold (1862). Helped found *Overland Monthly* (1868), in second issue of which appeared *The Luck of Roaring Camp,* which made him famous. Other well-known stories quickly followed: *The Outcasts of Poker Flat* (1869), *Tennessee's Partner* (1869), *The Idyll of Red Gulch* (1869), *How Santa Claus Came to Simpson's Bar* (1872), and the comic ballad *Plain Language from Truthful James* (1870). Accepted offer to write for *Atlantic Monthly* for a year and returned East (1871). Thereafter, however, the quality and popularity of his writing declined. Became U.S. consul in Germany and Scotland (1878–85), and settled in London for rest of his life. Harte's tales and ballads are notable for their humor and gusto and their Western local color.

EDITIONS: *Harte's Complete Works* (10 vols. Boston and New York 1929). *Stories and Poems and Other Uncollected Writings by Bret Harte* ed. Charles M. Kozlay (Boston and New York 1914).

REFERENCES: Margaret Duckett *Mark Twain and Bret Harte* (Norman, Okla. 1964). Richard O'Connor *Bret Harte: A Biography* (Boston 1966). George R. Stewart *Bret Harte: Argonaut and Exile* (Boston and New York 1931).

HARTLEY, Marsden (Jan. 4, 1877 – Sept. 2, 1943). American painter. Born Lewiston, Me., he called himself "the painter from Maine," though he traveled extensively and adopted a number of styles. Studied at Cleveland School of Art, then in New York at Chase School (1898) and at National School of Design (1901). Exhibited first with Alfred Stieglitz at Photo Secession Gallery, New York (1909). Stieglitz helped him go to Paris (1912) and Germany (1913), where he was strongly influenced by abstract-expressionist style of Wassily Kandinsky,

Franz Marc, and others of the Munich Blue Rider group. Martial atmosphere of Berlin on eve of World War I inspired him to paint brilliant series of abstract still lifes of German military emblems like *Portrait of a German Officer* (1914, Metropolitan Museum, New York). Back in U.S., Hartley evolved his own style of quieter cubist abstractions (1916–17), then a new objective style when the tumultuous scenery of the Southwest became the subject for interpretative landscapes like *New Mexico Recollections No. 11* (1922–23, Babcock Galleries, New York). After ten years of wandering around Europe, he settled in Aix-en-Provence (1926–28), renounced expressionism, and became converted to Cézanne and what he called "the great logicians of color." After more travels, he came home to Maine (1937) to live chiefly in Corea, and turned to a rugged primitive style in painting the mountains, forests, rocks and water of his native state. He is thought to be at his best in these New England landscapes of the '30's, which owe something in inspiration to Cézanne but express their own somber power and symbolism. He died in Ellsworth, Maine.

REFERENCES: Elizabeth McCausland *Marsden Hartley* (Minneapolis, Minn. and London PB 1952). Jerome Mellquist *The Emergence of an American Art* (New York 1942).

HASSLER, Hans Leo (Oct. 25/26, 1564 – June 8, 1612). German composer. Born Nuremberg. Taught music by his father, an organist. Went to Venice as pupil of Andrea Gabrieli (1584–85); was first important German composer to study in Italy. After serving as private organist to Count Octavianus Fugger in Augsburg (1585–1600), returned to Nuremberg to become the town's musical director as well as organist at the Frauenkirche. Appointed organist to the elector of Saxony (1608); accompanied him to Frankfurt for imperial election (1612), and died there of tuberculosis. Hassler was affected by Venetian music even before his study with the Gabrielis, who exerted strong influence on his style. He composed both secular and sacred works, including madrigals, motets, chorale arrangements, Masses, and organ pieces. His song "Mein Gemüth ist mir verwirret" is used in J. S. Bach's *St. Matthew Passion* as the chorale "O Haupt voll Blut und Wunden."

HAUPTMANN, Gerhart (Nov. 15, 1862 – June 8, 1946). German dramatist, poet, and novelist. Born Obersalzbrunn, Silesia, son of a hotelkeeper. Studied art in Breslau, Jena and Rome. After marrying wealthy German woman (1885), wrote for theatre, achieving immediate fame with *Vor Sonnenaufgang* (1889), an important German naturalist play, followed by *Das Friedensfest* (1890), *Einsame Menschen* (1891), and *Die Weber* (1892), the best of this genre and still performed. Socialist naturalism gave way to romantic symbolism and fantasy in *Hanneles Himmelfahrt* (1893), *Die versunkene Glocke* (1897), and *Und Pippa tanzt* (1906). Internationally famous and recipient of numerous public honors, he received Nobel prize (1912). Also wrote tragedies and comedies like *Der Biberpelz* (1893), a travel book, the novels *Der Narr in Christo, Emmanuel Quint* (1910), *Atlantis* (1912), *The Heretic of Soana* (1918), and the epic poem *Till Eulenspiegel* (1928), based on an old legend. After the 1920's his work declined in quality and popularity, and politically he shifted from being a liberal Social-Democrat to serving in the Nazi regime under Hitler. His reputation as the outstanding modern German playwright rests on his plays before World War I. He died in Agnetendorf, Silesia.

EDITION: Ludwig Lewisohn ed. *The Dramatic Works of Gerhart Hauptmann* (9 vols. New York 1912–1929). REFERENCE: Hugh F. Garten *Gerhart Hauptmann* (New Haven, Conn. and London 1954).

HAWKSMOOR, Nicholas (1661 – Mar. 25, 1736). English architect. Born Nottinghamshire. Went to London at eighteen as pupil and personal clerk of Sir Christopher Wren. As Wren's assistant at Chelsea Hospital (1682–90), Greenwich Hospital (1698–1736), Kensington Palace (1690–1715), St. Paul's Cathedral (completed, 1710), and else-where, he not only worked out his master's designs but also made small contributions of his own. Collaborated with Sir John Vanbrugh on Castle Howard, Yorkshire (1699–1714), and Blenheim (1705–15). Major independent works: Easton Neston, Northamptonshire (c.1695–1702); the London churches St. Anne's, Limehouse (1712–24), St. Mary Woolnoth (1716–19), St. George's, Bloomsbury (1720–30), and Christ Church, Spitalfields (1723–29), which he designed while surveyor to the churches commission of 1711; parts of Queen's College and All Soul's College at Oxford; towers of Westminster Abbey (from 1723). Hawksmoor's baroque style was romantic and imaginative; he was one of the earliest designers of picturesque Gothic. He died in London.

REFERENCE: Kerry Downes *Hawksmoor* (London 1959). H. S. Goodhart-Rendel *Nicholas Hawksmoor* (London 1924).

HAWTHORNE, Nathaniel (July 4, 1804 – May 19, 1864). American writer. Born Salem, Mass., of Puritan family. Attended Bowdoin College (1821–25). Published *Fanshawe* anonymously (1828); contributed stories to the *Token* and *New England Magazine*, later collected in *Twice-Told Tales* (1837, enlarged 1842). Worked at Boston Custom House (1839–41), then joined briefly transcendentalists' experiment at Brook Farm. Married Sophia Peabody (1842) and settled in Old Manse, Concord, continuing to write tales collected in *Mosses from an Old Manse* (1846). Surveyor of port of Salem (1846–49). Produced first novel, *The Scarlet Letter* (1850), gaining immediate fame. *The House of the Seven Gables* (1851), *The Blithedale Romance* (1852), and *The Snow Image and Other Twice-Told Tales* (1852) secured his reputation. In the Berkshires, where he knew Melville, produced *A Wonder Book for Girls and Boys* (1852) and *Tanglewood Tales for Girls and Boys* (1853), retelling classical myths and among his most popular books. In return for campaign biography, *The Life of Franklin Pierce* (1852), appointed consul to Liverpool (1853–58), which provided material for *Our Old Home* (1863). Vacation in Italy (1858–59) formed background for last novel, *The Marble Faun* (1860). Died at Plymouth, N.H.

EDITIONS: *The Complete Works of Nathaniel Hawthorne* ed. George P. Lathrop (12 vols. Boston 1883). *The American Notebooks* ed. Randall Stewart (New Haven 1932). *Complete Novels and Selected Tales* ed. Norman H. Pearson (New York 1937).

REFERENCES: Newton Arvin *Hawthorne* (New York 1961). Millicent Bell *Hawthorne's View of the Artist* (New York 1962). Julian Hawthorne *Nathaniel Hawthorne and His Wife* (2 vols. Boston 1885). Henry James *Hawthorne* (London and New York 1887, also PB). Harry Levin *Power of Blackness: Hawthorne, Poe, Melville* (New York 1950, also PB). F. O. Matthiessen *American Renaissance* (London and New York 1941, also PB). Randall Stewart *Nathaniel Hawthorne: A Biography* (New Haven and London 1948). Mark Van Doren *Nathaniel Hawthorne: A Critical Biography* (New York 1949 and London 1950). Hyatt H. Waggoner *Hawthorne: A Critical Study* (Cambridge, Mass., and London 1955).

✎

NATHANIEL HAWTHORNE
BY CURTIS HARNACK

For a dozen years following graduation from Bowdoin, Nathaniel Hawthorne sequestered himself in an uncle's house in Salem and struggled to become a writer. Seldom venturing out by day, he was steeped in isolation; "We do not even *live* at our house!" he remarked. Dissatisfied with his literary efforts, he burned the manuscript of *Seven Tales of My Native Land* and only two of these stories survive. But gradually his tales won acclaim and "the world found me out in my lonely chamber and called me forth." Marriage to Sophia Peabody further drew him into the mainstream, and a central theme in his fiction was to be the nurturing effect of love and human interdependence. In his notebooks he wrote: ". . . we are not endowed with real life, and all that seems most real about us is but the thinnest substance of a dream — till the heart be touched. That touch creates us."

Hawthorne's form of short story is a blend of the traditional narrative tale and the essay (plot events striving to enforce a meaningful point) which has characterized the short story ever since. As Edgar Allan Poe pointed out in his famous review of *Twice-Told Tales*, from reading Hawthorne one could see that the short story form had its own peculiar characteristics, such as that every word must count toward producing the desired effect, that it must be read in one sitting, and that only poetry possessed higher demands in terms of language. Hawthorne is most successful when symbolism is perfectly aligned with his Gothic imagination, as in *Young Goodman Brown*, a tale of a witches' sabbath; or in *Ethan Brand*, where the doomed hero searches for the unpardonable sin. In his tales of lost innocence, *The Gentle Boy* and *My Kinsman, Major Molineux*, the vividness of scene remains so strong that "meaning" cannot reduce the stories to the allegorical syndromes which overintellectualize such works as *Rappaccini's Daughter* and *The Celestial Railroad*.

Many of Hawthorne's stories convey a peculiar sense of having private meaning which the reader can only guess at, something almost apart from the tale being told. This elusiveness, which so interested Henry James, whose biography of Hawthorne is still perhaps the best, has beguiled modern psychologically oriented readers into attempting to capture the "real" Hawthorne behind his fictive mask; it is ironical that this activity suggests a major concern of Hawthorne himself, who viewed humanity as constantly in disguise, attempting to hide base motives and ugly postures from one another, and from eternity. Hawthorne in his essay on the Custom House says he intends to "still keep the inmost Me behind its veil." He continues to elude sleuthing biographer-critics because the secret hunted is manifest everywhere in his volumes: his work is a projection of his inner tensions and preoccupations — which is true of all artists — and these matters are "solved" only in the work itself; no one's life has the completion or turn that can be given a work of art.

Hawthorne's masterpiece is *The Scarlet Letter,* which is extraordinarily pared down and charged with life. He depicts the inner states of his doomed Puritan characters, Hester Prynne, the womanly, vibrant adulteress; Reverend Arthur Dimmesdale, her secret lover; and Roger Chillingsworth, her husband. The tangle of relationship is so orchestrated that every significant aspect is exposed before the final agony and expiation, when the minister dies in Hester's arms. Perhaps only symbolic little Pearl, that Victorian cutie-child, is a mistake, for Hawthorne plays too easily with the ironies and double meanings that surround the waif of sin. In *The Scarlet Letter* guilt and sin are allied with moral values that transcend the milieu described. Good and evil are forces in perpetual combat, and it is man's poignant condition that he must forever be thrust into the middle of the unending struggle.

Hawthorne viewed himself as a romance teller, knowing that such an inclination ran counter to the aims of the realistic novel. Romance "has fairly a right to present that truth (of the human heart) under circumstances, to a great extent of the writer's own choosing or creation." He

wanted that freedom. But works such as *The House of the Seven Gables* and *The Marble Faun* seem wrapped in the gauze of fancy and cluttered with sentimentality. Even his witty satire on socialist life at Brook Farm, *The Blithedale Romance,* falters and finally becomes hopelessly entangled in the inappropriate dictates of the literary convention of the romance.

His total output was small, for in middle life he experienced a failure of energy or imagination — or both. The romancer should "dream strange things, and make them look like truth," but perhaps the times loomed oppressively for such activity. The Civil War, coming when his health was impaired, was shattering for him, especially since he was a Democrat and took his politics seriously (even having written the official campaign biography of Franklin Pierce): "The Present, the Immediate, the Actual, has proved too potent for me . . . . It takes away not only my scanty faculty, but even my desire for imaginative composition, and leaves me sadly content to scatter a thousand peaceful fantasies upon the hurricane that is sweeping us all along with it."

Hawthorne was reluctant to reduce the inscrutable to a single answer or comfortable system (a disposition he shared with Herman Melville, who was so attracted to Hawthorne personally and to his work that he dedicated *Moby Dick* to him), since to do so would be to lessen the totality of the perceived truth. Thus he remained mercurial in his religious and philosophical thrusts, and "pessimism" alternated with gaiety. The only constant factor for Hawthorne was that the borderline between the "real" and the "not real" never seemed decisive; the so-called invisibles, existing by way of memories, psychological inclinations, and family history, were every bit as solid as the apparently firm, bustling world of mid-nineteenth-century America; and in the long run, more true.

HAYDN, Franz Joseph (Mar. 31, 1732 – May 31, 1809). Austrian composer. Born at Rohrau, Lower Austria. Training began early at a relative's school in Hainburg (1738–39) and at the choir school of St. Stephen's Cathedral, Vienna (1740–49). Wrote first string quartets for patron Count Fürnberg (1755), who obtained for him appointment as music director to Count Morzin, for whom Haydn wrote first symphony (1759). Married Anna Keller (1760). Appointed kapellmeister to Prince Esterhazy (1761–90), during which time he wrote Masses, operas, overtures, symphonies, sonatas, chamber music. Friendship with Mozart began c.1781. During two visits to London (1791–92 and 1794–95) wrote and conducted twelve *London* symphonies at the top of his style, and was received with intense enthusiasm. Settled in Vienna (1795) and produced the two oratorios *The Creation* (1797–98) and *The Seasons* (1799–1801). He died in Vienna. During his last years Haydn received honors and acclaim from governments and institutions throughout Europe. He is considered the chief founder of the Viennese classical school.

EDITION: *Collected Correspondence and London Notebooks* ed. H. C. Robbins Landon (London and New York 1959).

REFERENCES: Michel Brenet *Haydn* (tr. New York 1926). Karl Geiringer *Haydn: A Creative Life in Music* (New York 1946 and London 1947, also PB). Rosemary Hughes *Haydn* (London and New York 1950). H. C. Robbins Landon *Haydn Symphonies* (Seattle PB 1969).

✍

FRANZ JOSEPH HAYDN

BY MICHAEL STEINBERG

The most touching of Haydn's letters is one he wrote at seventy to the choral society in the little town of Bergen on the Baltic isle of Rügen. They had performed his oratorio, *The Creation*, and had written to thank him for the joy the task had given them. The composer wrote in his turn: "You give me the welcome assurance — and this is the greatest comfort of my declining years — that I am often the source from which you, and many other families receptive to heartfelt emotion, derive pleasure and satisfaction in the quiet of your homes. How soothing this reflection is to me! Often, as I struggled with obstacles of every kind opposed to my works — often, as my physical and mental powers sank, and I had difficulty in keeping to my chosen course — an inner voice whispered to me: 'There are so few happy and contented men here below — on every hand care and sorrow pursue them — perhaps your work may some day be a source from which men laden with anxieties and burdened with affairs may derive a few moments of rest and refreshment.' This, then, was a powerful motive to persevere, this the reason why I can even now look back with profound satisfaction on what I have accomplished in my art through uninterrupted effort and application over a long succession of years."

Haydn's artistic aim is at once simple and sublime. He composes to bring a touch of happiness into the lives of Baltic islanders or sophisticated Londoners, but the implications of the "In nomine Domini" and "Laus Deo" that he puts on the first and last pages of all his musical manuscripts are no less real to him. He shares with Handel, and perhaps with Verdi, that common touch, that ability to say the grandest and deepest things in the simplest phrases and gestures. Think what the first measures of "Hallelujah!" in *Messiah* are made of: think of the greatness and the daring simplicity of "And there was light" in *The Crea-tion*.

Like Handel, Haydn today has not the audience he once commanded. The standard adjectives for him in the listener's dictionary of *idées reçues*, "charming" and "delightful," will not do. The very simplicity of the surface of his music began soon after his death to deceive people into assuming that his procedures were essentially simple-minded. Even Schumann likened the appearance of a Haydn symphony at a concert to a visit from an old family friend whom we respect, whom we are always glad to see, but who really hasn't anything new to tell us. He is charming and delightful, of course, but unlike many who have those appealing and welcome qualities, Haydn is, as well, a composer of highly sophisticated and, in the late choral works, even stupendous, music, an artist capable of realizing his conceptions on the grandest possible scale.

The trouble with Haydn's music is that there is nothing to do about it except listen to it. Haydn has neither Mozart's sex appeal nor Beethoven's way on the soapbox, and he does not invite daydreams. His life was not colorful, and he was sufficiently successful for us not to be tempted to feel sorry for him. His marital unhappiness is too prosaic to titillate (he had a pathetic affair with a worthless Italian singer, employed, as he was, by the Esterházy family; and a touching one that meant a great deal to him with Rebecca Schroeter, a musician's widow, in London when he was sixty). He was not deaf, neither did he die young.

Then, his music is not colorful in richness of detail like Mozart's. Its strength and its humor are architectural. His seductiveness is that of a great musical intelligence. Not all are susceptible to such blandishments, but the deep and perhaps uniquely refreshing delight of his music is there for those who will listen, really listen, stretching perception and memory to the full.

Franz Joseph Haydn was born in Rohrau, Austria, March 31, 1732. After studies in Vienna and posts there and in Bohemia, in 1761 he entered the service of the Esterházy family, who would be astonished to know that we remember them only for Haydn's sake. Haydn retained his title and salary even when the musical establishment at Esterház was disbanded in 1790, though after 1795 he again wrote occasional compositions for the family, notably the Masses of the last years. He visited London in 1791–92 and again in 1794-95, and while he was in Vienna between the two journeys, he taught the young Beethoven, recently moved there from Bonn. He was active for a few more years, and then, at seventy, he suddenly became an old man, claiming afterwards that it was his effort at finishing his oratorio *The Seasons* that had finished him off. He lived in retirement now, tormented by his failing memory, and by musical ideas pursuing him "to the point of torture" — "if it is an allegro, my pulse beats faster, I cannot sleep; if an adagio, I find my pulse beating slowly; my imagination plays upon me as if I were a keyboard" — but for whose working out he could not summon the concentration and strength. He died on May 31, 1809, just as the French occupation of Vienna had begun. His lifetime had spanned a long and remarkable period of musical history: he was born just before Bach began work on the *B Minor Mass;* and as he lay dying, Beethoven was in a cellar a few streets away, a pillow over his head to protect the last shreds of hearing against the French bombardment, and struggling with the sketches of the *"Emperor" Concerto*.

Haydn composed in all genres, but he was at his greatest in the string quartet, of which the first examples come from about 1755 and the last, unfinished, one from 1803, and in the symphony, the first of them written about 1759, and the last, for London, in 1795. When he no longer wrote symphonies, he found himself in a new and marvelous flowering as a composer of Masses, oratorios, and a *Te Deum,* between 1796 and 1802. The trios for piano, violin, and cello, many of them from the nineties, are another group of works in which his mind's play can be enjoyed at its wittiest. Opera and concerto, the two genres in which Mozart is most characteristically himself and at his greatest, do not stimulate Haydn's imagination. Externalized theatre had little appeal for him: the drama and the humor is in the play of ideas, a play, often, of the subtlest sort. Haydn's music is characteristically economical rather than lavish, lean in sonority rather than lush. His model was the intellectual, severe, and fantastic Carl Philipp Emanuel Bach (Mozart's was the gracefully Italianate younger brother, Johann Christian). At Esterház, Haydn could work undisturbed by fashion, and the availability of the players and singers there provided him with a continuing, living laboratory in which he could try his ideas. By the beginning of the 1780's, Haydn was a famous man, perhaps more than he realized, whose music was widely published (he was generally shrewd, and not invariably quite honest, in his business dealings), and who was getting commissions from places as far away as Paris and Cadiz. Still, London was a turning point in Haydn's life because it brought him for the first time into personal contact with a larger audience, and a knowing, appreciative one. He loved being lionized, and far from spoiling his character, it made him a stronger man. In his music, too, he grew more progressive and bold right until the time he stopped composing.

One of his most precious resources was his friendship with Mozart, who was twenty-four years younger and whom he outlived by eighteen years, whom he loved deeply, in whom he recognized a gift of a greater order than his own. Mozart dedicated six string quartets to Haydn in thanks for what he had learned from the older man's music; if we follow Haydn's music from early days to late, we can hear that the old man learned from the young one. They became friends in 1781 and shared the excitement of the discovery of Bach and Handel, but the peculiarly Mozartean richness and tenderness and warmth in Haydn's late music is most vividly experienced in the works written after Mozart's death in 1791. Haydn would have been glad that the music at the memorial service in the Schottenkirche a fortnight after his death was Mozart's.

HAZLITT, William (Apr. 10, 1778 – Sept. 18, 1830). English critic and essayist. Born Maidstone, Kent, son of Unitarian minister. Entered Unitarian New College, Hackney (1793), but soon abandoned theological studies for art, then literature. Became friend of Coleridge and Wordsworth (1798) and of Charles Lamb (1804). First work: *On the Principles of Human Action* (1805). Married Sarah Stoddart (1808; divorced 1822). Settled in London (1812) and achieved recognition as contributor to the *Edinburgh Review,* the *Examiner,* and other periodicals. Collections of his essays, chiefly in field of literary and art criticism, include *The Round Table* (1817), *Characters of Shakespeare's Plays* (1817), *A View of the English Stage* (1818),

Table Talk (1821), and *The Plain Speaker* (1826). From 1813, gave several series of lectures on English literature. *Liber Amoris* (1823) is an account of his unhappy affair with a young girl, Sarah Walker (1820–22). Married a widow, Mrs. Isabella Bridgewater (1824), who left him after a year. Died in London. Hazlitt was one of the first to recognize the genius of Keats. A critic of great intelligence and uncompromising honesty, he developed a style remarkable for its plainness and vigor.

EDITION: *Complete Works* ed. A. R. Waller and Arnold Glover (13 vols. London 1902–1906); reissue ed. P. P. Howe (21 vols. London 1930–34).

REFERENCES: Herschel C. Baker *William Hazlitt* (Cambridge, Mass. and London 1962). Percival P. Howe *The Life of William Hazlitt* (London 1922, new ed. London 1947). Catherine M. Maclean *Born Under Saturn: A Biography of William Hazlitt* (London 1943 and New York 1944).

H.D. *See* **DOOLITTLE, Hilda.**

HEARN, (Patricio) Lafcadio (Tessima Carlos) (June 27, 1850 – Sept. 26, 1904). Greek-Anglo-Irish-Japanese author of works in English. Born Leukas, Ionian Islands. From 1856, ward of Irish great-aunt; attended Jesuit schools in France and England before sent by her to U.S. (1869). Struggled to make living as journalist first in Cincinnati, then in New Orleans (1877–87). His first book, *One of Cleopatra's Nights*, was translations of Gautier stories. It was followed by *Stray Leaves from Strange Literature* (1884) and *Some Chinese Ghosts* (1887), collections of tales adapted from foreign literature in the macabre and exotic vein which was Hearn's forte. Also wrote the narrative *Chita: A Memory of Last Island* (1889), travel sketches *Two Years in the French West Indies* (1890), and novel *Youma* (1890). Went to Japan (1890), where he spent rest of his life. Married daughter of a Samurai family, Setsu Koizumi (1891), acquired citizenship, and taught at Imperial University of Tokyo (1894–1903). Wrote several works revealing acute under-

standing of character, customs and legends of his adopted country, including *Glimpses of an Unfamiliar Japan* (1894), *Kokoro* (1896), *In Ghostly Japan* (1899), *Shadowings* (1900), *Japanese Fairy Tales* (1902) and *Japan: An Attempt at an Interpretation* (1904).

REFERENCE: Elizabeth Stevenson *Lafcadio Hearn* (New York 1961).

HEINE, Heinrich (Dec. 13, 1797 – Feb. 17, 1856). German poet and writer. Born Düsseldorf, of Jewish parents. Studied law at universities of Bonn and Göttingen (1819–25), receiving law degree (1825). Influenced to try hand at literature by teacher August Wilhelm von Schlegel. Published first poems, *Gedichte* (1822), inspired by unrequited love for girl cousin. Two verse tragedies, *Almansor* and *William Ratcliff,* followed (1823). Converted to Christianity (1825). *Buch der Lieder* (1827) made him famous, also his evocative travel sketches *Reisebilder* (4 vols. 1826–31). A passionate liberal, he was attracted by the French Revolution and went to Paris (1831), remaining for rest of his life. His essays on German thought from Luther to Hegel and on German romantic poets, which appeared in *Revue des Deux Mondes* and *Europe Littéraire* were collected (1834–35 and 1836). Also continued to write the biting satirical love poems and exquisite lyrics of which he was a master: *Deutschland, Ein Wintermärchen* (1844), *Neue Gedichte* (1844), *Romanzero* (1851), *Letzte Gedichte* (1869). Married Crescence Eugénie Marat (1841), a shopgirl, who cared faithfully for him during last eight years of invalidism as a paralytic. Other prose works include autobiographical sketches or *Confessions* (1854), essays on German folklore. Heine is best known for his lyrics and ballads, some of the finest in all literature, many like *Die Lorelei* set to music, and characterized by his own special romantic irony that has influenced poets across the world.

TRANSLATION: *The Complete Works of Heinrich Heine* tr. Charles G. Leland and others (13 vols. London and New York 1892–1905).

REFERENCES: Max Brod *Heinrich*

Heine: The Artist in Revolt (tr. London 1956 and New York 1957, also PB). Eliza M. Butler Heinrich Heine: A Biography (London 1956 and New York 1958). Laura Hofrichter Heinrich Heine (tr. London 1963 and New York 1964). William Rose Heinrich Heine: Two Studies of His Thought and Feeling (London and New York 1956).

HEMINGWAY, Ernest (Miller) (July 21, 1899 – July 2, 1961). American writer. Born Oak Park, Ill., son of a doctor who took him on hunting and fishing trips to Horton Bay, Michigan, background of his first stories, like Big Two-Hearted River. After graduating from high school, Hemingway worked as reporter on Kansas City Star (1917). Went to Italy (1918) as Red Cross ambulance driver, then served in Italian army and was seriously wounded. The experience became material for one of his finest novels, A Farewell to Arms (1929). Returned to U.S. and married Hadley Richardson (1918), who bore him a son. Divorced her to marry Pauline Pfeiffer (1927), then Martha Gellhorn (1940), and Mary Welsh (1946). After working for Toronto papers (1919–20), went to Europe again as correspondent for Toronto Star, and in Paris met Gertrude Stein and Ezra Pound. First publications were stories: Three Stories and Ten Poems (1923) and In Our Time (1924). First novel, The Torrents of Spring (1926), burlesqued Sherwood Anderson, an early influence on Hemingway's writing. Success came with The Sun Also Rises (1926), followed by the stories Men Without Women (1927), the study of bullfighting Death in The Afternoon (1932), and after an African safari The Green Hills of Africa (1935). During the Spanish Civil War he served as a correspondent (1937–38), using the experience in a play The Fifth Column, published with short stories as The Fifth Column and the First Forty-nine Stories (1938), and in the novel For Whom the Bell Tolls (1940). In Key West, Fla., then Cuba, continued to write: Across the River and into the Trees (1950) and The Old Man and the Sea (1952), which won the 1953 Pulitzer prize and helped win him the Nobel prize (1954). After intervals of hospitalization, Hem-

ingway shot himself at Ketchum, Idaho. His Paris memoirs, A Moveable Feast, appeared posthumously (1964); also a novel, Islands in the Stream (1970).

REFERENCES: Carlos Baker Hemingway: The Writer as Artist (3rd ed. Princeton, N.J. and Oxford 1963, also PB) and Ernest Hemingway: A Life Story (New York and London 1969). Sheridan Baker Ernest Hemingway (New York 1967, also PB). Charles A. Fenton The Apprenticeship of Ernest Hemingway: The Early Years (New York 1954 and London 1955, also PB). Leicester Hemingway My Brother, Ernest Hemingway (Cleveland and London 1962, also PB). A. E. Hotchner Papa Hemingway: A Personal Memoir (New York and London 1966, also PB). Robert P. Weeks ed. Hemingway: A Collection of Critical Essays (Englewood Cliffs, N.J. 1962, also PB). Philip Young Ernest Hemingway: A Reconsideration (2nd ed. University Park, Pa. 1966, also PB).

✍

ERNEST HEMINGWAY

BY ROBERT MANNING

"In the late summer of that year," begins A Farewell to Arms, "we lived in a house in a village that looked across the river and the plain to the mountain. In the bed of the river there were pebbles and boulders, dry and white in the sun, and the water was clear and swiftly moving and blue in the channels." One cannot estimate how many would-be writers, in a long generation since these lines were written by Ernest Hemingway, have looked at them, clean with discipline and pregnant with the sense of individual sensation, and then crumpled their own efforts with a sigh, and started over.

The impact of Hemingway's work — and his life — must be measured first in the novels, the short stories, and the nonfiction works like The Green Hills of Africa and Death in the Afternoon. The measure must also take into account the rest of the iceberg, his impact on the writers and the writing of the twentieth century. Very few other writers of the age — Proust is one, Joyce and Faulkner others — earned this second kind of fame, elusive, not sharply definable, not always accorded, but at least as profound in its meaning as that of their printed prose.

Hemingway was twenty-seven when his first short stories were published in 1925. His formal schooling had ended with graduation from high school in Oak Park, Ill., but his greater education had come in the Michigan woods, where he tramped and hunted and fished with his father, the affluent Dr. Hemingway; in the days of his service (and severe wounding by shellfire) as an ambulance driver on the Italian front in World War I; in the boulevards and an austere carpenter's loft on Paris's Left Bank, where, in the words of the poet Archibald MacLeish, Hemingway "whittled a style for his time from a walnut stick." He was married then to the first of what were to be four wives, had fathered the first of his three sons.

The stories, *In Our Time,* were an immediate sensation. Soon came *The Sun Also Rises,* with which Hemingway, even if indebted to Gertrude Stein for the label the Lost Generation, stamped it indelibly on an era. As the first successes were followed by his later novels and the short stories of the 1930's (among them the memorable *The Snows of Kilimanjaro, The Short Happy Life of Francis Macomber*), younger writers began to pay him the homage of imitation. He became, in technique and in the kind of moral choices he posed, the most profound influence on American writing of the '30's; as a stylist and craftsman he transfixed a majority of the younger authors and, by seeming to mix his own life and values with those of the characters in his books, he became, in

the perfect description of Alfred Kazin, "the bronze god of the whole contemporary literary experience." Beyond the imitators were others who were affected in reverse by the Hemingway impact, writers who made conscious, sometimes convulsive efforts to avoid imitation, to reach over and beyond — in manner as well as content — what today is still easily defined as "the Hemingway style."

Writing was always hard for Hemingway, and until his fading days, when he talked and too frequently wrote material that seemed a sad parody of the real Hemingway, he achieved his art through intense, painful dedication; two or three hundred words made a good day's work. He suffered from insomnia and nightmares for most of his life, and though he more than once referred to his father's suicide as the act of a coward, talked on several occasions of killing himself.

His comprehension of man's instinct for aggression led him to a lifetime preoccupation with the necessity for coping with that instinct, within oneself and within others. As a romantic activist, he nurtured his own demeanor of stoical fortitude and derring-do into the stuff of his fiction. "Writing," he used to say, "is inventing out of knowledge." He prided himself in, indeed became sometimes bombastic about, his knowledge of nature, of animal and marine life, of the weather, the ski slopes, the racetracks, the gamelands of Africa; his facility as a wing shot or a marlin catcher, his medical and military knowledge.

Hemingway was a big man (weighing from two hundred to two-sixty in the course of his adult life), strong and handsome. He was a nervous person, and oddly accident-prone for one with such a determination to take risks. He was very much a man's man, a heavy drinker for most of his life, obviously attractive to, and attracted by, women. He claimed to have had any woman he ever wanted. Capable of charm and generosity to those close to him or to young aspiring artists and writers, he was capable too of dark spurts of cruelty and jealousy toward those who crossed him or those whose success might seem to equal or overshadow his.

Writing and the physical life, both were necessary to Hemingway. In his fifties, years of hard living and accidents began to slow him down physically. By the time he won the Nobel prize in 1954, after publication of his last novel, *The Old Man and the Sea*, it was plain that there was little of the early art left in him. Either incapacity would have been enough to reduce for him the value of living, for both body and mind to falter was intolerable.

He lived for years outside his country (France, Italy, Austria, Africa) or on the periphery (in Key West) for almost all his adult life. Cuba became "home" for Hemingway in 1939, where he lived in his beloved Finca Vigia and fished in his boat, the *Pilar*. In 1960 he and his wife Mary moved into his shooting and fishing lodge in Ketchum, Idaho, intending someday to return to Cuba. But that did not come to pass. His physical and mental health deteriorated badly. Like Nick Adams in one of the great Hemingway short works, *Big Two-Hearted River*, he had come to a moment when "he felt he had left everything behind, the need for thinking, the need to write, other needs. It was all back of him." Early on the morning of July 2, 1961, he loaded one of his shotguns, held the barrels against his forehead, and killed himself.

HENLEY, William Ernest (Aug. 23, 1849 – July 11, 1903). English poet, critic, and editor. Born Gloucester, son of a bookseller, and attended Crypt Grammar School there. Invalided in the Edinburgh Infirmary for twenty months, where he met Robert Louis Stevenson, he wrote the poems that appeared as *In Hospital* (1875). Later included in *Book of Verses* (1888), they contained the famous *Invictus*. Henley went to London (1877), became editor of magazine *London,* to which he contributed poems and essays. Married Ann Boyle (1878). Edited *Magazine of Art* (1882–86) and the *Scots Observer* (1889), later the *National Observer*. Brought out the poems *Song of the Sword* (1892, second ed. *London Voluntaries* 1893), both included in *Poems* (1898). Later poetical works: *For England's Sake* (1900) and *Hawthorn and Lavender* (1901). Also collaborated with Stevenson on the plays *Deacon Brodie* (1880), *Beau Austin, Admiral Guinea* (both 1884), and *Macaire* (1894), and edited anthologies, including *Lyra Heroica* (1891), *Tudor Translations* (from 1892), *Dictionary of Slang* (with John S. Farmer, 1894–1904), and several other works, some in collaboration. He died at Woking.

REFERENCES: Jerome H. Buckley *William Ernest Henley* (Princeton, N.J. and Oxford 1945). John Connell *W. E. Henley* (London and New York 1949).

———

HENRI, Robert (June 25, 1865 – July 12, 1929). American painter. Born Cincinnati, Ohio. After studying under Thomas Anshutz, Thomas Eakins's pupil, at Pennsylvania Academy of the Fine Arts (1886–88), Henri went to Paris, where he attended École des Beaux Arts and Académie Julian. Back in Philadelphia (1891), his studio became a center for fellow artists William Glackens, John Sloan, and George Luks. After another sojourn in Paris, moved to New York (1899), where he taught at Chase School. Arranged historic exhibit (1908) of The Eight, the New York realists whom he led in revolt against academicism, later known as the Ash Can School. Exhibited there his *Laughing Boy* (1907, Whitney Museum, New York). Other major paintings: *Young Woman in Black* (Art Institute, Chicago), *Portrait of Mrs. Robert Henri* (1911, Metropolitan Museum, New York), *Girl with a Fan* (Pennsylvania Academy of the Fine Arts, Philadelphia). An outstanding teacher, Henri inspired students at various schools, including the Art Students League (1915–23), with his view that art must express life directly, or realistically. Among his pupils were George Bellows, Rockwell Kent, and Edward Hopper. Published *The Art Spirit* (1923), based on lecture notes and essays. Married twice. Died in New York.

REFERENCES: William Inness Homer, with assistance of Violet Organ *Robert Henri and His Circle* (Ithaca, N.Y. 1969). Nathaniel Pousette-Dart *Robert Henri* (New York 1922). Helen A. Read *Robert Henri* (New York 1931).

HENRY, O. (real name William Sydney Porter) (Sept. 11, 1862 – June 5, 1910). American short story writer. Born Greensboro, N.C.; attended local schools until age of fifteen, when he left to work in a pharmacy. Ill health forced him to go West (1882), spending two years on Texas ranch and four more as bookkeeper in Austin. Married Athol Estes (1887); secured job as teller in Austin bank (1891) and later ran weekly newspaper, the *Rolling Stone.* Became (1895) columnist for the Houston *Daily Post* but the following year was indicted for embezzlement by the Austin bank and fled the country, going first to Honduras, then wandering extensively around South America and, finally, Mexico. Reports of wife's failing health brought him back to Austin (1897), where following her death he was convicted of the embezzlement charge and sentenced to five years in the Ohio Penitentiary. Here he began writing and publishing the short stories which were to make him famous. Released after three years, he moved to New York, where he found the raw material for his prodigious output of stories and quickly followed his first volume, *Cabbages and Kings* (1904), with fourteen more collections, the most famous of which is probably *The Four Million* (the number of stories he thought New York contained). Although he was now remarried (Sara

Lindsay Coleman), wealthy, and famous, his health deteriorated until he succumbed to tuberculosis in New York. O. Henry's name is now most often associated with the genre of story he made his own: the compact, slick tale ending with a surprise twist. Some of the more famous single stories are *The Gift of the Magi, The Ransom of Red Chief,* and *The Cop and the Anthem.*

EDITION: *Complete Works* (2 vols. Garden City, N.Y. 1953; in single volume 1960).

REFERENCES: Robert H. Davis and Arthur B. Maurice *The Caliph of Bagdad* (New York and London 1931). Gerald Langford *Alias O. Henry* (New York 1957). E. Hudson Long *O. Henry: The Man and His Work* (Philadelphia, Pa. 1949, reprinted New York 1969, also PB).

HENRYSON (or Henderson), Robert (fl. 1475). Scottish poet. Almost nothing known of his life. Described in early editions as schoolmaster of Dunfermline. One of the "Scottish Chaucerians," his major works are *The Morall Fabillis of Esope the Phrygian,* a collection of thirteen beast fables in verse, notable for their wit and charm; *The Testament of Cresseid,* which describes the punishment of Cressida for her falseness, concluding with her death in a leper colony. Also wrote shorter poems, *Orpheus and Eurydice, The Pastoral, Robene and Makyne,* and others. *The Testament of Cresseid* was first published in Thynne's edition of Chaucer (1532); the first printed collection of his poems appeared in 1570.

EDITIONS: *Poems* ed. G. Gregory Smith (3 vols. Edinburgh and London 1906–14). *Poems and Fables* ed. H. Harvey Wood (2nd ed. Edinburgh 1958).

REFERENCES: John MacQueen *Robert Henryson: A Story of the Major Narrative Poems* (Oxford 1967). Marshall W. Stearns *Robert Henryson* (New York 1949).

HERBERT, George (Apr. 3, 1593 – Mar. 1, 1633). English poet. Born Montgomery Castle, Wales, of noble family. His mother, noted for piety and learning, was a friend of Donne. Educated at

Westminster School and Trinity College, Cambridge (B.A. 1613, M.A. 1616). His greatest academic honor, the office of public orator to the university (1620–27), promised illustrious public career, but instead he entered the church. Ordained deacon (1625) and priest (1630). Married Jane Danvers (1629). Appointed rector at Bemerton, Wiltshire (1630), he spent rest of his life there, serving with exemplary devotion as a rural parson. His poems, of the metaphysical school of Donne, were first published after his death as *The Temple* (1633). Intensely religious, they are characterized by imagery, sometimes homely, sometimes strained. His *A Priest to the Temple* (1652), is a prose tract on the duties of a parish priest.

EDITION: *Works* ed. F. E. Hutchinson (1941, new ed. Oxford 1967).

REFERENCES: Joan Bennett *Five Metaphysical Poets* (3rd ed. Cambridge, England, and New York 1964, also PB). Marchette Chute *Two Gentle Men: The Lives of George Herbert and Robert Herrick* (New York 1959 and London 1960). Arnold Stein *George Herbert's Lyrics* (Baltimore 1968). Joseph H. Summers *George Herbert: His Religion and Art* (Cambridge, Mass. and London 1954, new ed. Cambridge, Mass. 1968). Rosemund Tuve *A Reading of George Herbert* (Chicago and London 1952).

HERDER, Johann Gottfried von (Aug. 25, 1744 – Dec. 18, 1803). German philosopher and man of letters. Born Mohrungen, East Prussia, son of a schoolmaster. While studying theology at University of Königsberg, met Immanuel Kant and Johann Georg Hamann, and developed ideas which anticipated and deeply influenced German *Sturm und Drang* movement, literary nationalism, and romanticism. Stressing importance of folk poetry, ancient Hebrew poets, Ossian, and Shakespeare, he defined poetry as spontaneous, immediate expression and as the natural gift of all men rather than of the educated few. In Riga (1764–69), Herder taught, preached (following ordination, 1765), and published first works, *Fragmente über die neuere deutsche Literatur* (1767) and *Kritische Wälder* (1769).

Traveled to Paris (1769), where he accepted position of traveling tutor to a young nobleman; in Strasbourg he abandoned job (1770) and was for several months closely associated with Goethe, on whom his ideas had strong effect. Chief pastor at Bückeburg (1771–76); married Caroline Flachsland (1773). Through Goethe's influence, became general superintendent of the church district, court pastor, and consistory councilor at Weimar (1776), where he spent rest of his life. Greatest work: unfinished *Ideen zur Philosophie der Geschichte der Menschheit* (1784–91), a broad synthesis, presenting evolutionary philosophy of history. Others include *Von deutscher Art und Kunst* (1773) and *Volkslieder* (1778–79, later entitled *Stimmer der Völker in Liedern,* 1807), collection of folk poetry.

TRANSLATIONS: *Outlines of a Philosophy of the History of Man* tr. Thomas Churchill (London 1800, reprinted New York 1966). *God: Some Conversations* tr. Frederick H. Burkhardt (New York 1940, Indianapolis PB 1963).

REFERENCES: F. M. Barnard *Herder's Social and Political Thought: From Enlightenment to Nationalism* (Oxford 1965). Robert T. Clark *Herder: His Life and Thought* (Berkeley, Calif. 1955). Robert R. Ergang *Herder and the Foundations of German Nationalism* (1931, reprinted New York 1966). Joe K. Fugate *The Psychological Basis of Herder's Aesthetics* (The Hague 1966). Alexander Gillies *Herder* (Oxford and New York 1945). Robert S. Mayo *Herder and the Beginnings of Comparative Literature* (Chapel Hill, N.C. 1969).

HÉRÉDIA, José Maria de (Nov. 22, 1842 – Oct. 3, 1905). French poet. Born on coffee plantation in Cuba, son of Spanish father and French mother. Educated at Collège St. Vincent in Senlis, France, and at University of Havana (1859–61). Influenced by Leconte de Lisle and Parnassians, began writing verse. Returned to France (1861) and studied law in Paris, receiving license (1866). Married Louise Cecile Despaigne (1867), daughter of wealthy Cuban family, and began publishing sonnets in various Parnassian journals. Also translated Bernal Diaz del Castillo's *History of the Conquest of New Spain* (4 vols. 1877–87). Finally brought out book of his 118 sonnets, *Les Trophées* (1893), which received French Academy poetry prize, and Hérédia was elected to Academy (1894). That year published prose romance *La Nonne Alfarez*. Became literary director of *Le Journal* (1895), served as correspondent to *El Pais,* Buenos Aires (1901), and was made administrator of Arsenal Library (1901). Devoted last years to scholarly research, and edited André Chénier's *Bucoliques* (1905). Died at Château de Bourdonné, Seine-et-Oise, France. His sonnets are noted for their skillful technique and for the sensuous imagery evoked by Hérédia's Caribbean background.

REFERENCES: U. V. Chatelain *José Maria de Hérédia* (Paris 1930). M. Ibrovac *José Maria de Hérédia: sa Vie et son Oeuvre* (Paris 1923).

HERODOTUS (c.485–c.425 B.C.). Greek historian. Born Halicarnassus, Asia Minor. During 450's and 440's, traveled widely in Egypt, Phoenicia, Libya, Arabia, Mesopotamia, Scythia, Asia Minor, Thrace, Macedonia, and Greece, collecting historical, ethnological, and geographical data. Visited Athens, where he became friend of Sophocles and admirer of Pericles, before joining Athenian colony at Thurii, in south Italy (c.443). Died there or in Athens, which he probably revisited in early years of Peloponnesian War. Herodotus' basic purpose in his *History* (written in Ionic Greek; divided into nine books by the Alexandrians) is to give an account of the Graeco-Persian War of 490–79 B.C. and its preliminaries. Within this framework he provides, in a series of lengthy digressions, a wealth of legends, anecdotes, anthropological observations, and geographic description, covering the entire eastern Mediterranean area which had comprised the Persian empire at its height. The earliest prose writer and the first historian in Europe, Herodotus is known as the Father of History. His open-minded curiosity, his conscientious efforts toward accuracy, his lively, de-

ceptively simple style, and his coherence of purpose are outstanding traits.

TRANSLATIONS: *Herodotus* tr. J. Enoch Powell (2 vols. Oxford 1949). *The Histories* tr. Aubrey De Sélincourt (Harmondsworth, England, and Baltimore PB 1954).

REFERENCES: Aubrey De Sélincourt *The World of Herodotus* (London 1962 and Boston 1963, also PB). Terrot R. Glover *Herodotus* (1924, reprinted Freeport, N.Y. 1969). Walter W. How and Joseph Wells *A Commentary on Herodotus* (1912, latest ed. 2 vols. London and New York 1949–50). John L. Myres *Herodotus: Father of History* (1953, reprinted Oxford 1966). J. Enoch Powell *The History of Herodotus* (Cambridge, England, 1939, reprinted Amsterdam 1967). Joseph Wells *Studies in Herodotus* (Oxford 1923).

HERRICK, Robert (1591–October 1674). English lyric poet. Born London. Son of a goldsmith, he was apprenticed in the same trade under his uncle (1607). Entered Cambridge University (1613), enrolling first in St. John's College, then Trinity Hall (B.A. 1617, M.A. 1620). Ordained (1623). During years 1620–30, probably spent much time in London, associating with Ben Jonson and other poets and frequenting court society, while his poems, circulating in manuscript, won admiration. After accompanying duke of Buckingham as chaplain on expedition to Isle de Rhé (1627–29), received living of Dean Prior, Devonshire, where he spent rest of his life, save period 1647–62, when he was removed because of loyalist sympathies. Never married. Published only one collection of verse, *Hesperides* (1648), though other poems appeared in anthologies and song books. Inspired by Greek and Latin lyric poets, especially Horace, and by Ben Jonson, Herrick was interested above all in form, presenting conventional subjects (love, flowers, the transience of youth) with graceful simplicity.

EDITION: *Poetical Works* ed. Leonard Cyril Martin (Oxford and New York 1956), new ed. *Poems,* London and New York 1965).

REFERENCES: Marchette Chute *Two Gentle Men: The Lives of George Her-*

bert and Robert Herrick (New York 1959 and London 1960). Emily Easton *Youth Immortal: A Life of Robert Herrick* (Boston 1934). Frederic W. Moorman *Robert Herrick* (1910, reprinted New York 1962). Roger B. Rollin *Robert Herrick* (New York 1966).

HESIOD (Eighth century B.C.?). Greek poet. Son of a citizen of Cyme, in Aeolis, who migrated to Greece and settled at Ascra, in Boeotia. After their father's death, Hesiod and his brother Perseus engaged in a dispute over the estate, which led former to begin series of moral admonitions in verse. These resulted in hexameter poem *Works and Days*, a treatise on the practical and moral necessity for hard work, and on proper methods of farming. Also attributed to Hesiod is the *Theogony*, a genealogy of the gods, in which he attempts to work ancient traditions into a coherent system for the universe. His works are the earliest examples in Greek of didactic (*Works and Days*) and theological (*Theogony*) writing. He died in Orchomenus, Boeotia.

TRANSLATIONS: *Homeric Hymns, and Homerica* tr. Hugh G. Evelyn-White (Loeb Classical Library 1914, latest ed. Cambridge, Mass. 1967). *The Works and Days. Theogony. The Shield of Herakles* tr. Richmond Lattimore (Ann Arbor, Mich. and London 1959).

REFERENCES: Andrew R. Burn *The World of Hesiod* (2nd ed. New York 1966). Werner W. Jaeger *Paideia* (tr. 1939–44, latest ed. 3 vols. Oxford 1965, also PB). Friedrich Solmsen *Hesiod and Aeschylus* (1949, reprinted New York 1968). Peter Walcot *Hesiod and the Near East* (Cardiff 1966).

HESSE, Hermann (July 2, 1877 – Aug. 9, 1962). German-Swiss writer. Born Calw, Württemberg. Sent to classical school and theological seminary in order to prepare for father's career of Protestant missionary, he rebelled, working as mechanic and bookseller before success of first novel, *Peter Camenzind* (1904), enabled him to make living as writer. Married Maria Bernoulli (1904); they later separated. From 1912, lived in Switzerland, be-

coming Swiss citizen (1923). Received Goethe prize and Nobel prize for literature (both 1946). Died at Montagnola, Switzerland. Hesse's early work belonged to German romantic realist school. Beginning with *Demian* (1919, tr. 1923), however, his novels, lyrical and highly symbolic, show deep interest in psychoanalysis, Christian mysticism, and the teachings of Buddha and other Oriental philosophers. Subsequent major novels: *Klein und Wagner* (1920), *Siddhartha* (1922, tr. 1951), *Der Steppenwolf* (1927, tr. 1929), *Narziss und Goldmund* (1930, tr. *Narcissus and Goldmund* 1968), *Das Glasperlenspiel* (1943, tr. *Magister Ludi* 1949 and *The Glass Bead Game* 1969).

REFERENCES: Franz Baumer *Hermann Hesse* (tr. New York 1969). Mark Boulby *Hermann Hesse: His Mind and Art* (Ithaca, N.Y. 1967). Joseph Mileck *Hermann Hesse and His Critics* (Chapel Hill, N.C. 1958). Ernst Rose *Faith from the Abyss: Hermann Hesse's Way from Romanticism to Modernity* (New York 1965 and London 1966, also PB). Miguel Serrano *C. G. Jung and Hermann Hesse: A Record of Two Friendships* (London and New York 1966, also PB). Theodore Ziolkowski *The Novels of Hermann Hesse: A Study in Theme and Structure* (Princeton, N.J. 1965, also PB) and *Hermann Hesse* (New York 1966, also PB).

HEYWOOD, Thomas (c.1574–August 1641). English dramatist, poet and writer. Born in Lincolnshire. Probably studied at Emmanuel College, Cambridge. Sometime in 1590's went to London, where he became member, first of Philip Henslowe's company as actor and playwright, then of Queen Anne's Company. Died in London. Heywood wrote or helped write over two hundred plays, of which about two dozen survive. He worked in a wide variety of dramatic genres, but was most successful with domestic situations, as in his masterpiece, *A Woman Killed with Kindness* (written 1603, published 1607). Other plays include *Edward IV* (part I, 1600; part II, 1605), *The Fair Maid of the West* (1631), *The English Traveler* (1633), *The Royal King and the Loyal Subject* (1637).

Besides plays, wrote a court masque, *Love's Mistress* (1634), seven civic pageants (1631–39), a heroic poem *Troia Britannica* (1609); various miscellanies in prose and verse, pamphlets, translations, and *An Apology for Actors* (1612).

EDITIONS: *Dramatic Works* ed. R. Shepherd (1874, reprinted 6 vols. New York 1964). *A Woman Killed with Kindness* ed. R. W. Van Fossen (Cambridge, Mass. and London 1961).

REFERENCES: Frederick S. Boas *Thomas Heywood* (London 1950). Arthur M. Clark *Thomas Heywood: Playwright and Miscellanist* (Oxford 1931, reprinted New York 1967). Otelia Cromwell *Thomas Heywood: A Study in the Elizabethan Drama of Everyday Life* (1928, reprinted Hamden, Conn. 1969). Michel Grivelet *Thomas Heywood et le drame domestique élizabéthain* (Paris 1957). Mowbray Velte *The Bourgeois Elements in the Dramas of Thomas Heywood* (1924, reprinted New York 1966).

HILDEBRANDT, Johann Lucas von (Nov. 14, 1668 – Nov. 16, 1745). Austrian architect. Born Genoa of German parents, he studied architecture and military engineering, served as engineer in imperial army during three Piedmontese campaigns (1695–96). Settled in Vienna, was appointed court architect (1700) at height of baroque period, and enjoyed enormous success, receiving numerous commissions from Austrian nobility. Hildebrandt surpassed Fischer von Erlach in popularity even before latter's death (1723). His buildings, combining elements of Palladianism and of the north Italian late baroque style (in particular that of Guarini), are characterized by lightness and unusual decorative detail. His finest work is the Belvedere, Vienna, summer palace of Prince Eugene of Savoy (1714–23); among other Viennese buildings are Schönborn garden palace (1706–21); Daun-Kinsky palace (1713–16). Elsewhere he designed Schönborn castle near Göllersdorf (1710–17), Göttweig abbey on the Danube (begun 1719), Mirabell castle, Salzburg (1713–24). Died in Vienna.

Hildebrandt exerted a strong influence throughout central Europe during eighteenth century.

HINDEMITH, Paul (Nov. 16, 1895 – Dec. 28, 1963). German composer. Born Hanau. Father a musician; brother Rudolph a distinguished cellist. Attended Hoch Conservatory, Frankfurt (1909–17), and served in German army (1917–18). First success at Donaueschingen Festival (1921). Married Gertrud Ruttenberg (1924). Appointed professor at Berlin Hochschule (1927). His music was banned from public performance by Nazi government (1934); he left Germany (1937) and settled in U.S. (1939), where he became professor at Yale (1941–53) and Charles Eliot Norton lecturer at Harvard (1949–50). Professor at University of Zürich (1953–63). Died in Frankfurt. Major works: song cycle *Das Marienleben* (1924), operas including *Cardillac* (1926, revised version 1952) and *Mathis der Maler* (1934, produced 1938), choral music, madrigals, sonatas, and chamber works. Writings include *The Craft of Musical Composition* (1937–45) and *A Composer's World* (1952).

REFERENCE: William W. Austin *Music in the Twentieth Century* (New York 1966 and London 1967).

☞

PAUL HINDEMITH
BY ROBERT EVETT

Paul Hindemith was born into a bourgeois German family of the educated class. Thus, from the cradle, he enjoyed all of the privileges and pleasures of being brought up properly without the crippling disadvantages that attended the tin-suit aristocracy of the period. It appears that he had a good private life, but his career as a composer (and this began before the First World War) was — and continues after his death to be — stormy, disagreeable, and largely misunderstood. It was never Hindemith's intention to be a "composer." He thought of himself as an all-around musician with a talent which included, among many other things, a knack for musical composition.

In the beginning, Hindemith wrote extremely conventional music in a style very close to that of Brahms at his noblest best. Just after the First World War, he became dissatisfied with the style and technique of his youth. The result was a period of extraordinary turbulence and restlessness which went on for more than ten years and produced all of his worst music and some of his best. During these years, Hindemith became a darling of the International Society for Contemporary Music and the honored colleague of Stravinsky and Bartók. In the 1920's, any piece which deviated significantly from the harmonic usages of the past was thought to show considerable originality, and it was music that had a lot of wrong notes in it or was simply boring that brought Hindemith his first international acclaim. From this period, almost everything has been relegated to the dustbin by history or revised by the composer except the Third String Quartet and the *Kleine Kammermusik* from Opus 24. That the quartet is a triumph of the human imagination (and I'm not sure that this statement is open to dispute) would indicate, surely, that a great deal of what Hindemith was writing then was pretty good. He was a very productive young man, and a long look at the dustbin is in order.

At this time, when a great deal of serious music was disastrously serious, Hindemith introduced an element of levity. The man himself, otherwise an astonishingly brilliant person, was almost totally devoid of wit. What wrecks the First Violin Concerto is something very close to German bath-room humor, and even the genuinely funny work of his maturity, the *Weber Metamorphoses*, is forever at the point of being swamped in the quicksands of vulgarity.

In the late '20's, Hindemith gave up trying to be funny — almost, but not quite, for life. By 1930 he was well on the way to a *style noble* which, though quite different in sound and texture from the Brahmsian style of his youth, was to mark all of the music of his maturity. *Mathis der Maler,* the opera which was most characteristic of his new style, was presumably on his desk for some months before it was ready for performance in the fall of 1934. This is the famous Berlin performance that did not take place because the Nazis banned it. And this could have come as no surprise to anybody, because the opera is loaded with liberal ideology. In 1938, *Mathis* was finally performed in Zurich, and within a few weeks the opening chord — a D-flat major triad — was a shot heard round the world, as Hindemith had chosen this occasion to declare war on the Nazis and the musical establishment all at once. Hindemith had emerged as a new man and altogether as his own man. In the thirty vastly productive years left of his career, he never once betrayed himself.

The Nazi years were grim, and like so many Germans of his class, Hindemith was so incredulous of what was going on that he was slow to take definite action. He traveled for several years, and in 1941 went to Yale, where he stayed through the war and on into the '50's.

These were the years in which he wrote the Third Viola Concerto (*Schwanendreher*), *Nobilissima Visione,* and the Symphony in E-Flat. But they will be remembered as the sonata years, for it was then that he wrote the largest and infinitely the best sonata literature since Beethoven.

In 1944, the concerto for piano and strings known as *The Four Temperaments* introduced the final phase of his work, which was to consist primarily in maintaining an even technical and stylistic standard in which each succeeding work is quite like the one before. Current opinion had it that Hindemith was stagnating. But to say this is to forget that the composers he had most admired — the Flemish masters of the Renaissance, J. S. Bach, and even Bruckner — had done precisely the same thing. Once arrived at a high level of proficiency and a usable all-purpose style, these men had written poignantly original music in which the originality lay concealed beneath the surface. Hindemith was sufficiently the captive of his own stereotypes that many of his later works do not transcend the standard of purely technical excellence that he set for himself.

Hindemith did not become an American citizen until just after the Second World War. Since his Berlin days, he had written a number of books about music theory, some of them concise and useful, others forbidding. He had never had a proper opportunity to show off his beautiful English prose style until he was invited to deliver the Charles Eliot Norton lectures in poetry at Harvard in 1949 and '50. The result, his book *A Composer's World,* is probably the most coherent and unified sustained statement of aesthetic principles that a composer has ever made. Shortly after delivering the lectures, Hindemith returned to the German-speaking world — not to Germany proper, but to Zurich, where he taught and which he made the base of his operations as a conductor. It was shortly after a conducting engagement that he died, suddenly, of a circulatory disorder, at Christmastime in 1963. In a few months he would have been seventy.

In the years immediately following his death, Hindemith's reputation was subjected to unusually heavy attack and suffered unusually heavy damages. The word got out that he was neither a radical nor a seminal thinker, and that his position in the history of music is marginal. This is true in the sense that Hindemith made no contribution whatever to the technical development of his art and that whatever style he passed on to his followers remained his own private property. Some composers — Dufay, Peri, Stamitz — are important because of their enormous influence in shaping a trend. Hindemith was not one of these.

If Hindemith has a place in history which he has not earned on the merit of his works as such, it will be as the man who, given a perfect opportunity to go in and out with the tide, declined, thus placing a higher value on individuality than on the pressure to conform. The unresolved question is whether the body of his work is strong enough to support such a strong position.

HOBBEMA, Meindert (or **Meyndert**) (Oct. 31, 1638 – Dec. 7, 1709). Dutch landscape painter. Born and died in Amsterdam. All of his works show strong influence of his teacher and friend Jacob van Ruisdael. Married Eeltije Vinck, servant of the burgomaster of Amsterdam (1668), and through this connection obtained in same year a minor position with the Excise in the city. From this time, began to paint less. Died a pauper; popularity and influence came posthumously, especially in England. Hobbema's pictures of country roads, water mills, farmhouses, and ruined castles, always surrounded by dark trees, are noted for their subdued colors, delicate lighting effects, and tranquillity. *The Avenue, Middel-*

harnis (1689, National Gallery, London) is his most famous work. A typical landscape is *The Travellers* (1664, National Gallery, Washington).

REFERENCES: Wilhelm Bode *Great Masters of Dutch and Flemish Painting* (tr. 1909, reprinted Freeport, N.Y. 1967). Georges Broulhiet *Meindert Hobbema* (Paris 1938). Wolfgang Stechow *Dutch Landscape Painting of the Seventeenth Century* (New York and London 1966).

HOBBES, Thomas (Apr. 5, 1588 – Dec. 4, 1679). English philosopher. Born Malmesbury, Wiltshire, a clergyman's son. On receiving B.A. from Magdalen Hall, Oxford (1608), became tutor to William Cavendish, later 2nd earl of Devonshire, whose family remained Hobbes's patrons most of his life. Toured Europe with his pupil (1610). After producing translation of Thucydides (1629), traveled again in Europe (1629–30, 1634–37), and became ardent student of Euclidean geometry and of theories of Galileo, whom he met in Florence. Having supported absolute monarchy in *The Elements of Law, Natural and Politic* (circulated in manuscript 1640; modified later as *Of Human Nature* and *De Corpore Politico*, both 1650), Hobbes fled to Paris in fear of the parliamentarians (1640). Here he wrote series of treatises in political philosophy, culminating in *Leviathan* (1651), his prose masterpiece, which advocates absolute sovereign power in order to control man, whose life is "solitary . . . nasty, brutish, and short," and whose condition is one of "war of everyone against everyone." Hobbes's materialist philosophy offended exiled royalists and the church, and he returned to England (1651), where for rest of his life he engaged in disputes with scientists and theologians, and saw his books banned. Died at Hardwick, Derbyshire. Other important works: *De Cive* (1642), *De Corpore* (1655), *De Homine* (1658), *Behemoth* (1680). Hobbes's influence was great, especially on English philosophy.

EDITIONS: *Complete Works* ed. Sir William Molesworth (London 1839–45, reprinted 11 vols. Aalen, Germany, 1962). *Leviathan* ed. Michael Oake-shott (1946, latest ed. Oxford 1960 and New York 1965, also PB).

REFERENCES: Frithiof Brandt *Thomas Hobbes' Mechanical Conception of Nature* (tr. London and Copenhagen 1928). Keith C. Brown ed. *Hobbes Studies* (Cambridge, Mass. and Oxford 1965). M. M. Goldsmith *Hobbes' Science of Politics* (New York 1966). John Laird *Hobbes* (1934, reprinted New York 1968). Richard S. Peters *Hobbes* (2nd ed. Harmondsworth, England, and Baltimore PB 1967). Sir Leslie Stephen *Hobbes* (1904, new ed. Ann Arbor, Mich. and London 1961, also PB). Leo Strauss *The Political Philosophy of Hobbes* (tr. 1936, latest ed. Chicago 1963, also PB). Howard Warrender *The Political Philosophy of Hobbes* (London and New York 1957). J. W. N. Watkins *Hobbes's System of Ideas* (London and New York 1965, also PB).

HODGSON, Ralph (Mar. 12, 1871 – Nov. 3, 1962). English poet. Born Yorkshire. Little is known of his life. Lived briefly in America, was a journalist in London, and editor for several years of *Fry's Magazine*. Lectured on English literature at Sendai University, Japan (1924 and 1928). Through the private press of which he was co-owner, The Sign of the Flying Flame, he published his own poems and chapbooks. His poem *The Bull* won Polignac prize (1914). Hodgson wrote little poetry but is considered one of the purest lyricists of his time. Many of his poems have appeared repeatedly in anthologies, including *Eve, The Song of Honor, The Bells of Heaven,* and *Time, You Old Gypsy Man*. His collected *Poems* appeared in 1917. A ballad-like, singing quality, as well as a passion for animals, characterize his verse. From 1940 lived on a farm at Minerva, near Canton, Ohio, and published two volumes of verse privately. Received second annual award from National Institute of Arts and Letters (1946) and queen's gold medal for poetry (1954).

REFERENCES: W. H. Davies *Later Days* (London 1925 and New York 1926). Theodore Maynard *Our Best Poets, English and American* (New York 1922 and London 1924). William

Lyon Phelps *The Advance of English Poetry in the Twentieth Century* (1918, reprinted Port Washington, N.Y. 1970).

HOFMANNSTHAL, Hugo von (Feb. 1, 1874 – July 15, 1929). Austrian poet and dramatist. Born Vienna, son of a banker. Studied law and Romance languages at University of Vienna. While in teens, began publishing poems and verse dramas of great lyric beauty, notably *Der Tod des Tizian* (1892), *Der Tor und der Tod* (1893), and *Der Abenteurer und die Sängerin* (1899). Melancholy and nostalgic, perfect in technique, they made him famous as a leader of the neoromantic or symbolist movement, in revolt against naturalist school. At turn of century, abandoned lyric for larger dramatic forms. Many of his plays are best known as libretti for operas by Richard Strauss, with whom Hofmannsthal worked closely for rest of his life. These include *Elektra* (1903, music 1909), *Der Rosenkavalier* (1911), *Ariadne auf Naxos* (1912), *Die Frau ohne Schatten* (1919), *Die ägyptische Helena* (1928), *Arabella* (1933). Other important plays: *Jedermann* (1911), based on English morality play *Everyman; Das Salzburger grosse Welttheater* (1922), a mystery play based on Calderón; *Der Turm* (1925). Married in 1901. Died at home in Rodaun, a Viennese suburb, soon after the suicide of his eldest son.

TRANSLATIONS: *Selected Writings* ed. Michael Hamburger (3 vols. Princeton, N.J. 1952–63).
REFERENCES: Brian Coghlan *Hofmannsthal's Festival Dramas* (Cambridge, England, 1964). Hanns A. Hammelmann *Hugo von Hofmannsthal* (London and New Haven, Conn. 1957). Frederick Norman ed. *Hofmannsthal: Studies in Commemoration* (London 1963).

HOGARTH, William (Nov. 10, 1697 – Oct. 26, 1764). English painter and engraver. Born and died in London. After serving as apprentice to silverplate engraver, studied art at Sir James Thornhill's school at Covent Garden. Began designing plates for booksellers, then produced first signal work, illus-

trations for Samuel Butler's *Hudibras* (1726), and a series of paintings: *A Harlot's Progress* (1730–31), *A Rake's Progress* (1735, Soane Museum, London), and others. In the meantime, married Sir James Thornhill's daughter (1729). Though pictorial satire was his forte, gained reputation for portraits and family groups, including self-portrait with his dog Trump (1745, National Gallery, London). His social satire series included his masterpiece, *Marriage à la Mode* (1745, National Gallery), the engravings *The Enraged Musician* (1741), *Industry and Idleness* (1747), the painting *The March to Finchley* (Foundlings' Hospital, London). After the failure of his treatise on art, *Analysis of Beauty* (1753), Hogarth produced the prints of *The Election* series (1755–58, Soane Museum), *The Cockpit* (1759), and the vindictive portraits of John Wilkes and Charles Churchill, following a bitter quarrel. His reputation as a satirist remains unsurpassed.

REFERENCES: Frederick Antal *Hogarth and His Place in European Art* (New York and London 1962). Erick Berry *The Four Londons of William Hogarth* (New York 1964). Joseph Burke and Colin Caldwell ed. *Hogarth: The Complete Engravings* (London 1968). Georg C. Lichtenberg *The World of Hogarth* (tr. Boston and London 1966) and *Hogarth on High Life: Marriage à la Mode Series* (tr. Middletown, Conn. 1970). A. P. Oppé *The Drawings of William Hogarth* (London and New York 1948). Ronald Paulson *Hogarth's Graphic Works* (2 vols. New Haven, Conn. 1965). Peter Quennell *Hogarth's Progress* (London and New York 1955).

HOGG, James (the Ettrick Shepherd) (1770 – Nov. 21, 1835). Scottish poet. Born Ettrick, Selkirshire. Early became a shepherd and wrote verse. Sir Walter Scott helped him get a collection of his poems published, *The Mountain Bard* (1807), followed by *The Forest Minstrel* (1810). *The Queen's Wake* (1813) brought him recognition, and he came to know Byron, Wordsworth, Southey, and others. In 1816 he was granted a farm in Yarrow by the duke of Buccleuch, and remained there the rest of his life, farming and writing. Among his prose works are *The Three Perils of Man* (1822), *The Confessions of a Justified Sinner* (1824), and *Domestic Manners and Private Life of Sir Walter Scott* (1834). He also published an edition of Robert Burns in collaboration with William Motherwell (1834–35).

EDITIONS: *Selected Poems* ed. J. W. Oliver (Edinburgh 1940). *Private Memoirs and Confessions of a Justified Sinner*, introduction by André Gide (London 1947 and New York 1959, also PB).

REFERENCES: Edith C. Batho *The Ettrick Shepherd* (1927, reprinted New York 1969). Louis Simpson *James Hogg: A Critical Study* (Edinburgh and New York 1962). A. L. Strout *The Life and Letters of James Hogg, the Ettrick Shepherd* (Lubbock, Tex. 1946).

HOLBEIN, Hans, the Younger (1497/98–1543). German painter and engraver. Born in Augsburg, he studied painting with his father, Hans the Elder (c.1465–1524). Worked as religious painter, portraitist, decorator, book illustrator in Basel (1515–26), with interval in Lucerne (1517–19) and probable visit to Lombardy (1518–19). Married Elsbeth Schmid (1520). With introduction from Erasmus, whom he had delighted with his marginal drawings for *Praise of Folly* (1515, Kunstmuseum, Basel) and whose portrait he painted several times (best-known version 1523, Louvre, Paris), Holbein visited England as guest of Sir Thomas More (1526–28). Religious warfare made his second stay in Basel unpleasant (1528–32); returned to England for rest of his life, except for short official visits to the Continent. Became painter to court of Henry VIII (1536). Among his subjects besides the king were Anne of Cleves, Catherine Howard, Sir Thomas More. Holbein's portraits, with their solemnity and meticulous, brilliant rendering of costume, jewels, and *objets*, belong to the international mannerist school, but show a special gift for characterization. Other celebrated works include woodcut series *Dance of*

Death (cut c.1523–26, published 1538), *Madonna of Burgomaster Meyer* (1526, Darmstadt), *Nicholas Kratzer* (1528, Louvre), *The Artist's Family* (1528 or 1529, Kunstmuseum, Basel), *Georg Gisze* (1532, Staatliche Museum, Berlin), *The Ambassadors* (1533, National Gallery, London), *Christina of Denmark* (1538, National Gallery), *Henry VIII* (1540, National Gallery, Rome).

REFERENCES: Anthony Bertram *Holbein the Younger* (London 1948 and New York 1949). Arthur B. Chamberlain *Hans Holbein the Younger* (2 vols. London and New York 1913). James M. Clark *The Dance of Death, by Hans Holbein* (London 1947 and New York 1948). Paul Ganz *The Paintings of Hans Holbein* (tr. London 1950). K. T. Parker *The Drawings of Hans Holbein . . . at Windsor Castle* (London and New York 1945). Hans Reinhardt *Holbein* (tr. London and New York 1938). Roy Strong *Holbein and Henry VIII* (London 1967).

HÖLDERLIN, (Johann Christian) Friedrich (Mar. 20, 1770 – June 7, 1843). German poet. Born Lauffen, of long line of Protestant clergy. Expecting to enter the church, he attended Protestant seminary at Denkendorf, then at Maulbronn, where he studied intently Greek civilization. Entered University of Tübingen (1788), where he knew Hegel and Schelling. Left Tübingen (1793), and became friendly with Schiller, who helped him find a position as tutor. Lived briefly in Jena, moving in literary circle, and Schiller began publishing his work in his journals. Became tutor for children of banker Jakob Gontard in Frankfurt (1796) and fell deeply in love with his wife, Susette, who helped him finish novel *Hyperion* (begun 1793, published 1797–99). Dismissed from post, Hölderlin worked on drama on death of Empedocles until 1800. Suffered an attack of schizophrenia (1802); during spells of recovery he translated Sophocles and Pindar, but after 1806 lived rest of his life, largely insane, in the home of a carpenter in Tübingen. Hölderlin's ideal was a fusion of Hellenism and Christianity. He wrote odes and elegies in complex verse forms, characterized by sweeping rhythms. His reputation was not established until Stefan George and his group discovered him in the twentieth century. His poetry influenced Rilke, as well as George, and others.

TRANSLATIONS: *Some Poems of Friedrich Hölderlin* tr. Frederic Prokosch (Norfolk, Conn. 1943 and London 1947). *Selected Verse* tr. Michael Hamburger (Harmondsworth, England, and Baltimore PB 1961). *Hyperion* tr. Willard R. Trask (New York 1965, also PB). *Poems and Fragments* tr. Michael Hamburger (London and Ann Arbor, Mich. 1967).

REFERENCES: M. B. Benn *Hölderlin and Pindar* (The Hague 1962). Eliza M. Butler *The Tyranny of Greece Over Germany* (1935, new ed. London and Boston PB 1958). Marshall Montgomery *Friedrich Hölderlin and the German Neo-Hellenic Movement* (London and New York 1923). Edwin Muir *Essays on Literature and Society* (rev. ed. London and Cambridge, Mass. 1965). Ronald Peacock *Hölderlin* (London 1938). Lore S. Salzberger *Hölderlin* (New Haven, Conn. and London 1952).

HOLINSHED, Raphael (died c.1580). English historian. Probably a native of Cheshire; may have been educated at Christ's College, Cambridge. In London from about 1560, he was employed as translator by the queen's printer, Reginald Wolfe, who was preparing a history and geography of the world. After Wolfe's death (1573), Holinshed limited the range of the project. Aided by several others, including William Harrison (1534–1593), who supplied topographical sections, he published *Chronicles of England, Scotland, and Ireland,* a compilation from many sources (1577, enlarged edition 1587). The work was immediately popular, and is chiefly remembered as the source of a number of Elizabethan dramas, including Shakespeare's *Macbeth, King Lear, Cymbeline,* and other plays.

EDITION: *Shakespeare's Holinshed: An Edition of Holinshed's Chronicles,* 1587 ed. Richard Hosley (New York 1968).

HOLMES, Oliver Wendell (Aug. 29, 1809 – Oct. 7, 1894). American writer and physician. Born Cambridge, Mass., descendant of prominent Boston Brahmin families. Educated at Phillips Academy, Andover, and graduated from Harvard (1829). While studying briefly at Harvard Law School wrote several poems, of which the most famous was *Old Ironsides* (1830), responsible for saving the historic frigate *Constitution.* They and others were collected as *Poems* (1836), the year he received his M.D. from Harvard, having turned to medicine and studied two years in Paris. Appointed professor of anatomy at Dartmouth (1838), he returned to Boston to marry Amelia Lee Jackson (1840) and establish a practice there. Became first dean of Harvard Medical School (1842), then Parkman professor of anatomy and physiology there (1847) until his retirement (1882). Prominent in Boston literary circles, Holmes helped found (1857) the *Atlantic Monthly* (which he named), and for many years was its leading contributor, publishing the series of essays which became *The Autocrat of the Breakfast Table* (1858), *The Professor at the Breakfast Table* (1860), *The Poet at the Breakfast Table* (1872), and *Over the Teacups* (1891). He also contributed numerous poems, including *The Chambered Nautilus* and *The Deacon's Masterpiece, or The Wonderful "One-Hoss Shay,"* both appearing in the first volume of essays. Several volumes of poems were published in his lifetime, as well as novels, the most important being *Elsie Venner* (2 vols. 1861), a precursor of the modern psychological novel. Famous as a medical authority, he wrote two important medical publications: *Homeopathy and its Kindred Delusions* (1842) and *The Contagiousness of Puerperal Fever* (1843). Celebrated also as raconteur and lecturer, he died in Boston, survived by his son Oliver Wendell Holmes (q.v.), who became a famous justice of the Supreme Court.

EDITIONS: *Works* Riverside Edition (14 vols. Boston 1891–92). *Representative Selections* ed. S. I. Hayakawa and H. M. Jones (New York 1939).

REFERENCES: Mark A. DeWolfe Howe *Holmes of the Breakfast Table* (London and New York 1939). John T. Morse *Life and Letters of Oliver Wendell Holmes* (2 vols. Boston 1896). Eleanor M. Tilton *Amiable Autocrat* (New York 1947).

HOLMES, Oliver Wendell, Jr. (Mar. 8, 1841 – Mar. 6, 1935). American jurist and Supreme Court justice. Born Boston, son of physician and writer Oliver Wendell Holmes (q.v.). Graduated from Harvard (1861). Served with distinction in the 20th Massachusetts regiment during Civil War (1861–64), then returned to graduate from Harvard Law School (1866). On admission to bar (1867), joined a Boston law firm. Taught at Harvard (1870–73) while editing *American Law Review* (1870–73) and 12th edition of *Kent's Commentaries* (1873). Married Fanny Bowditch Dixwell (1872). Publication of his important work *The Common Law* (1881) led to appointment as professor of law at Harvard (1882–83). Served on Massachusetts Supreme Court (1883–1902), the last three years as chief justice. As justice of the U.S. Supreme Court (1902–32), he espoused a doctrine of judicial restraint and vigorously defended the citizen's guarantees under the Bill of Rights. Died in Washington, D.C.

EDITIONS: *Holmes-Pollock Letters: The Correspondence of Mr. Justice Holmes and Sir Frederick Pollock, 1874–1932* ed. Mark DeWolfe Howe (Cambridge, Mass. 1961). *Holmes-Laski Letters: The Correspondence of Oliver Wendell Holmes and Harold J. Laski, 1916–1935* ed. Mark DeWolfe Howe (Cambridge, Mass. 1963, also PB). *Holmes-Einstein Letters: The Correspondence of Mr. Justice Holmes and Lewis Einstein, 1903–1935* ed. J. B. Peabody (New York and London 1964). *The Common Law* (Boston 1881), ed. Mark DeWolfe Howe (Cambridge, Mass. and London 1963, also PB).

REFERENCES: Francis Biddle *Justice Holmes: Natural Law and the Supreme Court* (New York 1961). Catherine Drinker Bowen *Yankee from Olympus: Justice Holmes and His Family* (Boston 1944). Felix Frankfurter *Mr. Justice Holmes and the Supreme Court* (New York 1965, also PB). Mark De-

Wolfe Howe *Justice Oliver Wendell Holmes* (2 vols. Cambridge, Mass. 1957/63).

OLIVER WENDELL HOLMES, JR.
BY RICHARD H. ROVERE

"A sage with the bearing of a cavalier," Walter Lippmann wrote of the great jurist on the occasion of his seventy-fifth birthday. "He wears wisdom like a gorgeous plume." A sage is a man, generally well along in years, who wears wisdom, or sagacity, with a certain panache. Like most sages, Holmes was more original in expression than in thought. He was not a philosopher in any innovative sense but rather, like the likes of Montaigne and Dr. Johnson, a great apostle of common sense. It has been said that his was the profoundest intellect that ever dispensed or explicated Anglo-Saxon justice. This may well be so, but, even in jurisprudence, his gift was for logic and elucidation, not for invention or system building. It is not clear that he ever acknowledged this, and certainly he wished it to be otherwise. He hungered shamelessly for immortality, for celebration beyond the grave. He spoke of anticipating "the subtle rapture of a postponed power." No man, he said, "has earned the right to intellectual ambition until he has learned to lay his course by a star which he has not seen — to dig by divining rods for springs which he may never reach." But he did not ever really do this; he was no dowser; the revolutionary urges were alien to his profoundly skeptical mind and temperament. Metaphysics he regarded as "churning the void to make cheese." Most codified moralities, theologies, and antitheologies were "human criticism of or rebellion at the Cosmos, which to my mind is simply damning the weather."

What he did superbly was to state a case or extract an essence in a few clear and compelling words. "In compression of statement," Stimson Bullitt has written, "he was a rival of Tacitus and an equal of Bacon." He was in any case a splendid writer. There is a liveliness and tension and rub in the most casual of his letters and the least controversial of his opinions from the bench. He never spoke or wrote except crisply. He never committed a soggy sentence. Other men of his time labored and produced fat books to make some point that Holmes could clinch in a single declarative sentence. Toward the end of his life, for example, there was a modernist school of thought called "legal realism," in essence a revolt against the rule of *stare decisis.* The core of its doctrine had been most succinctly put by Holmes in 1897, in a now famous asseveration: "It is revolting to have no better reason for a rule of law than that so it was laid down at the time of Henry IV." Most of the rest of the case was summed up in these few — and also famous — words: "The common law is not a brooding omnipresence in the sky but the articulate voice of some sovereign or quasi-sovereign that can be identified . . . . [The law is] what the courts do in fact."

Holmes may or may not endure the centuries as Montaigne and Dr. Johnson have, or Tacitus and Bacon. One certain fact, though, is that he lived in that state of grace we call maturity as long as any man in the history of this republic. Holmes, who knew John Quincy Adams and Alger Hiss, was intellectually adult in adolescence, and he reached his middle nineties without being overtaken by senility. Aged nineteen, in the summer before Lincoln's election, he wrote a Harvard theme on Albrecht Dürer, that, many years after

his death, was cited by Wolfgang Stechow, an eminent German critic, as making Ruskin's essay on Dürer sound hazy, hasty, and trivial by comparison. Three quarters of a century later, he was cracking jokes with Felix Frankfurter and Harold Laski and advising the latter that Franklin Roosevelt was "a good fellow with rather a soft edge"; urging the soft-edged one to "form your battalions and fight"; shooting off prickly and sometimes indiscreet commentaries on current cases to his friend Sir Frederick Pollock; gossiping with Lippmann, while ogling Washington girls through his Georgetown window; reading Hemingway and talking on the radio. George Bernard Shaw started off as early as Holmes and was flashier all the way, but in most things he lacked Holmes's finish and judgment. ("He seems to me," Holmes said, "to dogmatize in an ill-bred way. . . . Of course, I delight in his wit.") "Maturity" was never the word for Shaw, but it was for Holmes, who had no flibbertigibbet phases, though he was sometimes prone to flipness, a quite different thing. It took him forty years to appreciate Lincoln, his one-time commander in chief. "Few men in baggy trousers and bad hats are recognized as great by those who see them," he explained, lamely, to a lady in 1909. He was on occasion wrong, but he was never foolish or banal. No platitude was ever known to cross his lips.

Perhaps the largest and most important thing about him was that he faced the dilemma of the modern mind — he snorted at phrases like this — unflinchingly, merrily, and responsibly, while such contemporaries as Henry Adams and John Jay Chapman either turned into cranks and helpless neurotics or averted their gaze and dwelt on other things. Holmes came to believe, at his learned father's knee, that "we're in the belly of the universe, not that it is in us." He found this anguishing, and he never stopped thinking about it, but he discovered a way of living with it. He was a moral and — though it did not come easily to him — a compassionate man, and he knew that he was so partly by choice, partly by breeding. All his values were, in any case, elected ones; a few he had deliberately chosen, the rest he deliberately accepted from his forebears, but none of them without reluctance and some grumbling. One reason he could not have been a philosopher was that it was part of his nature that he had to go through life believing no more than he had to believe. "All I mean by truth is what I can't help thinking," he said. He hated the bleakness of the world he saw by merely looking about and the even bleaker horizons that came into view when he looked hard. He could not avoid thinking that the "sacredness of human life is a purely municipal ideal of no validity outside the jurisdiction." But he accepted the municipal ideal as valid because his moral instincts told him to and because he enjoyed being part of the municipality. He simply decided, early in life to accept those values and moralities he found defensible on grounds other than certifiable truth. "Morality is simply another means of living," he wrote, "but the saints make it an end in itself." Still, he could not help thinking that some things *ought* to be sacred ("I do accept a rough equation between isness and oughtness") and he settled on some of these. Of free speech, he said that "in the abstract I have no very enthusiastic belief [in it, but] I hope I would die for it."

He remains by almost universal consent the greatest of American jurists. And he remains, in the judgment of many, one of the most splendid of our stylists and perhaps the one authentic sage to grace our literature.

HOMER (Homeros). (fl. probably 9th century B.C.) Greek poet. Virtually no indisputable facts are known about Homer. His language indicates that he was an Ionian Greek. The ancient Greeks attributed to him both the *Iliad* and the *Odyssey*, but modern scholars emphasize the immense complication of the problem of their authorship. The style of the epics suggests strongly that they were orally composed and transmitted, probably not being written down until the 6th century B.C. The so-called Homeric hymns are now believed to be not his. Traditionally he was blind. Seven cities (listed differently in different sources) claimed him as a native; Smyrna and Chios seem the most likely birthplaces. The *Iliad* and *Odyssey,* which deal with incidents during and after the Trojan War, may be considered the beginnings of the continuing tradition from which modern Western literature has developed. Homer's concern for his heroes' personalities rather than simply for their feats has had a profound and lasting effect on literature.

TRANSLATIONS: *Chapman's Homer* tr. George Chapman (1616) ed. Allardyce Nicoll (2nd ed. 2 vols. Princeton, N.J. 1967). *Iliad* tr. Alexander Pope (1715–20, ed. Maynard Mack 2 vols. London and New Haven, Conn. 1967); tr. Andrew Lang, Walter Leaf, and Ernest Meyers (1905, latest ed. New York 1950, also PB); tr. W. H. D. Rouse (latest ed. New York PB 1954); tr. E. V. Rieu (Harmondsworth, England, PB 1950); tr. Richmond Lattimore (2nd ed. Chicago 1962, also PB). *Odyssey* tr. Alexander Pope (1725–26, ed. Maynard Mack 2 vols. London and New Haven, Conn. 1967); tr. Samuel H. Butcher and Andrew Lang (1879, latest ed. New York 1959); tr. T. E. Shaw (T. E. Lawrence) (1932, latest ed. London and New York 1955, also PB); tr. E. V. Rieu (1950, latest ed. Harmondsworth, England, PB 1967); tr. Richmond Lattimore (New York 1967, also PB).

REFERENCES: C. M. Bowra *Tradition and Design in the Iliad* (London and New York 1930). Albert B. Lord *Singer of Tales* (Cambridge, Mass. and Oxford 1960, also PB). Cedric H. Whitman *Homer and the Heroic Tradition* (Cambridge, Mass. and Oxford 1958, also PB).

≥⃝

HOMER
BY GEORGE R. STEWART

To write about Homer is like fighting in the pitch dark with an opponent who probably is not there. But let me begin with a few ideas that seem reasonable to me, though they may not so seem to others who have opinions on the matter.

Homer, I believe, was a Greek of one of the cities on the coast of Asia Minor. He lived, as many ancient Greeks believed, about 800 B.C., by our reckoning. The poets of that time followed a wholly oral tradition, and in those cities, it seems likely, a whole mass of broken-down epic poems and ancient fragments and new lays were being sung by professional minstrels, such as several times appear as characters in the *Odyssey*. Each of these considered himself as qualified to tinker with the poetry.

Homer, probably one of these minstrels but certainly a great poet, apparently worked upon his mass of material, rejecting much of it, reworking parts, adding new sections. He did not finish with a neatly unified poem, because some of the ancient fragments were too fine to omit, even if they contradicted other parts of the story. Some of these inconsistencies are large, as in the way book II of the *Iliad* fails to mesh with book I. Other inconsistencies are minor, as when three emissaries are named in book IX and then are regularly mentioned with a verb form that means only two.

Still, Homer produced a very great poem. After he was dead, the minstrel poets moved in and muddled things up somewhat, but most of the great poem remained as the master had shaped it.

Homer may also have been, in the same way, the "author" of that other great poem the *Odyssey* — though personally I find the contrary arguments to be stronger. Superficially, one might say, that poem is like the *Iliad*, being developed out of the old epic tradition, with about the same vocabulary, displaying many of the stereotyped epithets, half-lines, and even full lines. But basically the *Odyssey*, magnificent in its own way, is not so much of an epic and is more of a "novel in verse," as it has often been called. It is also better unified, apparently much more a one-man production. Being like a novel, it translates easily, so that people who do not know Greek are likely to prefer it to the *Iliad*, which cannot be satisfactorily translated.

We have no reliable data on Homer's life, but a possible way to deduce something about him is to consider the most unusual features of the *Iliad* to be his. The ancient epic tradition, and even the minstrel poets, could account for the routine, and we can grant to them the meter, the structure of repeated and stereotyped half-lines with their epithets, and the conventional battle pieces.

In this connection there can be argument about the so-called "Homeric" similes. As the name indicates, they are characteristic of these poems, especially of the *Iliad*. At the same time, there is something highly conventional about them, with their monotonously marauding lions. They may well have been a part of the epic tradition, at which every minstrel was expected to show his skill.

To the personality of the master

himself, however, we may attribute the strange attitude toward war. Though combat is the very essence of epic, Homer is not happy with war. There is much bloody killing — probably a good deal of it, like the lengthy but pointless exploits of Diomedes, taken over from earlier poems. But constantly war gets such epithets as "direful," or "destructive," and commonly is described by the simple word "bad."

To Homer, second, I would attribute the curious attitude toward the gods. Perhaps he was not skeptical, but he was worse. He made his gods repugnant to decent-thinking people, so that they display themselves as vicious, lascivious, and treacherous bullies, and sometimes even ridiculous.

Third, Homer loved small touches in quite an un-epic way — as in the comparison about the little girl hanging on to her mother's skirt, or in the famous incident of the baby, Astyanax, who was frightened at his father's helmet plume.

Fourth, Homer was curiously prim and proper. There is scarcely a line in the *Iliad* that cannot meet the Victorian test of being fit to be read by a young girl. (The story of Aphrodite and Ares, which is somewhat erotic, is in the *Odyssey*.) Later Greeks imagined a homosexual tie between Achilles and Patroclus, but there is no suggestion of it in the *Iliad*. In other details also there is a kind of great decency. For instance, the sacrifice of the Trojan prisoners at the pyre of Patroclus must have been a part of the fixed tradition, not to be omitted. But it bothered the poet, and he took a half-line for reproof against Achilles — "he contrived bad deeds."

Finally, to the central planner we must ascribe the breadth of sympathy, almost unknown to other epics. In *The Song of Roland*, for instance, the op-posing Saracens are merely "bad guys." But Homer makes us feel for the Trojans almost as much as for the Achaeans — with some readers, even more so. Here one may wonder at a particular point (possibly biographical), that the name Homer actually is plain Greek for "hostage," and that he may have been significantly named, because as a boy he had spent some years as a hostage among "barbarians." Such a boy might have been kindly treated, and have learned to love a fatherly old king and expend his hero worship upon a chivalrous warrior. Then, in due time returned, he would have fought against his old friends, but he could never have forgotten what good people were among them. Who gets the last words in the *Iliad*? Not "manslaying Achilles," but "horse-taming Hector."

In such ways as these, we may think, a great poet impressed himself so deeply upon the ancient epic material that neither the lapse of years nor the fumbling of lesser men could ever eliminate or cover over the marks of the personality of the master.

HOMER, Winslow (Feb. 24, 1836 – Sept. 29, 1910). American painter. Born Boston, Mass. into old New England family. Apprenticed at nineteen to lithographer John Bufford. Opened his own studio (1857), moved to New York (1859), and illustrated commercially, notably for *Harper's Weekly* during Civil War, producing a series of drawings of camp life, also the oil *Prisoners at the Front* (Metropolitan Museum, New York). Won such success with his painting in oils (from 1862) that he was elected full member of National Academy of Design (1865). The next year traveled briefly in France. Took up watercolor (summer 1873) at Gloucester, Mass., and soon ceased commercial illustrating. Withdrew (1881) for two seasons to England's North Sea coast, then to Prout's Neck on Maine coast (1883), where he remained the rest of his life, with winter trips to Bahamas, Bermuda, and elsewhere, and summer trips to Adirondacks and northern woods. Homer's subjects were, in his earlier years, gay renditions of life on farms or at vacation resorts. He later depicted the sea, the woods, the mountains, and the people who live there. In this phase, his approach was virile and elemental. Among his finest works: *Eight Bells* (1886, Addison Gallery, Andover, Mass.), *Northeaster* (1895, Metropolitan Museum, New York), *The Lookout — All's Well* (1896, Museum of Fine Arts, Boston), *Gulf Stream* (1899, Metropolitan Museum).

REFERENCES: Philip C. Beam *Winslow Homer at Prout's Neck* (Boston 1966). James Thomas Flexner *The World of Winslow Homer* (New York 1966). Lloyd Goodrich *Winslow Homer* (New York 1959) and *Graphic Art of Winslow Homer* (Washington, D.C. 1969). Donelson F. Hoopes *Winslow Homer Watercolors* (New York 1969).

✍

WINSLOW HOMER
BY JAMES THOMAS FLEXNER

Winslow Homer's boyhood was part of America's Edenic phase. Europe with all its troubles seemed far away; prosperity mounted, bringing as much happiness as human frailty would accept; and a terrible bloody crisis that was rushing on the nation did not cause any premonitory shadows visible to a high-spirited boy rambling through woods and fields.

The college town, Cambridge in Massachusetts, where Homer grew up, was still a village. He dreamed through necessary hours in grade school and then resumed the rural sports which had been temporarily interrupted. His father, by losing the family money in a crackbrained effort to become rich, saved Winslow from the more serious academic trials of that local institution, Harvard. True, the alternative to college depressed Homer at first. Al-

though too young, or so he complained bitterly, to be drawn from "boyish play" — he was nineteen — he was apprenticed to a lithographer.

Fate had steered Homer into what was for him the perfect path. He wished to be an artist and believed that "if a man wishes to be an artist, he should never look at pictures." He wanted to work things out for himself, and he was being initiated in a trade that would enable him to do so, not theoretically but practically, in the presence of an audience, while at the same time he made his living.

Homer was soon drawing for woodblock reproduction in mass circulation periodicals like *Harper's Weekly*. While yet in his early twenties he became one of the most popular illustrators in the United States. He depicted gaieties of American life: elegant young ladies being frightened at a picnic by a swain waving a live lobster; pretty farm girls, in barns at cornhusking, struggling coyly to escape being kissed. And always the happy play of children.

When the Civil War struck, Homer was twenty-five. Covering some of the campaigns as a free-lance illustrator, he ignored — as far as he could — carnage, concentrating on the high jinks of the soldiery. In the middle of the conflict, he embarked on a conflict of his own: to teach himself, in the presence of nature, how to paint in oils. He was so successful at this personal task that within four years his fellow American artists awarded him their highest honor: full membership in the National Academy.

After the war, Homer made a ten-month trip to France. At the Louvre, he drew the pretty girl copyists but copied no pictures. He returned home with artistic richness stored in his memory, but his style in no basic way changed. He was painting in the manner of his American predecessors: not considering technique more important than subject matter as Europeans were inclined to do, but seeking to express what he saw as directly as possible by whatever technique would best and least obtrusively serve that end.

Homer wished the viewer to feel not that he was looking at a picture but that he was actually in the presence of nature. He sought naturalism through experiment. In this labor, he was greatly facilitated by his discovery of the possibilities of watercolor, a medium which was just rising to serious stature in Western art. With quick washes, he could catch, as he wandered through the landscape, evanescent visual effects that would have escaped more ponderous oil paints. He saw and expressed momentary aspects of nature that were being independently grasped by the impressionists who were rising in France. Homer's watercolors were in themselves delightful works of art, and with them he pioneered directions in which his oil painting more slowly followed.

Homer had turned his back on his memories of the war, reviving the subject matter of his prewar woodcuts. He showed Americans at play, or at work outdoors; belles strutting at watering places, New England milkmaids or huntsmen in the north woods. Increasingly, he viewed figures in landscape entirely freshly, noting, in particular, colors that actually existed in nature but had never been recorded before. As his work became less and less like the art in museums, his following became puzzled. His popularity waned. And then, at long last, the high-spirited optimism of youth failed to satisfy his more serious moods.

Although the pure pleasure of the entranced eye continued to light his rapid watercolors, he felt the need to dig in his oils for something more emotionally profound. He now suffered a period of sterility, during which he would disappear for months together from his friends. Finally, he exiled himself in a fishing village on the English coast of the North Sea, where he conducted painting experiments in a walled garden. On his return to America he abandoned the New York studios which had housed him for so long and settled at Prout's Neck, a rocky promontory on the coast of Maine.

The subject of his oils was now the battle of man with nature, usually of human beings with the sea. Eventually, people disappeared from his canvases; he painted great storms visualized as Herculean conflicts between sea and land. These were tragic pictures but never lachrymose, always imbued with strength, with elevation, with the glory of life even in conflict or defeat. No despair had frozen the springing in Homer's heart. He could still go off on boyish holidays. The watercolors he created as an old man in tropical climes are perhaps the gayest, the most brilliantly colored, the most freely executed in the history of art.

Living through many decades when other artistic conceptions, mostly imported from Europe, were fashionable in the United States, Homer continued to build, through personal experimentation, on the native American painting traditions of the second and third quarters of the nineteenth century. And, however paradoxical it may seem, the result was that his achievements paralleled, more than those of the imitators, the achievements of the greatest European artists of his time. Winslow Homer became, although in his own not the French idiom, an impressionist. In this critic's opinion, he was as great a painter as any individual member of the French impressionist group.

HONEGGER, Arthur (Oscar) (Mar. 10, 1892 – Nov. 27, 1955). Swiss-French composer. Born Le Havre, of Swiss parents. Received musical training in Paris, then at Zurich Conservatory (1909–11), and again in Paris at Conservatoire (from 1912), where he was particularly influenced by Vincent d'Indy. First important work, a sonata for violin and piano, appeared in 1916, followed by chamber, orchestral, and stage works. Became well known as member of group of composers called Les Six. Married pianist Andrée Vaurabourg (1926). Works include *Le Roi David,* a cantata (1921); the popular *Pacific 231,* an orchestral description of an American locomotive (1924); operas *Judith* (1926) and *Antigone* (1927); symphonic poem *Rugby* (1928); oratorio *Jeanne d'Arc au bûcher* (1938); five symphonies; ballet music; incidental music for plays, motion pictures, and radio dramas; songs. Died in Paris. Though associated with modern movement in French music, Honegger was more German in his approach. He made free use of polytonality and atonality, had a fondness for elaborate counterpoint, and most often strove for a mood of austerity and gravity. He is author of an autobiography, *Je suis compositeur* (1951, tr. *I Am a Composer* 1966).

REFERENCES: Marcel Delannoy *Honegger* (Paris 1953). Willy Tappolet *Arthur Honegger* (Neuchâtel, Switzerland 1939).

HONTHORST, Gerrit (or Gerard) van (Nov. 4, 1590 – Apr. 27, 1656). Dutch painter. Born and died in Utrecht. After studying under Abraham Bloemaert, spent ten years in Italy (1610–20), where he was decisively influenced by the naturalism and chiaroscuro of Caravaggio. On return to Utrecht, he married and joined painters' guild, of which he was dean four times. Honthorst achieved international renown as portrait and history painter: worked for Charles I in London (1628), painting *Charles I and Henrietta Maria with the Liberal Arts* (1628, Hampton Court); for king of Denmark (1635–41); and as court painter at The Hague (1637–52). Also famous for his genre scenes, usually of musicians, often illuminated by candlelight. An example is *The Procuress* (1625, Centraal Museum, Utrecht). Italian nickname Gherardo della Notte refers to this predilection for night scenes. Honthorst is important as transmitter of style of Caravaggio to northern painting; among those he influenced were Rembrandt and Hals.

REFERENCE: Jay R. Judson *Gerrit van Honthorst: A Discussion of His Position in Dutch Art* (The Hague 1959).

HOOCH (or HOOGH), Pieter de (1629–after 1683). Dutch painter. Born Rotterdam. Possibly after period of study under Nicolaes Berchem in Haarlem, he became (1653) servant and painter to Justus de la Grange, a resident of Delft and Leiden. Married Jannetje van der Burch, a girl from Delft (1654), and in following year was inscribed in Delft painters' guild. Moved (after 1660) to Amsterdam, where he was still living in 1677. A picture dated 1684 provides the last evidence of his activity; neither the place nor date of his death is known. His finest work, produced during the years at Delft and showing an affinity with that of his contemporary Vermeer, depicts simple domestic scenes, with housewives, maidservants and children. Rooms open into other rooms or to the outdoors, revealing half-seen vistas and subtly varied intensities of light. An example is the popular *Courtyard of a House in Delft* (1658, National Gallery, London). Later, in Amsterdam, de Hooch turned to more ambitious themes in order to please a wealthy and sophisticated clientele, with less artistic success. Over 320 of his paintings survive.

REFERENCES: Wilhelm Bode *Great Masters of Dutch and Flemish Painting* (tr. 1909, reprinted Freeport, N.Y. 1967). Jakob Rosenberg and others *Dutch Art and Architecture, 1600 to 1800* (Harmondsworth, England, and Baltimore 1966). Wilhelm R. Valentiner *Pieter de Hooch* (New York 1930).

HOOD, Thomas (May 23, 1799 – May 3, 1845). English poet and humorist. Born and died in London, son of a bookseller. Joined staff of *London Magazine* (1821–23), came to know Hazlitt, Lamb, and De Quincey. Produced in collaboration with friends satiric *Odes and Addresses to Great People* (1825) and two volumes of *Whims and Oddities in Prose and Verse* (1826–27). Edited the *Gem* (1829) in which his macabre *Dream of Eugene Aram* appeared. Began the *Comic Annual* (1830), to which he contributed profusely. Ill health obliged him to live abroad, where he continued his editorship. Returned to England (1840), edited the *New Monthly Magazine*, in which appeared his satire *Miss Kilmansegg* (1841–43), then *Hood's Magazine* (from 1844). His best-known poem, *The Song of the Shirt* (1843), was a serious poem about factory conditions of his time. Last poems were also serious: *The Bridge of Sighs* (1844), *The Elm Tree*, and others. His son, Thomas, known as Tom (1835–1874), was a humorist and editor of comic papers and *Tom Hood's Comic Annual* (from 1867).

EDITIONS: *Works* ed. Thomas Hood, Jr. and F. F. Broderip (1882–84, reprinted 11 vols. New York 1968). *Complete Poetical Works* ed. Walter Jerrold (1906, reprinted London and New York 1935).

REFERENCES: Laurence Brander *Thomas Hood* (London and New York 1963, also PB). John Clubbe *Victorian Forerunner: The Later Career of Thomas Hood* (Durham, N.C. 1968). Walter Jerrold *Thomas Hood: His Life and Times* (1907, reprinted New York 1969). John C. Reid *Thomas Hood* (London 1963 and New York 1964).

HOPKINS, Gerard Manley (July 28, 1844 – June 8, 1889). English poet. Born Stratford, Essex. At Balliol College, Oxford (1863–67), was converted from Anglicanism to Roman Catholicism (1866). Entered Society of Jesus (1868), worked in parishes in London, Oxford, Liverpool, Glasgow. Taught classics at Stonyhurst College, Lancashire; became professor of Greek at Dublin University (1884). Died of typhoid fever in Dublin. During his lifetime, most of his poetry was read only in manuscript by his friends, including Robert Bridges, who after his death published some in anthologies and later the collected *Poems* (1918). Much of his correspondence, journals, and sermons have been subsequently published.

EDITIONS: *Poems* ed. Robert Bridges (Oxford 1918; 2nd ed. enlarged 1930; 3rd ed. enlarged, ed. Bridges and W. H. Gardner, 1948). *The Letters of Gerard Manley Hopkins to Robert Bridges* (1935, new ed. London and New York 1955), *The Correspondence of Gerard Manley Hopkins and Richard Watson Dixon* (1935, new ed. London and New York 1955), and *Further Letters of Gerard Manley Hopkins, Including His Correspondence with Coventry Patmore* (1938, 2nd ed. London and New York 1956), all ed. Claude Colleer Abbott. *Journals and Papers* ed. Humphry House and Graham Storey (London and New York 1959) and *Sermons and Devotional Writings* ed. Christopher Devlin (London and New York 1959) together constitute a revised and enlarged 2nd ed. of *Note-Books and Papers* ed. Humphry House (London 1937). *A Hopkins Reader* ed. John Pick (1953, rev. ed. Garden City, N.Y. PB 1966).

REFERENCES: W. H. Gardner *Gerard Manley Hopkins* (1944–49, latest ed. 2 vols. London and New York 1966) and *Gerard Manley Hopkins: A Study of Poetic Idiosyncrasy in Relation to Poetic Tradition* (2nd ed. 2 vols. London and New York 1962). Alan Heuser *The Shaping Vision of Gerard Manley Hopkins* (London 1958, reprinted Hamden, Conn. 1968). Bernard Kelly *The Mind and Poetry of Gerard Manley Hopkins, S.J.* (London and Boston 1935). G. F. Lahey, S.J. *Gerard Manley Hopkins* (London 1930, reprinted New York 1969). W. M. A. Peters, S.J. *Gerard Manley Hopkins: A Critical Essay Toward the Understanding of His Poetry* (London and New York 1948). Elsie E. Phare *The Poetry of Gerard Manley Hopkins: A Survey and Commentary* (1933, reprinted New York 1967). John Pick *Gerard Manley Hopkins: Priest and Poet* (1942, 2nd ed. London and New York PB 1966). Norman Weyand ed. *Immortal Diamond: Studies in Gerard Manley Hopkins* (1949, reprinted New York 1969).

✍

GERARD MANLEY HOPKINS
BY RICHARD EBERHART

Hopkins had an oddness of language which together with his extreme passion gave his poetry a force which speaks directly to us today. He was ahead of his time instead of mirroring it.

The life of Hopkins is a subdued drama. Early in his life he encountered his great conflict. The conflict was whether to go over to the Roman Catholic Church.

When he became a Jesuit priest he renounced the possibility of marriage. He made another great discovery about himself, that religion was higher than art. He thus had the courage to destroy his early poems.

The church was wise in trying to find the best niche for the religious talents of Hopkins. They tried him out as a preacher but he was not to become a Donne. He was shifted around and was placed where he was best suited as a teacher. His knowledge of Greek and Latin made him well suited to teaching. He died in 1889 in Ireland at the early age of forty-four.

It must be remembered that during his life he was not known to the public as a poet. He was highly and deeply regarded by his perceptive poetic friends, Robert Bridges, Richard Watson Dixon, and Coventry Patmore. The letters to and from these make engrossing reading.

Robert Bridges lived to be old, dying in 1930 at eighty-six, having published *The Testament of Beauty* as late as 1930. It is to Bridges that we owe the presence among us of Hopkins. Bridges became poet laureate, his work known to the world. He must have recognized that his friend Hopkins was the better poet. Finally, in 1918, he brought out the first edition of Hopkins's poems, with a delicate poem to his friend included. The sensuousness, the immediacy, the Christian depth, and the new grammatical inventions of Hopkins inflamed readers of poetry at once, but it took about ten years for his startling new poetry to become somewhat generally known. Then there was a flood of books and articles on Hopkins's work and style. Up to the time of World War II the tide of interest in Hopkins was rising; since then it has leveled off to his acceptance as an established master.

Perhaps the most dramatic aspect of the subdued drama of his life was his return to poetry, after years of service to the church as a priest.

There was a sea disaster when the *Deutschland* sank en route from Bremen to England. Many died, but among the drowned were five Franciscan nuns. Protestant critics with a sense of irony remark that he was not so concerned with the scores of others who lost their lives as with the few nuns. He was given permission to write a poem on the subject, which released the complex, difficult poem *The Wreck of the Deutschland* and launched him on the career of his mature work. The denial of poetry for so long resulted in a passionate release of energies for some years, giving us his major poems, including the "dark night of the soul" poems, the "terrible sonnets," his ultimate questionings of and submission to the Christian commitment. He broke his seven-year poetic silence in 1875.

We can only think of Hopkins in a few aesthetic pieces as not primarily a

Christian poet. *Spring and Fall* with the lines

> Margaret, are you grieving
> Over Goldengrove unleaving?

which ends

> It is the blight man was born for,
> It is Margaret you mourn for

has the uncompromising sternness of Hardy. *Binsey Poplars, Felled 1879* is an aesthetic poem with sensuous and musical properties learned from Swinburne, but with its own unmistakable ardor and sensibility.

Heaven-Haven, with the epigraph "A nun takes the veil," is an aesthetic gemlike short poem of two quatrains with three beats in the first, second and fourth lines, line three in each stanza being long with five beats. The variations in rhythm are effective. The nun desires to go

> Where springs not fail,
> To fields where flies no sharp
>   and sided hail
> And a few lilies blow.

It was a stroke of genius that gave him "sided" for hail. He had first had it "unbridled hail."

The Leaden Echo and the Golden Echo (Maidens' song from St. Winifred's Well), with its difficult and intriguing syntax, I would place in an aesthetic category as it goes from the notion of despair to some ultimate notion of "Yonder," although after the despair of the Leaden Echo the idea of the Golden Echo is to "Give beauty back, beauty, beauty, beauty, back to God, beauty's self and beauty's giver."

The frustrated will of Hopkins went through loving one's suffering to complete subjection to Christ's will. In *Carrion Comfort* the rebellious Christian still rebels. In the next poem, No. 65, he is even more rebellious; which has in its last six lines

> O the mind, mind has mountains;
>   cliffs of fall
> Frightful, sheer, no-man-fathomed.
>   Hold them cheap
> May who ne'er hung there.

and

>   Here! creep,
> Wretch, under a comfort serves in
>   a whirlwind: all
> Life death does end and each day
>   dies with sleep.

No. 69 in its last six lines has

> I am gall, I am heartburn. God's
>   most deep decree
> Bitter would have me taste: my
>   taste was me;
> Bones built in me, flesh filled,
>   blood brimmed the curse.
> Selfyeast of spirit a dull dough
>   sours.

The final poem, No. 74, with a Latin inscription, sometimes called the "Time's eunuch" sonnet, shows the resolution of his will, the admission that God is just if He contends with man, makes man contend with Him. If Hopkins did not have to contend with God his central problem would vanish, and with it the most probing parts of his poetry. He makes the nice opposition that if God were his enemy, who is instead indeed his friend, how could God worse thwart him? "The sots and thralls of lust" thrive better than he, Christian, who spends "life upon thy cause." Were it not for his will-problem and his God-struggle the palpable beauty of the world would suffice for the adoration of man and for his. He concludes by saying though birds build he does not build, but strains, "Time's eunuch," and that he does not breed "one work that wakes." His final submission is in the last line: "Mine, O thou lord of life, send my roots rain."

God's Grandeur and *The Windhover: To Christ Our Lord* are profound religious poems, the latter having intrigued critics for decades with its complex grammar, the ambiguities of "Buckle," Christ on the Cross equated with the buckling of the bird. *Hurrahing in Harvest* has ambiguities too.

Hopkins is at his most sensuous in *Spring* and in *The Starlight Night.* There is the splendid rocking rhythm of *Inversnaid,* the original notion in *Pied Beauty* that pied things, fathered-forth by God and worthy of praise, are more beautiful than single perceptions. "Rose-moles all in stipple upon trout that swim" make one never want to look for a plain trout in water thereafter. *Felix Randal,* about the farrier once hardy-handsome but now broken by sickness, although given "our sweet reprieve and ransom," could not have imagined in health his doom

> *When thou at the random grim*
> *forge, powerful amidst peers,*
> *Didst fettle for the great grey dray-*
> *horse his bright and battering*
> *sandal!*

Hopkins was not a formal thinker, but he invented terms which have puzzled critics and lovers of his poetry to this day. Throughout his letters there are probably not more than twenty references to his terms instress and inscape.

When he mentions an "instress and charm of Wales" we learn from further references that instress refers to the feeling he has for a landscape or a sit-

uation. It is the personal charge of energy and of empathy going out from the self to the seen or the known. Inscape, on the other hand, is a quality, a peculiarity, perhaps he means an essence of a thing outside of the self, a truth of the world.

In the uses of these words in his letters, Hopkins not being a systematic thinker, there is some confusion, as his meanings are not clear-cut and sometimes contradict each other.

One of his most notable innovations was to go back to pre-iambic. From Anglo-Saxon verse he developed the four-beat line, but he elaborated upon this with a studied system of what he called outrides and other devices which make his poetry unique. He also gained tightening of syntax by omission of words. "There lives the dearest freshness deep down things" is a memorable Hopkins line because of the canceling of the expectation of hearing some such word as "within" before the end, which would render the line prosaic. He had a matchless ear for linguistic subtleties.

Through denial Hopkins won to the fruition of his great affirming verse, never knowing fame in his lifetime. His deepest dedication was to Christ.

———

HOPPER, Edward (July 22, 1882 – May 15, 1967). American painter. Born Nyack, N.Y. Studied under Robert Henri at Chase School, where he knew George Bellows. Concentrated on etching (1915–24), then returned to oils, receiving recognition when he exhibited watercolors and oils at one-man show at Museum of Modern Art (1933). His subjects are generally scenes of city streets, run-down old houses, Cape Cod landscapes, lighthouses. Among his paintings: *Manhattan Bridge Loop* (1928, Addison Gallery, Andover, Mass.), *Early Sunday Morning* (1930, Whitney Museum, New York), *Night Hawks* (1942, Art Institute of Chicago). He was elected to National Institute of

Arts and Letters (1944). Died in New York.

REFERENCES: Guy Pène Du Bois *Edward Hopper* (New York 1931). Lloyd Goodrich *Edward Hopper Retrospective Exhibition* (New York 1950) and *Edward Hopper* (New York 1964).

HOPPNER, John (Apr. 4, 1758 – Jan. 23, 1810). English painter. Born in London, of German parents, and died there. As a child, was chorister in royal chapel. Small allowance from George III enabled him to study painting; entered Royal Academy (1775), where he took silver medal for drawing from life (1778) and gold medal for history painting (1782). First exhibited at Academy (1780). Married daughter of Mrs. Patience Wright, an American who sculptured portraits in wax and whose home was frequented by such men as Garrick, Benjamin West, and Benjamin Franklin (1782). Began painting portraits, achieved immediate success, and became portrait painter to prince of Wales (George IV) (1789). Elected associate of Royal Academy (1792), Royal Academician (1795). The portraits of the prince of Wales, duke and duchess of York, Lord Rodney, and Lord Nelson in state apartments of St. James's Palace, and of countess of Oxford (1798, National Gallery, London), are among Hoppner's best works. A follower of Sir Joshua Reynolds, he was rivaled in popularity only by the king's painter, Sir Thomas Lawrence.

REFERENCE: E. K. Waterhouse *Painting in Britain: 1530–1790* (Harmondsworth, England, 1953).

HORACE (in full, **Quintus Horatius Flaccus**) (Dec. 8, 65 B.C. – Nov. 27, 8 B.C.). Roman poet. Born at Venusia, in Apulia. His father, a freedman, provided him with an aristocrat's education in Rome. While continuing studies in Athens, he was recruited as officer in Brutus's army (44 B.C.), but returned to Italy after the defeat at Philippi (42). Supported himself as *scriba quaestorius* (minor government clerk) and began writing verses. Made acquaintance of poets Virgil and Varius, and of Maecenas, Augustus's minister,

who by his generosity to poets gained their talent for indirect propaganda for the new government. From c.38 Horace, financially secure under patronage of Maecenas and Augustus, lived quietly as a writer, dividing his time between Rome and a farm in Sabine hills given him by Maecenas. Never married. Died in Rome. Works: *Epodes,* chiefly in iambic meters, based on Archilochus (published 30 B.C.); *Satires,* in hexameters (book I, c.35 B.C.; book II, c.30 B.C.); *Odes,* in Greek lyric meters (books I–III, 23 B.C.; book IV, c.13 B.C.); *Carmen Saeculare,* a Sapphic hymn for the secular games of 17 B.C.; *Epistles,* in hexameters, similar in form and content to *Satires* (book I, 20 B.C.; book II, c.13 B.C.); *Ars Poetica,* a discussion of poetry, in hexameters (date disputed).

TRANSLATIONS: *Complete Works* in Latin with interlinear English translation (New York 1961). *Collected Works* tr. Lord Dunsany and Michael Oakley (latest ed. London and New York 1961). *The Odes* tr. James Michie (New York and London 1963, also PB).
REFERENCES: Archibald Y. Campbell *Horace: A New Interpretation* (London 1924). Steele Commager *The Odes of Horace: A Critical Study* (New Haven, Conn. 1963, also PB). Eduard Fraenkel *Horace* (Oxford 1957, also PB). Tenney Frank *Catullus and Horace* (1928, reprinted New York 1965). Jacques Perret *Horace* (tr. New York 1964, also PB). Niall Rudd *The Satires of Horace* (Cambridge, England, 1966). Henry D. Sedgwick *Horace: A Biography* (1947, reprinted New York 1967). William Y. Sellar *The Roman Poets of the Augustan Age: Horace and the Elegiac Poets* (2nd ed. Oxford 1899, reprinted New York 1965). Lancelot P. Wilkinson *Horace and His Lyric Poetry* (2nd ed. reissued Cambridge, England, 1968, also PB).

☞

HORACE
BY REX WARNER

The period during which Horace lived, the events of his own life, and the views that have been taken of him seem full of contradictions. He started as the son of an ex-slave and ended as the valued friend of the greatest men in the state, including the emperor. He fought with Brutus for "liberty," saw it extinguished, and was grateful to the new regime. His poetry is entirely new, and yet much of it is imitated from the Greek. He has been loved for his "golden mediocrity" and for his common sense, and also for a magic and a grandeur that can be found nowhere else. Some romantic critics, presumably on the assumption that poets should die or come close to dying either for love or "liberty," have accused him of insincerity in his emotions and timeserving in politics. In fact everything which he tells us about himself (and he tells us more than any other classical poet) shows us a man of deep feeling, of courage and of genuine honesty.

Both Horace and Virgil have been charged with adulation of a dictator (a thing that offends modern tastes) and it is indeed somewhat difficult to understand their admiration for Augustus, whose enormous political ability was not matched, as in the case of Julius Caesar, by magnanimity and generosity (qualities which, after all, made the Ides of March possible). But there is no doubt that the feelings of the poets were sincere. Their language is not more extravagant than that used by English poets of Queen Elizabeth, and was inspired by the same hope or belief in the present and in the future. After three generations of civil war, such a hope was natural and such a belief not ill-founded.

Both Virgil and Horace were valued by Augustus and by their patron Maecenas for their political poetry, which among other things served to give a shape and a moral justification (much needed) for the new, and in fact revolutionary, regime. And they were rightly valued. Their patriotic verse is sincere, morally sound, beautiful, and in no way jingoistic. Though it certainly expresses a longing for peace and quiet, it expresses much more than this. Even when, in his *Ode After Actium,* Horace is following the prevailing propaganda line in misrepresenting Antony and Cleopatra as drunken and degenerate Orientals, he closes the poem with verses that give to Cleopatra all the dignity which she has in Shakespeare. Both Horace and Virgil show in their political verse a quality of timelessness that goes beyond the particular occasion. We are more moved by the self-chosen and distant suffering of Regulus than by the victories that may or may not be won in the east by Augustus.

The same quality of timelessness distinguishes in different ways all the odes. In his love poems Horace is less immediately personal than Catullus, but certainly not less moving. Both here and in the lighter odes — celebrations of a festival, a friend's return, a lovers' quarrel — he may remind one more of the Shakespeare of the songs and of the great dramatic lines than of anyone else. And it is above all on the four books of *Odes* that his reputation as one of the world's greatest poets rests.

Horace is fully conscious of this himself. He knows that here he has made "a monument more lasting than bronze," just as Thucydides knew that his work was "a possession forever." This is a fact, and for it he gives the credit to the muse. If he takes any credit to himself, it is for being the first to naturalize the Greek lyric meters in Latin. Here his achievement was astounding. Like Milton, he has found no worthy imitators. His early works include the *Epodes,* iambic poems written in the manner of Archilochus, which were composed in the years following the battle of Philippi before he became acquainted with Virgil and, through him, Maecenas. These poems, like the two books of *Satires* (in hexameters, and written in the same period) are witty, caustic, often, as we would say, "concerned," sometimes obscene, and often strangely moving. It was not until 23 B.C., some ten years after Maecenas had given him the famous Sabine farm, that he published the first three books of *Odes*. In these he uses the meters of Alcaeus, Sappho, and many others with consummate skill and mastery. Nothing like this had appeared in Roman poetry before, and the very unfamiliarity of the thing may account for the fact that the *Odes* did not immediately secure the wide audience that they have always enjoyed since.

The fourth book of *Odes* did not appear until about 13 B.C. In the interval Horace wrote the two books of *Epistles*, in hexameters. From these and from the earlier *Satires* a very clear picture of the poet himself emerges, and it is a picture which most people have found endearing. It is of a good friend, a modest, witty, affectionate, middle-aged man, rather short, one who has largely outgrown his early propensities as a great lover of girls and boys, but whose emotions are fresh, clear and vigorous, a man interested, but not to the exclusion of pleasure, in philosophy, enormously interested in the technique of poetry, independent, wise, tolerant and, if sometimes irascible, quick to recover his good humor.

There is no reason to suppose that this picture is not a true one. What it leaves out is what a modest self-appraisal must always leave out — that this delightful friend and drinking companion was also one of the greatest poets who has ever existed.

The greatness no doubt, in some way, proceeds from the character, but transcends it. And as the easy conversational and witty hexameters of the *Epistles* are ideally adapted to modest self-confession, comment and criticism, so the elaborate structure of the *Odes* seems to concentrate, intensify, and in sudden moments miraculously diffuse a great depth of sympathy, experience and understanding. If the passion is generalized, it is the more profound for that. If the tone is playful, there is often a strange sadness beneath the play. It is because of these wholly poetic and otherworldly qualities, rather than for his urbanity, his good sense and good fellowship, that Horace is most truly admired and loved.

———

HOUDON, Jean Antoine (Mar. 20, 1741 – July 15, 1828). French sculptor. Born Versailles, son of a servant. Studied art early, receiving prix de Rome for sculpture at twenty. In Rome (1761–69), he executed statues of St. Bruno, Minerva and others. On return to Paris made excellent portrait busts of Benjamin Franklin, Molière, Jean Jacques Rousseau, of which the finest is the magnificent seated *Voltaire* (1781, Comédie Française, Paris). Also famous is the graceful *Diana Nue* (Louvre, Paris). Traveled to U.S. with Franklin (1785), where state of Virginia commissioned him to execute a statue of George Washington (Capitol, Richmond). On same trip he modeled busts of eminent Americans, including Thomas Jefferson (Museum of Fine Arts, Boston) and John Paul Jones (Naval Academy Museum, Annapolis, Md.). Though Houdon was out of fashion for a time after the French Revolution, his popularity returned under Napoleon, when he was commissioned to model the statue of Cicero for the French Senate chamber. Also created busts of Napoleon and Empress Marie Louise. Died in Paris.

REFERENCES: Gilbert Chinard *Houdon in America* (Baltimore and London 1930). Georges Giacometti *La Vie et l'oeuvre de Houdon* (2 vols. Paris 1929). Élisa Maillard *Houdon* (Paris 1931). Louis Réau *Houdon, sa vie et son oeuvre* (2 vols. Paris 1964).

HOUSMAN, A(lfred) **E**(dward) (Mar. 26, 1859 – Apr. 30, 1936). English poet and scholar. Born Fockbury, Worcestershire. Educated at St. John's College, Oxford (1877–81). After failing final examinations went to work in London patent office, but devoted free time to classical studies. Became professor of Latin at University College, London (1892), then at Trinity College, Cambridge (1911). First book of poems, *A Shropshire Lad* (1896), made him famous, but next volume, *Last Poems,* appeared only in 1922. *More Poems* followed (1936) and *Collected Poems* (1939). Housman claimed that the chief sources of his simple, lyrical verse were "Shakespeare's songs, the Scottish border ballads, and Heine." Small as his volume of work was, it was important as a reaction against Victorian modes. The major part of his quiet life was concerned with classical scholarship, and he won academic eminence for his editions of Juvenal (1905), Lucan (1926), and especially Manilius (1903–31), in which he vehemently attacks other scholars, notably the Germans. His critical work, *The Name and Nature of Poetry,* appeared (1933), and further poems and letters are in his brother's memoir (see below). He died in Cambridge.

EDITION: *Complete Poems* ed. Tom Burns Haber, Centennial Edition (New York 1959).

REFERENCES: A. S. F. Gow *A. E. Housman: A Sketch* (Cambridge, England, and New York 1936). Tom Burns Haber *A. E. Housman* (New York 1967). Laurence Housman *A. E. Housman: Some Poems, Some Letters, and a Personal Memoir* (London 1937) and, as *My Brother, A. E. Housman* (New York 1938, reprinted Port Washington, N.Y. 1969). Norman Marlow *A. E. Housman: Scholar and Poet* (Minneapolis and London 1958). Christopher Ricks ed. *A. E. Housman: A Collection of Critical Essays* (Englewood Cliffs, N.J. 1968, also PB). George L. Watson *A. E. Housman: A Divided Life* (London 1957 and Boston 1958). Percy

Withers *Buried Life: Personal Recollections of A. E. Housman* (London 1940).

HOWARD, Henry. *See* **SURREY, Earl of.**

HOWELLS, William Dean (Mar. 1, 1837 – May 11, 1920). American novelist, editor, and critic. Born Martin's Ferry, Ohio. Largely self-educated, studying only briefly at various local schools. Entered journalism, and while working as news editor for *Ohio State Journal* in Columbus wrote a campaign biography of Lincoln (1860). Was rewarded with consulate at Venice (1861–64), where he married Elinor Meade (1862). Returning to New York, worked briefly on *Nation,* then became assistant editor of *Atlantic Monthly* in Boston (1866), editor in chief (1871–81). Having published some poetry and two travel sketches, *Venetian Life* (1866) and *Italian Journeys* (1867), produced his first novel, *Their Wedding Journey* (1872). It was quickly followed by others, including *A Foregone Conclusion* (1875), *The Lady of the Aroostook* (1879), and *The Undiscovered Country* (1880), dealing with international themes. After leaving the *Atlantic,* Howells turned to realistic portrayals of American manners and morals, producing his greatest works: *A Modern Instance* (1882), *The Rise of Silas Lapham* (1885), *Indian Summer* (1886), and others. Moved towards socialism beginning with *A Hazard of New Fortunes* (1890), a novel dealing with New York, where he now lived. While continuing to write novels at a rapid pace, he took over the Editor's Easy Chair in *Harper's Monthly Magazine* (1892), and wrote not only comedies and volumes of poetry but also works of criticism, including *Criticism and Fiction* (1891). Widely respected as America's foremost literary figure, Howells's last years were filled with travels and honors, including degrees from Oxford, Harvard, and Yale, and for several years the presidency of the American Academy of Arts and Letters. He died in New York, having left an important influence on the school of American realism.

EDITIONS: *Life in Letters of William Dean Howells* ed. Mildred Howells

(1928, reprinted 2 vols. New York 1968). *Selected Writings* ed. Henry Steele Commager (New York 1950).

REFERENCES: Van Wyck Brooks *Howells: His Life and World* (New York and London 1959). Edwin H. Cady *William Dean Howells: Dean of American Letters* (2 vols. Syracuse, N.Y. 1956/58). George C. Carrington, Jr. *The Immense Complex Drama: The World and Art of the Howells Novel* (Columbus, Ohio 1966). Everett Carter *Howells and the Age of Realism* (1954, reprinted Hamden, Conn. 1966). Delmar G. Cooke *William Dean Howells: A Critical Study* (1922, reprinted New York 1967). Oscar W. Firkins *William Dean Howells: A Study* (1924, reprinted New York 1963).

≈

WILLIAM DEAN HOWELLS
BY GRANVILLE HICKS

In 1912, when the seventy-fifth birthday of William Dean Howells was being observed by his illustrious contemporaries in and out of the arts, Henry James wrote a letter to be read at the congratulatory banquet. After speaking as one craftsman to another of Howells's gifts as a novelist, James attempted to sum up the achievements of his old friend: "Stroke by stroke and book by book your work was to become, for the exquisite notation of our whole democratic light and shade and give and take, in the highest degree *documentary;* so that none other, through all your fine long season, could approach it in value and amplitude." But "documentary" was not for James an altogether complimentary word, and he went on: "You may remember perhaps, and I like to recall, how the great and admirable Taine, in one of the fine excursions of his French curiosity, greeted you as a precious painter and a sovereign witness. But his appreciation, I want you to believe with me, will yet be carried much further, and then — though you may have argued yourself happy, in your generous way, and with your incurable optimism, even while noting yourself not understood — your really beautiful time will come."

Most of those participating in the festivities — including, perhaps, as James hinted, Howells himself — must have been astounded by the suggestion that there could be a more beautiful time than this for a man whom the President of the United States had chosen to honor with his presence. In half a century he had published nearly one hundred books, and though he would have acknowledged that some were trifles, he knew how much substance there was in the best of them. In the opinion of the majority of his literate countrymen he was, and long had been, the greatest of living American novelists. Moreover, as assistant editor and then, for a decade, editor of the *Atlantic Monthly,* and after that as a regular contributor to *Harper's,* he had had more influence on the literary taste of the American middle class than any other person of his time.

He had lived, in more ways than one, an exemplary American life. Born in the Middle West, son of a printer, he was largely self-educated, but from an early age he had literary ambitions, which centered his attention on New England. When, as a young man, he visited Boston, Cambridge, and Concord, and talked, both as journalist and as worshipful disciple, with Lowell, Holmes, Hawthorne, Thoreau, and Emerson, he had found his spiritual home. In the same year, 1860, he wrote a campaign biography of Abraham Lincoln, chiefly for distribution in Ohio, and was given the consulship in Venice as his reward. Although this, his first visit to Europe, strengthened his conviction of American superiority, especially in morals, he was always and increasingly conscious of his debt to European culture. When he left Venice in 1864, married to the woman with whom he was to live, apparently happily, for almost fifty years, he had written enough to attract the attention of editors and publishers. Beginning humbly, as an American should, he rose rapidly to an eminence he maintained for decade after decade.

By the time of his seventy-fifth birthday, however, there was a muttering of dissatisfaction with the dean of American letters, as he was often called, which was to become a roar and would eventually drown out his voice, seemingly forever. Discontent was directed chiefly against the attitude that had most commended him to his admirers — his almost unqualified adherence to what a later generation was to denounce as Victorian prudishness. In *Criticism and Fiction* (1891), for example, he had said that literature "was all the more faithfully representative of the tone of modern life in dealing with love that was chaste, and with passion so honest that it could be openly spoken of before the tenderest society bud at dinner." He, for one, he declared, would not write "things for young girls to read which you would be put out-of-doors for saying to them," nor would he deny himself "the pleasure — and it is a very high and sweet one — of appealing to these vivid, responsive intelligences."

There were scores of such observations that the young rebels could hurl back at Howells, so that he was nearly buried before his death in 1920. What the rebels forgot was that Howells had stood for honesty as well as what he believed to be decency, and that in case of conflict he had almost invariably put honesty first. Not only had he urged his fellow countrymen to read Tolstoy, Hardy, even Zola; he had championed Ed Howe, Stephen Crane,

Hamlin Garland, H. H. Boyesen, Frank Norris, Charles Chesnutt, Abraham Cahan, and virtually every other young American novelist who was pressing against the barriers of Victorianism. He deplored "the Southwestern, the Lincolnian, the Elizabethan breadth of parlance" that Mark Twain practiced in conversation, but this diminished neither his affection nor his admiration for the man who, he said, would "bask in the same light as Cervantes and Shakespeare." The man who wrote *My Mark Twain* was not wholly a prude.

The rebels taught us that realism was primarily a matter of candor, a willingness to present and examine all the aspects of life that the Victorians had tried to ignore and about which they had commanded writers to be silent. That was not, of course, what Howells had meant by realism while he was waging his fifty years' war on its behalf. In one of his early novels, *Their Wedding Journey*, Howells wrote, "Ah, poor Real Life, which I love, can I make others share the delight I find in thy foolish and insipid face?" He was challenging not only the frankly romantic novelists, Scott and his myriad of disciples, but also such contemporaries as Dickens and Thackeray, who, as he saw it, found it necessary to improve on "real life" to hold their readers. Says a character in *The Rise of Silas Lapham*: "The novelist who could interpret the common feelings of the common people would have the answer to 'the riddle of the painful earth' on the tip of his tongue."

The critics could argue that the "real life" Howells saw was a small part of American reality, and that was true, although it is to his credit that he saw more and more as the years passed. They said, too, that he wrote dull books about dull people, and sometimes he did. They said, finally, that his theory of realism led him to see only the surfaces of life, and here they were largely wrong. Whatever else may be true of the man who created Bartley Hubbard and Marcia Gaylord, Silas Lapham, Dryfoos and Lindau in *A Hazard of New Fortunes*, Northwick in *The Quality of Mercy*, Jeff Durgin in *The Landlord of Lion's Head*, and Dylks in *The Leatherwood God*, his knowledge of men and women was not superficial.

Henry James's "really beautiful time" did come, although not until thirty years after his death, but Howells's time hasn't come and probably never will. He seems to be the kind of writer who speaks less and less clearly to people as the passage of the years works its ever swifter and swifter alterations in our society. If he is kept alive at all, it will be by the scholars, but if he is unlikely to be widely read, he deserves to be gratefully remembered.

HUDSON, William Henry (Aug. 4, 1841 – Aug. 18, 1922). English novelist and naturalist. Born Quilmes, Argentina, of American parents, and educated privately. As a child on the pampas, developed his celebrated love of nature and knowledge of bird life. After father's death, left Argentina to settle permanently in England (1869). Employment as private secretary and, after marriage to Emily Wingrave (1876), running a boardinghouse failed to relieve his poverty. Two novels, *The Purple Land* (1885) and *A Crystal Age* (1887), though some of his best work, were poorly received, but his naturalist works, *Argentine Ornithology* (2 vols. 1888–89, written in collaboration with Philip L. Sclater), *The Naturalist in La Plata* (1892), and others brought recognition and a civil list pension (1901). His best-known work, *Green Mansions* (1904), is a romantic novel set in the Venezuelan jungles. Its publication in U.S. (1916) brought him

great popularity there. It was followed by series of nature books and stories (many on Latin American themes). *Far Away and Long Ago* (1918) is autobiographical. Died in London. A bird sanctuary established in Hyde Park as a memorial (1925) contains Jacob Epstein's sculpture of *Rima*, the half-bird, half-human heroine of *Green Mansions*.

REFERENCES: Robert Hamilton *W. H. Hudson: The Vision of Earth* (London 1946). R. E. Haymaker *From Pampas to Hedgerows and Downs: A Study of W. H. Hudson* (New York 1954). Morley Roberts *W. H. Hudson: A Portrait* (London and New York 1924). Ruth Tomalin *W. H. Hudson* (1954, rep. New York 1969).

HUGO, Victor Marie (Feb. 26, 1802 – May 22, 1885). French poet, playwright, and novelist. Born Besançon, son of an army officer who became a general of the empire. Family traveled to Corsica, Naples, and Madrid, where he studied, then finally settled in Paris. His literary ability was noticed early: honorable mention from the Academy for a poem at fifteen. After being granted royal annuity for *Odes et poésies diverses* (1822), he married Adèle Foucher and continued producing works which placed him in forefront of romantic movement, notably the celebrated preface to *Cromwell* (1827). Wife's attachment to the critic Sainte-Beuve drove him into liaison with actress Juliette Drouet (1833), who remained his mistress until her death in 1883. Elected to the Academy (1841) and made a peer of France (1845). Became increasingly involved with political affairs until his active opposition to Louis Napoleon forced him into exile (1851), first to Brussels, then the Channel Islands. Remained on Guernsey until advent of Third Republic made return to Paris possible (1870). Elected to Senate (1876), he spent his last years championing republicanism and writing voluminously. Died in Paris. Was given a state funeral and buried in the Panthéon.

A partial list of his important works includes novels *Notre-Dame de Paris* (1831), *Les Misérables* (1862), and *Quatre-Vingt-Treize;* plays *Hernani* (1830), *Le Roi s'amuse* (1832), *Lu-*

crèce Borgia (1833), and *Ruy Blas* (1838); poetry *Odes et Ballades* (1826), *Les Orientales* (1829), *Les Feuilles d'automne* (1831), *Les Voix intérieures* (1837), *Les Châtiments* (1853), *Les Contemplations* (1856), and *La Légende des siècles* (three series: 1859, 1877, 1883).

REFERENCES: J. B. Barrère *Hugo, l'homme et l'oeuvre* (1952, new ed. Paris 1967). Elliot M. Grant *The Career of Victor Hugo* (Cambridge, Mass. and Oxford 1945). Richard B. Grant *The Perilous Quest: Image, Myth, and Prophecy in the Narratives of Victor Hugo* (Durham, N.C. 1968). Henri Guillemin *Victor Hugo par lui-même* (Paris 1951). André Maurois *Olympio* (tr. New York and London 1956).

✍

VICTOR HUGO
BY ROBERT BALDICK

Though he lived a long life in the glare of welcome publicity, and has since been the subject of countless studies, Victor Hugo still remains a puzzling figure, so vast that he discourages anything but piecemeal analysis, so many-sided that he baffles the understanding of simpler mortals. To begin with, there was a flagrant discrepancy between the public image and the private individual. In the 1830's, the leader of the wild and hairy romantics, the apostle of unfettered liberty in literature, was a smooth-chinned, soberly dressed bourgeois, who took such infinite pains over shaving — carefully stropping his razor, warming it for a quarter of an hour, and washing his face with rose water — that he drove his friends wild with exasperation. Similarly, in the 1870's, the awe-inspiring Grand Old Man of Letters, the white-bearded author of *L'Art d'être grand-père*, was an insatiable satyr, tumbling into bed every day with one or other of a wide range of complaisant women, from leading actresses to humble chambermaids. If this were all, if the only conflict in

Hugo were between the public and the private man, there would be no real problem: none of us is what he seems to be.

But in Hugo the private man himself was a mass of contradictions. As a youth he did everything in his power to avoid doing military service, but as a middle-aged man he behaved with exemplary courage in the street fighting of 1848. He was generous enough to ease the terms of a publisher who had gone through a difficult period, but so mean that he kept his family and his aged mistress on skimpy allowances at a time when he was a millionaire twice over. He went into exile rather than accept the dictatorship of Louis Napoleon, but after his initial attacks on the Second Empire he was careful not to offend a government which might have banned his books and stopped his income. One could go on indefinitely quoting apparent inconsistencies of this sort — apparent because taken together, they form the unity of his character; taken together, they fall into the fundamental pattern of his life and work, the antithetical pattern of black and white, cunning and spontaneity, meanness and generosity. It was a pattern laid down at birth by his parents: his impulsive, passionate, sensual, warmhearted father, and his careful, determined, clearheaded mother. Time and again during his life he would find himself beginning to stagnate in a carefully calculated, hard-earned success — literary, political or personal — only to be rescued and redeemed by a sudden generous impulse, a passionate movement of the heart. But every time the impulse would harden into an attitude, the spontaneous gesture would stiffen into a muscular tic, the warm words would turn into cold clichés.

Thus the early letters in which he

acclaimed the talents of writers he admired became stereotyped forms which he dispatched to all and sundry, hailing every petty scribbler as a potential genius; his first love letters, with their lyrical references to God, nature and immortality, became trite formulas in which God, nature and immortality were merely code words designed to stir the feelings of impressionable women; and his first generous gifts to the poor became routine alms offerings which, however lavish they might be — and at one period of his life a third of Hugo's household budget went to charity — were no longer dictated by the heart. As time went by, in fact, Hugo consciously or unconsciously adopted one after another of a whole series of poses — Lover, Father, Politician, Peer, Outlaw, Mystic, Grandfather and Grand Old Man — in which the outside world and even Hugo himself believed. To quote Cocteau's penetrating witticism, "Victor Hugo was a madman who believed himself to be Victor Hugo," or, to be more accurate perhaps, he was a madman who believed each of a succession of attitudes to be Victor Hugo.

By the end of his life the ultimate Hugolian pose — that of the Demigod — had gained general acceptance, and when Hugo told an adoring workman, "I am only a man," nobody believed him. There was indeed something divine about a man in whom the creative impulse never failed, even on his deathbed; for in his final delirium he produced a perfect Alexandrine on his and every man's death agony — *"C'est ici le combat du jour et de la nuit"* — and his dying words arranged themselves naturally into a last Hugolian antithesis: *"Je vois de la lumière noire"* (I can see a black light). It was as a god, too, that he was taken to his grave, in a funeral of unparalleled

magnificence, with the route from the Étoile to the Panthéon hung with crepe and lined with emblems of his works, a procession of two million mourners, the Arc de Triomphe draped in black, and in the midst of all these splendors, eclipsing them with its characteristic, antithetical, theatrical simplicity, the dead man's coffin borne along on the pauper's hearse he had asked for.

As a demigod, a poseur, a mythmaker, Hugo knew no equal; but how was he, and how is he now, to be rated as a poet? For it is as a poet that he must ultimately be judged: as the lyricist of *Les Feuilles d'automne,* the satirist of *Les Châtiments,* the epic poet of *La Légende des siècles,* and the visionary of *Les Contemplations.* His novels are really only grandiose expressions in prose of his humanitarian ideas and poetic imagination, while if some of his dramas have survived (notably *Ruy Blas*) it is not for their crude symbolism or tragicomic contrasts but because of the splendid poetry they contain.

In 1885 it was too soon to tell: the force of his personality and his legend swayed critics too strongly one way or another. But over seventy years later, when André Gide was composing his *Anthology of French Poetry,* he asked himself who was the greatest of all French poets, and arrived at the answer: "Victor Hugo, alas." Most readers who know something of Hugo's life and work will probably echo that "alas" for different reasons. We may dislike his personality, which is apparent in all his work, and notably the horrifying egoism exemplified in his signet ring motto: EGO HUGO. We may be irritated by his naïve nineteenth-century faith in progress, in human perfectibility, in himself. We may consider his mysticism spurious, his style obvious and vulgar. But we cannot deny the beauty of his poetry or the universality of its appeal. If it is commonplace, it is magnificently commonplace, achieving what François Mauriac once called "a heroic banality." Which is why we admire it and why we also shake our heads over it.

HUME, David (Apr. 26, 1711 – Aug. 25, 1776). Scottish philosopher and historian. Born Edinburgh. At twelve, attended Edinburgh University for a few years, then went to France (1734), where he lived with Jesuits at La Flèche and wrote *A Treatise of Human Nature* (1739–40). On poor reception of this work, retired to family estate in Berwickshire to write *Essays Moral and Political* (1741–42), an immediate success. Served as judge advocate to General James St. Clair on diplomatic mission to France (1746), then to Vienna and Turin (1748–49); meanwhile *Philosophical Essays*, later entitled *Enquiry Concerning Human Understanding*, a simplified version of the earlier *Treatise*, appeared (1748). Settled in Edinburgh (1751), where he lived for next twelve years and produced *Enquiry Concerning the Principles of Morals* (1751) and *Political Discourses* (1752). Last major work was an exhaustive *History of England* (1754–62), a standard text for years. While serving as diplomatic secretary in Paris (1763–65), knew Rousseau, whom he brought back to England; but friendship was of brief duration. Served as undersecretary of state (1767–68). His autobiography appeared posthumously (1777). He died in Edinburgh. Hume's brilliant logic carried further the skepticism of Locke and looked ahead to the positivism and utilitarianism of nineteenth-century thought. Neither by reason nor by experience can we arrive at either physical or moral laws, he believed; causal relation derives from "the association of ideas," and other similar mechanisms.

EDITIONS: *A Treatise of Human Nature* (1888, latest ed. Oxford 1964, also PB) and *Enquiries* (2nd ed. 1902, latest ed. Oxford 1966, also PB), both ed. L. A. Selby-Bigge. *Dialogues Concerning Natural Religion* ed. Norman Kemp Smith (2nd ed. London and New York 1947, also PB).

REFERENCES: Anthony H. Basson *David Hume* (Harmondsworth, England, PB 1958). Antony Flew *Hume's Philosophy of Belief* (London and New York 1961). Peter Gay *The Enlightenment: An Interpretation* (2 vols. London and New York 1966/69). John Laird *Hume's Philosophy of Human Nature* (1932, reprinted Hamden, Conn. 1967). Ernest C. Mossner *The Life of David Hume* (Edinburgh and Austin, Tex. 1954). John A. Passmore *Hume's Intentions* (1952, rev. ed. London and New York 1968). H. H. Price *Hume's Theory of the External World* (1940, reprinted Oxford 1963). Norman Kemp Smith *The Philosophy of David Hume* (London and New York 1941, also PB). John B. Stewart *The Moral and Political Philosophy of David Hume* (New York 1963).

HUMPERDINCK, Engelbert (Sept. 1, 1854 – Sept. 27, 1921). German composer. Born Siegburg. Studied under Ferdinand Hiller in Cologne (1872–76), and under Franz Lachner and Joseph Rheinberger in Munich (1877–79). A Mendelssohn scholarship enabled him to go to Italy (1879), where he met Wagner; assisted him in production of *Parsifal* at Bayreuth (1880–81). After several years of travel in Italy, France and Spain, settled in Frankfurt, where he was professor of composition at Hoch Conservatory (1890–96). Had gained recognition with *Humoreske* for orchestra (1880); his masterpiece, the children's opera *Hänsel und Gretel* (1893), won him worldwide fame. Moved to Berlin (1900), where he was head of the Master School for Musical Composition and member of the Senate of the Royal Academy. Died at Neustrelitz. Humperdinck's musical style owes much to Wagner; in *Hänsel und Gretel*, for which alone he is remembered, he achieves a unique blend of simplicity of feeling and harmonic complexity.

HUNT, (James Henry) Leigh (Oct. 19, 1784 – Aug. 28, 1859). English poet and essayist. Born Southgate, Middlesex, son of a clergyman from Barbados.

Educated at Christ's Hospital School, London (1791–99). *Juvenilia* (1801), collection of verse, attracted some notice. Achieved recognition as drama critic, and brought out *Critical Essays on the London Theatre* (1807). Edited his brother John's liberal newspaper, the *Examiner* (1808–21), and was imprisoned (1813–15) for libeling the prince regent. Married Marianne Kent (1809) and settled in Hampstead (1815), where he entertained leading literary figures interested in political and social reform. These included Keats and Shelley, whose genius he proclaimed in the *Examiner* and the *Indicator* (1819–21). In Italy (1822–25) joined Byron and Shelley, and edited the journal *Liberal* (1822–23). On return to England, published his *Poetical Works* (1832), edited various periodicals and an anthology of English poetry, *Imagination and Fancy* (1844). Best-known of Hunt's poems are *The Story of Rimini* (1816) and short lyrics *Abou Ben Adhem* and *Jenny Kissed Me*. Prose works include *The Town* (1848) and *Autobiography* (1850). Died at Putney. Hunt is chiefly remembered as champion of poetry of Keats, Shelley, and Tennyson.

EDITIONS: *Poetical Works* ed. Sir Humphrey Milford (London and New York 1923). *Autobiography* ed. J. E. Morpurgo (London and New York 1949). *Dramatic Criticism, 1808–1831* (New York 1949 and Oxford 1950) and *Literary Criticism* (New York 1956 and Oxford 1957) ed. Lawrence H. and Carolyn W. Houtchens.

REFERENCES: Edmund Blunden *Leigh Hunt* (1930, reprinted Hamden, Conn. 1970). Louis Landré *Leigh Hunt* (2 vols. Paris 1935–36). Marie H. Law *The English Familiar Essay in the Nineteenth Century* (1934, reprinted New York 1965). G. D. Stout *The Political History of Leigh Hunt's Examiner* (St. Louis, Mo. 1949).

HUNT, (William) Holman (Apr. 2, 1827 – Sept. 7, 1910). English painter. Born and died in London. After attending private schools, took a job and studied art at night school. Left business (1843) and entered Royal Academy schools, where he came to know John Millais and Dante Gabriel Ros-

setti, with whom he founded Pre-Raphaelite Brotherhood (1848), the purpose being to paint nature honestly, as observed. Began exhibiting at Royal Academy (1846), and showed his first Pre-Raphaelite painting *Rienzi* (1849). Though his work was severely criticized, John Ruskin, influential as art critic, came to his defense. His chief work is the painting of Christ as *The Light of the World* (1854, Keble College, Oxford). Another version was painted 1904 (St. Paul's Cathedral, London). His interest in religious subjects led him to travel in Palestine for authentic backgrounds. Hunt was one of the artists chosen to illustrate Alfred Tennyson's poems (1857), and was author of *Pre-Raphaelitism and the Pre-Raphaelite Brotherhood* (2 vols. 1905).

REFERENCES: T. S. R. Boase *English Art, 1800–1870* (Oxford 1959). A. C. Gissing *William Holman Hunt: A Biography* (London 1936). Robin Ironside and John Gere *Pre-Raphaelite Painters* (London and New York 1948).

HUXLEY, Aldous (Leonard) (July 26, 1894 – Nov. 22, 1963). British novelist and essayist. Born Godalming, Surrey, grandson of Thomas Henry Huxley and grandnephew of Matthew Arnold. Attended Eton, where defective eyesight interrupted education, but went on to receive B.A. from Balliol College, Oxford (1915). Married Maria Nys (1919). On staffs of *Athenaeum* and *Westminster Gazette* (1919–21), where he knew John Middleton Murry and D. H. Lawrence. Published collection of short stories, *Limbo* (1920), followed by successful novel *Crome Yellow* (1921). Other novels include *Antic Hay* (1923), *Those Barren Leaves* (1925), *Point Counter Point* (1928), *Brave New World* (1932), *Eyeless in Gaza* (1936), *After Many a Summer Dies the Swan* (1939), *Time Must Have a Stop* (1944), *Brave New World Revisited* (1958), *Island* (1962). Contemporary satire characterizes them as well as the short stories, which include *Mortal Coils* (1922) and *Brief Candles* (1930). Also prolific writer of essays: *On the Margin* (1923), *Along the Road* (1925), *Jesting Pilate* (1926), *Ape and Essence* (1948), *Heaven and Hell* (1956). After living in Italy (1923–30) and southern

France, where he saw D. H. Lawrence, whose letters he edited (1933), he settled in California, became interested in mysticism and Hindu philosophy. Compiled anthology *The Perennial Philosophy* (1946) and wrote of experiences experimenting with drugs, *The Doors of Perception* (1954). Author also of biography and history, *Grey Eminence* (1941) and *The Devils of Loudun* (1952), works of poetry, and two plays. Died in Los Angeles.

EDITION: *Letters of Aldous Huxley* ed. Grover Smith (New York 1970).

REFERENCES: John Atkins *Aldous Huxley* (1956, rev. ed. London 1967 and New York 1968). Peter Bowering *Aldous Huxley: A Study of the Major Novels* (London 1968 and New York 1969). Jocelyn Brooke *Aldous Huxley* (London 1954, also PB). Julian Huxley ed. *Aldous Huxley 1894–1963* (London and New York 1965). Laura Huxley *This Timeless Moment: A Personal View of Aldous Huxley* (New York 1968 and London 1969). Jerome Meckier *Aldous Huxley: Satire and Structure* (New York and London 1969).

HUXLEY, Thomas Henry (May 4, 1825 – June 29, 1895). English biologist and essayist. Born Ealing, Middlesex, son of a schoolmaster. Studied medicine at Charing Cross Hospital (M.D. 1845). During voyage to South Seas and Australia as surgeon on H.M.S. *Rattlesnake* (1846–50), made studies in marine biology, sending to England papers on his findings which resulted in election to Royal Society (1851) and the award of its medal (1852). From 1854 to 1885, pursued distinguished career as educator. Married Henrietta Anne Heathorn (1855). After appearance of Charles Darwin's *Origin of Species* (1859), Huxley became chief public advocate of the evolutionary theory, engaging in celebrated disputes with leading figures of the day. A brilliant lecturer and prolific essayist, he was the leading popularizer of science and advocate of Darwinism and agnosticism in the Victorian age. Works include *Zoological Evidences as to Man's Place in Nature* (1863), *Lay Sermons* (1870), *Essays and Reviews* (1870), *Science and Culture* (1881), *Evolution and Ethics* (1893). Served on ten royal commissions (1862–84) and on London school board (1870–72); was secretary (1871–80) and president (1883–85) of Royal Society. He died at Eastbourne, Sussex, and was survived by two famous grandsons, biologist Julian Huxley (1887–) and novelist Aldous Huxley (q.v.).

EDITIONS: *Collected Essays* (9 vols. London and New York 1893–98). *Scientific Memoirs* ed. Sir Michael Foster and E. Ray Lankester (5 vols. London and New York 1898–1903).

REFERENCES: Ronald W. Clark *The Huxleys* (New York and London 1968). Leonard Huxley *Life and Letters of Thomas Henry Huxley* (2 vols. London 1900, rev. ed. 3 vols. 1913). William Irvine *Apes, Angels, and Victorians: The Story of Darwin, Huxley, and Evolution* (New York 1955).

HUYSMANS, Joris Karl (real name Charles Marie Georges Huysmans) (Feb. 5, 1848 – May 12, 1907). French novelist. Born Paris, descendant of family of Dutch painters. Educated at the Lycée St. Louis, then held position in government welfare office for thirty years. A frequenter of the Théâtre du Luxembourg, he began writing prose poems under influence of Baudelaire and produced *Le Drageoir aux épices* (1874). Using the pseudonym J. K. Huysmans, he then wrote a naturalist novel based on his first love affair, *Marthe* (1876), which was followed by the more successful novel *Les Soeurs Vatard* (1879). Working as an art critic, he helped the impressionist cause with his articles in *Le Voltaire* (1879), *La Reforme* (1880), and *L'Art Moderne* (1883). His fame chiefly rests, however, on the novel *A Rebours* (1884, tr. *Against Nature* 1959), a portrait of the aesthete Jean Des Esseintes, who became the prototype of the fin-de-siècle decadent. An interest in occultism was reflected in *Là-Bas* (1891) and his reconversion to Catholicism (1892) in *En Route* (1895). Resigning from his bureaucratic position in 1898, Huysmans became an oblate at the Benedectine Abbey of St. Martin at Légugé, but when the monastery was disbanded he returned to Paris to write *L'Oblat* (1903, tr. *The Oblate* 1924).

He died there of cancer, having been made an officer of the Legion of Honor shortly before.

REFERENCES: Robert Baldick *The Life of J. K. Huysmans* (Oxford 1955). Henry Brandreth *Huysmans* (London and New York 1963). James Laver *The First Decadent: Being the Strange Life of J. K. Huysmans* (London 1954 and New York 1955). Helen Trudgian *L'Esthétique de J. K. Huysmans* (Paris 1934).

————————

HYDE, Edward. *See* CLARENDON, Earl of.

IBSEN, Henrik (Johan) (Mar. 20, 1828 – May 23, 1906). Norwegian dramatist. Born Skien, son of businessman who went bankrupt (1836). Became pharmacist's assistant at sixteen; studied briefly at Christiania (Oslo) University. First published play, *Catiline* (1850), followed by nine others during next twelve years. Associated with Bergen Theatre (1851–57), then settled at Oslo as director and dramatist. Married Susannah Thoreson (1858); they had one son. Financial worry and public indifference led to twenty-seven-year exile (1864–91), mainly in Rome, Dresden, Munich. Achieved recognition with *Brand* (1866) and *Peer Gynt* (1867). *A Doll's House* (1879) won universal acclaim, followed by *Ghosts* (1881), *An Enemy of the People* (1882), *The Wild Duck* (1884), *Rosmersholm* (1886), *The Lady from the Sea* (1888), and *Hedda Gabler* (1890). After his return to Norway, produced *The Master Builder* (1892), *Little Eyolf* (1894), *John Gabriel Borkman* (1896), and *When We Dead Awaken* (1899). Died in Oslo; accorded state funeral.

TRANSLATIONS: *Collected Works* ed. William Archer (12 vols. London and New York 1906–12). *The Oxford Ibsen* ed. J. W. McFarlane (7 vols. London and New York 1960–66).

REFERENCES: Muriel C. Bradbrook *Ibsen the Norwegian: A Revaluation* (1946, rev. ed. London and Hamden, Conn. 1966). Bergliot Ibsen *The Three Ibsens* (tr. London 1951 and New York 1952). Halvdan Koht *The Life of Ibsen* (tr. New York and London 1931). Janko Lavrin *Ibsen: An Approach* (new ed. London 1950, reprinted New York 1969). George Bernard Shaw *The Quintessence of Ibsenism* (1891, rev. ed. London and New York 1913, PB 1958). P. F. D. Tennant *Ibsen's Dramatic Technique* (Cambridge, England, 1948, reprinted New York 1966). Hermann J. Weigand *The Modern Ibsen: A Reconsideration* (New York 1925 and London 1926, PB 1960). Adolph E. Zucker *Ibsen the Master Builder* (New York 1929 and London 1930).

❧

HENRIK IBSEN
BY
JOHN GASSNER

For several decades Henrik Ibsen was a culture hero of the modern European intelligentsia and the theatre's most influential playwright. History could not have chosen, if "history" could choose, a more unlikely candidate for international eminence.

Ibsen was born toward the end of the third decade of the nineteenth century in the small Norwegian town of Skien. His background was that of the Scandinavian petty bourgeoisie, and he sank in the social scale by the time he was eight years old, when his father became bankrupt and the déclassé family lived exiguously on a farm for some seven years. He was fifteen when the Ibsens returned to Skien, but their economic circumstances remained straitened. Leaving home at the age of sixteen, he became an apprentice for some three years in an impoverished pharmacy in the nearby shipping town of Grimstad, where he had to share a bedroom with his employer's little sons. This was a period of plain drudgery, relieved only by an affair with a servant girl ten years his senior who made him at the age of eighteen an unenthusiastic father to an illegitimate child.

A relatively congenial three-year period followed when he became an assistant pharmacist in a more flourishing shop. He acquired intellectual friends in Grimstad, produced radical poetry, and in 1849 wrote his first play, *Catiline,* in which he espoused liberal principles. It was the first Norwegian dramatic work to be published in seven years.

The young provincial, who soon moved to the capital Christiania (now Oslo) to study medicine, quickly renounced it in favor of philosophy and literature, became a man of the modern world. He concerned himself with the Hungarian revolution of 1848, with support for Denmark against the rising power of Prussia, and with trade-unionism, writing for a socialist publication, which was duly suppressed in 1851. In that year, during which he became associated with a newly founded progressive theatre in Bergen, he also traveled abroad for the first time on a small stipend that enabled him to attend the Copenhagen Royal Theatre and the Dresden Court Opera.

When he returned to stage-manage and write for the Bergen Theatre, he still had a considerable distance to travel before he would serve the cause of modern theatre. In his early work he continued to write romantic historical plays, mainly under the inspiration of the Norse sagas, though with an element of psychological conflict in the case of *Lady Inger of Østrat.*

Yet Ibsen did not have to postpone becoming a truly modern dramatist until he had developed the famous realistic form and style of his so-called middle period at the age of fifty. Ibsen actually became an important writer and significant realist once he attained the peak of his poetic talents and ambitions in the two dramatic poems *Brand* and *Peer Gynt.* Each of these imaginative works, still numbered among his masterpieces, was written as an episodic "romantic" play. But in each he launched a vigorous modern attack on the bourgeois spirit of compromise and opportunism of the 1860's. This fact is one of the many paradoxes of the man and his work without which one cannot understand either.

Ibsen was complex and contradictory as a man. Although he set most of his plays in Norway and dealt mostly with provincial characters as well as backgrounds, he spent most of his productive life in central Europe and Italy. He was a rebel against middle-class society, but took pride in displaying the decorations he received at the height of his career. Although he was acclaimed as an exponent of liberalism, he put no trust in the national liberal party in Norway and satirized its leaders, including its chief literary figure, Bjørnstjerne Bjørnson. He was both praised and denounced as a champion of feminism after the publication of *A Doll's House* in 1879. Yet his portraits of would-be emancipated women after *A Doll's House* are of failures; his Rebecca in *Rosmersholm* and the eponymous heroine of *Hedda Gabler* bring down disaster on the men they have tried to influence and ultimately commit suicide.

After earning international fame and notoriety with his attacks on conventional beliefs in *A Doll's House* and *Ghosts* and climaxing his call for truth with a barrage against social complacency and vested interest in *An Enemy of the People,* he gave the world a poignant defense of the value of illusions in *The Wild Duck* and a devastating exposé of the misguided character who destroys them. Ibsen did not pretend to solve problems with his problematical characters, and provided no programs for society while exposing its hypocrisies. Without failing to imply a need for reformation, he trusted no one — no individual, party, or class — to effectuate it. He was constitutionally incapable of idolatry whether in the cause of reform or even the cause of art. The protagonist of Ibsen's last play, *When We Dead Awaken,* who sacrificed life and love to art, is as much a failure as the tragic hero of *John Gabriel Borkman,* who sought only wealth and power.

The paradoxes and contradictions in Ibsen's work are not easily exhausted and they are never unimportant. He early became one of the leading modern Scandinavian poets, but he began to establish the rule of prose drama in the European theatre by the time he was fifty. Moreover, he had no sooner accomplished this with half a dozen plays written between 1877 and 1887 than he began to favor more or less symbolic playwriting, as in *The Lady from the Sea, The Master Builder, Little Eyolf,* and *When We Dead Awaken.* But this inclination did not prevent his producing during this last creative period his most powerful realistic drama, *Hedda Gabler.* Complexities and snarls appeared in the weave of all his mature work even if friends and enemies persisted in overlooking them. But Henry James, who did not overlook them, considered him an enigmatic writer; and Bernard Shaw, who tried to come to terms with Ibsen by attributing to him in *The Quintessence of Ibsenism* a tricksy mind like his own, was compelled to concede that there was much more to the northern giant of the theatre than blithe Shavianism.

Hardly a play is without its complicating contrasts, ambiguities, and ironies. Thus Mrs. Alving, the hapless mother in *Ghosts* who tried to observe respectability, was rewarded for her Victorian probity with a paretic son, who is about to succumb to softening of the brain. The orphanage she erected as a monument to the memory of her licentious husband burns down, and the pastor who once forbade her to leave her husband, and has refused to insure the orphanage against fire as a mark of distrust in God, now finds himself blackmailed into subsidizing a "sailor's home," actually a bordello, for the drunkard who accidentally set the building on fire. The idealist in *An Enemy of the People,* Dr. Stockmann, is a simpleton or, as Ibsen himself defines him, a "*Strudelkopf.*" The *dramatis personae* of the later written plays are likewise compounded of multiple strains. For all of Hedda Gabler's aristocratic tastes, she has a provincial and bourgeois dread of scandal; for all her sexual curiosity, an abhorrence of sex; and for all her cowardice combined with pretensions to grandeur, a final desperate sense of honor, to which she sacrifices her life.

Ibsen died in 1906 after years of failing health and mental debility, but his reported last words, "To the contrary," epitomize his highly individualistic temperament and art, his determination to see life in the round and in depth, and his saturnine penetration into the nature of man and the world he makes. His mature disposition kept him aloof even from the problems he observed and the sympathies and causes to which he inclined with half a heart but with an invariably critical intelligence. This inherent dividedness is, in fact, the essence of his consistency as a dramatist who created "drama of ideas" rather than dramatized sentiment or propaganda, and who rarely subordinated organically achieved characters to the claims of an ideal or an idea.

INDY, (Paul Marie Theodore) Vincent d' (Mar. 27, 1851 – Dec. 2, 1931). French composer. Born Paris, of aristocratic family. Studied music under Antoine Marmontel, Albert Lavignac, and (from 1872) César Franck, whose friend and chief disciple he became. Succeeded him on his death as president of Société Nationale de Musique (1890). Trip to Bayreuth (1876) made him a confirmed Wagnerian, and he determined to reform French music, then dominated by Gounod, Massenet, Saint-Saëns, and to create a French national style. He initiated revival of Rameau and Gluck, who with Bach and Franck deeply influenced his work. Compositions include symphonic trilogy *Wallenstein* (1874–84), *Le Chant de la Cloche* (1883), *Fervaal* (1895), *L'Étranger* (1898), *Symphonie sur un chant montagnard français* (1886), the symphonic variations *Istar* (1896), chamber music, piano pieces, songs. With Félix Alexandre Guilmant and Charles Bordes, founded Schola Cantorum (1894); became director (from 1911) and taught there rest of his life. Visited U.S. (from 1906), conducting own compositions with Boston Symphony Orchestra. Directed orchestra class at Paris Conservatoire (from 1912). D'Indy's teaching methods are embodied in his widely influential *Cours de composition musical*, in collaboration with Auguste Sérieyx (3 vols. 1903–33). Also wrote biographies of César Franck (1906) and Beethoven (1911). Married twice. Died in Paris.

REFERENCES: Norman Demuth *Vincent d'Indy, 1851–1931: Champion of Classicism* (London 1951). Camille Saint-Saëns *Outspoken Essays on Music* (tr. London and New York 1922). Léon Vallas *Vincent d'Indy* (2 vols. Paris 1946/50).

INGRES, Jean Auguste Dominique (Aug. 29, 1780 – Jan. 14, 1867). French painter. Born Montauban, son of a sculptor who gave him early instruc-

tion. Studied under Joseph Roques and Jean Briant in Toulouse (1791–96); entered Jacques Louis David's studio (1797) and École des Beaux Arts (1799) in Paris. Major influences on his style: classical art and, especially, Raphael. Having won Grand Prix de Rome (1801), he lived in Rome (1806–20), then in Florence (1820–24). Married Madeline Chapelle (1813); after her death (1849) he married Delphine Ramel (1851). Returning to Paris, won immediate fame at Salon with *Vow of Louis XIII* (1824, Montauban cathedral). Received numerous official commissions and became leader of classicists in opposition to romantics under Delacroix. After serving as director of French Academy in Rome (1835–41), spent rest of life in Paris. Celebrated works: *Oedipus and the Sphinx* (1808, Louvre, Paris), *Jupiter and Thetis* (1811, Musée Granet, Aix-en-Provence), series of female nudes called *Baigneuses* or *Odalisques* (beginning 1807), *The Apotheosis of Homer* (1827, Louvre), *La Source* (1856, Louvre), portraits, including one of *Madame d'Haussonville* (1845, Frick Collection, New York) and two of *Madame Moitessier* (1851, National Gallery, Washington, D.C.; 1856, National Gallery, London). Ingres was a classicist in his belief that line should be the basis of art and he was an exquisite draftsman. Yet the romantics acclaimed him for the sensuality and exoticism of his *Odalisques*. The Musée Ingres was founded in Montauban (1867).

REFERENCES: Agnes Mongan and Hans Naef *Ingres Centennial Exhibition: Drawings, Watercolors, and Oil Sketches from American Collections* (Meriden, Conn. 1967). Walter Pach *Ingres* (New York and London 1939). Gaëtan Picon *Ingres* (tr. Geneva 1967). Robert Rosenblum *Ingres* (London and New York 1967). Georges Wildenstein *Ingres* (1954, 2nd ed. London and New York 1956).

INNESS, George (May 1, 1825 – Aug. 3, 1894). American painter. Born Newburgh, N.Y., son of a merchant, and raised in Newark, N.J. Apprenticed to engraver at sixteen, but soon devoted time to painting. Exhibited *Afternoon* at National Academy of Design (1844) and opened own studio. Largely self-taught. In Italy at various periods, accompanied by wife Elizabeth Hart (married 1850), also to Paris (1854), when strongly influenced by Barbizon school. Returned to U.S. to settle first in Medfield, Mass., then Montclair, N.J. Early works somewhat stiff and full of detail in Hudson River school manner, but with *The Lackawanna Valley* (1855) began a freer style that developed, as a result of the Barbizon influence, in the classical breadth and control, the native freshness and airy sparkle of *Peace and Plenty* (1865, Metropolitan Museum, New York), *Harvest Scene* (1867), *Evening at Medfield* (1875, Metropolitan Museum). His paintings became increasingly lyrical and spiritual, reflecting his conversion to Swedenborgianism (1860's). Elected to National Academy (1868). His later emphasis on atmosphere, as opposed to form, in *Coming Storm* (1878, Addison Gallery, Andover, Mass.) and *Niagara Falls* (1884), relate him to the impressionists. The serene lyricism of his Eastern landscapes makes him outstanding among the American painters of his period. Died at Bridge of Allan, Scotland. His son, George Inness, Jr. (1854–1926), also a painter, shared a studio with his father before moving to Paris (1895–99), where he exhibited at the Paris Salon, receiving gold medal (1900). Elected to National Academy (1899) and made officer of Académie Française (1902). Among his most notable paintings are *The First Snow of Cragsmoor* and *Shepherd and Sheep* (both in Metropolitan Museum).

REFERENCES: George Inness, Jr. *The Life, Art, and Letters of George Inness* (New York 1917). LeRoy Ireland *The Works of George Inness* (Austin, Texas 1965). Elizabeth McCausland *George Inness: An American Landscape Painter* (New York 1946).

IRVING, Washington (Apr. 3, 1783 – Nov. 28, 1859). American writer. Born New York, son of a wealthy merchant. After attending private schools, entered law office (1798), but became involved in literary life, writing series of satires on New York society for brother Peter's *Morning Chronicle* under pseudonym Jonathan Oldstyle, Gent. (1802–1803). After two years abroad for his health, returned and passed bar examination (1806), but again turned to writing, establishing reputation as one of the Nine Worthies who published *Salmagundi* (1807–1808), satirical papers modeled on Addison's *Spectator*. Published brilliantly satiric *History of New York* under pseudonym Diedrich Knickerbocker (1809); in same year, his fiancée Matilda Hoffman died. Entered brothers' importing business (1810), leaving America (1815) to take charge of Liverpool branch. Bankrupt (1817), he returned to literature under pseudonym Geoffrey Crayon and published his most successful work, *The Sketch Book* (1820), a collection of tales including *Rip Van Winkle* and *The Legend of Sleepy Hollow*. An immediate success, it was followed by companion volume *Bracebridge Hall* (1822). After some time in Germany and France, Irving became diplomatic attaché in Spain (1826), where he gathered material for his scholarly *History of the Life and Voyages of Christopher Columbus* (1828), for *A Chronicle of the Conquest of Granada* (1829), and for *The Alhambra* (1832), a collection of Spanish legends. After a post with the American legation in London (1829), returned to America (1832). Long trip through West for the government resulted in *A Tour on the Prairies* (1832). After further diplomatic service in Spain (1842–46) settled at Sunnyside, country home on the Hudson, for remainder of his life. Here he completed *The Life of Washington* (5 vols. 1855–59). Irving was the first American writer to achieve international fame.

EDITIONS: *Works* (21 vols. New York 1863–66). *Selected Writings* ed. Saxe Commins (New York 1945).
REFERENCES: William L. Hedges *Washington Irving: An American Study, 1802–1832* (Baltimore 1965). George S. Hellman *Washington Irving, Esquire* (New York and London 1925). Pierre M. Irving *The Life and Letters of Washington Irving* (1863–64, reprinted 4 vols. Detroit 1967). Edward Wagenknecht *Washington Irving: Moderation Displayed* (New York 1962). Stanley T. Williams *Life of Washing-*

ton Irving (2 vols. New York and London 1935).

IVES, Charles Edward (Oct. 20, 1874 – May 19, 1954). American composer. Born Danbury, Conn., son of a bandleader whose band played Ives's first piece (1888). Graduated from Yale (1898), where he studied composition with Horatio Parker and organ with Dudley Buck. Became clerk in insurance company, and at same time worked as organist in churches around New York. Pursued double career as composer and businessman, forming insurance agency partnership (1907) with Julian Myrick. Married Harmony Twichell (1908). Stopped composing (1923) and retired from business because of ill health (1930). Died in New York. Major works were mostly written between 1906 and 1916, but recognition did not come until decades later. His third symphony (1901–1904) was first performed in 1947 and received the Pulitzer prize as well as special commendation by Music Critics Circle. His second piano sonata, *Concord, Massachusetts, 1840–1860* (1909–15), is generally considered his finest work; he published it at his own expense (1919). In addition to orchestral and instrumental music, Ives composed 114 songs (published 1922). An innovator, he experimented in sound, rhythm, and tonal relationship, and made use of allusions and themes from the hymns and American folk music of his youth.

EDITION: *Essays Before a Sonata* (New York 1962, also PB).

REFERENCE: Henry and Sidney Cowell *Charles Ives and His Music* (London and New York 1955, PB 1969).

JAMES, Henry (Apr. 15, 1843 – Feb. 28, 1916). American novelist. Born New York, son of a wealthy Swedenborgian philosopher and younger brother of philosopher William James. Educated at private schools in America and Europe. After brief period at Harvard Law School (1862), began writing stories and reviews, publishing first story (unsigned) in *Continental Monthly* (1864). Thereafter became frequent contributor to journals, and first novel, *Watch and Ward*, was serialized in *Atlantic Monthly* (1871). After a period in Paris he settled in London (1876). Experience in both America and Europe gave him material for the international theme of his early works: *Roderick Hudson* (1876), *The American* (1877), *The Europeans* (1878), *Daisy Miller* (1879) — the story that made him famous — and *The Portrait of a Lady* (1881). Novels of 1880's, *The Bostonians* (1886), *The Princess Casamassima* (1886), and *The Tragic Muse* (1889) were less successful, and in early 1890's he made a disastrous bid for fame in the theatre. Resigned to unpopularity, he returned to novels and stories, producing such celebrated works as *What Maisie Knew* (1897), *The Turn of the Screw* (1898), *The Awkward Age* (1899), and the novels of his major phase, *The Wings of the Dove* (1902), *The Ambassadors* (1903), and *The Golden Bowl* (1904). James was also a master of the tale, wrote over a hundred, including *The Aspern Papers* and *The Beast in the Jungle*. Recorded a lengthy visit to America in *The American Scene* (1907), but continued to make England his home, becoming a British subject (1915) and winning the Order of Merit. Also author of two biographies and two auto-biographical works, *A Small Boy and Others* (1913) and *Notes of a Son and Brother* (1914). The fragment of another, *The Middle Years*, appeared posthumously (1917). Died in London; ashes buried in Cambridge, Mass.

EDITIONS: *Novels and Tales* New York Edition (latest ed. 26 vols. New York 1961–64). *Complete Tales* ed. Leon Edel (12 vols. Philadelphia and London 1962–64). *Complete Plays* ed. Leon Edel (Philadelphia and London 1949). *Notebooks* ed. F. O. Matthiessen and Kenneth B. Murdock (New York 1947 and London 1948, PB 1961). *Selected Letters of Henry James* ed. Leon Edel (New York 1955 and London 1956).

REFERENCES: Oscar Cargill *The Novels of Henry James* (New York 1961). Frederick W. Dupee *Henry James* (2nd ed. Garden City, N.Y. PB 1956). Leon Edel *Henry James* (4 vols. Philadelphia and London 1953/62/69; one further volume scheduled) and *Henry James: A Collection of Critical Essays* (Englewood Cliffs, N.J. 1963, also PB). Ford Madox Ford *Henry James: A Critical Study* (1913, reprinted New York 1964). H. Montgomery Hyde *Henry James at Home* (London and New York 1969). Dorothea Krook *The Ordeal of Consciousness in Henry James* (Cambridge, England, and New York 1962, also PB). F. O. Matthiessen *Henry James: The Major Phase* (London and New York 1944, also PB). Richard Poirier *The Comic Sense of Henry James* (London and New York 1960, also PB). S. Gorley Putt *Henry James: A Reader's Guide* (London and Ithaca, N.Y. 1966, also PB).

HENRY JAMES

BY

HORTENSE CALISHER

No one will ever know the private life of Henry James. The James family circle, that ample panoply starting with the Swedenborgian, Fourierist father who kept his children as usefully as possible out of their native Albany and in Europe, has become a classic instance of the nineteenth-century family of culture, connections, and means. Together with James's own Harvard years, early saturation in Back Bay mores, and the glorious dining-out period in London, which culminated in British citizenship, the "life" becomes in turn one of the "high society" legends of our literature — as well as a picture of a writer who, with every dowry for either the novelist of manners or even of society in the Balzacian sense, insisted on becoming more. Fasten on him the label of younger brother forever preceded by the brilliantly psychological, philosophic William in whose "adaptive skin" Henry wished he might live, add to this the "obscure hurt" of the physical accident which kept Henry noncombatant in the Civil War and who knows if not the wars of the sexes also, top these with a bachelor's devotion to a depressed sister, and a perhaps blighted one to Minny Temple, the cousin who died of TB in their youth — and what a scoop we have had, for the Freudian sieve! We have had the facts of a Victorianly documented life collated with its very hours, historical *and* personal, and we have James's own help, in such formal recollections as *A Small Boy and Others, Notes of a Son and Brother* — as well as in a lifelong habit of the most trenchant personal allusion, marred only by the artist's will toward general truth. Everybody who writes of James imitates

that, in the end. Yet as Percy Lubbock, editing the letters, said: "Within . . . was a cycle of vivid and incessant adventure known only to himself." In the end we come to that obscuring darkness which half purposefully surrounds all great artists, time and their own prescience forcing us into another light — the great irradiation of the work.

There, once we accede to the famous "subjects": raw America against refined Europe (*The American, The Europeans*); that parade of gracefully or pitiably innocent girls whose sensibilities are the stage for this or other dramas of the moral temperament in society (*Daisy Miller, The Portrait of a Lady, The Wings of the Dove*); depth studies of good-and-evil, in which children are the arena and victim, collusive collaborators as well, or the "detached observer" at its proudest (*The Turn of the Screw, The Awkward Age, What Maisie Knew*); irony (*The Spoils of Poynton, The Bostonians*) — and after we concede that this latter contains a lesbian portrait as sharp as those extraordinary studies of adultery in the masterpieces of the late period, *The Ambassadors, The Golden Bowl* — may we then at last go on to that profound intermingling, the texts themselves? Now that we are inured to forty-page prefaces, so enthralling, and so much shorter than the books, can we stand upon the personal judgment, as James did always?

When I went to college in the 1930's, we were scarcely taught James, in favor of his genteel shadow, Howells. By accident I came upon more, and went mad with joy for what seemed even to me a peculiar reason. I had already read much in nineteenth-century prose, and except for the Russians, it was all fairy stories, especially Dickens, unable as he was to sift his

Gothic realities from his sentimental ones — appreciation of that would not come until middle age. But in the long, loping parentheses of James, I seemed to find a replica of how thought really thinks, a counterpart of the real psychological processes of my own brain. This was to be almost the exact attraction of his prose to the critics, especially the Freudians, who would swarm to it as they would to Proust. I was least taken with James wherever, as in Milly Theale, he assigned to women a terrifying innocence which didn't jibe with my inner knowledge — precisely as Salinger's pimpleless little sisters, and Hemingway's Dianas of the sleeping bag, were to amuse me later. But wherever his preoccupation was either with a good-and-evil whose roles were so rightfully never clearly assigned, or with the weighing of the soul in society, which is also a preoccupation of youth — I was with him. The localization, America versus Europe, didn't seem more than that, and still doesn't; the subject is eternal. A few years on, those same critics would take up Forster's *Howard's End;* James had taught them to *see* the subject. But I knew none of this. To me he seemed merely, as he does now, the most hard-minded writer I had yet encountered among us. I did not yet know that in the American novel, whose virtues tend toward poetic giantism, hard-mindedness — which has nothing to do with hard language — is rarely a total quality, more usually evincing itself only in those narrower realists who cannot make James's fuller use of it. No wonder the romanticists of the "hard-boiled" hate James.

James's vision departed enormously from his world yet was dangerously akin to it; as these unite and intently alternate, an artist is measured. It was a risky vision, at times in language magnificently eccentric from *within*, all the more significantly so because James is the last great novelist in English before those frontal assaults on the nature of language itself, which were shortly to come. He is one of the last to use the sentence as a vehicle of meaning primarily, rather than as an aggressive motif in the form of the whole, with as much weight as a line in a poem. In that sense, no one could now mimic him. To equate Jamesian language merely with long sentences is to mistake what he does. His sentences are more in the nature of long *meanings*; at their best, a vibrato hangs over the cumulus of actual words, adding an intangible exactly as occurs so much more familiarly in music, or poetry. Yet he never fell into poetic language or rhythm, per se. His victory was to be able to do what poetry does — in prose. To those who see prose as an art separable from poetry, and *equal* to it, his work, like that of the Turgenev he admired, has a particular importance — enraging those who think style is separable from meaning, or believe prose to be a subordinate art.

He is also — and here by the opposing strictures of his time and ours — one of the last to treat character as in itself stable enough to treat, not as a mere intersection of society and milieu, or else the stock character *of* the milieu rather than of human nature per se. To see the modern change, one need think only of Hemingway — for whom "character" is really the lyric expressiveness of human beings in or against their environment, or of Faulkner, where it blends in dynamic symphony with the environment. Or of those modern French writers who, working themselves by infinitely small cinematic steps up the staircase of the milieu, will find Zola looking down at them, at the top.

James was still able to separate people from their placement in life, so that the discriminatory blendings of art might then begin. The same objectivity made him a matchless explainer of the radical problems of art — and the best critic of his own work. "The effort really to see and really to represent is no idle business in face of the *constant* force that makes for muddlement. The great thing is indeed that the muddled state too is one of the very sharpest of the realities."

Meanwhile, at this moment some shaghaired young creature, ignorant of all this — or of those more adult pleasures to be found in any writer who so gleefully confirms our secret conviction that man is the most anthropomorphic of the animals — is staring at that other James wherein other writers also find encouragement — at his extraordinary affirmation of human consciousness. Here, James never for one moment underestimated the intelligence of his readers. There are some who will never forgive him for it.

JAMES, William (Jan. 11, 1842 – Aug. 26, 1910). American philosopher and psychologist. Born New York, son of a wealthy Swedenborgian philosopher, elder brother of novelist Henry James. Educated at American and European schools, he briefly studied art under William Morris Hunt before entering Lawrence Scientific School of Harvard University (1861). Went on to Harvard Medical School, where, after joining Louis Agassiz's exploration of Amazon (1865) and taking courses in Germany (1867–68), he took his degree (1869). Taught physiology, psychology, philosophy at Harvard (1872–1907). Married Alice Howe Gibbons (1878); they had four children. After publishing first book, *The Principles of Psychology* (1890), began studies in religion and

ethics, leading to famous Gifford lectures at Edinburgh University (1901), published as *The Varieties of Religious Experience* (1902). Next came period in which he elaborated and modified philosophy of pragmatism, introducing a concept of relativism that became widely influential. Acknowledged as foremost American philosopher of the time on appearance of *Pragmatism: A New Name for Some Old Ways of Thinking* (1907). Later works include *The Meaning of Truth* (1909), *A Pluralistic Universe* (1909), *Essays in Radical Empiricism* (1912). Died at summer home in Chocorua, N.H.; buried in Cambridge, Mass.

EDITIONS: *The Letters of William James* ed. Henry James, Jr. (Boston 1920, reprinted Mamaroneck, N.Y. 1969). *Collected Essays and Reviews* ed. Ralph Barton Perry (1920, reprinted New York 1969). *The Writings of William James* ed. John J. McDermott (New York 1968). *The Moral Philosophy of William James* ed. John K. Roth (New York 1969, also PB).
REFERENCES: Gay Wilson Allen *William James: A Biography* (New York and London 1967, also PB). A. J. Ayer *The Origins of Pragmatism* (London and San Francisco 1968). Théodore Flournoy *The Philosophy of William James* (tr. 1917, reprinted Freeport, N.Y. 1969). Arthur O. Lovejoy *The Thirteen Pragmatisms and Other Essays* (Baltimore and Oxford 1963). F. O. Matthiessen *The James Family* (New York 1947). Edward C. Moore *William James* (New York 1966, also PB). Ralph Barton Perry *The Thought and Character of William James* (2 vols. Boston 1935 and Oxford 1936; briefer version Cambridge, Mass. and Oxford 1948, PB 1964). John Wild *The Radical Empiricism of William James* (Garden City, N.Y. 1969).

JEFFERS, (John) Robinson (Jan. 10, 1887 – Jan. 20, 1962). American poet. Born Pittsburgh, Pa. After graduating from Occidental College (1905), studied medicine, forestry, and other subjects at universities of Southern California, Washington, and Zurich. First poetry volume, *Flagons and Apples* (1912). Married Una McCall Kuster (1913) and retired to a house and tower on California coast at Carmel, where save for occasional travels he spent rest of his life. Jeffers's basic theme is the worthlessness of man, whom he rejects in favor of strong and beautiful nature:

Cut humanity out of my being,
That is the wound that festers.

From the Greek classics he derived inspiration for themes and models. Works include *Tamar and Other Poems* (1924), *Roan Stallion* (1925), *Cawdor and Other Poems* (1928), *Dear Judas and Other Poems* (1929), *Descent to the Dead* (1931), *Thurso's Landing and Other Poems* (1932), *Give Your Heart to the Hawks* (1933), *Solstice and Other Poems* (1935), *The Double Axe and Other Poems* (1948). Adapted Euripides' tragedies *Medea* and *Phaedra* for modern stage under titles *Medea* (1946) and *The Cretan Woman* (1954). *Hungerfield and Other Poems* won Pulitzer prize (1954).

EDITIONS: *Selected Poems* (New York PB 1965). *Selected Letters* ed. Ann N. Ridgeway (Baltimore 1968).

REFERENCES: Brother Antoninus *Robinson Jeffers: Fragments of an Older Fury* (Berkeley, Calif., 1968). Melba B. Bennett *The Stone Mason of Tor House: The Life and Work of Robinson Jeffers* (Los Angeles 1966). Frederic I. Carpenter *Robinson Jeffers* (New York 1962, also PB). Lawrence Clark Powell *Robinson Jeffers: The Man and His Work* (1934, reprinted New York 1969). Radcliffe Squires *The Loyalties of Robinson Jeffers* (Ann Arbor, Mich. 1956 and Oxford 1957, also PB).

JEFFERSON, Thomas (Apr. 13, 1743 – July 4, 1826). American writer, third President of the United States. Born in Shadwell, Virginia; father a successful planter, mother from distinguished Virginia family. Educated in private schools and at College of William and Mary (1760–62); studied law (1762–67), and practiced until 1774. Married Martha Wayles Skelton (1772; she died 1782). Served in Virginia House of Burgesses (1769–74). Contributed forcefully to patriot cause with his pamphlet *A Summary View of the Rights of British America* (1774), which em-

phasized natural rights and formulated idea that Parliament had no authority over the colonies. Member of Continental Congress (1775–76), he was chosen to draft Declaration of Independence (1776). As member of Virginia legislature (1776–79), achieved sweeping reforms in land system and role of church, in accordance with his democratic ideals. Served as governor of Virginia (1779–81); wrote *Notes on the State of Virginia* (1781–83, published 1784–85), a remarkable work of natural history which with Declaration made him famous on both continents. Again member of Continental Congress (1783–84). In France as diplomat (1784–89), he became Benjamin Franklin's successor as minister. While Secretary of state (1790–93), engaged in famous dispute (1791) with Alexander Hamilton: Hamilton wished to concentrate power, Jefferson to diffuse it. Became leader of new anti-Federalist faction self-named Republican. Vice-President of United States (1797–1800); President (1801–1809). The secret of his power was his idealism, his belief in the perfectibility of mankind and in a republic based on agrarian democracy. Louisiana Purchase greatest achievement of his administration (1803); organized Lewis and Clark expedition to explore the new empire (1804–1806). The first American architect of his generation, Jefferson designed his Virginia home, Monticello (1770–1806), the Virginia statehouse (1785–96) for new capital at Richmond, modeled after Maison Carré, Nîmes, and the first work of classic revival in America. Also designed country estates of friends, and — crown of his architectural career — the University of Virginia (completed 1824), which he founded (1819). The classic forms of Roman republicanism were his inspiration for the new buildings in America. As president of American Philosophical Society (1797–1815) he promoted advances in science, public education, the arts. Died at Monticello, the same day as John Adams, aged ninety-one, on the fiftieth anniversary of the adoption of the Declaration of Independence.

EDITIONS: *The Writings of Thomas Jefferson* ed. Paul L. Ford (10 vols.

Philadelphia 1892–99). *The Papers of Thomas Jefferson* ed. Julian P. Boyd and others (52 vols. scheduled, Princeton, N.J. and Oxford 1950–).
REFERENCES: John Dos Passos *The Head and Heart of Thomas Jefferson* (Garden City, N. Y. 1954 and London 1955). Thomas Fleming *The Man from Monticello: An Intimate Life of Thomas Jefferson* (New York 1969). Fiske Kimball *Thomas Jefferson: Architect* (1916, reprinted New York 1968). Adrienne Koch *The Philosophy of Thomas Jefferson* (1943, reprinted Gloucester, Mass. 1957, also PB) and *Jefferson and Madison* (New York 1950, PB 1964). Karl Lehmann *Thomas Jefferson: American Humanist* (New York 1947, rev. ed. Chicago PB 1965). Dumas Malone *Jefferson and His Time* (4 vols. Boston and London 1948–70, also PB; one further volume scheduled) and *Thomas Jefferson as a Political Leader* (Berkeley, Calif. and Cambridge, England, 1963). Edwin T. Martin *Thomas Jefferson: Scientist* (New York 1952, PB 1961). Merrill D. Peterson *The Jefferson Image in the American Mind* (New York 1960, also PB). Nathan Schachter *Thomas Jefferson* (2 vols. New York 1951, one-vol. ed. 1957).

JEWETT, Sarah Orne (Sept. 3, 1849 – June 24, 1909). American writer. Born and died in South Berwick, Me.; educated at Berwick Academy. After reading Harriet Beecher Stowe, resolved to portray Maine life in realistic fiction. Published *Jenny Garrow's Lovers* (1868), followed by *Mr. Bruce* (1869), in *Atlantic Monthly*. A protégée of Howells, she gained recognition with short story collection *Deephaven* (1877). Continued publishing stories in *Atlantic*, *Century*, and *Harper's*. Collections and novels include *Country By-Ways* (1881), *A Country Doctor* (1884), *A Marsh Island* (1885), *Tales of New England* (1890), *The Tory Lover* (1901). Her masterpiece, *The Country of the Pointed Firs* (1896), one of the best pieces of nineteenth-century regional fiction, captured the disappearing New England order of farms and fishing towns with pictorial clarity, realism, and sympathy. During four trips abroad (1882, 1892, 1898, 1900) with friend Annie Fields she met Tennyson, Rossetti, Arnold, du Maurier, Kipling, and Henry James. Always drawn back to Boston and Maine coast and to friends Howells, T. B. Aldrich, Whittier, Holmes, Emerson, Longfellow, and Willa Cather, on whom she exerted strong influence. Received first Litt.D. awarded to a woman by Bowdoin College (1901). Her poems appeared in *Verses* (1916).

EDITION: *Letters* ed. Annie Fields (Boston 1911).
REFERENCES: Richard Cary *Sarah Orne Jewett* (New York 1962, also PB). F. O. Matthiessen *Sarah Orne Jewett* (Boston 1929, reprinted Gloucester, Mass. 1965). Margaret F. Thorp *Sarah Orne Jewett* (Minneapolis PB 1966).

JIMÉNEZ, Juan Ramón (Dec. 24, 1881 – May 29, 1958). Spanish poet. Born Moguer, Andalusia. Studied at Jesuit College in Puerto de Santa María, near Cadiz, and University of Seville (1896–98). Became a journalist, moving to Madrid (1901), where he knew Rubén Darío, Unamuno, and other intellectuals. Early volumes of poetry, showing influence of French symbolists and of Darío, include *Rimas* (1902), *Arias tristes* (1903), *Jardines lejanos* (1904, *Distant Gardens*), *Elegías puras* (1908), *Elegías intermedias* (1909), *Elegías lamentables* (1910), *Baladas de primavera* (1910), *La Soledad sonora* (1911, *Sonorous Loneliness*). After trip to United States, where he married Zenobia Camprubí (1916), returned to Madrid. *Diario de un poeta recién casado* (1917, *Diary of a Newly Married Poet*), containing prose and verse, marked beginning of mature period, in which he strove for a *poesía desnuda* ("naked poetry"), with short lines, simplified form, and purity of expression. Early in Spanish Civil War (1936), left Spain for America, living in United States, Cuba, and Puerto Rico. Later poetry includes *Sonetos espirituales* (1942), *Voces de mi copla* (1945), *Belleza* (1945), *Romances de Coral Gables* (1948), *Animal de fondo* (1949). Prose work *Platero y yo* (1914, tr. *Platero and I* 1956) has become a classic. Received Nobel prize for literature (1956). Died in San Juan, Puerto Rico.

TRANSLATIONS: *Platero and I* tr. William and Mary Roberts (Oxford 1956 and New York 1957). *Selected Writings* tr. H. R. Hays (New York 1957, also PB). *Three Hundred Poems* tr. Eloise Roach (Austin, Tex., 1962).

REFERENCES: Leo R. Cole *The Religious Instinct in the Poetry of Juan Ramón Jiménez* (Oxford 1967). Paul R. Olson *Circle of Paradox: Time and Essence in the Poetry of Juan Ramón Jiménez* (Baltimore 1967). Howard T. Young *The Victorious Expression: A Study of Four Contemporary Spanish Poets* (Madison, Wis. 1964, also PB) and *Juan Ramón Jiménez* (New York PB 1967).

JOHN, Augustus (Edwin) (Jan. 4, 1878 – Oct. 31, 1961). British artist. Born Tenby, Wales. While student at Slade School in London (1894–98) showed great precocity, and by 1899 was having drawings accepted by New English Art Club. Taught at Liverpool University (1900–1902). Roamed through British isles, painting gypsy life; later traveled extensively in Europe and America. By outbreak of World War I was well known as portraitist and colorful personality. Served in France as an official war artist, and painted many leading personalities of the peace conference. John's fame rests on his portraits of literary and artistic figures, many of them his friends; with open, swift brushstrokes and vivid color he presented them in spontaneous attitudes. Among his subjects were George Bernard Shaw (1914, Fitzwilliam Museum, Cambridge), Madame Suggia (1923, Tate Gallery, London), Dylan Thomas (c.1936–40, National Museum of Wales, Cardiff). Elected Royal Academician (1928); awarded Order of Merit (1942). Married twice. Died at Fordingbridge, Hampshire. Wrote two autobiographical works, *Chiaroscuro: Fragments of an Autobiography* (1952) and *Finishing Touches* (1964).

REFERENCES: Lord David Cecil *Augustus John: Fifty-two Drawings* (London and Greenwich, Conn. 1957). Stephen Longstreet *The Drawings of Augustus John* (Alhambra, Calif. 1967, also PB). John Rothenstein *Augustus John* (3rd ed. London and New York 1946).

JOHN OF THE CROSS, Saint (Spanish name San Juan de la Cruz, original name Juan de Yepes y Álvarez) (June 24, 1542 – Dec. 14, 1591). Spanish poet. Born Fontiveros, Avila. Studied with Jesuits, became Carmelite friar (1563), and after four years at University of Salamanca was ordained priest (1567). Helped promote Carmelite reforms of St. Teresa and participated in founding of discalced Carmelite monasteries. Kidnapped and imprisoned by unreformed Carmelites (1577–78). Attained office of vicar provincial of Andalusia (1585–87), but was deprived of position by opponents in reform movement. Died at Úbeda, Jaén. Canonized (1726); made a doctor of the church (1926). St. John's fame as one of Spain's greatest lyric poets rests on three mystical poems, *La Noche oscura del alma* (*Dark Night of the Soul*), *La Llama de amor viva* (*Flame of Divine Love*), and *El Cántico espiritual,* which, with the equally important prose commentaries accompanying them, provide a beautiful and instructive account of the mystical experience. They were published, together with short poems, as *Obras espirituales* (1618).

TRANSLATIONS: *Collected Works* ed. Kieran Kavanaugh, tr. Otilio Rodriguez (Garden City, N.Y. 1964). *Poems* ed. and tr. John F. Nims (1959, rev. ed. New York 1968).

REFERENCES: Father Crisógono de Jesús Sacramentado *The Life of St. John of the Cross* (tr. London 1958). Léon Cristiani *St. John of the Cross: Prince of Mystical Theology* (tr. New York 1962). E. Allison Peers *Spirit of Flame: A Study of St. John of the Cross* (London 1943 and New York 1944) and *Handbook to the Life and Times of St. Teresa and St. John of the Cross* (London and Westminster, Md. 1954).

JOHNSON, Lionel Pigot (Mar. 15, 1867 – Oct. 4, 1902). English poet and critic. Born Broadstairs, Kent. Educated at Winchester (1880–86) and New College, Oxford (1886–90). Settled in London, living as ascetic recluse and contributing essays and reviews to *National*

Observer, Academy, Daily Chronicle, Pall Mall Gazette, and other periodicals. Johnson's two chief enthusiasms were the Roman Catholic Church, which he entered (1891), and Irish political and literary movements; from 1893, visited Ireland often. Illness and alcoholism ended his life early, in London. Publications include *The Art of Thomas Hardy* (1894), *Poems* (1895), *Ireland, with Other Poems* (1897), *Post Liminium*, a book of essays edited by Thomas Whittemore (1911), *Poetical Works*, with introduction by Ezra Pound (1915), *Complete Poems*, edited by I. Fletcher (1951). All of Johnson's verse shows influence of Walter Pater. Formal and intellectual, it nonetheless expresses profound religious feeling.

EDITION: *Complete Poems* ed. Iain Fletcher (London 1953).

REFERENCES: Osbert Burdett *The Beardsley Period* (1925, reprinted New York 1969). Holbrook Jackson *The Eighteen Nineties* (1913, new ed. New York 1925 and London 1927, PB New York 1966).

JOHNSON, Samuel (Sept. 18, 1709 – Dec. 13, 1784). English poet, critic, essayist and lexicographer. Born Lichfield, Staffordshire, son of a bookseller. Attended Lichfield grammar school and Pembroke College, Oxford (1728–29), leaving without a degree because of poverty. Married Mrs. Elizabeth Porter, a widow twenty years his senior (1735; she died 1752), and set up a school at Edial near Lichfield. When this enterprise failed, he moved to London (1737) to write for *The Gentleman's Magazine*. First attracted notice with poems *London* (1738) and *The Vanity of Human Wishes* (1749), both imitations of satires by Juvenal, and with *The Life of Mr. Richard Savage* (1744), his friend. While working on the great *Dictionary of the English Language*, which established his fame (1755), published essay series *The Rambler* (1750–52), *The Adventurer* (1753–54), then *The Idler* (1758–60) and later the novel *Rasselas, Prince of Abyssinia* (1759). Royal pension (1762) freed him from necessity of hack writing, and allowed him time for friends. Met James Boswell (1763); founded The Club with Burke and others (1764). Met (1765) Mrs. Hester

Thrale, who became his close friend and memoirist. That year Dublin University awarded him honorary degree, as did Oxford later (1775). With Boswell toured the Hebrides (1773), which resulted in his *Journey to the Western Islands of Scotland* (1775) and Boswell's *Journal of a Tour to the Hebrides* (1785). Later major works: edition of Shakespeare with the celebrated preface (1765) and *Lives of the English Poets* (1779–81). Also author of numerous pamphlets, sermons, prayers, translations. Died in London.

EDITIONS: *Works* Yale Edition (New Haven, Conn. and Oxford 1958–). *Poems* ed. D. Nichol Smith and E. L. McAdam (1941, latest ed. Oxford 1962). *Lives of the English Poets* ed. Arthur Waugh (latest ed. 2 vols. London and New York 1942–46). *Johnson: Prose and Poetry* ed. Mona Wilson (1950, latest ed. London PB 1966 and Cambridge, Mass. PB 1967). *Letters* ed. R. W. Chapman (3 vols. Oxford 1952). *Johnson's Dictionary: A Modern Selection* ed. E. L. McAdam, Jr. and George Milne (New York and London 1963).

REFERENCES: Walter Jackson Bate *The Achievement of Samuel Johnson* (New York and London 1955, also PB). Edward A. Bloom *Samuel Johnson in Grub Street* (Providence, R.I. 1957). James Boswell *Life of Samuel Johnson, Together with Boswell's Journal of a Tour to the Hebrides, and Johnson's Diary of a Journey into North Wales* ed. George Birkbeck Hill and L. F. Powell (6 vols. Oxford 1934–50). B. H. Bronson *Johnson Agonistes and Other Essays* (New York and Cambridge, England, 1946). James L. Clifford *Young Sam Johnson* (London and New York 1955, also PB). *Johnsonian Miscellanies* ed. G. B. N. Hill (1897, 2 vols. reprinted New York 1966 and London 1967). M. J. C. Hodgart *Samuel Johnson and His Times* (London 1962 and New York 1948, PB 1963).

☞

SAMUEL JOHNSON

BY

WALTER JACKSON BATE

Johnson began life with almost everything against him. A tubercular infection when he was a baby left him blind in one eye and with very poor sight in the other. It also permanently scarred his face. Almost from birth until he was six, one arm was kept open, running with an "issue" of blood. He remembered overhearing an aunt say of him that she "would not have picked such a poor creature in the street." He was reared in poverty. He fought his way to Oxford, where he was able to stay for little more than a year. On his return to his native town of Lichfield, at the age of twenty, he fell into a state of despair and melancholy so acute that it seemed to himself and to others that he was losing his mind. One of the ironies in literary history is that its greatest exponent of sanity — of good sense wrung from concrete experience — should have begun his life thus. In order to get control of himself, he would force himself in a single day to walk through the muddy roads to Birmingham and back — a distance of thirty miles. These attempts to jolt himself out of self-absorption were typical of his life, from now till the end.

Everything, in short, had to be earned. After his marriage, he tried to conduct a small school, then trudged to London, roamed the streets, and became closely acquainted with the large floating body of the London poor. At the same time, during these years, he acquired a range of knowledge that led Adam Smith to say that "Johnson knew more books than any man alive." His inspired hackwork ranged from discussions of Chinese architecture to Sir Isaac Newton's proofs of the existence of God, from trade to metaphysics; and the two volumes of his reports on the debates of the House of Commons (which were not at that time officially reported) contain some of the finest political speeches of the mid-century, though Johnson half made them up — he was never in the gallery of the House but once. Working fitfully in an attic, he also compiled the first great English dictionary, "beating the track of the alphabet," as he said, "with sluggish resolution." In this pioneer work, from which all later dictionaries in English descend, he wrote, with little help, the definitions of over 40,000 words and illustrated them with over 100,000 quotations, many of them drawn from memory.

Meanwhile he had written his first major poem, *London* (1738), and then the powerful and condensed *The Vanity of Human Wishes* (1749). The latter has fascinated English poets and critics ever since it appeared, for there is nothing else quite like it. But the work that established his reputation during these years — aside from the *Dictionary* — consisted of about three hundred essays he wrote in periodicals: *The Rambler* (1750–52), *The Adventurer* (1753–54), and *The Idler* (1758–60). Concluding this period of his distracted life, he wrote the philosophical novel *Rasselas* (1759), dashed down in the evenings of one week to pay for the expenses of his mother's funeral. A terrible collapse occurred. Fitfully, through what Boswell called a "Caesarean operation," he brought out his edition of Shakespeare (1765) and its famous preface (the first great critique of Shakespeare), which Adam Smith justly described as "the most manly piece of criticism ever published in any country."

After his middle years, he put writing aside for a while, except to help other people, or to write some political pamphlets. This is the Johnson we have come to know through Boswell and the other memoirs (Fanny Burney, Sir John Hawkins, Mrs. Thrale, and a score of others): Johnson in his later years, unrivaled as a conversationalist, and the leading spirit of the famous club (called simply The Club) that included some of the finest minds in England (Burke, Gibbon, Reynolds, Smith, Garrick, Goldsmith, and others). In his final years, he virtually invented the art of literary biography when, at the request of some booksellers, he wrote *Lives of the Poets* (1779–81) — the introductions to fifty-two poets (Milton to Gray) for the period 1660–1760.

Within a half-century after his death, a stock reaction to Johnson developed that continued until the Second World War. Widely asserted, and then repeated without examination, was the contention that his own writing was not what we prized but rather the accounts of him as a person, especially Boswell's great *Life*. In our own generation, we are turning more to Johnson's own writing, rediscovering much that we feel, to use a phrase of his, that we can "put to use." But a distinction between "Johnsonians" and "Boswellians" still persists. Between them are often fundamental differences of mind and temperament, though the former more often subsume the latter than vice versa.

Whether we turn directly to his own writing, or simply to the fascinating collection of memoirs about him, what draws us to him is his perennial power to shake the insignificances out of a subject, and to cleanse our minds for the reception of what, in a memorable phrase, he called "the stability of truth." (He cleared my mind, said Sir Joshua Reynolds, of "a great deal of rubbish").

No writer in the language except Shakespeare has appealed to a wider variety of readers than Johnson. There are special reasons in each case, ranging from the trivial to the significant.

Taking for granted all the differences between the two men, we may also note a few qualities that they had in common — compassion, humor, good sense, a wide but clairvoyant knowledge of human nature, a strong imagination operating upon and by means of fact, and an uncanny readiness of language. We subsume these and perhaps other qualities when we say that what they share is *relevance* to almost every aspect of life: relevance and immense quotability. Whatever we experience, we find that they have been there before us, and we meet them on their way back (as the Greek epigrammatist said of Plato). Above all, we find that they have been there before us not as mere onlookers but as active participators; and what they say is put in a way we never want to forget. This honesty to the wealth of human experience, and the ability to word it, is what mankind seems to have agreed to value most during the past two millennia, however much we differ (or think we ought to differ) on what else we want. If a writer lacks it, men will in time leave him to the specialist. But given it, men will not only return to him but will forgive almost everything else.

———

JOINVILLE, Jean, Sire de (c.1224 – July 11, 1317). French historian. Born Champagne. Of noble family, he became seneschal of count of Champagne, Thibaut IV. Accompanied Louis IX on seventh crusade (1248–54), during which he shared the king's captivity and became his close friend. After his return, divided his time between court and his estates. Refused to join eighth crusade, pronouncing it ill-advised. Joinville's *Histoire de St. Louis* (completed 1309) provides a valuable account of the life and character of Louis IX and of the seventh crusade, is vividly informative on life in feudal France, and gives an engaging picture of the author himself, revealing his kindliness, humor, and human weaknesses.

TRANSLATIONS: *The History of St. Louis by John, Lord of Joinville, Seneschal of Champagne* tr. Joan Evans (London and New York 1938). *The Life of Saint Louis* tr. René Hague (London 1955).
REFERENCE: Gaston Paris *Jean, Sire de Joinville* (Paris 1897).

JONES, Inigo (July 15, 1573 – June 21, 1652). English architect and scenographer. Born London, son of a clothmaker. Went to Italy, perhaps as protégé of earl of Pembroke, but dates and movements are unknown. Returned to England to design masques for James I; from 1605 into 1640's staged continuous series of court masques. Visited Paris (1609) and traveled again in Italy (1613–14), where he studied remains of Roman architecture and Renaissance buildings of Palladio. Succeeded to office of surveyor to the crown (1615), an appointment which made him architect of any important state building project and responsible for maintenance and alteration of royal residences. His most important works are the Queen's House at Greenwich (1616–35), the Banqueting House at Whitehall (1619–22), the restoration of St. Paul's cathedral, London (begun 1634). He probably also advised on private residences both in London and in the country. Died in London. Jones is responsible for the introduction of Italian Renaissance principles to English architecture; his own tendency towards Palladianism largely determined the style of the English Georgian period.

REFERENCES: *Some Designs of Mr. Inigo Jones and Mr. Wm. Kent* (1744, reprinted Farnborough, England, 1967). J. Alfred Gotch *Inigo Jones* (London 1928, reprinted New York 1968). Allardyce Nicoll *Stuart Masques and the Renaissance Stage* (London 1937, reprinted New York 1964). Roy Strong *Festival Designs by Inigo Jones* (London 1967). John Summerson *Inigo Jones* (Harmondsworth, England, PB 1966).

INIGO JONES
BY
MARGARET WHINNEY

Inigo Jones was one of the greatest of English architects, and one of the most mysterious. In the eighteenth century, when his prestige was enormous, he was regarded as the man "who to adorn his country, introduced and rivaled Greek and Roman architecture." Exaggerated though that estimate may be, it contains a germ of truth, for Jones's buildings had a purity quite unknown in England before his day. In the reign of Elizabeth I, many Englishmen, both patrons and builders, were aware that the architecture of antiquity (which to them meant Rome, since Greece was virtually unknown) had a heroic quality which belonged to a golden age; and that architects in Italy, by using antique forms, were producing buildings which were much admired. Such Englishmen attempted to use antique forms, columns, the entablature above them, or triangular pediments, but they thought of them as decoration only, and did not grasp the rigorous system of proportions which governed every part of an antique building. Jones was beyond question the first Englishman to understand the idea of integrated design, and by about 1616 was applying it to his own buildings.

The mystery lies in how and why he arrived at this knowledge. His origins were humble, and though he certainly traveled in Italy before 1603, and was there long enough to acquire fluent Italian, it is not certainly known why or how he went. Nevertheless, on this first journey Jones does not seem to have been primarily interested in either antique or Italian Renaissance architecture. His first recorded employment in England is in 1603, working for the earl of Rutland as a picture maker; and in 1605 his career at the English court opened, not as an architect, but as the designer of the scenery and costumes for *The Masque of Blackness* for the queen.

Jones's work as a masque designer was of great importance in the history of the English theatre, for he introduced movable scenery and the proscenium arch, neither of which had played any part in the Elizabethan stage. The flavor of these lavish court entertainments is hard to capture, even though a large number of Jones's drawings for them still remain in the collection of the duke of Devonshire at Chatsworth House. The earlier ones, with words by Ben Jonson, show fantastic architecture which suggests an interest in France rather than Italy, and some highly complicated scene changes. Later he was to quarrel with Ben Jonson, who found Jones overbearing; and in the last masques, created for Charles I, the ever-changing spectacle, lit by the flicker of torches, must have been of ravishing beauty, fulfilling Jones's own description of them as "nothing else but pictures with light and motion."

Even in the early masque designs his exceptional skill as a draftsman is evident, but it became even more fluent after the important journey to Italy in 1613–14, when we know from his sketchbook that he studied, for instance, the etchings of Parmigianino, and also met Guercino. On this journey, too, he paid close attention to architecture, studying antique buildings, the reconstructions of them by the great Italian, Andrea Palladio, and also Palladio's own buildings in Vicenza. His annotated copy of Palladio's book *I Quattro Libri dell'Architettura* (1575) is, with the rest of his library, at Worcester College, Oxford.

On his return he became surveyor to the crown, and though he had produced a few immature designs before this time, his career as an architect really now begins. But again, it is not easy to assess, for of almost forty projects known from drawings or documents, only seven now remain, and some of these are fragments of the whole. Fortunately, in the Queen's House at Greenwich, the Banqueting House at Whitehall, and the Queen's Chapel at St. James's, three of his masterpieces remain, though none precisely as he left them.

All three reveal that he had now assimilated completely the concept of proportion, applied to the whole and to details alike. He borrowed freely from Italian architects, chiefly from Palladio, though he often simplified his borrowings. The Queen's House is a Palladian villa transferred to English soil, adjusted to fit a difficult site, but within as well as without mathematical proportions were (before later alterations) everywhere observed. The Banqueting House is an Italian palazzo in Whitehall. The two-storied exterior (since refaced) on a high basement, with Ionic and Corinthian columns enforcing the rhythm, is superb both in design and in detail, and the interior was nobly restored in 1965. Some fifteen years after it was built, Jones devised a great but abortive scheme for a vast new palace, but it is open to doubt if these permutations on the design of the Banqueting House would have had the dignity of the single building. The Queen's Chapel, small but monumental with its curved, coffered ceiling, has the gravity of a temple turned to Christian use, though the exterior does not show a temple form.

Jones was, however, to use a temple exterior of great severity for the church of St. Paul, Covent Garden

(1631), which still exists though much restored. He probably also designed, but did not himself execute, the "piazza" of uniform houses above open loggias in which it formerly stood, and his interest in uniform street architecture, later to become so characteristic of London, also found scope in the layout of Lincoln's Inn Fields. His grandest use of classical architecture can no longer be seen, for the great Corinthian portico which he added to the west end of St. Paul's cathedral was destroyed in the Great Fire of London in 1666. It must certainly have been without rival in northern Europe.

Jones was not a country house architect and no existing house can safely be attributed to him, though the small, simple, boxlike designs (known from drawings) for town houses may perhaps have been repeated in the country. But he was certainly responsible, with his assistant, John Webb, for the splendid interior decoration of the Double and Single Cube Rooms (after 1649) at Wilton House, Wiltshire. These are rich with gilded carving, elaborate doorcases and painted ceilings, but we know from a note written as early as 1614 that he approved richness in an interior, whereas outside a building should be "solid, proportionable according to the rules, masculine and unaffected." There can be no doubt that it was the way in which he carried out these precepts that earned the admiration of the eighteenth century, and made him the most influential of English architects.

JONGKIND, Johan Barthold (June 3, 1819 – Feb. 9, 1891). Dutch painter and etcher. Born Lattrop, near Rotterdam. Studied at The Hague under Andreas Schelfhout, and in Paris under L. G. Isabey and François Picot (1846–55). Exhibited at Paris Salon (1848 and 1852). After stay in Netherlands (1855–60), returned to Paris. Here he met Madame Fesser, an artist, who lived with him (from c.1863) and who rescued him from alcoholism and despair. During visits to Honfleur (1862 and 1865), met Eugène Boudin, the painter most often compared with him, and Monet. Settled at Côte-St.-André, Isère (1878), where he died. Jongkind is an important transitional figure in development of impressionism. In paintings (from c.1860 on) of the Seine, Dutch canals, Parisian streets, and seacoasts, he approached the methods of impressionists for rendering transitory atmospheric and lighting effects.

REFERENCE: Paul Signac *Jongkind* (Paris 1927).

JONSON, Ben (probably June 11, 1572 – Aug. 6, 1637). English dramatist and poet. Born in or near London, posthumous son of a clergyman. Studied under William Camden at Westminster School, where he learned the classics. After working briefly in stepfather's trade of bricklaying, joined army and fought in Flanders, returned to England, married, and worked as actor and playwright. First triumph in theatre *Every Man in His Humour* (1598); in same year killed actor Gabriel Spencer in a duel, but was released. *The Poetaster* (1601) satirized various literary contemporaries. Later works include classical tragedy *Sejanus* (1603) and the great comedies *Volpone* (1606), *Epicoene* (1609), *The Alchemist* (1610), and *Bartholomew Fair* (1614). Advanced by patrons, he collaborated with Inigo Jones on court masques, and received a royal pension (1616). After publication of his *Works* and unsuccessful production of *The Devil Is an Ass* (both 1616), popularity and productivity declined, but he retained great influence over younger writers. Died in London, buried in Westminster Abbey. Biographical material on Jonson contains several gaps and controversial dates, notably concerning his early years, his marriage (possibly to Anne Lewis, 1594), and his children. Much information dates from 1618, when Jonson took walking tour to Scotland and was entertained by Drummond of

Hawthornden, who recorded his conversation.

EDITIONS: *Works* ed. C. H. Herford and Percy and Evelyn Simpson (11 vols. Oxford 1925–52). *Complete Plays* (Everyman's Library 1910, latest ed. 2 vols. London and New York 1962). *Poems* ed. G. B. Johnston (London 1954 and Cambridge, Mass. 1965, also PB). *Bartholomew Fair* ed. E. A. Horsman (London 1960). *The Alchemist* ed. F. H. Mares (London 1967).

REFERENCES: Jonas A. Barish *Ben Jonson and the Language of Prose Comedy* (Cambridge, Mass. and Oxford 1960) and ed. *Ben Jonson: A Collection of Critical Essays* (Englewood Cliffs, N.J. 1963, also PB). H. W. Baum *The Satiric and the Didactic in Ben Jonson's Comedy* (Chapel Hill, N.C. 1947 and Oxford 1948). O. J. Campbell *Comicall Satyre and Shakespeare's Troilus and Cressida* (San Marino, Calif. 1938). Marchette Chute *Ben Jonson of Westminster* (New York 1953 and London 1954, also PB). John Hollander *Introduction to Ben Jonson* (New York 1961). Gabriele B. Jackson *Vision and Judgment in Ben Jonson's Dramas* (New Haven, Conn. 1968). Robert E. Knoll *Ben Jonson's Plays: An Introduction* (Lincoln, Nebr. 1965). Stephen Orgel *The Jonsonian Masque* (Cambridge, Mass. and Oxford 1965). Edward B. Partridge *The Broken Compass: A Study of the Major Comedies of Ben Jonson* (New York 1958). Wesley Trimpi *Ben Jonson's Poems: A Study of the Plain Style* (Stanford, Calif. 1962).

BEN JONSON
BY
ALFRED HARBAGE

The first notice of Jonson as writer comes in 1597, when he was jailed as coauthor of a play alleged to be libelous. He was then twenty-five, and had toured with provincial actors after bearing arms in Flanders, where he killed a Spaniard in a personal sortie. He had also, though the least domestic of men, had children by a wife he succinctly described as "a shrew, yet honest." Earlier it had been his traumatic lot to be put to bricklaying by his stepfather after becoming fiercely devoted to classical learning under Camden at Westminster School. His life continued stormy, marked by personal feuds (one of them lethal), several imprisonments, a twelve-year span of defiant conversion to Catholicism (then illegal), and a series of theatrical, scholarly, and critical "wars," some fought single-handed. Toughest of contenders, he survived, to die at sixty-five as a national celebrity — literary dictator and, in effect, poet laureate, more richly rewarded in money and prestige than any earlier English author. Toward the end, though immobilized by weight, wine bibbing, and paralysis, he was lionized by the "sons of Ben," a shoal of aristocratic young writers indebted to the poet who, "brought up poorly," had raised himself by his bootstraps to the peak of Parnassus.

His success is the more amazing in view of the dismal standing of professional authorship in his day, and his lack of good looks or good manners. He was gross, voracious, truculent, and vain, relying on frontal assault to make others take him at his own price. This proved less exorbitant than at first appeared. He was superbly gifted, with intellectual energy, literary acumen, and command of language. Elizabethan drama was prevailingly romantic, heroic, humane when he entered the lists, and in campaigning for the kind in which he believed he could excel, realistic, satiric, "classical," he dealt Shakespeare glancing blows, but it is absurd to suppose that he was blind to the genius of the reigning playwright. There were mossy seams in his own craggy nature, and some of the best things ever said about Shakespeare were said by him.

Much of Jonson's voluminous writing, dramatic, nondramatic, quasi-dramatic, was collected in *Works* edited by himself. After a success with *Every Man in His Humour,* played by Shakespeare's company in 1598, he took the bit in his teeth and wrote *Every Man Out of His Humour, Cynthia's Revels,* and *The Poetaster,* antipopular comedies which proved (understandably) unpopular. His "correct" Roman tragedy *Sejanus,* like his later *Catiline,* won only a delayed *succès d'estime.* Through the reign of his patron James I (1603–25), he joined in a querulous partnership with the able set designer Inigo Jones to create yearly masques for the court. *The Hue and Cry After Cupid* (1608) offers a good example of his finely wrought speeches, dialogues, and songs, but the masques in general have faded with the splendor of the royal balls they framed. His folk pastoral *The Sad Shepherd* is an original and appealing fragment, his later comedies *The Devil Is an Ass* and *The Staple of News* good but prolix, his last three comedies bad. The works of enduring general interest are a sheaf of lyrical and occasional poems, his critical *obiter dictu,* and the comedies of his prime: *Every Man in His Humour* and *Eastward Hoe* (written with Marston and Chapman), and the less genial but more powerful *Volpone, The Alchemist, Epicoene, or The Silent Woman,* and *Bartholomew Fair.*

In its fully realized form, Jonsonian comedy is unique and should not be viewed in the context of the ideal, human, or sophisticated comedies of Shakespeare, Molière, or Congreve. It presents farcical intrigue in a bourgeois milieu composed of a few colorless "straight" characters and a host of colorful crooked ones, the latter symbolizing social aberrations and psychological obsessions, dubbed by Jonson "humors." While derived from the "new comedy" of Menander, Plautus, and Terence, and deferring more or less consistently to neoclassical prescriptions of form, it is more nearly akin in spirit to the boisterous destructiveness of the "old comedy" of Aristophanes. In fact, medieval grotesquerie lies under the classical skin, and we are reminded of details in the paintings of Bosch and the Pieter Bruegels. The "plots" are really situations, exploited without restraint, or even rationality, and as the immoral scoundrels prey upon the amoral fools, the satire is too brutal to have much social significance. But the episodes are so hilariously ingenious, and the language, whether prose or verse, so nervous and compact of vivid detail, that a kind of demonic energy is generated. We are exhilarated as by poetry — the ugly sublime. Our laughter would be intolerable if directed at human beings, or even their reasonable facsimiles in other forms of drama, but our victims here have a saving unreality. The plays effect a catharsis of malice and hostility.

William Drummond of Hawthornden in his *Conversations* gives us a vivid if unflattering contemporary portrait of Jonson. The modern appraisals by T. S. Eliot and Edmund Wilson are acute but dampening, the first making us feel guilty if we do not enjoy Jonson, the second if we do. Much contemporary criticism is brilliantly analytical but so cerebral that it depresses, especially when its tone is somber and scolding as the critics hold aloft the Jonsonian torch in defiance of Shakespearean bullies. In *Bartholomew Fair* appears a puppet show, with comment by Zeal-of-the-Land Busy. As dramatic criticism it leaves something to be desired, but it is so funny that it pulls us back to the Fair. Perhaps here is our cue. Commentators need not try to be funny, but we should be more aware of the distinction between defining what amuses us and demonstrating that we are amused — by the one who, at the very least, must be reckoned the king of puppeteers, creator of the greatest Punch and Judy show on earth.

JORDAENS, Jacob (May 19, 1593 – Oct. 18, 1678). Flemish painter. Born and died in Antwerp, and spent an uneventful life there. Son of a prosperous merchant, he was from an early age a pupil of Rubens's teacher Adam van Noort, whose daughter Catharina he married (1616). Jordaens was a prolific baroque painter of religious and historical subjects of genre and portraits, all of which he treated with earthiness and love of the commonplace. Successor to Rubens as most popular painter in Flanders, he considerably resembles the latter in style. Though he lacks Rubens's strong sense of composition, his paintings communicate sensuous delight with their rich glowing colors and robust figures. Well-known works include two early paintings of *Adoration of the Shepherds* (National Museum, Stockholm, and Musée de Peinture et Sculpture, Grenoble), *The Satyr and the Peasant* (Musées Royaux des Beaux Arts, Brussels), decorative paintings at Huis ten Bosch, near The Hague (1652), and *Jesus Among the Doctors* (1663, Museum of Mainz).

REFERENCES: Horst Gerson and E. H. ter Kuile *Art and Architecture in Belgium, 1600–1800* (Harmondsworth, England, and Baltimore 1960). Leo van Puyvelde *Jordaens* (Paris 1953). Max Rooses *J. Jordaens: His Life and Work* (tr. London and New York 1908).

JOSEPHUS, Flavius (original name Joseph ben Matthias) (c. A.D. 37–95). Jewish historian. Born Jerusalem, of aristocratic family. Studied Hebrew and Greek, then became a Pharisee. After serving as delegate to Nero in Rome (A.D. 64), was appointed governor of Galilee and (from 66) took part in Jewish revolt against the Romans. When the stronghold he defended at Jotapata was taken (67), won favor of

Roman general Vespasian by prophesying that he would become emperor. Later freed, he settled in Rome after fall of Jerusalem, adopted Vespasian's surname Flavius, received pension and citizenship. Here he wrote *The Jewish War* (75–79), an important historical document, and *Antiquities of the Jews* (93–94), a history of the Jews from the Creation to A.D. 66. Other works are his autobiography and two essays eloquently defending the Jews against the anti-Semitic Alexandrian scholar Apion. He died in Rome.

TRANSLATIONS: *Works* tr. Henry St. John Thackeray and others (Loeb Classical Library 9 vols. Cambridge, Mass. and London 1926–65). *The Jewish War* tr. G. A. Williamson (Harmondsworth, England, and Baltimore PB 1959).
REFERENCES: Leon Bernstein *Flavius Josephus: His Time and His Critics* (New York 1938). R. J. H. Shutt *Studies in Josephus* (London 1961). Henry St. John Thackeray *Josephus: The Man and the Historian* (1929, reprinted New York 1968). G. A. Williamson *The World of Josephus* (London 1964 and Boston 1965).

JOSQUIN DES PRÉS. *See* DES PRÉS, Josquin.

JOYCE, James (Augustine) (Feb. 2, 1882 – Jan. 13, 1941). Irish novelist and poet. Born Dublin. Received classical Jesuit education at Clongowes Wood College (1888–91), Belvedere College (1893–99), and University College, Dublin (1899–1902). Left for Paris (1902), but returned (1903) to see his dying mother and remained two years, teaching school and beginning work on autobiographical novel *Stephen Hero* (surviving portions published 1944). Moved again to Continent (1904) with Nora Barnacle (whom he married 1931) and worked as language teacher in Pola and Trieste. While Joyce was attempting to publish short story collection *Dubliners*, a book of verse, *Chamber Music*, appeared (1907). *Dubliners* was published in 1914, the year *A Portrait of the Artist as a Young Man* (rewritten version of *Stephen Hero*) began to appear serially in London journal the *Egoist*. Suffering from chronic, severe eye disease, he underwent (from 1917) numerous eye operations and periods of total blindness while he was writing. Moved to Zurich (1915) and began work on *Ulysses*, portions of which appeared in the *Little Review*, a New York periodical (1918–20), until halted by court order. Joyce settled in Paris (1920), where Sylvia Beach's bookstore Shakespeare and Company published *Ulysses* (1922). It was banned in U.S. until Judge John M. Woolsey's celebrated court decision (1933). Now the focal point of literary avant-garde circles, Joyce worked for seventeen years on *Finnegans Wake* (1939). After fall of France (1940), returned to Zurich, where he died.

EDITIONS: *A Shorter Finnegans Wake* ed. Anthony Burgess (New York and London 1967). *Letters* ed. Stuart Gilbert and Richard Ellman (3 vols. London and New York 1957/66). *Critical Writings* ed. Ellsworth Mason and Richard Ellman (London and New York 1959, also PB). *Giacomo Joyce* ed. Richard Ellman (New York and London 1968).
REFERENCES: Sylvia Beach *Shakespeare and Company* (New York 1959 and London 1960, also PB). Samuel Beckett and others *Our Exagmination Round His Factification for Incamination of Work in Progress* (1929, new ed. New York and London 1962). Bernard Benstock *Joyce-Again's Wake* (Seattle and London PB 1965). Frank Budgen *James Joyce and the Making of Ulysses* (1934, new ed. Bloomington, Ind. PB and London PB 1960). R. H. Deming ed. *Joyce and the Critical Heritage* (2 vols. New York 1970). Leon Edel *James Joyce: The Last Journey* (New York 1947). Richard Ellman *James Joyce* (New York and London 1959, also PB). Gisele Freund and V. B. Carleton *James Joyce in Paris: His Final Years* (New York 1965 and London 1966). Stuart Gilbert *James Joyce's Ulysses* (2nd ed. New York and London 1952, also PB). S. L. Goldberg *The Classical Temper* (London 1961). Stanislaus Joyce *My Brother's Keeper* (London and New York 1958, also PB) and *Dublin Diary* (London and Ithaca, N.Y. 1962). Patricia Hutchins *James Joyce's World* (London and New York 1957). Hugh Kenner *Dublin's Joyce* (London 1955 and Bloomington, Ind. 1956, also

PB). Harry Levin *James Joyce: A Critical Introduction* (2nd ed. Norfolk, Conn. and London 1960, also PB). Wyndham Lewis *Time and Western Man* (London 1927). A. Walton Litz *The Art of James Joyce* (New York and London 1961, also PB). Marvin Magalaner and Richard M. Kain *Joyce: The Man, the Work, the Reputation* (New York 1956 and London 1957, also PB). J. Mitchell Morse *The Sympathetic Alien: James Joyce and Catholicism* (New York and London 1959). Margaret C. Solomon *Eternal Geomater: The Sexual Universe of Finnegans Wake* (Carbondale, Ill. and London PB 1969). William Y. Tindall *James Joyce* (New York 1950, also PB) and *A Reader's Guide of Finnegans Wake* (New York and London 1969, also PB).

JAMES JOYCE
BY
LEON EDEL

James Joyce created two large and highly original works: *Ulysses*, a modern "epic" of alienated urban man, and *Finnegans Wake*, a linguistic dream book woven out of myth and fable — man's eternal imaginings. He also created a large legend for himself. Poets in the past have complained of the world's indifference. Joyce called this indifference a conspiracy. His martyr-sensibility turned friends into enemies, his expatriation into "banishment." He harbored imaginary grudges, and by way of "silence, exile and cunning" revenged himself on friends and foes alike by planting hidden barbs in his writings. He was one of the great "injustice collectors" of literary history. He invited the contumely of the world so that he might vent his rage upon it. The world finally obliged. It banned his book — and defeated his anger by giving him renown. It could not fathom his labyrinths, but it called him a genius, since he possessed answers to his own brilliant riddles. Almost from the first it acknowledged his necromancy of words. Not since the days of Milton (some said) had there been an ear as sensitive to the music of the English language.

His work is a mixture of genius and charlatanry: the imagination of a poet harnessed to the mind of a pedant and journalist. *Ulysses* is the *reductio ad absurdum* of the naturalist movement; conceived as a mythopoetic picture of man's daily Odyssey in Dublin — or any city — and invoking the myth of the Wandering Jew, it resolved itself into a mixture of styles and methods, showpieces of realism, hidden meanings, pseudo-erudition. The birth of a child in one episode provides Joyce with the occasion for parodies of the evolution of English literature, an inventory of general obstetrical lore, a recounting of the Darwinian theory while imitating the mounting intoxication of a group of medical students. *Ulysses* is uncanny in its prophecy of the vocal-visual of television, its use of modern "camera" angles, its language of advertising: a harbinger of pop art. Joyce's sharpest instruments were those of mimicry and parody; he mocks (as Flaubert did in *Bouvard et Pécuchet*) the received language and ideas of the West. In spite of its great vitality and originality, its inventories and parodies, *Ulysses* ends by giving us a city choked in its own rubbish, a great irrelevant picture of the quotidian.

Reflected in the solipsistic wanderings of Joyce's two protagonists — the would-be artist Stephen Dedalus and the literal-minded advertising solicitor Leopold Bloom — is Joyce's divorce from his fellow men. He was a poet whose reality was words rather than people. A superstitious, self-absorbed, inward-turned, ritualized being, full of fears and phobias, Joyce (aided by his verbal instrument) could render as no

one before him man's dialogues with himself. "We walk through ourselves," he says in *Ulysses*, "meeting robbers, ghosts, giants, old men, young men, wives, widows, brothers-in-love. But always meeting ourselves." This sense of his being shut in, gave him a mastery of the inner monologue; and with it he inaugurated the avant-garde phase of the twentieth-century novel — the fiction of the "stream of consciousness." Here his influence was deeply felt, and on writers as different as Virginia Woolf and William Faulkner.

His letters, the unhappy scribbles of a gifted pen, reveal penury, suffering, improvidence, self-indulgence, drunkenness, hate: they speak for a Joyce-against-the-world who reconverted this into a legend of the world against Joyce. Yet Russell and Yeats had befriended him in his youth; and his difficulties with publishers were no greater than those of any untried writer with a sheaf of verses and tales under his arm. Almost alone among literary artists, Joyce asked the world to recognize his genius before he had given proof of it.

His early verses were muted and minor; his single play (*Exiles*) is watered-down Ibsen — for Joyce could people the stage only with Joyce. His tales published as *Dubliners*, are vivid, ironic pictures of his bourgeois Catholic life in Ireland. Mannered and marred by preciosity, they leave us with neither the feeling of the vitality of a Maupassant nor the humanity of a Chekhov. Joyce's most original work of this earlier time was his *Portrait of the Artist as a Young Man*, a reworking of an earlier unpublished novel he had called *Stephen Hero*. Here Joyce's ability to capture inner experience enabled him to describe the development of an artistic sensibility by means of perceptual experience and the inner crisis of adolescence. With an economy of art, and in a sustained, poetic narrative, this novel remains Joyce's least idiosyncratic work, the one most accessible to the public.

Celebrated, endowed — but as improvident as ever — Joyce spent the last two decades of his life writing his night-book *Finnegans Wake,* a work that drew on the wit and humor of the unconscious. It is a pastiche of many languages, a written Tower of Babel. Many of its passages recall the word salads of schizophrenia, save that Joyce's salads possess method as well as madness. The book has exquisite moments of incantation and reverie, evocations of whimsical tenderness and a kind of Chaplinesque self-mockery. But as always there is excess and surfeit, and much pedantry. The word juggler never knew when to stop.

Joyce's work, for all its insistence upon the literal and upon "reality," is profoundly subjective and personal. He pulled the world into himself and reorganized it into monstrous mazes like ancient systems of casuistry. Scholars and pedants drawn into the systems have endless delight in the code breaking and puzzle solving. Those who prefer not to be caught up in them still can recognize the obsessive brilliance of Joyce's mind, and his endless linguistic diversions. There is however a kind of moral flabbiness in the work, an enormous self-indulgence. Behind the acrobatics, the comic genius, the vaudeville, one discerns a picture of a terrible despair. The Joycean word music reaches us as a kind of dirge, sung over the flotsam and jetsam of civilization.

***

JUVENAL (Decimus Junius Juvenalis) (c. A.D. 60–c.140). Roman satirist. Little reliable information exists concerning his life. Born probably in Aquinum, he lived in poverty in Rome as client of the rich, and was a friend of Martial. His sixteen satires in hexameters, published in five books (c.100–127) describe with forceful outrage the degenerate life of the Romans, chiefly as he observed it during reign of Domitian (81–96). Most famous are *Satire I,* which exclaims that "indignation will produce verses" on the evils of the time; *III,* the model for Samuel Johnson's *London,* which describes the wretched conditions in Rome, such as high costs, dangerously ill-constructed tenements, noise, crime; *VI,* on immorality and decadent luxury; *X,* known as *The Vanity of Human Wishes* from Johnson's imitation, where appears the familiar phrase "bread and circuses" as the people's sole desire, and in which Juvenal cites the ideal goal as *"Mens sana in corpore sano."* His satires, in contrast to the good-natured ridicule of Horace's, are full of moralistic, bitter denunciation. For their power and superb rhetoric, they have served as models, especially in English literature, and are frequently quoted.

TRANSLATIONS: *Satires* tr. Hubert Creekmore (New York 1963); tr. Peter Green (Harmondsworth, England and Baltimore PB 1967); tr. Rolfe Humphries (Bloomington, Ind. 1958).

REFERENCES: I. G. Scott *The Grand Style in the Satires of Juvenal* (Northampton, Mass. 1927). Gilbert Highet *Juvenal the Satirist* (London 1954, also PB).

KABAPHES, Konstantinos Petrou. *See* CAVAFY, C. P.

KAFKA, Franz (July 3, 1883 – June 3, 1924). Czech writer. Born Prague, of well-to-do Jewish parents. Domineering father may have been responsible for the sense of guilt evident in K., the hero of Kafka's novels. He received law degree from German University of Prague (1906), then went to work in insurance office in Prague. Only a few of his stories were published during lifetime, including *Der Verwandlung* (1915, tr. *The Metamorphosis* 1948) and *In der Strafkolinie* (1919, tr. *The Penal Colony* 1948). Contracted (1917) tuberculosis, which eventually caused his death in sanatorium in Klosterneuburg, Austria. Engaged twice; also lived with Dora Dymant during his last year. Most of Kafka's work was published posthumously, against his express wishes, by his friend Max Brod, who put together the manuscripts of the unfinished novels: *Der Prozess* (1925, tr. *The Trial* 1937), *Das Schloss* (1926, tr. *The Castle* 1930), and *Amerika* (1927, tr. 1938). Other works include *The Diaries,* edited by Max Brod (2 vols. 1948–49), *Parables* (tr. 1947), and two volumes of letters (1952–54).

REFERENCES: Max Brod *Franz Kafka: A Biography* (tr. 2nd ed. New York 1960, also PB). Wilhelm Emrich *Franz Kafka: A Critical Study of His Writings* (tr. New York 1968). Angel Flores ed. *The Kafka Problem* (1946, rev. ed. New York 1963). Paul Goodman *Kafka's Prayer* (New York 1947). Erich Heller *The Disinherited Mind* (1952, new ed. New York 1957 and London 1959, also PB). Heinz Politzer *Franz Kafka: Parable and Paradox* (1962, rev. ed. Ithaca, N.Y., also PB). Herbert Tauber *Franz Kafka: An Interpretation of His Works* (tr. 1948, reprinted Port Washington, N.Y. 1968).

∿

FRANZ KAFKA
BY
GEORGE STEINER

When Franz Kafka died in 1924 he had published a few stories and one or two fragments of work in progress. Forty years later a partial list of translations and editions of his work, of Kafka biography and commentary, ran to more than four hundred pages and more than thirty languages. During his lifetime and for twenty years after, Kafka was remembered by a handful of friends as a marvelously secret being whose few known works were inaccessible to all but scattered survivors of the lost culture of German-Jewish Prague. Yet in the late 1950's — when Kafka could still, ought still to have been alive — W. H. Auden could say, as if stating an obvious truth, "Had one to name the author who comes nearest to bearing the same kind of relation to our age as Dante, Shakespeare and Goethe bore to theirs, Kafka is the first one would think of."

Does this metamorphosis (that word itself being Kafka's), this change of an intensely private, local act of imagination into the idiom of an age correspond to the actual meaning of the work? Would Kafka have wanted it?

This is a very difficult question. Notoriously, Kafka allowed his friend and executor Max Brod the option of destroying all his unpublished writings. According to Kafka's instructions *The Trial, The Castle* and *America* could simply have vanished. Nothing in his guarded, shadowy references to his own art points to any common lust for survival, let alone world glory: "Private vestiges of my human weakness are printed and even sold, because my friends . . . have set their minds on making literature of them, and because I am not strong enough to destroy these testimonials of my solitude." Here the term *literature* may be the key.

Kafka regarded his enterprise as something radically different from literature in the ordinary sense. He alluded with stinging distaste to the pretensions and mendacities of literary ambition. To him as to Kierkegaard, one of the very few presences who in any real degree influenced Kafka, the act of writing was a dread necessity, a visitation from some hidden, man-consuming place of truth. To write in the only vein that mattered was to run the risk, at almost every word, of self-mutilation, of being harried by the counterattacks of a world unwilling to be negated or probed by re-creation. It was to relinquish, with terrible lucidity, the blessed chaos of ordinary existence, of love, in plain fact, of life itself. Kafka's long illness, his successive renunciations of marriage (the *Letters to Milena* are the most incomplete, the most moving of modern love letters), the careful welcome he prepared for solitude and death — these were deliberate down payments, security offered against "the impossibility of not writing." A truth, a perception purchased at less than the cost of the world was merely *literature*.

That work wrested at such cost from his own being should today be our vulgate might not have seemed to Kafka an unqualified reward. Has this most singular of seers been "distorted to a fantastic shadow on the wall of time"?

No doubt there are several Kafkas. The Prague insurance assessor steeped in local humor and acting as a satirist of a particular Austro-Hungarian political and social context is one part of the constant mask. The spinner of Talmudic parables, the recently emancipated Jew who translates into a secular idiom the conventions of secrecy, the habits of riddling allegory inherited from rabbis and cabbalists is another. But the world impact of Kafka's fictions, the fact that his tribunals and mazes have become passwords to our century, point to a central vision. In his uncanny aloneness Kafka stumbled, as it were, across the threshold of our general condition. He found for it an expressive myth both simple as is a child's drawing of terror and encompassing as is Dante's metaphor of the voyage.

That expressive myth is the tragicomic confrontation of structure and monad, of complex assemblage and naked man. The structure can be an unfathomable edifice of legality as in *The Trial*, a continent of the absurd as in *Amerika*, a total bureaucracy as in *The Castle*. In *The Penal Colony* it is a machine, part printing press, part instrument of torture. In *The Metamorphosis* Kafka miraculously implants the monad inside the structure: Gregor is encased by the shard and delicate articulations of the beetle. In Kafka's last tale, *The Burrow*, a labyrinthine honeycomb first shelters and then entombs a lone, harried lodger.

However intimate its spiritual and psychosomatic roots (there is, obviously but not very significantly, a

"Freudian," a pathologically conditioned Kafka), this mythic form proved prophetic. Kafka foresaw, in an act of clairvoyance more telling than explicit prophecy or political argument, the world of the death camps; he heard the knock of the faceless policemen on the night door; he saw human beings transmuted to vermin and swept into garbage, exactly as Gregor is at the end of the story. No actual narrative of the Stalinist purges is more authentic than *The Trial*. No record of Auschwitz conveys so much of the obscene intimacies of torturer and victim as does *The Penal Colony*. It is in Kafka even more than in Marx that we find the controlling insight of our historical epoch — the absolute extension to man of the logic of mass production, the transformation of politics with their potential of anarchic challenge into the inertial, self-perpetuating motion of technology.

The waiting rooms in our anonymous hospitals, the punch cards on which our lives are programmed, the visas we hunger for in vain, the Chinese walls we have built across our cities, all these are a Kafka scenario. We recognize them as his, we diminish before them to the stature of the "little man," of the harried monad whom Kafka and Chaplin have made our mirror. Such is the shaping truth of Kafka's vision that one sometimes wonders whether he did not, unwittingly, help bring on what he foresaw. One thing is certain — and no other writer, in any language, has done this: this secluded spirit, almost anonymous as are the distant classics, claims for his own, and has very nearly appropriated, a letter from everyman's alphabet. Set down K. — and the rest follows.

KANDINSKY, Wassily (Dec. 4, 1866 – Dec. 17, 1944). Russian painter, founder of abstract expressionism. Born Moscow. Studied law at Moscow University (1886–93) and served briefly on faculty there before going to Munich (1896) to study painting at Azbé School and Royal Academy. Traveled in Europe and North Africa (1903–1908), then returned to Munich to live with painter Gabrielle Münter in Murnau, a village outside Munich (1909–14). There Kandinsky produced the first nonrepresentational paintings (1910), thereby initiating one of the major artistic movements of the twentieth century. Organized his work henceforth into three series: *Improvisations, Compositions*, and *Impressions*. They are characterized by dynamic movement, vivid color, violent line, and exuberance. Founded, with Franz Marc, the Blue Rider (Der Blaue Reiter) group (1911), and formulated theory of abstract art in *Über das Geistige in der Kunst* (1912, tr. *Concerning the Spiritual in Art* 1914). Lived in Russia from outbreak of World War I until 1921, and founded Museum of Pictorial Culture. Returned to Germany, and was appointed professor at Bauhaus (1922). With Paul Klee, Lyonel Feininger, and Alexei von Jawlensky founded the Blue Four group (1924). When Hitler closed the Bauhaus (1933), moved to Paris, where he lived until his death. Exhibited in London (1938), in Paris and New York. Married twice. Last period of his work characterized by geometric forms and balanced compositions in quiet colors, but the vigor and imaginative variety of his invention still prevailed.

EDITION: *Rückblicke* (1913, tr. *Reminiscences* in *Modern Artists on Art* tr. Robert L. Herbert New York 1965).

REFERENCES: Alfred H. Barr *Masters of Modern Art* (New York 1954). Will Grohmann *Wassily Kandinsky: Life and Work* (tr. New York 1958). J. Lassaigne *Kandinsky: A Biographical and Critical Study* (tr. New York 1964).

KAZANTZAKIS, Nikos (Feb. 18, 1883 – Oct. 26, 1957). Greek writer. Born Herakleion, Crete. Received B.A. from University of Athens (1906), studied law there, then went to Paris, where he studied philosophy under Henri Bergson. After period of withdrawal and asceticism, turned to life of political action, became director general of Greek Ministry of Public Welfare (1919–27), president of Union of Socialist Workers (1945), and minister of state (1945–46). As journalist and as cultural adviser to various governments and organizations, Kazantzakis made extensive travels throughout the world. Spent last years in France, where he served as director of UNESCO Bureau of Translation (1947–48). Married twice. Died at Freiburg-in-Breisgau, Germany. Kazantzakis is best known internationally as author of epic poem *The Odyssey: A Modern Sequel* (1938, tr. 1958) and novels *Zorba the Greek* (1943, tr. 1953), *The Greek Passion* (1948, tr. 1954), *The Last Temptation of Christ* (1951, tr. 1960), and others. His enormous literary output also includes philosophical essays and plays.

REFERENCES: Eleni Kazantzakis *Nikos Kazantzakis: A Biography* (tr. New York 1968). Pandelis Prevelakis *Nikos Kazantzakis and His Odyssey: A Study of the Poet and the Poem* (tr. New York 1961).

KEATS, John (Oct. 31, 1795 – Feb. 23, 1821). English poet. Born London, eldest child of a livery stable keeper. At school in Enfield (1803–10) became friend of Charles Cowden Clarke, the headmaster's son, who encouraged his early learning. Orphaned (1810), the Keats children's affairs were turned over to guardians. John was apprenticed to a surgeon (1810), registered as medical student at Guy's Hospital, London (1815), qualified licentiate of Society of Apothecaries (1816). His sonnet *O Solitude* appeared in Leigh Hunt's *Examiner* (May 1816), and that autumn, when he wrote the sonnet on Chapman's Homer and joined Hunt's literary circle, marks the beginning of his wholehearted commitment to poetry. Published first volume of verse, *Poems* (1817), and *Endymion* (1818). That year he began *Hyperion,* met Fanny Brawne, later his fiancée, and nursed his brother Tom until his death, in December, from tuberculosis. Wrote (1819) his great odes and *To Autumn,* included in *Lamia, Isabella, The Eve of St. Agnes, and Other Poems* (pub-

lished July 1820). Seriously ill with tuberculosis, he sailed for Italy with painter Joseph Severn that September and died the following February in Rome, where he is buried. Other important works include *La Belle Dame Sans Merci* (1819), the sonnets *When I Have Fears* and *Bright Star,* a second unfinished version of *Hyperion* (1819), and the incomparable *Letters*.

EDITIONS: *Poetical Works* ed. H. W. Garrod (2nd ed. London and New York 1958, also PB). *Letters* ed. Hyder E. Rollins (2 vols. Cambridge, Mass. and Cambridge, England, 1958). *The Keats Circle: Letters and Papers* ed. Hyder E. Rollins (2nd ed. 2 vols. Cambridge, Mass. and Oxford 1965).

REFERENCES: Walter Jackson Bate *John Keats* (Cambridge, Mass. and Oxford 1963, also PB) and ed. *Keats: A Collection of Critical Essays* (Englewood Cliffs, N.J. 1964, also PB). Douglas Bush *John Keats* (New York and London 1966, also PB). Robert Gittings *John Keats* (London and Boston 1968, also PB). Aileen Ward *John Keats: The Making of a Poet* (London and New York 1963, also PB).

🖝

JOHN KEATS
BY
ROBERT GITTINGS

Keats is the poet of immediate identification with the object or sensation described. This follows from his idea of the nature of a poet, itself a rationalization of his own personal temperament. Contrasting himself, not altogether accurately, with the more detached or "egotistical sublime" poet, such as Wordsworth, he defined his own way of composition as a complete absorption in the essence of his subject. At their best, Keats's poems seem to be a passing on of experience without any intervention by the poet, an almost nonliterary process. Yet the paradox of his brief writing life, at most six years, is how intensely literary it was. "The greatest men in the world were the Poets, and to rank among them was the chief object of his ambition," a fellow student noted. "My occupation is entirely literary," he himself wrote at the height of his powers.

His poetry begins encumbered by reading; nearly all his juvenile work is feeble imitation. He remained susceptible to literary influence, sometimes to a dangerous degree. *Isabella, or The Pot of Basil,* which he himself came to reject, was written in a conscious attempt to copy the style of older poets such as Chaucer and Shakespeare, and to avoid modernisms, as the poem itself announces; *Lamia,* though a fine technical achievement, has the air of a hybrid, partly owing to the intense study of Dryden's couplets which led to its composition. What saved Keats was his voracious appreciation of life itself, a quality that appears more and more in his letters, which shake off their literary models far more swiftly than his poems. Allied to this was his craving for thought, a search for first principles in everything, a "burning" of mental energy which his friends noticed, and which even led him to suspect philosophy to be a finer activity than poetry. He could exclaim, "O for a Life of Sensations rather than of Thoughts" — using "Sensations" in the sense of concrete experiences — but within six months realize the "difference of high Sensations with and without knowledge," and come down emphatically on the side of knowledge. Keats's letters are the record of an astonishingly quick growth to maturity.

His poems, in their turn, show a similar progress. As a person he was overwhelmed, "annihilated" in his own word, by every new influence; but as an active creator, he tried to shape each fresh experience to his idea of poetry. In spite of his early love of Spenser, in imitation of whom he wrote his first lines, his laborious study of Milton and a passionate identification with Shakespeare, his poetic guide was Wordsworth, who appears more often in Keats's letters than any other poet, and whose ideas and expressions pervade Keats's best poems. Though rejecting half of what Wordsworth had written, and partly repelled by his personality when they met, Keats recognized in the older man his idea of what poetry should be, vivid concrete sensations at the service of deep creative thought. In his own description of human life as a "Mansion of Many Apartments," Keats praised Wordsworth's genius as explorative of the "dark passages" of man's profoundest experience. At the same time, his verdict that Wordsworth had reached this eminence because of the general advance in the history of human intellect contains, perhaps, Keats's own confidence that he himself would ultimately outdo his master.

In poetic technique, Keats evolved a style completely his own, which found its true voice, by an early freak, in his sonnet *On First Looking into Chapman's Homer,* written before he was twenty-one. The violent attacks on *Endymion* in *Blackwood's Edinburgh Magazine* and the *Quarterly Review,* far from discouraging him as used to be thought, probably determined him all the more to infuse into the poems he then wrote the principles of prosody and melody in verse, which he had already worked out. The internal assonances and linked vowel sounds which strikingly mark the opening of *Hyperion* come to a triumphant expression in the narrative *The Eve of St. Agnes.* Meanwhile his philosophic meditation, brought to its highest pitch in his theories of spiritual growth, which he named "the vale of Soul-making," was matched by a poetic technique expressed in the great odes of spring and summer 1819, *To Psyche, On Melancholy, To a Nightingale* and *On a Grecian Urn,* together with their later companion piece, the poem *To Autumn.* They are the poems in which Keats's finest thought and essential nature find totally their poetic expression. At the same time, his recasting of the unfinished *Hyperion* into a personal and spiritual narrative, *The Fall of Hyperion: A Dream,* though itself unfinished, forecasts the type of poetry he might have achieved but for his death, and is itself a huge technical advance to a freedom and certainty never heard before in his work, except in the magical *La Belle Dame Sans Merci.*

The dramatic pattern of Keats's life has tended to obscure judgment about his work. On the other hand, the events of his life were in many senses the food on which he nourished his poems, which are often, as was recognized in his own time, a form of disguised autobiography. His resilient, thoughtful, and heroic character, in a life full of stress, shines through all his letters, which now seem a body of achievement comparable with his poems. Keats, in spite of his abundantly human nature, has the quality that makes legends, summed up in his own words on Shakespeare: "Shakspeare led a life of Allegory; his works are the comments on it."

KEMPIS, Thomas à. *See* THOMAS À KEMPIS.

KENT, William (c.1685 – Apr. 12, 1748). English architect, landscape gardener, and painter. Born Bridlington, Yorkshire. Group of patrons sent him to Rome (1709–19), where he collected art works for their houses, studied painting, and met future patron and friend, the earl of Burlington. Returned to England with Burlington, who employed him as interior decorator. Through him Kent was commissioned to decorate interiors at Kensington Palace (1722–25) and appointed master carpenter of the king's works (1726). Later became master mason and deputy surveyor of the king's works (1735) and principal court painter (1739). As architect, usually conformed to Palladian principles for exteriors of his buildings, while designing interiors of heavy baroque magnificence; and at Esher Place, Surrey (c.1730), provided first English example of Gothic revival. Famous buildings include Holkham Hall, Norfolk (1734), his masterpiece; 44 Berkeley Square, London (1742); Horse Guards building, Whitehall, London (1750–58). As garden designer, Kent initiated the landscape school, introducing concept of informal, "natural" grounds as contrast to severe architecture. Examples of his gardens are at Stowe, Buckinghamshire, and Rousham, Oxfordshire. Died in London.

REFERENCES: *Some Designs of Mr. Inigo Jones and Mr. Wm. Kent* (1744, reprinted Farnborough, England, 1967). Margaret Jourdain *The Work of William Kent* (London 1948 and New York 1949). Sacheverell Sitwell *British Architects and Craftsmen* (3rd ed. London and New York 1947).

KIERKEGAARD, Søren (Aabye) (May 5, 1813 – Nov. 11, 1855). Danish philosopher and theologian. Born and died in Copenhagen; son of a wealthy wool merchant. Studied at Copenhagen University (1830–40). On breaking his engagement to Regina Olsen (1841) departed for Berlin, then settled permanently in Copenhagen (1843). In *Either/Or* (1843, tr. 1944), his first important work, he investigated problems of "aesthetic" versus "ethical" consciousness; in *Fear and Trembling* (1843, tr. 1939) the categories are extended into the specifically religious; faith is understood as an absolute relation of the individual with God, involving a teleological suspension of the ethical and a decisive acceptance of the absurd. A feud with the radical Danish journal *Corsair* (1846) caused him intense bitterness. His last years were spent in a violent quarrel with the church of Denmark. Kierkegaard is known as the founder of modern existentialism. Major works, published in many editions in English, include *Philosophical Fragments* (1844, tr. 1936), *The Concept of Dread* (1844, tr. 1944), *Stages on Life's Way* (1845, tr. 1940), *Concluding Unscientific Postscript* (1846, tr. 1941), *The Sickness Unto Death* (1849, tr. 1941), and *Training in Christianity* (1850, tr. 1941).

REFERENCES: James D. Collins *The Mind of Kierkegaard* (Chicago 1953 and London 1954, also PB). Thomas H. Croxall *Kierkegaard Commentary* (London and New York 1956). Louis Dupré *Kierkegaard as Theologian* (tr. New York 1963 and London PB 1964). Vernard Eller *Kierkegaard and Radical Discipleship* (Princeton, N.J. 1968). Jerry H. Gill ed. *Essays on Kierkegaard* (Minneapolis PB 1969). Kenneth Hamilton *The Promise of Kierkegaard* (Philadelphia 1969, also PB). Johannes Hohlenberg *Søren Kierkegaard* (tr. London and New York 1954). Regis Jolivet *Introduction to Kierkegaard* (tr. London 1950 and New York 1951). Walter Lowrie *Kierkegaard* (London and New York 1938, new ed. 2 vols. New York PB 1962) and *A Short Life of Kierkegaard* (Princeton, N.J. 1942 and Oxford 1943, also PB). Peter P. Rohde *Søren Kierkegaard: An Introduction to His Life and Philosophy* (tr. London and New York 1963).

SØREN KIERKEGAARD
BY
JOHN UPDIKE

Perhaps because he lived in the toy metropolis of Copenhagen, a little man with a dandy's face and a crooked back strolling zigzag along the sidewalk, we presume to love him; or perhaps it is his voice — that extraordinary insinuant voice, imperious and tender, rabid and witty — that excites our devotion. He wrote, in a sense, as a lover, having spurned marriage, and the torrent of volumes that follows his break with his fiancée abounds with lover's stratagems: with flirtatious ambiguities,

elaborate deceits and impersonations, fascinating oscillations of emphasis, all sorts of erotic "display." Apart from his passionate literary production of the 1840's, his life knew few events: his struggle with his father, the attack by the *Corsair,* the attack upon Christendom. A life of antidotes. His "aesthetic" holiday of café conversation, brothels, and the Royal Theatre served as an antidote to the dour household of his theologically obsessed father. His father died, and Kierkegaard began to write like a slave. His first title, *Either/Or,* established the note of zigzag and alternation; each pseudonymous "aesthetic" work was accompanied on publication date by "edifying" discourses under his own name. The two campaigns of publicity in which he was involved — defensive against the *Corsair,* offensive against the church — seem thrust and counterthrust in his war with "the herd." His final, suicidal burst of energy, a public execration of all earthly manifestations of Christianity including a deathbed rejection of the Eucharist, was perhaps the subtlest antidote of all — an atoning re-enactment of his father's gesture when, as an eleven-year-old shepherd boy on the Jutland heath, Michael Kierkegaard (in the words of his youngest son's journal) "stood upon a hillock and cursed God."

Yet to make of Kierkegaard a case history and to view his ideas — as does Josiah Thompson in *The Lonely Labyrinth* — as maneuvers in a self-administered, and eventually futile, therapy is to excuse ourselves from his truth and his heroism. Heroism not so much of labor (for this was an industrious century) or of personal suffering (for in fact Kierkegaard, though he bemoans his mysterious "thorn in the flesh" for page after page, never impresses us as a martyr; like his slightly younger American contemporary Thoreau, he is a bachelor comfortable among willfully chosen privations), but heroism in facing down the imperious tradition of German idealistic philosophy: "Now if we assume that abstract thought is the highest manifestation of human activity, it follows that philosophy and the philosophers proudly desert existence, leaving the rest of us to face the worst. . . . [Philosophy] is disinterested; but the difficulty inherent in existence constitutes the interest of the existing individual, who is infinitely interested in existing. Abstract thought thus helps me with respect to my immortality by first annihilating me as a particular existing individual and then making me immortal, about as when the doctor in Holbert killed the patient with his medicine — but also expelled the fever."

It is no criticism to say that Kierkegaard is not a systematic philosopher like Hegel; it was his mission to be the anti-Hegel. "I am anything but a devilish good fellow at philosophy," his pseudonym Johannes Climacus admits. "I am a poor, individual existing man, with sound natural capacities, not without a certain dialectical dexterity, not entirely destitute of education. I have been tried in life's *casibus* and cheerfully appeal to my sufferings." To be human is *inherently* to be a problem; he certified what the romantics had merely suspected, that sickness is a prerequisite of wisdom. "With the help of the thorn in my foot I spring higher than anyone with sound feet." Philosophy, in his day the monarchial overscience, has become in ours the humblest of semantic inquiries, or else personal testimony. What seems strange is how the atheists Sartre, Camus, and Heidegger have given currency to terms — "the absurd,"

"the leap," "dread," "despair" — that Kierkegaard coined to pay his way into heaven; but, writing of Christianity as "an actualization of inwardness," Kierkegaard asserted that only two kinds of people could know anything about it, those who accept it and those who "in passion" reject it — "the happy and the unhappy lovers."

It is to would-be believers, above all, that Kierkegaard speaks. Behind all the fireworks and jockeying, the flights of poetry and dramatic imagination, the exegetical brilliance and the casually bestowed abundance of psychological insight, he is conducting, and the religiously inclined reader is desperately following, a search for the "Archimedean point" outside the world, from which the world can be lifted, admitting, like a crack of light in a sealed cave, the possibility of faith, that is to say, of escape from death. The assertion that "subjectivity is truth" provides such a point, though a rather slippery one. The concept of "the paradox," all too violently felt as the "crucifixion of intellect," accords with ancient Christian formulae, and gives a certain Promethean aura to alogism. And "the leap" does seem to be the way, both in particle physics and human affairs, that things move, rather than Hegel's deterministic "mediation."

Although he posited, in *Fear and Trembling*, a "knight of faith," Kierkegaard did not himself become that knight. The theology of his last years is dismaying in its ferocity. And his copious oeuvre seems unbalanced, incomplete, subjective to a fault. It remained for Karl Barth to build upon the basis of God's otherness (a concept Kierkegaard phrased, tragically, as "God's inhumanity") an inhabitable theology; it remained for Kafka, though the Dane's journals abound in miniature fables, to develop Kierke-gaardian sensations into real fiction, into epic symbols. Kierkegaard, whose emphasis was ever upon "the individual" and who wanted this citation as his epitaph, lives in history not as an author or thinker attached to his work like a footnote, but as a man incarnated in his books, a human knot that refuses to be unraveled, a voice asking to be loved.

KINGSLEY, Charles (June 12, 1819 – Jan. 23, 1875). English novelist, poet, and clergyman. Born Holne Vicarage, Devon, son of a clergyman. After graduating from Magdalene College, Cambridge, and taking orders (1842), became curate at Eversley, Hampshire, where he spent most of his life. Married Frances Grenfell (1844). First publication, *The Saint's Tragedy*, a blank verse drama (1848). In same year, helped F. D. Maurice in founding Christian Socialist movement and began to contribute to its journal, *Politics for the People*. *Yeast* (1848) and *Alton Locke* (1850), novels of social consciousness aimed at improving the lot of the working classes, brought him recognition. Historical novels *Hypatia* (1853), *Westward Ho!* (1855), and *Hereward the Wake* (1866) were extremely popular. Also wrote well-known children's story *The Water Babies* (1863). Appointed chaplain to the queen (1859) and canon of Westminster (1873). Was professor of modern history at Cambridge (1860–69). His bitter attacks on Roman Catholicism provoked Newman's *Apologia Pro Vita Sua* (1864). Died at Eversley, Hampshire. Known as a leading proponent of social reform, he was also one of the few clergymen to accept Darwin's theory of evolution. His brother Henry (1830–1876), also a writer, is best known for his novel *Ravenshoe* (1861).

EDITION: *Life and Works* ed. Frances Grenfell Kingsley (London 1880–85, reprinted 19 vols. New York 1968–69).
REFERENCES: Janet E. Courtney *Freethinkers of the Nineteenth Century* (1920, reprinted Freeport, N.Y. 1967). Robert B. Martin *The Dust of Combat:*

A Life of Charles Kingsley (London 1959 and New York 1960). Margaret F. Thorp *Charles Kingsley, 1819–1875* (Princeton, N.J. and London 1937, reprinted New York 1969).

KIPLING, (Joseph) Rudyard (Dec. 30, 1865 – Jan. 18, 1936). English writer. Born Bombay, India. Taken to England (1871), he spent five unhappy years in foster home, then received inferior education at United Services College of Westward Ho!, North Devon (1878–82). Returned to India (1882), where he made a name for himself as journalist, poet (*Departmental Ditties*, 1886), short story writer (*Plain Tales from the Hills* and six subsequent collections, 1887–89). After traveling around the world (1889), came to England and published *The Light That Failed* (1891), *The Naulahka* (1892, with Charles Wolcott Balestier), and *Barrack-Room Ballads* (1892). Married an American, Charles Balestier's sister Caroline (1892); they settled in Brattleboro, Vt., where he wrote travel sketches and books for children: *The Jungle Book* (1894), *The Second Jungle Book* (1895), and *Just-So Stories* (1902). Returned to England (1896) and, after traveling primarily for journalistic purposes, including reporting on the Boer War), settled permanently at Burwash, Sussex 1902). Here he produced his finest novel, *Kim* (1901), the children's books *Puck of Pook's Hill* (1906) and *Rewards and Fairies* (1910), and other works including poetry. The most popular author of his day, Kipling was the first Englishman to receive the Nobel prize for literature (1907). He died in London.

EDITIONS: *Collected Works* Burwash Edition (28 vols. London and New York 1941). *A Choice of Kipling's Verse* ed. T. S. Eliot (1941; PB New York 1962 and London 1963).
REFERENCES: Charles E. Carrington *The Life of Rudyard Kipling* (New York 1955). Louis Cornell *Kipling in India* (London and New York 1966). Bonamy Dobrée *Rudyard Kipling* (New York PB 1967). George Orwell *Dickens, Dali, and Others* (New York 1946). Andrew Rutherford ed. *Kipling's Mind and Art* (Edinburgh 1964). Edmund

Wilson *The Wound and the Bow: Seven Studies in Literature* (London and New York PB 1957).

✍

RUDYARD KIPLING
BY
BERNARD BERGONZI

To describe Kipling as a highly paradoxical writer may be, on the face of it, to utter a truism that could apply to many original writers who do not easily accommodate themselves to conventional criticism. Yet the contradictions inherent in Kipling's life and work have been evident ever since the poems and short stories of the brilliant young Anglo-Indian captured the imagination of English readers in the 1890's. Even though he came to seem the assertive laureate of British imperialism — an impression amplified by certain malicious caricatures of Kipling by Max Beerbohm — and to have gone on in later years, notably just before and during the First World War, to deliberately cultivate this self-assumed role, the truth was always more complex. As a young man whose formative years had been spent in the Indian empire, Kipling was able to stand somewhat apart from the conventional responses of English patriotism. He was, in short, anything but a literary Blimp. One may refer, for instance, to one of his most bitter poems, *The Islanders*, in which he castigates the English love of sport, which most of his fellow countrymen preferred to defending their country against a possible invasion: the poem contains a memorable onslaught on "the flanneled fools at the wicket and the muddied oafs at the goal." In a lighter vein, the autobiographical school stories in *Stalky & Co.* show the derision with which the young Kipling regarded the cult of compulsory games.

At the heart of the Kipling paradox is the role he favored of the anti-intellectual intellectual, the man of sensitivity and wide reading who preferred the company of men of action, the writer who was most at home with soldiers or the intelligent but philistine civil servants who ran the Indian empire at the end of the nineteenth century. Kipling's entry into literature was via journalism rather than by a conventional literary training; this apprenticeship gave him an early sense of verbal economy, whilst he learnt more profound lessons about the art of fiction from the French naturalists, whom he read when they were very much a minority taste in England. One of his dominant characteristics as a writer was his lifelong admiration for skill, for a craft well mastered, whether it was that of the engineer or the soldier or the writer. The extraordinary skill with which Kipling constructed his short stories, and his feeling for words, will be apparent even to those who do not relish his content. Again, although Kipling's imperialist attitudes may sometimes have echoed the strident assertions of the British popular press, he always regarded the empire in a deeply serious way as the occasion for unselfish service and dedication as much as for any form of material privilege (although, as Orwell pointed out, he ignored the economic basis of imperialism). In such a work as *Puck of Pook's Hill*, which is ostensibly a children's book, he makes clear both his profound feeling for the British past and his melancholy awareness of the parallels between the British and Roman empires, and the sense that the one may follow the other into decline.

Kipling's kind of artistic seriousness, though real enough, was very unlike that of the great innovators of the modern movement; the surface of his art always provided forms of narrative interest and accessible sentiment which ensured him a tremendous following among unliterary readers. There is a sense in which the author of, say, the *Jungle Books* or *If* and *Gunga Din* could afford to ignore the rather baffled maneuvers of modern literary critics, who feel that Kipling is an evidently important figure who needs to be reassessed and "placed," but who is so ideologically antipathetic to the habitual assumptions of the liberal sensibility that they do not quite know where to begin. Admittedly, Edmund Wilson helped to make Kipling look more like a proper man of letters, with a pattern of interesting weakness beneath the assertive façade, when in a very influential essay, *The Kipling that Nobody Read,* published in 1941, he subjected Kipling to a Freudian examination and discovered the sources of his art in the traumas of a singularly wretched childhood. Mr. Wilson's Kipling is a strikingly different figure from that caricatured by Max Beerbohm, and far more approachable to modern readers; since his essay appeared some useful critical work has gone on in the assessment of Kipling's prose, and much of it is conveniently collected in *Kipling's Mind and Art,* edited by Andrew Rutherford (Edinburgh 1964). (Kipling's poetry, on the other hand, though still popular amongst the unsophisticated, is not of a kind to respond to current critical approaches; T. S. Eliot ambiguously described it as "great verse" rather than poetry.)

Yet although a formalist approach can find much to occupy itself with in the close examination of the texture of Kipling's prose and the thematic patterns of his fiction, the ideological challenge remains. It was aggressively posed by Sartre in his *What Is Literature?* when he asserted that prose literature is necessarily an instrument of freedom and that no good novel has been written in the interests of social or racial oppression. Kipling was not a conscious advocate of oppression, but he advanced oppressive attitudes, and his imagination did encompass some remarkably brutal states of feeling. And yet he clearly was a writer of great originality and distinction. If one cannot solve the Kipling problem, then one must learn to live with it, and the best way of doing so was perhaps suggested by George Orwell. Acknowledging all that was repellent and perverse in Kipling's view of reality, he claimed that much of his strength came from his solid grasp of the social virtues of action and responsibility, which, as Orwell remarked, are qualities too often ignored or taken for granted by liberals. Despite his rhetoric, Kipling does have important things to say about basic and perennial human attributes.

———

KIRCHNER, Ernst Ludwig (May 6, 1880 – June 15, 1938). German painter. Born Aschaffenburg. Studied architecture at Dresden Technical School (1901–1905) and painting in Munich (1903–1904). His discovery of Polynesian and Negro art (1904) and the work of Norwegian painter Edvard Munch, influenced him. In Dresden (1905), Kirchner helped found Die Brücke (The Bridge), the group of young artists who began German expressionism. They gained in influence after their first exhibitions (1906), and moved to Berlin (1911), where Kirchner painted series of street scenes, in a violent, emotional style, with pronounced distortion of perspective and form, intense color, and nervous line. Served in army during World War I, but suffered nervous collapse and moved to Davos, Switzerland (1917). Here he remained until his death by suicide, painting mountain landscapes in a more serene, solid style, and working in woodcuts. He was influential during this period chiefly in Swiss circles, especially after the Nazis confiscated over six hundred of his works (1937).

REFERENCES: Annemarie Dube-Heynig *Kirchner: His Graphic Art* (London and Greenwich, Conn. 1966). Donald E. Gordon *Ernst Ludwig Kirchner* (Cambridge, Mass. 1968). Will Grohmann *E. L. Kirchner* (tr. New York 1961 and London 1962). Bernard Myers *The German Expressionists* (New York 1957 and London 1958). Peter Selz *German Expressionist Painting* (Berkeley, Calif. and Cambridge, England, 1957).

KLEE, Paul (Dec. 18, 1879 – June 29, 1940). Swiss painter. Born München-buchsee, near Bern; father a German musician, mother Swiss. Attended school in Bern, then went to Munich to study art (1898–1901). After trip to Italy, returned to Bern (1902), where he played violin in city orchestra and produced first etchings. Exhibited in Munich (1906) with some success; married pianist Lily Stumpf same year, and remained in Munich until 1920. Exhibited etchings and drawings in second Blue Rider show (1912) and at salon organized by Herwarth Walden's avant-garde enterprise Der Sturm in Berlin (1913). His reputation continued to grow. A trip to Tunisia (1914) was a turning point; he "discovered" color: "Color and I are one; I am a painter," he wrote in his diary. Worked first in watercolor, then (after 1918) in oil. Served in army during World War I (1916–18), then taught at Bauhaus (1921–31), where published his *Pedagogical Sketchbook* (1925). Exhibited in Berlin (1929) and at Museum of Modern Art, New York (1930). Taught at Düsseldorf Academy (1931–33) until dismissed by Nazis, whereupon he returned to Bern. Retrospective exhibition there (1935) was the first of many in Europe and the U.S. He died at Muralto-Locarno, Switzerland. Klee's special quality is his intuitive feeling for the primal movement of life, expressed in the way he captures the evanescent forms of nature in the act of creation. "Becoming is superior to being," he wrote, and "Art does not re-produce the visible, rather it makes visible. . . . As a child plays at being a grown-up, so the painter imitates the play of those forces which created and still are creating the world." Klee combines supreme draftsmanship with marvelous inventiveness and a poetic vision that plumbs the mystery of man and the universe. Of his more than nine thousand works, some of the best known are *Villa R* (1919, Kunstsammlung, Bern), *Twittering Machine* (1922, Museum of Modern Art, New York), *Landscape with Yellow Birds* (1923, private collection, Switzerland), *Pastoral (Rhythms)* (1927, Museum of Modern Art, New York), *Blue Night* (1937).

EDITIONS: *Diaries of Paul Klee (1898–1918)* ed. Felix Klee (Berkeley, Calif. 1964 and London 1965, also PB). *The Inward Vision: Watercolors, Drawings and Writings by Paul Klee* (New York 1958). *Pedagogical Sketchbook* (1944, New York and London 1953, also PB). *The Thinking Eye* (tr. 2nd ed. New York 1964).

REFERENCES: Merle Armitage ed. *Five Essays on Klee* (New York 1950). Carola Giedion-Welcker *Paul Klee* (tr. New York and London 1952). Will Grohmann *Paul Klee* (tr. London and New York 1954) and *Paul Klee: Drawings* (tr. 1960, new ed. London 1967). Werner Haftmann *The Mind and Work of Paul Klee* (tr. London and New York 1954, also PB). Felix Klee *Paul Klee: His Life and Work in Documents* (tr. New York 1962). Nello Ponente *Paul Klee: Biographical and Critical Study* (tr. Geneva and London 1960). Gualtieri di San Lazzaro *Klee: A Study of His Life and Work* (tr. New York 1959).

KLEIST, (Bernd) Heinrich (Wilhelm) von (Oct. 18, 1777 – Nov. 21, 1811). German writer. Born Frankfort on the Oder, of Prussian military family. Entered Prussian army (1792–99), but left it to study mathematics and philosophy at University of Frankfurt. Reading Kant caused him to abandon further study, and after a period of travel he took up writing. Produced tragedy *Die Familie Schroffenstein* (1803), followed by the masterly comedy *Der Zerbrochene Krug* (*The Broken*

Jug) (1806) and *Amphytrion* (1807), inspired by Molière. While in Berlin, then occupied by Napoleon's troops, Kleist was arrested as spy and imprisoned in France (1807), afterward living in Dresden (1807–1809), where he published literary periodical *Phöbus*, to which he contributed short stories. Produced tragedies *Penthesilea* (1808) and *Prinz Friedrich von Homburg* (1811), the romantic drama *Das Käthchen von Heilbronn* (1810), and his greatest work, the novella *Michael Kohlhaas* (1811). Too passionately nationalistic for occupied Germany, Kleist was not recognized in his time, and in despair over failure of last venture, the political newspaper *Die Abendblätter* (*Evening News*) (1810–11), he arranged a suicide pact with Henrietta Vogel on the shore of Wannsee, near Potsdam. Since his death, Kleist's reputation has grown to the stature of Goethe and Schiller. Basically a romantic, he is highly individualistic in his studies of the tormented soul in conflict with itself and with fate. His psychological realism anticipated that of the twentieth century, when he has gained full recognition.

TRANSLATIONS: *The Prince of Homburg* tr. Charles E. Passage (New York PB 1956). *The Marquise of O — and Other Stories* tr. Martin Greenberg (New York 1960 and London 1963, also PB). *Amphitryon* tr. Marion Sonnenfeld (New York PB 1962). *The Broken Jug* tr. John T. Krumpelmann (New York PB 1962).
REFERENCES: Sigurd Burckhardt *Drama of Language: Essays on Goethe and Kleist* (Baltimore 1969). John Gearey *Heinrich von Kleist: A Study in Tragedy and Anxiety* (Philadelphia 1968). Richard March *Heinrich von Kleist* (Cambridge, England, and New Haven, Conn. 1954). Walter Sitz *Heinrich von Kleist: Studies in His Works and Literary Character* (Philadelphia and Oxford 1962). Ernst L. Stahl *Heinrich von Kleist's Dramas* (1948, rev. ed. Oxford 1961).

KLIMT, Gustav (July 14, 1862 – Feb. 6, 1918). Austrian painter. Born and died in Vienna. Studied at School of Decorative Art in Vienna (1876–83). Early works, in a naturalistic style, include murals in Vienna Burgtheater (1886–88) and on staircase of Kunsthistorisches Museum (1890–92). Was a founder and first president of the Vienna Secession (1897); at this point formed his characteristic style, richly ornamental and linear, with emphasis on the two-dimensional surface. Soon recognized as the foremost painter of art nouveau in Vienna. Withdrew from Secession (1905). Visited Belgium and England (1906), Paris (1909). Won first prize at International Exhibition in Rome (1911); was made honorary member of Vienna and Munich academies (1917). Monumental murals include the allegories *Philosophy* (1900), *Medicine* (1901), and *Jurisprudence* (1903) for University of Vienna, and *Beethoven Frieze* (1902, in fragments in private collections, Vienna). Examples of his smaller works are *Portrait of Frau Fritza Riedler* (1906), *Portrait of Frau Adele Bloch-Bauer* (1907), and *The Kiss* (1908), all in Österreichische Galerie, Vienna. Klimt's work formed basis of early expressionism in Austria.

REFERENCES: Fritz Novotny and Johannes Dobai *Gustav Klimt* (with a catalogue raisonne of his paintings) (New York and London 1968) and *100 Selected Drawings* (New York PB 1970).

KNELLER, Sir Godfrey (originally Gottfried Kniller) (Aug. 8, 1646/49 – Nov. 7, 1723). Anglo-German portrait painter. Born Lübeck. Studied in Amsterdam under Bol and probably Rembrandt before going to Italy (1672), where he began to paint portraits. Settling in England (1674), he was assured of success after painting Charles II (1678). Succeeded Sir Peter Lely as principal painter to the king (1680), and was also favored by James II, William III, and Queen Anne. Knighted (1692) and created baronet (1715), he enjoyed enormous social and artistic eminence. Married Mrs. Susannah Graves, a widow (1704). Died in London; buried in Westminster Abbey. Kneller painted virtually every prominent figure of his day. Most famous series are of members of Kit-Cat Club (1702–18, National Portrait Gallery, London). Like Lely, he painted series of Hampton Court "Beauties" (1690–91) and of Admirals (1701–10, National Maritime Museum, London). He is admired more for his likenesses than for artistic imagination. Often left task of filling details of draperies and backgrounds to his many assistants.

REFERENCES: G. H. C. Baker *Lely and Kneller* (London and New York 1922). Ellis K. Waterhouse *Painting in Britain, 1530–1790* (1953, 3rd ed. Harmondsworth, England, 1969). Margaret D. Whinney and Oliver Millar *English Art, 1625–1714* (Oxford 1957).

KOLLWITZ, Käthe (née Schmidt) (July 8, 1867 – Apr. 22, 1945). German graphic artist and sculptor. Born Königsberg, East Prussia. Studied art in Berlin and Munich, and settled permanently in Berlin after marriage (1891) to Karl Kollwitz, a physician who practiced in the city's working-class district. Gerhart Hauptmann's play *The Weavers* (1893) inspired her first important print series, *Der Weberaufstand* (1894–98). Käthe Kollwitz's subsequent work depicts the sufferings of the poor; realistic and compassionate, they are dominated by motifs of mother and child, death, and war. Well known are the print series *Peasant War* (1902–1908), woodcut series *War* (1920–24) and *Proletariat* (1925), eight lithographs *Death* (1934–35), and many self-portraits. The first woman elected to Berlin Academy (1919), she served as director of the academy's master classes for graphic arts from 1928 until her dismissal by Nazis (1933). She was forbidden to exhibit (1936), but remained in Germany throughout World War II. Died in Moritzburg castle, near Dresden.

TRANSLATION: *The Diary and Letters of Käthe Kollwitz* ed. Hans Kollwitz, tr. Richard and Clara Winston (Chicago 1955).

REFERENCES: Herbert Bittner *Kaethe Kollwitz: Drawings* (New York 1959 and London 1960). August Klipstein *The Graphic Work of Käthe Kollwitz* (New York 1955). Stephen Longstreet *The Drawings of Kaethe Kollwitz* (Alhambra, Calif. 1967, also PB). Carl Zigrosser *Prints and Drawings of Käthe Kollwitz* (New York PB 1969).

KOTZEBUE, August (Friedrich Ferdinand) von (May 3, 1761 – Mar. 23, 1819). German writer. Born Weimar. Studied and practiced law at Jena, then went to St. Petersburg (1781), where he worked for government and wrote first of many successful plays, *Menschenhass und Reue* (1781, tr. *The Stranger* 1798). Served as chief dramatist of court theatre in Vienna (1797–99), then on return to Russia (1800) was arrested by Czar Paul I as political suspect and sent to Siberia. The czar released him the next year and appointed him director of German Theatre in St. Petersburg. Lived in Weimar and Berlin (1801–1806), editing a journal critical of the romantic movement. After a stay in Russia (1806–17), settled again in Germany as paid agent of Czar Alexander I, and founded reactionary weekly *Literarisches Wochenblatt* in Mannheim (1818). It aroused the wrath of the radical student movement, and the following year he was assassinated by a student. Extremely prolific, Kotzebue wrote 211 plays in all, including comedies that influenced European theatre and melodramas that were among the first to be written. He was the most popular dramatist of his time. Also wrote novels, historical and autobiographical works. Was married three times. His son Otto von Kotzebue (1787–1846), navigator and explorer, discovered a number of Pacific islands and the sound in Alaska that bears his name.

REFERENCES: A. W. Holzmann *Family Relationships in the Dramas of August von Kotzebue* (Princeton, N.J. and Oxford 1936). Charles Rabany *Kotzebue, sa vie et son temps* (Paris 1893).

KYD, Thomas (1558–1594). English dramatist. Born London, son of a scrivener. Attended Merchant Taylors' School, and probably worked in his father's profession before beginning career as dramatist. Was a friend of Christopher Marlowe, with whom he shared lodgings for a time. Died in London. Kyd's fame rests on a single play, *The Spanish Tragedy* (produced 1592, printed 1594), an Elizabethan tragedy of revenge that enjoyed great success and influenced the development of English drama. Borrowing from Seneca the devices of the ghost, revenge for a kinsman's murder, and elaborate rhetoric, Kyd used a sixteenth-century Spanish setting, brought acts of violence onstage, and created dramatic situations of unprecedented tension and power. Various features of *The Spanish Tragedy*, such as the play-within-the-play staged by the hero to further his ends, and the hero's derangement following the murder of his son, are echoed in Shakespeare's *Hamlet*. Kyd may in fact have been the author of an earlier version (now lost) of *Hamlet* which Shakespeare is known to have built upon. Kyd also wrote *Soliman and Perseda* (c.1588), and other works are attributed to him.

EDITIONS: *Works* ed. Frederick S. Boas (1901, reprinted Oxford 1967). *The Spanish Tragedy* ed. Philip Edwards (London and Cambridge, Mass. 1959, also PB).

REFERENCES: Howard Baker *Induction to Tragedy* (1939, reprinted New York 1965). Philip Edwards *Thomas Kyd and Early Elizabethan Tragedy* (London and New York 1966, also PB). Arthur Freeman *Thomas Kyd: Facts and Problems* (Oxford 1967). Peter B. Murray *Thomas Kyd* (New York 1969).

LA BRUYÈRE, Jean de (Aug. 16, 1645 – May 10, 1696). French moralist and satirist. Born Paris, of bourgeois family. Studied law and enrolled at Paris bar, but preferred life of retirement to practice. With an inheritance, bought absentee post in revenue department at Caen (1673). Through efforts of Bossuet, entered service of powerful Condé family (1684), first as tutor, then as secretary, remaining with them until his death at Versailles. La Bruyère is remembered for one remarkable work, *Les Caractères de Théophraste, traduits du grec, avec les caractères ou les moeurs de ce siècle* (1688), in which through portraits and aphorisms he points out the stupidity, immorality, and arrogance of the ruling classes, and protests against social injustice. It was an immediate success, edition followed upon edition, each of which La Bruyère enlarged by adding sketches to his original 390 and the 30 by Theophrastus. Final version (1696) contained some 1100 sketches; their brilliance, wit, and lucid style influenced Voltaire and other eighteenth-century writers. Keys to *Les Caractères* circulated, identifying individuals depicted, and provoking much hostility, which delayed his election to the French Academy until 1693, as did his support of the ancients in quarrel with moderns.

TRANSLATION: *Characters* tr. Henri Van Laun (1885, rev. ed. London and New York 1963).

REFERENCES: Edmund Gosse *Three French Moralists* (London 1918, reprinted Freeport, N.Y. 1967). Gustave Michaut *La Bruyère* (Paris 1936). Pierre Richard *La Bruyère et ses Caractères* (1946, rev. ed. Paris 1965).

LACHAISE, Gaston (Mar. 19, 1882 – Oct. 18, 1935). French-American sculptor. Born Paris, son of a cabinetmaker. Studied at École Bernard Palissy and École des Beaux Arts before becoming designer of art nouveau objects for René Lalique (1904). Met future wife, Isabel Nagle, an American (1905), and followed her to United States (1906). Worked first in Boston under academic monument sculptor H. H. Kitson, then settled in New York (1912) where he spent rest of his life. Lachaise slowly gained reputation as avant-garde sculptor after exhibiting one work at Armory Show (1913) and being given one-man shows at Bourgeois Galleries (1918 and 1920) and Alfred Stieglitz's gallery (1927). He received commissions for ornamental architectural sculptures, such as reliefs for American Telephone and Telegraph Building and the International and RCA buildings in Rockefeller Center (all in New York). Besides numerous portrait busts, he produced celebrated female figures of monumental proportions, including *Floating Woman* (1927) and *Standing Woman* (1932), both in Museum of Modern Art, New York.

REFERENCES: Albert E. Gallatin *Gaston Lachaise* (New York 1924). Lincoln Kirstein *Gaston Lachaise* (New York 1935). Hilton Kramer and others *The Sculpture of Gaston Lachaise* (New York 1967, also PB).

LACLOS, (Pierre Ambroise François) Choderlos de (Oct. 19, 1741 – Nov. 5, 1803). French writer. Born Amiens to family of minor nobility. Trained at École d'Artillerie de La Fère (1759–63), he became a professional soldier, and held rank of captain when he published his famous novel *Les Liaisons dangereuses* (1782). This analytical study in evil, in the epistolary form of Samuel Richardson's *Clarissa* (greatly admired by Laclos), depicts the amorality of French high society in last years of the ancien régime. It influenced Stendhal, Baudelaire, and other nineteenth-century writers, and in assessment of society values could apply to today. It is considered a progenitor of the modern novel: Martin Turnell calls Laclos "one of the first great analysts of the human heart." Laclos married Marie du Perré (1786). Retired from military and entered service of duc d'Orléans (Philippe Égalité) (1788), with whom he was arrested during the Terror and forced to flee (1789). Returned to Paris (1790), and rose steadily in the revolutionary administrative and military hierarchy, despite brief imprisonment (1793). Under regime of Napoleon, became general (1800), and died at Taranto during Italian campaign. Also author of now obscure nonfiction works.

TRANSLATION: *Dangerous Acquaintances* tr. Richard Aldington (1924, latest ed. New York PB 1960).

REFERENCES: Émile L. Dard *Le Général Choderlos de Laclos, auteur des Liaisons Dangereuses* (Paris 1936). A. and Y. Delmas *À la Recherche des Liaisons Dangereuses* (Paris 1964). Dorothy R. Thelander *Laclos and the Epistolary Novel* (Geneva 1963). Martin Turnell *The Novel in France* (London 1950 and New York 1951, also PB). Roger Vailland *Laclos par lui-même* (Paris 1953).

LA FAYETTE, Marie Madeleine Pioche de la Vergne, comtesse de (Mar. 16, 1634 – May 25, 1693). French novelist. Born and died in Paris; her family was of the lesser nobility and enjoyed royal favor. Spent first sixteen years at court, and studied with Gilles Ménage. Married François Motier, comte de La Fayette (1655), lived with him in Auvergne, raising two children; then established herself in Paris (1665). Her salon was frequented by Molière, Boileau, and other literary eminences of the day. Among her close friends were Madame de Sévigné, La Rochefoucauld, and Princess Henrietta of England. Madame

de La Fayette produced a masterpiece, *La Princesse de Clèves* (1678), a novel about a marriage with a problem. The sensitivity and psychological realism with which it is told anticipate the modern novel. She also wrote the novelle *La Princesse de Montpensier* (1662), *Zayde* (or *Zaïde*) (1670), and *La Comtesse de Tende* (1724).

TRANSLATION: *The Princesse de Clèves* tr. Harry Ashton (Cambridge, England, and New York 1925, also PB); tr. Nancy Mitford (London 1950 and New York 1951, PB 1963).

REFERENCES: Harry Ashton *Madame de La Fayette, sa vie et ses oeuvres* (Cambridge, England, 1922). Charles Dédéyan *Madame de La Fayette* (2nd ed. Paris 1965). Helen K. Kaps *Moral Perspective in La Princesse de Clèves* (Eugene, Oreg. 1969). Émile Magne *Le Coeur et l'esprit de Madame de La Fayette* (Paris 1927).

LA FONTAINE, Jean de (July 8, 1621 – Apr. 13, 1695). French poet. Born Château-Thierry, of bourgeois family. Studied theology and possibly law, but was drawn to neither. Marriage to an heiress, Marie Héricart (1647), failed through his neglect and extravagance, and they separated (1658). He settled in Paris, where he began literary career with adaptation of Terence's *Eunuchus* (1654), and soon after started putting into verse fables from Aesop, which became popular. Financial difficulties made him dependent on wealthy patrons, including Nicolas Fouquet, the superintendent of finances, the marquise de la Sablière, and the marquis d'Hervart, in whose Paris home he died. He published his tales in verse adapted from Boccaccio, Ariosto, and others, *Contes et Nouvelles* (1664–71), but his major work is the *Fables*, published in twelve books (1668–94). Like the *Contes*, they are noted for narrative skill, acute and witty observation, and free variations in verse form, and immediately became a classic. A friend of Racine, Boileau, Molière, La Rochefoucauld, Madame de Sévigné, and Madame de La Fayette, La Fontaine was elected to the Académie Française (1683) despite royal opposition based on his irreligious and unconventional character.

TRANSLATIONS: *The Fables* tr. Sir Edward Marsh (1931, new ed. London and New York 1952). *Fables* tr. Marianne Moore (New York 1954, also PB).

REFERENCES: J. D. Biard *The Style of La Fontaine's Fables* (Oxford and New York 1967). Pierre Clarac *La Fontaine, l'homme et l'oeuvre* (1947, rev. ed. Paris 1959). Jean Giraudoux *Les Cinq Tentations de La Fontaine* (Paris 1938). Ferdinand Gohin *L'Art de La Fontaine dans ses fables* (Paris 1929). Margaret Guiton *La Fontaine: Poet and Counter-Poet* (New Brunswick, N.J. 1961). Monica Sutherland *La Fontaine* (London 1953).

LAFORGUE, Jules (Aug. 16, 1860 – Aug. 20, 1887). French writer. Born Montevideo, Uruguay, of French parents; brought up by relatives at Tarbes, France (1866–76), where he attended lycée. Moved to Paris; earned living as secretary to editor of *Gazette des Beaux Arts* and began to write poetry. Produced most of his works while in Germany as reader to Empress Augusta (1881–86). Married Leah Lee, an Englishwoman (1887), then returned to Paris, to die a few months later of tuberculosis. Laforgue's symbolist poetry appeared in four volumes: *Les Complaintes* (1885), *L'Imitation de Notre-Dame la Lune* (1886), *Le Concile féerique* (1886), and *Dernier Vers* (1890). One of the greatest poets of lyrical irony and an inventor of vers libre, he had strong effect on Ezra Pound, T. S. Eliot, and the imagist poets. Short stories published as *Moralités légendaires* (1887); art criticism, showing keen insight into nature of impressionism, appeared in symbolist reviews and later in *Mélanges posthumes* (1923).

REFERENCES: Warren Ramsey *Jules Laforgue and the Ironic Inheritance* (London and New York 1953). Pierre Reboul *Laforgue* (Paris 1960). François Ruchon *Jules Laforgue: sa vie, son oeuvre* (Geneva 1924).

LA FRESNAYE, Roger de (July 11, 1885 – Nov. 27, 1925). French painter. Born Le Mans, of aristocratic Norman family. In Paris (1903–1908), studied at Académie Julian, École des Beaux Arts, and Académie Ranson, where he was influenced by Maurice Denis, Paul Sérusier, and others of the Nabis group. Later became admirer of Cézanne, and for a time associated with cubists, exhibiting with them at Salon des Indépendants, Salon d'Automne, and Section d'Or. However, in contrast to the scientific approach of Braque and other cubists, La Fresnaye developed a personal style in which forms were not always broken up in orthodox cubist manner. He suggested real perspective and also abandoned the somber palette of his early cubist phase for rich, brilliant color, and helped introduce a synthesis into the cubist experiment. During World War I he served in infantry. Afflicted with tuberculosis, he settled in Grasse (1919). His illness made it increasingly difficult for him to paint, and at forty he died there. Among his notable paintings are *The Artillery* (1912, private collection, Chicago), *Conquest of the Air* (1913, Museum of Modern Art, New York), *Seated Man* (1914, private collection, Paris).

REFERENCES: Raymond Cogniat and Waldemar George *Roger de La Fresnaye: Oeuvre complète* (Paris 1950). Germain Seligman *Roger de la Fresnaye* (London 1969).

LAMARTINE, Alphonse (Marie Louis de Prat) de (Oct. 21, 1790 – Feb. 28, 1869). French poet, statesman, and man of letters. Born Mâcon, of minor aristocracy. Educated at home and at Jesuit College, Bellay (1803). At Aix-les-Bains (1816), met and fell in love with Mme. Julie Charles, who died 1817. She became chief inspiration for his poems *Méditations poétiques* (1820), which were a great success. Both this volume, which included *Le Lac*, and *Nouvelles Méditations* (1823) strongly influenced romantic movement in France. Married Mary Ann (Marianne) Birch, and moved to Naples to serve in legation; later became chargé d'affaires in Florence (1825–28). Produced *La Mort de Socrate* (1823), *Harmonies poétiques et religieuses* (1830), and was elected to French Academy (1830). Supported revolution of 1830 and went into politics; was elected to Chamber of Deputies (1833–38), where he distinguished himself as an orator. Published *Voyage en Orient* (1835), outcome of visit to

Middle East (1832–33), *Jocelyn* (1836), and part of an epic, *La Chute d'un ange* (1838). His *Histoire des Girondins* (8 vols. 1847) helped incite revolution of 1848, after which he became head of the provisional government, but was defeated in election of December 1848. Thenceforth retired from politics and spent remaining years writing histories, autobiographical works, novel *Graziella* (1852), 28-volume *Cours familier de littérature* (1856–69) in vain effort to pay off his enormous debts. Died in Paris.

TRANSLATIONS: *Graziella* tr. James B. Runion (Chicago 1892). *Jocelyn* tr. Hazel Patterson Stuart (New York 1954).

REFERENCES: Albert J. George *Lamartine and Romantic Unanimism* (New York and Oxford 1940). Henri Guillemin *Lamartine, l'homme et l'oeuvre* (Paris 1940) and *Connaissance de Lamartine* (Fribourg, Switzerland, 1942). Marquis de Luppé *Les Travaux et les jours d'Alphonse de Lamartine* (Paris 1942). H. Remsen Whitehouse *The Life of Lamartine* (1918, reprinted 2 vols. Freeport, N.Y. 1969).

LAMB, Charles (Feb. 10, 1775 – Dec. 27, 1834). English writer. Born London. Educated at the charity school Christ's Hospital (1782–89), where fellow students included Leigh Hunt and Coleridge. Became clerk in South Sea House (1789) and later at East India Company (1792), where he remained for thirty-three years. In 1796, the year he published four sonnets in Coleridge's *Poems on Various Subjects*, Lamb's sister Mary in a fit of madness killed their mother. He spent the rest of his life taking care of her, and never married. Early works were unsuccessful — including poetry collection *Blank Verse* (with Charles Lloyd, 1798), which contains *The Old Familiar Faces;* melodramatic novel *A Tale of Rosamund Gray* (1798); and two plays, *John Woodvil* (1802) and *Mr. H.* (1806) — but some recognition came with publication of his children's book *Tales from Shakespeare* (1807), written with his sister. Other works for children and an anthology, *Specimens of English Dramatic Poets, Who Lived About the Time of Shakespeare* (1808), followed. Lamb is now chiefly known, however, for the essays which appeared in *London Magazine* (1820–25) under his pseudonym Elia. Collected as *Essays of Elia* (1823) and *Last Essays of Elia* (1833), they are among the most charming "personal" or "familiar" essays in English literature. On such matters as *The Praise of Chimney-Sweepers, Christ's Hospital Five and Thirty Years Ago,* and *Witches and Other Night Fears,* they express Lamb's mildly eccentric humor and love of life. He is also famous for his letters. He died at Edmonton, Middlesex.

EDITIONS: *The Works of Charles and Mary Lamb* (7 vols. London and New York 1903–1905) and *The Letters of Charles Lamb, to Which Are Added Those of His Sister Mary Lamb* (3 vols. London and New Haven, 1935), both edited by E. V. Lucas.

REFERENCES: George L. Barnett *Charles Lamb: The Evolution of Elia* (Bloomington, Ind. PB 1964). Edmund Blunden *Charles Lamb and His Contemporaries* (1933, reprinted Hamden, Conn. 1967). Marie H. Law *The English Familiar Essay in the Early Nineteenth Century* (1934, reprinted New York 1965). E. V. Lucas *Life of Charles Lamb* (5th ed. 1921, reprinted New York 1968). F. V. Morley *Lamb Before Elia* (London and New York 1932).

LANCRET, Nicolas (Jan. 22, 1690 – Sept. 14, 1743). French painter. Born and died in Paris. First studied under history painter Pierre Dulin and at Royal Academy; but after failing in competition for history painters (1711) became student of Claude Gillot, painter of *fêtes galantes.* While in Gillot's studio (1712–17) met Watteau, a fellow pupil, who influenced him profoundly. Admitted to French Academy as a painter of *fêtes galantes* (1719), Lancret devoted himself to this genre and became immensely popular, receiving numerous official commissions and enjoying the patronage of leading collectors. His elegant, charming scenes of balls and outdoor parties, though superficially resembling those of Watteau, lack the degree of delicacy and the subtle message for which Watteau is particularly admired. Lancret is estimated to have produced 787 paintings, among them *The Dancer La Camargo* (1730, National Gallery, Washington, D.C.), *The Pleasure Party* (1735, Musée Condé, Chantilly), *The Four Seasons* (1738, Louvre, Paris), and *Dance in a Park* (1738, Wallace Collection, London), as well as drawings and illustrations for La Fontaine's *Contes*.

REFERENCE: Georges Wildenstein *Lancret* (Paris 1924).

LANDOR, Walter Savage (Jan. 30, 1775 – Sept. 17, 1864). English writer. Born Warwick, son of a doctor. Hot temper resulted in his expulsion from both Rugby (1791) and Trinity College, Oxford (1794). Published *Poems* (1795) and achieved recognition with *Gebir*, a long narrative poem (1798), followed by *Poetry by the Author of Gebir* (1802). After his marriage to Julia Thuillier (1811), he resided in Llanthony, Wales, until local quarrels and financial difficulties forced him to leave (1814). Lived abroad, mainly in Italy (1815–35), returning to England after formal separation from his wife (1835). Convicted for libel (1858), he again left the country, settling for rest of his life in Florence, Italy, where the Brownings cared for him and where Swinburne visited him. Landor's important prose works, all developments of the Greek prose dialogue, are *Imaginary Conversations* (1824–62), *The Citation and Examination of William Shakespeare* (1834), *Pericles and Aspasia* (1836), and *The Pentameron* (1837). His lyric poems display the restraint and dignity of the Greek and Latin writers he revered.

EDITIONS: *Complete Works* ed. T. Earle Welby and Stephen Wheeler (London 1927–36, reprinted 16 vols. New York 1969). *Selected Poems* ed. Geoffrey Grigson (London 1964 and Carbondale, Ill. 1965). *Selected Imaginary Conversations* ed. Charles L. Proudfit (Lincoln, Nebr. 1969).

REFERENCES: Malcolm Elwin *Savage Landor* (New York 1941) and *Landor: A Replevin* (London 1958). E. W. Evans *Walter Savage Landor: A Critical Study* (1892, reprinted Port Washington, N.Y. 1970). John Forster *Walter Savage Landor: A Biography* (2 vols. Boston and London 1869). Robert Pinsky *Landor's Poetry* (Chicago 1968). Robert H. Super

Walter Savage Landor: A Biography (New York 1954 and London 1957).

LANDSEER, Sir Edwin Henry (Mar. 7, 1802 – Oct. 1, 1873). English painter. Born London, son of engraver and writer John Landseer, who provided early training. On Benjamin Haydon's advice (1815), studied Elgin marbles and wild animals at Exeter Change, and learned anatomy through dissection. Exhibited two animal pictures at Royal Academy (1815), where he became student (1816). By 1820 he had attained considerable reputation. Elected associate of Royal Academy (1826), Royal Academician (1831). The quality of Landseer's work declined in later years as he indulged in sentimentality, investing animals with human emotions for humorous or pathetic effect. Well-known paintings include *The Stag at Bay* (1846, private collection, Dublin), *Dignity and Impudence* (1839) and *Shoeing the Mare* (1844, both Tate Gallery, London). Bronze lions at foot of Nelson monument in Trafalgar Square (1867) are Landseer's work. He was a favorite of Queen Victoria and the most popular English artist of his day. Knighted (1850). Offered presidency of Royal Academy (1865), he declined it for reasons of health. Died in London.

REFERENCES: Algernon Graves *Catalogue of the Works of the Late Sir Edwin Landseer* (London 1875). James A. Manson *Sir Edwin Landseer* (London and New York 1902). Frederick G. Stephens *Sir Edwin Landseer* (3rd ed. London and New York 1880). M. F. Sweetser *Landseer* (Boston 1879).

LANGLAND, William (c.1330–c.1400). English poet. Chiefly on basis of autobiographical passages in his poem *Piers Plowman* (in full, *The Vision of William Concerning Piers the Plowman*), it is conjectured that he was born in the West Midlands and trained as a priest, took minor orders, was married, had a daughter, and led a vagabond life, becoming acquainted with all classes of society. *Piers Plowman*, a long allegorical dream vision in unrhymed alliterative verse, exists in three distinct versions (c.1362, c.1377, and c.1387–1400). Some scholars contend that more than one author is involved. Although chiefly remembered for his satirical attacks on the corruptions of the clergy, Langland also exposes the folly and ignorance of the lower classes and, most important, espouses an ideal of a perfect life based on the simplicity and humility of Scriptural example.

EDITIONS: *The Vision of Piers Plowman* tr. Henry W. Wells (1935, reprinted New York 1968). *Piers the Ploughman* tr. J. F. Goodridge (1959, rev. ed. Harmondsworth, England, and Baltimore PB 1968).
REFERENCES: Robert J. Blanch ed. *Style and Symbolism in Piers Plowman: A Modern Critical Anthology* (Knoxville, Tenn. 1969, also PB). Morton W. Bloomfield *Piers Plowman as a Fourteenth-Century Apocalypse* (New Brunswick, N.J. 1962). E. Talbot Donaldson *Piers Plowman: The C-Text and Its Poet* (1949, new ed. Hamden, Conn. and London 1966). Robert W. Frank *Piers Plowman and the Scheme of Salvation* (1957, reprinted Hamden, Conn. 1969). John Lawlor *Piers Plowman* (London and New York 1962). D. W. Robertson, Jr. and B. F. Huppé *Piers Plowman and Scriptural Tradition* (Princeton, N.J. 1951 and Oxford 1952). Elizabeth Salter *Piers Plowman: An Introduction* (2nd ed. Oxford 1969).

LANIER, Sidney (Feb. 3, 1842 – Sept. 7, 1881). American poet, musician, and critic. Born Macon, Ga. into distinguished Southern family. Developed strong musical interests in childhood. Attended Oglethorpe College (1856–60); after graduation served in Confederate army until his capture and imprisonment (1864–65) at Point Lookout, Md. Here he contracted tuberculosis. Returning to Macon, Lanier published first book, *Tiger Lilies*, a war novel (1867), and in same year married Mary Day. Eventually settled in Baltimore (1873) as first flutist in Peabody Orchestra. Here he produced several potboilers for juveniles and gained national recognition for his poems, which appeared in magazines and were first collected in 1877. Lanier's verse, which includes *Corn, The Symphony,* and *The Marshes of Glynn,* is noted for its or-

nateness and melodic qualities. From his work as lecturer in English literature at Johns Hopkins University (1879–81) came *The Science of English Verse* (1880), a prose treatise on relation of poetry to music, and *The English Novel* (1883). Died in Lynn, N.C.

EDITIONS: *Works* Centennial Edition ed. Charles R. Anderson and others (10 vols. Baltimore 1945). *Poems and Letters* ed. Charles R. Anderson (Baltimore PB 1969).
REFERENCES: Lincoln Lorenz *The Life of Sidney Lanier* (New York 1935). Edwin Mims *Sidney Lanier* (1905, reprinted Port Washington, N.Y. 1968). Edd W. Parks *Sidney Lanier: The Man, the Poet, the Critic* (Athens, Ga. 1969). Aubrey H. Starke *Sidney Lanier: A Biographical and Critical Study* (1933, reprinted New York 1964).

LARDNER, Ring(gold) (Wilmer) (Mar. 6, 1885 – Sept. 25, 1933). American writer. Born Niles, Mich. After graduating from Niles high school, spent term at Armour Institute of Technology in Chicago and held various jobs before becoming reporter on South Bend (Ind.) *Times* (1905). Made his name as a sports writer, specializing in baseball, for newspapers in Chicago, St. Louis, and Boston (1907–19). Meanwhile, began writing the short stories satirizing baseball players which, first printed in the *Saturday Evening Post* and later collected as *You Know Me, Al* (1916), brought widespread fame. Satirized full range of American types in subsequent short story volumes, notably *Gullible's Travels* (1917), *Treat 'Em Rough* (1918), *How to Write Short Stories* (1924), *What of It* (1925), *The Love Nest* (1926), and *Round Up* (1929), his humor growing ever more darkly sardonic. Wrote a mock autobiography, *The Story of a Wonder Man* (1927), and collaborated on two successful plays, *Elmer the Great* (1928, with George M. Cohan) and *June Moon* (1929, with George S. Kaufman). Married Ellis Abbott (1911); they had four sons. Died after years of illness at East Hampton, N.Y.

EDITIONS: *Collected Short Stories* (New York 1941). *The Ring Lardner*

Reader ed. Maxwell Geismar (New York 1963, also PB).

REFERENCES: Donald Elder *Ring Lardner: A Biography* (Garden City, N.Y. 1956). Otto Friedrich *Ring Lardner* (Minneapolis PB 1965). Walton R. Patrick *Ring Lardner* (New York 1963, also PB).

LA ROCHEFOUCAULD, François, 6th duc de (Sept. 15, 1613 – Mar. 17, 1680). French writer. Born Paris, heir of a powerful and ambitious line. Following his marriage to Andrée de Vivonne (1628), led a violent, restless life as soldier, politician, and lover of several prominent women. Participated in Anne of Austria's intrigues against Louis XIII and Richelieu, and later, with the prince of Condé, in the Fronde. Severely wounded in a riot at the Porte St.-Antoine (1652), he retired to his estates (1653) and began his *Mémoires sur la régence d'Anne d'Autriche* (completed 1662). Returning to Paris (1656), he frequented the salons of Madame de Sévigné and Madame de Sablé. Formed attachment to Madame de La Fayette (c.1665), which endured until his death, in Paris. His great work, *Reflexions ou sentences et maximes morales*, appeared in five authorized editions (1665–78) during his lifetime. In this series of finely whetted epigrams, La Rochefoucauld expresses his pessimistic view that man is ruled by self-love, and hence by self-delusion. "Our virtues are most frequently but vices in disguise" is a characteristic maxim.

TRANSLATION: *Maxims* tr. Louis Kronenberger (New York 1959, also PB).

REFERENCES: Morris Bishop *The Life and Adventures of La Rochefoucauld* (Ithaca, N.Y. 1951 and Oxford 1952). Edmund Gosse *Three French Moralists* (London 1918, reprinted Freeport, N.Y. 1967). Émile Magne *Le Vrai Visage de La Rochefoucauld* (3rd ed. Paris 1923). M. F. Zeller *New Aspects of Style in the Maxims of La Rochefoucauld* (Washington, D.C. PB 1954).

LASSUS, Roland de (Latin Orlandus Lassus, Italian Orlando di Lasso) (c.1532 – June 14, 1594). Dutch composer. Born Mons, in Hainault. As choirboy in church of St. Nicholas, Mons, he sang so beautifully that he was thrice kidnapped, the third time by agents of Ferdinando Gonzaga, viceroy of Sicily. Parents consented to his remaining in viceroy's service (1544), and subsequent decade in Italy greatly influenced his style. Served as *maestro di cappella* at St. John Lateran, Rome (1553–54). Returned to Antwerp (1555–56), then joined court of Duke Albert V of Bavaria in Munich, where, except for visits to Venice (1567–68) and to French court at Paris (1571), he remained rest of his life. Married lady of the court, Regina Weckinger (1558), became kapellmeister (c.1563), and was knighted by Emperor Maximilian II (1570). His prolific output of 1250 works covers a wide range of both secular and sacred musical forms, the finest example of which is generally thought to be his motets. His oeuvre includes 53 masses, Italian canzone, French chansons, German lieder, and two celebrated cycles, the seven *Psalmi Davidis poenitentiales* and the twelve *Prophetiae Sibyllarum*. Noted for his expressiveness, versatility, stylistic daring and cosmopolitanism, Lassus, with his contemporary Palestrina, is considered one of the greatest composers of the Renaissance.

REFERENCES: Charles van den Borren *Orlande de Lassus* (3rd ed. Paris 1930). Alfred Einstein *The Italian Madrigal* (tr. 3 vols. Princeton, N.J. and Oxford 1949). Gustave Reese *Music in the Renaissance* (1954, rev. ed. New York 1959).

LA TOUR, Georges de (Mar. 19, 1593 – Jan. 30, 1652). French painter. Born Vic-sur-Seille in Lorraine, where he lived all his life. After his marriage (1617), moved to Lunéville, where he became painter to the duke of Lorraine and, after Lorraine's occupation by France, painter to Louis XIV. Died at Lunéville. La Tour's religious and genre pictures show the influence of such Dutch Caravaggesque painters as Honthorst and Hendrick Terbrugghen. His early works (1620's), such as *The Fortune Teller* (Metropolitan Museum, New York) and *The Sharper* (Collection Landry, Paris), are minutely descriptive and set in daylight. In the 1630's he began to paint nocturnal scenes, such as *The Newborn* (Musée des Beaux Arts, Rennes), in which forms are dramatically illuminated by a candle or hidden light source, as well as such important daylight scenes as *The Hurdy-Gurdy Player* (Musée des Beaux Arts, Nantes) and *St. Jerome* (National Museum, Stockholm), still with meticulous realism. His night scenes after 1640 discarded extraneous detail and reduced figures to simple, almost geometric forms. Famous examples are *St. Joseph the Carpenter* (Louvre, Paris) and *St. Sebastian Mourned by St. Irene* (Staatliche Museen, Berlin). La Tour fell into obscurity after his death, and it was not until 1915 that his paintings began to be correctly ascribed to him.

REFERENCES: Marcel Arland and Anna Marsan *Georges de La Tour* (Paris 1953). Anthony Blunt *Art and Architecture in France, 1500–1700* (Harmondsworth, England, 1953 and Baltimore 1954). S. M. M. Furness *Georges de La Tour of Lorraine* (London 1949 and Boston 1951). Paul Jamot *Georges de La Tour* (2nd ed. Paris 1948). François Georges Pariset *Geroges de La Tour* (Paris 1949).

LATROBE, Benjamin Henry (Boneval) (May 1, 1764 – Sept. 3, 1820). American architect and engineer. Born Fulneck, near Leeds, England, son of a Moravian clergyman. He was educated in Germany, then returned to England and carried on unsuccessful architectural practice before emigrating to America (1796). In Norfolk, Va., he became engineer of James River and Appomattox canal. Built Richmond penitentiary (1797), Bank of Pennsylvania in Philadelphia (1798–1800), the first Greek revival building in America, and the Philadelphia waterworks (1798–1801), his major engineering project. Besides contributing significantly to the classic revival, Latrobe introduced Gothic style to American residential architecture with Sedgeley, a home outside Philadelphia (1798–99). Appointed by Jefferson to post of surveyor of public buildings in Washington (1803), he assumed supervision of uncompleted Capitol, designed White House exterior porticoes, and produced many other Washington buildings. After burning of Capitol by British (1814), returned to supervise rebuilding until 1817. Built first cathedral in U.S., the Roman Catholic cathedral in Baltimore (1805–21). Married twice. Died of yellow fever in New Orleans. Among Latrobe's pupils were William Strickland and Robert Mills. His son, Benjamin Henry Latrobe (1806–1870), was chief construction engineer with Baltimore and Ohio Railroad.

REFERENCE: Talbot F. Hamlin *Benjamin Henry Latrobe* (London and New York 1955).

LAUTREC. *See* TOULOUSE-LAUTREC.

LAWRENCE, D(avid) H(erbert) (Sept. 11, 1885 – Mar. 2, 1930). English writer. Born Eastwood, Nottinghamshire, son of a coal miner and a refined Nottingham woman. Through scholarships, attended Nottingham high school and, after brief period as clerk and elementary schoolteacher, Nottingham University (graduated 1908). Group of poems (1909) and short stories appeared in Ford Madox Ford's *English Review*, followed by first novel, *The White Peacock* (1911). Eloped (1912) with Frieda von Richthofen Weekley, wife of Nottingham professor, to Europe, where he finished book of poems, *Love Poems and Others* (1913) and one of his most important novels, the autobiographical *Sons and Lovers*. Lawrence and Frieda returned to England and were married (1914), but from outbreak of World War I were hounded by authorities because of Frieda's German origin. Resentment of this, of obscenity charge leveled at novel *The Rainbow*, and disaffection with industrial society sent the Lawrences to Italy (1919). *Women in Love* appeared 1920, then the travel sketches *Sea and Sardinia* (1921). Urged by Mabel Dodge (Sterne, later Luhan) to visit her in Taos, N.M., Lawrence left for America (1921), traveling by way of Ceylon and Australia, where he wrote novel *Kangaroo* (1923). Remained the better part of three years, off and on, in the Southwest, where the rugged terrain and the Indian sun and earth religion attracted him. Mabel Dodge Luhan wrote of that period in *Lorenzo in Taos* (1932). Visited Mexico, wrote there *The Plumed Serpent* (1926) and *Mornings in Mexico* (1927). Illness forced him to return to New Mexico, thence voyaged to England and Italy, where he wrote and published (in Florence) the controversial *Lady Chatterley's Lover* (1928). The last years before Lawrence succumbed to tuberculosis and died (in Vence, France) he produced *The Lovely Lady and Other Stories,* (1933), *Last Poems* (1932), which contains *The Ship of Death,* and the ultimate expression of his philosophy, *Apocalypse* (1931). His ashes are buried in the Taos mountains.

EDITIONS: *Letters* ed. Aldous Huxley (London and New York 1932). *The Collected Letters of D. H. Lawrence* ed. Harry T. Moore (2 vols. London and New York 1962).

REFERENCES: Horace Gregory *D. H. Lawrence: Pilgrim of the Apocalypse* (1933, new ed. New York PB 1957 and London PB 1958). F. R. Leavis *D. H. Lawrence: Novelist* (London 1955 and New York 1956, also PB). Harry T. Moore *D. H. Lawrence: His Life and Works* (1951, rev. ed. London PB 1963 and New York 1964) and *The Intelligent Heart: The Story of D. H. Lawrence* (1954, enlarged edition New York 1962, also PB). Edward Nehls ed. *D. H. Lawrence: A Composite Biography* (3 vols. Madison, Wisc. 1957–59).

✍

D. H. LAWRENCE
BY ROBERT GORHAM DAVIS

"Start with the sun," D. H. Lawrence wrote in the conclusion to his final book, *Apocalypse,* "and the rest will slowly, slowly happen." "The rest" is a vivid personal relationship with everything else in the cosmos, with earth, flowers, beasts, wife, child, nation, mankind. For *Apocalypse,* the sun is "a great heart whose tremors run through our smallest veins. The moon is a great gleaming nerve-center from which we quiver forever."

In one of Lawrence's last stories, called *Sun,* an American woman goes to the south of Europe at the advice of her doctors. She spends her days quite naked with her young boy in olive groves by the sea. Occasionally snakes sun themselves nearby. Her conscious self becomes secondary, almost an onlooker. Her true self is a "dark flow from her deep body to the sun." At the end she is poised in uneasy balance between her pallid, correct, emotionally timorous husband, and the dark, quick, sure-fingered, vital farm-worker with whom she has come into a state of intense, wordless polarity.

It is a situation that occurs over and over in Lawrence's fiction, and its key terms — "deep," "dark," "mindless," "vital," and "polarity" — are heavily weighted with doctrine. But behind the doctrine, which he put together from Frazer, Jung, Blavatsky, Nietzsche, and innumerable other writers on anthropology and myth, was highly relevant personal experience. His marvelous metaphors could draw as they did on Greek archaeology, Egyptian myth, Etruscan ruins, and Navaho dances because of what he learned to see and feel as a boy on the farms and in the collieries of the mining district where he was born. Within his own family, as he described it in *Sons and Lovers,* were some of the destructive tensions for which his later teachings offered cures — the conflict between his genteel, ambitious mother and her drunken, chthonic, dark-bearded miner husband, and the rivalry between the mother and equally aspiring young women for the love of the son.

Lawrence wrote *Sons and Lovers* after he had eloped to Germany with Frieda, daughter of Baron von Richthofen. She left three small children and a husband fourteen years older than herself with whom she had had a disappointing marriage. Lawrence was furious with her when she longed for her children. He promised that out of their love he would build prophetically a new world that would benefit the children and everyone else. But she knew that he was still guiltily preoccupied with his mother and his mother's death: "A sad old woman's misery you have chosen, you poor man, and you cling to it with all your power. I have tried, I have fought, I have nearly killed myself to get you in connection with myself and other people, early I proved to myself that I can love, but never you —"

In the emotionally stormy period after the marriage, Lawrence was two men. He was the small, dark, vital man who in so many of his fictions up through *Lady Chatterley's Lover* rescues a woman from a stultifying marriage and brings her to a new kind of fulfillment which can be described adequately only in religiomythical terms. But he was also a mother-dominated son, impaired and divided in his feelings for others. It required Frieda's combinations of strengths, including her motherliness, to rescue him, and biographers debate whether she actually ever did. But this conflict of selves provided the range of sympathies a novelist requires, and explains the fantasy element of some of his erotic scenes and ideas. Homoeroticism is a further complication. The idea of a polarized energizing flow applies between men and men as well as between men and women. This often takes directly physical form, as in the famous wrestling scene of *Women in Love.*

In the four years of greatest creativity that followed his elopement with Frieda in 1912, Lawrence recast *Sons and Lovers,* reported with violent immediacy the triumphs and torments of his marriage in the poems of *Look, We Have Come Through,* and returned to it in a more distanced and symbolic way

— a symbolism of flowers and moon, of rabbits and cows and horses — in *The Rainbow* and *Women in Love.*

The portrait of the mine director Gerald Crich in *Women in Love* shows Lawrence's increasing social rebelliousness, his Blakean reaction against mechanization, which grew steadily deeper in him as he and Frieda were badgered by the English authorities during the war years. As a result he left England and wandered widely in the early Twenties, to many places in southern Europe, to Ceylon, Australia, the United States and Mexico, testing out different modes of life at first hand. The results of this social preoccupation were the "leadership" novels, *Aaron's Rod, Kangaroo,* and *The Plumed Serpent,* the directly doctrinal treatises, *Psychoanalysis and the Unconscious, Fantasia of the Unconscious, Studies in Classic American Literature, Apocalypse,* and the marvelous evocations of place in his travel essays and poems. Begun in England during the war but revised radically in the United States, *Studies in Classic American Literature* taught a younger generation of American critics like Henry Nash Smith and Leslie Fiedler to see their own literature in an entirely new light.

None of the leadership novels was as satisfactory as *Sons and Lovers* or *Women in Love.* Lawrence never found what he was seeking. The doctrines he experimented with were not sufficiently grounded in personal experience. After coming close to fascism at several points, he realized that a mechanistic-military totalitarianism had seized upon modern leadership theories; he returned to hopes of tenderness instead. The best of these novels was *The Plumed Serpent* because it infused into fantasies of a revived Aztec theocracy in Mexico the profound emotions Lawrence had himself felt among the Indians of New

Lawrence, Thomas

Mexico. Their rituals and dances came closest to realizing communally the cosmic sense Frazer and Jung had taught him.

After finishing *The Plumed Serpent* Lawrence became seriously ill with tuberculosis, and never recovered as man or writer. *Lady Chatterley's Lover* reverts to the earlier triangular treatments of sexual awakening, but it was written in a period when Lawrence himself, according to Frieda, was impotent. The sex seems too much in the head, which is exactly where Lawrence said sex ought not to be. Some of the sex scenes become self-consciously ritualized travesties of what in earlier novels had seemed so revelatory and so right. Lost is the sense of balance which Lawrence — in his hortatory essay on novel writing — holds absolutely essential to an art which is to stay alive. But in some of the prophetic short stories, like *The Escaped Cock*, where the material itself also is mythical, a greater harmony prevails. Most moving of all is the melancholy deep acceptance which finds its music in the final poems.

In all the writing from the early *The White Peacock* to the last poems the dominant images remain the same. Lawrence is one of the greatest descriptive writers in English because of his fascinated responsiveness to the world and to other people. His superb presentational power of communicating this responsiveness is at once a satisfaction and a provocation, a testing of the reader's own capacity for life and experience and a persisting challenge to a society and education which inhibits or destroys the capacity. This double effect has given Lawrence as man and writer a special place in modern letters and evoked a vast body — often brilliant and creative in itself — of controversial criticism and biography.

LAWRENCE, Sir Thomas (May 4, 1769 – Jan. 7, 1830). English painter. Born Bristol. Began career as prodigy by drawing portraits of patrons of his father's inn (1773–82). In Bath (1782–87), supported family as professional portraitist in pastels. Received almost no formal education or artistic training. Went to London (1787), where he began working in oil. Exhibited portrait at Royal Academy (1789) which procured introduction to Queen Charlotte. His portrait of her (1790, National Gallery, London), together with *Miss Farren* (1790, Metropolitan Museum, New York), exhibited at Royal Academy, ensured his success. Elected associate of Royal Academy (1791), Royal Academician (1794). Succeeded Reynolds as principal portrait painter to George III (1792). Knighted by prince regent (1815), he was sent to Continent to paint allied victors of Napoleonic wars (1818). Portraits of *Archduke Charles* (1818, Windsor Castle) and *Pope Pius VII* (1819, Windsor Castle) are often considered his masterpieces. On return to England (1820), succeeded Benjamin West as president of Royal Academy. Died, a bachelor, in London. Other major works: *The Family of Sir Francis Baring* (1807, collection of earl of Northbrook), *Mrs. Wolff* (1815, Art Institute, Chicago), *George IV* (1819, Vatican Museums, Rome). Lawrence's highly popular portraits are in great romantic style, flattering, glittering, and facile.

REFERENCES: Kenneth Garlick *Sir Thomas Lawrence* (London 1954 and Boston 1955). Douglas Goldring *Regency Portrait Painter: The Life of Sir Thomas Lawrence* (London 1951).

LAWRENCE, T(homas) E(dward) (Aug. 15, 1888 – May 19, 1935). British soldier and writer. Born Tremadoc, Caernarvonshire, Wales, son of an Irishman. Family moved to Oxford (1896), where he attended school and Jesus College (1907–11). Interest in archaeology took him to Syria and Palestine (1909), where he studied Arabic and wrote *Crusader Castles* (1909–11). Again in Mesopotamia (1911–14) on British Museum expedition. At outset of World War I served on British Intelligence staff in Egypt, then joined

Arab army as liaison officer under Faisal al Husein, who commanded Arab rebels against the Turks. With Faisal and General Allenby helped capture Jerusalem (Dec. 9, 1917) and Damascus (Oct. 3, 1918). Lawrence of Arabia, as he had become known, then returned to England and attended Paris Peace Conference (1919); later became adviser on Arab affairs in Middle East conference (1921), but embittered and disappointed at outcome withdrew from Colonial Office (1922) and enlisted as private in tank corps, then as T. E. Shaw in air force (1926), where he became aircraftsman, until retirement ten years later. In Karachi, Pakistan, he published *Revolt in the Desert* (1927), an abridged version of *The Seven Pillars of Wisdom* (privately printed 1926, published 1935), the monumental, extraordinary account of his wartime experiences with the Arabs. Also published a translation of Homer's *Odyssey* (1932) and wrote a book on his service in the Royal Air Force (*The Mint*, 1955). Died as a result of a motorcycle accident at Clouds Hill, Dorset.

REFERENCES: Richard Aldington *Lawrence of Arabia: A Biographical Enquiry* (London and Chicago 1955, new ed. London 1969). Jean Béraud-Villars *T. E. Lawrence, or The Search for the Absolute* (tr. London 1958 and New York 1959). Robert Graves *Lawrence and the Arabian Adventure* (London 1927 and Garden City, N.Y. 1928). Basil H. Liddell Hart *Colonel Lawrence of Arabia: The Man Behind the Legend* (1934, enlarged edition London 1936 and New York 1937). Anthony Nutting *Lawrence of Arabia: The Man and the Motive* (London and New York 1961). Stanley Weintraub *Private Shaw and Public Shaw: A Dual Portrait of Lawrence of Arabia and G.B.S.* (London 1962 and New York 1963).

LEAR, Edward (May 12, 1812 – Jan. 29, 1888). English artist and poet. Born Highgate, near London, youngest and twenty-first child of a stockbroker. Forced to earn living by drawing from age of fifteen. While working for London Zoo (1832), where he produced the remarkable *Illustrations of the Family of the Psittacidae* (1832), met Edward Stanley, earl of Derby, who became his friend and engaged him to draw his menagerie at Knowsley Hall for four years. Here, Lear made up nonsense rhymes to entertain the earl's children, which eventually brought him great popularity when published as *A Book of Nonsense* (1846), illustrated with his drawings. *More Nonsense* followed (1871) and *Laughable Lyrics* (1877). About 1835, Lear took up landscape painting and began his extensive travels, in the course of which he learned to write and speak seven languages. His watercolors, which are really drawings, are important for their accuracy; he is considered one of the finest natural history draftsmen of all times. In his ornithological drawings he rivaled James Audubon. Spent two years touring India and Ceylon (1873–75) with Lord Northbrook, British viceroy, turning out some fifteen hundred drawings. Thereafter, settled in San Remo on the Italian Riviera, where he died. Suffered from epilepsy all his life, which partially accounted for the continual anxieties expressed in his journal, his shyness and loneliness. He is remembered for his wonderful nonsense poetry concerning the immortal Jumblies, the Yonghy-Bonghy-Bò, the Owl and the Pussycat, and other beloved characters; for his use of the limerick; and for his word inventions, such as the famous "runcible" spoon. He also wrote travel books, including *The Illustrated Journal of a Landscape Painter* (1869).

EDITIONS: *The Complete Nonsense of Edward Lear* ed. Holbrook Jackson (London 1947 and New York 1951, also PB). *Letters of Edward Lear* ed. Lady Strachey (1907, reprinted Freeport, N.Y. 1970). *Later Letters of Edward Lear* ed. Lady Strachey (London and New York 1911).

REFERENCES: Angus Davidson *Edward Lear: Landscape Painter and Nonsense Poet* (1938, reprinted London and New York 1968). Philip Hofer *Edward Lear as a Landscape Draughtsman* (Cambridge, Mass. and Oxford 1967). Vivien Noakes *Edward Lear: The Life of a Wanderer* (London 1968 and Boston 1969).

LECONTE DE LISLE, Charles Marie René (Oct. 22, 1818 – July 17, 1894). French poet. Born at St. Paul on Réunion Island, east of Madagascar, where his father was a sugar planter. Studied law at Rennes University (1837–43). Settled in Paris (1845) to write for Fourierist journals, particularly *La Phalange* and *La Démocratie pacifique*. When his republican hopes were dashed with coming of Second Empire, turned to poetry and doctrine of *l'art pour l'art,* and led the influential Parnassian movement. Formconscious, impersonal, and detached from contemporary issues, Leconte de Lisle's poetry reflects the pessimism of a disillusioned socialist. He often took as his subjects legends of ancient civilizations, particularly Greek, Indian, and Norse. Married Anne Adelaïde Perray (1857). With establishment of Third Republic, his financial difficulties were eased by appointment as assistant librarian to the Senate (1872). Elected to French Academy (1886). Published four books of verse during his lifetime: *Poèmes antiques* (1852), *Poèmes et poésies* (1855), *Poèmes barbares* (1862), and *Poèmes tragiques* (1884). Another volume, *Derniers Poèmes,* was published posthumously (1895). Died at Louveciennes.

REFERENCES: Irving Brown *Leconte de Lisle: A Study on the Man and His Poetry* (New York 1924). Edmond Estève *Leconte de Lisle, l'homme et l'oeuvre* (Paris 1923). Alison Fairlie *Leconte de Lisle's Poems on the Barbarian Races* (Cambridge, England, and New York 1947). Pierre Flottes *Leconte de Lisle, l'homme et l'oeuvre* (Paris 1954). Irving Putter *The Pessimism of Leconte de Lisle* (2 vols. Berkeley, Calif. PB 1954/61).

LE CORBUSIER (real name Charles Édouard Jeanneret-Gris) (Oct. 6, 1887 – Aug. 27, 1965). Swiss architect. Born La Chaux-de-Fonds, near Geneva. Studied at local art school, where one of his teachers, the painter Charles L'Eplattenier, encouraged interest in architecture. First buildings erected in Switzerland (1904–1906). After period of travel and study throughout Europe, settled in Paris (1917), where he first concentrated on painting, founding purist movement with Amédée Ozenfant, who also joined him in publishing avant-garde review *L'Esprit Nouveau* (1920–25). From 1922 Le Corbusier devoted himself to architecture. Among major works: Ozenfant house, Paris (1922–23), plans for palace of League of Nations (1927, not used), Savoye house, Poissy (1928–30), Swiss hostel at Cité Universitaire, Paris (1932), city planning schemes for Algiers, São Paulo, Rio de Janeiro, Buenos Aires, Barcelona, Geneva, Stockholm, Antwerp, Nemours (all 1930's), ministry of health and education building, Rio de Janeiro (1936), apartment block called Unité d'Habitation, Marseilles (1947–52), Chandigarh, capital city of Punjab (begun 1950), Ronchamp chapel in the Vosges, France (1955). Le Corbusier's impact on twentieth-century architecture is tremendous, especially since World War II. He revolutionized use of steel and reinforced concrete, developed concept of a house as "a machine for living," made enormously important contributions in field of urban planning and especially mass housing. Of widespread influence is his work *Vers une Architecture* (1923, tr. *Towards a New Architecture* 1959). Le Corbusier was also a gifted sculptor and abstract painter. Married Yvonne Gallis. Died at Roquebrune–Cap Martin, France.

EDITION: *Complete Works* ed. Willy Boesiger and others (7 vols. New York and London 1910–66).

REFERENCES: Maurice Besset *Who Was Le Corbusier?* (tr. Cleveland, Ohio 1969). Peter Blake *Le Corbusier: Architecture and Form* (Harmondsworth, England, PB 1963 and Baltimore PB 1964). Françoise Choay *Le Corbusier* (London and New York 1960, also PB). Norma Evenson *Le Corbusier: The Machine and the Grand Design* (New York 1969, also PB). Stamo Papadaki ed. *Le Corbusier: Architect, Painter, Writer* (New York 1948).

LEDOUX, Claude Nicolas (Mar. 21, 1736 – Nov. 19, 1806). French architect. Born Dormans-sur-Marne. Early works show influence of his teacher Jacques François Blondel and of Jacques Ange Gabriel. The houses he designed for Madame du Barry, the dancer Marie Madeleine Guimard, and other members of Parisian high society made his reputation, and from 1775 he received numerous royal commissions. That year marks beginning of his most inventive phase, in which he departed from tradition, exercising liberally his imagination in his designs. Important works include royal saltworks at Arc-et-Senans (1775–79), theatres of Besançon (from 1775) and Marseilles (from 1784), offices of Ferme Générale (1783), Parisian tollhouses (1784–89; four of them survive). Deprived of commissions after Revolution, Ledoux concentrated on his theoretical work *L'Architecture considérée sous le rapport de l'art, des moeurs et de la législation* (1804), in which he presented designs for an ideal city, "Chaux," which looked forward to Bauhaus functionalism, as well as unrealized plans for spherical, cylindrical, and pyramidal houses. Died in Paris.

REFERENCES: Yvan Christ *Projets et divagations de Claude Nicolas Ledoux, architecte du roi* (Paris 1961). Emil Kaufmann *Three Revolutionary Architects: Boullée, Ledoux, Lequeu* (Philadelphia PB 1952) and *Architecture in the Age of Reason* (Cambridge, Mass. 1955, also PB).

LE FANU, Joseph Sheridan (Aug. 28, 1814 – Feb. 7, 1873). Irish writer. Born Dublin, of French Huguenot descent and grand-nephew of dramatist Richard Brinsley Sheridan. While student at Trinity College, Dublin (1833–37), began contributing to *Dublin University Magazine*, of which he became staff member (1837), later editor and owner (1872). Was proprietor and editor of *Evening Mail* from 1839 to end of his life, making it a powerful Conservative organ and one of Ireland's major newspapers. Married Susan Bennett (1844); after her death (1858) became a recluse and began to produce the novels, mostly dealing with the supernatural, for which he is known. These include *The House by the Churchyard* (1863) and *Uncle Silas* (1864). His shorter ghost stories, some written as early as his student days, were collected in *In a Glass Darkly* (1872), *The Purcell Papers*

(1880), and other volumes. Died in Dublin.

REFERENCES: Nelson Browne *Sheridan Le Fanu* (London 1951). Stewart M. Ellis *Wilkie Collins, Le Fanu, and Others* (1931, reprinted Freeport, N.Y. 1968).

LÉGER, Fernand (Feb. 4, 1881 – Aug. 17, 1955). French painter. Born Argentan, Normandy, of peasant stock. Studied architecture at Caen, then in Paris (1900). Worked as architectural draftsman and studied painting in studios of Léon Gerôme and Gabriel Ferrier. Influenced at first by Cézanne, he then joined cubists, created sensation with *Nudes in the Forest* at Salon des Indépendants (1911) and with one-man show at Galerie Kahnweiler (1912). Following military service in World War I, developed characteristic style inspired by machine and industrial motifs, seen in such famous paintings as *The Card Players* (1917, Rijksmuseum Kröller-Müller, Otterlo), *The City* (1919, Museum of Art, Philadelphia), *Three Women* (*Le Grand Déjeuner*) (1921, Museum of Modern Art, New York), and *The Big Parade* (1954, Guggenheim Museum, New York). Léger traveled extensively and during World War II lived in U.S., the civilization of which influenced him deeply. A man of his age, he was completely original in all he created. Designed theatre and film sets, and created the first animated film (*Le Ballet mécanique*, 1924), stained-glass windows, sculpture, ceramics, mosaics (notably that for the façade of Notre Dame in Assy, 1946), murals (including those for United Nations General Assembly auditorium, 1952), book illustrations, and tapestry cartoons. Married twice. Died at Gif-sur-Yvette, Seine-et-Oise. There is a Musée Léger at Biot, Côte d'Azur.

REFERENCES: Douglas Cooper *Fernand Léger et le nouvel espace* (text in French and English, New York and London 1949). Robert L. Delevoy *Léger* (tr. Geneva 1962). Pierre Descargues *Fernand Léger* (Paris 1955). Katherine Kuh *Léger* (Urbana, Ill. 1953). André Verdet *Fernand Léger: le dynamisme pictural* (Geneva 1955).

LEHMBRUCK, Wilhelm (Jan. 4, 1881 – Mar. 25, 1919). German sculptor. Born Meidereich, near Duisburg. A miner's son, he studied art through scholarships at the Arts and Crafts School (1895–99) and Academy of Art (1901–1907) in Düsseldorf. Traveled to Italy and Paris (1905). First exhibited at Salon of 1907 in Paris, where he lived from 1910 to outbreak of World War I, when he moved to Berlin. Lehmbruck's work of 1905–10, such as *The Bather* (1905, Kunstakademie, Düsseldorf) and *Mother and Child* (1907, Folkwang Museum, Essen), shows influence of Rodin. Also influenced by Aristide Maillol's classicism as in *Standing Woman* (1910, Museum of Modern Art, New York) and *Frau Lehmbruck* (collection of Frau A. Lehmbruck, Stuttgart). The sculptures of Lehmbruck's mature phase are attenuated and angular, their mood melancholy and reflective. Characteristic is *Kneeling Woman* (1911, Museum of Modern Art, New York), one of his finest works. Others of this period include *Standing Youth* (1913, Museum of Modern Art, New York), *The Fallen* (1915–16, collection of Frau A. Lehmbruck, Stuttgart), *Seated Youth* (1918, Kunstakademie, Düsseldorf). Lehmbruck committed suicide in Berlin.

REFERENCES: August Hoff *Wilhelm Lehmbruck* (New York 1969). Erwin Petermann ed. *Die Druckgraphik von Wilhelm Lehmbruck* (Stuttgart and New York 1964). Paul Westheim *Wilhelm Lehmbruck* (London 1958 and New York 1959).

LELY, Sir Peter (real name Pieter Van der Faes) (Sept. 14, 1618 – Dec. 7, 1680). Dutch-English painter. Born probably at Soest, near Utrecht; trained in Haarlem. As portrait painter in suite of William of Orange he went to England (1641), where he remained for rest of his life, finding official favor alike under kings and Commonwealth. By 1650's he was most popular portraitist in England; appointed principal court painter to Charles II; knighted (1679). A gifted imitator and an astute judge of the taste of the moment, he developed in England a manner derivative of Van Dyke, adopting a tone of severity during the Commonwealth, and replacing this with elegance and sensuality to suit taste of Charles II. Well-known works are series of *Windsor Beauties* (1660's, Hampton Court) and *Admirals* (1666–67, National Maritime Museum, London), which inspired Sir Godfrey Kneller in his series, and portrait of Nell Gwyn (Metropolitan Museum, New York).

REFERENCES: C. H. Collins Baker *Lely and the Stuart Portrait Painters* (2 vols. London 1912 and Boston 1913). C. H. C. Baker and W. G. Constable *English Painting of the Sixteenth and Seventeenth Centuries* (London and New York 1930). Ronald B. Beckett *Lely* (London and Boston 1951). Margaret D. Whinney and Oliver Millar *English Art, 1625–1714* (Oxford 1957).

LE NAIN, Antoine (c.1588 – May 25, 1648), Louis (c.1593 – May 23, 1648), and Mathieu (1607 – Apr. 20, 1677). French painters. The three brothers were born at Laon. Circumstances of their early life and training are unknown; by 1630 they had established a studio in Paris, where, unmarried and working closely together, they spent the rest of their lives. All three were admitted to French Academy (1648). Primarily influenced by Dutch and Flemish art, they are known for their scenes of domestic and peasant life, the realism of which makes them unique in French seventeenth-century painting. Though the Le Nains often collaborated, signing works without initials, their styles have been distinguished as follows: Antoine was known for small family scenes; Louis, the most powerful and gifted, for such large peasant scenes as *The Forge* (Louvre, Paris), *The Cart* (1641, Louvre), *The Peasant Supper* (c.1640, Louvre), and *The Peasant Family* (c.1642, Louvre); Mathieu the most experimental brother, was noted for his strong chiaroscuro effects, as in *Le Corps de Garde* (c.1643, Berckheim Collection, Paris) and *The Backgammon Players* (Louvre).

REFERENCES: Anthony Blunt *Art and Architecture in France, 1500–1700* (Harmondsworth, England, 1953 and Baltimore 1954). Paul Fierens *Les Le Nain* (Paris 1933). Paul Jamot *Les*

Frères Le Nain (Paris 1922). Toledo Museum of Art *The Brothers Le Nain* (Toledo, Ohio 1947).

L'ENFANT, Pierre Charles (Aug. 2, 1754 – June 14, 1825). French-American architect. Born Paris, son of a painter to king of France. Studied painting, engineering, architecture before enlisting at his own expense in Continental army during American Revolution (1777). After being wounded at Savannah, Ga. (1779) and imprisoned at Charleston, S.C. (1780–82), he rose to rank of major (1783). Settled in New York (1784), remodeled (1787) the old city hall into the temporary Federal Hall, where Washington was inaugurated President (1789). The President then commissioned L'Enfant to design national capital on Potomac River. His plan (1791), reminiscent of Versailles, included radiating streets, beautiful parks and squares, and broad avenues, but his disregard for cost and for authority of the city commissioners led to his dismissal (1792). Most of his subsequent projects were also suspended because of his extravagance and willfulness. Spent last years on minor jobs while attempting to obtain remuneration for his work at Washington, D.C. Ultimately his was the chief plan chosen in development of the city. Never married. Died in poverty at Green Hill, Prince Georges County, Md., but was eventually (1909) reburied in Arlington National Cemetery.

REFERENCES: Hans Paul Caemmerer *The Life of Pierre L'Enfant, Planner of the City Beautiful, the City of Washington* (Washington 1950). Elizabeth S. Kite ed. *L'Enfant and Washington, 1791–1792* (Baltimore 1929).

LE NÔTRE, André (Mar. 12, 1613 – Sept. 15, 1700). French landscape architect. Son of Louis XIII's head gardener of the Tuileries, he was born and died in Paris. Apprenticed at thirteen to painter Simon Vouet, who taught him laws of perspective; he also studied architecture. Succeeded father (1637) at Tuileries. After designing, for Louis XIV's minister of finance Nicolas Fouquet, the famous gardens at Château de Vaux-le-Vicomte (1657), Le Nôtre became director of royal gardens. His designs, in which nature is transformed into precise geometry and becomes a logical architectural extension of the building it surrounds, express the spirit of French rationalism. His creations were known as *"les jardins de l'intelligence."* Versailles (begun 1662) was his masterpiece; other famous gardens include those at St.-Cloud, Fontainebleau, St.-Germain-en-Laye, Chantilly, Marly-le-Roi. Consulted by the great and powerful in England and Italy, his principles were dominating influence in Europe during first half of eighteenth century. Examples of this influence are St. James's and Hampton Court parks, England, the Vatican, and several villa gardens in Rome.

REFERENCES: Lucien Corpechot *Parcs et jardins de France; les jardins de l'intelligence* (Paris 1937). Ernest de Ganay *André Le Nostre, 1613–1700* (Paris 1962). Jules Guiffrey *André Le Nostre* (Paris 1912).

LEÓN, Fray Luis (Ponce) de (c.1527 – Aug. 23, 1591). Spanish poet and theologian. Born Belmonte, Cuenca. After schooling in Madrid and Valladolid, went to Salamanca (1543), where he entered Augustinian order (1544). From 1561 held chairs in theology at university there, except during imprisonment. As a result of academic rivalries and because he translated *The Song of Songs* into Spanish, León was denounced and on order of the Inquisition imprisoned (1572). Later absolved (1576), he returned to Salamanca. His most notable prose works are *De los Nombres de Cristo* (1583, additions 1585 and 1595, tr. *The Names of Christ* 1955), a Platonic discussion of the nature of Christ, and *La Perfecta Casada* (1583, tr. *The Perfect Wife* 1943), a handbook on the duties of a wife. León is especially remembered as a humanist whose poems (not published until 1631) include exquisite Renaissance lyrics as well as translations and imitations from the classics, Hebrew, and Italian. He died at monastery of Madrigal, Avila.

EDITIONS and TRANSLATIONS: *Original Poems* ed. Edward Sarmiento (in

Spanish; Manchester, England, 1953). Selections in *An Anthology of Spanish Poetry* ed. Angel Flores (New York 1961). *Lyrics of Luis de León* tr. Aubrey F. G. Bell (London 1928).

REFERENCES: Aubrey F. G. Bell *Luis de León* (Oxford 1925). Adolphe Coster *Luis de León* (2 vols. New York 1921–22). James Fitzmaurice-Kelly *Fray Luis de León* (Oxford 1921). Alain Guy *La Pensée de Fray Luis de León* (Limoges 1943).

LEONARDO DA VINCI (Apr. 15, 1452 – May 2, 1519). Italian painter and scientist. Born Vinci, Tuscany, illegitimate son of Florentine notary. Apprenticed to Andrea del Verrocchio (c.1466–72), remaining as his assistant until c.1477. Early works include landscape background and lefthand angel of Verrocchio's *Baptism of Christ* (c.1474, Uffizi, Florence), *Annunciation* (Uffizi), unfinished *Adoration of the Magi* (1481, Uffizi). In service of Ludovico Sforza, duke of Milan, as court painter and engineer (c.1482–99). First *Virgin of the Rocks* (begun 1483, Louvre, Paris); second version (begun c.1494, National Gallery, London). Fresco *The Last Supper*, in refectory of cloister of S. Maria delle Grazie, Milan (1496–98), is now much damaged. Leonardo returned to Florence (1500–1506, with interruptions), where he designed and partly executed a mural of *The Battle of Anghiari* (begun 1503) for Florentine Palazzo della Signoria. Now lost, it exerted great influence, especially through copies of its executed central portion. At about same time he painted the now lost *Leda and the Swan,* of which copies abound, and *Mona Lisa* (Louvre). In Milan at court of Charles d'Amboise, French governor (1506–13), where he painted *The Virgin and Child with St. Anne* (Louvre), and from 1513 to 1517 in Rome, where he probably painted *St. John the Baptist* (Louvre). Went to France (1517) on invitation of Francis I, who gave him title *"premier peintre, architecte, et méchanicien du roi."* He died at the Château de Cloux, near Amboise. Of major importance are his notes, drawings, and manuscripts (which include *Treatise on Painting* and treatises on

scientific subjects), preserved in various archives, museums, and libraries.

TRANSLATIONS: *The Notebooks of Leonardo da Vinci* ed. and tr. Edward McCurdy (1938, latest ed. New York 1954). *Treatise on Painting (Codex Urbinas Latinus 1270)* ed. and tr. A. Philip McMahon (2 vols. Princeton, N.J. and Oxford 1956). Erwin Panofsky *The Codex Huygens and Leonardo da Vinci's Art Theory* (London 1940). *Leonardo da Vinci on Painting* ed. Carlo Pedretti (Berkeley, Calif. and London 1964). *The Literary Works of Leonardo da Vinci* ed. Jean Paul Richter (3rd ed. 2 vols. London and New York 1970).

REFERENCES: Sir Kenneth Clark *Leonardo da Vinci: An Account of His Development as an Artist* (2nd ed. Cambridge, England, 1952, also PB). Sir Kenneth Clark and Carlo Pedretti *Leonardo da Vinci: Drawings* (2nd ed. 3 vols. London and New York 1968–69). R. Langton Douglas *Leonardo da Vinci: His Life and His Pictures* (Chicago 1944). Ludwig Goldscheider *Leonardo da Vinci: Paintings and Drawings* (8th ed. London and New York 1967). Ludwig H. Heydenreich *Leonardo da Vinci* (2 vols. London and New York 1954).

✐

LEONARDO DA VINCI
BY JUERGEN SCHULZ

Leonardo's career is a series of contrasts and contradictions that make him one of the most enigmatic figures of all time, despite the fact that he has left a fuller legacy of personal papers and contemporary accounts than almost any other figure of the Renaissance.

Born an illegitimate child, reared in a provincial hamlet, and trained in what was then the artisan's craft of painting, he rose by virtue of his talents to become a consort of princes, popes, and kings. Yet at the end of his life he had almost abandoned painting, to which he owed his fame, and had quit Italy, the theatre of his successes. Endowed with a brilliant, curious mind that led him to apply techniques of scientific observation to every phenomenon of the natural world, and to develop insights and inventions without precedent in his time, his research remained unknown to his contemporaries, and his discoveries were left to be rediscovered, independently, by scientists of the seventeenth and eighteenth centuries.

His career began at Florence, where within a short time of beginning his apprenticeship he rose to become the leading assistant in the studio of his master Verrocchio. By the time he was twenty-nine, in 1481, he was independently and successfully competing with established artists for state and religious commissions. His paintings of the period share certain characteristics with late fifteenth-century Florentine painting in general — excitement, overcrowding, circumstantial naturalistic description, and diffuseness in the representation of the subject — but distinguish themselves by their search for large organizational rhythms, their excellence of drawing and profoundness of sentiment. Yet at this point of his career Leonardo abandoned Florence, leaving a major work unfinished (*Adoration of the Magi,* in the Uffizi), to become court artist in the distant and artistically undeveloped city of Milan.

His seventeen years in the service of Ludovico Sforza, duke of Milan, were the most settled and productive period of his life. During it he gradually abandoned the precious painting style of his youth, and developed a new style that had all the earmarks of High Renaissance painting. In the London *Virgin of the Rocks,* begun c.1494, and the famous *Last Supper* (at Milan) of 1496–98, he substituted drama for excitement, severity for copiousness, abstract compositional rationalism for additive naturalistic observation, and

economy and grandeur for episodic multiplicity.

With the French capture of Milan in 1499, Leonardo returned to Florence. His brief residence there, from 1500 to 1506, was an artistic event of the greatest importance, for it introduced artists such as the young Raphael and Michelangelo to his Milanese style. He received commissions for a colossal battle mural in the council hall of the Florentine republic and an altarpiece in the church of the Servites, but he did not stay to finish the former and never began the latter. Instead, he explored the compositional possibilities of a subject he had already attempted once before, at Milan (the *Virgin and Saint Anne;* the composition is lost), produced a portrait and a mythological painting for private patrons (the *Mona Lisa,* in Paris, and a *Leda,* now lost), and engaged himself for engineering works such as mapping and fortifying conquered territories for the infamous Cesare Borgia, and diverting the Arno River for the Florentine republic.

In 1506 he returned to Milan, now under the administration of a French military government. There he completed the London *Virgin of the Rocks* and attempted yet a third time the subject of the *Virgin and St. Anne* (the painting is now in Paris). Much of his time, as the surviving notebooks show, went to scientific observation and speculation. Already toward the end of his first residence in Milan, he had begun systematically to pursue scientific investigation into the anatomy of the human body, the structure of plants, and the laws of optics. These activities had intensified during his return to Florence and his second stay in Milan, while the subjects of inquiry had subtly changed. During the second Florentine period he had observed the movements of water, the flight of birds, and the currents of the air. During the second Milanese period he studied problems of motion transfer, meteorology, geology and physiology. Increasingly his interest was drawn to dynamic rather than static phenomena; even his studies of geological formations show him rendering rock strata as the frozen remains of titanic upheavals.

A reflection of these changing interests can be sensed in his paintings. The central group he projected for the uncompleted Florentine battle scene (called *The Battle for the Standard,* it is known today only from copies) is cast in the monumental, compact, sculptural style of Leonardo's maturity. But the fierce movements and expressions of the group give the scene a terrifying and daemonic ferocity that has little in common with the grave sensibility of the High Renaissance. In the third *Virgin and St. Anne,* the strong modeling and sculptural form of Leonardo's previous work is gone. Shadow glides over the forms like wind over water, everything seems to tremble with slight movement, and form is insubstantial.

Leonardo left occupied Milan in 1513, to spend the bulk of the next three years in Rome, lodged in the Vatican as a guest of the cardinal nephew of Pope Leo X. He produced four small cabinet pictures, of which only a *St. John the Baptist* survives (Paris), experimented with varnishes and paint media, and practiced cruel transformations on lizards, which he turned into miniature dragons by grafting false wings into their bodies. The years 1513–16 are the high point of the Roman High Renaissance, during which Michelangelo was working on the Julius tomb, and Raphael on the Vatican *stanze* and tapestries. That Leonardo in such an environment, with the prospective patronage of the pope

at his command, should have achieved so little, must have been a matter of choice rather than fate.

Late in 1516 Leonardo took service with King Francis I of France. There, in the royal châteaux of the Loire, he spent his last three years. A visitor to his studio at Cloux in 1517 was shown three paintings, the *Mona Lisa,* the *Virgin and St. Anne,* and the *St. John* — all works Leonardo had brought with him from Italy. He was told that the artist's right hand was paralyzed and that Leonardo could no longer work well. But since Leonardo was left-handed, the obstacle must have been an inner and not a physical one. His chief works from these years are a series of extraordinary drawings, representing uranic cataclysms such as no eye has ever seen: whirlpools of water course through the sky and over the earth, explosions of rock hurl boulders into the air, and cities crumble and are washed away. It is as if the fascination with movement and flux had become a nightmare.

There is evidence that during his later years Leonardo sought to put in order his voluminous scientific papers and to compose four great treatises, on painting, architecture, anatomy, and mechanics. But this task also he never completed. Only some outline for the *Treatise on Painting* seems to have been conceived by him. The actual realization of the treatise, by the extraction of apposite passages from the multitude of his papers, was carried out after his death by a pupil.

The baffling fragmentariness of Leonardo's achievement and restlessness of his life have been a source for speculation from the sixteenth century to our time. Freud, in a celebrated study that is largely vitiated by misinformation, sought to explain Leonardo's personality and career exclusively from psychological considerations. The artist's solitary character, which could not brook competition, but preferred provincial cities as a residence and mediocrities as assistants, was certainly shaped by psychological needs. But the basic development of Leonardo's art and thought suggests an intellectual as well as a psychological dilemma.

His fundamental commitment to rational inquiry did not serve any comprehensive philosophy or outlook. The only abstraction he allowed himself was mathematics. More than once he contrasted in his writings the certainty of mathematical statements with the uncertainty of other processes of cognition. But mathematics was to him no more than a technique for quantifying and analyzing the elements of an individual problem; it was not a technique for system building. The philosophical system of the medieval Scholastics, which interpreted the natural world as a reflection of a hierarchical divine order, had been unmade in the fifteenth century. The philosophical system of the Enlightenment, which saw in the natural world the expression of a mathematical order, had not yet evolved. Leonardo himself did not have the power of synthesis to fill that gap. Thus, the multiplicity of observations recorded in his ever swelling notebooks became in the end an uncontrollable mass of material, the only common denominator of which was seemingly process or flux. "As every divided kingdom falls," Leonardo wrote in a notebook of his last years, "so every mind divided between many studies confounds and saps itself."

LEONCAVALLO, Ruggiero (Mar. 8, 1858 – Aug. 9, 1919). Italian composer. Born Naples, where he graduated from the conservatory (1876). His first opera, *Tommaso Chatterton,* was about to be performed in Bologna (1878) when the producer absconded, and Leoncavallo was thereupon forced to support himself by giving lessons and playing the piano in cafés. After years of travel, he returned to Italy (1887) with *I Medici,* first part of projected trilogy on Italian Renaissance. Before it was staged (1893), however, *I Pagliacci* was produced triumphantly with Arturo Toscanini as conductor in Milan (1892). A major example of Italian operatic realism (or *verismo*), it is Leoncavallo's only enduring composition. None of his later works — *La Bohème* (1897), *Chatterton* (produced 1896), *Zaza* (1900), or *Der Roland* (1904) — had real success. Leoncavallo also wrote two symphonic poems, *Nuit de mai* (after Musset's poem) and *Serafita* (after Balzac's novel). He died at Montecatini, near Florence.

LEOPARDI, Count Giacomo (June 29, 1798 – June 14, 1837). Italian poet and scholar. Born Recanati, near Ancona, of wealthy noble family. Educated at home, largely self-taught. Intense study of classics, Italian, and history overtaxed his frail constitution, causing him to contract severe spinal disease; he plunged into profound melancholy which affected his entire life. By sixteen had written verse, two tragedies, critical studies on Latin and Greek literature, translations from Horace, Virgil, and Greek odes. Friendship with writer Pietro Giordano inspired Leopardi to write two of his best romantic lyrics, *All'Italia* and *Sopra il Monumento di Dante* (1818). Always miserable at home, Leopardi made trips to Rome (1822–23), Milan, Bologna, Pisa, and Florence (1825–28), then left Recanati for good (1830), finally settling in Naples (1833), where he died of cholera. An unhappy love affair in Florence produced some of his greatest poems, including *La Ginestra* (1836), considered his masterpiece. His poetry in the collections *Canzoni* (1824), *Versi* (1826), which includes the apologia for suicide *Bruto minore,* and *Canti* (1831, 1835, 1845), expresses profound despair and disillusionment that combined with a classical style make him one of the great nineteenth-century Italian poets, whose influence was enormous. His best-known prose work,

Operette morali (1827, tr. *Essays, Dialogues, and Thoughts*), contains studies in his philosophy of pessimism.

TRANSLATIONS: *Poems* tr. Jean Pierre Barricelli (New York 1963). *Poems and Prose* ed. Angel Flores (Bloomington, Ind. 1966, also PB). *Selected Prose and Poetry* tr. Iris Origo and John Heath-Stubbs (London and New York 1966). *Canti* tr. John H. Whitfield (Manchester, England, PB 1967).

REFERENCES: Iris Origo *Leopardi: A Study in Solitude* (1935, enlarged edition London 1953 and New York 1954). G. S. Singh *Leopardi and the Theory of Poetry* (Lexington, Ky. 1964). John H. Whitfield *Giacomo Leopardi* (Oxford 1954).

LERMONTOV, Mikhail Yuryevich (Oct. 15, 1814 – July 27, 1841). Russian poet and novelist. Born Moscow; after his mother's death (1817), brought up by wealthy grandmother. Entered Moscow University (1830), where he read Byron intensely. Expelled for disciplinary reasons (1832), he was enrolled in military school in St. Petersburg; received commission (1834). Poem on death of Pushkin expressing anticourt sentiment (1837) caused a sensation and resulted in his being transferred to regiment in Caucasus. Returned to St. Petersburg a year later, a celebrated poet. Banished to Caucasus again after duel with son of French ambassador (1840), he was killed at Pyatigorsk in a duel with a fellow soldier. Lermontov's poetry, at first heavily influenced by Byron and Pushkin, developed toward simplicity and realism. Ranked second only to Pushkin's in Russian literature, his verses include *A Song About Czar Ivan Vasilyevich, His Young Bodyguard, and the Valiant Merchant Kalashnikov* (1837), *Mtsyri* (1840, *The Novice*), and *The Demon* (1841). His major prose work is the novel *A Hero of Our Time* (1840). The first Russian novel of psychological realism, it presents in the figure of the "hero," Grigoriy Alexandrovich Pechorin, an important development of the type introduced by Pushkin, further explored by successive Russian writers, and termed by Turgenev the "superfluous man."

TRANSLATIONS: *A Hero of Our Own Times* tr. Eden and Cedar Paul (1940,

new ed. London and New York 1958). *A Hero of Our Time* tr. Vladimir and D. Nabokov (Garden City, N.Y. and London PB 1958). *The Demon and Other Poems* tr. Eugene M. Kayden (Yellow Springs, Ohio 1965). *Selected Poetry* tr. C. E. L'Ami and Alexander Welikotny (Winnipeg PB 1965). *A Lermontov Reader* ed. and tr. Guy Daniels (New York 1965, also PB).

REFERENCES: C. E. L'Ami and Alexander Welikotny *Michael Lermontov* (Winnipeg 1967). Janko Lavrin *Lermontov* (London and New York 1959). John Mersereau *Mikhail Lermontov* (Carbondale, Ill. 1962). Henri Troyat *L'Étrange Destin de Lermontov: biographie* (Paris 1952).

LESAGE, Alain René (May 8, 1668 – Nov. 17, 1747). French playwright and novelist. Born Sarzeau, Britanny, to a family recently ennobled. Educated at Jesuit college at Vannes, he went to Paris (1692) to study law, but soon gave it up for writing. Married Marie Élisabeth Huyard (1694). After producing a series of translations, won success with a comedy, *Crispin, rival de son maître* (1707), produced in same year as his first novel, *Le Diable boiteux*, adapted in part from a Spanish tale. Best-known play is *Turcaret* (1709), a biting satire on French financiers. Lesage's masterpiece, the picaresque novel *Gil Blas de Santillane* (1715–35), presents a wide-ranging satirical tableau of early eighteenth-century France. Too proud and too jealous of his privacy to solicit a seat in the Académie Française, Lesage was the first known French writer to live by his pen, without patronage. Died at Boulogne.

TRANSLATIONS: *Gil Blas de Santillane* tr. Tobias Smollett (1749, new ed. London and New York 1928). *Turcaret* tr. W. S. Merwin, in Eric Bentley *The Classical Theatre* Vol. IV (Garden City, N.Y. PB 1961).

REFERENCES: Léo Claretie *Lesage, romancier* (Paris 1890). Charles Dédéyan *Lesage et Gil Blas* (2 vols. Paris 1965). Eugène Lintilhac *Lesage* (Paris 1893).

LESSING, Gotthold Ephraim (Jan. 22, 1729 – Feb. 15, 1781). German man of letters. Born Kamenz, Saxony, son of Protestant pastor. Educated at the Fürstenschule, Meissen, and at Leipzig University (1746–48). By 1748 was publishing reviews and had produced several plays. Settling in Berlin, he made reputation as literary journalist, wrote comedies and essays. Published collected edition of his works (6 vols. 1753–55). His play *Miss Sara Sampson,* produced with great success (1755), was the first German *bürgerliches Trauerspiel,* or tragedy of middle-class domestic life; it represented a total break with French drama and the beginning of modern German theatre. With Moses Mendelssohn and C. F. Nicolai, published critical journal *Briefe, die neueste Literatur Betreffend* (1759–65), contributing famous series of essays (1759–60) which proclaimed superiority of Shakespeare to Corneille and other writers of *tragédie classique.* While secretary to governor of Breslau (1760–65), wrote *Laokoon* (1766), treatise on aesthetics. In Hamburg (1767–69), produced comedy *Minna von Barnhelm* (1767) and wrote *Hamburgische Dramaturgie* (1767–69), series of critical essays on drama. From 1770, was librarian to duke of Brunswick at Wolfenbüttel. Married Eva König (1776; she died in 1778). Died in Brunswick. Major late works: *Briefe antiquarischen Inhalts* (1769) and *Wie die Alten den Tod gebildet* (1769), critical essays; tragedy *Emilia Galotti* (1772); *Nathan der Weise* (1779), a dramatic poem urging racial and religious tolerance; *Die Erziehung des Menschengeschlechts* (1780), a treatise on religion. Lessing was the chief German exponent of Enlightenment ideals of truth, reason, progress, and intellectual liberty. There are various recent German editions of whole works, and various English translations of individual or selected works.

REFERENCES: Henry B. Garland *Lessing: The Founder of Modern German Literature* (1937, 2nd ed., reprinted London and New York 1963). Michael M. Metzger *Lessing and the Language of Comedy* (The Hague 1966). John G. Robertson *Lessing's Dramatic Theory* (1939, reprinted New York 1965).

LE VAU, Louis (1612 – Oct. 11, 1670). French architect. Born and died in Paris. Made his name as designer of town houses on Ile St.-Louis, including Hôtel Lambert. Succeeding Jacques Lemercier as architect to Louis XIV (1654), Le Vau was commissioned to make additions to royal Château de Vincennes (1654–60). For minister of finance, Nicolas Fouquet, he designed Château de Vaux-le-Vicomte (1657–61), whose gardens made André Le Nôtre famous. Vaux-le-Vicomte, with its exquisitely proportioned two-story salon, is considered Le Vau's masterpiece. He continued work of enlarging the Louvre (1660's) and the Tuileries (from 1664), and designed the core of the Palais de Versailles, later extended by Jules Mansart and Jacques Ange Gabriel. Also designed church of St. Sulpice (1655) and Collège des Quatre-Nations (from 1661), now Institut de France. Le Vau is distinguished for brilliantly developing French baroque architecture.

REFERENCE: Anthony F. Blunt *Art and Architecture in France: 1500–1700* (Harmondsworth, England, 1953 and Baltimore 1954).

LEVER, Charles James (Aug. 31, 1806 – June 1, 1872). Irish novelist. Born Dublin, son of prosperous architect. Studied medicine at Trinity College, Dublin (1822–27), and at Göttingen, receiving degree at Trinity (1831). Married Kate Barker (1833). From 1834 began writing for *Dublin University Magazine,* which he later edited (1842–45), and in which first appeared his highly successful novel *The Confessions of Harry Lorrequer* (1837). It was the first of a series of lively tales of army life that includes *Charles O'Malley* (1840), *Jack Hinton the Guardsman* (1843), and *Tom Burke of "Ours"* (1844). After practicing medicine in Brussels (1837–42), returned to Dublin until 1845, when he went abroad again. Became British consul at La Spezia, Italy (1857–67), then at Trieste (1867–72), where he died. His later novels were serious and lacked the rollicking vitality of the earlier ones, and were therefore less popular.

REFERENCES: William J. Fitzpatrick *The Life of Charles Lever* (2 vols. London 1879). Lionel Stevenson *Dr. Quick-silver: The Life of Charles Lever* (1939, reprinted New York 1969).

LEWIS, (Harry) Sinclair (Feb. 7, 1885 – Jan. 10, 1951). American writer. Born Sauk Centre, Minn., son of small-town doctor. Educated locally, at Oberlin (Ohio) Academy, and at Yale (graduated 1908). Then traveled, worked at odd jobs, wrote a number of stories for popular magazines, and produced novel *Our Mr. Wren* (1914). Like its four successors it went unnoticed. However, *Main Street* (1920), an exposé of small-town Midwestern America, became an outstanding success and was followed by Lewis's four other major novels: *Babbitt* (1922), *Arrowsmith* (1925), for which he was offered the Pulitzer prize and refused, *Elmer Gantry* (1927), and *Dodsworth* (1929). Married Grace Hegger (1914). After their divorce (1925), married well-known journalist Dorothy Thompson (1928). Was the first American to win Nobel prize for literature (1930). Received honorary degree from Yale (1936). But his career began to decline to a long string of minor novels, and estrangement from his wife, ending in divorce (1942). Died of a heart attack in Rome. His caricature-like characters and his tendency to simplify human situations have caused Lewis to be compared with Dickens. As one of the great depicters of the 1920's, he captured unerringly the speech and mores of American middle-class life.

REFERENCES: D. J. Dooley *The Art of Sinclair Lewis* (Lincoln, Neb. 1967, also PB). Grace Hegger Lewis *With Love from Gracie: Sinclair Lewis* (New York 1955). Mark Schorer *Sinclair Lewis: An American Life* (New York 1961); ed. *Sinclair Lewis: A Collection of Critical Essays* (Englewood Cliffs, N.J. 1962, also PB). Carl C. Van Doren *Sinclair Lewis: A Biographical Sketch* (1933, reprinted Port Washington, N.Y. 1969).

LEWIS, (Percy) Wyndham (Nov. 18, 1884 – Mar. 7, 1957). English artist and writer. Born of English parents at sea in Bay of Fundy, off Maine; brought to England while an infant. Attended Rugby (1897–98) and Slade School of Art in London (1898–1901). Exhibited paintings in London from about 1909; founded the vorticist movement (1914), an offshoot of cubism and futurism which included as members Ezra Pound, Jacob Epstein, and others; and expounded his artistic theories in the magazine *Blast* (1914–15). Later paintings, though naturalistic, maintain harsh and metallic quality of vorticist works. Lewis's books, chiefly in vein of angry satire, include novels *Tarr* (1918); trilogy *The Human Age*, consisting of *The Childermass* (1928), *Monstre Gai* (1955), and *Malign Fiesta* (1955); *The Apes of God* (1930); *The Revenge for Love* (1937); *Self-Condemned* (1954); and nonfiction works *The Art of Being Ruled* (1926), *Time and Western Man* (1927), the autobiographical *Rude Assignment* (1950), and *The Writer and the Absolute* (1952). Married Anne Hoskyns (1929). Lived in Canada and United States during World War II. Returned to England (1948); lived in London rest of life.

REFERENCES: Geoffrey Grigson *A Master of Our Time: A Study of Wyndham Lewis* (London 1951). Charles Handley-Read ed. *The Art of Wyndham Lewis* (London 1951). Hugh Kenner *Wyndham Lewis* (London and Norfolk, Conn. 1954). Geoffrey A. Wagner *Wyndham Lewis: A Portrait of the Artist as the Enemy* (New Haven and London 1957).

LEYDEN. See LUCAS VAN LEYDEN.

LICHTENBERG, Georg Christoph (July 1, 1742 – Feb. 24, 1799). German physicist and satirist. Born Oberramstadt, near Darmstadt. Educated at Göttingen University (1763–69) and became professor of physics there (1769–99). Made important scientific contributions, especially in field of electricity, discovering a phenomenon called Lichtenberg's figures. Lived in England (1774–75), which resulted in *Briefe aus England* (1776–78, *Letters from England*), one of his best-known works. Edited *Göttinger Taschenkalender,* a journal disseminating the Enlightenment philosophy (1778–99), and wrote Swiftian satires, noted for their aphoristic style, on the *Sturm und Drang* writers, the physiognomist Johann Lavater, and other contemporaries. Another important work is *Ausführliche Erklärung der Hogarthischen Kupferstiche* (1794–99, tr. *The World of Hogarth: Lichtenberg's Commentaries on Hogarth's Engravings*, London and Boston 1966). Died at Göttingen.

REFERENCES: Carl Brinitzer *A Reasonable Rebel: Georg Christoph Lichtenberg* (tr. New York and London 1960). Joseph P. Stern *Lichtenberg: A Doctrine of Scattered Occasions, Reconstructed from His Aphorisms and Reflections* (Bloomington, Ind. 1959).

LIEBERMANN, Max (July 20, 1847 – Feb. 8, 1935). German painter. Born and died in Berlin; studied art there (1866–68) and in Weimar (1868–72). His first exhibited painting, *Women Plucking Geese* (1872, National Gallery, Berlin), caused a scandal because of its honest, realistic treatment of homely subject matter. Went to France (1873), where he was greatly influenced by Barbizon painters, particularly Millet. Equally important in formation of his style were summers spent in Holland, from 1879 to outbreak of World War I, during which he studied work of Hals. Liebermann's mature paintings, predominantly genre scenes, show his two aims as an artist: the study of light and the depiction of the life of humble people. After 1890, his works show influence of Manet and Degas. Settling in Berlin (1884), he became leader of German impressionists, and was chosen president of Berlin Secession, a group of antiacademic painters (1899). Liebermann's importance lies in his introduction to Germany of current trends in French painting. Major works include *Old Folks' Home in Amsterdam* (1880), *An Asylum for Old Men* (1881), *The Cobbler's Shop* (1881), *The Flax Spinners* (1887), *Mending the Nets* (1889, Kunsthalle, Hamburg).

REFERENCE: Karl Scheffler *Max Liebermann* (2nd ed. Wiesbaden 1953).

LINCOLN, Abraham (Feb. 12, 1809 – Apr. 15, 1865). American statesman. Born near Hodgenville, Ky., of uneducated pioneer parents. Spent youth on frontier farm in Indiana (1816–30); largely self-educated, he received only about a year's schooling. Settled in New Salem, Ill. (1831–37), where he took various jobs and ran for state legislature (elected 1834), serving until 1841. Obtained attorney's license (1836); moved to Springfield, Ill. to practice law (1837); rose to be one of the state's finest lawyers. Married Mary Todd (1842). William Herndon became his law partner (1844). Served term in Congress as Whig (1847–49), then retired from politics until he emerged as opponent of Kansas-Nebraska Bill (1854) and prominent member of antislavery Republican party (1856). Seeking Senate seat, engaged Democratic opponent Stephen A. Douglas in the seven famous debates on slavery (1858) that, though he lost the election, established Lincoln's national reputation. This was further enhanced by dignity and eloquence of the antislavery Cooper Union speech (Feb. 27, 1860). Elected President (1860). Determined above all to preserve the Union, Lincoln made a stand at Fort Sumter, and the Civil War began when Sumter was fired on (1861). Thereafter came his greatest, most memorable speeches and writings: the Emancipation Proclamation (1862, final version 1863), the Gettysburg Address, letter to Mrs. Bixby (Nov. 21, 1864) and numerous other letters, the Second Inaugural ("With malice toward none, with charity for all") (1865), speech on Reconstruction (April 1865). His writings are characterized by sensitivity to the occasion and audience, by an intrinsically American flavor, homespun simplicity, lucid and trenchant expression, profundity of thought. The grandeur and personal dignity of his language reflects more than anything his intensive reading of Scripture. He was shot by actor John Wilkes Booth while attending a play at Ford's Theatre in Washington, D.C., and died the following morning. With time he has become almost legendary; uncounted anecdotes are attributed to him, and the literature on him continues to mount with every decade.

EDITION: *The Collected Works of Abraham Lincoln* ed. Roy P. Basler (9 vols. New Brunswick, N.J. 1953–55).

REFERENCES: Albert J. Beveridge *Abraham Lincoln, 1809–1858* (2 vols. Boston and London 1928). William H. Herndon and Jesse W. Weik *Life of Lincoln: The Historical and Personal Recollections of Abraham Lincoln* (1888, latest ed. Cleveland, Ohio 1949). Jay Monaghan *Lincoln Bibliography: 1839–1939* (2 vols. Springfield, Ill. 1943–45). John G. Nicolay and John Hay *Abraham Lincoln: A History* (10 vols. New York 1890). James G. Randall *Lincoln the President* (4 vols. New York and London 1945–55, also PB). Carl Sandburg *Abraham Lincoln: The Prairie Years* (2 vols. New York 1926, also PB) and *Abraham Lincoln: The War Years* (4 vols. New York 1939, also PB). Benjamin P. Thomas *Abraham Lincoln: A Biography* (New York 1952 and London 1953).

LINDSAY, (Nicholas) Vachel (Nov. 10, 1879 – Dec. 5, 1931). American poet. Born and died in Springfield, Ill. Studied at Hiram College, Ohio (1897–1900), Chicago Art Institute (1900–1904), and New York Art School (1904–1905). Lacking success with his drawings, took up poetry, and began walking tours of South and West (1906), lecturing, preaching his "gospel of beauty," and reciting his poems in return for food and lodging. During winters, earned living by lecturing for Y.M.C.A. in New York and Springfield, and for Illinois Anti-Saloon League. Won fame on appearance of *General William Booth Enters into Heaven* in *Poetry* magazine (1913); this and *The Congo* are his best-known poems. Lindsay's reputation was at its height during his lifetime, when he read, or rather chanted, his verses to the public. Noted for forceful rhythms, onomatopoetic effects, and for portrayal of American folkways, his best work was written before 1920 and collected in *General William Booth Enters into Heaven and Other Poems* (1913); *The Congo* (1914); *The Chinese Nightingale* (1917), which includes *The Ghost of the Buffaloes; The Daniel Jazz* (1920); and *The Golden Whales of California* (1920). Among prose works

are *A Handy Guide for Beggars* (1916) and *The Golden Book of Springfield* (1920). Married Elizabeth Conner (1925).

EDITION: *Collected Poems* (rev. ed. 1925, reprinted New York 1960).

REFERENCES: Mark Harris *City of Discontent: An Interpretive Biography of Vachel Lindsay* (Indianapolis 1952 PB 1963). Edgar Lee Masters *Vachel Lindsay: A Poet in America* (1935 reprinted New York 1969). Eleanor Ruggles *The West-going Heart: A Life of Vachel Lindsay* (New York 1959).

LIPPI, Fra Filippo (or Lippo) (c.1406 – Oct. 9, 1469). Italian painter. Born Florence. Orphaned in childhood and given over to Carmelite friars of S. Maria del Carmine, Florence, he became a monk there (1421). The frescoes of Masaccio and Masolino in Brancacci chapel of the Carmine influenced him powerfully, as seen in his earliest known work, the fresco *Reform of the Carmelite Rule* (c.1432). Leaving the monastery (1432), he worked for a time in Padua before returning to Florence, where he soon won patronage of Cosimo de' Medici. Made rector of S. Quirico at Legnaia, near Florence (1442), but was dismissed for misconduct (1455). Appointed chaplain at convent of S. Margherita in Prato (1456), from which he eloped with a nun, Lucrezia Buti, who became mother of painter Filippino Lippi (c.1457–1504). The couple were released from their vows in order to marry (1461). Lippi died at Spoleto. Frescoes in choir of cathedral at Prato, depicting lives of SS. Stephen and John the Baptist (1452–64), are considered his greatest achievement; among other well-known works are numerous Madonnas including *Tarquinia Madonna* (1437, National Gallery, Rome), *Coronation of the Virgin*, altarpiece for S. Ambrogio, Florence (1441–47, Uffizi, Florence). A highly popular and influential painter, Lippi gave his figures the monumentality of Masaccio's and imbued them with emotional warmth. He was the teacher of Botticelli.

REFERENCES: Edward C. Strutt *Fra Filippo Lippi* (London 1901). Giorgio Vasari *Lives of the . . . Painters, Sculptors, and Architects* ed. and tr.

Gaston de Vere (10 vols. London 1912–15).

LISZT, Franz (Ferencz) (Oct. 22, 1811 – July 31, 1886). Hungarian composer and pianist. Born Raiding, Hungary, to family of noble descent. His father gave him his early musical training and supervised the precocious boy's career as concert pianist, taking him all over Europe and enabling him to study with Karl Czerny, Antonio Salieri, Anton Reicha, and others. At fourteen, Liszt produced a one-act opera, *Don Sanche*. On his father's death (1837) he settled in Paris, the great music center of the time. Formed a liaison (1833) with the brilliant, liberal countess Marie d'Agoult, with whom he eloped (1835) and by whom he had three children, one of them, Cosima (Dec. 25, 1837 – Apr. 1, 1930), to become wife of Richard Wagner (after marrying Hans von Bülow). Concert tours took him to Russia and other countries until 1847; he and the countess began to drift apart in 1839. Second phase of his career began with his position as kapellmeister at court of Grand Duke Carl Friedrich at Weimar (1848–58). Here he furthered the work of young, advanced musicians, and himself embarked on prolific period as composer. From 1848 also dates liaison with Princess Carolyne von Sayn-Wittgenstein. After failure of marriage plans with her (1861), Liszt lived in retirement, received orders as an abbé (1865), and divided his time teaching and composing between Weimar, Rome, and Budapest. Died at Bayreuth. His oeuvre includes twelve symphonic poems, the form of which he invented, fifteen Hungarian rhapsodies, two symphonies, three oratorios, many works for piano, and piano transcriptions from opera and other orchestral compositions. In his lifetime he was chiefly famous as a virtuoso, a supremely gifted pianist, but he was also important as a harmonic innovator who looked forward to the romanticism of the nineteenth century and the tonal experiments of the twentieth century. Liszt also wrote books and essays on music.

REFERENCES: Walter Beckett *Liszt* (London and New York 1956). Ernest Newman *The Man Liszt* (1934, reprinted London 1969 and New York 1970). Humphrey Searle *The Music of Liszt* (2nd ed. New York PB 1966). Sacheverell Sitwell *Liszt* (1934, rev. ed. London 1955 and New York 1956, also PB). Alan Walker *Franz Liszt: The Man and His Music* (New York 1970).

LIVY (real name Titus Livius) (c.59 B.C. – A.D. 17). Roman historian. Born and died at Patavium (Padua), but spent most of life in Rome, where he moved in fashionable circles and was a favorite of Emperor Augustus. Though he also wrote on philosophy and rhetoric, Livy's one surviving work is his great history of Rome (*Ab Urbe Condita Libri*) from its founding by Aeneas (753 B.C.) to death of Drusus, brother of Emperor Tiberius (9 B.C.). The work consisted of 142 books, of which thirty-five are extant: I–X (up to 293 B.C.) and XXI–XLV (218–167 B.C.); only tables of contents for the other books survive. Livy gathered his material largely from ancient annalists. His aim was not so much historical accuracy as to inspire his contemporaries with the qualities of greatness that characterized the outstanding Romans of the past. His narrative skill and vivid descriptive passages make him still highly readable.

TRANSLATIONS: *History of Rome* tr. B. O. Foster and others (Loeb Classical Library, 14 vols. Cambridge, Mass. and London 1919–63). *History of Rome: Selections* tr. Moses Hadas and Joe P. Poe (New York 1962).
REFERENCES: Hippolyte Taine *Essai sur Tite-Live* (8th ed. Paris 1910). Patrick G. Walsh *Livy: His Historical Aims and Methods* (Cambridge, England, 1961).

LOCHNER, Stefan (c.1410–c.1451). German painter. Born at Meersburg on Lake Constance. He is assumed to have spent some time in the Netherlands, probably in workshop of Robert Campin (presumed Master of Flémalle), before settling in Cologne, where he appears in records from 1442. Lochner's masterpiece is *The Patron Saints of Cologne* (1440's, cathedral of Cologne), a triptych of the *Adoration of the Magi* and, on the wings, SS. Ursula and Gereon. Other works include *The Last Judgment* (c.1440; central panel, Wallraf-Richartz Museum, Cologne; inner sides of wings, Städelsches Kunstinstitut, Frankfurt-am-Main; outer sides, Alte Pinakothek, Munich); *Madonna with Violets* (c.1443, Cologne, Erzbischöflisches Diözesan-Museum); *Presentation in the Temple* (1447, Landesmuseum, Darmstadt); *Madonna in the Rose Bower* (Wallraf-Richartz Museum, Cologne). Lochner died, probably of plague, in Cologne. His painting is noted for exquisite color, fluid lines, depth of mystical feeling, and abundant naturalistic detail.

LOCKE, John (Aug. 29, 1632 – Oct. 28, 1704). English philosopher. Born Wrington, Somerset, of middle-class family. Educated at Westminster School (1647–52) and Christ Church, Oxford (B.A. 1656, M.A. 1658). Became lecturer there in Greek, rhetoric, and philosophy (1661–64), meanwhile studying sciences, particularly medicine. Became friend and adviser of Lord Ashley (Sir Antony Ashley Cooper, future earl of Shaftesbury) and received various public posts under his patronage. Elected fellow of Royal Society (1668). Traveled and studied in France (1675–79). Followed Shaftesbury into exile in Holland (1683–89). Here he completed his great *Essay Concerning Human Understanding* (1690), which was published after his return to England at accession of William III, and which made him famous throughout Europe. Died, unmarried, at Oates, Essex. Other works include *Two Treatises on Government* (1690), *Some Thoughts Concerning Education* (1693), and *The Reasonableness of Christianity* (1695). Locke was a founder of the Enlightenment in England and France and a major influence on all later philosophy and political theory. In his *Essay*, he denied existence of innate ideas, developing an empiricist theory of knowledge. In his political writings, believing, unlike Hobbes, in man's natural goodness, he defended the individual's rights to life, liberty and property, and formulated policy of checks and balances as used in U.S. Constitution.

EDITIONS: *An Essay Concerning Human Understanding* ed. Alexander Campbell Fraser (latest ed. 2 vols. New York PB 1959). *Two Treatises of Government* ed. Peter Laslett (2nd ed. London 1967 and New York 1968).

REFERENCES: Richard I. Aaron *John Locke* (2nd ed. Oxford 1955, also PB). Maurice Cranston *John Locke: A Biography* (London and New York 1957). John M. Dunn *The Political Thought of John Locke* (London and New York 1969). Peter Gay *The Enlightenment: An Interpretation* (2 vols. New York 1966/69). J. W. Gough *John Locke's Political Philosophy* (Oxford 1950). D. J. O'Connor *John Locke* (London 1952, reprinted New York PB 1967). John W. Yolton *John Locke and the Way of Ideas* (1956, reprinted Oxford 1968) and ed. *John Locke: Problems and Perspectives* (London and New York 1969).

LOCKHART, John Gibson (July 14, 1794 – Nov. 25, 1854). Scottish writer. The son of a clergyman, he was born at Cambusnethan, Lanarkshire, and educated at universities of Glasgow and Oxford. Studied law and was admitted to Scottish bar (1816), but never practiced. Attracted wide notice as contributor of criticism and satire (under pseudonym Peter Morris) to *Blackwood's Magazine* (from 1817). Became friend of Sir Walter Scott (1818), whose eldest daughter, Sophia, he married (1820). As editor of *Quarterly Review* (1825–53), Lockhart was responsible for its becoming one of the leading critical journals of the period. He produced four novels, including *Adam Blair* (1822); a volume of translations; *Ancient Spanish Ballads* (1823); and several biographies. Of these, the *Life of Sir Walter Scott* (7 vols. 1837–38) is Lockhart's finest work and one of the great biographies in the English language. He also wrote lives of Robert Burns (1828) and Napoleon (1829). Died at Abbotsford, Roxburgh.

REFERENCES: Andrew Lang *The Life and Letters of John Gibson Lockhart* (2 vols. London and New York 1896). Marion Lochhead *John Gibson Lockhart* (London and New York 1954).

Gilbert Macbeth *John Gibson Lockhart: A Critical Study* (Urbana, Ill. 1935).

LONDON, Jack (real name John Griffith London) (Jan. 12, 1876 – Nov. 22, 1916). American writer. Born San Francisco, grew up along Oakland waterfront. Completed grammar school (1889) and became an oyster pirate (1891), a seaman on a sealing schooner in the north Pacific (1893, source of his first publication, article entitled *Typhoon off the Coast* of Japan, 1894), and a hobo, serving time for vagrancy in Erie, Pa. Joined Socialist Labor Party (1896); spent one semester at University of California. Joined gold rush to Klondike (1897–98). Married Bess Maddern (1900, divorced 1905). First book: *The Son of the Wolf* (1900). Won worldwide fame and popularity with *The Call of the Wild* (1903), followed by *The Sea-Wolf* (1904). Served as Russo-Japanese War correspondent (1904); married Charmian Kittredge (1905). Sailed his ship Snark halfway around world (1907); built Wolf House in Sonoma Valley, pioneering in modern agriculture and livestock breeding. Died of overdose of morphine there (near Santa Rosa, Calif.). A prodigious worker, he gained enormous popularity and wealth from his writings. His fifty volumes of novels, short stories and essays drew on personal experience and are noted for their dramatic action and sometimes brutal power. His major motifs, visceral primitivism and individualism, reveal influences of Spencer's evolutionism, Marxian socialism and Nietzsche's superman. Best-known work also includes *The Iron Heel* (1907), *Martin Eden* (1909) and *John Barleycorn* (1913), both semi-autobiographical.

EDITION: *Writings* Bodley Head Edition (London and Chester Springs, Pa. 1963–   ).

REFERENCES: Philip S. Foner *Jack London: American Rebel* (1947, rev. ed. New York 1964, also PB). Charmian London *The Book of Jack London* (2 vols. London and New York 1921). Joan London *Jack London and His Times* (New York 1939, reprinted Seattle 1969, also PB). Richard O'Connor *Jack London: A Biography* (Boston 1964 and London 1965). Irving Stone

Sailor on Horseback: The Biography of Jack London (Boston 1964).

LONGFELLOW, Henry Wadsworth (Feb. 27, 1807 – Mar. 24, 1882). American poet. Born Portland, Me., son of Stephen Longfellow, distinguished lawyer and congressman, and Zilpah Wadsworth. Brought up in cultivated atmosphere, he early contributed poems to local paper. Attended Bowdoin College (1822–25), and after three years' study abroad became professor of modern languages there (1829–35). Married Mary Potter (1831; she died 1835). Smith professor of modern languages at Harvard (1836–54). Produced volume of essays *Outre-Mer: A Pilgrimage Beyond the Sea* (1835), modeled on Irving's *The Sketch Book*, followed by poems *Voices of the Night* (1839). *Ballads and Other Poems* (1842), including *The Wreck of the Hesperus, The Village Blacksmith*, and *Excelsior*, secured his reputation as major American poet. Numerous volumes followed, including *Evangeline* (1847), *The Song of Hiawatha* (1855), *The Courtship of Miles Standish* (1858), *Paul Revere's Ride* (1860), and *Tales of a Wayside Inn* (1863, 1872, 1873). Married Frances Appleton (1843), whose father gave the couple Craigie House, Cambridge, where six children were raised (commemorated in *The Children's Hour*, 1860). After tragic death of wife by burning (1861), Longfellow turned to translating Dante's *Divine Comedy* (1865–67). Continued to write poetry and received honorary degrees from Oxford and Cambridge Universities (1868–69). After death in Cambridge was first American to be honored by a bust in Westminster Abbey. The most popular American poet of his time, he was widely translated. Influenced by lyricism of German romantic poets, he masterfully interpreted the Old World to the New, and drew on American colonial history for the themes of his best-loved poems, which also dwelt on the beauty of nature and details of common life. He was noted for his accomplished sonnets, use of hexameters, and the purity and simplicity of his lyricism. Also made scholarly contributions in the field of comparative literature.

EDITIONS: *Works* ed. Samuel Longfellow (14 vols. Boston 1886–1891). *Letters* ed. Andrew Hilen (2 vols. Cambridge, Mass. and Oxford 1967).

REFERENCES: Newton Arvin *Longfellow: His Life and Work* (Boston 1963, also PB). Herbert S. Gorman *A Victorian American: Henry Wadsworth Longfellow* (1926, reprinted Port Washington, N.Y. 1967). Samuel Longfellow *Life of Henry Wadsworth Longfellow* (1891, reprinted 3 vols. New York 1969). Lawrance R. Thompson *Young Longfellow, 1807–43* (1938, reprinted New York 1969). Edward C. Wagenknecht *Henry Wadsworth Longfellow: Portrait of an American Humanist* (New York 1966).

LONGHI, Pietro (1702 – May 8, 1785). Italian painter. Born and died in Venice, son of a silversmith who gave him his early training. After studying under Veronese history painter Antonio Balestra, Longhi tried to make his mark with large-scale historical and religious subjects. Unsuccessful in that sphere, he entered studio of Giuseppe Maria Crespi in Bologna, and thereafter limited himself to producing the small, charming, delicately colored scenes of contemporary Venetian life for which he is remembered. Examples are *The Toilette, The Concert, The Tailor,* and *The Dancing Master* (all in Accademia, Venice). Married Caterina Maria Rizzi (1732). Selected to be among first members of the Accademia (1756), he taught there until 1780. Longhi's gently satiric portrayal of the domestic life of wealthy Venetians is often compared to that of his contemporary, the playwright Carlo Goldoni. His son Alessandro (1733–1813) was a successful portrait painter and author of *Compendio delle vite de' pittore veneziani* (1762), a valuable source book for history of Venetian eighteenth-century painting.

REFERENCES: Germain Bazin *Baroque and Rococo Art* (New York 1966). Michael Levey *Painting in Eighteenth-Century Venice* (London and New York 1959). Terisio Pignatti *Pietro Longhi* (tr. London and New York 1969).

LONGINUS, name assigned in some manuscripts to author of the Greek treatise *On the Sublime* (c. 1st century A.D.), who is no longer identified with Cassius Longinus (c.213–273), Greek philosopher and rhetorician who taught at Athens and became friend and political adviser of Queen Zenobia of Palmyra. A valuable work of literary criticism, *On the Sublime* is chiefly concerned with defining the characteristics of the lofty style. In essence, these are grandeur of thought, inspired passion, and technical mastery. To illustrate his assertions, the author quotes widely from ancient literature, and thus records a number of writings that would otherwise be lost, including an ode by Sappho. Long in obscurity, *On the Sublime* became an important source of standards for European classicism after appearance of Nicolas Boileau's translation (1674).

TRANSLATIONS: *On the Sublime* tr. D. A. Russell (London and New York 1964); tr. John Warrington (with Aristotle's *Poetics* and Demetrius' *On Style,* London and New York 1963).

LOPE DE VEGA. *See* **VEGA.**

LORCA, Federico García (June 5, 1899 – Aug. 19, 1936). Spanish poet and dramatist. Born into wealthy farming family in village of Fuente Vaqueros, Andalusia. Educated in Granada and Madrid. After traveling through Castile (1917), settled in Madrid (1919) for fifteen years. Wrote poetry, collected and transcribed old folk songs. Recognition came with publication of *Libro de poemas* (1921, *Book of Poems*), *Canciones* (1927, *Songs*), and the widely celebrated *Romancero gitano* (1928, *Gypsy Ballads*). Began writing plays, producing *Mariana Pineda* (1927). Spent a year (1929–30) at Columbia University, New York. Harlem inspired *Poeta en Nueva York* (1940, *Poet in New York*). Returned to Spain (1930) and began producing plays with his own theatre company, La Barraca, touring many Spanish towns (1932). Toured Argentina and Uruguay (1933–34), lecturing and reading poetry. Wrote poem *Lament for the Death of a Bullfighter* (1935); his best-known plays include *Boclas de sangre* (1933, *Blood Wedding*), *Yerma* (1934), and *La Casa de Bernarda Alba* (1936, *The House of . . .*). Shortly after the outbreak of the Spanish Civil War, García Lorca was arrested near his natal village by Falangists and killed.

EDITION: *Obras completas* ed. Arturo del Hoyo (1957, 8th ed. Madrid 1965). TRANSLATIONS: *Poems of F. García Lorca* tr. Stephen Spender and J. L. Gili (Oxford and New York 1939). *Three Tragedies* tr. James Graham-Luján and Richard L. O'Connell (Norfolk, Conn. PB 1956). *Five Plays: Comedies and Tragicomedies* tr. James Graham-Luján and Richard L. O'Connell (Norfolk, Conn. PB 1967). *Poems* ed. and tr. J. L. Gili (Harmondsworth, England, PB 1967). REFERENCES: Arturo Barea *Lorca: The Poet and His People* (tr. London 1944 and New York 1949). Roy Campbell *Lorca: An Appreciation of His Poetry* (Cambridge, England, and New Haven, Conn. 1952, PB 1961). Manuel Durán ed. *Lorca: A Collection of Critical Essays* (Englewood Cliffs, N.J. 1962, also PB). Edwin Honig *García Lorca* (1944, rev. ed. Norfolk, Conn. PB 1963 and London 1968). John B. Trend *Lorca and the Spanish Poetic Tradition* (Oxford and New York 1956).

☞

FEDERICO GARCÍA LORCA
BY FRANCIS FERGUSSON

Lorca is that very unusual phenomenon in our time, a natural poet at home with the ballad, the modern lyric, and (rarest of all) the theatre. His art is deeply rooted in his native Spain, but it has many qualities which poets in other countries, in the two decades following World War I, were looking for. Synge and Yeats, for instance, were seeking in Ireland the mutually fertilizing relation to their folk traditions which Lorca actually had in Spain. Cocteau's recipes for "poetry of the theatre" as distinguished from the *symboliste* lyric, "poetry of the word," were realized in Lorca's plays. T. S.

Eliot was always trying to reassert the vitality of the classics in his criticism and in his plays and poems; but Lorca, with a minimum of doctrine, could use Greek and Spanish classics in plays and poems which reached far beyond the small circle interested in poetic drama. He soon had a very large audience in Spanish-speaking countries, and his works are still performed in good theatres all over the world.

It is perhaps the Spanish tradition of balladry (together with Lorca's unanalyzable genius, of course) that best accounts for his unique success. The ballad is a popular form everywhere, but in Spain it has also nourished the learned drama of Spain's golden age and the art of so sophisticated a poet as Góngora — which Lorca himself explained in one of his few critical essays. The poets in English-speaking countries who aspired to the theatre in Lorca's time found it very difficult to proceed from the modern lyric to the larger form of drama, in which narrative and character are essential. But the Spanish and gypsy ballads that Lorca knew as a child are not only "poetry" but also narrative and drama. Their stories are themselves poetry; Aristotle noticed more than two thousand years ago that the right story may produce some of the tragic effect even before the dramatist has found the words to embody it. Lorca was playing about with the staging of popular songs and ballads, devising his own sets, costumes and musical settings, while he was still a boy. From that early play to the tragic drama of his maturity, when he was fully aware of all the sources and stratagems of his art, the path seems to have been both natural and direct.

In this country Lorca is best known for poems like *Lament for the Death of a Bullfighter* and plays like *Blood Wed-*

ding and *Yerma,* which owe much of their power to the unchanging life of the Spanish peasantry and the poetic traditions which emerged from it. The *Lament* might be described as a folk rite, in close and intricate relation to that immemorial ritual game, the bull-fight itself, and it owes much also to ballad forms and attitudes. The two plays are not (so far as I know) derived from particular ballads, but both are on ballad-like themes and both depend for their tragic economy and inevitability upon the meager, unyielding peasant ways of life. In our up-to-date industrial society it proves very difficult to find tragic themes with any objective necessity, perhaps because it is so easy for us to avoid ultimate confrontations by changing our jobs, our mates, or our air-conditioned apartments. But Lorca's peasants cannot escape: they have to face their destinies. They have that quality of people who never leave the provinces where they were born, which Stark Young admiringly described as "narrow but very deep."

Several of Lorca's plays are based on sophisticated elements in his Spanish tradition. *Mariana Pineda,* an early play about a patriotic martyr, is inspired by nineteenth-century genre painting. *Doña Rosita the Spinster, or The Language of Flowers* is a most knowing and delicate evocation of Spanish Victorianism. *Don Perlimplin* is an extremely skillful transposition of a classical farcical situation, that of the old man married to a lusty young wife (which Cervantes dramatized with bawdy gusto in one of his interludes), into a romantic, boldly theatrical poem of love and death. *The House of Bernarda Alba,* written near the end of his career, is another play based on the rigid customs of a small country town, but unlike *Blood Wed-*

ding and *Yerma,* with their lavish use of verse, music, and spectacle, it strictly respects the conventions of nineteenth-century realism. For that reason it is comparatively easy to produce in this country.

The basic conceptions of Lorca's plays are always poetic, plastic, and musical. That includes *Bernarda Alba,* for its photographic realism is as consciously used for theatrical-poetic purposes as the convention of genre painting is in *Mariana Pineda.* More than any of his contemporaries (with the possible exception of Cocteau) Lorca was at home with painting (in which he was a gifted amateur) and music (in which he had almost professional competence), and that made him unusually sensitive to style and period in all the arts. He was a theatrical virtuoso like the great producers of the time, a Jacques Copeau or a Max Reinhardt, but this exuberant theatricality does not in my opinion make him any the less an authentic, original dramatist. He can use the other arts precisely because he always senses the dramatic motive in the painter's use of form and color, the musician's use of sound and rhythm; and so he knows in what plastic or musical styles his characters' motives are best expressed.

Lorca found himself and nourished himself by means of the ancient Spanish traditions, but that did not prevent his being acutely aware of the industrial, commercial, cosmopolitan, and traditionless modern city, and from time to time he tried to cope with it in his work. *If Five Years Pass* is about a young man in such a city, and in that play he uses devices reminiscent of Kafka's, and others which show that he had absorbed the surrealism of his friend Dali. *Poet in New York* comes straight from his dismaying experience of that city in 1929–30. The book is strikingly analogous to E. E. Cummings's diary of his trip to Russia at about the same time, *Eimi*, which presents Stalin's "unworld" as the visible death of all that the poet holds dear. *Poet in New York* shows aspects of Lorca's art not to be found in the Spanish work — an unexpected kinship, for instance, between his Daliesque "magic realism" and the dreaminess of his nursery rhymes.

Even in his own time Lorca was not very "modern." He was not identified like his contemporary Brecht with a political creed, being *engagé* only with the perennial life of his people. He would look even less up-to-date from the point of view of our current avantgarde establishment. Like all of his generation he is somewhat in eclipse at the moment, but it is safe to say that his work, like all authentic poetry, will long outlive the superficial vagaries of literary fashion.

LORENZETTI, Pietro (c.1280–c.1348) and his brother **Ambrogio** (c.1290–c.1348). Italian painters. Very little is known of their lives. They worked together on various projects and were chiefly active in Siena, though Ambrogio spent several years in Florence. Since there is no mention of the Lorenzettis after 1347, they are thought to have died in the great plague of 1348. The two underwent similar artistic development. Producing at first works whose color effects and emphasis on surface linear pattern link them with Duccio, they grew increasingly interested in rational perspective, solid forms, and realistic detail, probably under influence of Giotto. Their art represents a synthesis of Gothic, Sienese, and Florentine styles. Pietro's works include frescoes in lower church at Assisi (date disputed), altarpiece for S. Maria del Carmine, Siena (1329, Pinacoteca, Siena), *Crucifixion* (church of S. Francesco, Siena), and *Nativity of the Virgin* (1342, Museo dell' Opera del Duomo, Siena). Ambrogio, whose scientific approach to perspective and

whose evident scholarship in classical antiquity anticipate the Renaissance, is noted for *Good and Bad Government*, frescoes in Palazzo Pubblico, Siena (1337–39), and *Presentation in the Temple* (1342, Uffizi, Florence).

REFERENCES: Enzo Carli *Sienese Painting* (Greenwich, Conn. 1956 and London 1958). E. T. De Wald *Pietro Lorenzetti* (Cambridge, Mass. and Oxford 1930). George Harold Edgell *A History of Sienese Painting* (New York 1932). George Rowley *Ambrogio Lorenzetti* (2 vols. Princeton, N.J. 1958 and Oxford 1959).

LORRAIN, Claude (real name **Claude Gellée** or **Gelée**) (1600 – Nov. 21, 1682). French painter. Born Chamagne, in Lorraine, he was in Rome by c.1613, where he entered service of painter Agostino Tassi. Through Tassi, Claude had contact with northern landscape tradition of Adam Elsheimer and Paul Bril, but the style he evolved is markedly individual. After a journey to Lorraine (1625–27), he returned to Rome, where he spent rest of his life. By end of 1630's, Claude enjoyed enormous popularity. Partly to guard against forgery of his works, he made a record, *Liber Veritatis* (1635–82, Duke of Devonshire Collection, Chatsworth, England), consisting of 195 exquisite drawings of his paintings and names of their purchasers. Claude was the founder of the romantic style of landscape painting, which had such importance throughout the eighteenth century and first half of the nineteenth. While he usually provided his pictures with Biblical or classical subject matter, his figures are small and insignificant, and attention is devoted to idealized scenery and to effects of light and atmosphere, evoking a particular time of day. Examples are *The Trojan Women Setting Fire to the Greek Fleet* (Metropolitan Museum, New York) and *Seaport at Sunset* (Museum of Fine Arts, Boston).

REFERENCES: Marco Chiarini *Claude Lorrain: Selected Drawings* (University Park, Pa. 1968). Pierre Courthion *Claude Gelée, dit Le Lorrain* (Paris 1932). A. M. Hind *The Drawings of Claude Lorrain* (London and New York 1925). Marcel Roethlisberger *Claude*

Lorrain: The Paintings (2 vols. New Haven, Conn. 1961) and *Claude Lorrain: The Drawings* (2 vols. Berkeley, Calif. 1968).

LOTI, Pierre (real name Louis Marie Julien Viaud) (Jan. 14, 1850 – June 10, 1923). French novelist. Born Rochefort; of Huguenot family. Trained in navy class of Lycée Henri IV, Paris, and at École Navale, Brest (1865–67), Loti spent most of his life in the navy, retiring with rank of captain (1910). His wide-ranging voyages to foreign ports provided exotic settings for his novels, which are subjective, imbued with melancholy and pessimism, and emphasize the power of the primitive. Success came with second novel, set in Tahiti, *Rarahu* (1880, reprinted as *Le Mariage de Loti* 1882), which was followed by *Le Roman d'un Spahi* (1881) and *Mon Frère Yves* (1883, *My Brother Yves*). His masterpiece about Breton fishermen, *Pêcheur d'Islande* (1886, tr. *An Iceland Fisherman* 1886), won the Prix Vitet from the French Academy. Other works include *Madame Chrysanthème*, set in Japan (1887), *Ramuntcho*, a Basque story (1897, tr. 1897), *Les Désenchantées* (1906, *Disenchanted*). Loti was elected to the French Academy (1891), defeating Zola. Died at Hendaye, France.

REFERENCES: Edmund B. D'Auvergne *Pierre Loti: The Romance of a Great Writer* (1926, reprinted Port Washington, N.Y. 1970). Claude Farrère *Loti* (Paris 1930). Pierre Flottes *Le Drame intérieur de Pierre Loti* (Paris 1937). Albert L. Guerard *Five Masters of French Romance* (New York 1916). Nicolas Serban *Pierre Loti, sa vie et son oeuvre* (Paris 1924). Robert de Traz *Pierre Loti* (Paris 1948).

LOTTI, Antonio (c.1667 – Jan. 5, 1740). Italian organist and composer. A musician's son, he was born probably in Venice, and studied there under Giovanni Legrenzi, *maestro di cappella* to the doge. Produced an opera, *Giustino*, before he was sixteen. Lotti received a series of appointments at St. Mark's Cathedral: chorister (1687), deputy organist (1690), second organist (1692), first organist (1704), *maestro di cappella* (1736). He is best known for his church music, particularly for a *Miserere* which is still performed at St. Mark's every Maundy Thursday. Though working in the traditional contrapuntal style, he employed modern harmonies and achieved remarkable expressiveness. Lotti also produced twenty-one operas, four oratorios, madrigals, and songs, including the familiar *Pur dicesti*. He was married to a Bolognese singer, Santa Stella. Died in Venice.

LOTTO, Lorenzo (c.1480–1556). Italian painter. Born Venice. Nothing is known of his early life or training, and the eccentric nature of his art has led to a number of conflicting theories on its sources. Lotto led a restless existence, living at various times in Treviso, the Marches, Rome, Bergamo, Loreto, and Venice. Retired to a monastery at Loreto (1552), where he died. Early works are strongly influenced by Giovanni Bellini. They include *Portrait of Bishop Bernardo de' Rossi* (1505, Museo di Capodimonte, Naples), altarpiece in parish church at S. Cristina al Tivarone (1505–1506), *St. Jerome in the Wilderness* (1506, Louvre, Paris), Recanati polyptych (1506–1508) and *Madonna and Saints* (1508) in Villa Borghese, Rome, *Marriage of St. Catherine* (Alte Pinakothek, Munich). Lotto may have met Dürer in Venice (1505–1506); from that time his work shows affinities with German painting. After a period in Rome (1509–12), he came under influence of Raphael and others. His somber palette took on bright, golden hues, his compositions became more lively. Pontormo and the mannerists later influenced him in use of violent color. Among later works: *The Entombment* (1512, Pinacoteca Comunale, Iesi); three altarpieces in Bergamo, at churches of S. Bartolomeo (1516), S. Bernardino (1521), and S. Spirito (1521); *Susannah and the Elders* (1517, Collection Contini Bonacossi, Florence); *Portrait of Prothonotary Apostolic Giuliano* (c.1520, National Gallery, London); frescoes in chapel of Villa Suardi at Trescore (1524), with legends of St. Clare and St. Barbara; *Portrait of Andrea Odoni* (1527, Hampton Court, England); *St.*

Nicholas of Bari (1529, church of S. Maria del Carmine, Venice); *St. Antoninus of Florence Giving Alms* (1542, SS. Giovanni e Paolo, Venice).

REFERENCES: Bernard Berenson *Lorenzo Lotto* (3rd ed. New York and London 1956). Piero Bianconi *All the Paintings of Lorenzo Lotto* (tr. 2 vols. New York and London 1963).

LOUŸS, Pierre (real name Pierre Louis) (Dec. 10, 1870 – June 4, 1925). French novelist and poet. Born Ghent, Belgium, of French parents. Educated in Paris at École Alsacienne, Lycée de Sailly, and the Sorbonne. Founded the review *La Conque* (1891), to which Gide, Swinburne, Mallarmé, and Valéry contributed. Became associated with the Parnassian and symbolist poets; married Louise, daughter of José Maria de Hérédia (1899). Early poems collected in *Astarté* (1891). His next volume, *Chansons de Bilitis* (1894), contained prose poems on Sapphic love. *Aphrodite* (1896), a sensual novel set in ancient Alexandria, made him famous. His other major novel is *La Femme et le Pantin* (1898). Died in Paris. Louÿs's work, with its classical erudition, emphasis on style, and sensuousness, belongs to the Parnassian school.

TRANSLATIONS: *Collected Works* ed. M. S. Buck and J. Cleugh (New York 1932). *Aphrodite* tr. Frances Keene (New York 1960 and London 1961). *Mother's Three Daughters* tr. S. d'E. (New York 1969, also PB).
REFERENCES: Robert Cardinne-Petit *Pierre Louÿs intime, le solitaire du Hameau* (Paris 1942). Claude Farrère *Mon Ami Pierre Louÿs* (Paris 1955).

LOVELACE, Richard (1618–1657). English poet. Of an old Kentish family, he was born either at Woolwich, Kent, or in Holland, where his father was in Dutch military service. Educated at Oxford. The model courtier and a favorite of Queen Henrietta, Lovelace sided with the king during civil wars. While imprisoned for presenting a royalist petition to Parliament (1642), wrote *To Althea, from Prison* ("Stone walls do not a prison make"); it is for this poem and one other, *To Lucasta, Go-*

ing to the Wars ("I could not love thee, dear, so much, / Loved I not honor more"), that Lovelace is remembered. Following king's defeat he left England to serve in French army, and on his return was again imprisoned (1648–49). Having lost his fortune in the king's cause, he died in poverty, in London. Lovelace's elegant lyrics appeared in two collections, both entitled *Lucasta* (1649 and 1659).

EDITION: *Poems* ed. C. H. Wilkinson (1925, reprinted Oxford 1953).
REFERENCE: Cyril Hughes Hartmann *The Cavalier Spirit and Its Influence on the Life and Work of Richard Lovelace* (London and New York 1925).

LOWELL, Amy (Feb. 9, 1874 – May 12, 1925). American poet, critic, and biographer. Born and died in Brookline, Mass.; related to James Russell Lowell. Educated privately. First book, *Dream Drops* (1887), fairy tales, was privately printed. Published first volume of poetry, *A Dome of Many-Colored Glass*, (1912). In England (1913), she associated with Ezra Pound and the imagists. *Sword Blades and Poppy Seed* (1914) experimented with innovations of "unrhymed cadence" and "polyphonic prose," as did *Men, Women and Ghosts* (1916) and *Can Grande's Castle* (1918). At the same time she made imagists famous through her three-volume anthology *Some Imagist Poets* (1915/1916/1917). Chinese and Japanese influence is evident in *Pictures of the Floating World* (1919), *Legends* (1921), and *Fir-Flower Tablets* (1921). Critical works include *Six French Poets: Studies in Contemporary Literature* (1915) and *Tendencies in Modern American Poetry* (1917). Also wrote biography, *John Keats* (1925). Lecturing and reading (1915–25), she became a leading spokesman for the new poetry and modern European trends. Influenced by imagism and the French symbolists, her own poetry is especially noted for individuality, vivid movement and blazes of color. Received numerous academic awards; *What's O'Clock* (1925) posthumously awarded Pulitzer prize (1926).

EDITION: *Complete Poetical Works* (Boston 1955).

REFERENCES: S. Foster Damon *Amy Lowell: A Chronicle* (Boston 1935, reprinted Hamden, Conn. 1966). Horace Gregory *Amy Lowell: Portrait of the Poet in Her Time* (New York 1958). Clement Wood *Amy Lowell* (New York 1926).

LOWELL, James Russell (Feb. 22, 1819 – Aug. 12, 1891). American poet and man of letters. Born and died in Cambridge, Mass.; member of distinguished New England family. Educated at Harvard (B.A. 1838, LL.B. 1840). Married Maria White (1844), with whom he shared devotion to poetry and the abolitionist cause. Achieved recognition as romantic poet and critic with *A Year's Life and Other Poems* (1841), *Poems* (1844, 1848), *A Fable for Critics* (1848), and *The Vision of Sir Launfal* (1848); and as satirist with the humorous *Biglow Papers* (1846, 1848) in dialect. Meanwhile, he published about fifty antislavery articles in periodicals. After first wife's death (1853), married Frances Dunlap (1857). While Smith professor of modern languages at Harvard (1855–76), Lowell also edited the *Atlantic Monthly* (1857–61), to which he attracted major New England authors, and, with Charles Eliot Norton, the *North American Review* (1864–72). Served as minister to Spain (1877–80) and England (1880–85). After Civil War, Lowell concentrated on criticism and scholarship. Later works include *Commemoration Ode* (1865), *Among My Books* (1870–76), *My Study Windows* (1871), the poems *Heartsease and Rue* and *Political Essays* (both 1888).

EDITIONS: *Complete Writings* (includes *Letters* and biography by Horace E. Scudder) ed. Charles Eliot Norton (16 vols. Boston 1904). *James Russell Lowell: Representative Selections* ed. Harry H. Clark and Norman Foerster (New York 1947).
REFERENCES: Richmond C. Beatty *James Russell Lowell* (Nashville, Tenn. 1942, reprinted Hamden, Conn. 1969). Martin B. Duberman *James Russell Lowell* (Boston 1966, also PB). Leon Howard *Victorian Knight-Errant: A Study of the Early Literary Career of James Russell Lowell* (Berkeley, Calif.

1952 and Cambridge, England, 1953). Horace E. Scudder *James Russell Lowell: A Biography* (Boston 1901, reprinted 2 vols. Grosse Pointe, Mich. 1968).

LOWRY, (Clarence) Malcolm (July 28, 1909 – June 27, 1957). English novelist. Born Merseyside, Cheshire, son of wealthy cotton broker and grandson of Norwegian sea captain of legendary repute. Educated at the Leys School, Cambridge, Lowry then voyaged to the Far East for a year, later recording the experience in first novel *Ultramarine* (1933). Attended Cambridge University (1929–32), where he was considered one of the best undergraduate writers. After publication of novel went to Spain, where he married Jan, an American. She returned to U.S.; he lived in Paris with writer James Stern, then went to U.S., where he worked on movie scripts in Hollywood, and to Cuernavaca, Mexico. Met Margerie Bonner (1938), who became his second wife. They moved first to British Columbia, then settled near Toronto, Canada, where he completed *Under the Volcano* (1947), now recognized as a masterpiece. Set in Cuernavaca, the theme is Dantesque — the fall of man, depicted with the intensity and stylistic grandeur of Melville, as envisioned in the last day of the hero, a tragic figure, an alcoholic like Lowry himself, isolated in his own hell. The Lowrys were forced to leave their cabins when local authorities took their land for a public park. They left for Italy, then England, where he died in Ripe, Sussex. Posthumously published works: collection of short stories *Hear Us O Lord from Heaven Thy Dwelling Place* (1961), *Selected Poems* (1962), *Selected Letters* (1965), and novels *Dark as the Grave Wherein My Friend is Laid* (1968) and *Lunar Caustic* (1968).

EDITION: *Under the Volcano*, reissue with introduction by Stephen Spender (Philadelphia 1965 and New York PB 1966). *October Ferry to Gabriola* ed. Margerie Lowry (Cleveland 1970).
REFERENCE: Perle S. Epstein *The Private Labyrinth of Malcolm Lowry: Under the Volcano and the Cabbala* (New York 1969).

LUCAS VAN LEYDEN (real name Lucas Hugensz) (1494–1533). Dutch painter and engraver. Born and died in Leiden. A child prodigy, he studied under his father, Huygh Jacobsz, and Cornelis Engelbrechtsz, winning a reputation for such engravings as *The Temptation of St. Anthony* (1509), *Ecce Homo, The Milkmaid*, and *The Return of the Prodigal Son* (all 1510). Married Lijsbet van Boschuysen (1515). In Antwerp met Dürer (1521), who exerted strong influence on both his engravings and his paintings, such as *The Last Judgment* (1526, Leiden Museum). His powerful realistic perception, already developed by 1508 (*The Chess Players* and *Self-Portrait*), characterizes such works as *The Worship of the Golden Calf* and *Moses Striking Water from the Rock* (both c.1527, Museum of Fine Arts, Boston). His treatment of figures and use of homely detail have credited him with being the founder of Dutch genre painting.

REFERENCES: Sir Martin Conway *The Van Eycks and Their Followers*. M. J. Friedländer *From Van Eyck to Brueghel* (London 1956).

LUCIAN (or Lucianus) (c. A.D. 125 – 200). Greek satirist. Born Samosata, in Syria (now Samsat, Turkey). Originally apprenticed to a sculptor, he traveled widely, then settled in Antioch (c.162) to become a rhetorician, having acquired thorough knowledge of classical Greek. Later traveled again in Asia Minor, Greece, Italy, Gaul, and spent an interval in Athens, studying philosophy. Died in Egypt, where he was an official under the Roman administration. The major figure of the revival of Greek literature in the Roman Empire, Lucian produced rhetorical exercises, biography, criticism, and philosophical and satirical works, using many prose forms. Most popular are his dialogues, among them *Dialogues of the Gods*, which satirize mythology; *Dialogues of the Dead*, expositions of human vanity; *Dialogues of the Hetaerae*, describing life of Greek courtesans; and *Sale of Lives*, which satirizes various schools of philosophy. Other important works are the treatise *How History Should be Written* and *The True History*, a fantastic tale parodying untrustworthy accounts of foreign travel, which influenced such later writers as Rabelais, Voltaire, and Swift.

TRANSLATIONS: *Works* ed. and tr. Austin M. Harmon and others (Loeb Classical Library 8 vols. Cambridge, Mass. 1847–69). *Selected Works* tr. Bryan P. Reardon (Indianapolis 1965, also PB).

REFERENCES: Francis G. Allinson *Lucian: Satirist and Artist* (London and Boston 1926, reprinted New York 1963). Jacques Bompaire *Lucien écrivain: imitation et création* (Paris 1958). Marcel Caster *Lucien et la pensée religieuse de son temps* (Paris 1937). Jacques Schwartz *Biographie de Lucien de Samosate* (Brussels 1965).

✍

LUCIAN OF SAMOSATA
BY DUDLEY FITTS

It is impossible to speak with any certainty about the personal history of this great satirist. Lucian is a mysterious figure; deliberately so, it would seem. In writing about himself he is copious, but elusive and self-contradictory, as though he did not relish the idea of being recognized and catalogued. Nevertheless, we can be sure that he was born c. A.D. 125 in the Syrian city of Samosata. His parents were poor, he tells us, and he was apprenticed to an uncle whose trade was statuary. He abandoned this unpromising profession and took to the life of a wandering student, traveling from one to another of the great Ionian centers of civilization, hellenizing whatever traces might yet remain of his Syrian descent, and acquiring a brilliant and flexible mastery of the Greek language. For a time he seems to have practiced law, probably in Antioch. Certainly he was in Antioch in the year 162–163, when the emperor Lucius Verus visited that city, and he wrote a rather cloying panegyric on the current imperial mistress, one Panthea. He became widely known as a *rhetor* — we have no equivalent for the term, but may imagine a combination of public entertainer, declaimer, commentator on social and cultural matters, homespun philosopher (Will Rogers? Art Buchwald?) turned satirist. He lived and performed in Asia Minor, in Greece, in Italy, and in Gaul; and there is no reason to disbelieve the tradition that at the time of his death in the year 200 he was employed as a minor government official in Egypt. The record ends as mistily as it began.

The voluminous writings that have come down to us under his name raise similar uncertainties. Because he was so popular, because his particular kind of cynical wit — the disillusioned man of the world — must have attracted imitators by the swarm, much of our "Lucian" would seem to be the work of others riding upon his fame. There is no doubt, however, about the authenticity of the great pieces: the *Dialogues*, ranging from tiny conversations of a social or mythological cast to lengthy, fully developed philosophico-satirical affairs in a formidable parody of the Platonic manner; the very amusing essay *How to Write History*, still as pertinent as when it was written; *The True History*, a romance that foreshadows *Gulliver's Travels* and, disturbingly, certain science fiction phenomena of our own time; a series of exquisitely composed "prelusions," little pieces designed to be recited before the chief oration or dialogue of the day's entertainment. He wrote a verse tragedy, complete with choral odes, on the subject of the gout. It is possible that he is behind a romance that descends to us in truncated form, *Lucius, or The Ass*, which tells the story elaborated and apotheosized in the Latin of Apuleius' *Metamorphoses*. We should add one startling tour de force, an essay *On the Syrian Goddess*, a travelogue written in the five-hundred-year-old language

(Ionic) and style (archaic) of Herodotus, a masterpiece of parody and at the same time a source of value for the scientific antiquarian. These are the enduring works. Of the genuine pieces remaining, none is quite without interest, of course; and even among the spurious ones there is much that he would probably not wholly disdain.

Lucian is a satirist, but not a moralist. True, his pose is generally that of the reasonable plain citizen disgusted by the hypocrisy and self-serving of officialdom, whether it be governmental, or academic, or theological. It is necessary, no doubt, that a social satirist assume this air of conscious virtue, but it can become tiresome very quickly. When Lucian drops this virtuous mask and relies upon the lightning-like agility of his wit, he cannot be resisted. This wit is perfectly armed with the weapon of parody, running the gamut from gentle imitation to outrageous caricature. Even when there is little satirical animus, as in *The True History*, which, aside from a genial jab at the writers of best-selling travel books, is a super-romance to end all super-romances, it is this sense of the outrageous that makes it possible for the hero to live for months in the belly of a whale; to be present as a correspondent at the heavenly war between the Sunites and the Moonites, those astral armies; to visit the Abode of the Blessed Dead, Elysium, and interview such notable ghosts as Homer, and sneak out from under Penelope's very nose a love letter from Odysseus to Calypso. This kind of extravagance is Lucian at his best, even though the social sting is absent; certainly it is instructive to see how Swift, for example, took so much of *The True Story* for his own great romance, adding the sting of "savage indignation." Yet there will always be readers to prefer the less extravagant mode of the *Dialogues*. Some of these are slight to the point of evanescence — small colloquies among the Olympian gods, perhaps, or representative sea deities with their attendant nymphs and nereids. Others, equally small, take us among the dead — here is Swift again — and let us listen to the chapfallen moralities of fleshless skulls. (Hamlet, too, knew his Lucian.) In the full-scale dialogues, there is no one, human or divine, whose intervention would seem out of place. We watch Paris-Alexandros judge the first beauty contest and award the prize of the Golden Apple to Aphrodite, rather than to Hera or Athena; we travel by Styx ferry to listen to Alexander the Great, Hannibal, and other notable mass murderers; we encounter and are expected to approve of such bitter cynics as Timon of Athens and Menippus. And all of this in a style whose purity and elegance and ease are the despair of emulators and the abject dismay of the translator. As a writer, a technician, Lucian is close to the very top. As an entertainer, he *is* at the very top. We may forgive him for not being a first-rate thinker.

LUCRETIUS (Titus Lucretius Carus) (c.99 B.C. – c.55 B.C.). Roman poet. No certain facts exist regarding his life. His one work, *De Rerum Natura* (*On the Nature of Things*), is a lengthy didactic poem in hexameters, divided into six books, directed to overcoming man's superstitious fear of death and the gods. The theories expounded are those of Epicurus. Beginning with the premise that the universe is entirely made up of atoms, Epicurean doctrine refutes immortality because the soul as well as the body is made up of atoms, both controlled by the laws of nature. The gods exist but have no concern with mortal matters. Splendidly eloquent in language and rich in imagery, *De Rerum Natura* had great influence on Virgil.

TRANSLATION: *De Rerum Natura* ed. Cyril Bailey, with translation and commentary (1947, reprinted 3 vols. Oxford 1963).
REFERENCES: D. R. Dudley ed. *Lucretius* (London and New York 1965). George D. Hadzsits *Lucretius and His Influence* (1935, reprinted New York 1963). John Masson *Lucretius: Epicurean and Poet* (2 vols. London and New York 1907–1909). Edward E. Sikes *Lucretius: Poet and Philosopher* (Cambridge, England, and New York 1936). A. P. Sinker *Introduction to Lucretius* (Cambridge, England, and New York 1937). David West *The Imagery and Poetry of Lucretius* (Edinburgh and Chicago 1969).

LULLY, Jean-Baptiste (Italian, **Giovanni Battista Lulli**) (Nov. 28, 1632 – Mar. 22, 1687). French composer. Born Florence of humble family, he was brought to Paris (1646) as servant to Mademoiselle d'Orléans, cousin of Louis XIV. His musical talents were discovered, and he entered the king's orchestra (1652), soon became its conductor. Appointed composer to the king (1661), he introduced a new sprightliness and rapid rhythm to the style of the court dances. Appointed *maître de musique de la famille royale* (1662), he also that year married Madeleine Lambert, daughter of the *maître de musique de la cour*. Became friends with Molière and composed (1663–71) the music for several of his comedies, including *Le Bourgeois Gentilhomme* (1670). As director of the Paris Opéra (1672–87), Lully found his true calling; abandoning the Italian style, he founded a new national French opera, promoting dramatic action over superficial musical effects, and developed the French overture. Also introduced ballet into his operas, and composed at least thirty ballets for which he won great repute. Best known among his operas are *Alceste* (1674), *Atys* (1676), and *Armide* (1686). Died in Paris.

REFERENCES: Eugène Borrel *Jean-Baptiste Lully* (Paris 1949). Donald J. Grout *A Short History of Opera* (2nd ed. New York 1965). Henry Prunières *Lully* (2nd ed. Paris 1927).

LYDGATE, John (c.1370–c.1450). English poet. Born Lydgate, Suffolk. Became a monk in Benedictine abbey of Bury St. Edmunds, where he spent his whole life, apart from eleven years as prior of Hatfield Broadoak, Essex (1421–32), during which period he also visited Paris and Italy. Lydgate greatly admired Chaucer, whom he imitated. An extremely prolific writer, his works consist chiefly of long narratives of little poetic value. They include *The Troy Book* (1412–21); *The Story of Thebes* (c.1420), written as supplement to *The Canterbury Tales; The Pilgrimage of the Life of Man* (1426), a translation from the French of Guillaume de Deguilleville; *The Fall of Princes* (1431–38), an adaptation of Boccaccio's *De Casibus Virorum*. Also wrote versified saints' lives, and secular and religious lyrics. Esteemed in his own day, Lydgate has few readers today.

EDITIONS: Most of his works have been published by Early English Text Society. Also *Poems* ed. John Norton-Smith (Oxford 1966, also PB).

REFERENCES: Henry S. Bennett *Chaucer and the Fifteenth Century* (Oxford 1947). Eleanor P. Hammond *English Verse Between Chaucer and Surrey* (1927, new ed. New York 1965). Alain Renoir *The Poetry of John Lydgate* (Cambridge, Mass. and London 1967). Walter F. Schirmer *John Lydgate: A Study in the Culture of the Fifteenth Century* (tr. Berkeley, Calif. and London 1961).

LYTTON. *See* **BULWER-LYTTON, Edward George.**

MACAULAY, Thomas Babington, 1st Baron Macaulay (Oct. 25, 1800 – Dec. 28, 1859). English writer and statesman. Born Rothley Temple, Leicestershire, son of Zachary Macaulay, prominent abolitionist. Attended Trinity College, Cambridge (1818–21), elected fellow of Trinity (1824). Literary renown came with appearance of essay *Milton* in *Edinburgh Review* (1825), to which he contributed frequently until 1845. Called to the bar (1826), he entered Parliament (1830), became zealous reformer. As member of Supreme Council of India (1834–38), reformed the colony's educational system and drew up a penal code (1837). Returned to England and continued to serve in Parliament until 1856; appointed secretary of war (1839–41) and paymaster of the forces (1846–47). Published volume of poems *Lays of Ancient Rome* (1842), which was followed by *Essays* (1843). Greatest fame as well as immense wealth came with publication of his masterwork, *The History of England from the Accession of James the Second* (5 vols. 1849–61). Though its limitations and political bias were evident in Macaulay's day, the history continues to be admired for its superb dramatic style, clarity, and profound sense of history. Macaulay received numerous honors and was made a peer (1857). Died at Holly Lodge, Kensington; buried in Westminster Abbey.

EDITION: *History of England . . .* ed. Charles Harding Firth (6 vols. London 1913–15).

REFERENCES: Richmond C. Beatty *Lord Macaulay: Victorian Liberal* (Norman, Okla. 1938). Arthur Bryant *Macaulay* (London 1932 and New York 1933). Charles Harding Firth *Commentary on Macaulay's History of England* (London and New York 1938). G. O. Trevelyan *The Life and Letters of Lord Macaulay* (1876, new ed. 2 vols. London 1961).

MacDOWELL, Edward Alexander (Dec. 18, 1861 – Jan. 23, 1908). American composer. Born New York, where he studied piano under Juan Buitrago, Pablo Desvernine, and Teresa Carreño before going to Paris to attend Conservatoire (1876–78). Continued studies in Germany, where a major influence was exerted by Joachim Raff, who taught him composition at Frankfurt Conservatory and introduced him to Liszt (1882). On Liszt's invitation, MacDowell played *First Modern Suite* for piano at Allgemeiner Musikverein concert (1882). During next few years, established reputation in Europe with orchestral works *Hamlet and Ophelia* (1885), *Lancelot and Elaine* (1888), and *The Saracens and the Lovely Alda* (1891), and the *Second Piano Concerto* (1890). Married former pupil Marian Nevins (1884); settled in Boston (1888). Accepted chairmanship of new department of music at Columbia University (1896), but resigned (1904) after much publicized dispute with new administration over curriculum. Died in New York. MacDowell's music is more influenced by German romanticism than American nationalism. Well-known works include *Indian Suite* for orchestra (1897) and piano compositions *Woodland Sketches* (1896), *Sea Pieces* (1898), and *New England Idyls* (1902). After his death, his widow (1857–1956) established the MacDowell Colony at Peterborough, N.H., for composers, artists, and writers to work in seclusion and also enjoy each other's society.

REFERENCES: Lawrence Gilman *Edward MacDowell* (New York 1908). John Howard Tasker *Our American Music* (3rd ed. New York 1954).

MACHADO DE ASSIS, Joaquim Maria (June 21, 1839 – Sept. 29, 1908). Brazilian writer. Born Rio de Janeiro, son of Negro house painter and his Portuguese wife. Received little formal education, but from adolescence kept himself in a literary milieu, working as typesetter, proofreader, translator, and journalist before becoming famous as writer of fiction and poetry. From 1873, supported himself as bureaucrat in agriculture ministry. Married Carolina de Novaes, aristocratic Portuguese lady (1869). Machado founded Brazilian Academy of Letters (1897) and served as its president until his death in Rio de Janeiro. Generally considered the greatest of Brazilian writers, he is best known for three realistic novels marked by psychological insight and a pessimistic view of the human condition: *Memórias póstumas de Braz Cubas* (1880, tr. *Epitaph of a Small Winner* 1952), *Quincas Borba* (1892, tr. *Philosopher or Dog?* 1954), and *Dom Casmurro* (1900, tr. 1953). Poetry volumes include *Crisálidas* (1864), *Phalenas* (1870), *Americanas* (1875), and *Poesias completas* (1901), which includes his best poems, *Occidentais*. Also in translation is *The Psychiatrist and Other Stories* (1963).

REFERENCES: José Bettencourt Machado *Machado of Brazil: The Life and Times of Machado de Assis* (New York 1953). Helen Caldwell *The Brazilian Othello of Machado de Assis: A Study of Dom Casmurro* (Berkeley, Calif. 1960).

MACHADO Y RUIZ, Antonio (July 26, 1875 – Feb. 22, 1939). Spanish poet. Born Seville. Educated in Madrid at Institución Libre de Enseñanza, a liberal school founded by university professors who had denied allegiance to crown and church. Went to Paris (1899), where during next few years he associated with Rubén Darío and other modernist poets. Taught French at Instituto de Soria (1907–10). Married Leonor Izquierdo Cuevas (1909); after her death (1912), studied with Henri Bergson in Paris before continuing teaching career in Baeza (1912–19), Segovia (1919–32), and Madrid (from 1932). A staunch loyalist during Spanish Civil War, Machado fled to France when republic fell (1939), and died at Collioure, Pyrénées-Orientales. His poetry is known for its austerity, its profound religious and philosophical concerns, and its portrayal of Castile.

TRANSLATIONS: *Eighty Poems* tr. Willis Barnstone (with Spanish text; New York 1959). *Castilian Ilexes: Versions from Antonio Machado* tr. Charles Tomlinson and Henry Gifford (London and New York 1963). *Juan de Mairena* tr. Ben Belitt (Berkeley, Calif. 1963).

REFERENCES: Alice J. McVan *Antonio Machado* (with translations of selected poems, New York 1959). John B. Trend *Antonio Machado* (Oxford 1953). Howard T. Young *The Victorious Expression: A Study of Four Contemporary Spanish Poets: Miguel de Unamuno, Antonio Machado, Juan Ramón Jiménez, Federico García Lorca* (Madison, Wis. 1964).

MACHAUT (or MACHAULT), Guillaume de (c.1300 – Apr. 1377). French medieval poet and composer. Born Machaut, in the Ardennes. Entered service of John of Luxembourg, king of Bohemia, as chaplain and secretary (1323), accompanied him on his campaigns in central and eastern Europe, and received through him a canonry at Reims (1337). After John's death (1346), he lived mainly at Reims for rest of his life, and was patronized by John the Good of France, Charles the Bad of Navarre, and other nobles. Guillaume wrote several long poems which influenced Chaucer, including *Jugement dou roi de Navarre, Dit dou Vergier,* and *Voir Dit,* all on courtly love; and *Confort d'Ami,* which offers consolation and advice to Charles of Navarre, imprisoned by the king of France. Chiefly known, however, for his motets, ballades, lais, virelais, rondeaux, and chants royaux, the music and words of which he composed, and which affected the development of the French lyric. Also wrote church music.

EDITIONS: *Poésies lyriques* ed. Vladimir F. Chichmaref (2 vols. Paris 1909).

Oeuvres ed. Ernest Hoepffner (3 vols. Paris 1908–21).

REFERENCES: A. Machabey *Guillaume de Machault: la vie et l'oeuvre musical* (2 vols. Paris 1955). G. Reese *Music in the Middle Ages* (New York 1940).

MACHIAVELLI, Niccolò (May 3, 1469 – June 22, 1527). Italian statesman and writer. Born Florence, to a distinguished family. From 1498 until return of the Medici (1512), worked in chancellery of the Florentine republic and as secretary to committee in charge of war and foreign affairs. Had both administrative and diplomatic duties, traveled to France and Germany, and knew political leaders throughout Italy, including Cesare Borgia, model for *The Prince*. Married Marietta Corsini (1501). Introduced conscription in Florence (1506) as substitute for expensive, unreliable mercenary army. When the Medici resumed control of Florence (1512), Machiavelli was accused of conspiracy (1513), imprisoned and tortured, then banished from Florence. Retired to his farm at San Casciano, where he wrote his major works. *Il Principe* (1513, *The Prince*) discusses the qualities and action essential to the absolute ruler. *The Discourses on the First Ten Books of Livy* (completed 1519) present the theory that politics are above moral law, the object being to secure and retain power by any means, hence the concept Machiavellianism. Other major works: *Dell' Arte Guerra* (1519–20, *The Art of War*), *History of Florence* (1525), a comedy *Mandragola* (1518). Machiavelli returned to Florence (1520), where he held minor posts under the Medici, and where he died.

REFERENCES: Federico Chabod *Machiavelli and the Renaissance* (tr. London 1958). John R. Hale *Machiavelli and Renaissance Italy* (London 1961). Dorothy Erskine Muir *Machiavelli and His Times* (London and New York 1936). Roberto Ridolfi *The Life of Niccolò Machiavelli* (tr. Chicago 1963). Pasquale Villari *The Life and Times of Niccolò Machiavelli* (tr. 1878–83, new ed. New York 1969). John H. Whitfield *Machiavelli* (London 1947).

MacNEICE, Louis (Sept. 12, 1907 – Sept. 3, 1963). Irish poet. Born Belfast. Educated in England at Marlborough School and Merton College, Oxford (1926–30). Married Giovanna Marie Thérèse Ezra (1930, divorced 1936). Became lecturer in classics at Birmingham University (1930–36) and lecturer in Greek at Bedford College, London (1936–40). From 1941, he was a scriptwriter and producer for British Broadcasting Corporation, and except for various visits abroad, including eighteen months in Athens as director of British Institute (1950–51), he lived in London until his death. With his first collections, *Blind Fireworks* (1929) and *Poems* (1935), achieved recognition as member of group of poets of social protest which included W. H. Auden and Stephen Spender. Witty, detached, and elegant, full of forceful imagery, MacNeice's poetry concerns itself with contemporary life. Among later verse collections are *The Earth Compels* (1938), *Autumn Journal* (1939), *Plant and Phantom* (1941), *Springboard* (1944), *Ten Burnt Offerings* (1952), *Visitations* (1958), *Solstices* (1961). Prose works include travel books *Letters from Iceland* (1937, written with Auden) and *I Crossed the Minch* (1938); critical studies *Modern Poetry* (1938) and *The Poetry of W. B. Yeats* (1941). Also wrote verse translations of Aeschylus' *Agamemnon* (1936) and Goethe's *Faust* (1951).

EDITION: *Collected Poems* ed. E. R. Dodds (London 1966).

REFERENCE: John Press *Louis MacNeice* (London 1965).

MAETERLINCK, Maurice (Polydore Marie Bernard), Count (Aug. 29, 1862 – May 6, 1949). Belgian writer. Born Ghent. Educated at local Jesuit school and University of Ghent; admitted to bar (1886). On visit to Paris (1887) met Villiers de L'Isle-Adam and other symbolists and resolved to become a writer. His early works, the poetry collection *Serres chaudes* (1889) and such plays as *La Princesse Maleine* (1889; tr. 1892) and *Pelléas et Mélisande* (1892), belong to a symbolist school and demonstrate his strongest trait, a mysticism largely inspired by Novalis and Emerson. Maeterlinck's works, with their atmosphere of omnipresent death, mystery, and unreality, had greatest influence in period before World War I. He settled in France (1896). Received Nobel prize for literature (1911); was made a count by Belgian king (1932). Soon after World War I, ended long association with actress Georgette Leblanc to marry Renée Dahon. Made numerous lecture tours; lived in U.S. (1940–47). Died in Nice. Major writings include philosophical works *Le Trésor des humbles* (1896, tr. *The Treasure of the Humble* 1897), *La Sagesse et la destinée* (1898, tr. *Wisdom and Destiny* 1898), *Le Temple enseveli* (1901, tr. *The Buried Temple* 1902), *Le Double Jardin* (1904, tr. *The Double Garden* 1904), *L'Intelligence des fleurs* (1907), and *La Mort* (1913); series of books on naturalism, beginning with *La Vie des abeilles* (1901, tr. *Life of the Bee* 1901); the plays *Monna Vanna* (1902), *L'Oiseau bleu* (1908, tr. *The Blue Bird* 1909, his most popular work), *Les Fiançailles* (1912, tr. *The Betrothal* 1912), *Marie-Magdeleine* (1913), and the memoirs *Blue Bubbles* (1949). Maeterlinck's principal works are available in numerous English versions.

REFERENCES: M. E. M. Clark *Maurice Maeterlinck: Poet and Philosopher* (London 1915). W. D. Halls *Maurice Maeterlinck* (Oxford 1960). Patrick Mahony *Magic of Maeterlinck* (Hollywood, Calif. 1951). Una Taylor *Maurice Maeterlinck: A Critical Study* (1915, reprinted New York 1968).

MAGNASCO, Alessandro (1667 – Mar. 12, 1749). Italian painter. Born Genoa. Trained in studio of his father, also a painter; then moved to Milan (c.1681), where he was apprenticed to Venetian painter Filippo Abbiati, and began his career with a series of portraits, now lost. In Milan, became friend of Sebastiano Ricci, through whom he influenced Venetian eighteenth-century painting. Magnasco's mature works show small, attenuated figures, usually monks, nuns, hermits, or gypsies, in dark, romantic landscapes or gloomy interiors with mysterious lighting, creating hallucinatory effect. His perception and brushwork look forward to impressionism, and his bitter irony anticipates Goya and Daumier. Mag-

nasco returned to Genoa (1705), then became court painter to grand duke of Tuscany in Florence. Lived again in Milan (1711–35), then in Genoa, where he died.

REFERENCES: Germain Bazin *Baroque and Rococo Art* (New York 1966). Armando Ferri *Alessandro Magnasco* (Rome 1922). Benno Geiger *Alessandro Magnasco* (Bergamo 1949).

MAHLER, Gustav (July 7, 1860 – May 18, 1911). Austrian composer and conductor. Born Kalischt, Bohemia, son of Jewish shopkeeper. At Vienna Conservatory (1875–78) was a devotee of Wagner and became personally influenced by Bruckner. When first major composition *Das klagende Lied* (1880) failed to win a prize, Mahler began career as increasingly successful opera conductor in Austrian and German towns, culminating with triumphant period as director of Imperial Opera in Vienna (1897–1907). Married Alma Maria Schindler (1902). Now world-famous, he became conductor of New York Metropolitan Opera (1907–11) and New York Philharmonic Society (1909–11). Collapsed from strain of overwork, and shortly afterwards died in Vienna. His work, consisting entirely of symphonies and songs, falls into three periods: the early phase of *Lieder eines fahrenden Gesellen* (*Songs of a Wayfarer*, 1883–85); songs from the German folk collection *Des Knaben Wunderhorn* (*The Youth's Magic Horn*, 1888); and first four symphonies, which employed songs; the second phase, more abstract, of songs on poems by Friedrich Rückert, including *Kindertotenlieder* (*Songs on the Deaths of Children*, 1901–1904), and symphonies five to seven; the last phase, of the great song cycle *Das Lied von der Erde* (*The Song of the Earth*, 1907–10) and symphonies eight, nine, and ten (unfinished), in which Mahler greatly expanded the length of the symphonic form, its emotional range, and the role and color of voice and instruments. His music is the profound personal expression of his intense spiritual experiences.

REFERENCES: Alma M. Mahler *Gustav Mahler: Memories and Letters* (tr. London and New York 1946). Donald

J. Mitchell *Gustav Mahler: The Early Years* (London 1958). Dika Newlin *Bruckner, Mahler, Schoenberg* (New York 1947). Hans P. Redlich *Bruckner and Mahler* (London and New York 1955). Bruno Walter *Gustav Mahler* (tr. New York 1958).

MAILLOL, Aristide (Joseph Bonaventure) (Dec. 25, 1861 – Oct. 5, 1944). French sculptor. Born Banyuls-sur-Mer. Studied painting at École des Beaux Arts, Paris (1882–86), where he came under influence of Gauguin and turned to more decorative art forms such as wood carving and tapestry making. Opened tapestry workshop in his native town, and married one of the girls he employed as weavers (1895). Maillol took up sculpture at turn of century. His massive female nudes, influenced by Greek archaic and fifth-century art (especially after a visit to Greece in 1909), combine naturalism with classical idealism. Solid, impassive, and perfectly balanced, his sculptures constitute a direct reaction against the dramatic impressionist techniques of Rodin, and a return to formal values. Fine examples are his Cézanne monument commissioned (1912) by Aix-en-Provence (Tuileries, Paris) and *River* (Museum of Modern Art, New York). Maillol died in an automobile accident near Banyuls-sur-Mer.
REFERENCES: Judith Cladel *Aristide Maillol: sa vie, son oeuvre, ses idées* (Paris 1937). John Rewald *Maillol* (London 1939 and New York 1943). Waldemar-George (pseud.) *Aristide Maillol*, with biography by Dina Vierny (tr. Greenwich, Conn. 1965).

MALLARMÉ, Stéphane (Mar. 18, 1842 – Sept. 9, 1898). French poet, essayist, and translator. Born Paris. Educated at lycée in Sens. Went to England (1862) to learn the language, taking with him a German girl, Marie Gerhard, whom he married a year later. Became teacher of English, first in the provinces at Tournon (1863), Besançon (1866), Avignon (1867), and finally in Paris (1871). While in the provinces, he published eleven poems in *Le Parnasse contemporain* (1866) and began work on *Hérodiade* (never completed) and *L'Après-midi d'un Faune* (1876). However, provincial life made him hunger for the literary activity of the capital, and by 1875 he was settled at 89 Rue de Rome. Here he became center of a *cénacle* which was to include such admirers as Gide, Claudel, and Valéry, and was eventually acknowledged leader of the symbolist movement. Mallarmé spent his last years as a revered master, especially after praise of his work in Huysmans's novel *À Rebours* (1884), publication of *Poésies Complètes* (1887), translations of Poe (1888), and *Verset Prose* (1892). Only after retirement from teaching (1894) could he devote himself entirely to literature, and only four years later he died in his summer cottage at Valvins, near Fontainebleau.

TRANSLATIONS: *The Poem Itself* ed. Stanley Burnshaw (New York and Harmondsworth, England, PB 1967). Robert Greer Cohn *Towards the Poems of Mallarmé* (Berkeley, Calif. 1965). *Mallarmé: Selected Prose Poems, Essays and Letters* tr. Bradford Cook (Baltimore 1956).
REFERENCES: Wallace Fowlie *Mallarmé* (Chicago 1953). Guy Michaud *Mallarmé* (tr. New York 1965). H. Mondor *La Vie de Mallarmé* (Paris 1941).

❧

STÉPHANE MALLARMÉ
BY STANLEY BURNSHAW

To write about Stéphane Mallarmé, however briefly, is to hint at much of what is meant by "modern" in poetry, not merely "symbolism" and the revolutions in syntax and referents but "angelism" and something more. After decades in elected obscurity to all but a circle, Mallarmé's innovations suddenly exploded on the French world of letters (1884), with reverberations that reached even England. Nowadays it has become quite usual to hear glib remarks about his unparalleled influence, yet the number of people who can or are willing to experience his poetry remains negligible: there is still no body of verse more exacting or resistant.

Despite the remarkable illuminations of many individual poems, a reader has to learn to accommodate his mind to the phrases and lines, projecting himself in an unprecedented way on the sounds, images, and echoes of the words that their author hoped would "light up by mutual reflections like a virtual trail of fire on precious stones."

Part of the reason is suggested in Mallarmé's decision "to paint not the thing but the effect it produces." But the famous phrase means little outside the context of his poetics in its slow, pained unfolding. Like some of his peers, the adolescent Mallarmé yearned (in Lamartinian verses) for a more exalted reality than the usual one he knew; but it was not until after he had assimilated Baudelaire, then Gautier, Théodore de Banville, Villiers de L'Isle-Adam, and — more important — Poe, that he could grow sure of his own direction. Yet as early as his twentieth year he was telling the literary world that "Whatever is sacred, whatever is to remain sacred must be clothed in mystery"; that poets must make their work "accessible only to exceptional spirits . . . by inventing an immaculate language, a series of sacred formulae."

Born in Paris, Mallarmé as a child experienced two griefs which led him later to speak of his work as a sacrificial offering: the death of his mother when he was five, of his older sister a decade later. The loss of his father (1863), by contrast, brought him some freedom. Given a small inheritance, he was able to marry the twenty-five-year-old German governess with whom he had made an unidyllic sojourn in London six months before. In November 1863 the couple set out for the small city on the Rhône where Mallarmé was to begin the schoolteacher's career that he would detest throughout his next three decades. After three years at Tournon, he was shifted to Besançon and then, happily, to Avignon, where he soon found companionship among the Provençal poets.

That these eight years in the provinces were of crucial consequence can be seen not only in the titles of the poems that engaged him — some of his finest lyrics as well as the longer *Hérodiade* and *The Afternoon of a Faun*. Ironically, this rich productivity gives no hint of the crisis that was invading him. Laboring by day at a harassing job, he devoted the energy he had left toward achieving a poetic line that would be "composed not of words but of intentions," in which "all the words should efface themselves before sensations." Intermittently plagued by fears of creative impotence, often exhausted by insomnia, he was also at times tormented by physical pain — "during moments of respite I would throw myself like a desperate maniac on my poem's unattainable Overture [to *Hérodiade*]; it is singing inside my head but I cannot get it down." Two years after settling in Avignon, where he had longed to live, he found himself "in a state of crisis that cannot go on." By February 1869 he was unable to hold a pen: "The simple act of writing brings hysteria to my head."

However one conceives of this experience — or of the efficacy of his writing *Igitur* as the cure — one fact lies at the center: Mallarmé had been forcing himself to the brink of collapse with his uncompromising regime of depersonalization. Convinced that individuality was an illusion, he struggled to break through, and when appearances had finally dissolved, he confronted a void ("In *delving so deeply in my verse,* I have run into . . . Nothingness"). Yet the void was not the end ("I died and came back to life"). It was to emerge in his mind as nothing other than the All. "Having found Nothingness," he assures a friend, "I found the Beautiful." "I am no longer the Stéphane that you knew — but an aptitude of the spiritual universe for seeing and developing itself through what I was." "My mind *is moving in the Eternal.*" Whether his metaphysical basis prove to have been Plato, Hegel, or simply his own, Mallarmé proceeded to build a unique edifice, disposing throughout the work its recurrent symbols — flower, for example: "I say: a flower! and from that forgetfulness to which my voice consigns all contours . . . musically the suave idea itself arises [*idée même et suave*] that is absent from all bouquets." Having, as he believed, not invented but uncovered the system of the universe, he could finally dedicate himself to composing "the Book, for I am convinced that there is only One . . . the Orphic explanation of the Earth, which is the poet's sole duty and the true function of literature."

In May 1871, Mallarmé was able to resettle in Paris — "kinder, more polite, and madder than ever," said Leconte de Lisle, "with absolutely unintelligible prose and verse." Fifteen years later he was the acknowledged Master. His Tuesday evenings at home had become the great event for writers and artists, who received his words like those of an oracle. Yet it was not until 1892 that a volume of his poems became widely available; it was not until after his death that the larger world would hear of his strivings or begin to consider its achievement.

"To *name* an object," he had insisted, "is to suppress three quarters of the enjoyment of a poem, which is made up of gradual guessing; the dream is to *suggest* it." Yet with all the dedicated guesswork of Mallarmé specialists, much mystery remains (in the final *A Throw of the Dice*, for example, which Gide thought "the most extreme point to which the human spirit has ventured"). Moreover, for the nonspecialist who is eager to know more than the marvelous lines or phrases that keep singing in his head, tireless rereading will not bring him into the poetry unless he is able to accept it on its own terms. And equally, to accept a creative mind which could celebrate both the erotic Faun and the fiercely virginal Hérodiade, which sought "the divine transposition of the fact into the ideal" while also maintaining that "to be really a man or nature when thinking, one must think with all one's body." Words and word clusters reflect upon one another. They point in all directions, inviting multiple, conflicting interpretations — and always seeming to touch on the situation of the poet-artist-seer. Could it have been otherwise in a writer who had come to disparage his published poems as "chance inspirations" "of momentary value" — at best preparatory exercises for the Great Work that he feared he could never complete but of which he still strived to realize a fragment?

MALORY, Sir Thomas (? – Mar. 12/14, 1471). English writer. Modern research, still in dispute, tends to identify him with Sir Thomas Malory of Newbold Revell, in Warwickshire. He represented Warwickshire in Parliament of 1445, but soon thereafter seems to have become a confirmed criminal. Jailed eight times before 1460, he was charged with a number of unsavory crimes, including church plundering, extortion, and rape. Probably imprisoned again in 1468, he completed (1469 or 1470) his *Book of King Arthur and His Noble Knights of the Round Table* (given title *Le Morte d'Arthur* when it was published by William Caxton, 1485), a collection of Arthurian tales drawn chiefly from French romances. Buried near

Newgate, London, he probably died a prisoner. Written at the close of the Middle Ages, *Le Morte d'Arthur* is distinguished by its vigorous and eloquent prose and a firm control of narrative and structure that looks forward to modern fiction.

EDITION: *Works* ed. Eugène Vinaver (2nd ed. 3 vols. Oxford 1967).

REFERENCES: William Matthews *The Ill-Framed Knight* (Berkeley, Calif. 1966). Edmund A. Reiss *Sir Thomas Malory* (New York 1966). Eugène Vinaver *Malory* (Oxford 1929).

MANDELSTAM, Osip Emilyevich (Jan. 15, 1891 – c. Dec. 27, 1938). Russian poet. Born Warsaw, son of a Jewish businessman. Brought as a child to St. Petersburg, where he attended Tenishev School. After graduating (1907), visited Paris, and spent two terms (1910) at University of Heidelberg studying Kantian philosophy and Old French. On return, entered University of St. Petersburg and joined literary circles, attracting attention with group of poems in the review *Apollon* (1910). Member (from 1912) of Acmeist group of poets, led by Anna Akhmatova, who strongly influenced him. Mandelstam's poetry, most of which appeared in two collections of less than a hundred short poems, *Stone* (1913) and *Tristia* (1922), reflect life in art and literature, rather than direct experience. Chiefly concerned with form and technique, it is impersonal and erudite. Though opposed to Bolsheviks, Mandelstam remained in Russia after revolution. Married Nadezhda Yakovlevna Khazina (1922). From 1925, concentrated on prose, publishing collection under title *The Egyptian Stamp* (1928). His epigram on Stalin, "After each death, he is like a Georgian tribesman, putting a raspberry in his mouth," led to his arrest (May 1934). After three years in exile at Voronezh, he was released (1937), then arrested again (1938) and sent to Siberia, where he died soon after.

TRANSLATION: *The Prose of Osip Mandelstam: The Noise of Time, Theodosia, The Egyptian Stamp* tr. with critical and biographical essay by Clarence Brown (Princeton, N.J. 1965).

REFERENCES: Nadezhda Yakovlevna Mandelstam *Memoir* (London and New York 1970). Leonid I. Strakhovsky *Craftsmen of the Word: Three Poets of Modern Russia: Gumilyov, Akhmatova, Mandelstam* (Cambridge, Mass. 1949).

MANET, Édouard (Jan. 23, 1832 – Apr. 30, 1883). French painter. Born and died in Paris; of wealthy bourgeois family. After attending Collège Rollin (1842–48), sailed on naval training ship to Rio de Janeiro (1848–49). Upon return, decided to give up naval career and become a painter. Entered studio of Thomas Couture (1850); studied old masters in the Louvre and in museums of Europe. First submission to Salon, *The Absinthe Drinker* (1859, Ny Carlsberg Museum, Copenhagen), was rejected, but subsequent entries, notably *The Guitarist* (1860, Metropolitan Museum, New York), were accepted and praised. Throughout his life Manet sought public approval, although such masterpieces as *Déjeuner sur l'herbe* and *Olympia* (both 1863, Louvre, Paris) met with violent resentment. The impressionist group came to regard him as a leader, and he in turn was influenced by them during the 1870's. Other major works include *La Musique aux Tuileries* (1862, Tate Gallery, London), *The Dead Toreador* (1864, National Gallery, Washington), *The Fifer* (1866, Louvre), *Bar at the Folies Bergère* (1882, Courtauld Institute, London). Married Suzanne Leenhof (1863). Was a close friend of Zola, Baudelaire, Mallarmé, and other writers.

REFERENCES: Pierre Courthion *Manet* (New York 1961). George H. Hamilton *Manet and His Critics* (New Haven and London 1954). Nanne Coffin Hansen *Edouard Manet* (Philadelphia 1967). John Rewald *The History of Impressionism* (New York 1949, rev. ed. 1962). Nils Gösta Sandblad *Manet: Three Studies in Artistic Conception* (Lund, Sweden 1954). Pierre Schneider *The World of Manet* (New York 1968).

✍

MANET

BY WILLIAM C. SEITZ

Although he was the focus of outrage and controversy during his lifetime,

Manet is today acclaimed as one of the greatest of nineteenth-century painters. He was surely one of the most fluent, direct, and elegant manipulators of oil and pastel in the history of these media. In Manet's dexterous hands the most inconsequential motif — a flower or two, a few pieces of fruit, and in one delightful instance a single stalk of asparagus — could become pure poetry of butterfly-light brushwork, luminous color, and precise tone relationships. Perhaps more than any other master, Manet was the "perfect" painter, whose works can be admired, irrespective of subject, as one does the performance of a dancer or musician. Yet unless expanded, this formalistic view is so limited as to be false, for few painters present such unusual problems of interpretation.

Little is known of Manet's inner motivation, yet he nevertheless occupies a historical position as the archetype of the avant-garde artist. The most sophisticated criticism seems unable either to verify or dismiss all of the implicit meanings, innuendos, possible intentions and aesthetically subversive implications that seem to be contained within his art. He became a radical leader, in all probability, unintentionally. The son of a government official, Manet was never a bohemian, was elegant and aristocratic in manner and dress, and solicitous of the approval of the academicians by whom he was denounced. Although he showed an aptitude for drawing by the time he was eleven, his family wished him to study law. As a compromise he agreed to enter the Naval Academy, and was permitted to study art seriously only after failing the entrance examination twice. In 1850, followed by his friend Antonin Proust, he entered the studio of Thomas Couture, now remembered chiefly by an immense canvas in the Louvre,

Romans of the Decadence. After his academic training Manet did not discard tradition. His derivations from Velázquez, Goya, Raphael, Giorgione, Titian, Tintoretto, Hals, and other old masters anchor one pole of his art securely in the past.

Despite his retrospective predisposition, Manet can be seen as the inheritor of the realism championed by Courbet. During the Sixties he fulfilled Baudelaire's characterization of Constantin Guys as "the painter of modern life," and in the Seventies — taking a step which his younger contemporary Degas would not — he made the break to open brushwork, high-keyed color, and even, under the influence of Monet, to painting in the open. Yet he never wholly adopted the impressionist style, nor did he abandon the rich blacks he had discovered in Hals, Velázquez and Goya. The idea of Manet as a brilliant transitional figure between realism and impressionism, though not untrue, is also limited and overly deterministic.

In such early paintings as *The Guitarist* (1860) and *The Old Musician* (1862), painted before he had visited Spain, Manet assembles what are almost charades of Spanish paintings. Their ostensible subjects are drained of the original meanings to become motifs — even pretexts. His real themes are not the mocked or dead Christ, the bullring, or even the Spanish dancers that he saw in Paris, but the rich dark tones, saturated hues, and translucent backgrounds of Spanish art. Another view of Manet — for which *Mlle. Victorine in the Costume of an Espada* (1863) or the magnificent, boldly simple *The Fifer* (1866) are telling arguments — sees him as a "pure" painter, cavalierly dealing historic deathblows to the old subject matter, and elevating color, brushwork, and arrangement to become the end as well as the means of painting — an interpretation supported by the interest Manet showed, as did Whistler and other artists by the Sixties, in the abstract qualities of Japanese prints.

Yet the idea of Manet as subverting subject matter for medium and form is also incomplete. As early as 1862, in *Concert in the Tuileries Gardens,* he concentrated on the subtlest nuances of an entirely contemporary subject, and included portraits of himself and his friends in the crowd. His concern for modern actuality, indeed, was intensified during the same years that he was parodying the old masters. Paintings of current life and history, along with a series of dazzlingly animated portraits in oil and pastel of Zola, Mallarmé, Clemenceau, Berthe Morisot, George Moore, artists, musicians, actors, actresses and anonymous sitters, are the thread which unifies his complicated development.

Discussions of the resentment that greeted Manet's most ambitious works such as *Luncheon on the Grass,* shown in the Salon des Refusés in 1863, and the masterpiece *Olympia,* painted in 1863 but not exhibited until 1865, have become a staple of the mass media and scarcely demand additional comment. Part of the wave of hostility directed toward these great paintings was based on their flat color patterns and elimination of transitional tones, but the strongest criticism was directed toward their subjects. One cannot help but conclude that both pictures were intended, if only subliminally, to irritate a bourgeois public. During the reign of Napoleon III it was provocative to paint, as Manet did in *Luncheon on the Grass,* two modern couples picnicking in a park, the men fully clothed, one woman partially dressed and the other nude; and, in *Olympia,* a beautiful but brazen courtesan clad only in

jewelry and one slipper, a black cat standing erect at the foot of her bed and a Negro servant delivering a bouquet. That these works were based on revered prototypes by Giorgione, Raphael and Titian only sharpened the barbs that Manet so expertly placed in the flesh of bourgeois hypocrisy and prudery.

The argument that Manet was uninterested in content is further undermined by *The Execution of Maximilian* (1867), a painting of an event from current history. This puzzling composition, in the Städtische Kunsthalle, Mannheim, is plainly derived from Goya's *The Third of May, 1808,* but its dramatic confrontation is entirely lacking. Manet's picture is cold both in color and interpretation, and the uniforms of the firing squad are French rather than Mexican. There are three other oils of this controversial subject, as well as a lithograph that was suppressed by police censorship. In 1864 Manet had represented the naval battle of the *Kearsarge* and the *Alabama* off Cherbourg, an episode of the American Civil War, and in 1871, like a war reporter, he was to record grim scenes of Paris during the Commune.

Manet's painting during the 1870's is a magnificent fusion, articulated with his almost unbelievable skill, of what he had learned through the art of the past, the new impressionist color and brushwork, penetrating observation of contemporary life, and an exquisite but nevertheless virile sensibility. Although the works of this period are more extroverted, Manet's preoccupation with devious content does not entirely disappear: a one-legged man on crutches darkens a gay impressionist study of a Paris street decorated for a national festival; probing glances and intent gestures appear in otherwise casual subjects. The questions such peculiarities raise cannot always be answered, but they demonstrate that Manet's art is complex and multi-leveled, and that his personal attitudes were involved and paradoxical. His manner of painting, advanced though it was, belongs solidly to the nineteenth century. He prefigures the twentieth, however, not only in the battle he waged against philistine critics and the middle-class public, but also in his social and aesthetic hypersensitivity, traits typical of avant-garde artists in all media.

MANN, Thomas (June 6, 1875 – Aug. 12, 1955). German writer. Born Lübeck, son of a prosperous grain merchant who twice served as mayor of the city. After father died (1890), family moved to Munich, and Thomas, after completing studies at a military school, joined them (1894). That year while working as a clerk he sold his first story, *Gefallen* (*Fallen*). Went to Rome (1898) with brother Heinrich (1871–1950), who also became a novelist (best-known work *Professor Unrat*, 1905, tr. *The Blue Angel* 1932). Thomas began writing novel *Buddenbrooks;* in meantime his first collection of stories, *Little Herr Friedmann*, appeared (1898). Back in Munich he worked for journal *Simplicissimus* and completed *Buddenbrooks* (1901, tr. 1924), which soon became an international success. Two novellas, *Tristan* and *Tonio Kröger* (1903, tr. 1914), appeared next. Married Katja Pringsheim (1905). Novella *Der Tod in Venedig* (1913, tr. *Death in Venice* 1925) and his masterpiece *Der Zauberberg* (1924, tr. *The Magic Mountain* 1927) were widely acclaimed and led to his winning Nobel prize for literature (1929). Now one of the foremost German writers, he left Nazi Germany (1933); settled first in Switzerland, then in United States (1938), where he became a citizen (1944). Mann was greatly influenced by Goethe, who inspired the historical novel *Lotte in Weimar* (1939, tr. *The Beloved Returns* 1947) and version of Faust legend *Doktor Faustus* (1947, tr. 1948). Also produced tetralogy *Joseph und seine Bruder* (*Joseph and His Brothers* 1933–43), *Stories of Three Decades* (1936), and *Essays of Three Decades* (1947). Returned to Germany (1949), received numerous honors, settled in Zurich, Switzerland (1952), where he wrote *The Confessions of Felix Krull* (1954), and where he died. Work includes other novels, essays and studies. Of his six children, both Erika and Klaus have distinguished themselves as writers.

REFERENCES: James Cleugh *Thomas Mann: A Study* (London 1933). Ignace Feuerlicht *Thomas Mann* (New York 1968). Henry Hatfield *Thomas Mann* (New York 1951) and *Thomas Mann: A Collection of Critical Essays* (New York 1964). Erich Heller *The Ironic German: A Study of Thomas Mann* (Boston 1958). James M. Lindsay *Thomas Mann* (Oxford 1954 and New York 1955). *The Stature of Thomas Mann: A Critical Anthology* Charles Neider, ed. (New York 1947). Richard H. Thomas *Thomas Mann: The Mediation of Art* (London and New York 1956). Hermann Weigand *The Magic Mountain: A Study of Thomas Mann's Novel Der Zauberberg* (Chapel Hill, N.C. 1964).

✍

THOMAS MANN
BY HOWARD NEMEROV

Of Thomas Mann I find it especially hard to say much in a little space, perhaps because since boyhood I have admired his works so very much, even while sometimes acknowledging those doubts of which Erich Heller gives so convincing an account in his *Dialogue on The Magic Mountain*. Mann stands for me as an illumination singular in its purity of the truth that a great modern artist must be a monster, absorbing the whole world and transforming it by means of his few obsessions into the illusion of the whole world again. So much thoroughness, so much explicitness, so drastic an analysis! and at the end all is magic and mystery still.

Through the vast range of his stories and settings, through his powerful grasp of the particulars of the many knowledges, these obsessions remain clear and form his thematic center, his peculiar realm of the problematic. The kinds of question he examines through a long and splendid development remain visibly constant from *Buddenbrooks* through *Doctor Faustus*, from mythological Egypt *in illo tempore* to mythological Europe enthralled by the demonisms and dynamisms of the twentieth century. Of this thematic center I shall try to give a swift overview.

The genetic inheritance of Mann's artist heroes, like his own, comes as the result of a series of opposites: from the father, all that is Northern, stern, mercantile, puritanical; from the mother, all that is Southern, relaxed, artistic, passionate, and indulgent. Through the whole range of his fictions, art is regarded as a seduction from the clear duties of life, a giving-in, a giving-over of the self to a realm dubious, enthralling, disgraceful, yet necessary with its own unique and untranslatable necessity. In art there are nightmare, disease, criminality, madness, and death; but also exaltation — "heightened metabolism" — power, courage, and even grace. To the perils of this course the artist must expose himself at the cost of health, reason, even life — but especially at the cost of love. And what saves him, if anything does — what saves Mann himself if it saves all but none of his heroes, the lone exception being Tonio Kröger — is, oddly but appropriately, the bourgeois virtue of the forbidden father: *work.*

For a writer so much at home in the realm of the aesthetic and the morally questionable, this one commandment — work! — appears strangely as an absolute which must never be questioned. Mann's heroes are protected by routine, and the disasters which form their stories almost without exception overtake them when — and because — they go on a vacation. If this vacation be in the northward direction and the direction of home, as with Tonio Kröger, they may get away with it, experiencing their revelation at no greater cost than that of a certain dreamlike embarrassment; but if it is in a southward direction, and away from home, the result will be devastation, disease, madness, diabolism, whether they are then reborn or whether they die. Indeed, in Mann's stories, to go south *is* to go to the devil: Aschenbach to Venice, Castorp to his mountain, Joseph to Mizraim, Leverkühn to Italy and the pact with Satan.

Only toward the end of his life, speaking of Chekhov and finding as always in his subject chiefly himself, did Mann become explicit about this: "If the truth about life is by nature ironical, then must not art itself be by nature nihilistic? And yet art is so industrious! Art is, so to speak, the very paradigm of all work, it is work itself, and for its own sake." Developing the point with reference to Chekhov, he breaks in a few lines later: "Chekhov has fellow sufferers today, too, writers who do not feel at ease with their fame because they are 'amusing a forlorn world without offering it a scrap of saving truth' . . . These writers, too, are unable to say what the value of their own work is; nevertheless, they go on working, working to the end."

Mann goes on to speak of the protective, talismanic, regenerative powers of work in terms proper to his essay. But in his novels, it must be said, what work protects against is life itself, and the abruption of work leads dramatically through a disastrous love affair, often involving a child, to the death of artist or of child. In several of the early stories this prohibition against love, and penalty for daring to love, shape the action, Aschenbach's fatal love for Tadzio in *Death in Venice* being the best example. *The Magic Mountain* gives a more fragmented or dissociated version: Hans Castorp's love for Madame Chauchat, the immediate cause of his disease, refers itself to an early passion for a schoolmate; while the chief epiphany of the novel, his vision in the snow, makes the charm of an idyllic world depend upon a secret chamber where in darkness hags dismember and devour children. In the late novel *Doctor Faustus* the motif becomes explicit: Leverkühn's nephew is destroyed by Leverkühn's love for him.

Through the many metamorphoses of this central relation of artist and child I think to see in abstractest terms one of the poignant and recurring questions of modern literature: May the artist ever grow up and resume his rightful place among the fathers, or must his revolt be doomed from its beginning to irresponsible folly and he himself be numbered forever among the children? The subject is a secret presence throughout Mann's oeuvre, as it is an open one in Joyce and in Kafka. And for the most part Mann's answer would appear to be no. The artist can never re-enter with full adult authority the world of action. When Castorp goes back to the flatland it is as a private soldier, and in the infantry. Leverkühn in adult life duplicates as far as possible the scenes and even the persons that surrounded him in childhood. Joseph, though he gains great authority in the world, and though he is the adequate hero of a very great story, does not receive the father's blessing at the end; that belongs to the more serious and more limited Judah.

But I should not leave the subject without at least mentioning one happier resolution of this critical question. *The Confessions of Felix Krull*, origin-ally a memoir left unfinished in 1911 but resumed at the end of the author's life and left, alas, unfinished again — we have one volume of a projected three — seems to represent that transvaluation of all values that stands the whole world on its head to make it right again, the satyr play that in the Greek theatre crowned as it concluded the tragic sequence, dealing in the same persons, the same materials, but now in a spirit of absolute license and irreverence. If heretofore the artist for Mann had been *like* a child, *like* a criminal, and guilty on that account, the solution at the last is to embody the spirit of art in one who actually *is* a child and actually *is* a criminal, and who consequently has no reservations, and especially no feelings of remorse, about being both the one and the other. Here, it may be, is epitomized the wisdom of art, to which representing is "a higher and holier thing than merely being," and of which the artist said: "The wisdom meant was a tragically ironic one, which out of artistic instinct, for the sake of culture, holds science within bounds and defends life as the highest value on two fronts at once: against the pessimism of the calumniators of life, the apostles of an afterlife or of Nirvana; and against the optimism of the rationalists and reformers who preach their fables of justice and happiness on this earth for all men, and who prepare the way for a socialist uprising of the slaves."

Mann says that in description of a proposition Nietzsche inherited from Schopenhauer. Or so he says. But, again, that is the way with those great monsters, the great artists. Everything they touch becomes them.

MANSART (or MANSARD) (Nicholas) François (Jan. 23, 1598 – Sept. 23, 1666) and Jules Hardouin (April 1646 –

May 11, 1708). French architects. FRAN-
ÇOIS was born and died in Paris, son of
a master carpenter, and probably
trained by Salomon de Brosse, who certainly influenced him. He had designed
a number of châteaux and Paris
houses by 1635, when Louis XIII made
him royal architect. One of the supreme
exponents of French classicism, he exerted deep influence throughout seventeenth century and again in later
eighteenth. Works include château of
Balleroy (begun c.1626); additions to
château of Blois (1635); a series of
houses (1635–55): Hôtel de la Vrillière
(1635); château de Maisons-Laffitte,
near Paris (1642–51); Hôtel Mazarin
(1643–45); the superb church Val-de-
Grâce, Paris (1645); alterations to
Hôtel Carnavalet (1655–61). He popularized, but did not invent, the so-called
mansard roof. JULES HARDOUIN, François's grandnephew by marriage,
adopted his surname. Born in Paris, he
studied under the elder Mansart and
under Libéral Bruant. From mid-1670's
he was the favorite architect of Louis
XIV, and is best known for work on
Palace of Versailles (1678–1700),
which includes Galerie des Glaces,
Orangerie, Grand Trianon, palace
chapel. Other major works, all in Paris,
include Place des Victoires (1685–86),
Place Vendôme (1699), Dôme de Hôtel
des Invalides (1692–1704). Mansart's
style combines elements of classicism
and the baroque. Died at Marly.

REFERENCES: Reginald T. Blomfield
*A History of French Architecture,
1661–1774* (2 vols. London 1921).
Anthony F. Blunt *François Mansart
and the Origins of French Classical
Architecture* (London 1941) and *Art
and Architecture in France, 1500–1700*
(London 1953 and Baltimore 1954).

MANSFIELD, Katherine (real name
Kathleen Mansfield Beauchamp) (Oct. 14,
1888 – Jan. 9, 1923). British writer.
Born Wellington, New Zealand,
daughter of a successful businessman,
and received early schooling there. Sent
to London (1903) to attend Queen's
College. Returned to New Zealand
(1906), but was so disaffected that
she returned to London (1908) to devote herself to writing. Made disastrous
marriage (1909) with a young musician, George Bowden, whom she left
after a few days. Pregnant by another
man, she went to Germany to have the
child, but it was stillborn. Sketches
written at this time were collected with
other stories in her first book, *In a German Pension* (1911). Late that year
she met John Middleton Murry, then at
Oxford, and when he came to London
as a literary journalist they lived together. They married (1918) when
Bowden divorced her. In the meantime,
she was grief-stricken over the death
of her brother Leslie early in World
War I, and oppressed by discovery that
she had incurable tuberculosis. Nevertheless she continued to write, winning
recognition with *Bliss and Other Stories*
(1920) and *The Garden Party and
Other Stories* (1922). But literary efforts and restless searches for healthful
climates were finally abandoned (1922)
when she entered the Gurdjieff Institute at Fontainebleau, where she died
early in 1923. That year saw the publication of *The Dove's Nest and Other
Stories,* which established her reputation as a writer of acute awareness and
subtlety, a brilliant craftsman, and an
inspiring experimenter with narrative
devices. Katherine Mansfield is now
considered one of the founders of the
modern short story. Posthumously published works: *Poems* (1923), *Something Childish and Other Stories* (1924),
Selected Stories (1929), *The Aloe*
(1930), *The Journal of Katherine Mansfield* (1927), *The Letters of Katherine
Mansfield* (1929), *The Scrapbook of
Katherine Mansfield* (1939), *Katherine
Mansfield's Letters to John Middleton
Murry: 1913–1922* (1951).

REFERENCES: Anthony Alpers *Kath-
erine Mansfield: A Biography* (New
York 1953 and London 1954). Sylvia
Berkman *Katherine Mansfield: A Criti-
cal Study* (New Haven 1952). Ruth E.
Mantz and John Middleton Murry *The
Life of Katherine Mansfield* (London
1933).

MANTEGNA, Andrea (1431 – Sept. 13,
1506). Italian painter. Born Isola di
Carturo; apprenticed by his father, a
woodworker, to Paduan painter Francesco Squarcione (c.1441). Important
early influences were Filippo Lippi,
Donatello, Andrea del Castagno, Uc-

cello, and antique sculpture. Left Squarcione's studio the year (1448) he began first major work, frescoes in Ovetari chapel of church of the Eremitani, Padua (completed c.1455; nearly all destroyed in World War II). Married Nicolosia, sister of Giovanni Bellini (c.1453–54). One of Mantegna's greatest works is the *S. Zeno Altarpiece* (completed 1459; main triptych in church of S. Zeno, Verona; predella panels now in Louvre, Paris, and in Tours Museum). Became court painter to Gonzaga family at Mantua (1459), remained there for rest of his life, with occasional visits to other Italian cities. Later works include *St. George* (Accademia, Venice); *St. Sebastian* (Louvre, Paris); the frescoes in Camera degli Sposi, Gonzaga palace, Mantua (completed 1474), landmarks in Renaissance illusionistic painting; nine canvases of *The Triumph of Caesar* (1485–92, Hampton Court, England); *Madonna della Vittoria* (1495–96, Louvre); *St. Sebastian* (Ca d'Oro, Venice); *Dead Christ* (Brera, Milan); *Parnassus* (1497, Louvre, Paris); *Minerva Expelling the Vices from the Garden of Virtue* (1502, Louvre).

REFERENCES: Renata Cipriani *All the Paintings of Mantegna* (tr. 2 vols. New York 1964). Paul Kristeller *Andrea Mantegna* (tr. London and New York 1901). Millard Meiss *Andrea Mantegna as Illuminator: An Episode in Renaissance Art, Humanism, and Diplomacy* (New York 1957). Erika Tietze-Conrat *Mantegna: Paintings, Drawings, Engravings* (London and New York 1955).

MANZONI, Alessandro (Francesco Tommaso Antonio) (Mar. 7, 1785 – May 22, 1873). Italian novelist and poet. Born Milan; of aristocratic family. Entered literary circles of Milan (1801–1805) and Paris (1805–1807), and wrote first poems. Married Henriette Blondel (1808). When she became converted from Calvinism to Catholicism (1810), Manzoni himself underwent a conversion to a fervent belief in Catholicism, which became a strong element in his work. His finest poems are the five *Inni sacri* (*Sacred Hymns*, 1812–22, best known of which is *La Pentecoste*) and *Il Cinque Maggio* (1822, *The Fifth*

of May), on the death of Napoleon. Also wrote two historical tragedies, *Il Conte di Carmagnola* (1820) and *Adelchi* (1822). Greatest fame, however, came from immensely popular historical novel *I Promessi Sposi* (*The Betrothed*, 1825–27), which has been widely translated. An ardent supporter of Italian independence and unification, Manzoni participated with son in Milanese revolt of 1848, later became a senator (1860). After first wife's death (1833), married Teresa Borri (1837). He died in Milan. His great admirer, Giuseppe Verdi, wrote *Requiem* (1874) in his honor.

TRANSLATION: *The Betrothed* tr. Archibald Colquhoun (London 1951).
REFERENCES: Archibald Colquhoun *Manzoni and His Times* (London 1954). Bernard Wall *Alessandro Manzoni* (New Haven, Conn. and Cambridge, England, 1954).

MARCUS AURELIUS ANTONINUS (original name Marcus Annius Verus) (Apr. 20, 121 – Mar. 17, 180). Roman emperor. Born Rome, of aristocratic family. His aunt was the wife of Emperor Antoninus Pius, who adopted him (138) and whose daughter Faustina he married (145). Studied rhetoric under Cornelius Fronto, but was more interested in Stoic philosophy and the law. On succeeding Antoninus as emperor (161), he took unprecedented step of selecting a colleague, Lucius Verus, also an adopted son of Antoninus; Marcus held supreme authority, however, and ruled alone from Verus's death (169) until 177, when he named his son Commodus joint emperor. Marcus spent most of his reign waging frontier wars in Middle East and in central and southeast Europe; in domestic sphere, he took measures to aid the poor and to end various legal inequities; however, he also severely persecuted the Christians, especially in Gaul. One of the world's great Stoics, he expressed their philosophy in his *Meditations*, written in Greek. Died at Vindobona (now Vienna).

TRANSLATION: *Meditations* tr. A. S. L. Farquharson (2 vols. Oxford 1944).
REFERENCES: Anthony R. Birley *Marcus Aurelius* (London 1966). A. S. L.

Farquharson *Marcus Aurelius: His Life and His World* ed. D. A. Rees (2nd ed. Oxford 1952). Henry D. Sedgwick *Marcus Aurelius* (New Haven, Conn. 1921).

MARENZIO, Luca (1553 – Aug. 22, 1599). Italian composer. Born Coccaglio, near Brescia. Probably served (1560's) as choirboy in cathedral of Brescia. Sometime in 1570's he went to Rome, where he entered service of Cardinal Luigi d'Este (1578–86). After a sojourn in Florence (1588–89), where he worked for the Medici, he returned to Rome and enjoyed patronage of Cardinal Cinzio Aldobrandini and other nobles. Visited court of Sigismund III in Poland (1595–96). Died in Rome. Marenzio is considered the finest Italian madrigalist of his generation. His works first appeared in England, in Nicholas Yonge's *Musica Transalpina* (1588). Also wrote villanelle, motets, and church music.

REFERENCES: Denis Arnold *Marenzio* (London and New York 1965). Alfred Einstein *The Italian Madrigal* (tr. 3 vols. Princeton, N.J. 1949). Hans Engel *Luca Marenzio* (Florence 1956).

MARIN, John (Cheri) (Dec. 23, 1870 – Oct. 1, 1953). American painter. Born Rutherford, N.J. After a year at Stevens Institute of Technology, Hoboken, and four years' work as architectural draftsman, studied at Pennsylvania Academy of Fine Arts, Philadelphia (1899–1901), and Art Students League, New York (1901–1903). Spent most of period 1905–11 in Europe, exhibiting in Paris at Salon d'Automne (1908 and 1910) and Salon des Indépendants (1909). First exhibit (1909) at Alfred Stieglitz's Photo-Secession "291" Gallery, New York, began lifelong association between the two; Stieglitz's annual exhibitions of Marin's works established his reputation in 1920's. Married Mary H. Hughes (1914). His paintings reveal influences of Whistler, impressionism, and cubism, as well as an intuitive sense of abstraction and expressionism. Chiefly watercolors of New York City and Maine coast, such as *Woolworth Building* (1912 and 1913) and *Maine Islands* (1922, Phillips Collection, Washington, D.C.), they are known for their luminous color and dynamic movement, and for use of a kind of abstract shorthand to indicate waves, mountains, and pine trees, evoking immediacy of visual experience. Died at Addison, Maine.

EDITION: *The Selected Writings of John Marin* ed. Dorothy Norman (New York 1949). *John Marin* ed. Cleve Gray (New York 1970).

REFERENCES: Emanuel M. Benson *John Marin: The Man and His Work* (Washington, D.C. 1935). MacKinley Helm *John Marin* (Boston 1948). Frederick S. Wight *John Marin* (Berkeley, Calif. 1956).

MARIVAUX, Pierre Carlet de (Feb. 4, 1688 – Feb. 12, 1763). French playwright, novelist and essayist. Born and died in Paris. Studied law (1710–13), but preferred fashionable literary circles and wrote novels (1712–14), some romantic, some burlesques of the romantic. Married Colombe Bollogne (1717; she died c.1723). Marivaux's popular essays on contemporary life appeared in *Le Mercure de France* (1717–20), then in his own periodicals, notably *Le Spectateur Français* (1722–24). In 1720, the year he was ruined by bankruptcy of French West India Company, he began theatrical career with *Arlequin poli par l'amour*. Of thirty-four plays (1706–57) the best are *La Double Inconstance* (1723), *Le Jeu de l'amour et du hasard* (1730), *Le Legs* (1736), and *Les Fausses Confidences* (1737). He was an innovator of dramatic form, creating a highly personal style, witty and analytical, known as *le marivaudage*. His two major novels, *La Vie de Marianne* (1731–41) and *Le Paysan parvenu* (1735–36), are noted for psychological realism. Elected to French Academy (1743).

TRANSLATION: *The Virtuous Orphan, or The Life of Marianne* tr. Mary Mitchell Collyer (Carbondale, Ill. 1965).

REFERENCES: Marcel Arland *Marivaux* (Paris 1950). E. J. H. Greene *Marivaux* (Toronto 1965). Kenneth N. McKee *The Theater of Marivaux* (New York 1958).

MARLOWE, Christopher (c. Feb. 26, 1564 – May 30, 1593). English playwright and poet. A shoemaker's son, he was born in Canterbury (baptized Feb. 26), educated there at King's School and at Corpus Christi College, Cambridge (B.A. 1584, M.A. 1587). Moved to London and joined the "university wits," who included Robert Greene, John Lyly, Thomas Nashe, Thomas Lodge, and became attached to earl of Nottingham's theatrical company. Won fame with first play, *Tamburlaine* (part I acted c.1587, parts I and II published 1590), followed by *Dr. Faustus* (acted c.1588; published 1604, and in different version 1616), *The Jew of Malta* (acted c.1589, published 1633), *Edward II* (acted c.1592, published 1594), and lesser plays. The first great English dramatist, Marlowe influenced Elizabethan theatre, including early plays of Shakespeare, and established blank verse as a dramatic style. He also translated Ovid's *Amores* (c.1597) and Lucan's *Pharsalia* (1600), and wrote the poem *Hero and Leander,* completed after his death by George Chapman, as well as the famous lyric "Come live with me and be my love," which appeared in *The Passionate Pilgrim* (1599). Marlowe moved in the London underworld, was known as an atheist, seems also to have been engaged in secret service work. He was killed in a tavern brawl in Deptford.

EDITION: *Works and Life* ed. R. H. Case (1930–33, new ed. 6 vols. New York 1966).

REFERENCES: John Bakeless *The Tragicall History of Christopher Marlowe* (2 vols. Cambridge, Mass. 1942). Frederick S. Boas *Marlowe: A Biographical and Critical Study* (Oxford 1940). Una M. Ellis-Fermor *Christopher Marlowe* (London and Cambridge, Mass. 1925). Paul H. Kocher *Christopher Marlowe* (Chapel Hill, N.C. 1946). Harry Levin *The Overreacher: A Study of Christopher Marlowe* (Cambridge, Mass. 1952). Charles Norman *The Muses' Darling: The Life of Christopher Marlowe* (New York 1946). A. L. Rowse *Christopher Marlowe: A Biography* (London 1964). J. B. Steane *Marlowe: A Critical Study* (Cambridge 1964). Frank P. Wilson *Marlowe and the Early Shakespeare* (Oxford 1953).

CHRISTOPHER MARLOWE
BY DAVID KALSTONE

Born in 1564, the year of Shakespeare's birth, Christopher Marlowe died at the age of twenty-nine, murdered at a tavern in Deptford. The work of his greater contemporary would seem oddly thin if we knew only the plays he had written by 1593, but Marlowe's career by that date had acquired a kind of completeness. Like Keats, another poet who was to die in his twenties, he showed in his last works new powers, but rather than making surprising departures, these plays represent a fresh understanding of familiar strengths. The poet who began a literary career translating Ovid's *Amores* ended by creating a character, Dr. Faustus, who adapts Ovid desperately as he prepares to be dragged down to hell:

O lente, lente currite noctis equi!
The stars move still; time runs;
 the clock will strike;
The devil will come, and Faustus
 must be damned.

Behind that cry is a writer now fully aware of the pleasures and perils of a vivid literary imagination.

Before he left the university, Marlowe had not only translated parts of Ovid and Lucan, but had probably already completed *The Tragedy of Dido, Queen of Carthage* with its resounding prophecies of Roman conquest:

But bright Ascanius, beauty's bet-
 ter work,
Who with the sun divides one ra-
 diant shape,
Shall build his throne amidst those
 starry towers
That earth-born Atlas, groaning,
 underprops.
No bounds but heaven shall bound
 his empery.

Aeneas is encouraged by the Carthaginian queen to retell the story of the Trojan War, to be in other words his own Virgil: "Remember who thou art. Speak like thyself." Here, one feels, lay the literary enticements of the piece for the young man writing his first play — to create a heroic speaker, to bring to the stage heroic blank verse of the sort Surrey had brought to the printed page in his translated portions of the *Aeneid* half a century before. At climactic moments Marlowe's play includes whole lines of Virgil's Latin, untranslated. And the excitements of Dido's tragedy launched him into rhetoric unmistakably his:

> *I'll frame me wings of wax like*
> * Icarus,*
> *And o'er his ships will soar unto*
> * the sun,*
> *That they may melt and I fall in*
> * his arms.*

Ambition took a freer form than recreating the *Aeneid* and the destiny of Rome. In *Tamburlaine* Marlowe had his great success, announcing to London audiences his intention to move away from "jigging veins of rhyming mother wits," the jingles of earlier English plays, to heroic plays in which the warrior, like Marlowe's Aeneas, is also to be his own historian. One is to *hear*

> *the Scythian Tamburlaine*
> *Threat'ning the world with high*
> * astounding terms*
> *And scourging kingdoms with his*
> * conquering sword.*

What audiences remember from *Tamburlaine* is the scale of his boasts ("I hold the Fates bound fast in iron chains") and the round savoring of exotic conquests:

> *Is it not brave to be a king, Techelles?*
> *Usumcasane and Theridamas,*
> *Is it not passing brave to be a*
> * king,*
> *And ride in triumph through Persepolis?*

Tamburlaine is conquered only by death; but in part II, the sequel the public demanded, Marlowe suggests in growing violence — bloodier destruction, firing a town as the funeral pyre of Tamburlaine's dead wife Zenocrate and drawing her cortege in the wake of the hero's conquests — the possible disorders of the heroic personality. The play has drawn confused reactions from some modern critics who wish to find on Marlowe's part a simple endorsement or criticism of its overreaching protagonist. Surely this is the wrong question to ask of Marlowe's first successful plays — of *The Jew of Malta* as well as the two parts of *Tamburlaine*. The pleasure of bringing such creatures of appetite to light, of discovering their voices, fills the plays, either with dreams of conquest or of Barabas the Jew's wealth, resonant and bursting in the blank verse lines:

> *Bags of fiery opals, sapphires, amethysts,*
> *Jacinths, hard topaz, grass-green*
> * emeralds,*
> *Beauteous rubies, sparkling diamonds.*

These make up the poet's pleasure as well, enclosing "infinite riches in a little room."

Marlowe's exhilaration comes equally from the literary luxury of bringing Ovid alive, whether in the pageants and metamorphoses which Gaveston and his king want to act out in *Edward II*, or in the erotic play of the two sestiads he completed of his *Hero and Leander,* a poem so richly hyperbolic that George Chapman, who completed it, damped down the vivid, wittily indulged fantasy of Marlowe by introducing the offended and moderating allegorical figure of Ceremony. What Chapman sensed as missing was some distancing frame, a standard by which the tragedy of Hero and Leander might be judged and understood. In the plays as well — in *Tamburlaine, The Jew of Malta,* and *Edward II* — the pleasures of animation, of breathing large life into pageants of appetite, take precedence over the pleasures of structure or artistic and moral distance. To see Barabas, the Jew of Malta, against Shylock in *The Merchant of Venice* is to understand how Marlowe is not interested in "placing" his characters, not interested in creating, as Shakespeare does, a counter-society of wealth whose values provide rich and imaginative alternatives to Shylock's spoilsport greed. To view Tamburlaine against a Shakespearean conqueror like Othello is to understand how Marlowe's figures do not summon up their perfect antagonists who, like Iago, draw forth and make visible the blind spots of their heroes. Nor in *Edward II* is there any alternative standard by which to judge the pleasure-loving king and Mortimer, the Machiavellian rebel — that is, a perspective as clear as the vision of the gardeners or John of Gaunt's vision of the sceptered isle in Shakespeare's *Richard II.* Marlowe creates voices which Shakespeare is to take up — the hero, the poet king, the merchant adventurer — but Marlowe either places his protagonists above society or involves them in societies as appetitive as themselves, allowing them to play out their fantasies to the full. Our only way of judging Tamburlaine is to sense his growing destructiveness;

our only way of judging Barabas is to see him turning into a grotesque, a humorous figure of a revenger:

> *I walk abroad 'a nights*
> *And kill sick people groaning un-*
> *   der walls.*
> *Sometimes I go about and poison*
> *   wells. . . .*

It is with *Edward II* that Marlowe becomes interested in a hero who comes close to articulating the nature of his own tragedy. The deposed king himself gives us some perspective on his own appetites and those of the crude *politique* Mortimer:

> *But what are kings when regiment*
> *   is gone,*
> *But perfect shadows in a sun-*
> *   shine day?*

But it is for *The Tragical History of the Life and Death of Doctor Faustus* that Marlowe is most justly praised. Here the fantasies remain vivid: Faustus's dreams include most of the dreams of Marlowe's earlier characters: power, wealth, Ovidian pleasures — all won through the magic of learning. But the fantasies are also most judiciously placed, held in tense balance against the misplaced concreteness of the scholar's desires. We sense the way learning is distorted by desire when we hear Faustus slipping easily from an exposition of the Christian doctrine of original sin into a fashionable Italianate fatalism which justifies any action: *"Che serà, serà." Faustus* is a play in which the pageant master turns upon himself. The doctor of Wittenburg, having made his pact with Mephistophilis, can produce his shows, a combination of prank and revival of historical figures — Alexander, Helen of Troy. The climactic vision of Helen is invitation to further imaginings:

> I will be Paris . . .
> Yea, I will wound Achilles in the heel
> And then return to Helen for a kiss.

But Marlowe tests another light, Christian judgment, the end of time, as a way of revealing the limitations of his master of fantasy. It is strange that Marlowe, whose earliest work was energetically outside the framework of Christian judgment, should finally return to it, not necessarily to adopt its articles of belief, but certainly as a source of his richest vision of the pleasures and dangers of earthly imaginings. Of equal importance with Marlowe's movement from heroic subjects to the more reflective problems of intellectual appetite is a change in the lens through which he viewed experience: his discovery of conflict not between conquering hero or plotting villain and their ruined victims, but within the self. Understanding the damage done to the self demanded new voices for his tragic characters, like Faustus, who are heroes and victims in one.

MAROT, Clément (c.1496 – Sept. 1544). French poet. Born Cahors, son of court poet Jehan Marot. Entered service of sister of king, Marguerite d'Angoulême, future Marguerite de Navarre (1518). After serving in Italian campaign, entered household of King François I, as valet de chambre and court poet (1526). Published collection of poems on court life, *L'Adolescence clémentine* (1532). Because of his Lutheran sympathies, Marot suffered imprisonment a number of times; he wrote the satire *L'Enfer* on one of these experiences (1526). When the king initiated persecution of the Protestants (1534), Marot fled to Navarre (1535), to Ferrara, Italy (1536), to Venice (1537), thence to Lyon, where he was forced to abjure Protestantism. Returned to court (1539–42) and, influenced by Petrarchan forms of verse, composed the first sonnets in French and made verse translations of the Psalms. New persecutions (1542) forced him to flee to Geneva, to Chambéry, thence to Turin, Italy, where he died. A spirited innovator, Marot expressed his wit and imagination in a variety of forms such as epistles, ballades, rondeaux, epigrams, elegies.

EDITION: *Oeuvres complètes de Clément Marot* ed. C. A. Mayer (4 vols. London 1958–1966).

REFERENCE: Pierre Villey *Marot et Rabelais* (Paris 1923).

MARRYAT, Frederick (July 10, 1792 – Aug. 9, 1848). English naval officer and novelist. Born London; his father was a member of Parliament, chairman of Lloyd's, and landowner in West Indies. Entered navy at fourteen, thus beginning an adventurous and distinguished career. Was made a companion of the Order of the Bath for his services in First Burmese War (1824–26); devised a code of flag signals (1817) which earned him membership in French Légion d'Honneur (1833). Married Catherine Shairp (1819); of their eleven children, a daughter, Florence (1838–1899), became a popular novelist. On retirement from navy (1830), Marryat, already author of a first novel, *The Naval Officer* (1829), devoted himself to literature. His lively tales of adventure, taken from personal experience and full of humor, found immediate and lasting popularity. The best known is *Mr. Midshipman Easy* (1836); others include *The King's Own* (1830), *Peter Simple* (1834), and *Jacob Faithful* (1834). Most familiar boys' books are *Masterman Ready* (1841–42) and *The Children of the New Forest* (1847). Edited *Metropolitan Magazine* (1832–35), in which many of his novels appeared. Died at Langham, Norfolk.

REFERENCES: Florence Marryat *The Life and Letters of Captain Marryat* (2 vols. London 1872). Oliver Warner *Captain Marryat: A Rediscovery* (London 1953).

MARSTON, John (c.1575 – June 25, 1634). English poet and playwright. A lawyer's son, he was baptized at Wardington, Oxfordshire. After taking B.A. at Brasenose College, Oxford (1594), he joined the Middle Temple, but soon abandoned law studies for a literary career. First published an erotic poem, *The Metamorphosis of Pygmalion's Image,* together with *Certain Satires* (1598), attracting notice later in same year with *The Scourge of Villainy,* a second group of satires. His modern reputation rests on his plays, notably the two-part tragedy *Antonio and Mellida* and *Antonio's Revenge* (published 1602) and two bitter, satirical comedies, *The Malcontent* (1604) and *The Dutch Courtesan* (1605). A leading rival of Ben Jonson in the War of the Theatres, Marston later collaborated with him and George Chapman in *Eastward Ho* (1605), a comedy whose satiric references to Scots resulted in brief imprisonment of the authors. Marston stopped writing plays when he took holy orders (1609); held living of Christchurch, Hampshire (1616–31). Died in London.

EDITIONS: *Plays* ed. H. Harvey Wood (3 vols. Edinburgh 1934–39). *Poems* ed. A. Davenport (Liverpool 1961).
REFERENCES: A. J. Axelrad *Un Malcontent élizabéthain: John Marston* (Paris 1955). Anthony Caputi *John Marston, Satirist* (Ithaca, N.Y. 1961). Philip J. Finkelpearl *John Marston of the Middle Temple: An Elizabethan Dramatist in His Social Setting* (Cambridge, Mass. 1969). Brian Gibbons *Jacobean City Comedy: A Study of Satiric Plays by Jonson, Marston and Middleton* (Cambridge, Mass. 1968).

MARTIAL (Marcus Valerius Martialis) (A.D. c.40–c.104). Roman epigrammatic poet. Born Bilbilis, Spain. Went to Rome (64), where he associated with fellow Spaniards Lucan, Seneca, and Quintilian, and lived in uneasy dependence on patrons, eventually becoming popular but not wealthy. He had friends in the emperors Titus, Domitian, and Nerva, and enjoyed increased social standing after conferral of an honorary military tribunate and, though he seems never to have married, of the *ius trium liberorum* (privileged status given to fathers of three children). Returned to Bilbilis (98), where he spent last years on an estate given him by a Spanish patroness, Marcella. His work falls into four parts: the *Liber de Spectaculis* (*Book on Spectacles,* 80), short verses commemorating Titus's dedication of the Flavian amphitheatre (the Colosseum); the *Xenia* (*Guest Gifts*) and *Apophoreta* (*Gifts to Take Home*) (84–85), intended to be inscribed as mottoes on gifts presented at the Saturnalia; and the *Epigrams,* appearing at intervals between 86 and 102.

TRANSLATIONS: *Sixty Poems of Martial in Translation* tr. Dudley Fitts (New York 1967). *Martial: Epigrams* tr. Walter C. A. Ker (Loeb Classical Library 1919–20, rev. ed. 2 vols. Cambridge, Mass. 1968). Many others exist.
REFERENCES: John Wight Duff *Martial: Realism and Sentiment in the Epigrams* (Cambridge 1929). Paul Nixon *Martial and the Modern Epigram* (New York 1927).

MARTIAL
BY DUDLEY FITTS

A Spanish provincial by birth, urban and Roman by choice, Valerius Martial gives us in his brief poems a vivid and incalculably valuable picture of the capital of the world during the last quarter of the first century of our era. His works as they have come down to us consist of some fifteen hundred *epigrammata* — that is to say, pieces written "upon" an event or "for" an occasion, or "about" persons or objects, either as individuals or as types. Martial was not an innovator. The epigram as a literary form was already firmly established when he took it over from the Greeks and his immediate Latin predecessors. His genius was that of the perfecting exploiter: in his hands the tiny occasional poem became an instrument of the most versatile adaptability, capable of extraordinary range, with an almost unlimited richness of tone. The epigram as he used it was generally what we should call "light verse," but at its best it could be much more than a graceful personal exercise. Catullus, among others, had shown the way; but it was Martial's fourteen books that set the form as a medium of social and satiric comment, a form that has kept its characteristic tonality from his day down to ours.

Epigram: originally it was an inscription — hence its brevity. To us, the word means the quick saying with a sting in its tail. Its essence is a play of wit. It may be friendly, even genial, but usually it is an attack: the impulse is somehow destructive, born of indignation — personally abusive at the lower levels, generalized and ethical at the higher. We owe this concept to Martial and his disciples, largely because of his memorable handling of the more uninhibited modes of attack; but his work as a whole shows that this scandalous element, what we may call the Educated Comic Valentine, is only an important minor phase of his activity. The poems in question, which make up perhaps a fifth of his output, characteristically attack vicious excess rather than vice itself. The manner is ridicule, and the target is likely to be hyperbolized into something monstrous. Deviations, sexual and other, are the objects of Martial's scorn, as are physical abnormalities and deficiencies, not excepting the inevitable ones of disease and old age. He demolishes a whole gallery of stock types: misers, adulterers, pederasts, informers, niggardly patrons, sycophants, catamites, rival poets, whores, gluttons, flannel-brained tycoons. He can be tremendously funny, he can be disgusting, and occasionally he can be automatic and tedious. These are the poems that have given him his notoriety, but they should not be allowed to obscure the rest of the picture.

Flavian Rome must have been a kind of infernal paradise for a man with a moralistic bias and an inclination to writing satire. Domitian himself, most disheartening of emperors and the object of Martial's abject adulation, is the sick symbol of a sick age. The muckraker did not have to strain his muscles; there was enough offense to keep a right-minded man — Martial's gloomy friend Juvenal, for example — raging grumpily through poems that sometimes seem as though they would never end. But Martial was no Juvenal. It is not so much the satirist that persuades us in his verses as it is the amused reporter. Satire implies a moral stance, and Martial's seems to have been ambiguous, at best. His jibes at vice, like his jokes at the expense of physical deformity, arise from his finding the subject matter funny. Juvenal, a mean spirit and a far less accomplished artist than Martial, had the *saeva indignatio* that drives the true satirist, but there is very little of this indignation in Martial. He will utter the conventional clichés deploring the degeneracy of the age, and he will adduce the evidence, assuring us meanwhile that although his pages are smutty, his personal behavior is spotless. He will seem to take a moral stand, but really he is no moralist. He records.

What he records is Rome, the City. If we were to discard all of the ribald and otherwise festive epigrams — though God forbid that we should! — there would still be left one of the most absorbing descriptions of metropolitan life ever composed by a single author. The range is enormous. *Nil urbani alienum* — nothing, so long as it is Rome, so long as it makes possible a vivacious comment, escapes this inquisitive and delighted mind. True, much of the record is of interest now only to the historian, the archaeologist, or some other specialist. Moreover, many of the poems were written for the moment — anniversary poems, dedications, pleas for financial help, verses to accompany birthday and festival gifts, and the like. Topical verse always runs the risk of dying with its occasion, and these failures — if that is what they are — attend any writer who wants to reflect as much as Martial does of his time. Yet even in the poems most limited by occasion we are conscious of a superb technical control, a management of language and image that is enough in itself to hold us; and when this art is concerned with matters of timeless interest, there is no escaping its compulsive power.

In the dedication of one of his early volumes, a book admittedly of trifles, Martial observes, *"Nos haec novimus esse nihil"* — These poems, I confess, are nothing. The self-abasement of artists should seldom be taken at its face value: it is a part of the game. It is interesting, though, that some seventeen centuries later one of Martial's descendants should have used this phrase for a very Martial-like work: it serves as epigraph for John Gay's *The Beggar's Opera*. This kind of *nihil* has a way of surviving. If we have enough Latin, we can read Martial. Without Latin we lose him, on the whole: his brilliant conciseness makes him the despair of translators. We have him still, however, in the secular epigrams of the sixteenth and seventeenth centuries — Donne, for example, and most notably Ben Jonson and Robert Herrick.

MARTIN DU GARD, Roger (Mar. 23, 1881 – Aug. 22, 1958). French novelist and dramatist. Born Neuilly-sur-Seine, into family of lawyers. Educated in Paris at lycées Condorcet and Janson-de-Sailly and at École des Chartes,

graduating as archivist-paleographer (1905). Married Hélène Foucault (1906). First novel, *Devenir!* (1908), was unsuccessful; recognition came with *Jean Barois* (1913, tr. 1949), which explored the effects of the Dreyfus case and whose protagonist suffers conflict between inherited Catholic faith and scientific materialism. After serving in motor transport unit throughout World War I, wrote his masterpiece, *Les Thibaults* (1922–40, tr. *The World of the Thibaults* 1939–41), a cyclical novel in eight parts which develops from the chronicle of a middle-class family to a profound, wide-ranging study of French society and its changing values in the early twentieth century. Awarded Nobel prize for literature (1937). Other works include the peasant farces *Le Testament du Père Leleu* (1914) and *La Gonfle* (1928), naturalist drama *Un Taciturne* (1931), novella *Confidence africaine* (1931), and *Vieille France* (1933, tr. *The Postman* 1954), mordant sketches of French village life. Spent his last eighteen years working on a novel, *Le Journal du colonel de Maumort,* unfinished at his death and still unpublished. Died at Bellême, Orne.

REFERENCES: Denis Boak *Roger Martin du Gard* (London and New York 1963). Clément Borgal *Roger Martin du Gard* (Paris 1958). Robert Gibson *Roger Martin du Gard* (London 1961). David L. Schalk *Roger Martin du Gard: The Novelist and History* (Ithaca, N.Y. 1967).

MARTINI (or DI MARTINO), Simone (c.1284–1344). Italian painter. Born Siena. Stylistic traits indicate training under Duccio and study of French Gothic works, the latter having brought to his art a graceful refinement not seen in work of other Italians of the period. Earliest documented work is fresco of the *Maestà* (*Madonna in Majesty*) in Palazzo Pubblico, Siena (1315), which brought him renown. Much sought after, he traveled to Naples, Pisa, Orvieto, Assisi, and Florence to fulfill commissions. Often worked in collaboration with Lippo Memmi, whose sister Giovanna he married (1324). Summoned to papal court in Avignon

(1339), he spent rest of his life there, becoming friend of Petrarch, for whom he painted portrait of Laura (now lost). The most influential Sienese painter after Duccio, Simone is known for the splendor and harmony of his colors and for his decorative linear rhythms. The *Annunciation* triptych (1333, Uffizi, Florence) is his most celebrated work; others include *St. Louis of Toulouse Crowning King Robert* (c.1317, Museo di Capodimonte, Naples), *Madonna and Saints* polyptych (1319, Museo Nazionale, Pisa), frescoes of scenes from life of St. Martin in St. Martin's chapel, lower church of S. Francesco, Assisi (1320's), and equestrian portrait of *condottiere* Guidoriccio da Fogliano (1328, Palazzo Pubblico, Siena).

REFERENCES: G. H. Edgell *A History of Sienese Painting* (New York 1932). Giovanni Paccagnini ed. *Simone Martini* (tr. London 1957). Curt H. Weigelt *Sienese Painting of the Trecento* (New York 1930).

MARTINU, Bohuslav (Dec. 8, 1890 – Aug. 28, 1959). Czech composer. Born Polička, East Bohemia; trained at Prague Conservatory. While he was working as violinist in Czech Philharmonic Orchestra (1913–23), his ballet *Istar* (1921, performed 1922) and symphonic poem *Vanishing Midnight* (1922, performed 1923) were given in Prague. Moved to Paris (1923), where he remained until 1940. Studied composition with Albert Roussel, and by late 1920's had established reputation in Europe and America. Married Charlotte Quennehen (1931). Having fled German invasion (1940), Martinu settled in U.S. (1941–46), later dividing his time between America and Europe. Died at Liestal, Switzerland. His works, which are modern and individual while drawing often on Czech folk music, include ballets, operas, film and radio music, piano pieces, songs, and choral, orchestral, and chamber pieces. Noteworthy are operas *The Miracle of Our Lady* (1933, Brno 1934) and *Juliette* (1936–37, Prague 1938), and the *Concerto Grosso* (1938), *Sixth Symphony* (*Fantaisies Symphoniques*, 1955), and *Memorial to Lidice* (1943) for orchestra.

REFERENCE: Miloš Šafránek *Bohuslav Martinu: The Man and His Music* (New York 1944).

MARVELL, Andrew (Mar. 31, 1621 – Aug. 18, 1678). English writer. Born Winestead, Yorkshire. Educated at Hull Grammar School and Trinity College, Cambridge (B.A. 1639). Returning from travels on Continent (1642–46), he was attracted to Cromwell's cause (*An Horatian Ode upon Cromwell's Return from Ireland*, 1650), and worked as tutor to Mary, daughter of Lord Fairfax, at Nun Appleton in Yorkshire (c.1651–52). Many of his finest poems, such as *Upon Appleton House*, the *Mower* group, *To His Coy Mistress*, and *The Garden*, may come from this period. While tutor to Oliver Cromwell's nephew William Dutton (1653–57), Marvell wrote *The Bermudas*, *The First Anniversary*, and *On the Death of Oliver Cromwell*. He was Milton's colleague in office of Latin secretary to John Thurloe, the secretary of state, from 1657 to Restoration, and from 1659 until his death was member of Parliament for Hull. An opponent of the policies of Charles II, Marvell was known in his own day as politician, pamphleteer (*An Account of the Growth of Popery and Arbitrary Government in England*, 1677), and satirist (*Last Instructions to a Painter*, 1667; *The Rehearsal Transposed*, 1672–73) rather than as poet. Died in London. First collection of his poems appeared in 1681.

REFERENCES: Joan Bennett *Five Metaphysical Poets* (Cambridge, England, and New York 1964, also PB). Muriel C. Bradbrook and M. G. Lloyd Thomas *Andrew Marvell* (Cambridge, England, 1940 and New York 1941). Rosalie L. Colie *My Ecchoing Song: Andrew Marvell's Poetry of Criticism* (Princeton, N.J. 1969). Pierre Legouis *Andrew Marvell: Poet, Puritan, Patriot* (tr. 2nd ed. London and New York 1968, also PB). John M. Wallace *Destiny His Choice: The Loyalism of Andrew Marvell* (Cambridge, England, and New York 1968).

ANDREW MARVELL
BY FRANK KERMODE

Andrew Marvell was a Yorkshireman and a bachelor, two conditions predisposing a man to prudence and taciturnity, though not the enemies of ardor. We may therefore believe Aubrey when he says that the Member for Hull "was in his conversation very modest, and of very few words: and though he loved wine he would never drink hard in company, and was wont to say that he would not play the goodfellow in any man's company in whose hands he would not trust his life. He had a general acquaintance." However, Aubrey adds that in order to "exalt his muse" — for Aubrey a muse of satire or Latin panegyric — Marvell drank, presumably alone.

Although he wrote a good deal of verse, and much more prose, we still recognize this uncommunicativeness in Marvell; it is hardly helped by occasional glimpses of him in a passion, or misbehaving. He brawled in the House of Commons, got a reputation in France for being "a notable English Italo-Machiavel," and as a young man briefly renounced the Calvinism of his home for Roman Catholicism. He left Trinity under something of a cloud. At the time of his death he was under suspicion, justly enough as it happens, of writing against the king. At the same time, he was harboring undischarged bankrupts in his house; which is why his housekeeper Mary Palmer, when he died, claimed to be his widow, in order to recover five hundred pounds he had deposited on their behalf. Had she not done so his poems, which she published to lend color to her story, might have remained unpublished.

As a politician Marvell was capable of both extraordinary detachment and dangerous commitment. He said of the Commonwealth victory that "the cause was too good to have been fought for"; meaning that it would have come of itself, or by the pressure of history, without a war which could rot the fruit on the tree. Yet after the Restoration he took considerable risks, refusing the king's bribes and venting his satirical and patriotic spleen as well on the government as on the Dutch, its enemies. (Though he knew Europe, including Russia, there is a touch of plain English chauvinism in him.) He wanted constitutional monarchy, or even a republic; and what is characteristic is that he could blend short-term political activity with the mature historical perspective of a political philosopher. Thus, and by the potency of his opposition to all extremism, he gained his fame as one who devoted what his epitaph called his "wit and learning" and his "singular penetration and strength of judgment" to the cause of freedom. He was in the following century a model of true patriotism to Whig and Tory alike, as he was later to Wordsworth.

Like Milton, with whom he worked for Cromwell, Marvell knew at first hand the sources of power. He knew Thomas Fairfax and Cromwell, and studied at close hand the political expedients of Charles II, the death of whose father he rendered so judiciously and so memorably in the great *Horatian Ode*. He had felt the threat of power, in his own life and in Milton's. All this he interpreted as one able to hold in a single thought the confusions of a present power struggle and the great sweep of imperial and republican tradition. The *Ode*, which perfectly enacts this strenuous act of intelligence, survived its moment to become the greatest political poem in the language; so delicate its balance that neither contemporaries nor we can be sure to which party it leans. If he understood the *realpolitik* of Cromwell, "the war's and fortune's son," he also understood the justice of the king's "ancient rights." For all its controlled eloquence the *Ode* has something of that taciturnity, of prudence raised to the level of political wisdom.

Although we have chosen another Marvell than the politician to admire — preferring the author of a group of pastoral and garden poems which attracted little attention for more than a century after his death — our Marvell is still a man of mature and powerfully ambiguous mind. We recognize wit and penetration, but also taciturnity; his muse may be exalted, but Marvell will not put the life of his poem in our hands. What the increasingly extravagant scholarly debate (*To His Coy Mistress* is a refutation of Hobbes, etc.) implies is an essential reserve in the poems, which are not only much more lucid but also much more obscure than, say, Donne's. Most of them have, like the *Horatian Ode,* a place in some long tradition of civility; they are delicate, allusive, eloquent. Marvell understood that the world changes, but he also understood continuities. Virgil's shepherd, studying his reflection in a calm sea, becomes Marvell's Mower, mirrored in the polished blade of a scythe, "as in a crescent moon the sun"; it is evidence of a tradition reclaimed, an exquisite modernism. So do the images of Caesar and Augustus flicker over the surface of the *Horatian Ode.*

With this kind of power the poet's range is very great. Hence the puzzling harmonics of *The Nymph Complaining,* that most original blend of *fauxnaif* and serious simplicity; hence the learned purity of the Mower and the self-delighting poetic jokes of *Upon Appleton House.* The satires are a mass of witty allusions to politics and war; the lyric poetry alludes, with a wit not hostile to a peculiar enchantment of language which we elsewhere recognize, though only fitfully in Jonson, Carew, and Lovelace. Occasionally, as in *The Garden,* the wit is so delicate, the reserve so profound, that critics ransack the history of ideas to explain it.

You cannot thus explain so highly developed a mind, so highly developed an instrument. The passage in the *Ode* describing the emergence of Cromwell from rural retirement to the highest command is full of poised surprise that a man who had lived:

As if the highest plot
To plant the bergamot,

Could with industrious valor climb
To ruin the great work of time,
And cast the kingdom old
Into another mold.

Thus, from the tinkle of pastoral to the drum roll of an emperor crossing his Rubicon, changing the world and history; thus the voice changes from garden wit to civilized magniloquence. We value Marvell for what Eliot called, in the finest essay written about him, an "equipoise, a balance and proportion of tones," a wit and seriousness appropriate to every subject; we feel in him not only the mysteriousness of a full personality but, as Eliot said, "the quality of a civilization."

MASACCIO (real name **Tommaso di Giovanni di Simone Cassai**) (Dec. 21, 1401 – c.1428). Italian painter. Born San Giovanni Valdarno, Tuscany. First recorded as painter when he joined the guild in Florence (1422). Earliest known work: *Virgin and Child with St. Anne* (Uffizi, Florence), painted in collaboration with Masolino da Panicale. He knew and was influenced by Donatello and Brunelleschi, and was considered with his new style of realism one of founders of modern painting. Painted (1426) altarpiece for church of the Carmine in Pisa (now dismembered; central panel, *Virgin Enthroned,* in National Gallery, London). Greatest works are the frescoes of *Life of St. Peter* for Brancacci chapel of S. Maria del Carmine, Florence. While the chapel was painted in collaboration with Masolino, the celebrated scenes *Expulsion of Adam and Eve, Peter Baptizing, Tribute Money, St. Peter's Shadow Healing the Sick,* and *Peter Distributing Goods* are by Masaccio. They exerted a profound influence on subsequent Renaissance painting. Died in Rome.

REFERENCES: Luciano Berti *Masaccio* (University Park, Pa. 1967). Eve Borsook *The Mural Painters of Tuscany* (London 1960). Philip Hendy *Masaccio: Frescoes in Florence* (New York and London 1957). Ugo Procacci *All the Paintings of Masaccio* (New York 1962 and London 1969).

≥

MASACCIO
BY CREIGHTON GILBERT

Masaccio is tagged, and rightly so, as one of the great painters of the ages, but he is not one of those with whom the public is usually familiar. Many who are slightly acquainted with the name may recall that he died very young, or perhaps that he was a master of the new Renaissance technique of perspective (which is true but not in the sense generally assumed). Others remember two of his works, the *Expulsion of Adam and Eve,* which evokes a shocking violence of feeling in action, and the *Tribute Money,* which seems, at the opposite extreme, to present an almost academic static grandeur of robed dignitaries. The highly unitary quality of Masaccio's art is to be found between these two impressions.

Born in a village in Florentine territory, Masaccio was the elder of two sons whose mother was widowed twice while he was still a child. The boys'

only male relative other than their aged grandfather was their older stepsister's husband, who was an artist. It is very likely that they were apprenticed to him and went with him to the city when Masaccio was perhaps sixteen. He joined the painters' guild at twenty, not a precocious act in Renaissance terms. His earliest large work, the *Trinity* fresco in the Dominican church of S. Maria Novella, done almost certainly when he was twenty-three, was paid for by the "mayor" (*gonfaloniere*) of Florence, arranged for by the convent prior, and probably much influenced by another friar, Alessio, who belonged to the rich and potent Strozzi family and was an admiring friend of the architect Brunelleschi, since it shows thorough knowledge of Brunelleschi's new perspective technique. These circumstances, recently ascertained, cast doubt on the tradition that Masaccio was always poor and suggest rather that he was a success from the start; in fact we have record of work he was doing, under favorable conditions, during all the rest of his short life, except for one six-month period which is unknown.

More important, the same circumstances suggest Masaccio's attachment as early as this to the emerging group of extraordinary modern Florentine artists to which the main phase of his career is tightly linked. This group, strongly intellectual in approach and associated with humanist intellectuals, was led by Brunelleschi, and the classic image of it is in the letter written to him in 1436 by Alberti, the humanist writer and architect, praising Brunelleschi himself, their "very good friend" the sculptor Donatello, the other sculptors Ghiberti and Luca della Robbia, and Masaccio, for the artistic revolution. Masaccio's appearance here as the only painter, in the dedication of a book on painting, suggests that the founders of the group regarded him as someone talented enough to translate their attitudes into his medium. Masaccio's personal acquaintance with Donatello is on record, and in fact Donatello's use of perspective in his own sculpture makes it possible that Masaccio in the *Trinity* picked it up from him and only indirectly from Brunelleschi.

The patrons of the *Trinity* wished to expound the double nature of Christ as God (second person of the Trinity) and man (Crucified), and the artist illustrates this by overlapping parts of two standard images, in the systematic, diagrammatic way often used by artists of earlier generations in work for the Dominicans, suitable to the order's scholastic and preaching traditions. But the rather abstract visual schemes, like tables of organization, in such earlier work as Nardo di Cione's *Last Judgment* or Andrea Bonaiuti's *Triumph of St. Thomas and the Church*, the major older cycles at S. Maria Novella, could not be repeated in the new realism, and Masaccio diagrams in terms of boxes of systematically related perspective spaces. There is a nice parallel here with Jan van Eyck at the same date, who poured traditional religious symbols which he inherited into his favorite new imagery of realistic objects. Both used the most obviously modern aspect of their style as the hidden vehicle to carry nonvisual meanings. This explains further why the insistent architectonic perspective of the *Trinity* never recurs in Masaccio's other work. Elsewhere he gives perspective a minor role as an underpinning, coated over rather than shown off as it was by most of his contemporaries. It is common to call perspective the key to the new style (partly because a technical key is readily acceptable) and common to call Masaccio its greatest painter; the result is

a great interest in analyzing Masaccio's perspective, so that studies of the *Trinity* abound in which there is no suggestion that it is unique in his work.

In the *St. Peter* frescoes of the Brancacci chapel it is instead the human figure that dominates. Produced with a thick pasty paint in blended colors, mainly red, yellow, and flesh color, it is always warm-blooded. (The darkening of the *Tribute Money* by smoke from a fire has reduced this effect and supported the "academic" impression.) Lines and edges are minimized, so that the figures are not separated from the space. Thus we are greeted by a flowing and active humanity, the people are ready to move, physically strong, and even seem chiefly to be tough workers. The space by contrast is shown gray or white, but bounded all the way around; there are no infinite horizons. Thus the scenes are closed systems, the figures are in reciprocal balance with their space, the violent Adam and Eve for the *Expulsion,* for example, are bracketed by the gate through which they have just walked. Thus figures are stronger than environment but firmly held inside it; there is an equipoise of active mass and passive void, man and his world, organic person and geometric space. It recalls the then popular Stoic doctrine that man cannot overcome his fate but can prevent it from overcoming him by understanding it rationally. Masaccio's people stand at the center of an always ordered space, Donatellian creatures in a Brunelleschian cosmos. They are the first complete images of postmedieval, modern man, the focus of his own analysis.

MASCAGNI, Pietro (Dec. 7, 1863 – Aug. 2, 1945). Italian operatic composer. Born Leghorn. Studied there at Instituto Luigi Cherubini, and at Milan Conservatory. Finding academic discipline unbearable, he left Milan (1884) and for some years toured with itinerant opera companies as conductor before settling at Cerignola, where he gave piano lessons and managed municipal music school. Entered his one-act opera *Cavalleria rusticana* in a competition sponsored by the music publisher Sonzongo (1889); it won first prize, and on its first performance (Rome, 1890), made Mascagni a celebrity. Based on a play by Giovanni Verga, *Cavalleria rusticana* initiated the style known as *verismo* (realism). It is Mascagni's only enduring work. He was director of conservatory at Pesaro (1895–1903), toured widely as conductor, and was elected member of Royal Academy of Italy (1929). Died in Rome.

MASSENET, Jules Émile Frédéric (May 12, 1842 – Aug. 13, 1912). French composer. Born Montaud, Loire, son of an ironmaster and musically talented mother who gave him his early training. Entered Paris Conservatoire (1853) and won grand prix de Rome (1863) with cantata *David Rizzio*. During three years in Rome, he met Liszt, and married a pupil, Mademoiselle Sainte-Marie. Began career as operatic composer with *La Grand' Tante* (1867). His comic opera *Don César de Bazan* (1872), oratorio *Marie Magdeleine* (1873), and opera *Hérodiade* (1881) established his reputation. His greatest and lasting success was *Manon* (1884), based on novel *Manon Lescaut* by Abbé Prévost. Other popular operas included *Le Cid* (1885), *Werther* (1892), *Thaïs* (1894), *Sapho* (1897), *Le Jongleur de Notre Dame* (1902), *Don Quichotte* (1912). As a teacher and the most popular operatic composer of his day, Massenet exerted widespread influence throughout his lifetime. His style is noted for lyrical, sometimes sentimental melodies; he is also remembered for his incidental music and songs. Was made chevalier (1876) and grand officier (1899) of the Légion d'Honneur, and in 1878 became youngest member ever elected to the Académie des Beaux Arts. Died in Paris.

TRANSLATION: *My Recollections,* completed by Xavier Leroux, tr. H. Villiers Barnett (Boston 1919).
REFERENCES: H. T. Finck *Massenet and His Operas* (New York and London 1910). James Harding *Massenet* (London 1970). L. Schneider *Massenet* (Paris 1926).

MASSINGER, Philip (1583 – Mar. 1640). English playwright. Born Salisbury, son of Arthur Massinger, former fellow of Merton College, Oxford, and a future member of Parliament. Massinger entered St. Alban Hall, Oxford (1602), but left without a degree and went to London, where he became friend and collaborator of John Fletcher (from 1613), Thomas Dekker, and other dramatists. From c.1620 worked alone, aided financially by various patrons among the nobility, including Philip Herbert, 4th earl of Pembroke. Died in Southwark, London. Fifteen of his own plays survive, the most successful of which are the comedies *A New Way to Pay Old Debts* (c.1625) and *The City Madam* (1632), noted for their political and social satire. Best-known of his tragedies and tragicomedies, ingenious in plot construction but weak in characterization, are *The Duke of Milan* (produced c.1618), *The Bondman* (1623), *The Renegado* (1624), *The Roman Actor* (1626), and *The Maid of Honor* (1632).

EDITION: *Plays* ed. Francis Cunningham (London 1868).
REFERENCES: R. H. Ball *The Amazing Career of Sir Giles Overreach* (1939, reprinted New York 1968). Alfred H. Cruikshank *Philip Massinger* (Oxford 1920). Thomas A. Dunn *Philip Massinger: The Man and the Playwright* (London 1957). H. J. Makkink *Philip Massinger and John Fletcher: A Comparison* (New York 1927). Baldwin Maxwell *Studies in Beaumont, Fletcher, and Massinger* (1939, new ed. New York 1966).

MASSYS (also spelled MATSYS, MESSYS, METSYS), Quentin (or Quinten) (c.1466–1530). Flemish painter. Born Louvain, where, according to tradition, he practiced blacksmith's trade until desire to win the affection of an artist's daughter drove him to take up painting. His teacher is not known, but his style suggests training by one of Dirk Bouts's sons or other followers. Moved to Antwerp, where he joined painters' guild (1491) and spent rest of his life. Massys's major religious works are the *St. Anne Altarpiece* (1509, Musées Royaux des Beaux Arts, Brussels) and triptych of the *Deposition* (1511, Musée Royal des Beaux Arts, Antwerp). Also painted genre subjects, such as *The Money Changer and His Wife* (1514, Louvre, Paris), and portraits, notably that of Erasmus (1517, National Gallery, Rome). His precise detail and expressive faces reflect Flemish tradition, while influence of Italian Renaissance painters, especially of Leonardo, becomes increasingly evident in later works.

REFERENCES: Sir Martin Conway *The Van Eycks and Their Followers* (London and New York 1921). Max J. Friedlaender *From Van Eyck to Bruegel* (tr. London 1956) and *Early Netherlandish Painting* (tr. 14 vols. New York 1967).

MASTERS, Edgar Lee (Aug. 23, 1869 – Mar. 5, 1950). American poet, novelist, and biographer. Born Garnett, Kans., a lawyer's son. Grew up in Petersburg and Lewiston, Ill., near Spoon River; spent a year at Knox College, Galesburg, Ill., and when admitted to the bar (1891) had already published stories and poems in various periodicals. Settled in Chicago (1892), where he practiced law until 1923 and continued to write, publishing (from 1898) several books of poetry and plays in verse. Married Helen Jenkins (1898, divorced 1923); Ellen Coyne (1926). Inspired by the epigrams from the *Greek Anthology*, he wrote his masterpiece, *Spoon River Anthology* (1915), a collection of free-verse epitaphs spoken by the people buried in a Midwestern village graveyard, and revealing sardonically the truth of their inner lives, typical of rural America. Though its pessimism was attacked, it brought Masters fame and success, and he produced a sequel, *The New Spoon River* (1924). Subsequent, less successful publications include poetry collections, novels based on his youth, biographies of Lincoln (1931), Vachel Lindsay

(1935), Walt Whitman (1937), and Mark Twain (1938), and an autobiography *Across Spoon River* (1936). Died at Melrose Park, Pa.

REFERENCE: Horace Gregory and Marya Zaturenska *A History of American Poetry, 1900–1940* (1946, reprinted New York 1969).

MATHER, Cotton (Feb. 12, 1663 – Feb. 13, 1728). American theologian and historian. Born and died in Boston. His father Increase Mather and grandfathers Richard Mather and John Cotton were all prominent colonial divines. Educated at Harvard (B.A. 1678) M.A. 1681). Became his father's colleague in the North or Second Church, Boston (1685), and minister (from 1723). Married three times; of his fifteen children, only two survived him. Mather's preaching and his book *Memorable Providences Relating to Witchcraft and Possessions* (1689) may have precipitated Salem witchcraft trials (1692), although he opposed execution. A formidable scholar and scientist, he was one of the first Americans elected to the Royal Society (1713) and a leader in campaign for smallpox inoculation in New England (1721). Mather produced over 450 books, including *The Wonders of the Invisible World* (1693) concerning the Salem trials; his best-known work, *Magnalia Christi Americana* (1702), an ecclesiastical history of New England; *Bonifacius* (1710), an essay on philanthropy that influenced Franklin; and *Manuductio ad Ministerium* (1726), important for its chapter on "Poetry and Style." His *Diary* (7 vols. 1911–12) is a chronicle of spiritual development.

REFERENCES: Ralph and Louise Boas *Cotton Mather: Keeper of the Puritan Conscience* (1928, reprinted Hamden, Conn. 1964). Thomas J. Holmes ed. *Cotton Mather: A Bibliography* (Cambridge, Mass. 1940). Samuel Mather *Life of the Very Reverend and Learned Cotton Mather* (1729, rev. ed. New York 1969). Barrett Wendell *Cotton Mather: The Puritan Priest* (1891, new ed. New York 1963, also PB).

MATISSE, Henri (Émile Benoît) (Dec. 31, 1869 – Nov. 3, 1954). French artist.

Born Le Cateau, Picardy. After studying law in Paris (1887–89) and practicing, he took up painting during convalescence from an illness (1890). Studied at Académie Julian, Paris (1891–92), then under Gustave Moreau at École des Beaux Arts (1892–97), and copied the old masters in the Louvre. Married Amélie Payrayre (1898). From 1897 became influenced first by impressionists and neo-impressionists, then from 1901 by Cézanne; gradually evolved his own concept of structural role of color. At Salons d'Automne and des Indépendants (1905 and 1906), exhibited with group called Les Fauves (wild beasts), including Georges Braque, André Derain, Maurice de Vlaminck, and Raoul Dufy. His exhibited paintings included *Woman with the Hat* (1905, Hass Collection, San Francisco) and *Joy of Life* (1905–1906, Barnes Foundation, Merion, Pa.). From 1908 won international renown, exhibiting in New York (1908) at Stieglitz Photo-Secession "291" Gallery and with *Blue Nude* at Armory Show (1910). Influenced (1910) by Near Eastern art exhibit at Munich. Best-known paintings include *The Dance* and *Music* (both 1910, Hermitage, Leningrad); *Moorish Café* (1912–13, Hermitage); *Red Studio* (1911), *The Moroccans* (1916), *Piano Lesson* (1917, all Museum of Modern Art, New York); *Music Lesson* and *Three Sisters* (both 1917, Barnes Foundation, Merion, Pa.). From 1916 Matisse lived mainly in southern France. Work of last years was famous *papiers découpés*, brilliantly colored cut paper compositions sometimes verging on pure abstraction. Also decorated Dominican chapel of the Rosary, Vence (1948–51). Died in Nice.

REFERENCES: Alfred H. Barr, Jr. *Matisse: His Art and His Public* (1951, reprinted New York 1966). Gaston Diehl *Henri Matisse* (Paris 1954). Raymond Escholier *Matisse: A Portrait of the Artist and the Man* (tr. London and New York 1960). Roger Fry *Henri Matisse* (London and Paris 1935). Jean Guichard-Meili *Matisse* (tr. New York and London 1967, also PB). Jacques Lassaigne *Matisse* (tr. London and New York 1959). William S. Lieberman *Matisse: Fifty Years of His Graphic Art* (New York 1956). Giuseppe Marchiori *Matisse: The Artist and His Time* (New York 1967).

MATISSE
BY JOHN GOLDING

Perhaps the fact that Matisse was some ten to twenty years older than most of his great contemporaries explains the fact that he is the painter in whose work the transition from French art of the nineteenth century into that of the twentieth can most clearly be seen. By the time that he emerged as an independent modern master, actively involved in the Fauve movement, he had reflected in his art every significant development from Manet onwards. The thoroughness of his approach, and his refusal to commit himself until he felt completely in control of all his resources, are characteristic of his whole approach to art and life.

Because his art is saturated with color and light, and so often appears effortless in its execution, the view of Matisse as an intuitive, hedonistic painter of the senses quickly developed; and it was a view that he did his best to encourage. But to accept his art on this level is to apprehend only half his talent. For he was also one of the most rigorously intellectual of painters. From the first, the vivid immediacy of his work was balanced by, and indeed sometimes superimposed onto, a disciplined, highly reasoned substructure. This intellectual astringency was to give his work, at its best, enormous strength and precision; very occasionally it could lead to a certain uneasy sensation of coldness underlying an apparently inviting and easily accessible surface appeal.

Fauvism burst upon the Salon d'Automne in 1905, and Matisse was immediately acknowledged as its leader.

But he was not, paradoxically, the most representative or typical Fauve painter. If we want to catch the movement's buoyancy, its optimism and impetuosity, we must turn to the work of Vlaminck. Its restlessness, its eclecticism, and its occasional lack of direction are reflected in the art of Derain. For if Fauvism was the first important pictorial movement of the twentieth century, it was, simultaneously, a period of transition, a final paroxysm of postimpressionism. Only in the work of Matisse did Fauvism totally transcend or transform its sources, and he used it, quite consciously, as the springboard to his own personal and inimitable style.

The impressionists had viewed the world through a colored web of atmospheric light. Matisse, drawing on his experience of the art of Cézanne, Van Gogh, Gauguin, and the neo-impressionists, now sought to produce a sensation of light that would emanate directly and artificially from the canvas itself. To this end he adopted a heightened, often arbitrary or unnaturalistic palette. And during the succeeding years, with inexorable logic, he pursued Fauvism's desire to release color from its representational role through to its logical conclusions. The result was a series of masterpieces of startling originality, initiated by the celebrated *Harmony in Red* of 1908–1909, which flowed out for ten years in an unbroken sequence, works which confirm his reputation as the greatest colorist that the twentieth century has yet produced. The accuracy of the coloristic relationships in his painting he constantly checked against the visual sensations he experienced in nature and in the world around him. And perhaps the ultimate triumph of his art lay in his ability to evoke by the use of flat, often unnaturalistic and unmodulated areas of colors, spatial relationships of extraordinary accuracy and subtlety.

Matisse was a man who saw both art and life in terms of complementaries. Thus the most arbitrarily colored canvases run concurrently with others in which the colors of nature have been muted or only very slightly heightened. Throughout his life he was constantly looking for new methods, new sources with which to enrich the decorative splendors of his art; elements borrowed from Spanish shawls, Persian illuminations, Russian icons, Moroccan textiles and pottery and the dappled patterns of exotic foliage all found their way into his pictorial repertoire. Yet the most sumptuously decorative works exist side by side with the most austere and economical. The Twenties and Thirties are dominated by works that are intimate and naturalistic in character, but the experimental strain reasserted itself regularly in a succession of "problem" paintings designed to infuse new life into familiar themes.

If in middle age Matisse tended to turn his back on the exciting new developments that were taking place in contemporary painting, the late *papiers découpés* placed him once more in the mainstream of modern art. The cut-and-pasted-paper technique may have been particularly suitable to an artist who was now forced to spend long stretches of time in bed, but it brought forth works of astonishing originality and vitality. Matisse had always been primarily a colorist, and now, experimenting with areas of bright, unmodulated color, with no drawn or painted bounding outline, and with crisp, often jagged edges, he produced a series of vivid, highly abstracted images which were to leave a profound impression on much subsequent art. "To cut to the quick in color," he said, "reminds me of direct cutting in sculpture." Never before had color been used so boldly, so physically and yet so mysteriously. These works, and the quiet, philosophical conclusions which he drew from them in his chapel at Vence, make a splendidly affirmative end to his career.

MAUGHAM, W(illiam) Somerset (Jan. 25, 1874 – Dec. 16, 1965). English author. Born Paris, where his father was solicitor to British embassy. Orphaned at ten and raised by an uncle, a vicar, he entered King's School, Canterbury (1887) and attended lectures at Heidelberg University (1891), when he decided to become a writer. However, he returned to London to study medicine at St. Thomas's Hospital and practiced as intern in Lambeth slums, the background for his first novel, *Liza of Lambeth* (1897). Threatened with tuberculosis, he moved first to south of France, then to Paris, where he took up writing in earnest. Achieved first theatrical success with *Lady Frederick* (1907), which ran simultaneously with his *Jack Straw, Mrs. Dot,* and *The Explorer* (1908). His autobiographical novel, *Of Human Bondage* (1915), is considered a classic and his finest work. It was followed by a steady output of short stories (including the famous *Miss Thompson* in *The Trembling of a Leaf,* 1921), comedies of manners, and novels. *Ashenden, or The British Agent* (1928) is based on his experiences as an intelligence officer in Switzerland during World War I. Married the widow Lady Wellcome (1915; divorced 1927). Settled at Villa Mauresque, Cap Ferrat, Alpes Maritimes (1928), remaining there most of his life until his death. Other major works: *The Moon and Sixpence* (1919), novel based on the life of Paul Gauguin; *The Painted Veil* (1925), novel; *Cakes and Ale* (1930), satirical portrait of two artists, presumably Thomas Hardy and Hugh Walpole; *The Razor's Edge* (1944), story of a young American's spiritual quest; *The Summing Up* (1938) and *A Writer's Notebook* (1949), personal reflections and reminiscences expressing his skeptical and worldly philosophy of life.

REFERENCE: Laurence Brander *Somerset Maugham: A Guide* (Edinburgh and New York 1963). Richard A. Cordell *Somerset Maugham, A Writer for All Seasons: A Biographical and Critical Study* (2nd ed. Bloomington, Ind. 1969). Robin Maugham *Somerset and All the Maughams* (London and New York 1966, also PB). Wilmon Menard *The Two Worlds of Somerset Maugham* (Los Angeles 1965). M. K. Naik *William Somerset Maugham* (Norman, Okla. 1966). Karl G. Pfeiffer *William Somerset Maugham: A Candid Portrait* (New York and London 1959).

MAUPASSANT, (Henri René Albert) Guy de (Aug. 5, 1850 – July 6, 1893). Born at Château de Miromesnil, near Dieppe, of noble family; mother from childhood knew Gustave Flaubert. Educated at lycée in Rouen, served in Franco-Prussian War, then worked for nearly ten years as a government clerk in Paris in ministries of the navy and of public instruction. At this time (1873–80) also served literary apprenticeship to Flaubert, and concentrated on pointed observations of the bureaucrats who surrounded him and who were later to figure in many of his stories. His first short story, *Boule de suif,* appeared (1880) in *Les Soirées de Médan,* a collection of tales by Émile Zola and followers. Numerous collections of Maupassant's stories followed, including *La Maison Tellier* (1881), *Mademoiselle Fifi* (1882), *Contes de la Bécasse* (1883). In 1883 he produced his first novel, *Une Vie* (*A Woman's Life*), then *Bel-Ami* (1885), and his best work in novel form, *Pierre et Jean,* the preface of which sets forth his literary theories, evolving from the naturalist toward the psychological approach. He continued to write novels, stories, travel pieces, and articles until his rapidly deteriorating health (caused in part by syphilis) developed into mental disorder. After his brother died in an asylum (1889), he tried twice to commit suicide to save himself from the same fate, but was committed (1892) and died insane in Passy, Paris, the following year.

TRANSLATIONS: *Complete Short Stories,* new translations (New York 1955). *Short Stories* tr. Marjorie Laurie (reissue London 1956).

REFERENCES: Artine Artinian *Maupassant Criticism in France* (1941, reprinted New York 1969). Paul Ignotus *The Paradox of Maupassant* (London 1967 and New York 1968, also PB). Henry James *Maupassant* in *Partial Portraits* (1888, new ed. New York 1969). Frank O'Connor *The Lonely Voice: A Study of the Short Story* (New York PB 1965). Francis Steegmuller *Maupassant: A Lion in the Path* (New York 1949). Edward D. Sullivan *Maupassant the Novelist* (Princeton, N.J. 1954).

✒

GUY DE MAUPASSANT
BY WALLACE STEGNER

Few writers have managed to make major literary reputations out of the short story. Maupassant is one of the few. Though he wrote at least five stories long enough to be called novels, produced poems and travel books, and collaborated on a play, he is remembered primarily for his 360-odd short stories, written with unbelievable speed during a career that lasted barely more than a decade. It was as a creator of *contes* and *nouvelles,* both of which translate into English as short stories, that he influenced writers as various as James, Chekhov, Maugham, and Babel.

Temperament, training, and circumstances (and even, as James remarked, his own limitations) collaborated to shape him. He inherited both the *couleur locale* of Mérimée and the naturalism of Zola. He had ready to his use the robust tradition of the *fabliau,* with its snickering interest in low life and sexuality. He served an apprenticeship in precise observation (described in the preface to his novel *Pierre et Jean*) under his mother's friend Gustave Flaubert. He lived in a period of proliferating newspapers with an insatiable appetite for the short, pointed stories he was qualified to write. And he had, one guesses, hurts enough to

give him motivation: hatred of a brutal and irresponsible father, and an incurable disease, the syphilis that he contracted as a young man and that killed him at forty-three. (Is there something about wasting diseases that sets the mind toward short and certainly completable forms? One thinks of Chekhov and Katherine Mansfield, who like Maupassant knew that they did not have unlimited time.)

Henry James, opposing his essentially impressionist sensibility to the naturalism that Maupassant espoused, complained that if you had to sit all day trying to say how a particular tree or cab horse struck you, it probably hadn't struck you. He complained also, while admiring the precision and clarity of Maupassant's stories, that he was deficient in motivations — that he told us all he knew. The stricture, by and large, is justified — and it helps explain why Henry James had difficulty with the short story and Maupassant wrote it as naturally as he breathed. He saw with great clarity the small characteristic, the tiny episode, the telling relationship, the perverted motive, and he focused on it — wrung it, as James said, "either until it grimaces or until it bleeds."

His subjects are more various than James gave him credit for. Norman peasants and sailors, known from boyhood, occur by the score, generally in postures of avarice, clownishness, or bestiality (*A Piece of String, A Deal, Madame Husson's May King, The Devil*). The petty bourgeois, whether of Paris, Rouen, or the small towns of Normandy, are nearly as numerous (*A Country Outing, Uncle Jules, A Family Matter, A Night Out, The Necklace*). Local color of the Mérimée sort persists (*The Olive Orchard, A Vendetta*), and there are imitations of the fantastic tales of Poe (*The Horla,* sometimes cited as evidence of paretic degeneration, but actually as tight and controlled as any story Maupassant wrote).

Suffusing and coloring all his subjects is a sexuality so pervasive that critics derive from it conflicting theories. Thus Francis Steegmuller finds Maupassant's stories filled with cuckolds and takes them to be vengeful blows struck at a hated father. But Frank O'Connor finds the stories full of whores and concludes that a leitmotif of Maupassant's creature life is the celebration of this "submerged population," comparable to Turgenev's serfs and Chekhov's clerks, teachers, and country doctors.

Whatever the ultimate artistic intention, no reader can miss the cynicism of these stories, a cynicism emphasized by their extraordinary concision and their air of ironic disinterestedness. The "objectivity" commonly attributed to Maupassant is methodological only. He generally withholds authorial comment; he rarely, in Chekhov's phrase, "shows his hands and feet." But when one of his hatreds is being displayed (peasant greed, bourgeois hypocrisy, Germans of all descriptions) the omniscient author may poke his face through the arras and jeer. *Boule de Suif*, one of Maupassant's great stories, is so far from objective that it drips scorn. So do *Mademoiselle Fifi*, *The Capture of Walter Schnaffs*, and many others.

What has been called objectivity in Maupassant is generally simply a reversal of moral assumptions. Boule de Suif, a whore, is more generous and decent than the respectable and religious people she travels with, and more patriotic than the avowed patriot. In *Madame Husson's May King*, the drunk has a sounder notion of how to live in Gisors than the conventional citizens do. In *The Model*, a girl gets the man she wants, but on all the wrong terms.

In *Rose*, a woman's fear of rape turns into pique that a man with opportunities didn't take advantage of them.

Irony is Maupassant's method, a sardonic overturning of conventions is his theme, economy and clarity are his abiding virtues. One hardly thinks of going to him, as one goes to Chekhov, for sensitive and compassionate humanity. What compassion he has is narrow and savage; it expresses itself as scorn of what he despises. That makes him less easy to love than Chekhov, whose stories are consistently expressions of love rather than hate. When Maupassant shows through his stories he shows as an imperfect and even vengeful human being. But within his limitations he did do what he said an artist should do: "Make . . . something fine in the form that shall suit you best, according to your temperament." The particular way we see the world, James said, is our own particular illusion about it, and the great artists are those who make the world accept their illusion. Not consistently, but over and over again, and for the moment, Maupassant persuades us to accept his illusion that cunning, ferocity, greed, and coarseness are more common among men than we hope they are.

MAURIAC, François (Oct. 11, 1885 – Sept. 1, 1970). French writer. Born Bordeaux into prosperous, landed middle-class family. Father died when Mauriac was an infant, and he was raised by intensely pious Catholic mother. Went to Paris (1906); published first book of poems, *Les Mains jointes* (1909) at own expense. Turned to fiction and wrote *L'Enfant chargé de chaines* (1913, *Young Man in Chains*). That year married Jeanne Lafon. Served with a medical unit in World War I. First novels to win success: *Le Baiser au lépreux* (1922, *A Kiss for the Leper*) and *Génitrix* (1923), both translated under title *The Family* (1930). Writing chiefly of French provincial families, he spares nothing in his portrayal of his characters' meanness, avarice, destructive hatred and envy, the continuing conflict between man's struggle with evil and his desire for God's grace, and the frustration of stifling bourgeois conventions. He has been compared with Racine in his dramatic presentation of a psychological crisis. Major novels: *Le Désert de l'amour* (1925, tr. *The Desert of Love* 1929), *Thérèse Desqueyroux* (1927), and *Le Noeud de vipères* (1932, tr. *The Knot of Vipers* 1933), considered his masterpiece. Later novels more serene: *Le Mystère Frontenac* (1933, tr. *The Frontenacs* 1961), *La Pharisienne* (1941, tr. *Woman of the Pharisees* 1946), and his last immensely popular work, *Un Adolescent d'autre fois* (1969, tr. *Maltaverne* 1970). Also wrote numerous studies, including *Jean Racine* (1928), *Blaise Pascal et sa soeur Jacqueline* (1931), and a life of Jesus (1936, tr. 1937), as well as plays, his most popular being *Asmodée* (1938). A militantly anti-Communist journalist, Mauriac wrote for *Figaro* after World War II. His memoirs appeared in 1959 (tr. 1960). His immense gifts as a novelist of limpidly classical style and profound understanding of human psychology won him many honors, including membership in French Academy (1933) and Nobel prize for fiction (1952). He died in Paris.

REFERENCES: Martin Jarrett-Kerr *François Mauriac* (New York 1954). Cecil Jenkins *Mauriac* (New York 1965). Henri Peyre *French Novelists of Today* (1955, revised and enlarged edition New Haven and Oxford 1967, also PB).

MAUROIS, André (real name Émile Salomon Wilhelm Herzog) (July 26, 1885 – Oct. 9, 1967). French writer. Born Elbeuf, Normandy, son of a textile manufacturer. Educated at Rouen lycée and Caen University. Married Janine de Szymkiewicz (1912; she died 1924) and Simone de Caillavet (1926). Worked in father's factory until World War I. Published first book, *Les Silences du Colonel Bramble* (1918, tr. 1919), based on experience as liaison officer with British army; a sequel, *Les Discours du Docteur O'Grady,* followed

(1921, tr. 1922). *Bernard Quesnay* (1927, tr. 1928) is based on his factory experiences. *Climats* (1928, tr. *The Atmosphere of Love* 1929) is considered his finest novel. Maurois was chiefly distinguished as a biographer and man of letters, and famous for such studies as *Ariel: The Life of Shelley* (1923, tr. 1924), *Disraeli: A Picture of the Victorian Age* (1927, tr. 1928), *Byron* (1930, tr. 1930), *Voltaire* (1932, tr. 1932), *The Edwardian Era* (1933, tr. 1933), *Dickens* (1934, tr. 1935), *Chateaubriand* (1938, tr. 1938), also histories *The Miracle of England* (1937, tr. 1940) and *The Miracle of France* (1948, tr. 1949). Elected to French Academy (1938). Wrote *Tragedy in France* (tr. 1940) and *Why France Fell* (tr. 1941). During World War II served first as captain in French army attached to British GHQ; then, after period in U.S. described in autobiographical works *I Remember, I Remember* (tr. 1942) and *From My Journal* (tr. 1948), served from 1943 as volunteer with Allied forces in North Africa. Returned to Paris (1946), where he remained until his death. Other works include biographies of Marcel Proust (1949, tr. 1950), George Sand (*Lélia,* 1952, tr. 1953), Victor Hugo (*Olympio,* 1954, tr. 1955), also *Les Trois Dumas* (tr. *The Titans* 1957), *Sir Alexander Fleming: The Discoverer of Penicillin* (tr. 1959), and *Prometheus: The Life of Balzac* (tr. 1965); numerous collections of essays, such critical studies as *De Proust à Camus* (1963, tr. 1968), and histories of the U.S. and U.S.S.R. An elegant, perceptive writer, Maurois was highly honored in France, England and the U.S. His *Memoirs* were published posthumously.

REFERENCES: Georges Lemaitre *Maurois: The Writer and His Work* (rev. ed. 1968). L. Clark Keating *André Maurois* (New York 1969).

MAYAKOVSKY, Vladimir Vladimirovich (July 19, 1893 – Aug. 14, 1930). Russian poet and playwright. Born Bagdadi (now Mayakovsky), Georgia, U.S.S.R. Moved to Moscow, and after a year at school joined Bolshevik party at fourteen. Imprisoned nearly a year, he was released at fifteen to study art in Moscow, but soon turned to writing poetry and became one of leaders of Russian futurism. Achieved recognition with long poem, *A Cloud in Trousers* (1915). Became official poet of Communist government (1917). Produced *Backbone Flute* (1915), *War and the World* (1915–16), the long narrative poem *150,000,000* (1919–20), *About This* (1923), *Vladimir Illyich Lenin* (1924), *Korosho!* (1927), and his two most famous satirical plays, *The Bedbug* (1928–29) and *The Bathhouse* (1929–30). Founded (1923) the literary group Left Front (LEF) and the futurist journal *LEF*, succeeded by *New LEF* (1925). Considered the greatest Soviet poet, Mayakovsky exerted tremendous influence on modern Russian poets including Pasternak, Yevtushenko, and Voznesensky. In 1930 in Moscow he committed suicide, the reasons for which were probably personal, leaving unfinished one of his finest poems, *At the Top of My Voice*.

TRANSLATIONS: *The Bedbug and Selected Poetry* ed. Patricia Blake tr. Max Hayward and George Reavey (New York 1960 and London 1961, also PB). *Poems* ed. H. Marshall (New York and London 1965).

REFERENCES: C. M. Bowra *The Creative Experiment* (1949, new ed. London 1967 and New York 1968, also PB). David Burliuk and others *Vladimir Mayakovski, 1894–1930* (New York 1940). Alexander S. Kaun *Soviet Poets and Poetry* (1943, reprinted Freeport, N.Y. 1968). Lawrence L. Stahlberger *The Symbolic System of Majakovskij* (The Hague 1964).

McINTIRE, Samuel (Jan. 1757 – Feb. 6, 1811). American architect and woodcarver. Born Salem, Mass. Trained by his father, a housewright. Married Elizabeth Field (1778). Helped to design the Jerathmeel Peirce house, Salem (1779), thereby making his reputation. Became chosen designer of the Salem shipping merchants for their mansions and is known as "the architect of Salem." While his early houses are massive in effect, those from 1793 and after show the influence of Bulfinch, who introduced into American design and decoration the graceful, elegant, and refined Adam style. Examples are the Theodore Lyman house, Waltham

(begun 1793), and, all in Salem, the Elias Hasket Derby mansion on Essex Street (1795–99, destroyed 1815), John Gardner house (also called Pingree house, 1805), South Church (begun 1804, destroyed 1903), Assembly House (begun c.1782, remodeled 1796), Court House (1785, demolished 1839), Hamilton Hall (c.1805–1807). McIntire also specialized in carving interior woodwork and furniture; characteristic motifs are eagles, urns, medallions, festoons of drapery, rosettes, laurel sprays, fruit baskets. He died in Salem.

REFERENCES: Frank Cousins and Phil M. Riley *Wood Carver of Salem: Samuel McIntire, His Life and Work* (Boston 1916). Sidney Fiske Kimball *Mr. Samuel McIntire, Carver: The Architect of Salem* (1940, reprinted Gloucester, Mass. 1966). B. W. Labaree ed. *Samuel McIntire: A Bicentennial Symposium* (Salem, Mass. 1957). Mabel M. Swan *Samuel McIntire, Carver, and the Sandersons, Early Salem Cabinet Makers* (Salem, Mass. 1934).

MELVILLE, Herman (Aug. 1, 1819 – Sept. 28, 1891). American writer. Born New York City, descendant of English and Dutch colonial families. Attended schools there and in Albany, where his father moved after failing in business (1830). After various jobs, including teaching school at Pittsfield, Mass., Melville shipped as a cabin boy to Liverpool (1839), describing the voyage later in *Redburn* (1849). Spent eighteen months on a whaler in the South Seas (from 1841), jumped ship in the Marquesas, escaped his Typee captors, shipped to Tahiti and thence to Hawaii, returning to U.S. on an American frigate (1844), the experience of which served as basis for *White Jacket* (1850). His South Sea experiences provided material for the immensely popular narratives of adventure *Typee* (1846) and *Omoo* (1847). Married Elizabeth Shaw (1847) and settled in New York, where he skirted literary circles and continued writing novels, including *Mardi* (1849) and *Pierre* (1852). From 1850 lived on a farm near Pittsfield, where he became friends with Hawthorne and where he wrote his masterpiece *Moby-Dick* (1851). After travels to Europe and the Holy Land (1856–

57), lectured occasionally for three years on South Seas, classical art, and travel. Handicapped by illnesses, he sold farm (1863) and returned to New York, where for nineteen years (from 1866) he held post as customs inspector, and where he died. Late works include *The Piazza Tales* (1856), including *Benito Cereno* and *Bartleby the Scrivener;* a satire *The Confidence Man* (1857); *Battle Pieces* (1866), a series of Civil War poems; *Clarel* (1876), a long philosophical poem; and *Billy Budd,* a novelette completed just before his death (published 1924). His *Letters* were published in 1960.

REFERENCES: Newton Arvin *Herman Melville* (New York and London 1950, also PB). Richard V. Chase *Herman Melville: A Critical Study* (New York 1949) and ed. *Melville: A Collection of Critical Essays* (Englewood Cliffs, N.J. 1962, also PB). William H. Gilman *Melville's Early Life and Redburn* (New York and London 1951). Leon Howard *Herman Melville: A Biography* (Berkeley, Calif. 1951 and Cambridge, England, 1952, also PB). Harry Levin *Power of Blackness* (New York 1960, also PB). Jay Leyda *The Melville Log: A Documentary Life of Herman Melville, 1819–1891* (1951, new ed. New York 1969). F. O. Matthiessen *American Renaissance* (New York 1941). Lewis Mumford *Herman Melville: A Study of His Life and Vision* (1929, rev. ed. New York and London 1963, also PB). Milton O. Percival *A Reading of Moby Dick* (Cambridge, England, 1950, reprinted New York 1967). Constance M. Rourke *Roots of American Culture and Other Essays* (New York 1965, also PB). William Ellery Sedgwick *Herman Melville: The Tragedy of Mind* (1944, reprinted New York 1962). Raymond Weaver *Herman Melville: Mariner and Mystic* (New York 1921).

✍

HERMAN MELVILLE

BY LEWIS MUMFORD

The rise and fall of Herman Melville's reputation, the appreciation and depreciation of his work, his literary entombment during the last thirty years of his life and his resurrection and beatification today — all this might well have formed a chapter of a typical Melvillian satire. Both the stony rejection and the present effusive acceptance of his work have some of the melodramatic exaggeration that characterized his novel *Pierre,* the book that, not altogether without cause, turned his early public away from him.

To his own generation Melville was known as "the man who had lived among the cannibals." And in view of what recent biographic research and close literary analysis have accomplished, he might now be described as a man who was later fattened by cannibals, to be served up, duly eviscerated and carved, at a prolonged academic luau. The scholarly Happars and Typees who have performed this ritual sacrifice, hoping to acquire some of their victim's potency, have feasted well. But though the scraped bones remain, Melville, alas! has disappeared.

Perhaps the time has come to bring this dismembered Melville, our American Osiris, back to life; and the first step is to meet him face to face and listen closely to what he himself has to say. Almost with his first words, one realizes that he was a born writer, with a shrewd eye, a quick ear, a detached gaze; and no matter what his eventual disappointments and failures, his early life had been a full one — full of hardships, tensions, near-disasters, but also rich in exotic adventures, immensely stimulating to his receptive mind.

Melville's first six books, more than half the works he published in his lifetime, drew on the experiences of the lustrum between 1839 and 1844. Uneducated in a formal sense — a whaling ship, he proudly said, was his Yale College and his Harvard — his sea voyages by merchantman, whaler, and man-of-war turned out to be just the sort of nourishment he needed, with their mixture of toil, danger, reverie, and quiet rapture, with shipmates who might recite Camões's *Lusiad,* and a warship's library that, astonishingly, offered him Elizabethan classics. But he had listened, too, to the living speech of sailors and could spin a yarn with the best of them.

Though Melville finally returned to dry land; he never mentally left the sea with its storms and its calms, its brutalities and terrors, its enmities and comradeships. The sea became his image of reality, undefinable, illimitable, ungraspable, unfathomable. Tormented by that mystery he dove again and again, seeking to sound bottom; and for this quest, the whale was his preordained symbol. But there is another side to Melville; for he had an eye for earthy pleasures that makes him akin to the Dutch realists he enjoyed, like Teniers and Steen; and with his traditional Dutch appetite for food and drink, he had an insuppressible exuberance and high spirits which at first enabled him to mock his disappointments and survive his worst defeats. The tragic and the comic Melville are present in some degree in every work, even in what purported to be a boy's account of his first venture at sea, *Redburn.* In his grimmest stories, like *Bartleby,* a touch of quizzical humor still remains, and that humor flickers over the blackest pages of *Pierre* and *The Confidence Man.* Though Melville owes many debts to English writers from Chaucer and Shakespeare to Smollett and Carlyle, his sense of the comic, as Constance Rourke justly pointed out, is in the American frontier tradition as much as Audubon's practical jokes.

With *Mardi,* his third book, a new Melville emerged, one who gave rein to both fantasy and philosophic reflection, skimming through the pages of history, brooding over politics and religion, bringing to the surface some of those deep sea denizens of the mind that explode when they are hauled into the air. Though *Mardi* is overladen and incoherent, in the act of writing it Melville discovered an untapped literary resource and a so far ill-charted realm — his own unconscious. *Mardi* started Melville on his great voyage of spiritual exploration which daringly opened a whole new continent in *Moby-Dick,* foundered on the hidden rocks of *Pierre,* floated away on the sluggish Mississippi currents of *The Confidence Man,* reached port, barnacled and battered, in his long poem *Clarel,* and finally raised a faded tattered flag and fired a last salute in *Billy Budd.*

Before the climactic achievement of *Moby-Dick,* Melville wrote a coda to his actual adventures in *White Jacket,* an account of his voyage home in a United States frigate from Hawaii. Because it offers so few knots for the academic mind to untie, *White Jacket* is perhaps the least appreciated of Melville's works; yet the qualities that make *Moby-Dick* great are visible in *White Jacket* — all except the daemonic vision, the many-faceted symbolism, and the mythic projection. *White Jacket* is a Hogarthian portrait gallery, in which Jack Chase, captain of the maintop, is as freshly lovable as Hogarth's *Shrimp Girl,* while the character of Mr. Surgeon Cuticle, performing his ghastly operation, is in turn satirically operated on by a knife as merciless as Swift's. As for the prose, the account of White Jacket's fall into the sea shows a mastery of color and cadence equal to the best in *Moby-Dick.*

With *Moby-Dick,* Melville's imagination described its widest arc, released by his fresh encounter with the tragedies of Shakespeare and by his discovery of a like-minded contemporary in Nathaniel Hawthorne, whose dark intuitions reinforced Melville's own.

Moby-Dick as a work of art belongs to no accepted genre, for it is by turns a straightforward narrative of maritime adventure, a reckless Elizabethan tragedy close to the satanic, a desperate but heroic pre-Freudian plunge into the unconscious, and at the same time a compendium of useful historical information on the whaling industry in all its aspects, and a studious disquisition worthy of Buffon on the natural history of the whale. Beneath it all, *Moby-Dick* is a parable on human life and cosmic existence, with special reference to all that baffles and cripples the spirit of man. Such a work has no single theme and cannot be judged by its parts: it must be experienced as a whole; for only by letting one part modify and enrich the other, not discarding any as superfluous or irrelevant, does the book fully come to life. On those terms it is a masterpiece.

On the surface, Melville had attempted the impossible — to bring together the hitherto divided, isolated, or neglected aspects of human experience, the angelic and the daemonic, the transcendent and the pragmatic, the cosmic and the domestic, the Platonic and the Baconian, the romantic and the utilitarian, the adventurous and the calculating, all enveloped in a myth that seeks, like its tormented author, to bring light into the darkness and darkness into the light. The ship's crew, gathered from the ends of the earth, from Polynesia and Persia, from Africa and Nantucket, is mankind itself, whose ultimate fate is now in the hands of those mad captains who have cut themselves off from human loves and loyalties in their pursuit of the White Whale. The harmonious resolution of these disparate and incommensurable aspects of human experience proved too much for Melville and would have been equally so to Dante

had he not in *The Divine Comedy* built on a historic religious myth, already solidified and accepted. So, as Melville himself pointed out, the great structure of *Moby-Dick* remains unfinished, like the tower of Cologne cathedral. It is only within the reader's mind that all the parts can be brought together to form a living whole.

Each generation will carry its own inner probings and self-revelations into *Moby-Dick;* and no one interpretation can possibly encompass its full significance. The human issues Melville posed for himself in *Moby-Dick* were unanswerable on the terms he himself set, for neither Woman nor Love plays any part in the central fable: except for little Pip, whose love and loyalty almost overcome Ahab's paranoid fantasies and make him abandon his mad pursuit, the life-nurturing forces are repressed or absent. To overlook Melville's characterization of Ahab as a madman is to belittle the sanity of his creator.

Some two decades later Melville attempted a further resolution of the human dilemma in his long reflective poem *Clarel;* but he failed to see that the story of *Moby-Dick* itself, as Ishmael had told it, was the true resolution. For though *Moby-Dick* presents the spectacle of senseless power, blind, overwhelming, seemingly malign, against which Ahab's sterile hatred and "fatal pride," themselves cast in the satanic image, are impotent, what finally emerges from the whole story is the undaunted soul of man. Here in the person of the narrator, alone in the wide ocean, facing the utter loss of the ship and the crew, and the miscarriage of Ahab's purposes, but still able to retain what has happened in his own consciousness, the story rises to a triumphant conclusion. Not Ahab but Melville himself, as Ishmael, is the hero: for in him the spirit of man survives and has the last word.

MEMLING (or **MEMLINC**), **Hans** (c.1430 – Aug. 11, 1494). Flemish painter. Born Seligenstadt, near Frankfurt am Main. From c.1465 until his death, lived in Bruges, where he joined painters' guild (1467), married Anne de Valkenaere (c.1480), and became prosperous. Received commissions from England, Germany, Spain, and Italy, in addition to fulfilling heavy local demand which necessitated use of apprentices. His style, which shows no change from his first dated work, the *Donne Triptych* (1468, National Gallery, London) to his last, reveals strong influence of Roger van der Weyden. A sense of deep religious feeling and tenderness dominates Memling's work, which is also known for its luminous color and minute detail. Among his masterpieces are *Last Judgment*, altarpiece in church of St. Mary, Danzig (1472–73); *The Mystic Marriage of St. Catherine*, altarpiece in St. John's Hospital, Bruges (1479); diptych with *Virgin and Child* and portrait of the donor, Martin van Nieuwenhove (1487), and *St. Ursula Shrine* (1489), both in St. John's Hospital, Bruges; *Madonna with Angels* (1490, National Gallery, Washington); and many superb, lifelike portraits, notably that of Guillaume Moreel (c.1483, Musées Royaux des Beaux Arts, Brussels).

REFERENCES: Sir Martin Conway *The Van Eycks and Their Followers* (London and New York 1921). Georges Henri Dumont *Hans Memling* (tr. New York PB 1966). Erwin Panofsky *Early Netherlandish Painting* (2 vols. Cambridge, Mass. 1953).

MENANDER (c.343 B.C.–c.291 B.C.). Greek playwright. Born and died in Athens; presumably of prominent Athenian family. Was pupil of Theophrastus and friend of Epicurus. Founder of the New Comedy, Menander wrote over a hundred plays, which differed from Aristophanes' comedy in using lighthearted humor in place of virulent satire against persons and politics, and realism in plot and characterization, based on the domestic life of ordinary Athenians. Through his influence on the Romans Plautus and Terence, his close imitators, the modern comedy of manners developed. While the titles of eighty of his plays are recorded, only fragments of originals survive and one complete comedy, *Dyskolos* (*The Misanthrope*), recently discovered in Egypt.

TRANSLATIONS: *Principal Fragments* ed. and tr. F. G. Allinson (Cambridge, Mass. 1951). *The Rape of the Locks* tr. Gilbert Murray (London and New York 1942). *The Arbitration* tr. Gilbert Murray (London and New York 1945). *The Bad-Tempered Man, or The Misanthrope* tr. Phillip Vellacott (Oxford 1960).

REFERENCE: T. B. L. Webster *Studies in Menander* (2nd ed. Manchester, England, 1960).

MENCKEN, H(enry) L(ouis) (Sept. 12, 1880 – Jan. 29, 1956). American writer and editor. Born and died in Baltimore, son of prosperous businessman of German stock. Educated at private schools there and at Baltimore Polytechnic; then entered family tobacco business. After father's death (1899), secured position on Baltimore *Morning Herald* and soon became its editor (1905). When the paper folded (1906), he joined the Baltimore *Sun*, remaining with it until he gave up his regular column (1941). He was coeditor with George Jean Nathan of the *Smart Set* (1914–23), and editor of the *American Mercury* (1924–33). Produced a volume of verse (1903), a critical study, *George Bernard Shaw: His Plays* (1905), and *The Philosophy of Friedrich Nietzsche* (1908), but it was his literary and social criticism that made him famous and a widely influential figure during 1920's. A mordant satirist of the American middle class, dubbed the "booboisie," he deplored the Puritan and genteel tradition in American letters, championing such naturalist writers as Theodore Dreiser and Sinclair Lewis. He published six series of his essays, *Prejudices* (1919–27), several volumes of reminiscences (*Happy Days*, 1940; *Newspaper Days*, 1941; *Heathen Days*, 1943), and *A Book of Burlesques* (1916). His most enduring contribution, however, is *The American Lan-*

guage (four revisions and two supplements, 1919–48), an invaluable collection and study of American idioms and expressions. He married Sarah Powell Haardt (1930; she died 1935).

REFERENCES: Charles Angoff *H. L. Mencken: A Portrait from Memory* (New York 1956, also PB). Carl Bode *Mencken* (Carbondale, Ill. 1969). William Manchester *Disturber of the Peace: The Life of H. L. Mencken* (New York and London 1951, also PB). Sara Mayfield *The Constant Circle: H. L. Mencken and His Friends* (New York 1968).

_____

MENDELSOHN, Eric (Mar. 21, 1887 – Sept. 15, 1953). German architect. Born Allenstein, East Prussia. In Munich, where he attended university (M.A. 1911), associated with expressionist artists of Blaue Reiter group, and their influence is particularly clear in his early architectural sketches. After serving in World War I, set up practice in Berlin (1918). Married Louise Maas (1915). Won fame with Einstein Tower at Potsdam (designed 1919, completed 1925); a major example of art nouveau, the structure is known for its curved, sculptured contours. Moved toward a more severe functionalism with Herpich fur store, Berlin (1924); Schocken department stores, Stuttgart (1926–27) and Chemnitz (1928); Metalworkers' Union administration building, Berlin (1929); Columbus House, Berlin (1931). Lived in England (1933–37), where he designed De La Warr Pavilion at Bexhill (1933–34), and in Palestine (1937–41), where he designed Hadassah University Medical Center, Jerusalem (1936–38), Anglo-Palestine Bank, Jerusalem (1937–38), and many other buildings. Moved to U.S. (1941); settled (1945) in San Francisco, where he lived for rest of his life. American works include Maimonides Hospital (1946–50) and Leon Russel residence (1950–51), both in San Francisco, and series of synagogues and Jewish community centers in St. Louis, Cleveland, Baltimore, Grand Rapids, St. Paul, and Dallas.

REFERENCES: Wolf von Eckardt *Eric Mendelsohn* (London and New York 1960, also PB). Arnold Whittick *Eric Mendelsohn* (2nd ed. London and New York 1956).

_____

MENDELSSOHN (-BARTHOLDY), (Jakob Ludwig) Felix (Feb. 3, 1809 – Nov. 4, 1847). German composer. Born Hamburg, son of a wealthy banker and grandson of philosopher Moses Mendelssohn. Family moved to Berlin (1811), where Felix received excellent education from private tutors and studied piano under Ludwig Berger, violin under Wilhelm Henning, and composition under C. F. Zelter. Made public debut as pianist (1818) and by 1820 was actively composing. Important early works include octet for strings (1825) and overture to *A Midsummer Night's Dream* (1826). Inaugurated Bach revival by giving first performance since Bach's death of *St. Matthew Passion* (Berlin Singakademie, 1829). In same year, made first of many conducting tours in England, where he became particularly influential. Conducted Gewandhaus concerts in Leipzig (1835–47), making it the music center of Germany, and founded Leipzig Conservatory (1842–43) with Robert Schumann and others. Married Cécile Jeanrenaud (1837). Died in Leipzig. Major works include *Reformation* (1830–32), *Scottish* (1830–42), and *Italian* (1831–33) symphonies; *Hebrides (Fingal's Cave) Overture* (1830–32); *St. Paul* (1836) and *Elijah* (1846) oratorios; incidental music to *A Midsummer Night's Dream* (1843); violin concerto in E minor (1844); *Variations sérieuses* (1841) and *Songs Without Words* (1832–45) for piano.

EDITION: *Letters* ed. Gisella Selden-Goth (New York 1945 and London 1947).

REFERENCES: John Horton *The Chamber Music of Mendelssohn* (London 1946). Heinrich E. Jacob *Felix Mendelssohn and His Times* (tr. Englewood Cliffs, N.J. 1963). Philip Radcliffe *Mendelssohn* (London and New York 1954, PB 1963). Stephen S. Stratton *Mendelssohn* (1901, rev. ed. London 1934). Eric Werner *Mendelssohn: A New Image of the Composer and His Age* (tr. New York and London 1963).

FELIX MENDELSSOHN
BY DONALD MINTZ

In the conventional view, Felix Mendelssohn-Bartholdy was an earnest, happy man who lived an earnest and happy — though short — life. He left a small body of pleasant and exceptionally well made music and a rather large amount of inferior stuff.

That view is a misreading of Mendelssohn's life and character, a misreading, it must be added, that was encouraged by the distortions imposed on his letters by pious heirs. It is probably also a misreading of his music; it is in any event a simplification that ignores both the curious musical conditions of the composer's time and his efforts to deal with them.

No doubt Mendelssohn was in many respects a happy man. He was also an incredibly facile musician: a remarkable sight reader; a violinist who needed very little practice to maintain dexterity; a composer with a great ability to foresee the progress of a work without extensive sketching (though the sketches and drafts reveal that this ability has generally been overestimated); the possessor of an enviable musical memory; and so on through the list of musical virtues that so impress those who must work more slowly and laboriously.

Yet the equation of facility with superficiality and the suggestion that either or both tend to be components of happiness is surely wrong so far as Mendelssohn is concerned.

Those of his letters that have been printed as they were written (or nearly so) indicate that the celebrated gaiety had a strong manic aspect; and grim depression, the inevitable obverse, is likewise apparent. Moreover, the position of a baptized Jew in the Germany of Mendelssohn's time was far from comfortable. Eric Werner in his *Mendelssohn* (1963) has shown the extent to which this social phenomenon affected the composer.

The nature of Mendelssohn's music is more complex and controversial; inevitably, so too is the question of its place today. The matter has been made yet more complicated by the nineteenth century's tendency to read a composer's personality into his music (and the reverse), a tendency that still prevails, though possibly in a form more sophisticated than that of earlier formulations.

If, for instance, one assumes that the *Italian Symphony* is a happy piece by a happy man, the daemonic aspects of the final movement are likely to remain hidden. And indeed, most conductors force the movement to fit *a priori* (and perhaps largely unconscious) assumptions that in their crudest form have to do with happy peasants and similar nonsense.

Likewise, the *Fingal's Cave Overture* has been degraded to the status of a "pop" concert curtain raiser, a bit of salon-like genre painting, pleasant enough but little more. The rather odd, brooding quality of the opening, which should be plain enough from the static and repetitive melodic line and the movement of the harmonic roots, is suppressed.

Yet interpretive artists are not fools; much of the music does in fact contain elements that give some support to the conventional approaches.

First, Mendelssohn wrote a good deal of relatively modish music, particularly for piano, that has nothing whatever to say to our century. The existence of such embarrassments, however understandable, tends to diminish a composer's reputation for profundity.

Second, many aspects of Mendelssohn's style were conservative in terms of his time. His orchestra, by and large, is Beethoven's. He disliked what he considered noise and so remained unaffected by such things as Berlioz's and Meyerbeer's expansion of the orchestra. Within this restriction, however, his scoring is exceptionally imaginative and distinctly of its time. His piano writing, however, tended to be old-fashioned, a tendency he deplored. His dissonance treatment is likewise relatively cautious, compared for instance, to Schumann's. So too are his harmony and large-scale tonal schemes. Finally, Mendelssohn seems to have pursued notions of balance and symmetry that recall the aesthetic of the end of the eighteenth century.

But, like all German instrumental composers of his generation, he was trapped by singularly unfortunate historical circumstances. It was assumed that music was supposed somehow to progress; at the same time, it was difficult to see just how one could move forward within the received forms, which seemed to have been exhausted by Beethoven.

As a young man, Mendelssohn attempted to grapple directly with Beethoven's late works. The piano sonata, Op. 6, for instance, is clearly indebted to Beethoven's Op. 101. The A minor string quartet, with its anguished fugue, its "motto" theme and its elaborate, cyclic structure, is a thoroughly mature — and successful — effort to enter the world of the late Beethoven quartets.

But Mendelssohn changed direction. It must have seemed to him unprofitable to try to work in the Beethoven line, though there are some indications that, like Schubert, he was turning to the problem at the time of his death.

For the most part, Mendelssohn "solved" the dilemma by evading it; the Beethoven tradition was ignored. Older styles, however, were thoroughly explored, particularly those of the baroque and late Renaissance, and to some extent, at least, Mendelssohn attempted to adapt these for modern use. He also tried his hand at the style of contemporary Italian music; an exceptionally lovely *Kyrie* for soprano, a piece that sounds like Rossini, was first published in a dissertation about Mendelssohn as a church composer.

It is possible that studies in the Italian style had some influence on his mature compositions. The so-called Widow Scene in *Elijah* seems somewhat in this manner if one is not trapped into thinking of the oratorio as a chunk of Victorian piety with a few good tunes.

At the moment, Mendelssohn's position is being re-evaluated. A substantial number of previously unpublished works have been printed and the best of the youthful symphonies for strings have gained admirers. It seems likely that ultimately a good deal of the received wisdom about works that have remained in the repertory will be seen as received foolishness, and the music will be revealed as deeper than previously thought.

But a sense of a lack of fulfillment will probably remain. After all, the Beethoven dilemma was there, and from today's point of view, evasion seems a poor tactic.

MEREDITH, George (Feb. 12, 1828 – May 18, 1909). English novelist and poet. Born Portsmouth, Hampshire. His father, a tailor, went bankrupt (1838), and the boy became a ward in chancery (1841). After attending Moravian school at Neuwied on the Rhine (1842–44), he was briefly apprenticed to a London lawyer (1847) before trying journalism (1848). Married Mrs. Mary Nicolls, daughter of Thomas Love Peacock (1849). His first novel, *The Ordeal of Richard Feverel* (1859), which displays his characteristically intellectual and satiric style, found a distinguished audience in Carlyle, Swinburne, and Rossetti, but was withdrawn by the publishers as immoral. His wife left him (1858), and after her death (1861) Meredith wrote poem sequence based on the disintegration of their marriage, *Modern Love* (1862). Married Marie Vulliamy (1864). Served as correspondent during Austro-Italian War (1866), and on return edited *Fortnightly Review* and worked as reader for a publishing house before settling at Box Hill, Surrey (1868). Emerging from obscurity through success of novels *Beauchamp's Career* (1876), *The Egoist* (1879), and *Diana of the Crossways* (1885), he adopted the role of sage, making Box Hill one of the literary centers of England. His major poetry too was written after 1880; *Poems and Lyrics of the Joy of Earth* (1883), *Ballads and Poems of Tragic Life* (1887), *A Reading of Earth* (1888), *A Reading of Life* (1901) are some of the volumes. His famous lecture *On the Idea of Comedy and the Uses of the Comic Spirit* (delivered 1877, published 1897) sets forth his theories of literature, including his concept of objective yet tolerant comedy versus the sentimentality popular in current fiction. Became president of Royal Society of Authors (1892), and received Order of Merit (1905). Died at Box Hill.

REFERENCES: William Chislett *George Meredith: A Study and an Appraisal* (1925, reprinted New York 1966). J. H. E. Crees *George Meredith: A Study of His Works and Personality* (1918, reprinted New York 1967). Jack Lindsay *George Meredith: His Life and Work* (London 1955). J. B. Priestley *George Meredith* (London and New York 1926). V. S. Pritchett *George Meredith and English Comedy* (New York 1970). Siegfried Sassoon *Meredith* (London and New York 1948, reprinted 1969). Lionel Stevenson *The Ordeal of George Meredith: A Biography* (2nd ed. New York 1967). George M. Trevelyan *The Poetry and Philosophy of George Meredith* (1906, reprinted New York 1966).

MÉRIMÉE, Prosper (Sept. 28, 1803 – Sept. 23, 1870). French writer. Born in Paris, the son of a well-known painter, and educated there at Lycée Impérial and École de Droit. His first published works were a pair of successful mystifications: *Le Théâtre de Clara Gazul* (1825), a series of mock-romantic closet plays supposedly written by a Spanish actress, and *La Guzla* (1827), a collection of poems purportedly translated from the Serbian. He next published a historical novel, *La Chronique du règne de Charles IX* (1829). During following year, Mérimée traveled through Spain, where he became acquainted with Eugénie de Montijo, later empress of France. Upon his return, entered naval ministry, and in 1834 became inspector of historical monuments, a position that took him on frequent travels to various parts of the Continent. These trips provided exotic settings for the numerous short stories and novellas for which he is best known, including *Mateo Falcone* (1829), *Colomba* (1840), and *Carmen* (1847), later made into the famous opera by Bizet. Elected to French Academy (1844); made a senator when Eugénie became empress (1853). Died at Cannes. In contrast to his stories, known for their detachment, irony, and classical restraint, Mérimée's correspondence, notably the *Lettres à une inconnue* (addressed to his friend Jenny Dacquin; published 1873), shows sympathy and tenderness.

TRANSLATION: *The Writings of Prosper Mérimée* ed. George Saintsbury (8 vols. London 1906).
REFERENCES: Robert Baschet *Mérimée, 1803–1870: du romantisme au Second Empire* (Paris 1959). André Billy *Mérimée* (Paris 1959). Frank Paul Bowman *Prosper Mérimée: Heroism, Pessimism, and Irony* (Berkeley, Calif. 1962). George H. Johnstone *Prosper Mérimée: A Mask and A Face* (London 1926). Paul Léon *Mérimée et son temps* (Paris 1962). Sylvia Lyon *The Life and Times of Prosper Mérimée* (New York 1948). Pierre Trahard *La Jeunesse de Prosper Mérimée, 1803–1834* (Paris 1925), *Prosper Mérimée de 1834 à 1853* (Paris 1928), *La Vieillesse de Prosper Mérimée, 1854–1870* (Paris 1930).

METASTASIO, Pietro (real name Pietro Antonio Domenico Bonaventura Trapassi)

(Jan. 3, 1698 – Apr. 12, 1782). Italian poet and librettist. Born Rome. As a child he was apprenticed to a goldsmith, but precocious literary talents attracted attention of critic Gianvincenzo Gravina, who educated him and left him an inheritance. Early writings, including poems and a tragedy, *Giustino,* written when he was fourteen, appeared in 1717. Settling in Naples (1719), he entered literary and aristocratic circles, becoming protégé of singer Marianna Bulgarelli, called La Romanina. She introduced him to leading composers and encouraged him to write his first *melodramma* (musical drama), *Didone abbandonata* (1723). This and subsequent melodramas, including *Adriano in Siria* (1731), *Demetrio* (1732), *L'Olimpiade* (1733), *Demofoonte* (1733), *La Clemenza di Tito* (1734), and *Attilio Regolo* (1740), were set to music by all major composers of the period, their graceful, glittering language suiting ideally the eighteenth-century vocal style. Appointed court poet to Emperor Charles VI (1730), he spent rest of his life in Vienna.

REFERENCE: Charles Burney *Memoirs of the Life and Writing of the Abate Metastasio* (1796, 2nd ed. 3 vols. New York 1970).

METSU, Gabriel (1629 – Oct. 1667). Dutch painter. Born Leiden, son of a painter; may have studied there under Gerard Dou. By 1657 he was in Amsterdam, where his marriage (Apr. 12, 1658) and burial (Oct. 24, 1667) are recorded. Metsu painted genre scenes of quiet activity in middle-class domestic life. His muted colors and subtle lighting effects suggest the work of his contemporary Jan Vermeer. Among his paintings: *The Sick Child* (Rijksmuseum, Amsterdam); *The Letter Received* (Alfred Beit Collection, London); *The Visit to the Nursery, The Music Lesson, The Artist and His Wife* (all Metropolitan Museum, New York); *The Intruder* (National Gallery, Washington); *The Duet* and *The Music Party* (both National Gallery, London); *The Vegetable Market at Amsterdam* (Louvre, Paris).

REFERENCE: W. Bode *Great Masters of Dutch and Flemish Painting* (London 1909, 1926).

MEYERBEER, Giacomo (real name Jakob Liebmann Beer) (Sept. 5, 1791 – May 2, 1864). German composer. Born Berlin, son of a wealthy banker. First attracted notice as piano prodigy; studied composition under C. F. Zelter and Bernard Weber in Berlin and Abbé Vogler in Darmstadt. His early German operas proving unsuccessful, Meyerbeer went to Italy for further study (1815). Here he won immediate popularity with six operas in manner of Rossini (1817–24). In Paris from 1826, he studied French music and culture. Was also preoccupied in these years with his father's death, his own marriage, and the deaths of two of his children. With *Robert le Diable* (1831), Meyerbeer established the French grand opera style, the spectacular scenic effects and dramatic recitative in the French tradition, the florid arias, composed to show off the virtuoso, from Italian tradition, and the plot material in the current romantic literary taste. *Les Huguenots* (1836), his best-known work, was followed by *Ein Feldlager in Schlesien* (1844), *Le Prophète* (1849), *L'Étoile du nord* (1854), *Le Pardon de Ploërmel,* later known as *Dinorah* (1859), and *L'Africaine* (1865). Appointed general music director of Berlin by King Friedrich Wilhelm IV (1842), he lived there for long periods, but died in Paris.

REFERENCES: L. Dauriac *Meyerbeer* (2nd ed. Paris 1930). Arthur Hervey *Meyerbeer and His Music* (London 1913).

MICHELANGELO BUONARROTI (Mar. 6, 1475 – Feb. 18, 1564). Italian artist. Born Caprese, Tuscany, into an old Florentine Guelph family. Grew up in and near Florence. After brief apprenticeship to Domenico Ghirlandajo (1488–89), spent time in Medici gardens supervised by Donatello's pupil Bertoldo di Giovanni. Taken into household of Lorenzo de' Medici (1490–92), he met the leading intellectuals of the day, who were neo-Platonists. The two monumental sculptures, *Bacchus* (Museo Nazionale, Florence) and the

Pietà (St. Peter's, Rome), that made him famous date from his first visit to Rome (1496–1501). After his return to Florence, the huge marble *David* (1501–1504, Accademia, Florence) added to his fame. Also painted *Doni Tondo* (*The Holy Family;* c.1504, Uffizi, Florence). Summoned to Rome to design and execute tomb of Pope Julius II (1505), he had to interrupt project to fresco the Sistine chapel ceiling (1508–12). The tomb, which includes figure of *Moses* (c.1515–16), was completed, after many revisions, in 1545 (S. Pietro in Vincoli, Rome). In Florence (1520–34), created the Medici chapel (new sacristy) in S. Lorenzo, with its funerary monuments, also the Laurentian Library. Spent his last thirty years in Rome, where he wrote his finest poetry, frescoed the altar wall of the Sistine chapel (*Last Judgment,* 1534–41) and the walls of the Pauline chapel (*Conversion of St. Paul* and *Crucifixion of St. Peter,* 1542–50), and carved *Pietà* (1550–55, Florence cathedral) and *Rondanini Pietà* (1555–64, Castello Sforzesco, Milan). From 1546, he was chief architect to St. Peter's, Rome.

TRANSLATIONS: *Complete Poems and Selected Letters of Michelangelo* tr. Creighton Gilbert (New York 1963, 3rd ed. 1970). *Letters* tr. and ed. E. Ramsden (2 vols. London 1963).

REFERENCES: J. S. Ackerman *The Architecture of Michelangelo* (2 vols. 1961, rev. ed. New York 1967). Ascanio Condivi *Michelangelo Buonarroti* (1553; tr. Charles Holroyd 2nd ed. London 1911). Charles de Tolnay *Michelangelo* (6 vols. Princeton, N.J. 1943–70 and *Art and Thought of Michelangelo* (New York 1964). Ludwig Goldscheider *Michelangelo: Paintings, Sculptures, Architecture* (4th ed. London and Greenwich, Conn. 1963). John Addington Symonds *The Life of Michelangelo Buonarroti* (2 vols. London 1892, new ed. New York 1928).

✍

MICHELANGELO
BY CREIGHTON GILBERT

In our century the very word Michelangelo calls up a conventional image of the human figure represented in monu-mental grandeur. Familiar traditional personages such as Adam, Moses, David, and God the Father convey their overtones to invented ones like the Libyan sibyl, Dawn, "Il Penseroso," or Minos. We attribute the same scale and power to the psychological qualities of these figures and to their creator, tragically seeking and mourning. This viewpoint is indeed a partial truth. It is much influenced by the nineteenth-century romantic idea of great art, in which Michelangelo, especially as a painter, was again recognized as a genius after two centuries of relatively slight praise. Today, however, many observers are developing a new approach to Michelangelo which seems to be less exciting but perhaps richer in characterization.

The early works of Michelangelo, from his first drawings and carvings at about sixteen until he was about twenty-seven, make a longer list of separate works than do those of the following fifty years of his long life. Most of them are small, but they also include the great *Pietà* in St. Peter's and the colossal *David*. But they were practicable because they were not meant as parts of great sets, the typical pattern later on. They also have an un-Michelangelesque character of smooth simplicity. The young Michelangelo, emerging from a very rich local tradition of sculpture, was the most talented young man of his generation but not a revolutionary at all. His work is impressive most perhaps because of its heavy density, evoking serious importance, which contrasts somewhat with the more detailed or thin styles current just before, but this is also a bow to a greater predecessor a little earlier still, Donatello. Michelangelo is willing enough to show off his expertness and polish, and active surface interest is retained along with the gravity of form in the textures of the *Pietà* or the *Bacchus*'s virtuosity of pose. At twenty-five he was gaining recognition as the best sculptor in Florence, which was a good deal.

What probably did most to change all this was the impact of Leonardo da Vinci. In 1500 Leonardo came home to Florence after twenty years away, and his "modern art" was devastating to young artists. Florence had indeed been falling into complacency. For Michelangelo, Leonardo was most important, perhaps, in his insistence on the sense of living processes and movement, as seen in twisting human bodies or jumping horses or plant forms or anatomical dissections or anywhere. Although the young Michelangelo's static massiveness is plausible in any carver of statues, the great Michelangelo we know calls for a capacity to accept the lesson of Leonardo's vitality without losing at all the dense volume that one would assume was incompatible with it. The result is the first series of huge works, the lost *Battle of Cascina,* the frescoes of the Sistine ceiling, and the *Moses,* which is the chief fragment created for the project of Pope Julius II's tomb. Figures such as the *Moses* or elements of the ceiling such as the famous *Creation of Adam* or *Jeremiah* illustrate thoroughly this key to the unique capacities of their artist, the infusion of the potentials of motion and life into the huge hulks. The result is an impressive monumentality, a force and awesomeness, that makes them to us his most familiar and typifying works. This quality was probably encouraged further by the great scale of the projects of which they are part, and thus was helped into being by the most Michelangelesque of patrons, Pope Julius II, that remarkable exemplar of what we think of as the Renaissance pope.

So much is this our favored Michelangelo that we have tended against many visual obstacles to see the same qualities in the work of the 1520's dominated by the Medici tombs. Yet these figures shift largely toward lithe, thin, and decorated forms. Their place is in a chapel also designed by Michelangelo, whose thin elastic articulation, unsettled, shifting, and ambiguous, is not so much full of agonized tensions as of witty tricks. The same applies to the other great Medici project of the same years, the library and its stair hall. The self-trained architect here starts from the fact that a stairway is spatially ambiguous and antagonistic to Renaissance harmony of proportion (*where is a person who is climbing stairs?*) and that the stairwell has a related eccentricity of height-width proportions. With that stimulus he invented what we now see as the perfect example of mannerist architecture, full of intellectual contradictions and paradoxes against our accepted notions of the rational and classical. This too illustrates not the worried mannerism of psychic pressure that can be found in a painter of the time like Pontormo, but, even more in contrast, the fashionable elegant mannerism of another painter like Parmigianino. It does so for reasons similar to Parmigianino's stimuli, that it is essentially a court art, designed to accommodate the adulation and luxury of a newly absolutist dynasty. Even though this is a heresy against the romantic idea of the serious sincere artist to which we usually attach Michelangelo, it may increase still more our recognition of his versatility.

Michelangelo between the ages of sixty and ninety matches the accepted image rather better. He lived quietly in Rome and became intensely devout, as did many others in this age of the Council of Trent. He did not produce much sculpture, and at first concentrated on painting, especially the *Last*

Judgment. But after passing seventy he was concerned chiefly with architecture and poetry, his two nonmanual arts. His statements are not only serious, but in their essentials open and simple. They may deal with complicated matters, but are plainly articulated, even, sometimes, at the risk of banality. A finished statue like *Leah* may look dull, a sonnet may be literally a traditional prayer. But the open square of the Capitoline Hill and the main parts of St. Peter's, both huge but understated contributions to the social environment, are the final objects of his attentive care.

MICHELET, Jules (Aug. 21, 1798 – Feb. 9, 1874). French historian. Born Paris. A poor printer's son, he worked his way through Collège de Charlemagne and University of Paris; became professor of history at Collège Rollin (1821) and lecturer at École Normale (1827). First publications were a translation of Giambattista Vico's *Scienza nuova* and an abstract of modern history using Vico's methods (both 1827). Appointed chief of historical section of National Archives (1831). While professor at Collège de France (from 1838), vigorously expressed liberal, anticlerical views in his lectures and in such works as *Étude sur les jésuites* (1843), *Le Prêtre, la femme et la famille* (1844), and *Le Peuple* (1846); was dismissed for refusing allegiance to Second Empire (1851). In his great work, the *Histoire de France* (1833–67), Michelet used his literary gifts and fertile imagination to achieve "a resurrection of the life of the past." Among his other works are the brilliant but opinionated *Histoire de la Révolution française* (1847–53) and series of books on nature, including *L'Oiseau* (1856) and *L'Insecte* (1858). Married Pauline Rousseau (1824; she died 1839); Athanaïs Mialaret (1849). Michelet died at Hyères, Provence.

TRANSLATIONS: *History of France* tr. G. H. Smith (2 vols. New York 1847). *History of the French Revolution* tr. Charles Cocks (Chicago 1967).

REFERENCES: Jean-Marie Carré *Michelet et son temps* (Paris 1926). Daniel Halévy *Jules Michelet* (Paris 1928). Gabriel Monod *La Vie et la pensée de Jules Michelet* (2 vols. Paris 1923). Anne R. Pugh *Michelet and His Ideas on Social Reform* (New York 1923). Paul Viallaneix *La Voie royale: Essai sur l'idée de peuple dans l'oeuvre de Michelet* (Paris 1959). Edmund Wilson *To the Finland Station* (New York 1940, PB 1953).

MIDDLETON, Thomas (Apr. 1580 – July 1627). English dramatist. Born London. Matriculated at Queen's College, Oxford (1598); by 1600 or 1601, when he returned to London, had published several poems. Began career as playwright by collaborating with Thomas Dekker, John Webster, and others on comedies for producer Philip Henslowe. From 1613, composed masques and pageants for civic ceremonials, and was appointed city chronologer (1620). Married twice; made his home in Newington Butts, a London suburb, and was buried there. Middleton's plays include satirical comedies of London life *A Mad World, My Masters* (acted c.1604, published 1608), *Michaelmas Term* (acted c.1605, published 1607), *A Trick to Catch the Old One* (acted c.1606, published 1608), *A Chaste Maid in Cheapside* (acted c.1613, published 1630), *The Roaring Girl* (with Dekker; acted c.1604–10, published 1611); tragedies *Women Beware Women* (acted c.1621, published 1657), *The Changeling* (with William Rowley; acted 1622, published 1653); tragicomedies *A Fair Quarrel* (with Rowley; acted c.1616, published 1617), *The Witch* (acted c.1610–16, published 1778), *The Spanish Gipsy* (with Rowley; acted 1623, published 1653); and political satire *A Game at Chess* (1624).

EDITIONS: *Works* ed. Alexander Dyce (5 vols. London 1840); ed. A. H. Bullen (8 vols. 1885–86, latest ed. New York 1964).

REFERENCES: Richard H. Barker *Thomas Middleton* (New York 1958). Wilbur D. Dunkel *The Dramatic Technique of Thomas Middleton in His Comedies of London Life* (1926, reprinted New York 1967). T. S. Eliot *Elizabethan Essays* (1934, new ed. New

York 1964, also PB). Brian Gibbons *Jacobean City Comedy: A Study of Satiric Plays by Jonson, Marston and Middleton* (Cambridge, Mass. and London 1968). Samuel Schoenbaum *Middleton's Tragedies: A Critical Study* (New York and London 1955).

MIES VAN DER ROHE, Ludwig (Mar. 27, 1886 – Aug. 17, 1969). German-American architect and designer. Born Ludwig Mies in Aachen, Germany (he added mother's name), son of master mason and stonecutter who taught him elements of architecture. After attending trade school in Aachen, became apprentice first to draftsman, then at nineteen to Bruno Paul, leading furniture designer, in Berlin; assistant to Peter Behrens (1908–11), the teacher of Le Corbusier and Gropius, and Germany's most progressive architect. Opened his own office (1913), then served in German army in World War I, building roads and bridges in the Balkans. After the war, directed Novembergruppe, an association that promoted modern art, and became first vice president of Deutscher Werkbund (1926–32), founded to integrate art and industry. His finest European achievements of the period were the German pavilion at Barcelona International Exposition (1929, now destroyed) and Tugendhat house at Brno, Czechoslovakia (1930). He also established his reputation in Berlin with designs for glass and steel skyscrapers (1919–20), which with his designs for houses exerted widespread influence. His chair designs also famous: the MR (1926), the Barcelona (1929), the Tugendhat (1930). Directed Bauhaus (1930) before Nazis closed it down. Through architect Philip C. Johnson, Mies came to U.S. (1937); eventually became head of School of Architecture at Illinois Institute of Technology, Chicago (1940–58), for which he designed campus and buildings. Also built two apartment houses on Lake Shore Drive (1948–51). One of his most famous buildings, the Seagram building (New York City, 1956–58) in association with Philip Johnson, is characteristic of his spare, severely disciplined style, featuring glass and concrete surface, meticulous detail.

"Less is more" was a favorite maxim. Believing that a building should be a "clear and true statement of its times," and following his basic principles of order, logic, and clarity, Mies more than anyone helped create the distinctive twentieth-century industrial style. Other important buildings of his: Chicago Federal Center, Lafayette Park, Detroit (1960); National Gallery, Berlin (1968). He died in Chicago. Mies received many honors and published *The Art of Structure* (New York 1965).

REFERENCES: Peter Blake *Mies van der Rohe: Architecture and Structure* (Harmondsworth, England, and Baltimore PB 1964). Werner Blaser *Mies van der Rohe: The Art of Structure* (tr. New York and London 1965). Arthur Drexler *Ludwig Mies van der Rohe* (New York and London 1960, also PB). Ludwig Hilberseimer *Mies van der Rohe* (Chicago and London 1956). Philip C. Johnson *Mies van der Rohe* (2nd ed. New York 1954, also PB).

MILL, John Stuart (May 20, 1806 – May 8, 1873). English philosopher, economist, and reformer. Born London, son of historian and economist James Mill, who was an associate of Jeremy Bentham in the development of utilitarianism and founder of philosophical radicalism. Given an extremely thorough and accelerated education by his father, John spent a year of study in France (1820–21) with family of Sir Samuel Bentham, brother of Jeremy, and read law before taking position under his father in East India Company (1823), where he rose rapidly to become chief examiner. Strongly influenced by Bentham's doctrines, he founded a discussion group, the Utilitarian Society (1822), and became leader of the philosophical radicals. Wrote for periodicals and published *System of Logic* (1843), *Principles of Political Economy* (1848), *On Liberty* (1854), *Considerations on Representative Government* (1861), and other works which expound utilitarian theories of ethics, government, and economics, adding a new emphasis on human needs and welfare. In social reform, Mill was greatly influenced by his wife, the former Harriet Hardy, widow of John Taylor (they married 1851; she died

1858). As member of House of Commons (1865–68), he voted with the radicals and independently advocated such reforms as woman's suffrage. Spent most of last years in Avignon, France, where he died. His famous *Autobiography* appeared posthumously (1873, complete edition 1924).

EDITION: *Collected Works* (13 vols. Toronto and London 1963–69).

REFERENCES: Richard P. Anschutz *The Philosophy of John Stuart Mill* (2nd ed. Oxford 1963). Alexander Bain *John Stuart Mill: A Criticism, with Personal Recollections* (1882, reprinted New York 1969). Karl Britton *John Stuart Mill* (2nd ed. New York PB 1969). Élie Halévy *The Growth of Philosophical Radicalism* (tr. 1928, new ed. Boston PB 1960). Emery E. Neff *Carlyle and Mill: An Introduction to Victorian Thought* (1924, rev. ed. New York 1964). Michael St. John Packe *The Life of John Stuart Mill* (London and New York 1954). Sir Leslie Stephen *The English Utilitarians* vol. III (1900, reprinted 3 vols. New York 1968).

MILLAIS, Sir John Everett (June 8, 1829 – Aug. 13, 1896). English painter. Born Southampton. Trained in London under Henry Sass (1838–39) and from the age of eleven at the Royal Academy, where he won all the prizes. His first Academy painting was *Pizarro Seizing the Inca of Peru* (1846, Victoria and Albert Museum, London). With Holman Hunt and D. G. Rossetti founded Pre-Raphaelite Brotherhood (1848). Major works of Millais's Pre-Raphaelite phase (1848–59), characterized by rich color, faithful rendering of nature down to the minutest detail, and unconventional approach to composition, include *Isabella* (1849, Walker Art Gallery, Liverpool), *Christ in the House of His Parents* (1850, Tate Gallery, London), *The Huguenot* (1852, Art Gallery, Birmingham), *Ophelia* (1852, Tate Gallery, London), *The Blind Girl* (1856, Art Gallery, Birmingham). Later he concentrated on landscapes, fashionable portraits, and sentimental subjects, and the quality of his work declined. Married Euphemia Gray (1855), whose marriage to John Ruskin had been annulled. Millais became Royal Academician (1863), officer of Légion

d'Honneur (1878), baronet (1885), president of Royal Academy (1896). Died in London.

REFERENCES: Robin Ironside and John Gere *Pre-Raphaelite Painters* (London 1948). Mary Lutyens ed. *Millais and the Ruskins* (London 1967). John G. Millais *The Life and Letters of Sir John Everett Millais* (2 vols. London and New York 1899). Marion H. Spielmann *Millais and His Works* (London 1898).

MILLAY, Edna St. Vincent (Feb. 22, 1892 – Oct. 19, 1950). American poet. Born Rockland, Me. Began writing poetry early, publishing *Renascence* (1912) and book of poems upon graduating from Vassar College (1917). Lived several bohemian years in Greenwich Village, expressing social protest and feminine emancipation of the 1920's, and often using pseudonym Nancy Boyd for stories and articles. Published *Figs from Thistles* (1920) and became active in theatre as actress and director, producing the fantasy *Aria de Capo* (1920) and verse play *The King's Henchman*, made into an opera by Deems Taylor (1927). After a sojourn in Paris with other expatriates, published *Second April* (1921) and won (1923) Pulitzer prize for *The Harp Weaver*. Married Eugen Boissevain (1923) and moved to a farm in upper New York State, where she died. Her numerous volumes of poems include *Fatal Interview* (1931), *Wine from These Grapes* (1934), *There Are No Islands Any More* (1940), *Collected Sonnets* (1941), *The Murder of Lidice* (1942), *Collected Lyrics* (1943), and the posthumous *Mine the Harvest* (1954). She also translated, with George Dillon, Baudelaire's *Les Fleurs du Mal* (*Flowers of Evil*, 1936). She was a member of the American Academy of Arts and Letters.

REFERENCES: Elizabeth Atkins *Edna St. Vincent Millay and Her Times* (1936, new ed. New York 1964). Jean Gould *The Poet and Her Book: A Biography of Edna St. Vincent Millay* (New York 1969). Miriam Gurko *Restless Spirit: The Life of Edna St. Vincent Millay* (New York 1962).

MILLET, Jean François (Oct. 4, 1814 – Jan. 20, 1875). French painter. Born Gruchy, near Cherbourg, of peasant stock. After two years of art lessons in Cherbourg (1834–36), went to Paris to study with Paul Delaroche (1837–39). From 1840, exhibited at Salon. Married Pauline Ono (1841; she died 1844); Catherine Lemaire (1845). At the time, Millet painted portraits and religious, classical, and genre subjects in various derivative styles. Settled (1849) at village of Barbizon near forest of Fontainebleau, where he, Charles Daubigny, Theodore Rousseau, and other painters founded Barbizon school. Here Millet began to paint the scenes of peasant life which, greeted hostilely at first as vulgar and socialistic, from the 1867 Universal Exposition brought him enthusiastic recognition. The sincerity of his realism, the power and dignity of his figures, and his simple bold compositions were profoundly admired. His major works include *The Sower* (1850, Metropolitan Museum, New York), *The Gleaners* (1857) and *The Angelus* (1859, both in the Louvre, Paris), *The Potato Planters* (1862, Museum of Fine Arts, Boston), *The Man with a Hoe* (1863, San Francisco). He died at Barbizon.

REFERENCES: Julia Cartwright Ady *Jean François Millet: His Life and Letters* (London 1896 and New York 1902). Léonce Bénédite *The Drawings of Jean François Millet* (London 1906). Étienne Moreau-Nélaton *Millet raconté par lui-même* (3 vols. Paris 1921). Alfred Sensier *Jean François Millet: Peasant and Painter* (tr. Boston 1881). Charles S. Smith *Barbizon Days* (1902, reprinted Freeport, N.Y. 1969).

MILTON, John (Dec. 9, 1608 – Nov. 8, 1674). English writer. Born and died in London; father a scrivener and amateur musician. Educated at St. Paul's School and Christ's College, Cambridge (B.A. 1629, M.A. 1632). After travels abroad, especially in Italy (1637–39), settled in London and began teaching. From an early age wrote poetry, composing his great ode *On the Morning of Christ's Nativity* at twenty-one. Prodigiously learned, he wrote poems in Italian, Latin, and Greek, as well as English. Published *Comus, a Masque* (1637), *Lycidas* (1638), and first volume of poems, containing *L'Allegro, Il Penseroso,* and other lyrics (1645). Married (1642) first of three wives, Mary Powell, who left him after about a month. Published (1643) his controversial pamphlet *The Doctrine and Discipline of Divorce,* followed by tracts on the same subject and also pamphlets *On Education* (1644) and *Areopagitica* (1644). Wife returned (1645), and bore him four children before she died (1652). He married Katherine Woodcock (1656; she died 1657) and Elizabeth Minshull (1663). From 1641 he was largely occupied with political pamphleteering and activity with the Parliamentary government. Just after execution of Charles I, published *The Tenure of Kings and Magistrates* (1649), resulting in his appointment as secretary of foreign tongues to council of state, a post held until the Restoration (1660). During his service his eyesight, never strong, failed him completely (1652). His masterpiece *Paradise Lost* appeared (1667), *History of Britain* (1670), *Paradise Regained* with *Samson Agonistes* (1671), and the celebrated pamphlet *Of True Religion, Heresy, Schism, Toleration, and What Best Means May Be Used Against the Growth of Popery* (1673). A year later he died of gout in London.

EDITIONS: *Complete Poetical Works* ed. Douglas Bush (Boston 1965 and London 1966). *Complete Prose Works,* general editor D. M. Wolfe (5 vols. New Haven, Conn. 1953–   ).
REFERENCES: David Daiches *Milton* (London and New York 1957, also PB). John S. Diekhoff *Milton's Paradise Lost: A Commentary on the Argument* (1946, new ed. New York 1963) William Empson *Milton's God* (London 1961, new ed. 1965). Helen L. Gardner *A Reading of Paradise Lost* (London 1965). James Holly Hanford *John Milton, Englishman* (New York 1949 and London 1950, also PB) and *A Milton Handbook* (4th ed. New York 1946). C. S. Lewis *A Preface to Paradise Lost* (1942, rev. ed. London 1960 and New York 1961, also PB). David Masson *Life of Milton* (7 vols. London and New York 1859–1894). Kenneth Muir *John Milton* (2nd ed. London 1960). Bala-

chandra Rajan *Paradise Lost and the Seventeenth-Century Reader* (1947, new ed. London and New York 1962, also PB). E. M. W. Tillyard *Milton* (rev. ed. London 1966, also PB) and *Studies in Milton* (1950, new ed. London and New York 1960). A. J. A. Waldock *Paradise Lost and Its Critics* (Cambridge, England, 1947, also PB).

☞

JOHN MILTON
BY I. A. RICHARDS

Traditionally, man is of interest because he was made in the image of God. Recent, more venturesome theology seems sometimes ready to invert this proposition and hold that God is of interest as an image of man. These same twin speculations are surely as much invited by the Satan who salutes us whenever we look searchingly into our spiritual mirror.

Not a little of Milton's greatness comes from his creation of the Fallen One, the Enemy of Mankind, from whose sin man's fall in turn derives. Without *Paradise Lost* the figure of the Adversary would be relatively slight. So too for Adam and Eve and Paradise itself. But it is Satan who would lose most; dwindling towards a mere devil, a horrific or comic meddler, loathly rather than awesome. It is true that throughout *Paradise Lost* he declines, corroded by his grievance and hate. And in *Paradise Regained* he is another personage; the ruined seraph has become an expert salesman of careers. These changes, however, enhance rather than diminish his powers as an instrument through which we can learn about ourselves.

Temptation was always Milton's favorite theme. Comus's attempt on the Lady, the Serpent's easy success (*Paradise Lost* IX), Delila's dealings with Samson and the intricate gambits of *Paradise Regained,* read comparatively,

are extraordinarily revealing. The role of flattery in seduction, the need to divine the temptee's self-image, the dangers of misaimed appeals, the calculus of ambitions; of all this Milton's mastery is limitless. That side of a dramatist's genius he had in full.

Paradise Lost began as *Adam Unparadised,* drafts for a play on the Greek model. Fortunately Milton turned it into an epic, transforming the epic aim while closely respecting the traditional form. He kept, indeed extended, the scale, range, richness, universality of Homer and Virgil, but added — through his concern with ultimates of speculation — something which may in its turn be thought exorbitantly ambitious. His fiends are utmost triumphs of imagination; his celestials — and most of all their rulers — are dummies. No doubt Milton knew, as well as any of his critics, that the whole poem and all the parts of it can be no more than an image. But, as Shelley's Demogorgon puts it and finally: "the deep truth is imageless." To offer an image of it, as Milton does, is to incur heavy penalties. And when Omnipotence displays (perhaps inevitably) the character, passions, and behavior of a despot, the outcomes are beyond even Milton's powers of control. There is a desecration which either affronts or corrupts its audience.

Down in hell (book II, lines 558–561) the fiends

> . . . *reason'd high*
> *Of Providence, Foreknowledge,*
> *Will and Fate,*
> *Fixt Fate, free will, foreknowl-*
> *edge absolute,*
> *And found no end, in wand'ring*
> *mazes lost.*

Any fit audience, alas, must be as lost when it reads (X, 31; cf. III, 77–134):

> . . . *the most High*
> *Eternal Father from his secret*
> *Cloud,*
> *Amidst in Thunder [utter'd] thus*
> *his voice.*
> *Assembl'd Angels, and ye Powers*
> *return'd*
> *From unsuccessful charge, be*
> *not dismaid,*
> *Nor troubl'd at these tidings*
> *from the Earth,*
> *Which your sincerest care could*
> *not prevent,*
> *Foretold so lately what would*
> *come to pass,*
> *When first this Tempter cross'd*
> *the Gulf from Hell.*
> *I told ye then he should prevail*
> *and speed*
> *On his bad Errand, Man should*
> *be seduc't*
> *And flatter'd out of all, believing*
> *lies*
> *Against his Maker.*

Such utterance sanctions the very charges it describes as lies. It downgrades a thousand and more lines, turns the whole business of the confinement of Satan to hell, the posting of the Angelic Guard to bar his entry to paradise, the sending of Raphael down to warn Adam, etc., into an inconsiderate and silly charade. That the all-knowing should thus neglect what he foresees is behavior of a kind to justify Satan's initial revolt.

It threatens even the main action, which has, as a rule, been protected only through adroit disregard of these unhappy passages. Their consequences are too destructive for any mere "suspension of disbelief" (in Coleridge's phrase) to take care of them.

Satan's sin was that he "erst contended/With Gods to sit the highest" and "to the hight of Deitie aspir'd" (IX, 163–164, 167), moved thereto by envy.

Accordingly, in tempting Eve, he begins with the suggestion that she should (IX, 547)

> . . . *be seen*
> *A Goddess among Gods, ador'd*
> *and serv'd*
> *By angels numberless, thy daily*
> *train.*

It is the same line that Comus tries in vain on the Lady (*Comus*, 745):

> *Beauty is nature's brag, and*
> *must be shown*
> *In courts, at feasts, and high*
> *solemnities*
> *Where most may wonder at the*
> *workmanship.*

And it is with (IX, 716)

> *And what are Gods that Man*
> *may not become*
> *As they — participating God-like*
> *food?*
> . . . *Goddess humane, reach*
> *then, and freely taste —*

that he overcomes her.

It is notable that throughout this scene Eve shows no recollection whatever of the dream with which earlier he so disturbed her. Not though the language he uses in his borrowed Serpent form is alertingly close to that used in her dream, when (IV, 800) "Squat like a toad, close at the eare of Eve," he had spoken to her "With gentle voice, I thought it thine" (V, 37) and then as "One shap'd and wing'd like one of those from Heav'n/By us oft seen" (V, 55). What this wing'd shape says is: "Taste this, and be henceforth among the Gods/Thy self a Goddess, not to Earth confined" (V, 77).

The more we compare dream with actuality here the more our admiration will be moved. "In dreams begins responsibility" as we may learn from Yeats. We may be inclined to add: From dreams come *ir*responsibilities. Eve's self-persuasion (IX, 765–79), the dreamlike character of the scene, and her forgetfulness of her dream belong together. There is as much understanding of human nature here as even in Shakespeare.

> *Cromwell, I charge thee, fling*
> *away ambition:*
> *By that sin fell the angels.*

It is strangely and ironically fitting that this unsurpassed student of the workings of ambition, of overreaching, should himself have overreached in the designed demands of his poem and have been led thereby to an attempt, as the last line of *Dr. Faustus* has it, to practice more than Heavenly Power permits.

Of the earlier poems it may be remarked how often and how exquisitely they anticipate and are fulfilled in *Paradise Lost*. In *Lycidas*, the Invocation "Begin then, Sisters of the sacred well"; the account Phoebus gives of Fame that "lives and spreds aloft by those pure eyes,/And perfet witnes of all-judging Jove"; Peter's denunciation of the "Blind mouths" and "the grim Woolf with privy paw"; the "solemn troops and sweet Societies/That sing, and singing in their glory move"; and the promise too in the Sunset close are all foreshowings. So in *Comus* Hell is forefigured:

> . . . *evil on itself shall back*
> *recoyl,*
> *And mix no more with good-*
> *ness, when at last,*
> *Gather'd like scum, and setl'd to*
> *itself*

> *It shall be in eternal restless*
> *change*
> *Self-fed, and self-consum'd*

and Comus shudders at the Lady's words even as, at the sight of Eve,

> . . . *the Evil one abstracted*
> *stood*
> *From his own evil and for a time*
> *remaind*
> *Stupidly good, of enmity dis-*
> *arm'd.*

That *The Hymn* should resound with such preluding notes is not surprising. But even in *L'Allegro* we find Milton describing the verse which he beyond others was to write:

> *Such as the meeting soul may*
> *pierce*
> *In notes with many a winding*
> *bout*
> *Of lincked sweetnes long drawn*
> *out,*
> *With wanton heed, and giddy*
> *cunning,*
> *The melting voice through*
> *mazes running;*
> *Untwisting all the chains that ty*
> *The hidden soul of harmony*

And at the end of *Il Penseroso* he points to where all is leading:

> *Till old experience do attain*
> *To something like Prophetic*
> *strain.*

Prophesies these of *Paradise Lost*, with the summing up in *Samson Agonistes*:

> *His uncontroulable intent,*
> *His servants he with new ac-*
> *quist*
> *Of true experience from this*
> *great event*

With peace and consolation
hath dismist,
And calm of mind, all passion
spent.

In no fitter words than his own can Milton's constant aim and its achievement be celebrated.

MIRANDOLA. See PICO DELLA MIRANDOLA.

MISTRAL, Frédéric (Sept. 8, 1830 – Mar. 25, 1914). Provençal poet. Born and died in Maillane, Bouches-du-Rhône. A wealthy landowner's son, he was educated at Collège Royal of Avignon and University of Aix, where he took law degree (1851). Having no need to earn his living by a profession, he devoted himself to revival of Provençal language and customs, and with several friends founded (1854) a society for that purpose, called the Félibrige. Mistral's fame as the greatest poet in the langue d'oc since the Middle Ages rests chiefly on two long narrative poems, *Mirèio* (1859) and *Lou Pouèmo dóu Rose* (1897). Other works include *Calendau* (1867) and *Nerto* (1884), also long poems; verse tragedy *La Rèino Jano* (1890); two collections of lyrics, *Lis Isclo d'Or* (1876) and *Lis Oulivado* (1912); *Lou Tresor dóu Félibrige* (2 vols. 1878–86), a Provençal dictionary; *Moun Espelido* (1906), memoirs. Received Nobel prize for literature (1904). All Mistral's works have been translated into French, the better-known ones into English.

REFERENCES: Richard Aldington *Introduction to Mistral* (London 1956 and Carbondale, Ill. 1960). Charles A. Downer *Frédéric Mistral: Poet and Leader in Provence* (New York 1901). Tudor Edwards *The Lion of Arles: A Portrait of Mistral and His Circle* (New York 1964). Cuthbert M. Girdlestone *Dreamer and Striver: The Poetry of Frédéric Mistral* (London 1937). Robert Lafont *Mistral, ou l'illusion* (Paris 1954). Rob Lyle *Mistral* (Cambridge, England and New Haven, Conn. 1953).

MISTRAL, Gabriela (real name Lucila Godoy Alcayaga) (Apr. 7, 1899 – Jan. 10, 1957). Chilean poet. Born Vicuña. After attending Pedagogical College in Santiago, began at fifteen a career as village schoolteacher. Became known as poet when her *Sonetos de la muerte* (*Sonnets of Death*) won first prize in a poetry contest in Santiago (1914); thereafter her work appeared often in periodicals. She continued, however, to pursue her vocation as educator. Helped reorganize rural schools in Mexico (1922–24); spent many years in Europe working on Institute for Intellectual Cooperation of League of Nations and serving as Chilean consul in various cities; was visiting professor at Barnard, Vassar, and Middlebury colleges in United States (1931–32). Her verse, direct, emotional, deeply religious, often expresses a love for children tragically heightened by her unfulfilled maternal longings. Collections include *Desolación* (1922), *Ternura* (1925), *Tala* (1938), and *Lagar* (1954). Received Nobel prize for literature (1945). Died in Hempstead, New York.

TRANSLATION: *Selected Poems* tr. Langston Hughes (Bloomington, Ind. 1957).
REFERENCES: Margot Arce de Vázquez *Gabriela Mistral: The Poet and Her Work* (tr. New York 1964, also PB). Alice Stone Blackwell *Some Spanish-American Poets* (1929, rev. ed. New York 1968).

MODIGLIANI, Amedeo (July 12, 1884 – Jan. 25, 1920). Italian painter and sculptor. Born Leghorn. Studied at fine arts academies of Rome, Florence, and Venice (1901–1905). Moving to Paris (1906), he joined Montmartre artistic circles; at 1908 Salon des Indépendants, exhibited *La Juive* (1907, Collection Alexandre, Paris) and other paintings, showing influence of Cézanne, Gauguin, Toulouse-Lautrec, blue period of Picasso, and Matisse. Attracted some attention when his *Violoncellist* (1909, Collection Alexandre) was shown (1910). For next several years (1910–14) concentrated on sculpture: the primitivism and stylized simplification of his carved heads and figures reflect African art and work of Brancusi and Jacques Lipchitz. He then returned to painting and produced famous series of portraits and nudes characteristically distorted with elongated torsos, necks, and heads, broad, nearly flat areas of color, and expertly linear. After stormy affair with poet Beatrice Hastings (1914–16), who supported him, met Jeanne Hébuterne (1917), an art student, who bore him a daughter, Jeanne (1918). Despite her devoted care, Modigliani's health rapidly deteriorated through tuberculosis and addiction to drugs and alcohol. Died in Paris.

REFERENCES: Jeanne Modigliani *Modigliani: Man and Myth* (tr. London and New York 1958). Claude Roy *Modigliani* (tr. New York and London 1958). Franco Russoli *Modigliani: Drawings and Sketches* (tr. New York 1969). André Salmon *Modigliani: A Memoir* (tr. New York and London 1961). Pierre Sichel *Modigliani: A Biography* (New York and London 1967). James T. Soby *Modigliani: Paintings, Drawings, Sculptures* (3rd rev. ed. New York PB 1963). Alfred Werner *Modigliani* (New York 1966).

MOLIÈRE (real name Jean Baptiste Poquelin) (Jan. 15, 1622 – Feb. 17, 1673). French playwright and actor, director, producer. Born and died in Paris. Of bourgeois family, received a respectable education, but chose precarious, scandalous career of the stage. With Madeleine Béjart founded the Illustre Théâtre (1643), which went bankrupt (1645). Undiscouraged, he toured the provinces with his troupe for thirteen years. Stormed Paris with a curtain raiser, *Les Précieuses ridicules* (1659), a triumph, and set about re-establishing his troupe under patronage of Louis XIV's brother Philippe. Began (1662) most prolific and trying period of his life. Though chronically ill, he married Armande Béjart (Madeleine's sister), twenty years younger. Despite king's protection, he was constantly under fire from religious zealots for his alleged attacks on religion and morality in *L'Ecole des femmes* (*The School for Wives*, 1662), *Tartuffe* (1664) and *Dom Juan* (1665). Died while performing title role in *Le Malade imaginaire* (*The Imaginary Invalid*). Other major works: *Le Misanthrope* (1666), *Le Médecin malgré lui* (*The Physician in Spite of Himself*, 1666), *L'Avare* (*The Miser*, 1668), *Le Bourgeois Gentilhomme* (*The Would-be Gentleman*, 1670) with ballet music by Jean Baptiste Lully, *Les Femmes Savantes* (*The Learned Ladies*, 1672).

TRANSLATION: *Eight Plays* tr. Morris Bishop (New York 1957).

REFERENCES: R. Bray *Molière, homme de théâtre* (Paris 1954). P. Brisson *Molière: sa vie dans ses oeuvres* (Paris 1942). Lionel Gossman *Men and Masks: A Study of Molière* (Baltimore PB 1963). Jacques Guicharnaud ed. *Molière: A Collection of Critical Essays* (Englewood Cliffs, N.J. 1964, also PB). Will Grayburn Moore *Molière: A New Criticism* (1949, new ed. Oxford 1968, also PB). John Leslie Palmer *Molière: His Life and Work* (London and New York 1930, rev. ed. Denver, Colo. 1968). Arthur A. Tilley *Molière* (1921, reprinted New York 1968). Martin Turnell *The Classical Moment* (London 1947 and New York 1948).

✍

MOLIÈRE
BY MARTIN TURNELL

Molière was one of the most versatile as well as one of the greatest of comic dramatists. His work ranges from high comedy to the broadest farce. Many of the lesser plays like *Les Précieuses ridicules*, *L'École des maris* and *Le Bourgeois Gentilhomme* are a constant delight, but his immense reputation depends primarily on six masterpieces: *L'École des femmes*, *Tartuffe*, *Dom Juan*, *Le Misanthrope*, *L'Avare* and *Le Malade imaginaire*.

It was fashionable at one time to discover deep philosophical meanings in the plays. The reaction against this approach was led by Louis Jouvet, the greatest Molière actor of the century. In a lecture given in 1937 he delivered a frontal attack on what he called "the myth of Molière the moralist and philosopher," and insisted on the primacy of Molière the dramatist, who wrote to entertain. It is a good thing that somebody should remind the critics that plays are written to be acted, but like most reactions this one has probably gone too far.

In one of his *placets* or appeals to the king against the banning of *Tartuffe*, Molière himself declared that "the duty of Comedy is to correct men by entertaining them." Whether he was writing in his lightest or his most serious vein, he never lost sight of the dramatist's dual role. Of course he entertains us. Of course there is laughter in all the plays, but its nature varies according to the theme: there is the hearty carefree laughter of the farces, the subdued laughter of high comedy, and the very bitter laughter of *George Dandin*. For no great writer can be a pure entertainer, or be indifferent to his time. He is always a man endowed with *vision*. Comedy is simply a particular form of vision. What distinguishes it from tragedy is perhaps a basic optimism. The writer believes that he belongs to a stable order and that though human weaknesses spoil the fun, they are not mortal as they are in tragedy. It is a difference of ethos. In Molière "the imaginary cuckold" is a comic figure: in Lope de Vega and Calderón he is the monster who slaughters the innocent wife. Or compare the farcical ending of Molière's *Dom Juan* with the terrifying ending of the first of all the Don Juan plays: Tirso de Molina's *El Burlador de Sevilla*.

Molière was the great champion of the natural man and the implacable enemy of every form of convention or restraint which impeded or perverted the free development of personality. His main target was the bourgeoisie as the stuffiest and most restrictive section of society. The minor works make good-humored fun of individual foibles like preciosity or culture mongering which are absurd without being dangerous. In the great masterpieces foibles give place to vices, which if uncorrected could become a threat to society.

Long and solemn treatises have been written on Molière's personal beliefs. Whether he was a tepid believer or an out-and-out libertine, we shall never know. What is certain is that he was treated with extreme suspicion by the puritanical. *L'École des femmes* was widely regarded as an attack on Christian marriage. That was the start of the trouble. Much worse was to follow.

For Molière the cardinal vice of the age was hypocrisy or "imposture." *Tartuffe* was an attack on the sort of religious hypocrisy prevalent in the seventeenth century, and the protagonist was almost certainly based on a living model. The play was naturally interpreted as an attack on religion. Molière no doubt took an impish pleasure in baiting the "churchy," but it was not his principal aim. *Tartuffe* is an extraordinary sociological study of the effects not of religion, but of a decadent religiosity on the community. Molière does not show its effects on people in general. He chooses a particular unit and presents us with a picture of unsurpassed vividness of a prosperous middle-class family in the reign of Louis XIV. Each of the characters represents a different shade of religious opinion and is an essential strand in the pattern: Tartuffe himself with his hair shirt, his scourge, and his slimy manners; the foolish credulous Orgon; the puritanical mother; the urbane, reasonable brother; the worldly second wife, and the gorgeous servant. Like all the greatest creations the horrifying Tartuffe transcends the play: we meet his counterpart in every walk of life.

In spite of the switch from the middle classes to the aristocracy, *Dom Juan* is a companion piece: a study of a certain kind of arrogant unbelief which was as much a vice as the religiosity of *Tartuffe*. Molière obviously found his protagonist antipathetic, but there can be little doubt that he used him deliberately to ventilate provocative views which were not necessarily his own.

Le Misanthrope is the greatest of Molière's plays. It is also the most personal and the most difficult to interpret. On the surface it appears to be a comic story of the misfortunes of a man obsessed with the duty of plain speaking. Although it opens on a farcical note, it gradually sounds the deeper levels of perfidy or "imposture." For the perfidy attacked here is of the kind which warps and destroys one of the deepest of all human impulses: love. This in turn destroys the human being. Alceste, a partial portrait of the unhappily married dramatist, makes a bolt for the "desert."

Le Malade imaginaire is almost equally personal. It is an attack on another form of "imposture": the pretensions of doctors. The attack is scathing, but Argan is also a partial portrait of the sick Molière and Béralde of the healthy Molière trying to rally the sick Molière by demonstrating that his illnesses are "imaginary."

Molière is one of the greatest European dramatists because of his amazing insight into human nature, his vision of the contemporary scene, his superb dramatic skill, the extraordinary wit and vigor of his language, whether writing in verse or prose, and finally a joy in life which makes him endlessly stimulating and endlessly entertaining.

MOLNÁR, Ferenc (Jan. 12, 1878 – Apr. 1, 1952). Hungarian playwright and novelist. Born Budapest; of wealthy merchant family. Studied law at Budapest and Geneva universities, but never practiced; instead became a journalist. Achieved worldwide fame with a series of light, sophisticated comedies, beginning with *The Devil* (1907, tr. 1908) and including *Liliom* (1909, tr. 1921), his best work, source of Broadway musical *Carousel* (1945); *The Guardsman* (1910, tr. 1924); *The Swan* (1920, tr. 1929). Married actress Lili Darvas (1926). Moved to United States (1940), settling in New York, where he died. His novels, with the exception of *The Paul Street Boys* (1907, tr. 1927), proved less successful.

TRANSLATION: *The Plays of Ferenc Molnár* (New York 1929).

REFERENCES: Frank W. Chandler *Modern Continental Playwrights* (New York 1931). Emro J. Gergely *Hungarian Drama in New York: American Adaptations, 1908–1940* (Oxford and Philadelphia 1947).

MONDRIAN, Piet (Dutch name **Pieter Cornelis Mondriaan**) (Mar. 7, 1872 – Feb. 1, 1944). Dutch painter. Born Amersfoort. Having obtained two certificates for teaching drawing in state schools, he entered Academy of Fine Arts in Amsterdam (1892) and earned living as instructor and commercial artist while he explored various techniques in his still lifes, portraits, and landscapes. From 1908, was influenced by art nouveau and *fauvisme*; began painting in divisionist manner. In Paris (1912–14) came under influence of cubism, quickly evolving an independent, purely abstract variant, producing paintings composed entirely of horizontal and vertical strokes. In Holland on outbreak of war (1914), he remained there until 1919, when he returned to Paris. With Theo van Doesburg founded influential review *De Stijl* (1917); his articles therein and his treatise *Le Néoplasticisme* (1920) presented theory of painting in which the only elements used are horizontal and vertical lines, the three primary colors, and shades of black, white, and gray. Mondrian's principles, to which his own paintings from 1920 on conform, have exerted an incalculable influence on fine and applied arts of the twentieth century. He lived in London for two years (1938–40), then moved to New York, where he died.

REFERENCES: Frank Elgar *Mondrian* (tr. London and New York 1968).

Hans L. Jaffé *Mondrian* (New York 1969). Michel Seuphor *Piet Mondrian: Life and Work* (tr. New York and London 1956). L. J. F. Wijsenbeek *Mondrian* (tr. Greenwich, Conn. 1968 and London 1969).

MONET, Claude (Oscar) (Nov. 14, 1840 – Dec. 5, 1926). French painter. Born Paris; from 1845 in Le Havre. He worked there as a caricaturist and met Eugène Boudin, who persuaded him to paint landscapes. Moved to Paris (1859) and enrolled at Atelier Suisse, where he met Pissarro. After two years' military service in Algeria (1860–62), returned to Paris and entered Charles Gleyre's studio, where he met Renoir, Sisley, and Frédéric Bazille. Also knew Courbet, Cézanne, and Manet, who influenced his early paintings with their contrasts of light and dark: *Camille* (1866, Kunsthalle, Bremen) and *The Picnic* (1866, Pushkin Museum, Moscow). Began experimenting with new methods of capturing changing conditions of light and atmosphere, and started practice of painting outdoors. During Franco-Prussian War (1870–71) stayed in London and became influenced by Turner and Constable. Married his mistress Camille Doncieux (1870; she died 1879) and eventually settled in Argenteuil. In 1874 he and the new group of anti-academic painters held the famous exhibition where one of Monet's works, *Impression: Sunrise*, provided a hostile critic with the derogatory label of impressionism for the whole movement. Monet, considered the greatest of the impressionists, pursued his mastery of subtle gradations of light and color in such works as *Gare St. Lazare* series (1877, Louvre, Paris; Fogg Art Museum, Cambridge, Mass.). With Alice Hoschedé (whom he married, 1892) he settled at Giverny (1883) for rest of his life and, now accorded great acclaim, produced the famous series *Poplars* (1890), *Haystacks* (1891, two examples in Museum of Fine Arts, Boston), *Rouen Cathedral* (1892–95), *Mornings on the Seine* (1896–97), the *Thames* (1899–1904). From 1904 until his death he concentrated on the *Nymphéas* (water lilies), the late ones of which (1916, Musée de l'Orangerie, Paris), painted in shimmering colors, are considered to be the beginning of abstract art. Of Monet, Cézanne observed that he was "only an eye, but my God what an eye!"

REFERENCES: Raymond Cogniat *Monet and His World* (tr. London and New York 1966). Jean Leymarie *Monet* (2 vols. Paris 1964). Charles M. Mount *Monet: A Biography* (New York 1967). John Rewald *The History of Impressionism* (New York 1949, rev. ed. 1962). Denis Rouart and Léon Degand *Monet* (tr. New York 1958). William C. Seitz *Claude Monet* (New York and London 1960). Yvon Taillandier *Monet* (tr. New York 1963).

MONTAGU, Lady Mary Wortley (May 1689 – Aug. 21, 1762). English writer. Daughter of Evelyn Pierrepont, later duke of Kingston, she was born in London and baptized May 26. Married Edward Wortley Montagu, a Whig member of Parliament (1712); on his appointment to a post in the treasury (1714) the pair entered court circles, where Lady Mary's beauty and wit attracted much notice. Accompanied her husband on ambassadorial mission to Constantinople (1717–18), where she wrote the delightful Turkish letters. On her return introduced Turkish practice of smallpox inoculation to England. From 1715 was a friend of Pope, who with John Gay helped her compose *Town Eclogues* (pirated incomplete edition 1716, full edition 1747); she later quarreled with him and was frequently attacked in his satires. Leaving her husband and family (1739), Lady Mary settled on the Continent, living mainly in Italy until 1761. Died in London. She is best known for her letters (first published in 3 volumes, 1763), noted for graphic, informed descriptions of foreign lands, literary criticism, worldly wisdom, and entertaining and valuable gossip about famous contemporaries.

EDITIONS: *Letters and Works* ed. Lord Wharncliffe and W. Moy Thomas (4th ed. 2 vols. London 1893). *Complete Letters* ed. Robert Halsband (3 vols. Oxford 1965–67).

REFERENCES: Iris Barry *Portrait of Lady Mary Montagu* (Indianapolis and London 1928). Lewis S. Benjamin *Lady Mary Wortley Montagu: Her Life and Letters* (Boston and London 1925). Joseph W. Cove *The Admirable Lady Mary: The Life and Times of Lady Mary Wortley Montagu* (London and New York 1949). Robert Halsband *The Life of Lady Mary Wortley Montagu* (Oxford 1956 and New York 1960, also PB). Emily M. Symonds *Lady Mary Wortley Montagu and Her Times* (London and New York 1907).

MONTAIGNE, Michel Eyquem de (Feb. 28, 1533 – Sept. 13, 1592). French writer. Born at Château de Montaigne, near Bordeaux, into merchant family recently ennobled. He was taught to speak Latin before French as his native tongue; attended Collège de Guyenne at Bordeaux (1539–46), and subsequently studied law. While serving as a judge in Bordeaux (c.1555–70), met his only close friend, the humanist Étienne de La Boëtie, by whose death (1563) he was much affected. Married Françoise de La Chassaigne (1565). Montaigne's first publication was a translation of *Theologia Naturalis* of Raimond Sebond (1569). Resigning from his judicial post (1570), he retired to Montaigne, and from 1572 worked on his *Essays* (first edition of books I and II, 1580; final emended edition of books I, II, and III, 1595). A journey through Germany and Italy (1580–81) for his health is described in his *Journal du voyage* (discovered and published in 1774). Montaigne served as mayor of Bordeaux (1581–85) and occasionally as ambassador for Henry of Navarre. Died at Montaigne.

TRANSLATIONS: *Complete Works* tr. Donald M. Frame (Stanford, Calif. 1957 and London 1958). *Selected Essays of Montaigne in the Translation of John Florio* ed. Walter Kaiser (Boston 1964).

REFERENCES: Donald M. Frame *Montaigne's Discovery of Man* (New York and Oxford 1955), *Montaigne: A Biography* (New York and London 1965), and *Montaigne's Essais: A Study* (Englewood Cliffs, N.J. 1969). Virginia Woolf "Montaigne" in *The Common Reader* (London and New York 1925, also PB).

MONTAIGNE

BY WALTER KAISER

Perhaps no other author has left us so complete and vivid a portrait of himself as Michel de Montaigne. Even among artists, only Rembrandt has achieved his degree of dispassionate candor and penetrating honesty in self-delineation and, as a result, communicated so much of his essential being. Thus, though we readily acknowledge the charms of Montaigne's essays, the magnitude of their wisdom, and their abiding pertinence, what we remember best is the personality of the man who wrote them, and it is that personality, more than anything else, which has made his one of the best-loved books of all time.

Few of the world's great books have had a more casual birth than that of the *Essais*. When in 1571 Montaigne, having abandoned his legal career and courtly ambitions, retired to his estate, his avowed intention was merely to lead the leisured life of a country gentleman. A large part of that leisure he devoted to reading and "slippered contemplation," and, given his humanistic education and the fact that Latin was his first language, he naturally turned to the authors of classical antiquity. Almost by accident he began to keep a register of the thoughts such reading inspired — thoughts, he confesses, so orderless and purposeless that he wrote them down in the hope that one day they would be ashamed of themselves. Although these random jottings were to grow into his life's occupation, the informal, unpretentious quality of their origin continues to characterize them through three thick volumes, and in his own mind his written meditations were never more substantial or ambitious than the title he gave them: essays — that is to say, trials, attempts, experiments. The rambling, informal, vernacular style "of the marketplace" in which they are written, the absence of logical development which marks every essay, the constant digressions and contradictions and self-corrections, all reflect the author's unassertive purpose. "I do not teach," he insisted; "I recount." And his intention in the essays is no more than that, to recount what passes through his mind "from minute to minute" — his opinions, his conjectures, his doubts, his hopes, just as they come to him, however tentative, however inconclusive, however self-contradictory. "Myself I may contradict," he said; "the truth I do not."

Truth, indeed, is the perpetual goal of these essays, and he sought it wherever he thought it might lurk. When he first retired to his famous tower, Montaigne was attracted to the Stoic writers of antiquity. The earliest essays reflect his attempt to forge a moral philosophy out of their austere, exalted principles, but it was not long before he found such high-flown ideals somewhat terrifying, inaccessible, ultimately inhuman. "They want to get out of themselves and escape from the man," he concluded; "instead of changing into angels, they change into beasts." He recognized that his was neither an angel's conscience nor a horse's, but a man's, and he was content that it should be so. Abandoning the Stoics and the example of Cato the Younger, he turned instead to the more practical, humane wisdom of Plutarch and the intense dubieties of Sextus Empiricus. As Stoic idealism gave way to Pyrrhonic skepticism, he found that human reason, so praised by men like Seneca, was only an unreliable guide, a protean chimera with so many shapes that one could not catch hold of it; the experience of the senses, he concluded, was no different. Yet the deeply pessi-

mistic skepticism of this second phase of Montaigne's thought, the great document of which is his longest essay, *Apology for Raymond Sebond,* did not constitute his final vision of life. Rather, it freed him to accept a more positive, naturalistic vision, where nature became his guide and Socrates his hero. "The more simply we trust to nature, the more wisely we trust to her," he concludes, and a neo-Epicurean emphasis on the joys of existence comes flooding into the last essays. Realizing that "though we may mount on stilts, we still must walk on our own legs, and on the highest throne in the world we are still sitting only on our own bottom," he acknowledges human frailty and ignorance and urges us, in the end, to accept and follow our own nature; for "there is nothing so beautiful and legitimate as to play the man well and properly, no knowledge so difficult as to know how to live this life well and naturally, and the most savage of our maladies is to despise our own being."

This profound acceptance of his own humanity causes Montaigne, in the magnificent, symphonic essays of the third book, to return again and again to his true subject, himself — not out of any inflated self-esteem, but simply because, in a world where everything seemed uncertain and instable, that was the one thing he could best observe and understand. No author, he claimed, ever knew more about his subject than he did, since that subject was nothing other than himself. Though all of Montaigne's sorties in quest of truth start from the lofty edifices of ancient thought, they inevitably bring him back at last to his own humble threshold. If, as we read it, such extensive self-scrutiny seems so little egotistical, that is because Montaigne also realized that a book about one man was really a book about all men: that, as he memorably put it, "each man bears the entire form of the human condition." Because of this, as he went on year after year painting his own portrait for the reader, retouching, adding, correcting, registering every nuance of mood and thought, he managed, like Rembrandt, to confer upon his individual subject a universal significance. That is why, as Virginia Woolf has said, his self-portrait becomes, as we gaze into it, a mirror. That is also why it has attracted such a host of spectators over the years, who have seen there not merely Michel de Montaigne, not merely themselves, but the greater, profounder vision of what it means to be a man.

MONTESQUIEU, Charles Louis de Secondat, Baron de La Brède et de (Jan. 18, 1689 – Feb. 10, 1755). French philosopher and writer. Born Château de La Brède, near Bordeaux; of noble family of lawyers. Attended Oratorian Collège de Juilly (1700–1705); studied law in Bordeaux (1705–1708) and Paris (1708–13). Served in *parlement* of Bordeaux (1714–26). Married Jeanne de Lartigue (1715). From 1716 a member of Académie de Bordeaux, he devoted himself primarily to scientific researches during years preceding publication of his first literary success, *Persian Letters* (1721), a satirical portrait of French Regency society. Frequented the intellectual and social establishment of Paris between 1722 and 1728, year of his election to the Académie Française. After travels around the Continent (1728–29) and two years' residence in England (1729–31) spent most of his time at La Brède, pursuing the immense task of research and synthesis that resulted in *Considerations on the Causes of the Greatness of the Romans and Their Decline* (1734) and *The Spirit of the Laws* (1748), his efforts to show how the varying conditions of human experience generate laws, written and unwritten. Spent last years defending the latter work, censored by the Roman Catholic Church. Died in Paris.

TRANSLATIONS: *The Spirit of the Laws* tr. Thomas Nugent (latest ed. New York 1962, also PB). *Considerations . . .* tr. David Lowenthal (New York 1965, also PB). *Persian Letters* tr. J. Robert Loy (New York 1961, also PB).

REFERENCES: Joseph Dedieu *Montesquieu, l'homme et l'oeuvre* (Paris 1943). Émile Durkheim *Montesquieu and Rousseau* (tr. Ann Arbor, Mich. and London 1960, also PB). Henry J. Merry *Montesquieu's System of Natural Government* (Lafayette, Ind. 1969). Robert Shackleton *Montesquieu: A Critical Biography* (London 1961). Werner Stark *Montesquieu: Pioneer of the Sociology of Knowledge* (London 1960 and Toronto 1961).

✍

MONTESQUIEU
BY MORDECA JANE POLLOCK

Montesquieu is the slave of his image, cast for all time in a commemorative medal and reproduced for all time in all the textbooks. The learned magistrate appears in profile. His hair, toga, and aquiline nose are those of a Roman senator, a lawgiver of severe and noble countenance. But the medal suggests another age than Montesquieu's and the subject himself was less detached, more elegant, and more human.

Is this the author of the lethally frivolous *Persian Letters* and the social lion who wrote the erotic *Temple of Gnide*? Is this the man who conquered high society in Paris and London? The medal shows only the untroubled, official serenity of a man who has a monopoly on the truth. But the man's mind, his purpose, and his writings belie the image. For Montesquieu possessed the troubled lucidity of a compassionate man and a passionate researcher of facts.

France was falling apart and Montesquieu didn't like that. Montesquieu's youthful conceptions of right and wrong, justice and injustice were also at stake. To resolve this tension between his moral values and the facts of life, Montesquieu wrote the *Persian Letters*. In this brilliant and successful epistolary novel, two Persians make the long journey to France, and the ten years of their visit coincide with a breakdown in all domains of French life. Religious beliefs and piety, economic security, the good will and the good conduct of Frenchmen in public and private life are swiftly disintegrating. In letters they exchange with one another and in letters they write to friends at home, the two Persians discuss what they observe. They are by turns surprised, curious, critical, understanding, and indignant. One of them, Rica, describes the disturbingly funny pantomime of Parisian society, while the other, Usbek, speculates on the serious and profound issues at stake in what he has seen both at home and in France. But at the same time that the outsiders observe France, the reader has the pleasure of observing them. Usbek has left behind a harem full of wives along with a squadron of eunuchs to guard their chastity. While Usbek is writing with righteous wrath about the literal demoralization of French society, his wives are misbehaving with males, females, and eunuchs. Nobody in the novel is a hero. Neither Usbek nor the power merchants of French society realize that you can't run other people's lives for your own blind purposes, because people simply are not objects.

With the *Persian Letters*, Montesquieu did his countrymen the service of warning them that they were careering towards disaster. He also did them the service of bringing to maturity the epistolary novel in the French language. Montesquieu's handling of the genre lets us into the thoughts and preoccupations of the ten or so characters in his fiction: both the lucidity and the opacity of their minds play themselves out for the benefit of the reader. The benefit is double: the reader's opacity also comes into play, because the Persian outsiders tell the French what they really look like. What is more, the mosaic of the epistolary genre frees Montesquieu's indignation — as well as his doubts — from the chains of discursive language. He doesn't tell you that all is well in your household or that all is not well. You make your own decision and hopefully resolve to do a little better.

Montesquieu's writing of Roman history was also an act of liberation. By setting down the destiny of the Romans in clear and probing language, by using language to get to the root of things — the reasons why the Romans went to their own funeral — Montesquieu wanted to free his countrymen of the mistakes of their past and their present. When he wrote *The Spirit of the Laws*, Montesquieu acted upon his conviction that if we can find the deep causes that generate our laws, written and unwritten, if we can invest these causes with literary form and bring them into our consciousness, then we can free ourselves from blind destiny and guide our national destinies with a little bit of enlightenment and of sanity. With his escape from the dissertation form and from a linear fiction in the *Persian Letters*, Montesquieu had freed himself of the rigid values he had learned, and also of the totally skeptical attitude men and manners threatened to give him. So in *The Spirit of the Laws*, Montesquieu's refusal to write in Latin or in some adroit philosophical jargon carried through his desire to free his public from the theological version of the law and from the suspiciously clever viewpoint that might is right. Montesquieu's literary production — and that means his novel, his history, and his book on the laws — asserts the role of consciousness and free will in the most pressing realms of human experience — the way we live as families and as nations.

MONTEVERDI, Claudio (May 1567 – Nov. 29, 1643). Italian composer. Born Cremona, where he was baptized May 15. While a pupil of Marco Antonio Ingegneri, *maestro di cappella* of Cremona cathedral, he published his first work, a collection of sacred motets (1582). Spent twenty-two years in service of duke of Mantua (c.1590–1612); then from 1613 until his death was *maestro di cappella* at St. Mark's, Venice. Married Claudia Cattaneo, a singer (1599; she died 1607). Took holy orders (1632). Monteverdi's first opera, *Orfeo* (1607), was a success and is still performed. Other operas include *L'Arianna* (1608), from which only the famous *Lamento d'Arianna* survives; *Il Combattimento di Tancredi e Clorinda* (1624); *Il Ritorno d'Ulisse in patria* (1641); and his last and greatest opera *L'Incoronazione di Poppea* (1642). His madrigals appeared in nine collections (1587–1651). His religious music included three Masses and Vespers. He died in Venice.

REFERENCES: Denis Arnold *Monteverdi* (London and New York 1963). Denis Arnold and Nigel Fortune eds. *Monteverdi Companion* (London 1968). Henry Prunières *Monteverdi: His Life and Work* (tr. London 1926). Hans F. Redlich *Claudio Monteverdi: Life and Works* (tr. London and New York 1952). Leo Schrade *Monteverdi: Creator of Modern Music* (New York 1950 and London 1951, also PB).

✍

MONTEVERDI
BY ALAN CURTIS

Some composers are child prodigies, others are "late bloomers"; Monteverdi was both. While but a fifteen-year-old choirboy at Cremona, he was publishing motets with Gardano of Venice, one of the most distinguished music printers of Europe. His masterpiece, however, the incomparably fresh, vital and

passionate opera *L'Incoronazione di Poppea* was finished just in time for the Venetian carnival season of 1643, the year in which the seventy-six-year-old composer died.

He took his first permanent post at Mantua, starting around 1590 as *suonatore di vivuola* (an ambiguous term which may simply mean "violinist"). However, he seems to have worked mainly with singers; in fact, he married one in 1599. The most impressive musician already at the Gonzaga court was the noted vocal composer Giaches de Wert, who wrote the music to accompany a lavish production of *Il Pastor Fido* by Guarini in 1591. The performance was canceled, but Monteverdi would have learned much from the preparations; Guarini remained one of his favorite poets, as shown by the inclusion of many of his verses in the madrigal books from the third (1592) through to the last (1638), including the entire contents of the crucial Book V (1605).

His other court colleagues included Giovanni Gastoldi, Salomone Rossi, and Benedetto Pallavicino, whose death finally brought Monteverdi the position of *maestro di musica* in 1602. It had been a long wait. Monteverdi often rankled under the shabby treatment accorded their famous musicians by the Gonzagas, and his fame was growing fast. The fifth book of madrigals, the first to include the new *basso continuo*, the *stile concertato* (*Questi vaghi concenti*), and such sensuous, naturalistic, almost Caravaggesque compositions as *T'amo mia vita*, became known throughout Europe and was often reprinted. With his first opera, *La Favola d'Orfeo* (1607), in which he outdid the Florentines at their own invention, his reputation was established. He had brought the arcane new declamatory recitative to life, combining it with popular instrumental and vocal dances, madrigal choruses, etc., all in a superbly unified formal structure of simple and touching beauty.

Soon after the success of *Orfeo* came the shock of his wife's death, and he returned, in a state of collapse, to Cremona. The Mantuan court chronicler, coaxing his return for a new commission, wrote him that "this is the time to acquire the greatest fame which a man may have on earth, and all the gratitude of the Most Serene Prince." Undoubtedly counting more on the former than the latter, he did return. His enormous output of new music included the opera *L'Arianna*, now lost except for the beautiful lament. The title role was written for an eighteen-year-old with a magnificent voice, who had lodged with Monteverdi since her arrival five years earlier. Just before the premiere, she caught smallpox and died. For a second time Monteverdi retreated to Cremona. When commanded to return to Mantua, he replied, "I say that if I do not have a rest from working at music for the theatre my life will surely be short, for from my so considerable past labors I have been paid with a headache and itching so strong and rabid that neither cauteries nor cathartics nor bloodletting has made me better, and my father attributes the cause of my headache to overwork and the itching to the Mantuan air, which does not suit me, and suspects that the air alone will soon be the death of me."

The chance to be rid of the "Mantuan air" forever came in 1613, when the procurators of St. Mark's in Venice made a thorough, efficient, and intelligent search for a new *maestro di cappella*. Monteverdi was appointed at double his predecessor's salary, and he could later write that "there is no gentleman who does not esteem and honor me, and when I go and make a little music . . . I swear . . . the whole city runs to listen." What they heard was mostly church music, but of an unprecedented lavishness. Monteverdi headed what was probably the largest musical establishment in Italy, and there were not only Masses and motets required for St. Mark's but also music for special festivals at other churches and for state occasions. When Descartes in 1624 marveled at the annual Ascension Day celebration, with the doge in the golden *Bucintoro* sailing out to wed the Adriatic Sea, it was music by Monteverdi that he heard.

Somehow the maestro found time also to compose secular music, including such dramatic madrigals as *Lamento della Ninfa,* as well as ballets and even operas for patrons outside of Venice. At the end of an evening of madrigals in the Palazzo Mocenigo in 1624, he astonished the guests with a dramatic scene from Tasso, *Il Combattimento di Tancredi e Clorinda*. Because it was included in his *Madrigali guerrieri et amorosi* (1638), it happens to be preserved, but a vast amount of music, both sacred and secular, which he is known to have written while in Venice is now lost.

With the introduction of public opera in Venice in 1637, a new era of music history began. At first, Monteverdi sat in the wings, watching the efforts of younger colleagues or pupils such as Pier Francesco Cavalli, whose operas were a great success. Then the master himself entered the scene, cautiously, with a revival of *L'Arianna,* followed by *Le Nozze d'Enea* (now lost), *Il Ritorno d'Ulisse* (preserved only in a Viennese version probably much altered), and in final triumph, *L'Incoronazione di Poppea*.

While much revered in his lifetime, and not only in Italy, as the greatest composer of his day, less than half a century after his death Monteverdi was quite forgotten. With the rise of musical antiquarianism in the eighteenth and nineteenth centuries, he began again to be held in a certain chary respect, regarded as an important innovator but also as a destroyer of the Renaissance madrigal. This simpleminded attitude can be traced back to the literary controversy between a certain conservative composer-critic, Giovanni Maria Artusi, and Monteverdi's brother, who took up his defense. Today we would explain it simply as a generation gap, but it has taken many generations indeed to overcome the notion that Monteverdi singlehandedly slew, with malice aforethought, the valiant precepts of Renaissance polyphony. Even Verdi, so inherently vocal a composer, partook of the nineteenth-century penchant for Palestrina, advising students to avoid the study of Monteverdi's music because the part writing was bad!

Twentieth-century composers have had a less restricted view of what constitutes proper counterpoint and, perhaps in overcompensation, have scorned Artusi, archetype of the conservative critic, and rallied round Monteverdi, "the creator of modern music." In fact, Monteverdi has been championed by composers of the present more than almost any other composer of the past. Stravinsky has written: "I feel very close to him. But isn't he the first musician to whom we *can* feel very close? The scope of his music, both as emotion and architecture (parts of the same thing), is a new dimension compared to which the grandest conceptions, and the most estrual ardors and dolors of his predecessors, shrink to the status of miniatures. The man himself, in for instance Goretti's description of his habits of composing and conversation while at Parma, as well as in his own letters, with their moodiness, anxieties about shortage of time, complaints of migraines, sounds not only strikingly contemporary to me but even, if I may say so, rather *like* me."

MOORE, George (Augustus) (Feb. 24, 1852 – Jan. 21, 1933). Irish writer. Born Moore Hall, County Mayo, son of a member of Parliament. Educated at Oscott College, near Birmingham. Went to Paris (1873) to pursue career in art, enrolling in Académie Julian (1874). A cultivated dandy and frequenter of café society, he met most of the influential French painters and writers of the day. Returned to Mayo (1879) to manage his estate, spending part of each year in London. Moore adopted naturalist technique of Zola and the Goncourt brothers in his early novels, first of which was *A Modern Lover* (1883), followed by the more successful *A Mummer's Wife* (1885), and his best, *Esther Waters* (1894). Enthusiastic over the Irish Renaissance, he moved to Dublin and County Mayo (1899–1911), associating himself with W. B. Yeats, Lady Gregory, and others of the Abbey Theatre group. Began producing the work that he is most remembered for, the entertaining fictionalized autobiographical writings, valuable for their impressions of Paris café society and of the Irish Renaissance era: *Confessions of a Young Man* (1888), *Memoirs of My Dead Life* (1906), and the trilogy *Hail and Farewell*, comprising *Ave* (1911), *Salve* (1912), and *Vale* (1914). Returned to London (1911), where he lived the rest of his life. Later writings, highly stylized in contrast to early work, are interpretations of historical and legendary material, such as *The Brook Kerith* (1905) and *Héloise and Abelard* (1921).

REFERENCES: Malcolm J. Brown *George Moore: A Reconsideration* (Seattle 1955). Nancy Cunard *GM: Memories of George Moore* (London 1956). Joseph M. Hone *The Life of George Moore* (London and New York 1936). Charles Morgan *Epitaph on George Moore* (New York 1935). Graham Owens ed. *George Moore's Mind and Art* (Edinburgh 1968).

MOORE, Thomas (May 28, 1779 – Feb. 25, 1852). Irish poet. Born Dublin, son of a grocer. On graduating from Trinity College, Dublin (1799), went to London, where he entered Middle Temple and quickly won social and literary success with a translation, *Odes of Anacreon* (1800). Appointed registrar of the admiralty court at Bermuda (1803), he soon assigned his post to a deputy, and after a tour of United States and Canada returned to London (1804). After publishing *Epistles, Odes and Other Poems* (1806), brought out first series of *Irish Melodies* (1807–34), poems set to airs which he called "traditional" but which were mainly of the eighteenth century. These songs, his best-known works, secured his fame as an Irish national poet. Married Irish actress Bessie Dyke (1811). Became close friend of Byron, whom he visited during sojourn on Continent (1819–22). On return, settled at Sloperton Cottage, Wiltshire, where he died. Other works include the widely famous Oriental romance *Lalla Rookh* (1817), satires *The Twopenny Postbag* (1813), *The Fudge Family in Paris* (1818) and *The Fudges in England* (1835), his edition of *The Letters and Journals of Lord Byron*, which includes his life of Byron (1830), and his own *Memoirs*, edited by Lord John Russell (1853–56).

REFERENCES: Howard Mumford Jones *The Harp That Once — A Chronicle of the Life of Thomas Moore* (New York 1937). Seamus MacCall *Thomas Moore* (London 1935). L. A. G. Strong *The Minstrel Boy: A Portrait of Tom Moore* (London and New York 1937). Wilbraham F. Trench *Tom Moore* (Dublin 1934).

MORE, Hannah (Feb. 2, 1745 – Sept. 7, 1833). English writer. Born Stapleton, Gloucestershire, where her father was a schoolmaster. Became first a pupil, then a teacher, at a boarding school in Bristol kept by her three elder sisters, with whom she lived, unmarried, throughout most of her life. From 1773, spent much time in London, where she associated with David Garrick, Johnson, Burke, Reynolds, and the bluestockings, including Hester Thrale, and where, through Garrick's support, her plays *The Inflexible Captive* (1774) and *Percy* (1777) were successfully staged. Turning to religion and philanthropy, she retired from London to the countryside near Bristol, produced a series of widely read religious tracts, and founded schools and societies aimed at increasing literacy and piety among the poor. Her didactic novel *Coelebs in Search of a Wife* (1808) became enormously popular in England and the U.S. Her letters (published 1834) are highly readable. She died at Clifton.

REFERENCES: Mary A. Hopkins *Hannah More and Her Circle* (New York 1947). Mary G. Jones *Hannah More* (Cambridge, England, 1952, new ed. Westport, Conn. 1968).

MORE, Sir Thomas (Feb. 7, 1478 – July 6, 1535). English humanist. Born London, son of an eminent judge. Educated at St. Anthony's School, London, and in household of John Morton, archbishop of Canterbury; after two years at Oxford (c.1492–c.1494), studied law in London. While pursuing legal and public career (he entered Parliament in 1504), More continued Greek and Latin studies and formed friendships with Erasmus (who visited England in 1498) and other humanists. Married Jane Colt (1504 or 1505); they had four children. After her death (1511), he married a widow, Alice Middleton. Following death of Henry VII (1509), More rose to great prominence as public servant. He attracted attention of Henry VIII, becoming privy councillor and master of requests (1517), under-treasurer (1521), speaker of House of Commons (1523), and after fall of Wolsey, Lord Chancellor (1529). Steadfastly opposed to king's claim to supreme authority over the church, he resigned chancellorship (1532), refused to take oath of supremacy (1534), was imprisoned for a year, tried and convicted of treason, and beheaded, in London. A contemporary characterized him as "a man for all seasons." He was beatified (1886) and canonized (1935). More's masterpiece, *Utopia* (published in Latin, 1516), describes an imaginary commonwealth governed entirely by reason. Other writings, in Latin and

English, include *History of Richard III* (1513), anti-Lutheran tracts, and devotional works.

EDITION: *Complete Works* (Yale Edition, New Haven, Conn. 1963–   ).

REFERENCES: Russell Ames *Citizen Thomas More and His Utopia* (1949, reprinted New York 1969). Robert Bolt *A Man for All Seasons: A Play of Sir Thomas More* (New York 1963 PB and London 1964). Raymond W. Chambers *Thomas More* (London and New York 1935, also PB). Jack H. Hexter *More's Utopia: The Biography of an Idea* (Princeton, N.J. and Oxford 1952, PB 1965). Robbin S. Johnson *More's Utopia: Ideal or Illusion* (New Haven, Conn. 1969). William Nelson ed. *Twentieth Century Interpretations of Utopia* (Englewood Cliffs, N.J. 1968, also PB). Rainer Pineas *Thomas More and Tudor Polemics* (Bloomington, Ind. 1968). Ernest E. Reynolds *St. Thomas More* (London 1953 and New York 1954) and *The Field Is Won: The Life and Death of Saint Thomas More* (London 1968).

MOREAU, Gustave (Apr. 6, 1826 – Apr. 18, 1898). French painter. Born Paris, son of an architect. Studied at École des Beaux Arts, where under influence of Théodore Chassériau he developed his own symbolist style. His work also reflects admiration of Delacroix and Ingres. First picture shown at Salon was *Pietà* (1852). His favorite subjects are Biblical and mythological fantasies, exotically detailed with sumptuous trappings and mysterious lighting. His sense of magic makes his work a source of surrealism. He is chiefly known, however, as the teacher (at École des Beaux Arts, 1892–98) of Matisse, Rouault, and other painters eventually members of Fauves group. Made chevalier (1875) and officer (1883) of Légion d'Honneur. On his death in Paris, Moreau left his house and some eight thousand paintings and drawings to the state as a museum.

REFERENCES: Ragnar von Holten *L'Art fantastique de Gustave Moreau* (Paris 1960). John Rewald and others *Odilon Redon, Gustave Moreau, Rodolphe Bresdin* (New York 1962).

MÖRIKE, Eduard (Friedrich) (Sept. 8, 1804 – June 14, 1875). German poet and novelist. Born Ludwigsburg, Württemberg. Studied theology at Tübingen (1822–26), and after eight years as itinerant country curate settled at village of Cleversulzbach, Württemberg, as pastor (1834). Retired due to ill health (1843), but from time of his marriage to Margarete von Speeth (1851) until 1866 earned his living as lecturer in German literature at a girls' school in Stuttgart. Mörike's small literary output is noted for its variety. His best works are Gedichte (1838; augmented editions 1848, 1856, 1867), lyric poems in the romantic tradition, considered by some critics as surpassed only by those of Goethe. He also wrote narrative poems, ballads in folk song style, fairy tales, the romantic novel *Maler Nolten* (1832), and short stories, including *Mozart auf der Reise nach Prag* (1855). When he died, in Stuttgart, Mörike was little known; widespread recognition came when Hugo Wolf set some of his poems to music.

TRANSLATION: *Poems* tr. N. K. Cruickshank and G. F. Cunningham (London 1959).

REFERENCE: Margaret L. Mare *Edward Mörike: The Man and the Poet* (London and New York 1957).

MORISOT, Berthe (Jan. 14, 1841 – Mar. 2, 1895). French painter. Born Bourges, great-granddaughter of Honoré Fragonard. Dissatisfied with early classical training, she became pupil of Corot (1862–68). Met Edouard Manet (c.1869), who used her often as model and who exerted strong influence on her art, while she in turn urged him to paint outdoors and use light colors. She married his brother Eugène (1874), the year the impressionists, whom she joined from the beginning, held their famous exhibition. By 1879 she evolved her own style, closer to the impressionism of Renoir than to style of Manet, her subjects usually women and children and outdoor scenes, painted with freshness, delicacy, and acute sense of play of light. There are numerous examples of her work in the museums of Paris, Washington, D.C. (National Gallery), Chicago, Boston, London (Tate). Her letters and journals provide valuable records of history of impressionism. She died in Paris.

TRANSLATION: *Correspondence* ed. Denis Rouart and tr. Betty W. Hubbard (2nd ed. London 1960).

REFERENCES: Monique Angoulvent *Berthe Morisot* (Paris 1933). Ira Moskowitz ed. *Berthe Morisot: Drawings, Pastels, Watercolors, Paintings* (New York and London 1960). John Rewald *The History of Impressionism* (rev. ed. New York 1961, also PB).

MORLEY, Thomas (1557–c.1603). English composer. Little is known of his life. A pupil of William Byrd, he took a degree in music at Oxford (1588), became organist at St. Paul's Cathedral (1591), and a Gentleman of the Chapel Royal (1592). Published his *Canzonets* (1593), followed by madrigal collection (1594), the gay *Balletts* (1595), and *First Book of Consort Lessons* (1599) for instrumental sextet. His liturgical compositions include four services, responses, burial anthems, ten motets, psalms, and five anthems. He is author of the song *It was a lover and his lass* (published in *First Book of Airs,* 1600) for Shakespeare's *As You Like It.* Considered among the greatest of English madrigalists, his compositions are sprightly, deft and graceful, and include the celebrated *April is in my mistress' face* and *Since my tears and lamenting.* From 1598 he held a license to print songbooks and music paper, publishing his own and others' work. He also wrote one of the first English treatises on music, *A Plaine and Easie Introduction to Practicall Musicke* (1597, reprinted London 1952), an invaluable work on modal music. Believed to have married twice. He died in London.

REFERENCES: E. H. Fellowes *The English Madrigal Composers* (1921, 2nd ed. New York 1948) and *The English Madrigal* (1925, 3rd ed. London 1947). Catherine Murphy *Thomas Morley: Editions of Italian Canzonets and Madrigals* (Gainesville, Fla. 1964).

MORRIS, William (Mar. 24, 1834 – Oct. 3, 1896). English poet and craftsman. Born Walthamstow, Essex, son of well-to-do businessman. Educated at Marlborough (1848–51) and at Essex College, Oxford (1853–55), where he formed lifelong friendship with Edward Burne-Jones, a fellow medievalist. Settled in London (1856) as a painter and member of D. G. Rossetti's Pre-Raphaelite circle. His first volume of verse, *The Defence of Guenevere and Other Poems* (1858), had small success. Married Jane Burden (1859). The project of decorating and furnishing Red House, his new home at Upton, Kent, led to his founding (1861) a firm which eventually produced furniture, stained glass, tapestries, carpets, wallpaper, and textiles. Later he established the Kelmscott Press (1890), designing type and decorations for a series of books of which the finest was the 1896 *Chaucer.* Morris's work in the decorative arts had great effect on Victorian taste. His popular writings are the long narrative poems *The Life and Death of Jason* (1867) and *The Story of Sigurd the Volsung* (1877); *The Earthly Paradise* (1868–70), a collection of classical and medieval tales in verse; but his prose stories *A Dream of John Ball* (1888) and *News from Nowhere* (1891) and his collected essays and lectures are more vital. From 1884 he was active in the Socialist League, lecturing, writing, and organizing in its service as well as editing and financing its journal, *Commonweal.* Died at Hammersmith, London.

EDITION: *Collected Works* (24 vols. New York 1966).

REFERENCES: R. Page Arnot *William Morris: The Man and the Myth* (London and New York 1964). Paul Bloomfield *William Morris* (London 1934). Philip Henderson *William Morris: His Life, Work and Friends* (London and New York 1967). John W. Mackail *The Life of William Morris* (1899, reprinted London 1950 and 2 vols. New York 1968). May Morris *William Morris: Artist, Writer, Socialist* (1936), new ed. 2 vols. New York 1966). Edward P. Thompson *William Morris: Romantic to Revolutionary* (London 1955 and New York 1962). Paul R. Thompson *The Work of William Morris* (London and New York 1967). Ray Watkinson *William Morris as Designer* (London and New York 1967).

☞

WILLIAM MORRIS
BY LEWIS MUMFORD

To understand the life and work of William Morris, one must realize that his career began under the influence of the eighteenth-century Gothic Revival (Walpole, Chatterton, Blake) and came to a climax in the more robust Victorian setting of the Medieval Renaissance. In the first phase, he was spurred by his friendship while at Oxford with Dante Gabriel Rossetti, who awakened his interest in painting and so started him on his career as decorator and designer and master craftsman. This cup of friendship unfortunately held poison at the bottom, for Jane Burden, the girl Morris married, so quickened Rossetti's erotic dreams that she became his favorite model — in a relation close enough to corrode Morris's marriage.

The Medieval Renaissance, it is time to recognize, presents a close parallel to the Greco-Roman rebirth of the sixteenth century. Like the earlier movement, it was an attempt to bring back for conscious emulation the neglected manuscripts, books, paintings, and buildings of a vital and significant period. In contrast to the more formal aristocratic concerns of the Italian Renaissance, this Victorian movement sought to do justice to the popular arts and crafts of the high Middle Ages. This tradition had been cast aside by the classic humanists as barbarous and uncouth, and was now being ground out of existence by the advances of a materialistic civilization, committed to profit, power, and mechanical progress.

Morris had been awakened as a boy of eight to the wonder of Canterbury Cathedral; and the same passion that had led earlier poets to recover the folk ballads roused his admiration for the constructive arts of the Middle Ages.

John Ruskin's *The Stones of Venice* laid the solid foundation for Morris's lifework, both as a master craftsman and as a passionate critic of the existing industrial order. Ruskin's chapter "On the Nature of the Gothic" remained, in effect, his Bible. Though Morris had many colleagues and co-workers in the Medieval Renaissance, he became the dominant figure. Like Blake, he consciously linked his own vision of life with that of Geoffrey Chaucer.

Morris's career as poet opened with his first and best collection of verse, *The Defence of Guenevere and Other Poems*, in 1858: poems as sharp and vivid as the illuminations in a medieval manuscript, as magical as Keats's *La Belle Dame Sans Merci;* written as if by an eyewitness, indeed, one to the medieval manor born. But the feudal dreamworld of Morris, with its passionate loves, its desperate sorrows, its violent deaths, belongs to the Gothic Revival rather than to the more realistic Victorian Renaissance. Only toward the end of Morris's life, with his conversion to socialism, did he, in *The Dream of John Ball*, embrace the humbler world of rebellious peasants and urban craftsmen. Though most of Morris's poems in the anthologies come from his earliest volume, including such vivid embroideries as *Golden Wings*, George Moore's favorite, his first verses had little contemporary appeal, except to Browning and Swinburne. But they later influenced William Butler Yeats, who knew Morris in person in the Eighties.

Morris's copious output as a writer was partly due to his facility, already evident in adolescence, for turning his romantic daydreams into verse; and partly it was due to a need to ease the tormenting emotional pressures that developed in his marriage. With the publication in 1868 of his *The Earthly Paradise*, a series of ancient fables and fantasies, done over into easy, sleepy rhythms, with the coarse or unseemly passages in the original tales softened for reading aloud in the Victorian family circle, he achieved his first popular success.

Morris's own appetite for reality was not satisfied by these verses, or by his later prose romances, equally escapist. So in the Seventies he turned to the Norse sagas and sought, with the aid of an Icelandic scholar, to popularize, in translation, these harsher Northern equivalents of Homer. Here, as in his own translation of the Odyssey, he expressed his personal dislike for the "softer" Latin and Greek mind by using Anglo-Saxon words, inventing archaic turns of phrase, willfully clumsy, defiantly obscure. Though this part of Morris's writing still has its admirers, even his favorite *Volsung Saga* does not validate his method or justify his hopes.

William Morris's high standing as a writer derives not from his later poems and prose romances, but from his original reflections on the decorative and constructive arts in relation to modern society. Here his genius was indisputable, and the literary consequences of his industrial and political activities place him on the level of such Victorian masters as Newman, Arnold, and Ruskin. Like the great artists of the earlier Renaissance, Morris did not confine himself to a single specialized area: he was equally at home in glass, textiles, wallpaper, and typography. In all these departments, he led the counterattack against Victorian stuffiness, vulgarity, and commercialism.

Paradoxically, this backward-looking mind, who yearned for the medieval past, produced nothing but forward-looking disciples; for those who were most deeply influenced by Morris's spirit, with its insistence on simplicity, honesty, respect for materials and processes, above all, on the joy of handwork, became, like W. R. Lethaby and Barry Parker, the exponents of a humanized functionalism in the generation that followed. Morris's famous dictum, "Have nothing in your home that you do not know to be useful or believe to be beautiful," became the cornerstone of the new aesthetic.

It is this Morris, the master craftsman and designer, the seasoned historian of pre-machine technology in all its phases, at home with the Chinese potter, the Javanese weaver, the Persian rug maker, as well as with their medieval counterparts, whose literary achievements remain undiminished by time and change of taste. Toward the end of his life, he summed up his observations and his convictions in a series of essays, lectures, and speeches, to which his utopia, *News From Nowhere*, serves as a kind of neomedieval illumination. Even if every Morris print and wallpaper and tapestry should be lost, and if all his verses should vanish, the essential Morris would still be present in this robust, downright prose, whose style, in the rhythm of the spoken word, is free from studied quaintness or Nordic affectation. Here, too, is the mature Morris, whose passionate concern for joy in work, and justice in apportioning the rewards of work, led him to socialism: he wished to create a common environment of beauty, accessible to all, not a secluded aesthetic shelter for the privileged classes. While Morris came to understand the advantages of power-driven machines and approved their promise to lift the burden of depressing and unrewarding toil, he had no use for those who would sacrifice the pleasures of personal creativity to a trivial round of push-button duties, empty leisure, and consumptive gluttony.

Morris's utopia, *News from Nowhere*, was a projection of the life he had actually lived, collectively magnified, idealized, and universalized. For all its charm, this utopia remains too placidly innocent of the struggles and torments of his own life, too sanguine about overcoming the inertia of institutions and the recalcitrance and malignity of those in power, too unaware of human irrationality and perversity, to be either a credible picture of a happier future or a useful guide to it. But there was a deeper Morris who foresaw better than the conscious, Marx-guided revolutionary what actually lay ahead. This Morris sometimes revealed himself in his letters, and best of all, perhaps, in his coda to *The Dream of John Ball.* "Men fight and lose the battle, and the thing that they fought for comes about in spite of their defeat, and when it comes, turns out not to be what they meant, and other men have to fight for what they meant under another name." If ours is a generation that has learned this salutary truth, it may be ready to discover what Morris meant by linking the joy of work and the love of beauty to comradeship, friendship, and passionate sexual love.

MOZART, Wolfgang Amadeus (christened Johannes Chrysostomus Wolfgangus Theophilus) (Jan. 27, 1756 – Sept. 5, 1791). Austrian composer. Born Salzburg, son of Leopold Mozart, court composer and assistant kapellmeister to archbishop there. Leopold trained the child prodigy, who began composing at five, and took him at six with his virtuoso older sister Maria Anna on series of concert tours in major European cities and courts (1762–69). In 1768 Mozart composed his first operas, *Bastien und Bastienne* and, for Maria Theresa's son, the future Joseph II, *La Finta semplice*. After visiting Salzburg, Paris, and Munich in search of court positions (1773–79), he

returned to Salzburg as court organist to new Archbishop Colloredo. In Munich (1780–81), Mozart's production there of opera *Idomeneo* initiated period of his most prodigal achievement. Other operas followed: *Die Entführung aus dem Serail* (*The Abduction from the Seraglio,* 1782), *Le Nozze di Figaro* (*The Marriage of Figaro,* 1786), *Don Giovanni* (1787), *Così fan Tutte* (1790), *Die Zauberflöte* (*The Magic Flute,* 1791). He also wrote forty-one symphonies, over twenty concertos for clavier, innumerable chamber works in a variety of forms, church music including Masses and the *Requiem* which death prevented him from finishing. Having left the service of the archbishop (1781), he settled in Vienna for rest of his life. Met Haydn there who influenced his work, and married Constanze Weber (1782). The tragic early deaths of four of their six children and financial difficulties, little relieved by minor appointment to Joseph II (1787), darkened his last years, though his genius and energy continued undiminished.

REFERENCES: Eric Blom *Mozart* (London and New York 1935, also PB). Marcia Davenport *Mozart* (1932, rev. ed. New York 1956, also PB). Otto E. Deutsch *Mozart: A Documentary Biography* (tr. London and Stanford, Calif. 1965). Alfred Einstein *Mozart: His Character, His Work* (tr. London and New York 1945, also PB). C. M. Girdlestone *Mozart and His Piano Concertos* (London and Norman, Okla. 1948, also PB). Robert B. Moberly *Three Mozart Operas* (London and New York 1968). H. C. Robbins Landon and Donald Mitchell *The Mozart Companion* (1956, also PB). Walter J. Turner *Mozart: The Man and His Works* (1938, rev. ed. New York and London 1966, also PB).

✍

WOLFGANG AMADEUS MOZART
BY FRANK KERMODE

If you like to generalize about genius, avoid Mozart. His life is well documented — he was a European celebrity at the age of six, and a pretty copious letter writer — but there is little that suggests a man of intellectual or moral distinction. Like his friend Haydn, he showed, in conversation, "absolutely no sign of unusual power of intellect, and almost no trace of culture." This, the testimony of an admirer, is supported by Ludwig Tieck's memory of the composer as "small, rapid of movement, and with a stupid expression." The portraits, though all poor, bear out the last phrase. The powers which made Mozart part of our idea of human greatness were exhibited in one trade alone.

In this trade he followed his father Leopold, a man of superior formal education, who dropped out of the law and the church into this more menial occupation, and settled in Salzburg as a servant of the archbishop's court: teacher, minor composer, minor gentleman, uneasy in his social position, sometimes neglecting his duty to his patron, but always utterly devoted to the brilliant son whose quarrels with Archbishop Colloredo have preserved the name of the prelate as his own talents could not have done.

As the greatest of infant prodigies, Wolfgang suffered a celebrity out of proportion to his prospects. Virtuoso and composer, he was fated to a childhood of exhausting travel and ceaseless public exhibition. Before he was ten he had traveled to France and England; at fourteen he was a papal knight, entitled, like Haydn (who availed himself of the privilege), to call himself Chevalier. But if he could look back to the days when he sat on the knee of Maria Theresa, he had few comforts to look forward to. Not that he was ever less than famous; he died in semipoverty, but the world showed much concern. Though he grew more and more privately absorbed in a world of music where there were few or no companions, he accepted his kind of life in a commonplace manner, striking gentlemanly attitudes, worrying about money,

flirting, writing pointlessly obscene letters. His relationship with his father, strengthened by music, was often under pressure — he was scolded for his fecklessness and selfishness — and once broke down altogether; but this is normal enough. And he got over his disappointments in Paris, and the insults of the archbishop, who placed him at table between the valets and the cooks and had him literally kicked out by the court marshal. He was cheerful in a marriage that emerged from his muddled relationship with the Weber family, and was not all it should have been; he withstood the fickleness of the Viennese public for ten years, and wrote his greatest music for them. He was always dancing to somebody else's tune: always an entertainer, a showman even.

But in his own world language was not the vehicle of commands or insults; it was music, founded of course on the music of the day, but developed, as a language, to the point where only he could speak it, though others might partially understand. He told his father he was a composer, not a teacher or an entertainer; he meant to explore the possibilities of that language with an increasing intensity of study. He could learn from Haydn (as Haydn from him) and from Bach (here was music he had to *write down*); the series of quartets dedicated to Haydn, and the finale of the *Jupiter Symphony*, show what he learned. But not even in the almost revolutionary D minor clavier concerto did he altogether lose touch with the expectations and powers of a Viennese audience. In our time we should admire those powers, which were stretched but not defeated by an avant-garde genius.

Mozart, a keyboard virtuoso and connoisseur of virtuosos, probably never played a piano of the kind Beethoven used, and perhaps for that reason he wrote little of his best music for the solo clavier. Nor is his church music, except for the *Requiem* (his last work) among the things we best remember. When we exclude also the great mass of occasional music, for strings, wind bands, and so on — full of delights, but not the foundation of one's awed respect — we are left with the handful of great symphonies, a dozen chamber works, half a dozen clavier concertos, and, above all, the operas. What these works have in common, diverse as they are, is the Mozartian unity in complexity, their civil acceptance, and with it their intensive development of a common idiom. Orchestral players sometimes complained of the demands he made, but Mozart performed the D minor concerto without considerable rehearsal, and to an immediately pleased audience. This innovator, though of fantastic power, needed no revolutionary break with his contemporaries.

So with the operas; leaving out *opera seria* we have five masterpieces of the utmost originality, two German and three Italian. There had to be pre-existing forms, singers of the necessary kind (especially sopranos); and there had to be a suitable audience. For all that, the operas are personal, unique, even in their parodic and ironic elements. We may think to find in *Don Giovanni* some reflection of the tension in Mozart between the conventional morality of the man and the musician's powerful intuition of the tragedy and irony inherent in natural sexuality. Elvira is wonderfully endowed with music; but is it she who is too tragic for the occasion, or is the occasion too trivial for Mozart? Or one thinks of the marvelous *Così fan tutte* — the considered overstatement of *Come scoglio* and the duet between Ferrando and Fiordiligi, comic in situation, utterly

serious about the flowering of sexual attraction, so that few operatic surrenders match the authenticity of Fiordiligi's "Do with me what you will," though the context is ostensibly jocular. In Mozart music dissolves the boundaries of comedy and tragedy, buffoonery and heroism.

When he wrote *Così* and *Die Zauberflöte* he was a full man in the only way that counts. He had not long to live, and partly knew it, and he wrote endlessly, composing the music of a classic "final period" in his early thirties. Henceforth music was no longer a toy of the Colloredos. But, as a biographer remarked in his own time — he was complaining that even then an "unpracticed ear" could find Mozart difficult to follow — "it is fortunate that he attained to perfection when still young, and among the pleasing and pleasant Viennese Muses." Otherwise he might have grown hermetic; and for all the inwardness of his musical thought he never did, remaining always lucid and, when he chose, profound.

————————

MUIR, Edwin (May 15, 1887 – Jan. 3, 1959). Scottish writer. Born Deerness, Orkney Islands, son of a farmer. Moved to Glasgow, and at fourteen became clerk in a law office. Became a socialist, then (until he began writing poetry at thirty-five) a Nietzschean. Married Willa Anderson (1919) and went to London, became assistant editor of the *New Age,* later after travels in Europe coeditor of the *European Quarterly* (1934). Collaborated with his wife on translations from the German, including Kafka, which first made him known. Published *First Poems* (1925), *Chorus of the Newly Dead* (1926), *Variations on a Time Theme* (1934), *Journeys and Places* (1937), *The Voyage* (1946), *The Labyrinth* (1949), and *One Foot in Eden* (1956); his *Collected Poems 1921–1951* (1952) was expanded to *Collected Poems 1921–1958* (1960). His poetry is metaphysical, yet simple and direct in diction. After working for

British Council in Edinburgh during World War II, he became director of the British Institute in Prague (1945–48) and in Rome (1949–50); warden of Newbattle Abbey College, near Edinburgh (1950–55); Charles Eliot Norton professor of poetry at Harvard (1955–56). He died in Cambridge, England. Also noted for his works of criticism: *Latitudes* (1924), *Transition* (1926), *The Structure of the Novel* (1928), and *Essays on Literature and Society* (1949). He is the author of three novels, including *The Three Brothers* (1931), and his autobiography *The Story and the Fable* (1954).

REFERENCES: Peter H. Butter *Edwin Muir: Man and Poet* (Edinburgh 1966 and New York 1967). J. C. Hall *Edwin Muir* (London 1956). Daniel G. Hoffman *Barbarous Knowledge: Myth in the Poetry of Yeats, Graves, and Muir* (New York 1967). Willa Muir *Belonging: A Memoir* (London 1968).

MUNCH, Edvard (Dec. 12, 1863 – Jan. 23, 1944). Norwegian artist. Born Loyten; brought up in Oslo, where he attended State School of Art and Handcraft and joined bohemian painters whose naturalistic works were causing a stir. Frequent visits to Paris (1889–92) brought him in contact with post-impressionism and symbolism. Influence of Gauguin in particular is evident in his most famous painting, *The Cry* (1893, National Gallery, Oslo), and in *The Voice* (1893, Museum of Fine Arts, Boston), *Girls on the Bridge* (c.1899, National Gallery, Oslo), and other works of the period. While living in Germany, Munch gained immediate fame when the paintings he showed at Verein Berliner Künstler exhibition (1892) caused its closing. In Paris (1896) he joined the Nabis and group around Mallarmé, and exhibited *Frieze of Life* at Salon des Indépendants (1897). Lived in Germany until 1908, when he suffered a nervous breakdown, returning to Norway (1909) after stay in Copenhagen sanitarium. From 1916 settled at Ekely, estate outside Oslo, where he died. In his work before 1908, Munch expressed with forceful emotion his own psychic torments, man's universal terror, loneliness, and anxiety. His themes, symbolic use of color, and

linear patterns, especially in his lithographs and woodcuts, exerted enormous influence on German expressionism.

REFERENCES: Frederick B. Deknatel *Edvard Munch* (New York 1950). Johan Langaard and Reidar Revold *Edvard Munch* (tr. New York 1964) and *A Year by Year Record of Edvard Munch's Life: A Handbook* (Oslo 1961). Arve Moen *Edvard Munch: Graphic Art and Paintings* (3 vols. Oslo 1956–58). Werner Timm *The Graphic Art of Edvard Munch* (tr. Greenwich, Conn. 1969).

MUNRO, Hector Hugh. *See* **SAKI.**

MURILLO, Bartolomé Esteban (1617 – Apr. 3, 1682). Spanish painter. Baptized in Seville (Jan. 1, 1618). Apprenticed (1629) to painter Juan del Castillo, he was working independently by 1639, supporting himself by painting small religious pictures for export to South America. Visited Madrid (c.1648), evidently knew Velázquez. From 1645, the year also of his marriage to Beatriz de Cabrera y Sotomayor, Murillo was the most sought after religious painter in Seville, receiving numerous commissions from churches, convents, and monasteries. Founded Seville Academy of Painting (1660). Died in Seville. His religious paintings, known for their sweetness and warmth, soft "misty" atmosphere, and charming touches of realism, enjoyed enormous popularity throughout Europe during his own lifetime and in eighteenth and early nineteenth centuries. Also painted genre scenes, of which the best known are picturesque beggar boys, and excellent portraits. Among his major works: *Birth of the Virgin* (Louvre, Paris), *Knight of the Collar* (Prado, Madrid), *Flight into Egypt* (c.1645, Institute of Art, Detroit), *Grape and Melon Eaters* (Prado), *Girl and Her Duenna* (c.1670) and *Return of the Prodigal Son* (both National Gallery, Washington, D.C.), *Madonna and Child* (1673, Walker Art Gallery, Liverpool).

REFERENCES: A. F. Calvert *Murillo* (London and New York 1907). Charles B. Curtis *Velázquez and Murillo* (London and New York 1883). Santiago

Montoto *Murillo* (Barcelona 1932). G.
C. Williamson *Murillo* (London 1902).

MUSIL, Robert, Edler von (Nov. 6,
1880 – Apr. 15, 1942). Austrian novelist. Born Klagenfurt, son of a professor
of engineering. Educated at military
school, then studied engineering and
philosophy. After success of his first
novel, *Die Verwirrungen des Zöglings
Törless* (1906, tr. *Young Torless* 1955),
a study of adolescence, he gave up lectureship in civil engineering for writing. Married (1911) Martha Marcovaldi
(née Heimann). After working as librarian, then editor, and serving in
Austrian army (1914–18) and as civil
servant (1919–22), settled in Vienna
as full-time writer. Published two collections of short stories, *Vereinigungen*
(1911) and *Drei Frauen* (1924), masterly studies of feminine psychology,
an expressionist play *Der Schwärmer*
(1921), and a comedy *Vinzenz* (1924).
His masterpiece is the colossal unfinished novel *Der Mann ohne Eigenschaften* (3 vols. 1930–43, tr. *The Man
Without Qualities* 1953–60). Highly
intellectual, it analyzes with ironic wit
the decadent society of Vienna before
World War I, as symbolized by the
brilliant hero who cannot decide on a
career. Musil lived in Berlin (1931–33),
returned to Vienna, and at the time of
the Anschluss (1938) emigrated to
Switzerland. He died in Geneva.

TRANSLATIONS: *Tonka, and Other
Stories* (collected stories) (London
1955 and, as *Five Women,* New York
1966), *Young Torless* (New York and
London 1955, also PB), and *The Man
Without Qualities* (3 vols. London and
New York 1953–1960, also PB), all
translated by Eithne Wilkins and Ernst
Kaiser.
REFERENCE: Burton E. Pike *Robert
Musil: An Introduction to His Work*
(Ithaca, N.Y. 1961).

MUSSET, (Louis Charles) Alfred de (Dec.
11, 1810 – May 2, 1857). French writer.
Born and died in Paris; of aristocratic,
cultured family. Educated at Lycée
Henri IV and briefly studied law, then
medicine, but soon joined the romantic
literary set and brought out his first
volume of poems, the Byronic *Contes*

d'Espagne et d'Italie (1830). On failure
of his first theatrical venture, *La Nuit
vénitienne* (1830), resolved to write
plays solely to be read. Met George
Sand (1833); the two set off for a
winter in Italy (1833–34), separated
in Venice, and had a series of reconciliations and partings in Paris before final
break (1835). This liaison provided
main inspiration for Musset's famous
Nuits cycle (1835–37) and other love
poems, including *Souvenir* (1841), and
for autobiographical novel *Confession
d'un enfant du siècle* (1836). Among
his best plays are *Lorenzaccio* (1834),
On ne badine pas avec l'amour (1834,
No Trifling with Love), *Le Chandelier*
(1835), *Il ne faut jurer de rien* (1836,
One Never Can Tell), *Un Caprice*
(1837), *Il faut qu'une porte soit ouverte
ou fermée* (1845, *A Door Should Either
Be Open or Closed*), *On ne saurait
penser à tout* (1849, *One Can't Think
of Everything*). After successful performance (1847) of *Un Caprice*, Musset's plays were staged frequently.
Elected to Académie Française (1852).

TRANSLATION: *Complete Writings*
(10 vols. rev. ed. New York 1907).
REFERENCES: Maurice Allem *Alfred
de Musset* (rev. ed. Grenoble 1948).
Pierre Gastinel *Le Romantisme d'Alfred
de Musset* (Paris 1933). Charlotte Haldane *Alfred: The Passionate Life of
Alfred de Musset* (London 1960 and
New York 1961). Henry D. Sedgwick
Alfred de Musset (Indianapolis and
London 1931). Arthur A. Tilley *Three
French Dramatists: Racine, Marivaux,
Musset* (1933, reprinted New York
1967). Philippe Van Tieghem *Musset,
l'homme et l'oeuvre* (2nd ed. Paris
1967).

MUSSORGSKY (also spelled MUSORGSKI, MOUSSORGSKY), Modest (Petrovitch) (Mar 21, 1839 – Mar. 28, 1881).
Russian composer. Born Karevo, district
of Pskov, youngest son of wealthy landowner. As a child learned piano from
his mother. Attended cadet school in St.
Petersburg, then joined regiment of the
Imperial Guard. First piano piece,
Porte-Enseigne Polka (1852). Through
Alexander Dargomizhky, met Mily Balakirev (1857) and became one of "the
mighty Five": the five Russian composers (Balakirev, Borodin, César Cui,

Mussorgsky, Rimski-Korsakov) devoted to developing Russian national music. Began composing songs, lyric and folk. Completed the tone poem *A Night on the Bare Mountain* (1867) and his masterpiece, the opera *Boris Godunov* (1869, second version 1872); also *Pictures at an Exhibition* (1874), originally for piano. Died of alcoholism in St. Petersburg, leaving rough drafts of operas *Khovantchina* and *The Fair at Sorochinsk*. After his death Rimski-Korsakov prepared for publication and reorchestrated his works; in 1928 the Soviet Government began to publish the original texts.

REFERENCES: Michel D. Calvocoressi *Modest Mussorgsky: His Life and Works* (London and New York 1956, also PB). Jay Leyda and Sergei Bertensson *The Mussorgsky Reader: A Life of Modeste Petrovich Mussorgsky in Letters and Documents* (New York 1947). Montagu Montagu-Nathan *Masters of Russian Music: Moussorgsky* (London 1921). Oskar von Riesemann *Moussorgsky* (tr. 1929, reprinted New York PB 1970). Victor I. Seroff *Modeste Mussorgsky* (New York 1969).

✍

MODEST MUSSORGSKY
BY DALE HARRIS

Modest Mussorgsky's claims to greatness rest upon the merest handful of works: a set of piano pieces (*Pictures at an Exhibition*), a tone poem (*A Night on the Bare Mountain*), various songs (including three cycles, *Sunless*, *The Nursery*, and *Songs and Dances of Death*), two unfinished operas (*Khovantchina* and *The Fair at Sorochinsk*), and one completed opera (*Boris Godunov*). It is hard to think of another composer of similar stature with so few masterpieces to his credit. But Mussorgsky's worth has nothing to do with the creation of an oeuvre. His gifts were not protean; he showed little inclination for abstract music, none at all for developmental techniques. His artistic proclivities were at odds with the whole central European symphonic

tradition, a state of affairs which Mussorgsky acknowledged and ascribed to differences in national temperament, but which probably sprang from other causes. For it seems clear that, despite his dedication to the craft of music, Mussorgsky's ultimate aims as a composer were not really musical at all; they were philosophical. He always evaluated music in terms of its extrinsic significance. Aesthetic questions interested him only as they related to the attainment of truth. By truth, which Mussorgsky valued above any of the conventional musical virtues, he meant social awareness, engagement with life, the expression of fellow feeling. He was contemptuous of music making for its own sake.

Truth for Mussorgsky was bound up with nationalism. As a composer it was his avowed ambition to reveal the Russian character, individual and collective, psychological and societal. He wanted not merely to describe but to celebrate the life around him. From this came his preoccupation with folk music and, above all, with the direct representation of human experience. He excelled as a vocal composer because vocal music, in the way it unites the specificity of language and the abstractness of sound, was the genre that allowed him best to express his deepest artistic concerns. The Russian tongue determined the character of his music. Forged by Mussorgsky from the rhythms and intonations of ordinary, everyday speech (and influenced by his country's folk songs), his style was both startling and original. As a musician Mussorgsky mediated between the claims of beauty (or form) and the stronger claims of truthfulness (or content). His creative bent was for the dramatic, not the lyric, perhaps because his essential, truthful subject was man's inescapable confrontation by his fate: as in, for example, *Trepak,* the first of the *Songs and Dances of Death,* where a peasant, lost in the dark, snowy night, is embraced by Death, who dances with him while singing an invitation to eternal rest. Or the second act of *Boris,* where the Czar in his remorse is haunted by the murdered Czarevitch and tries in vain to shift the burden of guilt from himself to the will of the people. In dramatic situations like this, where his human sympathies were fully engaged, Mussorgsky showed an intuitive mastery of whatever technical means were necessary to express his feelings. Mussorgsky is probably the supreme example of the way in which native genius creates its own standards of proficiency.

Mussorgsky, who from his earliest days was destined by his wealthy, landowning parents for a military career, was a latecomer to the profession of music. Though he began to study the piano while still a child, he was already a subaltern in the Preobrazhensky regiment, and leading the life of a hard-drinking man-about-town, when, in 1857, he was introduced to Dargomizhky, and through him to the creators and patrons who were transforming Russia's artistic life. Developing a passion for music, he became a pupil of Balakirev, and shortly afterwards resigned his commission in order to devote all his energies to composing. He immediately identified himself with the group — The Five, as they eventually called themselves, or The Mighty Handful — who, intensely nationalistic and Slavophilic, sought to follow in Glinka's footsteps and create a Russian school of music. With Balakirev at their head, Mussorgsky, Borodin, Cui, and Rimsky-Korsakov set about the task, planning songs, operas, orchestral works. It was Mussorgsky's misfortune that poverty (his family had been ruined by the

liberation of the serfs in 1861), self-doubt, ill health, and finally dipsomania undermined his noble intentions. He died in 1881, not long after his forty-second birthday, leaving unfinished the two operas he had been working on simultaneously, *Khovantchina* and *The Fair at Sorochinsk. Boris Godunov* was the only opera he ever completed. Earlier on, he had abandoned work not only on the increasingly uncongenial subject of *Salammbô* (after Flaubert), but also on a word-for-word setting of Gogol's *The Marriage,* one act of which he actually finished.

It is not surprising that even by his advocates Mussorgsky was long thought to lack sufficient talent for the realization of his great gifts. To most of his contemporaries the fragmentariness of his efforts and the disdain he showed toward musical formulae (especially imported ones) made him seem merely amateurish. He was considered, in fact, a musical illiterate. It was with the very best motives that his friend Rimsky-Korsakov revised, reorchestrated, reshaped, in some cases completed, his work. To this day, *Boris* is hardly ever heard in Mussorgsky's own scoring — spare, austere, harmonically unexpected, occasionally clumsy, always powerful. Rimsky's version is sweeter, more conventional and smooth; it is much less audacious and much less moving. With its orchestral brilliance and sensuousness it is closer to pageantry than historical tragedy. But there is no easy solution to the textual problems of *Boris.* Mussorgsky himself revised his original conception in order to secure the opera's acceptance by the Maryinsky Theatre (where it was first performed in 1874). Even after its acceptance he made additional changes in response to criticisms. Quite simply, *Boris* has not come down to us in a definitive form. The wonder is that

Mussorgsky's operatic genuis seems to exist without reference to such considerations. In his supreme achievement Mussorgsky's overall dramatic and musical conception is profound enough, and original enough, to survive indeterminacy — as well as the misguided assistance of his friends.

NASH, John (1752 – May 13, 1835). English architect. Born London. After nearly ten years' apprenticeship under Sir Robert Taylor, he set up as architect and speculative builder in London, but went bankrupt (1783). Moved to Wales and established considerable reputation as designer of country houses there and in western England. Returned to London (1796) and formed partnership with landscape gardener Humphry Repton. Nash is remembered today as the favorite architect of George IV, who as prince regent became his patron (1798). He designed Regent's Park and Regent Street, Haymarket Theatre, London (1811–30); also remodeled the Royal Pavilion, Brighton, in so-called "Hindu" style (1815–23), and Buckingham Palace (1825–30; uncompleted and since considerably altered). An eclectic designer, Nash is particularly known for developing the neoclassic Regency style. He died at Cowes, Isle of Wight.

REFERENCES: Terence Davis *The Architecture of John Nash* (London 1960) and *John Nash: The Prince Regent's Architect* (London 1966 and Cranbury, N.J. 1967). John Summerson *John Nash: Architect to King George IV* (2nd ed. London 1949 and New York 1950).

NASH (or NASHE), Thomas (1567–1601). English writer. Born Lowestoft, Suffolk, son of a minister. Educated at St. John's College, Cambridge, after which he settled in London (c.1588) and associated with Robert Greene and the other writers known as University Wits. First published works were a preface to Greene's *Menaphon* (1589) and the satirical *Anatomie of Absurdities*

(1589). Became involved in Marprelate controversy, attacking the Puritans in pamphlets under pseudonym Pasquil (1589–90), which led to paper war with Gabriel Harvey (1591–99). Nash's most notable work, the picaresque romance *The Unfortunate Traveler, or The Life of Jack Wilton* (1594), is the first adventure novel in English, anticipating Defoe. Other writings include *Pierce Pennilesse, His Supplication to the Divell* (1592), a satire on contemporary vice, and *Summer's Last Will and Testament* (1600), a satirical masque. A lost comedy, *The Isle of Dogs* (1597), in which Nash collaborated, was suppressed as seditious and the authors were jailed. Died probably at Yarmouth.

EDITIONS: *Works* ed. R. B. McKerrow (5 vols. London 1904–1910, rev. ed. F. P. Wilson 5 vols. Oxford 1958 and New York 1967). *Selected Writings* ed. Stanley Wells (London 1964 and Cambridge, Mass. 1965).
REFERENCES: George R. Hibbard *Thomas Nashe: A Critical Introduction* (London and Cambridge, Mass. 1962). C. S. Lewis *English Literature in the Sixteenth Century* (Oxford 1954).

NERVAL, Gérard de (real name **Gérard Labrunie**) (May 22, 1808 – Jan. 25, 1855). French writer. Born and died in Paris. Mother died in his early childhood, which was spent in care of a great-uncle in the Valois country. Educated at Collège Charlemagne, Paris. At nineteen won recognition for translation of Goethe's *Faust*, part I, which Goethe himself praised. Joined romantic literary set (1828) centered about Victor Hugo, and made reputation for himself with his poems, plays, and translations of German romantics. Became obsessed (about 1834) with a passion for actress Jennie Colon, after whose rejection of him, marriage (1838) and death (1842) he suffered a nervous breakdown. Recovering, he began series of travels, out of which eventually came *Voyage en Orient* (1851). Interest in the occult and mysticism produced the study *Les Illuminées,* (1852). After another breakdown and a period in an asylum came his greatest work: the story *Sylvie* (1853), *Petits Châteaux de bohème* (1853), *Les Filles du feu* (1854), and the sonnets *Les Chimerès* (1854). The dreamlike fantasy and symbolism of his writings later influenced the symbolists and surrealists. *Aurélia,* his "document of madness" (begun 1854) was unfinished when he committed suicide by hanging.

TRANSLATION: *Selected Writings* tr. Geoffrey Wagner (New York 1957).

REFERENCES: R. M. Alberes *Gérard de Nerval* (2nd ed. Paris 1962). Albert Béguin *Gérard de Nerval* (2nd ed. Paris 1945). Leon Céllier *Gérard de Nerval* (2nd ed. Paris 1963). Aristide Marie *Gérard de Nerval, le poète et l'homme* (2nd ed. Paris 1955). Solomon A. Rhodes *Gérard de Nerval* (New York 1951 and London 1952). Jean Richer *Nerval: expérience et création* (Paris 1963).

NESBIT, Edith (Aug. 19, 1858 – May 4, 1924). English writer. Born London. Educated in France, Germany, and England. Married (1880) socialist journalist Hubert Bland, with whom she helped found the Fabian Society; they had four children. "E. Nesbit" earned money by turning out verses, articles, novels, and horror stories before discovering her true calling, and financial success, with a series of thirty stories for children. They included *The Story of the Treasure Seekers* (1899), *The Would-Be-Goods* (1901), *Five Children and It* (1902), *New Treasure Seekers* (1904), *The Phoenix and the Carpet* (1904), and *The Enchanted Castle* (1907). Humorous and unsentimental, the stories concern ordinary children, whose magical adventures take place against a quiet domestic background. After the death of her first husband

(1914), she married Thomas Tucker, a marine engineer (1917). Died at New Romney, Kent.

REFERENCES: Anthea Bell *E. Nesbit* (London 1960 and New York 1964). Doris Langley Moore *E. Nesbit: A Biography* (London 1933, rev. ed. Philadelphia 1966 and London 1967). Noel Streatfield *Magic and the Magician: E. Nesbit and Her Children's Books* (London and New York 1958).

NEUMANN, (Johann) Balthasar (Jan. 1687 – Aug. 18 or 19, 1753). German architect. Born Eger, Bohemia, and baptized January 30, 1687. Settled in Würzburg (1711) and was trained as civil and military engineer and architect by Andreas Müller. Had worked for several years as engineer when appointed (1719) by the prince bishop of Würzburg to build a new palace — the Residenz of Würzburg, one of the greatest palaces of the baroque era. He evolved the design after consultation with many southern German and French architects, particularly Gabriel Germain Boffrand, and supervised not only its construction (completed 1744) but also its decoration by an international staff of painters (including Tiepolo), sculptors, and other artists and craftsmen. His other palaces and castles include Bruchsal (1728–33) and Werneck (1733–45); outstanding examples among his numerous churches are Vierzehnheiligen (1743–72), Neresheim (1747–92), and Käppele, near Würzburg (1747–50). Married Maria Schild (1725). Died in Würzburg.

NEWMAN, John Henry (Feb. 21, 1801 – Aug. 11, 1890). English religious leader. Born London. His father, a banker, and his mother were Anglicans. Attended Trinity College, Oxford (B.A. 1820) and was elected fellow of Oriel College (1822). Ordained deacon (1824), priest (1825), and appointed vicar of St. Mary's, the university church (1828); he also held several university posts. His religious views grew increasingly high Anglican, and after hearing Rev. John Keble's "National Apostasy" sermon (1833) he became a leader of the

Oxford movement. He wrote twenty-four of the movement's *Tracts for the Times* (1833–41), including the controversial *Tract 90* on the Thirty-nine Articles (1841), which led to his resignation from St. Mary's (1843). Joined Roman Catholic Church, (1845), becoming a priest (1847). Lived in Birmingham, where he founded oratory of St. Philip Neri, from 1848, except for four years in Dublin as rector of new Catholic University (1854–58). Besides numerous volumes of collected sermons, Newman's major works in prose include *An Essay on the Development of Christian Doctrine* (1845); *The Idea of a University* (1852), a notable contribution to educational theory; his autobiography, considered a literary masterpiece, *Apologia pro Vita Sua* (1864), written in rebuttal to an attack by Charles Kingsley. *Verses on Various Occasions* (1868) includes his finest poem, *The Dream of Gerontius* (1866), his early verses, *Lead Kindly Light* (1833) and other hymns for the *Lyra Apostolica*, and such sonnets as *Substance and Shadow*. He also wrote two religious novels. Made cardinal by Pope Leo XIII (1879). Died in Birmingham.

EDITIONS: *Collected Works* (40 vols. London 1874–1921). *Letters and Correspondence of John Henry Newman During His Life in the English Church* . . . ed. Anne Mozley (2 vols. London 1891).

REFERENCES: Louis Bouyer *Newman* (tr. London and New York 1958, also PB). A. Dwight Culler *The Imperial Intellect: A Study of Newman's Educational Ideal* (New Haven, Conn. and Oxford 1955, also PB). Charles S. Dessain *John Henry Newman* (London 1966). Charles F. Harrold *John Henry Newman: An Exposition and Critical Study of His Mind, Thought and Art* (1945, reprinted Hamden, Conn. 1966). Christopher Hollis *Newman and the Modern World* (London 1967 and Garden City, N.Y. 1968). Sean O'Faolain *Newman's Way: The Odyssey of John Henry Newman* (London and New York 1952). Meriol Trevor *Newman: The Pillar of the Cloud* (2 vols. London and Garden City, N.Y. 1962). Jan Hendrik Walgrave *Newman: The Theologian* (tr. London and New York 1960). Wilfrid P. Ward *The Life of John Henry, Cardinal Newman* (1912, new ed. 2 vols. London and New York 1927).

NIETZSCHE, Friedrich Wilhelm (Oct. 15, 1844 – Aug. 25, 1900). German philosopher. Born Röcken, Saxony, son of a Lutheran pastor. Studied classical philology at universities of Bonn and Leipzig; appointed professor at University of Basel (1869). In Switzerland he became close friend of Wagner, whom he extolled in second part of his first book, *The Birth of Tragedy from the Spirit of Music* (1872, tr. 1910). The two broke with each other, however, on Wagner's establishing a chauvinistic, anti-Semitic cult at Bayreuth. After his resignation from the university (1879) due to poor health, Nietzsche spent a solitary and ascetic life, living in Switzerland in summer and Italy in winter. In his major works, *Thus Spoke Zarathustra* (1883–84, tr. 1909), *Beyond Good and Evil* (1886, tr. 1907), *The Genealogy of Morals* (1887), *Twilight of the Idols* (1889), *Antichrist* (1895), and *Ecce Homo* (1908) — the last three written in 1888 — he rejected Christian and middle-class morality and developed the concepts of the "will to power" and the Superman. Insane from 1889 until his death at Weimar, Nietzsche lived under the care of first his mother, then his sister. Unrecognized until the last years of his life, he deeply influenced twentieth-century philosophy and literature.

REFERENCES: Crane Brinton *Nietzsche* (Cambridge, Mass. and Oxford 1941, also PB). Arthur C. Danto *Nietzsche as Philosopher* (New York 1965, also PB). R. J. Hollingdale *Nietzsche: The Man and His Philosophy* (London and Baton Rouge, La. 1965, also PB). Karl Jaspers *Nietzsche: An Introduction to the Understanding of His Philosophical Activity* (tr. Tucson, Ariz. 1965, also PB). Walter A. Kaufmann *Nietzsche: Philosopher, Psychologist, Antichrist* (3rd ed. Princeton, N.J. 1968, also PB). George A. Morgan, Jr. *What Nietzsche Means* (Cambridge, Mass. 1941, also PB). Erich F. Podach *The Madness of Nietzsche* (tr. New York and London 1931).

NOLDE, Emil (real name Emil Hansen) (Aug. 7, 1867 – Apr. 15, 1956). German artist. Born in Nolde, Schleswig, of peasant stock. In 1890's studied wood carving and drawing, first with Frederich Fehr, Munich, then with Adolf Holzel, Dachau (1899), when he leaned toward impressionism. Attended Académie Julian, Paris (1900), and produced rich impressionist works such as *Harvest Day* (1904, Fehr Collection, Bern). Joined briefly the Brücke movement (1906), acquired woodcut technique. Cofounder of New Berlin Secession (1910), and began to paint his great religious works: *The Life of Christ* (1911–12, National Gallery, Berlin) and the triptych of *St. Mary of Egypt* (1912, Kunsthalle, Hamburg). Joined ethnological expedition to Russia, China, Japan, and Polynesia (1913–14) and became profoundly influenced by primitive art, especially its demoniac essence. Now painted such still lifes as *Wooden Figure and Mask* (1914, Kunstmuseum, Basel). Married twice: Ada Vilstrup (1902–46); Jolanthe Erdmann (1948). Received honorary degree from Kiel University (1925) and was appointed to Prussian Academy of Art (1931). His brooding, mystical landscapes, seascapes, and flower pictures were considered degenerate art by the Nazis; he was forbidden to paint, but continued to produce canvases prolifically until his death in Seebüll near Denmark, where there is a Nolde foundation. Of his work Bernard Myers writes in *The German Expressionists* "No other painter expressed as forcefully as he the underlying emotive and intuitive character of expressionism, its anguish, and its religious feeling; no other has left so strong an impression of a demonic, spasmodic quality and an explosive fury." His autobiography appears in German in four volumes (Berlin 1931–1961).

REFERENCES: Werner Haftmann *Emil Nolde* (tr. New York 1959 and London 1960) and *Emil Nolde: The Forbidden Pictures* (tr. New York and London 1965). Bernard S. Myers *The German Expressionists* (New York and London 1963). Peter Selz *Emil Nolde* (Garden City, N.Y. 1963). Martin Urban *Emil Nolde: Flowers and Animals, Watercolors and Drawings* (tr. New York 1966).

NORRIS, Frank (real name Benjamin Franklin Norris, Jr.) (Mar 5, 1870 – Oct. 25, 1902). American novelist. Born Chicago, son of wealthy jewelry manufacturer. Family moved to San Francisco (1884). Norris studied art there and in Paris. Returned to study at University of California, Berkeley, and at Harvard, where he began the novel *Vandover and the Brute* (posthumously published 1914) and *McTeague* (1899), a powerful naturalistic story of slum life in San Francisco. Served as correspondent for San Francisco *Chronicle* and *Collier's* in South Africa during Boer War (1895–96); edited San Francisco *Wave* (1897), in which his novel *Moran of the Lady Letty* (1898) was serialized, and covered Spanish-American War in Cuba for *McClure's* (1898). Thereafter worked as reader for Doubleday, Page in New York, and discovered Theodore Dreiser's *Sister Carrie* (1900). That year married Jeannette Black and moved back to San Francisco, where he died. His finest work is the unfinished trilogy *Epic of the Wheat*. *The Octopus* (1901) deals with the struggle between wheat growers and magnates of the railroad (the octopus); *The Pit* (1903) concerns speculators and the Chicago wheat exchange; *The Wolf* (unwritten) was to follow the dispersal of the wheat to Europe. Written with Zolaesque naturalism, the last works contributed to the "muckraking" movement, and helped establish the realist tradition in twentieth-century American fiction.

REFERENCES: William B. Dillingham *Frank Norris: Instinct and Art* (Lincoln, Nebr. 1969, also PB). Maxwell Geismar *Rebels and Ancestors* (Boston and London 1953, also PB). Ernest Marchand *Frank Norris: A Study* (1942, new ed. New York 1964). Donald Pizer *The Novels of Frank Norris* (Bloomington, Ind. 1966). Charles C. Walcutt *American Literary Naturalism* (Minneapolis and Oxford 1956). Franklin Walker *Frank Norris: A Biography* (1932, reprinted New York 1963).

O'CASEY, Sean (Mar. 30, 1880 – Sept. 18, 1964). Irish playwright. Born Dublin, into lower-class Protestant family. Fatherless in infancy and raised in slums, he was largely self-taught from 1893, and at eighteen worked as a laborer. Interested in Irish nationalist and labor movements, he became member of Irish Citizen Army and organizer of Irish Transport Workers' Union strike (1913). Also active in Sinn Fein movement and Easter Rebellion (1916). His first Abbey Theatre production, *The Shadow of a Gunman* (1923), was followed by *Cathleen Listens In* (1923) and *Juno and the Paycock* (1924), winner of the Hawthornden prize (1926). His controversial play about the Easter Rebellion, *The Plough and the Stars* (1926), caused riots at the opening and established him as a leading Irish playwright. Filled with irony and humor, his plays reflect the political temper of the times and the misery and violence of Dublin slum life. Moved to England (1926) and married (1928) Eileen Reynolds (stage name Eileen Carey). Among later works: *The Silver Tassie* (produced London 1929, Dublin 1936), *Within the Gates* (1934), *The Star Turns Red* (1939), *Purple Dust* (1944), *Red Roses for Me* (1947), *The Bishop's Fire* (1955), and *The Drums of Father Ned* (1959). Also wrote six volumes of fictionalized autobiography: *I Knock at the Door* (1939), *Pictures in the Hallway* (1942), *Drums Under the Window* (1945), *Inishfallen, Fare Thee Well* (1949), *Rose and Crown* (1952), *Sunset and Evening Star* (1954). He died in Torquay, England.

EDITION: *Collected Plays* (4 vols. London 1949–51).

REFERENCES: Ronald Ayling ed. *Sean O'Casey* (London 1969, also PB). *Saros Cowasjee Sean O'Casey: The Man Behind the Plays* (Edinburgh and New York 1963). Gabriel Fallon *Sean O'Casey: The Man I Knew* (London and Boston 1965). Robert G. Hogan *The Experiments of Sean O'Casey* (New York 1960). Jules Koslow *Sean O'Casey: The Man and His Plays* (1950, rev. ed. New York PB 1966). David Krause *Sean O'Casey: The Man and His Work* (New York and London 1960, also PB).

O'CONNOR, Frank (real name Michael O'Donovan) (1903 – Mar. 10, 1966). Irish writer. Born Cork, where he attended Christian Brothers school. Began writing, mostly in Gaelic, at early age. Worked as librarian in Cork and Dublin, where he was also director of the Abbey Theatre. Active (early 1920's) in the Irish republican movement. His first published work was a volume of short stories, *Guests of the Nation* (1931), followed by *The Saint and Mary Kate* (1932), *Dutch Interior* (1939), and *Crab Apple Jelly* (1944), all written with precise craftsmanship and great sensitivity to Irish speech. Although best known for his short stories, he also published verse, *Three Old Brothers* (1936) and *Time's Pocket* (1938), and translations from the Irish, *A Lament for Art O'Leary* (1940) and *The Midnight Court* (1945). Later books include *The Mirror in the Roadway* (1956), *Domestic Relations* (1957), *A Set of Variations* (1969), and the autobiographical *An Only Child* (1961) and *My Father's Son* (1968). He first married Evelyn Bowen (1939) and later an American, Harriet Rich (1953). Died in Dublin.

REFERENCE: Maurice Sheehy ed. *Studies on Frank O'Connor* (New York 1969).

OFFENBACH, Jacques (real name Jacob Eberst) (June 20, 1819 – Oct. 5, 1880). German-French composer. Born Cologne, son of a cantor in synagogue there. Sent to Paris to study cello at the Conservatory (1833–37) and became member of Opéra Comique orchestra (1837). Married Herminie de Alcain (1844), became conductor of Comédie Française (1849). From 1853 began composing, and managed his own theatre, Bouffes Parisiens (1855–66), where he produced his operettas. In Vienna during Franco-Prussian War (1870), after which he returned to Paris and managed Théâtre de la Gaîté (1873–75). Presented series of concerts in America (1876–77), writing up his experiences as *Notes d'un musicien en voyage* (1877). He directed the Théâtre Lyrique in Paris from that date until his death; he composed more than ninety works, best known of which are *Orphée aux enfers* (1858), *La Belle Hélène* (1865), *Barbe-Bleue* (1866), *La Vie Parisienne* (1866), *La Grande Duchesse de Gérolstein* (1867), *Madame Favart* (1878). His light, satirical style, full of sparkling and tuneful lyrics, reached its apotheosis in the four-act opéra comique *Les Contes d'Hoffmann* (*The Tales of Hoffmann*), on which his international fame rests. It was produced posthumously (1881).

REFERENCES: Siegfried Kracauer *Orpheus in Paris: Offenbach and the Paris of His Time* (tr. London 1937 and New York 1938). Louis Schneider *Offenbach* (Paris 1923). Sacheverell Sitwell *La Vie Parisienne: A Tribute to Offenbach* (London 1937 and Boston 1938).

OLMSTED, Frederick Law (Apr. 26, 1822 – Aug. 28, 1903). American landscape architect. Born Hartford, Conn. Studied agriculture and engineering at Yale (1842–43), then practiced scientific farming before touring in Europe to study agricultural methods and landscape gardening. Published *Walks and Talks of an American Farmer in England* (1852). Between 1852 and 1856 did firsthand research on effects of slavery on the South, publishing *A Journey in the Seaboard Slave States* (1856), *A Journey Through Texas* (1857), and *A Journey in the Back Country* (1860), all three condensed as *The Cotton Kingdom* (2 vols. 1861). Made (1856) first of several trips to study parks in Europe, and was appointed (1857) superintendent of New York's Central Park and architect of it with Calvert Vaux as assistant, completing the work by 1861. Married brother's widow, Mary Cleveland Olmsted (1859). Appointed by President Lincoln to U.S. Sanitary Commission (1861–63), resigning to become first commissioner of Yosemite National Park and Mariposa Grove. Designed landscape for U.S. Capitol, the Columbian Exposition in Chicago (1893), and the campuses of Stanford University and University of California, Berkeley. Among parks he designed besides Central Park: Prospect Park, Brooklyn; South Side Park, Chicago; Riverside Park, Riverside, Ill.; Mount Royal, Montreal; Belle Isle Park, Detroit; Niagara Falls Reservation; Franklin Park, Boston. He died in Waverly, Mass. Olmsted was America's first professional landscape architect, a pioneer in conservation and city planning. Instrumental in establishing functional principles of landscape design, he also predicted the growth of the suburbs and provided model solutions in plans for Berkeley, Calif., and Riverside, Ill. His son, Frederick Law Olmsted, Jr. (1870–1957), designed the Boston metropolitan park system (1898–1920) and others in Baltimore and Washington, D.C.

REFERENCES: Julius G. Fabos and others *Frederick Law Olmsted, Sr.: Founder of Landscape Architecture in America* (Amherst, Mass. 1968, also PB). Frederick Law Olmsted and Theodora Kimball eds. *Frederick Law Olmsted: Landscape Architect, 1822–1903* (2 vols. New York 1922–28).

O'NEILL, Eugene (Gladstone) (Oct. 16, 1888 – Nov. 27, 1953). American playwright. Born New York, son of actor James O'Neill. After a year at Princeton (1906), spent five years wandering in Europe and South America, then had to enter tuberculosis sanatorium (1912), where he read plays and decided to write them. Ibsen and Strindberg especially influenced him. Spent year studying with George Pierce Baker at Harvard (1914). The Provincetown Players produced his first one-act plays, beginning with *Bound East for Cardiff* (1916). First full-length play, *Beyond the Horizon* (1920), awarded Pulitzer prize; so also were *Anna Christie* (1922), *Strange Interlude* (1928), and *Long Day's Journey into Night* (1956). First American playwright to win Nobel prize (1936). Married three times, twice divorced: Kathleen Jenkins, 1909; Agnes Bolton, 1918; actress Carlotta Monterey, 1929. Died in Boston. Other notable plays include *The Emperor Jones* (1921), *The Hairy Ape* (1922), *Desire Under the Elms* (1924), *The Great God Brown* (1926), *Mourning Becomes Electra* (1931), *The Iceman Cometh* (1946), *Ah! Wilderness* (1933), *A Touch of the Poet* (1957).

REFERENCES: Doris Alexander *The Tempering of O'Neill* (New York 1962). Oscar Cargill and others *O'Neill and His Plays* (New York and London 1961, also PB). Barret H. Clark *Eugene O'Neill: The Man and His Plays* (rev. ed. New York 1947, also PB). John Gassner ed. *O'Neill: A Collection of Critical Essays* (Englewood Cliffs, N.J. 1964, also PB). Arthur and Barbara Gelb *O'Neill* (New York and London 1962, also PB). Clifford Leech *Eugene O'Neill* (New York 1965). John H. Raleigh *The Plays of Eugene O'Neill* (Carbondale, Ill. 1965). Louis Sheaffer *O'Neill: Son and Playwright* (Boston 1968). Sophus K. Winther *Eugene O'Neill* (2nd ed. New York 1961).

✍

EUGENE O'NEILL
BY HAROLD CLURMAN

It has been said that Eugene O'Neill never wrote a proper English sentence. More devastating than this is the quip: "He was a great playwright who never wrote a good play."

Admirers of O'Neill need not take umbrage at the various criticisms, true or false, of O'Neill's work. His language *is* crude, he *was* a confused thinker, some of his plays *are* absurd. These charges do not seriously diminish his stature as an important dramatist.

Before O'Neill's emergence in 1915 the American theatre was barely adult. Such dramatists as Ibsen entered the stage stealthily or defiantly through the support of isolated minorities. A light Maugham comedy was held to be the height of sophistication; the peak of "problem" drama was attained through Pinero. Our most advanced playwrights — Clyde Fitch, Augustus Thomas, Edward Sheldon — wrote romances, comedies, and historical, social, and "psychological" plays so timid and flimsy (apart from a rudimentary technical proficiency) that their revival today could only be contemplated for purposes of lampoon.

Though not a didactic artist, O'Neill was the first American dramatist to justify Shaw's definition of the theatre as "a factory of thought, a prompter of conscience, a school of social conduct, an armory against despair and dullness and a temple of the Ascent of man." He dramatized preoccupations which were at once profoundly personal and objectively significant. His experiments in form and exploration of material cover a wider range than that of any other American playwrights of his or our day. He never swerved from the deeply felt duty to fashion from the experience of his life dramatic forms of general relevance. The intensity of his impulse verges on the religious.

O'Neill described the central character of his first full-length play *Beyond the Horizon* as a young man with "a touch of the poet." Though O'Neill gained a reputation among his early critics as a powerful (or "sordid") realist, his efforts to reach beyond the bounds of naturalism were insistent. In the last act of his autobiographical play *Long Day's Journey Into Night,* after Edmund (the young O'Neill) has spoken of his feeling for the sea, Tyrone (the author's father, the actor James O'Neill) murmurs, "Yes, there's the makings of a poet in you all right," to which Edmund replies, "The *makings* of a poet . . . I couldn't touch what I tried to tell you just now. I just stammered. That's the best I'll ever do . . . Well, it will be faithful realism, at least." O'Neill's "stammer" has proved the most eloquent and significant in American drama. And it is not too much to claim that he achieved more than a "touch" of poetry.

We perceive this not simply through the allegory of such ambitious but unfulfilled plays as *Lazarus Laughed,* in which Lazarus rises from the grave to proclaim that there is no death, or *The Fountain,* in which we see Ponce de León in quest of eternal youth ("Life is a fountain, forever leaping, failing, falling, ever returning"), but also through his entirely realistic plays. *Desire Under the Elms,* for example, is not as some believe a Strindbergian sex drama — involving incest, infanticide — but a sort of parable. At stake is the possession of the "farm" (America) and the struggle of the generations for that possession, a struggle between the older which established it and the younger which inherited it. The affair between old Ephraim's wife and her stepson is motivated to begin with by the desire for the acquisition of property and is deviated by the realization of a love which supersedes greed.

Emperor Jones is not a study of the black man's psychology but a stage poem of atavistic forces in humankind generally. Realism yields to expressionism in *The Hairy Ape,* which is both a legend of alienation and at the same time a "ballad" which sings of the American worker convinced that it is he who makes the machine of industry run and yet is haunted by the knowledge of his exclusion from the fruits of the civilization which it produces: his manhood is ignored. When O'Neill writes of a sanatorium in *The Straw,* what remains in our memory is not the naturalistic detail but the sense of aspiration which never withers in humanity even in the face of inevitable disaster.

The essence of O'Neill's work is wrought from the stuff of his own life. His was a torn spirit. He bitterly resented and inordinately admired his father. He craved his mother's love desperately and could not overcome the feeling that she had failed him. Wracked by disbelief he groped toward positive affirmation. He suffered guilt due to some ancient sin which he could not altogether identify. At the beginning perhaps he may have thought it social. Later he saw it as something intrinsic to existence which required the healing power of a faith he could not find.

"What the hell was it I wanted to buy, I wonder . . . ?" old Tyrone asks himself in *Long Day's Journey into Night.* And Mary, his wife, wandering through the night, carries a long-forgotten wedding dress (symbol of her innocence) and asks, "What is it I'm looking for? I know it's something I've lost."

O'Neill could not return to the church of his forebears, though he sorely felt the need of a sustaining belief. Between the desired yea and the persistent nay he remained a tortured soul. His characters constantly abuse one another and immediately after abjectly beg forgiveness. They speak in two voices. That is why O'Neill's use of the inner monologue (as in *Strange Interlude*) and of the mask (in several plays) is not merely an aesthetic device but a response to an organic need.

The conflict in O'Neill projected itself as a bitter view of America itself. *The Great God Brown* dramatizes the tension and mutual wound between the American as artist and the American as businessman: their envy, attraction, their separate failure and their dream of woman — ideally the all-accepting, all-healing Earth Mother. *A Touch of the Poet* presents the struggle between the American immigrant and his native-born offspring, the outmoded dream and culturally bequeathed grace of the one, the successful and the ever-to-be frustrated drive of the other. "What shall it profit a man," O'Neill forever quoted the Teacher, "if he gain the whole world and lose his own soul?" America was a failure, O'Neill believed, because it had betrayed its ideal; it had never in practice adhered to a binding principle, tradition, or faith.

Though not always complete as dramatic entities, O'Neill's plays hold us, apart from their content, for two reasons. They stand on well-grounded pillars of strong action — melodrama in fact — and far more effectively they are the embodiments of his spiritual obsessions. The combination gives them a hypnotic, indeed a hallucinatory power. That is why they still live as the one sure American contribution to the world literature of the theatre.

ORLÉANS. *See* CHARLES, duke of ORLÉANS.

OROZCO, José Clemente (Nov. 22, 1883 – Sept. 7, 1949). Mexican artist. Born Zapotlán (now Ciudad Guzmán), Jalisco. Studied agronomy, then architectural drawing (1904–1908). Studied art at Academia de San Carlos (1906–14), and was influenced strongly by expressive graphics of José Guadalupe Posada. A product of the Mexican Revolution (which began 1910), Orozco stressed the human rather than the political element. By 1914 he was producing caricatures for a pro-revolution paper, and from 1922 his work depicted revolutionary scenes and themes. His first important mural assignment, at Escuela Nacional Preparatoria, Mexico City (1923–27), was followed by mural at Escuela Industrial of Orizaba. In U.S. (1927–32), he executed three series of frescoes: at Pomona College, Claremont, Calif.; New School for Social Research, New York City; and Dartmouth College, Hanover, N.H., where his scenes from the history of the Americas in brilliant color, vigorous movement, and sculpturesque forms are among his finest work. Back in Mexico City he painted large mural, *Catharsis* (1935), for Palacio de Bellas Artes. Called to Guadalajara (1936), he executed frescoes for the university and for Hospicio Cabañas, where he depicted the history of Mexico with recourse to symbolism for which he is noted. His last years were spent on murals at Jiquilpan (1940); *Dive Bomber and Tank* (1940) panels for New York City Museum of Modern Art; mural for Palacio de Justicia (1941), visionary religious murals for church of Jesús Nazareno (1942), and murals for Escuela Normal (1947), all in Mexico City, where he died. Orozco ranks as one of Mexico's Big Four with Rivera, David Siqueiros, and Rufino Tamayo.

TRANSLATION: *An Autobiography* tr. Robert C. Stephenson (Austin, Tex. 1962).

REFERENCES: McKinley Helm *Man of Fire: José Clemente Orozco* (New York 1953). Bernard Samuel Myers *Mexican Painting in Our Time* (New York 1956). Alma Reed *Orozco* (New York and London 1956).

ORTEGA Y GASSET, José (May 9, 1883 – Oct. 18, 1955). Spanish philosopher. Born and died in Madrid, son of newspaper editor. Educated at University of Madrid and in German universities, especially Marburg. Influenced by Nietzsche, Max Scheler, and Wilhelm Dilthey. Returned to Madrid (1910), became professor of metaphysics, and married Rosa Spottorno-Topete; they had three children. First book: *Meditations on Quixote* (1914). Published his widely read *España invertebrada* (1921, tr. *Invertebrate Spain* 1937) and became editor of influential magazine, *Revista de Occidente* (1923). Achieved worldwide fame through *The Revolt of the Masses* (1930, tr. 1932). An active antimonarchist, he was an intellectual leader of the Spanish republican movement, and member of the constitutional assembly until 1936, when he left Spain, a voluntary exile, to live first in France, then Buenos Aires. Finally returned to Spain (1949). His philosophy is concerned with man, not in the abstract, but in definite historical and social circumstances. His most significant contribution was to bring Western philosophical ideas into Spanish intellectual life, thereby stimulating it.

REFERENCE: José Ferrater Mora *Ortega y Gasset: An Outline of His Philosophy* (1957, rev. ed. New Haven, Conn. PB 1963).

ORWELL, George (real name Eric Arthur Blair) (June 25, 1903 – Jan. 21, 1950). British writer. Born Motihari, India, where his father worked in Bengal civil service. After attending Eton (1917–21), served with Indian Imperial Police in Burma (1922–27). Returned to Europe, struggled to be a writer, and sought out experiences of poverty, described in first book *Down and Out in Paris and London* (1933). While working as schoolmaster and bookseller's assistant (1933–35) wrote novels which established small English reputation: *Burmese Days* (1934), *A Clergyman's Daughter* (1935), *Keep the Aspidistra Flying* (1936). Wrote for Left Book Club a study of the depression in England and his reaction to the situation, *The Road to Wigan Pier* (1937). Fought on Republican side in Spanish Civil War as described in *Homage to Catalonia* (1938), and published a further novel, *Coming Up for Air* (1939). From the early 1930's was increasingly active as journalist and essayist, and two collections of essays (*Inside the Whale*, 1940; *Critical Essays*, 1946) were published before his death. Achieved international fame through his novels *Animal Farm* (1945) and *1984* (1949). His essays and journalism have been reprinted in various volumes such as *Shooting an Elephant* (1950), the nearest to complete being the 1968 edition listed below. Was twice married: to Eileen O'Shaughnessy (1936; she died in 1945), with whom he adopted a son, Richard; and to Sonia Brownell (1949). Orwell died in London.

EDITION: *The Collected Essays, Journalism and Letters of George Orwell* ed. Sonia Orwell and Ian Angus (4 vols. New York and London 1968).

REFERENCES: John Atkins *George Orwell: A Literary and Biographical Study* (London 1954 and New York 1955). Robert A. Lee *Orwell's Fiction* (Notre Dame, Ind. 1969). Richard Rees *George Orwell* (London 1961 and Carbondale, Ill. 1962, also PB). Edward M. Thomas *Orwell* (London 1965 and New York 1968). George Woodcock *The Crystal Spirit* (Boston 1966 and London 1967, also PB). Forthcoming study by Peter Stansky and William Abrahams.

GEORGE ORWELL
BY PETER STANSKY

In the essay *Why I Write* Orwell declared that "one can write nothing readable unless one constantly struggles to efface one's personality. Good prose is like a windowpane." As a generalization, this is arguable; applied to Orwell himself, it is misleading, for while he is one of the best and most readable writers of his time, his personality is all over his prose — in which respect he is no different from Shaw or Lawrence or Forster — and his windowpane is not the clear colorless glass it appears to be but a glass tinted with Orwellian colors. It is the proof of his skill as a prose writer, and the appeal of his personality, that when we look through the pane we are persuaded we are seeing the truth as it actually is, rather than the truth as he believed it to be.

The memoirs of Orwell by his friends make clear how self-revealing, but also how reticent, he could be, in his life, and in his writing. Much of what he wrote, whether fiction or nonfiction, is a kind of edited autobiography, and it is almost impossible as one reads to separate the man from his work. The defects of the novels of the 1930's, their inconsistencies and improbabilities, represent a failure to assimilate the elements of autobiography into the fiction — the experience of life that was going on almost simultaneously with the attempt to record it. But Orwell's personality is compelling and ineffaceable, and it is the presence of the writer in whatever guise he may choose to assume — except perhaps *A Clergyman's Daughter* — that gives these novels their undeniable vitality. Still, in the 1930's his best books are nonfiction, where he can write directly of life as he saw it among the dispossessed (*Down and Out in Paris and London*), the working class (*The Road to Wigan Pier*), and the soldiers of the Republic in the Spanish Civil War (*Homage to Catalonia*). It was only some years later that he hit upon the form best suited to him as a novelist of ideas, the fable, and achieved his masterpiece of fiction, *Animal Farm*, where style and content are perfectly in accord.

Of course the most obvious example of Orwell's determination to reveal only so much of himself and no more is that he should be known to us not as Eric Blair, his real name, but as George Orwell, the nom de plume he adopted at the time of the publication of *Down and Out in Paris and London* (1933). A good deal more was at stake than the mere taking of a pseudonym. What needs to be emphasized is the use that George Orwell made of the experience of Eric Blair, both in his work and in his life. There was always in Orwell the residue of Eric Blair; he remained Eric to those who knew him before 1936; he never changed his name legally. The creation of Orwell was an act of will by Blair, and it was carried on at almost every level of his existence, affecting not only his prose style but also the style of his daily life. Becoming George Orwell was his way of making himself into a writer at which he brilliantly succeeded, and of unmaking himself as a gentleman, of opting out of the genteel lower-upper-middle class into which he was born and going down a class, at which he had only an equivocal success. He got on well with tramps, who took him as an Etonian down on his luck, which he was, and with his comrades in the Spanish Civil War, who were impressed with his air of authority and recognized him as a leader, but he did not appear to have a circle of friends among the workers, even at his local pub in Islington.

The enduring result of the creation was that it allowed Eric Blair to come to terms with his world. Eric Blair was the man to whom things happened; George Orwell the man who wrote about them. Much of his life, especially before 1936, was an attempt to escape from the system into which he had been born, and which inexorably provided him with an education, an accent, and a standard of judgment that might be turned against him. The system he felt had almost crushed him in his prep school days, and towards the end of his life he left a grim record of them in *Such, Such Were the Joys*. Cyril Connolly, who was at school with him at St. Cyprian's, thought him a "true rebel" there, but in his own mind Orwell was sure he was damned: "I had no money, I was weak, I was ugly, I was unpopular, I had a chronic cough, I was cowardly, I smelt." That he felt was the judgment of St. Cyprian's and by inference of the system. Even after he went to Eton, and from there to the Imperial Police in Burma, he continued to believe that it was an unalterable judgment, and that your place in the world did not depend on your own efforts but on "what you were." This mood continued to afflict him until his return from Burma in 1927; and his novels, including *Animal Farm* and *1984*, accept the omnipotence of the system, while his heroes are its victims.

Yet Orwell made himself a happier man than he had ever dreamed of being, and a powerful writer also. It was here that he was best served by his creation. Much as Orwell in conversation with friends would pick and choose what he would reveal of himself, so Blair, through Orwell, could pick and choose among the elements of his past. Ironically, many of the qualities that contribute to the Orwell personality and style as we are familiar with them in his work are precisely the qualities Blair had thought despicable in his schooldays. Eric Blair saw himself as a smelly, impoverished member of the lower-upper-middle class who because of his being bright enough for a scholarship and coming from a suitable Anglo-Indian background had received an inappropriate gentleman's education. But George Orwell was an idiosyncratic socialist, who, no matter how badly he dressed or austerely he lived, would never lose the air of authority in his prose which marks a public school "old boy." Orwell could transform the upper-class values that Blair resented and infuse them with the egalitarianism he envied among the miners in Wigan and learned at first hand as a soldier among soldiers in Spain. Eric Blair looked back unforgivingly on the world before 1914 — it was that world that had sent him to his prep school — while George Orwell could believe it was superior to what came after it, and recorded the period nostalgically in *Coming Up for Air*. And if Eric Blair was enraged by the hypocrisies endemic to a boys' school in England of the First World War, George Orwell was moved to a simple and intense patriotism during the Second World War when England was endangered.

There were moments when Blair and Orwell were at one: in the comradeship of the Spanish Civil War, and in the inspiriting early years of the blitz when it was possible to believe in a brave new England to come. They were moments of honor and decency, in which Blair and Orwell could participate and feel at ease. But such moments could not last: they would be undone by the Stalinists, as in Spain, or by the thought police, as in *1984*. Then the struggle would be resumed, between the patriot and the radical, the idealist and the skeptic, the sahib and the victim. Out of the tension came the masterpieces *Homage to Catalonia, Animal Farm,* and the essays.

OSTADE, Adriaen van (Dec. 10, 1610 – May 2, 1685). Dutch painter. Born and died in Haarlem. Occasionally went to Amsterdam, where he married his second wife (1634). Member of painters' guild in Haarlem and became its dean (1662). Studied with Frans Hals, but particularly influenced by Adriaen Brouwer who also painted scenes of everyday peasant life. From 1640 Ostade was influenced by Rembrandt, turning from the tavern drinkers and smokers, peasants dancing and gaming of earlier works to calmer figures, to a richer tonality and more contrast of light and dark. His finest work is in this period, includes *The Slaughtered Pig* (1643, Stadelisches Kunstinstitut, Frankfurt) and *Cottage Dooryard* (National Gallery, Washington). He painted over a thousand pictures; influenced Jan Steen. His younger brother ISAAC VAN OSTADE (1621–1649), born and died in Haarlem, was a pupil of Adriaen Brouwer, and is especially known for his landscapes and winter scenes such as those in National Gallery and Wallace Collection, London; Louvre, Paris; Metropolitan Museum, New York.

OTWAY, Thomas (Mar. 3, 1652 – Apr. 10, 1685). English dramatist. Born at Trotton, Sussex, son of a clergyman. Educated at Winchester School and Christ Church, Oxford, which he left (1672) to pursue unsuccessful stage career in London. Developed lifelong unrequited love for the actress Mrs. Elizabeth Barry, who appeared as heroine in most of his dramas. His first play, *Alcibiades* (1675), in rhymed verse, was well received. Even more so was *Don Carlos* (1676), also in rhymed verse. It was followed by two adaptations, *Titus and Berenice* from Racine and *The Cheats of Scapin* from Molière (both 1677), and his own Restoration comedy *Friendship in Fashion* (1678). His plays were all produced by the famous actor Thomas Betterton. Returned to London after a brief military stint in Holland to write the comedies *The Soldier's Fortune* (1681) and *The Atheist* (1684). Maturity also produced the tragedies in blank verse on which his fame rests: *The Orphan* (1680) and in particular *Venice Preserved* (1682). His tragedies, more in the tradition of Racine than of Shakespeare, have plots of classic simplicity and abundant passion, with the heroine's role fully developed. Otway died destitute in an alehouse in London.

EDITION: *Complete Works* ed. J. C. Ghose (London 1932).

REFERENCES: Bonamy Dobrée *Restoration Tragedy* (1929), reprinted Oxford 1954). Edmund Gosse *Seventeenth-Century Studies* (1883, new ed. New York 1914). Roswell G. Ham *Otway and Lee: Biography from a Baroque Age* (1931, reprinted New York 1969). Aline M. Taylor *Next to Shakespeare* (Durham, N.C. 1950 and Cambridge, England, 1951).

OVID (Full name Publius Ovidius Naso) (Mar. 20, 43 B.C. – c. A.D. 17). Roman poet. Born Sulmo (modern Sulmona) to landowning family of equestrian rank. Studied law and rhetoric in Rome and Athens, then traveled in Sicily and Asia Minor before settling in Rome as member of cultivated society. Became an instant celebrity with the first of his erotic poems, *Amores*, which was followed by the *Heroides*, fictitious love letters addressed by legendary heroines, and *Ars Amatoria* (*The Art of Love*) in three books, which gives instruction on lovemaking and caused a sensation. While completing the first of his mythological writings, *Metamorphoses*, his greatest work, which in fifteen books retells Greek and Roman myths, Ovid for reasons never made clear was exiled to Tomi, an outpost on the Black Sea (A.D. 8) for the rest of his life. There he finished *Fasti*, a poetical calendar of Roman festivals, and composed his last series of poems expressing the sorrows of exile, including *Tristia* and *Epistulae ex Ponto*. The *Metamorphoses* in particular inspired much medieval and later art and literature, and has been extensively translated, as have the *Amores* (first by Christopher Marlowe) and *Ars Amatoria*.

TRANSLATIONS (all in the Loeb Classical Library series): *Metamorphoses* tr. Frank Justus Miller (latest ed. 2 vols. Cambridge, Mass. 1966). *The Art of Love, and Other Poems* tr. J. H. Mozley (latest ed. Cambridge, Mass. 1962). *Tristia* and *Ex Ponto* tr. A. L. Wheeler (latest ed. Cambridge, Mass. 1959). *Heroides* and *Amores* tr. Grant Showerman (latest ed. Cambridge, Mass. 1947).

REFERENCES: Hermann F. Fraenkel *Ovid: A Poet Between Two Worlds* (1945, reprinted Berkeley, Calif. 1969). Brooks Otis *Ovid as an Epic Poet* (Cambridge, England, 1966). Edward K. Rand *Ovid and His Influence* (1925, reprinted New York 1963). John C. Thibault *The Mystery of Ovid's Exile* (Berkeley, Calif. and Cambridge, England, 1964). Lancelot P. Wilkinson *Ovid Recalled* (Cambridge, England, 1955).

OWEN, Wilfred (Mar. 18, 1893 – Nov. 4, 1918). English poet. Born at Oswestry, Shropshire. Educated at Birkenhead Institute and Shrewsbury Technical School; matriculated at London University (1911) but lack of finances kept him from attending, and he became lay assistant to the vicar at Dunsden, Oxfordshire. Went to France (1913) became tutor in English at school of languages in Bordeaux, then took post as tutor in a family there. At outbreak of World War I he returned to England

and joined the Artists' Rifles (1915). Commissioned in Manchester Regiment, he left for the front (1916); returned wounded six months later and spent five months at Craiglockhart War Hospital, Edinburgh, where he met Siegfried Sassoon. Sent to the front again (1918) where, a month after being awarded the Military Cross for gallantry, he was killed in action, just a week before the armistice. Although a few of his poems had been published in magazines, he was virtually unknown until Sassoon collected his work in *Poems* (1920). Their subject, in the words of his preface, is "War and the pity of War. The Poetry is in the pity. All a poet can do is warn." His passionate utterance and experimental style, making use of assonance instead of rhyme, exerted tremendous influence on the young poets of the next generation, and his reputation as a major poet has grown with time.

EDITION: *Collected Poems* ed. C. Day Lewis, includes memoir by Edmund Blunden (London 1963 and New York 1964, also PB).

REFERENCES: W. Harold Owen *Journey from Obscurity: Memoirs of the Owen Family: Wilfred Owen, 1893–1918* (3 vols. London and New York 1963–65). D. S. R. Welland *Wilfred Owen: A Critical Study* (London 1960). Gertrude M. White *Wilfred Owen* (New York 1969).

PAGANINI, Niccolò (Oct. 27, 1782 – May 27, 1840). Italian violinist and composer. Born Genoa. An obedient child prodigy (first violin concert at nine) driven by an ambitious father, at fourteen he became rebellious and dissolute, a gambler and philanderer. Both extremes ruined his health (1804). Resuming a serious concert career (1805), he rapidly became popular virtuoso in Italy and director of music (1805–13) for Maria Bacciocchi, princess of Lucca (Napoleon's sister). Had a stormy liaison (1815–28) with singer Antonia Bianchi; their son Achillino was born 1826. First concert in Vienna (1828) began series of triumphant, profitable tours: the German provinces, Paris (1831), the British Isles (1831–32). A controversial showman, often accused of charlatanism, even of diabolism, he fully exploited both his Mephistophelian appearance and uncanny technical virtuosity. After semi-retiring to an estate near Parma, he gave rare recitals. Financial reverses (1836) further weakened his shaky health. Four years later, near Nice, he died of a disease of the throat, probably cancer, after a legendary deathbed performance on his Guarnerius. His major contribution was as a performer rather than composer, but among his memorable works are twenty-four caprices for violin solo, Op. 1 (themes used for piano by Schumann, Liszt, Brahms, Rachmaninoff); *Moto Perpetuo* and *Witches' Dance* (*Le Streghe*), both virtuoso showpieces.

REFERENCES: Lillian Day *Paganini of Genoa* (1929, new ed. London 1966). Geraldine I. C. De Courcy *Paganini the Genoese* (2 vols. Norman, Okla. 1957). Jeffrey Pulver *Paganini: The Romantic Virtuoso* (2nd ed. New York 1969).

Stephen Stratton *Nicolo Paganini* (London and New York 1907).

PAINE, Thomas (Jan. 29, 1737 – June 8, 1809). American writer. Born Thetford, Norfolk, England, son of a Quaker stay maker. After grammar school he held numerous jobs, including a position as exciseman from which he was dismissed for agitating for higher wages in Parliament. Married twice: to Mary Lambert (1759; she died soon afterward) and to Elizabeth Ollive (1771; they separated legally 1774). Sailed for America (1774) with letters of introduction from Benjamin Franklin, whom he met in London. An editor of the *Pennsylvania Magazine* and contributor to the *Pennsylvania Journal,* he became involved in the revolutionary struggle and wrote (1776) his famous pamphlet *Common Sense,* which urged independence and exerted a powerful influence. Enlisted in Continental army and wrote series of revolutionary pamphlets *The Crisis* (1776–83), the first of which begins with the celebrated line "These are the times that try men's souls." Left army to serve as secretary of the committee on foreign affairs of the Continental Congress (1777–79); then became clerk of the Pennsylvania Assembly (1779–81). After the war New York awarded him a farm at New Rochelle, and here he continued his writings on various subjects. Left for England (1787) to launch his scheme for iron bridge construction. While there replied to Edmund Burke's critical *Reflections on the French Revolution* with his *Rights of Man* (in two parts, 1791/92), advocating a similar revolution in Britain, for which he was prosecuted. He escaped to France, where he was elected to the National Convention as member from Calais. At the trial of Louis XVI he voted against execution, and was arrested and imprisoned (1793), but upon the fall of Robespierre released. His deistic treatise *The Age of Reason, Being an Investigation of True and Fabulous Theology* (in three parts: 1794, 1795, and 1807) was adversely received as an attack on religion and alienated his friends abroad and in America, to which he returned (1802). Lived for a time on his farm where, having died in New York, he was buried. His remains were moved to England (1819) by William Cobbett. A man of intellect and a writer of vigor, Paine was regarded as a great lover of liberty and admired by Washington, Jefferson, and Franklin, especially for his outstanding services in the American cause.

EDITION: *The Writings of Thomas Paine* ed. Moncure D. Conway (1902–1908, reprinted 2 vols. New York 1969).

REFERENCES: Alfred O. Aldridge *Man of Reason: The Life of Thomas Paine* (Philadelphia 1959 and London 1960). Moncure D. Conway *The Life of Thomas Paine* (1892, new ed. New York 1968). William E. Woodward *Tom Paine: America's Godfather* (New York 1945 and London 1947).

PALESTRINA, Giovanni (Pierluigi da) (c.1525 – Feb. 2, 1594). Italian composer. Born Palestrina, of the Pierluigi family. Although he spent some of his youth in Rome (as a chorister at S. Maria Maggiore, 1537; as a music student, 1540), his career really began in Palestrina when he became choirmaster-organist there (1544). Married Lucrezia de Goris (1547). Appointed (1551) choirmaster of Cappella Giulia in Rome by Pope Julius III (former bishop of Palestrina), to whom he dedicated his first book of Masses (1554). Published first book of madrigals (1555) and for next dozen years served as music director of St. John Lateran (1555–60), then of S. Maria Maggiore (1561–67). During this period (c.1563), supposedly persuaded Council of Trent not to proscribe contrapuntal music as profane. First book of motets appeared (1563). From 1567 to 1571 concerned

himself with miscellaneous musical enterprises, some secular, including serving the Cardinal d'Este at his villa at Tivoli. From 1571 until his death, music director of Cappella Giulia. The various epidemics in Rome of 1572–80 carried off two of his three sons, two brothers, and his wife (1580). After briefly considering the priesthood, he married before the year was out a rich widow, Virginia Dormuli, and successfully ran her inherited fur business while continuing to compose. His liturgical works (including 93 Masses, hundreds of motets) are polyphonic, written for unaccompanied voices, related to plainsong; his secular works, over a hundred madrigals, are based on French or Dutch chansons. With his contemporary Orlandus Lassus, Palestrina is considered one of the greatest Renaissance composers. Died in Rome, buried at St. Peter's (his remains were later moved to an unknown location).

REFERENCES: H. K. Andrews *An Introduction to the Technique of Palestrina* (London 1958). Henry Coates *Palestrina* (London and New York 1938). Knud Jeppesen *The Style of Palestrina and the Dissonance* (tr. 1927, 2nd ed. Oxford 1946, PB 1969). Zoe K. Pyne *Giovanni Pierluigi da Palestrina: His Life and Times* (London and New York 1922). Gustave Reese *Music in the Renaissance* (1954, rev. ed. New York 1959).

PALLADIO, Andrea (real name Andrea di Pietro della Gondola) (Nov. 30, 1508 – Aug. 19, 1580). Italian architect. Born Padua, where he was apprenticed to a stonecutter until 1524. Moved to Vicenza and worked as stonemason; then was given an education by poet and scholar Giangiorgio Trissino and taken to Rome to study ancient and Renaissance art. Married Allegra, daughter of Marcantonio Marangon (c.1534). Began (1540's) career as professional designer of villas in neighborhood of Vicenza, where he received his first major public commission: reconstruction of medieval town hall, the Basilica (work begun 1549). Among his famous villas of 1550's and 1560's are Palazzo Chiericati, Villa Capra (or Rotonda), and Palazzo Valmarana, all at Vicenza; Villa Barbaro at Maser; Villa Foscari

(La Malcontenta) at Fusina. In late years built churches in Venice of which major examples are S. Giorgio Maggiore (begun 1565) and Il Redentore (begun 1576). Before his death in Venice he finished design for Teatro Olimpico, Vicenza, completed by Vincenzo Scamozzi. Palladio also wrote *Le antichità di Roma* (1554), a small guidebook to the ancient monuments, and *I quattro libri dell'architettura* (*Four Books of Architecture*, 1570). The latter set forth his principles of design, included drawings of many of his own plans, and spread his influence throughout the world. Palladianism reached its height during the eighteenth century.

TRANSLATION: *The Four Books of Architecture* tr. Nicholas Dubois (1715, new ed. New York 1965).

REFERENCES: James S. Ackerman *Palladio* (Harmondsworth, England, 1966 and Baltimore PB 1967) and *Palladio's Villas* (Locust Valley, N.Y. 1967). Franco Barbieri *Palladio's Basilica in Vicenza* (tr. University Park, Pa. 1969). Camillo Semenzato *The Rotonda of Andrea Palladio* (tr. University Park, Pa. 1968). Rudolph Wittkower *Architectural Principles in the Age of Humanism* (3rd ed. London 1962 and New York 1965, also PB).

✍

PALLADIO
BY JAMES S. ACKERMAN

If we measured the importance of an architect in terms of his influence, Palladio would be the unchallenged master of all time. In every country of the western world, thousands of churches, houses, and public buildings display their debt to his inventiveness in façades symmetrically arranged about a central pedimented columnar portico. It was Palladio who inspired the American building style of much of the pre- and post-revolutionary period: Thomas Jefferson used his *Four Books of Architecture* (1570) in designing his home in Monticello and the University of Virginia; George Washington's Mount Vernon took from Palladio the curving colonnades before the river front; the first designs for the National Capitol and the Boston State House depended on the British eighteenth-century revival of Palladian architecture — a revival that occurred in almost every country of northern Europe as a reaction to the overrefined and courtly elegance of the rococo style.

Unlike most Renaissance architects, who were trained in the ateliers of painters, Palladio started his career as a stonemason. He was hired in this capacity by Giangiorgio Trissino, a humanist writer of Vicenza, who sensed Palladio's talent and took him into his school for young aristocrats, gave him the rudiments of a classical education and, in 1541, took him to Rome to study the monuments of antiquity. Architects had been borrowing ideas from Roman remains for a century, but Palladio was the first to look at them as an archaeologist, and to attempt to draw plausible reconstructions of them in their original condition. When he returned to work for the gentlemen of Vicenza and Venice, who were themselves steeped in classical learning, he created a new kind of architecture that combined the splendor of imperial Rome with the achievements of a brilliant older generation of Roman architects that included Bramante, Raphael, Michelangelo, Antonio da Sangallo, and Guilio Romano. To this combination he added the ingredient that makes his work unique: proportion.

Palladio conceived the manipulation of numerical proportions as a means not only of creating pleasing façades and interior spaces, but of integrating all parts of a building. He would relate the plan of a room to its elevation, side rooms to central rooms, central rooms to the total perimeter, and all of these to the façade by a system of ratios borrowed from musical theory. In a sequence of rooms, he would bind the dimensions of each to its neighbor by simple ratios — for example, one 12′ × 12′ (1:1), the next 12′ × 18′ (2:3), and the third, 18′ × 30′ (3:5) — corresponding to musical intervals as measured on a monochord, and the result is as pleasing to the eye as it would be to the ear. The system was applied within a rigorously ordered symmetrical scheme in which the major features of the plan and façade were placed at the center, and dependent elements mirrored one another on either side: where there is a stairwell or tower on the left, there is one on the right. So the building would have the symmetry of the human body: a central spine, nose, and mouth; and lateral legs, eyes, ears. The unconscious awareness of this metaphor increases our delight in Palladio's designs.

Palladio was most inventive and influential in the design of villas. There had been little building in the Venetian countryside in the generation preceding his first villas. Not only had the *terraferma*, as the mainland territory of Venice was called, been devastated by war, but large portions of it were flooded by rivers and the ocean. In the 1540's vast projects of reclamation were started as the Venetian nobility began to turn its resources from overseas trade to agriculture. Palladio's clients needed a type of country estate that was not a rustic retreat but a glorified farm that should combine stable, storehouses, and grain lofts with the splendors of Roman architecture. Palladio met the challenge with a quite new kind of villa, elegant yet practical, in which a central living block, often preceded by a pedimented portico modeled on the Roman temple, was flanked by low wings serving farm functions. To save expense, the walls, columns, and decoration were made of brick,

then stuccoed and painted, which permitted a new range of color; stone was used only for framing apertures and for capitals and bases of columns. Nevertheless, few were finished according to the designs illustrated in the *Four Books;* generally, only the central block was built. Some nineteen survive in whole or part, and many are ornamented with fresco cycles of allegorical scenes portraying contemporary life or mythological subjects. The most impressive are Villa Barbaro at Maser, decorated by Veronese, Villa Emo at Fanzolo, still owned by the descendant of Palladio's client, and Villa Rotonda in Vicenza, an exception in being designed as a pleasure pavilion rather than a farmhouse.

Palladio's palaces, mostly in Vicenza, were based on the types popular in contemporary Rome, but are unique in their orderly symmetrical planning and in the references to ancient architecture, such as the entrance atrium and the peristyle court. Again, few were completed as they appear in the *Four Books,* a misfortune that is apparent in the court of the Thiene palace in Vicenza, with its two-story arcades, which though less than half complete is one of the most majestic sights of Renaissance architecture.

In Vicenza's public square, Palladio built the arcades of the huge medieval Basilica, and part of a civic loggia named for the presiding officer of the Venetian Republic. The former design solved with great skill problems of buttressing the interior building and of compensating for its irregularities, but it was not really original. The bays of the upper story with their central arched opening flanked by narrower and lower linteled openings came, in honor of the Basilica, to be called "Palladian," though the motif was used by Bramante half a century earlier. The loggia of 1571 is characteristic of Palladio's late work in its ample forms and richness of texture and ornament which makes the most of the play of light over the surface.

Every visitor to Venice recalls Palladio's two major churches, which face the city from across the Giudecca canal — San Giorgio Maggiore and Il Redentore (Redeemer) — as brilliant incidents in that magical environment. Their façades of white Istrian stone, often imitated in later Venetian churches, adapt the Roman temple portico and pediment to the three-part arrangement of the Renaissance church. The interiors, bare of ornament and mural painting, are ample theatres for a moving play of light.

The great majority of Palladio's imitators in later centuries learned of his architecture through editions of his book rather than by visiting the hinterlands of Venice. Because his style was grounded in concepts of planar composition and proportion, elements of it could be transmitted effectively in rather crude woodcut illustrations. But just for this reason, the followers almost always missed the color, the subtlety, and the geniality of the originals.

Though the columns and pediments of Palladio's architecture no longer are relevant to building today, many of our designers are still, consciously or not, heirs of his legacy of mathematical order.

PALMER, Samuel (Jan. 27, 1805 – May 24, 1881). British artist. Born London, the son of a bookseller, who educated him and encouraged him to paint. By 1819 had exhibited at Royal Academy, but only in mid-1820's did his visionary style develop. John Linnell (whose daughter Hannah he married, 1837) introduced him (1824) to William Blake, a major influence. Settled in Shoreham, Kent (1827); from 1827 to 1832 he exhibited only two works: *The Deluge* and *Ruth Returned from the Gleaning* (1828, Victoria and Albert Museum, London). Took up watercolor and (1850) etching. Interest in Milton inspired his eight watercolor illustrations for *L'Allegro* and *Il Penseroso* (1868–87). But the subjects of his paintings were chiefly scriptural (*Repose of the Holy Family*, 1824–25, Ashmolean Museum, Oxford) or pastoral, *In a Shoreham Garden*, 1829, and *The Bright Cloud*, 1834, both in Victoria and Albert Museum). His style is noted for great precision and mystical intensity in his depiction of nature. Influenced by medieval art, he blended landscape and symbol, and was the last of the great school of landscape painters that included Claude Lorrain and Turner. He died in Reigate, Surrey.

REFERENCES: Lord David Cecil *Visionary and Dreamer: Two Poetic Painters, Samuel Palmer and Edward Burne-Jones* (London 1969 and New York 1970). Geoffrey Grigson *Samuel Palmer: The Visionary Years* (London and Boston 1947) and *Samuel Palmer's Valley of Vision* (London 1960). Carlos Peacock *Samuel Palmer: Shoreham and After* (New York and London 1969). Raymond Lister *Samuel Palmer and His Etchings* (New York 1969).

PARKMAN, Francis (Sept. 16, 1823 – Nov. 8, 1893). Born Boston into prominent "Brahmin" family. Early developed love of wilderness and Indians. While sophomore at Harvard conceived plan of writing history of France and England in North America. Before graduating (1844), toured Europe, and on return published travel sketches in the *Knickerbocker*. After receiving degree at Harvard Law School (1846), traveled from St. Louis to the West, gathering material for *The California and Oregon Trail* (1849), the fourth edition of which as *The Oregon Trail* (1872) was to become a classic. On return to Boston (1846) suffered severe nervous breakdown, but persisted in work as a historian despite recurring attacks. Published *History of the Conspiracy of Pontiac* (2 vols. 1851) and began the work which established his reputation, *Pioneers of France in the New World* (1865). These were the first of a series of histories dealing with colonial struggles for domination of North America. Others: *The Jesuits in North America in the Seventeenth Century* (1867), *La Salle and the Discovery of the Great West* (1869), *The Old Regime in Canada* (1874), *Count Frontenac and New France under Louis XIV* (1877), *Montcalm and Wolfe* (2 vols. 1884), *A Half-Century of Conflict* (1892). Poor health having turned him to gardening, he also wrote *The Book of Roses* (1866), and was professor of horticulture at Harvard (1871–72). Died at Jamaica Plain, near Boston.

EDITIONS: *Works* Frontenac Edition (20 vols. Boston 1899–1905). *The Parkman Reader* ed. Samuel Eliot Morison (Boston 1955 and London 1956, also PB). *The Letters of Francis Parkman* ed. Wilbur R. Jacobs (2 vols. Norman, Okla. 1960). *The Journals of Francis Parkman* ed. Mason Wade (2 vols. New York 1947).

REFERENCES: Howard Doughty *Francis Parkman* (New York 1962). Otis A. Pease *Parkman's History: The Historian as Literary Artist* (1953, reprinted Hamden, Conn. 1968). Mason Wade *Francis Parkman: Heroic Historian* (New York 1942).

✍

FRANCIS PARKMAN

BY MARCUS CUNLIFFE

Given his outward circumstances, Francis Parkman need never have done a day's hard work. He was born into that circle of assured and prosperous Boston families which Oliver Wendell Holmes was to characterize as "Brahmin." His father was a polished Unitarian minister, his grandfather a rich merchant. Various stages in his life — attendance at Harvard, presidency of Hasty Pudding, a grand tour in Europe, a law school interlude, an appropriate marriage — seemed preordained. Add to these the composition of an unsuccessful novel (*Vassall Morton*, 1856), a fondness for flower growing that led him to write *The Book of Roses* (1866), weak eyesight, a pronounced tendency to nervous prostration (which, as with his acquaintance Henry James, kept

him out of the Civil War): add all these and we have the makings of a portrait of a fastidious dilettante, a Bostonian worthy of closed and complacent horizons, cushioned and debilitated by the possession of an inherited income.

There are in fact aspects of Parkman that fit such a picture. The only formal position he occupied, briefly, was a Harvard chair of horticulture. Harvard remained his alma mater to an almost cloying extent. He served as an overseer of Harvard and a fellow of its corporation. He dedicated one of his books to his classmates, and another to the college. Though he traveled fairly far and often, Boston was emphatically his home. His opinions on topics of the day, which he was now and then provoked to declare publicly by means of pamphlets or letters to newspapers, were the opinions proper to a well-established gentleman of conservative leanings. Parkman, for instance, was hostile to abolitionism, woman suffrage, conspicuous moneymaking and Democratic politics. He regarded President Lincoln as "feeble and ungainly"; he was convinced that the Union would go on losing battles until it purged itself of "demagoguery" and selected its commanders from among the gentry. Having exactly lived out his allotted span, he died (in 1893), not far from the house he owned at 50 Chestnut Street — the hub of the hub of the universe — that had once belonged to his father.

An awareness of such factors may explain why until recently Parkman's importance as a historian has been conceded yet not enthusiastically appraised. Literary and historiographical surveys have paid tribute to him as among the foremost American historians — perhaps as *the* foremost. But in assigning him "classic" status they have, we might say, taken him as read: in other words, absolved the student from reading him. It has been vaguely supposed that his narrative method made him irrelevant for historians committed to more analytical approaches; that his descriptions of warfare and exploration belonged to the "drum-and-trumpet" era of historical writing; that in seeking to be dramatic he exaggerated the role of certain of his heroes; and that he was biased. Readers eager to be assured that the American West was the true home of democracy might take comfort from Frederick Jackson Turner. They would not find much in Francis Parkman. Even in his first, most popular book, the autobiographical *The Oregon Trail* (1849), a Western buff would be disconcerted to discover how unromantically Parkman viewed the majority of Indians or settlers among whom he sojourned.

This neglect of Parkman has now been redressed in excellent studies by such sympathetic scholars as Otis Pease, David Levin, Howard Doughty, Samuel Eliot Morison, and William R. Taylor. What intrigues them all, and must fascinate any sensitive reader, is the relation of the man to his work. The conditions of Brahminism both disabled and invigorated him. Complete indolence was not psychologically permissible in Parkman's Boston — at least not unless one opted out by living in Europe, as did a playboy uncle of his. But what careers were open to the patriciate? Politics and business were unthinkable. Law was too arid for one of Parkman's restive temperament. Medicine was ruled out (another uncle, Dr. George Parkman, brought notoriety to the family through being murdered by a professor at the Harvard Medical School). The ministry likewise held no appeal for young

Parkman, who later in life admitted to being a "reverent agnostic"; if evangelicalism was too crude to attract him, Unitarianism was too pallid.

There remained the profession of letters. But in common with such other Bostonians as W. H. Prescott and John L. Motley, Parkman lacked the talent or the inclination for imaginative writing. His temperament favored the ascertainable fact, the framework of actuality. A robust boy, he developed a passion for the pockets of wild landscape still to be found in the vicinity of Boston, and abundantly present in the forest wilderness of northern New England. While an undergraduate he therefore began to address himself to his lifelong theme: the history of the wanderings and conflicts of the French and English nations in North America. In exploring such a theme he could satisfy his desire to be respectably active; he could seek recognition as an author, yet avoid the more effeminate, drawing-room connotations of belles lettres; and he could indulge the martial and patriotic impulses still strong in one whose ancestors had fought at Ticonderoga and at Lexington.

The American wilderness was to be his great escape, his assertion of a manliness not incompatible with gentlemanliness. Parkman thus pioneered a route followed later by Harvard patricians like Theodore Roosevelt and Owen Wister. The literary outcome — eight volumes of history, culminating in *A Half-Century of Conflict* (1892) — was the more extraordinary because, after the arduous travels chronicled in *The Oregon Trail*, Parkman suffered a neurasthenic collapse, aggravated by eyestrain, that incapacitated him for long periods. It is tempting to suppose that the visitations of this ailment — which he called "the Enemy" — supplied Parkman with an unconscious means of disqualifying himself from personal involvement in the clamantly active America of his own day. What is more certain is that he re-created his own frustrations and aspirations in the stories of his principal characters. Most of them — La Salle, Champlain, Frontenac, Montcalm, Wolfe — were gentlemen as well as men of action. They endured appalling hardships, dangers, disappointments, betrayals: Coriolanuses with a tincture of Captain Ahab, sustained by the sheer effort of individual will, the ingrained habit of aristocratic courage. Time ran against most of them. Some, like the murdered La Salle, lay in unmarked graves. They knew the bitterness of defeat, and of victories without consequence.

It is a dark, compulsive saga, redeemed by the sense of human gallantry — "grace under pressure," in Hemingway's phrase — and by Parkman's remarkable ability to evoke the precise look and feel of a scene. His one novel is marred by self-pity and melodrama. His histories, though they may be interpreted as a gloss upon the problems of a Boston gentleman in a vulgar era, are raised far above querulous personal concerns. Ancestral voices speak through him, accurately, vividly, without bluster or bathos. The hypochondriac Brahmin, blinds drawn against the painful light, recovers his past, America's past, as devotedly as that other hypochondriac artist, Marcel Proust, recovered the lost French civilization of Combray.

PARMIGIANINO, Il (real name Girolamo Francesco Maria Mazzola or Mazzuoli) (Jan. 11, 1503 – Aug. 24, 1540). Italian painter. Took name from birthplace, Parma. Raised by uncles, both painters. First important work, the *Marriage of St. Catherine* (1521, S. Maria, Bardi), shows influence of Correggio, and prefigures his rejection of High Renaissance tenets. Handsome and precocious, he moved to Rome (1524), presenting as credentials to Pope Clement VII self-portrait reflected in convex mirror (1523, Kunsthistorisches Museum, Vienna). One of the early mannerists, he produced *Vision of St. Jerome* (1526–27, National Gallery, London), and other paintings that also show influence of Raphael and Michelangelo. After the sack of Rome (1527) by Charles V, he escaped to Bologna, where he perfected his mannerist vision, revising nature into improbably graceful, attenuated, luminous forms, as in *Madonna with St. Margaret and Other Saints* (1528–29, Pinacoteca Nazionale, Bologna). He was also one of the first Italian etchers. Returning to Parma (1531), he became obsessed with alchemy, increasingly more eccentric personally and distracted artistically, although *Madonna del Collo Lungo* (1535, Uffizi, Florence) is of this period. Having undertaken redecoration of S. Maria della Steccata, he managed to complete only one series of frescoes and was prosecuted for breach of contract. At thirty-seven, poverty-stricken in nearby Casalmaggiore, he died. His mannerist paintings and etchings exerted strong influence in Italy and northern Europe.

REFERENCES: Sydney J. Freedberg *Parmigianino: His Works in Painting* (Cambridge, Mass. and Oxford 1950). A. E. Popham *The Drawings of Parmigianino* (London and New York 1953). John Shearman *Mannerism* (Harmondsworth, England, 1967, also PB). Giorgio Vasari *Lives of the . . . Painters, Sculptors and Architects* (1550) Vol. V ed. and tr. Gaston de Vere (10 vols. London 1912–15).

PASCAL, Blaise (June 19, 1623 – Aug. 19, 1662). French philosopher. Born Clermont, Auvergne, son of a magistrate of old ennobled family. After mother died, moved to Paris (1631). Educated by father, he early showed striking aptitude for mathematics, and at sixteen wrote a treatise on conic sections. Two Jansenist friends of the family converted him to their doctrine of predestination through divine grace (1646). Death of his father (1651) inaugurated a period of both scientific and social activity, in course of which he produced a second treatise. It ended abruptly upon Pascal's experiencing an "ecstasy" in the night of November 23, 1654. Thereafter he became associated with Port-Royal, convent of the Jansenist group, for whom he wrote the eighteen *Lettres provinciales* (1656–57), a polemic against the Jesuits. An increasingly painful illness as well as prolific scientific and literary activity marked the subsequent years. Death prevented him from finishing his other great literary achievement, *Apologie de la religion chrétienne,* the notes from which were collected posthumously as the *Pensées.* The influence of Pascal's theology and thought on the paradox of man is far-reaching. Many of his *Pensées* remain famous, such as "Man is but a reed, the weakest in nature, but he is a thinking reed"; "Man is neither angel nor beast; and the misfortune is that he who would act the angel acts the beast"; "The heart has its reasons which reason knows nothing of." He died in Paris.

TRANSLATIONS: *Pensées* tr. William F. Trotter (1931, latest ed. New York 1965, also PB). *The Provincial Letters* tr. Thomas McCrie (1850, new ed. London 1904). Both translations published in one volume by Modern Library (New York 1941).
REFERENCES: Morris Bishop *Pascal: The Life of Genius* (1936, reprinted New York 1968). Jack H. Broome *Pascal* (London 1965 and New York 1966). Émile Cailliet *Pascal: The Emergence of Genius* (2nd ed. New York and London 1961, also PB). Romano Guardini *Pascal for Our Time* (tr. New York 1966). Jean Mesnard *Pascal: His Life and Works* (tr. London and New York 1952). Ernest Mortimer *Blaise Pascal: The Life and Work of a Realist* (New York and London 1959). Jean Steinmann *Pascal* (tr. London 1965 and New York 1966). Hugh F. Stewart *The Secret of Pascal* (Cambridge, England, and New York 1941). Clement C. J. Webb *Pascal's Philosophy of Religion* (Oxford 1929).

PASTERNAK, Boris (Leonidovich) (Feb. 10, 1890 – May 30, 1960). Russian writer. Born Moscow, son of painter Leonid Pasternak and pianist Rosa Kaufman. Through influence of composer Scriabin, studied music in early years. Educated at Moscow University (1909–13) and University of Marburg, Germany (1912), where he studied philosophy. Published first collection of poems, *A Twin in the Clouds* (1914); gained recognition with *My Sister, Life* (1922), *Themes and Variations* (1923), and other volumes of verse in 1920's. Except for visits to Germany (1923), the Caucasus (1930–31), and Paris (1935), spent all his life in or near Moscow. At height of Stalinist regime, Pasternak's poetry was officially banned for his nonpolitical position. During this period he published translations, largely from Shakespeare. Published new poems, *On Early Trains* (1943) and *The Terrestrial Expanse* (1945). From 1946 worked on his novel *Doctor Zhivago* (tr. 1958), only excerpts of which were published in U.S.S.R.; Italian translation appeared (1957). Awarded Nobel prize (1958), he was forced by severe political pressure from Soviet authorities to refuse it. However, the Western world hailed *Doctor Zhivago* as a masterpiece, a narrative full of philosophical reflection, human passion, and Christian spirituality, set against the history of Russia from the revolutions of 1905 and 1917 into World War II. The appendix contains his latest and greatest lyrics, in a simpler, more classical style than his early experimental verse. He also wrote the stories *Aerial Journeys* (1925) and an autobiographical memoir, *Safe Conduct* (1931). He died at Peredelkino.

TRANSLATION: *Poems* tr. Eugene M. Kayden (2nd ed. Yellow Springs, Ohio, 1964). *I Remember: Sketch for an Autobiography* tr. David Magarshack (London and New York 1959).
REFERENCES: Robert Conquest *The Pasternak Affair* (London 1961 and Philadelphia 1962). Robert Payne *The Three Worlds of Boris Pasternak* (New York 1961 and London 1962, also PB). Dale L. Plank *Pasternak's Lyric: A Study of Sound and Imagery* (New York 1965). Renato Poggioli *The Poets of Russia, 1890–1930* (Cambridge, Mass. and Oxford 1960). Mary F. and Paul Rowland *Pasternak's Doctor Zhivago* (Carbondale, Ill. 1967, also PB).

Gerd Ruge *Pasternak: A Pictorial Biography* (tr. London and New York 1959).

PATER, Walter (Horatio) (Aug. 4, 1839 – July, 30, 1894). English writer. Born London; educated at King's School, Canterbury, and Queen's College, Oxford (B.A. 1862). Made fellow (1864) of Brasenose College, Oxford, where, except for visits to London and travels on the Continent, he remained for rest of his life. Renown came to the classics tutor with his collection of essays on art and poetry, *Studies in the History of the Renaissance* (1873). Enormously popular with young aesthetes, who saw in its somewhat hedonistic and subjective theories a landmark of the aesthetic movement, it became one of the most influential books of its day, hailed by such writers as Oscar Wilde and George Moore. A historical novel, *Marius the Epicurean* (1885), proved equally successful and, somewhat to his embarrassment, Pater came to be considered an apostle to the decadents of the Eighties and Nineties. A bachelor, he quietly continued his scholarly studies, producing *Imaginary Portraits* (1887), the novel *The Child in the House* (1894), as well as volumes of critical essays including *Appreciations, with an Essay on Style* (1889), *Plato and Platonism* (1893), and the posthumous *Miscellaneous Studies* (1895). After a brief illness he died in Oxford.

EDITION: *Works* (8 vols. London and New York 1900–1901).
REFERENCES: Arthur C. Benson *Walter Pater* (1906, reprinted Detroit 1968). Ruth C. Child *The Aesthetic of Pater* (1940, reprinted New York 1969). Arthur Symons *A Study of Walter Pater* (London 1932). Anthony Ward *Walter Pater: The Idea in Nature* (London 1966). Thomas Wright *Life of Walter Pater* (1907, reprinted 2 vols. New York 1969).

PATINIR (PATENIER or PATINIER), Joachim (de) (c.1485–c.1524). Flemish painter. Born possibly in Bouvignes. Joined painters' guild in Antwerp (1515), where he lived for rest of his life. Married first Françoise Buyst, then Jeanne Noyts (1521). Albrecht Dürer attended the wedding and drew his por-

trait. Influenced by Hieronymous Bosch and Jan van Eyck, Patinir was the first Flemish painter to focus primarily on landscape rather than on the figures depicted in them. He specialized in religious subjects set in fantastic scenery — tiny figures of saints among rocks and grottoes or ruins with mountains in the distance, imaginative fantasy mixed with naturalistic detail. Only a few paintings are signed, all dates unknown. This, together with the number of Patinir's imitators and the fact that often he supplied only backgrounds for figures painted by others, makes authentication of his paintings problematic. Among his best-known works are *Baptism of Christ* (Kunsthistorisches Museum, Vienna), several paintings of *St. Jerome* (Prado, Madrid; Louvre, Paris; Metropolitan Museum, New York), and two of *The Flight into Egypt* (Musée Royal des Beaux Arts, Antwerp; Prado, Madrid).
REFERENCES: Sir Martin Conway *The Van Eycks and Their Followers* (London and New York 1921). Max J. Friedlaender *Landscape, Portrait, Still Life: Their Origin and Development* (tr. Oxford and New York 1949, also PB) and *From Van Eyck to Breugel* (3rd ed. New York 1969, also 2 vols. PB). Robert A. Koch *Joachim Patinir* (Princeton, N.J. 1968).

PATMORE, Coventry (Kersey Dighton) (July 23, 1823 – Nov. 26, 1896). English poet. Born Woodford, Essex, son of a writer. Privately educated. Worked as assistant librarian of British Museum (1846–65). Married Emily Augusta Andrews (1847; she died 1862), daughter of Congregational minister. His first volume of poems was poorly received, but put Patmore in touch with Pre-Raphaelites, to whose periodical, *Germ*, he contributed. Also wrote for *Edinburgh Review*. More poems appeared (1853) with greater success. They were followed by *The Betrothal* (1854), *The Espousals* (1856), *Faithful Forever* (1860), and *The Victories of Love* (1862), four parts of *The Angel in the House* (1862), his best-known work, a celebration of love in marriage, admired by his friends Tennyson, Ruskin, Browning, and Carlyle. Converted to Roman Catholicism (1864). Married

Marianne Caroline Byles (1865; she died 1880). His later works include the odes *The Unknown Eros* (1877), collected articles *Principle in Art* (1899), *Religio Poetae* (1893), and religious meditations, *Rod, Root and Flower* (1895). Married Harriet Robson (1881). Died at Lymington, Hampshire.

EDITION: *Poems* ed. Frederick Page (London and New York 1949).

REFERENCES: Osbert Burdett *The Idea of Coventry Patmore* (London 1921). Edward J. Oliver *Coventry Patmore* (New York 1956). Frederick Page *Patmore: A Study in Poetry* (Oxford 1933, reprinted Hamden, Conn. 1970). Derek Patmore *The Life and Times of Coventry Patmore* (London 1949 and New York 1950). John C. Reid *The Mind and Art of Coventry Patmore* (New York and London 1957).

PEACOCK, Thomas Love (Oct. 18, 1785 – Jan. 23, 1866). English novelist and poet. Born Weymouth, Dorset, son of a London merchant whose death (1788) caused family to move to Chertsey. Though his only formal schooling consisted of six years at Englefield, Peacock was self-educated and widely read. After a clerkship in London (1800), he began to write poetry, published *The Monks of St. Mark's* (1804) and *Palmyra and Other Poems* (1806). Became secretary to a naval officer (1808), spent a winter at sea, and began long poem *The Genius of the Thames* (1810). Knew many of the romantic poets, especially Shelley, went on walking tours, and began the writing that established him, the delightful satirical novels *Headlong Hall* (1816), *Melincourt* (1817), and *Nightmare Abbey* (1818). One of the great comic writers of his time, Peacock used the device of the motley gathering in an old house, thereby creating caricatures of great personalities and lampooning the theories and ideas he considered farfetched. Took a post (1819) in examiner's office of the East India Company; married Jane Gryffydh (1820; she died 1852). They had four children; his eldest daughter became first wife of George Meredith. He continued to write novels: *Maid Marian* (1822), a burlesque of Robin Hood; *The Misfortunes of Elphin* (1829), satire on the Welsh;

and *Crotchet Castle* (1831). Thereafter as examiner he was too busy to write. After retirement (1856), he embarked on *Memorials of Percy Bysshe Shelley* (1858–62) and his last novel, *Gryll Grange* (1860). He died at his cottage at Lower Halliford, Chertsey.

EDITION: *Works* ed. H. F. B. Brett-Smith and C. E. Jones (10 vols. London and New York 1924–34).

REFERENCES: Carl Dawson *Thomas Love Peacock* (New York and London 1968, also PB). Howard W. Mills *Peacock: His Circle and His Age* (Cambridge, England, 1968). J. B. Priestley *Thomas Love Peacock* (1927, new ed. London and New York 1966). Carl Van Doren *Life of Thomas Love Peacock* (1911, reprinted New York 1966).

PEALE, Charles Willson (Apr. 15, 1741 – Feb. 22, 1827). American artist. Born Queen Anne County, Md. Worked as saddlemaker in Annapolis (1762), but his revolutionary activities alienated his loyalist creditors, and he gave up trade for portrait painting. A group of Annapolis citizens sent him to London (1767) to study with Benjamin West, and upon return (1769), he rapidly became the leading painter of the colonies. Painted (1772) the first of his sixty portraits of George Washington, seven from life, including full-length portrait of 1778–79 (Museum of Art, Philadelphia) and the 1784 one at Yorktown (Annapolis). Moved to Philadelphia (1776), his home thereafter, and served in Continental army, continuing to paint portraits. Served in the Pennsylvania Assembly (1779–80) as one of the Furious Whigs. He and his sons established in Philadelphia the museum of natural history (1784–1802), which became the prototype for later similar museums. *Exhuming the Mastodon* (1806, Peale Museum, Baltimore) records one of Peale's archaeological undertakings. During his lifetime he painted about eleven hundred portraits, his subjects including most of the prominent figures of the time. Equally versatile and energetic in his private life, he had three wives (Rachel Brewer, 1762; Elizabeth de Peyster, 1791; Hannah Moore, 1805) and seventeen children. Among these were Rembrandt Peale (1778–1860), most gifted of the sons in portraiture and miniatures; Raphaelle (1774–1825), noted for still lifes; Rubens and Titian, both naturalists. At eighty-one, Peale portrayed his brother James, a miniature painter, in *Lamplight Portrait of James Peale* (1822, Institute of Arts, Detroit). Artist, museum curator, inventor, patriot, this protean American died at eighty-five in Philadelphia on Washington's birthday.

REFERENCES: Wolfgang Born *Still Life Painting in America* (New York and London 1947). Robert Plate *Charles Willson Peale* (New York 1967). Charles Coleman Sellers *Charles Willson Peale* (New York 1969) and *Portraits and Miniatures by Charles Willson Peale* (Philadelphia 1952).

PEELE, George (c.1558–c.1597). English playwright and poet. Birthplace possibly Devonshire. Raised and educated at Christ's Hospital, a London orphans' home where his father was head bookkeeper. Went to Pembroke College, Oxford (1571, B.A. 1577, M.A. 1579), and stayed on until 1581, when he and his wife, Anne Cooke, moved to London. There he continued to lead a life of dissipation, struggling to make a living as a playwright and occasional actor, and consorting with such University Wits as Robert Greene, Thomas Kyd, Thomas Nash, and Christopher Marlowe. Reputed to have written many plays; the chief authentic ones are *The Arraignment of Paris* (1584), a pastoral play in verse; *King Edward the First* (1593), a chronicle play; *The Old Wives' Tale* (1595), notable as a source of Milton's *Comus; The Love of King David and Fair Bethsabe* (1599), in blank verse. His plays are full of charming lyrics. He died of syphilis in London.

EDITION: *Works* ed. A. H. Bullen (1888, reprinted 2 vols. Port Washington, N.Y. 1966).
REFERENCES: Leonard R. N. Ashley *Authorship and Evidence: A Study of Attribution and the Renaissance Drama, Illustrated by the Case of George Peele* (Geneva 1968). P. H. Cheffaud *George Peele* (Paris 1913). D. H. Horne *The Life and Minor Works of George Peele* (New Haven, Conn.

and Oxford 1952). G. K. Hunter *Lyly and Peele* (London 1968, also PB).

PÉGUY, Charles (Jan. 7, 1873 – Sept. 5, 1914). French writer. Born Orléans; the legend of the city's heroine Joan of Arc was a pervasive influence on the child, who was raised by his mother, an impoverished chair mender. After lycée (on scholarship) and military service (1892–93), studied philosophy at École Normale Supérieure, Paris. Described himself (1895) as "converted" from religion to his own personal version of socialism. *Jeanne d'Arc*, a three-part philosophical drama, and *De la Cité socialiste*, a notable article, appeared (1897). That year married Charlotte Baudouin and quit the university; she helped him open the Librairie Socialiste in the Latin Quarter. His successful struggle to persuade the Socialists to support Dreyfus in the celebrated case of 1898 nevertheless left Péguy disenchanted with the party. Founded (1900) *Cahiers de la Quinzaine (Fortnightly Notebook)*; during its fifteen years of publication it listed as contributors Anatole France, Henri Bergson, Jean Jaurès, Romain Rolland, and exerted a deep influence on French intellectual life. Reconverted to Catholicism, as testified in *Clio I* (1909), *Un Nouveau Théologien* (1911), *Clio II* (1912); wrote poetry, publishing such works as *Le Mystère de la charité de Jeanne d'Arc* (1910) and *Ève* (1913), last long poem. Served in the army once more, and met his death at forty-one in action in the battle of the Marne.

TRANSLATIONS: *Basic Verities* tr. Julian Green (New York and London 1943, PB 1965). *Men and Saints: Prose and Poetry* tr. Anne and Julian Green (New York 1944 and London 1947). *God Speaks* (New York 1945) and *Mystery of the Charity of Joan of Arc* (New York and London 1950), both tr. Julian Green. *Mystery of the Holy Innocents and Other Poems* tr. Pansy Pakenham (New York and London 1956). *Temporal and Eternal* tr. Alexander Dru (New York and London 1958).
REFERENCES: Alexander Dru *Péguy* (London 1956 and New York 1957). Daniel Halévy *Charles Péguy and Les Cahiers de la Quinzaine* (tr. London

1946 and New York 1947). Nelly Jussem-Wilson *Charles Péguy* (New York and London 1965). Romain Rolland *Péguy* (2 vols. Paris 1945). Hans A. Schmitt *Charles Péguy: The Decline of an Idealist* (Baton Rouge, La. 1967). Yvonne Servais *Charles Péguy: The Pursuit of Salvation* (Cork, Oxford, and Westminster, Md. 1953). Marjorie Villiers *Charles Péguy: A Study in Integrity* (London 1965 and New York 1966).

PEPYS, Samuel (Feb. 23, 1633 – May 26, 1703). English diarist. Born and died in London, son of a tailor. Educated at St. Paul's School and Magdalene College, Cambridge. Married (1655) Elizabeth St. Michael, fifteen-year-old daughter of a French Huguenot. His cousin, Sir Edward Montagu, a firm royalist, supported him, and with the Restoration of 1660 secured for him a position in the navy office. By 1668 Pepys had become a prestigious naval official with a considerable estate, and was a friend of the duke of York (later James II). Made secretary of the admiralty (1673), sat in Parliament (1679). Became a victim of the Popish Plot frenzy and was imprisoned briefly in the Tower (1679), but was vindicated and the case dismissed (1680). Joined Lord Dartmouth on Tangier expedition (1683–84), was again made secretary of the admiralty, again sat in Parliament (1684), and became president of the Royal Society (1684–86). The major naval authority of his time, he retired with the accession of William of Orange (1689) and proceeded to publish *Memoirs Relating to the State of the Royal Navy* (1690). It was not until 1825 that a part of his famous *Diary: Jan. 1, 1660 – May 31, 1669* was published by Magdalene College, followed by complete edition (1893–99). Written in shorthand and ending only because of his growing blindness, it is a candid self-portrait and invaluable chronicle, covering the early days of the Restoration, the Great Plague (1665), the Fire of London (1666), and the entry of the Dutch fleet into the Thames (1667).

EDITION: *Diary of Samuel Pepys* ed. Henry B. Wheatley (10 vols. 1893–99, latest ed. 3 vols. London 1962). *The Diary of Samuel Pepys: A New and Complete Transcription* ed. Robert Latham and William Matthews (vols. I–III 1660–62, Berkeley, Calif. 1970).
REFERENCES: Arthur Bryant *Samuel Pepys* (3 vols. Cambridge, England, and New York 1933–39, also PB). Cecil S. Emden *Pepys Himself* (London and New York 1963). Percival Hunt *Samuel Pepys in the Diary* (Pittsburgh, Pa. 1958 and Oxford 1960, also PB). Percy Lubbock *Samuel Pepys* (London and New York 1909). Joseph R. Tanner *Mr. Pepys* (New York 1924 and London 1925). Leslie A. Wilcox *Mister Pepys's Navy* (Cranbury, N.J. 1968). John Harold Wilson *The Private Life of Mr. Pepys* (New York 1959 and London 1960).

PÉREZ GALDÓS, Benito (May 10, 1843 – Jan. 4, 1920). Spanish novelist and playwright. Born Las Palmas, Canary Islands, and attended the English school there. Went to Madrid to study law; then shifted to a career in literature. The seventy-seven novels he wrote — noted for their exuberance, accurate portrayal of the passions of the period in which they were set, and unforgettable characters — were the result of meticulous research, and established his reputation as the father of the modern Spanish novel. His forty-six-volume *Episodios nacionales* (1873–1912), a fictional re-creation of the history of nineteenth-century Spain from the battle of Trafalgar to the restoration of the Spanish monarchy (1876), shows forcefully how history affects the little man. His other vast novel cycle, *Novelas españolas contemporáneas* — romances dealing with contemporary life and its religious and social problems — begins with *Doña Perfecta* (1876, tr. 1960) and includes his better-known, finer works: *Gloria* (1877), *Fortunata y Jacinta* (1886–87), *La Familia de León Roch* (1878, tr. *León Roch* 1886). *Marianela* (1878, tr. 1951), *Tormento* (1884, tr. *Torment* 1952) and *Angel Guerra* (1891). Pérez Galdós also wrote twenty-one plays, less successful than the novels, of which *Electra* (1901) and *El Abuelo* (1904, tr. *The Grandfather* 1910) are the best known. Made a member of the Royal Spanish Academy (1897), he also entered politics as an anticlerical liberal, serving as delegate with republican party. Blindness ended his political career (1912). A bachelor, he died in Madrid.

REFERENCES: Hyman C. Berkowitz *Benito Pérez Galdós: Spanish Liberal Crusader* (Madison, Wis. 1948). Sherman H. Eoff *The Novels of Pérez Galdós* (St. Louis, Mo. 1954). Salvador de Madariaga *The Genius of Spain* (1923, reprinted Freeport, N.Y. 1968). Michael Nimetz *Humor in Galdós: A Study of the Novelas Contemporáneas* (New Haven, Conn. 1968). Theodore A. Sackett *Pérez Galdós: An Annotated Bibliography* (Albuquerque, N. Mex. 1968). Robert J. Weber *The Miau Manuscript of Benito Pérez Galdós* (Berkeley, Calif. PB 1964).

PERGOLESI (originally Draghi), Giovanni Battista (Jan. 4, 1710 – Mar. 16, 1736). Italian composer. Born Iesi, near Ancona, son of a surveyor. Family name replaced by Pergolesi (of Pergola). Only survivor of four children, he was frail and limped, perhaps an early symptom of the tuberculosis that would kill him at twenty-six. After studying music in Iesi, he trained as a violinist at the Conservatorio dei Poveri di Gesù Cristo in Naples (1726–31). The next five years saw the composition of oratorios, sacred drama, instrumental music, and the production of four *opere serie*, including *Salustia* (1732) and *L'Olimpiade* (1735); two *opere buffe*, *Lo Frate 'nnamorato* (1732) and *Flaminio* (1735); and three intermezzi (light entr'actes), including his most famous work, *La Serva padrona* (1733), which became the prototype of the genre in Italy for decades. After his death, and pauper's burial, at Pozzuoli (near Naples), his reputation expanded beyond Naples and Rome. One reason was his *Stabat Mater* (supposedly completed as he lay dying); another was the 1752 Paris production of *La Serva padrona*. Its immense popularity provoked *la guerre des bouffons*, the brouhaha between partisans of Pergolesi's Italian style and supporters of the French opera à la Lully and Rameau. Many imitations and forgeries appeared in this period — the Pergolesiana that continues to confuse musicologists and musicians. The Pergolesi that Stravinsky used in his ballet *Pulcinella* (1920) is largely inauthentic.

PERUGINO (real name **Pietro di Cristoforo di Vannucci**) (c.1446–1523). Italian painter. Born Città della Pieve, near Perugia, he became the outstanding representative of the Umbrian school. According to Vasari, he studied first under Piero della Francesca in Arezzo, later under Andrea del Verrocchio in Florence. The *Adoration of the Magi* (c.1475, Umbrian National Gallery, Perugia) stems from the early years. His growing reputation led to a commission from the Vatican (1481) to decorate the Sistine chapel, and he executed there the famous, monumental fresco *Christ Delivering the Keys to St. Peter*. At the height of his powers (1488–1500), Perugino in this prolific period produced the *Nativity* triptych (1491, Villa Albani, Rome), the portrait of *Francesco dell 'Opere* (1494, Uffizi Gallery, Florence), the *Pietà* (1495, Pitti Palace, Florence), *Apollo and Marsyas* (c.1497, Louvre, Paris), *St. Sebastian* (Louvre, Paris), the *Pavia Altarpiece* (1499, National Gallery, London), and the *Crucifixion* (completed 1496, S. Maria Maddalena dei Pazzi, Florence), generally considered his masterpiece. In incorporating the basic architectural elements of the room into his design of this fresco, it is a supreme example of his space composition. At its best, Perugino's style is characterized by simplicity, clarity, and grace. Its influence is evident in the work of his greatest pupil, Raphael. To his last declining years belong the allegorical frescoes in the Collegio del Cambio, Perugia (1497–1500) and *The Combat Between Love and Chastity* (1505, Louvre, Paris). Perugino died of the plague while working near Perugia.

REFERENCES: Bernard Berenson *The Italian Painters of the Renaissance* (latest ed. 2 vols. London and New York 1968, also PB). Raimond van Marle *The Development of the Italian School of Painting* (19 vols. The Hague 1923–38). Giorgio Vasari *Lives of the . . . Painters, Sculptors and Architects*

(1550) vol. IV ed. and tr. Gaston de Vere (10 vols. London 1912–15).

PETRARCH (in Italian, Francesco Petrarca) (July 20, 1304 – July 18, 1374). Italian poet and scholar. Born Arezzo, where his mother had taken refuge from political unrest in Florence. Family moved to Incisa, then Pisa (1310) and Carpentras, near Avignon (1312). Studied humanities privately, then law for four years at University of Montpellier and three years at Bologna, where he also wrote his first Latin verses. Settled at papal court in Avignon (1326), where he took minor orders in the church and met Laura (1327, real identity unknown), the object of his devotion even after her death (1348) and the inspiration for his vernacular poetry, sonnets and odes, later collected in *Canzoniere*, aside from the unfinished *Trionfi* (begun c.1353), his only book in Italian. Became chaplain to Cardinal Giovanni Colonna (1330), the first of many patrons whose favors and commissions enabled him to travel extensively (starting in 1333) and write leisurely. Fathered an illegitimate son in Rome (1337), and six years later by the same unknown woman a daughter with whom he spent his last years. Established himself in south of France, at Vaucluse (1337–53) to study and write, with occasional travels and stays elsewhere. Crowned poet laureate in Rome (1341); became occasional secretary and ambassador to Visconti in Milan (1353–61); lived in Padua, Venice, and Pavia, retiring to Arquà (1370), where he died. Famous now for his *rime sparse* (scattered rhymes) and for being the founder of humanism, his fame among his contemporaries rested on his Latin scholarship. Works include *De Vita Solitaria* (1345), *De Remediis Utriusque Fortuna* (completed by 1361), *Africa* (begun c.1338), a self-analysis in the form of a dialogue between himself and St. Augustine, and *Epistolae Familiares* (last years).

TRANSLATIONS: *Sonnets and Songs* tr. Anna Maria Armi (New York 1946, also PB). *Testament* ed. and tr. Theodor E. Mommsen (Ithaca, N.Y. and London 1957). *Four Dialogues for Scholars* ed. and tr. Conrad Rawski (Cleveland 1966). *Triumphs* (Chicago 1962), *Prose Letters of Petrarch* (New York 1951), and *Petrarch at Vaucluse: Letters in Verse and Prose* (Chicago and Cambridge, England, 1958), all translated by Ernest H. Wilkins.

REFERENCES: Aldo S. Bernardo *Petrarch, Scipio and the Africa: The Birth of Humanism's Dream* (Baltimore and Oxford 1962). Morris Bishop *Petrarch and His World* (Bloomington, Ind. 1963 and London 1964). L. W. Forster *The Icy Fire: Four Studies in European Petrarchism* (Cambridge, England, 1969). E. H. R. Tatham *Francesco Petrarca* (2 vols. London and New York 1925). John H. Whitfield *Petrarch and the Renascence* (1943, reprinted New York 1965). Ernest H. Wilkins *Studies in the Life and Works of Petrarch* (Cambridge, Mass. 1955), *Petrarch's Eight Years in Milan* (Cambridge, Mass. 1958), *Petrarch's Later Years* (Cambridge, Mass. 1959), and *Life of Petrarch* (Chicago 1961, also PB).

PETRONIUS ARBITER (real name Gaius Petronius) (d.66 A.D.). Roman writer. Recorded by Tacitus as an able proconsul of Bithynia and later acting consul in Rome. A favorite of Nero's, he was famous as an aesthete and voluptuary and as the court's *arbiter elegantiae* — judge of taste and manners. This incited the envy of Nero's adviser Tigellinus, who accused him of treason. Arrested at Cumae and ordered to commit suicide, Petronius arranged to die leisurely, spending his last hours cataloguing the emperor's bizarre vices. His reputation rests chiefly, however, on the *Satyricon*, of which he is almost certainly the author. Only parts of books XV and XVI of this picaresque romance in prose and verse survive, of which the most celebrated is the *Cena Trimalchionis* (*The Banquet of Trimalchio*), describing the vulgar exhibitionism of a nouveau riche freedman. Besides the grotesque detailing of the comic characters, the work presents a vivid picture of first century A.D. provincial life, making use of the colloquial Latin spoken by the common people. Petronius's extraordinary talent for depicting the vice and depravity of the age won him the title of "writer of the purest impurity" (*auctor purissimae impuritatis*).

TRANSLATIONS: *Satyricon* tr. William Burnaby (1694, latest ed. New York 1969); tr. William Arrowsmith (Ann Arbor, Mich. 1959, also PB).

REFERENCES: Gilbert Bagnani *Arbiter of Elegance: A Study of the Life and Works of C. Petronius* (Oxford PB 1954). J. P. Sullivan *The Satyricon of Petronius: A Literary Study* (London and Bloomington, Ind. 1968) and ed. *Critical Essays on Roman Literature: Satire* (London 1963 and Bloomington, Ind. PB 1968).

PHIDIAS (Pheidias) (498 – 432 B.C.). Greek sculptor. Born Athens, son of Charmides. He was pupil of Athenian Hegias. None of his work survives, except as recorded in ancient writings or in imitations. For Cimon he made statuary group at Delphi (c.465); his work thereafter was under Pericles (in power 445–431). The two men were linked throughout their careers, in glory and ultimately in political downfall. Director of the creation of the great temples, colonnades, and statuary of Periclean Athens, Phidias probably designed the Parthenon sculptures (metopes, frieze, pediments). He executed the gigantic bronze Athena Promachos, visible on the Acropolis from miles at sea; the ivory and gold Athena Parthenos (dedicated 438) inside the Parthenon; and the sixty-foot Zeus of the temple at Olympia — the Olympian Zeus — regarded as one of the Seven Wonders of the World, later removed by Theodosius I to Constantinople (destroyed by fire, 475 A.D.). Ancient critics praised his work for its intangible moral values, the effect of his vision of serene power and majesty. Honored by the Athenians, he was later sent by Pericles' enemies into exile at Elis. Not known whether he died there, or as a political prisoner in Athens.

REFERENCES: Maxime Collignon *Phidias* (Paris 1886). Ernest A. Gardner *Six Greek Sculptors* (1910, reprinted Freeport, N.Y. 1967). Henri Léchat *Phidias et la sculpture grecque au cinquième siècle* (Paris 1924). G. M. A. Richter *The Sculpture and Sculptors of the Greeks* (1929, rev. ed. New Haven, Conn. and London 1950). Charles Waldstein *Essays on the Art of Pheidias* (Cambridge, England, and New York 1885).

PICABIA, Francis (Jan. 22, 1879 – Nov. 30, 1953). French painter. Born and died in Paris. Father a Cuban, mother French. Studied at École des Beaux Arts. After impressionist period emerged as influential leader of avantgarde. Example of new abstract style: *Edtaonisl* (1913, Art Institute of Chicago). In Armory Show (1913). From 1911 friend of Marcel Duchamps, founder of Dadaist movement, who inspired Picabia to found in Barcelona *391* review (1917–24), expressing antiartistic theories parallel to Dadaism. Returned to Paris (1918), joined Dada group, contributing to review edited by Tristan Tzara and to *Dada Anthology*, while serving as link between German Dadaists in Zurich and French group. However, he followed (1921) André Breton into surrealist movement, began to exhibit with Miro, Max Ernst, and Dali. Designed setting and costumes for ballet *Relâche* (1924) for Ballets Suédois. But after painting abstract works and inventing a series of "ironic machines," he suddenly reverted to representational art, retiring to the Riviera until 1945, when he took up abstraction again. Exhibited in Paris in late 1940's, and a retrospective exhibition of his work was held at Galérie Furstemberg, Paris, in 1956. Noted for his steady creativeness, independence, and unquenchable curiosity that led to experimentation, even during his last years.

REFERENCES: Marie de la Hire *Francis Picabia* (Paris 1920). Robert Motherwell *The Dada Painters and Poets* (New York 1951). Maurice Raynal *History of Modern Painting*, vol. III (tr. London 1950). Michel Seuphor *L'Art abstrait, ses origines, ses premiers maîtres* (Paris 1949).

PICO DELLA MIRANDOLA, Count Giovanni (Feb. 24, 1463 – Nov. 17, 1494). Italian philosopher. Born Mirandola, near Ferrara, youngest son of the prince of Mirandola. Studied the humanities at home; canon law, at fourteen, in Bologna; Aristotelian philosophy in Padua; and acquired Aramaic, Arabic, and Hebrew in the course of his scholarly travels in Italy and France. In 1486 the handsome young nobleman went to Rome, where he expounded his nine hundred theses (drawn from Arabic, Hebrew, Greek, and Roman philosophies) and proposed to defend them in a public speech, as was the custom. Innocent VIII and a papal commission, however, forbade him, declaring thirteen of the theses to be heretical. He retreated to Paris, but at invitation of Lorenzo de' Medici returned to Florence (1488), where he remained the rest of his life, although absolved of any taint of heresy by Alexander VI (1493). Became involved in circle of Ficino and his Platonic Academy, but later was influenced by Savonarola. Renounced his inherited lands (1491), planning to give up all worldly goods and become an itinerant preacher, a plan unfulfilled at his death at thirty-one. His collection, *Commentationes Joannis Pici Mirandulae,* edited by his nephew, appeared (1495–96; parts later translated by Thomas More, c.1510). It includes *Heptaplus,* his mystical discourse on *Genesis* (he was one of the first Christians to adopt a cabalistic interpretation of the Scriptures); his treatise *On Being and One (De Ente et Uno)*; and a disquisition on the church's enemies, particularly astrologers, which was to influence the astronomer Kepler in the seventeenth century.

REFERENCES: Joseph L. Blau *The Christian Interpretation of the Cabala in the Renaissance* (1944, reprinted Port Washington, N.Y. 1965). Pierre Marie Cordier *Jean Pic de la Mirandole* (Paris 1957). Avery Dulles *Princeps Concordiae: Pico della Mirandola and the Scholastic Tradition* (Cambridge, Mass. 1941). Edgar Wind *Pagan Mysteries in the Renaissance* (1958, rev. ed. New York and London 1968, also PB).

PIERO DELLA FRANCESCA (real name Pietro di Benedetto dei Franceschi) (c.1420 – Oct. 12, 1492). Italian painter. Born and died in Borgo San Sepolcro, near Arezzo, son of a shoemaker. Little is known of his early years; he worked in Florence under Domenico Veneziano and in 1440's was back in Borgo painting the polyptych of *The Madonna of Mercy* (Pinacoteca Comunale, Borgo

San Sepolcro). Later he executed frescoes in Ferrara, now lost, and in Rimini: *Sigismondo Malatesta* (1451, Tempio Malatestiano, Rimini). Began (1452) his masterpiece, frescoes illustrating *The Legend of the True Cross* (completed 1466, S. Francesco, Arezzo). Employed by Duke Federico, he made repeated visits to Urbino, where he probably painted *The Flagellation of Christ* (Galleria Nazionale, Urbino), *The Madonna and Child, Angels, Saints, and Federico da Montefeltro* (Brera Museum, Milan), and the statuesque *Sinigallia Madonna* (c.1475, Galleria Nazionale, Urbino). The calm monumentality of his style is unmistakable and unsigned works such as *The Baptism of Christ* (c.1445) and *The Nativity* (c.1475, both National Gallery, London), *The Resurrection* (c.1460, Pinacoteca Comunale, Borgo San Sepolcro) and *Hercules* (c.1460, Gardner Museum, Boston) are easily identified. Piero's works are characterized by their motionless solemnity and seraphic texture. He was also a very considerable mathematician.

REFERENCES: Kenneth Clark *Piero della Francesca: Complete Edition of the Paintings* (2nd ed. London and New York 1969). Roberto Longhi *Piero della Francesca* (tr. New York and London 1930). Lionello Venturi *Piero della Francesca* (tr. New York and London 1954).

✐

PIERO DELLA FRANCESCA
BY JOHN RUSSELL

From time to time there is among great painters a sleeping beauty newly awakened: someone whose long slumber is matter for incredulity in later ages. How could people possibly not have known of Vermeer? Was not Georges de La Tour there for all to see? That kind of thing. We are astonished that our great-grandparents did not know of such painters: or that, knowing them, they missed the point.

Piero della Francesca is in this class. Among people today who care for painting there can be few who do not put him among the six or seven greatest names in European painting. He is for us the first and the greatest of classical painters: the man who brought a *lucida ordo* into the complexities of human experience and, in doing so, made it easier for us to live. Yet for a great many years he passed almost unnoticed. Ruskin mentions him only once, in a winsome allusion to the source of his name. Piero was ideal material for an essay in Pater's *Renaissance,* but Pater seems not to have known it. Heinrich Wölfflin wrote his canonical *Classic Art* in the 1890's without so much as a mention of Piero. Sir Charles Eastlake, director of the National Gallery in London, was a jump or two ahead of Ruskin and Pater and Wölfflin; but when Piero's *Baptism* came up at the Uzielli sale in London in 1861 he said that because of its ruinous state "I am at this moment undecided whether to place it in the National Gallery (where it cannot have a good place) or to take it myself."

Eastlake's successors have overruled him, and the *Baptism* today has a place second to none in the National Gallery. And since the publication of Kenneth Clark's book in 1951, Piero has been, with Cézanne, the painter of all painters who stands highest in the esteem of English-speaking readers. There is in this, if not "poetic justice," justice at any rate of a sentimental kind. Piero never pushed himself to the front. He was born a shoemaker's son, in a little town of Borgo San Sepolcro. He could have lived in a great city — Florence — and brought it new luster. He could have lived at a ducal court — Urbino — which was probably the most civilized thing of its kind in European history. He valued the associations which could be formed at such places, and one of them — his friendship with Leon Battista Alberti — was probably as important to him as anything that ever

happened outside of his studio. But in the end he seems always to have gone back to Borgo San Sepolcro, where he played a useful but not preponderant role on the town council. What he looked like nobody knows, but Marco di Longaro, a lantern-maker from Borgo San Sepolcro, has come down in history because as a small boy he "used to lead by the hand Master Piero della Francesca, an excellent painter, who was blind."

All this could suggest some kind of rustic sage, a voluntary provincial who had chosen to disengage himself from metropolitan concerns. And it is true that insofar as there is in Piero's work a basic human type, that type has the strong neck, the strong calf, and the broad and open countenance of the person who lives much in the open and has no time for politicking. Piero was undoubtedly a man of peace: the *Victory of Heraclius* at Arezzo was one of his rare failures. But he knew, instinctively, all that there was to know about *les grands:* and when he came to paint the Queen of Sheba's visit to King Solomon he drew infallibly, at a fifteen years' distance, on the bearing of the Emperor Paleologus as he had passed through the streets of Florence in 1439.

He had the kind of total comprehension which makes us trust in him, unreservedly. Berenson could have had Piero in mind — though he did not — when he wrote to his sister in 1892 that "Architecture and manners are perhaps more closely connected than any two other expressions of the human personality." The incidental architecture in Piero's paintings is, in effect, as much the mirror of the man as anything else in the work, and one can say this as much of the curious, brick-built, magpie-haunted lean-to in *The Baptism* as of the way in which the unnamed palace in *The Flagellation* makes celestial eye-music. In this, as in all things, Piero never forced: the more we study his paintings the more we come to think that even the very great things in later art may not come from quite so pure a source. We find ourselves harboring, in fact, certain most seditious opinions: one of them is that after the three standing figures in *The Flagellation* Raphael's philosophers in *The School of Athens* look devious and official. One may even think, in Arezzo itself, that after Piero's *Death of Adam* even Rembrandt on old age looks sentimental.

Piero had, of course, a parallel life. He was a great mathematician as well as a great painter, and one result of this was that he was in on the birth of perspective. Perspective is now a part of the demonology of art, and generally derided as a fraudulent box of tricks and a betrayal of the true nature of painting. So it takes a little effort of the historical imagination to realize that in Piero's day perspective meant primarily a vastly greater assurance in the handling of complex subjects. Piero believed in exact measurement — *commensuratio* — as one of the three fundamentals of art; and if we give ourselves into his hands without reservation, it is partly because we know that in his paintings every thing is precisely judged in its relation to every other thing. Piero takes our ramshackle world and gives it back to us in perfect working order.

This could have resulted in a kind of meticulous toytown, a compartmented dollhouse of no universal resonance. But it is Piero's achievement that after more than five hundred years his references are our references: it is in his work that E. M. Forster's "Only connect" is apotheosized. He has the supreme artist's gift of acquiring a new pertinence for each generation. No one knows, for instance, what Piero meant to say in *The Flagellation*. (Conceivably he would have agreed with Degas that "The artist who insists on dotting every *i* ends up as a bore.") But no one who has any feeling for life as it has actually been lived in the last forty years will have missed out on one interpretation: that for every three men who are still free to stand beneath the sun in disputation, a fourth man, somewhere, is being tortured.

What might have been mere moralizing is redeemed, in Piero's case, by austere and measured statement — and, equally, by his use of the still unhackneyed science which put everything, as we say, "in perspective." Nothing is forgotten, in Piero. He had Tolstoy's eye for the detail which reminds us that even the most august development in human affairs is subject to the kind of incident which classic art later concealed. (In Racine, who sneezes?) *The Nativity*, in the National Gallery, London, is a late Piero, and the scholars will tell us that the Christ-child is derived from Hugo van der Goes, while the drapery of the angelic orchestra brings back to life the Greek sculptors (whose work Piero had never seen), just as in Kenneth Clark's view Piero's *Madonna of Monterchi* "reminds us of the finest Buddhist sculpture in its calm detachment." Piero in this sense takes upon himself the whole burden of human experience, past, present and future; but he never, for all that, gets tight or stiff. Among the images that stay with us from *The Nativity* none is more vivid than the one which later painters would have tidied away: that of the cow which thought nothing of the whole proceedings and let go with an uncontrollable yawn, a braying exhalation like a vacuum cleaner cut off at full throttle. The man who could make us accept that yawn as part of one of the most seraphic scenes ever painted has my vote, any time, as Perpetual President of European painting.

PIERO DI COSIMO (real name Piero di Lorenzo) (c.1462–1521). Italian painter. Born and died in Florence. The son of a goldsmith, he studied under Cosimo Rosselli, whom he probably assisted on his frescoes in Sistine chapel, Rome (1481). Was chiefly influenced by Filippo Lippi, Ghirlandajo, and Luca Signorelli. His mature works reveal an anticlassical, eccentric, and imaginative spirit; they combine close study of nature in the landscape backgrounds with romantic, sometimes bizarre fantasy, as in *Hunting Scene* (Metropolitan Museum, New York) and the mythological scenes *Discovery of Honey* (Art Museum, Worcester, Mass.), *Discovery of Wine* (Fogg Museum, Cambridge, Mass.), *The Fight Between the Lapiths and the Centaurs,* and *Death of Procris* (both in National Gallery, London). Under influence of Leonardo da Vinci, Piero's style after 1500 grew more in accord with Renaissance classical ideals. Late works include *Perseus Freeing Andromeda* (Uffizi Gallery, Florence) and *Legend of Prometheus* (Alte Pinakothek, Munich). Most famous of his portraits is that of *Simonetta Vespucci* (Musée Condé, Chantilly, France).

REFERENCES: R. Langton Douglas *Piero di Cosimo* (Chicago and Cambridge, England, 1946). Sydney J. Freedberg *Painting of the High Renaissance in Rome and Florence* (2 vols. Cambridge, Mass. and London 1961).

PINDAR (c.518 B.C. – c.438 B.C.). Greek poet. Born Cynoscephalae, of aristocratic family. Educated in nearby Thebes, later in Athens. After a period at the court of Hieron of Syracuse, Sicily (476–474), he lived mainly in Thebes, though he had patrons in many cities. Considered Greece's greatest lyric poet, Pindar's extant complete works are all triumphal odes, or epinicia. Forty-four survive, celebrating victories in the athletic games; there are fourteen Olympian, twelve Pythian, eleven Nemean, and four Isthmian odes, each ode embodying an appropriate myth, narrated in a high moral, religious tone, and quoting such maxims as "The issue is in God's hands." Numerous fragments in other genres of poetry survive. Pindar's work is characterized by rich verbal eloquence and metrical complexity. He was influential throughout antiquity, and widely imitated, but not rediscovered until the Renaissance, by Ronsard and Joachim du Bellay in France and in England by Milton. The Pindaric ode was a popular form during seventeenth and eighteenth centuries.

TRANSLATIONS: *Works* tr. Lewis R. Farnell (3 vols. London 1930–32). *Odes* tr. Richmond Lattimore (Chicago 1947, also PB).

REFERENCES: C. M. Bowra *Pindar* (Oxford 1964). Reginald W. B. Burton *Pindar's Pythian Odes: Essays in Interpretation* (Oxford 1962). Jacqueline Duchemin *Pindare, poète et prophète* (Paris 1956). John H. Finley *Pindar and Aeschylus* (Cambridge, Mass. and Oxford 1955). Mary A. Grant *Folktale and Hero Tale Motifs in the Odes of Pindar* (Lawrence, Kans. 1968). Gilbert Norwood *Pindar* (Berkeley, Calif. and Cambridge, England, 1945).

PINTURICCHIO or PINTORICCHIO (real name Bernardino di Betto di Biago). (c.1454 – Dec. 11, 1513). Italian painter. Born Perugia. Little is known of his early life. Assisted Perugino (1481–84) with his Sistine chapel (the *Baptism of Christ* is attributed to him). Was commissioned by Pope Alexander VI to paint frescoes of *Life of San Bernardino* in S. Maria in Aracoeli, Rome, and in Borgia apartments of Vatican (1492–94), both richly decorative in blazing color and ornamental motif. Returned to Umbria (1495), painted altarpiece for S. Maria de' Fossi, Perugia (now in Pinacoteca there), and other works in Orvieto and Spoleto. His most celebrated achievement is the frescoes commissioned by Cardinal Francesco Piccolomini, afterward Pope Pius III, for library of Siena cathedral 1503–1509), marvelously architectonic decoration depicting scenes from life of cardinal's uncle Pope Pius II. The young Raphael, who accompanied Pinturicchio to Siena, may have assisted him. Last work was the *Way to Calvary* (1513, Palazzo

Borromeo, Milan). He was noted more for his decorative sense and space composition than for form and movement. He died in Siena.

REFERENCES: Bernard Berenson *The Italian Painters of the Renaissance* (latest ed. 2 vols. London and New York 1968, also PB). Giorgio Vasari *Lives of the . . . Painters, Sculptors and Architects* (1550) ed. and tr. Gaston de Vere (10 vols. London 1912–15).

PIOMBO. *See* **SEBASTINO DEL PIOMBO.**

PIRANDELLO, Luigi (June 28, 1867 – Dec. 10, 1936). Italian writer. Born Girgenti, Sicily, son of a mine owner. Studied at universities of Rome and Bonn, where he obtained doctorate in philology (1891). Settled near Rome (1893), writing verse and short stories (*Amori senza amori*) and two novels. Married Antonietta Portulano (1894); she became insane but was not committed until just before her death in 1918. By that time, Pirandello had written his finest novels, including *Il fu Mattia Pascal* (1904, tr. *The Late Mattia Pascal* 1923), hundreds of short stories, and his first successful play, *Right You Are If You Think You Are* (1917). The themes of these works were those of his life — madness, jealousy, death. In his own words he was "opposed to social hypocrisies and conventions," and his psychologically penetrating analysis of society led him to concentrate on the nature of reality and illusion and self-identity, which are explored in his masterpieces *Henry IV* (1922) and *Six Characters in Search of an Author* (1921, tr. 1922). At the same time he experimented with dramatic form, achieving a unity between dramatic structure and ideas that produced a tremendous impact on modern theatre. Awarded Nobel prize for literature (1934). He died in Rome.

TRANSLATIONS: *Naked Masks: Five Plays* ed. Eric Bentley (New York 1952, also PB). *Short Stories* tr. Frederick May (London 1965, also PB). REFERENCES: Robert Brustein *The Theatre of Revolt* (Boston 1964). Walter Starkie *Luigi Pirandello* (3rd ed. Berkeley, Calif. 1965, also PB). Domenico

Vittorini *The Drama of Luigi Pirandello* (New York 1957).

PIRANESI, Giovanni Battista (Oct. 4, 1720 – Nov. 9, 1778). Italian etcher and architect. Born near Venice. Educated there by stonemason father and architect-engineer uncle. Studied etching in Rome (1740–44) and published first major work, *La Prima Parte di architettura* (1743). Settled permanently in Rome (1745). As student had envisioned series of etchings of monuments of ancient and Renaissance Rome; in 1748 began the famous series of 135 *Vedute di Roma* (*Views of Rome*), which appeared singly until his death. Other works include the twenty-seven plates of *Carceri* (*Prisons*), fantastic, macabre creations in architecture (1750); *Le Antichità Romane* (1756); studies of the ruins of Pompeii and Paestum (1777–78). As architect his major achievement was the rebuilding of S. Maria Aventina (1764–65). Also published *Diverse Manieri d'adornare i cammini* (1769), eccentric designs for interior decoration which influenced Louis XIV, Adam, and Empire styles, just as the dramatic contrasts in light and shade of his etchings and his romantic conception of ruins influenced eighteenth-century architecture. His son Francesco was his curator, collecting lifework of two thousand plates (published in twenty-nine folio volumes, Paris 1835–37). Piranesi received numerous honors, was productive until his death in Rome.

REFERENCES: Henri Focillon *Giovanni Battista Piranesi* (1918, new ed. Paris 1963). Arthur M. Hind *Giovanni Battista Piranesi* (1922, new ed. London and New York 1967). Aldous Huxley *Prisons* (London 1949). A. Hyatt Mayor *Giovanni Battista Piranesi* (New York 1952 and London 1953). Hylton Thomas *The Drawings of Giovanni Battista Piranesi* (New York and London 1954).

PISANELLO (real name Antonio Pisano) (c.1395–1455). Italian artist. Born Pisa, trained in Verona probably under Stefano da Zevio. Worked on frescoes (1415–22) begun by Gentile da Fabriano in the doges' palace, Venice (all destroyed); Gentile's style dominates Pisanello's early works such as the frescoes in S. Caterina, Treviso. Worked (1420's) in Mantua and Verona, painting Nicolò di Brenzono's monument in S. Fermo Maggiore there (1424). Continued Gentile's series of frescoes (also destroyed) in St. John Lateran, Rome (1431–32), and painted St. George legend for Pellegrini chapel, S. Anastasia, Verona (1437–38). Pisanello produced the first Renaissance portrait medal, depicting the emperor of Constantinople (1438), and became chiefly known as a medalist, as well as a draftsman. Many of his immensely varied drawings, exquisite studies of animals, costumes, etc., survive, notably in the Vallardi Codex (Louvre, Paris), a collection of fifteenth-century drawing. The purity of line shows draftsmanship on the verge of the Renaissance. Other major works: *Madonna with SS. Anthony and George* (1438–45) and *Vision of St. Eustace* (c.1435, both in National Gallery, London). He died in Rome.

REFERENCES: G. F. Hill *Pisanello* (London and New York 1905) and *Pisanello Drawings: A Selection* (New York 1965, PB). Enio Sindona *Pisanello* (New York 1964).

PISANO, Andrea (real name Andrea da Pontedera) (c.1290–1348/9). Italian architect and sculptor. Born Pisa, son of a notary. Though probably trained as a metalworker, nothing is known of his work before 1329. He designed (1329–36) reliefs of scenes from life of John the Baptist for the south bronze doors of the baptistery in Florence (whose north and east doors were made by Ghiberti in the next century). Architectural composition and gesture are Giottesque, but the intimate grouping of each relief is distinctive of Andrea. He also presumably contributed to the marble reliefs on the cathedral campanile. In Pisa (1343–47) he designed the tomb of Simone Saltarelli in S. Caterina, and in Orvieto the marble *Maestà* (1347, Museo dell'Opera del Duomo) for the cathedral. Despite his small extant output Andrea Pisano is important, both for his restrained naturalism and for being the first artist to use Giotto's narrative technique in relief carving.

REFERENCES: John Pope-Hennessy *Italian Gothic Sculpture* (London and New York 1955). Giorgio Vasari *Lives of the . . . Painters, Sculptors and Architects* (1550) ed. and tr. Gaston de Vere (10 vols. London 1912–15). John White *Art and Architecture in Italy: 1250–1400* (Harmondsworth, England, and Baltimore 1966).

PISANO, Nicola (c.1220–c.1283) and Giovanni (c.1250 – after 1314). Italian sculptors and architects. Whatever his origin, NICOLA settled in Pisa, where he produced the remarkable hexagonal marble pulpit in the baptistery (1260). He was powerfully influenced by Roman sarcophagi and vases in the Campo Santo (cemetery) of the cathedral. Aided by his son GIOVANNI, Nicola also executed the octagonal pulpit in Siena cathedral (1266–68); though based on the Pisa pulpit, the figures became increasingly individual and involved in the scene depicted. Giovanni also collaborated with Nicola on the three-tiered bronze and marble fountain in the piazza at Perugia (1278), but corrosion has made it hard to distinguish their styles. To Nicola is attributed the expressive *Deposition* on the façade of S. Martino, Lucca. Giovanni's principal works include the magnificent façade of Siena cathedral (1284–95), the hexagonal pulpit in S. Andrea, Pistoia (completed 1301), the round pulpit in Pisa cathedral (completed 1310), and *Madonna and Child* in Padua (Arena chapel, c.1305). All his carving displays great dramatic power and vigorous movement. Nicola was the first Italian sculptor to combine classical models with the northern Gothic style; Giovanni carried Nicola's style to its highly charged maturity.

REFERENCES: Michael Ayrton and Henry Moore *Giovanni Pisano: Sculptor* (London and New York 1970). G. H. and E. R. Crichton *Nicola Pisano and the Revival of Sculpture in Italy* (Cambridge, England and New York 1938). John Pope-Hennessy *Italian Gothic Sculpture* (London and New York 1955). John White *Art and Architecture in Italy: 1250–1400* (Harmondsworth, England and Baltimore, 1966).

PISSARRO, Camille (July 10, 1830 – Nov. 13, 1903). French painter. Born St. Thomas, Virgin Islands, West Indies. Sent to Paris (1841) to study at Savary's school in Passy. Returning to St. Thomas (1847), he soon became bored with his job, fled to Caracas (1852) with Danish painter Fritz Melbye, and began painting. Went to Paris (1855); attended Académie Suisse and became influenced by Corot, first exhibiting at the Salon of 1859. Moved away from Corot influence, began participating in Salon des Refusés (1863). At the time lived with Julie Vellay, whom he married (1870). They had seven children, five of whom became painters, including Lucien (1863–1944), an impressionist landscapist. Pissarro became influenced by Monet, and while in England during Franco-Prussian war (1870) studied Turner and Constable. Returned to Pontoise, where Cézanne joined him (1872–74), and under his influence moved further toward an impressionist style. Exhibited with impressionist group in the first show of 1874 and all subsequent ones. He was greatly esteemed by his fellow painters. Increasing recognition became true fame when an exhibition of his works was held in Paris (1883), followed by shows in other countries. He met (1885) Georges Seurat and Paul Signac, and with them began experimenting in a pointillist technique, which he eventually abandoned (c.1890), returning to former style. Successful now, he purchased a house at Eragny (1892) and began his celebrated views of Paris (1893, most of the boulevard scenes in 1897) and Rouen. *Côtes de Boeufs near Pontoise* (1877, National Gallery, London) and *Entrance to a Village* (1872, Louvre, Paris) are typical examples of country scenes at the height of his impressionist powers. He died in Paris.

TRANSLATION: *Letters to His Son Lucien* tr. Lionel Abel (New York 1943 and London 1944).
REFERENCES: William S. Meadmore *Lucien Pissarro* (London 1962 and New York 1963). L. R. Pissarro and L. Venturi *Camille Pissarro: son art, son oeuvre* (2 vols. Paris 1939). John Rewald *Camille Pissarro* (London and New York 1963) and *The History of Impressionism* (2nd ed. New York 1961, also PB).

PLATO (c.428 – 347 B.C.). Greek philosopher. Born Athens, into prominent aristocratic family. Early attracted to politics, but deflected from political career by the events of his young manhood: an oligarchic government initiated a reign of terror in Athens, followed by a democratic one that condemned his friend Socrates to death. After Socrates' death (399 B.C.), Plato spent some years traveling, visited court of Dionysius I, tyrant of Syracuse, Sicily (387), and became involved in Syracusan politics. Hoping to teach the royal family the principles of philosophical rule, he made two more trips to Sicily (367 and 360), but his efforts failed disastrously. Meantime, he had founded the Academy in Athens (387), the philosophical school that occupied him for the rest of his life, and where he wrote his works: the twenty-five *Dialogues* and thirteen *Letters* (the letters possibly not all genuine). The dialogues vary in tone and subject; Plato can be severe and logical, witty and relaxed, or lofty and poetic. Some concern definitions: of justice (*Republic, Gorgias*); knowledge (*Theaetetus*); piety (*Euthyphro*). Others deal with relationships: between virtue and knowledge (*Protagoras*), body and soul (*Phaedo*). Socrates is the principal figure in all but one of the dialogues; Plato himself never appears, which makes it difficult to determine which concepts are his own and which Socrates'. This applies especially to the so-called Theory of Ideas. The chronology of the dialogues is uncertain, but those based closely on Socrates' life and trial, such as the *Apology*, are probably early. The *Republic*, which reflects Plato's interest in politics, is from the years 370–360; the *Laws*, also political, is probably his last work. He died in Athens.

TRANSLATIONS: *The Collected Dialogues, Including the Letters* tr. Lane Cooper and others, ed. Edith Hamilton and Huntington Cairns (New York 1961). *The Portable Plato* (containing *Symposium, Phaedo,* and *The Repub-*

lic) tr. Benjamin Jowett, ed. Scott Buchanan (New York 1948, also PB).

REFERENCES: Ernest Barker *Greek Political Theory: Plato and His Predecessors* (5th ed. London and New York 1960, also PB). R. H. S. Crossman *Plato Today* (2nd ed. London and New York 1959). Raphael Demos *The Philosophy of Plato* (1939, reprinted New York 1966). Paul Friedlaender *Plato* (tr. 3 vols. New York 1958–69). John Gould *The Development of Plato's Ethics* (Cambridge, England, 1955). G. M. A. Grube *Plato's Thought* (1935, reprinted London and Boston PB 1958). Alexander Koyré *Discovering Plato* (tr. New York and Oxford 1945, also PB). Sir David Ross *Plato's Theory of Ideas* (2nd ed. Oxford 1953). Paul Shorey *What Plato Said* (Chicago and Cambridge, England, 1933). Friedrich Solmsen *Plato's Theology* (Ithaca, N.Y. and Oxford 1942). A. E. Taylor *Plato: The Man and His Work* (7th ed. London 1960) and *Socrates* (1933, new ed. London and Boston 1951, also PB).

PLAUTUS, Titus Maccius (c.254–184 B.C.). Roman dramatist. Born Sarsina, Umbria. Very little is known of his life. He is thought to have had theatrical connections because of his mastery of stage technique. Only two firm dates stand out in his chronology: in 200 B.C. *Stichus* was produced at the plebeian games, and in 191 *Pseudolus* at the dedication of a Palatine temple. Of the 130 plays originally attributed to him, it seems only about forty were actually his; of these only twenty comedies and a fragment of another are extant and authentic, all written during last part of his life. His original humor, entertaining and colloquial dialogue, satirical characterization, and plot with interludes of song and dance made him the leading dramatist of ancient Rome. His popularity continued through Cicero's time, faded, and revived during the second century. Unlike the work of Menander and the Greek dramatists of the New Comedy (c.320–350 B.C.), who provided the plots, characters, settings, and costumes for Plautus, his comedies were preserved and reemerged in the Renaissance, when Ariosto used them as models, Molière wrote adaptations (*L'Avare,* based on

Aulularia, is an example), and Shakespeare based *The Comedy of Errors* on Plautus's *Menaechmi* and Falstaff on the character of *Miles Gloriosus*.

TRANSLATION: *Plautus, with an English Translation* tr. Paul Nixon (Loeb Classical Library, 5 vols. London and Cambridge, Mass. 1916–38).

REFERENCES: William Beare *The Roman Stage* (3rd ed. London 1964 and New York 1965, also PB). George E. Duckworth *The Nature of Roman Comedy* (2nd ed. Princeton, N.J. 1967). Wallace M. Lindsay *Early Latin Verse* (1922, reprinted London and New York 1968). Gilbert Norwood *Plautus and Terence* (1932, reprinted New York 1963). Erich W. Segal *Roman Laughter: The Comedy of Plautus* (Cambridge, Mass. and Oxford 1968). Frederick A. Wright *Three Roman Poets: Plautus, Catullus, Ovid* (London and New York 1938).

PLINY THE ELDER (full name Gaius Plinius Secundus) (A.D. 23 – Aug. 24, 79) and **PLINY THE YOUNGER** (full name Gaius Plinius Caecilius Secundus) (A.D. 61/62–c.113). The elder Pliny, a Roman writer, was born in Como. He moved to Rome in his youth and pursued a short career as an advocate. While prefect of the Roman cavalry in Germany (47–57) he produced his earliest work, a military manual on cavalry use of the javelin, and a twenty-book study of all Roman-German wars. Under Vespasian he was appointed procurator in Spain, serving also in Africa, Gaul, and perhaps the Middle East (c.65–70). Was stationed as prefect of the Roman fleet at Misenum, Campania (74). An indefatigable and prodigious scholar, his lifetime compulsion was the excerpting and digesting of all writings available to him. His only extant work, the thirty-seven-book *Natural History* (77), although a "storehouse of ancient error" in its quasi-scientific documentation of myths and marvels such as unicorns, is a unique compendium of ancient scientific scholarship in areas ranging from astronomy to medical botany to zoology. In many cases it is the sole source of information on certain aspects of Roman cultural life and manners. Not preserved was his thirty-one-book his-

tory of the Roman world. Pliny the
Elder died of asphyxiation on the beach
at Castellammare di Stabia during the
eruption of Vesuvius that buried Her-
culaneum and Pompeii. His dramatic
death was later described by his nephew
and adopted son, PLINY THE YOUNGER,
Roman author and administrator.
Born also in Como, early an orphan,
he was educated in Rome. At eighteen he began the practice of law, establishing a reputation as prosecutor
first in civil and then in political courts.
Rose steadily through the ranks of
Roman administrators: became praetor
(93) and consul (100), occasioning his
Panegyricus to Trajan; headed the military, then the senatorial treasuries
(94–100); administered the drainage
board of Rome (104–106). Sent (110)
by Trajan to Asia Minor to investigate
corruption in the province of Bythynia,
whose governor he became (c.112) and
where he died a year later. His fame
rests on his collected *Letters* (*Epistulae*), which appeared in ten volumes
(I–IX, 100–109; X, posthumously).
These "letters written with special
care," each examining a single historical, social, moral, or literary subject,
are invaluable in historical reconstruction of the period.

PLINY THE ELDER
   TRANSLATION: *Natural History* ed.
and tr. Harris Rackham and William
H. S. Jones (Loeb Classical Library, 10
vols. Cambridge, Mass. 1938–63).
   REFERENCE: Herbert N. Wethered
*The Mind of the Ancient World: A
Consideration of Pliny's Natural His-
tory* (London and New York 1937).

PLINY THE YOUNGER
   TRANSLATION: *Letters* tr. William
Melmoth (1746), rev. W. M. L. Hutchinson (Loeb Classical Library, latest
ed. 2 vols. Cambridge, Mass. 1961–
63).
   REFERENCES: Eugène Allain *Pline le
Jeune et ses héritiers* (3 vols. Paris
1901–1902). Adrian N. Sherwin-White
*The Letters of Pliny: A Historical and
Social Commentary* (Oxford 1966). Se-
latie E. Stout *Scribe and Critic at Work
in Pliny's Letters* (Bloomington, Ind.
1954).

───────────

PLUTARCH (c. A.D. 46–c.125). Greek
biographer and philosopher. Born Cha-

eronea, in Boeotia. Educated in Athens.
Traveled widely throughout Roman empire and lived in Rome (c.69–70) before settling in his native town, where
he taught and served as a magistrate
and priest of Apollo. While his religious views approached monotheism,
Plutarch's philosophy was a mixture
of Platonic, Pythagorean, Aristotelian,
and Stoic ideas. His philosophical writings, the *Moralia* (*Morals*), range
widely over religion, ethics, education,
science, psychology, literature, history,
ethnology, and zoology. About seventy-
eight titles survive, less than half of
the total, and include essays with such
titles as *On Fortune, On Virtue and
Vice, On Curiosity, On Superstition, On
the Education of Children*. But Plutarch
owes his immortality to the monumental *Parallel Lives*, forty-six paired biographical studies of illustrious Greeks
and Romans, and four separate biographies. In the *Lives* he is both a
shrewd interpreter of history and a
masterly portrayer of character, his
purpose being to provide models of behavior to be either emulated or avoided.
Rich with anecdotal detail, dramatic
scenes, quotations, and Plutarch's own
critical comments, the *Lives* served all
of Europe for centuries as the principal source of classical antiquity. From
the French of Jacques Amyot, Sir
Thomas North made a translation
called *Lives of the Noble Grecians and
Romans* (1579) that strongly influenced Elizabethan prose and gave
Shakespeare material for *Coriolanus,
Julius Caesar, Antony and Cleopatra*,
and *Timon of Athens*.

   TRANSLATIONS: *The Lives of the Noble Grecians and Romans* tr. John Dryden (1683–86), rev. Arthur Hugh
Clough (1864, new ed. New York
1932). *Plutarch's Lives* tr. Bernadotte
Perrin (Loeb Classical Library, 11 vols.
Cambridge, Mass. 1915–28). *Moralia*
tr. F. C. Babbitt and others (Loeb
Classical Library, 16 vols., vols. 1–15
Cambridge, Mass. 1927–69).
   REFERENCES: R. H. Barrow *Plutarch
and His Times* (London and Bloomington, Ind. 1967). J. R. Hamilton *Plutarch: Alexander, A Commentary* (Oxford 1969). Roger Miller Jones *The
Platonism of Plutarch* (Menasha, Wis.
1916). H. Armin Moellering *Plutarch*

on *Superstition* (rev. ed. Boston 1963). John Oakesmith *The Religion of Plutarch* (London 1902). Katharine M. Westaway *The Educational Theory of Plutarch* (London 1922).

POE, Edgar Allan (Jan. 19, 1809 – Oct. 7, 1849). American writer. Born Boston, where his actor parents were performing. After their deaths, which left Edgar, his brother and sister destitute, he was informally adopted by John Allan, wealthy merchant of Richmond, Va., and his wife. With the Allans he went to England (1815), where he attended school; they returned to Richmond (1820). A good student at the University of Virginia, he withdrew because of gambling. Quarreled bitterly with Allan and went to Boston, where he published anonymously *Tamerlane and Other Poems* (1827). That year entered U.S. Army, then West Point (1830), but a year later was dismissed. While in New York, published *Poems by Edgar A. Poe* (1831), containing *Israfel, To Helen,* and *The City in the Sea.* Alienated from Allan, he went to live with his aunt Mrs. William Clemm in Baltimore (1831–35) and began writing for magazines. His story *Ms. Found in a Bottle* won a prize, which led to the first of editorial posts on the *Southern Literary Messenger* and other magazines. Married his thirteen-year-old cousin Virginia Clemm (1836; she died 1847). In New York on journalistic work (1837–38) he published *The Narrative of Arthur Gordon Pym* (1838); in Philadelphia he published *The Fall of the House of Usher* (1839), followed by his first collection, *Tales of the Grotesque and Arabesque* (1840). Became literary editor of *Graham's Magazine* (1841–42), to which he contributed poems, stories, and brilliant criticism. In New York again, wrote *The Raven* (1844), which became his most famous poem, known across the world. Published more *Tales* (1845), poems, and criticism. After his wife's death, he deteriorated physically and emotionally, but produced some of his finest work: the metaphysical prose poem *Eureka* (1848), *Ulalume* (1847), *Annabel Lee* and *The Bells* (1849). Found unconscious in a Baltimore street, he died in a hospital there.

Best known in his lifetime as a critic, Poe's international reputation as a poet was first established in France, by Baudelaire, later by Mallarmé and the symbolists, whom he deeply influenced with his highly charged imagination, his obsession with beauty and melancholy, and use of musical effect. His stories have exerted wide influence, and because of his "ratiocinative tales" *The Murders in the Rue Morgue* (1841), *The Mystery of Marie Roget* (1842–43), and *The Purloined Letter* (1845), he is recognized as the founder of the modern detective story.

EDITION: *Collected Works* ed. Thomas Ollive Mabbott (Cambridge, Mass. 1969–   ).

REFERENCES: William Bittner *Poe: A Biography* (Boston 1962 and London 1963). Edward H. Davidson *Poe: A Critical Study* (Cambridge, Mass. and Oxford 1957). Joseph Wood Krutch *Edgar Allan Poe: A Study of Genius* (1926, reprinted New York 1965). Una B. Pope-Hennessy *Edgar Allan Poe, 1809–1849: A Critical Biography* (London and New York 1934). Arthur H. Quinn *Edgar Allan Poe: A Critical Biography* (1941, reprinted 2 vols. New York 1969). Robert Regan ed. *Poe: A Collection of Critical Essays* (Englewood Cliffs, N.J. 1967, also PB). Edward Shanks *Edgar Allan Poe* (London and New York 1937). Edward C. Wagenknecht *Edgar Allan Poe: The Man Behind the Legend* (New York 1963). Frances Winwar *The Haunted Palace: A Life of Edgar Allan Poe* (New York 1959). George Edward Woodberry *Life of Edgar Allan Poe* (1909, reprinted 2 vols. New York 1965).

POLLAIUOLO, Antonio (c.1431–1498) and Piero (c. 1444–c.1496). Italian artists. Born probably in Florence, sons of a poulterer. ANTONIO was trained as a goldsmith; he received many commissions but little of his work survives. Also designed embroideries for vestments (Cathedral Museum, Florence), armor, crucifixes, and worked on the papal tombs in Rome, where he died. Frequently collaborated with PIERO, who was principally a painter. Piero painted six of the Virtues for the council chamber of the Mercatanzia (1469, Uffizi Gallery, Florence).

His only signed and dated work is *Coronation of the Virgin* (1483, S. Agostino, San Gimignano). He died in Florence. Both brothers worked on *Apollo and Daphne* and *Martyrdom of St. Sebastian* (1475, National Gallery, London), noted for its clear composition and careful anatomy. Antonio's engraving *Battle of the Nudes* (c.1470, Uffizi Gallery, Florence) and dramatic bronze statuette *Hercules and Antaeus* (c.1480, Museo Nazionale, Florence) are equally brilliant anatomical studies. The monumental effigy and tomb of Sixtus IV (1484–93, St. Peter's, Rome) show him at his most sophisticated; for the tomb of Innocent VIII (1494–97, St. Peter's) he used Piero's designs for reliefs of the Virtues, but showed his originality in depicting the pope as a seated figure.

REFERENCES: J. G. Phillips *Early Florentine Designers and Engravers* (Cambridge, Mass. 1955). John Pope-Hennessy *Italian Renaissance Sculpture* (London 1958).

POLLOCK, Jackson (Jan. 28, 1912 – Aug. 11, 1956). American painter. Born Cody, Wyo., son of a farmer. Studied painting at Manual Arts School, Los Angeles (1925–27), then went to New York and studied under Thomas Hart Benton at Art Students' League (1929–31). Worked on WPA Federal Art Project, New York (1938–42). Peggy Guggenheim, who championed him henceforth, held his first one-man show (1943) at her Art of This Century Gallery. His early work showed influence of American Indian sand painting, of Albert Ryder's seascapes, and of Mexican muralists José Clemente Orozco and Diego Rivera. Through Picasso and the surrealists he evolved a personal abstract style, freely rhythmic and linear, expressing profound emotional intensity. Married Lee Krasner (1944), who encouraged him in his "dripping" form of calligraphy, executed on a huge canvas spread on the floor. "I need the resistance of a hard surface," wrote Pollock. "On the floor I am more at ease. I feel nearer, more a part of the painting, since this way I can walk around it, work from the four sides and literally be *in* the painting. . . . I continue to get fur-

ther away from the usual painter's tools such as easel, palette, brushes, etc. I prefer sticks, trowels, knives and dripping fluid paint or a heavy impasto with sand, broken glass and other foreign matter added." Pollock became a leading figure in the New York School of abstract expressionism, and is now acknowledged as one of the towering artists of the twentieth century, an innovator in method and concept of space, and an extraordinary craftsman. His best works include *Male and Female* (1942), *Pasiphae* (1943), *Cathedral* (1947), *Number One* (1949), *Autumn Rhythm* (1950), *Blue Poles* (1953), *White Light* (1954). He died in an automobile accident on Long Island, N.Y. Photographer Hans Nemuth made a short film of his work (1950).

REFERENCES: James Biddle and Bernice Rose *Jackson Pollock: Works on Paper* (New York 1969). Sidney Janis *Abstract and Surrealist Art in America* (New York 1944). Francis V. O'Connor *Jackson Pollock* (New York PB 1967). Frank O'Hara *Jackson Pollock* (New York 1959). Bryan Robertson *Jackson Pollock* (London and New York 1960).

PONTORMO, Jacopo da (real name Jacopo Carrucci) (May 24, 1494 – 1556/7). Italian painter. Born Pontormo, near Empoli, the son of a painter. A pupil of Piero di Cosimo, by 1512 he was working as Andrea del Sarto's assistant. He was influenced by del Sarto and Fra Bartolommeo in early works such as the *Visitation* fresco (1514–16, Santissima Annunziata, Florence). His own style emerged in the altarpiece for S. Michele Visdomini, Florence (1518); its restlessness makes it a forerunner of mannerism. He produced unconventional frescoes such as the mythological ones for the Medici villa at Poggio a Caiano (1520–21); for the *Passion* cycle in the Certosa of Galluzzo (1523–24) he borrowed ideas from Dürer's engravings. Influenced by Michelangelo in the late 1520's, his style became more harmonious, as in the *Deposition* (1525–28, S. Felicita, Florence), but the *Visitation* (c.1528, parish church, Carmignano) is purely individual. Few of his later works survive, though drawings such as those of the frescoes of S. Lorenzo, Florence remain, showing

him as a highly accomplished draftsman. He also painted a number of
sensitive portraits, including *Alessandro de'Medici* (1535, Museum of Art,
Philadelphia), *Giovanni della Casa*
(1540–44, National Gallery, Washington) and *Portrait of a Woman* (1543–
45, Uffizi Gallery, Florence). Pontormo
was a principal innovator of the mannerist style. He died in Florence.

REFERENCES: F. M. Clapp *Pontormo:
His Life and Work* (New Haven, Conn.
1916). Janet C. Rearick *The Drawings
of Pontormo* (2 vols. Cambridge, Mass.
1964).

POPE, Alexander (May 21, 1688 – May
30, 1744). English poet. Born London
of Roman Catholic parents. Barred
from formal education by ill health
and his faith, was self-taught and notably precocious. Deformed by an early
illness (Pott's disease, a spinal tuberculosis), he never married. Settled
(1719) at Twickenham, outside London, where he remained rest of his life.
Published four *Pastorals* (1709), and
achieved recognition with *An Essay on
Criticism* (1711) and *The Rape of the
Lock* (1712, enlarged 1714). First
taken up by Addison and the Whigs,
later shifted to the Tories and joined
the Scriblerus Club with Swift, Gay,
Arbuthnot, Bolingbroke, and others.
Published (1715) first volume of his
very remunerative translation in heroic couplets of the *Iliad* (completed 6
vols. 1720), one of the great poems of
the age. Translated the *Odyssey* (1720–
25) in collaboration with William
Broome and Elijah Fenton (published
1725–26). Also published an edition of
Shakespeare (1725), criticized by Lewis
Theobald, who as a result became the
first hero of *The Dunciad,* a satire on
dullness in three books which appeared
anonymously (1728). (Colley Cibber
replaced Theobald as the hero in the
enlarged edition of 1743.) One of the
most widely quoted English poets, Pope
is especially famous for the heroic
couplet. Later major works: *An Essay on Man* (1733–34), *Moral Essays*
(1731–35), *Imitations of Horace, Satires and Epistles* (1733–38), and *Epistle to Dr. Arbuthnot* (1735), one of his
most brilliant and mordant poems, con-

taining the famous portraits of Addison, Lord Hervey, and critics.

EDITIONS: *Works* gen. ed. John Butt
(10 vols. London 1939–61, also PB in
one volume, abridged). *Poetical Works*
ed. Herbert Davis (London and New
York 1966).

REFERENCES: Norman Ault *New
Light on Pope* (1949, reprinted Ham-
den, Conn. 1967). Reuben A. Brower
Alexander Pope: The Poetry of Allusion
(New York and London 1959, PB 1969).
Bonamy Dobrée *Alexander Pope* (1951,
reprinted New York 1969, also PB).
John A. Jones, Jr. *Pope's Couplet Art*
(Athens, Ohio 1969). George Wilson
Knight *The Poetry of Pope: Laureate of
Peace* (1954, new ed. New York and
London PB 1965). Judith O'Neill ed.
Critics of Pope (Coral Gables, Fla. and
London 1968). Rebecca P. Parkin *The
Poetic Workmanship of Alexander Pope*
(1955, new ed. New York 1966). Peter
Quennell *Alexander Pope: The Educa-
tion of Genius* (London and New York
1968, also PB). George W. Sherburn
The Early Career of Alexander Pope
(1934, reprinted London and New York
1963). Geoffrey Tillotson *On the Poetry of Pope* (2nd ed. Oxford 1950)
and *Pope and Human Nature* (Oxford
1958).

☙

ALEXANDER POPE

BY MARTIN SEYMOUR-SMITH

Few reputations have changed in the
past sixty years as startlingly as that
of Alexander Pope. When George Pas-
ton (E. M. Symonds) published her
1909 biography he was still generally
regarded as a viper, no poet, but, as
Arnold called him, "a classic of our
prose." Now he is seen as a very great
poet indeed: a moral genius whose borrowings are no longer thefts but "allusions"; as a man he was "much loved
and loving." To evince distaste for his
character or to refuse to recognize him
as a supreme poet is thought of as a
grave critical failing. No poet has been
so clear a victim of extremes.

Pope was a dwarf and a cripple,

which is doubtless why he was predominantly a satirist; furthermore, he was all his life a member of the Roman Catholic Church, which since 1688, the year of his birth, had been a much despised minority. Despite these handicaps, or more probably because of them, he succeeded in putting himself on equal terms with nearly all the most powerful and gifted men of his time. Whatever may be said against his personality, he undoubtedly inspired admiration and affection in such men as Swift, Bolingbroke, Gay, and Arbuthnot, although the first two ultimately had cause to blame him for double-dealing.

The poetaster William Walsh, disciple of Dryden, early told Pope that "there was one way left of excelling": to be wholly "correct." Pope, although his passion was to excel rather than to be correct, took his advice to heart. For him, correctness meant what would most delight and flatter the best minds of his age. His youthful *Pastorals* (1709) show little feeling for nature but are what Pope designed them to be: promising. *An Essay on Criticism* (1711) is a derivative and critically meaningless mosaic of current attitudes; but it sets the tone for his future performance in that it is beautifully executed and highly elegant — intellectually tawdry, it nevertheless breathes "class."

The mock epic *The Rape of the Lock* (1712, 1714) is Pope's finest poem: in it he is basically concerned with taste and with style, both of which he fully understood. Without trying to be profound, he frankly sets out to please, and he pleases. Furthermore, this is his first satire — and it was as a satirist that he excelled. In *The Rape of the Lock*, there is none of the vituperation that vitiates parts of the later satires.

Pope's superlative skill was matched by an impeccable sense of taste. He knew intuitively, and it is to his credit that he did so, who were the greatest men of his age. (If he was wrong about Defoe, then so was the incomparably more serious Swift.) Thus he early transferred his allegiance from Addison's Whig Little Senate to the Tory group around Swift, Bolingbroke, and the physician Arbuthnot, with whom he founded the Scriblerus Club, out of whose gay proceedings *The Dunciad* grew. He set out to dazzle each one of these men, and almost succeeded. Only Swift, as a close examination of their correspondence reveals, remained somewhat ironically equivocal in his attitude; when he stayed with him in 1727 Pope's understandable fussings over his bad health drove him to sudden flight.

As *An Essay on Man* (1733) indicates, Pope's intellectual position, if it can be described as such, was that of a conventional deist. But he remained a nominal Roman Catholic, cleverly taking advantage of the official wilderness into which this put him to maintain friendships with Whig magnates as well as with the Tories who were his main choice. There is no suggestion that his religion meant anything to him.

The modern view of Pope as a great moralist and as an upholder, chiefly in *The Dunciad,* of high literary standards is contradicted by the facts of his life. For, although he possessed rare courage in physical adversity, and genuine charm and taste (and he always had, too, an endearing desire to be pleasant in society), he was also one of the most thoroughgoing hypocrites that English literature has ever known.

Now extolled by critics as the enemy of Grub Street, of bad writing and bad writers, it was the methods of Grub Street that he secretly used in order to get his revised, falsified, and selected letters printed — so that he might then issue a "corrected" and "authorized" edition. He cheated and deceived the aging Swift into issuing a volume of their letters (which he himself had printed, whilst publicly uttering threats against the printer) and then piously accused him of vanity. In these affairs, which are so complex that they can never now be completely disentangled, Pope employed a variety of agents, ranging from Richard Savage to the foolish Lord Orrery.

It is frequently stated that these were the accepted methods of Pope's age, which was of course the great age of letter writing; but no writer, not even one from Grub Street, lavished the care Pope did on his own letters, or falsified and cheated his friends on such a scale. The letters of the two greatest letter writers of the century, Lady Mary Wortley Montagu and Lord Chesterfield, were not published until after their deaths. Pope's revision of his letters for publication was quite acceptable; but the extent of his trickery over them has no parallel in his or any other age.

The so-called biographical fallacy apart, common sense should tell us that it is unlikely that such a man would be especially distinguished as a moralist; and Pope was not. His poetry should be appreciated for what it does achieve, not for the abstractions that critics recklessly project into it: for its technical perfection within narrow limits, its amoral, aesthetic superiority, its essentially heartless but comforting and superb elegance — as in the *Epistle to Dr. Arbuthnot,* an apology for himself which is as magnificently tasteful and enjoyable as it is breathtakingly disingenuous. The real Pope is neither the vituperative hunchback of the Victorians nor the so-called Mozartian and Keatsian moral philosopher of the twentieth-century critics: he is a touching, very human mixture of kindness and viciousness, charm and cunning, fear and ambition, who wrote perhaps the most dignified and accomplished light verse and some of the most vicious and witty satire of all time.

PORTA. *See* BARTOLOMMEO, FRA.

PORTER, William Sydney. *See* HENRY, O.

POULENC, Francis (Jan. 7, 1899 – Jan. 30, 1963). French composer. Born and died in Paris. Studied piano with Ricardo Viñes and composition with Charles Koechling. His music shows influence of Ravel, Chabrier, Satie, and Stravinsky. As one of the group of young Parisian composers known as Les Six, his works were first performed in 1918. Held (1934) the first of his joint recitals with tenor Pierre Bernac, with whom he toured Europe and the United States. Poulenc wrote piano pieces and incidental and chamber music, but achieved most success in his vocal works, notably *Litanies à la Vierge noire de Rocamadour* (1936), a Mass (1937), *Four Motets* (1938–39), the cantata *Figure humaine* (1943), *Stabat Mater* (1951), *Dialogues des Carmelites* (1957), *La Voix humaine* (1958), and songs on poems by Ronsard, Apollinaire, Éluard, and others. Urbane and neoclassic, these works display a great melodic gift.

EDITIONS: *Entretiens avec Claude Rostand* (Paris 1954). *Correspondance, 1915–63* ed. Hélène De Wendel (Paris PB 1967).

REFERENCE: Henri Hell *Francis Poulenc* (tr. London and New York 1959).

POUSSIN, Nicolas (June 1593 or 1594 – Nov. 19, 1665). French painter. Born Les Andelys, Normandy, of peasant stock. After twelve years in Paris and other parts of France (1612–24), he settled in Rome, spending the rest of his life there, except for an interlude in Paris (1640–42) as first painter to

Louis XIII. The work of his early years in Rome reveals diversified tendencies. *The Martyrdom of St. Erasmus* (1628) in a baroque vein established his reputation. Mature style begins about 1630, the year of his marriage to Anne Marie Dughet. Other important examples of his work are the two series of *Seven Sacraments* (the first begun c.1636, the second painted 1644–48), his many *Holy Family* paintings, and his landscapes with classical themes, such as the *Arcadian Shepherds* (1650, Louvre, Paris) and *Birth of Bacchus* (1657, Fogg Art Museum, Cambridge, Mass.). The first French painter to win international fame since the Middle Ages, and the founder of French classical art, Poussin inspired such later artists as David, Ingres, Cézanne, and Picasso.

REFERENCES: Sir Anthony Blunt *Nicolas Poussin* (London and New York 1967). Walter F. Friedlaender *Nicolas Poussin: A New Approach* (New York 1965). Walter F. Friedlaender and Sir Anthony Blunt *The Drawings of Nicolas Poussin: A Catalogue Raisonné* (London 1939–53).

✍

NICOLAS POUSSIN
BY SIR ANTHONY BLUNT

The case of Poussin is the rare one of an artist who attained great imaginative heights by the conscious application of rational methods. All through his career, he sought balance and harmony rather than violence and intensity, explicit statement rather than suggestive hints, and perfection rather than brilliance of technique. At the height of his career in the 1640's and early 1650's, reason also dominated his choice of subject — and a quite specific kind of reason, too, for in those years he was a wholehearted adherent of the doctrine of Stoicism and his paintings can be regarded almost as expositions of Stoic ethics. Their underlying theme is the heroic virtue of those Greeks and Romans whom the Stoics most admired: Diogenes for the simplicity of his way of life, Scipio Africanus for his continence, Phocion for his passionate adherence to the truth, Coriolanus for preferring death to revenge even on a city which he thought had ill-treated him, Cato the Younger for committing suicide rather than submit to a tyrant. These and other examples of Stoic virtue provided the themes for Poussin's paintings and drawings and were also the subject of his reading, for he constantly quotes tags from Stoic writers in his letters and makes confession of the Stoic faith with its belief in the power of man to dominate circumstance by the application of reason and self-control. This Stoicism, however, did not conflict with his Christianity, and he seems to have found in the doctrines and practice of the early church a synthesis of the two creeds to which he gave expression in his series of paintings of the Seven Sacraments (on loan at the National Gallery of Scotland, Edinburgh).

Poussin, however, extended the severity of Stoic morals to his art, and it is this fact that gives his paintings of the middle years an almost puritanical severity and simplicity. Diogenes and Phocion were his models in this field as well as in the conduct of life, for both had given the example of that concentration on essentials and that artistic economy which Poussin deemed essential to all great art: Diogenes, who threw away his last piece of domestic furniture — his drinking cup — on seeing a boy drinking water from a stream in his hand, and Phocion, who when asked what he was brooding over before addressing the assembly answered: "I'm thinking what I can leave out of my speech."

That there was poetry in Poussin was clear from his earlier paintings, idylls or elegies recounting the loves of the gods, or triumphs showing the feasts of the satyrs and maenads in honor of Bacchus, painted with a palette learned from Titian and other great Venetians. These paintings with their lyrical charm and their immediate appeal to the eye will always be among Poussin's most widely loved works, and rightly so, because never again did he attain such freshness and directness of expression. But he himself felt that this was not enough and, like Renoir in the 1880's, he deliberately taught himself a new and stricter discipline. He threw away all those charms which appealed to the eye and the senses and learned the new and severe moral and artistic code which dominated his thought and his painting for more than fifteen years.

In the last ten years of his life, however, his conception of his art changed again and he reached a new kind of vision in which were assimilated the poetry of his early paintings and the wisdom of his middle years without its harshness. He turned back to classical mythology for his themes, but he treated them in a quite new way, not as love stories but as allegories — very strange allegories, in which Jupiter, Apollo, and Bacchus are no longer rivals in love but symbols of life and energy: Apollo, the sun and the source of warmth, pursuing Daphne, the symbol of cold and dampness; Jupiter, sending his mysteriously born son, Bacchus, to infuse into the earth the vitality symbolized by the vine. These late paintings do not have the gaiety of Poussin's early mythological compositions, but they have a profoundly moving and poetical quality, wholly removed from the world of the senses and existing purely in the realm of the imagination.

Poussin would not himself have described them so, for he never uses the word imagination in his letters and talked only of reason; but for him reason was the *logos* of the Stoics, which was the great creative force of the universe, and which in a sense subsumed both reason and imagination. There would, therefore, not have been for him any contradiction between the beliefs of his early and middle years and those of his old age; he had simply penetrated more deeply into the mysteries of the *logos*.

Poussin was an intellectual artist who painted for intellectuals, and many of the allusions in his art which were common knowledge in his circle are to us strange and obscure, but although an understanding of the meanings implicit in his compositions leads to a fuller appreciation of his intentions, the exquisite harmony of the forms and the appeal of the color — whether sensuous as in the early paintings, clear-cut as in the middle years, or subtle and restrained as in the late works — are so carefully adapted to his themes that they convey, as if by a sort of equivalence, the core of his message, even if the individual words have not been spelled out.

In his youth he was full of fire; but in his later years he became remote and withdrawn, feared rather than loved by other artists because he was sharp in his judgments of those who did not live up to the highest standards — but, it must be added, he applied these standards with exactly the same severity to himself and his art. He worked slowly, preparing each composition with endless preliminary sketches and spending longer over the execution of a six-foot canvas than his contemporaries would have taken over frescoing a ceiling — he called himself "the tortoise of painting," but not entirely without pride — and hating to finish a painting because, with further searching, he might have found a solution infinitesimally better. He was a perfectionist and his works are few in number, but they must rank with the greatest achievements of European painting.

PRAETORIUS, Michael (real name Schultheiss or Schultz) (Feb. 15, 1571 – Feb. 15, 1621). German musician. Born Kreuzberg (Thuringia). Most famous of musicians to use latinized form of his German name. After serving as choirmaster in Lüneburg, was choirmaster and secretary (from 1604 until his death) to duke of Brunswick at Wolfenbüttel. Best-known work is his collection of church songs, *Musae Sioniae* (9 vols. 1605-10), some for eight to twelve voices, Venetian double choir style, and some in four-part style. Although he was a prolific composer, his greatest reputation is for his invaluable historical work *Syntagma musicum* (1615-20), whose three published volumes are (I) a Latin treatise on music theory, (II) an illustrated description of instruments, and (III) an exposition of ancient, secular, and religious music, musicians, and technique. The fourth part on counterpoint was not completed.

PRAXITELES (c.390–c.330 B.C.). Greek sculptor. Born Athens, son of sculptor Kephisodotus. Together with his older contemporary Scopas, he was a leader of the later Attic school. He worked chiefly in marble, but also used bronze. Although there are references in ancient writings to about sixty works by him, few, if any, originals survive. Some scholars consider the partially mutilated *Hermes with the Infant Dionysus* (Heraeum, Olympia) and the *Apollo, Marsyas, and the Muses* (National Museum, Athens) to be the work of Praxiteles himself. Other works survive as Roman copies: the *Satyr* (Capitol, Rome), *Apollo Sauroktonus* (Vatican Museum, Rome), and *Aphrodite* from Arles (Louvre, Paris). His most celebrated work was the *Aphrodite of Cnidus* (copy in Vatican Museum), considered one of the first nude female figures of Greek sculpture. There are also Roman copies of several Erotes and Satyrs. Praxiteles represents the culmination of classical Greek sculpture. He is unsurpassed in modeling of heads and handling of surface. Grace of form, strength, and joyous spirit are his outstanding characteristics.

REFERENCES: Rhys Carpenter *Greek Sculpture* (Chicago and Cambridge, England, 1960). G. M. A. Richter *The Sculpture and Sculptors of the Greeks* (1929, rev. ed. New Haven, Conn. 1950 and Oxford 1951).

PRESCOTT, William Hickling (May 4, 1796 – Jan. 28, 1859). American historian. Born Salem, Mass.; of prominent New England family. Graduated from Harvard (1814). Severe eye injury through an accident in his junior year caused nearly total blindness, and he abandoned study of law. After two years abroad seeking a cure he settled in Boston, married Susan Amory (1820), and determined on a literary career. Published (1831) a review in *North American Review*, first of a series collected in *Biographies and Critical Miscellanies* (1845). During 1820's his interest shifted to history, and aided by readers, he schooled himself with iron-willed intensity. Embarked (1829) on his first major project and produced the three-volume *History of the Reign of Ferdinand and Isabella the Catholic* (1838), which was so successful in the U.S. and Europe that he devoted the rest of his life to the history of Spain in the Old World and New. *History of the Conquest of Mexico* (3 vols. 1843), his masterpiece, and *History of the Conquest of Peru* (2 vols. 1847) are among the most popular histories in English, combining dramatic narrative and superb language with historical acumen. Oxford awarded him a degree (1850) and he was received by Queen Victoria. In the middle of the third volume of an epic project, *History of the Reign of Philip the Second, King of Spain* (10 vols. planned, two published, 1855), he suffered a stroke and died in his Beacon Street home in Boston.

EDITION: *Works* ed. W. H. Munro (22 vols. Philadelphia and London 1904).

REFERENCES: Howard F. Cline and others *William Hickling Prescott: A Memorial* (Durham, N.C., and Cambridge, England, 1959). C. Harvey Gardiner *William Hickling Prescott: A Biography* (Austin, Tex. 1969). Samuel Eliot Morison *William Hickling Prescott* (Boston 1958). Harry T. Peck *William Hickling Prescott* (1905, reprinted New York 1969). George Ticknor *Life of William Hickling Prescott* (Boston 1864).

PRÉVOST, Abbé (real name Antoine François Prévost d'Exiles) (Apr. 1, 1697 – Nov. 25, 1763). French novelist. Born Hesdin, Artois, into lawyer's family. Years from age of sixteen to twenty-three spent alternately as soldier and Jesuit novice. Became Benedictine monk (1721), ordained (1726). Went to Paris (1728) to publish first four volumes of *Mémoires et aventures d'un homme de qualité* (7 vols. 1728–31), and that year left the order. To avoid arrest he fled to England, later to Holland (1730); was converted to Protestantism. Published last volumes of *Mémoires* (1731). The seventh, *Histoire du Chevalier des Grieux et de Manon Lescaut* (tr. 1831), was condemned as immoral by French authorities. It is the story of an aristocrat who forsakes everything for his passion for a demimondaine, with the result that they ruin each other's lives. From *Manon Lescaut* derive such great nineteenth-century romantic works as the plays *Marion Delorme* by Victor Hugo and *La Dame aux camélias* by Alexandre Dumas *fils*, and the operas *Manon* by Massenet and *Manon Lescaut* by Puccini. In England (1732), Prévost founded *Pour et Contre* (20 vols. 1733–40), a journal of English events and letters for the French public, then returned to France to become chief chaplain of prince de Conti (1736) and editor of *Journal Étranger* (1755). A devoted Anglophile, he translated into French the novels of Samuel Richardson, thereby influencing development of the novel in France. Died of apoplexy at home in Chantilly.

TRANSLATION: *Manon Lescaut* tr. L. W. Tancock (Harmondsworth, England, PB 1951).

REFERENCES: Claire Éliane Engel *Le Véritable Abbé Prévost* (Monaco 1958). Henry Harrisse *L'Abbé Prévost* (Paris 1896). George R. Havens *The Abbé Prévost and English Literature* (1921, reprinted New York PB 1965). Henri Roddier *L'Abbé Prévost, l'homme et l'oeuvre* (Paris 1955).

PRIOR, Matthew (July 21, 1664 – Sept. 18, 1721). English poet. Born Wimborne, Dorset, son of a carpenter. Thanks to Charles Sackville, Lord Dorset, was educated at Westminster School and St. John's College, Cambridge (graduated 1686). Achieved recognition with first publication, *The Country Mouse and the City Mouse* (1687), a burlesque of Dryden's *The Hind and the Panther,* written in collaboration with the Hon. Charles Montague. Aided by Lord Dorset, Prior began a long diplomatic career as secretary to ambassador at The Hague, was employed in negotiations for treaty of Ryswick (1697). Returned to England (1699) and at Queen Anne's accession joined Tories (1702), entered Parliament, and later served in Paris on peace negotiations, playing a leading role in treaty of Utrecht (1713), known as "Matt's Peace." Upon queen's death was imprisoned (1715–17). Returned to writing poetry and brought out a collection (1718) which included the long poems *Alma, or The Progress of the Mind* and *Solomon on the Vanity of the World* in three books of heroic couplets. Died at Wimpole Hall, Cambridgeshire; buried in Westminster Abbey.

EDITION: *Literary Works* ed. H. Bunker Wright and Monroe K. Spears (2 vols. Oxford 1959).
REFERENCES: Francis Bickley *Life of Matthew Prior* (London and New York 1914). Charles K. Eves *Matthew Prior: Poet and Diplomatist* (New York 1939). Samuel Johnson *Lives of the Poets* (London 1779–81). L. G. Wickham Legg *Matthew Prior: A Study of His Public Career and Correspondence* (Cambridge, England, 1921).

MATTHEW PRIOR
BY BERTRAND H. BRONSON

With no advantages of birth or wealth, Prior attained twofold eminence early in life. By a double stroke of luck, he got the best liberal education possible in his day. His uncle, a London wine seller, no doubt looking toward his own future advantage, put him into famous Westminster School under the celebrated Dr. Busby. There he absorbed Latin and Greek like a sponge, and did not stop reading when he came home to learn his uncle's business. At that critical moment, the earl of Dorset, a great patron of art and himself something of a poet ("To all you ladies now at land / We men at sea indite"), noticed him reading Horace in the shop, and was so struck by his lively intelligence that he promptly underwrote his further education at Cambridge. At St. John's College, Prior met abundance of good company, made friends easily, grew conversant with the manners of the well-born, and was welcomed in great houses. He began to be known as a talented and witty verse writer, turning out numerous songs, epigrams, anacreontics, odes, verse epistles: courtly compliments and graceful tributes to ladies and gentlemen. With one of his close friends, the Honorable Charles Montague, he composed a comical travesty of Dryden's *The Hind and the Panther* that hit the fashionable taste with a wave of mischievous laughter. The authors found themselves suddenly famous.

They were not to be forgotten. Within three years, Prior went to The Hague as secretary to the English embassy; won the confidence of King William; continued thereafter his diplomatic career at Ryswick and Versailles; in the new reign of Queen Anne became an M.P., and eventually rose to be ambassador to the French court during the negotiations leading to the Peace of Utrecht. During these reigns, he was the de facto court poet, and wrote many formal pieces on state occasions. He aspired, however, to be named in the roster of poets of lasting, philosophic interest. When the Whigs, returning to power upon the death of Anne, put him under close custody for over two years with charges of treason, he managed to keep his head — in both senses — and devoted himself to poetry, laboring especially at two long works, one humorous, the other grave. The former is *Alma*, racy, irresponsible, learned; the latter, *Solomon*, is a philosophic monologue proving that "All is vanity." Both were read and reread throughout their own century, but find few readers today.

Prior's best work, undoubtedly, is to be found, not in his ambitious poems, but in his *jeux d'esprit*. These he composes with a felicity that seems like casual inspiration, but is the quintessence of art. He has a hypersensitive ear for the cadences of cultivated discourse, the careless elegance, the idiomatic turn of phrase, the well-bred colloquialism, the vibrant harmonics and timbre of voices in play, the assumption of easy familiarity.

Illustrations define his qualities better than descriptive phrases, but there is little space here for quotation. It is hard to forgo his *Epitaph* on sauntering Jack and idle Joan, two human ciphers whose lives added up to exactly zero:

> *Without love, hatred, joy, or fear,*
> *They led — a kind of — as it were:*
> *Nor wished, nor cared, nor*
>   *laughed, nor cried:*
> *And so they lived, and so they*
>   *died.*

Written with an almost weightless pen are two exquisite poems to children of quality, the one a tiny letter in verse to little Margaret Cavendish Holles-Harley; the other to a five-year-old from her forty-year-old admirer, in part as follows:

> *Nor quality, nor reputation,*
>   *Forbid me yet my flame to tell,*
> *Dear five years old befriends my*
>   *passion,*
>   *And I may write till she can*
>   *spell . . .*
>
> *For, as our different ages move,*
>   *'Tis so ordained (would Fate*
>   *but mend it!)*
> *That I shall be past making love,*
>   *When she begins to comprehend*
>   *it.*

At a different level of airy grace are the Chloe poems, especially three called *A Better Answer, An Ode* ("The merchant, to secure his treasure"), and *A Lover's Anger.*

In anapestic meter, Prior writes some charming verses picturing his life at The Hague ("While with labor assiduous"); and in the same measure another autobiographical poem, the ballad of *Down-Hall*, in which he captures the garrulous chitchat of his landlady on his way into the country:

> *By my troth! she replies, You grow*
>   *younger, I think:*
> *And pray, Sir, what wine does the*
>   *gentleman drink? . . .*
>
> *Why things, since I saw you, most*
>   *strangely have varied,*
> *The ostler is hanged, and the*
>   *widow is married.*
>
> *And Prue left a child for the par-*
>   *ish to nurse:*
> *And Cicely went off with a gentle-*
>   *man's purse.*

Another poem in the same meter, but rhyming in triplets, is one of his happiest characterizations: *Jinny the Just*, a poignant, homely, and unstilted, but deeply felt, tribute to an old friend and companion. It cannot be abridged without loss.

In a more polished style is the brilliant compliment to the Lady Katherine Hyde called *The Female Phaeton*. Happier still is the famous poem in octosyllabic couplets *An English Padlock*, containing some of his quickest dialogue. Sounding a profounder note are the Horatian stanzas written on Mézeray's *History of France*, beginning, "Whate'er thy countrymen have done." Such verses as the foregoing are the perfection of delicately modulated English speech, moving rhythmically to its own sufficient music.

But perhaps the most remarkable of Prior's poetic achievements, and in their kind unsurpassed, are the four tales *The Ladle, Paulo Purganti, Hans Carvel,* and *Protogenes and Apelles.* They are written, as Dr. Johnson said, "with great familiarity and great sprightliness: the language is easy, but seldom gross, and the numbers smooth, without appearance of care." As he also gently allows, three of them "are not over-decent"; but the present generation is not likely to mind that. The verve, the pace, the narrative skill, the unerring tact in detail, the deftness of characterization, the happiness of phrase and word, are inimitable. The prating housekeeper of Protogenes; the delicious description of the farmstead in *The Ladle*; the desperate fencing and fending of the doctor in *Paulo Purganti* against his prudish but lustful wife; and the kindred anxieties of the old husband in *Hans Carvel*:

> *He bought her sermons, psalms,*
>   *and graces;*

And doubled down the useful places;

the marvelous pen sketch of his young wife, "a lass of London mould":

Handsome? enough; extremely gay:
Loved music, company, and play . . .

But when no very great affair
Excited her peculiar care,
She without fail was waked at ten;
Drank chocolate, then slept again:
At twelve she rose; with much ado
Her clothes were huddled on by two . . .
Next, how to spend the afternoon,
And not come home again too soon;
The 'Change, the City, or the Play,
As each was proper for the day:
A turn in summer to Hyde Park,
When it grew <u>tolerably</u> dark.

For such economy of phrase, so light a touch, such harpsichordal clarity, such accuracy in capturing by ironic hint a whole gamut of social and personal values, where else can we turn?

PROKOFIEV, Sergey Sergeyevitch (Apr. 23, 1891 – Mar. 5, 1953). Russian composer. Born Sontsovka. Trained in piano by his mother, he wrote piano score for an opera, *The Giant* (1900), followed by another opera *On Desert Islands* (1902). Studied with Reinhold Glière, Moscow (1902), under whom he wrote a piano symphony and two operas, *Feast During the Plague* (1903) and *Ondine* (1904). Entered St. Petersburg Conservatory (1904), studying composition with Rimsky-Korsakov and Anatol Liadov, piano with Anna Essipova, conducting with Nicholas Tcherepnin. Graduated 1914, having written ten four orchestral pieces, including *Scythian Suite,* a piano concerto, four piano sonatas, piano cycle *Sarcasms,* and an opera. Received Anton Rubin-

stein prize as pianist for performance of his first piano concerto. Early works display dynamic power, abundance of irony, aggressive rhythms. *Classical Symphony* (1916–17) combines rapid modulatory shifts with classic Mozartian structure. During Revolution (1918) left Russia, via Japan, for American concert tour. Conducted his opera *The Love for Three Oranges,* and third piano concerto (Chicago 1921). Settled in Paris (1922), where he produced ballets in close association with Sergei Diaghilev: *Chout,* or *Buffoon* (1920), *Le Pas d'acier* (1921), *L'Enfant prodigue* (1928). Settled in Moscow (1933), producing a variety of works: symphonic fairy tale *Peter and the Wolf* (1936); ballet *Romeo and Juliet* (1935–36); opera *War and Peace* (1941–52); the fifth, sixth, and seventh (last) symphonies; several piano sonatas; incidental music for Pushkin's *Boris Godunov* (1936) and the films *Lieutenant Kijé* (1933) and *Alexander Nevsky* (1938). Died in Moscow. In later years he was severely criticized by Soviet press for his "modernistic" techniques. Despite occasional experiments with polytonality and atonality, Prokofiev never left the tonal system. A master of bold rhythms, asymmetrical patterns, unexpected harmony, he greatly influenced a younger generation of Soviet composers.

REFERENCES: Lawrence Hanson *Prokofiev: A Biography in Three Movements* (New York and London 1964). Israel V. Nestyev *Prokofiev* (tr. Stanford, Calif. 1960 and Oxford 1961). Victor I. Seroff *Sergei Prokofiev, A Soviet Tragedy: The Case of Sergei Prokofiev, His Life and Work, His Critics, and His Executioners* (New York 1968).

PROPERTIUS, Sextus (c.50 B.C. – c.16 B.C.) Roman poet. Little is known of his personal life. Born to wealthy family in or near Assisi. Lost father early in childhood, and estate through agrarian confiscation after battle of Philippi and return of Octavian to Rome. In spite of near poverty acquired a good education in Rome and was urged to become an advocate, but preferred a career of light literature and gallantry. May have married and fathered at least one child. Foppish in dress, of delicate constitution, inclined to melancholy and superstition in later years, he was member of circle of Maecenas and a friend of Ovid and Virgil. Died probably in Rome. His collected elegies (4046 lines), modeled somewhat after those of the Alexandrine poets Callimachus and Philetas, are usually divided into four books and fall into three categories: amatory and personal (dedicated to his mistress of six years, "Cynthia," the courtesan Hostia), political and social, and historical. Propertius is considered a master of the elegiac form; though his poems are flawed by their obscurity, uneven workmanship and a tendency to pedantry, they also reveal imagination, freshness of conception, range and boldness of vocabulary, humor, delicacy of description and emotion.

TRANSLATIONS: *Propertius* tr. H. E. Butler (Loeb Classical Library, 1912, latest ed. London and Cambridge, Mass. 1952). *Poems* tr. Constance Carrier (Bloomington, Ind. 1963, also PB). *Poems* tr. A. E. Watts (Boston 1967, also PB).

REFERENCES: P. W. Damon and W. Helmbold *Structure of Propertius* (2 vols. Berkeley, Calif. PB 1952). D. R. Shackleton Bailey *Propertiana* (Cambridge, England, and New York 1956).

PROUDHON, Pierre Joseph (Jan. 15, 1809 – Jan. 16, 1865). French writer. Born Besançon, of peasant stock. Studied briefly at university there. At nineteen entered printing trade, and as proofreader-compositor received a self-education in theology, Latin, Greek. Won a prize from University of Besançon (1838) for a philological essay, which financed further education in Paris. His interests turned to theoretical politics and economics, and he published (1840) *Qu'est-ce que la Propriété? (What is Property?)* "Property is theft!" he answered himself, advocating the abolition of finance capitalism for a system based on individual productivity without government control. Prosecuted, tried, and acquitted on charges of revolutionary opinions (1842). Published *The Philosophy of Misery* (1846); in 1847 Karl Marx, who dismissed him as a mere middle-class reformer, responded with *The Misery of Philosophy*. After the revolution of 1848, Proudhon

served briefly and unsuccessfully in the Assembly and founded the Banque du Peuple; its failure resulted in his prosecution and imprisonment (1849–52). During a parole married Euphrasie Piégard (1849). Publication (1858) of *De la Justice dans la révolution et dans l'église* (3 vols.) resulted in another trial and three-year sentence, from which he fled to Belgium. Amnesty granted (1862) enabled him to come back to Paris, where he lived uneventfully until his death. His funeral was attended by six thousand. Although his theories were inconsistent and he had no party affiliations (Trotsky called him "the Robinson Crusoe of socialism"), he influenced revolutionary thought throughout Europe.

REFERENCES: D. W. Brogan *Proudhon* (London 1934). John Hampden Jackson *Marx, Proudhon, and European Socialism* (London 1957 and New York 1958, also PB). S. Y. Lu *The Political Theories of P. J. Proudhon* (New York 1922). Alan Ritter *The Political Thought of Pierre Joseph Proudhon* (Princeton, N.J. 1969). George Woodcock *Pierre Joseph Proudhon* (London and New York 1956).

PROUST, Marcel (July 10, 1871 – Nov. 18, 1922). French novelist. Born Paris; educated at Lycée Condorcet. Son of a wealthy physician, he was strongly attached to his mother (who was Jewish), particularly after he developed asthma at age of nine. Brilliant and witty, he early became a frequenter of fashionable literary salons, writing occasional short pieces. After a year's service in the army (1889), he made a brief attempt to study law and then became honorary assistant at the Mazarine library. He was also an active Dreyfusard. Published first book, a collection of pieces, *Les Plaisirs et les jours* (1896, *Pleasures and Days*). Suffering from increasingly severe attacks of asthma, he retained his image as the witty dilettante, but after his mother's death (1905) he spent some time in a sanatorium, and remained a semi-invalid for rest of his life. It was under these conditions that he set out to write his monumental work, *À la Recherche du temps perdu* (1913–27, tr. *Remembrance of Things Past* 1922–32), a long novel in seven parts, three of which were published posthumously. The first part, *Du Côté de chez Swann* (1913, tr. *Swann's Way* 1928), attracted little notice, but the second volume, *À l'Ombre des jeunes filles en fleur* (1918, tr. *Within a Budding Grove*), won the Prix Goncourt (1919) and made him famous. The other volumes: *Le Côté de Guermantes* (1921, tr. *Guermantes Way*), *Sodome et Gomorrhe* (1921, tr. *Cities of the Plain*), *La Prisonnière* (1923, tr. *The Captive*), *Albertine disparue* (1925, tr. *The Sweet Cheat Gone*), *Le Temps Retrouvé* (1927, tr. *The Past Recaptured*). Drawing heavily upon his own experiences, the novel is at once a portrait of French society and an intensely personal study of wasted youth and human relations. He died in Paris just after its completion. The manuscript of an earlier unfinished novel was discovered after World War II and published as *Jean Santeuil* (1951, tr. 1955). The critical work *Contre Sainte-Beuve* was published in 1954.

TRANSLATIONS: *Remembrance of Things Past* tr. C. K. Scott Moncrieff and Stephen Hudson (1922–31, latest ed. 12 vols. London 1960–67 and 2 vols. New York 1960). *By Way of Sainte-Beuve* tr. Sylvia Townsend Warner (London 1958). *Jean Santeuil* tr. Gerard Hopkins (London 1955 and New York 1956, also PB). *Pleasures and Days* tr. Louise Varèse (Garden City, N.Y. PB 1957). *Letters of Marcel Proust* tr. and ed. Mina Curtiss (New York 1949 and London 1950, also PB).

REFERENCES: Richard H. Barker *Marcel Proust: A Biography* (New York 1958 and London 1959, also PB). Leo Bersani *Marcel Proust: The Fictions of Life and Art* (London and New York 1965, also PB). Germaine Brée *Marcel Proust and Deliverance From Time* (tr. 2nd ed. New Brunswick, N.J. 1969) and *The World of Marcel Proust* (Boston 1966 and London 1967). Wallace Fowlie *A Reading of Proust* (Garden City, N.Y. 1964 and London 1968). André Maurois *The Quest for Proust* (tr. London and New York 1950). George Painter *Proust: The Early Years* (London and Boston 1959) and *Proust: The Later Years* (London and Boston 1965, also PB).

MARCEL PROUST
BY JOHN GROSS

Suppose one were compelled to write a publisher's testimonial for Proust, recommending his work to the reluctant common reader in the language of handouts and blurbs. It would not be a particularly demanding assignment: without feeling that one was creating a false impression, one could talk of memorable characters and dramatic situations, of passion, humor, even suspense. One could freely invoke famous names, too, since radical an innovator though he was, Proust was also in many ways a traditionalist, whose writing displays most of the major virtues of his great nineteenth-century predecessors. He has the psychological acumen of a Stendhal, the social grasp of a Balzac, the evocative power and the satirical edge of a Flaubert. *Un Amour de Swann*, read "just for the story," can bear comparison with almost any of the classic love affairs of fiction; the last illness of Marcel's grandmother can bear comparison with almost any of the classic death scenes; Charlus, Françoise, Swann, the duchesse de Guermantes are figures who have long since found their way into the general mythology of world literature, and they are only the most extended portraits in a gallery which also includes dozens of other less elaborate but hardly less substantial studies of varying social types, of diplomats, artists, fashionable grandees, savants, actresses, demimondaines, pious maiden aunts. For if it were nothing else, *À la Recherche du temps perdu* would still command attention as a brilliant panorama of the epoch of Dreyfus and the First World War, an anatomy of upper-class French society with all its internal rivalries. shifting alliances, intricate subdivisions.

It is, of course, many other things as

well, and in fact our hypothetical blurb would probably next proceed to stress the sheer range of Proust's artistry, the triumphant way in which he manages to combine seemingly disparate effects. He is, for example, both a magician, who casts a dreamlike glamour over everything he describes, and a relentless moralist, intent on stripping away the last illusions of ambition and self-regard. Or again, the sensuous and pictorial vividness of his narrative style is matched by a correspondingly powerful analytical intelligence, a mastery of unsuspected analogies and fine distinctions — so much so that it was possible for an early admirer like Joseph Conrad to characterize his achievement as "analysis pushed to the point at which it becomes creative." Aphorisms came as naturally to him as images; his similes and parenthetical asides again and again blossom into subtle general disquisitions on love, egoism, old age, and half the other great perennial themes of literature. On more exotic themes, too: to take only the most obvious instance, homosexuality, a territory which as far as fiction goes he was virtually the first to open up.

An impressive enough rollcall of recommendations, and one which makes no pretense of being complete. Yet at the same time how easy it would be, if one confined oneself to routine terms of reference, to play the devil's advocate, to draw up an indictment against Proust considered as a conventional novelist. The aristocracy and their hangers-on, the rich and their parasites — how narrow his social world really is, for all its apparent density, and how snobbish his presuppositions! And the smothering neurotic jealousy — is there all that much to be learned in the end from a moralist who takes so constricted a view of human nature, who in the course of his investi-

gations gradually comes to see almost every adult relationship through the distorting medium of homosexual unfulfillment? Nor is it simply a question of those episodes which deal directly with Proust's erotic obsessions; there are many other places in the book as well where his outlook is morbid or precious or unnervingly passive, where he must surely induce a feeling of claustrophobia in anyone but the most fully acclimatized Proustian.

Certainly these limitations are not enough in themselves to outweigh the virtues which have already been listed. But taken in conjunction with the demands which Proust makes on his readers, they represent a formidable deterrent. Demands in terms of time and concentration: immense digressions, proliferating subordinate clauses, hairsplitting refinements and elaborations which in any other writer would be dismissed as outrageously prolix. It is hard not to feel, indeed, that there is something deliberately exorbitant about the whole undertaking. Wasn't it an essential part of Proust's nature to keep demanding more and more attention, like a plaintive invalid or a spoiled child?

The price is worth paying only if *À la Recherche* is judged as a whole, and valued not for this or that incidental merit but for what makes it unique: a unifying vision, quite unlike that of any earlier novelist, which acts on the reader like a drug, liberating his imagination and stirring up forgotten depths. Such a vision can only be experienced, not described, but essentially it might be summed up as a revelation of what Proust himself insisted was *la vraie vie*, the inner life of instinct, archetype, unpremeditated cross-reference, fugitive ideal which persists underneath the everyday surface world of habit and calculation. And it is the persistence which needs to be emphasized. To some extent, no doubt, it is the function of every work of art to put us in touch with our buried selves; the novelty of *À la Recherche* lies not so much in its isolated moments of intensity as in the pattern, the rhythm, the conscious attempt to elucidate an unconscious design.

Equally, it has to be stressed that Proust saw his subject as *la vraie vie*, not *ma vraie vie*. Those critics who describe his book as a "creative autobiography" are doing him a disservice. *"L'ouvrage de l'écrivain,"* he wrote, *"n'est qu'une espèce d'instrument optique qu'il offre au lecteur afin de lui permettre de discerner ce que, sans ce livre, il n'eût peut-être pas vu en soi-même."* And in his case, at least, the miracle works. Reading him is like reading two books simultaneously, one about the narrator's past, one about our own — so that Combray, for instance, is both a unique, lovingly delineated little town in nineteenth-century France, and the place where we all grew up. The souvenirs of egoism are converted into common property, and Proust's one true justification lies precisely in the fact that he has transcended autobiography and achieved the impersonality of art.

PUCCINI, Giacomo (Dec. 22, 1858 – Nov. 29, 1924). Italian composer. Born Lucca; represented fifth generation of a local dynasty of church musicians. Studied at Milan Conservatory (1880–83). Attracted considerable attention with his first opera, *Le Villi* (1883), and rose to international fame with *Manon Lescaut* (1893, based on novel by Abbé Prévost, 1731), and *La Bohème* (1896, based on Henry Murger's novel *Scènes de la vie de Bohème*, 1847–49). Settled in Torre del Lago, Tuscany (1891–1921), then moved to Viareggio. Married Elvira Gemignani (1904). *Tosca* (1900, based on melodrama by Victorien Sardou, 1887) was followed by *Madame Butterfly* (1904) and *La Fanciulla del West* (1910, based on David Belasco's play *The Girl of the Golden West,* 1905). Other works include *La Rondine* (1917) and *Il Trittico* (1918, *The Triptych*, comprising three one-act operas, *Il Tabarro, Suor Angelica,* and *Gianni Schicchi*). He had almost finished *Turandot* (performed 1926, its score completed by Franco Alfano) when he was stricken with throat cancer. He died in Brussels.

REFERENCES: William Ashbrook *The Operas of Puccini* (London and New York 1968). Mosco Carner *Puccini: A Critical Biography* (London 1958 and New York 1959). Dante del Fiorentino *Immortal Bohemian: An Intimate Memoir of Giacomo Puccini* (New York and London 1952). George R. Marek *Puccini* (New York 1951 and London 1952). Richard Specht *Giacomo Puccini: The Man, His Life, His Work* (tr. London and New York 1933).

✍

PUCCINI
BY DIANA TRILLING

In the downgrading of opera by people who undertake to be guardians of the pure and serious in art, Puccini has been a conspicuous victim. For some time now in America advanced musical opinion has regarded him as the composer who perhaps most thoroughly represents the meretricious appeal of romantic opera. *Madame Butterfly, Tosca, La Bohème:* the very names of these most famous of his works are made synonymous with sentimentality and superficiality, and the works themselves consigned to the limbo of middlebrow popularity.

In the light of this opinion it is amusing to recall that Puccini was the best-loved composer of James Joyce, himself so crucial a figure in our advanced culture. There are no fewer than seven references to Puccini's music in Richard Ellman's collection of the Joyce letters: Joyce begged that his wife, Nora, acquaint herself with the arias he found so full of "languor and longing," and he addresses her as his "little Butterfly." But it is of course precisely the languor and longing in Puccini's music, its unabashed lyricism and its commitment to dramatic narrative that diminish Puccini's authority for the modernist.

Ours is manifestly not a lyrical or narrative age, nor even an age that is readily responsive to the personal emotions, or certainly not to those once believed to be appropriate to a heroic or dramatic conception of the individual possibility. It is perhaps a clue to the traditionalism which underlies Joyce's genius of innovation and which supports the ultimateness of his investigations of feeling that Joyce could so warmly appreciate a composer who, though he lived and wrote well into the twentieth century, when Toscanini gave many of his operas their first performances, was always in essence a nineteenth-century man and artist.

Puccini was himself not at all an innovative talent and he had little imagination of anything more ultimate than the limitations life puts on human hope: nothing he said had not already been explored in the literature and even in the music of his predecessors. But what he brought to opera that was uniquely his was his extraordinary force of personal emotion which he was able to transmute into melody. Except for his single, brilliantly successful venture into comedy, *Gianni Schicchi*, all of his operas are concerned with the tragic hindrances to love. Although only in *Tosca* and to a lesser degree in *Manon Lescaut* is personal tragedy precipitated by politics, in all his operas the sexual passion is shown in dangerous, often fatal conjunction with some malign condition of life which intervenes between the individual and the attainment of his desires. In *La*

Bohème it is the malignity of disease, in *Turandot* the cold power of will, in *Butterfly* the hard division between nations and races, in *Suor Angelica* and in *La Rondine* as well the tyranny of social convention, in *Il Tabarro* a claustral poverty and jealousy, in *La Fanciulla del West* the power of the law. The drama to which Puccini's gift of song was best suited was always that of love desperately threatened by those private and public circumstances which legislate against personal fulfillment.

From Mosco Carner's careful biography we learn of a tragic episode in Puccini's life which must surely have had its effect on his work. In mid-career, already a composer of world fame, Puccini was accused unjustly by his half-crazed wife of having had an affair with a young girl employed in their household, whom she hounded to suicide. Carner suggests, with cogency, that the dead girl became the model for Liu in *Turandot*, the servant girl who kills herself to protect her beloved master, and that his wife was the inspiration both for the heartless princess in the same opera and for the cruel aunt in *Suor Angelica*. But Puccini obviously had no need of this direct instruction in the intimate connection between love and death; it was an expectable part of his equipment as a romantic artist. As he wrote in a letter, "I still want to *make people weep* . . . Love and grief were born with the world." The essential communication of his work is a traditional one: it is that of the preordained and doomed struggle between the individual and the overpowering world, in which the triumph of man is measured not by the victory that is bound to elude him but by the passion of his intention.

Musically, this conflict between the individual aspiration and the external circumstances of life is expressed in Puccini's operas by a complex interplay between solo voice and orchestra: in moments of great dramatic tension Puccini characteristically will allow the individual voice its brief passage of seeming triumph, only to withdraw this ascendancy from the individual and vest it finally in the orchestra. A familiar example of this strategy is Rodolfo's cry of anguish at Mimi's death, in which the voice is suddenly and terrifyingly isolated only to be orchestrally overwhelmed as the opera ends. But an at once subtler and bolder demonstration of the same process is the suicide scene in *Suor Angelica,* where the heroine holds the stage alone and silent while the unimpeded orchestra reiterates the exquisite music of her tormented love.

The little-performed *Suor Angelica* is Puccini's only opera which looks to a religious apotheosis; and written wholly for female voices, it makes the plainest admission of Puccini's sympathy for women as the chief carriers of human aspiration and of the heroic impulse. No male character in Puccini's operas is equal to the transcendent role in which he would be cast by the woman he loves or who loves him. In *Butterfly* it is Pinkerton's faithlessness that gives us the full measure of Butterfly's devotion. Mario, in *Tosca,* endures the torture inflicted on him but it is Tosca who commits the murder which is meant to set her and Mario free. In *La Bohème,* Rodolfo's lightminded selfishness, although not the cause of Mimi's death, is the unhappy counterpoint to her loyalty to him. The female voices in Puccini, now tender and submissive, now ringing and soaring over the orchestrated threats of the world, undoubtedly represent the natural instrument of his compelling lyrical gift. But they also remind us of an earlier mode

of dramatic thought in which it was women who spoke most persuasively on behalf of the life of heroic feeling.

PUGIN, Augustus Welby Northmore (Mar. 12, 1812 – Sept. 14, 1852). English architect. Born London, son of French architect and archaeologist Augustus Charles Pugin (1762–1832), who lived there. Worked in his father's office. After conversion to Catholicism (1833), executed numerous designs for churches, monasteries, convents, and schools, and became leader in English Gothic revival. With Sir Charles Barry worked on designs for Houses of Parliament at Westminster (1837–42), executed designs for St. George's cathedral, Southwark (1845), the cathedral of Killarney, Ireland, and a number of residences. Published several studies, including *Contrasts, or A Parallel Between the Architecture of the Fifteenth and Nineteenth Centuries* (1836) and *The True Principles of Christian Architecture* (1841). Died at the home he designed for himself at Ramsgate.

REFERENCES: Peter Ferriday ed. *Victorian Architecture* (London 1963 and Philadelphia 1964). Henry Russell Hitchcock *Early Victorian Architecture in Britain* (2 vols. New Haven, Conn. 1954 and London 1955). Michael Trappes-Lomax *Pugin: A Mediaeval Victorian* (London 1932).

PURCELL, Henry (c.1659 – Nov. 21, 1695). English composer. Born probably in London, son of Thomas Purcell, long in the king's service. Was a choirboy of Chapel Royal from early age until his voice broke, then became assistant keeper of the instruments (1673). Appointed composer to the king's violins (1677), succeeded his teacher John Blow as organist at Westminster Abbey (1679), and became one of Chapel Royal's three organists (1682). Appointed organmaker and keeper of king's wind instruments (1683). Married (c.1681); three of his six children died in infancy. From 1680 began composing for the theatre: incidental music for numerous plays, including Dryden's *King Arthur* (1691), Shakespeare's *The Fairy Queen* (from *A Midsummer*

Night's Dream) (1692), and *The Tempest* (c.1695) ("Arise, ye subterranean winds"), and Dryden's *The Indian Queen* (1695) ("I attempt from love's sickness to fly"). Wrote one opera, *Dido and Aeneas* (1689), and a great deal of occasional music: odes, welcome songs, anthems for his royal patrons. Among most famous: *My Heart Is Inditing*, anthem written for coronation of James II (1675). First instrumental music (published 1683): twelve sonatas of three parts. A master of church music, he excelled in melody, form, harmony, and counterpoint. One of finest religious works is *Ode for St. Cecilia's Day* (1694). He died at Westminster, is buried in the Abbey.

REFERENCES: Dennis Arundell *Henry Purcell* (London 1927). William H. Cummings *Purcell* (1881, reprinted New York 1968). Arthur K. Holland *Henry Purcell* (London 1932). Imogen Holst ed. *Henry Purcell, 1659–1695: Essays on His Music* (London 1959). Robert E. Moore *Henry Purcell and the Restoration Theatre* (Cambridge, Mass. and London 1961). Jack A. Westrup *Purcell* (4th ed. London and New York 1965). Franklin B. Zimmerman *Henry Purcell: His Life and Times* (New York and London 1967).

PUSHKIN, Alexander Sergeyevich (June 6, 1799 – Feb. 10, 1837). Russian poet. Born Moscow, into family of impoverished nobility; descended on mother's side from an Abyssinian prince. Educated at home and at Imperial Lyceum, Tsarskoye Selo, later named for him. Began publishing poetry at fifteen. Started (1817) three-year service in foreign office in St. Petersburg, where in spite of strenuous social life he continued writing. His long narrative poem *Ruslan and Ludmila* (1820) won him acknowledged leadership in Russian poetry, but some revolutionary epigrams resulted in his exile to Bessarabia. During exile he visited the wild, primitive Caucasus, which inspired the Byronic *The Captive of the Caucasus* (1821) and other poems. Allowed back in St. Petersburg (1826) by new Czar Nicholas I after Decembrist revolt (1825). Finished tragedy *Boris Godunov* (1825) and completed *Eugene Onegin* (1830), a novel in verse, gen-

erally considered his masterpiece. Married the youthful Natalia Goncharova (1831). Despite pressures of new responsibilities, financial difficulties, demanding court life, and three children, Pushkin continued to write: the poem *The Bronze Horseman* (1833), prose tale *The Queen of Spades* (1833), fairy stories, *The Captain's Daughter* (1836), a historical novel. In the course of a duel (1837) defending his wife's honor, he was mortally wounded. Pushkin became and still is the poet most beloved of his countrymen, and ranks foremost in Russian literature.

TRANSLATIONS: *Poems, Prose, and Plays* ed. Avrahm Yarmolinsky (New York 1936). *Complete Prose Tales* tr. Gillon R. Aitken (London and New York 1966, also PB). *Eugene Onegin* in verse tr. Vladimir Nabokov (4 vols. Princeton, N.J. 1964). *Letters of Alexander Pushkin* ed. J. T. Shaw (3 vols. Philadelphia 1964).

REFERENCES: Samuel H. Cross and Ernest J. Simmons eds. *Centennial Essays for Pushkin* (1937, reprinted New York 1967). Janko Lavrin *Pushkin and Russian Literature* (1947, reprinted New York 1969). David Magarshak *Pushkin: A Biography* (London 1967 and New York 1968, also PB). D. S. Mirsky *Pushkin* (1926, reprinted New York PB 1963). Ernest J. Simmons *Pushkin* (Cambridge, Mass. and Oxford 1937, PB 1964). Henri Troyat *Pushkin* (tr. New York 1970). Walter N. Vickery *Pushkin: Death of a Poet* (Bloomington, Ind. 1968). Avrahm Yarmolinsky *Pushkin in English* (bibliography; New York 1937).

☙

ALEXANDER PUSHKIN
BY SIMON KARLINSKY

Alexander Pushkin was born into an aristocratic Russian family in which French poetry was a household article in daily use. At the age of twelve he entered an exclusive boarding school where he was the most outstanding member of an unbelievably talented class that gave Russia many of her nineteenth-century poets, statesmen, and rebels. At sixteen Pushkin saw his poetic genius recognized by the reigning literary luminaries, and when, at twenty-one, he published his narrative poem *Ruslan and Ludmila,* he became celebrated throughout Russia, and his most illustrious older contemporary, Zhukovsky, graciously conceded the young poet's supremacy in Russian poetry.

For some impulsive and youthful revolutionary verse Czar Alexander I exiled Pushkin to the Riviera-like Black Sea coast. Nicholas I allowed him to return to Moscow and St. Petersburg, but harassed him with petty censorship and restrictions and prevented him from traveling abroad. In the 1820's each new lyric or verse tale by Pushkin seemed a revelation to the eager reading public. In the next decade, as the poet's genius deepened and matured, he turned largely to prose and began slipping from the public's favor. He died at thirty-seven, victim of a senseless and petty affair of honor.

In subsequent decades, the circumstances of his death and of his earlier exile gave rise to a whole vast scholarship dedicated to the cult of Pushkin as a martyr of czarist tyranny. This particular legend, raised to the status of a major national myth by the end of the nineteenth century, obscured Pushkin's poetry for less literate Russian readers or replaced the poetry as the central object of interest. The myth is supported by the ever-popular industry of simplistic biography, reproductions of sentimental academic paintings — *Pushkin the Inspired Child-Poet, Pushkin and His Peasant Nanny, The Death of Pushkin* — and, in the twentieth century, propagandistic cinema. When in 1897 the great Russian philosopher Vladimir Soloviev dared publish an article in which, with all reverence for Pushkin's memory, he pointed out that the poet himself was to a large degree

responsible for the duel that terminated his life and that his persecution by the authorities was mild when compared to that suffered at other times by Dante, Byron or Dostoevsky, Soloviev's essay was received as an outrage and an insult to national honor by Russians of most diverse factions. In fact Soloviev's remarkable essay has not been reprinted anywhere since 1911.

Because he never stated a clear-cut political or spiritual credo, Pushkin has been claimed by every subsequent literary, political, and even religious movement in Russia, by the monarchists as well as Communists, by atheists and by mystics. Primarily, of course, he belongs to Russian literature and his position as its central, most overwhelmingly momentous phenomenon was never challenged by any of the tremendous nineteenth- and twentieth-century literary figures that followed him. Gogol and Turgenev, Dostoevsky and Chekhov, Mayakovsky and Pasternak, Anna Akhmatova and Vladimir Nabokov all acknowledge Pushkin as their master and teacher. An occasional dissenting opinion by a major Russian writer — Tolstoy, Bunin — is inevitably motivated by some extraliterary consideration.

Foreigners have been repeatedly puzzled by this unanimous acclaim. There is in Pushkin that very unique fusion of thought and verbal music that has resisted the efforts of the most able foreign translators. The slightest tampering with Pushkin's own words and his most subtle and original ideas and insights become platitudes, the brilliance of his style fades into haziness, and the miraculous precision of his prose sprawls out into unimpressive verbosity. Every Pushkin poem translated into another language turns into a more or less elegant frog cruelly deprived of whatever made her a princess in the original incarnation. Puzzled by all this, some foreign critics have asserted that the Russians like Pushkin so much merely because he was their first writer of note who singlehandedly created the Russian literary language. This could not be more wrong as either literary history or literary judgment.

It is the modesty and simplicity in which Pushkin's brilliance, virtuosity, and depth are garbed that makes it mandatory that this writer be read in his own language. Only in the original do *Eugene Onegin* — and what other literature has a major novel that is at the same time one of the world's greatest poems? — *Boris Godunov, The Queen of Spades, The Captain's Daughter*, and *The Bronze Horseman* make their magical impact unhampered by the pseudohistorical clichés of Russian scholarship, the platitudinous translators, and the distorting prism of operatic adaptations. For, whatever their musical and dramatic virtues, Mussorgsky's *Boris Godunov* and Tchaikovsky's *Eugene Onegin* are utter artistic betrayals of the Pushkin originals, with their precision, transparency, and joy. Now, if one could imagine a Pushkin opera with an English libretto written jointly by Jane Austen and Coleridge, with music that was an amalgam of Mozart's *Don Giovanni* and Stravinsky's *Jeu de cartes* (or *Dumbarton Oaks Concerto*) and with settings by Jan Vermeer — then perhaps one's non-Russian-speaking friends could get some notion of what this poet's unique flavor is like.

In his impassioned defense of Pushkin written in 1940, Igor Stravinsky stated: "In justice, his name should be revered on the same plane with those of Dante, Goethe, Shakespeare." Generations of Russians who have returned to Pushkin again and again with reverence and gratitude would vouch for that statement. It is well worth mastering Russian just to be able to read Pushkin.

Or one can simply forget translations or language study and listen to Mozart's *G Minor Quintet* or the *A Major Piano Concerto*. One will find there better than anywhere else the same polished elegance, the same sunlit clarity, and the same sudden intimations of the tragic aspects of existence that form the most precious essence of Pushkin's poetry.

PUVIS DE CHAVANNES, Pierre Cécile (Dec. 14, 1824 – Oct. 10, 1898). French painter. Born Lyons. Originally intending to be an engineer, Puvis turned to painting after visiting Italy, and studied under Henri Scheffer in Paris. His early work, influenced by Delacroix and Couture, was rejected by the Salons until 1858, but with Théophile Gautier's support he came to be recognized and sold (1861) his pictures *War* and *Peace* to the state (Musée de Picardie, Amiens). His principal works were murals for public buildings, chiefly religious and mythological in subject matter, such as *Life of St. Genevieve* (1874–98, Panthéon, Paris), *Science, Art, and Letters* (1887, Sorbonne, Paris), and *Summer* and *Winter* (1889–93, Hôtel de Ville, Paris). Puvis also executed the mural *Pastoral Poetry* for Boston Public Library (1895–98). Other paintings include *Hope* (1872, Louvre, Paris), *The Poor Fisherman* (1881, Palais de Luxembourg, Paris), and *The Happy Land* (1882, Musée Bonnat, Bayonne). His style is classical in inspiration, employing flat planes and figures, spacious settings, and cool pale colors. He died in Paris.

REFERENCES: René Jean *Puvis de Chavannes* (1914, new ed. Paris 1933). André Michel and J. Laran *Puvis de Chavannes* (tr. Philadelphia and London 1912). Marius Vachon *Puvis de Chavannes* (Paris 1895). Léon Werth *Puvis de Chavannes* (Paris 1926).

QUEVEDO Y VILLEGAS, Francisco Gómez de (baptized Sept. 26, 1580 – Sept. 8, 1645). Spanish writer. Born Madrid. His father was secretary to the queen and his mother a lady-in-waiting. Quevedo's clubfoot, as well as the somber atmosphere of the court of Philip II, partly account for his pessimistic, cynical view of life. Educated at Jesuit College in Madrid and Alcalá University, where he excelled in theology, law, classics, and languages. Appalled at corruption in court of Philip III, he began to write satirical verse and pamphlets. Killed a dueling opponent (1611) and fled to Italy. Served as agent of duke of Osuna (1613–20) until forced to return to Spain after duke's attempt to overthrow the republic of Venice failed. Confined to his estate in Torre de Juan Abad. Upon accession of Philip IV (1621) he was given honorary post at court and devoted himself exclusively to writing. At age fifty-two married a widow of noble family, only to be separated from her after a few months. In disgrace once more, presumably for his satirical allusions to the king's favorite El Conde-Duque de Olivares, he was imprisoned in the monastery of St. Mark at León (1639–43). Released upon Olivares' fall, he retired to Torre de Juan Abad. Died at Villanueva de los Infantes. Best known for his paradoxical, punning *Los Sueños* (1627) and the picaresque novel *La Historia de la vida del Buscón* (1626), whose grotesque atmosphere and Machiavellian characters may have influenced Goya's *Caprichos* and *Disparates*. Also the author of quantities of verse, which established him as a major poet, collected posthumously in *El Parnaso espanol y musas castellanas* (1648) and *Las Tres Ultimas Musas castellanas* (1670), the political satire *La Hora de todos y fortuna con seso* (1635–45), a Christian Stoic treatise *La Vida de Marco Bruto* (1631).

TRANSLATIONS: *The Works of Don Francisco de Quevedo*, translator anonymous (3 vols. Edinburgh 1798). *The Choice Humorous and Satirical Works* tr. Sir Roger L'Estrange, John Stevens, and others, ed. Charles Duff (London and New York 1926). *The Scavenger* tr. Hugh A. Harter (New York 1962). *Visions* tr. Sir Roger L'Estrange (Carbondale, Ill. and Arundel, England, 1963).

REFERENCE: Cyril B. Morris *The Unity and Structure of Quevedo's Buscón* (Hull, England, PB 1965).

———————

RABELAIS, François (c.1494–c.1553). French writer. Born La Devinière, near Chinon, into family of lawyers. Probably studied at Angers. Became a Franciscan monk (c.1521) in order to pursue humanist studies. Transferred to Benedictines (1523), but when University of Sorbonne forbade study of Greek, he left the cloister (1527). After traveling, entered University of Montpellier to study medicine (1530). Practiced in Lyon (1532–34), intellectual center of France, and published learned translations. His robust, earthy satire *Pantagruel* (1532), published under anagram name Alcofrybas Nasier, became immediately popular and was condemned by the Sorbonne for obscenity. Left for Rome (1534) as physician to patron Jean du Bellay, bishop of Paris, later cardinal, and there developed keen interest in classicism. Returned to Lyon and published story of Pantagruel's father *Gargantua* (1534), now printed first. Violently satirical of French theologians, scholasticism, politics, manners, it was also condemned by the Sorbonne, and Rabelais had to leave Lyon. Taught and practiced medicine (1536–46), brought out *Third Book of Pantagruel* (1546), the censorship of which forced him to flee to Metz. Again with du Bellay in Rome (1548–50), returned to serve briefly as vicar of Meudon and Jambet (1551), and published *Fourth Book of Pantagruel* (1552). Not known where he died. A *Fifth Book* (1564) attributed to him is regarded as suppositious. Rabelais's extraordinary flair for storytelling, his broad satire, lusty humor, and erudition were immediately acclaimed in his own time. A famous translation by Sir Thomas Urquart and Peter Anthony Motteux appeared (1653–94).

TRANSLATION: *The Histories of Gargantua and Pantagruel* tr. J. M. Cohen (Harmondsworth, England, 1955 and Baltimore PB 1969).

REFERENCES: M. M. Bakhtin *Rabelais and His World* (tr. Cambridge, Mass. 1968). Huntington Brown *Rabelais in English Literature* (New York 1967 and London 1968). D. B. Wyndham Lewis *Doctor Rabelais* (1957, reprinted New York 1968). Albert Jay Nock and C. R. Wilson *Francis Rabelais: The Man and His Work* (New York and London 1929). Jean Plattard *The Life of François Rabelais* (tr. 1931, reprinted London 1968 and New York 1969). John Cowper Powys *Rabelais: His Life* (London 1948 and New York 1951).

RACHMANINOFF, Sergei Vassilievich (Apr. 1, 1873 – Mar. 28, 1943). Russian composer and pianist. Born on estate near Novgorod; of well-to-do family. Studied piano at St. Petersburg Conservatory (1882–85), then at Moscow Conservatory, graduating as pianist (1891), as composer (1892), and winning gold medal for his opera *Aleko*. Went on long concert tour in Russia. At twenty composed *C Sharp Minor Prelude*, which rapidly became famous. Also won lasting success with his *Second Piano Concerto* (1901). Married Natalie Satina (1902). Conductor at Bolshoi Theatre (1904–1906). Visited U.S. (1909) and wrote *Third Piano Concerto* there. Worked in Moscow until Revolution (1917), then lived in Switzerland and U.S., giving piano recitals. He died in Beverly Hills, Calif. Rachmaninoff was one of the world's great piano virtuosi. As a composer he was technically gifted and, influenced by Tchaikovsky, derived his style from nineteenth-century romantics. Among his works: three symphonies, the opera *Francesca da Rimini* (1904–1905), the brilliant *Rhapsody on a Theme by Paganini* (1934), four piano concertos, numerous pieces for piano, and over seventy songs. Much of his work is still popular throughout the world.

REFERENCES: Watson Lyle *Rachmaninoff: A Biography* (London 1939). A. Gronowicz *Sergei Rachmaninoff* (tr. New York 1946). John Culshaw *Sergei Rachmaninoff* (London and Chester Springs, Pa. 1949). Sergei Bertensson and Jay Leyda *Sergei Rachmaninoff: A Lifetime in Music* (New York 1956).

RACINE, Jean (Dec. 22, 1639 – Apr. 21, 1699). French dramatist and poet. Born La Ferté-Milon; of family of civil servants. Orphaned (1643) and educated by Jansenists at Port-Royal (1649–53). An ode, *La Nymphe de la Seine* (1660), was favorably received. With Molière's encouragement, produced tragedy *La Thébaïde* (1664), which failed, and a successful one, *Alexandre le Grand* (1665). Broke with Port-Royal, which disapproved violently of theatrical activities. *Andromaque* (1667) established his supremacy as a dramatist. Followed by eight other tragedies, culminating in his greatest masterpiece, *Phèdre* (1677). Lover of Thérèse du Parc and Marie Champmeslé, two of his leading actresses. After *Phèdre,* appointed king's historiographer, retired from the theatre, and married Catherine de Romanet (1677), who bore him seven children. At Madame de Maintenon's request wrote two Biblical tragedies, *Esther* (1689) and *Athalie* (1691), for performance by pupils at her girls' school. Last years spent writing religious poems and short history of Port-Royal, where he was buried.

TRANSLATIONS: *Phaedra and Other Plays* (Harmondsworth, England, and Baltimore PB 1963) and *Andromache and Other Plays* (Harmondsworth, England, and Baltimore PB 1967), both translated by John Cairncross. *Phaedra* tr. Robert Lowell (New York 1961 and London 1963). *Five Plays* tr. Kenneth Muir (New York 1960). *Complete Plays* tr. Samuel Solomon (2 vols. New York 1967).

REFERENCES: Roland Barthes *On Racine* (tr. New York 1964). Geoffrey Brereton *Jean Racine: A Critical Biography* (London and New York 1951). A. F. B. Clark *Jean Racine* (1939, reprinted New York 1969). Jean Giraudoux *Racine* (tr. Cambridge, England, 1938). J. C. Lapp *Aspects of Racinian Tragedy* (Oxford 1956, also PB). T. Maulnier *Racine* (Paris 1936). François Mauriac *La Vie de Jean Racine* (1928, new ed. Paris 1962). Martin Turnell *The Classical Moment* (London 1947). E. Vinaver *Racine and Poetic Tragedy* (tr. Manchester 1955).

☙

JEAN RACINE

BY MARTIN TURNELL

A contemporary has left us a fascinating glimpse of Corneille, very old, very lonely, very grand, shaking his head solemnly over a performance of *Britannicus* and complaining that Racine dwelt too much on the weaknesses of human nature. It helps us to understand the immense impact of Racine on the theatre of his day and the differences between the two dramatists which divided polite society into two hostile camps.

Corneille, like Molière, was a pupil of the Jesuits, Racine a pupil of the Jansenists. We must not underestimate the influence of Jansenism on Racine's work. It went deep. The Jesuits laid great emphasis on free will. Jansenist teaching was strongly colored by the Protestant doctrine of original sin. The Fall had led to the complete ruin of human nature, which was incapable of any good without the direct intervention of grace. The Jansenists also leaned toward the doctrine of predestination, which added to the gloom.

Corneille's protagonists are fighters. They use their willpower to the full to withstand the ravages of original sin. When faced with a moral dilemma they stand back, take stock, and decide on the right course of action. Even if they lose their lives in the process, they end up better men than they started. The conflict is genuinely purgatorial. In Racine it is plain hell. In most of his plays it is not a *moral* conflict, but a clash of personalities who are determined to batter the beloved into submission or smash a rival. The drama starts with the proverbial *coup de foudre*. A man catches sight of a girl, or a girl of a man. The damage is done. They are "predestined" to disaster from the very first line. They at once become the victims of an irresistible passion which sweeps aside all the moral imperatives and sends the lovers hurtling down the dizzy slope to destruction. The dagger or the poison cup that ends their lives is no more than consummation on the *physical* plane of the total ruin which has already taken place on the *psychological* plane.

Racine's beginnings were modest. His first two plays were competent, but if he had written nothing more they would have vanished without trace. In *Andromaque* he made that leap which is the unmistakable sign of genius and produced a masterpiece which occupies the same place in his oeuvre as *Le Cid* in Corneille's.

The setting is the aftermath of the Trojan War. Oreste arrives in Epirus as ambassador of Greece. His mission is to persuade King Pyrrhus to marry Hermione, the Greek princess to whom he is betrothed. It is a ruse. He himself is in love with Hermione and is secretly hoping to get her on the rebound. There is nothing heroic about the characters, who never allow the plighted word to deflect them from their goal. Pyrrhus jilts Hermione and marries Andromaque, the widow of Hector. At Hermione's instigation Oreste murders the sovereign to whom he is accredited. Hermione kills herself out of remorse. Oreste goes mad.

Racine strikes a deeper note in *Britannicus,* which was written while he was still suffering from the shock of Thérèse du Parc's death. The love interest is there. The innocent young lovers make their first appearance and provide a comment on the wickedness of their elders, but this is not the most spectacular part of the play.

Britannicus is dominated by the family feud: the ruthless struggle between Néron and his appalling mother Agrippine — one of Racine's most stupendous creations. He throws off her yoke and murders his cousin Britannicus, who is his rival in love. The combination Néron-Narcisse is a symbol of the sheer evil at work in everyday life, reflecting, perhaps, the dramatist's own experience of the sinister Paris underworld.

In *Bérénice* and *Mithridate*, both influenced by Corneille, Racine did introduce a moral conflict. It breaks the protagonists in *Bérénice*. In *Mithridate*, where father and son are rivals for the hand of Monime, the young lovers are saved by the lecherous old king's suicide. *Bajazet* is the most violent of all the plays: Roxane murders her man rather than let her rival get him. Although *Iphigénie* is the first play since *La Thébaïde* with a religious motif, we have to await *Phèdre* for a development of the moral tendencies of *Britannicus*.

Jules Lemaître called *Phèdre* the first stage in Racine's conversion. The doctrine of predestination is translated into sexual terms. Phèdre is hopelessly and helplessly in love with her stepson. There is no grace in the world ruled by Venus, the pagan goddess not of love but of sexuality. Phèdre can do nothing; she cannot even control her homicidal jealousy when she discovers at almost the same moment that her husband, believed dead, is living and her stepson is in love with another woman. But unlike the protagonists of the earlier plays, she is destroyed less by the forces of passion than by an overwhelming sense of guilt.

The impression of Jansenism is most marked of all in *Athalie*. It is scarcely an exaggeration to describe the middle-aged queen as a Jansenist who has lost the faith and on whom unbelief has the same corrosive effect as sexual passion in the secular plays.

It is difficult, said Vinaver, to explain the originality of a writer who claimed none, who merely tried to do better than his predecessors. Violent passion was not new and there had been penetrating psychologists before Racine. The novelty lies in the contrast between extreme violence and the tightness of the form, between the primitive passions simmering just below the surface of civilized society and the versification which reflects the outer shape of that society. There may often be no moral conflict, but Racine's alexandrine, unlike the turgid rhetoric of his lesser contemporaries, provides a moral standard which places the characters' actions in their proper perspective. Nor is that all. What makes Racine unique is the magic voice. The more we study him, the more he imposes himself, the more compelling the voice becomes: the authentic undiluted voice of a master first heard in *Andromaque*.

RADIGUET, Raymond (June 18, 1903 – Dec. 12, 1923). French poet and novelist. Born Parc-St.-Maur, near Paris. Little is known about his childhood or education except that by fourteen he had written some outstanding poems. In Paris (1919) he met and became protégé of the poet Jean Cocteau. Resisting Nunism, Dadaism, and surrealism, then in vogue, he contributed poems to *Sic* and other magazines, writing in a neoclassical, orthodox style. First book was a collection of poems, *Les Joues en feu* (1920), fol-

lowed by another poetry collection, *Devoirs de vacances* (1921). Largely abandoning poetry for the novel, he published his penetrating study of adolescent love, *Le Diable au corps* (1923, tr. *The Devil in the Flesh* 1932), from which a remarkable French film was made (1950). Another novel of emotions, *Le Bal du comte d'Orgel* (posthumously published 1924; tr. *The Count's Ball* 1929), immediately followed. Both were highly acclaimed by literary figures, and especially aroused the enthusiasm of Aldous Huxley and Cocteau. Radiguet died in Paris of typhoid fever at twenty, leaving, in addition to the poems and the two short novels, an unproduced play and a number of essays.

TRANSLATIONS: *Count d'Orgel* tr. Violet Schiff, preface by Jean Cocteau (1952, new ed. London and New York PB 1969). *The Devil in the Flesh* tr. Kay Boyle, introduction by Aldous Huxley (London 1949 and New York 1950).
REFERENCES: André Germain *De Proust à Dada* (Paris 1924). W. D. Noakes *Raymond Radiguet: une étude* (Paris 1968). Maurice Sachs *The Decade of Illusion, 1918–28* (New York 1933).

RAEBURN, Sir Henry (Mar. 4, 1756 – July 8, 1823). Scottish painter. Born Stockbridge, near Edinburgh, son of successful manufacturer. Orphaned at early age, he was educated as a scholar of Heriot's Hospital. Apprenticed to goldsmith James Gilliland (1771), who encouraged his attempts to paint miniatures. Studied with David Martin, then the leading Edinburgh portraitist, but was mainly self-taught. His earliest known portrait, of George Chalmers (1776, Town Hall, Dunfermline, Scotland), reveals deficiencies of training. His marriage (1780) to wealthy widow Ann Edgar Leslie gave him financial leeway to seek further instruction. On advice of Joshua Reynolds he studied in Rome (1885–87). Edinburgh, when he returned, was emerging as lively center of art and letters, and he soon took his place as portraitist of virtually all its leading figures: Sir Walter Scott, Hume, Boswell, Adam Smith, among many. Between 1790 and 1800 "the Scottish Reynolds" did his best work;

Lady Raeburn (1790, collection of Countess Mountbatten) and *Sir John and Lady Clerk* (1790, collection of Sir Alfred Beer) date from this period, though the famous *The Macnab* is later (c.1805–10, Messrs. John Dewar, London). Held his first London exhibit in 1793. A brilliant conversationalist, described as "one of the best liked men of his day," he enjoyed a comfortable old age filled with honors: president of the Edinburgh Society of Artists (1812); Royal Academician (1815); knighted and appointed His Majesty's Limner in Scotland (1822). He died in Edinburgh of a sudden "mysterious atrophy."

REFERENCES: William Raeburn Andrew *Life of Sir Henry Raeburn, R. A.* (2nd ed. London 1894). Sir Walter Armstrong *Sir Henry Raeburn* (London and New York 1901). R. S. Clouston *Sir Henry Raeburn* (London and New York 1907). James Greig *Sir Henry Raeburn: His Life and Works* (London 1911). National Gallery of Scotland *Raeburn Bicentenary Exhibition* (Edinburgh 1956).

RALEGH (or RALEIGH), Sir Walter (c.1552 – Oct. 29, 1618). English writer. Born Hayes Barton, Devon. Educated at Oriel College, Oxford. Served with Huguenot army in France (1569). With half brother Sir Humphrey Gilbert engaged in voyages of discovery and expeditions against Spanish in West Indies (1578). A favorite of Queen Elizabeth's, he was knighted (1584), gained wealth and positions of honor. Sent five expeditions to North America (1584–89), including one that resulted in lost colony of Roanoke Island, N.C. Introduced potatoes and tobacco from New World into England and Ireland. Lost favor with queen (1592) because of his involvement with Elizabeth Throckmorton, one of her attendants and subsequently his wife, and imprisoned in Tower. Freed, he sailed for the Orinoco (1595) in search of gold. Fought triumphantly at Cádiz (1596) and Fayal, Azores (1597), thereby regaining lost favor, and returned to court (1597). Upon accession of James I (1603), his enemies caused him to be charged with treason and committed to the Tower. Here for Prince Henry he began *History of the World*, completed one volume (1614). Released (1616) to lead ill-fated expedition for gold in Guiana, he ignored royal orders by attacking and burning Spanish settlement San Tomás, and on return (1618) was at Spanish ambassador's demand beheaded in Old Palace Yard, Westminster. The author of political pamphlets, essays, and philosophical treatises, he also wrote poetry (much of which is lost), including elegy to Elizabeth, *Cynthia, the Lady of the Sea,* the introductory sonnet to his friend Edmund Spenser's *The Faerie Queene* ("Methought I saw the grave where Laura lay"), *The Lie* ("Go, Soul, the body's quest"), *The Nymph's Reply to the Passionate Shepherd,* and the lines beginning "Even such is time" found at Westminster after his death. Among his prose writings: *A Report of the Truth of the Fight About the Isles of the Azores* (1591) and *The Discovery of the Empire of Guiana* (1596).

EDITIONS: *Works* ed. William Oldys and Thomas Birch (8 vols. 1829, reprinted New York 1965). *The Poems of Sir Walter Ralegh* (1929, new ed. London and Cambridge, Mass. 1951, also PB) and *Selected Prose and Poetry* (London and New York 1965) ed. Agnes M. C. Latham.

REFERENCES: J. H. Adamson and H. F. Folland *The Shepherd of the Ocean: An Account of Sir Walter Ralegh and His Times* (Boston 1969). Muriel C. Bradbrook *The School of Night: A Study in the Literary Relationships of Sir Walter Ralegh* (1936, reprinted New York 1965). Philip Edwards *Sir Walter Ralegh* (London 1953). Edmund Gosse *Raleigh* (London and New York 1886). Sir Philip Magnus *Sir Walter Ralegh* (1952, reprinted London and Hamden, Conn. 1968). Walter F. Oakeshott *The Queen and the Poet* (London 1960 and New York 1962). Increase N. Tarbox *Sir Walter Ralegh and His Colony in America* (1884, reprinted New York 1967). Edward Thompson *Sir Walter Ralegh: The Last of the Elizabethans* (London 1935 and New Haven, Conn. 1936). Willard M. Wallace *Sir Walter Ralegh* (Princeton, N.J. 1959 and Oxford 1960). Norman L. Williams *Sir Walter Ralegh* (London 1962 and Chester Springs, Pa. 1963, also PB).

RAMEAU, Jean Philippe (Sept. 25, 1683 – Sept. 12, 1764). French composer and theorist. Born Dijon, where his father was church organist. Originally prepared for law, but took up music at eighteen. Visited Italy (1701), then began years as organist in various provincial cities, as well as Paris (1705–1708), where he settled permanently (1722). Quickly established his reputation with *Traité de l'harmonie* (1722), first of seven major theoretical treatises on harmonics and acoustics. Married (1726) young Marie Louise Mangot, a singer. Seven years later he acquired a rich patron, the financier-courtier Le Riche de la Poupelinière, and began to write operas (twenty-two in all), of which the best known are *Hippolyte et Aricie* (1733) and *Castor et Pollux* (1737). An innovator in harmony as well as theory, he also composed chamber music and keyboard pieces. By 1745, with lavish performances of his work at Versailles, he was a national hero. His last years, however, were troubled with controversy, as partisans of French versus Italian operatic styles fought "la guerre des bouffons," and Rousseau with the Encyclopedists attacked both his music and his theories. He died in Paris of typhoid fever.

REFERENCES: Jacques Gardien *Jean-Philippe Rameau* (Paris 1949). Cuthbert M. Girdlestone *Jean-Philippe Rameau: His Life and Work* (1957, rev. ed. New York PB 1970). Paul-Marie Masson *L'Opéra de Rameau* (Paris 1930). Arthur Pougin *Rameau, essai sur sa vie et ses oeuvres* (Paris 1876).

RAPHAEL (real name **Raffaello Santi** or **Sanzio**) (c. Apr. 1483 – Apr. 6, 1520). Italian painter and architect. Born Urbino. His father, Giovanni Santi, was painter at famous court of Federico of Montefeltro there. By 1500 was working with Perugino, probably on frescoes in Collegio del Cambio, Perugia. Painted *Knight's Dream* (National Gallery, London) at this time. During next decade he emerged as the prodigy of the High Renaissance, moving through influences of Piero della Francesca, Leon Battista Alberti, Leonardo, and Michelangelo, as he worked in Florence, Perugia, and Urbino before settling permanently in Rome (c.1508). His Florentine period (1504–1508) produced the famous Madonnas, including the *Sposalizio* (*Marriage of the Virgin*) (1504, Pinacoteca di Brera, Milan) and *La Belle Jardinière* (1507, Louvre, Paris). In Rome, Pope Julius II commissioned him to fresco the Stanza della Segnatura (1509–11) and Stanza d'Eliodoro (1511–14) in the Vatican — at the same time Michelangelo was painting ceiling of Sistine chapel. Raphael also painted his greatest altarpiece, the *Sistine Madonna* (c.1512, Dresden Gemäldegalerie), and designed (1515) ten tapestries for the Sistine chapel (cartoons in Royal Collection, Victoria and Albert Museum, London). Among his many superb portraits are *Julius II* (1511, Uffizi, Florence) and *Baldassare Castiglione* (1516, Louvre, Paris). His last major painting was the *Transfiguration* (incomplete at his death, commissioned 1517, Vatican). Raphael became the most important practicing architect in Italy from the time of Bramante's death (1514), responsible for progress on St. Peter's, the design of S. Eligio degli Orefici, several palaces, and two chapels for banker Agostino Chigi. Universality is the outstanding quality of this great genius of the High Renaissance.

REFERENCES: *Complete Works of Raphael* (New York 1969). Luciano Berti *Raphael* (tr. New York 1961 and London 1962). Ettore Camesasca *All the Frescoes of Raphael* (tr. 2 vols. New York and London 1963) and *All the Paintings of Raphael* (tr. 2 vols. New York and London 1963). Oskar Fischel *Raphael* (tr. 2 vols. London 1948 and Boston 1951). Sir Charles J. Holmes *Raphael and the Modern Use of the Classical Tradition* (London and New York 1933). Ulrich A. Middeldorf *Raphael's Drawings* (New York 1945). Vilhelm Wanscher *Raffaello Santi da Urbino: His Life and Works* (London 1926).

RAVEL, Maurice Joseph (Mar. 7, 1875 – Dec. 27, 1937). French composer. Born Ciboure, near Pyrenees border. Musical training began early; he entered Paris Conservatoire at fourteen, wrote *Serenade grotesque* at eighteen. Despite competing unsuccessfully several times for

Prix de Rome, he nonetheless gained an early reputation as a composer, scoring a triumph with *Jeux d'eau* (1901) for piano. *Sonatina* (1905) and *Miroirs* (1905) followed. Composed one-act opera *L'Heure espagnole* and *Rapsodie espagnole* for orchestra (both 1907). Piano suite *Gaspard de la nuit* followed (1908). Wrote ballet *Daphnis and Chloë* (1912) for Sergei Diaghilev's Ballet Russe. Works thereafter included *Trois Chansons de Mallarmé* (1913), *Le Tombeau de Couperin* (1917), *Tzigane* (1915), *La Valse* (1920), *L'Enfant et les sortilèges* (1925), the ballet *Boléro* (1928) for Ida Rubinstein. Also composed numerous piano pieces and chamber music. Led a life of seclusion. Died (in Paris) following a brain operation to cure an incapacitating neurological condition of many years' duration.

REFERENCES: Norman Demuth *Ravel* (London 1947 and New York PB 1962). Roland Manuel *Maurice Ravel* (tr. London 1947 and New York 1948). Rollo H. Myers *Ravel: Life and Works* (London and New York 1960). Victor I. Seroff *Maurice Ravel* (New York 1953). H. H. Stuckenschmidt *Maurice Ravel: Variations on His Life and Work* (tr. Philadelphia 1968).

✎

RAVEL
BY ROBERT EVETT

During his public life, a composer, if he has any integrity, can expect from time to time to rise and fall in the esteem of his colleagues, or the public, or whatever variety of opinion he values most. If his ultimate destiny is to sink like a stone, he will be a happier man if he has no premonition of this while he is alive.

Ravel had a particularly bad time of it. His career, which began with some good but not really distinguished piano pieces when he was about twenty-three, was over by 1932 when he was still under sixty — after less than thirty years of real work. What was worse, he suffered from a degenerative nervous disorder which made the last five years of his life especially unpleasant because he knew what was happening to his faculties.

It was Ravel's misfortune to be thirteen years younger than Debussy and to be compared constantly with the older man. The fact is that they were different in temperament and frequently different in sound. But between 1901, the year of *Jeux d'eau*, and 1912, the year of *Daphnis and Chloë*, the two composers briefly found their styles tangent in point of sonority. A few years later, Debussy was to die horribly after executing the sombre *En Blanc et noir* and the relatively austere late sonatas. Ravel was to affect the neoclassicism of *Le Tombeau de Couperin*, the trio, and the left-hand concerto, all of which make sense in terms of his evolution. Some odd pieces (the violin sonata, *Les Chansons madécasses*, and the G major concerto) do not follow a straight line from his other works.

Ravel was fond of claiming an exaggerated debt to older composers — notably Gounod and Chabrier, who had been powers in France when he was growing up — and Satie, a heretic, who was, in his old age, a Bolshevik, trying to raise money for Lenin and set up a soviet in Paris. In the brilliance of his orchestration and the harmonic coloring of some of his fake Spanish pieces, Ravel was influenced by Chabrier. Gounod must have been introduced as smoke screen to conceal Ravel's debt to Debussy, which was already clear in his dissonant and tonally imaginative *Menuet antique* (1898). As for Satie, he was an afterthought. True, there was a slight lessening of density in Ravel's textures after the First World War, but nothing to suggest a Satiesque plainness.

The most celebrated incident in Ravel's life grew out of his long career as a student at the Conservatoire, where he competed repeatedly for the Prix de Rome. After losing three times, he was refused a chance to compete a fourth time, on the grounds that he had passed the age limit of thirty. Ravel was already on his way to becoming an eminent man and was in no mood for hanky-panky. Besides, his view (and that of his friends) was that, at thirty, he was still within the acceptable age limit. In the scandal that followed, the director of the Conservatoire, Théodore Dubois, was deposed and replaced by Fauré.

A major participant in the row was Debussy, and because of his aid to Ravel, it has often been suggested that they were good friends. There was no reason that this should have been so. There was a significant age difference between the men, and besides that, they found themselves rivals. Debussy was as generous as he could or should have been. Ravel, for his part, repaid the courtesy by making a marvelous two-piano arrangement of Debussy's *Nocturnes*, and they remained on generally good professional terms.

A variation in their development was that Debussy's interior journey was endlessly slow. He was thirty-one before he got around to the *String Quartet*. Ten years later, with *Pelléas*, his style was still in formation, with the result that virtually all of his best music was written after he was forty.

Ravel, on the other hand, was a genuine enfant terrible. In France, the stylistic developments of Fauré and Debussy had given him the opportunity to fall into a kind of music that he wrote well and with ease. The result is that more than half of the works in his catalog — including the most spectacular piano pieces, the *Quartet* and the opera *L'Heure espagnole*, the most brilliant orchestra music except for

Boléro and *La Valse* — were written before he was thirty-five. He wanted to do everything superbly well, and for him, "sincerity" evidently consisted in technical perfection.

In works like *Le Tombeau de Couperin* and *Valses nobles et sentimentales* Ravel conveyed the most profound and deeply touching tender emotions. But in most of his music, the excitement and brilliance come first. And in some of his later music — the "blues" from the violin sonata, the tonally amorphous sections of *Chansons madécasses* — he appears to be following fashion instead of leading it. The sonata is a strong piece, and the "blues" from it survives the dating process very well — but it is dated, much more so than the other two movements. As for the G major concerto, it is dated to the point of banality. Whether this is a tactical error or a symptom of his growing illness would be difficult to say, but when it was written it was already an academic exercise.

By the time of his death, Ravel had joined the "safe" moderns — Rachmaninoff, Strauss, Sibelius, the Stravinsky of *Firebird* — as a man who made the symphony orchestra sound marvelous and could be listened to with pleasure by people of no highly cultivated taste. For a man of fashion, it must have been hard to take this unfair verdict of history while the music was still being written. The size of the royalty checks may have made it easier to bear.

READE, Charles (June 8, 1814 – Apr. 11, 1884). English novelist and playwright. Born Ipsden House, Oxfordshire, into wealthy family. Educated privately, obtained B.A., Magdalen College, Oxford (1835), then went to London to study law at Lincoln's Inn. Admitted to bar (1843) but never practiced law. Independently wealthy, traveled extensively in Europe, returning to London (1849) to begin career as dramatist. First production, a comedy, *The Ladies' Battle* (1851), quickly followed by almost twenty more. At suggestion of Laura Seymour, the famous actress and his housekeeper (from 1854), turned to fiction by transforming his most successful play *Masks and Faces* (written with Tom Taylor, 1852) into the novel *Peg Woffington* (1853). After first long novel, *It Is Never Too Late to Mend* (1856), wrote more than twenty, at first historical romances, and then painstakingly researched "novels with a purpose," in which he attacked abuses in Victorian society. Although he wanted to be remembered as a dramatist, he is known today for *The Cloister and the Hearth* (1861), considered one of the finest English historical novels. An amateur violinist, he collected and wrote about Cremona violins. He died in London.

REFERENCES: Malcolm Elwin *Charles Reade* (1931, reprinted New York 1969). Walter C. Phillips *Dickens, Reade, and Collins: Sensation Novelists* (1919, reprinted New York 1962). John Francis Quinn *Charles Reade: Social Crusader* (New York 1946). C. L. and Compton Reade *Charles Reade, Dramatist, Novelist, Journalist: A Memoir* (2 vols. London and New York 1887). A. C. Swinburne *Miscellanies* (3rd ed. London 1911).

REDON, Odilon (Apr. 22, 1840 – July 6, 1916). French artist. Born Bordeaux. Influenced by the printmaker Rodolphe Bresdin, who created a world of fantastic imagery. Redon settled in Paris after Franco-Prussian War, and brought out first volume of lithographs, *Dans le Rêve* (1879), based on his own visionary imagery. Other volumes followed whose titles suggest their imaginative and often literary content: *À Edgar Poe* (1882), *Les Origines* (1883), *Hommage à Goya* (1885), *La Nuit* (1886), *La Tentation de St. Antoine* (1888), *Les Fleurs du mal* (1890), *Songes* (1891), *L'Apocalypse* (1899). First exhibition of charcoal drawings (1881) also helped establish his reputation. Participated in first Salon des Indépendants (1884). From 1886 became closely associated with the symbolists through

his friend Stéphane Mallarmé. After 1889 began painting in oil, extraordinary still lifes of exquisite form and color such as *The Large Green Vase* (c.1908, Museum of Fine Arts, Boston) and visionary subjects like *Le Silence* (Museum of Modern Art, New York) and *Les Yeux clos* (1890, Louvre, Paris). Held his first comprehensive one-man show in 1894. Died in Paris. His journal, *À Soi-même* appeared posthumously (1922).

REFERENCES: Roseline Bacou *Odilon Redon* (2 vols. Geneva 1956). Klaus Berger *Odilon Redon: Fantasy and Colour* (tr. London and New York 1965). André Mellerio *Odilon Redon* (Paris 1913, reprinted New York 1968). John Rewald and others *Odilon Redon, Gustave Moreau, Rodolphe Bresdin* (New York 1962, also PB). Alfred Werner *The Graphic Works of Odilon Redon* (New York PB 1969).

✍

ODILON REDON
BY CARLTON LAKE

Odilon Redon was a quiet, contemplative artist whose work is as disquieting as any in modern times. A lonely, thought-filled childhood encouraged him to formulate early a dream imagery that became the basis of his art. As a result he was able to create a highly original body of work totally untouched by what was going on in art all around him: by either the all-powerful official art of the Salon or the vigorous, assertive, revolutionary art the impressionists were bringing into being.

Redon's art is that of a visionary. The impressionists had "too low a ceiling" for him. "Real parasites of the object," he called them. He used the object — flowers, for example — as a point of departure, the outer shell of layers of mood and suggestion. More recent painters have used distortion or simplification to create new forms derived from but distinct from their model. Not so Redon, whose flowers we identify at once — the peony, red poppy, cornflower, daisy, nasturtium, mimosa, anemone, against their beige or black background. But for all their naturalism, their individuality is such that we could never mistake Redon's flowers for another's; nor, having known Redon's, could we ever find others anything but pale and dull. Their color, their arrangement, even their scent, is unique. At their most colorful and appealing they are ominous. The treachery and imminent disintegration of the material universe are implicit in their bright intensity. Less subtle painters, like the German expressionists, scream their threats of decay and death. Redon makes us sense the sinister across the overtones.

Music was one of the great forces in Redon's life; its influence far outweighed that of his formal art training. He had been disillusioned early by his studies at the Beaux Arts and had looked elsewhere — to Michelangelo, Leonardo, Rembrandt, Goya, and Delacroix — for nourishment. His approach to art was essentially that of the autodidact. He came to his most characteristic media — charcoal, lithography, pastel — as a result of his need to find media which could contain and express his vision, in contrast to the more usual procedure of adopting a medium and then working within the discipline it imposes.

Redon did not work in color to any extent until about 1895, but what he accomplished in his charcoal drawings — the five or six hundred of them that he created on chamois-toned or blue paper between 1862 and 1898 — could not have been achieved by other means. His "researches into chiaroscuro and the invisible," as he referred to them, cried out for charcoal; only its infinitely subtle gradations could have expressed what he called his "abstract line." The charcoal "trembles" and "vibrates," he noted during his early experiments.

In the work of no other artist is the use of shadow so important. When Redon began to work in lithography — the first of his thirteen albums of lithographs appeared in 1879 — he did so because the medium offered him about the same possibilities as charcoal with the added advantage of enabling him to reproduce his work in quantity. The official Salon had refused to allow him to show his charcoal drawings there. And so his portfolios of lithographs, many of which duplicated charcoal drawings he had been unable to sell, introduced him to a public he had no other means of reaching. At first Redon found the new medium "intractable," but he soon overcame its strangeness and it is doubtful if anyone, before or since, has exploited its possibilities as effectively as he did. His black and white and his extraordinarily varied gamut of grays are as rich and evocative as most other artists' full palette.

"All my originality," Redon wrote, "consists in bringing to life improbable beings in accordance with the laws of probability." Among these improbable beings are the spider with its human smile, the human head served up as a centerpiece, the eyeball and the poppy floating serenely through space, Caliban sleeping under a tree, as minute, luminous, disembodied winged heads hover over him. Yet these visions are neither less believable nor more disturbing than the more conventional elements of Redon's universe. Redon's trees, for example, are constructed as nature intended, but, like his flowers, they have an added quality — an animistic pulsation through which we experience their aliveness.

How did Redon achieve this seamless blending of the rational and the irrational? His work was grounded in natural forms; as for the other kind, he believed in *them* just as deeply. "After an attempt to copy minutely a stone, a blade of grass, a hand, a profile . . . I feel a mental ebullition . . . I then have need to create, to let myself go in the representation of the imaginary. Nature blended and steeped thus becomes my source and my leaven . . ."

In his own day Redon was venerated by a small but elite group of writers and artists. Mallarmé was one of his early admirers. Huysmans, Gourmont, and Gide honored him; Gauguin and Émile Bernard also. The Nabis — Bonnard, Vuillard, Paul Sérusier, Albert Roussel, Maurice Denis — considered him their master. Nearer our time the surrealists looked back to Redon for inspiration and example in their exaltation of the fantastic. Long before Dalí, Redon planned to "put the logic of the visible at the service of the invisible." And well before Chagall, he set floating violinists into orbit above a topsy-turvy earth.

Redon was often tempted by literary themes. He interpreted (rather than illustrated) Poe, Baudelaire, and Flaubert, and he made essays in the direction of more abstract works such as the *Pensées* of Pascal and Mallarmé's hermetic poem *Un Coup de dés jamais n'abolira le hasard*. All his work has a strongly ideational basis. He was constantly striving to express in it the conquest of "light over dark," in the symbolic sense. Such symbols as Jacob and the angel, the winged horse, Saint George and the dragon, recur frequently.

Literary themes, symbols, and ideas almost invariably end by consigning a painter to oblivion. The fact that Redon still seems such a rich source of plastic invention, which no amount of literature has been able to submerge, is almost the highest tribute that could be paid him. The history of modern art furnishes very few comparable examples.

REGER, Max (Johan Baptist Joseph Maximilian) (Mar. 19, 1873 – May 11, 1916). German composer. Born Brand, Bavaria, son of a teacher who gave him his early musical training. Organist at Weiden Roman Catholic church (1886–89). Became pupil of Hugo Rieman (1890). Remained in Weiden composing prolifically (1898–1901), then went to Munich, marrying Elsa von Bagensky a year later. Among his finest keyboard works are *Fantasy and Fugue on B–A–C–H.* (op. 46) and *Variations and Fugue* (op. 73) for organ; *Variations on a Theme by Bach* (op. 81) and *Passacaglia and Fugue* (op. 96) for piano. His first orchestral work was the *Sinfonietta* (op. 90, 1906). After 1907 taught at Leipzig Conservatory and wrote choral music, full-scale works such as the violin concerto (op. 101), the piano concerto (op. 114), and the *Comedy Overture*, also chamber music and songs. Became director of court orchestra at Meiningen, where he composed more orchestral music: *Romantic Suite, Böcklin Suite,* and *Variations and Fugue on a Theme by Mozart.* Though considered an innovator in his lifetime, Reger's music is in tradition of his great predecessors Bach, Beethoven, and Brahms. He died in Leipzig.

REMBRANDT (full name Rembrandt Harmensz van Rijn) (July 15, 1606 – Oct. 4, 1669). Dutch painter. Born Leiden, son of a miller. Entered Leiden University (1620), soon left to become pupil of Jacob von Swanenburgh, then of Pieter Lastman in Amsterdam (1624). In Leiden again he had a flourishing studio (1625–1631/32), period of earliest known paintings, such as *Clemency of Titus* (1626, Utrecht Museum). Settling permanently in Amsterdam, he won fame with group portrait *The Anatomy Lesson of Dr. Tulp* (1632, Mauritshuis, The Hague);

became leading portraitist in Holland, received important commissions for religious paintings, and married wealthy Saskia van Uylenburgh (1634). Among works of Rembrandt's successful years: *Self-Portrait with Saskia* (1635, Gemäldegalerie, Dresden), *The Blinding of Samson* (1636, Frankfurt Museum), and *The Militia Company of Capt. Frans Banning Cocq* (1642, Rijksmuseum, Amsterdam, known as *The Night Watch*). About the time of Saskia's death (1642) Rembrandt's popularity began to wane, and he spent remaining years in financial straits, but continuing to work. Hendrickje Stoffels was his companion from c.1645 until her death (1662). Among the great later works: *The Deposition* (c.1653, National Gallery, Washington), *Aristotle Contemplating the Bust of Homer* (1653, Metropolitan Museum, New York), *The Syndics of the Cloth Guild* (1662, Rijksmuseum). His numerous portraits include the self-portraits of 1629 (Gardner Museum, Boston), 1659 (National Gallery, Washington), and 1669 (Mauritshuis, The Hague), *Jewish Merchant* (c.1650, National Gallery, London), *Jan Stix* (1654, Six-Stichting Collection, Amsterdam), *Woman with an Ostrich-Feather Fan* (c.1650, National Gallery, Washington). His most famous etchings are *Three Trees* (1643) and *Christ Healing the Sick* (1649, known as the *Hundred Guilder Print*). Rembrandt died in Amsterdam.

REFERENCES: Abraham Bredius revised by Horst Gerson *Rembrandt: The Complete Edition of the Paintings* (3rd ed. London and New York 1969). Kenneth Clark *Rembrandt and the Italian Renaissance* (New York and London 1966, also PB). R. H. Fuchs *Rembrandt in Amsterdam* (New York 1969). Horst Gerson *Rembrandt Paintings* (tr. London and New York 1968). Bob Haak *Rembrandt: His Life, His Work, His Time* (tr. London and New York 1969). Julius S. Held *Rembrandt's Aristotle, and Other Rembrandt Studies* (Princeton, N.J. 1969). Michael Kitson *Rembrandt* (London 1969). Jakob Rosenberg *Rembrandt: Life and Work* (3rd ed. London and New York 1968, also PB). Seymour Slive *Drawings of Rembrandt* (2 vols. New York PB 1965). Christopher White *Rembrandt as an Etcher: A Study of the Artist at Work* (2 vols. London and University Park, Pa. 1969).

✍

REMBRANDT

BY JOHN WALKER

Holland has never produced outstanding sculpture, poetry, or drama, and yet Holland did produce one genius preeminent as sculptor, poet, and dramatist. That Rembrandt's sculpture was carved with light and shade, that his poetry and drama were written with pigment and acid, is not significant. For Rembrandt the medium was definitely not the message. Nor can he really be considered a Dutch painter. His work proved the truth of Whistler's axiom that art knows no nationality. In his full maturity his work belongs to the Mediterranean tradition, which is essentially plastic, rather than to the northern tradition, the goal of which has always been realistic representation, the total visual effect.

Rembrandt's insight into Italian art is in part the explanation of his unique position among Dutch artists. Many painters from Holland studied in Italy, but they grasped only the superficial externals of classical art. Almost all we know of Rembrandt's first teacher, Jacob von Swanenburgh, for example, is that he had journeyed to Italy. The Italian sojourn of his subsequent masters, Pieter Lastman and Jan Pynas, reinforced this interest in the Mediterranean world. But Rembrandt at first was no more aware than these minor painters of the lessons to be learned from the great Italian artists. In his early work, he was merely more accomplished than a number of his contemporaries. Consequently for a time he was one of the most popular painters in Holland, a popularity that lasted until there occurred that ominous portent of change, the criticism of *The Night Watch* in 1642. It was a first break with his patrons, an augury not only of subsequent misunderstanding of Rembrandt's noblest work, but of the decline of discriminating patronage itself, corroded by middle-class taste.

The decrease in commissions during the transitional years, from about 1642 to about 1650, gave Rembrandt the opportunity for a more thorough study of classical art. Bankruptcy was still to come, and Rembrandt remained in possession of his collections, until they were sold for debt in 1657–58. They included much classical sculpture, particularly Roman portrait busts, as well as Italian pictures and engravings. These he copied, and his drawings after Mantegna, Carpaccio, and Gentile Bellini have been preserved.

The influence of such models explains the astonishing transformation of Rembrandt's style during the years from about 1642 to his death. His early work is characterized by a porcelain-like finish, a microscopic exactness in the delineation of the features, and, in figure painting, a heavily concentrated spotlight effect strongly emphasizing the central figures. In this theatrical way of painting — tending sometimes toward the melodrama of the *Samson* (1636) of Frankfurt, sometimes toward the sensuousness of the *Danaë* (1636) of Leningrad — everything is extravagant, even to architectural accessories. Swarms of Lilliputian figures gather in fantastic edifices, as in the *Simeon in the Temple* (1631) of The Hague, or sway in turbulent masses, as in the *Christ before Pilate* (1634) of the National Gallery, London. The promise of the early work lies chiefly in the simplest of the monochromatic studies, such as *The Philosopher*, also in the National Gallery, London, since in these the deep shadows eliminate details and

concentrate attention on the solids and voids of the design.

Shortly after 1642, however, Rembrandt's light becomes more widely diffused, and later when it was again occasionally concentrated, it is less for dramatic than for plastic effect. Details are gradually eliminated; compositions change from diagonal to horizontal and vertical designs; and baroque ornamentation disappears. Instead of intensely dramatic illustration, the pictorial form is infused with a mood as intangible and yet all-pervading as a mood created by music. Toward the middle of the century the handling also changes. The early, enamel-like surfaces had suggested the tactility of the whole form, for Rembrandt was never without a certain tactile sense, but later a thick crumbling paste conveyed, also, the density of the different volumes. This thick pigmentation, in which the paint texture itself becomes expressive, gives a rough appearance to the flesh, so that to achieve a harmony of surface, figures are often dressed in bejeweled and heavily embroidered costumes. Compared to these late paintings, form in other Dutch pictures seems of an almost egglike fragility. Vermeer, for instance, always creates a three-dimensional effect, but his volumes fail to suggest the touch-resistance of compact atoms, the density of substance Rembrandt renders so irresistibly that one's finger tips tingle with the same intense tactile impulse one feels before certain pieces of sculpture, the bronzes of Donatello, for example. And since it is light that molds form out of darkness, local color in these late works is subordinate to the effect of light. Thus Rembrandt's palette was gradually limited in its dominant tone to low intensities of the spectrum from yellow to red.

The same extraordinary surge of

creative power is to be found in Rembrandt's graphic work. His early etchings are compactly modeled with strong contrasts of light and shade. Little by little the illumination becomes more diffused and the economy of line increases. Though these lines are broken, overlayed, tangled as never before in art, each stroke is essential, none can be eliminated without destroying the recession of planes exactly as they occur in the retinal impression.

In landscape Rembrandt's etchings and drawings mark a limit of Western art. Only the Chinese have gone further. By eliminating the niggling detail that plagued other Dutch artists, Rembrandt conveys the stark simplicity of the flat countryside of Holland, penetrates to the essence of each glimpse of tree clumps, muddy roads, windmills, and cottages. The result is a sublimation of natural beauty that reaches a climax in such etchings as *The Three Trees* of 1643 and the *Goldweigher's Field* of 1651.

Though bankruptcy, loneliness, and diminished fame seem only to have increased Rembrandt's creative strength, such adversities explain the pervading sadness of his late work. Unfortunately this mood of austere and epic sorrow did not appeal to patrons, who demanded cheerful, not melancholy likenesses, pleasant not gloomy scenes; nor were the tradesmen and shopkeepers of Holland impressed by his portrait style, by his method of giving his sitters the majestic presence that one feels before great actors in the traditional roles of high tragedy. Rembrandt, indeed, would have been better understood by Venetian patrons accustomed to dramatic painting in the grand manner than by his compatriots who were increasingly absorbed in the modish elegance of the drawing-room comedies of Terborch, and the petty realism of the contemporary dramas of Gerard Dou.

REMINGTON, Frederic (Sackrider) (Oct. 1/4, 1861 – Dec. 26, 1909). American artist and sculptor. Born Canton, N.Y., son of newspaper publisher. Attended military school and Yale for two years, then headed West (1880) and worked as cowboy and ranch cook. Began lifelong work of recording pictorially the Old West because he knew that the railroad was coming and that "the wild riders and the vacant land were about to vanish forever." Was largely self-taught as an artist. Returned to New York (1888), began selling drawings to *Harper's Weekly*, and illustrated series of articles by Theodore Roosevelt for *Century Magazine* (published as book, *Ranch Life and the Hunting Trail*, 1888). Settled in East, summered in West. Awarded silver medal at Paris Exposition (1889). Joined army in war against the Sioux (1890), which he depicted for *Harper's*. Also illustrated Longfellow's *Hiawatha* (1890), Francis Parkman's *The Oregon Trail* (1892), as well as his own books, *Pony Tracks* (1895) and others. Sent by Hearst to Cuba as artist-correspondent in Spanish-American War (1898). Continued to work prolifically until his death near Ridgefield, Conn. In his dramatic paintings, studies, sketches, and powerful small bronzes such as *Bronco Buster,* Remington captured the whole era of the Old West.

REFERENCES: Harold McCracken *Frederic Remington: Artist of the Old West* (Philadelphia 1947) and *Drawings of Remington* (New York PB 1970). R. W. G. Vail *Frederic Remington: Chronicler of the Vanished West* (New York 1929).

RENI, Guido (Nov. 4, 1575 – Aug. 18, 1642). Italian painter. Born and died in Bologna. Apprenticed as child to Flemish painter Denys Calvaert; left him (c.1595) to study with the Carracci. Won competition for decorative frescoes celebrating visit of Pope Clement VIII to Bologna (1598). Shortly after 1600 made first of many visits to Rome, where he came under influence of Caravaggio. His most famous work, the *Aurora* fresco (1613) in the Rospigliosi palace, was commissioned by his patron Scipione Cardinal Borghese. Also painted frescoes in various Roman churches and for Pope Paul V in Vatican. Among other celebrated works are Hercules series painted for duke of Mantua (1617–21, Louvre, Paris) and several paintings of the subject *Ecce Homo* (National Gallery, London, and Louvre). Spent latter part of life in Bologna, executing numerous commissions for altarpieces. Long admired for his idealization of beauty and baroque use of themes from antiquity, Reni since the nineteenth century has been criticized for excessive emotion, verging on sentimentality.

REFERENCE: Rudolf Wittkower *Art and Architecture in Italy* (Harmondsworth, England, 1958).

RENOIR, Pierre Auguste (Feb. 25, 1841 – Dec. 17, 1919). French painter. Born Limoges, son of a tailor. Soon after his birth, the family moved to Paris, where he began by painting porcelain, then fans and banners. Entered studio of Charles Gabriel Gleyre (1861), where he met and was influenced by impressionists Monet, Sisley, and Bazille; left after a year to work independently with them. Exhibited with impressionists at Salon of 1864, and at later Salons with them, but continued to exhibit at Salons without them until 1890. Achieved popular recognition in the 1870's, producing such famous paintings as the *Moulin de la Galette* (1876, Louvre, Paris) and portraits such as *Madame Charpentier and Her Children* (1878, Metropolitan Museum, New York). Married Aline Charigot (1881); they had three sons. Visited Algeria and Italy (1881–82). Plagued by arthritis, settled in Provence (1890), where he spent rest of his life, continuing to paint with brush strapped to his arm. From his early impressionist pictures of groups in and out of doors, dancing, boating, and so forth, he concentrated on nudes, portraying with tender warmth exquisite flesh tones. Died at Cagnes-sur-Mer. Other well-known works include the *Luncheon of the Boating Party* (1881, Phillips Collection, Washington), *Le Bal à Bougival* (1883, Museum of Fine Arts, Boston), and *Les Parapluies* (c.1884, National Gallery, London). Also created such sculptures as the bronze *Washerwoman* (1917, Museum of Modern Art, New York). Renoir's son Jean (b. 1894) has achieved fame as a film writer and director.

REFERENCES: Albert C. Barnes and Violette de Mazia *The Art of Renoir* (1935, reprinted Merion, Pa. 1959). François Daulte *Renoir: Watercolors and Pastels* (New York and London 1959). William Gaunt *Renoir* (Greenwich, Conn. 1962). Lawrence Hanson *Renoir: The Man, the Painter, and His World* (New York 1968). Walter Pach *Pierre Auguste Renoir* (New York 1960). Vassily Photiadès *Renoir Nudes* (tr. New York 1964). Jean Renoir *Renoir, My Father* (tr. Boston and London 1962, also PB). John Rewald *Renoir: Drawings* (1946, new ed. New York 1958 and London 1959). Michael Robida *Renoir: Children* (tr. New York 1962).

RENOIR

BY QUENTIN BELL

A brutal, a filthy painter; he paints the body of a woman as though it were a mass of decomposing flesh green and purple with putrefaction. Such, broadly speaking, was the general opinion of Auguste Renoir amongst the critics and cultivated public who first saw his paintings. Even I have met old people who still found his flesh colors unbearably offensive (this makes me what they call "a link with the past").

That other innovators should have disgusted a public which found beauty in Meissonier and Bouguereau is not so incomprehensible. Van Gogh was a rude enough fellow to be sure, tearing at his paint like a wild beast devouring a carcass, Toulouse Lautrec certainly looked on the ugly side of things, and even Degas is, at times, brutal. But Renoir . . .

And make no mistake, I am not talking about the hotly colored, rolypoly nudes that wriggle around in his later paintings. When Renoir painted these, struggling heroically with a brush strapped to his crippled hand, the public had learned to respect him. No, it was the lyrical evocations of Paris in the 1870's, charming in theme, melodious in color, full of shimmering light and easy movement, pictures of foliage, flowers, fruit, and sunlight breaking through gentle rain, pretty girls in charming dresses (with never an ugly face in any crowd) — it was these which excited the rage, the mockery, and the disgust of the cultivated public.

Time, which observes so much, can also illuminate. The shutters which darkened the vision of our grandparents have grown transparent, so much so that today it is only with an effort, a sensible shift of vision, that we can at all understand what it was that made Renoir's strong complementary colors, the swift asperities of his brushwork so shocking when his paintings were first shown to the public. For us, indeed, Renoir's fault — if he has one — lies not in any kind of brutality but in the lack of it. His attitude towards his art is, by our standards, unusual, for he paints with the mild rationality of a convinced hedonist, looking only at that which is pleasant and inoffensive, perfectly willing, in his pursuit of that which is agreeable, to accept that which is pretty. There is no pain, no heroic passion in his art; never was there a less tormented genius or one who failed more completely to live up to that image of depression, depravity, and despair which the public likes to think of as being typical of the creative artist. He is, in fact, so abnormally normal that we may doubt whether he is a genius at all, for genius, we apprehend, ventures to the very frontiers of insanity. And in fact it must be conceded that Renoir is not among the titans: he is not a Rembrandt or a

Cézanne; he is, as Roger Fry put it, the "master of the commonplace." But within the limits implied by such a classification he was as great as an artist can be, great enough, at all events, to make us pause, question some of our assumptions, and wonder whether, in the face of his achievements, our predilection for the sterner emotions is not, in a way, cowardly. That Renoir lived in a territory which is now forbidden to all — or very nearly all — but the profane, is made strikingly clear when one considers the products of a trade, an aesthetically disreputable commerce, in what we may call pseudo-Renoirs. These are pictures which were painted yesterday by artists who have a pretty good notion of what an undiscerning public will buy tomorrow. Seeing in Renoir an artist whose work is now enormously expensive, they extract from it that which is most clearly marketable: viz., the fringes, rosy cheeks, wide-spaced dark eyes, tiptilted infantile noses, becomingly replete bodies, feathery trees, and dappled illumination. The recipe is easily made up. If we take it we may appreciate the difference which exists between a noble vintage and the cheapest booze that was ever compounded from gooseberries and treacle.

Clearly the difference between Renoir and his pasticheurs is the essential thing in him — his genius. But it is not something purely personal and peculiar to Renoir himself; it is also, in some measure, a national quality, a capacity for being pretty without being silly. It is a rare gift anywhere, but it is particularly rare amongst the Teutons, the Spaniards, the English-speaking peoples, and even the Italians. Perhaps Rubens could achieve it, but even Rubens had not the sense and delicacy of the French. That which in other nations would be sentimental, banal, or prurient can be expressed by that remarkable nation with a nice sobriety, a chaste simplicity of manner which we cannot imitate. This is even true of the relatively minor painters of the French eighteenth century and we find this quality of grave unembarrassed sensuality magnificently exemplified in the work of Boucher and Fragonard, who were Renoir's legitimate ancestors.

Like every considerable artist of his century, Renoir does not simply inherit an artistic patrimony; he invests it in a new enterprise. Like so many of the great pictorial traditionalists, he was an innovator. What he retained was a certain calm honesty of mind which allowed him in a cozy, puritanical, and sentimental age to look with scientific but affectionate curiosity at natural appearances. Thus he painted frankly, and to his contemporaries his frankness seemed like brutality. He told the truth at a time when it was customary to tell lies; in consequence he seemed to be abominably rude. Hence the vituperation of the critics and hence, since truth endures while manners change, our admiration.

———

RESTIF DE LA BRETONNE, Nicolas Edme (Oct. 23, 1734 – Feb. 3, 1806). French writer and printer. Born Sacy, near Auxerre, to farming family. Was destined for church but became apprenticed (1751) to a printer in Auxerre. Went to Paris (1755) and worked at Imprimerie Royal (1759–66). Married Agnès Lebègue (1760). Began printing and publishing novels (1767), winning reputation with *Le Pied de Fanchette* (1768). Drawing on his own bohemian experiences amid lowest strata of Parisian society, he produced racy realistic novels that earned him the title "Rousseau of the gutter," as well as the admiration of the literary salons of the day. The tone of his work is moralizing and cynical rather than prurient; he also wrote with com-passion of the mores and miseries of the poor. His works include *Le Pornographe* (1770), *Le Paysan perverti* (1776), *Les Parisiennes* (1787), the autobiographical *Monsieur Nicolas, ou Le Coeur humain dévoilé* (1796). Died in Paris.

TRANSLATIONS: *The Corrupted Ones* tr. Alan Hull Walton (London 1967). *Monsieur Nicolas, or The Human Heart Laid Bare* tr. Robert Baldick (New York 1967). *Nights of Paris* tr. Linda Asher and Ellen Fertig (New York 1964).

REFERENCES: Marc Chadourne *Restif de la Bretonne, ou Le Siècle prophétique* (Paris 1958). C. R. Dawes *Restif de la Bretonne* (London 1946). Charles A. Porter *Restif's Novels* (New Haven, Conn. 1967).

———

REYES, Alfonso (May 1, 1889 – Dec. 27, 1959). Mexican writer. Born Monterrey, Mexico. After receiving law degree from University of Mexico (1913), entered Mexican foreign service, accepting a post in Paris embassy (1913–14). Throughout his life, combined distinguished career as a diplomat with career as poet, essayist, scholar, and humanist. Served as ambassador to Argentina (1927, 1936–37) and Brazil (1930–36); repeatedly represented Mexico in Pan-American conferences. His poetry, graceful, witty, and urbane, captures the spirit of Spanish America. It includes the ambitious *Vision de Anáhuac* (1917), a tableau of the Mexico of the Conquistadores; *Huellas* (1922); the lyrical tragedy *Ifigenía Cruel* (1924); *Romance del Río de Enero* (1933); *Yerbas del Tarahumara* (1934); *Golfo de Mexico* (1935). Among his prose works: editions of the Spanish classics, such as Ruiz de Alarcón and Lope de Vega; numerous essays, including the collection *El Suicida* (1954); critical studies of aesthetics and literary theory, among them *Cuestiones estéticas* (1910), *La Experiencia literaria* (1941), *La Crítica en la edad ateniense* (1941), and *El Deslinde* (1944). Also translated into Spanish a wide variety of writers from Homer to Chesterton. Elected president and member of governing board of Colegio de Mexico (1940), he also received honorary degrees from many foreign universities and Mexico's national prize for arts and sciences (1945) for work on classical criticism. Died in Mexico City. Although little known in the English-speaking world, Reyes is considered one of the towering Spanish-American men of letters in the twentieth century.

TRANSLATIONS: *Mexico in a Nutshell and Other Essays* tr. Charles Ramsdell (Berkeley, Calif. and Cambridge, England, 1964). *The Position of America and Other Essays* tr. Harriet de Onis (New York 1950).

REFERENCES: M. A. Arango *Tres Figuras representivas de Hispanoamerica en la generación de vanguardia o literatura de postguerra* (Bogota 1967). Hispanic Institute in the United States *Alfonso Reyes: Vida y obra, bibliografía, antología* (New York 1956). M. Olguin *Alfonso Reyes, ensayista: Vida y pensamiento* (Mexico City 1956). J. W. Robb *Patterns of Image and Structure in the Essays of Alfonso Reyes* (Washington, D.C. 1958).

REYNOLDS, Sir Joshua (July 16, 1723 – Feb. 23, 1792). English painter. Born Plympton, near Plymouth, son of a clergyman. Apprenticed (1740) to Thomas Hudson, well-known London portraitist, he soon enjoyed modest success painting portraits in Devonshire and London. First important work, *Captain John Hamilton* (1746, duke of Abercorn, London). After three years' study in Italy (1750–52), Reynolds settled in London for rest of his life; there his *Commodore Augustus Keppel* (1753, National Maritime Museum, London) marked beginning of enormous popularity in literary and society circles. Reynolds painted over two thousand portraits and historical works. Among the former are several portraits of *Dr. Johnson, Nelly O'Brien* (1760–62, Wallace Collection, London), *Garrick as Kiteley* (1768, Windsor Castle), *Mrs. Siddons as the Tragic Muse* (1784, Huntington Art Gallery, San Marino, Calif.), *Duchess of Devonshire and Her Daughter* (1786, trustees of the Chatsworth Settlement, Derbyshire). The friend of Johnson, Goldsmith, Burke, Gibbon, and David Garrick, he founded the Literary Club (1764). When Royal Academy was founded (1768), Reynolds was elected president and knighted. Delivered (1769) first of annual addresses to Academy, later published as *Discourses.*

EDITION: *Discourses on Art* ed. Robert R. Wark (San Marino, Calif. 1959 and New York 1966).

REFERENCES: Algernon Graves and W. V. Cronin *A History of the Works of Sir Joshua Reynolds* (4 vols. London 1899–1901). Frederick W. Hilles *The Literary Career of Sir Joshua Reynolds* (1936, reprinted Hamden, Conn. 1967). Derek Hudson *Sir Joshua Reynolds: A Personal Study* (London 1958). Mark Roskill *English Painting from 1500 to 1865* (London 1959). John Steegman *Sir Joshua Reynolds* (London and New York 1933). Ellis K. Waterhouse *Reynolds* (London 1941). R. H. Wilenski *English Painting* (4th ed. London 1964).

✍

SIR JOSHUA REYNOLDS
BY QUENTIN BELL

If all Reynolds's pictures had vanished we should probably suppose that he was not a very good painter. The story of his life is too prosperous, his character was too affable, too courteous, too urbane, to suggest genius; he had none of the divinely ill-tempered and unreasonable savagery which makes his great adversary, William Blake, so popular. Moreover he was English and he was an academician.

Fortunately, his pictures have not vanished. There are a great many — rather too many in fact; for when Reynolds attempts the sublime, or when he is coy, or when he paints simpering bodiless putti, he is hard to defend. But Reynolds at his best is one of the greatest of masters and also one of the most perplexing and fascinating characters in the history of art, for he unites such opposite qualities. He, the first president of the Royal Academy, was at once the most academic and the least academic of painters.

Academic theory as it then existed

was based upon an idea not unlike that of the abstract artists of our own day. Painting should not consist in a mere representation of nature. The visible world was to be no more than a starting point which the painter, like the great dramatic poets, would translate into forms nobler, more regular, and more dignified than those which he could see in nature. The picture would be built from generalized concepts, abstracted and divorced from the common world of material things and composed in accordance with the laws of pictorial harmony. Thus Correggio had worked, thus Guido, Raphael, and the Carracci. The Royal Academy was to foster this, the highest form of art, and give to England a school which might resemble and perhaps surpass the great schools of Italy. It had in truth some other and less exalted objects; but for Reynolds himself this was its great purpose. It was a purpose that could not be realized — indeed, we can see now that it was bound to fail — but it was not ignoble.

The fifteen *Discourses* which Reynolds delivered to the Academy were intended to explain and uphold the academic ideal. In the main, they follow the lines laid down by all the academic theorists of Europe from Alberti onwards. But from the first, Reynolds fails to be consistent. His predecessors were dogmatic, he is skeptical; they based their arguments upon authority, he upon reason. Worse still, from an academic point of view, he cannot quite bring himself to follow the academic canon which makes of Florence and Rome the sole capitals of art. Reynolds was too deeply attached to the Venetians to take so narrow a view and indeed he could appreciate artists who had no place at all in the academic scheme of things. It is this distaste for dogmatic assertion, this generous enthusiasm for all kinds of painting, together with a certain very unacademic humility, which makes Reynolds, unlike other theorists, so very readable.

Reynolds's occasional infidelities to the reigning deities of academic taste were not the result of a radically and fundamentally eccentric taste but rather of an affection for the art of painting too great to be contained within one channel. On the whole, he admired that which he felt he ought to admire. The great aesthetic experience of his life was of a thoroughly orthodox kind; his beliefs and tastes were, to a very great extent, fixed in Italy and, to apply his own phrase to himself, "all Rome and the works of Michelangelo in particular were to him an Academy." He would, in fact, have liked, if it had been possible, to be another Michelangelo or, as he put it in his last *Discourse:* "It will not, I hope, be thought presumptuous in me to appear in the train, I cannot say of his imitators but of his admirers. I have taken another course, one more suited to my abilities, and to the taste of the times in which I live." That course was portrait painting.

The trouble about portrait painting is that it breeds insincerity. The artist, in attempting to give a sitter the kind of image of himself that he requires, is false to his own conceptions, and it is one of the many tragedies of British painting that several generations of patrons have wanted to look like paintings by Reynolds and that British artists have attempted to oblige by working, as far as they could, in the manner of the master. Reynolds, like Gainsborough, had the great advantage that he could be himself. He was sincere, enthusiastic even, in his acceptance of the social ideal that his sitters valued. To some extent he invented it, and although this could, on occasion, make him sentimental — for sentimentality was then the fashion — it also enabled him to present an image of dignity and social felicity, of class and of character, in which both he and his patrons believed.

The image of himself which Reynolds presented to English society was slightly different from that which Gainsborough has left us; Gainsborough is a shade more aristocratic, more seductive, and less admirable; there is more glass and glitter, more obvious charm in his sitters. Reynolds is more serious and more domestic; his ideals are those of the sober and cultivated professional men, with a leaven of gifted women who gathered around Dr. Johnson. He feels the influence of the polite comedy, the comedy of Sheridan and Goldsmith, of the polite novels of Fanny Burney, of that important section of society which was a little softer in its manners, a little more philanthropic than any that could have existed at the beginning of the century.

The great principle of that society was the balance of two opposing forces: dignity and intimacy. It is this which Boswell achieves in his *Life of Johnson*. Sir Joshua, a more stately and much more reputable character than Boswell, has the same gift. When he paints Lord Heathfield, we feel that we know him well and that Reynolds was hardly less great as a psychologist then Rembrandt himself, and yet the defender of Gibraltar, with the key to the Mediterranean secure in his great hands, is a monument. Or again, in the portrait of Mr. Watkyns Wynne and his mother, Reynolds's acuteness goes very deep and is not altogether kind. They are a wonderfully stupid pair and we know the exact quality of their dimness and yet that crass, obstinate quality is united with a superb aplomb, a kind of grand insensibility which is truly awful and yet, because of its grandeur, impressive.

How does Reynolds manage to combine these opposite qualities in so miraculous a way? By a thousand subtle and almost imperceptible strokes of the brush; but also by using his Italian education, by applying his academic theories. It is the design of the pictures, the perfect rightness of the placing of the figures against the landscape, the precise angle with arm outstretched in which the young man holds his three-cornered hat that gives majesty to that which would otherwise be no more than perceptive.

Reynolds, in fact, could paint things both as they were and as they ought to have been; nature is there, alive and undisturbed by an art of the most formal, the most architectonic regularity. To make a virtue of such inconsistency was a very notable achievement, and only Reynolds could have done it.

RIBERA, Jusepe (José) de (nicknamed Lo Spagnoletto) (Feb. 17, 1591 – Sept. 2, 1652). Spanish painter. Born Játiva, Valencia, son of a shoemaker. Nothing is known of his early life. He traveled round Italy and settled in Naples for rest of his life; there he married Caterina Azzolino (1616). Influenced by Caravaggio, the Carracci, and Guercino; religious subjects preoccupied him. His earliest extant painting is probably the *Crucifixion* (c.1618, Colegiata, Osuna). Dramatic movement and realistic detail characterize his best-known painting, the *Martyrdom of St. Bartholomew* (1630 or 1639, Prado, Madrid). About 1635 his style took on light and vivid color, in such pictures as the *Immaculate Conception* (1635, Augustinian convent, Salamanca). After 1640 he reverted to the Caravaggesque style in portrayal of penitential saints and groups such as *The Holy Family with St. Catherine* (1648, Metropolitan Museum, New

York). Completed (1651) two of his greatest canvases, the *Institution of the Eucharist* (S. Martino, Naples) and *Last Supper* (National Museum, Naples). These late works are imbued with serene mysticism. Ribera's naturalism sometimes led to morbidity, but the dramatic austerity of his vision is unquestionable.

REFERENCES: Elizabeth du Gué Trapier *Ribera* (New York 1952). Rudolf Wittkower *Art and Architecture in Italy: 1600–1750* (Harmondsworth, England, 1958).

RICHARDSON, Henry Hobson (Sept. 29, 1838 – Apr. 27, 1886). American architect. Born St. James Parish, La. After graduating from Harvard (1859), studied architecture at École des Beaux Arts, Paris. Returned to America after Civil War (1865); settled first in New York, then in Brookline, Mass. (1874), where he remained until his death. Richardson departed from contemporary Gothic revival in architecture and created a style known as Richardsonian Romanesque, best seen in his first major work, Trinity Church, Boston (designed 1872, built 1873–77). Having initiated the Romanesque revival, he developed a highly individual, bold style, characterized by unornamented exteriors and skillful incorporation of varied materials. Great examples of this style are the Marshall Field Wholesale Store, Chicago (1885–87, demolished 1930), and the Allegheny County courthouse and jail, Pittsburgh (1884–88). Among other notable buildings are the Brattle Square (now First Baptist) Church, Boston (1870–72); Sever Hall (1878–80) and Austin Hall (1881–83), Harvard; Ames Monument, near Cheyenne, Wyo. (1879–80); and many distinguished, shingled private houses, such as the Bryant House, Cohasset, Mass. (1880), and Stoughton House, Cambridge, Mass. (1882–83). In the 1890's Richardson's work especially influenced the Chicago school of architects, among them Louis Sullivan and Frank Lloyd Wright.

REFERENCES: H. R. Hitchcock *The Architecture of H. H. Richardson and His Times* (1936, rev. ed. Hamden, Conn. 1961, PB 1966) and *Richardson as a Victorian Architect* (Baltimore 1966). Lewis Mumford *The South in Architecture* (1941, new ed. New York 1967). Mariana G. Van Rensselaer *Henry Hobson Richardson and His Works* (1888, reprinted Park Forest, Ill. 1967, PB New York 1969).

RICHARDSON, Samuel (1689 – July 4, 1761). English novelist. Born Derbyshire. Received little schooling, and at age of seventeen was apprenticed to a printer. By 1719 had his own prospering business. Married Martha Wilde (1721), and after her death (1731), Elizabeth Leake. Died in London. His three novels are portraits of moral dilemma. *Pamela* (1740–44) was the first novel of sentiment, in which virtue is rewarded. The moral triteness and humorlessness is transcended by the realism of the writing, Richardson's attention to detail, and his psychological insight. *Clarissa* (1747–48), his masterpiece, displays the same qualities on a grander scale. Fielding parodied him in *Shamela* (1741), so in reply to *Tom Jones* Richardson wrote *Sir Charles Grandison;* unfortunately his rival hero, though a gentleman, was also a prig. The novels were immensely successful, and Richardson suffered from piracies as well as parodies. He introduced the epistolary novel to English fiction. His fame spread to Europe and influenced Rousseau and Goethe. His success depended not on story or narration, which are tedious and tendentious; as Dr. Johnson observed, "You must read him for the sentiment."

EDITION: *Complete Novels* (19 vols. Oxford 1930).

REFERENCES: John Carroll ed. *Samuel Richardson: A Collection of Critical Essays* (Englewood Cliffs, N.J. 1969, also PB). Brian W. Downs *Richardson* (1928, reprinted New York and London 1969). Morris Golden *Richardson's Characters* (Ann Arbor, Mich. 1963). Alan D. McKillop *Samuel Richardson: Printer and Novelist* (1936, reprinted Hamden, Conn. 1960). Clara L. Thomson *Samuel Richardson* (London 1900, reprinted Port Washington, N.Y. 1970).

RICHTER, Johann Paul Friedrich (also known as Jean Paul) (Mar. 21, 1763 – Nov. 14, 1825). German writer. Born Wunsiedel, Bavaria; educated at Leipzig (1781–84). Served as tutor and schoolmaster in Töpen and Schwarzenbach; published first book (1783). Married Caroline Mayer (1801) and settled permanently in Bayreuth (1804), devoting himself exclusively to writing. Relieved of financial anxieties (from 1808) by annual pension from government. Little known outside of Germany, his humor and fertile imagination nonetheless won him the admiration of Thomas de Quincey and Thomas Carlyle, who translated some of his works and wrote two essays on him. Best-known books are the romantic novels *Hesperus* (1795, tr. 1865), *Life of Quintus Fixlein* (1796, tr. 1827), *Siebenkäs* (1796, tr. 1845), *Titan* (1800–1803, tr. 1862), and *Felgeljahre* (1804–1805, translated by Carlyle as *Wild Oats*); and a treatise on art, *Die Vorschule des Aesthetik* (1804). Before dying of dropsy in Bayreuth, he edited all his books, published in sixty-five volumes (1826–28).

REFERENCES: Edward V. Brewer *New England Interest in Jean Paul Friedrich Richter* (Berkeley, Calif. PB 1943). Joseph Firmery *Étude sur la vie et les oeuvres de Jean Paul Friedrich Richter* (Paris 1886). J. C. Hayes *Laurence Sterne and Jean Paul* (New York PB 1942). John W. Smeed *Jean Paul's Dreams* (London and New York 1966).

RIEMENSCHNEIDER, Tilman (c.1460 – July 8, 1531). German sculptor. Born Osterode, Harz Mountains, Saxony, he was in Würzburg by 1483, where he became a citizen (1485) by marrying widow of a goldsmith. Active in city government, he became councilman (1504) and burgomaster (1520), but was imprisoned (1525) for his sympathy with peasants' insurrection (1524–25). Little is known of his work after this time; he died in Würzburg. Many of his sculptures, in stone and wood, are in and around Würzburg. His figures are graceful, delicate, and expressive. His earliest documented work is the altarpiece of St. Mary Magdalene, in the parish church of Münnerstadt (1490–92). A famous sculpture is the limestone statue of *Adam and Eve* (1491–93, Mainfrankisches Museum, Würzburg). Other well-known works are the marble monument for Bishop Rudolf von Scherenberg (1496–99, Würzburg cathedral) and the marble sarcophagus for Emperor Henry II and his wife Kunigunde (1499–1513, Bamberg cathedral). Limestone relief *The Lamentation* (1519–23, parish church of Maidbroon) is considered his last work. Riemenschneider won considerable reputation throughout Europe for his wood carvings, an example of which is *Adoration* (1505–1506, British Museum, London).

REFERENCES: Arthur Burkhard *Two Late-Gothic German Sculptors: Hans Leinberger and Tilman Riemenschneider* (Cambridge, Mass. 1933). Carl Streit *Tilman Riemenschneider, 1460–1531* (Berlin 1888).

RILKE, Rainer Maria (Dec. 4, 1875 – Dec. 29, 1926). Austrian poet. Born Prague. Had an unhappy childhood, spending five years (ending 1891) in military academy. Attended universities of Prague, Munich, and Berlin. Published first volume of poems, *Leben und Lieder* (*Life and Songs*) (1894). Visited Italy (1898). His travels to Russia (1899 and 1900), where he met Tolstoy, influenced him profoundly, as is evident in the short stories *Geschichten vom lieben Gott* (1904, tr. *Stories of God* 1932). Married briefly to sculptor Clara Westhoff (1901–1902); they had a daughter, Ruth. First won recognition with the poems *Das Buch der Bilder* (1902, *The Book of Images*), followed by *Das Stundenbuch* (1905, tr. *The Book of Hours* 1961). As secretary to Rodin (1905–1906), he gained much inspiration from the sculptor regarding creative work; completed (1907) a study of Rodin (*Das Rodin-Buch*). Also published poem *Tale of the Love and Death of Cornet Christopher Rilke* (1906, tr. 1948), a popular success. A new phase, less mystical, more aware of reality, began with the poems *Neue Gedichte* (1907–1908, tr. 1957) and the autobiographical novel *The Notebook of Malte Laurids Brigge* (1910, tr. 1930; also known as

The Journal of My Other Self). From 1910 to 1912 lived as guest of Princess Marie von Thurn und Taxis-Hohenlohe at Duino, near Trieste, where he began writing the ten *Duino Elegies* (1923, tr. 1963) and produced *Das Marien-Leben* (1913, tr. *Life of Virgin Mary* 1951). After sojourn in Paris (1913), returned for military service in Austria during World War I. Always solitary, finally settled (1919) in small tower of Muzot, in Sierre, Switzerland, completing before his death by blood poisoning *Sonnets to Orpheus* (1923). *Späte Gedichte* was published posthumously (1934).

TRANSLATIONS: *Selected Works* tr. G. Craig Houston and J. B. Leishman (2 vols. London and New York 1954–60). *Poems, 1906–26* tr. J. B. Leishman (London and Norfolk, Conn. 1957). *Duino Elegies* tr. J. B. Leishman and Stephen Spender (New York and London 1939, PB New York 1963). *Letters* tr. Jane B. Greene and M. D. Norton (2 vols. New York 1945–48, PB 1969). REFERENCES: H. W. Belmore *Rilke's Craftsmanship* (Oxford and Hollywood, Fla. 1954). Eliza M. Butler *Rainer Maria Rilke* (Cambridge, England, and New York 1941). Siegfried Mandel *Rainer Maria Rilke: The Poetic Instinct* (Carbondale, Ill. 1965). Eudo C. Mason *Rilke, Europe, and the English-Speaking World* (Cambridge, England, 1961). Federico Olivero *Rainer Maria Rilke: A Study in Poetry and Mysticism* (Cambridge, England, 1931). Heinz Frederick Peters *Rainer Maria Rilke: Masks and the Man* (Seattle and Nottingham, England, 1960). Nora Purtscher *Rilke: Man and Poet* (London 1949 and New York 1950). William Rose and G. Craig Houston eds. *Rainer Maria Rilke: Aspects of His Mind and Poetry* (London 1938). J. R. von Salis *Rainer Maria Rilke: The Years in Switzerland* (tr. Berkeley, Calif. and London 1964, also PB).

☞

RAINER MARIA RILKE
BY ARTHUR GREGOR

"Beloved Rilke! I saw in him, I loved in him — the tenderest and most spiritual man I knew — a man who more than anyone else possessed all the wonderful anguish and secrets of the spirit . . ." Thus said Paul Valéry of a major Middle European poet in whom a great tradition fulfilled itself, and in whose work are embodied the artistic and spiritual ambitions of a profound culture that is perceptible today in little else than the works it brought forth. This was the essentially bourgeois culture of nineteenth-century Middle Europe, which had inherited and made part of its way of life centuries of cultural achievements. It was a culture in which the sense of experience and perception was still human, and into which the shifts produced by an externalizing machine age had not yet intruded. The tone of this culture was reverential, its heroes were men of the spirit, the fabric of life that sustained it was based on accepting the frailty of human existence. It was a culture that courted the subtle and that distrusted the obvious. Thus, poetic by nature, it counted on its celebrants to give it voice and, from its respect for poets, asked much of them. Rilke, who bespoke the spiritual quality of his period, was perhaps the last of these. Straining never to fail in his grasp of the hierarchy of human values, he was never a social rebel, but to the last a spokesman of man's highest endeavors, and to the last a celebrant of human existence. He was, both in his life and in his work, what for centuries Central Europe had meant by *the poet*.

Rilke's life was marked by a ruthless dedication to his calling. That he looked on his task as a mission is made clear in his letters. To prepare himself for it he cultivated his need for solitude. As early as 1898 he opens a poem with the line *"Du meine heilige Einsamkeit"* (You, my holy solitude). Though Rilke and his wife Clara had a close relationship — as is evidenced by their vast correspondence — they lived apart. Rilke saw their daughter Ruth only intermittently. He regarded personal associations as a means for sharpening and safeguarding individuality. The true obligation to those one loved was to help the individual experience his existence as fully as possible.

Although Rilke had published several slim volumes — verse, stories, plays — when he was in his early twenties, it was not until he returned from his trips to Russia, in 1899 and 1900, that his important work began. He was by then struggling for mastery of reality and unity of existence, and the life of the heart he had found in Russia proved a release of his own devotional nature and enabled him to write *The Book of Hours, The Book of Images,* and *Stories of God.* "Write" ill describes his activity in creation. He was constantly preparing for those periods of grace during which his poems came to him; indeed, he preferred to view his major works as things that were "dictated" to him; and the speed with which they were bodied forth is perhaps unprecedented in literary history.

Memory and images, the richness of things that filled the landscape of human drama and of history, figure prominently in Rilke's work as examples of continuity and tradition. But in his attempt to experience the unity of existence, and to find the right symbols through which this could be conveyed, he discarded traditional methods. The strict religious structure within which the saints climbed to a transcendent awareness Rilke could not accept. The ladder of his ascent was poetry itself — the dream-component, or the realization, of the world experience.

In his attempt to find a verbal equivalent for his spiritual insight, Rilke never resorted to distortions. In the great *Duino Elegies* and *Sonnets to Orpheus* he used language with increased directness, discovering an internal life in words to convey his innermost vision and his acclaim of existence. To the Rilke of these last and major works what was visible was visible consciousness. Consciousness being centered in human experience, the external world is seen as an inner experience or a human statement. Thus in the *Elegies* he offers a landscape wherein life is acted out not as a mere worldly occurrence divorced from the inner man, but as a human experience in which what is outward and what is inward are merged. From his letters it is evident that he had long planned the *Elegies* — the first was "given" to him at Duino on the Adriatic in 1912; but they were not completed until 1922 and then within a few days in February. On the other hand, he seems not to have been entirely aware of the magnitude of the *Sonnets,* which he saw as the "natural overflow" of the *Elegies* and which he also wrote during February 1922.

The *Sonnets* are perhaps the purely lyrical counterpart of the more dramatic and rhapsodic *Elegies.* In their economy and loftiness, the *Sonnets* have perhaps never been equaled in German literature. They conclude with the supreme affirmation — philosophic, religious, above all poetic — of the human reality: *Und wenn dich das Irdische vergass, / zu der stillen Erde sag: Ich rinne. / Zu dem raschen Wasser sprich: Ich bin* (And if the earthly has forgotten you, tell the still earth: I am flowing. To the rapid water say: I am). The *Sonnets* are the testament not only of Rilke's great art but of the great art of the lyric. The *Elegies,* on the other hand, are the testament not just of Rilke's humanity but of the humanity at the core of

Europe's religious impulse, as contained in its greatest creative acts. This is the reverential feeling for life which the culture that had bred Rilke bestowed upon him as its outstanding poetic spokesman.

RIMBAUD, (Jean Nicolas) Arthur (Oct. 20, 1854 – Nov. 10, 1891). French poet. Born Charleville and educated there. Severe upbringing by mother (whom he referred to as "la mère Rimb") after father deserted family (1860) probably one of the reasons for his repeated attempts to run away. Influenced by his teacher Georges Izambard, began writing poetry early and published first verse at fifteen. Had already written *Le Bateau ivre* when he made his way to Paris (1871) and met Verlaine, with whom he formed a very strong, presumably homosexual relationship. Returned to Charleville (March 1872), to write last poems in verse and begin prose poems published by Verlaine as *Les Illuminations* (1886). In London with Verlaine until April 1873, when he again returned home to write *Une Saison en enfer*. Rejoined older poet briefly only to make final break with him when wounded by pistol shot during quarrel in Brussels. After finishing *Une Saison,* and conceivably the remainder of the *Illuminations,* Rimbaud renounced literature and wandered extensively in Europe. Spent last eleven years in Africa, exploring, gunrunning, and possibly slave trading, but never achieved financial success he desired. A tumor on his knee forced him back to Marseilles, where his leg was amputated; three months later he died.

TRANSLATION: *Complete Works with Selected Letters* tr. Wallace Fowlie (Chicago and London 1966, also PB).
REFERENCES: H. de Bouillane de Lacoste *Rimbaud et le problème des Illuminations* (Paris 1949). Marcel Coulon *Le Problème de Rimbaud* (Paris 1923). René Étiemble and Yassu Gauclère *Rimbaud* (3rd ed. Paris 1966). Wallace Fowlie *Rimbaud* (Chicago 1966, also PB). Wilbur M. Frohock *Rimbaud's Poetic Practice* (Cambridge, Mass. and Oxford 1963). C. A. Hackett *Rimbaud* (London and New York 1957).

Henry Miller *The Time of the Assassins: A study of Rimbaud* (New York PB 1962). Edgell Rickword *Rimbaud: The Boy and the Poet* (1924, rev. ed. Castle Hedingham, England, 1963). Enid Starkie *Arthur Rimbaud* (4th ed. New York PB 1968).

≈

RIMBAUD
BY MARTIN TURNELL

In 1923 Marcel Coulon published a book called *The Problem of Rimbaud.* The title was ominous. Rimbaud was a highly controversial figure during his lifetime. Since his death the problems have multiplied and the controversy has grown much more acrimonious. A leading authority celebrated the poet's centenary by denouncing critics with whom he disagreed as "turds." Rimbaud's poetry possesses what is known as an extraliterary appeal. This has turned his admirers into a collection of bitterly warring factions. There is no longer one Rimbaud: there are a dozen Rimbauds. His patronage has been claimed by people of every shade of opinion and belief. There have been Catholic, Marxist, freethinking, surrealist, and existentialist Rimbauds. The result is not simply confusing; there is a real danger of his one slim volume of poetry being smothered under a mountain of tendentious commentary.

Three of the problems are genuine: the interpretation of the poetry, the state of the texts, and the dates of composition. Rimbaud is one of the most difficult poets who ever lived. The difficulties and obscurities cannot be reduced to a single aspect of style. The *Illuminations* exemplify every form of obscurity known to criticism. They are difficult because of the elusiveness of the central experience, the references to events in the poet's private life, their syntax, their imagery, their structure. The difficulties are aggravated by a text which in places is manifestly corrupt.

Rimbaud is not only one of the greatest of French poets; he also introduced a revolutionary theory of poetry. Its aim was not to please or instruct: it was to "change life." He enlarges on it in the celebrated *lettre du voyant* addressed to his friend Paul Demeny in May 1871, when he was sixteen years old. "I say," he wrote, "that one must be a *visionary*, make oneself a *visionary*. The Poet makes himself a *visionary* by a long, immense and reasoned *derangement* of *all the senses*," and in that way "arrives at the *unknown*."

This brings us to the third and most complicated problem of all. Rimbaud's poetry divides into three parts: *Poésies, Illuminations, Une Saison en enfer.* The early verse poems were written between 1869 and 1872, *Une Saison en enfer* between April and August 1873. The *Illuminations* were thought to have been written in 1872. It all seemed plain sailing. The early verse poems were a frontal attack on the contemporary world which had to be demolished to enable the poet to reach the "unknown." In *Le Bateau ivre*, one of the most splendid of them, he actually describes a solitary sea voyage in a "drunken boat" in which he sees "what men believe that they have seen." The *Illuminations* were pure vision. Then he suddenly discovered that his "visions" were really "hallucinations" which were leading not to the "unknown," but to madness. *Une Saison* was a spiritual autobiography in which he abandoned the pursuit and returned to "rugged reality." It was, in fact, a farewell to poetry. Rimbaud wrote no more: he took up gunrunning in Africa instead.

This view received a rude shock in 1949 when the late Bouillane de Lacoste, an amateur graphologist, tried to prove by the handwriting of the manuscripts and the dubious testimony of Paul Verlaine that the *Illuminations* were composed after *Une Saison en enfer*. His theory is not so disturbing as it once appeared. If correct it would mean only that Rimbaud overcame his fear of madness and after his farewell to one kind of vision returned to the pursuit of a different kind in the *Illuminations*. There is no certain answer. My own view is that the traditional version is substantially correct, that the bulk of the *Illuminations* were written before *Une Saison* and the remainder during the year 1874: a year which Rimbaud spent mainly in England with the poet Germain Nouveau and about which we have virtually no information.

In spite of their dissensions, the majority of critics agree that the *Illuminations* are Rimbaud's greatest, as they are certainly his most influential, work. They contain forty prose poems and two poems in free verse. We have, unhappily, no idea of the order in which they were composed or in which the poet would have published them. The poem called *After the Flood* is usually placed by editors at the beginning. It describes what was evidently intended to be a new world — the world of "vision" — emerging from a flood which reminds us of the biblical Flood. Rimbaud's flood has played havoc with everyday conceptions of "reality" and some of the poems, with their novel imagery, read like extracts from a work of science fiction. The poem called *Sale*, usually placed at or near the end of the collection, suggests a general liquidation — the "sale" or renunciation of all the marvels belonging to the visionary world.

"I live on Rimbaud," a young Frenchman once said to me. It explains Rimbaud's strange hold on us or what I described as his extraliterary appeal. The literal meaning of the mature poems is anyone's guess: about their effect there can be no doubt at all. He was trying in his greatest work to do that impossible thing: to arrive at a direct apprehension of reality without the intermediary of a concept. It was because of the impossibility that so many of the poems end in darkness and failure. It does not detract from their significance. The test of great poetry is not what it *says*, but what it *does* to us. Rimbaud's poetry was essentially a work of liberation. Its value lies in its power of modifying, and not merely modifying but reorganizing, our sensibility. For to submit to the new mode of seeing, to enter the fabulous world of the *Illuminations*, to walk the "crystal streets," ride in the "diamond carriages," is to undergo a process of liberation from our stereotyped ways of seeing and feeling which is permanent. Nothing can ever look quite the same again.

RIMSKI-KORSAKOV, Nikolai Andreievitch (Mar. 18, 1844 – June 21, 1908). Russian composer. Born Tikhvin, near Novgorod, into aristocratic family. Attended naval academy, St. Petersburg (graduated 1862). Met (1861) Balakirev, which led him to compose in earnest, and he wrote his first symphony (1862–65) while still in the navy. Appointed professor of composition at St. Petersburg Conservatory (1871), also conducted in Europe. Married gifted pianist Nadezhda Nikolaievna Purgold (1873). Devoted himself to program music, and composed *Spanish Capriccio* (1887), *Scheherazade* (1888), which Diaghilev used for the Russian Ballet, and *Easter Overture* (1888). Turning to opera, wrote sixteen in all, largely based on Russian subjects, of which the best known is *Le Coq d'Or* (*The Golden Cockerel*, 1906–1907). Also wrote over eighty songs based on folk themes. Became one of The Five — group of Russian

nationalist composers — with Mussorgsky, Borodin, and others. Also orchestrated operas by Borodin and Mussorgsky. Among his pupils were Glazunov and Stravinsky. Died in St. Petersburg.

REFERENCES: Gerald Abraham *Studies in Russian Music* (1936, reprinted Freeport, N.Y. 1968) and *Rimsky-Korsakov: A Short Biography* (London 1945 and Chester Springs, Pa. 1949). N. A. Rimski-Korsakov *My Musical Life* (tr. New York and London 1942). Victor I. Seroff *The Mighty Five* (New York 1948). Mikhail Osipovich Zetlin *The Five: The Evolution of the Russian School of Music* (tr. New York and London 1959).

RIVERA, Diego (Dec. 8, 1886 – Nov. 25, 1957). Mexican painter. Born Guanajuato. Educated in Mexico City at Liceo Católico Hispano-Mexicano (1892–98) and at San Carlos Academy of Fine Arts (1896–1902). His first exhibition (1907) led to a government scholarship to Spain. From there he traveled throughout Europe, spending most of his time in Paris, where he was closely associated with Cézanne and Picasso, and took up the political ideas of Russian Communists in exile. On his return to Mexico (1922), was commissioned to paint murals for Ministry of Education in Mexico City (completed 1930). These frescoes, with their massive, simplified figures based on Mayan and Aztec sculptural forms, glorifying peasants and workers, set the tone for his subsequent work. Rivera next undertook decoration of chapel in National School of Agriculture at Chapingo (1926–27), generally considered his masterpiece. Visited Moscow (1927–28). Married artist Frida Kahlo (1929). Painted frescoes in San Francisco, Detroit, and New York (1930–40) — the mural for Rockefeller Center was rejected for including portrait of Lenin — and decorations for numerous other government buildings in Mexico. Died in Mexico City. His autobiography written with Gladys March, *My Art, My Life: An Autobiography*, appeared in 1960.

REFERENCES: MacKinley Helm *Modern Mexican Painters* (1941, reprinted Freeport, N.Y. 1968). Laurence Schmeckebier *Modern Mexican Art* (Minneapolis and Oxford 1939). Bertram D. Wolfe *The Fabulous Life of Diego Rivera* (1963, reprinted New York 1969, also PB).

ROBBIA, Luca Della (1399/1400 – Feb. 23, 1482). Italian sculptor. Born and died in Florence. Decisively influenced by Ghiberti. Entered guild of stone-masons and wood-carvers (1432), in which he held various offices. Established as major Florentine artist of Renaissance by 1431, when outstanding work, the Cantoria or Singing Gallery (completed 1438) for Florence cathedral, was commissioned. This series of ten marble relief panels displays the purity and sweetness characteristic of all Luca's works. Other marble sculptures include reliefs of arts and sciences for campanile of cathedral (1437–39) and reliefs for altar of St. Peter in cathedral (1439). Also collaborated with Michelozzo on bronze doors of north sacristy of cathedral (1446–69). He is best known, however, for figures and reliefs in polychrome terra-cotta glazed like faience, a technique (begun with white reliefs on blue ground) that he perfected and applied for first time to monumental sculpture. Best-known works in this medium include *Resurrection* (1442–45) and *Ascension* (1446–51) above portals of cathedral. He also decorated numerous altars and ceilings, and assisted by his pupils produced many Madonnas, tympanum groups, and medallions. He founded large workshop for production of glazed terra-cotta pieces known as Della Robbia ware. He was succeeded as director by nephew ANDREA DELLA ROBBIA (1435–1525), who is also noted for the ten Foundling Children on Brunelleschi's loggia of Ospedale degli Innocenti, Florence (1463–66). Andrea's sons Giovanni Della Robbia (c.1469–1529) and Girolamo Della Robbia (1488–1566) collaborated with him and enlarged the workshop production.

REFERENCES: Maud Cruttwell *Luca and Andrea della Robbia and Their Successors* (London and New York 1902). Allan Marquand *Luca della Robbia* (Princeton, N.J. 1914).

ROBINSON, Edwin Arlington (Dec. 22, 1869 – Apr. 6, 1935). American poet. Born Head Tide, Me., brought up in Gardiner, Me. Attended Harvard (1891–93) as a special student, and lived most of his mature life in New York. His first book of poems, *The Torrent and the Night Before* (1896) was privately published. His next works, *The Children of the Night* (1897) and *Captain Craig* (1902), impressed Theodore Roosevelt, who procured for him a post as clerk at the New York Custom House (1905–10). Robinson then (1911) began to devote summers to writing poetry at the MacDowell Colony, Peterborough, N.H. Won recognition with narrative poem *The Man Against the Sky* (1916), and began Arthurian trilogy with *Merlin* (1917). *Tristram* (1927) won the Pulitzer prize, as did *Collected Poems* (1921) and *The Man Who Died Twice* (1924). Robinson also received numerous honorary degrees, poetry prizes, the gold medal of the National Institute of Arts and Letters (1929). Died in New York. Other works include *The Town Down the River* (1910), *Lancelot* (1920), *The Three Taverns* (1920), *Avon's Harvest* (1921), *Dionysus in Doubt* (1925), *Sonnets, 1889–1927* (1928), *Amaranth* (1934), and *King Jasper* (1935).

EDITION: *Collected Poems* (1937, reprinted New York 1966).

REFERENCES: Wallace L. Anderson *Edwin Arlington Robinson: A Critical Introduction* (Boston 1967, also PB). Ellsworth Barnard *Edwin Arlington Robinson: A Critical Study* (1952, reprinted New York 1969). Louis O. Coxe *Edwin Arlington Robinson: The Life of Poetry* (New York 1969, also PB). Edwin S. Fussell *Edwin Arlington Robinson* (Berkeley, Calif. 1954 and Cambridge, England, 1955). Hermann Hagedorn *Edwin Arlington Robinson: A Biography* (New York 1938). Lloyd R. Morris *The Poetry of Edwin Arlington Robinson* (1923, reprinted New York 1969). Emery Neff *Edwin Arlington Robinson* (1948, reprinted New York 1968). Chard P. Smith *Where the Light Falls: A Portrait of Edwin Arlington Robinson* (New York 1965). Yvor Winters *Edwin Arlington Robinson* (Norfolk, Conn. 1946).

EDWIN ARLINGTON ROBINSON
BY J. V. CUNNINGHAM

Robinson was a man almost without biography who became a legend to his friends. He was decent, reticent, likable, and contrary — he himself called it selfish. He was not going to work for a living. He would do nothing but write poetry, except at times prose fiction or drama for their economic potentialities. But in this he failed; prose was not his language. And unsuccessful prose he ultimately transmuted to poetry. The prose sketch of 1894, "in a lighter vein," "of a philosophic tramp . . . looking for rest" becomes in a few years *Captain Craig.*

To think of oneself as a poet has serious consequences, even if one's dignity precludes the Dionysiac role of a Hart Crane. The professed poet must keep writing, "scrivening to the end against his fate," for it is the justification of his life. So he wrote too much, and when written out he could not swear off. Again, the role is jealous of all other roles. Without an independent income and a secure place in society, loneliness, dispossession, chronic indigence follow. Finally, the role is vatic; the poet must intuit and communicate a meaning in the universe. So he kept asking the inadmissible question, What is it all about? — especially considering the pain. That it was unanswerable he thought guaranteed the question. He spoke again and again of the Light, which was now the Grail, now a woman, now "The light behind the stars," and always something that blurs "man's finite vision with misty glimmerings of the infinite." He believed in love and in belief with "a kind of optimistic desperation."

Tobacco, alcohol, and Wagner were his passions and his stay. The first he occasionally, but never seriously, gave up. The second, apparently under the persuasion of friends, he did for long periods, which is remarkable, for he drank whiskey straight by the tumblerful. The last he never wearied of.

At twelve or thirteen he came under the influence of a local osteopath who had forsaken all else to write sonnets and the French forms. Now, metrical speech is a language which, like all languages, must be learned young or never. And as a language it must have an audience; this the doctor and a cultivated local poetic circle provided, so that in his later career he never faltered in meter, and at his most involved and obscure is still speaking to an audience.

At twenty-one, after three years of helping around the home place and doggedly writing, he entered Harvard College, "the object of almost the only patriotism I possess," as a special student. It was the making of the poet; for there is an educated ease with ideas and experience and a breadth that is denied to the self-tutored. It is interesting that later in the decade Frost and Stevens were also special students at Harvard.

After two years he returned home, the family dead, dying, or physical and spiritual wrecks. Four years later, at twenty-seven, he left home, finally settling in New York. The dissipation of the family fortune — he had tacitly expected to live on a modest patrimony — and a stubborn worldly incompetence reduced him at the age of thirty to absolute poverty, a life of cadging, and ten months' employment as a timekeeper on a construction job. The job finished, he was supported until his fiftieth year by public and private patronage: by a sinecure at the New York Custom House arranged by President Theodore Roosevelt, by the contributions of his friends, ultimately made systematic, and by summer residence at the MacDowell Colony. At fifty-one, when the

Collected Poems was awarded the first of his three Pulitzer prizes, he could finally live on what his poetry made, and with the extraordinary success of *Tristram* in 1927 he was able to repay many of his debts and remain financially secure. Thereafter he wrote long poems, one a year until his death, which were bought primarily by public libraries and gave him a steady income. The principal other event of these years was the First World War and the destruction of the world he had known, which he translated into the Arthurian legend, "And there was darkness over Camelot."

He lived during his mature life among the moderately wealthy and cultured and with the outcast and miscast. He belonged to the former by breeding, to the latter by experience, imagination, and compassion. And he wrote of both. Yet little that he wrote was a direct transcription of experience. He had a life of fantasy in which Tilbury Town was and was not Gardiner, Maine, and those who come no more to Calverly's had their own existence, transpositions or opposites of himself and his friends. Though celibate he wrote with insight and some tedium of sexual passion. And he knew we do not really know about others; we do not know about him.

Toward the end of his life he concluded: "As lives go, my own life would be called, and properly, a rather fortunate one." Most commentators have not thought so, but it seems true. He died of cancer at sixty-five.

Though he wrote too much, he wrote much that was distinctive and good, and even in the dull wastes there are fragments. He commanded from the beginning the full range of late Victorian styles, from the flat naturalistic prose line (and his own special roundabout pentameter), through incanta-

tory jingle and the tightly rhymed stanzas of the light verse tradition, to the full diapason of romantic rhetoric:

> *Something of ships and sunlight,*
> * streets and singing,*
> *Troy falling, and the ages com-*
> * ing back,*
> *And ages coming forward.*

He had a gift for simile:

> *The stillness of October gold*
> *Went out like beauty from a*
> * face,*

and especially for the abstract simile: the recurrent cadger

> *Familiar as an old mistake,*
> *And futile as regret.*

He could secure the commonplace with the right epithet:

> *At someone's tinkling afternoon*
> * at home.*

He could manage unobtrusive profundity:

> *Love builds of what Time takes*
> * away,*
> *Till Death itself is less than*
> * Change.*

and mark the quiet defeat of life:

> *. . . nor was there anything*
> *To make a daily meaning for*
> * her life . . .*
> *But the blank taste of time.*

ROCHESTER, John Wilmot, second earl of (Apr. 10, 1647 – July 26, 1680). English poet. Born near Woodstock, Oxfordshire; his father, Henry Wilmot, first earl, was a close associate of Charles II during civil wars. Upon father's death (1658) succeeded to title. A precocious child, he entered Wadham College, Oxford, at thirteen (M.A. 1661). After traveling to France and Italy, he returned to court (1664), became a favorite of the king's. Notorious for leading dissolute life, frequently banished from court for his escapades but always recalled for his charm, he was imprisoned (1665) for abducting heiress Elizabeth Malet, whom he married (1667). Fathered four children by his wife and one by a mistress, Elizabeth Barry, whom he trained as an actress. Served with distinction as naval volunteer in attack on Dutch ships, Bergen (1665). A gentleman of the king's bedchamber (1667), he was appointed keeper of Woodstock Park, Oxfordshire (1675), where he remained until his death. Before a later feud, John Dryden dedicated *Marriage à la Mode* to him (1673); George Etherege made him the model for his *Man of Mode* (1676). His health ruined by debauchery, he died after a religious conversion (June 29, 1680), when he sent for Bishop Gilbert Burnet and repented his misspent life. Among the Restoration wits Rochester stands out as a considerable poet and gifted satirist. His works include lyrical love poems; a posthumous play, *Valentinian;* and numerous satires, among which are his denunciation of rationalism, *A Satyr Against Mankind,* and his *History of Insipids,* an attack on the government of Charles II.

EDITIONS: *The Collected Works of John Wilmot, Earl of Rochester* ed. John Hayward (London 1926). *The Complete Poems of John Wilmot, Earl of Rochester* ed. David M. Veith (New Haven, Conn. 1968). *Poems* ed. Vivian de Sola Pinto (London and Cambridge, Mass. 1953, PB 1964). REFERENCES: Gilbert Burnet *Some Passages of the Life and Death of John Wilmot, Earl of Rochester* (1680, reprinted Hildesheim, Germany, 1968). Samuel Johnson *Lives of the Poets* (London 1779–81). Charles Norman *Rake Rochester* (New York and London 1954). Vivian de Sola Pinto *Enthusiast in Wit: A Portrait of John Wilmot, Earl of Rochester, 1647–80* (London and Lincoln, Nebr. 1962). Johannes Prinz *John Wilmot, Earl of Rochester: His*

Life and Writings (Leipzig 1927, reprinted New York). David M. Veith *Attribution in Restoration Poetry* (New Haven, Conn. 1963).

RODIN, Auguste (Nov. 12, 1840 – Nov. 17, 1917). French sculptor. Born Paris; of humble family. Educated at École Impériale, he decided at twenty to become a sculptor. Lived (from 1864) with Rose Beuret, who bore him a child; he married her in 1917, the year of his death. Entered studio of sculptor Albert Ernest Carrier-Belleuse, a lasting influence. Went to Italy (1875); inspired by Michelangelo's work to execute the male nude *The Age of Bronze* (1876, the cast in Tate Gallery, London; the bronze in Luxembourg Gardens, Paris), which created a furore at the 1877 Salon. Extended his range (1879) by producing ceramics and engravings. The 1880's and 1890's were his most productive and creative years. Among his famous works: *John the Baptist* (1880), the great group *The Burghers of Calais* (1884–86, Calais), *The Kiss* (1886, Tate Gallery, London), *The Thinker* (1888, Rodin Museum, Paris), *The Hand of God* (1904, Tate Gallery, London), monuments to Victor Hugo and Balzac, and the unfinished bronze doors called *The Gate of Hell,* inspired by Dante's *Inferno.* By 1900 his fame was immense; he was showered with honors, and commissions for sculpture portraits came from numerous great figures, including Georges Clemenceau and G. B. Shaw. Rodin's conception of sculpture was to render an idea in bronze or marble; he used the whole range of human emotion from brooding concentration to erotic passion to do so. Originals and copies of his work are in the Musée Rodin, Paris. He died at Meudon. REFERENCES: Bernard Champigneulle *Rodin* (tr. London and New York 1967). Robert Descharnes and J. F. Chabrun *Auguste Rodin* (tr. New York and London 1967). E. C. Geissbuhler *Rodin: Later Drawings* (Boston 1963). Rainer Maria Rilke *Auguste Rodin* (tr. New York and London 1945). Sommerville Story *Rodin* (London and New York 1939). Yvon Taillandier *Rodin* (tr. New York 1967).

ROETHKE, Theodore (May 25, 1908 –
Aug. 1, 1963). American poet. Born
Saginaw, Mich.; family of German
origin. Childhood memories of large
greenhouse owned there by his father
and uncle later inspired numerous
poems, including *Transplanting* and
Child on Top of a Greenhouse. Educated at local schools, University of
Michigan (1925–30), and Harvard
(1930–31); his work was first published
while he was at Harvard. Dropped out
of graduate school because of financial
difficulties and took teaching post at
Lafayette College (1931–35). Next
taught at Michigan State (1935–36),
where he suffered first nervous breakdown; continued to write and teach
despite intermittent recurrences during
rest of life. Taught at Pennsylvania
State (1936–43), where he published
well-received first book *Open House*
(1941), and at Bennington (1943–
46). Awarded Guggenheim fellowship
(1945), he spent year in Saginaw
writing *The Lost Son and Other Poems*
(published 1948), which established
his reputation as a leading poet. Moved
to University of Washington (1947).
Married Beatrice O'Connell (1953) and
lived in Italy briefly thereafter. Received two *Poetry* prizes (1947, 1951),
and the Pulitzer prize (1954) for *The
Waking*. Other works: *Praise to the
End!* (1951), *Words for the Wind*
(1957), *I Am, Says the Lamb* (1961),
The Far Field (1964), *Collected Verse*
(1965). Died from coronary occlusion
in Bainbridge, Washington.

REFERENCES: Karl Malkoff *Theodore
Roethke: An Introduction to the Poetry*
(New York 1966). Ralph J. Mills, Jr.
Theodore Roethke (Minneapolis PB
1963) and ed. *On the Poet and His
Craft* (Seattle 1965, also PB) and
Selected Letters of Theodore Roethke
(Seattle 1968). Allan Seager *The Glass
House: The Life of Theodore Roethke*
(New York 1968). Arnold Stein ed.
Theodore Roethke: Essays on the Poetry
(Seattle 1965, also PB).

☞

THEODORE ROETHKE
BY STANLEY KUNITZ

The poet of my generation who meant
most to me, in his person and in his
art, was Theodore Roethke. To say, in
fact, "poet of my generation" is to
name him. Immediately after Frost and
Eliot and Pound and Cummings and
Hart Crane and Stevens and William
Carlos Williams, it was difficult to be
taken seriously as a new American
poet; for the title to "the new poetry"
was in the possession of a dynasty of
extraordinary gifts and powers, not the
least of which was its stubborn capacity for survival. When Roethke was a
schoolboy in Michigan in the Twenties,
these poets had already "arrived." For
a long time, in the general view, they
remained the rebels and inventors.

Roethke took his own work seriously
indeed. Lashed by his competitive and
compulsive temper, he committed himself fully to the exhausting struggle for
recognition — a desperately intimate
struggle that left its mark on him.
Only a few years before his death, he
could refer to himself sardonically as
"the oldest younger poet in the U.S.A."

More than a third of a century has
passed since he blew into my life like
the "big wind" of one of his poems. I
was living in the Delaware Valley then.
He came, unannounced, downriver
from Lafayette College, where he was
instructor in English and — more satis-
fying to his pride — tennis coach. My
recollection is of a traditionally battered jalopy from which a perfectly
tremendous raccoon coat emerged, with
my first book of poems tucked under
its left paw. The introductory mumble
that followed could be construed as a
compliment. Then he stood, embar-
rassed and inarticulate, in my doorway,
waiting to gauge the extent of my
hospitality. The image that never left
me was of a blond, smooth, shambling
giant, irrevocably Teutonic, with a cold
pudding of a face, somehow contradicted by the sullen downturn of the
mouth and the pale furious eyes: a

countenance ready to be touched by time, waiting to be transfigured, with a few subtle lines, into a tragic mask.

Our evenings in the years that followed seemed to move inexorably towards a moment of trial for both of us when he would fumble for the crinkled manuscript in his pocket and present it for approval. During the reading of his poem he stiffened in an attitude of excruciating tension and suspicion. Roethke was not easy on his friends, but neither was he easy on himself. In the proper season, when conversation became dangerous, we would fight it out on the courts for what we liked to boast, with a bow to Joyce, was the lawn tennyson championship of the poetic world. For all his six-foot-three, two-hundred-plus-pound bulk and his lumbering gait, he was amazingly nimble on his feet and ruthless at the kill, with a smashing service and a thunderous forehand drive. The daemon in him played the game just as it wrote the poems. Whatever he did was an aspect of the same insatiable will to conquer self and art and others. He could not bear to lose. If you managed to beat him by cunning and luck, you could not expect to be congratulated by him: he was more likely to smash his racket across his knees. After the steady deterioration of his body had forced him to abandon the game — his knees in particular gave out — he retreated into croquet and badminton, which he played with the same rapture and *Schrecklichkeit*.

As a young man he felt humiliated and disgraced by the periodic mental breakdowns that were to afflict him all his life. There were outbreaks and absences and silences that he had to cover up, partly because he realized what a threat they offered to his survival in the academic world. He was one of the supreme teachers of poetry,

but not until he came — after Bennington — to the University of Washington in 1947 did he have any assurance of tenure.

By the time of his arrival in Seattle, Roethke had found the means of transforming his ordeal into language. Eventually, he more than half believed that the springs of his disorder, his manic-depressive cycles, were inseparable from the sources of his art, and he could brag of belonging to the brotherhood of mad poets that includes William Blake, John Clare, and Christopher Smart, with each of whom he was able to identify himself as "lost." His affection for Dylan Thomas had much the same base; but on the other hand, some of his longest friendships, including those with Louise Bogan and W. H. Auden, signified his unswerving admiration for those who stood in his mind as representatives of a sacred discipline.

When *The Lost Son* — the book of his that I continue to think of as the great one — was published in 1948, I wrote of it in *Poetry*: "The ferocity of Roethke's imagination makes most contemporary poetry seem pale and tepid in contrast. Even the wit is murderous. . . . What Roethke brings us is news of the root, of the minimal, of the primordial. The subhuman is given tongue, and the tongue proclaims the agony of coming alive, the painful miracle of growth." One of Roethke's remarkable powers is that of the compassionate flow of self into the things of his experience. His poems become what they love.

> I study the lives on a leaf: the
> little
> Sleepers, numb nudgers in cold
> dimensions,
> Beetles in caves, newts, stone-
> deaf fishes,

Lice tethered to long limp sub-
terranean weeds,
Squirmers in bogs,
And bacterial creepers . . .

He is our poet of transformations, and his imagination is populated with shapeshifters who are aspects of his own being, driven to know itself and yet appalled by the terrible necessity of self-knowledge. The life in his poems emerges out of stones and swamps, tries on leaves and wings, struggles towards the divine. "Brooding on God," he wrote towards the end, "I may become a man." He could turn even his stammerings into art.

No other modern poet seems so directly tuned to the natural universe: his disturbance was in being human. The soul trapped in his ursine frame gathered to itself a host of "lovely diminutives." This florist's son never really departed from the moist, fecund world of his father's greenhouse in Saginaw.

When I asked him, in 1953, for an autobiographical statement, he wrote, in part: "I have tried to transmute and purify my 'life,' the sense of being defiled by it, in both small and formal and somewhat blunt short poems, and, latterly, in longer poems which try in their rhythms to catch the very movement of the mind itself, to trace the spiritual history of a protagonist (not 'I,' personally), of all haunted and harried men; to make in this series . . . a true and not arbitrary order which will permit many ranges of feeling, including humor."

He found it possible, increasingly, to incorporate a wild sort of laughter into his flights. "I count myself among the happy poets," he would say, knowing that the laughter and the fierceness and the terror were indivisible. In "this matter of making noise that rhymes"

— his phrase — he dared to seek a combination of vulgarity and nobility, and he put his stamp on the mixture.

In the spring of 1960, Roethke gave his last reading in New York at the Poetry Center, where I introduced him. He had a high fever, and backstage he was jittery, sweating copiously as he guzzled champagne — "bubbly," he called it. On stage, for the first portion of his program he clowned and hammed incorrigibly, weaving, gyrating, dancing, shrugging his shoulders, muttering to himself intermittently, and now and then making curiously flipper-like or foetal gestures with his hands. But gradually, as the evening wore on, he settled into a straight dramatic style that was enormously effective and moving. When he came to his new "mad" sequence, headed by the poem that begins, "In a dark time the eye begins to see," his voice rang out with such an overwhelming roll of noble anguish that many in the audience wept.

As we filed out of the hall, a friend remarked on Roethke's strange affinity to that other lost and violent spirit, Jackson Pollock. "How true!" I thought. And I heard myself repeating a rather enigmatic phrase that I had picked up from the painter Franz Kline when he was reminiscing once about his late companion: "He divined himself."

ROLFE, Frederick William (known as **Baron Corvo**) (July 22, 1860 – Oct. 26, 1913). English writer. Born London, son of a piano manufacturer. Left school at fifteen, was converted to Roman Catholicism (1886), but failed repeatedly to enter priesthood. Took up painting, tutoring, photography, and writing. Published *In His Own Image* (1901) containing legends of saints, six of which had appeared in the *Yellow Book* (1898) under the title *Stories Toto Told Me. Chronicles of the House of Borgia* (1901) was followed by his famous romanticized autobiography *Hadrian the Seventh* (1904), in which the hero is a rejected would-be priest who becomes pope. Brilliant and eccentric, it is full of witty malicious studies of those whom Rolfe hated. He spent his last disreputable, debt-ridden years in Venice, where he died. His friends and enemies of those years are portrayed in a posthumous novel, *The Desire and Pursuit of the Whole* (1934).

REFERENCES: A. J. A. Symons *The Quest for Corvo* (1934, new ed. London and East Lansing, Mich. 1955, also PB). Cecil Woolf and Brocard Sewell *New Quests for Corvo: A Collection of Essays by Various Hands* (Chester Springs, Pa. 1961, also PB).

ROMNEY, George (Dec. 15, 1734 – Nov. 15, 1802). English painter. Born Dalton-in-Furness, Lancashire, son of a cabinetmaker. Married Mary Abbott (1756). Apprenticed to painter Christopher Steele (1755–57), then established himself in Kendal, Westmorland. Moved to London (1762), and won a Royal Society of Arts prize for his *Death of Wolfe* (1763). Became a popular and fashionable portrait painter, ultimately (except for Reynolds) the most sought-after portraitist in England. Studied in Italy (1773–75). Met the future Lady Hamilton (Emma Hart) (1782), and painted her over fifty times in character roles such as *Lady Hamilton as a Bacchante* (c.1783, Mrs. Tankerville Chamberlayne Collection). In addition to graceful portraits, he executed thousands of sketches reminiscent of Fuseli and Blake. After 1799, poor health forced him to return to Kendal, where he died. *Mr. and Mrs. William Lindow* (1772, Tate Gallery, London) and *Mrs. Robinson* (1781, Wallace Collection, London) are characteristic of his charming style.

REFERENCES: Arthur B. Chamberlain *George Romney* (New York and London 1910). John Romney *Memoirs of the Life and Works of George Romney* (London 1830). T. H. Ward and W. Roberts *Romney* (2 vols. London and New York 1904).

RONSARD, Pierre de (Sept. 11, 1524 – Dec. 27, 1585). French poet. Born Château de la Poissonière (near Ven-

dôme). Served (1536) as page at French court, then to Scottish king James V (1538–40). Career at court and on missions abroad to Germany, Flanders, and elsewhere ended by his deafness. Took up scholarly life at humanist Collège de Coqueret (1544–50), where he became chief of group of young poets known as La Pléiade. They eschewed medieval tradition for classical models. Ronsard published his *Odes*, of Horatian and Pindaric inspiration (1550), followed by *Amours de Cassandre* (1552) in Petrarchan mode, the less formal *Amours de Marie* (1555) in alexandrine verse, and the philosophical *Hymnes* (1555–56), which won him the title of *poète-philosophe*. Named court poet to Charles IX (1560–74), engaged in religious and political polemics, such as *Discours sur les misères de ce temps* (1560), and published unfinished national epic, *La Franciade* (1574). Best known are the lovely lyrical *Sonnets pour Hélène* (1578), which include "*Quand vous serez bien vieille, au soir à la chandelle . . .*" Died at his priory, St. Cosme. His erudition, lofty poetic ideal, and lyrical gifts exerted strong influence in England among Elizabethans.

TRANSLATIONS: *Selected Poems* tr. Charles Graves (Edinburgh 1924). *Songs and Sonnets of Pierre de Ronsard* tr. Curtis Hidden Page (2nd ed. Boston 1924). *Sonnets pour Hélène* tr. Humbert Wolfe (London and New York 1934). *Lyrics of Pierre de Ronsard, Vandomois* tr. Charles Graves (Edinburgh 1967).

REFERENCES: Elizabeth Armstrong *Ronsard and the Age of Gold* (Cambridge, England, 1968). Morris Bishop *Ronsard, Prince of Poets* (London and New York 1940, PB 1959). Gustave Cohen *Ronsard, sa vie et son oeuvre* (1924, new ed. Paris 1956). D. B. Wyndham Lewis *Ronsard* (London and New York 1944). Marcel Raymond *L'Influence de Ronsard sur la poésie française, 1550–85* (1927, new ed. Geneva 1965). Donald Stone, Jr. *Ronsard's Sonnet Cycles: A Study in Tone and Vision* (New Haven, Conn. 1966).

ROSA, Salvator (July 1615 – Mar. 15, 1673). Italian artist and poet. Born Naples, into family of painters. Studied with uncle, Domenico Greco, and with Aniello Falcone. Went to Rome (1635) and established reputation with *Prometheus* (Corsini Palace, Rome). Wrote (1639) satire on Bernini which so antagonized him that Rosa left for Medici court in Florence. Here he met Lucrezia Paolina, whom he married (1673). Returned to Rome (1649) and began painting battle scenes and landscapes such as *The Philosopher's Grove* (Pitti Palace, Florence), *Landscape with Figures*, and *Mercury and the Dishonest Woodsman* (both National Gallery, London). Later turned to allegories and historical subjects such as the macabre *L'Umana Fragilità* (c.1657, Fitzwilliam Museum, Cambridge, England) and *Temptation of St. Anthony* (Pitti). His reputation rests, however, on his wild romantic landscapes, desolate and storm-rent, peopled with witches or bandits or soldiers. These influenced many English painters. After 1660 Rosa became an engraver of great originality. Famous also for his satirical poems. He died in Rome.

REFERENCES: Rudolf Wittkower *Art and Architecture in Italy, 1600–1750* (Harmondsworth, England, 1958). Ottilie G. Boetzkes *Salvator Rosa* (New York 1960).

ROSENBERG, Isaac (Nov. 25, 1890 – Apr. 19, 1918). English poet and artist. Born Bristol; moved to London at early age. Educated at board schools in Stepney in East End. Apprenticed at fourteen to Carl Hentschel, an engraving firm; further trained in engraving at Slade School (1911–14), where he won several prizes. He also had a painting exhibition at Whitechapel Gallery. Began writing poetry and privately printed *Night and Day* (1912); first published poem appeared in *Georgian Poetry* (1916–17), followed by *Moses: A Play* (1916). Returning from a visit to his sister in South Africa, where he went for his health, Rosenberg enlisted in World War I, and was killed in action. His military experience inspired most of his best-known poetry, appearing in *Youth* (1918) and *Poems* (1922). Siegfried Sassoon describes him as "a poet of movement. Words which express movement are often used by him

and are essential to his natural utterance." The same energy is found in his imagery, and use of light and shade to convey expression.

EDITIONS: *Collected Works* (London 1937) and *Collected Poems* with foreword by Siegfried Sassoon (New York and London 1949), both edited by Gordon Bottomley and Denys Harding.
REFERENCE: Denys Harding *Experience into Words* (London 1963 and New York 1964).

ROSSETTI, Christina Georgina (Dec. 5, 1830 – Dec. 29, 1894). English poet. Born and died in London, daughter of Gabriele Rossetti, Italian poet and political exile, and sister of Pre-Raphaelite poet and painter Dante Gabriel Rossetti. A devout High Anglican, she refused marriage to painter James Collinson (1850) and later to translator Charles Cayley (1861) on religious grounds. Published seven poems in Pre-Raphaelite journal *The Germ* (1850). Her first two collections, *Goblin Market and Other Poems* (1862) and *The Prince's Progress and Other Poems* (1866), established her reputation at home and abroad. *Commonplace and Other Short Stories* followed (1870). Serious attack of Graves' disease (1870–72) permanently impaired her health. From 1876 she lived in retirement, but continued to publish, chiefly devotional prose: *Annus Domini* (1874), *Seek and Find* (1879), *Time Flies*, containing both verse and prose (1885), and *The Face of the Deep* (1892). Other major works: *Sing-Song: A Nursery Rhyme Book* (1872, enlarged 1893) for children, *A Pageant and Other Poems* (1881), containing the fine sonnet sequence *Monna Innominata*. Her poetry, characterized by unusual lyricism, sensuous imagery and visualization, as well as technical skill, has earned her recognition as one of the outstanding Victorian poets.

EDITIONS: *Poetical Works of Christina Rossetti with Memoirs and Notes* (London and New York 1904) and *The Family Letters of Christina Georgina Rossetti* (1908, reprinted New York 1968), both edited by William M. Rossetti.

REFERENCES: Georgina Battiscombe *Christina Rossetti* (London 1965, also PB). Mackenzie Bell *Christina Rossetti: A Biographical and Critical Study* (London and Boston 1898). Margaret Sawtell *Christina Rossetti: Her Life and Religion* (London 1955). Eleanor W. Thomas *Christina Georgina Rossetti* (New York 1931). Marya Zaturenska *Christina Rossetti: A Portrait with Background* (New York 1949).

ROSSETTI, Dante Gabriel (May 12, 1828 – Apr. 10, 1882). English poet and painter. Born London, son of exiled Italian patriot and poet Gabriele Rossetti (professor of Italian at King's College, London) and brother of poet Christina Rossetti. Studied at King's College School, but left at fourteen to study art, eventually attending classes at the Royal Academy (1846). After a brief apprenticeship to painter Ford Madox Brown, he set up his own studio, and with friends Holman Hunt and John Millais organized the Pre-Raphaelite Brotherhood, which for inspiration looked to the Italian painters before Raphael. Subject matter and style combined romantic mysticism with meticulous detail. Rossetti also began to write poetry, much of which, including his best-known work, *The Blessed Damozel* (1847), appeared in the Pre-Raphaelite publication *The Germ* (1850). Became engaged (1851) to his model Elizabeth Siddal, but did not marry her until 1860, by which time she already suffered from tuberculosis. His translations from the Italian, *Dante and His Circle*, appeared (1861). His wife's death (1862) so affected him that he buried with her a sheaf of unpublished poems, which he was later persuaded to have exhumed (1869) and published in the famous *The House of Life* (1870), the work that established his reputation. Though increasingly successful in painting and poetry, he became addicted to chloral and suffered moods of depression and paranoia. *Ballads and Sonnets*, containing *The White Ship* and *The King's Tragedy*, appeared (1881), but drug addiction caused severe deterioration, and in late 1881 he made a heroic effort to give up chloral. Four months later, recuperating at Birchington, he died and was buried there.

EDITIONS: *Collected Works* ed. William M. Rossetti (1897, reprinted 2 vols. St. Clair Shores, Mich. 1969). *Letters* ed. Oswald Doughty and R. Wahl (4 vols. Oxford 1965–).
REFERENCES: Helen Rossetti Angeli *Dante Gabriel Rossetti: His Friends and Enemies* (London 1949). Arthur C. Benson *Rossetti* (London and New York 1904). Hall Caine *Recollections of Dante Gabriel Rossetti* (1882, new ed. London 1928). Oswald Doughty *A Victorian Romantic: Dante Gabriel Rossetti* (2nd ed. London and New York 1960). R. Glynn Grylls *Portrait of Rossetti* (London 1965). Kerrison Preston *Blake and Rossetti* (London 1944). William M. Rossetti *Dante Gabriel Rossetti as Designer and Writer* (London and New York 1889). Evelyn Waugh *Rossetti: His Life and Works* (2nd ed. London 1931).

ROSSINI, Gioacchino Antonio (Feb. 29, 1792 – Nov. 13, 1868). Italian composer. Born Pesaro, child of two musicians. Studied under various masters at Bologna, where a cantata of his won a prize and was publicly performed (1808). Produced in Venice (1810) his first opera, *La Cambiale di matrimonio;* at twenty-one he had written eleven more for theatres in Venice, Milan, Bologna, and Ferrara, and became the leading Italian operatic composer. From 1815 to 1823 he wrote for Domenico Barbaja, impresario for theatres in Naples, Milan, and Vienna, whose mistress, Spanish soprano Isabella Colbran, Rossini married (1822). From this period came *Il Barbiere di Siviglia* (*The Barber of Seville*, 1816), based on the play by Beaumarchais, probably his best-known work; *Otello* (1816); *La Gazza ladra* (*The Thieving Magpie*, 1817); *La Cenerentola* (*Cinderella*, 1817); *Semiramide* (1823–24), and others. After a tumultuously successful season in London (1823), he was appointed musical director of the Théâtre Italien in Paris (1824). After his masterpiece, *Guillaume Tell* (1829), he ceased to write opera, composing in remaining years of his life only a *Stabat Mater* (1832, completed 1847), the *Petite*

Messe solennelle (1864), and many songs and instrumental pieces. After first wife's death (1845), married Olympe Pélissier (1847). Lived in Italy (1836–55), then returned to Paris, living in a city apartment and a Passy villa which until his death were gathering places of the international artistic world. He died at Passy.

REFERENCES: Henri Beyle (Stendhal) *Life of Rossini* (1824, tr. London 1956 and New York 1957). Francis Toye *Rossini: A Study in Tragi-Comedy* (1934, new ed. New York 1947, PB 1963). Herbert Weinstock *Rossini: A Biography* (New York 1968).

&

ROSSINI
BY HERBERT WEINSTOCK

In 1860, Giuseppina Strepponi Verdi drafted in a letter copybook a reply to someone who had sent Rossini's love to her and Verdi. "Does Rossini really love us?" she wrote. "He is the eternal father of composers, past and present, but we had thought that the verb 'to love' did not exist in his dictionary." Strepponi was reacting not so much to the sixty-eight-year-old composer himself as to his reputation for cynicism and the royal-paternal attitudes to which retirement in an enduring aura of fame had brought him. Half a century earlier, Rossini had burst into the congealing world of eighteenth-century *opera seria* in command of an unexampled mixture of qualities: a heady combination of *joie de vivre* and lack of illusions; a command of rhythms revealingly brought to bear upon literary text and musical tempo; a gift for near melody that he could open out at will into full melody; the ability to make telling dramatic use of the orchestra as it expanded. He knew what was to be known about operatic singing in an era that had inherited surpassing techniques from unsurpassed teachers, the last *castrati*. He was not artistically polite, exuded energy that would not brook protocol and catatonic formalities, being too eager for audience-pleasing results to stop for propriety of means. Composing operas had been his métier: no Beethovian daemon had prodded him to world-capping summits.

Rossini had been born during the last decade of the eighteenth century, less than three months after the death of Mozart, before Schubert's birth, while Haydn and Cimarosa continued to create in Vienna (*Il Matrimonio segreto* had been heard for the first time on February 8, 1792; Rossini was born exactly three weeks later). Beethoven was about to go to Vienna from Bonn; Paisiello, who completed the Italian opera of the late eighteenth century, still was delighting Naples.

In 1810, aged eighteen, Rossini composed *La Cambiale di matrimonio*, which announced a new operatic order. Nineteen years and almost forty operas later, he closed his operatic career with *Guillaume Tell*, which went far toward establishing "grand opera," the special contribution of Paris to operatic romanticism. Although Rossini stayed mostly Italian and an eighteenth-century artisan, *Guillaume Tell* — following a year after Auber's *La Muette de Portici* — demonstrated the nineteenth century's operatic coming of age. It also made clear that another new dispensation would neglect many of the means by which Rossini had triumphed. Then it was that he gladly allowed reasons of health and disposition to decide his retirement from theatrical combat. (By then, however, because Italy was increasingly being left to one side of the main stream of operatic evolution, two other Italians of abounding talent — Gaetano Donizetti and Vincenzo Bellini — were able to perpetuate many of the peculiarly Italian, specifically Rossinian aspects of the styles that he had evolved.)

Rossini went on living for nearly forty years after *Guillaume Tell* — he was to discuss the theories of the *Gesamtkunstwerk* with Richard Wagner and Eduard Hanslick — but he had the talent to recognize that he and his operas had become the honored past. Posterity found it hard to forgive Rossini for that "great renunciation," for having composed between the ages of thirty-seven and seventy-six only the *Stabat Mater,* the *Petite Messe solennelle,* and a library-full of bonbons including the *Péchés de vieillesse.* Almost as though seeking revenge, until recently posterity seemed to have chosen to neglect his operas on serious and tragic texts, to perform only his swift *opere buffe,* and at times only the best of them, *Il Barbiere di Siviglia.*

By the time of his last opera, Rossini believed that the art of singing was moribund, if not dead. And so it was, if by "singing" we understand those difficult, delicate, hard-won techniques which the vanishing *castrati* had taught to others. New ways of singing would be demanded and produced, to be sure, for proper performance of *Tell* itself, of Meyerbeer, Wagner, Verdi, Puccini, and Richard Strauss. But Rossini, as usual, had been right: those techniques are useless for the operatic music that he had developed out of Pergolesi, Cimarosa, and Paisiello and had made available for other uses by Donizetti and Bellini. In our century, however, the emergence of such singers as Conchita Supervia, Giulietta Simionato, Maria Callas, Marilyn Horne, Joan Sutherland, Teresa Berganza, Beverly Sills, Cesare Valletti, and Alfredo Kraus has made it possible for many of the Rossini, Donizetti, and Bellini roles to be sung almost as conceived. Another transi-

tional shift in taste appears to be bringing the operas of the Italian first half of the nineteenth century back into the active repertoire.

In 1968, performances honoring the centenary of Rossini's death proved that today's opera-goers will respond with satisfaction when those documents of an intricate art come to life in avatars reasonably resembling their original selves. Out of the shadows cast by Verdi and Puccini are emerging, and being welcomed for the variety they bring to the pinguid "standard repertoire," not only such impolite Rossinian entertainments as *L'Italiana in Algeri, Il Turco in Italia, La Cenerentola,* and *Le Comte Ory,* but also reasonable simulacra (much too often lacking male bel canto singers to match the sopranos and the ladies of deeper voice) of *Mosè in Egitto, Otello, Semiramide, Guillaume Tell,* and their Donizettian and Bellinian successors.

Partially, that is, we are being enabled to hear what those operas were which held Italy, then Europe, then the world enthralled for decades. The processes of musicological inquiry, hopefully leading to accuracy in performance, are being applied to Rossini, Donizetti, and Bellini. And that practice is essential for the defalsification of operatic history (as well as for an undistorted picture of the origins of that huge master of another era, Giuseppe Verdi). We can only wonder if, and hope that, in this age of easier vocal success by less complex means adapted to other purposes, enough conductors, instrumentalists, and singers — particularly male singers — can be found willing to suffer the protracted, lonely training without which performance of the Italians of the first half of the nineteenth century always will disappoint, because without it we are offered misunderstood travesties of the originals. Upon the acquisition of those techniques, upon their informed and text-sensitive employment, depends the future of a whole operatic literature that brims with potential delights as it did more than a century ago.

ROSTAND, Edmond (Apr. 1, 1868 – Dec. 2, 1918). French dramatist and poet. Born Marseilles, son of a journalist. Attended Collège Stanislas, Paris, and prepared for law, but after publishing first collection of poems, *Les Musardises* (1890), devoted himself to writing. Also, that year, married the poet Rosemonde Gérard. His first play, *Les Romanesques* (1894, tr. *The Romances* 1899), produced at the Comédie Française, was a success; he continued writing romantic dramas, often tailoring them for specific leading actors. *La Princesse lointaine* (1895, tr. *The Faraway Princess* 1899) was written for Sarah Bernhardt, and his masterpiece *Cyrano de Bergerac* (1897, tr. 1923) for Benoît Constant Coquelin. It was widely translated and hailed as the last great popular historical romance. *L'Aiglon* (1900), based on the life of Napoleon's son the king of Rome, was also created for Bernhardt. Rostand received considerable fame and honors; was made commander of the Legion of Honor (1900) and member of Académie Française (1901). Failing in health, he built a villa in southern France, where he spent most of his remaining years. He died in Paris. Of his later plays *Chantecler* (1910), a barnyard fable, is most noteworthy. His son, Maurice Rostand, collaborated with his mother on two plays, *Un Bon Petit Diable* (produced as *A Good Little Devil*, New York, 1912) and *La Marchande d'allumettes* (1914).

TRANSLATION: *Plays of Edmond Rostand* tr. Henderson D. Norman (2 vols. New York 1921).
REFERENCES: Hobart Ryland *The Sources of the Play Cyrano de Bergerac* (New York PB 1936). Jean Suberville *Le Théâtre d'Edmond Rostand* (Paris 1919).

ROTHKO, Mark (real name Marcus Rothkovich) (Sept. 25, 1903 – Feb. 25, 1970). American painter. Born Dvinsk, Russia, son of a pharmacist. Family moved to Portland, Ore., when Rothko was ten. He aspired to be a labor leader, attended Yale (1921–23), then moved to New York. Inspired by visit to an art class, he decided to become a painter (1925). Studied with Max Weber at Art Students' League, painting realistic pictures and exhibiting with group (1929). Worked with WPA Federal Arts Project, New York (1936–37), and from 1945 painted abstracts, attracting attention of important critics and patrons. Of the abstract expressionist group, he pioneered in colorfield painting. Married Mary Alice Beistle (1945). In New York, held one-man shows (1945, 1946), and exhibited with celebrated show Abstract Painting and Sculpture in America (1951) at Museum of Modern Art, where he also held a retrospective exhibition (1961). Soft-edged rectangles floating in colored space characterize his art. Stanley Kunitz has described him "as a poet among the painters, a lyric imagination in the dominion of the abstract." The paintings (always unnamed) of the late 1950's, which will decorate a chapel in Houston, Tex., are dominated by black, brown, dark red, showing, as he said (1958), "a clear preoccupation with death." Rothko also taught, and was recipient of the Creative Arts Award, Brandeis University (1964) and an honorary degree from Yale (1969). He died by his own hand in New York City.

REFERENCES: Thomas B. Hess *Abstract Painting* (New York 1951). Andrew C. Ritchie *Abstract Painting and Sculpture in America* (New York PB 1951). Peter Selz *Mark Rothko* (Greenwich, Conn. PB 1961).

ROUAULT, Georges (May 27, 1871 – Feb. 13, 1958). French painter and engraver. Born and died in Paris, son of a cabinetmaker. Apprenticed as a stained glass maker (1885–90) and became interested in religious art. Studied with Gustave Moreau at École des Beaux Arts (1891). Associated for a time with the Fauves, with whom he exhibited. Painted Biblical subjects un-

til he began (1903) series of prostitutes, clowns, judges, peasants, and
working people, bitter expressions of
human misery and depravity. The sufferings of Christ were also his subjects, as in *Christ Mocked by Soldiers*
(Museum of Modern Art, New York)
and several *Crucifixion* paintings.
From this period (he did not date his
work) came such paintings as *Three
Judges* (Museum of Modern Art), *Circus Trio*, and *Afterglow Galilee* (both
Phillips Gallery, Washington). Later
paintings, calmer in emotional expression, include *Italian Woman* (1938,
Tate Gallery, London), *The Old King*
(1936, Carnegie Museum, Pittsburgh),
Le Clown Blessé (private collection,
Paris), and *Head of Clown* (1940–48,
Museum of Fine Arts, Boston). His
versatility led to his producing prints,
gouaches, enamels, tapestries, settings
for the Diaghilev ballet *Le Fils Prodigue*
(1929), and especially engravings, including the series published as *Miserere*
(1948). Also designed stained glass
windows for church of Plateau d'Assy.
The black leading and luminous color
of stained glass inspired much of his
work, which is considered among the
greatest religious art of the twentieth
century.

EDITION: *Souvenirs intimes* (Paris
1926).

REFERENCES: Pierre Courthion
Georges Rouault (London and New
York 1962). Giuseppe Marchiori *Rou-
ault* (New York 1967). James T. Soby
Georges Rouault: Paintings and Prints
(New York 1945). Lionello Venturi
Rouault (tr. New York and London
1959).

ROUSSEAU, Henri (May 21, 1844 –
Sept. 2, 1910). French painter. Born
Laval, Mayenne, and educated at lycée
there. After serving in army (1864–68,
1870), he settled in Paris and married
Clémence Boitard (1869). Held position in customs bureau until 1893,
hence his nickname, "le Douanier
Rousseau." At about forty he began
painting and exhibited at Salon des
Champs-Elysées (1885). Next year,
through Paul Signac, began exhibiting
regularly at Salon des Indépendants.
Carnaval du Soir (1886, Museum of
Art, Philadelphia) is of this period; its

atmosphere of otherworldliness and
haunting mystery, the exquisite detail
in the painting of the tree branches, is
characteristic of Rousseau's fantasy
pictures. He also painted simple, solid
"primitive" portraits, such as *Père Ju-
niet's Cart* (1908, private collection,
Paris) and *Pierre Loti* (1891, Kunsthaus, Zurich). After his wife's death,
he devoted himself entirely to painting. Associated with Gauguin, Redon,
and Seurat, and knew the critic Apollinaire. Married Rosalie-Josephine
Nourry (1899; she died 1903). It is
said that rejection repeatedly by the
woman he wished to make his third
wife contributed to his death (in
Paris). Among his well-known paintings are *Sleeping Gypsy* (1897, Museum of Modern Art, New York), the
Snake Charmer (1907, Louvre, Paris),
The Dream (1910, Museum of Modern
Art). Uninhibited by any technical
training, Rousseau seemed to translate
his visions directly onto canvas, as
though by inner compulsion. Indeed,
he said, "It is not I who paint, but
someone else who holds the brush."

REFERENCES: Adolphe Basler *Henri
Rousseau, sa vie, son oeuvre* (New
York 1927). Pierre Courthion *Henri
Rousseau le Douanier* (Geneva 1944).
Maurice Garçon *Le Douanier Rousseau
accusé naïf* (Paris 1953). Daniel C.
Rich *Henri Rousseau* (2nd ed. New
York 1946). André Salmon *Rousseau*
(tr. New York and London 1963). Dora
Vallier *Henri Rousseau* (New York and
London 1964).

ROUSSEAU, Jean Jacques (June 28,
1712 – July 2, 1778). French writer,
philosopher, and composer. Born Geneva, son of a watchmaker. Mother
died shortly after his birth. After two
apprenticeships, he left Geneva (1728),
wandered through southeastern France
and northern Italy, working as servant, music teacher, tutor, returning
often to visit at Annecy his patroness
and eventual mistress, Mme. Louise
Éléonore de Warens. In Paris (1742),
he published *Dissertation on French
Music* (1743). Served as ambassador's
secretary in Venice until 1744. Returned to Paris, and began lifelong
liaison with Thérèse Le Vasseur, with
whom he had five children. Associated

with Diderot and contributed to his *Encyclopédie*. Won first prize (1749) at Academy of Dijon for paradoxical *Discours sur les sciences et les arts* which brought him sudden fame. The sequel, *Discours sur l'origine de l'inegalite des hommes* (1754), argued against private property. Also composed opera *Le Devin du village* (1752). Returning to Geneva, he wrote the highly successful novel *La Nouvelle Heloïse* (1761) and *Émile* (1762), an anti-intellectual treatise maintaining that the ultimate goal of education should be to teach men to live. *Émile* and the theoretical *Du Contrat social* (1762) provoked official censorship, and Rousseau moved from one country to another (1762–1779), frequently at odds with his benefactors. In England he wrote his extraordinary autobiography, the highly personal *Confessions* (1766–67), which continues to be widely read. Returned to Paris (1770), worked as music copyist, wrote *Dialogues* (1774) and *Rêveries du promeneur solitaire*, beautifully descriptive of nature. Died at Ermenonville. Rousseau's theories emerge forcefully: that God, nature, and man are good; that evil arises not from original sin but from man's social environment and the inequalities brought about by ownership of property leading to discord. Rousseau advocated not revolution as an ideal but the small egalitarian state. He also brought to full flowering the romantic idealization and feeling for nature, which influenced deeply German and English romanticism. His works were first translated into English in a ten-volume edition (1773–74).

TRANSLATION: *Confessions* tr. J. M. Cohen (Harmondsworth, England, and Baltimore PB 1953). *The Social Contract and the Discourses* tr. G. D. H. Cole London PB 1955). *Émile* tr. Barbara Foxley (London and New York PB 1955).
REFERENCES: Irving Babbitt *Rousseau and Romanticism* (Boston 1919, also PB). J. H. Broome *Rousseau: A Study of His Thought* (London and New York 1963). Ernst Cassirer *The Question of Jean Jacques Rousseau* (tr. New York 1954, also PB). Frederick C. Green *Jean Jacques Rousseau:*

A Critical Study of His Life and Writings (New York and Cambridge, England, 1955). Ronald Grimsley *Jean Jacques Rousseau: A Study in Self-Awareness* (Cardiff, Wales, 1961). Jean Guehenno *Jean Jacques Rousseau* (tr. 2 vols. London and New York 1966). Ernest H. Wright *The Meaning of Rousseau* (London and New York 1929).

___

ROUSSEAU, (Pierre Étienne) Théodore (Apr. 15, 1812 – Dec. 22, 1867). French painter. Born Paris. Studied under Charles Remond, copied landscapes of Dutch masters and Claude Lorrain and painted his own wildly romantic landscapes from nature. First exhibited at Salon of 1831, and by late 1830's was established as leading landscapist. But his large *Descent of the Cattle* (1835, Musée de Picardie, Amiens) was rejected by 1836 Salon and he fell out of favor until 1848. His style became calmer, and he painted more peaceful scenes, particularly in Fontainebleau forest, such as *Edge of the Forest at Fontainebleau* (1848), *Springtime* (c.1852), *Oak Trees at Apremont* (1852), and *The Marsh in the Landes* (1854, all Louvre, Paris). Rousseau settled in Barbizon for rest of his life, where with J. F. Millet he headed the Barbizon school and founded the modern school of French landscape painting.

REFERENCES: Robert L. Herbert *Barbizon Revisited* (Boston 1962). J. W. Mollet *The Painters of Barbizon* (London and New York 1890). D. C. Thomson *The Barbizon School of Painters* (London 1902). Charles S. Smith *Barbizon Days* (1902, reprinted Freeport, N.Y. 1969).

___

ROWLANDSON, Thomas (July 1756 – Apr. 22, 1827). English painter and caricaturist. Born and died in London, son of prosperous merchant. Studied at Royal Academy and in Paris, returning to England at eighteen. By 1777 he was an established portrait painter and exhibited regularly at Royal Academy. He was best known, however, for his trenchant, sometimes coarse caricatures and his delightful drawings of contemporary English life. He traveled through England and Europe, sketching as he went; was particularly skilled at portraying crowds. His *Vauxhall Gardens* (1784) became a popular engraving; was followed by the series of drawings *The Comforts of Bath* (1798). For Rudolph Ackermann he produced plates for *The Miseries of Life* (1808), *The Tour of Dr. Syntax* (1812–21) and its sequels: *The English Dance of Death* (1815–16) and *The Dance of Life* (1816). Also illustrated for Ackermann the works of Smollett, Sterne, Swift, and Goldsmith. Collaborated with A. C. Pugin on *The Microcosm of London* (1808), bringing Pugin's architectural scenes to life. Produced many political drawings, especially cartoons travestying Napoleon. Rowlandson's humorous, richly imaginative, nimble drawings, often etched and colored by hand, chronicled Regency England at its liveliest.

REFERENCES: Adrian Bury *Rowlandson Drawings* (London 1949). Bernard Falk *Thomas Rowlandson, His Life and Art* (London 1949). Joseph Grego *Rowlandson the Caricaturist: A Selection from His Works* (2 vols. London and New York 1880). F. G. Roe *Rowlandson: The Life and Art of a British Genius* (London and New York 1947).

RUBENS, Peter Paul (June 29, 1577 – May 30, 1640). Flemish painter. Born Siegen, Westphalia. His father, a lawyer and magistrate, had been expelled as a Calvinist from Antwerp, whither the family returned after his death (1587). There Rubens attended a Jesuit school, acted as court page, and was apprenticed to several minor painters. Admitted to painters' guild (1598), he left for Italy (1600), where he spent eight years in service of the duke of Mantua, in the course of which he made diplomatic mission to Spain (1603). Upon return to Antwerp, he quickly became the city's foremost painter, and set up a large studio. Married Isabella Brandt (1609; she died 1626). In Madrid and London (1628–30) as diplomat in service to regent of the Netherlands. On his return, married sixteen-year-old Helena Fourment (1630), who became frequent subject and model in his paintings. He died in Antwerp. Among his most famous works are the *Raising of the Cross* (1610) and *Descent from the Cross* (1611–14), both in Antwerp cathedral; series of paintings for Marie de' Medici in Luxembourg palace (1622–25, Louvre, Paris); *Allegory of War and Peace* (1629, National Gallery, London); *Venus and Adonis* (c.1632–34, Metropolitan Museum, New York), *The Garden of Love, The Three Graces, The Judgment of Paris* (all c.1632–34, Prado, Madrid).

EDITION: *The Letters of Peter Paul Rubens* ed. and tr. Ruth Magurn (Cambridge, Mass. and Oxford 1955).

REFERENCES: Jacob Burckhardt *Recollections of Rubens* (tr. London and New York 1950) . Jennifer Fletcher *Peter Paul Rubens* (London and New York 1968). Julius S. Held *Rubens: Selected Drawings* (2 vols. London and New York 1959). John R. Martin ed. *Rubens: The Antwerp Altarpieces* (New York 1969, also PB). Leo van Puyvelde *The Sketches of Rubens* (tr. London 1948 and New York 1954). Max Rooses *Rubens* (tr. 2 vols. Philadelphia and London 1904). Wolfgang Stechow *Rubens and the Classical Tradition* (Cambridge, Mass. 1968 and Oxford 1969). Christopher White *Rubens and His World* (London and New York 1968).

✍

PETER PAUL RUBENS
BY SVETLANA ALPERS

Peter Paul Rubens was one of the most brilliant and generously endowed painters of any time. Although he grew up in Antwerp when it was but a provincial art center, Rubens undertook to educate himself in the accomplishments of past art by diligently copying the works of both northern and southern artists. He succeeded in solving the major problem that had faced northern artists since the time of Dürer, one hundred years before: how to deal with the tremendous achievements of Italian art. Rubens is usually treated as the major representative of the baroque style in Europe, but it is equally important to see him in the context of northern Europe, as the artist who was able to wed the monumental, idealized figures and grand narrative tradition of Italian art to the particularizing, descriptive tradition of the art of his native land. In this sense Rubens can be seen as the first great Renaissance artist in the north.

In an age when artists were truly international figures, traveling with ease and patronized in many countries, Rubens was among the most well-traveled and widely patronized. His works hung in the major churches and courts of Europe, where many have remained until this day. To name but a few examples, in addition to numerous works in and around Antwerp: his early altarpieces were in Mantua, Genoa, and Rome; the large series of works commissioned by Marie de' Medici to celebrate her life and reign hung in the Luxembourg palace in Paris; in London, Rubens's ceiling celebrating King James graced Inigo Jones's Whitehall Banqueting Hall; and near Madrid a great series of mythological and animal paintings decorated one of the hunting lodges of Philip IV. Unlike the other, more isolated geniuses of the age — Rembrandt, who never left Holland; Poussin, who painted for a small circle of Roman and French admirers; and Velazquez, who painted only for Philip IV — Rubens possessed the personality and energy as well as the grand artistic style suited to the tasks set by his great ecclesiastical and court patrons. In order to accomplish the Herculean tasks he was called upon to do, Rubens organized and directed a studio of many artists, who were trained to execute the finished works according to Rubens's instructions and designs.

Living during the Thirty Years' War, and through the Netherlands' struggle for independence from Spain, at a time, in other words, when the established institutions of church and state were trying to hold out against continuing assaults, Rubens came out firmly on the side of the establishment, defending its beliefs and catering to its tastes. The range of subjects he dealt with was broad, and in spite of the deeply troubled times in which he lived, the tone common to most of his works is one of affirmation and celebration. He celebrated the heroic figure of a crucified Christ looking confidently up toward heaven, and the self-certain St. Francis Xavier converting and healing the heathen in India, as well as Marie de' Medici, queen of France, and James of England confident of their wisdom in the face of all threats to their rule; the hulking Silenus, grand in spite of his drunkenness, or the beautiful Andromeda despairing in her final moments of captivity, as well as the deadly struggle between hunters and exotic beasts of the Nile, or the shepherd and his flock made golden by the sun setting on a Flemish landscape.

By virtue of his learning (Rubens knew Latin and most modern European languages and was a leading amateur antiquarian), his aristocratic bearing, and his manner of living (he remodeled his Antwerp house in imitation of an Italian palazzo), Rubens's life was of a piece with the public and affirmative nature of his art. He was one of those rare artists at one with himself, his art, and his society. It is a mistake to look beneath the surface of his art (or of his equally joyous life) for troubled depths that do not exist. The greatness of Rubens's art lies in its surface, but it is a greatness that depends not only on the sheer technical skill with which he organized a myriad of figures and orchestrated his brilliant colors, not only on the wit with which he combined historical, mythological, and Christian meanings in allegorical paintings, but also on the full, clear, and sympathetic manner in which he rendered the essential passions common to all men in all times. We are made to feel the terror, love, and grief of the mothers of the slaughtered children in the *Massacre of the Innocents,* or the first recognition of love between Atalanta and Meleager, or the varieties of faith manifested in the saints worshiping the Madonna and Child in the great altarpiece Rubens picked to surmount his grave — the splendid martial address of St. George, the repentant pose of the still sensual Magdalene, and the grand gesture of the august Jerome. The success of Rubens's greatest works depends on a frank and full handling of human passions and thus it is hardly surprising that in his great antiwar picture, the *Horrors of War* (an exceptional critique of his age for Rubens), the central image of the destruction and disharmony of war is the desertion of the desperate Venus by her lover, Mars.

Although from the vantage point of our age Rubens appears to be one of the last upholders of the great tradition of Italian narrative art, he was considered by many in his own time to be a revolutionary, destroying the established conventions and traditions of that art. The free and personal manner in which he handled the nude without regard to the ideal proprieties of art (his fat women and his men with bulging calves were commented on in his own day), and his emphasis on color, which since antiquity had traditionally been considered the easiest and least noble way for an artist to appeal to his viewers, were compared unfavorably with the ideal restraint of Poussin. It may seem remarkable to us, who find his art so far from reality, that Rubens, in his own time, was considered too much the realist and too little the idealist. This view of Rubens was in some sense confirmed in the reaction against Poussin and the great vogue for Rubens's art among French rococo artists of the first half of the eighteenth century. Watteau's *Fêtes Galantes* — which made a radical break with the elevated subject matter of a more traditional art by depicting ideal views of contemporary society and its mores — are indebted in subject matter to Rubens's *Garden of Love* and to his other pictures of aristocracy playing amorous games in parklike settings. Furthermore, Watteau, Fragonard, and others supported this break with traditional subject matter by working with a loaded brush and a lightened palette that owed much to the oil sketches Rubens made in preparing his large, finished works.

The last artist to champion Rubens was Delacroix, who in the early nineteenth century turned to the Flemish master once again as a reaction against a severe, neoclassic style — this time the art of David and his followers. Delacroix, himself both a revolutionary and a conservative, combined an admiration for Rubens's daring use of color with a reverence for his technical brilliance and his success in rendering the human passions, the latter being achievements which were, for Delacroix, among the hallmarks of the great old masters. It was in fact just because of their commitment to the established traditions of art in the face of the artistic revolutions of the nineteenth century that Delacroix and the Renaissance historian Jacob Burckhardt were moved to pay Rubens an exceptionally fine and appropriate tribute. Both called him the Homer of painters, and thus bore witness to the grandeur, frankness, and generosity of his depiction of human dramas — aspects of his art that our century has tended to lose sight of.

RUBINSTEIN, Anton Grigorievich (Nov. 28, 1829 – Nov. 20, 1894). Russian pianist and composer. Born Wechwotynez, into Jewish family who soon moved to Moscow. Early training by musician mother. Made debut as pianist at nine in Moscow; then performed in concert in Paris (1840). Won admiration of Mendelssohn, Chopin, and Liszt, who urged him to study in Germany. Studied theory in Berlin under Siegfried Wilhelm Dehn until 1848, when he returned to settle in St. Petersburg. Appointed court pianist there (1848). Founded St. Petersburg Conservatory (1862), serving as director (1862–67, 1887–91). Made concert tours in Europe from 1867, and in the U.S. (1872–73). For virtuoso brilliance he ranked with Liszt. Achieved less fame as composer. His works comprise operas, oratorios, piano concertos, solo piano pieces, and orchestral works such as *The Ocean Symphony.* His brother, Nicholas Grigorievich Rubinstein (1835–81), was also a brilliant pianist and teacher; he founded the Moscow Conservatory (1864), which he directed until his death.

REFERENCES: Catherine Drinker Bowen *Free Artist: The Story of Anton and Nicholas Rubinstein* (1939, reprinted Boston 1961). N. H. Dole *Famous Composers* (New York 1929).

RUISDAEL (or **RUYSDAEL**), Jacob van (c.1628 – Mar. 14, 1682). Dutch painter and engraver. Born Haarlem, son of art dealer. Received early training from his uncle Salomon van Ruysdael, well-known Haarlem landscape painter. Entered painters' guild there (1648). During 1640's painted and engraved landscapes and forest scenes noted for their simple realism and intimate feeling for nature. Early influenced by Cornelius Vroom, who shared his enthusiasm for painting trees. Soon Ruisdael became leader of new gen-

eration of landscape painters. After visit to Germany (1650), his paintings became increasingly monumental and dramatic, many reflecting elements of German landscape. Moved to Amsterdam (1659), where he painted famous forest scene, *The Morass* (c.1660, Hermitage, Leningrad). Formed lasting friendship with Hobbema, his apprentice and journeyman. Painted many mountain-waterfall landscapes and dramatic panoramas during 1660's, including *Waterfall in Rocky Landscape* (National Gallery, London) and *Wheatfields* (Metropolitan Museum, New York). Other paintings depict wide variety of landscapes, seascapes, river and town views. Among best-known works from period 1660–75 are *The Shore at Egmondaan-Zee* (National Gallery, London), *The Jewish Cemetery* (Detroit Institute of Art), *Mill at Wijk* (Rijksmuseum, Amsterdam), and *View of Haarlem* (Kunsthaus, Zurich). Made doctor of medicine at Caen, France (1676), and set up medical practice in Amsterdam. Died a bachelor at Amsterdam. Considered greatest Dutch landscape painter of seventeenth century.

REFERENCES: W. Bode *Great Masters of Dutch and Flemish Painting* (London 1926). Frank Cundall *The Landscape and Pastoral Painters of Holland* (London and New York 1891). Émile Michel *Great Masters of Landscape Painting* (tr. Philadelphia and London 1910). Wolfgang Stechow *Dutch Landscape Painting of the Seventeenth Century* (Greenwich, Conn. and London 1966).

RUSKIN, John (Feb. 8, 1819 – Jan. 20, 1900). English art critic and social theorist. Born London, son of wealthy wine merchant who took the boy on extensive travels abroad and had him privately tutored. Went to Christ Church, Oxford (degree 1842); won Newdigate prize (1839). Published (1843) what began as a defense of J. M. W. Turner, first of five-volume treatise on art, *Modern Painters* (1843–60), which immediately established him as one of most influential critics of his day. Married Euphemia Gray (1848); the unfortunate marriage was annulled (1854; she married painter J. E. Millais). Ruskin's interest in architecture led to his writing *The Seven Lamps of Architecture* (1849), followed by the famous *The Stones of Venice* (1851–53). Also from 1851 defended the Pre-Raphaelites in pamphlets and letters to *The Times*. Thereafter his writings turned more and more toward social reform. *Unto This Last* appeared (1860) in the *Cornhill Magazine*, attacking the unaesthetic waste of modern industry. Other articles followed, and then his own theories of social reform in *Sesame and Lilies* (1865), *The Crown of Wild Olive* (1866), *Time and Tide* (1867), and *Fors Clavigera* (1871–84), in the form of letters to workingmen and laborers. Ruskin supported such present-day accepted ideas as a national system of education, old age pensions, labor organization. As Slade professor of fine arts at Oxford (appointed 1870) he was the first professor of art in England, but his later years were marked by increasingly severe spells of mental illness. His autobiography, *Praeterita*, containing some of his finest prose, was left unfinished after onset of his permanent illness (1889). He died eleven years later at his country house in Coniston.

EDITIONS: *Works* ed. E. T. Cook and Alexander Wedderburn (39 vols. London and New York 1903–12). *Diaries* ed. Joan Evans and John Howard Whitehouse (3 vols. Oxford 1956–59). *The Genius of John Ruskin: Selections from His Writings* ed. John D. Rosenberg (New York 1963 and London 1964, also PB).
REFERENCES: John L. Bradley *John Ruskin: A Critical Introduction* (Boston PB 1969). W. G. Collingwood *The Life of John Ruskin* (9th ed. London 1912). Edward T. Cook *Life of John Ruskin* (1911, reprinted 2 vols. New York 1968). Joan Evans *John Ruskin* (London and New York 1954). John T. Fain *Ruskin and the Economists* (Nashville, Tenn. 1956). Luke Herrmann *Ruskin and Turner* (London 1968 and New York 1969). Derrick Leon *Ruskin: The Great Victorian* (1949, reprinted Hamden, Conn. 1969). Peter Quennell *John Ruskin: The Portrait of a Prophet* (London and New York 1949). John D. Rosenberg *The Darkening Glass: A Portrait of John*

Ruskin's Genius (New York and London 1961). Roger B. Stein *John Ruskin and Aesthetic Thought in America, 1840–1900* (Cambridge, Mass. 1967). R. H. Wilenski *John Ruskin* (1933, reprinted New York 1967).

RUSSELL, Earl Bertrand Arthur William (May 18, 1872 – Feb. 2, 1970). British philosopher. Born Ravenscroft, Monmouthshire. Grandson of John Russell (twice prime minister) and son of Lord Amberley. Educated privately and at Trinity College, Cambridge, of which he became a fellow (1895). Married (1894) Alys Pearsall Smith (divorced 1920; he had three later marriages). Meeting the logician Giuseppe Peano led to Russell's first major work, *The Principles of Mathematics* (1903). Collaborated with A. N. Whitehead on the formidable *Principia Mathematica* (1910–13), asserting that all mathematics could be deduced from a few logical axioms. A pacifist in World War I, he was deprived of his Trinity lectureship and later imprisoned. He continued to write philosophical works, such as *Introduction to Mathematical Philosophy* (1919), *The Analysis of Mind* (1921), *An Analysis of Matter* (1927), and the popularizing *History of Western Philosophy* (1945). In 1920's he took up lecturing and journalism; his books include *The A.B.C. of Relativity* (1925), *On Education* (1926), *Marriage and Morals* (1929), and *Religion and Science* (1935). In 1950's he campaigned for nuclear disarmament and in 1960's vigorously opposed U.S. invasion of Vietnam. In his last years he wrote a candid *Autobiography* (3 vols. 1967–69). Russell was a philosopher of the greatest importance, yet devoted much of his life to humanitarian political activity. He received the Order of Merit (1949) and the Nobel prize for literature (1950). He died at Penrhyndeudraeth, Merionethshire.

EDITIONS: Bertrand Russell *My Philosophical Development* (London and New York 1959). *The Philosophy of Bertrand Russell* ed. P. A. Schilpp (Chicago 1944).
REFERENCES: D. F. Pears *Bertrand Russell and the British Tradition in Philosophy* (London and New York

1967). Ralph Schoenman ed. *Bertrand Russell: Philosopher of the Century* (London 1967 and Boston 1968). Alan Wood *Bertrand Russell: The Passionate Sceptic* (London 1957 and New York 1958).

RUSSELL, George William. *See* AE.

RYDER, Albert Pinkham (Mar. 19, 1847 – Mar. 28, 1917). American painter. Born New Bedford, Mass. Damaged vision prevented him from proceeding further than grammar school. Moved to New York City (c.1870), where he studied art at National Academy of Design. Exhibited first painting there, *Clearing Away* (1873), and eventually became National Academician (1906). His original style, a romantic abstract approach to nature, developed from his highly personal vision. After several trips to Europe (1877–96), lived as a recluse in his New York studio continually reworking his small paintings, already of a somber palette, until they became thick and discolored with paint and other substances. His most fruitful period (1880–1900) produced his finest landscapes and marines, nocturnal moonlit scenes of a brooding, visionary quality, that include *Moonlight Marine*, *Toilers of the Sea* (both Metropolitan Museum, New York), *Jonah* and *The Flying Dutchman* (both National Gallery, Washington), and literary and allegorical paintings such as *The Race Track* (Museum of Art, Cleveland) and *Siegfried and the Rhine Maidens* (National Gallery, Washington). As his reputation grew, an enormous number of forgeries of his little more than 150 works were made. He never married; died in Elmhurst, New York.

REFERENCES: Lloyd Goodrich *Albert Pinkham Ryder* (New York 1959). Frederic Newlin Price *Ryder* (New York 1932). Frederic Fairchild Sherman *Albert Pinkham Ryder* (New York 1920).

✍

ALBERT PINKHAM RYDER

BY GERALD SYKES

If serious American painters were polled on the best of their kind, their vote would probably still go, as it has gone in the past, to Albert Pinkham Ryder. If disaffected American youth were polled on their favorite rebel (in the unlikely event that they were willing to examine the lives and works of their spiritual ancestors), their vote might also go to Ryder. He broke as recognizably with custom as any hippie of our own day, though with more decorum and more determination; and out of his quiet intransigence came some of our most memorable works of art. In spite of his frayed frock coat, he was a hero of revolt.

Without issuing any manifestos or making any sartorial innovations, he got out of his native New Bedford soon, at the age of twenty-three, by following a successful restaurateur brother to New York. In the pre-telephonic metropolis he studied art and eventually set up a studio that seems to have been as remote from the concerns of other men (and women) as a cabin in the Rockies. With the same single-minded devotion to his canvases he made four trips to Europe in his thirties and forties, only to return each time to New York with his style repurged of foreign influence (more potent then than domestic). Ryder was what we now call a loner — a loner who had to paint differently from anybody else. He took such traditional subjects as the Crucifixion, the Forest of Arden, the Man with the Scythe, and made them almost weirdly his own.

An important part of his originality was his affinity with night, an affinity that together with a faulty technique — the practice of painting too soon, too impetuously, on undried undersurface — now causes already nocturnal visions to recede into Stygian obscurity. Perhaps the New England reticence that made him propose only once to a woman (he heard her playing a violin in the same building, went to her place without an introduction, made impromptu the rashest declaration of a lifetime, and was whisked unprotesting by friends to Europe) contributed also to the cracks and the darkness that now mar such masterpieces as *Moonlight Marine* and *The Racetrack*. The desire to recede can be united to the desire to excel.

Ryder liked to stroll about New York, especially at night, and at full moon, when he said he "soaked in the moonlight" that later appeared in his small pictures. Since he dressed ordinarily like a tramp, in an old sweater and a fisherman's knitted skullcap, he did not fear being robbed on the waterfront. "I expect they can see that I have nothing worth stealing about me, and besides, I don't think these people are as bad as they are made out to be." When he grew older he said to a friend, "Come yourself. You are always welcome. But I don't want to meet any new people." At Christmastime he brewed perfume for children, whom he liked very much, and gave it to them in little jars. His studio became a Collier brothers junkpile of odds and ends, since he never let it be cleaned or painted, and never threw anything out. Paths had to be worn through rubbish, to permit him to move around. Because his cot was crowded, he slept on the floor.

He made no attempt to acquire money, but as his talent and his reputation grew he acquired friends who looked after him. One of them found a check for more than a thousand dollars in his cupboard, uncashed after several months. The mysteries of banking were then explained to him. He said, "The artist needs but a roof, a crust of bread and his easel, and all the rest God gives him in abundance. He must live to paint and not paint to live. He cannot be a good fellow." When his physical powers failed he was looked after by a neighboring carpenter and his art-loving wife. He died in their house on Long Island.

Almost twenty years before then his artistic powers had already failed. He originated no new pictures during the last two decades of his life, but was content to rework old beginnings. This seems to have been the price of his extreme unworldliness and his uncompromising withdrawal from the bourgeois society into which he had been born. He had narrowed his available world overmuch. He did not enjoy the aged fertility of a Titian or a Renoir.

In this respect, since his lifetime ran from 1847 to 1917 and that of Henry James about the same (1843–1916), he suggests a brief comparison with the novelist, who was a man of the world, who made enough by writing to renounce a legacy, who did some of his most original work in his later years. The more romantic, the more religious talent of Ryder, renouncing all but a sacred intuition, was destined to have a briefer span of productivity. Out of that briefer span, however, came some of the most mysterious works of any kind the New World has ever produced. They are receding, but their intensity, born of an almost bizarre self-sacrifice, endures.

SAARINEN, Eero (Aug. 20, 1910 – Sept. 1, 1961). American architect. Born Kirkkonummi, Finland, son of Eliel Saarinen, noted Finnish architect who emigrated to U.S. (1923). Studied sculpture in Paris (1930–31) and architecture at Yale (B.F.A. 1934), collaborating with his father from 1936 until the elder Saarinen's death (1950). First achieved independent recognition for his enormous stainless steel arch that won competition for Jefferson National Expansion Memorial, St. Louis (designed 1948, completed 1965). Won national acclaim for industrial campus at General Motors Technical Institute, Warren, Mich. (1951–55). Married sculptor Lillian Swann (1939; divorced 1953). Married art critic Aline B. Louchheim (1954). Famous for his designs for industrially produced furniture, Saarinen also achieved worldwide fame for his American embassy buildings in Oslo (1955–59) and London (1955–60). Most of his work is characterized by bold design and brilliant structural engineering. Among the most notable examples: chapel and auditorium, Massachusetts Institute of Technology, Cambridge, Mass. (1953–56); Ingalls Hockey Rink, Yale University (completed 1958); Trans World Airlines terminal, Kennedy International Airport, New York (completed 1962); Vivian Beaumont Theater, Lincoln Center, New York (completed 1963); and Dulles International Airport, Chantilly, Va. (1958–62). He died in Ann Arbor, Mich. Along with his father, Eero Saarinen is one of the leading figures in the development of modern architecture.

EDITION: *Eero Saarinen on His Work* ed. Aline B. Saarinen (New Haven, Conn. 1962).

REFERENCE: Allan Temko *Eero Saarinen* (New York 1962, also PB).

SACKVILLE, Thomas (1536 – Apr. 19, 1608). English poet, playwright, and statesman. Born Buckhurst, Sussex; of prominent family. Educated at St. John's College, Cambridge, and studied law at Inner Temple. Married Cicely Baker (1555). Entered Parliament (1558); gained favor with Queen Elizabeth, who made him Baron Buckhurst (1567). Collaborated with Thomas Norton on the work that made them famous, *Gorboduc* (1561), first English play in blank verse and probably the earliest Elizabethan tragedy. As poet, Sackville also took over a verse series, *A Mirror for Magistrates*, for which he wrote the celebrated *Induction* and *Complaint of Henry, Duke of Buckingham* (1563). His career as statesman was highly distinguished: he served on numerous diplomatic missions (1567–98), became member of Privy Council (1571), Knight of the Garter (1589), chancellor of the University of Oxford (1591), and lord treasurer of England (1599), the pinnacle of his career. After negotiating a peace with Spain, he was created 1st earl of Dorset (1604). Greatly esteemed as both author and politician, he died at a council meeting in Whitehall, London.

EDITIONS: *Works* ed. Reginald W. Sackville-West (London 1859). *Gorboduc* (vol. 1, *Specimens of Pre-Shakespearean Drama*) ed. John M. Manly (New York PB 1967).
REFERENCES: E. K. Chambers *The Elizabethan Stage* vol. III (4 vols. Oxford 1923). Wolfgang Clemen *English Tragedy Before Shakespeare* (tr.

London 1961 and New York 1962, also PB). Jacobus Swart *Thomas Sackville: A Study in Sixteenth-Century Poetry* (Groningen, Netherlands, 1949).

SADE, Donatien Alphonse François, Comte de (known as **Marquis de Sade**) (June 2, 1740 – Dec. 2, 1814). French writer and libertine. Born Paris, of aristocratic parents. Educated at military school, he served as captain during Seven Years War (1756–63). Shortly after marriage to Renée Pélagie Cordier de Launay de Montreuil (1763), he was imprisoned at Vincennes for debauchery. Condemned to death at Aix-en-Provence (1772) for crimes of poisoning and sodomy, he escaped and fled (1775) to Italy. After his return (1777) he was tried and imprisoned, first at Vincennes (1778–84), then at the Bastille (1784–89), and finally at the Charenton insane asylum (1789–90). Twenty-seven years of his life were spent under arrest, during which time he wrote sexually graphic novels and plays. Upon his initial release from Charenton (1790), he had several plays produced by the Comédie Française and published the novels *Justine, ou Les Malheurs de la vertu* (1791, tr. 1953, 1965), *Juliette* (1792, tr. 1968), *La Philosophie dans le boudoir* (1795, tr. 1953), and *La Nouvelle Justine* (1797). Arrested (1801) as author of the scandalous *Justine*, he was sent from prison to prison, ending up again at Charenton, where he died eleven years later. Long considered straight pornography, Sade's works were eventually revaluated and admired by literary critics and others. His theory of human nature, violently opposed in his own day, holds that sexual and criminal acts largely considered abnormal are natural human behavior. Indeed, Sade anticipates much of the theories of modern psychology, especially those of Freud. The term sadism derives from his name.

TRANSLATIONS: *The Marquis de Sade: The 120 Days of Sodom and Other Writings* compiled and tr. Austryn Wainhouse and Richard Seaver (New York 1966). *The Complete Marquis de Sade* ed. and tr. Paul L. Gillette (2 vols. Los Angeles PB 1966). *Selected Writings* tr. Leonard de Saint-Yves (London 1953 and New York 1954). *De Sade Quartet* (four stories from *Contes et Fabliaux*) tr. Margaret Crosland (London and New York 1963). *Selected Letters* ed. Margaret Crosland and tr. W. J. Strachan (London 1965 and New York 1966).

REFERENCES: Simone de Beauvoir *The Marquis de Sade: An Essay* (tr. London 1962). Jean Jacques Brochier *Le Marquis de Sade et la conquête de l'unique* (Paris 1966). Geoffrey Gorer *The Life and Ideas of the Marquis de Sade* (rev. ed. London 1953 and New York 1954, PB 1963). Pierre Klossowski *Sade mon prochain* (new ed. Paris 1967). Gilbert Lély *The Marquis de Sade: A Biography* (tr. London 1961 and New York 1962).

SAINTE-BEUVE, Charles Augustin (Dec. 23, 1804 – Oct. 13, 1869). French critic, poet, and novelist. Born Boulogne-sur-Mer three months after his father had died. Sent to Paris for education (1818); entered medical school (1823). Began contributing brilliant articles on sixteenth-century French theatre to *Le Globe*, then abandoned medicine for literary career and became enthusiastic member of group of young romantics surrounding Victor Hugo. Inspired by them, published volume of prose and poetry, *Vie, poésies et pensées de Joseph Delorme* (1829), followed by *Les Consolations* (1830). An autobiographical novel, *Volupté*, appeared (1834), based on his celebrated liaison with Mme. Adèle Hugo, which broke up the friendship between poet and critic. At that time Sainte-Beuve began writing his numerous literary "portraits," which eventually filled three volumes. Gave series of lectures (1837–38) on Jansenist movement, published as *Port-Royal* (1840), which established him as scholarly critic as well as journalist. Reputation heightened by lectures on Chateaubriand and his circle (published 1861). Best-known work is the fifteen-volume *Les Causeries du lundi* (*Monday Conversations*, 1851–62), his weekly columns for *Le Constitutionel* (begun 1849), followed by *Les Nouveaux Lundis* (13 vols. 1863–70). Honored early with a seat in the French Academy (1844) and later with a seat in the Senate (1865), Sainte-Beuve maintained his standing as the most influential critic of his day with an astonishing literary productivity halted only at his death in Paris.

TRANSLATION: *Selected Essays* tr. and ed. Francis Steegmuller and Norbert Guterman (Garden City, N.Y. 1963 and London 1965, also PB).

REFERENCES: Norman H. Barlow *Sainte-Beuve to Baudelaire: A Poetic Legacy* (Durham, N.C. 1964). George McLean Harper *Charles Augustin Sainte-Beuve* (Philadelphia and London 1909). Andrew G. Lehmann *Sainte-Beuve: A Portrait of the Critic, 1804–42* (Oxford 1962). Maxime Leroy *Vie de Sainte-Beuve* (Paris 1947). Harold Nicolson *Sainte-Beuve* (London and Garden City, N.Y. 1957).

SAINT-EXUPÉRY, Antoine de (June 29, 1900 – July 31, 1944). French writer and aviator. Born Lyons; educated at Jesuit schools and at Collège de Fribourg, Switzerland. Obsessed with aviation from an early age, he joined French Army Air Force (1921), but left to become a commercial pilot (1926), flying new air mail routes over North Africa, the South Atlantic, and South America. Wrote first novel, *Courrier-Sud* (1928, tr. *Southern Mail* 1933), based on these experiences. In Buenos Aires married a young widow, Consuelo Suncin (1931), and that year published second novel, *Vol de Nuit* (1931, tr. *Night Flight* 1932), which won the Prix Femina-Vie Heureuse. Served for a time as foreign correspondent and wrote *Terre des hommes* (1939, tr. *Wind, Sand, and Stars* 1939), which won French Academy's Grand Prix. At outbreak of World War II rejoined air force and, after being shot down, succeeded in reaching U.S. Published *Pilote de guerre* (1942, tr. *Flight to Arras* 1942), an account of his wartime experiences; then a fantasy for children, *Le Petit Prince* (1943, tr. *The Little Prince* 1943). But he soon felt compelled to return to his old squadron in North Africa, and left U.S. (1943). Grounded at first because of age and previous injuries, he served as instructor, then began making reconnaissance flights over southern France (1944), and during one of these missions disappeared. His *Citadelle* was published posthumously (1948, tr. *The Wisdom of the Sands* 1950). Saint-Exupéry's writings celebrate his faith in man and life, are philosophical, even mystical. His prose is at once poetic and incisive.

REFERENCES: Curtis Cate *Antoine de Saint-Exupéry* (New York 1970). André-A. Devaux *Saint-Exupéry* (3rd ed. Paris 1967). Luc Estang *Saint-Exupéry par lui-même* (Paris 1956). Jean-Claude Ibert *Saint-Exupéry* (Paris 1960). Jules Roy *Passion et mort de Saint-Exupéry* (Paris 1964). Richard Rumbold and Lady Margaret Stewart *The Winged Life: A Portrait of Antoine de Saint-Exupéry, Poet and Airman* (London 1953 and New York 1955).

SAINT-GAUDENS, Augustus (Mar. 1, 1848 – Aug. 3, 1907). American sculptor. Born Dublin, Ireland, son of a French shoemaker who brought him to New York in infancy. Trained there first, then in Paris as cameo cutter. Entered studio of sculptor François Jouffroy at École des Beaux Arts (1867). In Rome produced his first figure, *Hiawatha* (1872, present whereabouts unknown). Returning to U.S. (1872), expanded his skill in sculpture and into medallion making. Through architect Stanford White he met the artist John La Farge, whom he joined in working on decoration of St. Thomas Church, New York. Statue of Admiral Farragut (1881, Madison Square Park, New York) made Saint-Gaudens immediately famous and brought numerous commissions, such as the *Robert Gould Shaw Memorial* (1884, Boston Common), *Seated Lincoln* (1887, Lincoln Park, Chicago), *The Puritan* (Springfield, Mass.), *Adams Memorial* (1891, Rock Creek Cemetery, Washington, D.C.), *General Sherman Memorial* (1904, Central Park, New York). Saint-Gaudens also executed in bronze and marble many portrait medallions and bas-reliefs, such as those of Mrs. Stanford White (1884), the Jacob Schiff children (1888, Metropolitan Museum, New York), and William Dean Howells and his daughter Mildred (1898, National Portrait Gallery, Washington, D.C.). He died at Cornish, N.H., where he had a studio from

1885. His brother Louis Saint-Gaudens (1854–1913) also was a gifted sculptor.

REFERENCE: Louise Hall Tharp *Saint-Gaudens and the Gilded Era* (Boston 1969).

SAINT-SAËNS, (Charles) Camille (Oct. 9, 1835 – Dec. 16, 1921). French composer. Born Paris. Extremely precocious, he made his debut as pianist at ten and entered Paris Conservatoire at thirteen. His first symphony was performed in 1853. Served as organist at St. Merry (1853–57) and the Madeleine (1858–77), then retired to compose, conduct, and perform his own works. Began (1875) series of triumphant worldwide tours. After performing his own works in Dieppe late in 1921, he died while wintering in Algiers. A champion of instrumental music when it was unpopular in France, Saint-Saëns was later regarded as the embodiment of traditionalism. Strongly opposed work of Debussy and the modernists, and was famous for witty attacks on them. Among his numerous honors: membership in Institut de France (1881) and grand cross of the Légion d'Honneur (1913). A prolific composer, he developed a brilliant technique. Among his best-known works are the opera *Samson et Dalila* (1877), *Third Symphony* (1886), *Introduction and Rondo Capriccioso* (1863), and symphonic poems *Le Rouet d'Omphale* (1871) and *Danse macabre* (1874). He also composed the popular piano concertos in G minor (1868) and C minor (1875).

TRANSLATION: *Musical Memories* tr. Edwin Gile Rich (Boston 1919 and London 1921).

REFERENCES: Jean Chantavoine *Camille Saint-Saëns* (Paris 1947). Arthur Hervey *Saint-Saëns* (London and New York 1921). Watson Lyle *Camille Saint-Saëns: His Life and Art* (London and New York 1923).

SAINTSBURY, George (Edward Bateman) (Oct. 10, 1845 – Jan. 28, 1933). English literary critic and historian. Born Southampton. Educated at King's College School, London, and Merton College, Oxford (1863–66). Senior

classics master at Elizabeth College, Guernsey (1868–74), then headmaster of Elgin Educational Institute (1874–76). In London, began (1876) writing articles for *Academy, Saturday Review,* and other journals. Professor of rhetoric and English literature at Edinburgh University (1895–1915). He died at Bath. One of the most esteemed and prolific critics of his time, he wrote such books as *Dryden* (1881), *Short History of French Literature* (1882), *Elizabethan Literature* (1887), *Nineteenth-Century Literature* (1896), *Sir Walter Scott* (1897), *Periods of European Literature* (general editor 1897–1907), *Short History of English Literature* (1898), *Matthew Arnold* (1899), *History of Criticism* (1900–1904), *History of English Prosody* (1906–10), *The English Novel* (1913), *Notes on a Cellar Book* (1920), *A Scrap Book* (1922).

EDITIONS: *Short History of English Literature* (1898, new ed. New York and London 1929, also PB). *A History of English Prose Rhythm* (1912, reprinted Bloomington, Ind. 1965). *A History of the French Novel* (1917–19, reprinted 2 vols. New York 1964). *Collected Essays and Papers, 1875–1920* (1923–24, reprinted 4 vols. Freeport, N.Y. 1969). *George Saintsbury: The Memorial Volume* eds. John W. Oliver and Augustus Muir (London and New York 1945). *Saintsbury Miscellany* eds. John W. Oliver and Augustus Muir (New York and London 1947). *A Last Vintage: Essays and Papers* (London and New York 1950). *A History of English Prosody* (2nd ed. 3 vols. New York 1961).

REFERENCES: Oliver Elton *George Edward Bateman Saintsbury, 1845–1933* (London and New York 1933). Walter Leuba *George Saintsbury* (New York 1967). A. B. Webster *George Saintsbury* (London 1933). René Wellek *A History of Modern Criticism,* vol. IV (4 vols. New Haven, Conn. 1955–65).

SAINT-SIMON, Louis de Rouvroy, Duc de (Jan. 15, 1675 – Mar. 2, 1755). French memoirist and courtier. Born and died in Paris. Son of an aged nobleman raised to peerage by Louis XIII, he was impregnated with reverence for royalty, love of protocol, and dislike of the middle class. Served in cavalry (1691–1702); resigned in anger when he failed to receive promotion. Married Marie Gabrielle de Durfort (1695), daughter of the duc de Lorges. Though disliked at court, he went to Versailles, where he befriended the dauphin, the duc de Bourgogne. His political hopes crushed by dauphin's death (1712), he attached himself to future regent, the duc d'Orléans. After death of Louis XIV (1715), Saint-Simon, known for his arrogance and violent temper, received only a mediocre government position as member of council of regency and special ambassador to Madrid (1721). Realizing that his public career was over, he retired from court at regent's death (1723) and settled on his estate near Chartres. For rest of his life he worked on his *Mémoires,* his sole claim to fame, an immense tableau of court life under Louis XIV and during the regency. Begun 1694 and first published 1788, they were written mostly between 1739 and 1751. Despite his lofty disregard for grammar and his antibourgeois venom, their vivid detail, wealth of information, and skillful portraiture make the *Mémoires* a monument of French literature and an invaluable historical work.

TRANSLATIONS: *Memoirs Covering the Years 1691–1723* ed. and tr. Desmond Flower (New York 1959). *The Age of Magnificence: The Memoirs of the Duc de Saint-Simon* ed. and tr. Sanche de Gramont (New York 1963). *Historical Memoirs of the Duc de Saint-Simon: A Shortened Version* ed. and tr. Lucy Norton (2 vols London and New York 1967–).

REFERENCES: Emmanuel d'Astier *Sur Saint-Simon* (Paris 1962). François R. Bastide *Saint-Simon par lui-même* (Paris 1953). Gaston Boissier *Saint-Simon* (2nd ed. Paris 1899). Yves Coirault *L'Optique de Saint-Simon: essai sur les formes de son imagination and de sa sensibilité d'après les "Mémoires"* (Paris 1965). Herbert De Ley *Marcel Proust et le duc de Saint-Simon* (Urbana, Ill. 1966, also PB). André Le Breton *La Cómedie Humaine de Saint-Simon* (Paris 1914). Jacques Roujon *Le Duc de Saint-Simon, 1675–1755* (Paris 1958).

SAKI (real name Hector Hugh Munro) (Dec. 18, 1870 – Nov. 13, 1916). English writer. Born Akyab, Burma, son of an officer in the Burma police. Sent to live with aunts in England, he attended schools at Exmouth and Bedford, then returned briefly to Burma (1893–94). In London he wrote whimsical political satires for *Westminster Gazette,* adopting name Saki. Traveled in Balkans, Russia, Poland, and France (1902–1908) as foreign correspondent for *Morning Post,* then settled in London and concentrated on short story writing. Joined Royal Fusiliers in World War I, and was killed at Beaumont-Hamel, France. His reputation rests on the short stories in *Reginald* (1904), *Reginald in Russia* (1910), *Chronicles of Clovis* (1911), and *Beasts and Superbeasts* (1914), collected as *The Short Stories of Saki* (1930). Full of inventive fantasy and strange animals, they assail with trenchant humor and his characteristic whimsy social pretension and the complacent fatuity of adults, often viewed through the eyes of children or irreverent young men. Also wrote novels, including *The Unbearable Bassington* (1912), and plays, collected as *The Novels and Plays of Saki* (1933).

REFERENCE: E. M. Munro's biographical sketch in *The Square Egg* (London 1924, reprinted New York 1929).

SAND, George (real name Amandine Aurore Lucie Dupin Dudevant) (July 1, 1804 – June 8, 1876). French novelist. Born Paris, daughter of an aristocrat who died when she was four. Raised by grandmother on family estate at Nohant, she was largely educated there. Married Baron Casimir Dudevant (1822), and after bearing two children, left him (1831) to live the life of independence she believed in and to embark on literary career in Paris. At first collaborated with Jules Sandeau, then brought out the novel that made her famous, *Indiana* (1832), under the name George Sand. Other romantic novels followed: *Valentine* (1832), *Lélia* (1833), *Jacques* (1834), and others. Having fallen in love with Alfred de Musset (six years younger), she went to Venice with him (1834–35). But the liaison proved difficult, she had an affair with her doctor, Pietro Pagello, and eventually she and de Musset separated. The novel *Lettres d'un voyageur* (1834–36) recounts the story; other similarly inspired works emerged: Musset's *Les Nuits* (1835–37) and *Confession d'un enfant du siècle* (1836) and Sand's *Elle et lui* (1859). A dazzling member of French artistic circles, Sand met Frédéric Chopin (1837), and took him and her son to Majorca for an ill-fated winter made difficult by his tuberculosis, despite her ministrations. The affair lasted until 1846, during which time she wrote novels in strong socialist vein: *Mauprat* (1837), *Spiridion* (1838–39), *Le Compagnon du tour de France* (1840), *Consuelo* (1842, tr. 1846). *Un Hiver à Majorque* (1841) relates the experience with Chopin. Her last years were spent on the Nohant estate, where she produced the pastoral novels for which she is best known: *La Mare au diable* (1846, tr. *The Haunted Pool* 1890), *La Petite Fadette* (1848, tr. *Fanchon the Cricket* 1864), *François le champi* (1850, tr. *Francis the Waif* 1889), and others, full of freshness and charm. She died at Nohant.

REFERENCES: André Maurois *Lélia: The Life of George Sand* (tr. New York and London 1953). Marie Louise Pailleron *George Sand, histoire de sa vie* (3 vols. Paris 1938–53). Pierre Salomon *George Sand* (Paris 1953). Felizia Seyd *Romantic Rebel: The Life and Times of George Sand* (New York 1940). Edith Thomas *George Sand* (Paris 1959). Frances Winwar *The Life of the Heart: George Sand and Her Times* (New York and London 1945).

SANDBURG, Carl (Jan. 6, 1878 – July 22, 1967). American poet and biographer. Born Galesburg, Ill., son of Swedish immigrants. Left school at thirteen to roam the Midwest for six years, working as a day laborer. During Spanish American War served in Puerto Rico (1898) for eight months; then attended Lombard College, Galesburg (1898–1902), where a professor of English was responsible for private publication of his first book of poems, *In Reckless Ecstasy* (1904). Moved to Milwaukee, became organizer for Wisconsin Social-Democratic party, then secretary to mayor (1910–12) and feature writer for *Journal and Daily News*. Met and married Lillian Steichen there (1908). Went to Chicago (1912) to work as associate editor of *System;* later was editorial writer for Chicago *Daily News*. The magazine *Poetry* published (1914) a group of his poems, including *Fog, Grass,* and *Chicago,* which won the Levinson prize that year. *Chicago Poems* (1916), in which he used the American idiom skillfully and forcefully, brought both praise and indignation. During World War I served as correspondent for Newspaper Enterprise Association in Stockholm, where one of his three daughters was born. After the war he returned to Chicago and continued to write poems, with ever-increasing mastery, about the America he knew so well and loved, especially the prairie West and her common people whom, with Whitman, his chief influence, he has depicted with sensitive awareness of character and speech: *Cornhuskers* (1918), which won special Pulitzer award, *Smoke and Steel* (1920), *Slabs of the Sunburnt West* (1922), *Good Morning, America* (1928), *The People, Yes* (1936). For more than thirty years he had studied Lincoln, and spent eight years writing the monumental *Abraham Lincoln: The Prairie Years* (2 vols. 1926), which together with *The War Years* (4 vols. 1939) won him Pulitzer prize (1940). With Paul M. Angle wrote *Mary Lincoln: Wife and Widow* (1932). Began (1920) tours of lecturing and singing folksongs; published *American Songbag* (1927), where more than a hundred airs appeared in print for first time. Also wrote children's books, including *Rootabaga Stories* (1922), *Rootabaga Pigeons* (1923), *Potato Face* (1930); a novel, *Remembrance Rock* (1948); an autobiographical memoir, *Always the Young Strangers* (1952). His *Complete Poems* (1950) won another Pulitzer prize. *The Sandburg Range* (1957) was a selection of his poetry and prose. He received numerous honors and honorary degrees. The voice of both agricultural and industrial America, Sandburg is recognized as one of the great national poets in the country's history. He died in Flat Rock, N.C., where he had lived for some years.

EDITIONS: *Complete Poems* (New York 1950). *The Letters of Carl Sandburg* ed. Herbert Mitgang (New York 1968).

REFERENCES: North Callahan *Carl Sandburg: A Biography* (New York 1969). Karl W. Detzer *Carl Sandburg: A Study in Personality and Background* (New York 1941). Hazel Durnell *The America of Carl Sandburg* (Washington, D.C. PB 1965). Harry Golden *Carl Sandburg* (Cleveland, Ohio 1961). Joseph Haas and Gene Lovitz *Carl Sandburg: A Pictorial Biography* (New York 1967). Harry Hansen *Carl Sandburg: The Man and His Poetry* (Girard, Kans. 1925). Edward Steichen ed. *Sandburg: Photographers View Carl Sandburg* (New York 1966).

SANTAYANA, George (Dec. 16, 1863 – Sept. 26, 1952). Spanish-American philosopher, poet, and critic. Born Madrid; brought to the United States (1872) to be educated with three children of mother by a former marriage. Attended Boston Latin School and Harvard (B.A. 1886). Studied two years at University of Berlin, then received M.A. and Ph.D. from Harvard (1889). Member of Harvard philosophy department (1889–1912) with William James, Josiah Royce, and George H. Palmer. Among his students were T. S. Eliot, Conrad Aiken, and Felix Frankfurter. First work, *The Sense of Beauty* (1896), was followed by *The Life of Reason* (5 vols. 1905–1906: *Reason in Common Sense, Reason in Society, Reason in Religion, Reason in Art, Reason in Science*), which established him as a philosopher of the first rank. A skeptic, critical realist, and an Aristotelian, he held that matter was the only reality. Though raised as a Catholic, he was a nonbeliever; in *Interpretations of Poetry and Religion* (1900) he claims that religion is mostly the product of imagination. A legacy enabled him to retire and he left the United States for good (1912); he lived in France, Spain, and England until the end of World War I, when he settled permanently in Rome. *The Realms of Being* (*The Realm of Essence*, 1927; *The Realm of Matter*, 1930; *The Realm of Truth*, 1937; *The Realm of Spirit*, 1940) further expounds his philosophy that knowledge is faith in the unknowable. A writer of great literary skill and wide-ranging interests, Santayana also produced a novel, *The Last Puritan* (1935); a play, *Lucifer* (1899); a three-volume autobiography, *Persons and Places* (1944), *The Middle Span* (1945), and *My Host the World* (published posthumously 1953); poetry, *Sonnets and Other Verses* (1894) and *A Hermit of Carmel and Other Poems* (1901); and critical volumes such as *Three Philosophical Poets: Lucretius, Dante and Goethe* (1910), *Egotism in German Philosophy* (1916, revised 1940), and *Character and Opinion in the United States* (1920). Awarded the Nicholas Murray Butler gold medal by Columbia University (1945). Died in Rome in convent where he had found sanctuary during World War II.

EDITIONS: *The Works of George Santayana* (14 vols. New York 1936–37). *Letters of George Santayana* ed. Daniel Cory (New York 1955 and London 1956). *The Genteel Tradition at Bay* (New York and London 1931). *Persons and Places* (3 vols. New York 1944–53 and London 1944–48, also PB). *Character and Opinion in the United States* (1944, new ed. New York 1955, also PB). *Dialogues in Limbo* (New York 1948, also PB). *Dominations and Powers* (New York and London 1951). *Three Philosophical Poets* (New York PB 1953). *The Philosophy of George Santayana* ed. Paul A. Schilpp (2nd ed. New York 1951). *Essays in Literary Criticism of George Santayana* ed. Irving Singer (New York 1956). *Santayana's Aesthetics* ed. Irving Singer (Cambridge, Mass. 1957). *The Sense of Reality* (New York PB 1962). *The Wisdom of George Santayana* ed. Ira D. Cardiff (2nd ed. New York 1964, also PB). *Soliloquies in England* (Ann Arbor, Mich. PB 1967). *George Santayana's America: Essays on Literature and Culture* ed. James Ballowe (Urbana, Ill. 1967, also PB).

REFERENCES: Van Meter Ames *Proust and Santayana: The Aesthetic Way of Life* (1937, reprinted New York 1964). Willard E. Arnett *Santayana and the Sense of Beauty* (Bloomington, Ind. 1955, PB 1969). Jerome Ashmore *Santayana, Art and Aesthetics* (Cleveland, Ohio 1966). Richard Butler *Life and World of George Santayana* (Chicago

PB 1960) and *Mind of Santayana* (1955, reprinted New York 1968). Daniel Cory *Santayana: The Later Years* (New York 1963). George W. Howgate *George Santayana* (Philadelphia and London 1938).

SAPPHO (fl. early 6th century B.C.). Greek lyric poet. Born Lesbos, probably at Mytilene, where she seems to have spent all her life. Her family were aristocrats, and presumably suffered much from the democratic movements in Lesbos. Sappho is said to have been married and the mother of a girl, Cleis. What remains of her work, in the form of quotations by later critics, epigrams of dubious authenticity in the *Palatine Anthology*, and papyrus fragments, is written in the Aeolic dialect of Lesbos in a great variety of meters, and consists in the main of love lyrics and informal hymns.

TRANSLATION: *Sappho: A New Translation* tr. Mary Barnard (Berkeley, Calif. and Cambridge, England, PB 1958).

REFERENCES: C. M. Bowra *Greek Lyric Poetry: From Alcman to Simonides* (2nd ed. Oxford 1961). Denys L. Page *Sappho and Alcaeus: An Introduction to the Study of Ancient Lesbian Poetry* (Oxford 1955). David M. Robinson *Sappho and Her Influence* (1924, new ed. New York 1963).

✍

SAPPHO

BY DUDLEY FITTS

Sappho was born on the island of Lesbos towards the end of the seventh century before our era, and her *floruit* (the year 590 B.C. will do as a guess) is connected with Mytilene, the capital city. As a poet, a celebrant of love, she had an enormous reputation in antiquity. "Sappho was something to be wondered at," writes the geographer Strabo. "Never within human memory has there been a woman to compare with her as a poet." The passage of time has augmented that fame instead of dimming it, and so many romantic or scandalous rumors have

been added to it over the centuries that Sappho today is rather a legend and a symbol than a literary actuality. The situation is not eased by the fact that her poems, originally the basis for her reputation, have been almost entirely lost. The ancient critics credited her with nine books, which must have run to several thousand lines, but only one poem, a seven-stanza address to Aphrodite, has come down to us intact. The remainder is all fragments transmitted to us accidentally in the citations of old lexicographers and grammarians, with here and there a genuine literary critic, or else deciphered from shreds of papyrus dug out of the sands of Egypt. Some of these papyrus scraps are of considerable length, a matter perhaps of several mutilated stanzas; but more often we must be content with lacerations of lines, the survival of a phrase here, a word there — sometimes, indeed, only a syllable or less of an isolated word. This is fragmentary survival with a vengeance. Yet it has its advantages: the surrounding darkness and the fortuitous emphasis thus thrown upon a brief passage or a single unusual word tend to increase the radiance of a fame as long and generously established as Sappho's. There is so little material evidence that criticism is almost impossible. She has become what an ancient admirer called her: a divinity, the Tenth Muse.

The more garish parts of the legend are to be marveled at and discarded: vague and self-contradicting stories of sorcery, of political intrigue and travel abroad, of sexual complications culminating in a lovers' leap suicide. These are dreams. We know the names of her father and mother, we know that she had three brothers, we think we know that she married a rich man named Cercolas, a citizen of Andros; and she tells us that she has a daughter whose name is Cleis. She is said to have been small and dark, not at all beautiful. She is reputed to have been a kind of priestess in a feminine love cult, a deviation that took its name from her island, and it is clearly true that she celebrated the love of women in her poems. Certainly she was a Lesbian in more than a geographical sense to the poets who cracked jokes about her two hundred years later in the Old and Middle Comedy. But a reputation based upon comic repartee, even if your master of ceremonies is an Aristophanes, is scarcely to be taken seriously, especially when most of the evidence has vanished. Normal or abnormal, *femme damnée* or Tenth Muse, the only reality of Sappho is in her poetry.

The problem here, because of the fragmentary nature of the text, is to distinguish what she wrote from what she might have written. Reading translations of Sappho, even the best of them, we should remember that what we are reading is largely reconstruction based upon conjecture. Only the address to Aphrodite is probably whole, having been passed on to us with stylistic comment by Dionysius of Halicarnassus, who wrote during the reign of the emperor Augustus. Another poem, which had the good fortune to be paraphrased in Latin by Catullus, comes to us reasonably intact from "Longinus," whoever he may have been, who wrote a notable essay *On the Sublime*. After that, we move among mutilations of greater or lesser import. Yet enough remains, even in these *disjecta membra*, to reveal a poet of extraordinary grace and power. Possibly the grace has been more often perceived than the power. Partly because of a vulgar but still obtrusive idea that a woman poet is a "poetess" and that poetesses are delicate and feminine and "sweete-slyding,"

and partly because of the decadent aura of the Lesbian idea itself, Sappho has been seen rosily in an erotic mist, a dream of Algernon Swinburne's. It is something of a relief then to come upon the clear, sinewy strength of her verses. Again and again, in passages that are long enough to take hold of us, the impression is that of total awareness working with great subtlety upon total reality. The tone has been caught best, I think, by Mary Barnard, in her version of the opening of a love poem to a girl named Anactoria:

> *Some say a cavalry corps,*
> *some infantry, some, again,*
> *will maintain that the swift oars*
>
> *of our fleet are the finest*
> *sight on dark earth; but I say*
> *that whatever one loves, is.*

That is the clean Sapphic tone, far enough removed from the nightingale languors of the late Victorians. She is not always so stripped as this, but she is always direct and tactile, always delighting us with a twist of hard physical insight where a "poetess" would have given us a murmur or a swoon. Such, at any rate, is the impression of the scraps that have come down to us. The presence is that of a poet of a high order, possibly of the highest; but no argument can be based upon fragments existing out of context.

SARDOU, Victorien (Sept. 7, 1831 – Nov. 8, 1908). French playwright. Born and died in Paris. After abandoning a career in medicine, he devoted himself to writing. His first play was the unsuccessful *La Taverne des étudiants* (1854). Married Laurentine Léon (1858), through whom he met actress Virginie Déjazet, who starred in his first successful play, *Les Premières armes de Figaro* (1859). Firmly established his reputation with *Les Pattes* *de mouches* (1860, tr. *A Scrap of Paper* 1889). After his wife's death (1867), married Anne Soulié (1872). Elected to Académie Française (1877), he was extremely popular with audiences of his day, although contemporary and later critics scorned him. Much of his success was due to the actors and actresses who played his leading roles; many of his plays were written especially for Virginie Déjazet and Sarah Bernhardt. Like Eugène Scribe, he was a master of the well-made play; his expert but superficial craftsmanship inspired G. B. Shaw's derisive term "Sardoodledom." His works, which number over seventy, include the outstanding farce *Divorçons* (1880, tr. *Let's Get a Divorce* 1909); comedies of manners such as *Nos Intimes* (1861, tr. *Our Friends* 1879), *La Famille Benoîton* (1865); melodramas such as *Fédora* (1882, tr. 1883) and *La Tosca* (1887, the source of Puccini's opera); historical plays such as *Patrie!* (1869), *Thermidor* (1891), and the still popular *Madame Sans-Gêne* (1893).

REFERENCES: Jerome A. Hart *Sardou and the Sardou Plays* (Philadelphia and London 1913). Georges Mouly *La Vie prodigueuse de Victorien Sardou* (Paris 1931). Blanche Roosevelt (pseudonym of Mrs. B. R. T. Macchetta) *Victorien Sardou* (London 1892).

SARGENT, John Singer (Jan. 12, 1856 – Apr. 15, 1925). American painter. Born Florence, Italy, of well-to-do American parents; educated there, in Rome and in Nice. Entered École des Beaux Arts (1874) and studio of Carolus-Duran. After first trip to U.S. (1876), exhibited *Miss Watts* at Paris Salon (1877). Traveled to Spain and North Africa (1879–80) and came under lifelong influence of Velázquez. The famous *El Jaleo* (1882, Gardner Museum, Boston) comes from this period. In Paris began to establish reputation as portraitist. On trips to Boston, joined fashionable society and was in demand for portraits, painting works such as *The Daughters of Edward D. Boit* (1882, Museum of Fine Arts, Boston). In Paris his superb portrait of Madame Gautreau, *Madame X* (1884, Metropolitan Museum, New York), was so daring it caused a scandal that drove Sargent to

London. Here, he was promptly taken up by high society and flooded with commissions for portraits, among others of such famous persons as Ellen Terry, whom he painted as Lady Macbeth, and Robert Louis Stevenson (1884–87, Taft Museum, Cincinnati). Today a whole room at the Tate Gallery, London, is devoted to his characteristically luminous, polished portraits of the rich and fashionable. But he declined knighthood (1907) because he considered himself American. Among his famous American portraits are those of Theodore Roosevelt, John D. Rockefeller, Woodrow Wilson, and Edwin Booth. He also executed murals in Boston for the Public Library (1890–1916) and Museum of Fine Arts (1916–21). From 1910 he concentrated especially on watercolors, a medium in which he excelled. Served in Europe in World War I as artist for British government; *Gassed* was exhibited at Royal Academy (1919). World-famous and a recipient of numerous honors, Sargent spent his last years in Boston and London, and is buried at Brookwood, Surrey, England.

REFERENCES: Evan Charteris *John Sargent* (London and New York 1927). William Howe Downes *John S. Sargent: His Life and Work* (Boston 1925). Ellen Gross and James Harithas eds. *Drawings in the Corcoran Gallery of Art* (Alhambra, Calif. n.d., also PB). David McKibbin *Sargent's Boston* (Boston 1956). Charles M. Mount *John Singer Sargent: A Biography* (3rd ed. New York 1969). Richard Ormond *Sargent: Paintings, Drawings, Watercolors* (New York 1970).

SARMIENTO, Domingo Faustino (Feb. 15, 1811 – Sept. 11, 1888). Argentine statesman, educator, and writer. Born San Juan, Argentina. Opposed (1829) the Gaucho dictator Juan Manuel de Rosas, and was exiled to Chile on Rosas' return to power (1835). Here he developed a distinguished career in journalism, political philosophy and educational reform, and wrote his most famous work, *Facundo* (1845, tr. *Life in the Argentine Republic in the Days of the Tyrants*, 1961). Sarmiento returned to Argentina (1852), after Rosas' defeat, and rapidly rose to eminence in a political career; he was minister to U.S. (1864–68) and president of Argentina (1868–74) in an enlightened and progressive administration. Reorganized the school system of his country (1875–88), writing prolifically on educational theory. Died in Asunción, Paraguay.

REFERENCES: Allison W. Bunkley *The Life of Sarmiento* (Princeton, N.J. 1952). *A Sarmiento Anthology* tr. and ed. Stuart E. Grummon (Princeton, N.J. 1948).

SARTO, Andrea del (real name Andrea Domenico d'Agnolodi Francisco) (July 16, 1486 – Sept. 29, 1530). Italian painter. Born and died in Florence. Son of a tailor (*sarto;* hence his name). Apprenticed to painters Gian Barile and Piero di Cosimo; entered Florentine painters' guild (1508). Commissioned (1509) to paint frescoes in cloister of SS Annunziata, which show influence of Leonardo. Later he added *Procession of the Magi* (1511) and *Birth of the Virgin* (1514), both fine examples of High Renaissance painting. Made his reputation with series of frescoes on life of John the Baptist in church of the Scalzi (begun 1512). They were influenced by engravings of Dürer, recently brought to Italy. Married Lucrezia del Fede (1517), who frequently posed for his Madonnas. Invited to French court by Francis I (1518). At this time, his work showed marked interest in dramatic and sculptural effects, as in *Madonna of the Harpies* (1517, Uffizi, Florence) and *The Holy Family* (c.1515, Louvre, Paris). Among his other great works: *The Sculptor* (1524, National Gallery, London), the superb lunette *Madonna del Sacco* (1525, SS Annunziata), and the fresco *The Last Supper* (1526, S. Salvi, Florence). At his best del Sarto is compared with the Raphael of the Madonnas, and is considered one of the foremost Florentine painters of the sixteenth century. He is the subject of one of Browning's famous poems.

REFERENCES: Bernard Berenson *The Drawings of the Florentine Painters* (new ed. 3 vols. Chicago 1938). Sydney J. Freedberg *Andrea del Sarto* (2 vols. Cambridge, Mass. and Oxford 1963). H. Guinness *Andrea del Sarto* (London

1899). J. K. G. Shearman *Andrea del Sarto* (2 vols. Oxford 1965).

SASSETTA (real name Stefano di Giovanni) (c.1395–1450). Italian painter. Though probably trained in Siena, nothing is known of him until 1426, when he completed a polyptych of which fragments still survive (Pinacoteca Nazionale, Siena). His early works, with their bright colors and gold backgrounds, have all the elegance and richness of fourteenth-century Sienese art. But influenced by early Florentine Renaissance painters, he used a sense of space and a more naturalistic technique to express his mystical imagination, as in the monumental *Madonna della Neve* (1430–32, Collection Contini Bonacossi, Florence). From 1433 to 1437 he painted the decorative polyptych for S. Francesco, Cortona (Museo Diocesano, Cortona). The sections of his beautifully expressive altarpiece for S. Francesco, Borgo San Sepolcro (1437–44), are scattered across Europe (I Tatti, Settignano; National Gallery, London; Louvre, Paris). His last works, finished by Sano di Pietro, were frescoes for the Porta Romana, in Siena (1444–50), where he died. Some works formerly assigned to Sassetta, including a triptych in the Osservanza church near Siena, are now attributed to a Master of the Osservanza. It is the consummate combination of fantastical international Gothic with the new techniques of the Renaissance which gives Sassetta's art its greatness.

REFERENCES: Bernard Berenson *Sassetta* (Florence 1946). John Pope-Hennessy *Sassetta* (London and New York 1939).

SASSOON, Siegfried (Lorraine) (Sept. 8, 1886 – Sept. 1, 1967). English poet and writer. Born Brenchley, Kent. Parents separated when he was a child. Educated at Marlborough and at Clare College, Cambridge (two years). Served as army officer during World War I and, recuperating from a throat wound, began writing series of bitterly antiwar and antipolitical poems, *The Old Huntsman* (1917), *Counterattack* (1918), *War Poems* (1919); later, published *Satirical Poems* (1926). During the war, he was certified temporarily insane and sent to a sanitarium in Edinburgh. But later he not only disavowed pacificism but rejoined service as officer in Palestine, then in France, where he was again wounded. Besides his war poetry, he is famous for the three-volume autobiography in fictional form: *The Memoirs of George Sherston,* published separately as *Memoirs of a Fox-Hunting Man* (1928, winner of Hawthornden prize and James Tait Black Memorial prize), *Memoirs of an Infantry Officer* (1930), and *Sherston's Progress* (1936). Other autobiographical volumes include: *The Old Century and Seven More Years* (1938) and *The Weald of Youth* (1942). His *Collected Poems: 1908–1956* appeared in 1961. Also wrote under pseudonyms of Pinchbeck Lyre, Sigmund Sashun, and Saul Kain. Awarded C.B.E. (1951). Died at Heytesbury House, near Warmister, Wiltshire.

REFERENCES: F. J. Harvey Darton *From Surtees to Sassoon* (London and Boston 1931). Geoffrey Keynes *Bibliography of Siegfried Sassoon* (London 1962 and New York 1964). Michael Thorpe *Siegfried Sassoon: A Critical Study* (London 1966).

SATIE, Erik (Alfred Leslie) (May 17, 1866 – July 1, 1925). French composer. Born Honfleur, son of a Paris music publisher. After attending Paris Conservatoire for one term (1883–84), abandoned systematic study and played piano in various Montmartre cabarets. Published first piano pieces (1887), deliberately and humorously labeling them opus 62. After years of living in poverty and obscurity, resumed serious musical study at Schola Cantorum (1905–1908), studying composition with Albert Roussel and Vincent d'Indy. Often the serious intent of his music was concealed by absurdly witty titles, such as *Trois Pièces en forme de poire* (1903, *Three Pieces in the Shape of a Pear*). But his eccentricity, humor, harmonic innovations, and seemingly revolutionary theories won him numerous devoted admirers among musicians. Darius Milhaud, Henri Sauguet, and the conductor Roger Desormière organized the École d'Arcueil in his honor, named after the Paris suburb in which

he lived after 1898. He also influenced a group of young composers known as Les Six, whose members included Arthur Honegger, Georges Auric, Louis Durey, Germaine Tailleferre, Francis Poulenc, and Milhaud. His work often anticipated the impressionism of Ravel and Debussy, as in the piano pieces *Sarabandes* (1887) and *Gymnopédies* (1888, nos. 1 and 3 orchestrated by Ravel). His other works include the lyric drama *Socrate,* based on the dialogues of Plato (performed 1920); ballets *Parade* (1917), *Mercure* (1924), *Relâche* (1924); numerous piano pieces, among them *Gnossiennes* (1890); and songs. He died in Paris.

REFERENCES: Wilfred H. Mellers *Studies in Contemporary Music* (London 1948). Rollo H. Myers *Erik Satie* (London 1948, also PB). Roger Shattuck *The Banquet Years: The Arts in France, 1885–1918: Alfred Jarry, Henri Rousseau, Erik Satie, Guillaume Apollinaire* (1958, rev. ed. New York PB 1968 and London PB 1969). Pierre Daniel Templier *Erik Satie* (tr. Cambridge, Mass. 1969).

SAVILE, George, 1st marquis of Halifax (Nov. 11, 1633 – Apr. 5, 1695). English writer and statesman. Born Thornhill, Yorkshire, son of Sir William Savile, a prominent royalist in the Civil War. Spent early years traveling with a tutor in France and Italy, and at Rufford Abbey, Nottinghamshire, which he was to make his family's principal seat. Rose to high office under Charles II and James II, but was dismissed by James for opposing repeal of the test act and habeas corpus act (1685). In retirement during the next three years, he wrote the pamphlets on which his fame largely rests, including *Letter to a Dissenter* (1687), the *Anatomy of an Equivalent* (1688), and his best-known work, *The Character of a Trimmer* (1688), which defends the policy of moderation, compromise, and retention of tradition which had earned him the sobriquet of "the Trimmer." Halifax actively furthered the accession of William III, but resigned (1690) from his service. Married twice. Died in London.

EDITION: *The Complete Works of George Savile, First Marquis of Halifax* ed. Walter Raleigh (Oxford 1912, reprinted New York 1970).

REFERENCES: Helen C. Foxcroft *Life and Letters of Sir George Savile* (2 vols. London and New York 1898) and *A Character of the Trimmer* (Cambridge, England, 1946).

SCARLATTI, (Pietro) Alessandro (Gaspare) (May 2, 1660 – Oct. 24, 1725). Italian composer. Born Palermo, Sicily. Moved to Rome (1672), where he married Antonia Anzalone (1678; see DOMENICO SCARLATTI below). His first opera, *Gli Equivoci nell' amore* (1679), produced in Rome, won him appointment there as *maestro di cappella* to the abdicated Queen Christina of Sweden. Became *maestro di cappella* to viceroy of Naples (c.1690), and from 1702 to 1709 enjoyed patronage of Prince Ferdinando de' Medici in Florence and Cardinal Ottoboni in Rome. Also visited Urbino and Venice, where he supervised production of one of his finest operas, *Mitridate Eupatore* (1707). Resumed post in Naples, producing such outstanding operas as *La Principessa fedele* (1710) and *Il Tigrane* (1715). He died in Naples. Handel and other operatic composers were influenced by Scarlatti's operas of the Neapolitan school, of which he produced 115. He also wrote oratorios, sacred music, exquisite secular vocal music, chamber and keyboard works. He is remembered as the founder of classical music and the harmonic system later perfected by Mozart.

REFERENCES: Charles van den Borren *Alessandro Scarlatti et l'esthétique de l'opéra napolitain* (Paris 1921). E. J. Dent *Alessandro Scarlatti: His Life and Work* (1905, new ed. London and New York 1960).

SCARLATTI, (Giuseppe) Domenico (Oct. 26, 1685 – July 23, 1757). Italian composer. Born Naples, son of Alessandro Scarlatti (see above). Trained by his father and by Francesco Gasparini, he was first known as a writer of operas. In Rome (1709–20), he served as composer for the private theatre of Maria Cosima, queen of Poland, and as *maestro di cappella* for both the Portuguese ambassador and the Vatican. Ap-

pointed *maestro* of the royal chapel at Lisbon (1720), but returned to Italy twice: to see his father in Naples (1724) and to marry Maria Catalina Gentili in Rome (1728). When the Portuguese Infanta Maria Barbara, his pupil, was married to the heir to the Spanish throne (1729), she took Scarlatti with her to the court at Madrid, where he remained until his death. In Spain he composed the works for which he is famous, an enormous number of harpsichord sonatas.

REFERENCES: Ralph Kirkpatrick *Domenico Scarlatti* (1953, rev. ed. Princeton, N.J. and Oxford 1955, also PB). Sacheverell Sitwell *A Background for Domenico Scarlatti, 1685–1757* (London 1935).

DOMENICO SCARLATTI
BY ROBERT EVETT

If musical scholars were as suspicious a breed as Shakespearean scholars, there might be a movement to prove that Domenico Scarlatti never existed, or that his best pieces were written by somebody else — possibly the queen of Spain. The man left hardly any record of himself: one letter (inviting the duke of Huescar to come calling), a will, some signatures, and a very few musical autographs. Most of what we know about him comes from legal documents and gossip.

Until he was almost forty, Domenico seems to have been under the thumb of his eminent father Alessandro Scarlatti — then one of the great lions of Italian music. Alessandro was a purveyor of musical entertainment to the very rich, and guided his own career by the simple rule that a prince of the blood is a better financial risk than a prince of the church. When he was twenty, he was already music master to Queen Christina of Sweden (who was living in Rome). A pretty good start. And, as a man who contrived to support himself in great style, Alessandro did what he could to transmit success and the secrets of it to his son. Therefore, from his youth into his middle age, Scarlatti *fils* supported himself creating diversions, mostly operatic, for the dowager queen of Poland and the notorious libertine Cardinal Ottoboni, and — to round out his Italian career — as musical director of the Archbasilica of St. Peter. Then, when he was thirty-five, Domenico resigned his post and left Italy for good. By that time, he had written a great deal of operatic and liturgical vocal music. What has survived (and a lot of it hasn't) is perfectly all right, but slapdash and in no sense arresting.

Because so many documents were destroyed in the Lisbon earthquake of 1755, it is hard to say what happened next and when. Scarlatti did go west, and before he was forty he had taken the post of music master to Maria Barbara de Braganza. A frightfully ugly little girl, she was then the infanta of Portugal, and soon to become the queen of Spain.

If he had gone into a cloistered monastery, Scarlatti could not have been kept under wraps more securely than he was in the Portuguese and Spanish courts. Maria Barbara and her husband, Fernando VI, were music lovers. They were in a position to buy musicians, and this is just what they did. (They did not, in fact, buy Scarlatti, who was a gift from King João V of Portugal to his daughter.) But once they acquired a musician, his public career was over. He could look forward to a life of great security, following the court from one royal estate to the next, but his audience would be a private one.

The traveling must have been unpleasant, but there is no indication that life at court was particularly tedious. The musicians in the entourage were men of unusual endowments and,

allowing for occasional temperamental outbursts, they must have found each other stimulating. And the royal patrons were generous. Scarlatti's salary was large enough to allow him to keep a fine house in Madrid. The queen, in her will, bequeathed her music master two thousand doubloons — which was, and still is, a fortune in Spanish gold. (Scarlatti died before Maria Barbara, and nobody got the doubloons.) Furthermore, in 1738, Scarlatti was made a knight of the order of Santiago by João V. They checked his ancestry in a cursory way and, finding no heretics, Jews, or Moors in it, bestowed the cloak of the order on him, with special permission to "wear clothes of velvet and silk in any color, rings, jewels, chains and clothing of gold, inasmuch as the hat be of velvet."

It was in these circumstances that Scarlatti wrote the sonatas that constitute his major contribution to music and on which his reputation rests. There are 555 of them in Ralph Kirkpatrick's catalogue. It is impossible to state flatly when the composition of the series began, but in 1738, when he was fifty-three, Scarlatti published thirty of them under the title *Essercizi per gravicembalo*. The following year, a British publisher brought out an edition of the *Essercizi* with an additional twelve sonatas. Aside from these, most of the works have survived in beautiful manuscripts copied and bound in leather at the command of the queen.

It is hard to remember that these pieces were composed not only for the queen's pleasure, but also for her use. She must have been a most unusually accomplished performer by any standards. The Scarlatti sonatas are not only extremely idiomatic for the harpsichord; they are hard to play. Many, in fact most of them, are accessible only to the virtuoso. Of the eighteenth-century keyboard works that immediately suggest comparison — works of Couperin, Rameau, Handel, and the Italian crowd — none are as treacherous. J. S. Bach wrote pieces that are every bit as hard, but Scarlatti could not conceivably have known them.

Since Scarlatti could not possibly have started the sonata series before he was forty, and was still working hard right up to the time of his death at the age of seventy-two, it is proper to think of this literature as an old man's music — a source of encouragement to late starters everywhere. Much of Scarlatti's facility must be attributed to the fact that the composition of the sonatas made few demands on his imagination in point of form. Scholars, enthusiasts, and apologists can point out enormous differences between one piece and another, but the fact remains that they are all about the same length — five minutes, give or take a minute or two; and that almost all of them are divided at or near the middle by a caesura. And there are whole families of pieces that resemble each other closely. Of the D major sonatas, twenty-two fast ones are in ⅜ time. Faced with this combination of tempo, key, and meter, Scarlatti always went into the same whirling dervish routine.

The largest distinction of the sonatas is a stylistic one. A great deal — too much, I think — has been made of how much of Spain got into them: brassy sounds from outdoor processionals, hints of flamenco, etc. The real eccentricities are in the harmony, which is never completely predictable and, at its wildest, is extraordinarily audacious, as in one of the A minor sonatas (number 175 in the Kirkpatrick catalogue), which takes the dissonance as far as it was going to go before Stravinsky's *Sacre du printemps*. This can be explained by the fact that

the only ears to which he was responsible besides his own belonged to a king and queen whose taste he had helped form.

At Scarlatti's death, the queen paid his gambling debts and settled a pension of four thousand crowns a year on his family.

———

SCHILLER, (Johann Christoph) Friedrich von (Nov. 10, 1759 – May 9, 1805). German playwright, poet, and literary theorist. Born at Marbach in Württemberg, son of overseer of estate of Duke Karl Eugen. Eugen insisted young Schiller enter military academy, where he studied medicine and became regimental physician. First play, *Die Räuber* (1781), a brilliant attack on political tyranny, was a success when first performed in Mannheim (1782). Escaped military duty and, short of funds, living with friends, worked on poems and plays. *Louise Millerin* (1783) (renamed *Kabale und Liebe*, 1784) was best of early works. Founded literary periodical *Rheinische Thalia* (1785–93) and, again in financial trouble, was supported by Christian Gottfried Körner, for whom he wrote ode *An die Freude* (*Hymn to Joy*), choral finale of Beethoven's *Ninth Symphony*. *Don Carlos* (1787), first outstanding tragedy in blank verse, represents Schiller's movement from *Sturm und Drang* philosophy and search for political freedom to search for spiritual freedom. Schiller settled in Weimar (1787–92), became immersed in historical studies (most noteworthy was *Geschichte des Abfalls der vereinigten Niederlande*, 1788); named professor of history in Jena. Married Charlotte von Lengefeld (1789). Ill health prevented his further teaching; concentrated on Kant and aesthetic theory, producing some outstanding essays. Developed great friendship with Goethe through establishment of journal *Die Horen* (1794). During this period wrote reflective poems *Das Ideal und das Leben, Der Spaziergang, Die Macht des Gesanges*. Turned again to drama, produced his finest: the *Wallenstein* trilogy (1799), *Maria Stuart* (1800), *Die Jungfrau von Orleans*

(1801), *Die Braut von Messina* (1803), *Wilhelm Tell* (1804). Ennobled (1802). Died in Weimar. Considered one of Germany's greatest poets and dramatists.

TRANSLATIONS: *Wallenstein* tr. Charles E. Passage (New York and London 1958, also PB). *Mary Stuart* tr. Stephen Spender (London 1959). *Don Carlos* tr. Charles E. Passage (New York 1959, also PB). *Letters on the Aesthetic Education of Man* tr. E. M. Wilkinson and L. A. Willoughby (Oxford 1968). *Friedrich Schiller: An Anthology for Our Time* ed. Frederick Ungar (New York 1959, also PB).

REFERENCES: Thomas Carlyle *The Life of Friedrich Schiller* (1825; 1899 ed. reprinted New York 1969). John R. Frey ed. *Schiller, 1759–1959* (Urbana, Ill. PB 1959). Henry B. Garland *Schiller* (London 1949 and New York 1950) and *Schiller: The Dramatic Writer* (Oxford 1969). Bernt von Heiseler *Schiller* (tr. London 1962 and Chester Springs, Pa. 1964). Friedrich W. Kaufmann *Schiller, Poet of Philosophical Idealism* (Oberlin, Ohio 1942). William F. Mainland *Schiller and the Changing Past* (London 1957). Frederick Norman ed. *Schiller Bicentenary Lectures* (London 1960). Ernst L. Stahl *Friedrich Schiller's Drama, Theory and Practice* (Oxford 1954). A. Leslie Willson ed. *A Schiller Symposium* (Austin, Tex. 1960).

SCHLEGEL, August Wilhelm von (Sept. 8, 1767 – May 12, 1845) and (Karl Wilhelm) Friedrich von (Mar. 10, 1772 – Jan. 12, 1829). German critics. Both born in Hanover, sons of a Lutheran pastor. August, educated at Göttingen University, became a professor at Jena (1798) and Bonn (1818–45), where he died. Friedrich studied law, but turned to literature and lectured at Jena. In Paris (1802), he studied Oriental literature and lectured on philosophy. The brothers founded the journal *Athenäeum* (1798–1800), a breeding ground for the romantic movement. From 1798 to 1801 August translated superbly seventeen Shakespeare plays, aided by his wife Karoline (née Michaelis; they were married 1796, divorced 1804). He later translated Spanish, Portuguese, and San-

skrit texts. Expounded romantic view of literature in *Vorlesungen über Schöne Literatur und Kunst,* lectures given in Berlin (1801–1804). Became (1804) secretary to Madame de Stael. In Vienna he delivered his celebrated lectures *Über Dramatische Kunst und Literatur* (1809–11), extolling Shakespeare. In his late years at Bonn he turned to Oriental studies and pioneered Sanskrit scholarship. Friedrich also wrote on this subject: *Über die Sprache und Weisheit der Inder* (1808). He married Dorothea Veit, daughter of philosopher Moses Mendelssohn (1804). In addition to his early studies of classical literature, *Die Griechen und die Römer* (1797) and *Gespräch über die Poesie* (1798), he wrote many critical essays, including a famous analysis of Goethe's *Wilhelm Meister.* In 1798 he published *Fragmente,* a collection of brilliant aphorisms. Lectured in Vienna much of his life — *Die Philosophie der Geschichte* (1829), *Die Philosophie der Sprache* (1830) — and edited many journals. He died in Dresden. Both brothers published their collected poems (August, 1800; Friedrich, 1809), but their distinction lay in their role as proponents of German romanticism, thereby exerting profound influence on development of German literature.

REFERENCES: M. E. Atkinson *A. W. Schlegel as a Translator of Shakespeare* (Oxford 1958). Hans Eichner *Friedrich Schlegel* (New York 1970). Ralph Tymms *German Romantic Literature* (London 1955). Oskar F. Walzel *German Romanticism* (tr. New York and London 1932, also PB). L. A. Willoughby *The Romantic Movement in Germany* (Oxford 1930, reprinted New York 1966).

SCHLÜTER, Andreas (c.1664 – 1714). German sculptor and architect. Born Hamburg, son of sculptor Gerhard Schlüter, with whom he studied. After travels in Italy, entered service of king of Poland in Warsaw (1691), then went as architect and sculptor to Hohenzollern court in Berlin. There he built part of the royal palace, his decoration of which is the finest example of German baroque style. He also decorated the arsenal in Berlin, and is particularly noted for his equestrian group statue of Frederick William the Great Elector (1698–1703), Schloss Charlottenburg, Berlin, a masterpiece of German baroque sculpture. Also designed pulpit in the Marienkirche (Berlin) and tomb of Frederick I and Queen Sophia Charlotte in cathedral. Difficulties with construction of the Mint Tower for royal palace resulted in Schlüter's losing favor with King Frederick I (1706). Invited to serve Peter the Great of Russia (1714) in St. Petersburg, he died there soon after his arrival.

SCHNITZLER, Arthur (May 15, 1862 – Oct. 21, 1931). Austrian playwright and novelist. Born and died in Vienna. Son of well-known throat specialist who treated theatre people. Schnitzler studied medicine at University of Vienna (degree 1885), and began writing short plays at that time. Published series of one act plays, *Anatol* (1893, tr. 1911), concerning love affairs of young Viennese philanderer. The success of *Anatol* was followed by other lighthearted plays dealing with love and sex: *Liebelei* (1895, tr. *Playing with Love* 1914), *Reigen* (1903, tr. *Merry-Go-Round* 1953, filmed as *La Ronde* 1955), which firmly established his reputation. But with maturity he became preoccupied with more serious themes and problems between men and women, using his knowledge of Freudian psychology in exploring human relationships. *Zwischenspiel* (1906, *Intermezzo*), *Professor Bernhardi* (1912, tr.1927), concerned with anti-Semitism, *Der Einsame Weg* (1903, tr. *The Lonely Way* 1915), *Das Weite Land* (1911, tr. *The Vast Domain* 1923) belong to this period, as does the autobiographical novel *Der Weg ins Freie* (1908, tr. *The Road to the Open* 1923). Melancholy and skepticism characterize his later works, especially the last writings, of which *Flucht in die Finsternis* (1931, tr. *Flight into Darkness* 1931) is an example.

EDITION: *Stories and Plays* ed. and tr. Allen W. Porterfield (New York 1930 and London 1934).

REFERENCES: Henry C. Hatfield and Jack M. Stein *Schnitzler, Kafka, Mann* (Boston 1953). Solomon Liptzin *Arthur Schnitzler* (New York 1932). Herbert W. Reichert and Herman Salinger eds. *Studies in Arthur Schnitzler* (Chapel Hill, N.C. 1963, also PB).

SCHOENBERG, Arnold (Sept. 13, 1874 – July 13, 1951). Austrian composer. Born Vienna. Largely self-taught. Early works, in late romantic style, include chamber music and songs. Married Mathilde von Zemlinsky (1901). Completed and performed highly original *Pierrot Lunaire* (1912). Perfected method of composition with twelve tones (1923). After wife's death, married Henriette Kolisch (1925). Appointed to Prussian Academy of Arts (1925) but dismissed for breach of contract (1933). Re-embraced Jewish faith that year and emigrated to U.S. (1934). Appointed professor of music, University of California at Los Angeles (1936). Died at Brentwood, Calif. Principal works: early, *Verklärte Nacht, Gurrelieder, Pelleas und Melisande;* middle, piano pieces, op. 11 and 19, Five Pieces for Orchestra, *Pierrot Lunaire;* late, suite for piano, third and fourth quartets, violin concerto, piano concerto, *Moses und Aaron.*

EDITIONS: *Style and Idea* (New York 1950). *Letters* (New York 1965).

REFERENCES: Benjamin Boretz and Edward T. Cone *Perspectives on Schoenberg and Stravinsky* (Princeton, N.J. PB 1968). René Leibowitz *Schoenberg and His School* (tr. New York 1949). Dika Newlin *Bruckner, Mahler, Schoenberg* (New York and Oxford 1947). Anthony Payne *Schoenberg* (London and New York 1968). H. H. Stuckenschmidt *Arnold Schönberg* (tr. London and New York 1960). Egon Wellesz *Arnold Schönberg* (tr. London 1925, reprinted New York 1969). Karl H. Wörner *Schönberg's Moses and Aaron* (tr. London 1963 and New York 1964).

☞

SCHOENBERG

BY ROBERT EVETT

In applying for a Guggenheim fellowship (the application was rejected), Arnold Schoenberg wrote: "On September 13, 1944, I have become seventy years of age. At this date — according to regulations — I had to retire from my position as professor of music at the University of California at Los Angeles. As I was in this position only eight years, I will receive a 'pension' of $38.00 (thirty-eight) a month, on which I am supposed to support a wife and three children (13, 8 and 4 years old)."

Things, as they turned out, were not quite this bad. But the old man had every right to be bitter. He was an exile in a country which, in his opinion, was populated largely by Yahoos. His influence appeared to be declining. As late as 1949, he wrote: "My music is almost totally unknown in America and also in present-day Europe." Again, "My adherents . . . all rank Hindemith, Stravinsky and Bartók if not above me at least as on a par with me."

Trouble was never a stranger to Schoenberg. When he was sixteen, his father died, leaving him to support himself, and he did this very badly. For years he made a living orchestrating and copying an estimated six thousand pages of cheap Viennese theatre music. His only formal training consisted of a few counterpoint lessons with his friend (later his brother-in-law) the conductor Alexander von Zemlinsky.

Schoenberg's early triumphs, *Verklärte Nacht* and *Gurrelieder*, demonstrated that he was a consummate master of post-Wagnerian harmony — a highly sophisticated musical language rooted in almost three hundred years of Teutonic tradition. He was equipped by technique and also by temperament to become a junior Richard Strauss. Strauss evidently thought so at one time, and was instrumental in getting Schoenberg a teaching position. But by the spring of 1914, Strauss had said of Schoenberg: "I think he'd do better to shovel snow than to scribble on music paper." Schoenberg, for his part, said: "I have no intention of damaging Herr Strauss 'morally.' . . . He is no longer of the slightest artistic interest to me, and whatever I may once have learnt from him, I am thankful to say I misunderstood."

The cause of all this bad temper and backbiting was a stylistic leap that Schoenberg had made sometime between 1906 and 1909. In his new style, Schoenberg introduced a harmonic vocabulary which, though it grew logically out of the practices of the late German romantics, was more volatile, ambiguous, and elusive than anything that had come before it. Together with this came a melodic style that was really quite radical, characterized by an extremely wide range and, within it, great craggy leaps. It was probably the melodic substance that most put off the early listeners. Whatever the cause, by 1910 the public performance of a new work of Schoenberg's was more often than not the occasion for disorder in the concert hall. It was at about this time that the term "atonal" was invented and applied to the music of the Viennese school. Schoenberg resented the term, considered it erroneous and damaging, and at the age of seventy-three was still insisting, "A follower of my music should not say 'atonal.' "

By 1923 Schoenberg had evolved his method of composing with twelve notes. This much misunderstood system, which involves deploying the notes of the chromatic scale in an arbitrary series and repeating them in order, has always been substantially a harmonic device, the object being to produce the kind of coherence that is supplied by structural harmony in conventional music. In the hands of other, younger composers, the concept of serialism has gone through many transmutations and produced music with no recognizable similarity to the music of the past. Schoenberg himself, however, was imbued with tradition. Except for the rhetoric, his music is conventional more often than not.

Schoenberg was one of the first distinguished refugees from Hitler's Germany. In the fall of 1933 he was dismissed from the faculty of the Prussian Academy of Arts in Berlin. He came to the United States at the age of fifty-nine and for the rest of his life was remarkably productive. Though he was received with honors, commissions, and academic appointments, Schoenberg understood correctly that he was an enemy alien in Stravinsky territory. This knowledge was to vex him as long as he lived.

Schoenberg had a phenomenal gift for attracting people to him and for making friendships that lasted for forty or fifty years. He was also captious and quarrelsome to the end, and given to engaging in acrimonious letter writing without caring about the consequences. During the last years of his life he was sometimes nearly blind and often too sick to undertake any major projects, but never too far gone to defend himself. He quarreled with an editor of his book, *Style and Idea;* he accused his publishers of defrauding him; he had a magnificent public row with Thomas Mann.

In a late letter, he said, "I believe, when the movement of the reactionaries has died away, that music will return to composing with 12 tones." The extent to which this prophecy came true must have exceeded even Schoenberg's expectations, because Stravinsky, the old archenemy himself, became a twelve-tone composer, and with him a vast number of followers. For at least fifteen years after his death, Schoenberg was the dominant force in Western composition — sometimes directly, often indirectly, through his pupils. As more radical styles developed, his influence waned. There is no consensus about the enduring aesthetic merit of his work as yet. What is assured is the importance of his position as a historical figure.

SCHONGAUER, Martin (c.1450 – Feb. 2, 1491). German painter and engraver. Born Colmar, Alsace, son of a goldsmith. Attended Leipzig University (1465), but soon turned to art. Earliest works are drawings dated 1469; over fifty remain. Rogier van der Weyden and other Flemish artists influenced his painting, much of which is lost. Rich coloring and serene dignity characterize the work that survives: the *Virgin of the Rose Garden* (1473, St. Martin, Colmar), the *Orliac Altar* (divided between Musée d'Unterlinden, Colmar, Kunsthistorisches Museum, Vienna, and Staatliche Museen, Berlin), fragments of the *Last Judgment* frescoes (1489–91, Breisach cathedral), the small attributed *Nativity* (Alte Pinakothek, Munich). The 115 surviving copper engravings of exquisite craftsmanship were even more important than the paintings for their influence upon artists as different as Dürer and Michelangelo, who made a copy of the demonic *Temptation of St. Anthony.* Most depict religious scenes: series of life of the Virgin, the Passion of Christ, the Apostles, and individual subjects. The refinement and depth of his work make Schongauer the most outstanding German artist before Dürer. He died in Breisach.

REFERENCES: Max Geisberg *Martin Schongauer* (tr. New York 1928). Alan Shestack *Complete Engravings of Martin Schongauer* (New York PB 1969).

SCHOPENHAUER, Arthur (Feb. 22, 1788 – Sept. 21, 1860). German philosopher. Born Danzig, of a wealthy family, he traveled widely and studied philosophy at universities of Göttingen, Berlin, and Jena. Received doctorate (1813) at Jena for dissertation *Über die vier-*

fache Wurzel des Satzes vom zureichenden Grunde (1813, tr. *On the Fourfold Root of the Principle of Sufficient Reason* 1889). Settling in Dresden (1814), wrote his major work *Die Welt als Wille und Vorstellung* (1819, tr. *The World as Will and Idea* 1883), which led to lecture engagement at University of Berlin (1820). Emphatically opposed to the Hegelian optimism that dominated philosophy, Schopenhauer attracted little attention and few followers; embittered, he resigned. Settled as a recluse in Frankfurt-am-Main (1831), where he remained until his death. A misogynist and a misanthrope, he never married and discouraged friendships. His later writings, such as *Über den Willen in der Natur* (1836, tr. *Will in Nature* 1889), *Die beiden Grundprobleme der Ethik* (1841, tr. *The Basis of Morality* 1903), and *Parerga und Paralipomena* (1851), mostly elaborate his original thesis, stated in earlier works. Drawing upon Kant and Oriental thought, Schopenhauer developed a pessimistic philosophy which held an irrational will to be the active principle of the universe. Man can escape the will's ceaseless striving only by aesthetic contemplation or ascetic existence. Recognition and acclaim came to Schopenhauer only after 1848, when his pessimism corresponded with the mood of the times. His thought influenced many writers, philosophers, and psychologists, among them Thomas Mann, Friedrich Nietzsche, and Sigmund Freud.

TRANSLATIONS: *The World as Will and Idea* tr. Richard B. Haldane and J. Kemp (3 vols. 1883–86, new ed. Garden City, N.Y. PB 1961). *The World as Will and Representation* tr. E. F. J. Payne (Indian Hills, Colo. 1958 and London 1959). *On the Basis of Morality* tr. E. F. J. Payne (Indianapolis 1965, also PB). *Complete Essays* tr. Thomas Bailey Saunders (New York 1942 and London 1947). *The Living Thoughts of Schopenhauer* ed. Thomas Mann (London and New York 1939). *Essays from the Parerga and Paralipomena* tr. P. Bailey Saunders (London 1951).

REFERENCES: Frederick Copleston *Arthur Schopenhauer, Philosopher of Pessimism* (London 1946). Patrick

Gardiner *Schopenhauer* (Harmondsworth, England, and Baltimore PB 1963). Michael Kelly *Kant's Ethics and Schopenhauer's Criticism* (London 1910). Vivian J. McGill *Schopenhauer, Pessimist and Pagan* (New York 1931). Friedrich Nietzsche *Schopenhauer as Educator* (tr. Chicago PB 1965). William Wallace *Life of Arthur Schopenhauer* (London and New York 1890, reprinted New York 1902).

SCHUBERT, Franz (Peter) (Jan. 31, 1797 – Nov. 19, 1828). Austrian composer. Born and died in Vienna. Showed early promise in music. Joined court chapel choir (1808) and studied composition with Antonio Salieri. Wrote chamber music for private performance; became music master at Esterhazy summer residence (1818). It was not until the most famous singer of the day, Johann Michael Vogl, popularized his songs in Vienna that publishers were willing to take Schubert's work on a commission basis, but even then his financial rewards were slight. His attempts at opera were unsuccessful. He depended on help from a large circle of friends. Continually in ill health, he finally died of typhoid fever. Schubert's piano sonatas, string quartets, quintets, and symphonies are the core of his instrumental output. He virtually created the genre of the art song (*lied*), setting to music lyric poetry from Goethe, Schiller, Heine, and many others. Later major works: *Symphony no. 8 in B minor* (1822), *Die schöne Müllerin* (1823), *Die Winterreise* (1828), *Symphony no. 9 in C* (1828).

REFERENCES: Gerald Abraham ed. *Music of Schubert* (1947, reprinted Port Washington, N.Y. 1969). Maurice Brown *Schubert: A Critical Biography* (New York and London 1958) and *Essays on Schubert* (London and New York 1966). Richard Capell *Schubert's Songs* (2nd ed. New York 1966). Otto Erich Deutsch *Schubert: A Documentary Biography* (tr. New York and London 1947). Alfred Einstein *Schubert: A Musical Portrait* (New York and London 1951). Arthur Hutchings *Schubert* (3rd ed. London and New York 1956). Ernest G. Porter *Schubert's Song Technique* (London 1961 and Chester Springs, Pa. 1962). Marcel

Schneider *Schubert* (tr. New York and London PB 1960).

☞

FRANZ SCHUBERT
BY JOHN RUSSELL

"Schubertian" is one of the great European adjectives. It can be used with precision, though sparingly, of a footpath along water meadows, a side street in a market town, a garden restaurant trellised with vines, a mail van halfway up a mountain, or a countrified sitting room full of clean yellow cottons and furniture the color of old bamboo. It can be used of a weather report, a frog in a pond, or an attitude to the legend of Orestes. It can be used of a notion of human integrity, or a way of marking time in a waltz, or a reason for not getting up in the morning. It can be used of a dish (Bavarian *Dampfnudeln,* for instance), or of a conveyance, or of the capacity to amuse oneself without buying one's pleasures ready-made. It stands for natural genius of a kind that comes only once or twice in human history; but it also stands for qualities that should be within the reach of all of us — magnanimity, for instance, and constancy in private affections, an unenvious wonder at the achievement of others, and steadfastness in the face of bodily misfortune.

Not all this is given to us at once: "Schubertian" at sixteen and "Schubertian" at sixty are two quite different things. In childhood there is no problem: Schubert the inventor of tunes is the greatest there ever was. No one has had, as completely as he, the gift of the complete long-breathing musical sentence that can be lifted out of its context, and travestied in all kinds of ways, and still make delectable sense. His tunes work at all levels. The rondo theme of the D major piano sonata, op. 53, is, for instance, a marvel of high

art; but it can be belted out by the Carinthian Railway Workers' Silver Band and still change the world for us.

A year or two later, Schubert the disembodied spirit of music gives way to Schubert the ideal companion, the all-comprehending elder who has been everywhere before us as we stumble through the dark mazes of the heart. He it is who gives their true names to expectation and loss, yearning and fulfillment; and he puts into perspective the strange and dismaying fact that the great things and the small contrarieties can come about at the same time and come about in ways that no amount of sage counsel can foretell. He knew, better than anyone, how to distinguish true feeling from false; he never deceived himself, and he never deceives us; he is the metal by which alloys can be judged.

All this we can get from *Die schöne Müllerin* when we are still quite young. Schubert at such times reveals himself not as a simpleminded songbird, but as a man of quite exceptional intuitive intelligence, and as a dramatist in little who can get close in to every kind of emotional predicament and have something irreplaceable to say about all of them. His was a close-hauled, introspective art, free from the curse of competitive performance and aimed at a roomful of close friends: it did not occur to him to clamor for the attention of a hall packed with fee-paying strangers. He was not a great pianist, and he himself had very little voice, and he emphatically did not care for a spectacular or a histrionic style of performance. When he played in string quartets he did not ask either to lead the proceedings on first violin or to underpin them on cello: the equable and unobtrusive viola was his instrument. His was not music for display. "There is something in you," was the verdict of one great singer of the day, "but you are too little of an actor, too little of a charlatan. You squander your fine things without making the most of them."

These could be the traits of a minor master, too timid or too feeble to challenge the big men on their own ground. Schubert was touchingly and unaffectedly modest: "I still hope to make something of myself," he once said, "but who can write music after Beethoven?"; and in the last months of his life he was still taking lessons in fugue and counterpoint and planning to make a study in depth of Handel's oratorios. But the truth as it appears to us in middle life is that when Schubert wished to strike hard he could strike as hard as anyone. We can spend whole seasons in the opera house and not hear anything more compelling, in the way of drama, than the three minutes' traffic of *Der Erlkönig;* equally, we can watch the orchestra filing in for some piece of gigantomania by Mahler or Richard Strauss and know that for sheer unequivocal impact they are beaten before they begin by the scherzo from Schubert's C major quintet. Schubert did not need to quadruple the wind and reinforce the percussion; with the forces of a Viennese school orchestra, and at the age of eighteen, he could produce in his C minor symphony a structure before which Stravinsky at eighty-five was still filled with admiration.

Schubert in life was the personification of an easygoing good nature, but in his work there are no compromises. His friends remembered the times when he took a glass too many of strong young wine and could not get up from the table. But the rest of us remember the occasions on which Schubert outfaced the very worst that life has to offer and went on unde-terred. He never lost himself in generalities, but had a naturalist's exactitude: the raven in *Die Winterreise* turns our blood to ice, as it is meant to, but its wheeling flight is observed as exactly as if Audubon, and not Schubert, were turning his eyes up to the sky. In the next song in that same cycle, Schubert brings the fall of the leaf before us with the kind of inspired shorthand that Rembrandt used in his pen drawings. All this is not "art," and it is not "music-making," as those things are conceived of in polite society: it is life itself, dis-upholstered. Schubert takes us to the very edge, as Shakespeare does in the last pages of *King Lear.*

He himself would say, I think, that this is too somber an assessment. And it is certainly true that "Schubertian" applies to many of the pleasantest things in life, and above all to those which cost nothing, have no social cachet, and are owed simply to a general sympathetic alertness. Schubert was himself this alertness personified: so much so that when his surviving friends spoke of him thirty and even forty years after his death they would say over and over again that in his company they had been "the happiest people in Germany — no, in the whole world!" Listening to the great sixteen-bar tune which brings the *Octet* to an end, we believe them.

SCHUMANN, Robert (Alexander) (June 8, 1810 – July 29, 1856). German composer. Born Swickau, Saxony, son of a bookseller. Attended the Gymnasium (1820–28), then was sent to Leipzig to study law, but instead devoted himself to literature and music. Founded *Die Neue Zeitschrift für Musik,* which he edited (1834–44), a journal in which he expounded the most advanced musical trends, proclaiming the genius of Chopin (1834) and later Brahms. Studied piano with Friedrich

Wieck, whose daughter Clara he married (1840). His earliest pieces were for piano, such as *Papillons* (1829–31), *Carnaval* (1834), sonatas in F flat Minor (1835) and G Minor (1833–35), *Fantasia* in C (1836), *Kreisleriana, Études Symphoniques*. In 1840 he turned to composing some hundred and fifty songs, settings for poems by Heine, Goethe, Eichendorff, and others. His wife, a piano virtuoso, made Schumann famous by her concert tours throughout Europe. He also composed orchestral works of which the outstanding are piano concerto in A minor (1841–45), *Spring Symphony* (1841), and *Rhenish Symphony* (1850). An opera, *Genoveva* (1847–48), was not a success. In 1854, mental illness which had threatened him from adolescence required his entering a private sanitorium at Endenich, near Bonn, where he died.

REFERENCES: Gerald Abraham ed. *Schumann: A Symposium* (London and New York 1952). Joan Chissell *Schumann* (1948, rev. ed. London and New York 1967, also PB). Leon B. Plantinga *Schumann as Critic* (New Haven, Conn. 1967). Eric Sams *Songs of Robert Schumann* (London 1969). Robert H. Schauffler *Florestan: The Life and Work of Robert Schumann* (1945, new ed. Gloucester, Mass. 1963, also PB). Percy M. Young *Tragic Muse: The Life and Works of Robert Schumann* (1957, enl. ed. London 1961).

✍

SCHUMANN
BY DONALD MINTZ

Robert Schumann's tragedy is obvious: madness and confinement, and a relatively early death.

Some aspects of his triumph are equally obvious: the establishment of an influential musical journal, *Die Neue Zeitschrift für Musik*, despite considerable difficulties, the development of a viable and highly personal style in which he created works of unchallenged greatness, and his marriage to Clara Wieck over her father's objections, which were so strenuous that the couple resorted to court action to overrule them.

Yet the personal tragedy, overwhelming as it was, can be exaggerated. Though mental difficulties attacked Schumann early in life, both the volume and tone of his literary and musical work suggest that for most of his life, he worked, lived, and loved as well as any and better than most.

The triumph can also be exaggerated. Like Mendelssohn, who was about a year older, Schumann belonged to a generation that faced a stylistic crisis: how to go on after Beethoven had apparently used up the received forms. Schumann's musical journalism shows clearly that he perceived the problem, and it shows, too, that at least until fairly late in his life, he had little idea what the nature of the solution might be.

As a composer, he began with piano music. He wrote at the keyboard, short pieces mostly, but often short pieces that in one way or another were connected so as to form cycles. Sometimes the connections are sensed rather than heard, for it was normally Schumann's way to conceal them rather than to display his ingenuity in the manner of Beethoven.

Schumann loved mystification: imaginary, secret societies; private references in music; odd (or not so odd) mottoes prefixed to scores in a way that suggests some hidden meaning, perhaps musical, perhaps extramusical, perhaps both.

Fortunately for the analyst, *Carnaval* in a sense explains its own mystification. The permutations of the "dancing letters" of the cycle's subtitle are set out for all to see — and for all to pursue through the work. Though the use of the "letters" is generally more obvious than analogous motivic connections in later pieces, there are a few puzzles. But one has only to search out "A S (i.e. Es, German for E flat) C H (German for B natural)" or the permutations set out in the section called *Sphinxes* (which some pianists play and others do not), and all becomes clear.

Carnaval thus in effect establishes a formal principle and provides justification for somewhat arcane explanations of the seemingly mysterious process by which Schumann often holds together works which on the surface seem exceptionally heterogeneous.

But however that may be, the cycles of short pieces, however constructed, and longer works like the *Novelettes,* op. 21, with their blend of chain, rondo, and scherzo structures, do not solve the great post-Beethoven problem. On the contrary, they are an evasion, though a magnificent one.

In 1840, Schumann adopted still another evasive maneuver. He turned suddenly to song composition, though in earlier years he had expressed the notion that vocal music is inherently inferior to instrumental music.

Schumann had grown up in a literary rather than a musical milieu. His early ambitions seem to have been more literary than musical, and his sensitivity to literature was very great. In his years of piano composition, he had developed an advanced style that met the extreme demands for "expressiveness" that he and other progressives of his generation made on music. This "expressiveness" is generally viewed in terms of harmony; the number and type of chords available (in other words, the vocabulary) expanded rapidly; at the same time the empirical rules governing the contexts in which chords could be used became broader, which is to say that syntax became richer. But the view needs to be expanded to take into account the extent to which Schumann expanded the use of dissonance. He was surely the most dissonant composer since J. S. Bach. His equipment was thus perfect for the "expressive" song, and a remarkably high percentage of his songs have remained in the repertory.

Schumann is most problematic in two areas: the symphonies and the last, "neoclassical" works, whatever the medium for which they were composed.

The symphonies suffer from dense orchestration which in its time may have had some justification. Today, however, virtually every conductor has his own revisions, sometimes excisions to reduce the heavy doublings, but sometimes rather extensive reorchestrations.

The "neoclassical" works represent an attempt to take the received forms and adapt them to modern conditions. Schumann seems to have set stringent limiting conditions. The freedom with which he handled sonata form in the three relatively early piano sonatas is replaced by remarkably close adherence to the tonal rules of high classicism.

The strictness, paradoxically, is made possible by the richness of his style. By about 1851, Schumann had evolved so highly developed a short-range harmonic and melodic vocabulary that he found it possible to remain in a single key for a considerable length of time without sounding old-fashioned. In this sense, he may be said to have invented the style of Brahms. Surely, these last works — the two violin sonatas, for example — hit upon precisely the solution to the post-Beethoven problem that made it possible for Brahms to continue the German symphonic and chamber music tradition.

Yet these last instrumental works, like the late choral music, are generally neglected. The reasons probably have more to do with surrounding circumstances than with the music itself.

In the first place, many of them appeared posthumously in a world more interested in Wagner and his opponents than in the dead. Those opponents might have been expected to seize upon at least some of this music as if it were a weapon. In fact, the vocal music struck them as too "Wagnerian" for such polemical purposes, and it was not, of course, sufficiently "Wagnerian" for the Wagnerians.

Secondly, the cloud of madness hung over them. They were written, it was felt, at a time when Schumann was deteriorating in general (which was certainly true); therefore, the reasoning ran, they could not be good music (which does not in fact follow).

Though they also have real problems, these last works are a genuine triumph. And yet posterity has so far largely denied their composer his victory.

SCHÜTZ, Heinrich (Oct. 8, 1585 – Nov. 6, 1672). German composer. Born Köstritz, Saxony. Trained as a choirboy. Studied law at Marburg University, then (from 1609) studied under Giovanni Gabrieli in Venice, where he published book of eighteen madrigals (1611). Appointed director of elector of Saxony's chapel in Dresden (1617), he remained there until his death, except for travels to Italy (1628), Copenhagen (1633), and elsewhere. Married Magdalene Wildeck (1619; she died 1625). Most of his compositions are settings for religious texts in Latin and German. Monteverdi's influence is evident in brilliant writing for solo voice, but choral settings are distinctly German. His *Dafne* (1627, now lost) was probably the first German opera and the *Musikalische Exequien* (1636) the first German requiem. His mature works, the finest church music of the seventeenth century, include three *Symphoniae Sacrae* (1629, 1647, 1650), *Geistliche Konzerte* (1636, 1639), *Seven Words from the Cross* (c.1645), and

Christmas Oratorio (1664). Later style is more somber, as in settings for the Passions. Also composed motets and psalm settings. He combined Venetian antiphonal choirs with German baroque polyphonic style, and was first to link Italian and German schools in his composition, which exerted strong influence on German music.

REFERENCES: Hans Joachim Moser *Heinrich Schütz: His Life and Work* (tr. St. Louis, Mo. 1959). André Pirro *Schütz* (Paris 1924).

SCHWARTZ, Delmore (Dec. 8, 1913 – July 11, 1966). American poet. Born Brooklyn, N.Y. Educated at University of Wisconsin, New York University (B.A. 1935), and Harvard. Lecturer at N.Y.U., Kenyon College, Indiana University, Princeton, and Chicago. Married Gertrude Buckman (divorced); married Elizabeth Pollet (1949). An editor of *Partisan Review* (1943–55) and poetry editor of *New Republic* (1955–57), he also contributed to numerous magazines, including *Commentary, New Yorker*, and *Poetry*. Recognized while in college as an outstanding poet, he became known as one of the most gifted writers of his generation. Although his reputation rests primarily on his poetry, he also wrote many short stories and verse plays. Among his works are: *In Dreams Begin Responsibilities* (1938), containing a story, lyrics, and a play; a translation of Rimbaud's *A Season in Hell* (1939); the verse plays *Shenandoah* (1941) and *Genesis* (1943); *Vaudeville for a Princess and Other Poems* (1950); *Summer Knowledge* (1959), for which he was awarded the Bollingen prize (1960); two collections of stories, *The World Is a Wedding* (1948) and *Successful Love* (1962); and *Syracuse Poems* (1964). His work is characterized by remarkable craftsmanship and a deep irony, stressing the disintegrative aspects of the twentieth century. He died in New York.

SCOTT, Sir Walter (Aug. 15, 1771 – Sept. 21, 1832). Scottish poet, novelist, and historian. Born at College Wynd, Edinburgh, son of a lawyer and descendant of proud Border families. Educated at Edinburgh University. Called to the bar (1792), and continued law practice throughout his life. Married Margaret Charlotte Charpentier (1797). Entered printing business with James Ballantyne (1799). First works were translations from the German. His interest in old ballads and narrative poems resulted in the great collection *The Minstrelsy of the Scottish Border* (2 vols. 1802, 3 vols. 1803). He wrote *The Lay of the Last Minstrel* (1805), which made him famous as poet. His major poem, *Marmion* (1808), which contains the familiar *Lochinvar* ballad, followed, and in the same year he brought out an eighteen-volume edition of Dryden's poems with a *Life*. His most popular poem was *The Lady of the Lake* (1810); others: *Rokeby* and *The Bridal of Triermain* (1813), *The Lord of the Isles* (1815), and lesser known poems. Having gone into partnership with John Ballantyne (brother of James) as publisher and bookseller (1809) — a venture that went bankrupt — Scott began to produce historical novels anonymously, began the Waverley series with *Waverley* (1814), an immediate success. That year he also produced his nineteen-volume edition of Swift. His best-known novels include *Guy Mannering* (1815), *Old Mortality* (1816), *Rob Roy* (1817), *The Heart of Midlothian* (1818), *The Bride of Lammermoor* (1819), *Ivanhoe* (1819), *Kenilworth* (1821), *Quentin Durward* (1823), *Redgauntlet* (1824), *The Talisman* (1825), *The Fair Maid of Perth* (1828). Scott also wrote less successful dramatic works and numerous historical and antiquarian books. The bankruptcy of the firm (1826) left the partners deeply in debt, which Scott himself undertook to discharge by writing. The strain told on his health, shortening his life. He died at his estate, Abbotsford, where he had lived like a feudal laird since 1812. His son-in-law, John Gibson Lockhart, wrote his biography, one of the finest in the language. Scott exerted a profound influence on the development of the novel.

EDITIONS: There are innumerable editions of the Waverley Novels. *Letters* ed. Herbert Grierson and others (12 vols. London and New York 1932–37).

REFERENCES: John Buchan *Sir Walter Scott* (1932, reprinted Port Washington, N.Y. 1967). A. O. J. Cockshut *The Achievement of Walter Scott* (London and New York 1969, also PB). Donald Davie *The Heyday of Sir Walter Scott* (New York and London 1961). Herbert Grierson *Sir Walter Scott* (London and New York 1938). Francis R. Hart *Scott's Novels: The Plotting of Historical Survival* (Charlottesville, Va. 1966). John O. Hagden *Scott: The Critical Heritage* (New York 1970). Norman Jeffares ed. *Scott's Mind and Art* (New York 1970). Edgar Johnson *Sir Walter Scott: The Great Unknown* (2 vols. New York 1969). J. G. Lockhart *Memoirs of the Life of Sir Walter Scott* (7 vols. Edinburgh and Boston 1837–38). Hesketh Pearson *Walter Scott: His Life and Personality* (London and New York 1954). Alexander Welsh *The Hero of the Waverley Novels* (New Haven, Conn. 1963, also PB).

✍

SIR WALTER SCOTT
BY JANET ADAM SMITH

In 1707 was signed the act uniting the Parliaments of England and Scotland. The Scottish Members took the road south to Westminster; effectively, Scotland had lost her Parliament (though she kept her own church and her own legal system) and Edinburgh was no longer a seat of government. "The end of an old song" was the verdict of one Scottish signatory. Throughout the century, the poets were quick to react against this diminishment of Scotland. For Allan Ramsay (1686–1758), Robert Fergusson (1750–1774), and Robert Burns (1759–1796), to write in Scots was an act of patriotism; their poems were at once a description and a celebration of a peculiarly Scottish culture; while Ramsay with his collections of earlier Scottish poetry, Burns with his work on Scottish folk song, were also preservers of that culture.

Walter Scott, born in 1771, accepted the union with England more readily than these; by his day there was no clear alternative. But his drive as a writer also sprang from his sense of his country's lost political independence, his cherishing of her culture. In his first publication he too was a preserver; in *The Minstrelsy of the Scottish Border* (1802–1803) he presented the ballads which he and his helpers had collected in the Border country to which his family belonged, and where he soon afterwards made his home. There for the first time the reader could find ballads now as familiar as *The Wife of Usher's Well* and *Johnnie Armstrong*. In his own narrative poems, Scott was the celebrator of the legendary and heroic elements in the Scottish past: wizardry and feudal splendor in *The Lay of the Last Minstrel* (1805); in *Marmion* (1808), the catastrophe of Flodden Field in 1513, when the flower of Scotland was destroyed in battle with the English, among them the hero-king James IV; in *The Lady of the Lake* (1810), the battles and forays of the Highland clans.

When — partly, as he owned, because in narrative poetry Byron beat him — Scott turned to prose, his concern was still Scotland and his intentions more precise. He wished to put on record the old Scotland he had known and had heard of from his elders; he wished (as Maria Edgeworth had done in her novels for the Irish) to make Scotland interesting and sympathetic to the English; to introduce Scots men and women "to those of the sister kingdom, in a more favourable light than they had been placed hitherto, and tend to procure sympathies for their virtues and indulgence for their foibles" (General Preface to the Waverley Novels, 1829). Still the preserver and patriot, he was also to be the recorder and interpreter. The first novel, *Waverley* (1814), fulfills these aims. It is a record — realistic where *The Lady of the Lake* is picturesque and romantic — of the old Highland way of life: chieftains with private armies, an economy based on blackmail and cattle raiding, a morality of bravery and loyalty within the clan, of lawlessness and expediency outside it. The action takes place in 1745–46, when a Highland army under Prince Charles Edward Stewart made the last attempt to upset the 1707 settlement by war. So one of Scott's aims in *Waverley* was to persuade the English reader — apt to regard the Highlander as a breechless barbarian, who had scared the wits out of him when Prince Charlie's army marched into England in 1745 — that his late enemy belonged to a society that, if primitive, was also fascinating, as worthy of attention as the Red Indians of America, and all the more intriguing in that it was practically at the Englishmen's back door. And as such readers followed the Wizard of the North through the canon of the Scottish novels, ever more aspects of Scotland were opened to them: in *Guy Mannering* (1815), the free sporting life of the Border sheep farmers, the wild ways of the Galloway gypsies and smugglers, the manners — rational or bacchanalian, whether on or off duty — of the Edinburgh lawyers; in *Rob Roy* (1817), more about the Highland freebooters, and the rising mercantile class of Glasgow; in *The Antiquary* (1815), the humors of an east-coast port and neighborhood; in *The Heart of Midlothian* (1818), the state of Edinburgh shortly after the Union.

All these novels span a wide range of society and are concerned with a close network of relationships: between laird and gypsy, chieftain and clansman, lawyer and client, shopkeeper and customer, rebel and authority, servant and mistress, as well as between man and wife, father and children, girl and lover. Scott is a great creator of individuals, but they never stand alone. Dandie Dinmont, Dominie Sampson, Meg Merrilies, Bailie Nicol Jarvie, are marked by their trade, their profession, their place in society, their beliefs, and their country's history. David and Jeannie Deans of *The Heart of Midlothian* are not only peasants living near Edinburgh early in the eighteenth century; they are people in whom a Calvinist Presbyterianism has affected every view and action.

So this novelist — Scottish-bred in Edinburgh and on a Border farm, Scottish-educated at Edinburgh's Royal High School and University, practicing a Scottish profession as advocate, sheriff of Selkirk and clerk of the Court of Session — gave the world a living picture of his country. And as he wished to please his readers — and he needed to please, for his expansive way of life depended on his sales — here and there he laid his colors on thick; and as the novels were first read when wildness and peculiarity, of nature or of man, were to be appreciated, it was Scott's highly colored pictures of Highland scenes and ways, of the wild country of the Borders and Galloway, of gypsies and witches, of outlaws and eccentrics, that most impressed itself on his public. When he turned to subjects outside Scotland, the colors were even brighter and the romance more contrived. These are the elements in Scott which have worn badly: local color laid on for its own sake, antiquarianism, melodrama. The Scott who lives today is the novelist with a Tolstoyan sense of man in history, man in society: the author of half a dozen novels which, conceived in a profound patriotism, transcend their Scottishness and become of universal appeal.

SCRIABIN, Alexander Nikolaievitch (Jan. 6, 1872 – Apr. 27, 1915). Russian composer and pianist. Born and died in Moscow. The son of a lawyer, he abandoned a military career to study at the Moscow Conservatory (1888), winning gold medal (1892). Married Vera Isakovitch, a pianist (1897). Taught piano at Conservatory (1898–1904); thereafter concentrated on composition and concert tours, including a tour in U.S. (1906–1907). Early works show influence of Liszt and Chopin, especially in his preference for miniature forms, the best of which are found in the *Preludes*, op. 33, 44, and 48, the *Tragic Poem*, and the *Satanic Poem* (all 1903–10). He became increasingly absorbed in mysticism, a sense of which pervades late pieces such as *Vers la Flamme*, the *Dances*, op. 73, and the *Preludes*, op. 74. Of his ten piano sonatas, the last six in particular are charged with ecstatic mysticism and harmonic subtlety. His few orchestral works were influenced by Wagner, especially *The Poem of Ecstasy* (1908). *Prometheus: A Poem of Fire* (1910) uses a color organ in an attempt to blend light and sound. Scriabin based much of his music on a "mystic chord," built up in fourths.

REFERENCES: M. D. Calvocoressi and Gerald Abraham *Masters of Russian Music* (London and New York 1936). Arthur E. Hall *Scriabin* (New York and London 1918). Montagu Montagu-Nathan *Handbook of the Piano Works of A. Scriabin* (London and Boston 1916). Alfred J. Swan *Scriabin* (London 1923, reprinted New York 1969).

SCRIBE, Augustin Eugène (Dec. 24, 1791 – Feb. 20, 1861). French dramatist and librettist. Born and died in Paris. Son of a silk merchant. Educated there at Collège Sainte-Barbe. Began writing for the theatre in 1810, but success only came with the one-act vaudeville comedy *Une Nuit de la garde nationale* (1815). During the long career that followed, he wrote over four hundred plays — light, historical bourgeois comedies — and opera libretti. Known as the man who brought melodrama into the drawing room, and often criticized for his frequent use of collaborators (of whom the most important was Casimir Delavigne), he was nevertheless the most successful dramatist of his age, and was elected to the French Academy (1834). Retiring to his country estate at Séricourt, he continued writing even after he was no longer in vogue, but as the master of the *pièce bien faite* (well-built play) he influenced a series of later playwrights, including Dumas *fils*, Émile Augier, and Victorien Sardou. Among his chief works are *Le Mariage d'argent* (1827), *Bertrand et Raton* (1833), *Le Verre d'eau* (1840), *Une Chaine* (1841), and *Bataille des dames* (1851). He was successful also as an opera librettist for such works as François Boieldieu's *La Dame blanche* (1825), Auber's *La Muette de Portici* (1828), Meyerbeer's *Les Huguenots* (1836), Verdi's *Vêpres siciliennes* (1853), and Jacques Halévy's *Manon Lescaut* (1856).

REFERENCE: Neil Arvin *Eugène Scribe and the French Theatre* (1924, reprinted New York 1967).

SEBASTIANO DEL PIOMBO (real name Sebastiano Luciani) (c.1485 – June 21, 1547). Italian painter. Born Venice; nicknamed "del Piombo" after appointment as *piombatore papale* (keeper of the papal seals, 1531). Originally a musician, he turned to painting (c.1500) and was apprenticed first to Giovanni Bellini, then to Giorgione, by whom he was influenced. His first important work is the altarpiece of S. Giovanni Crisostomo, Venice. Called to Rome (1511), he decorated the wealthy Chigi family's Villa Farnesina, where he met Raphael. Also met Michelangelo, under whose influence he painted the *Transfiguration* and the *Flagellation* (begun 1516; frescoes, Borgherini chapel, S. Pietro in Montorio, Rome), the *Pietà* (c.1517, Museo Civico, Viterbo), and *The Raising of Lazarus* (begun 1516, National Gallery, London). During 1520's painted numerous altarpieces, such as the *Martyrdom of St. Agatha* (1520, Pitti, Florence), and portraits, notably *Andrea Doria* (1526, Doria Pamphili Gallery, Rome) and *Pope Clement VII* (1526, Museo di Capodimonte, Naples). Returned briefly to Venice (1528–29) after sack of Rome (1527), renewing friendships with Aretino, Jacopo San-

sovino, and Titian. After his lucrative appointment as piombatore (1531), he painted less and less. Invented a technique for painting on plaster walls with oils instead of fresco. Died in Rome.

REFERENCES: Sydney J. Freedberg *Painting of the High Renaissance in Rome and Florence* (2 vols. Cambridge, Mass. and Oxford 1961). Giorgio Vasari *Lives of the . . . Painters, Sculptors, and Architects* (1550) ed. and tr. Gaston de Vere (10 vols. London 1912–15).

SEDLEY, Sir Charles (1639 – Aug. 20, 1701). English poet, dramatist, and courtier. Born at Aylesford, Kent; inherited baronetcy (1655–56). Educated at Wadham College, Oxford. Married Katherine Savage (1657), who became insane; later took vows with Ann Ayscough (1672). Daughter of first marriage, Katherine Savage Sedley (1657–1717), became mistress of James II, who made her countess of Dorchester (1686). After restoration of Charles II (1660), Sedley became attached to his court, where he was famous for his wit, and belonged to notorious group of young profligates. He wrote two mediocre tragedies and three lively comedies: *The Mulberry Garden* (produced 1668), based in part on Molière's *L'École des maris; Bellamira* (1687), a ribald play considered his best; and *The Grumbler,* an adaptation of *Le Grondeur* (1691) of David Augustin de Brueys and Jean Palaprat. Dryden, a friend, represents Sedley as Lisideius in *Essay on Dramatic Poesy,* a defender of imitating French comedy in English. Sedley's literary reputation, however, is based on his graceful love lyrics. In latter part of his life he was seriously engaged in politics, sitting in Parliament during reign of William III. Died at home in Hampstead.

EDITION: *The Poetical and Dramatic Works of Sir Charles Sedley* ed. Vivian de Sola Pinto (1928, reprinted 2 vols. New York 1969).

REFERENCE: Vivian de Sola Pinto *Sir Charles Sedley, 1639–1701: A Study in the Life and Literature of the Restoration* (1927, reprinted New York 1969).

SENECA, Lucius Annaeus (c.4 B.C. – A.D. 65). Roman philosopher, dramatist, and statesman. Born Corduba (Córdoba), Spain, the son of a writer on rhetoric. Went to Rome in his childhood, studied law, rhetoric, and philosophy, and earned early fame as an orator. Banished to Corsica (41) by the emperor Claudius, he was recalled in 49 at the urging of Agrippina to become tutor to the young Nero. During the first years after Nero's ascension (54), Seneca was, with Afranius Burrus, virtual ruler. But the murders of Agrippina (59), to which he was a reluctant accessory, and of Burrus (62) undermined his position; he was ordered to retire, and, finally, to commit suicide. Died near Rome. In contrast to his greed and corruptibility as a politician, Seneca's writing embraces the Stoic creed. He wrote moral essays (the twelve so-called *Dialogues,* and others, notably *On Clemency* and *On Benefits*), and a satire, the *Apocolocyntosis,* on the deification of Claudius (54); but is best known for his nine tragedies, including *Medea, Thyestes, Hercules Furens.* With their atmosphere of gloom and horror, and their declamatory style, they exerted a major influence on the development of Renaissance tragedy.

TRANSLATIONS: *Tragedies* tr. F. J. Miller (Loeb Classical Library 1917, latest ed. 2 vols. Cambridge, Mass. 1953). *Seneca's Tragedies* (containing *Oedipus* tr. Alexander Neville; *Troas* tr. Jasper Heywood; *Agamemnon* tr. John Studley) ed. Eric C. Baade (New York 1969). *Moral Essays* tr. J. W. Basore (Loeb Classical Library 1951, latest ed. 3 vols. Cambridge, Mass. 1958). *The Stoic Philosophy of Seneca: Essays and Letters* ed. and tr. Moses Hadas (New York 1958 and London 1959, also PB).

REFERENCES: H. B. Charlton *The Senecan Tradition in Renaissance Tragedy* (Manchester, England, 1946). John W. Cunliffe *The Influence of Seneca on Elizabethan Tragedy* (1893, reprinted Hamden, Conn. 1965). R. M. Gummere *Seneca the Philosopher and His Modern Message* (1922, reprinted New York 1963). F. L. Lucas *Seneca and Elizabethan Tragedy* (1922, reprinted New York 1966). Clarence W.

Mendell *Our Seneca* (1941, reprinted Hamden, Conn. 1968). Leighton D. Reynolds *The Medieval Tradition of Seneca's Letters* (London and New York 1965).

SEURAT, Georges (Dec. 2, 1859 – Mar. 29, 1891). French painter. Born Paris. Studied at École des Beaux Arts there (1877–79). After a year's military service in Brest, he returned to Paris, and concentrated on drawings, exhibiting two at the Salon of 1883. His first great painting, *La Baignade* (1884, Tate Gallery, London) was rejected by the Salon of that year. He then with Paul Signac founded the Société des Artistes Indépendants. Though critics remained hostile, Seurat continued experimenting with light and color, adopting the pointillist method of using tiny dots of pure color to achieve a blended optical effect. Upon the exhibition of *Un Dimanche à la Grande Jatte* (1886, Art Institute, Chicago), his style was defended by the critic Félix Fénéon, who called it neo-impressionist, a name thereafter applied to Seurat, Signac, and their group. Other major works before Seurat's early death include *La Parade* (1888, Metropolitan Museum, New York), *Le Chahut* (1889, Kröller-Müller Museum, Otterlo), and *Le Cirque* (1891, Louvre, Paris). His mistress Madeleine Knobloch (portrayed in *Jeune Femme se poudrant,* 1890, Courtauld Institute, London) was recognized by his family soon after his death (in Paris).

REFERENCES: Pierre Courthion *Seurat* (New York 1968). Henri Dorra and John Rewald *Seurat* (Paris 1959). Roger Fry *Seurat* (London and Greenwich, Conn. 1965). Robert L. Herbert ed. *Seurat's Drawings* (New York 1964 and London 1965). William I. Homer *Seurat and the Science of Painting* (Cambridge, Mass. 1964). John Rewald *Georges Seurat* (2nd ed. New York 1946). Daniel C. Rich *Seurat and the Evolution of "La Grande Jatte"* (Chicago and Cambridge, England, 1935). John Russell *Seurat* (London and New York 1965, also PB).

SÉVIGNÉ, Marie de Rabutin Chantal, marquise de (Feb. 5, 1626 – Apr. 17,

1696). French letter writer. Born in Paris; of ancient Burgundian nobility. Orphaned at early age (1633) and brought up by her uncle, Christophe de Coulanges. Her excellent education was rounded out by the fashionable literary-aristocratic salons she frequented. Married Marquis Henri de Sévigné (1644); lived in Brittany until 1652, when her husband was killed in a duel, leaving her with a daughter (b.1646) and son (b.1648). She settled in Paris, occasionally journeying to provinces. When her daughter, having married Comte François de Grignan, left with him for Provence (1671), Madame de Sévigné inaugurated the famous correspondence, which lasted until 1694, when she went to live with her daughter's family. She died in Provence. Madame de Sévigné's lively, cultivated personality won her such friends as Madame de Lafayette, Mademoiselle de Scudéri, La Rochefoucauld, and La Fontaine. Her letters (first published 1726) record in witty, gossipy, spontaneous style all the news events and social and literary preoccupations of the court of Louis XIV for a quarter of a century. They are an invaluable document of the life of the times, as well as the subtle distillation of an unusual *esprit*.

TRANSLATION: *Letters* tr. Violet Hammersley (London 1955 and New York 1956).

REFERENCES: Harriet Ray Allentuch *Madame de Sévigné: A Portrait in Letters* (Baltimore 1963). Auguste Bailly *Madame de Sévigné* (Paris 1955). Jean Cordelier *Madame de Sévigné par elle-même* (Paris PB 1967). Jean Lemoine *Madame de Sévigné, sa famille et ses amis* (Paris 1926). Arthur Stanley (pseud.) *Madame de Sévigné: Her Letters and Her World* (London 1946).

SHADWELL, Thomas (c.1642 – Nov. 19, 1692). English dramatist and poet laureate. Born at Stanwell Hall, Norfolk, he entered Caius College, Cambridge (1656), left (1658) to study law. Married (c.1665) actress Ann Gibbs, who played leading role in his first comedy, *The Sullen Lovers* (1668), adapted from Molière's *Les Fâcheux*. Its success encouraged him to pursue career as comedian in tradition of Ben Jon-

son. Works include *Epsom Wells* (1673), *The Virtuoso* (1676), *The Squire of Alsatia* (1688), *Bury Fair* (1689). A controversy with Dryden over the merit of Jonson's comic powers turned serious when Shadwell's Whig sympathies in the political crisis of 1678–79 offended the Tory poet. Dryden's anti-Whig *The Medal* (1682) was rebutted by Shadwell's *The Medal of John Bayes, Satyr to His Muse*, and *The Tory Poets* (all 1682); Dryden then caricatured Shadwell as Og in *Absalom and Achitophel* and published the satire on him, *Mac Flecknoe* — "The rest to some faint meaning make pretense, / But Shadwell never deviates into sense" — (probably written late 1678, published piratically 1682, officially 1684). When William III came to power (1688), Shadwell became royal historiographer and replaced Dryden as poet laureate; he tried to use his influence, often unsuccessfully, to thwart Dryden's career. Suffered from gout in last years and died in London, presumably from overdose of opium to relieve the pain.

EDITION: *Complete Works of Thomas Shadwell* ed. Montague Summers (London 1927, reprinted 5 vols. New York 1968).

REFERENCES: Michael W. Alssid *Thomas Shadwell* (New York 1967). Albert S. Borgman *Thomas Shadwell: His Life and Comedies* (1928, reprinted New York 1969).

SHAHN, Ben (Sept. 12, 1898 – Mar. 14, 1969). American artist. Born Kovno, Lithuania, son of a cabinetmaker. Came to U.S. with family (1906); lived in Brooklyn. Apprenticed to lithographer (1913). Worked as lithographer while attending high school, New York University, City College of New York (1919–22), and National Academy of Design (1922). Married Tillie Goldstein (1922); they had two children. After her death he married Bernarda Bryson (1935). Traveled to Europe and North Africa to study art (1925, 1927–29). On return to New York, shared studio with photographer Walker Evans. First one-man show (1930). His desire to present social issues through art early expressed in twenty-three gouache paintings on the

Sacco and Vanzetti trial (1931–32) and fifteen paintings on the case of labor leader Thomas Mooney (1933). Assisted Diego Rivera on Rockefeller Center frescoes (1932). Employed as artist for Farm Security Administration (1935–38). From 1937 resident of Roosevelt, N.J., where he completed mural for garment workers' resettlement project. Executed large murals for Bronx Post Office (1939) and Social Security Building, Washington (1942). Contributed posters to government during World War II, and after the war to C.I.O. Achieved recognition here and abroad with one-man retrospective show at Museum of Modern Art (1948). Norton professor at Harvard (1956–57); the lectures led to his book *The Shape of Content* (1957). During last two decades Shahn used a wide variety of artistic processes — prints, serigraphs, paintings and posters. His work also became more abstract. Illustrated a series of religious works, including *The Alphabet of Creation* (1963), *Ecclesiastes* (1967), and *Haggadah for Passover* (1966, translation and notes by Cecil Roth). Wrote *Love and Joy About Letters* (1963). Designed a large mural — a return to the Sacco-Vanzetti theme — for Syracuse University (1965–66). Died in Roosevelt, N.J.

EDITION: *The Shape of Content* (Cambridge, Mass. 1957 and Oxford 1958).

REFERENCES: Martin H. Bush *Ben Shahn: The Passion of Sacco and Vanzetti* (Syracuse, N.Y. 1969, also PB). Kneeland McNulty *Prints of Ben Shahn* (Philadelphia PB 1967). Selden Rodman *Portrait of the Artist as an American: Ben Shahn* (New York 1951). James T. Soby *Ben Shahn: His Graphic Art* (New York 1957) and *Paintings of Ben Shahn* (New York 1963).

SHAKESPEARE, William (c.Apr. 23, 1564 – Apr. 23, 1616). English poet, playwright, actor. Born, baptized, and buried in Stratford-upon-Avon; son of respected, property-owning parents John Shakespeare and Mary Arden. Attended Stratford Grammar School until he left to help father's failing business (c.1577). Married Anne Hathaway (1582); they had three children:

Susanna (1583), twins Hamnet and Judith (1585). From 1585 to 1592 his exact whereabouts are unknown; by 1592 he was established in London as actor and playwright. First plays based on Roman models: *Comedy of Errors* (1589)* and *Titus Andronicus* (1589). Historical plays written throughout 1590's: *Henry VI, Part I* (1590–92), *Henry VI, Part II* (1590–91), *Henry VI, Part III* (1590–92), *Richard III* (1592–93), *King John* (1594–97), *Richard II* (1595–97), *Henry IV, Part I* (1596–97), *Henry IV, Part II* (1596–97), *Henry V* (1599). When plague closed the theatres (1592–93), he wrote the *Sonnets* (published 1609) and narrative poems *Venus and Adonis* (1593) and *The Rape of Lucrece* (1593), both dedicated to the Earl of Southampton. Plays of 1590's also include comedies, lyrical love plays, Roman tragedy: *The Taming of the Shrew* (1593), *Two Gentlemen of Verona* (1592–93), *Love's Labour's Lost* (1594), *A Midsummer Night's Dream* (1594–95), *Romeo and Juliet* (1595), *The Merchant of Venice* (1596), *The Merry Wives of Windsor* (1597), *Julius Caesar* (1599). Following three romantic comedies, *Much Ado About Nothing* (1598–99), *As You Like It* (1600), and *Twelfth Night* (1600–1602), he wrote the more serious comedies, *Troilus and Cressida* (1601–1602), *All's Well That Ends Well* (1602–1603), *Measure for Measure* (1604). Then came the great tragedies in rapid succession: *Hamlet* (1601–1602), *Othello* (1604), *King Lear* (1605), *Macbeth* (1606), and *Antony and Cleopatra* (1607). Two tragedies, *Timon of Athens* (1605–1609) and *Coriolanus* (1608), preceded his last group of plays, the romances *Pericles* (1608), *Cymbeline* (1609–10), *The Winter's Tale* (1611), and *The Tempest* (1611). There is some controversy about the authorship of *Henry VIII* (1613), but it is generally thought that Shakespeare collaborated with John Fletcher, who wrote the larger part. Most of Shakespeare's plays were performed by a repertory company called the Lord Chamberlain's Men (formed 1594; re-

---

* All dates are according to *The Reader's Encyclopedia of Shakespeare* ed. Oscar J. Campbell and Edward G. Quinn (New York 1966).

named the King's Men upon accession of James I, 1603), who built their own theatre, the Globe (1599). They also performed in the Blackfriars Theatre (1608–1609). Shakespeare had already retired to Stratford (1612) when the Globe was destroyed by fire (1613). The earliest collected edition of Shakespeare's plays is the First Folio (1623), edited by his fellow actors John Heming and Henry Condell. Divided into Comedies, Histories, and Tragedies, it contains thirty-six plays (including *Henry VIII*), seventeen of which had previously been printed in quarto form. *Pericles* (printed in quarto, 1609), the thirty-seventh, came into the canon with the Third Folio (1664). *The Noble Kinsmen,* the thirty-eighth, is generally considered a collaboration with Fletcher.

EDITIONS: *Complete Works* ed. Hardin Craig (London and New York 1951). *Complete Works* ed. G. L. Kittredge (Boston 1936). *The Penguin Shakespeare* ed. G. B. Harrison (37 vols. Harmondsworth, England, PB 1937–59). *The New Nonesuch Shakespeare* ed. Herbert Farjeon (1929, New York and London 1953). *The Pelican Shakespeare* general editor Alfred Harbage (38 vols. Baltimore PB 1956–67, reprinted 1 vol. Harmondsworth, England, and Baltimore 1969). *The First Folio of Shakespeare* ed. Charlton Hinman (New York 1968).

REFERENCES: C. L. Barber *Shakespeare's Festive Comedy* (Princeton, N.J. and Oxford 1959, PB 1963). A. C. Bradley *Shakespearean Tragedy* (1905, London and New York PB 1957). E. K. Chambers *William Shakespeare: A Study of Facts and Problems* (2 vols. Oxford 1930). Northrop Frye *Natural Perspective: The Development of Shakespearean Comedy and Romance* (New York 1965, also PB). Harley Granville-Barker *Prefaces to Shakespeare* (1927–46, latest ed. 4 vols. Princeton, N.J. 1965, also PB). Alfred Harbage ed. *Shakespeare: The Tragedies: A Collection of Critical Essays* (Englewood Cliffs, N.J. 1964, also PB). G. B. Harrison *Introducing Shakespeare* (3rd ed. Harmondsworth, England, and Baltimore PB 1966). G. Wilson Knight *Wheel of Fire* (4th ed. reissue London 1965 and New York 1966, also PB).

Wyndham Lewis *The Lion and the Fox: The Role of the Hero in the Plays of Shakespeare* (1927, new ed. London and New York 1966, also PB). Peter Quennell *Shakespeare: A Biography* (London and Cleveland 1963). A. P. Rossiter *Angel with Horns, and Other Shakespeare Lectures* (London and New York 1961). Ernest Schanzer *The Problem Plays of Shakespeare* (London and New York 1963, also PB). Theodore Spencer *Shakespeare and the Nature of Man* (2nd ed. New York 1949, also PB). E. E. Stoll *Art and Artifice in Shakespeare* (1933, reprinted New York 1962 and London 1963, also PB). E. M. W. Tillyard *Shakespeare's History Plays* (1944, latest ed. New York 1964, also PB). Derek Traversi *An Approach to Shakespeare* (3rd ed. 2 vols. London and New York 1969, also PB). W. K. Wimsatt, Jr., ed. *Samuel Johnson on Shakespeare* (New York and London 1960, also PB).

✐

WILLIAM SHAKESPEARE
BY HARRY LEVIN

The basic facts of Shakespeare's life are solidly established; but since they stand in modest contrast to the magnitude of his creative achievement, some farfetched efforts have been made to identify certain more pretentious names with the authorship of his works. None of those attempted identifications satisfies the conditions of the playwright's career nearly so well as what we know about Shakespeare from local records, legal documents, and contemporary testimonials. His framing circumstance was Stratford-upon-Avon, the market town in the heart of rural England which would retain an aspect of half-timbered picturesqueness in tribute to his memory. He was baptized and buried in its parish church; he frequently revisited his family; after his London success he purchased Stratford's most substantial house, to which he retired in his last years. His father, who had his ups and downs as a tradesman, was active in the town's affairs and lived to bear the escutcheon of a gentleman. Shakespeare's mother came from a household of prosperous Warwickshire farmers, whose name was that of a neighboring woodland, Arden. The Forest of Arden, reappearing as a typical locale of Shakespearean comedy in *As You Like It,* commemorates the poet's fondness for touching his native soil.

The range and depth of his writing should be sufficient to demonstrate that he was a well-educated man. Though he did not attend a university, he had an opportunity to study at the Stratford Grammar School, where the curriculum was strong in the Latin classics, Christian ethics, and rhetoric. He is also reported to have spent a brief interval as a country schoolmaster. The flavor of his earliest plays, notably the Plautine *Comedy of Errors* and the Senecan *Titus Andronicus,* would reveal an intensive literary training which was yet to be fully digested. At the age of eighteen he married Anne Hathaway, who was eight years his senior, and their elder daughter was born six months afterward. Twins were born to them two years later: another girl, and a boy who would die in childhood. Beyond the fact that Shakespeare left Stratford to seek his fortune at about this time, we have little personal information from his twenties. Yet his subsequent activities presuppose a theatrical apprenticeship which could only have taken place during these years of obscurity. It is evident that he found his way to London, that he took up the profession of acting, and that he tried his apprentice hand at playwriting with the early comedies and histories.

He emerged as a man of letters with two narrative poems in the erotic vein of Ovid, *Venus and Adonis* and *The Rape of Lucrece.* Both of them were dedicated to the young Earl of Southampton, whose courtly patronage he seems to have enjoyed. His *Sonnets,* probably written in the early 1590's and privately circulated for some years before publication, passionately celebrated the counterclaims of love and friendship. His true vocation, the drama, was too professional to be regarded as a branch of belles lettres. Plays, commissioned at from five to ten pounds apiece, belonged to the producing companies, whose interests were not served by publishing them. Many were printed as quartos, nonetheless, some of them unauthorized and garbled; but the body of Shakespeare's work did not appear until seven years after his death, when two of his partners edited the First Folio. From 1594 he was a shareholder in the leading troop which counted the lord chamberlain as its patron, and which came under royal sponsorship when King James succeeded Queen Elizabeth. Meanwhile it had built the Globe Playhouse as its public headquarters and acquired a private theatre at Blackfriars. Its principal actor, the famous Richard Burbage, created many of Shakespeare's title roles.

Shakespeare had learned his business from the inside. An actor-manager-playwright, like Molière, he combined the playwright's craftsmanship with the manager's sense of audience and the actor's gift for projecting himself into an endless variety of roles. During not much more than twenty active years in the theatre, he managed to turn out thirty-eight plays, developing and extending the potentialities of all the available dramatic modes. Echoes from the grandiloquent Marlowe, the melodramatic Kyd, and the aphoristic Lyly reverberate through his journeywork. Contributing to the popular sequence of Elizabethan history plays, he imposed an inner form on that episodic and pageant-like vehicle; he rendered it tragic in *Richard II*, comic in *Henry IV*, and well-nigh epical in *Henry V*. Out of his experiments with comedy and poetry, he refined a peculiarly lyrical style of his own, with which he could pass in the mid-1590's from the gossamer fantasies of *A Midsummer Night's Dream* through the conflicting values of *The Merchant of Venice* to a tragedy of love — heretofore the preserve of comedy — in *Romeo and Juliet*. Yet his sunniest comedies have their shadows: *Twelfth Night* revels in a house of mourning, and the sharp satirical thrust of *Measure for Measure* foreshadows the modern problem play.

Except for *Hamlet*, whose concern for the issue of succession reflects the intellectual unrest in the closing years of Elizabeth's reign, Shakespeare's major tragedies were written during the Jacobean period. Darkening introspection points the way toward a deepening exploration of the problem of evil. The emphasis is on the responsibility of the protagonist, on heroic complicity and guilt, in *Othello* and *Macbeth*. The scope enlarges in *King Lear* to an unflinching quest for some cosmic pattern, a problematic inquiry into the forces that shape man's destiny. Through the tragedies set in ancient Rome and inspired by Plutarch's *Lives* — *Julius Caesar, Antony and Cleopatra,* and *Coriolanus* — Shakespeare could set forth the relations between the state and the individual with greater freedom and sharper definition than in his patriotic chronicles. Though he died relatively young, his last plays move through an autumnal and mellow atmosphere which we associate commonly with the art of old age. Their preoccupation with time, with illusory marvels, and with treacheries resolved by happy endings has led them to be retroactively placed in the special category of romances. When Prospero in *The Tempest* renounces his magical craft, he may afford us a glimpse of Shakespeare himself, contemplating the phantoms to which he has given life.

SHAW, George Bernard (July 26, 1856 – Nov. 2, 1950). British dramatist, critic, and journalist. Born Dublin, of English parents, and received formal schooling until the age of fourteen, when he went to work as a clerk. Moved to London with his mother (1876) and began writing series of five novels (all unsuccessful), including *Immaturity* and *Cashel Byron's Profession*. Meanwhile, he had become interested in socialism, joined Fabian Society (1884), lectured widely, and became a leader. Brought into the society Beatrice and Sidney Webb; through them met Charlotte Payne-Townshend, whom he married (1898). Became music critic for the *Star* (1888–90) and *World* (1890–94), where he championed Wagner; then drama critic for *Saturday Review* (1895–98), where, having written *The Quintessence of Ibsenism* (1891), his enthusiasm was for Ibsen. During this period began writing for the theatre, producing *Widowers' Houses* (1892). His life thereafter is primarily a record of his numerous dramatic successes, including *Arms and the Man* (produced 1894), *Candida* (produced in both 1893 and 1897), *Mrs. Warren's Profession* (1902), *The Philanderer* (1905), *You Never Can Tell* (written 1895), which were published as *Plays: Pleasant and Unpleasant* (1898). That year he also published *The Perfect Wagnerite*. Other major plays: *The Devil's Disciple* (produced 1897), *Caesar and Cleopatra* (1899), *Captain Brassbound's Conversion* (1900), *Man and Superman* (1905), *Major Barbara* (1905), *Androcles and the Lion* (1912), *Pygmalion* (1913; later produced as a highly popular musical, *My Fair Lady*), *Heartbreak House* (1919). Of the later plays *Saint Joan* (1923) is outstanding. Others include *Back to Methuselah* (1921), *The*

Apple Cart (1928), *Too True to Be Good* (1932). Shaw gained a reputation for brilliant prefaces to his plays, and while continuing to write plays for the rest of his life, he also wrote numerous volumes of critical and political essays, including the famous *Intelligent Woman's Guide to Socialism and Capitalism* (1928). The autobiographical *Sixteen Self Sketches* appeared the year before his death at Ayot St. Lawrence, England. He received the Nobel prize for literature (1925). A number of volumes of correspondence have appeared: *Ellen Terry and Bernard Shaw: A Correspondence* (1931), Mrs. Patrick Campbell's *My Life and Some Letters* (1922), and others. The continuing popularity of his plays is evident on stage and in film.

EDITIONS: *Complete Plays with Prefaces* (6 vols. New York 1962). *Complete Plays* (London 1965). *Complete Prefaces* (London 1965). *Collected Letters* ed. Dan H. Laurence (4 vols. London and New York 1965–). *Shaw on Theatre* ed. E. J. West (New York 1958 and London 1960, also PB). *Shaw: An Autobiography* (vol. I 1856–98, vol. II 1898–1950) ed. Stanley Weintraub (New York 1970).

REFERENCES: Eric Bentley *Bernard Shaw* (2nd ed. London 1967, also PB). G. K. Chesterton *George Bernard Shaw* (1909, latest ed. New York PB 1956). Archibald Henderson *George Bernard Shaw: Man of the Century* (New York 1956). William Irvine *The Universe of G.B.S.* (1949, reprinted New York 1968). R. J. Kaufmann ed. *G. B. Shaw: A Collection of Critical Essays* (Englewood Cliffs, N.J. 1965, also PB). Desmond MacCarthy *Shaw's Plays in Review* (London and New York 1951). Richard M. Ohmann *Shaw: The Style and the Man* (Middletown, Conn. 1962). Hesketh Pearson *George Bernard Shaw: His Life and Personality* (1942, latest ed. New York PB 1963). J. Percy Smith *The Unrepentant Pilgrim* (Boston 1965 and London 1966). Stephen Winsten ed. *G.B.S. 90: Aspects of Shaw's Life and Works* (London and New York 1946).

SHELLEY, Mary Wollstonecraft Godwin (Aug. 30, 1797 – Feb. 21, 1851). English writer. Born and died in London.

Daughter of Mary Wollstonecraft Godwin, who died shortly after Mary's birth, and William Godwin. Brought up by Godwin and his second wife, the widow Mary Jane Clairmont, mother of Claire Clairmont (later Byron's mistress). In 1814, Mary fell in love with Percy Bysshe Shelley and eloped with him to Switzerland. After suicide of his wife, they married. Of their three children, two died in Italy (1818 and 1819). Having written a travel book, *Journal of a Six Weeks' Tour* (1817), she produced her first novel, *Frankenstein* (1818), which caused a sensation. After Shelley's death (1822), she edited his writings (1824–40) and wrote biographies, articles, the travel book *Rambles in Germany and Italy* (1844), and fiction to pay for the education of her surviving child, Percy (b.1819). Best novels of this period are *The Last Man* (1826) and the autobiographical *Lodore* (1835). Her own adventurous life and a vivid imagination contributed to her success as a novelist. Her journal and letters served as basis for Shelley biography.

EDITIONS: Frederick L. Jones ed. *Letters of Mary Wollstonecraft Shelley* (2 vols. Norman, Okla. 1944) and *Journal of Mary Wollstonecraft Shelley* (Norman, Okla. 1947).

REFERENCES: Rosalie Glynn Grylls *Mary Shelley* (London 1938). Elizabeth Nitchie *Mary Shelley: Author of Frankenstein* (New Brunswick, N.J. 1953).

SHELLEY, Percy Bysshe (Aug. 4, 1792 – July 8, 1822). English poet. Born near Horsham, Sussex, son of landed aristocrat. Educated at Eton, then at University College, Oxford, until his collaboration on a pamphlet, *The Necessity of Atheism,* caused his sudden expulsion. In London he met Harriet Westbrook, eloped with her to Edinburgh (1811), where they married; later had two children. While a disciple of social philosopher William Godwin, Shelley printed privately first major poem, *Queen Mab* (1813). He also fell in love with Godwin's daughter, Mary Wollstonecraft, and eloped with her to Switzerland (1814), causing a public scandal. After Harriet's death (she drowned herself, 1816) he married

Mary, but was refused custody of his and Harriet's children. (One of his three children with Mary — Percy, born 1819 — survived.) Having written *The Revolt of Islam* (1818, a revision of *Laon and Cynthia*, 1817), Shelley with his family left England for good (1818) and settled in Italy, where his era of greatest achievement began. He produced a tragedy, *The Cenci* (1819); his masterpiece *Prometheus Unbound* (1820), and the great lyrics *Ode to the West Wind, Ode to a Skylark, The Cloud, Ozymandias, Hellas.* Replied to Thomas Peacock's *Four Ages of Poetry* with *A Defense of Poetry* (1821, posthumously published), and wrote *Adonais* (1821), his elegy to Keats. This was the period of his Pisa Circle, a group of admirers who sometimes included Byron. A sailing accident in the Gulf of Spezia caused his death and that of his friend Edward Williams. He was cremated, and his ashes buried in the Protestant Cemetery, Rome. Among his other works are *Peter Bell the Third* (1819), a parody of Wordsworth, *Epipsychidion*, romantic expression of Platonism (1821), and numerous romantic lyrics, *Music, when soft voices die, To Night, When the lamp is shattered*, and others.

EDITIONS: *Complete Works* ed. Roger Ingpen and Walter E. Peck (1926–30, reprinted 10 vols. New York 1965). *Poetical Works* ed. Thomas Hutchinson (1904, latest ed. London and New York 1967, also PB). *Shelley's Prose* ed. D. L. Clark (1954, rev. ed. Albuquerque, N. Mex. 1966, also PB). *Letters* ed. Frederick L. Jones (2 vols. London and New York 1964).

REFERENCES: Carlos Baker *Shelley's Major Poetry: The Fabric of a Vision* (1948, new ed. New York 1961, also PB). Harold Bloom *Shelley's Mythmaking* (New Haven, Conn. and Oxford 1959, also PB). Edmund Blunden *Shelley: A Life Story* (1946, rev. ed. London and New York PB 1965). Kenneth N. Cameron *Young Shelley: Genesis of a Radical* (New York 1950 and London 1951, PB 1962). Desmond King-Hele *Shelley: The Man and the Poet* (London and New York 1960). G. M. Ridenour ed. *Shelley: A Collection of Critical Essays* (Englewood Cliffs, N.J. 1965, also PB). Neville

Rogers *Shelley at Work: A Critical Inquiry* (2nd ed. Oxford 1967). Newman Ivey White *Shelley* (2 vols. New York 1940 and London 1947; abridged as *Portrait of Shelley*, New York 1945). Humbert Wolfe ed. *Life of Percy Bysshe Shelley*, containing Thomas Jefferson Hogg *The Life of Shelley* (1858), Edward John Trelawny *The Recollections of Shelley and Byron* (1858), Thomas Love Peacock *Memoirs of Shelley* (articles 1858–62) (2 vols. New York and London 1933).

☞

SHELLEY
BY STEPHEN SPENDER

At the end of the nineteenth century, Shelley perhaps was, after Shakespeare, the greatest single influence in English poetry, which was predominantly "romantic." Browning's work originated in Shelley, Swinburne was influenced by him. He was the poet most loved of Thomas Hardy. He remained to the end an influence in Yeats.

However, like his Sensitive Plant, Shelley's reputation was always peculiarly liable to frost. In the last century he was to Matthew Arnold an "ineffectual angel." In the twentieth he seemed to D. H. Lawrence a white slug (because he addressed the Skylark as "Spirit! / Bird thou never wert" — thus slighting its sexuality).

His reputation once damaged is difficult to heal. For few of the poems stand integral and separate from the poet's opinions and biography. We all know that Shelley was an atheist and a rebel, influenced by Godwin and Rousseau, better even than we know that he was a mystic, a Hellenist, and interested in science. We know that Harriet, his first wife, fell victim to his views on free love — and drowned herself in the Serpentine; that he paid the debts of the philosopher Godwin, the father of Mary, his second wife. The image of Shelley's slight corpse in marble is surrounded in our minds with those of victims he rescued who then became, in turn, the victims of his mixture of idealism, altruism, and egotism.

Mary Shelley — with Shelley's withered heart in an envelope in her desk as she wrote — through her excessive piety in publishing every fragment and sketch by Shelley is perhaps largely responsible for drawing attention to his often careless writing. Yet speed is the very essence of his poetry. Like arrows of light, or like the prismatic raindrops of the rainbow, his images shoot in a radiant screen before our eyes, and when they blur it is either because his intellect has not caught up with his imagination or his imagination with his ideology.

We are today analytic New-Critical readers, and a good deal of Shelley we find simply unacceptable. However, there is a great difference between the Shelley — expelled from Oxford for his atheistic pamphlet — of *Queen Mab* and the mature, saddened yet visionary Shelley of *The Triumph of Life*. In the end intellect and imagination are fused without loss of rapidity. That Shelley was as conscious of the necessity of immediacy in his poetry as any writer of today's "projective" verse is shown in his prefatory lines addressed to Mary (who did not like the poem) to *The Witch of Atlas* — his masterpiece as a flight of pure imagination — which he wrote in three days. He criticizes Wordsworth for "Watering his laurels with the killing tears / Of dull, slow care," and then goes on to justify his own rapid style in words strangely similar to those in which D. H. Lawrence (writing to Edward Garnett) justified his own way of writing by comparing it to a butterfly sometimes in flight, sometimes settling on a flower, sometimes on a cow patch in the road:

> *The watery bow burned in the*
> *evening flame,*
> *But the shower fell, the swift*
> *Sun went his way —*
> *And that is dead. — Oh, let me*
> *not believe*
> *That anything of mine is fit to*
> *live.*

Lines that challenge, incidentally, the charge that Shelley was totally devoid of humor.

Our problem today is, without falling into the uncritical raptures of the Shelley-worshipers, to avail ourselves of the light of Shelley's genius. For he was a prophetic poet — a visionary as well as revolutionary, one of the very rare poets who combine intellectual power and intensity with lyricism. There is still a good deal that modern poets could learn from him: notably the ability to translate philosophic, scientific, and political ideas into translucent imagery. Here he stands midway between the Goethe of the second part of *Faust* — who poured all his erudition into poetry of great virtuosity — and Baudelaire incisively laying bare the social evils of his time.

Yeats is probably the only modern poet who learned the lesson of Shelley's rhythmic impetuosity. We underestimate Shelley's virtuosity and aesthetic skill because of occasional collapses due either to the weight of the ideas or to psychological reasons deeper than mere carelessness — his imperfect self-knowledge which causes him so often to resort to exclamations such as: "I fall upon the thorns of life! I bleed!"

An imagistic pattern that recurs in his poetry is of things being illuminated by their own refulgence: "A lovely lady garlanded in light / From her own beauty" or "The sly serpent, in the golden flame / Of his own volumes intervolved" or "Like a poet hidden / In the light of thought" — or, marvelously, that picture of Coleridge:

> . . . *He who sits obscure*
> *In the exceeding luster and the*
> *pure*
> *Intense irradiation of a mind,*
> *Which with its own internal*
> *lightning blind,*
> *Flags wearily through darkness*
> *and despair.*

There runs through all his poetry the effect of light giving light to light, fire setting fire to fire:

> *Life of life! thy lips enkindle*
> *With their love the breath be-*
> *tween them.*

Metaphors of visions dissolving into light are indeed so frequent that one might consider his poetry as a metaphor for the metamorphosis of poetry into sensations or ideas beyond words. This is of course contrary to our modern preoccupation with the idea that poetry is "about" words, or with experiences becoming words, not with words dissolving into transcendental sensations or experience. Shelley is a poet who, too often for our taste, uses language to work against language. His kind of purity is not Keatsian — pure poetry; it is — if one can conceive of such a thing — pure purity, thought purging itself of words and becoming the sensation of thought like light.

In poems like *The Cloud* and *To a Skylark,* he takes us on a trip through a dazzling series of metaphors, some of which turn out to be damp squibs, but some of which uplift the spirit. The words themselves are often thrillingly unexpected, but they do not allow us to hand around and look at them; they are there as conveyers of the metaphor, and of the thought beyond the meta-

phor. A peculiarity of his poetry is that a metaphor can make a vivid picture without our being sure what it refers to. An example criticized by T. S. Eliot in an English periodical for this reason became the subject of a fierce correspondence in the 1930's. Eliot asked what was the "sphere" referred to in these lines:

> *Keen as are the arrows*
> *Of that silver sphere,*
> *Whose intense lamp narrows*
> *In the white dawn clear*
> *Until we hardly see — we feel*
> *that it is there.*

Various suggestions — moon and planets and morning star — were made, which proved Eliot's point that Shelley's imagery can be difficult to identify with its source in nature. Yet Shelley probably knew more about the heavenly bodies than did Eliot; and it was not through ignorance that he produced an effect of vague luminosity, but with intent. The skylark's song is invisible and the images describing it hover between the seen and the unseen, the real and the ideal, the named and the nameless.

Shelley has indeed a variety of styles, and when he is being personal and intimate, as in the poems addressed to Jane Williams, he can move precisely and concretely among familiar things:

> *We pause amid the pines that*
> *stood*
> *The giants of the waste,*
> *Tortured by storms to shapes as*
> *rude*
> *As serpents interlaced . . .*

In *Prometheus Unbound* his imagination seems to enter into the geography and history of the world — the universe even. He gives the elements and civilizations and religions and myths voices in which they talk across icy gulfs to one another. He comes nearer to writing world poetry here than any other poet, except perhaps Goethe; and it is possible that one reason for his comparative neglect is that his cosmic imagination is still in advance of us.

SHERIDAN, Richard Brinsley (Nov. 4, 1751 – July 7, 1816). Brtish playwright and politician. Born Dublin, son of theatrical and literary parents. Attended Harrow (1762–69). Family moved to Bath (c.1771), where he met the young singer Elizabeth Ann Linley, daughter of composer Thomas Linley. They were married (1773) after an elopement and secret marriage in France aimed at protecting Elizabeth from another suitor's attentions. Sheridan, deciding on a dramatic career, began writing plays, and achieved sensational success with his first, *The Rivals* (1775). *St. Patrick's Day* and a musical comedy, *The Duenna*, for which his father-in-law supplied the music, followed in the same year; then his other great work, *The School for Scandal* (1777), and his last play, a burlesque, *The Critic* (1779). Having effectively revived the state of English comedy and also succeeded as part owner of the Drury Lane Theatre (from 1776), he decided to enter politics, in which he was active more than thirty years. Sat in Parliament (1780–1812), made a name as a brilliant orator, and distinguished himself in various cabinet posts: under-secretary for foreign affairs (1782), secretary to the Treasury (1783), treasurer of the Navy (1806). He moved in the most fashionable circles and was a member of the Literary Club, proposed by Samuel Johnson (1777). After his wife's death (1792) he married (1795) Jane Ogle, daughter of the dean of Winchester. His last years were darkened by financial troubles, especially when the Drury Lane Theatre was destroyed by fire, and he died (in London) in poverty. Acclaimed on his death as a great statesman and one of the most important writers of comedy in English literature, he was buried in Westminster Abbey.

EDITION: *The Plays and Poems of Richard Brinsley Sheridan* ed. Raymond Crompton Rhodes (1928, reprinted New York 1962).

REFERENCES: W. A. Darlington *Sheridan* (London and New York 1933). Lewis Gibbs *Sheridan* (1947, reprinted Port Washington, N.Y. 1970). Thomas Moore *Memoirs of . . . Sheridan* (1825, 1855 ed. reprinted 2 vols. New York 1968). W. F. Rae *Sheridan* (2 vols. London and New York 1896). Raymond Crompton Rhodes *Harlequin Sheridan: The Man and the Legends* (Oxford and New York 1933). Oscar Sherwin *Uncorking Old Sherry: The Life and Times of Richard Brinsley Sheridan* (New York 1960 and London 1961).

SHIRLEY, James (Sept. 18, 1596 – Oct. 29, 1666). English playwright and poet. Born and died in London. Attended Merchant Taylor's School (1608–12), and Oxford and Cambridge universities (B.A. 1617). Ordained an Anglican minister, he became a convert to Roman Catholicism and master of St. Albans Grammar School (1621–24). After success of first play, *Love Tricks* (1625), resigned this post, settled in London. Numerous successful plays followed, including his best-known, the tragedy *The Traitor* (1631), establishing him as London's most popular dramatist. In Dublin (1636–40), working for new theatre there, wrote several more plays. Altogether produced thirty-seven tragedies, comedies, and masques, as well as a volume of poems. Entered service of Queen Henrietta Maria (1642) when the Civil War broke out. After Puritans closed the theatres, Shirley lived quietly as a schoolmaster at Whitefriars, where he wrote *Grammatica Anglo-Latina* (1651). His death in London was precipitated by the Great Fire. Other major plays: *Hyde Park* (1632), *The Lady of Pleasure* (1635), *The Cardinal* (1641). Extremely conventionalized and influenced by Elizabethan predecessors, his plays were highly popular in his time, but are little read today.

EDITION: *The Dramatic Works and Poems of James Shirley* ed. William

Gifford and Alexander Dyce (6 vols. London 1833, reprinted New York 1966).

REFERENCES: Frederick S. Boas *An Introduction to Stuart Drama* (London and New York 1946). Robert S. Forsythe *The Relations of Shirley's Plays to the Elizabethan Drama* (1914, reprinted New York 1965). Arthur H. Nason *James Shirley, Dramatist* (1915, reprinted New York 1967).

SHOLOM ALEICHEM (real name Solomon Rabinovitch) (Feb. 18, 1859 – May 13, 1916). Yiddish short story writer and dramatist. Born Pereyaslavl; grew up in Woronka, Ukraine, the setting for his stories and novels. In Kiev, where he married Olga Loyeff (1883), with whom he had six children, he .wrote unsuccessfully in Russian and Hebrew, then turned to Yiddish (from 1883). Immediately acclaimed, he edited the literary annual *Die Yidishe Folksbibliotek* (1888–89), which attracted the best Yiddish writers. Financial losses forced him to depend entirely on writing for a living. Moved his family to Odessa (1890) and then to New York (1906), where he spent the rest of his life and enjoyed international fame. Among his collections of stories in a number of translations are *The Old Country* (tr. 1946), *Tevye the Dairyman* (written 1895–99, tr. 1949), and *Adventures of Mottel, the Cantor's Son* (1907–16, tr. 1953).

REFERENCES: Melech Grafstein *Sholom Aleichem Panorama* (London 1948). Sol Liptzin *The Flowering of Yiddish Literature* (New York 1964). Maurice Samuel *The World of Sholom Aleichem* (New York 1943, PB 1965). Marie Waife-Goldberg *My Father, Sholom Aleichem* (London and New York 1968).

✒

SHOLOM ALEICHEM
BY IRVING HOWE

Sholom Aleichem came at a major turning point in the history of the east European Jews: between the unquestioned dominance of religious belief and the appearance of modern ideologies, between the past of traditional Judaism and the future of Jewish politics, between a totally integrated culture and a culture that by a leap of history would soon plunge into the midst of modern division and chaos. Yet it was the mark of Sholom Aleichem's greatness that, coming as he did at this point of transition, he betrayed no moral imbalance or uncertainty of tone. In his humorous yet often profoundly sad stories, Sholom Aleichem gave to the Jews what they instinctively felt was the right and true judgment of their experience: a judgment of love through the medium of irony.

The world of Sholom Aleichem is bounded by three major characters, each of whom has risen to the level of Jewish archetype: Tevye the dairyman; Menachem Mendel the *luftmensch;* and Mottel the cantor's son, who represents the loving, spontaneous possibilities of Jewish childhood. Tevye remains rooted in his little town, delights in displaying his uncertain Biblical learning, and stays close to the sources of Jewish survival. Solid, slightly sardonic, fundamentally innocent, Tevye is the folk voice quarreling with itself, criticizing God from an abundance of love, and realizing in its own low-keyed way all that we mean, or should mean, by humaneness.

Tevye represents the generation of Jews that could no longer find complete deliverance in the traditional God yet could not conceive of abandoning Him. No choice remained, therefore, but to celebrate the earthly condition: poverty and hope. For if you had become skeptical of deliverance from above and had never accepted the heresy of deliverance from below, what could you do with poverty but celebrate it? "In Kasrilevke," says Tevye, "there are experienced authorities on the subject of hunger, one might say specialists. On the darkest night, simply by hearing your voice, they can tell if you are hungry and would like a bite to eat, or if you are really starving." Tevye, like the people for whom he speaks, is constantly assaulted by outer forces. The world comes to him, most insidiously, in the form of undesired sons-in-law: one who is poverty-stricken but romantic; another who is a revolutionist and ends in Siberia; a third — could anything be worse? — who is a Gentile; and a fourth — this *is* worse — who is a Jew, but rich, coarse, and unlearned.

Menachem Mendel, Tevye's opposite, personifies the element of restlessness and soaring, of speculation and fancy-free idealization in Jewish character. He has a great many occupations: broker, insurance agent, watchmaker, coal dealer, and finally — it is inevitable — writer; but his fundamental principle in life is to keep moving. The love and longing he directs toward his unfound millions are the love and longing that later Jews direct toward programs and ideologies. He is the utopian principle of Jewish life; he is driven by the modern demon. Through Tevye and Menachem Mendel, flanked by little Mottel, Sholom Aleichem creates his vision of the Yiddish world.

This world, as presented by Sholom Aleichem, is constantly precarious and fearful. Yet the vision from which it is seen remains a vision of absolute assurance, a vision controlled by that sense of Jewish humaneness which held the best of — even as it transcended — both the concern with the other world that had marked the past and the eagerness to transform this world that would mark the future. If Sholom Aleichem's work abounds in troubles, only rarely does it betray anxiety. The characteristic effect of his stories is laughter.

I doubt there has ever been a reader naïve enough to ask if Sholom Aleichem *really* believed in God. Whether the answer is yes or no (it's probably yes), the question is irrelevant. What Sholom Aleichem believed in was the Jews who lived with him and about him, most of them Jews still believing in God. God is there in his stories, not because He is God, not because there is any recognition or denial of His heavenly status, but simply because He figures as an actor in the life of the Jews. To put it more drastically, God is there because Tevye is there. But Tevye, does *he* believe in God? Another irrelevant question. Tevye believes in something more important than believing in God; he believes in talking to God. And Tevye talks to God as to an old friend whom one need not flatter or assuage. Tevye, to put it in American slang, gives Him an earful. God has become absorbed into the vital existence of the people.

Sholom Aleichem's Yiddish is one of the most extraordinary verbal achievements of modern literature, as important in its way as T. S. Eliot's revolution in the language of English verse or Berthold Brecht's infusion of street language into the German lyric. He uses a sparse and highly controlled vocabulary; his medium is so drenched with irony that the material which comes through it is often twisted and elevated into direct tragic statement — irony multiplies upon itself to become a deep winding sadness. Many of his stories are monologues, still close to the oral folk tradition, full of verbal byplay, slow in pace, winding in direction, but always immediate and warm in tone. His imagery is based on an absolute mastery of the emotional rhythms of Jewish life. There is also a strong element of fantasy, even surrealism: a tailor becomes enchanted, a clock strikes thirteen, a timid little

Jew looks at himself in the mirror and sees the face of a Czarist officer.

To say that Sholom Aleichem speaks for a whole culture is true, but that does not mean that he represents all the significant levels of behavior and class in that culture, thereby encompassing the style of life of the east European Jews in the nineteenth century. He does not command the range of a Balzac or even a Faulkner, and he does not present himself as the kind of writer who is primarily concerned with social representation. Nor does it mean that he advances the conscious program of that culture. Toward the dominant Jewish ideologies of the time Sholom Aleichem showed a characteristic mixture of sympathy and skepticism, and precisely this modesty enabled him to achieve a deeper relation to the *folksmassen* than any Jewish political leader. He never set himself up as cultural spokesman or institution, in the style of Thomas Mann at his worst; he had no interest in boring people.

Sholom Aleichem speaks for the culture of the east European Jews because he embodies — not represents — its essential values in the very accents and rhythm of his speech, in the inflections of his voice and the gestures of his hand, in the pauses and suggestions between the words even more than the words themselves. To say that a writer represents a culture is to imply that a certain distance exists between the two. But this is not at all the relationship between Sholom Aleichem and the culture of the east European Jews: it is something much more intimate and elusive, something for which, having so little experience of it, we can barely find a name. In Sholom Aleichem everything that is deepest in the ethos of the east European Jews is brought to fulfillment and cli-

max. He is, I think, the only modern writer who may truly be said to be a culture-hero, a writer whose work releases those assumptions of his people, those tacit gestures of bias, which undercut opinion and go deeper into communal life than values.

———

SIBELIUS, Jean (Julius Christian) (Dec. 8, 1865 – Sept. 20, 1957). Finnish composer. Born Tavastehus. Spent semester at University of Helsinki (1885), then entered Helsinki Conservatory, where he studied under Martin Wegelius (1886–89). After further study in Berlin and Vienna, settled in Helsinki (1891). Married Aino Jänefelt (1892) and was appointed to Conservatory faculty same year. His symphonic poems *Kullervo* (1892), *A Saga* (1892), and *Four Legends from the Kalevala*, including *The Swan of Tuonela* (1893–95), works inspired by native legends, made him famous as Finland's national composer. The Finnish senate granted him a yearly pension (1897); he retired (1904) to country home at Järvenpää, near Helsinki, where he remained until his death, emerging rarely. Visited U.S. (1914), taught briefly at New England Conservatory (Boston), and conducted premiere of his *Oceanides* at Norwalk, Conn., Festival. Other well-known works are symphonic poems *Finlandia* (1900), *Pohjola's Daughter* (1906), *Tapiola* (1925), and the seven symphonies (1898–1924). Also composed chamber music, songs, and piano pieces. Essentially romantic, Sibelius's music is at once intensely nationalistic, making use of the melodic patterns of folk music, and highly individual.

REFERENCES: Gerald Abraham ed. *Music of Sibelius* (New York and London 1947). Karl Ekman *Jean Sibelius: His Life and Personality* (tr. New York 1938). Cecil Gray *Sibelius* (2nd ed. London 1934). Harold E. Johnson *Jean Sibelius* (New York 1959 and London 1960). Robert Layton *Sibelius* (London and New York 1965). Nils-Eric Ringbom *Jean Sibelius* (tr. Norman, Okla. 1954). Simon Parmet *The*

Symphonies of Sibelius (tr. London 1959).

SICKERT, Walter Richard (May 31, 1860 – Jan. 23, 1942). English painter. Born Munich, son of Danish-born German draftsman who settled in England (1868). After several years on the stage, enrolled (1881) at Slade School, London, where he studied under Alphonse Legros. Became pupil of Whistler (1882) and in Paris (1883) met Degas, both of whom profoundly influenced his work. For the next fifteen years, though Sickert's headquarters were in London, he spent much time in Dieppe. Exhibited with the New English Art Club (1886). Opened art school in Chelsea (1893), but from 1895 to 1905 lived on the Continent, first in Venice, then Dieppe, and Paris. On return to London, as major British impressionist, he became focus of a group of painters, including Lucien Pissarro, Spencer Gore, Harold Gilman, and Augustus John, who formed the Camden Town and London groups (1911 and 1913). From the 1920's, devoted his time increasingly to teaching; painted often at Brighton and at Bath, where he died. Sickert was married three times. Elected an associate of the Royal Academy (1924), he became a Royal Academician (1934), resigning in 1935. Well-known paintings include *L'Ennui* (c.1913) and *Portrait of Victor Lecour* (1924).

EDITION: Walter Richard Sickert *A Free House! or The Artist as Craftsman* ed. Sir Osbert Sitwell (London 1947).

REFERENCES: Lillian Browse *Sickert* (London 1960). Robert Emmons *The Life and Opinions of Walter Richard Sickert* (London and New York 1941).

✍

WALTER SICKERT

BY QUENTIN BELL

He knew London in the years when Oscar Wilde, Max Beerbohm, and Whistler (his first master) were letting off verbal fireworks and teasing the philistines. But he also knew Paris; and whereas London was gay, flippant, foppish, and decadent, Paris was a sober place, an austere and industrious school of aesthetic virtue.

Given time and skill one might weave these generalizations into a paradox of some elegance; but the only point of making them is that, for Sickert, they contained a great deal of truth. Whistler and his circle — Whistler and his antagonists; it comes to much the same thing — were clever and ingenious, but they lacked solidity. The impressionists and Degas, and for Sickert it was Degas who mattered, had been trained in a hard school. They disdained those graces in which Whistler excelled, they had no truck with the fashionable exaggerations of art nouveau, and Degas, in particular, seemed to prize ugliness and to cultivate brutality.

Now the immortal element in Sickert was Parisian. That high seriousness and profound artistic integrity which places him head and shoulders above his friends of the New English Art Club results from a good French education. It is true that his verbal brilliance, his wit, his playacting (which he learnt upon the professional stage and never quite forgot) have been remembered by his friends and recorded in his writings; but who would bother about them if it were not for his paintings — his intensely serious and sincere paintings?

This does not mean that Sickert's literary work deserves to be forgotten. In fact, he is still very readable. He wrote at a gallop, careless of style, of grammar, and very often of the truth. And with a runaway verve and fluency, dragging up any boutade, anecdote, or locus classicus that will serve his argument or his mood. He can be charming, flippant, enlightening and, on occasion, devastatingly rude.

"Mr. Berenson, after making us feel small, and breaking our heads for years with his *'inis* and *'iccios,* [has come] down heavily and imprudently into the field of modern art, and plumped for Matisse, carrying with him deeply moved spinsters who had never heard of Monet, and breathless dowagers to whom Degas was nought! . . . how relieved were those of us, including the present writer, who had hitherto modest and chilly doubts as to the sufficient weight and length of our kilt of culture, when we saw Berenson prone and bare in the field of modern art, revealing deficiencies we had long suspected, but dared not hint at! *Ouf!* There is one at least whose works I shall not have to read!"

She was a saucy muse who inspired these remarks, wrongheaded too — wrong enough at all events to oblige Sickert to contradict himself on the subject of Matisse, though not, I think, on that of Berenson. Note how the opening of the last sentence is cast in a form which makes it appear to be translated from the French (*Ouf, voila un au moins* . . .); that too is typical of Sickert. These remarks were tossed, like a pinch of cayenne pepper into a jam omelet, being inserted, without apparent justification, into a review of Théodore Duret's *Histoire de Édouard Manet and de son oeuvre.* Thus he wrote, and thus he spoke.

Then, indeed, he was even more wildly discursive. He wandered happily from topic to topic. "Thérèse," he would say, waving an arm in the direction of Mrs. Sickert, "Thérèse will gather my parentheses together," and I have known him, while talking, ostensibly about the technique of painting in oils, launch into a spirited defense of a crook called Orton who claimed to be the long-lost heir of the Tichborne estate and had, declared Sickert, been "a thoroughly honest man sent to prison for signing his own

name." Undoubtedly he had a perverse genius for being in the wrong.

And yet, where painting was concerned, he was in the right. By this I mean that although he could say all sorts of foolish things about art and artists, he was not wrong about his own painting. Within his own terms he was perfectly sensible, logical, and consistent. He was not one of those who, like Corot, seem almost to have achieved masterpieces by accident. Sickert had learned the lessons of Degas very thoroughly and applied them very intelligently. He understood the danger, that danger which had been too much for Whistler, of being "artistic." In his finest period he knew perfectly well what he wanted to do and he did it perfectly.

He set out to paint what he called "reality." Reality, of course, means whatever we want it to mean. For Sickert it meant the average, the unhappy mean; for him the kitchen was more "real" than the drawing room, but the ash can was not more real than the kitchen. He turned away from all those pearls and all that satin, the marble fountains, shaven lawns, stately homes, and other paraphernalia of the life genteel in which his contemporaries rejoiced so freely and which he described as "the august site and the nicely got up young person"; but he also avoided the raggle-taggle and all too easily acceptable picturesque. He found what he wanted in the lives of the moderately seedy, the third-rate music hall, the ill-favored small-time tart, the shop-soiled bourgeoisie with its ornate lampshades, preposterous wallpapers, its stuffed birds, and the over-decorated detritus of late Victorian near-gentility. He could, when he pleased, address himself to the urban landscape of Venice or Dieppe, rendering it with beautiful exactitude, but his favorite territory was north London and, in particular, the great area of lace-curtained squalor which lies to the northwest of Bloomsbury.

In the same way, while insisting that he was a literary painter, Sickert avoided the dramatically or sentimentally obvious anecdote. In fact, he avoided anecdotes altogether; reality, to his way of thinking, abounds in situations, in scenes which convey a mood, but it does not play charades, it does not point its meaning, the artist must take what he sees even though that which he sees may be, and usually is, from a literary point of view, taciturn.

Thus he denies himself all the more easily appreciated forms of assistance that nature can provide, all the generally acceptable forms of beauty, monstrosity, and eloquence; and he does this, I think, because he is by nature an alchemist and there is nothing that a true alchemist less desires than gold, unless he has made it. As he himself put it: "The artist is he who can take a piece of flint and wring out of it attar of roses."

To describe how this was done one would have to paint a Sickert, to draw with miraculous economy, to possess an infallible instinct for the perfect interval, to relate tones with magical dexterity. At his best, Sickert could do all this, no one better. He understood his own aesthetic program and he carried it out with the utmost science.

Thus, when he fell foul of Roger Fry and his postimpressionist exhibition and when he declared that Cézanne was a fraud, the battle that he fought against the moderns, he who had been a leader of the moderns, was a battle, not of right against wrong, but of right against right. I am glad to say, for it is to the credit of everyone concerned, that his adversaries recognized this, even when he could not. He never lost either the friendship or the respect of the younger generation, nor did he ever stop teasing his juniors. And, when a still younger generation arose and "rediscovered him," claiming him as their leader and the genius of British art in our century, the ranks of Tuscany were present, cheering loudly with the rest.

SIDNEY, Sir Philip (Nov. 30, 1554 – Oct. 17, 1586). English poet, critic, soldier, statesman. Born Penshurst, Kent, eldest son of Sir Henry Sidney, Queen Elizabeth's lord governor in Ireland, and Mary Dudley; nephew of Robert Dudley the earl of Leicester. Educated at Shrewsbury School and Christ Church, Oxford (1567–71), Sidney traveled extensively abroad, sent first by his father and uncle to complete his education (1572–75) and later by Queen Elizabeth on a royal mission to Germany (1577). In Paris (1572) he visited English ambassador Sir Francis Walsingham, later to become his father-in-law, and met Hubert Languet, whose Protestant humanism greatly influenced his thought. Visit to father in Ireland (c.1576) led to meeting with Penelope Devereux, daughter of earl of Essex and the "Stella" of his sonnets, and resulted in *Discourse of Irish Affairs* (1577), a defense of his father's activities. Exiled from court for letter written to the queen opposing her marriage to the duke of Alençon and Anjou (1579), he devoted himself to writing. Major works written 1578–83 include *The Lady of May*, pastoral entertainment for the queen (1578); prose romance *Arcadia* (first version completed by 1580, revised 1584); critical essay *An Apology for Poetry* (or *Defense of Poesy*, 1581–83); *Astrophel and Stella* (1581–83), first of the important Elizabethan sonnet sequences. Having regained the queen's favor, he was knighted (1583) and married Frances Walsingham the same year. Elizabeth stood as godmother to their only child, Elizabeth (b.1585). Appointed governor of Flushing, Netherlands (1585), he became general of cavalry under Leicester sent to assist Dutch in war against Spanish. At battle of Zutphen (Sept. 22, 1586) he was fatally wounded. He died at Arnheim, Netherlands, and was buried in Old St. Paul's Cathedral, London. All of his works were published posthumously: *Arcadia* (1590 quarto, augmented folio 1593, authorized folio 1598), *Apology* (1595), *Astrophel and Stella* (1598).

EDITIONS: *The Complete Works of Sir Philip Sidney* ed. Albert Feuillerat (4 vols. Cambridge, England, 1912–26). *The Poems of Sir Philip Sidney* ed. William A. Ringler (London and New York 1962). *Selections from Arcadia and Other Poetry and Prose* ed. Thomas W. Craik (London 1965 and New York PB 1966). *Sir Philip Sidney: Selected Prose and Poetry* ed. Robert Kimbrough (New York PB 1969). *Astrophel and Stella* ed. Max Putzel (New York PB 1967).

REFERENCES: John Buxton *Sir Philip Sidney and the English Renaissance* (2nd ed. London and New York 1964). Thomas W. Craik *Sir Philip Sidney* (London 1965). Roger Howell, Jr. *Sir Philip Sidney: The Shepherd Knight* (London and Boston 1968). David M. Kalstone *Sidney's Poetry* (Cambridge, Mass. and Oxford 1965, also PB). Robert L. Montgomery *Symmetry and Sense: The Poetry of Sir Philip Sidney* (Austin, Tex. 1961). Kenneth Myrick *Sir Philip Sidney as a Literary Craftsman* (2nd ed. Lincoln, Nebr. PB 1965). Neil L. Rudenstine *Sidney's Poetic Development* (Cambridge, Mass. and Oxford 1967). Malcolm W. Wallace *The Life of Sir Philip Sidney* (Cambridge, England, 1915, reprinted New York 1967). Mona Wilson *Sir Philip Sidney* (2nd ed. London 1950).

SIR PHILIP SIDNEY
BY ROY LAMSON

Courtier, soldier, scholar, patron, diplomat, poet, novelist, critic, friend and associate of the intellectual elite of his age — all these things Sir Philip Sidney was. He embodied the perfect courtier of Castiglione.

In his public life, where we may clearly see his ambitions, his aims were practical. He saw himself as a courtier who served his queen, a man of affairs, a heroic man of war. From his private life came his art, so intellectually responsive to the continental literary climate of his time and yet teeming with innovation and with pride in the English language.

His heritage and his family connections were good. Born in Penshurst in Kent (the room of his birth is still shown to visitors), he was the eldest son of a faithful though little rewarded servant of Queen Elizabeth, Sir Henry Sidney, and of Lady Mary, eldest daughter of John Dudley, duke of Northumberland. In 1564 Philip and Fulke Greville, his biographer, entered Shrewsbury School together and became lifelong friends. Four years later he and Greville entered Oxford; during the plague of 1571 he left without a degree.

In 1572 he traveled in the suite of the earl of Lincoln to Paris, where he associated with the chief French writers and Protestant leaders. From Paris he went to Frankfort-am-Main, where he met the scholar and controversialist Hubert Languet, who became a master to him in literary and religious matters. Vienna, then Venice and Padua (for study in astronomy), were next in his travels; at Venice he became a friend of Tintoretto and of Veronese (for whom he sat for a portrait, now, unfortunately, lost).

After a further visit to Vienna and Poland, he was summoned home to carry on the life of a courtier and servant of the queen on official and diplomatic missions. On one of the queen's progresses to the residence of the earl of Essex, he is supposed to have seen for the first time Penelope Devereux, Essex's daughter, then a girl of thirteen, and later the "Stella" of his sonnets. In literary affairs Sidney was the center of a learned group including Sir

Edward Dyer, Edmund Spenser, and Fulke Greville, men of letters and affairs who were concerned with the new English poetry and the introduction of classical meters in English verse.

By chance, an important opportunity for Sidney to have leisure to write came in 1579, when the duke of Alençon and Anjou, brother of the French king and a leading suitor for the queen's hand, was visiting Elizabeth. In full view of the French ambassadors Sidney and the earl of Oxford quarreled over the use of a tennis court. The queen demanded that Sidney apologize to Oxford. Sidney refused, challenged Oxford, and left for Wilton to stay with his sister, the countess of Pembroke, herself the center of a literary circle, whose famous house was described as like "a college, there were so many learned and ingenious persons."

At Wilton, he began the early draft of *The Arcadia,* his prose pastoral romance, because, as he says in a letter to his sister, "you desired me to do it, and your desire to my heart is an absolute commandment." Before 1584 he also wrote *An Apology for Poetry,* his contribution to literary criticism. He was knighted in 1583, and in the autumn married Frances, a daughter of Sir Francis Walsingham, the famous secretary of state.

Sidney shared the Elizabethan desire to see the New World, and was actually planning in 1585 to sail with Drake on an expedition against the Spaniards in America, when the queen recalled him to serve the Protestant cause in the Netherlands against the Spaniards as governor of Flushing and as a military leader. On September 22, 1586, during an attack near Zutphen on a convoy of provisions for the forces of the duke of Alva, he received "a sore wound upon his thigh, three fingers

above his knee." The well-known story, told by Greville, that the wounded Sidney gave his own bottle of water to a dying foot soldier with the words "Thy necessity is yet greater than mine," is typical of the man even though it may be apocryphal. Sidney was ferried down the Issel to Arnhem, where he died on October 17, shortly before his thirty-second birthday. All England and Protestant Europe mourned the ideal English courtier of his age.

Sidney's renown as an Elizabethan gentleman drew him strongly to the hearts of his generation and those that followed, but his literary work, the product of his spare time, has given him an important place in English literature. As Kenneth Muir has said: "His *Defence of Poesie* is the first real English criticism; his *Astrophel and Stella* is one of the seminal works of the sixteenth century; and *Arcadia* is the first great masterpiece of English prose."

Except for two poems, none of Sidney's literary work was published in his lifetime. *The Countesse of Pembrokes Arcadia,* published in 1590, was a reworking by Sidney and his sister of the "old *Arcadia*" written at Wilton in 1580. Both versions show Sidney following the pattern of Renaissance romances in which prose narrative is interspersed with songs and eclogues. The work itself, a mixture of pastoral, chivalric, and heroic elements, often reflects Sidney's own experience, praising courage and the active, heroic life.

Astrophel and Stella (1591), consisting of 108 sonnets and eleven songs, is the most important and influential pioneer of the "new poetry" of the Eighties and Nineties of Elizabeth's reign. In these sonnets Sidney molds the conventions of Petrarch and his followers into new, vigorous, sometimes startling patterns, producing a strong sense of originality and variety combined with wit, irony, fine imagination, and dramatic skill. In *Astrophel and Stella*, "Stella" and Sidney himself emerge as central figures in a poetic dramatization which rivals Shakespeare's sonnets. The last of Sidney's works to be published, *The Defense of Poesy*, 1595 (a second edition is called *An Apologie for Poetrie*) is a defense of art against its narrow-minded detractors. Sidney, with Horace, sees delightful teaching as the end of poetry, and he supports English as a language for poetry.

In the English Renaissance, Sidney and his sister, the countess of Pembroke, "played the part of the Medici in Florence," says John Buxton. "The personality of Philip Sidney shaped the literature of his countrymen, as it set an example for them to cherish."

SIENKIEWICZ, Henryk (May 5, 1846 – Nov. 15, 1916). Polish novelist. Born Wola Okrzejska, near Lukow, Poland, of impoverished patrician family. Educated at University of Warsaw, he began writing critical articles while still a student (1869) and published his first novel, *Na Marne* (1872, tr. *In Vain* 1899). As correspondent for the *Gazeta Polska*, traveled to U.S. (1876–78), writing his *Listy z Podróży do Ameryki* (1876–78, tr. *Portrait of America* 1959) and publishing several successful short stories upon his return. Married three times: his first wife, Maria Szetkiewicz, died (1885); after annulment of his second marriage, to Maria Wolodkowicz, married Maria Babska (1904). Among his chief works: *Ogniem i Mieczem* (1883–84, tr. *With Fire and Sword* 1890), *Potop* (1886, tr. *The Deluge* 1891), and *Pan Wolodyjowski* (1887–88, tr. *Pan Michael* 1893), a monumental patriotic trilogy of seventeenth-century Poland; *Quo Vadis?* (1895, tr. 1896), a historical novel about Nero's Rome, an immensely popular work; his excellent psychological novel *Bez Dogmatu*

(1891, tr. *Without Dogma* 1899); and the historical novel *Krzyżacy* (1900, tr. *Knights of the Cross* 1900–1901). Recipient of the Nobel prize in literature (1905), Sienkiewicz was revered by the Polish people and became their unofficial spokesman during World War I, when he worked devotedly for Polish independence. He died in Vevey, Switzerland, while organizing relief for Polish war victims.

REFERENCES: Monica M. Gardner *The Patriot Novelist of Poland* (London 1926). Mieczyslaw Giergielewicz *Henryk Sienkiewicz* (New York 1968). Marja Kosko *Un Best-Seller, 1900: Quo Vadis?* (Paris 1960). Waclaw Lednicki *Henryk Sienkiewicz, a Retrospective Synthesis* (The Hague and New York 1960).

SIGNAC, Paul (Nov. 11, 1863 – Aug. 15, 1935). French painter. Born and died in Paris; of middle-class family. Through Jean Baptiste Guillaumin joined impressionists, became influenced by Monet. With Georges Seurat founded Société des Artistes Indépendants (1884), became president, and exhibited at its salon annually from 1908 to 1934. With Seurat was one of first painters to adopt technique of pointillism, using tiny dots of pure color to achieve the blended effect of light and reflection. Published treatise of neo-impressionist theory, *D'Eugène Delacroix au néo-impressionisme* (1899). One of first artists to live in St.-Tropez (from 1892), he painted chiefly coastal scenes of south of France, also of Brittany, Venice, Rotterdam, and Istanbul.

REFERENCES: G. Besson *Signac* (Paris 1950). Lucie Cousturier *Paul Signac* (Paris 1922). John Rewald *Post-Impressionism from Van Gogh to Gauguin* (2nd ed. Garden City, N.Y. 1962).

SIGNORELLI, Luca (1441/50 – Oct. 16, 1523). Italian painter. Born and died in Cortona. Probably a pupil of Piero della Francesca, who with Pollaiuolo influenced strongly his early work. First signed painting is a two-sided processional standard depicting the *Flagellation* and a *Madonna and*

Child (c.1474, Brera, Milan). Other early works include an *Annunciation* (S. Francesco, Arezzo) and two versions of the *Madonna and Child* (Museum of Fine Arts, Boston, and Ashmolean Museum, Oxford). Painted the commanding S. *Onofrio Altarpiece* (1484, Museo del Duomo, Perugia), the *Circumcision* (National Gallery, London), *Holy Family* (Uffizi, Florence) and *Adoration of the Magi* (1493–94, Louvre, Paris), and some portraits. The solemn frescoes of *St. Benedict's Life* for abbey of Monte Oliveto Maggiore, Siena (1497–98), were followed by his masterpiece, the *Last Judgment* series in S. Brizio chapel, Orvieto Cathedral (completed 1504). The apocalyptic conception, realistic rendering of infernal scenes of terrifyingly human devils inflicting torture, and handling of anatomy influenced Michelangelo. Other late works, less powerful and intense, include the *Crucifixion* (Uffizi, Florence), the *Assumption* and *Immaculate Conception* (1520–21, Museo Diocesano, Cortona). In his forceful treatment of anatomy, Signorelli was perhaps the greatest painter of the nude figure before Michelangelo.

REFERENCES: Maud Cruttwell *Luca Signorelli* (London 1899). Giorgio Vasari *Lives of the . . . Painters, Sculptors, and Architects* (1550) tr. Gaston de Vere (10 vols. London 1912–15).

SILVA, José Asunción (Nov. 27, 1865 – May 24, 1896). Colombian poet. Born and died in Bogotá; of aristocratic family. In Europe (1886), he associated with a literary group, returned to Bogotá to become one of the writers of *modernismo* — modern Spanish and Spanish-American poetry. Having at length found a publisher in France, he sent off his manuscript, only to lose it in a shipwreck. This and other misfortunes, joined with the death of a sister, so affected him that he committed suicide at the age of thirty-one. His poetry, tinged with melancholy and ironic pessimism, is notable for its haunting melodiousness and fluidity of form which influenced Rubén Darío and other Latin-American *modernistas*. Among his best known poems are *Nocturno III*, elegy for his sister, *Cre-*

púsculo (Twilight), and *El Día de Difuntos (The Day of the Dead)*.

SIMONE MARTINI. *See* **MARTINI, Simone.**

SISLEY, Alfred (Oct. 30, 1839 – Jan. 29, 1899). French painter. Born Paris, of English parents. Sent to London at eighteen to study business. On his return (1862), he decided on career as artist and entered studio of Charles Gleyre, where he met Renoir, Monet, and Frédéric Bazille, often painting with them out of doors. Still influenced by Courbet, Corot, and Barbizon school, he exhibited at Salon of 1866 (the year he married Marie Lescouezec), but thereafter gradually turned to impressionist colors and ideas. When war ruined his father's business (1870), Sisley suffered also financially just at the time his style was becoming mature. He was taken up by the dealer Durand-Ruel and exhibited with the impressionists (1874), but his situation remained precarious. His uneventful life is marked only by the several moves he made to Marly-le-Roi (1874), Sèvres (1877), Veneux-Nadon (1879), and Moret-sur-Loing (1882, for rest of his life), all of which became subjects for his landscapes which include *Sand Heaps* and *Street in Moret* (both in Art Institute, Chicago). He died penniless, scarcely recognized; but ironically, barely three months later his paintings (sold for his children's benefit) brought high prices and started a vogue which prompted the famous sale of 1900, when *Flood at Port-Marly* (1876, Louvre, Paris), probably his best-known work, was sold for 43,000 francs. Sisley is now considered a great landscapist and one of the purest exponents of impressionism.

REFERENCES: George Besson *Sisley* (Paris 1946). François Daulte *Sisley: Landscapes* (New York 1963). Gustave Geffroy *Sisley* (Paris 1923). John Rewald *History of Impressionism* (1946, rev. ed. Greenwich, Conn. 1961, also PB).

SITWELL, Dame Edith (Sept. 7, 1887 – Dec. 9, 1964). British poet. Born Scarborough, eldest child of an aristocratic family. Sister of writers Sir Osbert and Sacheverell Sitwell. Privately educated at Renishaw Hall, the family seat in Derbyshire; early influenced by Swinburne and French symbolists. Moved to London (1914). Edited *Wheels* (1916–21), an annual anti-Georgian verse anthology. *The Mother and Other Poems* privately published (1915). First performance of poem cycle *Façade* with music by William Walton (1922, later enlarged and revised 1926, 1942) excited violent criticism. Experimented with rhythm and imagist "sense transfusion" in *Bucolic Comedies* (1923); continued romantic elegiac tone in *The Sleeping Beauty* (1924), *Troy Park* (1925), and *Rustic Elegies* (1927). First serious satire of social corruption and human cruelty appeared in the poems of *Gold Coast Customs* (1929). Moved to Paris (1932), where she formed friendships with Gertrude Stein, Jean Cocteau, Pavel Tchelitchew. *Street Songs* (1942), *Green Song* (1944), and *The Song of the Cold* (1945), profoundly religious and full of understanding of human suffering, at last brought general acclaim. Living in London and at Renishaw during the 1940's, she worked periodically for the B.B.C. and edited anthologies. Made lecture tours in U.S. with Osbert (1948, 1950). Made Dame of the British Empire (1954), the year of her first *Collected Poems*. Became a Roman Catholic (1955). Awarded Foyle prize (1958). An impressive public figure, her last years were marked by many television appearances. Died in London. *Taken Care Of,* her autobiography, was published posthumously (1965). Other major works: *Alexander Pope* (1930), a biography; *Aspects of Modern Poetry* (1934); *I Live Under a Black Sun* (1937), a collage novel; *A Poet's Notebook* (1943); *Notebook on William Shakespeare* (1948); *Gardeners and Astronomers* (1953), poems; *Collected Poems* (1957); *The Outcasts* (1962), poems; and *The Queens and the Hive* (1962), biography of Elizabeth I and three other queens.

REFERENCES: C. M. Bowra *Edith Sitwell* (Monaco 1947). James D. Brophy *Edith Sitwell: The Symbolist Order* (Carbondale, Ill. 1968). John Lehmann *A Nest of Tigers: The Sitwells in Their Times* (London and Boston 1968). Rodolphe L. Mégroz *The Three Sitwells* (1927, reprinted Port Washington, N.Y. 1969). Elizabeth Salter *The Last Years of a Rebel: A Memoir of Edith Sitwell* (London and Boston 1967). Geoffrey Singleton *Edith Sitwell: The Hymn to Life* (London 1961). Max Wykes-Joyce *A Triad of Genius* (London 1953).

———

SKELTON, John (c.1460 – June 21, 1529). English poet, translator, rhetorician. Date and place of birth unknown. Educated at Cambridge, he won distinction in Latin grammar, rhetoric, and versification. Also attended Oxford (c.1488), Louvain (c.1488–93), Cambridge (1493). Translated Cicero's letters and Diodorus Siculus, acclaimed for his Latin scholarship by William Caxton (1490, preface to *Eneydos*) and Erasmus, who called him "the incomparable light and glory of English letters" (1499). Tutor to Prince Henry (later Henry VIII), he took holy orders (1498) and became rector of Diss, Norfolk (c.1504), by royal appointment. Early works include *The Bowge of Courte* (1499), an allegorical satire on Henry VII's court; *Speculum Principis* (1501), moral treatise for the prince; minor satires *Phillip Sparrow* (1508) and *Ware the Hauke* (1504–12). Served as Orator Regius for Henry VIII, for whom he wrote the morality play *Magnyfycence* (1516). Later works include *The Tunnynge of Elynour Rummyng* (1517), a humorous poem about tavern life, and three clerical satires directed against corruption of the church and mounting power of Cardinal Wolsey: *Speke, Parrot* (1521), *Colin Clout* (1522), *Why Come Ye Nat to Courte?* (1522). Wrote (1523) apologia for his poetic career, *Garlande of Laurell*. Died at Westminster, where he was buried in St. Margaret's, his parish church. Skelton's distinctive style of short rhyming lines, based on colloquial speech rhythms, is known today as "Skeltonic verse." Considered the only major English poet between Chaucer and Sir Thomas Wyatt.

EDITIONS: *Poetical Works* ed. Rev. Alexander Dyce (London 1843, reprinted 2 vols. New York 1965). *Complete Poems* ed. Philip Henderson (2nd ed. London and Toronto 1931). *John Skelton: A Selection from His Poems* ed. Vivian De Sola Pinto (London and New York 1950).

REFERENCES: H. L. R. Edwards *Skelton: The Life and Times of an Early Tudor Poet* (London and New York 1949). Stanley Eugene Fish *John Skelton's Poetry* (New Haven, Conn. 1965). Ian A. Gordon *John Skelton, Poet Laureate* (1943, reprinted New York 1970). William O. Harris *Skelton's Magnyfycence and the Cardinal Virtue Tradition* (Chapel Hill, N.C. 1965). Arthur Ray Heiserman *Skelton and Satire* (Chicago 1961). Leslie J. Lloyd *John Skelton: A Sketch of his Life and Writings* (Oxford 1938, reprinted New York 1969). William Nelson *John Skelton, Laureate* (1939, reprinted New York 1964).

SLOAN, John French (Aug. 2, 1871 – Sept. 7, 1951). American painter and etcher. Born Lock Haven, Pa. Studied briefly at Pennsylvania Academy of Fine Arts (1892–93) and worked as illustrator for Philadelphia *Inquirer* (1892–95) and Philadelphia *Press* (1895–1903). Married Anna Marie Wall (1901). Strongly influenced by Robert Henri, he began (1897) painting seriously and moved to New York (1904), supporting himself as illustrator. Won recognition as member of the Eight, a group of realists whose paintings of urban scenes became known as the "ashcan school." Chief organizer and later president (1918–44) of the Society of Independent Artists, he was also an active and popular teacher (1916–37), mostly at the Art Students' League of New York. In collaboration with Helen Farr, later his second wife (1944), he produced *The Gist of Art* (1939). His scenes of teeming city life, animated by a sense of character, humor, and movement, include *Sunday, Women Drying Their Hair* (1912, Addison Gallery, Andover, Mass.), *McSorley's Bar* (1912, Detroit Institute of Fine Arts), *Backyards, Greenwich Village* (1914, Whitney Museum, New York), *The Lafayette* (1928, Metropolitan Museum, New York). In his late fifties, Sloan abandoned the con-

temporary genre and began to study the nude figure, using a complex technique of underpainting, glazing, and linework. A leading figure in American modern art, he died in Hanover, N.H.

REFERENCES: Van Wyck Brooks *John Sloan: A Painter's Life* (New York and London 1955). Helen Farr *American Art Nouveau: The Poster Period of John Sloan* (Lock Haven, Pa. 1967). Lloyd Goodrich *John Sloan* (New York 1952). Peter Morse ed. *A Selection of Etchings by John Sloan from the Philadelphia Museum of Art* (Columbia, Mo. PB 1967) and *John Sloan's Prints* (New Haven, Conn. 1969). Bruce St. John ed. *John Sloan's New York Scene* (New York 1965).

SMART, Christopher (Apr. 22, 1722 – May 21, 1771). English poet. Born Shipbourne, Kent. Father was steward for William Viscount Vane until his death; family then moved to Durham, where Smart spent vacations and gained patronage of duchess of Cleveland. Educated at Durham School and Pembroke College, Cambridge; as fellow there, he lectured in philosophy and rhetoric until 1752. Moved to London (1753) and produced theatricals, edited humorous magazines, and wrote for John Newbery, whose stepdaughter, Anna Maria Carnan, he married. Published two volumes of *Poems* (1752, 1763), wrote satire *Hilliad* (1753), translated Horace (1756) and *Phaedrus* (1765). After 1756 he fell prey to religious mania, but though in and out of asylums wrote *A Translation of the Psalms and Hymns and Spiritual Songs* (1756), *Rejoice in the Lamb* (first published 1939), and the highly praised *Song to David* (1763), which was greatly admired by Pre-Raphaelites and reprinted in *London Magazine* (1820). In debt, he wrote last *Hymns for the Instruction and Amusement of Children* in King's Bench prison, where he died. Smart is considered a leading English devotional lyricist.

EDITION: *Collected Poems* ed. Norman Callan (1949, latest ed. 2 vols. London and Cambridge, Mass. 1967). *Jubilate Agno (Rejoice in the Lamb)* ed. W. H. Bond (Cambridge, Mass. 1954).

REFERENCES: Edward G. Ainsworth and Charles E. Noyes *Christopher Smart* (Columbia, Mo. 1943). Lawrence Binyon *The Case of Christopher Smart* (London and New York 1934). Sophia B. Blaydes *Christopher Smart as a Poet of His Time: A Re-appraisal* (The Hague 1966). Moira Dearnley *The Poetry of Christopher Smart* (London and New York 1968). Christopher Devlin *Poor Kit Smart* (London and Carbondale, Ill. 1961).

SMETANA, Bedrich (Mar. 2, 1824 – May 12, 1884). Czech composer. Born Leitomischl, Bohemia. The son of an amateur violinist, he received little formal musical training, but became a child prodigy as a pianist. Studied briefly with Josef Proksch, Prague, and became music master to family of Count Thun (1844–47). After opening piano school with the aid of Franz Liszt, married pianist Katharina Kolař (1848). Left Czechoslovakia for Göteborg, Sweden (1856), where he was conductor for the Philharmonic Society (1856–61) and composed his first three symphonic poems: *Richard III, Wallensteins Lager,* and *Hakon Jarl*. After his wife's death (1859), married Betty Ferdinandi (1860) and returned to Prague (1861), where the movement towards nationalism in the arts was gathering momentum. His first opera, the patriotic *The Brandenburgers in Bohemia,* opened at the new national opera house in Prague (1866), followed by his masterpiece, *The Bartered Bride* (1866). Acclaimed Bohemia's greatest composer, he was appointed director of the National Theatre, a post he held until 1874, when he became deaf. Among his other operas: *The Kiss* (1876), *The Secret* (1878), *Libussa* (written 1871, performed 1881). Returning to the symphonic poem, he wrote his nationalistic symphonic cycle *Má Vlast (My Country),* which contains the well-known *Vltava (The Moldau)* (1874). Suffered a complete mental breakdown (1883) and died in an insane asylum, Prague.

REFERENCES: Frantisek Bartos ed. *Smetana: Letters and Reminiscences* (tr. London 1956). Liam Nolan and J. B. Hutton *The Life of Smetana: The Pain and the Glory* (London and Mystic, Conn. 1968). Rosa Newmarch *The Music of Czechoslovakia* (London and New York 1942).

SMIBERT (or Smybert), **John** (1688 – Apr. 2, 1751). Scottish-American portrait painter. Born Edinburgh, son of a dyer. Moved to London, then to Italy, where he copied old masters and met Bishop George Berkeley (author of the celebrated line, "Westward the course of empire takes its way"), who offered him professorship of art at future college of Bermuda. Accordingly, Smibert sailed for the U.S. (1728), waited in Newport, R.I., and when plans for the college failed went to Boston, opened a studio (1730), and became one of first notable colonial portraitists. Among his works: *Bishop Berkeley and His Family* (Yale University, New Haven), *Governor John Wanton* (c.1735, Rhode Island Historical Society, Providence, R.I.), *Governor John Endicott* (Massachusetts Historical Society, Boston), *John Lowell* (Harvard University, Cambridge, Mass.), *Judge Edmund Quincy* and *Jonathan Edwards* (both, Museum of Fine Arts, Boston). Smibert married an heiress and settled in Boston for rest of his life. He exerted considerable influence on the succeeding generation of portrait painters, including Copley and Trumbull, and was architect of Fanueil Hall, Boston.

REFERENCE: Henry W. Foote *John Smibert, Painter: With a Descriptive Catalogue of Portraits* (Cambridge, Mass. 1950).

SMITH, David (Mar. 9, 1906 – May 23, 1965). American sculptor. Descendant of a pioneer blacksmith who settled in Decatur, Ind. Smith worked in factories assembling metal parts before he became interested in art; then studied painting at Art Students' League with Czech cubist Jan Matulka. In 1930's was exposed to abstract art through Stuart Davis and others. Impressed by Picasso's welded iron sculpture, he gradually moved from painting to sculpture, and began applying welding technique to steel and bronze. After working as a welder in defense plant during World War II, began in late 1940's to produce his finest sculpture: *Blackburn*

— *Song of an Irish Blacksmith* (1950, Estate of the Artist); *Hudson River Landscape* (1951, Whitney Museum, New York), an example of linear sculpture termed by Smith "drawing-in-space"; the series based on the human figure, *Agricola* and *Tank Totem* (1950's); the three major series of monumental geometric sculpture, *Voltri-Bolton, Zig, Cubi* (1960's, Marlborough-Gerson Gallery, New York). Through his use of the symbol and the geometrical structure, Smith's art is related to abstract expressionism. He died in Albany, following an accident.

SMITH, Sydney (June 3, 1771 – Feb. 22, 1845). English clergyman, satirist, wit. Born Woodford, Essex, son of a wealthy landowner. Educated at Winchester School and New College, Oxford, where he became a fellow (1791). Ordained an Anglican minister (1794) and became curate of Netheravon on Salisbury Plain. Went as a tutor (1798) to Edinburgh, and founded with Francis Jeffrey and others the *Edinburgh Review* (1802), which gained fame particularly for his brilliant contributions (1802–28). Married Catherine Amelia Pybus (1800). Returned to London (1803) and became well known as a preacher, lecturer, Whig politician, and wit. His *Peter Plymley Letters* (published anonymously, 1807–1808) in favor of Catholic emancipation cleverly satirized Protestant bigotry and ignorance, and enjoyed immediate success. Moved to Yorkshire as rector of Foston-le-Clay (where according to *Lady Holland's Memoir* he stated his living was "so far out of the way that it was actually twelve miles from a lemon"); made prebend of Bristol (1828) and canon residential of St. Paul's, London (1831). Died in London. Often compared to Swift and Voltaire, Smith was a master of wit and satire, noted for pithy remarks and observations such as, "Live always in the best of company when you read," or "Daniel Webster struck me much like a steam engine in trousers," and a recipe for a salad: "Let onion atoms lurk within the bowl /And, half suspected, animate the whole." A lover of justice and truth, he used his pen to attack the corrupt while championing the causes of the op-

pressed. His other works include *A Letter to the Electors upon the Catholic Question* (1826) and the *Singleton Letters* (1837–39).

EDITIONS: *Works* (3 vols. 1839; new ed. London 1869 and New York 1872). *Selected Writings* ed. W. H. Auden (New York 1956 and London 1957). *Letters* ed. Nowell C. Smith (2 vols. London and New York 1953). *A Memoir of the Rev. Sydney Smith by His Daughter, Lady Holland* . . . (2 vols. London 1855).

REFERENCES: G. W. Bullett *Sydney Smith: A Biography and a Selection* (London 1951). Osbert Burdett *The Reverend Smith, Sydney* (London 1934). Sheldon Halpern *Sydney Smith* (New York 1966). Hesketh Pearson *The Smith of Smiths, Being the Life, Wit, and Humour of Sydney Smith* (London and New York 1934).

SMOLLETT, Tobias (George) Mar. 1721 – Sept. 17, 1771). British novelist. Born near Dumbarton, Scotland; descended from Scottish lairds. Apprenticed to a Glasgow surgeon, he also attended University of Glasgow. Left for London (1739) to seek production of his first play, *The Regicide* (published 1749), but then sailed as a surgeon's mate (1740) on Admiral Edward Vernon's expedition against Spanish sea power in America. Settled in Jamaica, where he met his wife Anne (Nancy) Lassells. Returned to London (1744) as a surgeon. First novel, *Roderick Random* (1748), is partly based on his own adventures. Received M.D. from Marischal College, Aberdeen (1750), and left for France, gathering material for *Peregrine Pickle* (1751). Moved to Chelsea (1750), where he continued an enormous literary production: translations of Voltaire, Lesage, and Cervantes' *Don Quixote;* a four-volume history of England (1757–58) followed by a fifth (1760–65); chronicles of voyages (1756); a play, *Reprisal, or The Tars of Old England* (1757); the novel *Ferdinand Count Fathom* (1753). Also edited the *Critical Review* (1756–c.1762), the *British Magazine* (1760–67), where his novel *Sir Launcelot Greaves* (1762) appeared serially (1760–61), and the *Briton* (1762–63), an organ of the Tory party. Overworked and grieved by the loss of his daughter, he traveled to the Continent (1762–65), meeting Laurence Sterne, who nicknamed him "Smelfungus" in *A Sentimental Journey*. Returned to London (1765), publishing his *Travels Through France and Italy* (1766) and later *The History and Adventures of an Atom* (1769), a lively attack on contemporary English politics. Ill health forced him to return to Italy (1768), where he wrote *The Expedition of Humphry Clinker* (1771), based on a recent tour of Scotland and England. He died near Leghorn and is buried in the English cemetery there.

EDITIONS: *Works* ed. George Saintsbury (12 vols. London and Philadelphia 1895–1900). A new edition is now in progress at the University of Iowa Press. *The Letters of Tobias Smollett* ed. Lewis M. Knapp (Oxford and New York 1970).

REFERENCES: Fred W. Boege *Smollett's Reputation as a Novelist* (1947, reprinted New York 1969). Louis L. Martz *The Later Career of Tobias Smollett* (New Haven and Oxford 1942). George M. Kahrl *Tobias Smollett, Traveler-Novelist* (1945, reprinted New York 1968). Lewis M. Knapp *Tobias Smollett: Doctor of Men and Manners* (1949, reprinted New York 1963). Robert D. Spector *Tobias Smollett* (New York 1969).

TOBIAS SMOLLETT

BY JAMES L. CLIFFORD

Restless and always experimenting with new techniques, Tobias Smollett is perhaps the most difficult to place of all the early practitioners of the English novel. Although lacking the psychological depth of Richardson and Sterne, or the artistic control of Fielding, he nevertheless brought irresistible zest to the delineation of character, and some of his creations — Commodore Trunnion, Matthew Bramble, Winifred Jenkins, to name only a few — have a secure place in the galaxy of great comic figures. It is sometimes forgotten that in the early nineteenth century Smollett was often preferred to Field-

ing. Many of the great romantics were his youthful admirers, and Dickens actually thought *Peregrine Pickle* better than *Tom Jones*.

As his biographer Lewis M. Knapp has shown, Smollett's personality was extremely complex. At the same time that he aspired to be a rationalistic, aristocratic gentleman, he had violent emotions and was "passionate in speech, explosive in action, highly irascible in sarcasm and invective." Because he was a Scot in London, and thus never quite secure, he tended to be sensitive to imagined slights and lack of appreciation. And there was another sharp split. Like his contemporary Samuel Johnson, he combined a firm belief in social order and subordination with generous instincts and a deep sympathy for the poor. The story is told that once by accident he gave a beggar a guinea instead of a small coin. When the poor fellow hobbled after him trying to return it, Smollett was so touched by his honesty that he insisted on having the poor man keep the guinea and added another to it.

Smollett at first was a practicing surgeon, but soon was devoting most of his time to literary pursuits. A powerhouse of energy, he was occasional poet, unsuccessful dramatist, novelist, translator, compiler, editor, journalist — at times aided by a group of impecunious assistants whom he fed "beef, pudding, and potatoes, port, punch, and Calvert's entire butt-beer" on Sundays at his Chelsea house. His productivity as a man of letters is astonishing, and it is no wonder that his health began to give way before he was forty. Because of his acerbity he was involved in a number of serious lawsuits, and once spent almost three months in prison for libel, as the result of a caustic book review.

One theme runs through the best of

Smollett's works — an ardent delight in travel — and his *Travels Through France and Italy* is easily one of the best of its genre. V. S. Pritchett, who recommends the book without reservation, calls it the "first ill-tempered, captious, disillusioned and vigorously personal travel book in modern literature." If he was perhaps too stringent in his complaints about accommodations and local customs, and too determined not to parrot the gushing raptures of the connoisseurs of famous works of art — an attitude which led Sterne to nickname him "Smelfungus" — Smollett did provide fresh and perceptive comments which still make good reading.

The heroes of his novels, too, are constantly on the move. Roderick Random comes to London from Scotland, takes part in the ill-fated Carthagena expedition, as had Smollett himself, and later travels to Guinea and Buenos Aires. Peregrine Pickle visits Paris and the Low Countries. Ferdinand, Count Fathom, moves all over Europe, and Sir Launcelot Greaves is on a traditional quest. Humphry Clinker and his party visit Scotland and various parts of England.

The same restless spirit is apparent in Smollett's unwillingness to settle on any one narrative method, no matter how successful. At first attracted to the popular picaresque form, he tried combining this with various other devices, in differing degrees — at first with classical satire, melodrama, and mid-eighteenth-century sentiment — then with scenes of Gothic terror and pure Cervantean romance. After a promising start with *Roderick Random* and *Peregrine Pickle,* the next two novels — one with a monstrous unsympathetic hero, the other a slavish imitation of *Don Quixote* — were comparative failures. Then for his fifth and last, *Humphry Clinker,* he tried what was for him a completely new form, the Richardsonian epistolary technique. This time eschewing the picaresque, he concentrates on character portrayal, and in a remarkable manner makes each of the travelers inject his own personality into his letters. Less harsh than his earlier fiction, and with some of his richest comic effects, *Humphry Clinker* has generally been considered his masterpiece.

Smollett has often been criticized for his slapstick, low humor — for episodes such as Strap's blundering into the wrong bed with the customary riotous results, Peregrine's boring holes in his aunt's chamber pot, or Lismahago's descent down a ladder with bare posterior showing. But if he does at times violate good taste, he is never pornographic. He is following in the scatalogical tradition of Rabelais and Swift, who found comedy in places where society prefers to draw the curtain. All this, too, is part of Smollett's thirst for reality. The sordidness of life, the brutishness and vulgarity, he saw as an essential part of existence.

It has been customary to point out Smollett's avoidance of abstract ideas of philosophic depth. But this does not mean that he lacks moral purpose. He once wrote to a friend that his first novel was "intended as a satire on mankind," and he obviously held to this intention in subsequent works. His targets are the shams, the hypocrisy, the meanness and false values of society, and he prefers to expose them through exaggeration and satiric distortion, rather than by sober preaching.

Throughout he is lavish in Hogarthian caricatures, sometimes grotesque, at other times comic in the best sense. He sums up the evils and the vagaries of life, not perhaps with the subtlety of Sterne, but with infinite fertility. In the end, however, it is his robust style which carries the reader along. Smollett was a born storyteller. Despite a host of clichés and pompous passages, once he has his hero on the move, with some farcical scene or practical joke to describe, his verve is overwhelming.

SOANE, Sir John (Sept. 10, 1753 – Jan. 20, 1837). English architect. Born near Goring-on-Thames, son of a bricklayer. Entered London office of George Dance the Younger (1768); soon transferred to that of Henry Holland. Won gold medal at Royal Academy (1776) for design of a triumphal arch and, as winner of the king's traveling studentship (1778), traveled to Italy (1778–80). Worked chiefly as architect on country house (1780–88), then appointed, through support of the prime minister, William Pitt, architect to the Bank of England (1788), his largest and finest work. Various other government appointments followed, and he became (1802) a member of the Royal Academy. Succeeded Dance as professor of architecture there (1806); knighted (1831). Died in London. A leader of the classical revival in England, Soane developed a highly individual style, classical in spirit without imitation of classical detail. Among his most famous works are the Dulwich College Picture Gallery (1811), Pitzhanger Manor, Ealing (1800), and his own residence at 13 Lincoln's Inn Fields, London (1812), bequeathed to the state and now the Soane Museum.

REFERENCES: Arthur T. Bolton *The Works of Sir John Soane* (London 1924) and *The Portrait of Sir John Soane, 1753–1837* (London 1927). Dorothy Stroud *The Architecture of Sir John Soane* (London and Toronto 1961). J. N. Summerson *Sir John Soane, 1753–1837* (London and New York 1952).

SOCRATES (c.469 B.C. – 399 B.C.). Greek philosopher. Born and died in Athens. Son of Sophroniscus, a sculptor, and Phaenarete, a midwife, he apparently came from a family of some means. Late in life he married Xanthippe, whose shrewish character,

though probably exaggerated, is legendary. They had three sons, all of whom, according to Plato, proved insignificant. Little is known about the external events of Socrates' life. Interested in science as a young man, he studied under physicist Archelaus of Miletus. Served with distinction as a hoplite in Athenian army: perhaps at Samos (441–440), and during Peloponnesian War at Potidaea (432–430), where he saved Alcibiades' life, Delium (424), and Amphipolis (437–436, or 422). Although he never sought public office, he believed that a citizen must not refuse public duty. As a member of the Council of 500 (406–405), he was the only councilor at the trial of the Arginusaean generals to resist the unconstitutional collective condemnation of the generals. Showed the same courage in 404, when he defied the Thirty Tyrants' orders to arrest one of their political victims. Brought to trial for "impiety" (399), he was charged by the influential Anytus and prosecuted by the insignificant Meletus for religious heresies and for corrupting the youth. Condemned to death, he refused to consider an escape plan by his friend Crito and drank the hemlock thirty days after his condemnation. Socrates left no writings; our information about his personality and doctrine derives chiefly from Xenophon (*Memorabilia*) and Plato, his disciple (*Dialogues;* e.g. *Apology, Phaedo, Crito*). His major contributions were a new method of philosophical inquiry (the Socratic method); an emphasis on moral conduct and ethics; a conception of the soul as the seat of moral character, immortal and in harmony with an ordered universe based on a principle of good.

REFERENCES: John Burnet *Greek Philosophy: Thales to Plato* (1914, latest ed. New York and London 1964, also PB). Francis M. Cornford *Before and After Socrates* (1932, latest ed. Cambridge, England, 1962, also PB). Romano Guardini *The Death of Socrates: An Interpretation of the Platonic Dialogues: Euthyphro, Apology, Crito, and Phaedo* (tr. London 1948, also PB). Norman Gulley *The Philosophy of Socrates* (London and New York 1968). R. L. Levin and John Bremer

The Question of Socrates (New York
PB 1961). Plato Portrait of Socrates:
Being the Apology, Crito, and Phaedo
ed. R. W. Livingstone, tr. Benjamin
Jowett (London and New York 1938,
also PB). A. K. Rogers The Socratic
Problem (New Haven, Conn. and Oxford 1933). A. E. Taylor Socrates (London 1932 and New York 1933, PB
1953). Alban D. Winspear Who Was
Socrates? (2nd ed. New York 1960).
Xenophon Recollections of Socrates,
and Socrates' Defense Before the Jury
(tr. Indianapolis 1965, also PB).
Eduard Zeller Socrates and the Socratic Schools (tr. 3rd ed. London 1885,
reprinted New York 1962).

SOPHOCLES (c.496 B.C. – 406 B.C.).
Greek dramatist. Born Colonus, a village outside Athens; son of the wealthy
Sophillus, who gave his son the best
possible education. His master in music,
Lamprus, was the most distinguished
musician of the day. His youthful
beauty and skill in dancing and music
attracted attention, and at sixteen he
was chosen to lead the chorus in a
paean on the victory at Salamis. Won
first prize for drama (468) over
Aeschylus; thereafter about twenty
more prize-winning plays followed in a
career of unparalleled success. A civic-
minded Athenian, he was imperial
treasurer (443–442), and was elected
general probably twice. Died in Athens.
Extant from the 123 plays he is said to
have written are seven complete tragedies, Ajax (c.439), Antigone (c.441),
Oedipus Tyrannus (c.429), Trachiniae
(c.434), Electra (c.418–410), Philoctetes (409), and Oedipus at Colonus
(produced posthumously in 401), and
numerous fragments.

TRANSLATIONS: Among the many by
Sir Richard C. Jebb, Gilbert Murray,
Dudley Fitts, Robert Fitzgerald, and
others are The Complete Greek Trage-
dies tr. Richmond Lattimore and David
Grene (Chicago 1959, also PB).
REFERENCES: Sinclair M. Adams
Sophocles the Playwright (Toronto 1957
and Oxford 1958). William N. Bates
Sophocles, Poet and Dramatist (1940,
reprinted New York 1969, also PB).
C. M. Bowra Sophoclean Tragedy (Ox-
ford 1944, also PB). Alister Cameron

The Identity of Oedipus the King: Five
Essays on the Oedipus Tyrannus (New
York 1968). Gordon M. Kirkwood A
Study of Sophoclean Drama (1958, re-
printed New York 1968). Bernard M. W.
Knox The Heroic Temper: Studies in
Sophoclean Tragedy (Berkeley, Calif.
1964 and Cambridge, England, 1965).
F. J. H. Letters The Life and Work of
Sophocles (London and New York
1953). A. J. A. Waldock Sophocles the
Dramatist (Cambridge, England, 1951,
also PB). T. B. L. Webster Introduction
to Sophocles (2nd ed. London and New
York 1969). Cedric H. Whitman Sopho-
cles: A Study of Heroic Humanism
(Cambridge, Mass. and Oxford 1951).
Thomas M. Woodward ed. Sophocles:
A Collection of Critical Essays (Engle-
wood, Cliffs, N.J. 1966, also PB).

~

SOPHOCLES

BY REX WARNER

In the ninety years of his life Sophocles
saw and took part in events more
significant and rapid, more full of hope
and despair, of triumph and disaster
than have ever, perhaps, taken place in
the same period of time in history. He
came from a wealthy family and was
noted in his youth for his beauty and
his skill in dancing. It was he who was
chosen to lead the choir of young men
singing the hymn of victory after Salamis. His popular success as a dramatist was early and continuous. Unlike
Euripides, he was never placed third
in the dramatic competitions and only
very rarely second. He was the friend
of the greatest men of his age and held
at various times a number of important
official positions. In his early youth
and middle age he was a part of the
full brilliance of Athenian expansion
and invention. In his later years he saw
the decline and corruption of very
much of the ideal of his friend Pericles.
Yet in his last play, Oedipus at Colonus,
he wrote the most splendid hymn of
praise that has ever been written to a
city, and also, in another of the cho-

ruses, gave a picture of man's tragic lot which is as dark as anything to be found in *King Lear*. In the year after his death Aristophanes (in *The Frogs*) represents him as "good, kindly and easy in this world and the next." Someone may have said the same thing of Shakespeare, but the phrase would not clearly indicate the author of *King Lear* or *Othello*.

He is said to have written 123 plays. Only seven of these survive. It is thought that the earliest of these was the *Ajax*, probably produced about 439. The *Antigone* appeared about 441. It is said that its popularity accounts for Sophocles' appointment as general and colleague with Pericles in the war against Samos in 440. The Athenians certainly did some odd things, but it seems unlikely that for so important a campaign they would have chosen a commander solely on the strength of his literary reputation. The *Oedipus Tyrannus* appeared about 429, after the outbreak of the Peloponnesian War and the plague at Athens, and the *Trachiniae* about the same time. The *Electra* is variously dated between 418 and 410. The *Philoctetes* was produced in 409, after the disaster in Sicily, and the *Oedipus at Colonus* in 401, five years after the poet's death.

Sophocles' first victory (over Aeschylus) was won in 468, so, even if this victory was won at his first appearance, it will be seen that all the extant plays fall into his middle or late periods, by which time his style has developed its own individuality and has also, to some degree, been influenced by that of his younger contemporary Euripides. Certainly one does not find in Sophocles the "words as big as bulls, with crests and shaggy eyebrows" which Aristophanes (somewhat unkindly) attributes to Aeschylus, whereas we do find the clear use of antithesis in argument or

situation which is so prominent in Euripides.

But Sophocles' style is his own and, deceptively clear as it seems, is an extremely difficult one to translate or to explain. This is indicated by the great divergencies of opinion among critics. It was once fashionable to regard Sophocles as the perfectly well-balanced Greek — without the "exaggeration" of Aeschylus or the over-cleverness of Euripides, wise, brave, moderate and gentlemanly, somehow reminiscent of the gods in the statues of Phidias. This view seems to be derived from a German interpretation of the words of Aristophanes, and so far as the personal character of Sophocles is concerned may even be correct. It certainly does not explain his art.

Sophocles has also suffered from that misinterpretation of Aristotle which protests too much about the "tragic flaw." Many critics, convinced that without a "tragic flaw" a tragedy is impossible, and that the "flaw" we should be looking for is likely to be "pride," encourage us to believe that Antigone is guilty of pride in speaking sharply to her sister, as is Oedipus in being rather rude to Teiresias. They are therefore supposed, in some sense, to deserve their fates, and thus the ways of the gods are justified to men.

Such an interpretation makes nonsense of the plays and is in conflict with our feelings when we watch them. And one might note in the particular instance of Oedipus that in the last of the plays this old blind character not only does not admit to any "flaw" but vehemently rejects the idea that there ever was one, that he is much violent to his own son than he ever was to Teiresias, and that in the end he is rewarded by a kind of deification.

There may seem to be more sense in the view that what Sophocles is justifying is not the gods, but man. He makes no apologies for his grand, unbending characters — Ajax, Antigone, Oedipus, or Philoctetes. They are mortal, certainly, and they suffer, but they are heroic in the sense that Homer's Achilles is heroic and the gods are not. There is some truth in this view, but it also is exaggerated and it tends towards impiety. Though there certainly are many resemblances between the heroes of Sophocles and those of Homer, Sophocles is in a very different world and is interested in moral and political problems which are quite foreign to Homer — such as, for example, the contradiction between honor and expediency which we find in the *Philoctetes* and which, unknown to Homer's world, is a commonplace in fifth-century Athens. And though it is quite true that Sophocles, like Homer, glorifies the heroic in man, he does not, any more than Homer does, belittle the gods. In fact he is far more concerned with them than Homer is.

Sophocles does not fit into a neat critical framework any more easily than Shakespeare does. Some of the tragedies have "happy" endings. Others end as grimly as it is possible to imagine. Not even Yeats could pronounce the Oedipus at the end of *Oedipus Tyrannus* as exactly "gay." The gods are not "justified" as they are, with some difficulty, by Aeschylus; nor are they denounced, as they are (sometimes, though not always) by Euripides. As for men and women, suffering may end in a kind of beatitude, but this is not felt by Antigone, Haemon, or Deianeira. One may attempt to describe, as Aristotle does, the effects of the poetic truth which we seem to perceive, but the truth itself is only perceptible through the words and actions of the play itself. It is not the truth of prose argument or of critical analysis, being more profound than the one and more sublime than the other.

SOUSA, John Philip (Nov. 6, 1854 – Mar. 6, 1932). American composer and bandmaster. Born Washington, D.C., son of Portuguese father and German mother. Studied violin there with John Esputa and harmony with George Benkert (1864–67). At thirteen, played in U.S. Marine Corps Band; at sixteen, led a vaudeville orchestra. Played violin (1876–77) for Jacques Offenbach's special American tour. Leader of U.S. Marine Corps Band (1880–92), he organized his own band (1892), making several successful European tours (1900, 1901, 1903, 1905) and a world tour (1910–11). His talent for composing military marches and his brilliant band arrangements earned him the title of March King. Among his most celebrated marches: *The Stars and Stripes Forever* (1897), *Semper Fidelis* (1888), *The Washington Post* (1889), *The Liberty Bell* (1893). He also composed many operettas, including *El Capitan* (1896), *The Charlatan* (1897), *The Free Lance* (1906), and *The American Maid* (1913). Compiled for the Naval Department *National, Patriotic, and Typical Airs of All Lands* (1890); published instruction books for trumpet, drum, and violin; wrote five novels; published an autobiography, *Marching Along* (Boston 1928). His compositions also include symphonic poems, suites for band and for symphony orchestras, and numerous waltzes and songs. He died in Reading, Pa.

REFERENCE: *Through the Years with Sousa* (excerpts from his writings; New York 1910). Ann M. Lingg *John Philip Sousa* (New York 1954).

SOUTHEY, Robert (Aug. 12, 1774 – Mar. 21, 1843). English poet. Born Bristol, son of a linen draper, but at three went to live in Bath with aunt, Elizabeth Tyler. Attended Westminster School and Balliol College, Oxford (B.A. 1792). There supported French Revolution and made friends with Coleridge, whose pantisocracy scheme for a utopian community on the shores of the Susquehanna River in Pennsylvania aroused his enthusiasm. The plan fell through for lack of funds. In the meantime, both poets had secured wives in the Fricker sisters — Robert married Edith (1795). After a trip to Portugal, he began a prolific career in writing, turning out, besides essays and biographies, such long narrative poems as *Joan of Arc* (1796), *Thalaba the Destroyer* (1801), *Madoc* (1805), and *The Curse of Kehama* (1810). In the meantime he and Coleridge and their wives took a house at Keswick in the Lake District (1803), which Southey became sole owner of (1809). His highly successful *Life of Nelson* appeared in 1813, the year he reached the pinnacle of his literary career by being made poet laureate. His last years, however, were marked by personal tragedy: the deaths of two children and his wife's insanity. Two years after her death (1837) he married Caroline Ann Bowles, but his health had already broken and a few years later he died at Keswick. Besides his *Life of Nelson* and *Life of Wesley* (1820), and the classic fairy tale *The Three Bears*, a handful of Southey's lyrics are familiar today, such as *The Battle of Blenheim* (1798), *The Holly Tree*, and *The Inchcape Rock*, and the comic rhymes such as *The Devil's Walk*.

EDITIONS: *Poetical Works* (10 vols. London 1837–40 and New York 1839). *Life and Correspondence* ed. Charles C. Southey (6 vols. London and New York 1849–50, reprinted New York). *New Letters of Robert Southey* ed. Kenneth Curry (2 vols. New York 1965).

REFERENCES: Geoffrey Carnall *Robert Southey and His Age* (Oxford 1960). Edward Dowden *Southey* (1888, reprinted New York 1968). William Haller *Early Life of Robert Southey, 1774–1803* (1917, reprinted New York 1967). Jack Simmons *Southey* (1945, reprinted Port Washington, N.Y. 1968).

SOUTHWELL, Robert (c.1561 – Feb. 21, 1595). English poet, writer, and Catholic martyr. Born Horsham St. Faith, Norfolk, to Roman Catholic mother and Anglican father, he was educated by Jesuits in Douai and Paris. Ordained a Jesuit priest (Rome, 1584), he returned to England as a missionary (1586). Forced to live clandestinely because of Queen Elizabeth's anti-Catholic penal laws (1585), he became domestic chaplain to Lady Arundel (1589), whose husband, as a recusant, was imprisoned in the Tower for treason. Wrote letters of encouragement to the earl and other coreligionists, such as *An Epistle of Comfort to the Reverend Priests* (printed illicitly, 1587). He was apprehended while celebrating Mass in a Catholic household (1592), and although tortured severely, refused to reveal the names of fellow priests. After long imprisonment in the Tower, he was tried for treason (1595), condemned, and executed at Tyburn. His poetry, all published posthumously, includes *St. Peter's Complaint* (1595), his major work, and short devotional lyrics such as *The Burning Babe*. Among his prose writings: *Mary Magdalen's (Funeral) Tears* (1591) and *The Triumphs over Death* (1596). A religious poet comparable with George Herbert and Richard Crashaw, Southwell is a major figure of Catholic letters in Elizabethan England.

EDITION: *The Poems of Robert Southwell, S. J.* ed. James H. McDonald and Nancy P. Brown (Oxford and New York 1967).

REFERENCES: Christopher Devlin *The Life of Robert Southwell, Poet and Martyr* (1956, new ed. London 1967 and New York 1969). Pierre Janelle *Robert Southwell, the Writer: A Study in Religious Inspiration* (London and New York 1935). George Saintsbury *A History of Elizabethan Literature* (1906, reprinted London 1928).

SOUTINE, Chaim (1894 – Aug. 9, 1943). Russian-French painter. Born Smilovich, near Minsk, son of a poor tailor. Worked his way through school of Fine Arts in Vilna, where his talent impressed a doctor who sent him to Paris (1911). Enrolled at École des Beaux Arts, studied intently the masters, from Rembrandt to Cézanne. A patron whom he met through Modigliani sent him to Céret, near Perpignan (1919–22), where he painted his best-known work, about two hundred landscapes. These are charged with turbulent emotion, painted with violent distortion of form and unbridled use of pigment. Later he lived at Cagnes (until 1925), and painted portraits of choirboys and other subjects. From 1929 frequented the Château de Lèves, near Chartres, belonging to the collectors, Monsieur and Madame Castaing. During the Nazi occupation he hid in a village in Touraine, continuing to paint landscapes until his death under surgery in a Paris hospital. His intensity of feeling brings tremendous force to his landscapes, is sensed in the calmer portraits, including the *Self-Portrait* (1922–23, Musée d'Art Moderne, Paris). The Los Angeles County Museum of Art, Calif., held a large representative exhibition of Soutine's art in 1968.

REFERENCE: A. Forge *Soutine* (Paris 1965). Monroe Wheeler *Soutine* (New York 1950).

SPENSER, Edmund (c.1552 – Jan. 16, 1599). English poet. Born in London. Educated at Merchant Taylors' School there and at Pembroke College, Cambridge (B.A. 1573, M.A. 1576). Was in employ of bishop of Rochester and then of earl of Leicester, a powerful Elizabethan patron from whom he received only mild support. While in Leicester's household he met Sir Philip Sidney, to whom he dedicated *The Shepheardes Calender* (1579, reprinted four times in Spenser's lifetime). Became secretary to Lord Grey of Wilton, lord deputy of Ireland, whose severe policies he supported in some later writings (1580). Remained in Ireland throughout his life, except for visit to England (1590), at which time he published first three books of *The Faerie Queene.* Later published *Complaints* (1591), a collection of his minor verse, including early work; books IV, V, and VI of *The Faerie Queene* (1596), along with slightly revised versions of the first three books; and most of his important minor poems, including the bulk of his love poetry: *Colin Clouts Come Home Again* (1595), a long wide-ranging pastoral; *Amoretti and Epithalamion* (1595), a sonnet sequence and a poem celebrating Spenser's own marriage to Elizabeth Boyle (1594); *Fowre Hymnes* (1596), "of love," "of beauty," "of heavenly love," and "of heavenly

beauty"; and *Prothalamion* (1596), a "spousall verse" celebrating the marriage of the earl of Worcester's daughters. The Irish situation finally exploded into civil war, and when Spenser's Kilcolman castle was destroyed (1598) he fled to England with his family. He died shortly afterwards, and was buried near Chaucer in Westminster Abbey. A final fragment of *The Faerie Queene,* the "Mutability Cantos," was published in the first posthumous edition of the poem (1609).

EDITIONS: *The Works of Edmund Spenser* ed. Edwin Greenlaw and others (11 vols. Baltimore 1932–57). *Poetical Works* ed. James C. Smith and Ernest de Sélincourt (1910, latest ed. London and New York 1961, also PB).

REFERENCES: Paul J. Alpers *The Poetry of The Faerie Queene* (Princeton 1967). Josephine Bennett *The Evolution of the Faerie Queene* (1942, reprinted New York 1960). Edwin Greenlaw *Studies in Spenser's Historical Allegory* (1932, reprinted New York 1967). A. C. Hamilton *The Structure of Allegory in The Faerie Queene* (Oxford 1961). Graham Hough *A Preface to The Faerie Queene* (London 1962 and New York 1963, also PB). A. C. Judson *The Life of Edmund Spenser* (1945, reprinted Baltimore 1966). W. R. Mueller and D. C. Allen eds. *That Soueraine Light: Essays in Honor of Edmund Spenser, 1552–1952* (1952, reprinted New York 1967). William Nelson *The Poetry of Edmund Spenser* (New York 1963, also PB). William L. Renwick *Edmund Spenser: An Essay on Renaissance Poetry* (1925, latest ed. London 1961). T. P. Roche *The Kindly Flame* (Princeton, N.J. 1964).

✍

EDMUND SPENSER
BY PAUL J. ALPERS

Edmund Spenser was the first indubitably great poet of the English Renaissance. He and his patron, Sir Philip Sidney, sought to give England what Italy and France had already achieved, a body of literature to rival those of Greece and Rome. Emulation — a sense of admiring rivalry which made "imitation" so much more than slavish borrowing — was a powerful literary motive in the Renaissance: Spenser was very much of his time when he proposed, early in his career, to "emulate and overgo" Ariosto's great romance-epic, *Orlando Furioso*. His first work, *The Shepheardes Calender,* domesticated the classical eclogue in a virtuoso display of metrical forms and modes of diction, while his masterpiece, *The Faerie Queene,* was intended to be the English equivalent of the heroic poems of the ancient world. European and nationalistic motives were equally important in works like these. The unidentified "E.K." who wrote a preface and commentary to *The Shepheardes Calender* not only places Spenser in the tradition of Theocritus, Virgil, and their Renaissance imitators, but also insists on Spenser's indebtedness to Chaucer and on his linguistic patriotism, his reviving (in the fullest sense) old words that had fallen into disuse. By the same token, *The Faerie Queene* exemplifies the moral and didactic notions of the epic that are universal in the Renaissance: each book of the poem is devoted to a virtue with which one or more heroes are identified. At the same time, the poem is pervaded by patriotic subjects and themes. The hero of book I is not only the Christian knight of holiness, but the English St. George. One cannot read many cantos in *The Faerie Queene* without coming upon a piece of British history (real or mythological), praise of Queen Elizabeth, satire on the Roman Catholic Church, and the like.

Although he wrote in the heroic, pastoral, Petrarchan, and neo-Platonic modes characteristic of his century, Spenser is at the same time the last major poet in the tradition of medieval allegory. His view of man is profoundly undramatic. He assumes that what is most important about each of us is what we have in common, not the accidents (as he would have thought them) of personality, circumstance, and history that make each man a separate individual. Spenser's undramatic sense of man underlies every major aspect of *The Faerie Queene* — the choice of subjects and episodes; the proliferation of emblematic pictures and processions; the unselfconscious and masterful deployment of a generalizing and abstract vocabulary; the Spenserian stanza itself, which by virtue of its rhyme scheme and its long ninth line is a more massive, static, and inviolable unit than the *ottava rima* of Spenser's Italian masters, and which lends itself not to narrative continuities and changes of pace, but to the steady and untroubled progression that is characteristic of *The Faerie Queen*. The undramatic nature of *The Faerie Queene* is all the more striking when we consider that it was published in the decade in which Shakespeare (ten years younger than Spenser) wrote his first plays and Donne (twenty years younger) his first poems. Indeed, Spenser's work was to some extent historically anomalous. Sidney objected to the archaisms of *The Shepheardes Calender,* and Ben Jonson said of *The Faerie Queene* that "Spenser, in affecting the ancients, writ no language." But more than the linguistic surface of his poems was out of date when Spenser wrote. Hence there were many fewer seventeenth-century editions of *The Faerie Queene* than of Sidney's chivalric and pastoral romance *Arcadia,* which brilliant though it is now strikes us as a much narrower work. And although Spenser had a band of poetic disciples and deeply influenced Milton, he did not decisively affect the course of seventeenth-century poetry, as Donne and Jonson did. Of course

The Faerie Queene is a poem of the Renaissance, for it is secular in a way its medieval predecessors are not: it looks not to man's salvation and his eternal life, but to the realities of moral effort and conflict, of love, and of society more or less as we know them today. And yet the most precious quality of *The Faerie Queene* — the fusion of clear-sighted evaluation and trusting acceptance as the poem unfolds all that Spenser thought to be true of man and his life — comes from a tradition of seeing man *sub specie aeternitatis,* as if all his stories composed themselves into aspects of a single truth.

Given the relation of *The Faerie Queene* to its own age, it is not surprising that to later times it has appeared a more puzzling and specialized poem than it is. To the eighteenth century it was a "Gothic" work: its multiple narratives, allegorical mode, romantic and magical trappings, and archaic diction offended all neoclassical canons. Spenser found imitators, defenders, commentators, and editors in the eighteenth century, but even those who most admired *The Faerie Queene* treated it as an oddity. The romantic period naturally found the greatest of English romances more congenial to its taste and its notion of serious poetry; Spenser had a genuine influence on the work of Wordsworth, Keats, and Shelley. And yet the nineteenth-century view of Spenser as, in Hazlitt's words, "the poet of our waking dreams," is as narrow in its way as the neoclassical opinion it superseded. Even Charles Lamb's handsome epithet, "the poet's poet," has a limiting sense that is apparent in Hazlitt's reformulation of it: "Of all the poets, he is the most poetical.' There is considerable irony in the fact that for at least a century *The Faerie Queene* was praised for releasing the reader from the demands of the real world and opening up the groves and bowers of fairyland. Spenser, himself a public official, intended the poem to "fashion a gentleman or noble person in virtuous and gentle discipline." Not that he thought that a poem merely gives rules of behavior. His underlying conception is that in giving an understanding of man's nature it gives self-knowledge, and therefore can have a humanizing and civilizing influence on men in positions of power and responsibility. Of course our views of man (and our social positions) are very different from those of Spenser's first readers. But we can still see that the poem takes seriously man's moral and emotional life in a way that could not be acknowledged by critics who regarded its essential qualities as escapist and dreamlike. The essence of *The Faerie Queene* — the poised and generous intelligence with which it displays and enters into man's traditional wisdom about himself — is there for anyone who will encounter the poem, as Thoreau said we should encounter nature, "with a corresponding trust and magnanimity."

STAËL, Madame de (full name **Anne Louise Germaine Necker,** baronne de Staël-Holstein) (Apr. 22, 1766 – July 14, 1817). French writer. Born Paris, daughter of prominent Swiss banker Jacques Necker, finance minister to Louis XVI, and his wife Suzanne Curchod (earlier the fiancée of Gibbon), whose salon familiarized the child at an early age with the literary and political elite. Married, unhappily, to Swedish ambassador Baron Eric de Staël-Holstein (1786, divorced 1797), Madame de Staël soon became famous for her affairs. Her *Lettres sur le caractère et les écrits de J. J. Rousseau* (1788), express the liberal views of the day. During Reign of Terror she fled to family estate at Coppet on Lake Geneva, Switzerland, where she bore the first of two children by her lover Vicomte Louis de Narbonne. Returning to Paris, she established a salon that attracted important political and intellectual figures, and began (1795) her celebrated fifteen-year affair with Benjamin Constant. After publication of *The Influence of the Passions* (1796) and *The Influence of Literature on Society* (1800), as well as her first romantic novel favoring liberalism, *Delphine* (1802, tr. 1803), Napoleon, whom she once admired, resented her radical views and writings and exiled her with Constant (1803), again to Coppet, where she developed a brilliant salon and aided political exiles. Also embarked on several journeys — to Italy (1804), where she gathered material for second novel, *Corinne* (1807), and notably to Austria and Germany (1804, 1808) with August Schlegel, where her interest in the German romantic movement led to her greatest work, *De l'Allemagne*. A three-volume critical study (1813), it introduced German romanticism to French literature, becoming one of the source books of the romantic movement, although banned by Napoleon. In 1811, Madame de Staël married Albert de Rocca, a young soldier, and threatened by Napoleon's police, lived in exile with him until Napoleon's abdication (1814); then they returned to Paris, where she died. Considered the foremost woman of her age, she exerted a powerful influence on statesmen and men of letters, and in her life championed women's right to individualism.

TRANSLATIONS: *Ten Years' Exile* (tr. New York 1821, new ed. Fonthill, England, 1968). *Madame de Staël on Politics, Literature and National Character* tr. and ed. Morroe Berger (Garden City, N.Y. and London 1964, also PB). *Unpublished Correspondence of Madame de Staël and the Duke of Wellington* tr. Harold Kurtz (London 1965 and New York 1967). *De Staël–Du Pont Letters* tr. and ed. James F. Marshall (Madison, Wis. 1968).

REFERENCES: Wayne Andrews *Germaine: The Portrait of Madame de Staël* (New York 1963 and London 1964). Lady Charlotte Blennerhassett *Madame de Staël, Her Friends, and Her Influence in Politics and Literature* (tr. 3 vols. London 1889). Richmond Laurin Hawkins *Madame de*

Staël and the United States (Cambridge, Mass. 1930, also PB). J. Christopher Herold *Mistress to an Age* (Indianapolis 1958 and London 1959). D. G. Larg *Madame de Staël: Her Life Revealed in Her Work* (tr. London and New York 1926). Robert C. Whitford *Madame de Staël's Literary Reputation and the English* (1918, reprinted New York PB 1968).

STAËL, Nicolas de (1914 – Mar. 22, 1955). Russian-French painter. Born St. Petersburg, son of a czarist officer who took his family to Poland after the revolution. After the death of his father (1920) and mother (1922), de Staël was sent to Brussels, where he was educated at the Jesuit college St. Michel and later (1932–33) at the Académie Royale des Beaux Arts. Traveling widely and working mainly in watercolors, he settled for a time in Morocco (1936), and here met Jeannine Guilloux, his mistress for many years. Joined (1939) the Foreign Legion in Tunisia, but the following year was demobilized and settled in Nice. Here he painted several portraits of Jeannine and began his nonfigurative work, experimenting with surface texture of paint. Soon moved to Paris, where he became friendly with Braque and participated in the 1944 abstract painting exhibition at Galérie l'Equisse. His first one-man show was held the same year, followed by another in 1945. After Jeannine's death (1946), he married Françoise Chapouton, took a studio near Braque, became a French citizen (1948), and worked feverishly at painting. Received increasing acclaim, especially for the famous *Footballers* series (1952). After a trip to New York (1953) he bought a château in Vaucluse, but the following year settled in Antibes, where he committed suicide. Some of de Staël's best-known works are *Rue Gauguet* (1949), *Parc des Princes* (1952, private collection, Paris), *Bottles* (1952), *The Musicians* (1953), *Agrigento* (1954, private collection, Paris).

REFERENCES: André Chastel *Nicolas de Staël* (Paris 1968). Douglas Cooper *Nicolas de Staël* (New York 1961 and London 1962). R. V. Gindertael *Nicolas de Staël* (Basel 1966). Jean Guichard-

Meili *Nicolas de Staël: Peintures* (Paris 1966).

STEELE, Sir Richard (Mar. 1672 – Sept. 1, 1729). British essayist and dramatist. Born Dublin; on his parents' early death became ward of a distinguished uncle, Henry Gascoigne. Attended (1684) Charterhouse School and there met Joseph Addison. Both went on to Oxford, but Steele left without a degree (1694) and enlisted in a guards regiment. Stationed at the Tower by 1700, he wrote a moral work, *The Christian Hero* (1701), which was not popular. He decided to recoup his loss with a comedy, and the success of *The Funeral, or Grief à la Mode* (1701) prompted him to follow it with *The Lying Lover* (1703) and *The Tender Husband* (1705). That same year he married the elderly widow Margaret Stretch, and at her funeral (1706) met Mary Scurlock, whom he married (1707). Interested now in politics, he began writing essays, founded (1709–10) the famous journal *The Tatler* (under the pseudonym Isaac Bickerstaff), later joined Addison in producing *The Spectator* (1711–12, 1714). Also published *The Guardian* (1713), and the political periodical *The Englishman* (1713). Widely influential, these became the precursors of the modern newspaper and marked the advent of the bourgeois sensibility which was to dominate the age. This trend was clearly seen in Steele's last play, *The Conscious Lovers* (1722), which demonstrated the turn from Restoration to sentimental comedy. Knighted by George I (1715). Died at Caermarthen, Wales, where he retired (1724) because of debts.

EDITIONS: *Dramatic Works* ed. George A. Aitken (London 1903). *Correspondence of Richard Steele* ed. Rae Blanchard (1941, reprinted Oxford 1968).
REFERENCES: George A. Aitken *The Life of Richard Steele* (1889, reprinted 2 vols. New York 1968). Willard Connely *Sir Richard Steele* (1934, reprinted Port Washington, N.Y. 1967). Austin Dobson *Richard Steele* (London and New York 1886). Bertrand A. Goldgar *The Curse of Party: Swift's Relations with Addison and Steele* (Lincoln,

Nebr. 1961). John Loftis *Steele at Drury Lane* (Berkeley, Calif. and Cambridge, England, 1952). Calhoun Winton *Captain Steele: The Early Career of Richard Steele* (Baltimore 1964).

STEEN, Jan (Havickszoon) (1626 – Feb. 3, 1679). Dutch painter. Born and died in Leiden. Son of a wealthy brewer, he studied in Utrecht and in Haarlem under Adriaen Van Ostade and Jan Van Goyen, whose daughter Margaretha he married (1649). At various times a brewer and tavern keeper, he lived in The Hague (1649–54), Delft (1654–56), Warmond (1656–60), Haarlem (1661–70), and Leiden (1670–79). Four years after death of his first wife, married Maria von Egmont (1673). Elected dean of the painters' guild at Leiden (1674). Though he also depicted historical and Biblical subjects, Steen is best known as a genre painter. His many, many scenes of lower- and middle-class life, noted for their technical brilliance, humor, and vivid characterization, include *The Feast of St. Nicholas* and *The Happy Family* (Rijksmuseum, Amsterdam), *The Menagerie, The Painter's Family*, and *The Doctor's Visit* (Mauntshuis, The Hague).

REFERENCE: F. Schmidt Degener and H. E. van Gelder *Jan Steen* (tr. London 1927).

STEIN, Gertrude (Feb. 3, 1874 – July 27, 1946). American writer. Born Allegheny, Pa., to upper-middle-class family of German-Jewish extraction. Taken to Vienna and Paris as infant. Family moved to Oakland, Calif. (1879), where she attended elementary and high school. At Radcliffe (1893–97) after death of her parents she studied under William James, whose theories influenced much of her early writing. Studied medicine at Johns Hopkins (1897–1902), but left without a degree. Took up residence at 27 Rue de Fleurus, Paris, with brother Leo (1903). Acquired large collection of paintings and turned home into famous gallery and gathering place for young artists. Close friendships with Picasso and Matisse. First published works: *Three Lives* (1910), *Tender*

Buttons (1914), *The Making of Amer-icans* (1925). Did relief work during World War I with Alice B. Toklas, her companion and secretary since 1907. In Paris after war, became friend and hostess to the "lost generation" of American writers, including Heming-way, Faulkner, and Sherwood Ander-son. *The Autobiography of Alice B. Toklas* (1933) brought recognition in America and led to her American lec-ture tour (1934). Her play, "a sketch of the Spanish landscape," entitled *Four Saints in Three Acts,* was pro-duced in New York with score by Vir-gil Thomson (1934). Lived at country home in Bilignin during German oc-cupation of World War II. Out of her war experience wrote *Wars I Have Seen* (1944), *Yes Is For A Very Young Man,* a play (1944), *Brewsie and Wil-lie* (1946). Other major works: *The Geographical History of America* (1936), *Picasso* (1939), *Ida* (1941), *Paris France* (1940). A radical experi-mentalist with language who sought to fuse "the being with the continuous present" through her abstract, repeti-tive style ("Rose is a rose is a rose is a rose"), she has often been termed a "cubist writer." Died in Paris.

EDITIONS: *The Yale Edition of the Unpublished Writings of Gertrude Stein* ed. Carl Van Vechten (8 vols. New Haven, Conn. and Oxford 1951–58). *Gertrude Stein on Picasso* (New York 1970).

REFERENCES: Richard Bridgman *Ger-trude Stein in Pieces* (London and New York 1971). John Malcolm Brin-nin *The Third Rose: Gertrude Stein and Her World* (Boston 1959 and London 1960). Michael J. Hoffman *The Devel-opment of Abstractionism in the Writ-ings of Gertrude Stein* (Philadelphia 1965). Elizabeth Sprigge *Gertrude Stein: Her Life and Work* (London and New York 1957). Allegra Stewart *Gertrude Stein and the Present* (Cam-bridge, Mass. 1967). Donald Suther-land *Gertrude Stein: A Biography of Her Work* (New Haven, Conn. and Ox-ford 1951). Alice B. Toklas *What Is Remembered* (New York 1963).

STENDHAL (real name **Marie Henri Beyle**) (Jan. 23, 1783 – Mar. 23, 1842).

French writer. Born Grenoble, son of a lawyer. Educated by Jesuit priest and at École Centrale, Grenoble. Qualified (1799) for admission to École Poly-technique in Paris, but failed to take entrance examination. Instead, joined French army, was commissioned a lieutenant (1800) and sent to Italy, which made a lasting impression on him. Two years later returned to Paris, became involved in series of romantic intrigues, and took job in Marseilles (1805–1806). Returned to army, serv-ing several diplomatic missions to Po-land and Russia, but after Napoleon's abdication (1814), settled in Milan to write. First work, *Les Vies de Haydn, de Mozart et de Métastase* (1814), was followed by several undistinguished works. Expelled from Italy (1821) for his revolutionary sympathies, he re-turned to Paris, where he worked at various journalistic positions. An analy-tical study of love, *De l'Amour* (1822), was a commercial failure, but his con-troversial pamphlet *Racine et Shake-speare* (1823) became an important document in the romantic movement. The novel *Armance* (1827) aroused less enthusiasm than the guidebook *Promenades dans Rome* (1829). His first great novel, *Le Rouge et le noir* (1830, *The Red and the Black*—red meaning the army, and black meaning the church), caused a notoriety that perhaps deprived him of developing a public career. Instead, he spent his last years as a consular officer in the little town of Civitavecchia, near Rome. Here he wrote *Mémoires d'un touriste* (1838) and during a leave in Paris his other masterpiece, *La Chartreuse de Parme* (1839, *The Charterhouse of Parma*), also two autobiographical works published posthumously: *La Vie de Henri Brulard* (1890) and *Souvenirs d'égotisme* (1892). After he suffered a stroke (1841), his doctor ordered a leave in Paris, where he died the follow-ing year. The manuscripts he left in-cluded two unfinished novels, *Lamiel* (1889) and *Lucien Leuwen* (1894).

TRANSLATIONS: *The Charterhouse of Parma* (1925, latest ed. Garden City, N.Y. PB 1956) and *The Red and the Black* (1926, latest ed. New York 1964), both translated by C. K. Scott-Moncrieff. *Private Diaries of Stendhal* ed. and tr.

R. Sage (Garden City, N.Y. 1954 and London 1955, PB 1962).

REFERENCES: Robert M. Adams *Stendhal: Notes on a Novelist* (London and New York 1959, also PB). John Atherton *Stendhal* (Cambridge, England, and New York 1964). Victor H. Brombert ed. *Stendhal: A Collection of Critical Essays* (Englewood Cliffs, N.J. 1962, also PB) and *Stendhal: Fiction and the Themes of Freedom* (New York 1968, also PB). Peter Brooks *The Novel of Worldliness* (Princeton, N.J. 1969). Armand Caraccio *Stendhal* (tr. New York 1965, also PB). Howard Clewes *Stendhal: An Introduction to the Novelist* (London 1950 and New York 1951). Wallace Fowlie *Stendhal* (New York 1969). Frederick C. Green *Stendhal* (Cambridge, England, and New York 1939). F. W. J. Hemmings *Stendhal: A Study of His Novels* (Oxford 1964). Matthew Josephson *Stendhal, or The Pursuit of Happiness* (1946, reprinted New York 1969).

☞

STENDHAL

BY SEAN O'FAOLAIN

It has been said that in every fat man there is a thin man signaling to get out. If we apply this image to Stendhal we find ourselves, sooner or later, asking ourselves two questions at one and the same time. What private personality and ideas was he trying to release and express in his novels? And how, technically, did he manage this escape and transformation?

Stendhal's master ideas may be, very roughly, reduced to three. He was convinced that society in France after the fall of Napoleon and the restoration of the monarchy in 1815 had become so mean and corrupt as to offer no real scope to the man of spirit. He illustrated these gloomy feelings by the collateral conviction that the Italian people had a far fuller, braver, and more passionate involvement in life than his own countrymen. Above all he admired to distraction what he called southern "energy" — Napoleon its greatest exemplar. On this basis he developed as his theory of action the belief that no man of spirit in Europe after 1815 could proceed otherwise than by cherishing in secret the most lofty and honorable ideals while practicing in public a most devious, Machiavellian cunning in order to outwit the contemptible upstarts and Bourbon aristos among whom he had henceforth to live as an *emigrato all' interno* — an alien with a passport. It will be observed that I say *proceed,* not *succeed.* Stendhal was much too ironical a soul not to perceive that ideals plus cunning make bad bedfellows. It is the whole point of *The Red and the Black* that because its hero Julien Sorel lives like a man of spirit he must therefore — his society being what it is — end on the guillotine.

The second half of our question is by no means so easy: Stendhal's technique when he comes to the projection or dramatization of these ideas in his novels.

Does Stendhal first take the general and universal chaos of life as he observed or experienced it in his own time and place, break it down rationally and scientifically into its components — social, political, economic, and so on — as some modern sociologist might do, and as the realist Balzac so ably did; then analyze these components; and then put them all back together again into a novel?

Or, alternatively, does Stendhal, working as a purely instinctive, non-analytical writer, just roll all life up into one ball and then secrete or digest it into a series of imaginative and highly idealized self-projections called by the names of his heroes? In short, does he in general proceed according to the technique of an objective realist or of a subjective romantic?

This is, to be sure, an oversimplification, but some simplification sooner or later becomes forced upon us if for no other reason than to challenge his own repeated claims to be a scientific observer of men and an objective historian of his times.

I give one quick illustration of these claims from *The Charterhouse*. Having shown us the lovelorn Count Mosca and his beloved Contessa plotting her marriage with an impotent old duke as a cover for their secret love affair, Stendhal, the sole inventor of this outrageously unlikely stratagem, utters the following bland observations: "Why should the historian who follows faithfully all the most trivial details of the story that has been told to him be held responsible for what he records? Is it his fault," he asks, parsonically, "if his characters, led astray by passions which he, unfortunately for himself, in no way shares, descend to conduct which is profoundly immoral?"

The interpolation is revealing. It indicates a sudden loss of nerve. He is aware that in thus imagining for the year 1816 or 1817 a passion so devouring as to be possible only in Rome under the Borgias, he is revealing himself not as the objective historian of his times that he is pretending to be, but as the daring creator of a piece of poetic melodrama spun out of his fervent wish that life could always be like that. His pretension did not deceive Balzac. "All," he cried, in admiration (himself more than a bit of a melodramatist), "is so Italian as to make us want to take the coach and fly to Italy, there to seek out for ourselves *this drama and this poetry*."

In other words, Stendhal is not, as Balzac also shrewdly observed, recording individuals but creating *types*. He is spinning amalgams. He is doing very much what Joyce did when, against a minutely verifiable background of a real Dublin, he imagined that idealized mirror of himself, the artist as a young man. So with Stendhal, his Contessa is a composite vision of the *bellezza folgorante* (the beauty that blinds like lightning) of all the Italian women of his dreams. His Julien Sorel is an amalgam of what all French youth might be if they had been born under the energy-giving sun beyond the Alps. It is his constant technique.

Benedetto Croce perceived this visionary quality of Stendhal's mind very clearly when he insisted that this adored southern "energy" of his was not real energy — which always involves the controlling will — but an image of completely uncontrolled passion; and even more forcibly when he insisted that Stendhal's enchanting Italy never existed at all, being either a dream Italy or a dream of some world projected in terms of Italy; indeed, it was not even an "idea" of Italy so much as an emotional obsession about Italy as a symbol of the good life.

The surface of life had no appeal for Stendhal. As he eschews all direct descriptions, he distrusts all immediate observations. He knows the fallibility of the observing mind so well that he actually hates to put down his own observations about anything that is specially dear to him — on the ground that it spoils fruit to touch it. An entry in his diary says, about a day spent with his beloved Angelina Pietragrua: "But if I describe my feelings it distresses me — I am convinced that pure feeling leaves no memory." Meaning that pure feeling, impregnated by experience in the imagination's womb, is born only when all detailed memories of the love-act are forgotten. Another time he says, most revealing of all: "The timid man is led to observe, the bold man sees nothing." Meaning that the bold man penetrates deepest when he trusts blindly to his imagination.

No other novelist that I know has so completely succeeded with this technique except Dostoevsky, whose characters also undergo the same unexpected oscillations, the same irrational contradictions, the same sudden blinding moments of self-revelation, because they, also, live fully only within the heart, where their creator surprises them in those hours of crisis when all convention, all reason drops away and nothing is left but "pure feeling" — which is, of course, in the end his own "pure feeling" — born of his own passionate desires.

STEPHEN, Sir Leslie (Nov. 28, 1832 – Feb. 22, 1904). English essayist, biographer, critic, and editor. Born and died in London. Son of prominent government official. Educated at Eton, King's College, London, and Trinity Hall, Cambridge. Won tutoring fellowship there (1854), also took holy orders (1855), and remained in Cambridge teaching mathematics until 1864. Gave up holy orders (1862), became advocate of liberal school of John Stuart Mill, and eventually a spokesman for agnosticism, especially in *Essays on Free-Thinking and Plain Speaking* (1873). Visited America (1863) to observe the Civil War, made lifelong friend of James Russell Lowell, and on return wrote anonymously on behalf of the North, *"The Times" and the Civil War* (1865). Moving to London (1864), he quickly became prominent in literary circles and wrote numerous literary essays, published later in three collections called *Hours in a Library* (1874/76/79). Also produced first book, *Sketches from Cambridge by a Don* (1865), and a popular work on Alpine climbing (he was an expert), *Playground of Europe* (1871). Married Harriet Marian, daughter of William Makepeace Thackeray (1867; she died 1875). Edited *Cornhill Magazine* (1871–82). Established his reputation with his major work, *The History of English Thought in the Eighteenth Century* (2

vols. 1876). Achieved greatest fame, however, as a biographer for English Men of Letters series with *Samuel Johnson* (1878), *Alexander Pope* (1880), *Jonathan Swift* (1882), *George Eliot* (1902), and *Thomas Hobbes* (1904). Edited *Dictionary of National Biography* (1882–91). Received honorary degrees from Oxford, Cambridge, Harvard, Edinburgh, and was knighted (1902). Married Julia Prinsop (1878). Two of their four children became famous in their own right, Vanessa Bell and Virginia Woolf. His finest critical work, *English Literature and Society in the Eighteenth Century,* based on the Ford Lectures (1903), appeared the year he died (1904).

REFERENCES: Noel Annan *Leslie Stephen: His Thought and Character in Relation to His Time* (London 1951 and Cambridge, Mass. 1952). Janet E. Courtney *Freethinkers of the Nineteenth Century* (1920, reprinted Freeport, N.Y. 1967). Desmond MacCarthy *Leslie Stephen* (Cambridge, England, 1937). Frederic W. Maitland *Life and Letters of Leslie Stephen* (1906, reprinted London and Detroit 1968).

STERNE, Laurence (Nov. 24, 1713 – Mar. 18, 1768). English novelist and clergyman. Born Clonmel, Ireland, son of an impoverished British ensign. Spent childhood among the military, receiving little formal education until 1723, when he entered school near Halifax, Yorkshire. Entered Jesus College, Cambridge (1733, B.A. 1737), and entered the church (1737), becoming vicar of Sutton-in-the-Forest (1738) and prebendary of York (1741). Married Elizabeth Lumley (1741). Their daughter, Lydia, later edited her father's works. Ecclesiastical politics inspired his first satire, *A Political Romance* (1759, later renamed *The History of a Good Warm Watch-Coat*). The first two volumes (1760) of *The Life and Opinions of Tristram Shandy, Gentleman* (9 vols. 1760–67) followed and were immediately a national success. Sterne then decided to publish his sermons in two volumes as *The Sermons of Mr. Yorick* (1760; two more collections appeared 1766/69). Ill health took him to the Continent (1762–64, 1765–66), where he gathered material for seventh volume of *Tristram Shandy* and *A Sentimental Journey Through France and Italy* (1768). Devotion to Mrs. Elizabeth Draper, whom he met in 1767, inspired his *Journal to Eliza* (written 1767, published 1904) and *Letters from Yorick to Eliza* (published posthumously, 1775). Tubercular since childhood, he died of pleurisy in London.

EDITIONS: *Works* (7 vols. Oxford and Boston 1926–27). *Memoirs of Mr. Laurence Sterne: The Life and Opinions of Tristram Shandy, A Sentimental Journey, Selected Sermons and Letters* ed. Douglas Grant (London 1950 and Cambridge, Mass. 1951). *A Sentimental Journey Through France and Italy* ed. Graham Petrie (Harmondsworth, England, and Baltimore PB 1967). *The Life and Opinions of Tristram Shandy, Gentleman* ed. Ian P. Watt (Boston 1965, also PB).

REFERENCES: Arthur Hill Cash *Sterne's Comedy of Moral Sentiments: The Ethical Dimension of the Journey* (Pittsburgh, Pa. 1966). Wilbur L. Cross *The Life and Times of Laurence Sterne* (3rd ed. 1929, reprinted New York 1967). Ernest N. Dilworth *The Unsentimental Journey of Laurence Sterne* (1948, reprinted New York 1969). Lodwick Hartley *Laurence Sterne: A Biographical Essay* (Chapel Hill, N.C. 1968, also PB). Peter Quennell *Four Portraits: Studies of the Eighteenth Century* (1945, rev. ed. London and Hamden, Conn. 1965). John M. Stedmond *The Comic Art of Laurence Sterne: Convention and Innovation in Tristram Shandy and A Sentimental Journey* (Toronto 1967). Walter B. C. Watkins *Perilous Balance: The Tragic Genius of Swift, Johnson and Sterne* (1939, new ed. Cambridge, Mass. PB 1960).

LAURENCE STERNE
BY ROBERT GORHAM DAVIS

Reviewing in 1760 the first two volumes of Sterne's *Tristram Shandy*, the *London Magazine* exclaimed in an outburst of admiration and bewilderment (and with a use of dashes matching Sterne's own): "Oh rare Tristram Shandy! —

Thou very sensible — humorous — pathetick — humane — unaccountable! what shall we call thee? — Rabelais, Cervantes, What?" The English novel had just begun (Richardson's *Pamela* was published in 1740; Fielding's *Tom Jones* in 1749) and already Sterne had turned the form upside down and inside out. Two centuries later the "What?" is still hard to answer.

Not until the 1920's, with Joyce's *Ulysses*, did anyone write a novel so boldly and brilliantly experimental. But *Tristram Shandy* is far more unified than *Ulysses* by a consistently maintained style in which art, artifice, and personality are inextricably combined. Not until the phenomenological "anti-novels" of Butor, Sarraute, and Robbe-Grillet in France, did any fiction respond so thoroughly in form and content to a particular philosophy as did Sterne's — also an "anti-novel" — to Locke's *Essay Concerning Human Understanding*. But even here scholars disagree. Some say that Sterne is playing with a few simple psychological notions that he could have got from a dinner-table conversation. Others say that his work is a subtle and profound critique of Locke's philosophy, exposing its limitations.

The fictional Tristram Shandy, born in 1718, purports to be writing an autobiography. But by the beginning of the third volume, published in 1761, he has not yet brought himself into "this scurvy and disastrous world of ours." In the middle of volume four, he is a few hours old and so black in the face that he gets hastily christened before he might die. As autobiographer he knows that now he has 365 more days of his life to write about than when he began this work a year earlier, and he is not yet through the very first day of his life. But since time is so much a matter of psychology, he can sport with it even while it sports with him. He insists on putting in all the conditioning elements — especially the accidental ones — which make a man what he is. The homunculus which was to be Tristram had already been affected at the moment of conception by his mother's interrupting the act of love to ask his father, in the initial speech of the book, "Pray, my Dear, have you not forgot to wind the clock?" The clumsiness of Dr. Slop and the too tight knots with which a servant has tied up his bag of surgical instruments cause Tristram to be born with a flattened nose. His despairing father has always believed that a nose is the sign and even determinant of character. Finally the infant hesitating between life and death is named sad "Tristram" rather than magical "Trismegistus" because the "megistus" is too much for a rattled servant girl to remember.

The telling is full of digressions and interruptions: his father's learned disquisitions out of old books, Uncle Toby's military reminiscences and re-enactments of battles, even a sermon — one of Sterne's own — recited by Corporal Trim. Everyone rides a hobby. But these are never boring, because they are interrupted, too, in delightful Lockean demonstrations of the irrationality of associative processes. Most famous is the way news of her young master's death gets mixed up with a green satin nightgown in the mind of a maid, without lessening, ultimately, any of the pathos of the death. Sterne's composition, whether of a sentence, a paragraph or a book, is musical, and he always returns at exactly the right moment to the notes of one of his principal themes. The tale, the teller, the telling, and the one told to — at times a "Sir," at times a "Madam," at times his own Jenny — are always in his mind. He loves to discuss the form

of the book with the reader, and is not above drawing squiggles to explain the sequence, or leaving a page blank so that the reader can describe the Widow Wadman for himself.

It is part of the design of the book that the members of the Shandy household — true comic characters — should remain unchanged by accident or time. For his wit and learning, Sterne drew heavily on Swift, Rabelais, Montaigne, and the Burton of *The Anatomy of Melancholy*. His characters are closer to those of Cervantes, especially to the little group in the village who tried to bring Don Quixote back to his senses. For his own literary persona, which was as contradictory and yet as consistent as the book which embodied it, Sterne chose the name of Yorick, the jester who educated Hamlet.

Born to a soldier father who, ruined by an unfortunate marriage, died early, Sterne had to make his own way in the world, and chose the Church. As a "lousy prebendary" at York Cathedral his first writing was a satirical pamphlet on a church controversy in which he was involved. All his life he was high-spirited in the face of every kind of misery, including severe lesions of the lungs which brought him repeatedly to the point of death.

When the first two volumes of *Tristram Shandy* were an immediate dazzling success, he hurried to London. Because of his grace and gaiety, his social success matched the literary one. He was painted by Reynolds, befriended by Garrick, and entertained nightly for three months at the best tables in London, including that of the king's son. Later he was received the same way in Paris. He put his new knowledge of the world at the service of his writing, published his sermons under the name of Yorick, and without changing its basic character introduced

into successive volumes of *Tristram
Shandy* matters which he thought his
fashionable friends would enjoy. Some
of this was gaily suggestive, like the
Freudian disquisition on noses or inquiries into the exact effect of Uncle
Toby's wound in the groin. They displeased Dr. Johnson in that century and
disgusted Thackeray in the next.

Sterne's behavior was of a piece with
his wit. He lived often apart from his
wife and his cherished daughter Lydia,
and openly courted a long series of
pretty women. How far the affairs went
scholars do not know. Though sometimes criticized, Sterne carried out his
clerical duties conscientiously and was
invited to preach before distinguished
audiences in Paris and London.

His last romantic attachment was to
one Elizabeth Draper. Heartbroken
when she was forced to rejoin her husband in India, he wrote a journal to
his Eliza, imitating Swift's *Journal to
Stella*. He found more adequate expression for his feelings in *A Sentimental Journey Through France and
Italy*, published in 1768. Already, as
in the account of the death of Le
Fever in *Tristram Shandy*, he had, in a
pre-Wordsworthian, pre-romantic way,
evoked readers' sympathies for the
good, the naive, the young, the ill, and
animals as well as men. Now he let
such feelings be dominant in a partly
true, partly fictional travel journal
which gave the word "sentimental" its
vogue. In conscious contrast to Tobias
Smollett's recent travel book with its
ill-tempered responses to ugly ruins and
rapacious landlords, Sterne, though
grievously ill, wrote warmly, humorously, touchingly, about people he met
and liked. The book is simpler in
scheme than *Tristram Shandy* but uses
many of the same stylistic effects in
even subtler ways. It is characteristic
of Sterne's whole career, which still

sounds in our ears like a hauntingly
unresolved chord, that *A Sentimental
Journey* should begin with a tribute to
order, and end with a broken sentence,
an interrupted action, and a teasing,
naughty equivocation of which it is
left to us to make what we choose.

STEVENS, Wallace (Oct. 12, 1879 –
Aug. 2, 1955). American poet. Born
Reading, Pa. After studying at Harvard
(1897–1900), he attended New York
University Law School and was admitted to the bar (1904). Engaged in
general law practice until he joined
the Hartford Accident and Indemnity
Company (1916), serving as its vice-
president from 1934 to his death (in
Hartford). Married Elsie V. Kachel
(1909). Began his career as a poet with
contributions to *Poetry* magazine
(1914). His first book, *Harmonium*
(1923), which contains one of the best-
known of his poems, *Sunday Morning*,
was received with enthusiasm by critics. Other major volumes are *Ideas of
Order* (1935), *The Man with the Blue
Guitar* (1937), *Parts of a World* (1942),
Transport to Summer (1947), *The
Auroras of Autumn* (1950), *The Necessary Angel* (1951; essays), and *Opus
Posthumous* (1957). His *Collected
Poems* (1954) was awarded the Pulitzer
prize.

EDITIONS: *Collected Poems* (New
York 1954 and London 1955). *Letters
of Wallace Stevens* ed. Holly Stevens
(New York 1966 and London 1967).
Opus Posthumous ed. Samuel French
Morse (New York 1957 and London
1959).
REFERENCES: Daniel Fuchs *The
Comic Spirit of Wallace Stevens* (Dur-
ham, N.C. and Cambridge, England,
1963). Frank Kermode *Wallace Stevens*
(Edinburgh 1960 and New York 1961).
Samuel French Morse *Wallace Stevens:
Life as Poetry* (New York 1970). Rob-
ert Pack *Wallace Stevens:- An Ap-
proach to His Poetry and Thought*
(1958, reprinted New York 1968). Roy
Harvey Pearce and J. Hillis Miller eds.
*Act of the Mind: Essays on the Poetry
of Wallace Stevens* (Baltimore 1965).
Ronald Sukenick *Wallace Stevens:
Musing the Obscure* (New York and

London 1967, also PB). Helen Vendler *On Extended Wings: Wallace Stevens' Longer Poems* (Cambridge, Mass. 1969).

WALLACE STEVENS
BY PETER DAVISON

Stevens's work is less a poetry of emotion than a poetry of cognition: the servant not of the emotions but of the mind. His career had much the same quality. His undergraduate acquaintance with Professor Santayana seems not only to have furnished Stevens with a model for philosophical poetry but to have provided an example for detachment in personal life.

Stevens's ultimate biography has not yet been written, but both his poems and his letters have some of the equality of self-hypnosis. He was "an ascetic by virtue of all his rejections and also by virtue of his devotion to the real," as he himself wrote about Courbet. His personal and his business lives were kept so separate from his poetic life as to constitute separate worlds; and in his early letters to his wife he wrote often about the creation of another world for the two of them. "I believe that with a bucket of sand and a wishing lamp I could create a world in half a second that would make this one look like a lump of mud."

Wallace Stevens, like his contemporary Robert Frost, was late in maturing; but unlike Frost he was deliberate about it. He was engaged for five years before his marriage, and his only child was begotten fifteen years after that, after his first book, *Harmonium*, had been safely published. His early, somewhat timid ventures in the law bore little fruit until, at thirty-seven, he entered the insurance business, where he labored for the rest of his life — even for many years after he could have retired — living in Hart-ford and occasionally but with growing infrequency traveling south and west. Although his poetry is full of European tags and allusions, he never left this hemisphere.

He was not at ease with himself as a young man. Between his boyhood in Reading and his ultimate move to Hartford there stretches a mysterious and ill-documented era of lawyerly failure and poetic experiment in New York; but in those years he cautiously laid the base for his career, his marriage, and his poetry. His temperamental wariness seemed to suit the insurance business and enabled him to make a policy of his career and an accident of his life. Hence his leisurely development as a poet: he seemed unable to dedicate himself to the world of imagination until he had first mastered the common world.

Like so many American writers, Stevens was haunted by the loss of his childhood, and the search for paradise and perfection in his poetry takes its psychic origins from Reading, Pennsylvania, as surely as Mark Twain's quest for innocence leads to Hannibal, Missouri. Stevens clung to his early vision out of a kind of duty, and perhaps that is what eventually leached it of overt emotion. Like Mark Twain, he may have been alarmed by what he found when he got around to looking. After the publication of his first and finest work, *Harmonium*, in 1923, he ceased writing altogether for some seven years, whether out of discouragement, distraction, or despair of perfection. Then, at the age of fifty-two, he resumed, and the secret of his later poetic enterprise is embedded in the untiring fluency with which he composed for the rest of his life, repetitively seeking the changeless. Henceforward his private avocations as well as his poetic concerns would be objects: gardens, parks, zoos, views, music on records, paintings, *objets,* and books. The statement was always the same: "The Ultimate Poem is Abstract." "It is an illusion that we were ever alive."

Stevens's poetry is forbidding, fluent, elaborate, imperturbable, chaste, avuncular. "Having elected to regard poetry as a form of retreat," perhaps even as a form of worship, and having required himself to separate his factual life from his fictive life, he also shunned, as almost beneath the notice of poetry, certain varieties of resonance, conflict, and pain, and fixed his mind and talent exclusively on "the essential poem at the center of things." He was, in fact, an aesthetic puritan, who endowed poetry with such high seriousness that the mere poet ("the demon that cannot be himself, / That tours to shift the shifting scene") can be regarded only as a figure of brittle comedy, as in *The Man with the Blue Guitar,* or *Peter Quince at the Clavier,* or *Le Monocle de Mon Oncle,* or *The Comedian as the Letter C.* His wit, with all its sense of manipulative play, is directed at man and at language, never at nature or illusion.

His obsession was of course with the relation of the mind to objects and events and thence with what he called poetry. ("Poetry is the subject of the poem.") In pursuit of the Platonic vanishing point he developed an amazingly fluid, responsive, consistent, but at its worst, monotonous poetic style. Beneath its porcelain surfaces lies a sea in which the mind must sink and swim below the ceiling of the air. Perhaps its very self-containment, its airlessness, explains why Stevens's poetry has become a favorite subject for academic study. His images do not dominate his poetry, his poetry dominates its images, and the images serve him as talismans

of the ultimate vision, no matter how often he asserts the opposite, as in the famous early lines:

> *Beauty is momentary in the*
> *   mind —*
> *The fitful tracing of a portal;*
> *But in the flesh it is immortal.*

In practice Stevens turns increasingly to the abstract, and his language, while at best it incandesces in glimpses of subtlety and elegance (*Cuisine Bourgeoise, Esthetique du Mal,* and *The Rock,* to name a few of the finest later poems), at worst passes into remoteness and sterility. Stevens is often, despite all the exotic gaudiness of his language, less evocative than he purposes. No other important poet of his generation utilizes so seldom the dramatic opposition of characters and ideas, explores so infrequently the act of becoming, speaks with so single and cultivated and predictable a voice.

Stevens withheld from language — as in so many ways he withheld from his life — a full measure of vitality. The result is St. Elmo's fire in certain lines and verses; but how seldom we find in his work — and how often in the work of other major poets — a complete poem that moves through time and space like sculpture. He mouthed and chewed ceaselessly upon the real, without, it seems, often tasting it. His intelligence was enormous but obsessive, and after the dazzling achievement of *Harmonium* it spread out to encompass more and more examples of but a single idea, like a balloon that could grow forever larger without bursting. The later poetry is (the word keeps recurring) endless and endlessly evasive; to try to contain it is like trying to catch fog in a net.

The fairest evaluation of Stevens I know appears in an unerring poem of

John Berryman's, a poet as unlike Stevens as it is possible to be:

> He lifted up, among the actuaries,
> a grandee crow. Ah ha & he
> crowed good.
> That funny money-man.
> Mutter we all must as well as we
> can.
> He mutter spiffy . . .
>
> What was it missing, then, at the
> man's heart
> so that he does not wound? It is
> our kind
> to wound, as well as utter
>
> a fact of happy world. That meta-
> physics
> he hefted up until we could not
> breathe
> the physics . . .
> brilliant, he seethe;
> better than us; less wide.
> (Dream Song 219)

STEVENSON, Robert Louis (Nov. 13, 1850 – Dec. 3, 1894). English novelist, poet, essayist. Born Edinburgh, son of a successful engineer. He was early stricken with tuberculosis, but studied law and was admitted to the bar (1875), though he never practiced. Instead he began writing for journals: essays, which appeared later in *Virginibus Puerisque* (1881), and stories, published as *New Arabian Nights* (1882). Also traveled, in search of more favorable climates and adventure. First book, *An Inland Voyage* (1878), and the famous *Travels with a Donkey in the Cévennes* (1879) recount his experiences in Belgium and France, where he fell in love with Mrs. Fanny Osbourne. He followed her to California and, after her divorce, married her (1880). They spent the next decade moving from one health resort to another. At one he wrote the adventure novel *Treasure Island* (1883), primarily for his stepson Lloyd Osbourne. An instant success, it was followed by the beloved collection of children's po-

ems *A Child's Garden of Verses* (1885), the horror tale *The Strange Case of Dr. Jekyll and Mr. Hyde* (1886), and the adventure story *Kidnapped* (1886). Stevenson traveled extensively in America, stayed at Saranac, N.Y., for his health, where he wrote *The Master of Ballantrae* (1889). Exploring the South Seas, he finally bought the estate Vailima (1889) on the island of Samoa, where he spent the last five years of his life. Revered by the natives (who called him Tusitala, teller of tales), he wrote the controversial *A Footnote to History: Eight Years of Trouble in Samoa* (1892), and continued to produce books, often collaborating with his stepson Lloyd: *The Wrong Box* (1889), *The Wrecker* (1892), and *The Ebb-Tide* (1894). His last, possibly greatest novel, *Weir of Hermiston*, unfinished at his death, was published in 1896. Stevenson described to his friend Sidney Colvin his literary role: "With all my romance, I am a realist and a prosaist, and a most fanatical lover of plain physical sensations plainly and expressly rendered."

EDITIONS: *Complete Works* South Seas Edition (32 vols. New York 1925). *Collected Poems* ed. Janet Adam Smith (London 1950 and New York 1951). *Letters* ed. Sidney Colvin (1899, new ed. 4 vols. London and New York 1911). *R.L.S.: Letters to Charles Baxter* ed. DeLancey Ferguson and Marshall Waingrow (New Haven, Conn. and Oxford 1956).

REFERENCES: Graham Balfour *Life of Robert Louis Stevenson* (1901, reprinted 2 vols. Grosse Pointe, Mich. 1968). Elsie Caldwell *Last Witness for Robert Louis Stevenson* (Norman, Okla. 1960). G. K. Chesterton *Robert Louis Stevenson* (1927, new ed. New York 1955). David Daiches *Robert Louis Stevenson* (Norfolk, Conn. 1947 and Glasgow 1948). Edwin M. Eigner *Robert Louis Stevenson and Romantic Tradition* (Princeton, N.J. 1966). Joseph C. Furnas *Voyage to Windward: The Life of Robert Louis Stevenson* (New York 1951 and London 1952, PB 1962). Robert J. Kiely *Robert Louis Stevenson and the Fiction of Adventure* (Cambridge, Mass. 1964). Fanny and Robert Louis Stevenson *Our Samoan Adventure* (New York 1955).

STIEGLITZ, Alfred (Jan. 1, 1864 – July 13, 1946). American photographer and editor. Born Hoboken, N.J., son of German Jewish wool merchant. Attended New York City College (1879–81); then went to Germany, intending to become engineer, and entered Berlin Polytechnic Institute (1882). After his first photographs (1883), he shifted to photography and chemistry at the Polytechnic and University of Berlin (1884–90). Returned to U.S. (1890), settled in New York. Worked in photoengraving firm, from which he retired after five years to devote himself fully to photography and promotion of modern art. Edited series of magazines, *American Amateur Photographer* (1891–96), *Camera Notes* (1897–1902), and *Camera Work* (1902–17), the organ of Photo-Secession, the organization of pictorial photographers which he founded. Directed (1905–17) the famous 291 Gallery in New York, where he exhibited work of American and European photographers and introduced to America the work of such avant-garde artists as Cézanne, Picasso, Braque, and Brancusi. Also arranged the earliest known exhibitions of children's art (1912) and African Negro sculpture (1914). Subsequently directed the Intimate Gallery (1925–29) and An American Place (1929–46), both in New York, where he died. Two series of over four hundred prints each (1917–37) are often considered Stieglitz's greatest photographs: the portrait of Georgia O'Keeffe (his second wife) and the *Equivalents*.

REFERENCES: Doris Bry *Alfred Stieglitz* (Boston 1965). Waldo Frank, Lewis Mumford, Dorothy Norman, Paul Rosenfeld, and Harold Rugg eds. *America and Alfred Stieglitz: A Collective Portrait* (New York 1934). Dorothy Norman *Alfred Stieglitz: Introduction to an American Seer* (New York 1960). Herbert J. Seligmann *Alfred Stieglitz Talking: Notes on Some of His Conversations, 1925–1931* (New Haven, Conn. 1966).

ALFRED STIEGLITZ

BY HAROLD CLURMAN

Alfred Stieglitz's personality was manifold. "He was," to quote Edward Steichen, with whom he was closely associated between 1903 and 1917, "the father of modern photography and a fertilizing force in the development of modern art in America." He was not only a pioneer photographer but a man who did more than any other in our country to establish photography as a medium of personal expression. He did this not only by preachment and by his example but by the encouragement and exhibition of such men as Steichen, Clarence White, David Octavius Hill, Paul Strand, and numerous others.

Stieglitz was the first to show Henri Matisse's work in the New York of 1905. The same is true in regard to the work of Henri Rousseau (1910), Cézanne, Picasso (1911). He introduced Arthur Dove, Marsden Hartley, John Marin, Georgia O'Keeffe, Charles Demuth, Max Weber to us. He organized the first one-man Brancusi show anywhere. He was the first to publish Gertrude Stein.

Artists, journalists, critics, novelists, poets, and educators gathered around him. He acted as an inspiration, a beacon to light the way for men of sensibility struggling to bring to America a new vision of itself. He made them feel that what they had to offer was essential to us particularly at the moment of our country's coming of age as a great industrial power. Around him one could behold the extraordinary spectacle of such men as Waldo Frank, Lewis Mumford, Paul Rosenfeld, Sherwood Anderson, William Carlos Williams, Hart Crane, Alfred Kreymborg, Abraham Walkowitz, Duncan Phillips, Lionel Venturi *listening* to Stieglitz as he talked and talked and talked.

Occasionally the sense of his words was nebulous, his story-parables were sometimes puzzling, his maxims repetitive. Still the impression they left was unforgettable, not as doctrine or as aesthetics but as the emanation of an inextinguishable spirit of life in all its manifestations and of art as its crystallization, its flower. He was a seer, a great teacher.

After his studies and wanderings in Europe, Stieglitz moved about very little. Yet he seemed to be in contact with everything. He perceived the universe through the people he spoke to. He accepted everything except the fake, the shoddy, the coarse. He never railed at falsehood; he shed it as if nature had provided him with some miraculous insulation against it.

He had a marked romantic streak in him, and like all romantics he could irritate, bore, and for all his gentleness, seem at moments a solipsistic monster. One had to recall the facts of his career to realize that this was not so. To comprehend his stature, one had only to survey his work, in which romantic afflatus and a classic restraint achieve a synthesis.

Stieglitz's photographs are as direct as declarative sentences. They are straightforward, unambiguous, even "realistic." Yet one has but to glance at them to become aware that they cannot be properly described except in hyperbole and metaphor. Eschewing all artifice, they speak a language which transcends their subjects without prettifying or dramatizing them as "messages."

Stieglitz, who was a connoisseur in the visual arts — he appreciated such artists as Kandinsky, Braque, and Mondrian and many others outside the sphere of the American painters whose "cause" he espoused — often spoke of his photographs as if they were simply formal exercises. He once referred to his famous *The Steerage* (1907) as a study in perpendicular and horizontal lines and of *Sunlight and Shadows* (1889), a photograph of a German girl who had been his mistress, as an attempt to capture the transfigurations of light. But that is not how we see or feel them. That, one is convinced, is not why he made them or what they were meant to convey. His purely professional explanations in terms of composition, chiaroscuro and the like was Stieglitz's way of leaving the viewer free to see each of the photographs after his own bent.

Venetian Boy, a grim-faced ten-year-old ragamuffin, is a picture (taken in 1887) of integrity, endurance, the capacity to sustain suffering and to remain beautiful. It looks as if the door of the palace or church in the background had imparted all these qualities to the boy. The photo of the aforementioned German girl communicates a kind of tactile tenderness in the presence of humble and unconscious innocence. *The Terminal* (1892), in which we see an old-time horse-drawn streetcar conductor resting his animals as they steam from their labor in the snow, is a tribute to the mute honesty of hard work. *Night* (1896), which Stieglitz spoke of as merely an attempt (perhaps the first in the history of photography) to make a clear picture of a dark street (outside the Plaza Hotel), is an image of glamorous festivity twinkling in the gloom of old New York.

The Steerage is at once a portrait of patient fortitude, apprehension, and the drama of expectancy as the passengers are about to reach port. *Marin* (1920) reveals the dignity, the sturdiness, the quiet pride of the painter. *Mountain and Sky — Lake George* (1924) is a poem to the blessedness of nature and might be entitled *God's Handwriting! O'Keeffe's Hands with Thimble* (1919) is a picture of rhythmic grace in work as well as the delicacy of the subject's sensibility. In

Barn — Lake George (1920), weather-beaten wood and a cracked window-pane are lovingly contemplated for their unadorned, consistent staunch-ness. *New York Series — Spring* (1935) reflects the majesty of the city, erect, boastful, bloodless, and sad. A picture of *Hands* (1932) is a metaphor of female sexuality just as a cloud formation (Stieglitz called this series *Equivalents*) brings to mind a seminal flow, a river of life. Another cloud photo (1931) possesses something of an orgastic exaltation, and still another is an ecstatic sign of the life force forever mounting and renewing itself.

All the impulses of Stieglitz's personality finally coalesce: they form a *whole* man. In doubt, in pain, in love, and in perpetual solicitude for his friends and colleagues, Stieglitz never lost his religious respect for mankind. He was always able to give himself to all men everywhere, particularly to the artists whose travail celebrates existence.

Another master, Henri Cartier-Bresson, wrote the most concise summation of the older artist on the occasion of his death: "The purity and simplicity of Stieglitz is expressed through his work which is the fruit of a profound knowledge of the Humane."

STOWE, Harriet (Elizabeth) Beecher (June 14, 1811 – July 1, 1896). American writer. Born Litchfield, Conn., one of nine children of antislavery Calvinist minister Lyman Beecher and his first wife Roxana Foote; among other children were famous clergymen Edward and Henry Ward Beecher, also women's education pioneer Catharine Beecher, in whose school in Hartford Harriet was educated. Family moved (1832) to Cincinnati, Ohio, where Lyman Beecher headed Lane Theological Seminary. After teaching in Western Female Institute founded by Catharine, Harriet married (1836) Calvin Ellis Stowe (1802–1886), a professor at the seminary; they had seven children. Moved to Brunswick, Me., when he became professor at Bowdoin College (1850), and to Andover, Mass., when he went to Andover Theological Seminary (1852). Outraged at fugitive slave law (1850), and accustomed since childhood to writing, Harriet dramatized the condition of slavery in her first novel *Uncle Tom's Cabin, or Life Among the Lowly* (1852), which caused a sensation at home and abroad and was of incalculable influence in molding opinion against slavery. After another antislavery novel, *Dred: A Tale of the Great Dismal Swamp* (1856), she confined herself largely to novels of New England such as *The Minister's Wooing* (1859), *The Pearl of Orr's Island* (1862), and *Oldtown Folks* (1869). Lionized in England, which she visited (1853) after publication of *Uncle Tom's Cabin*, she formed a friendship with Byron's widow, and after two other trips to Europe (1856, 1859) shocked many readers on both sides of the Atlantic by publishing in an *Atlantic Monthly* article (1869) (and in *Lady Byron Vindicated*, 1870) charges that Byron had an incestuous relation with his sister. More tales of Oldtown followed, as well as the autobiographical *Poganuc People* (1878). Her last years were spent largely at a winter home on St. John's River in Florida, and in Hartford, the Stowes' home since Calvin's retirement (1864), where she died.

EDITION: *Writings* Riverside Edition (16 vols. Boston 1896–98).
REFERENCES: Alice C. Crozier *The Novels of Harriet Beecher Stowe* (London and New York 1970). Charles H. Foster *The Rungless Ladder: Harriet Beecher Stowe and New England Puritanism* (Durham, N.C. 1954 and Cambridge, England, 1955). Joseph C. Furnas *Goodbye to Uncle Tom* (New York 1956, also PB). Catherine Gilbertson *Harriet Beecher Stowe* (1937, reprinted Port Washington, N.Y. 1968). Constance M. Rourke *Trumpets of Jubilee* (1927, new ed. New York PB 1963). Charles E. Stowe *Life of Harriet Beecher Stowe* (Boston 1889). Edward C. Wagenknecht *Harriet Beecher Stowe* (New York 1965). Forrest Wilson *Crusader in Crinoline: The Life of Harriet*

Beecher Stowe (Philadelphia 1941 and London 1942).

✍

HARRIET BEECHER STOWE
BY HENRY NASH SMITH

Harriet Beecher Stowe might conceivably have been one of the "d——d mob of scribbling women" that Hawthorne complained about not long after the publication of *Uncle Tom's Cabin*. This first novel had quickly achieved international fame and it eventually became by far the best-selling American book of the century. In attacking the institution of slavery, Mrs. Stowe had exploited to the full the crude conventions of sentimental fiction — introducing gross villains such as the slave trader Haley and the plantation owner Simon Legree; a genteel heroine, Eliza Harris; and the angelic child Evangeline St. Clare, whose edifying death is described at excruciating length. Later Mrs. Stowe would present other improbably beautiful and virtuous heroines such as Mary Scudder in *The Minister's Wooing* and Tina Percival in *Oldtown Folks*. She had a weakness for literary fads — for example, the Byronism that appears in such charming but wicked men of the world as Aaron Burr and Ellery Davenport in these same novels; or the cult of the picturesque that is exemplified at tedious length by the half-insane runaway slave Dred in her second novel, who has brooded over the Bible until his mind is a jumble of Old Testament prophecies and New Testament apocalyptic imagery. Mrs. Stowe compares him to "one of those old rude Gothic doorways, so frequent in European cathedrals, where scriptural images, carved in rough granite, mingle themselves with a thousand wayward, fantastic freaks of architecture."

Nevertheless, the reader who refuses to be put off by these period trappings will discover beneath them a body of fiction that expresses better than anything else in our literature the culture of New England just after its climax in the Golden Day of Emerson and Thoreau, when the heroic past of the region had begun to be obscured by a nostalgic haze but had not entirely ceased to be a vital force in American life. The important thing about Mrs. Stowe is not her power as a propagandist or her tearful scenes of stereotyped sentiment but her profound insight into the religious experience of the Puritans, her shrewd observation of character (especially in minor figures, when she was less trammeled by convention), and her strong sense of history. Daughter of a Calvinist clergyman, she had grown up in a household where the lives and doctrines of Jonathan Edwards and other noted divines were constant topics of conversation. Yet she had gained perspective on her native region by living eighteen years in Cincinnati, where her husband was professor in a theological seminary, before returning with him to more congenial appointments at Bowdoin and then Andover.

The circumstances of her life provided her with the recurrent themes of her fiction, although she was seldom able to devise a plot that could do justice to what she wanted to say. A partial exception would have to be made for the pattern of the two journeys — southward to death for Tom, northward to freedom for George and Eliza Harris — that determines the structure of *Uncle Tom's Cabin*. But this chaotic masterpiece upsets all generalizations; it might almost be the result of demonic possession. Mrs. Stowe's effort to write a second novel about slavery was an embarrassing failure. Fortunately, she shifted to New England materials and produced a half-dozen volumes that might collectively bear some famous title out of the Puritan past such as *Wonders of the Invisible World* or *A History of Plimouth Plantation*. For her enduring concern was with the relation of the actual world to the realm of spirit, and it was in the annals of New England that she found this relation most copiously illustrated. She was proud, even to the point of arrogance, of participating in her people's special covenant with God. "It is impossible to write a story of New England life and manners for a thoughtless, shallow-minded person," she declared. "If we represent things as they are, their intensity, their depth, their unworldly gravity and earnestness, must inevitably repel lighter spirits, as the reverse pole of the magnet drives off sticks and straws." (The regional loyalty here is just as characteristic of Mrs. Stowe's writing as is the careless syntax and the naïveté about the operation of a magnet.)

Yet she found the burden of high Calvinism almost unbearable, particularly after the death of her eldest son Henry, who was drowned in 1857 while he was a freshman at Dartmouth. For she had, as she wrote her sister, "distressing doubts as to Henry's spiritual state." She tried to persuade herself that these doubts were "an attack of the Devil trying to separate me from the love of Christ," but with the deeper part of her mind she knew that the iron creed which had made New England great forbade her to believe that Henry was in heaven. Just as the death of her infant son Charles in 1849 had made her especially sensitive to the suffering of slave mothers separated from their children, her inability to accept the possibility that Henry was condemned to eternal torment provided the hidden energy for her subsequent career as a novelist. In book after book she sought to illustrate a theology of Christ's love and mercy in contrast with the Calvinist emphasis on God's sovereignty and justice.

This impulse coincided with the widespread evangelical trend that threatened to replace Calvinist austerity with a mindless emotionalism, as for example in the preaching of her famous clergyman brother, Henry Ward Beecher. Fortunately, her merits as a novelist extend far beyond her intense but narrow religious concerns. In addition to her grasp of New England history, she has a surprisingly robust comic gift, particularly in the portrayal of Negroes such as the slaves on the Shelby plantation in *Uncle Tom's Cabin* who delay the pursuit of Eliza Harris for several hours while they pretend they are trying to catch Haley's horse, or the majestic black tyrant Dinah, who presides over a cosmic disorder in the St. Clare kitchen. Equally delightful is the character of Miss Nervy, in *Oldtown Folks*, who expounds Latin grammar in a rich vernacular: "Massy, child! that 'ere is one o' the deponent verbs. 'T ain't got any active form." More than any other of our writers before Mark Twain, Mrs. Stowe recognized the literary potentialities of everyday speech, and found a way to use it without patronizing it. And until the advent of William Faulkner, whom in some ways she oddly resembles, no one except Mark Twain had surpassed her as the interpreter of an American region.

STRACHEY, (Giles) Lytton (Mar. 1, 1880 – Jan. 21, 1932). English biographer and critic. Born London, son of Richard Strachey, Indian administrator, and Lady Jane Strachey, brilliant essayist. Educated at Trinity College, Cambridge (1899–1903), he began his career by writing for literary periodicals in London. There, along with Virginia and Leonard Woolf, Clive Bell, Roger Fry, Arthur Waley, E. M. Forster, and others, he became a leading member of the Bloomsbury Group. Attracted general attention with *Eminent Victorians* (1918), a collection of biographies, and *Queen Victoria* (1921), his masterpiece. His other biographies include *Pope* (1925), *Elizabeth and Essex* (1928), and *Portraits in Miniature* (1931). As a critic, he wrote *Landmarks in French Literature* (1912), *Books and Characters* (1922), and *Characters and Commentaries* (1933). Unmarried, he died at Ham Spray House, near Hungerford. Strachey revolutionized the art of biography, painting realistic portraits of his subjects, "warts and all," rather than presenting a record of activities and events.

REFERENCES: Sir Max Beerbohm *Lytton Strachey* (Cambridge, England, and New York 1943). Michael Holroyd *Lytton Strachey: A Critical Biography* (2 vols. London 1967–68 and New York 1968). J. K. Johnstone *The Bloomsbury Group: A Study of E. M. Forster, Lytton Strachey, Virginia Woolf and Their Circle* (London and New York 1954). Charles R. Sanders *Lytton Strachey: His Mind and Art* (New Haven, Conn. 1957 and Oxford 1958). R. A. Scott-James *Lytton Strachey* (London and New York 1955, also PB).

STRAUSS, Johann, the Younger (Oct. 25, 1825 – June 3, 1899). Austrian composer. Born and died in Vienna. Named for his father, a renowned conductor and composer of waltzes. Embarked on musical career in opposition to his father. Secretly took violin lessons and studied composition with Joseph Drechsler. Formed his own orchestra (1844), which immediately rivaled his father's; he combined the two groups after his father's death (1849), playing and touring successfully throughout Europe and Russia. After leading summer concerts in Petropaulovski Park, St. Petersburg, he entrusted the orchestra to his brothers Josef and Eduard (1862), and became conductor of the court balls, Vienna (1863–70). His waltzes, on which his fame largely rests (he was known as the Waltz King), number over four hundred;

among the most popular are *The Blue Danube* (1867), *Artists' Life* (1867), *Tales from the Vienna Woods* (1868), and *Wine, Women, and Song* (1869). From 1871 he began writing operettas, among them *Indigo and the Forty Robbers* (1871), *The Carnival in Rome* (1873), the outstanding *Die Fledermaus* (*The Bat*, 1874), and *The Gypsy Baron* (1885). Visited the U.S. (1872), conducting fourteen concerts in Boston and four in New York. He was married three times: to Henrietta Treffz (1862), who died (1878); to Angelica Dietrich (1878), whom he divorced (1883); to Adele Deutsch (1883), who survived him. Greatly admired by Johannes Brahms and Richard Wagner, Strauss was the most brilliant member of a family of musicians; his waltzes have come to represent the elegance and grace of Viennese court life.

REFERENCES: David Ewen *Tales from the Vienna Woods: The Story of Johann Strauss* (New York 1944). Heinrich E. Jacob *Johann Strauss, Father and Son: A Century of Light Music* (tr. London and New York 1940). Jerome Pastene *Three Quarter Time: The Life and Music of the Strauss Family of Vienna* (New York 1951). Ada B. Teetgen *Waltz Kings of Old Vienna* (London 1939 and New York 1940).

STRAUSS, Richard (Georg) (June 11, 1864 – Sept. 8, 1949). German composer. Born Munich, son of an eminent hornist. Began music lessons at four; graduated from Munich University (1883). Performances of his *Symphony in D Minor* (1881), *Violin Concerto* (1883), and *Serenade for Wind Instruments* (1884) brought recognition. Conducted the Meiningen orchestra (1885–86) and became third conductor at Munich Opera (1886–89). While serving as hofkapellmeister at Weimar (1889–94), he produced his first major works in his characteristic style, *Don Juan* (1889) and *Tod und Verklärung* (1889). Appointed conductor of Berlin Philharmonic (1894–95), hofkapellmeister in Berlin (1898–1918), comusical director of the Vienna Opera (1919–24), and president of the Reichsmusikkammer (1933–35). Traveled throughout Europe and in the Near East as guest conductor. Married singer

Pauline de Ahna (1894). In retirement during World War II, he became a controversial figure as he took no stand against Nazism. Died at Garmisch-Partenkirchen. Major works are the tone poems *Till Eulenspiegel* (1895), *Also Sprach Zarathustra* (1896), *Don Quixote* (1898), *Ein Heldenleben* (1899); the operas *Salome* (1905), *Elektra* (1909), *Der Rosenkavalier* (1911), *Die Frau ohne Schatten* (1919). Strauss was one of the last of the German romantics, influenced by Wagner and Liszt. He was a master of the grand, rich orchestral effect.

REFERENCES: Norman Del Mar *Richard Strauss: A Critical Commentary on His Life and Works* (vol. I, London 1962 and New York 1963; vol. II, London and Philadelphia 1969). Ernst Krause *Richard Strauss: The Man and His Work* (tr. London 1965 and Boston 1969). William S. Mann *Richard Strauss: A Critical Study of the Operas* (London 1964 and New York 1966). George R. Marek *Richard Strauss: The Life of a Non-Hero* (New York 1967).

STRINDBERG, (Johan) August (Jan. 22, 1849 – May 14, 1912). Swedish dramatist and novelist. Born and died in Stockholm. Son of an arrogant, bankrupt aristocrat and a former barmaid, he grew up in a poor, unhappy home. Studied intermittently at University of Uppsala, leaving without a degree. Supporting himself as a painter, journalist, tutor, and librarian, he began to write. First important play, *Master Olaf* (1872, tr. 1915), influenced by Shakespeare and Ibsen, deals with Swedish Reformation. Won renown for his satirical novel about Stockholm society, *The Red Room* (1879, tr. 1913). Married Swedish actress Siri von Essen (1877), traveled restlessly abroad (1883–89), and became active in socialist movements. His misogyny, first suggested in his collection of short stories *Married* (1884, tr. 1912), influenced his naturalist dramas *The Father* (1887), *Miss Julie* (1888), *Creditors* (1888), and eventually led to his divorce (1891). Second marriage (1893), to Frida Uhl, Austrian journalist, ended in divorce (1896). Always verging on insanity, he abandoned socialism for a Nietzschean anarchic individualism, and after a

religious conversion (1894–96; described in *Inferno*, 1897) embraced a Swedenborgian mysticism. Experiments in expressionistic and symbolic drama followed, as in *The Dream Play* (1902), *The Road to Damascus* (3 parts, 1898–1904), *The Ghost Sonata* (1907), and his last play, the autobiographical *Great Highway* (1909). From 1899 he wrote a series of historical dramas, including the outstanding *Gustav Vasa* (1899). His third marriage (1901), to Norwegian actress Harriet Basse, also ended in divorce (1904), provoking the bitterness of his satirical novel *Black Banners* (1907). Expounded his philosophy in *Blue Books* (1907–12, selections tr. *Zones of the Spirit* 1913). Died of cancer. One of Sweden's greatest authors, Strindberg profoundly influenced both European and American playwrights, among them Sean O'Casey, Eugene O'Neill, and Luigi Pirandello.

TRANSLATIONS: *Six Plays* (Garden City, N.Y. PB 1955), *Five Plays* (Garden City, N.Y. PB 1960), and *Plays* (Chicago 1962 and London 1963), all translated by Elizabeth Sprigge. *Eight Expressionist Plays* tr. Arvid Paulson (Toronto 1965).

REFERENCES: Carl Dahlström *Strindberg's Dramatic Expressionism* (2nd ed. New York 1965). Eric O. Johannesson *The Novels of August Strindberg: A Study in Theme and Structure* (Berkeley, Calif. 1968). Franklin S. Klaf *Strindberg: The Origin of Psychology in Modern Drama* (New York 1963, also PB). Frank L. Lucas *The Drama of Ibsen and Strindberg* (London and New York 1962). Brita M. E. Mortensen and Brian W. Downs *Strindberg: An Introduction to His Life and Work* (1949, new ed. Cambridge, England, 1966, also PB). Elizabeth Sprigge *The Strange Life of August Strindberg* (London and New York 1949). Frida (Uhl) Strindberg *Marriage with Genius* (London 1937).

STUART, Gilbert (Charles) (Dec. 3, 1775 – July 9, 1828). American portrait painter. Born North Kingston, R.I., in his father's snuff mill. Grew up in Newport, where he studied painting with visiting Scotsman, Cosmo Alexander. Accompanied him briefly to Edinburgh (1772), returning after

Alexander's death. In London (1775–87) studied portraiture with Benjamin West and opened his own studio (1782); painted portraits of George III, the prince of Wales (later George IV), Sir Joshua Reynolds, and other notable figures. Won renown for *The Skater* (c.1782, National Gallery, Washington, D.C.), which shows influence of Gainsborough and Reynolds. Married Charlotte Coates (1786). After some time in Dublin (1787–92) returned to America, working in New York (1793), Philadelphia (1794–96), Germantown (1796–1803), and Washington, D.C. (1803–1805). Settled permanently in Boston (1805), where he had a studio until his death. The most celebrated portraitist of his day, Stuart painted such prominent people as John Adams, John Quincy Adams, Thomas Jefferson, James Madison, John Jay, and Jacob Astor. He is best known for his numerous portraits of George Washington, all replicas of three works done from life: the Vaughan bust portrait (1795, National Gallery), the Lansdowne full-length (1796, Pennsylvania Academy of the Fine Arts, Philadelphia), the unfinished Athenaeum Head (1796, Museum of Fine Arts, Boston). Other fine portraits are those of Mrs. Richard Yates (c.1793, National Gallery) and Mrs. Timothy Pickering (1818, Carnegie Institute, Pittsburgh). Stuart's work and advice influenced many younger painters, among them Thomas Sully, John Neagle, Samuel Morse, and John Wesley Jarvis.

REFERENCES: James T. Flexner *Gilbert Stuart: A Great Life in Brief* (New York 1955). John H. Morgan *Gilbert Stuart and His Pupils* (1939, reprinted New York 1969). Charles M. Mount *Gilbert Stuart: A Biography* (New York 1964). Lawrence Park *Gilbert Stuart: An Illustrated Descriptive List of His Works* (4 vols. New York 1926). William T. Whitley *Gilbert Stuart* (1932, reprinted New York 1969).

STUBBS, George (Aug. 24, 1724 – July 10, 1806). English painter. Born Liverpool. Began art studies under his father, a tanner, and later worked at engraving paintings from Lord Derby's collection. Established himself in Leeds as portrait painter, and also taught anatomy at York. Worked (1756–60) on his monumental study *Anatomy of the Horse* (1766). Throughout his life Stubbs painted the great racehorses of the time, such as *The Racehorses of George III* (Walker Art Gallery, Liverpool) and the families that owned them, as in *The Melbourne and Milbanke Families* (c.1770, J. Salmond Collection) and *Gentleman Holding a Horse* (National Gallery, London). He excelled in capturing dramatic moments, in such paintings as *White Horse Frightened by a Lion* (1770, Walker Art Gallery, Liverpool) and *Horses Fighting*, and in bucolic works such as *Mares and Foals in a Landscape* (c.1765, Tate Gallery, London). Also (from 1770) painted other animals and country scenes. Began (1790) a series of racehorse portraits, completed sixteen. In old age he started a second anatomical work, comparing the human body with the tiger and the common fowl. He was noted for exact likenesses of his subjects, invariably accurate in anatomy and behavior. Died in London.

REFERENCES: Sir Walter Gilbey *Life of George Stubbs* (London 1898). Basil Taylor *Animal Painting in England from Barlow to Landseer* (Harmondsworth, England, 1955).

SUETONIUS (full name Gaius Suetonius Tranquillus) (c. A.D. 69 – c.140). Roman biographer. Little known about his life except that before becoming secretary to Emperor Hadrian (119–121 or 122) he had practiced law. Of his works, which included Greek and Latin antiquarian, historical, grammatical, and scientific writings, only two collections of biographies have survived: fragments of *De Viris Illustribus* (*On Illustrious Men*, completed by 113), containing accounts of grammarians, rhetoricians, poets, orators, historians, and philosophers; and the almost complete *De Vita Caesarum* (*The Lives of the Caesars*, published c.121), from Augustus through Domitian. His biographical portraits of the Caesars, filled with anecdotes which he gathered from public and private sources, are exceptionally colorful, racy, and informative.

TRANSLATIONS: *Suetonius* tr. J. C. Rolfe (1924, latest ed. 2 vols. Cambridge, Mass. 1960). *The Twelve Caesars* tr. Robert Graves (Harmondsworth, England, 1957 and Baltimore PB 1960).

REFERENCES: Walter Dennison *The Epigraphic Sources of the Writings of Gaius Suetonius Tranquillus* (New York 1898). Alcide Macé *Essai sur Suétone* (Paris 1900).

SULLIVAN, Sir Arthur (May 13, 1842 – Nov. 22, 1900). English composer. Born London, son of a musician. Became chorister at Chapel Royal (1854), where he received his first musical instruction. Won Mendelssohn scholarship to Royal Academy of Music (1856), which entitled him to study at Leipzig Conservatory (1858–61). Organist at St. Michael's, London (1861), and professor of composition at Royal Academy of Music (1866), he devoted himself to composition after success of his incidental music for Shakespeare's *The Tempest* (produced 1862). First operatic production, *Cox and Box* (1867). Began (1871) his long and fruitful, if somewhat tempestuous, collaboration with librettist William S. Gilbert. Together they wrote fourteen operettas, ten of which are still produced by D'Oyly Carte Opera Company: *Trial by Jury* (1875), *H.M.S. Pinafore* (1878), *The Pirates of Penzance* (1879), *Patience* (1881), *Iolanthe* (1882), *Princess Ida* (1884), *The Mikado* (1885), *Ruddigore* (1887), *The Yeomen of the Guard* (1888), and *The Gondoliers* (1890). Despite the success of his operettas, for which he is remembered, Sullivan felt his best work was his serious music: cantatas *Kenilworth* (1864) and *The Golden Legend* (1886); oratorio *The Prodigal Son* (1869); overture dedicated to his father, *In Memoriam* (1866); grand opera *Ivanhoe* (1891). Among his other works: incidental music for Shakespearean plays; ballets, such as *L'Île Enchantée* (1864); hymns, including *Onward, Christian Soldiers* (1871); orchestral works, including the *Irish Symphony* (1866); numerous songs, among them *The Lost Chord* (1877). Conductor of the London Philharmonic Orchestra (1885–87) and the Leeds Festivals (1880–98), he received honorary degrees from Oxford and Cambridge, and

was knighted (1883). He died in London, was buried in St. Paul's Cathedral.

REFERENCES: Thomas F. Dunhill *Sullivan's Comic Operas: A Critical Appreciation* (London and New York 1928). A. H. Godwin *Gilbert and Sullivan: A Critical Appreciation of the Savoy Operas* (1926, reprinted Port Washington, N.Y. 1969). Isaac Goldberg *The Story of Gilbert and Sullivan, or The Compleat Savoyard* (New York 1928 and London 1929). Gervase Hughes *The Music of Arthur Sullivan* (London and New York 1960). Raymond Mander and Joe Mitchenson *A Picture History of Gilbert and Sullivan* (London 1962 and Chester Springs, Pa. 1965). Hesketh Pearson *Gilbert and Sullivan: A Biography* (London and New York 1935). Herbert Sullivan and Newman Flower *Sir Arthur Sullivan: His Life, Letters, and Diaries* (London and New York 1927).

SULLIVAN, Louis Henri or Henry (Sept. 3, 1856 – Apr. 14, 1924). American architect. Born Boston. Attended Massachusetts Institute of Technology (1872–73) and, after working for Chicago architect William Le Baron Jenney (1873), went to Paris (1874), where he studied at École des Beaux Arts and in atelier of Joseph Vaudremer. Joined firm of architect Dankmar Adler (1879), Chicago, forming successful partnership (1881–95), and became leader of Chicago school. Abandoned Victorian Gothic and Romanesque revival styles in the Chicago Auditorium (1886–89), the structural integrity and acoustics of which made him famous. Married Margaret Hattabough (1899; divorced 1917). In developing his organic theory, "Form follows function," Sullivan established a style that was at once functional and intrinsically American — characteristically in the skyscraper stressing the steel skeleton verticality. His finest designs include the Wainwright Building, St. Louis (1890–91), especially admired by Frank Lloyd Wright: Schiller Building (1891–92), Stock Exchange Building (1893–94), and the innovative, celebrated Transportation Building at the World's Columbian Exposition (1893), all in Chicago; Guaranty Building, Buffalo (1894–95); Bayard Building, New York

(1897–98), and several banks and memorials. Continued to develop his highly original views and principles in writings collected as *Kindergarten Chats* (1918) and in *The Autobiography of an Idea* (1924). Exerted profound influence on such disciples as Frank Lloyd Wright and Claude Bragdon. He died in Chicago.

REFERENCES: Albert Bush-Brown *Louis Sullivan* (New York 1960 and London 1961, also PB). Willard Connely *Louis Sullivan as He Lived* (New York 1960). Hugh Morrison *Louis Sullivan: Prophet of Modern Architecture* (1935, new ed. New York PB 1962). Sherman Paul *Louis Sullivan: An Architect in American Thought* (Englewood Cliffs, N.J. PB 1962). John Szarkowski *The Idea of Louis Sullivan* (Minneapolis 1956).

SULLY-PRUDHOMME, René François Armand (Mar. 16, 1839 – Sept. 7, 1907). French poet. Born Paris, of lower-middle-class family, he lost his father when only two and suffered from acute feelings of loneliness throughout his life. Forced to abandon scientific studies because of eye trouble, he worked as a law clerk in Paris (1860), where he began writing verse and essays; first published poem, *L'Art* (1863). Met Leconte de Lisle (1864), and contributed to *Le Parnasse contemporain* (1866, 1871, 1876), but remained somewhat aloof from the Parnassians because of differences in personal enthusiasms. First collection of poems, *Stances et poèmes* (1865), contained his well-known *Le Vase brisé*, and was followed by the sentimental lyrics of *Les Épreuves* (1866), *Les Solitudes* (1869), and *Les Vaines Tendresses* (1875). His later poetry, more rational and philosophical, is best represented by the two long poems *La Justice* (1878) and *Le Bonheur* (1888). Among his prose works: *Réflexions sur l'art des vers* (1892), *Que Sais-je?* (1895), *Testament poétique*, and *La Vraie Religion selon Pascal* (1905). Elected to the French Academy (1881), he was the first recipient of the Nobel prize in literature (1901). He died near Paris, at Chatenay.

REFERENCES: Edmond Estève *Sully-Prudhomme, poète sentimental et poète philosophe* (Paris 1925). Pierre Flottes *Sully-Prudhomme et sa pensée* (Paris 1930). Camille Hémon *La Philosophie de M. Sully-Prudhomme* (Paris 1907). Henri Morice *La Poésie de Sully-Prudhomme* (Paris 1920).

SURREY, Henry Howard, earl of (c.1517 – Jan. 19, 1547). English poet. Born possibly at Hundson, Hertfordshire, eldest son of Lord Thomas Howard. During early years learned Latin, Italian, Spanish, and made translations. Lived at Windsor as companion to Henry VIII's natural son the duke of Richmond (1530–32). Married Lady Frances de Vere (1532). False charge of aiding Catholic rebellion of 1536 led him to strike his courtier-accuser, for which he was confined at Windsor (1537–39). During this time probably wrote most of his poetry. First published poem (1542) was an epitaph for Sir Thomas Wyatt. Served in military campaigns in Scotland (1542), Flanders and France (1543–46). As field marshal won royal approval (1544). Returned to England (1546), where he was accused of treason (without grounds) by the powerful Seymours. After an unsuccessful attempt to defend himself Surrey was executed on Tower Hill. Most of his short poems first appeared in *Tottel's Miscellany* (1557), including translations of Petrarch and original sonnets with themes of love, death, and youthful memories. Surrey's translation of books II and IV of the *Aeneid* (also published 1557) marks the first use of blank verse in English. Known chiefly today for his role (along with Wyatt) in introducing Italian verse forms — chiefly the Petrarchan sonnet — to English.

EDITION: *The Poems of Henry Howard, Earl of Surrey* ed. Emrys Jones (Oxford 1964).

REFERENCES: Edwin Casady *Henry Howard, Earl of Surrey* (New York 1938). Hester Chapman *Two Tudor Portraits: Henry Howard, Earl of Surrey, and Lady Katherine Grey* (London 1960). C. S. Lewis *English Literature of the Sixteenth Century* (Oxford 1954).

SURTEES, Robert Smith (May 17, 1805 – Mar. 16, 1864). English novelist. Born near Newcastle-on-Tyne, he was educated at Durham Grammar School; later was articled to attorneys in Newcastle and London (1822–25). But mildly interested in the law, his real passion was hunting, and he contributed (from 1830) frequent articles to the *Sporting Magazine*. With Rudolph Ackermann, founded the *New Sporting Magazine* (1831), which he edited until 1836. Here appeared in serial form the humorous sporting tales of Mr. Jorrocks, the Cockney grocer whose escapades were later published as *Mr. Jorrocks's Jaunts and Jollities* (1838). An unsuccessful Conservative candidate for Parliament (1836), Surtees retired to his family's country estate after his father's death (1838) and led the life of a country gentleman. Married Elizabeth Jane Fenwick (1841). He died in Brighton. Among his other works: *Handley Cross* (1843), which continues the career of Jorrocks, *Hawbuck Grange* (1847), *Mr. Sponge's Sporting Tour* (1853), *Ask Mamma* (1858), and *Mr. Facey Romford's Hounds* (1865). Full of hearty humor and mordant satire, his works present a colorful picture of English hunting life. Many of them are enhanced by the spirited illustrations of John Leech.

REFERENCES: Edward W. Bovill *The England of Nimrod and Surtees, 1815–1854* (London and New York 1959). Leonard Cooper *R. S. Surtees* (London 1952). Anthony Steel *Jorrocks's England* (New York 1932). Frederick Watson *Robert Smith Surtees: A Critical Study* (London 1933).

SWEELINCK, Jan Pieterszoon (May 1562 – Oct. 16, 1621). Dutch organist and composer. Born Deventer, son of an organist of Amsterdam, where he spent most of his life and where he died. Married Claesgen Puyner (1590), a merchant's daughter. Reputedly the greatest organist of his time, he played at the Old Church, Amsterdam (1580–1621), and was a renowned organ teacher; 254 of his vocal compositions have survived, including *Chansons* (1592–94), *Rimes françoises et italiennes* (1612), 37 *cantiones sacrae*, and 153 psalms. He based these works on sixteenth-century techniques, always writing in a contrapuntal style, both in his lighthearted *chansons* and in solemn religious settings. Noted particularly for his instrumental music for organ and harpsichord, he founded the forms perfected by J. S. Bach. He was an early developer of fugue, and may be considered the inventor of chorale variations, in which he used double and triple counterpoint. Seventy-two instrumental works survive, including nineteen fantasies, thirteen toccatas, and twenty-four chorale variations. Also wrote secular variations based on popular tunes. Sweelinck was active just as the old polyphonic style was giving way to the classical style.

EDITION: *Complete Works* ed. Max Seiffert (10 vols. The Hague 1894–1901).
REFERENCE: Robert L. Tusler *The Organ Music of Jan Pieterszoon Sweelinck* (2 vols. Bilthoven, Netherlands, 1958).

SWIFT, Jonathan (Nov. 30, 1667 – Oct. 19, 1745). British writer. Born Dublin, posthumous son of Jonathan Swift, a distant cousin of John Dryden's. Having been raised by his uncles, he attended Kilkenny School (1663–82) and Trinity College, Dublin (B.A. 1686). Became secretary to Sir William Temple, Moor Park, Surrey (1689), through whom he met young Esther Johnson, the "Stella" of his *Journal to Stella* (1710–13) and his constant companion until her death (1728). Left England for Ireland (1693), where he was ordained Anglican deacon (1694) and priest (1695). Returned to Moor Park (1696) and stayed until Temple's death (1699), when he began editing his letters and memoirs (1700–1709). Works of this period include Pindaric odes and prose satires *The Battle of the Books* and *A Tale of a Tub* (both written c.1696, published 1704). Became vicar of Laracor, Agher, and Rathbeggan (County Meath), Ireland (1700), traveling frequently to London (1702–13), where he was involved in first Whig, then Tory, politics. In behalf of Irish clergy, sought "Queen Anne's bounty" (1707–12) for Irish church. Actively involved in Tory ministry (1710–14), he wrote a series of political pamphlets, among which is *The Conduct of the Allies* (1711). A friend of Addison and Steele, he contributed to the *Tatler*, occasionally to the *Spectator*, and along with Pope, Gay, and John Arbuthnot became member of the Scriblerus Club (1714). In London he became close friend of Esther Vanhomrigh, the *Vanessa* of *Cadenus and Vanessa* (1713). She followed him to Ireland, died shortly after he broke with her (1723). Appointed dean of St. Patrick's Cathedral, Dublin (1713), Swift left England after death of Queen Anne and downfall of Tories (1714) to settle permanently "in exile." Later works, concerned with English oppression of Irish, include the *Drapier's Letters* (begun 1724) and *A Modest Proposal* (1729). His most important satire, *Gulliver's Travels* (written to "vex the world rather than divert it"), was published anonymously in London (1726). Died in Dublin; buried in St. Patrick's, near Stella and beneath the epitaph he wrote for himself: "... *Ubi saeva indignatio ulterius cor lacerare nequit*" "Where savage indignation can lacerate his heart no more."

EDITIONS: *The Prose Works of Jonathan Swift* (14 vols. Oxford 1939–68) and *The Poetical Works of Jonathan Swift* (London and New York 1967), both ed. Herbert Davis. *Poems of Jonathan Swift* ed. Padraic Colum (New York PB 1962). *Correspondence* ed. Harold Williams (5 vols. Oxford 1963–65). *Gulliver's Travels and Other Writings* ed. Louis Landa (Boston PB 1960 and London 1965).

REFERENCES: Herbert Davis *Jonathan Swift: Essays on his Satire and Other Studies* (Gloucester, Mass. 1964, also PB). Denis Donoghue *Jonathan Swift: A Critical Introduction* (Cambridge, England, 1969). Irvin Ehrenpreis *Swift: The Man, His Works, and the Age* (2 vols. Cambridge, Mass. and London 1962 John Middleton Murry *Jonathan Swift: A Critical Biography* (London 1954). Ricardo Quintana *Swift: An Introduction* (London and New York 1955, also PB). Edward W. Rosenheim, Jr. *Swift and the Satirist's Art* (Chicago 1963). Walter B. C. Watkins *Perilous Balance: The Tragic Genius of Swift, Johnson and Sterne* (1939, new ed. Cambridge, Mass. PB 1960). Kathleen Williams *Jonathan Swift and the Age of Compromise*

(Lawrence, Kans. 1958 and London 1959, also PB).

☜

JONATHAN SWIFT
BY RICARDO QUINTANA

The truly formative years of Swift's life were those spent as a member of Sir William Temple's household at Moor Park, Surrey. Born in Dublin, a posthumous child of English parents not long resident in Ireland, Swift had his paternal uncles to thank for his education. His career at Trinity College, Dublin, though scarcely distinguished, had not been altogether as dismal as he was later to suggest. He was still in residence there, proceeding towards the master's degree, when the political disturbances which spread through Ireland in the wake of the revolution of 1688 drove him to England. Here he shortly found employment as a kind of secretary to Temple, a retired Whig statesman and foreign diplomat of distinction, now engaged in writing his memoirs and composing a number of polite essays. Undoubtedly Swift was ill at ease during his early days at Moor Park, but the young genius and the elderly man of taste eventually came to understand one another, and their association, though twice interrupted when Swift in dudgeon retired for brief periods to Ireland, ended only with Temple's death in 1699.

A wholly new life now opened up for him, but the personal characteristics evident in the notable figure of subsequent years had already been established, his intellectual and artistic temper determined once and for all. At Moor Park he had suffered the first symptoms of Ménière's disease, which was to assail him through life. Here he had first laid eyes on Stella — Stella, the eight-year-old daughter of one of the women employed in the Temple establishment, raven-haired, and to him, then as always, utterly captivating. He had taken orders in the Church of England, assenting completely to what the Anglicans liked to call their *via media,* their middle way of moderation and reasonableness between Puritan enthusiasm and Roman Catholicism. Thanks to Temple himself and to the exciting books in the Temple library, he had formulated the comprehensive theory of human behavior, historically and politically considered, which was to underlie his public writings. Most of all, he had learned the meaning and art of prose satire, and in *A Tale of a Tub,* not to be published until 1704, had as a matter of fact composed a work of incomparable brilliance, originality, and force.

Swift's career from this point on presents three readily distinguishable periods. Returning to Ireland shortly after Temple's death, he was preferred to a modest church living — the vicarage of Laracor — but in the course of the ensuing ten years made frequent trips to London, where he acted as an agent for the officials of the Irish Church, who were then seeking certain church benefits from the Whigs, at this time in control of the administration.

In 1710, however, the Tories were swept into office. Swift was a Whig by birth and training, but as a stout Anglican he had viewed with mounting apprehension the present Whig policy towards the established church. He soon allied himself with the Tory leaders and promptly became the most effective political writer of the period. When Queen Anne expired in the summer of 1714 and the Tories lost all power, Swift, overwhelmed by the disaster which had overtaken his friends, had no choice but to seek seclusion in Ireland.

Since 1713 he had been dean of St. Patrick's in Dublin. The post, a rich one, had come to him as a reward for his services to the Tory administration. Swift had hoped for better preferment — for a bishopric, and preferably a bishopric in England. However, he had made powerful enemies in the church and at court. A bishop he was never to be. And so it was to his deanery in Dublin that he returned after the great political reversal. The final period of his career can be thought of as from this point down to his death. He was utterly withdrawn at first, but by 1720 he had emerged from seclusion, roused to activity by the deplorable conditions throughout Ireland. He showered the country with his economic pamphlets, and through his series of *Drapier's Letters* he defeated the scheme of the English government for providing the hapless Irish with an overly plentiful supply of copper halfpence. Swift had become the Patriot Dean, Ireland's foremost public figure. Such he remained until, towards his seventieth year, his health began to fail visibly. His final years were ones of total incapacity resulting from a paralytic stroke, but to say, as so many have, that he died insane does not accord with the true facts.

There are many Swifts that we come to know, and all of them are provocative figures. There is Swift the man, beloved by his friends, hated and reviled by his enemies — a figure who has often been discerned against a background of strange shadows. Was there some mystery about his parentage? Apparently not, but there are those who still press the question. What were his relations with Stella? She and a companion, a Mrs. Dingley, had come to Ireland shortly after Temple's death. Swift was constantly in their company. Were he and Stella secretly married some time in 1716, as rumor had it? If they were, it is a fact that has never been established. And what part did Vanessa — otherwise Esther Vanhomrigh — play in all this? Swift had come to know her in London. Against his protests she had followed him to Ireland. Her passion for him is fully revealed in the letters she wrote him. But Swift? And Stella? To such questions we do not have the answers.

And we turn to Swift the public figure, to Swift the unexcelled publicist, to Swift the churchman, to Swift the verse writer (an authoritative minor poet, we now know), to Swift the greatest of all English satirists. *A Tale of a Tub, A Modest Proposal, Gulliver's Travels* have endured through all the climates of opinion which have come and gone since Swift wrote. There is infinite wit here — wit in the sense of comic energy and ceaseless imaginative ingenuity. But we are made to feel the passion that informs this wit, and it is the passion that we remember. Against all history, Swift asserted the integrity of the intellect and the dignity of the human spirit.

SWINBURNE, Algernon Charles (Apr. 5, 1837 – Apr. 10, 1909). English poet and critic. Born London; of old, distinguished family. Educated at home and at Eton (1849–53). While at Balliol College, Oxford (1856–59), met Burne-Jones, Morris, and Rossetti, and thus became associated with Pre-Raphaelites. Left Oxford without a degree and settled in London (1860). Published two blank-verse plays, *The Queen Mother* and *Rosamond* (1860), which attracted little attention; but *Atalanta in Calydon* (1865), a verse drama with choruses ("When the hounds of spring are on winter's traces") made him famous, and is considered his masterpiece. *Poems and Ballads* (1866) followed, containing *Laus Veneris, Dolores, The Garden of Proserpine,* and other sensual, pagan poems that incurred moral outrage. Swinburne expressed his enthusiasm for the republican ideals of Mazzini in *A Song of Italy* (1867) and *Songs Before Sunrise* (1871). Also wrote in same vein *Ode on the Proclamation of the French Republic* (1871). A second series of *Poems and Ballads* (1878) contained soberer poems, including *Ave atque Vale* for Baudelaire and *A Forsaken Garden.* Dissipation and self-neglect brought him near death (1879); he was rescued by his friend Theodore Watts-Dunton, who took him to his home in Putney. Swinburne was restored to health and spent the rest of his life there. His late poetical works include *Tristram of Lyonesse* (1882) and *A Tale of Balen.* As a critic Swinburne tended toward extreme opinions, wrote studies of the Elizabethans, William Blake, the Brontës, Dickens, and Victor Hugo.

EDITIONS: *Complete Works* ed. Sir Edmund Gosse and T. J. Wise (1925–27, reprinted 20 vols. New York 1968). *Letters* ed. C. Y. Lang (6 vols. New Haven, Conn. and Oxford 1959–62).

REFERENCES: Samuel C. Chew *Swinburne* (1929, reprinted Hamden, Conn. 1966). Thomas E. Connolly *Swinburne's Theory of Poetry* (Albany, N.Y. 1965). Jean Overton Fuller *Swinburne: A Critical Study* (London 1968). Sir Edmund Gosse *The Life of Algernon Charles Swinburne* (London and New York 1917). Humphrey Hare *Swinburne: A Biographical Approach* (London 1949). Clyde K. Hyder *Swinburne's Literary Career and Fame* (1933, reprinted New York 1963). Georges Lafourcade *Le Jeunesse de Swinburne* (2 vols. London and New York 1928) and *Swinburne: A Literary Biography* (1932, reprinted New York 1967). Harold Nicolson *Swinburne* (1926, reprinted Hamden, Conn. 1969). Robert L. Peters *The Crowns of Apollo: Swinburne's Principles of Literature and Art* (Detroit 1965). T. Earle Welby *A Study of Swinburne* (1926, reprinted Port Washington, N.Y. 1968).

☞

ALGERNON CHARLES SWINBURNE
BY MARTIN SEYMOUR-SMITH

Many readers born after 1900 can dispense with Swinburne. But he still pleases scholars and those who appreciate prosodic mastery, for his best poems still seem unique in this particular brand of musicality. Attempts to rehabilitate him are rarely heeded, but some kind of modified revival seems eventually inevitable. The difficulty in the way of a complete rehabilitation is that Swinburne's thinking never rose above that of a singularly gifted, overgrown Eton schoolboy, which is what he most resembled throughout his long life; for the last thirty years of it he found peace in submitting himself to the will of a commonplace but ferocious prefect, whose disguise as an admirer was only superficial.

It cannot be claimed that Swinburne's perpetual unripeness was altogether due to a bizarre appearance or a nervous temperament: these were in themselves not only the result of physical accident but also of an arrested constitution. The "tangled mass of red hair almost at right angles" — "unmistakable, unpoetical carrots" — the "excess of electric vitality" that caused him to flutter his hands and to scream when roused, the seriously held military ambitions — all these, if not the chinlessness and dead whiteness of skin, could have been controlled and modified. Instead they combined to produce an image of extreme ridiculousness. Thus, when he thought himself in love with Jane Faulkner, "Divine Boo," his proposal of marriage was so inappropriately melodramatic that the startled girl burst out into laughter. And *The Triumph of Time*, the poem into which he supposed himself to be pouring his grief, is as jejune as the behavior that inspired it.

At Eton, whose jealously preserved flogging traditions formed his sadomasochistic impulses into a drearily normal English Flagellation Complex ("Swish, swish, swish! O I wish, I wish I'd not been late for lock-up last night"), Swinburne was excellent at languages and at writing Greek and Latin verses. He paid for his literary precocity by, in one important sense, never growing up. Thus he could distort Blake, in a study written at thirty-one, into a crude apostle of art for art's sake in rather the same manner as he (then more naturally) distorted the subtleties of Middleton and Tourneur into mere feasts of horror at thirteen.

By the time he left Oxford without a degree in 1860, Swinburne had made friends of Benjamin Jowett and the Pre-Raphaelites. But no one could stabilize him. He even managed to disturb the tenor of life at Rossetti's house in Cheyne Walk, "part Bohemian doss-house and part zoo," by indulging in nude corybantic exercises, screaming, sliding naked down the banisters, becoming suddenly prostrate after small doses of alcohol, and quarreling violently with George Meredith.

His fervid republicanism and lifelong reverence for a triumvirate consisting of Landor, Mazzini and Hugo are not more intellectually significant than *The Whippingham Papers* or the engaging picture of him at Étretat in the autumn of 1868 that Maupassant has given us: the tree-lined drive leading to the farmhouse in which he stayed with his friend George Powell was called Avenue de Sade; bones and a mummified hand littered the tables; among other properties was "a life-size photograph of a soldier masturbating against a sheet of glass." But Swinburne's sense of justice and passion for freedom, although not distinguished by intellectual content, were sincere; some of his political poetry can still move.

Until 1877 Swinburne's father, a more sensible admiral than his son was drinker, continually rescued him, by snatching him away from London for recuperation in the country at the point when each of his bouts began to develop into crisis. When he died Swinburne slipped into a less interrupted decline. Had Theodore Watts (later Watts-Dunton) not kidnapped him and carried him off to a life of respectability at No. 2 The Pines, Putney, in 1879, he would not have recovered.

Behind his "clotted moustache" (a sinister triangular object that entirely hid his lips) and effacing manner, Watts possessed a will of steel. He did not long have to hide Swinburne's boots to prevent his issuing forth in search of brandy, causing him to cry, "O God, if there is a God, which there isn't, where are my damned boots?"; he had the now rapidly deafening sinner morally restored within a year, as a "nature poet" of decidedly less distinction than before. As a solicitor should, Watts did well out of the deal both in prestige and (after Swinburne's death) cash.

Swinburne's reputation was out of proportion to his intellectual but not to his technical merits. True, the once much-vaunted technique of most of the better-known poems eschews rhythmical subtlety; the organ-grinding master of the metrics of these can be praised only at a high pedagogical level: it is ultimately no more than a reflection of a consistently adolescent response to experience. But even here he cannot be entirely dismissed, for there is an emotional validity in his vast and overflowing energy that the most skeptical of readers must admire. Moreover, in certain less well-known poems, as well as in the famous *Atalanta in Calydon,* he achieves subtle variations of rhythm. The impressive *Hertha,* a long poem in which Swinburne came as near as he ever did to expressing thought in his poetry, is almost a major success.

Swinburne does, on the biographical

level, inspire pity: his sense of isolation in the late 1870's is truly tragic. He had a sweet helplessness. His enthusiasm for poetry, in a world bitterly hostile to it, was noble and has exercised a benign influence. His fiction — notably *Love's Cross Currents* — is wittily written. He is not always a reliable critic, but his pioneer work on behalf of the Elizabethan dramatists was salutary, and did much to bring them back into favor.

Finally, he had the potentialities of a good satirist. He was always an excellent parodist of his own excesses. Such early, Drydenesque lines as those on J. A. Froude,

> *First in manure of hot religion*
>   *hatched,*
> *And fattening on the titbits that*
>   *he snatched . . .*
> *The hybrid, fit for neither man*
>   *nor priest,*
> *Stalked into light, a ruminative*
>   *beast*

suggest that had he been able to direct all or most of his energy into the channel of satire, he might have sublimated much of the sexual immaturity that ruins lyrical poems such as *Dolores.* There is an intuitive intelligence and dignity here. He might in this way have achieved the intellectual and emotional authority that his readers, always sympathetic to him, have to regret he usually did not possess.

SYMONDS, John Addington (Oct. 5, 1840 – Apr. 19, 1893). English poet, biographer, historian. Born Bristol, son of a distinguished physician. Educated at Harrow and Oxford, where he became a fellow of Magdalen College (1862). After winning chancellor's prize for an English essay on the Renaissance (1863), his health collapsed and he traveled to Italy and Switzerland for rest. Married Janet North (1864) and devoted himself to literature. Settled at Davos-Platz, Switzerland (1877), where he worked until his death. His writings, largely concerned with the Renaissance, include *The Renaissance in Italy* (7 vols. 1875–86), his chief work; *An Introduction to the Study of Dante* (1872); biographies of Sir Philip Sidney (1886), Ben Jonson (1886), and Michelangelo (2 vols. 1892); translations of the *Sonnets of Michelangelo and Campanella* (1878) and the *Autobiography of Benvenuto Cellini* (2 vols. 1887). He also wrote travel books, including *Sketches in Italy and Greece* (1874) and *Italian Byways* (1883); literary essays, such as *Studies of the Greek Poets* (1873–76); a study of Walt Whitman (1893); and books of verse, best represented by *Many Moods* (1878) and *New and Old* (1880). He died in Rome, while visiting the city with his daughter, and is buried there in the Protestant cemetery.

EDITION: *The Letters of John Addington Symonds* ed. Herbert M. Schueller and Robert L. Peters (3 vols. Detroit 1967–   ).

REFERENCES: Van Wyck Brooks *John Addington Symonds: A Biographical Study* (New York and London 1914). Phyllis Grosskurth *John Addington Symonds: A Biography* (London 1964; published New York 1965 under the title *The Woeful Victorian: A Biography of John Addington Symonds*). Margaret Symonds *Out of the Past* (London 1925).

———

SYMONS, Arthur (Feb. 28, 1865 – Jan. 22, 1945). English poet and critic. Born Milford Haven, Wales, son of a Methodist minister; educated at private schools. At twenty-one he published his first work, *An Introduction to the Study of Browning* (1886), and followed it with a collection of poems, *Days and Nights* (1889), both of which received praise from Walter Pater. A frequent visitor to France, he was influenced by Baudelaire, Verlaine, and Mallarmé, and soon became a leading authority on French literature, and the symbolist movement in particular. Translating French authors, writing poetry (*Silhouettes*, 1892; *London Nights*, 1895) and critical articles, he

became influential in the literary scene of the 1890's. Served on staff of the *Athenaeum* (1891) and *Saturday Review* (1894). Finally became editor of the *Savoy* and produced his famous study *The Symbolist Movement in Literature* (1899). Married Rhoda Bowser (1901; she died 1936). While visiting Bologna, Italy (1908), he suffered the last of a series of nervous breakdowns, and spent two years in Italian and English sanitariums. He almost died from a severe attack of pneumonia (1909), but recovered and regained his sanity as well. Afterwards, he retired from editing and literary circles, settled in a house on the sea at Wittersham and continued writing critical studies such as *Charles Baudelaire* (1921), *A Study of Thomas Hardy* (1927), and reminiscences of the 1890's until his death.

EDITION: *Collected Works* (9 vols. London 1924).

REFERENCES: Roger Lhombreaud *Arthur Symons: A Critical Biography* (London 1963 and Philadelphia 1964). John M. Munro *Arthur Symons* (New York 1969).

———

SYNGE, John Millington (Apr. 16, 1871 – Mar. 24, 1909). Irish playwright. Born near Dublin to middle-class Protestant parents. Educated at Trinity College, Dublin (B.A. 1892), he studied music in Germany, then moved to Paris (1895) to study literary criticism. There he met Yeats (1896), who encouraged him to leave Paris for the Aran Islands and write about Irish peasant life. Made the first (1898) of five annual visits to the islands, immersing himself in the life his plays depict. They appeared in rapid succession: *The Shadow of the Glen* (1903), *Riders to the Sea* (1904), *The Well of the Saints* (1905), and *The Playboy of the Western World* (1907). Two of his plays were produced posthumously: *The Tinker's Wedding* (written 1902, performed 1909) and the unfinished *Deirdre of the Sorrows*, which he wrote on his deathbed (performed 1910). A director of the Abbey Theatre along with Yeats and Lady Gregory, Synge was a leading figure in the Irish literary revival. Also produced poems, translations of Petrarch, and the descriptive essays, *The Aran Islands* (1907), *In*

Wicklow, West Kerry and Connemara (1911). He died of Hodgkin's disease in Dublin.

EDITIONS: *Collected Works* ed. Robin Skelton (4 vols. London 1962–68). *The Aran Islands* with drawings by Jack B. Yeats (Dublin 1907 and Boston 1911). *The Aran Islands and Other Writings* ed. Robert Tracy (New York PB 1962).

REFERENCES: Francis Bickley *J. M. Synge and the Irish Dramatic Movement* (1912, reprinted New York 1968). Maurice Bourgeois *John Millington Synge and the Irish Theatre* (1913, reprinted New York 1965). Daniel Corkery *Synge and Anglo-Irish Literature* (1931, reprinted New York 1965). David H. Greene and Edward M. Stephens *J. M. Synge, 1871–1909* (New York 1959, also PB). Denis Johnston *John Millington Synge* (New York 1965). Alan Price *Synge and Anglo-Irish Drama* (London 1961 and Chester Springs, Pa. 1964). William Butler Yeats *Autobiography* (new ed. New York 1953 and London 1955, PB 1966) and *Synge and the Ireland of His Time* (Churchtown, Ireland, 1911).

JOHN MILLINGTON SYNGE
BY JOHN L. SWEENEY

"That enquiring man John Synge," as William Butler Yeats described him, was born in Rathfarnham near the city of Dublin on April 16, 1871. His father died when Synge was one year old. He and the four elder children were brought up by their mother in comfortable but not affluent circumstances. The source of their income was a small estate in County Galway, so the family was of the landed gentry in its own right as well as by descent and connections. Nevertheless, the ambience of Synge's upbringing was middle-class, suburban, and fervently Protestant.

During his childhood Synge had delicate health and attended school so briefly and intermittently that most of his early education was received from private tutors at home. The suburb in which he grew up is on the outskirts of Dublin near the hills which ring the city to the south. It is probable that his walks in these hills led him to his love of the natural scene. While still in his teens he became a naturalist, interested in insects and birds and a reader of Darwin and Charles Waterton.

Music was another early interest. Indeed it was his chief interest by the time he entered Trinity College in 1889. He also took to reading about Irish antiquities and studied Irish and Hebrew. In the summer of 1893, a half-year after his graduation, he set out for Germany to continue his musical studies. A year later he abandoned the idea of a musical career and in 1895 went to Paris to study at the Sorbonne. He had already written some verses and essays and was thinking of becoming a literary critic.

In Paris, in December 1896, Synge came to a happy turning point in his life through meeting W. B. Yeats. Yeats thought that the poems and essays which Synge showed him were lifeless and full of morbidity, but when he heard of Synge's wandering with his fiddle and of his studying Irish at college he gave the famous advice: "Go to the Aran Islands. Live there as if you were one of the people themselves; express a life that has never found expression."

David Greene, in the excellent Greene and Stephens biography, says that "Synge's visit to the Aran Islands in 1898 must be one of the most remarkable examples on record of how a sudden immersion in a new environment converted a man of ostensibly mediocre talent, a complete failure, in fact, into a writer of genius." Synge set down his response to the new environment in *The Aran Islands*. This masterpiece of attentive and sympathetic observation was completed in 1901 after three of his five annual visits to the islands. Synge had intended to familiarize himself with the speaking of Irish and made progress in that direction but he soon discovered that some of the islanders were bilingual. The slow, melodic, measured English into which they translated their thoughts was rich in Irish idiom and cadence. It came to Synge's ear as a revelation and became the language of his literature.

After Aran, Synge visited with West Kerry peasants and walked in the Wicklow hills and glens, his eye and ear always alert to the life and language of peasants and vagrants. His regional writings (*In Wicklow, West Kerry and Connemara*) candidly disclose the stream which his imagination tapped. These pieces about places and people stand with *The Aran Islands* and *The Playboy of the Western World* as firm evidence of Synge's genius.

Equipped with a fresh and vigorous idiom and with themes suggested by stories he had heard or read, and with the Irish theatre hungering for new plays, Synge began his brief but productive period as a dramatist. Between the years 1902 and 1909 four of his plays were produced in Dublin. A fifth, *The Tinker's Wedding,* was published but not performed during his lifetime, and a sixth, *Deirdre of the Sorrows,* was left unfinished. The first of his plays to be performed, *The Shadow of the Glen,* brought Synge into conflict with Irish nationalists, but his *Riders to the Sea* received general approval. Neither play is truly dramatic, but each has atmosphere and memorable language. *The Tinker's Wedding* and *The Well of the Saints* are slight entertainments. Their small strength is in language rather than in character or plot.

Synge's theatrical masterpiece, *The Playboy of the Western World,* was based on a happening he had heard of during a visit to the Aran Islands. The riots which interrupted the opening in January 1907 can be understood if it is remembered that the play was first produced at the Abbey Theatre during a time of intense nationalist feeling in Ireland. The inciters of the riots, blind to the play's lighthearted comicality, read into it an indictment of the Irish peasantry as approvers of parricide. However, resentment gradually subsided and *The Playboy* became one of the most admired pieces in the repertoire of the Abbey Theatre.

In the summer of 1906 Synge fell in love with twenty-year-old Molly Allgood, an actress of the Abbey company who under her stage name Maire O'Neill was to be the first Pegeen Mike in *The Playboy.* This love was compounded for him of ecstasy and anguish: she was young, lighthearted, courted by others; he was in failing health and aware of the imminence of death. His last play, *Deirdre of the Sorrows,* is entirely a play of love, the fear of love's ending, the horror of physical decline, and the safety of the grave as love's only surety. It is a poignant document, differing from his other plays in mood and setting. Synge died on March 24, 1909, leaving the play unfinished, but a year later it was produced with Molly in the title role. The last words which his Deirdre speaks are in striking contrast to Pegeen Mike's lament at the close of *The Playboy.* Deirdre dies asserting that her story "will be a joy and triumph to the ends of life and time." In terms of art these words are true also of the story of Pegeen Mike and her Playboy and of their creator, who gave to drama "the rich joy found only in what is superb and wild in reality."

TACITUS, Cornelius (c. A.D. 57 – c.117). Roman historian. Birthplace and parentage unknown. Married daughter of governor of Britain, Julius Agricola (78). Began distinguished political career in Rome, serving as praetor (88), as consul (97–98), and as proconsul of Asia (112–113). His first monograph, *Dialogue on Oratory* (c.80), was followed by the eloquent eulogy on his father-in-law, *Agricola* (98), and *Germania,* an account of the various tribes of Germany. His major works (which survive incomplete) are the *Histories* and the *Annals,* detailed accounts of the Roman emperors and their reigns. The *Histories* cover the years 69–96, the *Annals* (written later) the preceding period from the death of Augustus. Of the original probably twelve to fourteen books of the *Histories,* four books and part of a fifth survive, covering the reign of Galba and beginning of the reign of Vespasian. Of the *Annals* the surviving books deal with Tiberius, Claudius's last years, Nero's first years. A meticulous observer of Roman life, Tacitus aimed to write *sine ira et studio* (without passion or partisanship), but his sense of the tragedy of human ambition, of the degeneration of his age, and awareness of the horrors of Domitian's reign are felt throughout his narrative. As a stylist he rebelled against the rotund elegance of Cicero, and based his style on that of his predecessor, the historian Sallust. Tacitus's style is his own, however — rugged, uneven, full of archaic and poetic words, studded with epigrams, brilliantly mordant character studies, and his own moral observations. He is considered by many Rome's greatest historian.

TRANSLATIONS: *Complete Works of Tacitus* tr. A. J. Church and W. J. Brodribb (New York 1942). *The Annals of Imperial Rome* tr. Michael Grant (Harmondsworth, England, and Baltimore PB 1956). *The Histories* tr. Kenneth Wellesley (Harmondsworth, England, and Baltimore PB 1964).

REFERENCES: Donald Dudley *The World of Tacitus* (London and Boston 1968). Clarence W. Mendell *Tacitus: The Man and His Work* (New Haven, Conn. 1957 and Oxford 1958). Sir Ronald Syme *Tacitus* (2 vols. Oxford 1958). Bessie Walker *The Annals of Tacitus* (New York 1952 and 2nd ed. Manchester, England, 1960).

TAINE, Hippolyte Adolphe (Apr. 21, 1828 – Mar. 5, 1893). French critic, philosopher, historian. Born Vouziers, Ardennes, son of an attorney. Educated in Paris at the Collège Bourbon and École Normale Supérieure. Appointed instructor at University of Nevers (1851–52), he resigned because of political differences, and devoted himself to literature. Achieved recognition with publication of *Essai sur les fables de La Fontaine* (1853, revised 1860), and won prize from the French Academy for his *Essai sur Tite-Live* (1854). First expressed his deterministic theories on effect of heredity and environment on man in preface to his well-known *Histoire de la littérature anglaise* (4 vols. 1863–64). While serving as professor of aesthetics and history of art at École des Beaux Arts, Paris (1864–84), he further developed his determinism, which strongly influenced the theories of the naturalist school, in his major philosophical and psychological work, *De l'Intelligence*

(1870), and in several other philosophical studies. Married Mademoiselle Danuelle (1868), daughter of noted architect. Profoundly affected by France's defeat in the Franco-Prussian War (1870–71), he devoted the rest of his life to tracing the causes of France's political instability and even resigned his academic post to this end. The result was his great historical work *Les Origines de la France contemporaine* (6 vols. 1876–94). Elected to the French Academy (1878), he died in Paris before completing his work. Antiromantic and coldly rational, Taine embodied the late nineteenth century's ideal of scientific objectivity, and strongly influenced the study of philosophy, aesthetics, and literary criticism.

TRANSLATIONS: *On Intelligence* tr. T. D. Haye (London and New York 1871). *The Origins of Contemporary France* tr. John Durand (1876–94, new ed. 6 vols. New York 1931). *History of English Literature* tr. H. Van Laun (1883, reprinted 4 vols. New York 1965). *Notes on England* tr. Edward Hyams (London 1957 and Fair Lawn, N.J. 1958).

REFERENCES: François Aulard *Taine, historien de la révolution française* (Paris 1907). André Chevrillon *Taine: formation de sa pensée* (Paris 1932). André Cresson *Hippolyte Taine: sa vie, son oeuvre* (Paris 1951). Alvin A. Eustis *Hippolyte Taine and the Classical Genius* (Berkeley, Calif. 1951). S. J. Kahn *Science and Aesthetic Judgment: A Study in Taine's Critical Method* (London and New York 1953).

TALLIS (or TALLYS), Thomas (c.1505 – Nov. 23, 1585). English organist and composer. Probably a native of Leicestershire; held posts at Dover Priory, then at Waltham Abbey, Essex, until 1540. Made gentleman of the Chapel Royal (1542), later sharing post of organist with William Byrd. His sixteen motets with Byrd's eighteen appeared in *Cantiones Sacrae* (1575). Tallis's other works include a four-part *Magnificat,* numerous settings for Anglican services such as *Venite exultemus* and *Te Deum,* as well as anthems and hymn tunes; he has been called the father of English cathedral music. One of the first to compose settings for Eng-

lish liturgy, he also wrote secular music. He died in Greenwich.

EDITION: *Complete Keyboard Music* ed. Denis Stevens (New York 1953).
REFERENCE: Paul Doe *Tallis* (Oxford 1968).

TARKINGTON, (Newton) Booth (July 29, 1869 – May 19, 1946). American novelist and playwright. Born and died in Indianapolis. Son of prominent lawyer and friend of writer James Whitcomb Riley, who encouraged his early writing attempts. Educated at Phillips Exeter Academy, Purdue University (1890–91) and Princeton (1891–93), then returned to Indianapolis to write full-time. Won great popularity with his first novels *The Gentleman from Indiana* (1899) and *Monsieur Beaucaire* (1900). Lived briefly in New York (1900–1901), then was Republican member of Indiana legislature (1902–1903), and lived abroad most of 1903–12. Wrote plays almost exclusively (1907–11), many in collaboration with Harry Leon Wilson. After divorce (1911) from Louisa Fletcher (married 1902), he married Susannah Robinson and settled in Indianapolis (1912). His popular novels *Penrod* (1914) and *Seventeen* (1916) are humorous portrayals of boyhood in the Midwest. Received Pulitzer prizes for *The Magnificent Ambersons* (1918) and *Alice Adams* (1921), also novels of Midwestern life and character. *Tweedles* (1923) was his best-known play. Series of eye operations (1928–32) partially restored his failing sight and he continued to write, spending summers in Kennebunkport, Me. Among his other best works are plays *The Man from Home* (1908), *Mister Antonio* (1916), and *Up from Nowhere* (1919), all written with Wilson, and novels *The Conquest of Canaan* (1905), *The Turmoil* (1915), *The Plutocrat* (1927), and *Claire Ambler* (1928). A skillful storyteller, Tarkington portrayed a genteel urban Midwest with perceptive realism, humor, and endearing sentimentality.

REFERENCES: Asa Don Dickinson *Booth Tarkington, a Sketch* (Garden City, N.Y. 1926). Robert Holliday *Booth Tarkington* (Garden City, N.Y. 1918). James Woodress *Booth Tarking-*

ton, Gentleman from Indiana (Philadelphia 1955, reprinted New York 1969).

TASSO, Torquato (Mar. 11, 1544 – Apr. 25, 1595). Italian poet. Born Sorrento, son of Bernardo Tasso, poet and author of *L'Amadigi di Gaula.* Spent youth largely at court of Urbino and studied law at University of Padua. At eighteen won renown with his romantic epic in twelve cantos, *Rinaldo* (1562). Entered service and patronage of Cardinal Luigi d'Este (1565), traveling with him to court of Charles IX of France (1570). Moved to court of Luigi's brother, Duke Alfonso of Ferrara (1572), where he wrote the pastoral play *Aminta* (1573) and completed the masterpiece on which his fame rests, *Gerusalemme liberata* (1575, *Jerusalem Delivered*), an epic of the First Crusade, full of romantic, poetical episodes. As a result of friends' criticism of the manuscript, Tasso, whose health was failing and who had been wandering restlessly through northern Italy, began to suffer from persecution mania, requiring his confinement to an asylum (1579–85 and 1587). Still tormented by critical attacks, he rewrote his epic as the rigid *Gerusalemme conquistata* (1593) which succumbed to the strictures of the Counter-Reformation, thereby sacrificing all its lyrical beauty. He returned to Rome (1594), but died before Clement VIII could fulfill his plan to crown him laureate. He also wrote the unsuccessful tragedy *Il Re Torrismondo* (1587), almost two thousand lyrics and religious poems, and over seventeen hundred eloquent letters.

TRANSLATIONS: *Jerusalem Delivered* tr. Edward Fairfax (1600, reprinted Carbondale, Ill. and London 1962). *Aminta* tr. Ernest Grillo (London and New York 1924).

REFERENCES: William Boulting *Tasso and His Times* (1907, reprinted New York 1968). C. M. Bowra *From Virgil to Milton* (London 1945 and New York 1946). Charles P. Brand *Torquato Tasso: A Study of the Poet and His Contribution to English Literature* (Cambridge, England, and New York 1965). Mario Praz *The Flaming Heart* (New York 1958).

TAYLOR, Edward (c.1642 – June 24, 1729). American poet and Puritan teacher. Born near Coventry, Leicestershire, England, son of yeoman farmer. Childhood familiarity with farming and weaving became basis for imagery of much of his adult writing. His nonconformist religion caused difficulty in finding suitable employment during reign of Charles II, so he left teaching post at Bagworth and emigrated to Massachusetts Bay Colony (1668), with letters of introduction to Increase Mather and John Hull. Gained immediate admission to Harvard (matriculated 1671) and became close friend of Mather family and Samuel Sewall, his college roommate, later the famous jurist. Accepted pastorship of Congregational Church, Westfield, Mass. (1671), where he remained until his death. Married Elizabeth Fitch (1674) and after her death (1689) Ruth Wyllys (1692). His manuscripts of original poetry and sermons, which he requested not to be published, were kept by his descendants until a great-grandson gave quarto manuscript of *Poetical Works* to Yale Library (1883). Nevertheless, works not edited and published until 1939. Major works: *Preparatory Meditations* (dated 1682–1725), a series of poetic exercises on the sacrament of Communion; *God's Determinations Touching His Elect,* a long allegorical poem on God's purpose. Also left in manuscript a number of miscellaneous verses, a *Metrical History of Christianity,* and a group of sermons, fourteen of which were bound together, titled *Christographia* (written 1701–1703). Taylor is considered a metaphysical poet because of his unusual choice of metaphor which fuses concrete, familiar experience and profound, spiritual insight in his poetry. He is recognized now as perhaps the finest American poet of colonial times.

EDITIONS: *The Poems of Edward Taylor* ed. Donald E. Stanford (New Haven, Conn. 1960, 2nd abridged ed. PB 1963). *The Diary of Edward Taylor* ed. Francis Murphy (Springfield, Mass. 1964). *Christographia* (New Haven, Conn. 1962) and *Treatise Concerning the Lord's Supper* (East Lansing, Mich. 1966), both edited by Norman S. Grabo.

REFERENCES: Darrel Abel *American Literature: Colonial and Early National Writing* (Great Neck, N.Y. 1963). Norman S. Grabo *Edward Taylor* (New York 1961). Harold S. Jantz *The First Century of New England Verse* (1944, reprinted New York 1962). Kenneth B. Murdock *Literature and Theology in Colonial New England* (Cambridge, Mass. 1944).

TCHAIKOVSKY, Pëtr Ilich (May 7, 1840 – Nov. 6, 1893). Russian composer. Born Kamsko-Votinsk, district of Viatka. His father, a mine inspector, had no interest in music. Family moved to St. Petersburg (1850), where Tchaikovsky studied music and attended School of Jurisprudence until 1859. From 1861, having studied piano, he worked on theory with Nikolai Zaremba. Was influenced by Anton Rubinstein. Graduated from St. Petersburg Conservatory (1865) and became professor of harmony at new Moscow Conservatory (1866–78). His marriage (1877) was a disastrous failure and broke up after nine weeks. At that time he began correspondence with Nadezhda von Meck, who became his confidante and benefactor. Produced with little success the opera *The Voyevoda* (1869), then the orchestral piece *Romeo and Juliet* (1870), which is still popular. Began travels through western Europe; visited U.S. (1891); in England received honorary degree from Cambridge University (1893). Died of cholera in St. Petersburg. His other major works include *Marche slave* (1876), *Fourth Symphony* (1878), the operas *Eugene Onegin* (1879) and *The Queen of Spades* (1890), a violin concerto, two piano concertos, *1812 Overture* (1880), *Fifth Symphony* (1888), the ballets *Swan Lake* (1877), *The Sleeping Beauty* (1890), and *The Nutcracker* (1892), the *Sixth Symphony* (*Pathétique*) (1893). Though strongly Russian in his style, he was not one of The Five with Mussorgsky. He incorporated Russian elements into a romantic rather than nationalist style. His remarkable gift for melody influenced Rachmaninoff and such American composers as MacDowell.

REFERENCES: Gerald Abraham *Tchaikovsky: A Short Biography* (London 1945) and ed. *The Music of Tchaikovsky* (1946, reprinted Port Washington, N.Y. 1969). Edwin Evans *Tchaikovsky* (1906, rev. ed. New York and London 1966, also PB). John Gee and Elliot Selby *The Triumph of Tchaikovsky* (London 1959 and New York 1960). Lawrence and Elisabeth Hanson *Tchaikovsky: The Man Behind the Music* (London 1965 and New York 1966). Peter Tchaikovsky *Diaries* (tr. New York 1945). Herbert Weinstock *Tchaikovsky* (New York 1943 and London 1946).

✍

PËTR ILICH TCHAIKOVSKY
BY ROBERT GARIS

The first step in understanding serious music has often taken the form of an adolescent infatuation with Tchaikovsky, and no one has ever found it hard to understand why this should be so. The grandiose opening of the *First Piano Concerto,* the dramatic contrasts and conflicts of *Romeo and Juliet,* the electric vitality of the march in the *Pathétique,* the seductive melancholy of its finale — the meaning of musical events like these is as accessible as anything in music, and Tchaikovsky's broad themes seem to be what the word "melody" was invented for. But this accessibility has been costly to Tchaikovsky's reputation. For the second step in musical understanding is likely to be a violent, even angry repudiation of what had given so much pleasure before, a reaction unfortunately no harder to account for than the initial appeal.

No music has suffered more from overexposure than Tchaikovsky's, since overexposure has never taken a worse form than the luridly exaggerated style of performance in which this music is usually encountered. The disciplined continence of the performances by Toscanini, Beecham, Cantelli, and a few others faithfully represents Tchaikovsky's intentions and actually increases the intensity of the musical experience; but this correct style is still less frequently heard than the melodramatic explosions and the languishing sentimentalities which are mistaken for the true spirit of Tchaikovsky. Yet even the most tasteful performance might be wasted on young people whose reaction against Tchaikovsky is a by-product of their eager discovery of the classical masters. The greatest utterances of Bach, Mozart, and Beethoven are undeniably loftier and purer than anything in Tchaikovsky, and the musical thinking in Bach's counterpoint, and in Mozart's and Beethoven's sonata and concerto forms, offers a demonstrably greater challenge to the intellect. Moreover, in some of the greatest works of these composers one can make what is perhaps the most exciting discovery in music, the discovery that the most sublime musical meanings can be expressed with the least opulent musical resources. The first flush of enthusiasm for Beethoven's last quartets and sonatas can for a time produce an almost puritanical intolerance of even the best music of lesser composers: even Haydn and Schubert may be temporarily eclipsed by these supreme illuminations. But with Tchaikovsky it is the worst music that is most frequently heard, and the worst music can be very bad indeed. The banality of the *First Piano Concerto* is as unmistakable and as consistent as its popularity, and similar failures of taste occasionally, but very audibly, disfigure almost all of the other familiar works. It is not then surprising that intolerance should light particularly and with vengeance on Tchaikovsky, and that many serious and sincere music lovers should have written him off permanently as a composer whose music it is a sign of musical understanding to detest.

Responsible criticism should try to correct this injustice by carefully disentangling the good Tchaikovsky — which is wonderfully good — from the bad; but responsible criticism is even rarer in music than in the other arts. B. H. Haggin's perceptively discriminating praise has indeed had an important effect, though on a relatively small audience. Stravinsky paid a different kind of tribute by his lovingly scrupulous reworking of Tchaikovsky's melodies in *Le Baiser de la fée*; but this beautiful score is seldom performed and there is evidence that even the most faithful of Stravinsky's admirers and disciples discount his love for Tchaikovsky as an eccentricity of genius, if not even as an amusing expression of nationalist sentiment. Balanchine, another great artist devoted to Tchaikovsky, is also Russian by birth and therefore might be suspected of musical nationalism; besides, Balanchine is a choreographer, and no one has ever bothered to deny that Tchaikovsky wrote the world's best ballet music.

But in the 1950's there began to occur an enormously increased attention to and respect for the classical ballet; and this development, valuable in itself, may gradually bring about a re-evaluation of Tchaikovsky. When you listen to the music of *Swan Lake, The Sleeping Beauty,* or *The Nutcracker* in the theatre, thoughts of Beethoven's chamber music do not arise to confuse the issue; you are ready and willing to indulge yourself with the familiar charms; and if you are seriously interested in music you will then be receptive to Tchaikovsky's transmutation of charm, romance, and grace into high art. You will discover that the delightful Bluebird *pas de deux* in *The Sleeping Beauty* is danced to an exquisitely wrought little orchestral suite in which you cannot decide which element to admire most: the enchanting spontaniety of the musical ideas, the elegance and depth of the technique, or the instinct for musical order that shapes the four little sections into an inspired unity. The composer you may have repudiated as the very archetype of vulgarity and banality turns out to be master of a refined musical workmanship worthy of comparison with the best of Bach's suites. Actually the comparison is more dangerous to Bach than to Tchaikovsky; for in the three full-length ballets there is hardly a trace of the mechanical music-making with which Bach often keeps things jogging along when inspiration has flagged.

Having discovered the distinction of the ballet music, serious music lovers will be ready to enjoy some of the rest of Tchaikovsky's output, though they may express their pleasure in amusingly naive, almost shamefaced terms: one has often enough heard that the second movement of the *Pathétique* sounds so much like ballet music that Balanchine ought to do something with it. And Balanchine has, in fact, used several Tchaikovsky scores not originally intended for the ballet: *Serenade*, for instance, is set to the *Serenade in C for Strings*, op. 48, and *Ballet Imperial* and *Allegro Brillante* offer rare chances to hear the oddly neglected and very beautiful second and (uncompleted) third piano concertos. In choosing the *Third Symphony* for the "Diamonds" section in *Jewels*, Balanchine's musicianship rightly told him to omit the long first movement, for its structure demands a close and purely musical attention which makes it unsuitable for the ballet. But even with Tchaikovsky's most complex structures those who have come to love him at the ballet will enjoy a special advantage. Con-

sider the second subject of the first movement of the *Fourth Symphony*: the melodies in the woodwinds and strings share the mondaine elegance and grace of the ballet music, and listeners used to hearing Beethoven in the concert hall may be put off by a hint of the salon in this musical language. But those who have been educated at the ballet will be able to recognize not only the distinguished taste with which Tchaikovsky is using his characteristic musical vocabulary, but also the highly original powers of musical construction with which he is shaping these delightful melodies into a magnificently sustained and cumulative power and tension.

TELEMANN, Georg Philipp (Mar. 14, 1681 – June 25, 1767). German composer. Born Magdeburg. Largely self-taught as a musician. Entered University of Leipzig (1701) to study law, but devoted himself to music, founding student society Collegium Musicum and writing several operas for Leipzig Theatre. Organist at the Neukirche (1704), he became kapellmeister to Count Promnitz at Sorau (1704) and konzertmeister at court of Eisenach (1708), where he became friends with J. S. Bach and stood godfather to Carl Philipp Emanuel Bach. After some years as musical director at Frankfurt-am-Main, settled in Hamburg (1721), where he was cantor of the Johanneum and musikdirektor of the city until his death. A sojourn to Paris (1738–39), where he studied with Lully, inspired him with French musical ideas and style. Twice married, he had ten children; one grandson, Georg Michael Telemann (1748–1831), also became a musician. An extraordinarily versatile and prolific composer, Telemann could write in any desired style. His works include about forty operas, for Hamburg, Leipzig, and Weissenfels; church music, including twelve services for the church year, forty-four Passions, twelve funeral and fourteen wedding services; over six hundred overtures in the French style; chamber music; also cantatas, odes, and oratorios. Died in Hamburg. Although more prominent in his day than Bach, Telemann has only recently been "rediscovered."

TENIERS, David, the Younger (Dec. 14, 1610 – Apr. 25, 1690). Flemish painter. Born Antwerp, into large family of Flemish painters. Studied under his father, David the Elder. Became master in Antwerp painters' guild (1632–33) and later its dean (1645). Early influenced by Adriaen Brouwer. Painted *The Temptation of St. Anthony* (versions in Musée des Beaux Arts, Antwerp; Staatliche Museen, Berlin; Prado, Madrid) and other religious subjects (1633–36). Married Anna, daughter of Jan Brueghel (1637). Through this alliance came into contact with Rubens's circle. In 1640's painted *The Kitchen* (1644, Mauritshuis, The Hague) and other genre scenes. Also painted procession scenes set against rich, panoramic landscapes, such as *Village Fête* (1643, National Gallery, London) and *The Dance in Front of the Castle* (1645, Buckingham palace, London). Moved to Brussels (1651), where Archduke Leopold Wilhelm made him court painter and keeper of his art collection. Painted *The Picture Gallery of Archduke Leopold Wilhelm* (c.1653, Prado, Madrid) and made many small copies of paintings in the collection, 244 of which were engraved for *Theatrum Pictorium* (1660). Prospered under Leopold and his successors and hired many helpers to meet the demand for his works. Bought De Drie Torens (1662), a country house near Perck, whose towers appear in many of his later landscapes. Chief founder of Antwerp Academy (1665). Other major paintings: *The Guard Room* (1642, Hermitage, Leningrad), *The Marriage of the Artist* (1651, Edmund de Rothschild Collection, London), *Panorama of Valenciennes* (1656, Musée des Beaux Arts, Antwerp). Last years marred by financial and family troubles. Died in Brussels. One of the foremost Flemish genre painters, Teniers's works are marked by a Dutch-influenced love of tone and atmosphere.

REFERENCES: Léon Bocquet *David Téniers* (Paris 1924). Horst Gerson and E. H. ter Kuile *Art and Architec-ture in Belgium, 1600–1800* (Harmondsworth, England, and Baltimore 1960). Sir Paul Lambotte *Flemish Painting Before the Eighteenth Century* (London 1927).

TENNYSON, Alfred (First Baron Tennyson) (Aug. 6, 1809 – Oct. 6, 1892). English poet. Born Somersby, Lincolnshire; one of twelve children born to the rector there. Educated at home and at Louth Grammar School; entered Trinity College, Cambridge (1827), left without degree because of his father's death (1831). At Cambridge won chancellor's gold medal for his poem *Timbuctoo* (1829) and met Arthur Hallam, the close friend whose death (1833) inspired *In Memoriam* (written 1833–50). After publishing *Poems by Two Brothers* (1827) with his older brother Charles, he produced *Poems, Chiefly Lyrical* (1830) and *Poems* (1832). Grieved by Hallam's death, he began writing *In Memoriam*, but discouraged by the *Quarterly Review's* attack on his poetry (1833), he avoided publication of further work until 1842, when *Poems* (2 vols.) appeared and established him as the foremost Victorian poet. He was granted a civil list pension by Prime Minister Sir Robert Peel (1845). *The Princess* appeared in 1847 and *In Memoriam* in 1850. Succeeded Wordsworth as poet laureate (1850) and married Emily Sellwood (1850), his early fiancée. Settled at Farringford, Isle of Wight (1853); published *Maud* (1855), the first four of his twelve *Idylls of the King* (1859), *Enoch Arden* (1864), and *The Holy Grail and Other Poems* (1869). Wrote blank-verse dramas for the stage, among them *Queen Mary* (1875), *Harold* (1876), *Becket* (1884). Later volumes of poetry include *Ballads and Other Poems* (1880), *Tiresias and Other Poems* (1885), *Locksley Hall Sixty Years After* (1886), *Demeter and Other Poems* (1889), and *The Death of Oenone* (1892). Created a peer by Queen Victoria (1884). He died at his summer home near Haslemere, Surrey, and was buried in Westminster Abbey. His oldest son, Hallam (1852–1928), succeeded to the title and compiled the *Memoir* (below).

EDITIONS: *Complete Poetical Works* ed. W. J. Rolfe (Boston 1898). *Works* ed. Hallam, Lord Tennyson (London 9 vols. 1908 and New York 6 vols. 1908, one vol. 1913). *Selected Poetry* ed. D. Bush (New York 1951, also PB). *Poems of Tennyson* ed. Jerome H. Buckley (Boston PB 1958). *The Poems of Tennyson* ed. Christopher Ricks (London 1969), the standard annotated edition.

REFERENCES: A. C. Bradley *A Commentary on Tennyson's In Memoriam* (3rd ed. rev. London 1910). Jerome H. Buckley *Tennyson: The Growth of a Poet* (Cambridge, Mass. and London 1960, also PB). D. Bush *Mythology and the Romantic Tradition in English Poetry* (Cambridge, Mass. 1937, reprinted 1969). E. D. H. Johnson *The Alien Vision of Victorian Poetry* (Princeton 1952). John D. Jump ed. *Tennyson: The Critical Heritage* (London and New York 1967). John Killham ed. *Critical Essays on the Poetry of Tennyson* (London and New York 1960, also PB). Valerie Pitt *Tennyson Laureate* (London 1962, also PB). Sir Charles Tennyson *Alfred Tennyson* (1949, reprinted Hamden, Conn. 1968), the authoritative biography; Hallam, Lord Tennyson, *Alfred Lord Tennyson: A Memoir by His Son* (2 vols. London and New York 1897, reprinted New York 1969). George Watson ed. *The New Cambridge Bibliography of English Literature*, vol. 3 (Cambridge and New York 1969).

🖜

TENNYSON
BY DOUGLAS BUSH

In the later decades of his long life Tennyson's fame was of a kind and degree such as had come to no English poet before him; his unique eminence was crowned by the splendor of his burial in Westminster Abbey. But the earlier and larger portion of his enduring poetry was the work of a lonely, poor, and profoundly melancholy man. A temperamental inheritance of "black blood" was aggravated by both private and external circumstances. The young Alfred and his ten brothers and sisters had all the literary and outdoor pleasures of a self-sufficient family in a rural parsonage; but they lived under the strain created by the growing aberrations and violence of their brooding father, who had been disinherited by his father in favor of a younger son and forced into the church. Even as a boy Alfred could long for death.

In 1827, before he went up to Cambridge, Tennyson and his two poetical brothers got out a volume of poems. Alfred's echoes of Byron and Moore gave few signs of the precocious originality manifested in his juvenile play, *The Devil and the Lady*. The happiest part of his Cambridge life he owed to the Apostles, a group of intellectual undergraduates who were questioning conventional beliefs and ideas. One member, Arthur Hallam, a brilliant Etonian, became a close friend of the shy, unkempt country boy, a "gypsy Apollo," who was the poet of the group. In *Timbuctoo* (1829), a prize poem of unusual significance, Tennyson treated a theme of recent (and continuing) currency: the withering effect of science upon the great vine of "myth" by which man lives. A volume of 1830 included that primitive, massive creation, *The Kraken;* a poem of religious doubt and alienation, *Supposed Confessions;* and *Mariana,* Tennyson's first notable projection of a mental state (here the death wish) through scenic detail. In 1831 his father died and he left Cambridge without a degree, to live chiefly with his mother and sisters as the responsible head of a family of limited means. In the *Poems* of 1832 Tennyson faced a problem that had troubled Keats (and that also continues in our day), the problem of a poet's aesthetic detachment or social involvement. While in *The Poet* he had proclaimed a messianic role, now, in *The Hesperides* and *The Lady of Shalott,* he upheld detachment; *The Lotos-Eaters* might seem ambivalent; *The Palace of Art* achieved a compromise; in *Oenone,* a Theocritean version of *Mariana,* moral wisdom and action were set against the private allurements of beauty.

The always hypersensitive Tennyson was so bruised by some attacks on this volume that he shunned publication until 1842. During this "ten years' silence" he revised earlier poems and in others moved out into contemporary English life. We do not now much relish *Locksley Hall,* but for many young men with a social conscience (such as Charles Kingsley) it had a direct appeal like that of the English social poetry of the 1930's. However, the best poems of the 1842 volumes were occasioned by the most shattering event of Tennyson's life, the sudden death in Vienna of Arthur Hallam, in September 1833. That event affected him as Edward King's death had affected Milton: it crystallized all the prime questions about the meaning of the world and human life. But for Tennyson, in his age, a Christian answer was more difficult. In *The Two Voices* affirmation won a hard struggle against suicidal nihilism; and the two voices had separate expression in *Ulysses* and *Tithonus* (this finished later). Tennyson was almost always superb when he could render personal feeling through a classical mask.

The Princess (1847), a seriocomic medley, attested the poet's interest in the rising challenge of feminism, but for most readers it lives in some lyrics. *Tears, Idle Tears* subtly distills Tennyson's "passion of the past," the sense of time and loss that was a wellspring of his inspiration. He was indeed the supreme lyrist of the century, and during the seventeen years after Hallam's death he was composing the lyrics that eventually formed *In Me-*

moriam. The eddying moods of this spiritual "diary" (T. S. Eliot's word) reveal — to pass by the "lesser faith" in evolutionary progress — a general movement from overpowering grief, through recognition of geological time and change and "Nature, red in tooth and claw," to an ultimate faith in love as the principle of being. Poems and groups are linked by affinity and contrast and by such recurrent images as the clasping of hands; the language and rhythm have a ritualistic quality that undulates through many phases from fear and despair to mystical exaltation.

The year 1850 brought the publication of *In Memoriam,* Tennyson's long delayed marriage to Emily Sellwood, and his appointment as poet laureate in succession to Wordsworth. *Maud* (1855), his "little *Hamlet,*" Tennyson liked much better than many of his readers. Its plot recalled *Locksley Hall* and the old family feud and, it has been lately argued, the poet's attachment (1834–36) to Rosa Baring. The "monodrama" was a technical *tour de force.* The hero's violent railing at society and his lyrical raptures partook of the mid-century's "spasmodic" fashion, but his neurosis is also remarkably modern. And his final embracing of war as salvation is dramatically right, though the author — at the time of the Crimean War and later — was accused of jingoism.

Idylls of the King (1859–88) greatly enlarged Tennyson's popular if not his critical fame. Whatever our response to King Arthur's blend of social action and mystical faith, the negative part of the theme, the waste land of modern civilization, comes through impressively in the spurious religious excitements of *The Holy Grail* and the autumnal decay of *The Last Tournament.* But the *Idylls* as a whole suffer from the uneven significance of the tales, from diffuseness, and from over-refined stylization (which had only begun in the early *Morte d'Arthur*). Yet Tennyson's later years brought forth such poems as *Lucretius, Rizpah, The Ancient Sage*, a "very personal" confession of faith, and *Demeter and Persephone*, the most "mythic" of all his classical idylls. And he wrote historical plays; *Becket* had — just after its author's death — real success on the stage.

Tennyson was probably the century's most conscious and consummate craftsman in language and rhythm; his inlaid texture — along with his feeling for *lacrimae rerum* — has linked him with the Virgil he so nobly praised. Quite early he was linked, by both friends and foes, with Keats; but ornate opulence was only one of his many styles, which ranged from the incantatory magic of *The Hesperides* to the earthy dialect of *The Northern Farmer*. The notion that Tennyson was corrupted by popularity must be heavily discounted; his strengths and weaknesses were in him from the start. If he was not a profound philosophic poet, neither was he simply an artist or a mirror or comforter of his age; with his mind as well as his emotions he lived through a time of spiritual crisis, "the night of fear." Whatever his lapses, a body of great poetry remains.

TERBORCH, Geraert (also called **Gerard ter Borch**) (1617 – Dec. 8, 1681). Dutch painter. Born Zwolle, where he probably studied under his father, himself an artist. Visited Amsterdam (1632) for the first of many times. Studied under landscape painter Pieter de Molijn in Haarlem (1634). Became master of Guild of St. Luke, Haarlem (1635). Visited London (1635). Extensive travels to Rome, Naples, possibly Spain (1636–43). Painted (1640's) series of fine miniatures, including *Helena Van der Schalke as a Child* (c.1644, Rijksmuseum, Amsterdam). Attended peace conference at Münster, Germany (1645–48), where he made portraits of delegation members, the most famous of which is *Count Peñeranda* (c.1646, Museum Boymans–Van Beuningen, Rotterdam). *The Peace of Münster* (1648, National Gallery, London), is a masterly group portrait in Terborch's characteristic elegant, objective style. After living in Amsterdam, The Hague, and Kampen, he finally settled in Deventer (1654), where he married, became a citizen, and held honorary office in the city government. Painted group portrait of Deventer city regents (1667, Stadhuis, Deventer). Among genre pieces — notable for their psychological penetration and delicacy of color and texture — are *Parental Admonition* (c.1654, Staatliche Museen, Berlin), *The Letter* (c.1659, Buckingham palace, London), *The Music Lesson* (c.1675, Cincinnati Art Museum), *The Concert* (c.1675, Staatliche Museen). Died in Deventer. Known chiefly for the genre paintings and portraits in which he specialized, Terborch is ranked as one of the finest Dutch painters of the seventeenth century.

REFERENCES: Eugène Fromentin *The Masters of Past Time: Dutch and Flemish Painting from Van Eyck to Rembrandt* (tr. London and New York 1958). Neil Maclaren *The Dutch School* (London 1960). Jakob Rosenberg, Seymour Slive, and E. H. ter Kuile *Dutch Art and Architecture, 1600 to 1800* (Harmondsworth, England, and Baltimore 1966).

TERENCE (full name **Publius Terentius Afer**) (c.195 – 159 B.C.). Roman playwright. Born Carthage. Brought to Rome as a slave of the senator Terentius Lucanus, who educated and subsequently freed him. Terence's talents soon won him admission to the so-called Scipionic Circle, where former slave mingled on terms of friendship with the social and literary elite of Rome. Between 166 and 160 he wrote six comedies, all of which survive. He died returning from a trip to Greece. Terence's plays — *Andria* (166), *Heautontimoroumenos* (163), *Eunuchus* and *Phormio* (161), *Adelphi* and *Hecyra*

(160) — all derive from Greek New Comedy originals, and though written in Latin, are set in Greece with Greek characters. They are not translations, however; Terence alters freely, often fusing elements from two or more Greek originals to form his own plot. He uses the stock characters of comedy — the ingenious slave, amorous young man, strict father — but portrays them subtly and with a certain sympathy. His stories draw a moral, but seldom insist on it. His language is pure and refined, yet the exuberance of his great predecessor Plautus is lacking. Julius Caesar described his style well when he praised Terence's polish but deplored his lack of *vis comica* (comic force).

TRANSLATIONS: *The Comedies of Terence* tr. Frank O. Copley (Indianapolis 1967, also PB). *The Brothers and Other Plays* tr. Betty Radice (Harmondsworth, England, and Baltimore PB 1965). *Phormio and Other Plays* tr. Betty Radice (Harmondsworth, England, and Baltimore PB 1967).
REFERENCES: William Beare *The Roman Stage* (3rd ed. London and New York 1965, also PB). George E. Duckworth *The Nature of Roman Comedy: A Study in Popular Entertainment* (Princeton, N.J. and Oxford 1952). Gilbert Norwood *The Art of Terence* (Oxford 1923, reprinted New York 1965) and *Plautus and Terence* (1932, reprinted New York 1963).

THACKERAY, William Makepeace (July 18, 1811 – Dec. 23, 1863). English writer. Born Calcutta, India, where his father was collector of revenues. Sent to England (1817), he was educated at Walpole House, Chiswick, and Charterhouse. Entered Trinity College, Cambridge (1829), leaving without a degree (1830) to go abroad. Entered Middle Temple (1831) but abandoned law (1833) for literary career, becoming owner of and Paris correspondent for the short-lived *National Standard* (1833). Upon its failure, studied art, worked for a Paris newspaper, and became correspondent for the unsuccessful *Constitutional* (1836). In Paris married Isabella Shawe (1836), who bore him two daughters before their separation (1840) due to her insanity. Returned to London (1837), contrib-

uted frequently to *Fraser's Magazine, The Times,* and other London publications. Published *The Yellowplush Correspondence* (Fraser's, 1837–38), *Some Passages in the Life of Major Gahagan* (*New Monthly Magazine,* 1837–38). Under the pseudonyms Michael Angelo Titmarsh or George Savage Fitz-Boodle he wrote *A Shabby Genteel Story* (1840), *Paris Sketch Book* (2 vols. 1840), *The Great Hoggarty Diamond* (1841), *The Fitz-Boodle Papers* (1842–43), *The Irish Sketch Book* (1843). Began writing for *Punch* (1842). Among his most famous contributions: *Jeames's Diary* (1845–46), the burlesque *Mr. Punch's Prize Novelists* (1847), and his denunciation of pretentiousness, *The Snobs of England* (1846–47, reprinted as *The Book of Snobs* 1848). His most important novel, *Vanity Fair,* published in installments (1847–48), was followed by the semi-autobiographical *Pendennis* (1850), *The History of Henry Esmond, Esq.* (1852), and *The Newcomes* (1855). Having resigned from *Punch* because of political differences (1851), he began giving lectures to support himself: *The English Humorists of the Eighteenth Century* (1851, published 1853) and *The Four Georges* (1860). The comical fairy tale *The Rose and the Ring* appeared in 1855. Two lecture tours to America (1852, 1855) provided material for the sequel to *Henry Esmond, The Virginians* (1859). Became editor of *Cornhill Magazine* (1860), where his *The Adventures of Philip* appeared (1861–62) before his resignation (1862). He died in London. Thackeray also wrote numerous, often whimsical rhymes and ballads, including *Little Billee.*

EDITION: *Centenary Biographical Edition of the Works of Thackeray* eds. Anne Thackeray Ritchie and Leslie Stephen (26 vols. New York and London 1910–11).
REFERENCES: John W. Dodds *Thackeray: A Critical Portrait* (1941, reprinted New York 1963). Malcolm Elwin *Thackeray, A Personality* (London 1932). Lambert Ennis *Thackeray: The Sentimental Cynic* (Evanston, Ill. 1950). Margaret M. Goodell *Three Satirists of Snobbery* (Hamburg 1939). Gordon N. Ray *The Buried Life: A Study of the Relation Between Thackeray's Fiction*

and his Personal History (Cambridge, Mass. and London 1952), *Thackeray, The Uses of Adversity: 1811–1846* (New York 1955), and *Thackeray, The Age of Wisdom: 1847–1863* (New York 1958). George Saintsbury *A Consideration of Thackeray* (London 1931, reprinted New York 1968). Lionel Stevenson *The Showman of Vanity Fair: The Life of William Makepeace Thackeray* (1947, reprinted New York 1968). M. G. Sundell ed. *Twentieth-Century Interpretations of Vanity Fair* (Englewood Cliffs, N.J. 1969, also PB). Geoffrey Tillotson *Thackeray the Novelist* (Cambridge, England 1954. Reprinted London 1963). Geoffrey Tillotson and Donald Hawes eds. *Thackeray: The Critical Heritage* (London and New York 1968). Anthony Trollope *Thackeray* (1879, new ed. Detroit 1968). James H. Wheatley *Patterns in Thackeray's Fiction* (Cambridge, Mass. 1969).

✍

WILLIAM MAKEPEACE THACKERAY
BY JOHN W. DODDS

Thackeray came late to success as a novelist. He was thirty-seven years old before the publication of *Vanity Fair* in monthly parts in 1847–48 brought him to the crest of literary popularity and he began to hear himself mentioned in the same breath as Dickens. Indeed this was his first major work not written under a nom de plume. His early books and tales had been published under such pseudonyms as Michael Angelo Titmarsh and Major Goliah Gahagan. Before 1847 he had served a long literary apprenticeship as a humorist for *Punch* (for which he had written *The Snob Papers*), a book reviewer for various magazines, and a writer of travel books. He had written, too, such extravagant burlesques and satires as *Mr. Punch's Prize Novelists, Jeames's Diary,* and *The Yellowplush Papers. Barry Lyndon* (1844), by George Fitz-Boodle, had been his most creative work to date — a lively picaresque tale about a depraved rascal

who insists that he has been mistreated by fate.

In his early work, however, can be seen many of the qualities which found a place in his later great novels. Thus his hatred of snobs, his acute perception of life's cruelties and ironies and his clinical awareness of shabby and vulgar motives, his unerring sense of the ludicrous and the grotesque; but at the same time his love of honesty, simplicity, clarity, and good humor. One can even see here his tendency to digress and philosophize in the midst of his narrative, to record his own reaction to the scene he has just described.

The young Thackeray had attended Trinity College, Cambridge, for a year and a half. Never one to unhinge his mind by too much study, he left Cambridge to travel on the Continent. At twenty-one he came into a small fortune, which he rapidly dissipated in gambling. For a time he played with the idea of becoming a painter (he later illustrated many of his own stories) but soon gave up serious art for authorship. His early journalism and his humorous, satiric tales brought him little in the way of acknowledged success — a success he badly needed to support his young wife and his growing family. Domestic tragedy struck early; only a few years after their marriage his wife became insane — eventually to outlive her husband, but never to be cured.

Thackeray was devoted to his two daughters and to his wide circle of friends, but the other side of his genial, affectionate nature was an acute nervous sensibility. However much he socialized (he became quite a clubman) he was always lonely, and thought of himself as the jester who was gloomy behind the comic mask. Hence much of the retrospective wistfulness which runs through his novels. Thackeray's art, however frequent its amiable digressions and however keen its sense of the ridiculous, is always warmed by his affection for gentleness and honesty. It is sharpened, too, by a corollary hatred of selfishness, cruelty, and insincerity. This emerges in his novels in a pervasive irony by which he measures the gap between man's aspirations and his self-deceptions.

All this is seen in *Vanity Fair,* his story of early nineteenth-century upper-middle-class English society, extending over two decades and seen through the careers of two families. It is impregnated with Thackeray's ironic sense of contrast between the real and the apparent, for he knew that rascals often flourish while innocence suffers, and that virtue is frequently dull and rascality lively. Yet it seems strange that Thackeray should have been called "cynical" by some of his contemporaries — he, the creator of Amelia Sedley, over whose quivering sensitivity he spent a good deal of sentimental concern. It is true, nevertheless, that Becky Sharp really dominates the novel, and she is one of the great creations in literature. Unprincipled and cunning, but tolerant and charming and quite unmalicious, she serves as a catalyst to bring out the seaminess of other even less admirable characters. Thackeray couldn't approve of what she stood for, but he obviously had a lingering liking for her — as have many readers since.

Pendennis (1848–50), Thackeray's next major effort, confessedly autobiographical in part, treats the career of a well-meaning and generous but rather spoiled young man. The theme is really the education of Pendennis through a succession of love affairs and under the influence of his worldly uncle, Major Pendennis, until he reaches the haven of marriage. The story is diffuse, and the reader becomes irritated with Pen's stubborn and superficial opportunism, yet the novel is rich in many sustained characterizations.

Henry Esmond (1852), Thackeray's only novel to be written as a whole rather than in monthly parts, is a triumphant tour de force of historical writing, tightly organized. Turning back to the eighteenth century which he so much loved, Thackeray evoked brilliantly the atmosphere of Queen Anne's day. The plan is once again that of the memoir or "history." Esmond himself is quixotic and generous, but was capable, as Thackeray admitted, of being a most unheroic bore. Beatrix, a lesser Becky, is as brilliant as Henry is commonplace.

Thackeray's last great novel was *The Newcomes* (1853–55). Here again he works on a broad canvas, creating a whole fictional society. There is satire here, and a melancholy recognition of human frailty; much of the book is tragic in its implications. But Clive Newcome is more likable than Pendennis, and Clive's cousin Ethel Newcome, whom he finally has the good luck to win, is one of Thackeray's superb creations — a woman intelligent, high-spirited, and warm. Colonel Newcome, perhaps the best-remembered character in the story, belongs with the Don Quixotes, Sir Roger de Coverleys, and Samuel Pickwicks of fiction.

In Thackeray's last novels, *The Virginians* (1857–59) and *Philip* (1861–62), his creative energy was diminished; he seemed to be imitating himself at undue length. He was ill and tired and weary of life.

He died in his fifty-third year, but the fictional world he created is remarkable for its richness, depth, and resonance. The novels are written, too, in a prose style unfailingly felicitous — urbane, meditative at times but racy at other times, seemingly effortless and simple, with a luminous clarity. It is a style both subtle in its rhythms and sinewy — an intensely personal style, with the color of Thackeray's own rich and varied personality.

THOMAS, Dylan (Marlais) (Oct. 27, 1914 – Nov. 9, 1953). Welsh poet and prose writer. Born Swansea, South Wales. Educated at Swansea Grammar School, where his father taught English. Spent long childhood visits at aunt's farm in Llangain, later commemorated in his poem *Fern Hill*. Left school at sixteen and worked as reporter on *South Wales Evening Post* (1931–34). During this time wrote most of the poems in his first volume *18 Poems* (1934). Moved to London (1934), where he continued to write poetry and supported himself by book reviewing. Second volume, *Twenty-five Poems* (1936), established his reputation in England. Married Caitlin Macnamara (1937); they had two children, and lived in Laugharne, Wales. Published *The Map of Love* (1939), a book of poems and surrealistic short stories. American publication of *The World I Breathe* (1939) brought recognition there, augmented by *Portrait of the Artist as a Young Dog* (1940), a series of autobiographical sketches. During World War II moved to London and wrote scenarios for documentary films (1940–44). Worked for B.B.C. as performer, writer, and poetry commentator (1945–50); some of these essays-for-radio are collected in *Quite Early One Morning* (1954). A new tone of acceptance and use of Christian symbolism characterized *Deaths and Entrances* (1946), which includes *A Refusal to Mourn the Death, by Fire, of a Child in London* and *The Hunchback in the Park*. Visited Italy (1947) and Prague (1949). First American tour (1950) of readings a great success. Moved to the Boat House at Laugharne. Wrote *Do Not Go Gentle into That Good Night* (1952) for his father. Afflicted by failing health and financial difficulties. Made three more

American tours (1952–53). On his last trip directed the final production of *Under Milk Wood*, a "play for voices," in New York, where he died. Other works: *New Poems* (1942), *Selected Writings* (1946), *In Country Sleep* (1952), *Collected Poems* (1953). Generally considered one of the finest English-speaking poets of the twentieth century.

EDITIONS: *Collected Poems, 1934–1952* (London and New York 1966). *Letters to Vernon Watkins* ed. Vernon Watkins (London and New York 1957). *Selected Letters* ed. Constantine Fitzgibbon (London 1966 and New York 1967). *The Notebooks of Dylan Thomas* ed. Ralph Maud (New York 1967 and London 1968).

REFERENCES: John Malcolm Brinnin *Dylan Thomas in America* (Boston 1955 and London 1956, also PB). Charles B. Cox ed. *Dylan Thomas: A Collection of Critical Essays* (Englewood Cliffs, N.J. 1966, also PB). George Firmage ed. *A Garland for Dylan Thomas* (New York 1963 and London 1966, also PB). Constantine Fitzgibbon *The Life of Dylan Thomas* (London and Boston 1965, also PB). Ralph Noel Maud *Entrances to Dylan Thomas' Poetry* (Pittsburgh PB 1963 and Lowestoft, England, 1964). William Moynihan *The Craft and Art of Dylan Thomas* (Ithaca, N.Y. and Oxford 1966, also PB). Bill Read *The Days of Dylan Thomas* (New York 1964 and London 1965, also PB). Alphonsus Reddington *Dylan Thomas: A Journey from Darkness to Light* (New York 1968). Derek Stanford *Dylan Thomas: A Literary Study* (1954, rev. ed. New York PB 1964).

THOMAS, Edward (Mar. 3, 1878 – Apr. 9, 1917). English poet. Born London. Educated at Lincoln College, Oxford. Wrote popular travel books, biographies, and critical studies until Robert Frost came to England for two years (1912). The two became friends, and Thomas began to write poetry. Produced *Poems* (1917) just before he was killed in Flanders in World War I. *Last Poems* was published posthumously (1919). His work is marked by melancholy and a certain intensity of vision. His themes deal largely with nature, showing keen observation, especially of the English countryside.

EDITION: *Collected Poems* (1920, rev. ed. London 1936).

REFERENCES: R. P. Eckert *Edward Thomas: A Biography and a Bibliography* (London and New York 1937). Aldous Huxley *On the Margin* (London and New York 1923).

THOMAS À KEMPIS (real name Thomas Hammerken or Hemerken) (c.1380 – July 25, 1471). German priest and writer. Born Kempen, near Düsseldorf, son of a peasant. Educated at Deventer school, Netherlands, by Brothers of the Common Life. Entered new Augustinian convent of Mt. St. Agnes, Zwolle, Netherlands (1399), received priest's orders (1413), and became convent's subprior (1424). Among his numerous writings are several biographies, including life of Gerhard Groote, founder of the Brothers, treatises on monastic life, three collections of sermons, and hymns. His masterpiece is the famous *Imitatio Christi*, (*Imitation of Christ*, written 1380–1410), which has been translated into more languages than any other book save the Bible. Its simplicity of language, profound sincerity, and antiworldly religious humility account for its extraordinary popularity. The authorship has been disputed, but Thomas's claim remains the most solid. Died at Mt. St. Agnes.

TRANSLATIONS: *Imitation of Christ* tr. Richard Whitford (c.1530), revised Harold C. Gardiner (New York 1955, also PB).

REFERENCES: F. R. Cruise *Outline of the Life of Thomas à Kempis* (London 1904). Samuel Kettlewell *Thomas à Kempis and the Brothers of the Common Life* (2 vols. New York 1882). James Williams *Thomas of Kempen* (London 1910).

THOMPSON, Francis (Dec. 16, 1859 – Nov. 13, 1907). English poet. Born Preston, Lancashire, son of Roman Catholic physician. Educated at Ushaw College, a Catholic school (1870–77), but frail health and nervousness prevented his becoming a priest. Studied medicine at Owen's College, Manchester (1877–80). Severe illness led to his use of opium (1880). After failing medical examinations, went to London (1885), where he lived as a vagrant in extreme poverty. His poetry was first published in Catholic magazine *Merry England* (1888); its editor Wilfred Meynell befriended Thompson and helped him find a sanatorium to cure his addiction (1889). Declining health and further addiction caused him to move to Franciscan monastery in Wales (1893–97). Most famous poem, *The Hound of Heaven*, concerning a man rejected from the priesthood, appeared in his first volume, *Poems* (1893), which Wilfred and Alice Meynell helped him in publishing. Formed close friendship with Coventry Patmore, who strongly influenced his theological development and inspired his experimentation with quantitative meter. *Sister Songs* (1895) poorly received. *New Poems* (1897), which contained the fine poems *The Mistress of Vision* and *Orient Ode*, brought storm of public abuse for its difficult diction and obscure thought. Returned to London (1897), where he worked mostly as critic and reviewer until his death there of tuberculosis. Last years marred by ill health and extreme depression. A profoundly religious poet, Thompson portrayed his "sacramental view of the cosmos" in startling images and complex, multilevel symbols evocative of the seventeenth-century metaphysical poets. Also wrote essays, including one on Shelley (1909).

EDITION: *Complete Works of Francis Thompson* ed. Wilfred Meynell (3 vols. 1913, reprinted Freeport, N.Y. 1969).

REFERENCES: Agnès de la Gorce *Francis Thompson* (tr. London 1933). Everard Meynell *The Life of Francis Thompson* (5th ed. London and New York 1926). F. C. Owlett *Francis Thompson* (London 1936). John Cowie Reid *Francis Thompson, Man and Poet* (London 1959). Paul van Kuykendall Thomson *Francis Thompson: A Critical Biography* (New York 1961). John Evangelist Walsh *Strange Harp, Strange Symphony: The Life of Francis Thompson* (New York 1967 and London 1968).

THOMSON, James (Sept. 11, 1700 – Aug. 27, 1748). British poet. Born Ednam, Scotland, son of clergyman. Entered Edinburgh University (1715), where he completed an arts course (1719), studied theology (1720–24), and published a number of poems in *The Edinburgh Miscellany*. Went to London (1725), where he became a tutor. Publication of *Winter* (1726) won praise from such contemporary men of letters as Gay and Pope. It was collected with *Summer* (1727), *Spring* (1728), and *Autumn* (1730) as *The Seasons* (1730) which was well received. Thomson became a teacher (1726) at Watt's Academy in Little Tower Street and soon formed friendships with Richard Savage, Edward Young, and John Dyer. Wrote *Sophonisba*, a tragedy (produced 1730). Served as companion to Charles Richard Talbot on a grand tour of Europe (1730–31). On his return began his long political poem *Liberty* (1735), which traced the history of civil and religious freedom. Received pension from Frederick, prince of Wales (1737), and became frequenter of the court. Other well-known works are his masque *Alfred*, produced in collaboration with David Mallet (1740), containing the song *Rule Britannia; Tancred and Sigismunda*, another tragedy (produced 1745); and his well-known poem *The Castle of Indolence* (1748), modeled on Spenser. Appointed surveyor-general of the Leeward Islands (1744). Lived quietly in Richmond, Surrey, during the last years of his life and died there. Known chiefly for *The Seasons*, in which he repopularized blank verse and introduced nature as a self-sufficient theme in English literature.

EDITION: *Complete Poetical Works* ed. J. Logie Robertson (1908, latest ed. London and New York 1965).

REFERENCES: William Bayne *James Thomson* (Edinburgh and London 1898). Ralph Cohen *The Art of Discrimination: Thomson's The Seasons and the Language of Criticism* (Berkeley, Calif. and London 1964). Douglas Grant *James Thomson, Poet of The Seasons* (London 1951). G. C. Macaulay *James Thomson* (London 1907). Patricia Spacks *The Varied God: A Critical Study of Thomson's The Seasons* (Berkeley, Calif. 1959).

THOMSON, James (pseudonyms Bysshe Vanolis; B.V.) (Nov. 23, 1834 – June 3, 1882). British poet and essayist. Born Port Glasgow, Renfrew, Scotland, son of a seaman. Father's disablement (1840) impoverished the family. James placed in Royal Caledonian Asylum (1842), where he was educated. Admitted to military academy, Chelsea (1850). While teaching in regimental school in Ballincollig, Ireland (1851), he fell in love with Matilda Weller, whose death (1853) left a permanent scar on his already melancholy disposition. Served as army schoolmaster in England and Ireland (1855–62) and began writing poetry. First used signature B.V. (Bysshe Vanolis, because of reverence for Shelley and Novalis) in essays contributed to *London Investigator* (1859). Discharged from service (1862). Became solicitor's clerk in London, and contributed much verse and prose to the *National Reformer* (1862–74), including *Vane's Story* (1864) and *Weddah and Om-el-Bonain* (1866–67), two well-known fantasy poems. His political connections retarded his recognition as a poet even after his somber masterpiece expressing his despair, *The City of Dreadful Night*, was published (1874). Traveled to Colorado as secretary to mining company (1872) and to Spain as correspondent for *New York World* (1873). During "seven songless years" (1874–80), a period of failing health and mental disturbances, he produced mostly critical and journalistic pieces. First collection, *The City of Dreadful Night and Other Poems* (1880), at last brought recognition. *Vane's Story and Other Poems* (1880), *A Voice from the Nile* (1884), and prose volume *Essays and Phantasies* (1881) appeared before his death in London.

EDITIONS: *The Poetical Works of James Thomson* ed. Bertram Dobell (2 vols. London 1895). *The City of Dreadful Night and Other Poems*, with introduction by Edmund Blunden (London 1932).

REFERENCES: Kenneth H. Byron *The Pessimism of James Thomson ("B.V.") in Relation to His Times* (The Hague

1965). Bertram Dobell *The Laureate of Pessimism: A Sketch of the Life and Character of James Thomson ("B.V.")* (London 1910). Henry S. Salt *The Life of James Thomson* (1889, rev. ed. London 1914). William D. Schaefer *James Thomson, "B.V.": Beyond "The City"* (Berkeley, Calif. 1965). Imogene B. Walker *James Thomson: A Critical Study* (Ithaca, N.Y. and Oxford 1950).

THOREAU, Henry David (July 12, 1817 – May 6, 1862). American philosopher, poet, and naturalist. Born Concord, Mass., where his father had a pencil factory. Attended Concord Academy, learned surveying, and studied classics and Eastern languages at Harvard (graduated 1837). On return to Concord he began his *Journal;* it filled fourteen volumes when published (1906). Never married, and after a brief period as a schoolteacher, lived by lecturing, surveying, working as a handyman in Concord. Gave first lecture at Concord Lyceum (1838). A friend of Emerson, he lived with Emerson family for a time (1841–43, 1847–48), and contributed to the *Dial.* From July 1845 until September 1847 he lived in a hut beside Walden Pond, writing and studying nature. First book, *A Week on the Concord and Merrimack Rivers* (1849), was based on an excursion he and his brother John made (1839). *Walden, or Life in the Woods* followed (1854). On a trip to New York (1856) met Horace Greeley and Walt Whitman. Made several trips to Cape Cod and Maine. By the end of 1860 his health was failing, but he continued to write and even made a final expedition to Minnesota. Died of tuberculosis in Concord. Other major works: the essay *Civil Disobedience* (1849), *The Maine Woods* (1864), and *Cape Cod* (1865). Thoreau is now considered one of the most original thinkers among the transcendentalists.

EDITIONS: *The Writings of Henry David Thoreau* Walden Edition (20 vols. Boston 1906). *Walden and Other Writings* ed. Brooks Atkinson (New York 1937, also PB). *Collected Poems* ed. Carl Bode (Chicago 1943, enlarged ed. Baltimore 1964, also PB). *Correspondence of Henry David Thoreau* ed. Walter Harding and Carl Bode (New York 1958).

REFERENCES: Henry S. Canby *Thoreau* (1939, reprinted Gloucester, Mass. 1965). Walter Harding ed. *Thoreau: A Century of Criticism* (Dallas, Tex. 1954), *A Thoreau Handbook* (New York 1959, also PB), and *The Days of Henry Thoreau* (New York 1965). Henry B. Hough *Thoreau of Walden: The Man and His Eventful Life* (1956, reprinted Hamden, Conn. 1970). Joseph Wood Krutch *Henry David Thoreau* (New York 1948, PB 1965). Sherman Paul ed. *Thoreau: A Collection of Critical Essays* (Englewood Cliffs, N.J. 1962, also PB). Leo Stoller *After Walden: Thoreau's Changing Views on Economic Man* (Stanford, Calif. 1957 and Oxford 1958). Mark Van Doren *Henry David Thoreau: A Critical Study* (1916, reprinted New York 1961).

✍

HENRY DAVID THOREAU
BY EDWARD WEEKS

Intuitive and, in his contradictory way, dedicated to sincerity, an exaggerator in both scorn and humor, a worshiper of nature, a dissenter as impatient with the state as he was with moneygrubbers, Henry David Thoreau holds a special attraction for students: *Walden,* his most famous book, and his essay on civil disobedience speak to them; and, as Alfred Kazin says, they respond to "the absoluteness of his impatience with Authority, the natural vagabondage, the expectation of some different world just over the next horizon . . . they recognize in Thoreau a classic near their own age and condition."

Of French origin, Henry's grandfather, John Thoreau, landed in America, as Henry said, "sans souci, sans sous" (without worry, without a penny). Though the grandfather prospered, Henry's father was a bankrupt storekeeper who slowly acquired a reputation for making lead pencils; they were good pencils and Henry in his turn improved and sold them. Henry's mother Cynthia was determined that her children should be well educated, and it was her resourcefulness as much as the pencils that paid Henry's bills at Harvard. Her near poverty had sharpened her tongue; her son's fondness for lecturing to others was first cultivated at home.

At Harvard, Henry was a misfit. With his long, Indian-like tread, his downcast eyes and moist handshake (probably the result of his shyness), he was not marked for popularity. He mastered the Greek classics, used the library insatiably in his reading, but did poorly with the scores of essays he wrote for Professor Channing. It took Henry ten years to shake off the effect of Channing's rhetoric.

On his graduation in 1837 Henry was still a small-town boy of unknown potential, with schoolteaching his best bet. These were his assets: he had begun a journal, which would eventually run to thirty-two manuscript volumes; he had read Emerson's *Nature* and at once felt the attraction that was to make him an intimate in Emerson's household; and finally, his home town of Concord, thanks to Emerson, Margaret Fuller (the editor of the *Dial*), Hawthorne, Bronson Alcott, and the transcendentalists, was such a stimulant as he could have found nowhere else in America.

In his early twenties this stumpy, energetic, dark-haired youth with the long drooping nose who was saved from ugliness by his fine blue eyes and sensitive mouth is still searching. He can do anything with his hands but fancies himself a poet. The progressive school for twenty-five pupils at which he and his older brother Tom had enjoyed teaching was disbanded in 1839, and that summer the brothers took a leisurely trip on the Concord and Merrimack rivers, in a skiff of their building, sleeping in a pup tent, their staples the potatoes and melons from home. Both kept diaries which provide the text for Henry's first book ten years later. Their affection for each other was the dearest Henry had for any contemporary, and it was now tested by the discovery that they were in love with the same girl, Ellen Sewall. In turn each was rejected. Then Tom, through a casual infection, died suddenly from lockjaw in 1842. The rebuff followed by this terrible loss threw Henry more than ever on his own. When he was unable to buy a farm on credit, it was Emerson who took him in.

Emerson was the first to recognize Henry's genius, although he judged it limited, and it was through his friendship and patronage that Thoreau met as much of the sophisticated world as he did. Their difference in temperament is well suggested by the two rooms holding their memorabilia in the Concord Antiquarian Society, the one so full of mahogany, books, and busts, the other so frugal and austere. The cool decorum which prevailed at Emerson's home was sometimes disturbed by Henry's controversial questioning; Emerson also observed that "Henry never went through the kitchen without coloring," but seems not to have realized that the cause of it was Lidian, his comely wife. She was fifteen years Henry's senior, she laughed at him and liked him; they were drawn together by propinquity and by sorrow, for she lost her son Waldo the very month that Tom died. Henry wrote of her as "Sister," and they were careful to transcendentalize their relations, but in his *Journal* he could not disguise from himself that his feelings about her were sometimes other than fraternal.

The years with Emerson were the

most formative of Thoreau's life. In his hall bedroom at the top of the stairs he had a privacy denied him in the female chatter of his own home and in the library he assimilated more deeply than his patron the Hindu, Greek, and Persian philosophers who helped him set his values. He got from Emerson the magnetic assurance of one who believed profoundly in American originality; he throve on friction. Now on his walks as a "self-appointed inspector of snow-storms and rain-storms" he gathered those intuitions, judgments, and paradoxes which enrich his *Journal*. When Emerson purchased fourteen acres of pine and brier on Walden Pond, he offered Henry the chance to build a cabin on it, and such in 1845 became the providential setting for Thoreau's finest writing.

A Week on the Concord and Merrimack Rivers came first, and it was a young book, full of the dawn and dusk, the riverbanks still shadowed by the Indian and his ancient campgrounds, cheery encounters with bargemen and at evening the taste buds eager for a supper of horned pout, fresh bread, and muskmelon. But the *Week* is not all pastoral; through the excursion Thoreau interspersed poems and reflective pieces, some previously printed in the *Dial*, and these were distracting. Lowell, who praised the book, added that "We came upon them like snags that mar our Merrimacking dreadfully. We were bid to a river party — not to be preached at."

Thornton Wilder has called *Walden, or Life in the Woods*, "a manual of self-reliance," and certainly on its appearance in 1854 it was the most powerfully original American book yet written. It vibrates with vitality: Henry takes his early morning plunge in the pond, works in the bean patch, or walks to Sudbury measuring the giant chest-nuts as he goes — two and a half embraces for the largest; he makes a minute comparison of the neighboring ponds — White Pond, which is the mate of Walden, and as deep and as clear, and Sandy Pond in Lincoln, which is larger and shallower; he discourses on the water bugs, the difference in taste of the blueberry and huckleberry; he writes of the birds ("I found myself suddenly neighbor to the birds; not by having imprisoned one but by having caged myself near them"), and is transfixed by the magic stillness at sunset. Confident as never before, he declared his purpose in this famous passage: "I went to the woods because I wished to live deliberately, to front only the essential facts of life, and see if I could not learn what it had to teach, and not, when I came to die, to discover that I had not lived. I did not wish to live what was not life, living is so dear; nor did I wish to practice resignation." As Emerson said in his eulogy, "He saw as with microscope, heard as with ear trumpet, and his memory was the photographic register of all he saw and heard."

Thoreau "chose to be rich by making his wants few," and the affinity with nature in Walden has for its counterpoint a scathing evaluation of America's economic and moral development. Texas land, California gold, and the railroads opening the West were being exploited in a turbulent boom, the effect of which Henry deplored. Begun in the mid 1840's, *Walden* took nine years to ripen; Ticknor and Fields, Boston's best, published an edition of two thousand copies.

In 1847, when he had "exhausted the advantages of solitude," Henry moved back to the village, and that summer in his disapproval of the Mexican War he refused to pay his poll tax of one dollar. Like Alcott, he was arrested, spent a night in jail, and was exasperated when Aunt Maria bailed him out. From this came his lecture on *Civil Disobedience,* in which he assumed a democratic system and majority rule, admitted that a tyrannical government could overrule him, but insisted that he must somehow resist. He was thinking of his own integrity, as Henry Seidel Canby points out, not of mass rebellion, of which, as the Civil War approached, he disapproved.

In the afternoon of his career Thoreau found more comfort and respect. The process for graphite he had perfected was bringing the family a steady income and he was receiving modest fees for his lecturing and surveying. He found a walking companion in William Ellery Channing and together they explored the Maine woods, Cape Cod, and made a short visit to Canada, all observantly recorded in the *Journal.* His friendship with Lidian was cooling, for in her invalidism she was wrapped up in her family, but he still partook in the famous conversations at the Emersons, and the old fire blazes up in him again in indignation at the fate of John Brown. He insisted that the village come to hear his plea for Captain John Brown, which he delivered with "burning eyes," and such eloquence that it warmed the sympathy of many listeners there and when he repeated it to greater audiences in Boston. Had he lived in our time he would have been a conscientious objector, but had he read of Stalin's purge and of Auschwitz one wonders if he would still believe that a free society could put its trust in limited resistance.

THUCYDIDES (c.460–c.400 B.C.). Greek historian. Born Athens, the son of Olorus, and probably related to Cimon, whose pro-Spartan and "conservative" policies were successfully challenged by Pericles. Though he may well have been reared in a conservative milieu, as a young man he became an admirer of Pericles. Began to take notes for his history on the outbreak of the Peloponnesian War (431). Between 430–427 caught the plague, but recovered. Appointed general (424), he failed to save Amphipolis from the Spartan commander Brasidas; was exiled and did not return to Athens for twenty years. His history breaks off abruptly with the events of 404; presumably he died soon after. Thucydides' vision of history is based on a scientific appraisal of human nature. Outstanding features of his writing are its accuracy and impartiality, and the use of speeches attributed to important figures to express the personality and motives of each political group.

TRANSLATIONS: *The Peloponnesian War* tr. Thomas Hobbes (1629) ed. David Grene (2 vols. Ann Arbor, Mich. 1959 and London 1960). *Complete Writings: The Peloponnesian War* tr. Richard Crawley (New York 1951, also PB). *History of the Peloponnesian War* tr. Sir Richard Livingstone (London PB 1943); tr. Rex Warner (Harmondsworth, England, and Baltimore PB 1954).

REFERENCES: C. N. Cochrane *Thucydides and the Science of History* (London 1929, reprinted New York 1965). Francis M. Cornford *Thucydides Mythistoricus* (1907, reprinted London 1965 and New York 1969). John H. Finley *Thucydides* (1942, reprinted Ann Arbor, Mich. 1963, also PB). Peter J. Fliess *Thucydides and the Politics of Bi-Polarity* (Baton Rouge, La. 1966). David Grene *Greek Political Theory: The Image of Man in Thucydides and Plato* (Chicago 1965, also PB). G. B. Grundy *Thucydides and the History of His Age* (2nd ed. 2 vols. Oxford 1948). H. D. Westlake *Individuals in Thucydides* (London and New York 1968).

↧

THUCYDIDES
BY REX WARNER

Thucydides is often described as "the first scientific historian," and there is a sense in which this description is perfectly correct. Much more than Herodotus, he really tried to find out what in fact did happen, to be, as we say, "objective." As he says himself, "I have made it a principle not to write down the first story that came my way, and not even to be guided by my own general impressions; either I was present myself at the events which I have described or else I heard of them from eyewitnesses whose reports I have checked with as much thoroughness as possible." He also makes use of documentary evidence and certainly writes in these ways as one would expect a good historian to write today. But good, honest, "scientific" historians are not necessarily great historians, and we shall miss the real greatness of Thucydides if we merely give him credit for an exceptional objectivity.

A more enlightening phrase is used of him by Thomas Hobbes, who was one of his first and one of his very greatest translators into a modern language. He describes him as "the most Politick Historiographer that ever writ." And many will consider this judgment still true. For he is much more than a reporter, however accurate. He is certainly concerned to find out exactly what did happen, but his real interest is in why things went the way they did. He lived in the most political period of a state which was more acutely conscious of politics than has been any other state in history. He saw the greatness and he saw the fall of Athens and he was passionately concerned to find the reasons both for the greatness and for the decline.

"Passion" is not a word which we are apt to associate with an "objective" historian, yet it is a word which one must use of Thucydides. H. T. Wade-Gery, on the subject of Thucydides' prose, writes: "Its precision is a poet's precision, a union of passion and candor." This fine sentence might be applied to his work as a whole.

The poetical element in Thucydides is very like what we find in the great poets of his time and place, Sophocles and Euripides. Just as they were to some extent limited by the conventional cycle of stories thought suitable to tragedy, so he was limited by facts. His originality is shown, as theirs was, by emphasis, antithesis, and the passion for understanding. Until very recently it was an axiom that poetry, among its functions, should "make men better." Thucydides would certainly make this claim for his history. "It will be enough for me," he writes, "if these words of mine are judged useful by those who want to understand clearly the events which happened in the past and which (human nature being what it is) will, at some time or other and in much the same ways, be repeated in the future. My work is not a piece of writing designed to meet the taste of an immediate public, but was done to last forever."

His real theme, then, is something much wider than the war between Athens and Sparta. It is nothing less than human nature itself in the changing relationships of peace and war. And his story moves us like a beautifully constructed tragedy, not like a list of events. What we are really seeing is a clear and passionate picture of the greatness and the misery of man.

Thucydides falsified nothing in the story and the story is in itself dramatic. But the whole style and manner of thought of the historian seem almost incredibly well adapted to bring out the full force of the drama. Only very seldom does Thucydides refer to himself, and even his personal opinions will usually take such a form as "Human nature being what it is, it follows that . . ." Yet from the narrative itself, in particular from the speeches of the leading characters, and from the use of style and emphasis, it does not seem impossible to imagine the kind of man he was.

He was passionately devoted to the Athens of his early youth, the Athens of Pericles. He saw, as Pericles did, the utter incompatibility between the ways of life of Athens and Sparta. This is expressed over and over again, notably in the Corinthian analysis of the two powers — one static and slow, the other dynamic and restless — and in Pericles' funeral oration. There is no doubt that he prefers the ideal of Athens, but he fully recognizes its dangers and sees its almost inevitable deterioration after Pericles' death. But his understanding of the weakness and instability of an uncontrolled and self-seeking democracy does not lead him — as it did, to some extent, Xenophon and Plato — to overestimate the advantages of the opposed ideal. He knows that Spartan virtue and integrity are no more to be depended upon than Athenian enterprise and ambition. And in particular he sees that under the stresses of war, revolution, and the unpredictable, both sides are apt to lose their distinction and behave with equal savagery. The Spartans treat the Plataeans just as badly as, though with more hypocrisy than, the Athenians treat the Meleans.

The temper of Thucydides' mind seems to have been like that of Pericles and very unlike that of Cleon, that parody of Pericles. In other words he can see politics in the wider context of "nature," "reality," "men and gods." Not only Athens but civilization itself is fragile. There are many instances of this insight. In particular the account of the plague (coming directly after Pericles' funeral oration), the description of the appalling effects of the breakdown of law and order in Corcyra, and the whole story of the Sicilian expedition (coming directly after the Athenian massacre of the population of Melos). Nicias, who has led army and navy to destruction, is made pathetically to say that since all through his life he has worshiped the gods as he should and done his duty to men, he still has a strong hope for the future. He has none, and Thucydides' implied comment has nothing of cynicism in it, but very much of pity.

This humanity of Thucydides has seldom been sufficiently emphasized, perhaps because it is so much a part of him that it does not require to be expressed in sentimental or uplifting phraseology. And perhaps what most strikes a modern reader about him is the total absence of sentimentality, uplift, or insincerity. Indeed, the language of his speakers is so unlike that of modern political oratory that at first sight it may appear almost incomprehensible. A closer look may lead us to wish that politicians were still capable of saying what they really mean. But, as I have attempted to indicate, there is much more in Thucydides than just the ability to tell the truth, rare as this is. What is more important is that he seems to know and to feel the truth, and this is why his work remains, as he knew it would, "a possession forever."

THURBER, James (Grover) (Dec. 8, 1894 – Nov. 2, 1961). American writer and illustrator. Born Columbus, Ohio, he was educated in public schools there. Blinded in one eye by childhood accident. Attended Ohio State University (1913–18), but left without degree. State Department code clerk in Washington, D.C., and Paris (1918–20). Reporter for Columbus *Dispatch* (1920–24). In spare time wrote book and lyrics for five musical comedies produced at O.S.U. Married Althea Adams (1922). Reporter for *Chicago Tribune* in Paris (1924). Moved to New York (1925), working for *Evening Post*. Began writing humorous sketches which won him position of staff writer on the *New Yorker* (1927–33). Wrote *Is Sex Necessary?* with E. B. White, a well-received book in which his drawings were published as book illustrations for first time. His drawings soon became hallmark of the *New Yorker*. Collections of essays and illustrations which followed secured his reputation as a leading American humorist: *The Owl in the Attic* (1931), *The Seal in the Bedroom* (1932), *My Life and Hard Times* (1933), *The Middle-Aged Man on the Flying Trapeze* (1935). Divorced (1935) and married Helen Wismer same year. A play, *The Male Animal* (with Elliot Nugent), was produced on Broadway (1940) with great success. His sight was deteriorating, but even when practically blind (from 1946) he continued to write. Other major works: *My World — And Welcome to It* (1942), which contained *The Secret Life of Walter Mitty*, his best-known short story; *The Thurber Carnival* (1945); *The 13 Clocks* (1950); *The Thurber Album* (1952); *Thurber Country* (1953); *Thurber's Dogs* (1955); *The Wonderful O* (1957); *The Years with Ross* (1959), an account of his years on the *New Yorker*. Died in New York.

REFERENCES: Walter Blair *Horse Sense in American Humor* (1942, reprinted New York 1962). Malcolm Cowley *The Literary Situation* (New York 1954 and London 1955, also PB). Robert E. Morsberger *James Thurber* (New York 1964, also PB). William Murrell *A History of American Graphic Humor* (1938, reprinted 2 vols. New York 1967). Richard C. Tobias *Art of James Thurber* (Athens, Ohio 1969). Mark Van Doren *The Autobiography of Mark Van Doren* (New York 1958).

TIBULLUS, Albius (c.54 B.C.–18 B.C.). Roman poet. Born Pedum, near Praeneste. Probably of the equestrian rank, he was a close friend of Marcus Valerius Messala Corvinus, whom he allegedly accompanied on a campaign (c.30) to Aquitanian Gaul. A member of Messala's literary circle, he was also a friend of Horace, who addressed him as Albius in *Odes* I, 33, and *Epistles* I, 4. Divided his time between Rome and his country estate, located between Palestrina and Tivoli. Of the four books

of poetry in the *Corpus Tibullianum*, only books I, II, and part of book IV are his; the remainder are attributed to other members of Messala's circle. First two books contain, respectively, elegies to Delia and Nemesis, fictitious names for his mistresses. A tender and graceful master of the Latin love elegy, Tibullus also celebrates the beauties of country and family life. Stands with Cornelius Gallus, Propertius, and Ovid as a classical writer of Latin elegiacs.

TRANSLATIONS: *The Erotic Elegies of Albius Tibullus* tr. Hubert Creekmore (New York 1966). *The Poems of Tibullus* tr. Constance Carrier (Bloomington, Ind. 1968, also PB).

REFERENCES: John P. Elder in J. P. Sullivan ed. *Critical Essays on Roman Literature: Elegy and Lyric* (Cambridge, Mass. and London 1962). William Y. Sellar *The Roman Poets of the Augustan Age: Horace and the Elegiac Poets* (Oxford 1892, reprinted New York 1965).

TIECK, (Johann) Ludwig (May 31, 1773 – Apr. 28, 1853). German writer. Born Berlin, son of a craftsman. Attended Friedrich Werder Gymnasium, Berlin (1782–92), and universities of Halle, Göttingen, and Erlangen (1792–94). In Berlin (1794–99) began writing light stories for publisher C. F. Nicolai and published an epistolary novel, *William Lovell* (3 vols. 1795–96). In collaboration with W. H. Wackenroder, wrote *Franz Sternbalds Wanderungen* (2 vols. 1798), one of the first German romantic novels. Among folk tales and satiric plays published in *Volksmärchen* (3 vols. 1797) was the romantic story *Der blonde Eckbert*, which won admiration of the Schlegel brothers. At their invitation, moved to Jena (1799), center of early German romantics, where he met Goethe and Schiller. An adviser to A. W. Schlegel's great Shakespeare translation (1797–1810), he also collected and translated Elizabethan plays, *Altenglisches Theater* (2 vols. 1811). After seventeen years near Frankfurt an der Oder (1802–19), moved to Dresden, where he became adviser and critic to Court Theatre (1825). Summoned to Berlin by Frederick William IV of Prussia, he became a leading literary figure there until his death. Among major works: the novellas *Der Runnenberg* (1804), *Der Aufruhr in den Cevennen* (1826), and *Des Lebens Überfluss* (1839); the plays *Ritter Blaubart* (*Knight Bluebeard*, 1797), *Der gestiefelte Kater* (*Puss in Boots*, 1797), *Genoveva* (1799), *Kaiser Oktavianus* (1804), a medieval romantic drama in verse; a collection of medieval German lyrics, *Minnelieder aus dem schwabischen Zeitalter* (1803); a historical novel *Vittoria Accorombona* (1840). Tieck bridges the gap between the Enlightenment and romanticism in Germany.

REFERENCES: R. M. Immerwahr *The Esthetic Intent of Tieck's Fantastic Comedy* (St. Louis, Mo. 1953). A. E. Lussky *Tieck's Approach to Romanticism* (Leipzig 1925) and *Tieck's Romantic Irony* (Chapel Hill, N.C. 1932). Percy Matenko *Ludwig Tieck and America* (Chapel Hill, N.C. PB 1954). James Trainer *Ludwig Tieck: From Gothic to Romantic* (The Hague 1964). Edwin H. Zeydel *Ludwig Tieck, the German Romanticist: A Critical Study* (Princeton, N.J. 1935 and Oxford 1936).

TIEPOLO, Giambattista (real name Giovanni Battista) (Mar. 5, 1696 – Mar. 17, 1770). Italian painter. Born Venice, son of a merchant. Studied painting first with Gregorio Lazzarini, from whom he learned a grandiose, decorative style; also influenced by Paolo Veronese and Giovanni Piazzetta. Earliest known work is the *Sacrifice of Abraham* (1715–16, church of Ospedaletto, Venice). Married Maria Cecilia Guardi, sister of Francesco Guardi (1719); two of their nine children, Giovanni Domenico and Lorenzo, later became his assistants. Received important commissions to decorate palaces and churches in and around Venice (Udine, 1726; Milan, 1731 and 1740; Bergamo, 1732; Montecchio Maggiore, 1743), and was quickly recognized as the outstanding fresco painter in Italy. His Cleopatra frescoes in Palazzo Labia, Venice (1745), brought him international fame. Summoned by the prince bishop to Würzburg (1750), he decorated the ceilings and staircase of the Kaisersaal with such historical and allegorical subjects as the *Life of Frederick Barbarossa* and the *Investiture of*

Bishop Harold (1750–53) (oil sketches for them are in Gardner Museum, Boston). At invitation of Spanish king Charles III he went to Madrid (1762), accompanied by his two sons, and decorated the royal palace with the vast allegorical *Apotheosis of Spain* and ceiling frescoes *Spain and Her Provinces*. He died suddenly in Madrid. He also produced sketches, drawings, portraits, oil paintings, and etchings. His son, Giandomenico (1727–1804), was also a successful fresco painter, as well as his father's assistant and imitator. Among his well-known decorative works are the Villa Valmarana frescoes (1757), which reveal an interest in more down-to-earth subjects, such as carnivals, than the historical and allegorical subjects of his father's art, which also adorn the villa.

REFERENCES: Valentino Crivellato *Tiepolo* (tr. New York and London 1962). Detlev von Hadeln *Drawings of G. B. Tiepolo* (2 vols. Paris 1928). Michael Levey *Painting in Eighteenth-Century Venice* (London and New York 1959). Antonio Morassi *G. B. Tiepolo: His Life and Work* (tr. London and New York 1955) and *A Complete Catalogue of the Paintings of G. B. Tiepolo* (London 1962). J. Byam Shaw *The Drawings of Domenico Tiepolo* (Boston and London 1962).

✍

TIEPOLO
BY JUERGEN SCHULZ

Giambattista Tiepolo (not to be confused with his painter son Giandomenico) was the last and at the same time one of the greatest of his breed — the history painters in the grand manner of that period of painting, running in Italy from the late Middle Ages to the end of the baroque, which represents a sort of middle age of its own, between the conceptual, abstract art of the age of faith and the aesthetic, abstract art of modern times.

His range, in an age of specialization, was uncommonly large: he painted portraits, allegories, mythologies, historical scenes, genre, private devotional pictures, public altarpieces, wall and ceiling decorations; he made designs for mosaics, drawings for presentation, and etchings. His productivity was immense: over a thousand compositions in painting, drawing, and prints still survive today. He painted easily and quickly, and enjoyed working on a large scale. Venice was not a sufficient theatre for his talents and ambitions. After a decade of working for Venetian private patrons and religious bodies, he received in 1726 his first major commission outside the city, for a cycle of frescoes in the archiepiscopal palace of Udine. In 1731 he frescoed the palace of a Milanese nobleman, on the first of three prolonged stays in the Lombard capital. In 1736 the Swedish ambassador to Venice sought, unsuccessfully, to engage the artist for the decoration of the royal palace of Stockholm. In 1750 Tiepolo and his studio traveled to Würzburg, the capital of Franconia, to fresco the palace, or Residenz, of the prince bishop of the state. Numerous altarpieces and fresco cycles for the churches of Venice and provincial cities of the Venetian state fill the intervening years, along with fresco cycles and cabinet pictures for the palaces and country villas of Venetian noblemen. Finally, in 1761, he was engaged by King Charles III of Spain to fresco the state rooms of the royal palace of Madrid. Other commissions from Spanish patrons followed, including a suite of altarpieces for Aranjuez, and it is at Madrid, in 1770, that he died.

It can be seen that it was above all as a frescoist that Tiepolo was in demand abroad, just as frescoes and public works such as altarpieces formed the chief element of his production at home. History painting of this kind is an art that has almost vanished today. Modern pictures are painted to be en-joyed in solitude, or in a small company. History painting alone has as its function the making of an immediate, collective impression upon a large number of people gathered together to look at an imaginary episode acted, as if upon a stage. Beginning in the age of Giotto, the aim of history painters was to dramatize their subject by skillful editing of their story, and a naturalistic representation of setting, action, and expression. Tiepolo belongs at the end of this great tradition of pictorial dramatists, and it is in this genre that his chief achievement lies.

His earliest works show the artificial method of dramatizing action invented during the early baroque period. It is the expressive use of light and shade, whereby a few gleaming figures and forms stand out startlingly from a pervading darkness. At Venice it was favored especially by the older artist Piazzetta, who clearly exercised a strong influence on Tiepolo.

By the time of the Old Testament scenes of 1726–27 in Udine, however, Tiepolo's palette had lightened to the characteristic, cool, and silvery tonality of his maturity. Drama was wrung instead from the lively narration of the action. Tiepolo's gifts as a narrator are seldom remarked today, because the modern observer's eye fastens on the pictorial values of his light-struck, exquisitely colored, and brilliantly painted forms. But in scenes such as the story of *Rachel Hiding the Stolen Images*, in the Udinese cycle, the wrath of the searching father, the puzzlement of the unaware husband, and the duplicity of his wife, Rachel, who is hiding the images beneath her skirts, are characterized with the most astonishing mastery of human physiognomy. Characteristically, Tiepolo defines the roles of the protagonists with considerable wit, making the father seem ponderous, the husband innocent, and Rachel a young woman trading on her femininity. The protagonists are drawn together into a monumental group, and all about them appear the children and servants of Rachel's train — some occupied in their appropriate tasks, others watching the confrontation in the center with knowing or unknowing eyes. In them, as in the central figures, there is an extraordinary copiousness of narrative detail, set down for the sheer pleasure of communicating an observation. The observations are drawn from art as much as from life, for some of the figures and details of the setting are derived from Veronese and other artists of the Renaissance. But the imported motives are so completely assimilated to Tiepolo's personal style of representation and narration that they can hardly be recognized, and there is no semblance of eclecticism in the borrowing.

The illusionistic devices, for which Tiepolo was famous, and which became progressively more audacious as the artist aged, are similarly used to sharpen the narrative force of the representation and spice it with wit. A cycle of Homeric scenes of 1757, in the Villa Valmarana outside Vicenza, for instance, involves the whole space of the room in which it is painted. At one end of the room, the *Sacrifice of Iphigenia* is portrayed beneath a portico of painted columns that seemingly carries the real roof. Beneath the central opening stands the altar, on which the high priest is about to drive a knife through Iphigenia's breast, while a servant stands ready facing him, with a platter to receive the sacrificial blood. But both priest and victim look with awe toward the left, where a cloud bearing a deer appears, moving rapidly toward the altar. It is the substitute victim for the sacrifice, sent by

the goddess Diana. On the right stands Agamemnon, his face buried in his cloak, to hide the hideous sight of his daughter's sacrifice. Agamemnon and the servant remain unaware of the impending deliverance, while the priest and Iphigenia have not yet understood the meaning of the apparition. It is the very moment before the crisis of the story, when tension is at its peak. The miraculous deer is shown not within the painted portico, with all the other actors, but in front of it, moving in a space that is logically the real space of the room. On the facing wall, under a similar portico, Greek warriors are shown beholding the scene from across the room, while on the ceiling the goddess Diana is painted, gesturing commandingly toward the high priest. Thus, the story is completed by psychological relationships that likewise traverse the actual room, placing the beholder in the middle of the action, a veritable bystander at the climax of a piteous tale, and yet clearly aware that it is painted, a tour de force of illusionistic art.

The same technique of overlapping the painted and the real world is used to vivify the great allegorical cycles, such as the celebrated fresco of *Olympus and the Four Quarters of the World*, over the state staircase of the Würzburg Residenz. An imaginary architecture is painted around the edge of the ceiling, seemingly joined to the real walls of the room, and giving onto a painted sky that covers the bulk of the vault. The animated personifications that perch upon the painted architecture or float in the painted sky gesture and move towards one another, across the space of the very room itself, in such a way as to place the spectator in the selfsame world as they.

The high values of Tiepolo's palette, with their effect of streaming daylight, the rapid, bravura execution of the individual passages, these add to the impression of excitement and freshness that pervades all Tiepolo's works.

In the predominant, light tonality of his work, and certain other features such as the love for excited, irregular silhouettes, the preference for approximate rather than mathematical symmetries, and the avoidance of continous recessions into clearly defined distances, Tiepolo is typical of rococo painters in general. But his mastery and plain enjoyment of storytelling, his capacity to orchestrate vast casts of figures in illustration of a clear and dramatic theme, was unique among rococo painters. He summarized within his person and his work a century-old tradition of monumental history painting that was extinguished with his death.

TINTORETTO (real name Jacopo Robusti) (1518 – May 31, 1594). Italian painter. Born and died in Venice. Son of a dyer (*tintore*), whence his nickname (little dyer). Supposedly apprenticed briefly to Titian, he was essentially self-taught. A prolific painter of both cabinet and monumental pictures for private and public patrons, his most important works are large religious and secular mural cycles composed of canvas paintings and produced for Venetian churches, confraternities, and government offices. Dramatically conceived and dashingly executed figure compositions, they are characterized by exaggerated body movement, strong contrasts of light and shade, and irrational space constructions. Although he studied closely the work of central Italian mannerists and shared with them some of these characteristics, his impetuous technique and urgent dramatization of narrative scenes anticipate high baroque style and differentiate his work sharply from mannerist painting properly so called. Many of his mural cycles still remain in original site. Religious cycles number over a dozen, among them are six scenes from *Legend of St.*

Roch (1549–78), S. Rocco; choir paintings of *Adoration of Golden Calf* and *Last Judgment* (c.1558), S. Maria dell'Orto; four scenes from *Legend of St. Mark* for confraternity of that saint (1548–c.1586), now divided between Brera, Milan, and Accademia, Venice; thirty-one *Old Testament Scenes* and *New Testament Scenes* setting forth the mystery of holy sacraments by means of typological juxtaposition (1576–81), in great hall of confraternity of St. Roch; and choir paintings of *Gathering of the Manna* and *Last Supper* (1591–94), S. Giorgio Maggiore. Secular cycles decorate seven rooms of Ducal Palace, Venice. They include a painted ceiling (c.1562) and four *Allegories* (1578) for Salotto Dorato; four *Battle Scenes* and a colossal *Allegory of Venice Receiving Subject States* (1579–82) in ceiling of Sala del Maggior Consiglio; and *Battle of Zara* (1584–87) in Sala dello Scrutinio. Four of Tintoretto's eight children became painters and worked in his studio: Giovanni Battista, Marietta, Marco and Domenico. Only the last two survived their father and, together with their mother, continued Tintoretto's studio into the seventeenth century. Although bulk of work produced by the firm after Tintoretto's death is routine in style and inferior in quality, autograph works of Domenico show him to have been a considerable painter in his own right.

REFERENCES: Juergen Schulz *Venetian Painted Ceilings of the Renaissance* (Berkeley and Los Angeles 1968). Hans Tietze *Tintoretto: The Paintings and Drawings* (New York 1948 and London 1949).

TINTORETTO
BY JUERGEN SCHULZ

Within the context of the Venetian Renaissance, Tintoretto was a revolutionary artist and personality. He was born and trained outside the closed circle of artists, littérateurs, and noblemen who controlled the art world of mid-sixteenth-century Venice, and neither shared their tastes nor obtained their support. Against them he pitted an uncompromising sense of purpose and aggressive methods of self-promotion, and he prevailed to turn Venetian painting Tintorettesque for more than a generation.

He was born into a working-class family, and as an artist he was essentially self-trained. There is a tradition that for ten days he was an apprentice of Titian, who discharged the young man as soon as he became aware of his talent and felt its threat. Possibly he served as apprentice with another master after that. But neither Titian nor the putative second master were as formative for Tintoretto's style as was his intensive study of the compositional and figure style of the central Italian schools of his own time. His earliest history paintings, such as the *Miracle of St. Mark* of 1548 (Accademia, Venice), show him striving to set the action in a stage space, such as had become the norm in Rome and Florence at the beginning of the century. His early drawings (in the Berlin Museum; Uffizi, Florence; Christ Church College, Oxford) show him studying unceasingly and from infinitely varied angles the figure sculpture of Michelangelo, other central Italians, and the antique. It is reported that he worked out his compositions by setting up small wax figures on a model stage, and that he studied attitudes by placing small sculptural models before, above, and below him according to the desired angle, and drawing them by the light of carefully placed lamps. These very methods were not Venetian, but Florentine and Roman. Moved by a deep religiosity and an innate sense for passion and drama, he strove for mastery of a central Italian narrative style, dramatic in its naturalism and movement, expressively robust and active in its figure style. Yet his temperamental preference for excitement, and the coloristic and

technical resources of Venetian painting of his time, led him to develop an idiosyncratic figure style that went far beyond a simple imitation of the central Italian masters. His figures are shown in swift action and unstable poses, relief is dramatized through an exaggerated play of light and shade, and an expressive value is wrung from the very brushwork itself, with its discontinuities between flashing, thickly impasted highlights and broad, flatly painted areas of shadow.

During Tintoretto's learning years, running roughly from the late 1530's to the early 1550's, the dominant style of Venetian painting was that of Titian and Bonifazio. These artists had formed their style at the beginning of the century, when Venetian painting was undramatic, withdrawn, and sensuous in character. Although Titian in his middle age incorporated into his work some of the grandeur, drama, and movement of the central Italians, he continued to emphasize exquisite color, delicate finish, and controlled pattern in a way that Tintoretto rejected from the very start. The rejection was felt and resented by the older artists. We have some evidence for the disdain Titian felt for Tintoretto's art, and explicit criticism from Titian's friends the art critic Pietro Aretino and art historian Giorgio Vasari. Both, while approving the emotional force of Tintoretto's paintings, reprehended the artist's brilliant, improvisatory technique, which the former taxed as "hasty," and the latter as "a farce." Artists of a younger generation, on the other hand, such as the Veronese Cristoforo Sorte, regarded it as the sign of a superb mastery and directness.

The older artists not only represented an established style, but also controlled the distribution of major commissions by the republic and the public bodies of the state. Titian was official painter to the doge and a close friend not only of the voluble critic Aretino but also of the official sculptor and architect of the procurators of St. Mark, Jacopo Sansovino. Bonifazio was the preferred artist of the lesser magistracies of the republic. Although the story of Tintoretto's ten-day apprenticeship may be apocryphal, it is clear that he was not encouraged by Titian and had to make his way outside the establishment.

According to an early biographer, Tintoretto first earned his keep by working among the furniture painters who kept stalls under the porticoes of St. Mark's Square. He brought his style to public attention by seeking out well-situated palaces and offering to paint their façades free of charge. In 1549 he sought, as partial payment for a commission of the confraternity of S. Rocco, admission to its select membership, presumably as a way to enter the world of favors and connections through which the established artists exercised their control of patronage. His aggressive self-promotion encountered as much opposition as his artistic style. In the case of the confraternity, the members challenged the agreement for admission given by their officers. The artist's methods rankled still when he was famous and established. Thus, in 1564, when new decorations for the same confraternity were planned, the expense of which was to be borne by the members, one of them made the explicit reservation that if Tintoretto were chosen for the work, he would give nothing for it.

The emotional religiosity that impelled the young Tintoretto toward the expressive narrative style and figure art of central Italy continued to guide his development to the end of his career. His early work shows a growing

mastery of those elements of naturalistic space and dramatic plasticity that he sought to make his own. Thus, while the figures of the early *Miracle of St. Mark* are massed in awkward, unarticulated crowds at the very apron of the stage space in which they are set, in the *Removal of the Body of St. Mark* (Accademia, Venice) and the *Finding of the Body of St. Mark* (Brera, Milan) of 1563–65 even vaster spaces are effortlessly animated to their full depth by active figures, and distance is used expressively. Toward the end of the 1560's, however, Tintoretto began to allow himself distortions of normal relationships in space and of masses, heightening the importance of the figures as carriers of meaning and mood. Thus, the *Crucifixion* of 1569 (S. Cassiano, Venice) shows the crosses silhouetted dramatically against a darkening sky. The setting is confined to a narrow strip of ground at the bottom, from behind which a file of bystanders rises into view, similarly silhouetted against the sky. Thus, the ground seems to fall away steeply, and we are left with a setting that contains a minimum of space but eloquently conveys the isolation and loneliness of the dying Christ.

In the ceiling paintings of 1575–78, of the upper hall in the confraternity of S. Rocco, the landscape settings consist of improbable terraces of ground, pierced by impossible openings onto further landscapes. The actors are no longer disposed according to the exigencies of the stage, but rather space is constructed according to the needs of the actors. Figure movement is more intense and rhetorical, as if impelled by forces outside of and beyond the control of the individual will.

The cycle of Marian paintings of 1581–87 on the ground floor of the same building, and contemporary works such as the *Martyrdom of St. Catherine* (Accademia), have settings that can no longer be read as consistent wholes, but only as episodes of space linked decoratively by movement, light, and similar effects. Settings and figures are texturally made of the same stuff, and the figures wear trancelike expressions that show their actions belong to the world of miracle and faith, of which they are the vehicles.

The late work of the artist is difficult to isolate from among the abundant production of his studio. One of the very latest paintings that is certainly from his hand is the *Entombment* completed the year of his death, 1594 (S. Giorgio Maggiore, Venice). Here the scale of the figures varies according to their importance. None seem to stand or be supported in any earthly way. Rather they sway or float. Their substance is gossamer: without weight or density. None exclaim or show their grief. The death of Christ is a necessity, a silent ritual in which the actors participate with the same acquiescence as did the aged artist in the mystery for which it is the symbol.

TITIAN (real name **Tiziano Vecellio**) (c.1487/90 – Aug. 27, 1576). Italian painter. Born Pieve di Cadore, in the Alps. Trained at Venice under Giovanni Bellini; much influenced by Giorgione. Recognized locally from beginning of his career: received government commission (1507) together with Giorgione to fresco exterior of German Merchant Exchange, Venice; commissioned (1510) by confraternity of St. Anthony, Padua, to fresco interior of its meeting hall; appointed (1516) official painter to Doge, succeeding Giovanni Bellini. Chief works of early maturity are group of large altarpieces and a set of mythologies. The altarpieces include *The Assumption* (1516–18) and *Pesaro Madonna* (1519–26), both in S. Maria dei Frari, Venice), *The Madonna with SS. Aloysius and Francis* (1520, Museo Civico, Ancona),

The Resurrection Altar (1520–22, SS. Nazarus and Celsus, Brescia), and *The St. Peter Martyr Altar* (1525–30) for SS. John and Paul, Venice, now destroyed. The mythologies, painted for Duke Alfonso d'Este of Ferrara (1518–23), are now divided between Prado, Madrid, and National Gallery, London. Beginning with Titian's presentation to Emperor Charles V at Bologna (1530), his clientèle rapidly expanded, eventually including rulers and leading nobility of all of Catholic Europe. During 1530's he was especially patronized by Francesco Maria della Rovere, Duke of Urbino, for whom he produced among other works *The Venus of Urbino* (1538, Uffizi, Florence), and during 1540's by family of Pope Paul III, for whom he produced among other works the early version of *Danaë* (c.1546, Capodimonte, Naples). During same time was patronized by Charles V, and eventually his relationship with Charles and Charles's son Philip II grew to be most important of all. While his 1530 portrait of Charles (now lost) failed to please, the second (1532, Prado, Madrid) was a brilliant success. Named official painter to the emperor and counsellor of empire, with titles of Count Palatine and Knight of Golden Spur. Over next twenty-five years produced for Charles and Philip over two dozen portraits of their persons, families, and court members, and a small number of religious and mythological pictures, among which the best known are *The Allegory of Marriage*, said to be that of Marchese del Vasto (c.1538, Louvre, Paris), *Equestrian Portrait of Charles V* (1548) and *The All-Saints Altar*, called "La Gloria" (1553, both in Prado, Madrid). All were explicitly commissioned works. With beginning of 1550's, however, Titian started sending Philip both mythological and religious paintings unasked. They were gratefully received, richly rewarded, and include Titian's very finest late works. Among these late mythologies are *Danaë* and *Venus and Adonis* (1553–54, Prado, Madrid), *Diana and Actaeon* and *Diana and Callisto* (1556–59, on loan to National Gallery of Scotland, Edinburgh), *Europa and the Bull* (1559–62, Gardner Museum, Boston), and *The Death of Actaeon* (c.1565, collection of Lord Harewood, England).

Among these late religious works are *The Entombment* (1557–59, Prado, Madrid) and *The Martyrdom of St. Lawrence* (1564–67, monastery chapel of Escorial). Titian died in Venice. Of his three children by his common-law wife Cecilia, one, Orazio, became a painter and worked in his father's studio.

REFERENCES: J. A. Crowe and G. B. Cavalcaselle *The Life and Times of Titian* (2 vols. 2nd ed. London 1881). Erwin Panofsky *Studies in Titian: Mostly Iconographic* (New York 1969). Harold Wethey *The Religious Paintings* (New York and London 1969; vol. I of *The Paintings of Titian* in progress).

≪

TITIAN

BY JUERGEN SCHULZ

Titian, wrote Vasari in the sixteenth-century *Lives of the Artists,* was "favored as none of his equals ever were, and had from heaven nothing but favors and happiness." He was in fact endowed by fortune not only with extraordinary talent, long life (he lived to be over eighty), and social dexterity, but also with extraordinary circumstances in which to work. He lived in an age that offered a painter an unparalleled range of tasks in every medium and on every scale: religious imagery, secular allegory, pagan mythology, historical narrative, portraiture, and festival decoration. Moreover, by the death of Giorgione in 1510, and the departure for Rome of Sebastiano in 1511, he was left without serious rivals for more than a quarter century at the very beginning of his career, which allowed him to develop as an artist very much according to his own promptings and needs.

His first teacher was the aged Giovanni Bellini, from whom he learned to conceive of the painted image as a still geometry of colored planes. Within a short time he had fallen under the spell of Giorgione, also a former pupil of Bellini, who had developed the older master's style into a vehicle for expressing the shimmering, unstable surfaces of the natural world, producing paintings laden with mood and sensuous richness. The two styles remained normative for Titian throughout his long career, and his own artistic development followed a circular path that in the end carried him back to the principles with which he had first begun.

His earliest works, such as the frescoed scenes from the life of St. Anthony of Padua of 1510–11 (Scuola del Santo, Padua), show the Bellinesque tendency to pull out compositions and forms in the plane, and the enflamed colors and quivering landscape details of Giorgione. But they show also the marks of an individual temperament. The figures are more grandiose and the compositional rhythms larger than those of his teachers, the narrative is clearer, more concentrated and dramatic, and the motives include borrowings from Michelangelo and antiquity, where Titian could find an expressive figure style not to be learned at Venice itself.

For a brief time after the death of Giorgione he returned more closely to the plane geometry and withdrawn sentiment of Bellini's manner. Paintings like the *Sacred and Profane Love* of c.1515 (Borghese Gallery, Rome) show the motionless and flattened forms of the older artist, although with the characteristic monumentality of Titian. However, by 1516–18, in the altarpiece of the *Assumption* (S. Maria dei Frari, Venice), he was pursuing once again the goal of a dramatically expressive and animated style. In the succeeding three decades he borrowed more and more elements of the plastic, rhetorical figure art of central Italy, eschewing in the end even the sensuous coloring that was the traditional hallmark of Venetian painting. In force and grandeur these works of his middle age are the equal of those by his central Italian contemporaries, Michelangelo and Raphael. However, he never adopted the rigid compositional schemes of the Florentines and Romans. His groupings remained asymmetrical and labile, and natural forms participate as much as the figures in the intuitively balanced masses of his pictures. In the great St. Peter Martyr altarpiece of 1526–30 (formerly SS. Giovanni e Paolo, Venice), the writhing trees combine with the struggling figures on the ground to create a dramatic unity of action and setting that was altogether new in European painting. Thus, the style of Titian's maturity represents a translation of Giorgione's vision of a world in constant movement into the dramatic terms of the central Italian High Renaissance.

Even the most "Roman" of his works, paintings of the early 1540's like the *Ecce Homo* (Vienna), never entirely abandoned the Venetian tendency to link motives in the plane, and to create loose and shifting compositional groupings. It earned Titian disapproving criticism from his central Italian contemporaries when, in 1545–46, he visited Rome at the invitation of Pope Paul III. Upon his return to Venice, we find him reversing the development of the previous quarter century and returning step by step to the extreme planar simplifications and the exquisite colors of his earlier years.

Later works, such as the mythological and religious paintings he conceived for King Philip II of Spain (among them *Diana and Callisto* and *Diana and Actaeon*, 1556–59, National Gallery of Scotland, Edinburgh; *Europa and the Bull*, 1560–62, Gardner Museum, Boston; *Martyrdom of St. Law-*

rence, 1564–67, S. Lorenzo, El Escorial), show compositions that read primarily as surface pattern, and for their somber richness and beauty of coloring have been equaled by none. The stories are presented with the seriousness and directness characteristic of Titian's narrative from the beginning, but with a new sense of poignancy that is the legacy of his expressive style of the 1540's. Figure poses recall the dramatic force of those of his middle years, but are now subtly distorted to lie in the pictorial plane. The solidity of figures and objects is dissolved by a discontinuous brushstroke that makes each detail an abstract composition of color patches, and imposes a uniform texture on all forms regardless of their substance or distance.

In Venice itself these works represented an aberration, the private works of an aging artist. Younger painters, like Tintoretto and Veronese, continued Titian's earlier efforts to master the complexities of central Italian drawing and sculptural relief. But the decorative simplifications and especially the open brushwork that were the trademark of Titian's late style inspired the abbreviated facture and painterly style of artists like Rembrandt, Velázquez, Goya, and Manet, and have remained a fertile influence on European painting to this day.

As a portraitist Titian deserves special mention. Early in his career he developed a formula that met with international success for typifying his sitter as the representative of a class, the embodiment of an office or skill, or the representative of a human type. A history of the sixteenth century could be illustrated with Titian's portraits. They range from the *Emperor Charles V* of 1532 (Madrid), the incarnation of refinement, strength, and serene confidence, and *King Francis I of*

France of 1539 (Paris), the model of royal flair and energy, to the *Imperial Chancellor, Antoine Perrenot de Granvella* of 1548 (Nelson Gallery, Kansas City), the archetype of statesmanlike reserve and self-control, and the *Imperial Art Dealer, Jacopo della Strada* of 1568 (Vienna), the essence of self-importance, subservience, and craft.

Titian's far-flung connections in the social world of his day brought him sitters from the four corners of the known world. In 1533 he was appointed official painter to Emperor Charles V, on which occasion he was also raised to the nobility. He was called to attend upon the emperor during the latter's visits to Italy of 1536, 1541, and 1543, and to attend the imperial Diets at Augsburg in 1548 and 1550, in order to produce on each occasion likenesses of the emperor, members of his household, allies, followers, and even captives. The position of confidence he enjoyed was such that, according to later Venetian historians, he was even asked to report his impressions of the Diet of 1548 to the government of the republic on his return from Augsburg.

During the 1540's he functioned as the unappointed portraitist of the Farnese, the family of Pope Paul III, who sought furthermore to enlist him in their service on the model of his relationship with the emperor. The dukes of Ferrara, Mantua, and Urbino vied with one another to obtain from him portraits and subject pictures for their courts. These connections gave him entry to an international world of rulers and nobility, to a degree greater than that of any other artist of the Italian Renaissance.

Titian, a descendant of a family of timber merchants in the mountain country of provincial Venetia, exploited this power to the utmost for personal gain and authority. Throughout his life he continued to deal in timber in the family tradition, obtaining from his patrons favorable cutting privileges and exemptions from duty. In the artistic world of Venice, he asserted the position of an arbiter of taste and dispenser of patronage, in company with the sculptor and architect Jacopo Sansovino and the journalist and critic Pietro Aretino, who were personal friends. It was a position that he was able to defend against the younger generation of Tintoretto and Veronese until he was high in his old age, and that caused the latter to regard him as a pernicious influence in the very same years that he was creating his most personal works, which we view today as his most sublime achievement.

TOCQUEVILLE, Alexis (Charles Henri Maurice Clérel) de (July 29, 1805 – Apr. 16, 1859). French historian and statesman. Born Verneuil, of a Norman aristocratic family. After studying law in Paris, he followed his father into government service as a junior magistrate at Versailles (1827). Out of sympathy with the government after the July Revolution of 1830, he and his friend Gustave de Beaumont obtained leave of absence to study the American penal system. First result of a year (1831–32) in U.S. was their joint report *Du Système pénitentiaire aux États-Unis et de son application en France* (1832). Tocqueville's *De la Démocratie en Amérique* (vols. I–II, 1835; vols. III–IV, 1840) won him immediate fame and a seat in the Académie Française (1841); it has become a world classic (tr. *Democracy in America* 1835–40). On a trip to England (1835), married Miss Motley. Elected to the Chamber of Deputies (1839), he played a minor role until after the Revolution of 1848, when he became a member of the Constituent Assembly and of the committee which drafted the constitution of the Second Republic. From June to October 1849 served as minister of foreign affairs. After Louis Napoleon's coup d'etat (1851), he retired from politics to write *L'Ancien Régime et la révolution* (1856) and his *Recollections* (1893, tr. 1896). Died in Cannes.

TRANSLATIONS: *Democracy in America* tr. Henry Reeve (2 vols. New York 1945, also PB). *Recollections* ed. Jacob P. Mayer, tr. A. T. de Mattos (London 1948 and New York 1949). *The Old Régime and the French Revolution* tr. Stuart Gilbert (Garden City, N.Y. PB 1955).

REFERENCES: Seymour Drescher *Tocqueville and England* (Cambridge, Mass. and Oxford 1964) and *Dilemmas of Democracy: Tocqueville and Modernization* (Pittsburgh, Pa. 1968). Edward T. Gargan *De Tocqueville* (New York and London 1965). Richard Herr *Tocqueville and the Old Regime* (Princeton, N.J. 1962, also PB). Max Lerner *Tocqueville and American Civilization* (New York PB 1966). Jack Lively *The Social and Political Thought of Alexis de Tocqueville* (London and New York 1962). Jacob P. Mayer *Alexis de Tocqueville: A Biographical Study in Political Science* (tr. 1939, new ed. Gloucester, Mass. 1960, also PB). George W. Pierson *Tocqueville in America* (1929, new ed. Gloucester, Mass. 1960, also PB). Marvin Zetterbaum *Tocqueville and the Problem of Democracy* (Stanford, Calif. 1967).

~

ALEXIS DE TOCQUEVILLE
BY RICHARD HOFSTADTER

Tocqueville may be best thought of as a sociologist, perhaps the first great political sociologist of the modern era. This judgment will surely provoke disagreement: there are those who prefer to think of him as a historian or a political scientist, and those who will think of Tocqueville's style as being so radically unlike the style of any sociologist they can call to mind, contemporary or even classical, that the suggestion will seem bizarre. But, of course, Tocqueville was a sociologist with a difference. His way of developing a theme is so characteristically that of the French literary mind, his view of society retains so much of the moralist's manner, his way of approaching his subjects remains so impressionistic. It may be useful here to contrast him with Marx. Where Marx thought he was developing a "scientific" sociology, Tocqueville was candidly intuitive — though not without system. Both of them were responding to the industrial revolution and the early rise of modern democracy. But while for Marx the conception of class was the central theme — and for him a democracy could be truly achieved only after a class society was destroyed — for Tocqueville the central fact of the democratic era was the passion for status, and he saw clearly the tremendous paradox imported into modern political and social development by the tension between the striving for status and the striving for equality. "Democratic institutions awaken and foster a passion for equality which they can never entirely satisfy." Again, where Marx was the sociologist of the proletariat and of socialism, Tocqueville was the sociologist of the aristocracy and, in a certain qualified sense, of conservatism. Marx stems from the critical thought of the Enlightenment, and also, though he found a "scientific" corrective so necessary, from the utopian thought stimulated by the Enlightenment and by the French Revolution. Tocqueville owes little or nothing to utopian modes of thought: he seems rather to carry on the tradition of cool intelligence which we associate with Montaigne and Montesquieu. It seems important that he was a believing Catholic, since his sociological insights tend to go beyond the place and the moment and to rest on something universal in the human condition. The feeling of being embattled is alive everywhere in Marx's writing; in Tocqueville it is the sense of distance one feels most keenly, not because he has no values or commitments (far from it) but because his ears are always tuned to the music of the spheres.

One of the keys to Tocqueville's detachment, to his sense of distance, lies in the fact that he accepted the historical necessity of the values he disliked. Where Marx's "science" assured him that the future belonged to Marx, Tocqueville's intuition told him that the future most assuredly did not belong to Tocqueville. As an aristocrat, he stood for certain things — a kind of freedom, tradition, honor, and the creativity and leadership of great individuals — which his informed sense of the world told him would be replaced or diminished, perhaps in some cases eliminated, by democracy. But what distinguishes him from the reactionaries of his own era is that he wastes no time in lamentations over an *ancien régime* that cannot be restored, or in shrill denunciations of revolution. His intellectual life is an argument for accepting the pattern for the future, and for attempting only to educate, inform, and lead it. In this respect he still finds a role for a wise and flexible elite.

This explains why Tocqueville took so much trouble to see the United States at first hand, since he saw in American development the vanguard of the future, the nearest living realization of what the inevitable and unwanted democracy would be like. And this is why — with all due respect to his *The Old Régime and the French Revolution* — *Democracy in America* is his greatest work. It was not that he was primarily interested in the United States: he was interested in France, and in Europe. But he used the condition of America as a key to open the door to the future.

Tocqueville firmly believed that "the gradual development of the principle of equality is . . . a providential fact."

"It has," he said, "all the chief characteristics of such a fact: it is universal, it is lasting, it constantly eludes all human interference, and all events as well as all men contribute to its progress. . . . To attempt to check democracy would be . . . to resist the will of God," and the nations ought to make the best of the lot meted out to them by Providence. To try to stop the advance of democracy would be not merely futile but very likely ruinous. It should not be opposed, but, while there is still time, guided. The duty of leadership is "to educate democracy, to reawaken, if possible, its religious beliefs; to purify its morals; to mold its actions; to substitute a knowledge of statecraft for its inexperience, and an awareness of its true interest for its blind instincts."

Hence, in examining America, Tocqueville was able to hold his distaste for equality in check by his regard for what Marx would have called its historic necessity, and to rein in his fears for the future by his need for hope and by his awareness that any grand historical movement that is to be guided must be understood. What he found in America, as an anchor for his hopes, was that democracy, while inelegant and chaotic, and presumably fated not to achieve the highest reaches of human creativity, was astonishingly peaceful in its mode of development and that it had a goodly variety of minor virtues to compensate for its loss of a few heroic qualities. Having experienced, as he said in his *Recollections*, two revolutions in seventeen years, he was particularly responsive to the peaceful, nonrevolutionary pattern of American politics. "I have endeavored," he wrote a friend, "to abate the claims of aristocrats and to make them bend to an irresistible future; so that the impulse in one quarter and resistance in another being less violent, society may march on peaceably toward the fulfillment of its destiny." He saw in the United States the outlines of a future in which there would be less splendor, but also less misery; fewer acutely enjoyed pleasures, but more general comfort; a less distinguished cultivation of science, but also a better-educated general public. "The nation, taken as a whole, will be less brilliant, less glorious, and perhaps less strong; but the majority of the citizens will enjoy a greater degree of prosperity, and the people will remain peaceable, not because they despair of a change for the better, but because they are conscious they are well off already."

Something should be said about the style of Tocqueville's observations. He had not only his own love of paradox but also a strong sense for the perversity of the human species and the irregularities of conduct that this perversity engenders. He was singularly free from those mechanical errors that follow from the assumption that everything takes place, so to speak, according to reason. "For my part," he wrote in his *Recollections,* "I detest these absolute systems, which represent all the events of history as depending upon great first causes linked by the chain of fatality, and which, as it were, suppress men from the history of the human race. They seem narrow, to my mind, under their pretense of broadness, and false beneath their air of mathematical exactness." It was this freedom from mechanical juxtapositions that made it possible for him to penetrate those aspects of historical experience that proceed not smoothly from point to point, but by the sudden jumps of contradiction — "those impromptus," he called them, "which astonish and alarm us." Though it is

now a commonplace, he was one of the first modern thinkers to prepare us to see why revolutions are the work not of oppressed and despairing masses but rather of classes already significantly on the rise.

This keen sense for the pattern of events is often matched by a sense for styles of thought. See how, in recalling a conversation with Ampère, he goes to the heart of a style of thought that not only characterizes generations of French intellectuals but also touches perfectly upon the ways of some of the more unthinking literary radicals of our own age: "Unfortunately, he [Ampère] was inclined to carry the *esprit* of the salons into literature and the *esprit* of literature into politics. What I call *esprit* in politics consists in seeking for what is novel and ingenious rather than for what is true; in preferring the showy to the useful; in showing one's self very sensible to the playing and elocution of the actors, without regard to the results of the play; and, lastly, in judging by impressions rather than by reasons. . . . To tell the truth, the whole nation is a little inclined that way, and the French public very often takes a man-of-letters' view of politics."

Certainly Tocqueville is fallible; there are, of course, some things he misses and misinterprets, some things he exaggerates. There are moments when he at least *seems* to contradict himself in his comments on America. But on balance, after more than one hundred and thirty years, one is impressed again and again by the importance and durability of Tocqueville's insights. As one finds one's self plodding deliberately along the muddy bottoms of uncomprehended or half-comprehended historical problems, one looks up from time to time with wonder to see how Tocqueville's mind leaps and soars. Whatever word we are to fix upon as suggesting the very opposite of pedestrian — that is Tocqueville.

TOLSTOY, Leo Nikolaevich, Count (Aug. 28, 1828 – Nov. 7, 1910). Russian novelist. Of noble family, he was born at Yasnaya Polyana, his parents' estate, near Tula. Orphaned at nine and brought up by aunts, he received his early education from private tutors. Entered University of Kazan at sixteen; returned to estate (1847), but soon left to lead profligate life in Moscow and St. Petersburg. Followed his brother (1851) into army service in the Caucasus, where he wrote his first published work, *Childhood* (1852), part of autobiographical trilogy which includes *Boyhood* (1854) and *Youth* (1857). Participated in defense of Sevastopol (1854). Left army service (1855) and for several years divided his time between Yasnaya Polyana, where he engaged in projects to educate and emancipate his serfs, and St. Petersburg, where he associated with Turgenev and other writers. Traveled in western Europe (1857, 1860–61). After marriage to Sofiya Bers (1862), resided chiefly at his estate, writing *The Cossacks* (1863), *War and Peace* (1865–69), and *Anna Karenina* (1875–77). A religious conversion in the late 1870's, described in *A Confession* (1879), led to his condemnation of organized religion and government, war and private property, and to estrangement from his family. He became an enormously influential prophet and religious-anarchistic leader. Left home (1910), accompanied by his doctor and youngest daughter, and died at the railway station at Astapovo. Other major works are *The Death of Ivan Ilyich* (1884), *The Kreutzer Sonata* (1889), *Hadji Murad* (1896–1904), *Resurrection* (1899–1900).

TRANSLATIONS: *Tolstoy Centenary Edition* tr. Louise and Aylmer Maude (21 vols. London and New York 1928–37). *The Journal of Leo Tolstoi, 1895–1899* tr. Rose Strunsky (New York 1917). *The Private Diary of Leo Tolstoy, 1853–1857* tr. and ed. Louise and Aylmer Maude (Garden City, N.Y. 1927).

REFERENCES: John Bayley *Tolstoy and the Novel* (London 1966 and New York 1967, also PB). Isaiah Berlin *The Hedgehog and the Fox: An Essay on Tolstoy's View of History* (London and New York 1953, also PB). R. F. Christian *Tolstoy's War and Peace: A Study* (Oxford 1962) and *Tolstoy: A Critical Introduction* (Cambridge, England, 1969, also PB). Janko Lavrin *Tolstoy: An Approach* (1946, reprinted New York 1968). R. E. Matlaw ed. *Tolstoy: A Collection of Critical Essays* (Englewood Cliffs, N.J. 1967, also PB). Aylmer Maude *The Life of Tolstoy* (1908–10, rev. ed. 2 vols. London and New York 1931). Ernest J. Simmons *Leo Tolstoy* (Boston 1946 and London 1949, also PB). George Steiner *Tolstoy or Dostoevsky* (New York 1959 and London 1960, also PB). Henri Troyat *Tolstoy* (tr. New York 1967 and London 1968, also PB).

~

TOLSTOY
BY GEORGE P. ELLIOTT

Tolstoy is so various in himself and so much is known about him that defining him is as risky as characterizing a people, a heterogeneous, contumacious, divinely afflicted people. It is as much as one can do to imagine the actual man, to hold him steadily in imagination, for finally he himself seemed not to hold together; yet one must try to imagine him, for it was not till he had passed his eighty-second year that he broke apart. If he broke apart even then: taking a doctor friend and a devoted daughter with him he ran from home and wife, collapsed on the train, and died of pneumonia in the house of the stationmaster in a little town. Maybe he did not succumb to craziness, old age, and disease, but used them. Maybe there remained that in him which presided even over those pulling him to death, saying *Do it my way.*

Inconsistency, self-contradiction, absurd behavior, these we are used to in life and also in Tolstoy's stories, in which an unending series of unexpected actions erupt into our minds, keeping the characters alive. But Tolstoy himself! Who would have dared to invent him? No scheme holds so outrageous a man, certainly none of his own schemes. Not even *War and Peace* would be big enough to hold him.

As a young soldier he was praised by a general for intrepidity in the face of fire. As a middle-aged writer living "a correct, honorable family life," he awakened the household one night (as his eldest son recounts it) screaming for his wife; it was his custom to undress in one room and go down the hall to the bedroom he shared with her; this night, having no candle, he lost his way between one door and the other in the house where he spent his life; his wife came to him and took him to bed.

Young, he was enormously lustful. Later, he preached absolute chastity as the sexual ideal to be striven for. When he was nearly seventy he told a guest he had been a husband to his wife the night before but perhaps God would yet grant him strength to be chaste. When he was eighty-one he said that he had finally ceased to be troubled by sexual desire. As he was turning eighty-two, his wife of sixty-six, to whom he had been faithful for forty-eight years and who had borne him thirteen children, accused him of a homosexual attachment to a man of fifty-six.

The vain young aristocrat could be so snobbish that once he shocked his brother by saying that a respectable-looking gentleman driving past them was a scoundrel. "Why?" "Because he is without gloves." After his great religious crisis culminating in a conversion at the age of fifty-one, he preached a radical and heretical Christianity of nonviolence, chastity, communal property, brotherhood — in a word, humility. Nothing, not even the celebrated novels, made him so famous throughout the world and such a power in his own country as preaching humility.

He bitterly regretted the chasm of class that separated him from peasants, from the vast majority of his fellow countrymen, and he taught that their way of life was essentially superior to the sophisticated way because it was nearer nature. Not one of the peasants in his stories is comparable, as a living fictional personality, to scores of characters from the educated classes, and to the end, when his own peasants exasperated him, he was capable suddenly of becoming their barin again, cold, autocratic, cruel, making them cringe and slink off.

He taught that the meaning of life is love within each man and among men — *The Kingdom of God is Within You* — and that death is the joyous completion of life, and fear of death a superstition. In a letter to Chekhov, written in 1900, Gorki said: "Now when I heard him speak about Christ and saw his eyes — too clever for a believer — I know that he is indeed an atheist and a confirmed one." A few weeks later, Chekhov, who also loved Tolstoy and knew him well, wrote Gorki that he had just read *Resurrection:* "The novel made the impression of strength, richness, and breadth, and the insincerity of a man afraid of death and refusing to admit it and clutching at texts and holy Scripture."

No end to this cataloguing. One must say, with awe: he was a man of powerful appetites — sensual, emotional, intellectual, egoistic — and he strove for the opposite of each appetite, its denial or its counter. A radical and merciless questioner, one whom ideas seized and shook into action, he preached a simplified Christian faith, acquiescent, even passive, and increasingly throughout his life he tossed from an extreme of skepticism to an extreme of faith. To the born confidence of genius there was added in him the bred pride of a Russian aristocrat; after his conversion, he thought the root sin was assertion of the ego; down to the last week of his life, he meticulously recorded in his diaries the victories and perplexities and defeats of his own ego, which fascinated him as much as it did the rest of the world.

There is all that writing, and especially the three principal stories — *War and Peace* written in his late thirties, *Anna Karenina* in his late forties just before the conversion, and *The Death of Ivan Ilyich* shortly after it in his fifties. In these if not in his life, he was able harmoniously to order the actual variety and even greater abundance of possibility within himself. It is true that later, in *What Is Art?*, he depreciated his fiction — not its excellence, for he did not lose his judgment, but its importance. *War and Peace* was not useful, as *Uncle Tom's Cabin* was useful; therefore it was unimportant and he had better have spent his time at moral fables. Only a "Tolstoyan" yields to this argument; the rest of us turn to the three novels for both pleasure and truth, for that kind of enduring truth which survives the local instance. One use for his fiction, irrelevant to its literary and moral purposes but yet a source of truth, is to provide insights into what in this man, beyond his tensions, was continuous and coherent.

Above all, there is the gift of genius, about which one need say only that he accepted it.

There is the curiosity about the world and himself, the attentiveness, the unflagging observation, the prying even. He looked hard at whatever plain light revealed of behavior, and he intuited much that lay hidden in the irrational and unconscious. His concern to understand apparent reality was as intense as his pleasure in stories that figured forth hidden reality.

There is the vitality, the "life," which everyone speaks of, helplessly, who discusses his stories and him. The characters of his novels are full of fictional life, and reading those books fills you with life. All who knew Tolstoy were strongly affected by him, and even to read about him is to share Gorki's opinion: "One looks at him and it is frightfully pleasant to feel that one is also a man, to realize that man can be such as Leo Tolstoy." There was much death in Tolstoy, for it takes much death to kill a man that alive: he shuddered, and roared against it. Gorki said: "Even the unpleasant and hostile feelings which he roused were of a kind not to oppress but rather to explode the soul; they made it more sensitive and capacious."

There is Tolstoy's concern for life, which never ceased, so far as we know, to struggle with its cold antagonist. All life mattered and what was really there mattered, but the good mattered to him even more. Why live? What is the meaning of life? What is good here and now? Not being able to answer this question in all its forms nearly killed him in the middle of his journey, and answering it became an obsession. His whole contrary nature both asserted *it matters* and admitted the appalling opposite, the void of *nothing matters*. Not even the elaborate bastion of ideas and belief which he kept throwing up could always protect him; certainly it did not keep out that fear of the void and death which could make him howl and dodge. Nevertheless, when nothing else mattered, to think that *nothing mattered* always mattered to him desperately.

His death is a terrifying waste, a Lear's death, excruciating, yet one does not cry out against it, no harmonious fulfillment was possible, only that tossing pain, that intricate powerful bewildered love. The love failed him over and over again, darted now towards this opposite, now toward that; but it never died. His last distinguishable words were: "Truth . . . I love all . . . all of them." Shortly before, he had suddenly sat up in bed and called in a loud voice: "Escape, I must escape!" His love failed often, but his dream of love endured. When he was a child of five, his older brother Nikolai said he possessed a secret which, if it were known, would destroy all evil in men so that they would love one another in universal brotherhood and this secret was written on a little green stick hidden in the ground at the edge of a ravine not far from their home. Tolstoy, as he requested, was buried at the place of the green stick.

TOULOUSE-LAUTREC, Henri (Marie Raymond) de (Nov. 24, 1864 – Sept. 9, 1901). French painter and lithographer. Born Albi, (Tarn), France, son of Comte Alphonse de Toulouse-Lautrec and Adèle Tapié de Céleyran. From earliest childhood sketched animals, family, country life. Delicate health and accidents resulted in deformity from youth on. Studied briefly in Paris with René Princeteau, Léon Bonnat, and Fernand Cormon. Moved (1884) into studio of his own and began to frequent and draw the night haunts of Montmartre. Accepted by Salon des Indépendants (1889). Spent several months in a Neuilly asylum recovering from a breakdown brought on by alcoholism (1899). Paralysis struck (1901) and he died at family's Château de Malromé. Belated recognition came in 1922 with the assembling of a collection that became permanent exhibition of his work at the Albi Mu-

seum, now called Musée Toulouse-Lautrec.

REFERENCES: Jean Adhémar *Henri de Toulouse-Lautrec: Complete Lithographs and Drypoints* (New York and London 1965). André Fermigier *Toulouse-Lautrec* (tr. New York 1969, also PB). Philippe Huisman and M. G. Dortu *Lautrec by Lautrec* (tr. New York and London 1964). Maurice Joyant *Henri de Toulouse-Lautrec* (Paris 1926–27, reprinted 2 vols. New York 1968). Horst Keller *Toulouse-Lautrec, Painter of Paris* (tr. New York 1969). Jacques Lassaigne *Toulouse-Lautrec* (New York and London 1953). Gerstle Mack *Toulouse-Lautrec* (New York 1938). Fritz Novotny *Toulouse-Lautrec: Paintings, Drawings, Lithographs* (tr. New York and London 1969). Henri Perruchot *Toulouse-Lautrec: A Definitive Biography* (tr. London 1960 and Cleveland 1961, also PB).

☞

TOULOUSE-LAUTREC
BY CARLTON LAKE

"I have tried to make it true and not idealized. Perhaps that is a fault, because I don't spare the warts and I enjoy adding the hairs that sprout from them." Lautrec was sixteen when he wrote that in a letter from Nice to his friend Étienne Devismes. The "fault" was no fault; it was his grace and glory, but drawing and painting the truth as he saw it endeared him to few. Degas was an exception. "I see you're one of us," he said after his visit to Lautrec's exhibition at the Goupil gallery. But the official painters, the established reputations, recognized the threat presented by this wittiest and most honest of painters. And so did the collectors, the curators, and all the others who lived by pandering to the hypocrisies of the times.

What made Lautrec's departures from "good taste" and the entrenched aesthetic canons all the more unpardonable was the fact that he hadn't sprung from the usual nondescript background: his father, for whom hunting and hawking were the whole of life, and his painfully pious, over-protective mother had endowed him with the genes of one of the oldest and noblest of French families. It was also one of the most inbred. Marriage between first cousins (as in the case of Henri's parents) was commonplace, and the children didn't always survive. Henri did, but with a bone disease that stunted his growth and made his recovery from two falls lingering and incomplete. When he finally weaned himself from this tentacular family, he put down roots among its polar opposites in Montmartre to make a life of his own, and wrote to his Uncle Charles, "I feel myself held back by a great load of sentimental considerations that I must absolutely forget if I wish to achieve anything."

He had been, from the beginning, extraordinarily gifted as a draftsman, with a delicious wit that is almost never absent from the drawings and letters of even the pre-teen years. Whatever the prejudices of his background, his own work shows none. He examined everything with a clear eye and set it down with a forthrightness that could only be disturbing to the upholders of tradition, social inequities, and all the hand-me-down moralities. Unlike most of his contemporaries, Lautrec was never the propagandist. His whores and lesbians were painted without commentary. They are simply people, like his actresses, dancers or bicycle racers — citizens of a world he chose in preference to one based on pride, power, sham, and a kind of moral double entry bookkeeping. This suspension of all moral judgment gives a unique freshness to his portrayal of brothel scenes. There is neither censure nor eroticism in such paintings as *Au Lit, Le Baiser* (1892), *Au Salon* (1894),

Femme nue accroupie (1897), or *Femme retroussant sa chemise* (1901). They are total innocence in comparison to the lubricious Salon exhibits of painters like Bouguereau and Rochegrosse who fed the fantasies and insulated the illusions of the era. Lautrec spoke simply and directly of the facts of the times and that was unforgivable. But even when his subjects were less troubling — Jane Avril, Yvette Guilbert, May Milton, for example — there was always his line, his color, his technique in general to give offense to the *bienpensant*. The flatness of Japanese prints had been a strong influence, along with Degas, and Forain's journalistic bluntness, which became lighter and more nervous in Lautrec's hands. Lautrec's clear, bold colors, rarely mixed, are bathed in a harsh light that sets off his subject against the background in a sharp, sometimes brutal manner, more arresting than anything derived from traditional use of chiaroscuro and perspective. What counted for him was the human figure — or the animal — and its movement. In his lithography he was suggestive rather than explicit and he achieved more with less than any other artist of the western world. For that reason he could raise the poster to a creative eminence no one else was ever able to sustain.

Lautrec lived at a period when most articulate people kept journals and — at a nonliterary level, as in his own family — wrote unending letters to set down a continuing account of their daily activities. Throughout his work, Lautrec was doing just that: a great painter with the temperament of a writer and an insatiable curiosity about life in all its forms. Wherever he went — the Moulin Rouge, the Moulin de la Galette, the Cirque Fernando, the Divan Japonais, Aristide Bruant's Mirliton, Le Chat Noir, the Café Weber, the

Irish and American Bar, the Comédie Française, the Vélodrome Buffalo, or the brothels he and his friend Romain Coolus occasionally lived in — everything found its way into his work. He was the instinctive artist, the man who bears witness to his time. Thus his insistence on getting away from the traditional subject matter of art, the academic nudes, the official portraits, the mythological scenes full of the window dressing of third-rate imaginations. He had no pupils and left no disciples, but his influence on the great innovator of the next generation, Picasso, was determining, visible not only in Picasso's early work but more lastingly in Picasso's general attitude toward the painter's role. Picasso has said he paints "the way some people write their autobiography. The paintings, finished or not, are the pages of my journal. . . . It's the movement of painting that interests me." He could have been speaking for Lautrec.

In Lautrec's last years, alcohol was first his solace, finally his nemesis. As his strength ebbed, his world began to seem a less habitable place. In the end the umbilical cord proved the strongest bond and Henri, irreparably broken, dragged himself back to die in his mother's arms at the Château de Malromé, sobbing, with his last breath, "Mama, you, only you."

After Lautrec's death French officialdom did its best to keep him out of sight, just as it had resisted the great impressionist paintings of the Caillebotte bequest and Manet's *Olympia*. The Luxembourg Museum was offered its choice of the contents of Lautrec's atelier but a timid curator was too prudent to force the issue with an unsympathetic administration. In 1882 Lautrec's early teacher, the fashionable portraitist Léon Bonnat, had called his drawing "simply atrocious." He hadn't changed his mind in 1905 when, as president of the Council of Museums, he barred the door of the Luxembourg to the gift of even one relatively inoffensive portrait by Lautrec. But we all owe Bonnat a debt of gratitude: without his intransigence there would be no Musée Toulouse-Lautrec in Albi, now the repository of the rich family bequest, along with the others, including that of Lautrec's devoted friend Maurice Joyant, which logically followed.

TOURNEUR, Cyril (c.1575 – Feb. 28, 1626). English dramatist and poet. Possibly the son of Captain Richard Turnor, lieutenant governor of Brill, Netherlands. First published a satirical, allegorical poem, *The Transformed Metamorphosis,* in 1600. Apparently served in Low Countries, where he met the English general Sir Francis Vere, about whom he wrote *A Funeral Poem* (1609). Joined with John Webster and Thomas Heywood to write *Three Elegies on the Most Lamented Death of Prince Henry* (1612). After the cancellation of his appointment as secretary to the council of war, he sailed with Sir Edward Cecil on illfated Cádiz expedition (1625). Fell sick on return voyage and died at Kinsdale, Ireland. Remembered chiefly as a dramatist, author of *The Revenger's Tragedy* (1607) and *The Atheist's Tragedy* (1611), full of gloom and murder. *The Nobleman* (performed 1612) is now lost. A masterpiece of Jacobean drama, *The Revenger's Tragedy* is of questionable authorship. Published anonymously, it was attributed to Tourneur by bookseller Edward Archer (1656); scholars are not agreed whether Tourneur or Thomas Middleton was its author.

EDITIONS: *Works* ed. Allardyce Nicoll (1929, reprinted New York 1963). *The Atheist's Tragedy* ed. Irving Ribner (London and Cambridge, Mass. 1964). *The Revenger's Tragedy* ed. R. A. Foakes (London and Cambridge, Mass. 1966).
REFERENCES: T. S. Eliot *Elizabethan Essays* (1934, latest ed. New York 1964). Una Ellis-Fermor *The Jacobean Drama: An Interpretation* (5th ed. Lon-

don 1965, also PB). Peter B. Murray *A Study of Cyril Tourneur* (Philadelphia 1964 and Oxford 1965). S. A. and D. R. Tannenbaum *Cyril Tourneur: A Concise Bibliography* (New York 1946).

TRAHERNE, Thomas (c.1636 – Sept. 27, 1674). English poet. Born Hereford, son of a shoemaker, he was educated at Brasenose College, Oxford (B.A. 1656, M.A. 1661, B.D. 1669); ordained as clergyman (1660). Served as chaplain to Sir Orlando Bridgeman, lord keeper of the seal, from 1667. Unmarried, he died at Teddington, having published *Roman Forgeries* (1673). His *Christian Ethics* published posthumously (1675), was followed by anonymous publication of *A Serious and Pathetical Contemplation of the Mercies of God* (1699) and *Meditations and Devotions* (1717). Remained virtually unknown as a literary figure until 1896, when Bertram Dobell discovered a manuscript of his prose and poetry in a London bookstall. Edited by Dobell and published as *Poetical Works* (1903) and *Centuries of Meditations* (1908), the manuscript established Traherne as a religious writer of inspired vision and fervent intensity. Another manuscript, found to have been in British Museum since 1818, was published as *Poems of Felicity* (1910). In 1964 Yale University acquired and identified a 60,000-word manuscript entitled *Select Meditations*. A religious writer in the metaphysical tradition, Traherne emphasizes the purity of union between God and man, stressing the mystical powers of the imagination.

EDITIONS: *The Poetical Works of Thomas Traherne* ed. Gladys I. Wade (3rd ed. London 1932, reprinted New York 1965). *Poems, Centuries, and Three Thanksgivings* ed. Anne Ridler (London and New York 1966).

REFERENCES: A. L. Clements *The Mystical Poetry of Thomas Traherne* (Cambridge, Mass. 1969). Queenie Iredale *Thomas Traherne* (Oxford 1935 and New York 1936). James B. Leishman *The Metaphysical Poets: Donne, Herbert, Vaughan, Traherne* (Oxford 1934, reprinted New York 1963). Louis L. Martz *The Paradise Within: Studies in Vaughan, Traherne, and Milton* (New Haven, Conn. 1964). Keith W.

Salter *Thomas Traherne, Mystic and Poet* (London and New York 1964). Gladys I. Wade *Thomas Traherne* (London and Princeton, N.J. 1944).

TRAKL, Georg (Feb. 3, 1887 – Nov. 3, 1914). Austrian poet. Born Salzburg, Austria. While student of pharmacy in Vienna, produced his first mature poems (1910). After a year of military service (1910–11), moved between Salzburg, Vienna, and Innsbruck, indulging excessively in wine and narcotics. Deeply attached to sister Grete, a gifted pianist. Winter of 1912–13 in Vienna was a productive period, during which he wrote the long poem *Helian*. Received subsidy in July 1914 from Ludwig Wittgenstein, who considered him a genius, but the next month Trakl was drafted as reserve lieutenant-pharmacist in Austrian army, and on November 3 committed suicide in Cracow military hospital, Poland. His work, which has affinity with that of Rimbaud and Hölderlin, is thought to be "a vision of spiritual crisis in Europe," in the words of his translator-editor Christopher Middleton, "mysteries of death and love and regeneration enacting themselves as things fall apart and the center cannot hold."

TRANSLATION: *Selected Poems* tr. Robert Grenier and others, ed. Christopher Middleton (London 1968 and New York 1969, also PB).

TREVELYAN, George Macaulay (Feb. 16, 1876 – July 21, 1962). English historian. Born Welcombe, near Stratford-upon-Avon, son of Sir George Otto Trevelyan, historian and statesman, and grandnephew of Thomas Babington Macaulay. Educated at Harrow and Trinity College, Cambridge, he commanded the First British Ambulance Unit for Italy during World War I. Became regius professor of modern history at Cambridge (1927–40) and master of Trinity College (1940–51). Received Order of Merit (1930) and was appointed chancellor of Durham University (1949). Married Janet Penrose Ward (1904), a niece of Matthew Arnold. Died in Cambridge. His most ambitious works are a Garibaldi trilogy (*Garibaldi's Defence of the Roman Re-*

public, 1907; *Garibaldi and the Thou-sand*, 1909; *Garibaldi and the Making of Italy*, 1911) and his *England Under Queen Anne* (3 vols. 1930–34). His *History of England* (1926) is an outstanding single-volume British history. Other works include *England Under the Stuarts* (1904), *The Life of John Bright* (1913), *Lord Grey of the Reform Bill* (1920), *British History in the Nineteenth Century, 1782–1901* (1922), *English Social History: A Survey of Six Centuries* (1944), and *An Autobiography and Other Essays* (1949). Trevelyan greatly influenced a generation of historians, emphasizing history as part of a nation's literary heritage.

REFERENCE: J. H. Plumb *G. M. Trevelyan* (London and New York 1951, also PB).

TROLLOPE, Anthony (Apr. 24, 1815 – Dec. 6, 1882). English novelist. Born London, son of a barrister and a mother, Frances Trollope (1780–1863), who wrote novels to support the family and achieved considerable fame with *Domestic Manners of the Americans* (1832). He spent some time at both Harrow and Winchester, and at nineteen became a clerk in London Post Office. By 1841 was traveling postal inspector in Ireland, where he married Rose Heseltine (1844) and wrote first novel, *The Macdermots of Ballycloran* (1847). A failure, it was followed by two others, but his fourth attempt, *The Warden* (1855), a novel of clerical life, was so well received that he produced a sequel, *Barchester Towers* (1857) and four more novels, collectively entitled the Chronicles of Barsetshire. Now famous and financially secure, Trollope resigned from his post and stood (unsuccessfully) for Parliament (1868). The ensuing experiences resulted in a series of political novels (sometimes grouped as Parliamentary Novels), including *Phineas Finn* (1869) and *The Prime Minister* (1876). One of the most prolific writers in English literature, Trollope turned out altogether some sixty novels, four travel books, and eventually his *Autobiography* (published 1883). After moving to Harting Grange, Hampshire (1880), he returned to London (1882), where he died of a paralytic stroke.

REFERENCES: Bradford A. Booth *Anthony Trollope: Aspects of His Life and Art* (Bloomington, Ind. and London 1958). A. O. J. Cockshut *Anthony Trollope: A Critical Study* (1955, new ed. New York 1968, also PB). P.D. Edwards *Anthony Trollope* (London 1968 and New York 1969, also PB). Rafael Helling *A Century of Trollope Criticism* (1956, reprinted Port Washington, N.Y. 1967). Robert M. Polhemus *The Changing World of Anthony Trollope* (Berkeley, Calif. and Cambridge, England, 1968). Michael Sadleir *Trollope: A Commentary* (1928, rev. ed. London 1945 and New York 1947, PB 1961). Donald Smalley ed. *Trollope: The Critical Heritage* (London and New York 1969). Lucy P. and Richard P. Stebbins *The Trollopes: The Chronicle of a Writing Family* (New York 1945 and London 1946). Anthony Trollope *An Autobiography* (1883, latest ed. London and New York 1953).

✍

ANTHONY TROLLOPE
BY JOHN GROSS

Like Jane Austen or Dickens, Trollope is a novelist who has to be rescued from the addicts who have made a middlebrow cult of him before he can be taken as seriously as he deserves. Even today, in spite of several recent attempts to rehabilitate his work as a whole, he is far too often thought of solely as the chronicler of Barchester, and of the broader humors of Barchester at that. It still needs to be pointed out that, on the contrary, his finest achievements are mostly to be found among the more astringent, altogether less sedate novels of his later years; that socially his range extends well beyond the country house and the cathedral close; that, however conventional his general outlook, when it comes to anatomizing the living detail of behavior he is constantly surprising one with his flexibility and finesse. He can be a good deal more subtle, in fact, than many novelists who advertise subtlety as their stock in trade. And yet, although the popular estimate has to be substantially modified and revised, it would be sheer critical perversity to try and stand it completely on its head. Trollope was not a commonplace man, but as an artist the commonplace was his home ground, and no one is likely to get much enjoyment out of his work who doesn't respond to the traditional Trollopean virtues — amplitude, solid good sense, a certain robustness of feeling, a keen eye for the minor skirmishes and mildly absurd self-deceptions of everyday life.

The mystery, if there is one, lies in the degree rather than the essential nature of his appeal. How does he manage to invest ordinary people in unremarkable situations with so much dramatic interest? What is it that saves him from seeming merely trite, or offensively hearty, or smug? For an answer, one surely has to go no further than the autobiography which did his reputation so much harm when it first appeared, with its disclosures about his tradesman-like attitude to literature, but which in retrospect is really far more significant for what it reveals about his painful beginnings. An eccentric, hopelessly undependable father and a bullying elder brother ensured that even by the standards of a Victorian novelist Trollope had an exceptionally wretched childhood. He went to Winchester and Harrow, but arguably he would have been happier in a blacking factory; he grew up conscious of himself as ignorant, clumsy, unattractive, snubbed by his seniors and despised by his contemporaries. In another period, or with a different temperament, he might have taken refuge in daydreams of revenge, adopting the stance of a rebel and an outsider. Instead, he dreamed of social acceptance, though always of acceptance gained without sacrificing his self-

respect: normality became a challenge, and the ordinary world took on some of the fascination of a paradise from which he could never be quite sure that he wasn't irretrievably locked out. Henry James summed up the matter as well as anyone could, in words which have — understandably — often been quoted: "His great, his inestimable merit, was a complete appreciation of the usual." He appreciated it in the sense that it gave him pleasure, and also in the sense that he didn't take it for granted, that he had gauged to a nicety the power of social inertia, the pervasiveness of habit, the limited scale on which most human passions were ultimately forced to operate.

Given this general cast of mind, he naturally tends to excel at the minor variant rather than the startling exception. His clerics, squires, politicians almost always run true to type, but no two are exactly the same; even his conventional heroine is usually something more than an undifferentiated English rose, his conventional hero something more than a walking gentleman. And it is not only individual characters who are firmly realized; there is an equally strong sense of society as a whole, of the way in which its parts interlock and of the assumptions which hold it together. This is Trollope's real claim to be considered a political novelist. It may seem paradoxical that while he had what he called "an insane desire" to become an M.P., there should be so few political ideas or controversies in his parliamentary novels. But the truth is that he was committed to Parliament as an institution rather than to any one party, and fascinated by machinations rather than policies. In the same way the Barchester novels have nothing to say about theology, but a good deal to say about the sociology of religion; the later novels have nothing to say about economics, but a great deal to say about money.

Taken together, Trollope's works represent the nearest English equivalent to the *Comédie Humaine*. His world is smaller and safer than Balzac's: the Bishop is in his palace, the Duke of Omnium still rules at Gatherum Castle, everything has its allotted place in an almost feudalistic hierarchy. This was obviously not the whole story about mid-Victorian England — Barchester is a long way from Manchester — but there was enough truth in it to exculpate Trollope from the charge of unrestrained wishful thinking. Whatever the gains of the bourgeoisie, the England of his time was a country in which governments remained predominantly aristocratic, and the old squirearchical and Anglican forms still prevailed to an astonishing extent: throughout the period in which the Barsetshire series appeared, for instance, Oxford and Cambridge were still exclusively Church of England preserves. A generation later it would scarcely have been possible for a novelist of Trollope's caliber to put so much faith in the stability of the social order, and towards the end of his career he himself was increasingly assailed by doubts, voiced most notably in *The Way We Live Now,* with its savage picture of deepening social and financial corruption. There is psychological bitterness in the later novels as well, a new preoccupation with such themes as treachery and morbid jealousy. But the stable framework is only shaken, not shattered, and the dominant tone is still fairly charitable. Within the limits of the gentlemanly Victorian ethos, of which he is one of the most engaging representatives, Trollope can be a searching moralist, but he has a strong impulse towards forgiveness. He has the distinction, too, of being one of the few novelists who take as much interest in their good characters as their bad ones, partly because he doesn't underestimate the amount of effort which being good usually requires.

———

TURA, Cosmé (Cosimo) (c.1430–1495). Italian painter. Born and died in Ferrara. By 1452 was court artist to Duke Borso d'Este and became the leading Ferrarese painter. His earliest extant work is *Portrait of a Young Prince of Este* (Metropolitan Museum, New York). Pisanello and especially Mantegna were formative influences, although the angular postures and dramatic tension of his mature works are his own style. Characteristic are the paintings on organ door of Ferrara cathedral (1469). The monumentality of Piero della Francesca's figures exerted an influence on Tura. Animals and charming details of nature also appear in his painting. Completed *Roverella Altarpiece* (1474, central panel in National Gallery, London; other sections in Louvre, Paris, and Galleria Colonna, Rome). In later life Tura painted in a more energetic style a number of allegories and *St. Anthony* (1484, Galleria Estense, Modena.). Other works include *Pietà* (1468, Museo Correr, Venice); *Madonna in a Garden* (c.1471, National Gallery, Washington), and some tapestries.

REFERENCES: B. Nicolson *The Painters of Ferrara* (London 1950). Eberhard Ruhmer *Cosimo Tura: Paintings and Drawings* (London and New York 1958).

———

TURGENEV, Ivan Sergeyevich (Nov. 9, 1818 – Sept. 3, 1883). Russian writer. Born Orel, Russia, son of retired cavalry officer and domineering, wealthy, landed mother. Studied at universities of Moscow (1833), St. Petersburg (1834–37), and Berlin (1838–41), and became an enthusiastic Westernizer. Began literary career as a poet in tradition of Pushkin and Lermontov, and tried his hand at plays, best known of which is the comedy *A Month in the Country* (1850). Achieved fame with a series of masterly stories published first in the *Contemporary* (1847–52), then as the book *Notes of a Hunter: A Sportsman's Sketches* (1852). The attacks on serfdom in these stories, together with his enthusiastic obituary of Gogol in the same year, led to confinement at Spasskoe, his country estate. From 1845 he spent most of his time in Germany and France, following his mistress, Pauline Viardot-Garcia, a celebrated opera singer to whom he remained devoted all his life. Moving in the leading artistic circles of western Europe, he became an interpreter abroad of Russian literature and values, and gained an international reputation. The novel *Rudin* (1856) was followed by *A Nest of Gentlefolk* (1859), *On the Eve* (1860), and his masterpiece, *Fathers and Sons* (1862), in which nihilism is propounded, thereby arousing a fierce controversy in Russia. Other works include the short stories *First Love* (1870) and *Torrents of Spring* (1871), the novels *Smoke* (1867) and *Virgin Soil* (1877), and his last work *Poems in Prose* (1878–1882). He died in Bougival, near Paris.

TRANSLATIONS: *The Novels of Ivan Turgenev* tr. Constance Garnett (1894–1922, reprinted 15 vols. New York 1970). *The Plays of Ivan Turgenev* tr. M. S. Mandell (London and New York 1924). *Literary Reminiscences* tr. David Magarshak (New York 1958 and London 1959, also PB). *Fathers and Sons* tr. George Reavey (London 1950). *First Love* and *Rudin* tr. Isaiah Berlin (London 1950). *Letters: A Selection* ed. and tr. Edgar H. Lehrman (New York 1961).

REFERENCES: Richard Freeborn *Turgenev: The Novelist's Novelist* (London and New York 1960). Edward Garnett *Turgenev* (1917, reprinted Port Washington, N.Y. 1966). David Magarshak *Turgenev: A Life* (London and New York 1954). Avrahm Yarmolinsky *Turgenev: The Man, His Art, and His Age* (1926, rev. ed. New York 1959 and London 1960, also PB). Varvara N. B. Zhitova *The Turgenev Family* (London 1948).

✍

TURGENEV

BY V. S. PRITCHETT

Turgenev was the first of the great Russian writers of the nineteenth century to become well known outside his own country. He had been famous in Russia mainly because of his book, *A Sportsman's Sketches,* which had a powerful influence in the czar's decision to liberate the serfs; but his next works, *A Nest of Gentlefolk* and the superb *Fathers and Sons,* offended both the right wing and left wing in the new, revolutionary generation; he left Russia for Berlin, Baden, and Paris, where he bitterly attacked his countrymen, and rarely returned. He became a Westerner in life, as he was also a Westerner — as opposed to Slavophils like Dostoevsky — in his writing and in his political views. To Europeans he was the sensitive, cultivated aristocrat; to Russians he showed another face — passionate, scornful, and tormented. The friend of Flaubert and Henry James, he appeared to Russians as an expatriate landowner who had ratted and turned pure artist; who had turned his back on social and political commitments. For this reason his abhorrence of tyranny was too gentlemanly and superficial to be attractive to the socially conscious Russians, and was held to be too soothing to Europeans. The truth is that Turgenev's hatred of tyranny had a terrible private source. His mother had been a monster of Tartar ferocity to the people on her estates and above all to her sons. His will was broken young. And when he escaped from Russia and from her, he was once more to pass his life under the tyranny of his mistress, Pauline Viardot, the opera singer. Though he was to live another thirty years he declared that at thirty-five his life was finished.

This declaration points to the nature of his genius. Turgenev is the novelist of farewells; he is close to the ripple of change, the good-bye to the passing day. He is the novelist-poet of the moments after meetings and the moments before partings. First there is the budding of spring; then there is the sadness of autumn. There is no summer of fulfillment between. The poet-sportsman watches the young heart rise like a bird; he watches it fall, winged, to the common lot. The young and the old are his fullest characters: the homecoming and death of Bazarov, in his greatest novel, *Fathers and Sons,* and the mourning of his parents are among the most beautifully done things in Russian literature. At thirty-five Turgenev looked back on the Russia of his childhood among the serfs, whom he thought superior to their masters, and yet with nostalgia upon the life of the country house. That life, whether it was pleasant or disgraceful, sets the controlling scene and, because it was the center of conversation about the state of Russia, provides him with his leisurely, cultivated idiom. *A Nest of Gentlefolk* evokes the gentry class of that time. His famous long stories, like *Torrents of Spring, Mumu, First Love,* and *Rudin,* show us how the hours of the day flow through our lives. In no Russian novelist is one so aware of transience. He is a master of the instant, and a master of irony.

In *A Sportsman's Sketches,* he drew from real life as he met it when he was out shooting on his mother's estates, life as it came shapelessly and accidentally before his eyes. This is true also of his novels and stories. He was incapable of elaborate plot, which, in any case, he thought falsified experience. He relied on the observation of character and he always began with real people. He sees a man or woman, and like a sportsman, he stalks and watches. One is taken from the dusty carriage to the great house, one sees the landowners and the servants, the young lovers, and watches them change.

He is less a creator of character than one who watches given people expose themselves stage by stage and with contradiction. Who would believe that the central figure of *Rudin,* who sounds like a forceful idealist on the first day, would look like an idiot or a fraud on the next; that his romantic warmth should turn out to be cold and caddish in love; that, exposed as a futile egoist, he would yet end his life in a futile act of self-sacrifice? And that this sacrifice could be his attempt to give meaning to a wasted life? And that, nevertheless, when they look back upon Rudin, his friends feel that perhaps after all this wasted man was an exemplar? He is said to have been drawn from Bakunin. Each incident takes us deeper into the mystery of human character and each character finds something unexpected in his own nature. In *First Love,* the charming youth who is experiencing all the lyrical, jealous, and agonizing sensations of first love discovers his father is his rival. He is forced to see the terrible difference between early love and mature passion; he should now hate his father, but instead he is left in awe before the sight of an adult love that is violent and profound. At the crisis, the characters in Turgenev are always taken aback by what is in their own hearts. They have grown up morally.

Although character was Turgenev's ruling interest — and he is perhaps the supreme portrayer of Russian women — his methods were not analytical, as they are in the later Russian novelists. He does not intervene. He remains the detached observer. His art is to make life seem to do his work for him; his task is to be transparent, orderly, simple, and percipient. He is essentially a novelist of the tender membranes; and perhaps he is too much of the gentleman in his compassion. Yet he is not superficial. A powerful but discreet use of poetic symbolism gives depth to stories that might be said, but for that, to talk themselves away. Compare the use of the horse as a symbol of sexual passion in *Torrents of Spring* or *First Love* with D. H. Lawrence's. The latter's symbol is imposed; it is preached into us; in Turgenev, the first effect of the symbol is to take us naturally into ordinary scenes of Russian life; this enhances the force of the inner meaning as it gradually discloses itself. Life is always a disclosure and always in natural terms first. Turgenev does with great art what all later Russian realists were to learn from him. His marksmanship never fails in the social scene: "In the General the good nature innate in all Russians was intensified by that special kind of geniality which is peculiar to all people who have done something disgraceful." Of the General's wife: "There was always a tear in her left eye, on the strength of which Kalliopa Karlovna (she was, one must add, of German extraction) considered herself a woman of great sensibility."

The weakness of Turgenev's leisurely and almost biographical method is that he was forced to rely on what seems to us now the old-fashioned device of hearsay. A group of friends either meet to hear someone tell the tale or intervene at convenient points, to indicate events which have not been described, or to make comments that will push the story on. The method seems too essay-like to the modern novelist, who is inside his characters and not outside of them. Turgenev's detachment looks like an evasion. The fact is that his conversational commentary is the weak if interesting part of his narrative. A late novel like *Smoke*, which caused an uproar in Russia, has far too much generalizing and, in this case, denun-

ciatory talk; yet, even here, Turgenev told one of his most graceful and penetrating love stories.

The doctrinaires did not like Turgenev's detachment in his attitude to the Russian situation, his refusal to join, his dislike of personalities and movements. They disliked his attachment to Europe and did not believe Russia would have to be Europeanized. Was Turgenev so far wrong? It was a European who gave the revolution its Bible. These quarrels have now become academic. Participators — if they have genius — may be richer and fuller writers; but the observers, if they possess poetic genius, create those still and crystal-like works of art which have a lasting strength. In all his work Turgenev is the perceiver of human dignity.

TURNER, J(oseph) **M**(allord) **W**(illiam) (Apr. 23, 1775 – Dec. 19, 1851). English painter. Born London, son of a barber, he began his career as topographical draftsman. Studied at Royal Academy (1789–93) and began exhibiting watercolors (1790), oils (1796). Elected Associate Royal Academician (1799) and full member (1802), he was professor of perspective at Academy (1808–38). His first trip abroad (1802) produced *Calais Pier* (1803, National Gallery, London) and paintings of Alpine scenes. Traveled constantly in England and on Continent, making innumerable drawings, sketches for studio oils, and watercolors. Began imitating old masters (1800–20), especially Claude Lorrain, Titian, Nicolas Poussin, and Dutch sea painters. Modeled a collection of engravings, *Liber Studiorum* (1807–19), on Lorrain's *Liber Veritatis* (1777). Works of this period include *Somer Hill, Tunbridge* (1811, National Gallery of Scotland, Edinburgh). *England: Richmond Hill* (1819, Tate Gallery, London). First trip to Italy (1819) resulted in the purer, lighter coloring of *The Bay of Baiae* (1824, Tate Gallery) and *Ulysses Deriding Polyphemus* (1829, National Gallery). In the 1830's and 1840's his colors became more brilliant and intense, as reflected in *The Burning of the Houses of Parliament* (1835, Cleveland Museum), *The Fighting Téméraire* (1839, National Gallery), *The Slave Ship* (1840, Museum of Fine Arts, Boston), and *Rain, Steam, and Speed: The Great Western Railway* (1844, National Gallery). Three more trips to Italy (1828, 1835, 1840) evoked his great Venetian watercolors. A recluse throughout his life, he never married. Many of his works were displayed at his Queen Anne Street gallery until his death, when he bequeathed all the works in his possession to the state. He died in Chelsea and was buried with honors in St. Paul's cathedral.

REFERENCES: Martin Butlin *Turner: Watercolours* (London 1962 and New York 1965). Charles Clare *J. M. W. Turner: His Life and Work* (London and New York 1951). A. J. Finberg *Turner's Sketches and Drawings* (1910, reprinted New York 1968, also PB), *In Venice with Turner* (London 1930) and *The Life of J. M. W. Turner* (2nd ed. Oxford and Toronto 1961). John Gage *Color in Turner: Poetry and Truth* (New York and London 1969). Lawrence Gowing *Turner: Imagination and Reality* (New York 1966). Luke Herrmann *Ruskin and Turner* (London 1968 and New York 1969). Jack Lindsay *J. M. W. Turner, His Life and Work: A Critical Biography* (Greenwich, Conn. and London 1966). Graham Reynolds *Turner* (London and New York 1969, also PB). John Rothenstein and Martin Butlin *Turner* (London and New York 1964). John Ruskin *Modern Painters* (1843–60, latest ed. 5 vols. London and New York 1923).

✍

TURNER
BY WILLIAM C. SEITZ

J. M. W. Turner, often thought of as the greatest of all English artists, is most renowned for his light-permeated, unrestrainedly romantic landscapes and seascapes. He was unusually prolific, and at his death in 1851 some three hundred oils, finished and unfinished, and more than nineteen thousand watercolors and drawings were left to the British nation in a bequest from the artist. Many of these works remained in Turner's studio during his lifetime, and some were not exhibited publicly until the 1960's, when interest in Turner was heightened because of the appeal that the high-keyed color, fluidly modulated form, and apparent abstractness of his late works held for contemporary taste. It would be difficult to overemphasize the radical uniqueness of Turner's painting and, were it not for records left by offended critics, to imagine the shock it was to a public accustomed to Poussin, Claude Lorrain, the Dutch painters, Wilson, Gainsborough, Girtin, and Crome.

The son of a London barber, Turner had almost no formal education. Yet in 1790, after one year as an art student, he began exhibiting at the Royal Academy, and was elected a full academician by the time he was twenty-seven. The works he showed before 1800, mostly picturesque and topographical landscapes, were pleasing to current taste and therefore popular — a prelude, it must have seemed, to a successful but unexceptional career. Never shown until more than a century later, however, was a small but extraordinary group of river views painted between 1805 and 1810 that (inasmuch as they predate the outdoor studies of John Constable) may well be the first landscapes in oil ever completed in the open. Turner always continued the direct observation of natural phenomena, although he did not adopt the open air method that the French impressionists were to develop a half-century later. Except for drawings and rapid notations in watercolor, he remained a studio painter.

Turner's unconventional way of living, at times under an assumed name, has been overemphasized — in part because of a scurrilous biography by

G. W. Thornebury which appeared in 1861 but was almost immediately discredited. His eccentricities were those of an artist committed to his goals and fully cognizant of his genius. His life, punctuated by sketching trips in England, in the Alps and in Italy, was totally devoted to painting and to the optical studies, technical experiments, business activities, and continual return to nature it demanded. Turner was also motivated by a sweeping concept of man, nature, and destiny which he tried all his life to enunciate in the verses of a ponderous epic poem, *The Fallacies of Hope*. In his most ambitious early works such as *The Fifth Plague of Egypt* (1800), *Snow Storm: Hannibal and His Army Crossing the Alps* (1812) and *Dido Building Carthage* (1815), all of which he showed in Royal Academy exhibitions, Turner followed the tradition of history painting. As subjects he chose crucial events in which his essentially pessimistic view of man's achievements were manifest. But in contrast with more conventional history paintings, those of Turner do not focus on the human protagonists but on overpowering natural phenomena: thunderstorms and blizzards on the sea or in the mountains, symbolic sunrises and sunsets, descending darkness and moonlight. Years later in *The Burning of the Houses of Parliament* (1835), an immediately current event was transformed into an ideally Turneresque subject: a confrontation of fire and water. Against the night blue of the sky and river, the angry reds and yellows of the conflagration, doubled in area by their reflection in the Thames, swirl ravenously upward and leftward in a whirling spiral.

Many of Turner's finest works in watercolor record the exotic and evanescent image of Venice which, after his first trip to Italy in 1819, continued to be one of his major subjects. This medium was especially suitable for his imaginative yet accurate representations of the overwhelming power or tranquil radiance of nature. His method of handling oil pigment, it is important to recognize, arose from the fluidity and the potential for improvisation natural to watercolor. During the 1830's and 1840's — even in a machine-age subject such as *Rain, Steam, and Speed: The Great Western Railway* (1844) — solid form is pulverized by light, enshrouded in mist and spray, dissolved in reflections and refractions, or swept into a characteristic vortex of movement. Some of these late works seem to belong more to the twentieth than to the nineteenth century, for rather than being represented, their subjects are transmuted into pigment. In *Sun Setting over the Sea* (1840–45), not even the horizon line can be deciphered within the deep golden atmosphere where luminous vapor and water seem to fuse with the pigment in a new amalgam at once material, optical, and imaginative. Turner was one of the first to give improvisation a central function in the creation of form. He often sent works to exhibitions unfinished and completed them on the walls during the three days allowed for "varnishing," to the amusement of observers.

In 1816 the essayist and critic Hazlitt complained that Turner, whom he recognized as the best landscape painter of his time, made "pictures of the elements of air, earth, and water. The artist delights to go back to that first chaos of the world, or to that state of things when the waters were separated from dry land, and light from darkness. . . . All is without form and void." Inapplicable though these words now seem to the early works to which they referred, they augur the daring projection into the unknown of Turner's late work. Long before the impressionists, and more fully and imaginatively, he recorded the most extreme and fleeting effects of weather, time of day and night, light and atmosphere. The idiosyncratic emotionality of his fusion of form with content was not carried further until the time of the expressionists, and a fuller use of paint as a direct source for creation had to await the surrealists and abstract expressionists. Related to his innovations, and also prophetic of contemporary art, was Turner's willingness to sacrifice any number of details in the sweep of a theme, and to allow his subjects to melt into what Hazlitt called, quoting an anonymous critic, "pictures of nothing, and very like."

TWAIN, Mark (real name Samuel Langhorne Clemens) (Nov. 30, 1835 – Apr. 21, 1910). American writer. Born Florida, Mo., son of restless Virginian who dreamed of making a fortune in land speculation. Family settled in Hannibal, Mo. (1839). Clemens became printer's apprentice (1847), then successively journeyman printer, writer of humorous sketches, and steamboat pilot. On outbreak of Civil War, and after brief service as Confederate irregular, went to Nevada. Joined staff of Virginia City *Territorial Enterprise* (1862), adopting pen name Mark Twain (1863). *Jim Smiley and His Jumping Frog* appeared in New York *Saturday Press* (1865). Described trip to Europe and Holy Land (1867) in *The Innocents Abroad* (1869). Married Olivia Langdon (1870), and after brief period as newspaper editor in Buffalo, settled in Hartford, Conn. He wrote *Roughing It* (1872), *The Gilded Age* (1873, with Charles Dudley Warner), *Sketches: New And Old* (1875), *Tom Sawyer* (1876), *A Tramp Abroad* (1880), *The Prince and the Pauper* (1882), *Life on the Mississippi* (1883), *Huckleberry Finn* (1885), *A Connecticut Yankee in King Arthur's Court* (1889), and

Pudd'nhead Wilson (1894). Bankrupt due to business ventures (1894), he paid his debts by making lecture tour of the world (1895–96). Years from 1896 were marked by private griefs and public acclaim. During this period wrote *Joan of Arc* (1896), *Following the Equator* (1897), and *The Mysterious Stranger* (published 1916). Died in Redding, Conn.

EDITIONS: *The Writings of Mark Twain* ed. Albert Bigelow Paine (37 vols. New York 1922–25, reprinted 25 vols. Grosse Pointe, Mich. 1968). *Mark Twain's Notebook* ed. Albert Bigelow Paine (New York and London 1935). *Letters from The Earth* ed. Bernard De Voto (New York 1962, also PB). Mark Twain's papers are now being edited for publication by University of California Press.

REFERENCES: Van Wyck Brooks *The Ordeal of Mark Twain* (1920, rev. ed. New York 1933 and London 1934). James M. Cox *Mark Twain: The Fate of Humor* (Princeton, N.J. 1966). Bernard DeVoto *Mark Twain's America* (1932, rev. ed. Boston 1967, also PB). DeLancey Ferguson *Mark Twain, Man and Legend* (1943, reprinted New York 1966). William Dean Howells *My Mark Twain* (1910, new ed. Baton Rouge, La. 1967, also PB). Justin Kaplan *Mr. Clemens and Mark Twain* (New York 1966 and London 1967, also PB). Albert Bigelow Paine *Mark Twain: A Biography* (3 vols. New York and London 1912). Henry Nash Smith *Mark Twain: The Development of a Writer* (Cambridge, Mass. 1962 and Oxford 1963, also PB).

MARK TWAIN
BY JUSTIN KAPLAN

Two currents flow through the life of Mark Twain. One flowed away from Hannibal, Missouri; the other, back to Hannibal again. Out of the opposition of these currents, out of the turbulent dark waters, came one of the great styles and dazzling personalities of our literature, one of its few undisputed masterpieces, and half a dozen of its major books.

Samuel Clemens's first fifty years

swell the legend of the self-made man. At twelve he ended his formal schooling in Hannibal, where he had been brought at the age of four, and began work as a printer. At seventeen he left home for good, set out on his travels, and was in turn an itinerant typesetter, a river pilot, and for an unforgettable two weeks, a Confederate irregular. As a miner he never struck it rich in the Nevada Territory, but it was there, during the Civil War, that as a journalist he created the name and identity of Mark Twain, whose vocation was "to excite the *laughter* of God's creatures."

His first travel book, *The Innocents Abroad* (1869), made him famous, he prospered as a humorist on the lecture circuit and he became part owner of a newspaper in Buffalo. His marriage to Olivia Langdon, heiress to an Elmira coal combination, completed the decisive stage of his transition from the golden age of his Hannibal boyhood to what he would soon call the Gilded Age. The river rat and sagebrush bohemian became a gentleman and householder, the Western journalist a man of letters and property. During the three decades after his marriage his fame became international. He was the people's author, having reached a mass audience through the subscription book market, but he was also the idol and intimate of the rich, renowned, and titled. He was as much at home in London, Paris, Vienna, or Berlin as he was in his unmistakable, eye-catching mansion in Hartford, which dwarfed the cabin he had been born in to the size of a bird cage. He was capitalist, promoter, entrepreneur, and he invested both his psyche and his fortune in visionary enterprises, including the mechanical typesetter and the publishing house which eventually bankrupted him. In 1885, with the successful publication by his own firm of both *Huckle-*

berry Finn and the *Personal Memoirs* of his hero, General Ulysses S. Grant, Mark Twain reached the heights of a multiplex career as writer and businessman. All in all, it would seem that he had come as far as any man could possibly come from the drowsing white town of Hannibal.

But the central drama of Samuel Clemens's mature literary life was his discovery of his boyhood in Hannibal as the usable past. He began to make this discovery in his early and middle thirties as he explored the literary and psychological options of the comic identity, Mark Twain. Instead of severing his imagination from Hannibal, his triumphs in the East only reunited them. The first Sunday after his marriage he rained reminiscences of his boyhood day and night, and for the rest of his life, however involved he was with the insistent materialities of houses and machines, business ventures and publishing contracts, his imagination continued to dwell "down there" in Hannibal, with Tom and Huck. His image of Hannibal, as he evolved as a writer, became supple and comprehensive. Instead of purging the idyll of its frontier violence, of the pains of adolescence and the horrors of slavery, Mark Twain reshaped his idyll so that it embraced them. The river towns of *The Gilded Age* (1873) as well as *Pudd'nhead Wilson* (1894) mirror the possibilities of the human condition; and Huck and Tom, in Mark Twain's late notes for continuing their story, reflect some of his own sense of aging and desolation. Comparably, Mark Twain's style became a wonder of suppleness, moving freely from Huck's vernacular poetry to flights of savage invective and satire, at times laconic or eloquent, fierce or caressing, analytic or hyperbolic, always employing a complex rhetoric of comic invention, and, at its best, something incomparably and distinctively native.

Mark Twain's laughter had always been close to his sorrow, but when the opulent structure of his life gave way during the 1890's under a series of terrible blows — his business failures and bankruptcy, the sudden death of his favorite daughter, his fear that he was finished as a writer — he fell into a pronounced mood of despair and misanthropy which was to be as dramatic a manifestation of his late years as his white suits, his strolls on Fifth Avenue, his brilliance as a banquet speaker, his autobiographical dictations. At times he believed that his rags-to-riches, obscurity-to-fame story, which reminded some of his friends of *The Arabian Nights*, was a meaningless story of failure. During his darkest period he turned inward in the hope of solving what had become an intolerable sense of divisiveness and multiplicity, a sense suggested by the fact that Samuel Clemens often felt oppressed by his "conscience" and also shackled to humor by the fame of Mark Twain. But to the end he remained an enigma and a prodigy: "Everyone is a moon and has a dark side which he never shows to anybody," not even to himself.

All his life had been spent in divided and distinguished worlds. Frontier Hannibal had nurtured him, he was its celebrant and chronicler, and eventually he became the living symbol of America's vanished frontiers. Even so, his friend William Dean Howells said, he was "the most desouthernized southerner I ever knew." He came to be associated with the motorcar and steam yacht in place of the stagecoach and riverboat, and he sometimes wore a silk hat. But the subject matter of his fiction went farther and farther back into the past, and as a fiction writer he became an expatriate from his own times, just as in his person he became an expatriate from his own country (between 1878 and 1900 he spent about eleven years abroad) and complained of his "everlasting exile."

The representative of a broad spectrum of paradox, as writer, critic, and moralist, Mark Twain stood outside American society of his times and observed it with a bitter eye, but as a businessman he embraced its business values. Thus he flayed the shams and venalities of the Gilded Age, but he also lived deeply and hungrily in the age, and although he believed money corrupted absolutely, he was determined to be rich, not merely to get along. He identified himself with the masses and elevated the vernacular to literature, yet he sometimes courted the approval of high official culture, was often confused in his goals, and spent his inspiration in such genteel performances as *The Prince and the Pauper* and *Joan of Arc*. He was an exhibitionist who jealously guarded his privacies and sensitivities, an aristocrat who was a passionate foe of social injustice, and a grass-roots radical who, for all his denunciation of the "damned human race," is known the world over as a democrat and general friend of mankind.

UCCELLO, Paolo (real name **Paolo di Dono**) (1397 – Dec. 10, 1475). Italian painter. Born and died in Florence. Worked in metal under Lorenzo Ghiberti in shop where first Baptistery doors were made (1407). Became member of Painters' Guild (1415). In Venice (1425–30) worked on mosaics for S. Marco. Back in Florence devoted himself to study of perspective, in which he became one of the early masters. Painted frescoes of *Creation* scenes for cloister of S. Maria Novella. Commissioned (1436) to paint for the cathedral a fresco in imitation of an equestrian statue of Sir John Hawkwood, which is a fine example of foreshortening. In Padua (1445) he painted the *Giants* and was commissioned (1465) by confraternity of Holy Sacrament of Urbino to execute an altarpiece. *Hunt* (Ashmolean Museum, Oxford) belongs to same period. His major works, however, are the two frescoes in the Chiostro Verde of S. Maria Novella, *The Drunkenness of Noah* and *The Flood* (c.1450), and three battle scenes of the *Rout of San Romano* (c.1454–57, in Uffizi, Florence; Louvre, Paris; and National Gallery, London), which are remarkable for their feats of foreshortening.

REFERENCES: Paolo d'Ancona *Paolo Uccello* (tr. London 1960 and New York 1961). Enzo Carli *All the Paintings of Paolo Uccello* (tr. London and New York 1964). John Pope-Hennessy *Paolo Uccello: Complete Edition* (2nd ed. London and New York 1969).

UHLAND, (Johann) Ludwig (Apr. 26, 1787 – Nov. 13, 1862). German poet. Born and died in Tübingen. Studied law, classical and medieval literature there (1802–1808). First collection of poems, *Gedichte* (1815, *Songs*) was followed by patriotic ballads of *Väterlandische Gedichte* (1816, *Songs of the Fatherland*). Actively involved in politics from 1812. Married Emilie Vischer (1820), whose fortune enabled him to continue political and literary interests. Resigned chair of German literature at Tübingen (1833) when forbidden leave of absence to sit as a liberal in the Landtag. After appointment to Frankfurt national assembly (1848), began to withdraw from politics and devoted himself to German philology. Wrote two unsuccessful historical plays, *Ernst, Herzog von Schwaben* (1818) and *Ludwig der Bayer* (1819). Interest in philology led to *Über das altfranzosische Epos* (1812, *History of the Old French Epic*), and other historical studies. He is best known for his nationalist ballads and lyrics, many of which, such as *Guter Kamerad* (*The Good Comrade*) have become German folksongs and were translated by Longfellow.

TRANSLATIONS: *Poems of Ludwig Uhland* tr. Alexander Platt (Leipzig 1848). *Songs and Ballads of Uhland* tr. W. W. Skeat (London 1864).

UNAMUNO Y JUGO, Miguel de (Sept. 29, 1864 – Dec. 31, 1936). Spanish philosopher and writer. Born Bilboa; of Basque parentage. Educated at University of Madrid (1880–84). Became professor of Greek (1891) and later rector (1901–14) of University of Salamanca. First publication was collection of essays about Spanish traditionalism, *En Torno al casticismo* (1895), followed by novel *Paz en la guerra* (*Peace in War*, 1897) about Carlist siege of Bilboa. His *Poesías* (1907, *Poems* 1952) was followed by *Rosarios de sonetos líricos* (1911). Exiled to Fuerteventura, Canary Islands, for criticism of dictator Primo de Rivera (1924), he went to France (1925); returned to Spain on establishment of republic (1930) and was reinstated as rector of Salamanca (1931). An independent Republican deputy to the Cortes (1931–33), he at first supported the republic but finally denounced it and the opposition. He died in Salamanca. An original thinker, his theories derived from ideas of Bergson, Kierkegaard, and William James, and reflect both a preoccupation with life and death and a profound conflict between faith and reason. His major works: *Amor y pedagogia* (1902); *La Vida de don Quijote y Sancho* (1905, *The Life of Don Quixote and Sancho* 1927); his principal opus, *Del Sentimiento trágico de la vida en los hombres y los pueblos* (1913, *The Tragic Sense of Life in Men and Peoples* 1921), in which he reaches the culmination of his philosophy regarding faith and doubt; the novels *Niebla* (1914, tr. *Mist* 1928), *Abel Sánchez* (1917, tr. 1956), and *Tres Novelas ejemplares y un prólogo* (1920, *Three Exemplary Novels and a Prologue* 1930). A late philosophical work is *La Agonía del cristianismo* (1925, tr. *The Agony of Christianity* 1928). Also wrote the plays *Fedra* (1910) and *El Hermano Juan* or *El Mundo es teatro* (1934). Unamuno is one of the major philosophers of the twentieth century.

TRANSLATION: *Selected Works* ed. Anthony Kerrigan and others (3 vols. Princeton, N.J. and London 1967).

REFERENCES: Arturo Barea *Unamuno* (tr. Cambridge, England, and New Haven, Conn. 1952). José Ferrater Mora *Unamuno: A Philosophy of Tragedy* (tr. Berkeley, Calif. and Cambridge, England, 1962, also PB). José Huertas-Jourda *The Existentialism of Miguel de Unamuno* (Gainesville, Fla. PB 1963). Paul Ilie *Unamuno: An Existential View of Self and Society* (Madison, Wis. 1968). Julián Marías Aguilera *Miguel de Unamuno* (tr. Cambridge, Mass. 1966). M. T. Rudd *The Lone Heretic: A Biography of Miguel de Unamuno y Jugo* (Austin, Tex. 1963).

UNDSET, Sigrid (May 20, 1882 – June 10, 1949). Norwegian novelist. Born Kallundborg, Denmark, daughter of a noted Norwegian archaeologist whose early death (1893) left family in poor circumstances. Worked as a secretary (Oslo, 1898–1908), publishing first novel, *Fru Marta Oulie* (1907). Achieved first success with *Jenny* (1911), novel of art students in Rome. Married painter Anders C. Svarstad (1912; they had three children, were separated 1926). Achieved world fame with historical novel of medieval Norway, *Kristin Lavransdatter* (3 vols. 1920–22, tr. 1923–27), which won Nobel prize for literature (1928). Another massive work, *Olav Audunsson* (4 vols. 1925–27, tr. *The Master of Hestviken* 1928–30) also incorporated medieval themes. Later works, marked by her conversion to Roman Catholicism (1924) and a return to contemporary settings, include: *Gymnadenia* (1929, tr. *The Wild Orchid* 1931), *Den Braendende Busk* (2 vols. 1930, tr. *The Burning Bush* 1932), *Ida Elisabeth* (1932, tr. 1933), and *Den Trofaste Hustru* (1936, tr. *The Faithful Wife* 1937). Upon German invasion of Norway (1940), she escaped to the United States. Returned to Norway (1945) and died in Oslo. Author of short stories, essays, and poems, she also wrote a book on Norwegian saints and the autobiographical *Elleve Aar* (1934, tr. *The Longest Years* 1935).

REFERENCES: Nicole Deschamps *Sigrid Undset, ou La Morale de la passion* (Montreal 1966). Alrik Gustafson *Six Scandinavian Novelists* (1940, reprinted New York 1969). Harry Slochower *Three Ways of Modern Man* (1937, reprinted New York 1968). Andreas H. Winsnes *Sigrid Undset: A Study in Christian Realism* (tr. London and New York 1953).

UTRILLO, Maurice (Dec. 25, 1883 – Nov. 5, 1955). French painter. Born Paris, illegitimate son of painter Suzanne Valadon, who was also model for Renoir, Degas, and Toulouse-Lautrec. Legally adopted by Spanish writer Miguel Utrillo (1891). Self-taught, he took up painting as therapy for his alcoholism, exhibiting first at Salon d'Automne (1909). At this time he painted in impressionist style, as in *Church of St. Hilaire* (Tate Gallery, London) and *Rooftops of Montmagny* (1907, Musée d'Art Moderne, Paris). Produced his finest paintings 1908–16, chiefly townscapes such as *Abbey of St. Denis* (1910, Phillips Collection, Washington), *La Porte St. Martin* and *Place du Tertre* (both 1911, Tate Gallery). This was his "white period," so called from the zinc white he used in depicting the weathered walls of houses. Scenes of Montmartre were his favorite subjects, sometimes painted from picture postcards, and embodying the atmosphere of the old narrow streets and squares. His later work repeats itself, lacks the freshness and vigor of the earlier. He married Lucie Pauwels (1935). Died at Dax, in Landes.

REFERENCES: Peter De Polnay *Enfant Terrible: The Life and World of Maurice Utrillo* (New York 1969). Guy Dornand *Utrillo* (tr. New York PB 1965). Waldemar George *Utrillo* (tr. New York 1960). Paul Pétridès *L'Oeuvre complet de Maurice Utrillo* (4 vols. Paris 1959–69). Alfred Werner *Utrillo* (New York 1969).

VALÉRY, Paul (Ambroise Toussaint Jules) (Oct. 30, 1871 – July 20, 1945). French poet and critic. Born Sète, on the Mediterranean, son of a customs officer. Attended lycée (1884) and university (1888) in Montpellier. Met Mallarmé and other symbolists in Paris (1891), where he settled the following year. Worked as civil servant in the French War Office (1897–1900), then as private secretary to director of Havas News Agency (1900–22). Married Jeanne Gobillard (1900). His early poems had appeared in various reviews, but he had written very little verse since 1892. A brief valedictory intended for a projected collection of his early work grew into a long poem, La Jeune Parque (1917); this, together with a new collection Charmes (1922), is his major poetical production. His first collection of prose for the general public was Variété, which was followed at intervals by Variété II, III, IV, and V (1924–44), as well as by a number of dialogues. Elected to French Academy (1925); president of Committee for Intellectual Cooperation of League of Nations (1936); professor of poetry at Collège de France (1937). Died in Paris; accorded a state funeral.

TRANSLATIONS: Collected Works ed. Jackson Matthews (15 vols. Princeton and London, vols. I–XIV 1956–70). Selected Writings ed. J. Laughlin (1950, latest ed. New York PB 1964). Self-Portraits: The Gide/Valéry Letters tr. June Guicharnaud, ed. Robert Mallet (Chicago 1966).

REFERENCES: Maurice Bémol La Méthode critique de Paul Valéry (Paris 1960). Jean Hytier The Poetics of Paul Valéry (tr. Garden City, N.Y. PB 1966). W. N. Ince The Poetic Theory of Paul Valéry: Inspiration and Technique (Leicester, England, 1961 and New York 1964). Agnes E. Mackay The Universal Self: A Study of Paul Valéry (London 1961). Henri Mondor Précocité de Valéry (Paris 1957) and Propos familiers de Paul Valéry (Paris 1957). Marcel Raymond Paul Valéry et la tentation de l'esprit (1946, new ed. Neuchâtel, Switzerland, 1964). Francis Scarfe The Art of Paul Valéry (London 1954). Norman Suckling Paul Valéry and the Civilized Mind (London and New York 1954). Pierre O. Walzer La Poésie de Valéry (Geneva 1953).

✍

PAUL VALÉRY
BY MALCOLM COWLEY

He was not yet twenty-one and already he had published dozens of poems in little magazines. He was admired by other beginning writers, two of whom, André Gide and Pierre Louÿs, had become his closest friends. A well-known critic had said that his name would soon "be fluttering on men's lips." It was the sort of prophecy that might have intoxicated a young poet, but Valéry found it absurd and revolting. He was beginning to have doubts about his vocation. On the night of October 4, 1892, while he was staying at his aunt's house in Genoa, there was a terrific rainstorm. "An appalling night," he was to say in a memorandum to himself — "spent lying on the bed — storm everywhere — my room dazzlingly bright at each stroke of lightning — And my whole future was played out in my head. I was between myself and myself."

During the "night of Genoa," as it came to be called, two things had died in him. One was the notion of being a Poet — that is, a man whose acute sensibility is aroused by concrete objects — and the other was the dream of becoming a literary personage. He did not "stop writing for twenty years," as the story used to be told; he wrote almost every day, and at times he even wrote for publication. Two of his most impressive works in prose, *An Introduction to the Method of Leonardo da Vinci* and *An Evening with Mr. Teste*, appeared respectively in 1895 and 1896; but he regarded such works, like the four short poems he published at intervals, as nothing more than exercises based on principles discovered in the course of his central endeavor.

The aim of that endeavor was not at all vague — "My nature abhors the vague," he used to say — but it is hard to explain. During the "night of Genoa" he had wrenched himself away from concrete experiences and had entered the realm of abstract principles; even his handwriting testified to the change. "Let us assume that thought in general is a kind of music," he said in a letter from which I translate freely. "My ideal would be to construct its scales and its system of harmony." If he succeeded in that effort, perhaps it might lead to a further achievement; perhaps he might emulate Leonardo by making himself universal or, in his own words, by finding "the central attitude from which all the enterprises of learning or science and all the operations of art are equally possible, and a successful cooperation between analysis and action is singularly probable."

Meanwhile he was living modestly in a Parisian world where he had some famous friends — eventually a wife and children too — but where he dreamed of remaining as anonymous as his imagined Mr. Teste. The problem of supporting a family was solved in 1900 when he was hired as a reader by the director of the Havas News Agency, an invalid who liked to hear and discuss the masterpieces of seventeenth-century French prose; it was pleasant work and did not claim too much of Valéry's time. Every morning he rose at five o'clock, drank a cup of warmed-over coffee, and *thought* — that was his central occupation — while making entries in a big notebook. Eventually there would be 257 of those notebooks, running in an unbroken series from 1894 to a few days before his death in 1945. They contain his thoughts on such subjects as attention, dreams, waking, words, and literature, besides his efforts to express all the operations of the mind — his own mind — in mathematical formulas; indeed, they are a complete record of his intellectual preoccupations, with very little mention of the events in his daily life.

Some of those events were dramatic and paradoxical, as is widely known. At the moment when his dream of becoming anonymous seemed likely to be realized, almost everyone having forgotten the name that was to have fluttered on men's lips, some of his friends — notably Gide and Louÿs — entreated him to collect the poems he had written before he was twenty-one. "I owe almost everything to friendship," he would later tell the French Academy. In this case he yielded to friendship, but only on condition that he should first write one new poem, of thirty or forty lines, as a prologue or epilogue to his early work. He spent four years on the poem, which grew to more than ten times its planned length and was published separately in 1917: *La Jeune Parque*. With a sense of release he then wrote another volume of new poems, *Charmes*, besides collecting and revising the early ones. All sorts of honors were suddenly heaped on his head. All sorts of requests poured in, usually for essays or public lectures, and he accepted as many commissions as he could carry out. As if by inadvertence and in less than ten years, he reached and passed both the goals he had forsaken during the "night of Genoa." He was a Poet, regarded in France as the greatest of his time, and he was easily the first of literary personages — so much so that his funeral was a national ceremony, with military honors, held in the presence of General de Gaulle.

This man who had published very little until the age of forty-five, and almost nothing during what should have been his twenty most productive years, left behind him an immense quantity of published writing. The English translation of his prose works, prepared for the Bollingen Series under the editorship of Jackson Matthews, is in fifteen volumes. After long reflection Mr. Matthews decided to omit the poetry. All poetry is untranslatable, or so we often hear, but Valéry's poems are more than that: they are unadaptable. Much of their effect depends on the reader's knowledge of classical French prosody and of the special vocabulary developed by the French symbolists. Either their music or their meaning is lost in English. I might add in all candor that the poems in French have always appealed to me much less than they have compelled my admiration.

The Bollingen translation also omits the 257 notebooks, which the French have published in facsimile. This again seems to me a wise omission. The note-

books are of absorbing interest to students of Valéry, but, with their mixture of topics, their algebraic formulas, and their phrases that the author did not bother to clarify since he was writing for himself, they dishearten the general reader. At times they disheartened Valéry himself, and he wrote after reading them over, "There sleeps the labor of my best years. I say the labor, not the works. The works are there too, potentially, but only my own eye can recognize them." The potential was never to be actualized. Although he planned to use the notebooks as material for an *Intellectual Comedy* that might stand beside *The Human Comedy* — perhaps *The Divine Comedy* — Valéry died before the masterwork was even started.

But his labor on the notebooks was by no means wasted. It disciplined his mind; it furnished an immense stock or even system of ideas, together with the right words to express them; and it gave him a point of view from which, in his public years, he could discern common principles in all sorts of apparently unrelated activities. "Will you give us your opinions on architecture, Monsieur Valéry?" "Will you address the Congress of Surgeons?" "Will you write a paper on photography? . . . on philosophy? . . . on Degas? . . . on the dance?" He regarded each of these invitations as a challenge to the reasoning power he had spent so long in cultivating; the problem in each case was to seize hold of an unexpected subject and transform it into a concept that belonged in his own system of thinking. Some of those occasional pieces are superb: for example, his address to the surgeons, which modulates into a series of bold speculations on science and mankind. To me the best essays, however, are those dealing with his intellectual or literary heroes, especially Leonardo and Mallarmé. I translated a book of those essays in 1926, then retranslated some of them along with others in 1958, so that I have lived with them for more than forty years. Sometimes on rereading them I find myself still puzzled by a passage in which I know perfectly what every word should mean. Sometimes I am shocked again by an opinion, for this author dislikes everything that is copied from life or that rises from the subconscious. Always I am held by the exact but graceful language, the breadth of vision, and the interplay of well-meditated ideas. Valéry did create a music of ideas, and the best of his essays — which are also the best of our time — are as soundly constructed as a Beethoven sonata.

VALLEJO, César (Mar. 16, 1892 – Apr. 15, 1938). Peruvian poet. Born Santiago de Chuco, a mestizo of Indian and white origin, he identified himself with the sufferings of the underprivileged. Voiced the plight of the exploited Andean Indians in the poems *Heraldos negros* (1918). Imprisoned on false charges (1920), he wrote a part of *Trilce* (1922) while in jail, one of his finest works, highly experimental in form and full of the tragic sense. Left Peru permanently for Europe (1923), and, an avowed Communist, joined the Republicans in Spanish Civil War. Wrote *Tungsteno* (1931), a novel about the Indians. Two volumes of poems appeared after he died in poverty (in Paris): *Poemas humanos* (1939), considered his masterpiece, and *España, aparta de mi este cáliz* (1940). Of *Poemas humanos,* M. L. Rosenthal has written, "They are poems of cruel suffering, physical and mental, which yet have a kind of joy of realization in their singular music, harshness, humor, and pain. They are clear as brookwater; you can see through them to the specific awareness and feeling, the sharply exuberant self, green and alive, growing at the bottom, while at the same time they are elusive and changing. . . . The technical range of these poems . . . is striking in its variety and its functional virtuosity. They are sometimes tightly formal structures and sometimes quite improvisational ones, and they move easily between colloquial directness and the most exquisitely pure and imaginative language reaching toward complex and concentrated effects." Vallejo is a leading figure of great influence in contemporary Latin American literature.

TRANSLATION: *Poemas Humanos / Human Poems* tr. Clayton Eshleman (New York 1969).

VAN AELST, Willem (c.1625–c.1683). Dutch painter. Born Delft, son of a notary. Was taught painting by his uncle Evert van Aelst. Lived in France (1645–49), and then in Italy, employed for some time as court painter to grand duke of Tuscany. Returned to Holland (1656), finally settling in Amsterdam. His last known painting is of 1683. Van Aelst's pictures are still-life studies, of fruit and flowers, fish and dead game. Blue is the dominant color in his paintings. He often depicted an asymmetric arrangement of flowers, as in a picture of 1651 in Musée des Augustins, Toulouse, and another of 1663 in the Mauritshuis, The Hague. In his game pieces, he painted his subjects as if in bright daylight, using his finesse and high color sense to suggest the rich plumage of the birds. His fruit pieces are works of great elegance: peaches or grapes are arranged round a jug or goblet, with a velvet curtain draped over the table. Van Aelst was a master of the exquisitely finished still-life painting. Other examples of his work are found in galleries in Berlin, Dresden, Munich, Copenhagen, Stockholm, and Florence (Pitti Palace).

REFERENCE: Ingvar Bergström *Dutch Still-Life Painting in the Seventeenth Century* (London and New York 1956).

VANBRUGH, Sir John (Jan. 1664 – Mar. 26, 1726). Architect and playwright. Born and died in London. Served in English army and was imprisoned on charges of espionage in France (1690–92). His first play, *The Relapse, or Virtue in Danger* (1696), a success, was followed by _Aesop,_ and his finest work, _The Provoked Wife_ (both 1697). In witty caricature and cynicism, Vanbrugh ranks with the most popular of the Restoration dramatists; was a member of the famous Kitcat club. Although he died leaving an unfinished play, completed and revised by Colley Cibber, and produced as _The Provoked Husband_ (1728), Vanbrugh increasingly became involved with architecture. Designed Castle Howard, Yorkshire (1702), for the earl of Carlisle, a grand example of English baroque (Nicholas Hawksmoor designed the interior). Vanbrugh built a theatre (1702) which produced operas and plays, including his own _The Confederacy_ (1705). Appointment as comptroller of the office of works (1702) led to his being commissioned to design with Hawksmoor Blenheim Palace at Woodstock, a grateful nation's gift to the duke of Marlborough. Vanbrugh ran into financial difficulties, and the duchess, although using his plans, dismissed him. He built other manor houses for the landed aristocracy, notably Seaton Delaval, Northumberland (1718), one of the most daring and theatrical of his creations. Though strongly influenced by Palladio, Vanbrugh used medieval detail such as the fortress towers at Lumley near Durham (1721), which inspired the baroque Grimsthorpe, Lincolnshire (1723), and his own house, near Greenwich, Vanbrugh Castle (1721). Knighted by George I (1714) and appointed comptroller of royal works (1715). His impressive originality as architect inspired the late eighteenth-century picturesque style.

EDITION: _Complete Works, plays_ ed. Bonamy Dobrée, _letters_ ed. Geoffrey Webb (4 vols. London and New York, 1927–28).

REFERENCES: Christian Barman _Sir John Vanbrugh_ (London and New York 1924). John Summerson _Architecture in Britain, 1530–1830_ (5th ed. Harmondsworth, England, 1969). Laurence Whistler _Sir John Vanbrugh: Architect and Dramatist_ (London 1938 and New York 1939) and _The Imagination of Vanbrugh and His Fellow Artists_ (London 1954).

VAN DE VELDE. _See_ **VELDE.**

VAN DYCK (or **VANDYKE**), Sir Anthony (Mar. 22, 1599 – Dec. 9, 1641). Flemish painter. Born Antwerp, son of a prosperous merchant. He had already set up his own studio and taken pupils when admitted to the painters' guild (1618). Became assistant, then close collaborator, of Rubens. By 1620 enjoyed a high reputation and was summoned to England to paint James I. Traveled in Italy (1621–27), studied particularly works of Venetians, and painted a series of remarkably distinguished portraits of Genoese nobility, notably that of Marchesa Elena Grimaldi (National Gallery, Washington, D.C.). Returning to Antwerp (1627), he painted some of his finest religious works, including _The Vision of St. Augustine_ (Antwerp). As sought after as Rubens, he also painted stately portraits of the patricians and artists of Antwerp. Invited to England by Charles I (1632) as court painter — he painted, for example, _Five Children of Charles I_ (1637, Royal Collection, Windsor Castle), was knighted, and spent the rest of his life in luxury, mainly at the English court. In the Netherlands again (1634–35), he painted more portraits and such religious paintings as the _Deposition_ (Antwerp). Married Lady Mary Ruthven (1639). Died at his house in Blackfriars, London, and was buried in St. Paul's. The painter supreme of the aristocracy, Van Dyck, while remaining true to his subjects, succeeded in endowing them with an elegance and dignity which played an influential role in developing a courtly manner for aristocratic subjects themselves, as well as a style for those who would paint them. Perhaps his most famous portrait is of _Charles I in Hunting Dress_ (c.1635, Louvre, Paris).

REFERENCES: Lionel Cust _Anthony Van Dyck: An Historical Study of His Life and Work_ (London 1900). Michael Jaffé _Van Dyck's Antwerp Sketchbook_ (2 vols. London 1966). Marie Mouquoy-Hendrick _L'Iconographie d'Antoine Van Dyck_ (Brussels 1956). Alfred Michiels _Van Dyck et ses élèves_ (2nd ed. Paris 1882). Leo van Puyvelde _Van Dyck_ (2nd ed. Brussels 1959).

Margaret D. Whinney and O. Millar *English Art, 1625–1714* (Oxford 1957).

VAN GOGH, Vincent (Mar. 30, 1853 – July 29, 1890). Dutch painter. Born Groot Zundert, Holland, son of a Protestant minister, and educated in nearby Zevenbergen. Obtained position with Goupil art gallery (1869); transferred to branch in London (1873), where he fell in love with but was rejected by Ursula Loyer. Transferred to Paris branch (1875), but became obsessed with religious and social questions and was dismissed. After teaching in the south of England, decided upon his religious calling and went to Amsterdam (1877) to work for admission to theological college, but gave up theological studies (1878). Thereupon enrolled in evangelical training school in Brussels and became lay preacher in poor mining district of Borinage, Belgium. His zeal led him to such lengths of asceticism that the authorities relieved him of his duties (1879); he went into a period of despair, and at last decided to devote himself to painting (1880). After leading a deeply troubled life in Brussels and The Hague he returned home to Nuenen and concentrated only on art, producing his first major work, *The Potato Eaters* (1885, Van Gogh Foundation, Amsterdam). Left for Paris (1886) to live with devoted brother Theo, and became influenced by the impressionists, painting frequently in pointillist style. Exhibited at Salon des Indépendants (1888), then moved south to Arles, where he painted some of his best-known works of the countryside and the town such as *Outdoor Cafe at Night, Arles* (1888, Kröller-Müller Museum, Otterlo), and developed his principles of suggestive color and brushwork. Already troubled by nervous disorders, he fell out with Gauguin, now staying with him, and slashed his own ear (afterwards painting the remarkable *Self-Portrait with Bandaged Ear*, 1889, Courtauld Institute, London), and finally, though in the midst of his most productive period, asked to be confined to the asylum at St.-Rémy. He continued painting prolifically, and in 1890 appeared the first enthusiastic appraisal of his work (by Aurier in the *Mercure de France*). But after moving to Auvers to the care of Dr. Gachet, he shot himself, and died two days later. He was buried in Auvers, and Theo, who died six months later, was eventually buried beside him.

EDITION: *Complete Letters* (3 vols. London and Greenwich, Conn. 1958).

REFERENCES: Alfred H. Barr, Jr. and Charles M. Brooks, Jr. *Vincent van Gogh* (New York 1935, reprinted 1966). Douglas Cooper *Drawings and Watercolors by Vincent van Gogh* (New York 1955). J. B. De La Faille ed. *Vincent van Gogh: His Paintings and Drawings* (New York 1970). Frank Elgar *Van Gogh: A Study of His Life and Work* (tr. New York and London 1958, also PB). Charles Estienne *Van Gogh* (tr. New York and London 1953, also PB). A. M. Hammacher *Genius and Disaster: The Ten Creative Years of Vincent van Gogh* (New York 1969). Julius Meier-Graefe *Vincent van Gogh: A Biographical Study* (tr. New York 1933 and as *Vincent: A Life of Vincent van Gogh* London 1936). Carl Nordenfalk *The Life and Work of Van Gogh* (tr. New York and London 1953). Mark Edo Tralbaut *Vincent van Gogh* (New York 1969).

VAN GOGH
BY MARK ROSKILL

The idea that van Gogh was both simpleminded and crazy still survives, but only, today, at the level of popular myth. If nothing else did, van Gogh's correspondence with his brother Theo and artist-friends — now published in English as the *Complete Letters* — would be bound to show the careful reader the misconception in both cases.

The picture of simplemindedness is contradicted in the first place by the sheer wealth and extent of van Gogh's reading; by his extraordinary articulateness in expressing his ideas; and by the very calculated way in which he constantly kept his brother informed of his plans and practical progress, and thereby assured himself of the financial support on which he was completely dependent. But what lies behind the misconception here is, perhaps, rather the idea of van Gogh's artistic isolation.

Because of the premium placed in modern times — beginning actually in van Gogh's day — on individuality and personal, revolutionary innovation, any modern artist must to a large extent work by himself and develop on his own. And van Gogh, after his two years (1886–88) in the metropolitan center of Paris, which he found too oppressive to bear, did spend the rest of his life off the artistic map, so to say: first at Arles in the south of France, then at nearby St.-Rémy, and finally at Auvers outside Paris. His dreams of an artistic community in the south equally came to nothing, after the sad debacle of Gauguin's stay with him at the end of 1888. Throughout this time, however, through the friends he had made in Paris, his correspondence and reading and his brother's activities as a dealer, van Gogh remained very well informed and aware of all that was going on in Paris and around. And his art of those years belongs correspondingly in the main artistic and intellectual currents of the time. All of the major developments, such as symbolism in particular, have their echoes or analogues in van Gogh's achievement.

As for the question of madness, the repeated attacks to which van Gogh was subject from the end of 1888 on, and which eventually drove him to his death, should by no means lead one to suppose that there is any real, direct similarity between his work and the art of the insane. There have been various medical and psychiatric hypotheses as to the nature of those attacks, but none of them is really satisfactory, and the problem remains unsolved. Naturally there is, in a general sense, a relationship between those attacks — the feelings and pressures out of which they came — and the

character of van Gogh's art; one sees this particularly in the choice, from the beginning, of themes and motifs that were intensely charged with an inner and personal significance, and in what van Gogh said or revealed about such subjects in his letters. But what is certain is that van Gogh's late works — with one or two exceptions, notably the famous *Crows Over a Wheatfield* — were not done during the periods of attack, but rather in between, when he was completely in charge of himself, or during the weeks of recovery. And the evidence of the works themselves points correspondingly to van Gogh's complete control over what he was doing. The deep, accelerated perspectives of the Arles landscapes, which seem to tie down and hold together a stretch of nature that would otherwise warp or topple down towards the spectator, and the exaggerated, swirling rhythms of such St.-Rémy paintings as the *Starry Night* and the *Olive Trees* — these are elements that van Gogh adopted with complete self-awareness and a lucid deliberateness. He "knew what he wanted"; and the art was, in fact, itself a means of control.

Though van Gogh sold only one or two paintings during his lifetime, he did attract attention even before his death — as the exhibition situation opened up inside and outside France — from the fellow artists and critics most closely involved. His "rediscovery," however, came in the early years of this century with the expressionist generation of painters — the Fauves in France and the Brücke in Germany. For them what mattered was the way that van Gogh had shown of doing things, rather than what he had actually done: the distortions and the expression of inner, subjective feeling which his example sanctioned. He became in this way, like Nietzsche in literature, a figurehead for a whole movement.

The results in time were twofold: first, the detachment of van Gogh's last three years in France (1888–90) as his "great period" and the tendency to read into each painting the drama and psychic urgency of the artist's feelings at the time (though van Gogh made it clear that he wanted his works to speak in themselves, without any such background); and secondly, an amplification of the importance of the works from the early years in Holland (1880–85) — the clumsiness of figure drawing in these works and the concern which they show with the harsh dignity of peasant life being seen as positive virtues.

Today, perhaps, a more sober view is in order. The years in Holland were essentially a period of apprenticeship — to the old masters whom van Gogh revered, particularly Rembrandt and Millet, and to the nineteenth-century Dutch line of landscape painting also. Symbolism, when van Gogh introduced it at this time, tends to be overcontrived or literary; but by the *Potato Eaters* (1885) he was working towards a more subtle and indirect kind of suggestiveness, based on his affiliation to the romanticism of the earlier nineteenth century. In Paris, from the impressionists and postimpressionists, he discovered color and a freer technique and was able to find his way through and beyond impressionism (of the 1870's) by transmuting everything that he successively picked up into personal terms of handling and approach to subject matter. But at Arles he was still learning — as he saw himself. The moving directness of his portraits, the "flaming" vision of the landscape of Provence — images so familiar now that one cannot any too easily make a proper evaluation of them — are still accompanied by unresolved qualities of structure and presentation. And the same holds true for the St.-Rémy works, some of which have in addition, or in compensation, a somewhat forced simplism. It was only, perhaps, at Auvers in the last months of his life that van Gogh fully succeeded in reconciling the crispness and flattening that he adopted from the Japanese print and the quality of allusive suggestion — and then in works that are not the best known, such as the figures against backgrounds of wheat and grasses. It is something of a cliché today to say of an artist who died young (van Gogh was thirty-seven) that he was just reaching the height of his powers and achievement at the time of his death; but in van Gogh's case this would appear to be true.

VAN GOYEN, Jan Josephszoon (Jan. 13, 1596 – Apr. 27, 1656). Dutch painter and etcher. Born Leiden, where he studied under several masters and married Annetje Willems van Raelst (1618); studied also in Haarlem. Settled at The Hague (1631); there he became dean of the painters' guild, prospered, and died. One of the first landscape painters to subordinate detail to atmospheric effect and space, he established a new course for Dutch landscape art. Best-known works are his vistas of towns, such as the *Panorama of The Hague* (The Hague) and *View of Dordrecht* (Rijksmuseum, Amsterdam).

REFERENCE: Wolfgang Stechow *Dutch Landscape Painting of the Seventeenth Century* (Greenwich, Conn. and London 1966).

VAN LEYDEN, Lucas. *See* LUCAS VAN LEYDEN.

VARESE, Edgar (Dec. 22, 1885 – Nov. 8, 1965). Franco-American composer. Born Paris, he studied science before attending the Paris Schola Cantorum

(1904), where d'Indy and Albert Roussel were his teachers. While still a student, he won the first Bourse Artistique, awarded by the city of Paris. Founded choirs in Paris and Berlin before leaving for the U.S. (1917) to conduct in New York and to found the International Composers' Guild (1921). His first performed work, *Hyperprism* (1926), was a determinedly avant-garde piece which startled the audience with its new sonorities. Other orchestral works followed, including *Amériques* (1926), *Arcana* (1927), and *Intégrales* (1931). Varese declared that he "dedicated himself to glorifying in music the modern triumphs of pure science," which explains some of his titles: *Ionization* (1931) for thirteen percussion players, *Metal* (1937) for soprano and orchestra, and *Density 21.5* (1936) for solo flute. Varese considered his music "organized sound" and stressed that he did not use sounds impressionistically but as an intrinsic part of the structure; hence his music is nonthematic and dissonant. In later works such as *Déserts* (1954) and *L'Homme et la machine* (1958) he used electronic music and recorded sounds.

REFERENCES: Henry Cowell ed. *American Composers on American Music* (Stanford, Calif. 1933). Fernand Ouellette *Edgard Varèse* (tr. New York 1968).

VASARI, Giorgio (July 30, 1511 – June 27, 1574). Italian architect, painter, and art historian. Born Arezzo. Settled in Florence, where he studied under Luca Signorelli, Andrea del Sarto, and Michelangelo, deriving from latter a mannerist style. Best known in his day for his paintings, Vasari's most notable work is the frescoes in the Palazzo Vecchio, Florence (begun 1554), executed under patronage of the Medici family. Of his architectual works, the Uffizi palace, Florence (begun 1560), is a fine example of mannerism in architecture. He also founded the Accademia del Disegno in Florence, and designed the Palazzo dei Cavalieri di S. Stefano, Pisa, and a monument to Michelangelo in S. Croce. He is most famous today for his great work *Le Vite de' piu eccellenti architetti, pittori e scultori italiani* (*The Lives of the Most Eminent Italian Architects, Painters, and Sculptors,* 1550). Traveled widely in Italy to gather material for the work, whose revised and enlarged second edition (1568) is more valuable than the first. The only source for information on innumerable subjects, *The Lives of the Artists* is meticulously accurate and voluminous in detail. Vasari married Niccolosa Bacci (1549), and died in Florence.

TRANSLATION: *Lives of the . . . Painters, Sculptors and Architects* (1550) tr. Gaston de Vere (10 vols. London 1912–15) from edition annotated by Gaetano Milanesi (9 vols. Florence 1878–85).

VAUGHAN, Henry (Apr. 17, 1622 – Apr. 23, 1695). British poet. Born and died in Llansantffraed, Brecknockshire, Wales; of ancient Welsh family. Educated privately and at Jesus College, Oxford (1638–40). Married twice. After brief law practice in London, returned to Brecknock (1642) at outbreak of Civil War. Published *Poems, with the Tenth Satire of Juvenal Englished* ("The Vanity of Human Wishes" satire, 1646). *Olor Iscanus* (*Swan of Usk*) followed (1651). Became powerfully influenced by George Herbert's poetry, and began to write in a profoundly mystical and religious vein. Best known of his poetry is *Silex Scintillans* (1650, enlarged 1655), which includes "They are all gone into the world of light." In prose he wrote *The Mount of Olives, or Solitary Devotions* (1652). His special quality is his intense spiritual vision, and mystical affinity with nature. He is known as the Silurist because his native county of Brecknock was once inhabited by the ancient Silures of south Wales. He was not recognized until the nineteenth century, when *The Complete Works* were edited by Dr. A. B. Grosart (1871) and by E. K. Chambers as *Poems of Henry Vaughan, Silurist* (1896).

EDITIONS: *Works* ed. L. C. Martin (2nd ed. Oxford 1957). *Complete Poetry* ed. French Fogle (New York 1965, also PB).

REFERENCES: Joan Bennett *Five Metaphysical Poets* (3rd ed. Cambridge, England, and New York 1964, also PB).

Edmund Blunden *On the Poems of Henry Vaughan* (London 1927, reprinted New York 1969). R. A. Durr *On the Mystical Poetry of Henry Vaughan* (Cambridge, Mass. and Oxford 1962). Ross Garner *Henry Vaughan: Experience and Tradition* (Chicago and Cambridge, England, 1959). Elizabeth Holmes *Henry Vaughan and the Hermetic Philosophy* (1932, reprinted New York 1967, also PB). Francis E. Hutchinson *Henry Vaughan: A Life and Interpretation* (Oxford 1947). E. C. Pettet *Of Paradise and Light: A Study of Vaughan's Silex Scintillans* (Cambridge, England, and New York 1960). Helen C. White *The Metaphysical Poets: A Study in Religious Experience* (New York 1936 and London 1937, PB 1962).

VAUGHAN WILLIAMS, Ralph (Oct. 12, 1872 – Aug. 26, 1958). English composer. Born Down Ampney, Gloucestershire. Attended Trinity College, Cambridge (1892–95), where he received D.Mus. degree (1901); also Royal College of Music, London (until 1896). Studied with Max Bruch in Berlin (1897–98), and with Ravel in Paris (1909). At the turn of the century, a revival of Elizabethan music, Purcell's works, and especially English folk song unlocked his talent. Recognition came with performance of cantata *Toward the Unknown Region* (1907). After serving with British army in World War I, became professor of composition at Royal College of Music and conducted the London Bach Choir (1920–28). Received Order of Merit (1935). Married twice. Died in London. Important works are the nine symphonies, notably the *London* (1914) and *Pastoral* (1922); choral compositions and songs; and small orchestral pieces such as *Fantasia on Greensleeves* and *Fantasia on a Theme by Tallis* (1910). His music is known for its distinctively national style; in later work he adopted advanced harmonic techniques.

REFERENCES: James Day *Vaughan Williams* (London and New York 1961). Hubert Foss *Ralph Vaughan Williams* (London and New York 1950). Frank Howes *The Music of Ralph Vaughan Williams* (London and New York 1954). Elliott S. Schwartz *The Symphonies of Ralph Vaughan Williams* (Amherst, Mass. 1965). Ursula Vaughan Williams *R.V.W.: A Biography of Ralph Vaughan Williams* (London and New York 1964).

VEGA, Lope de (full name Lope Felix de Vega Carpio) (c.Nov. 25, 1562 – Aug. 27, 1635). Spanish dramatist and poet. Born and died in Madrid. Educated at University of Alcalá (c.1577), he was banished from Madrid for libel against a mistress (1588), whereupon he joined the Armada and married by proxy Isabel de Urbina (the Belisa of many of his poems). In Valencia (1589–90), then the center of dramatic activity, he began writing plays. After his first wife's death (1595), married Juana de Guardo. Throughout both marriages and even after becoming a priest (1614), he had numerous love affairs and fathered several illegitimate children. But his life was ridden with tragedy: the death of his second wife (1613); the blindness, insanity, and death of his last mistress; the death of his favorite son and abduction of his youngest daughter (both in 1634). An enormously prolific writer, he wrote over fifteen hundred plays, of which nearly five hundred survive. Ranging in theme and genre from heroic tragedy to comedies of manners and cloak-and-dagger intrigue, they include *Peribáñez* (c.1610), *Fuente Ovejuna* (c.1612–14, *The Sheep's Well*), *El Mejor alcalde el rey* (1620–23, *The King the Greatest Mayor*), *El Caballero de Olmedo* (c.1620–25, *The Knight of Olmedo*), and *El Castigo sin venganza* (1631, *Punishment Without Revenge*). In his *Arte nuevo de hacer comedias* (1609, *The New Art of Writing Plays*) he set forth his dramatic precepts and defended his conscious disregard of the neoclassical unities. Among his numerous nondramatic works: the pastoral romance *Arcadia* (1598), inspired by Jacopo Sannazaro; the epic *La Hermosura de Angelica* (1602, *The Beauty of Angelica*), after Ariosto's *Orlando;* his autobiography *La Dorotea* (1632); and the lyrics *Rimas humanas* (1602) and *Rimas sacras* (1614). Of literary historical interest is his poetical *Laurel de Apolo* (1630), in which Apollo crowns the Spanish poets on Helicon. Historically Lope de Vega occupies the place in Spanish drama that Shakespeare does in English, and is considered "the Phoenix of Genius" in Spain.

TRANSLATION: *Five Plays* tr. Jill Booty (New York and London 1961, also PB).

REFERENCES: Francis C. Hayes *Lope de Vega* (New York 1967). S. Griswold Morley and Courtney Bruerton *The Chronology of Lope de Vega's Comedias* (London and New York 1940). Jack H. Parker and Arthur M. Fox *Lope de Vega Studies, 1937–1962: A Critical Survey and Annotated Bibliography* (Toronto PB 1964). Hugo A. Rennert *The Life of Lope de Vega* (1904, reprinted New York 1968). Rudolph Schevill *The Dramatic Art of Lope de Vega* (1918, reprinted New York 1964).

VELÁZQUEZ, Diego Rodriguez de Silva y (June 6, 1599 – Aug. 6, 1660). Spanish painter. Born Seville, of Portuguese origin. Studied under Francesco Pacheco, whose daughter he married (1618). Introduced at court in Madrid (1622), where he became the lifelong friend of King Philip IV and was appointed court painter (1623). Greatly admired Rubens, who visited Madrid (1628) and became his friend. Went to Italy (1629–31), where he produced *The Forge of Vulcan* (Prado, Madrid) and *Joseph's Coat* (Chapter House, Escorial, Spain). Famous earlier works include, from his Sevillian period, the *bodegones* (genre scenes), and from his first years at court, *Los Borrachos Bacchus*, 1629, Prado). In 1630's and 1640's produced equestrian portraits and others of the king and queen, the heir Don Balthasar, and El Conde-Duque de Olivares; a series of portraits of court dwarfs; the *Surrender at Breda* (1634, Prado); and, before 1648, the *Rokeby Venus* (National Gallery, London). From a second trip to Italy (1649–51) date the portraits of *Juan de Perera* (1649, Wildenstein Collection, New York) and *Innocent X* (1650, Doria palace, Rome and two landscapes, *Views of the Villa Medici*. Late works include portraits of court ladies, *Las Meniñas* (1656, Prado), and *The Spinners* (Prado). Died in Madrid.

REFERENCES: Karl Justi *Diego Velázquez and His Times* (tr. London 1889). Enrique Lafuente Ferrari *Velázquez*

(New York and London 1960). José López-Rey *Velázquez: A Catalogue Raisonné of His Oeuvre* (London 1963) and *Velázquez' Work and World* (London and Greenwich, Conn. 1968). Elizabeth du Gué Trapier *Velázquez* (New York 1948).

☞

VELÁZQUEZ
BY SVETLANA ALPERS

Of all the great baroque painters, Velázquez enjoys the greatest general popularity today. The pleasure which his works give is directly related to the fact that since the middle of the last century he has seemed to many viewers the most "modern" artist of his time. While Rubens — to oversimplify this view — championed the established beliefs and institutions of his day in traditional allegorical, mythological, and historical terms, and while Rembrandt invented new pictorial means to study the inner passions of men, Velázquez looked at the world around him, recording clearly and directly what he saw, be it peasant, dwarf, or king. The nineteenth century saw in Velázquez's early *bodegones* (for example, *The Water Carrier* or *The Old Woman Cooking Eggs*) an interest in realistic subject matter that was a precursor of Courbet's revolutionary realism, and it saw in his lightened palette and dependence on color and light rather than linear means to define form a precursor of the impressionists' insistence on truth to the visual world. Although tastes in art have changed since Velázquez's first nineteenth-century biographer, William Stirling-Maxwell, writing in 1855, praised him for having anticipated the photograph, excitement about Velázquez's sheer imitative skill has survived to be celebrated today even in the Prado, where a huge mirror is hung opposite *The Maids of Honor*, so as to seduce the visitor into imagining that it reflects not a painting but a real scene.

There is inevitably some distortion when an artist of another age is understood in the light of contemporary art. To see Velázquez as a realist is to recognize certain important characteristics of his art and of the art of his age: even in his own time he, along with Caravaggio and the Dutch school, was attacked by conservative critics for what was considered a tasteless embracing of low subject matter and an overly naturalistic style. But in order to explain how a seventeenth-century artist could have painted in so realistic and, by implication, modern a manner, a majority of writers since the nineteenth century have assumed that Velázquez was in conflict with the world in which he lived and with its ideals. To some, the frank and intimate portrait Velázquez gives us of King Philip IV growing from an ungainly youth into a sick and aged man reveals a rebellion against the court and the ideal status of the king, while a mythological work such as that depicting Bacchus with his entourage of simple peasants reveals a satiric disrespect for the gods of antiquity.

The error of this view is its assumption that in seeing the world steadily and seeing it whole Velázquez was necessarily seeing through it. Far from leading the life of a rebel, he lived in harmony with the established world of the court. From the age of twenty-four, when he was appointed court painter, Velázquez lived at the court and worked only for Philip IV. The relatively small number of works by Velázquez's hand is testimony to the demanding nature of his court service (his duties included purchasing works for the court and supervising their arrangement), and the fact that almost all of his greatest works are to be found in Madrid testi-

fies to the exclusive nature of his patronage.

This involvement in court life enabled Velázquez to paint other members of the court with ease and familiarity. Thus the immediacy of the king's presence in a portrait by Velázquez, the frankness with which the small eyes, the Hapsburg lips, and the protruding chin are handled, is the result not only of Velázquez's descriptive skill but of his place in the court. Velázquez presents the king not only as a king but as a particular individual. It is largely in order to preserve the delicate balance between these two elements that he often employs the device of placing the realistically depicted monarch in a severely simplified and, as it were, unrealistic setting, with the effect of removing him from the real world. All of Velázquez's portrait subjects share this essential quality of being depicted as particular individuals, as well as according to their positions in the world. Thus the five-year-old Balthasar Carlos prancing on his huge horse is a proud and excited little boy as well as a prince. And in some of his most remarkable portraits, even the pathetic, deformed court dwarfs and fools (who were commonly the butt of jokes in the Renaissance and were kept at the court as entertainers) are treated with full dignity as human beings — not because Velázquez held revolutionary egalitarian views, but because they too had a place in the circumscribed world of the court. Significantly, it is this entire world, not just the royal members, that Velázquez celebrates in the famous *Maids of Honor*.

Although he was primarily a portrait painter, Velázquez's job at court also required him to paint traditional religious, mythological, and historical subjects. The problem of how to draw on direct observations of the real world while depicting such ideal subjects was one shared by many seventeenth-century artists who were most consciously trying to give new life to that great tradition of Renaissance art whose premises were at once imitative and idealizing. Although their solutions differed, most of the leading artists of the time found little difficulty in producing ideal images of church, state, and the antique gods. To Velázquez, however, the handling of such elevated subjects and figures posed peculiar problems. His difficulty lay partly in his training — Spain was but a provincial art center which received much of its knowledge of the idealizing tradition of Italian art at second hand — but more significantly it lay in the fact that Velázquez's strength as an artist was in the realistic rendering of people and objects. Far from being attacks on the gods, Velázquez's early ideal figures — for example, the awkward nude Apollo at the forge of Vulcan, or the incongruous Bacchus among the peasants — reveal a difficulty, such as we never find in the works of Rubens, Bernini, or Poussin, in producing and presenting ideal figures.

Velázquez's successful solution to this problem produced works that are unique in presenting heroic public actions in astoundingly intimate and realistic terms. The formal act of the *Surrender at Breda*, which is announced by the celebrated massing of lances and the battlefield smoking in the distance, is actually rendered through the relationship of the two generals. The intimate nature of this moment is conveyed by the inattentive troops and the horse who, rather than honoring the surrender, inappropriately turns his back on it and lifts his hind leg. In a similar mode, Velázquez presents Mercury's slaying of Argus as he watches over Io as what is almost a sinister scene of cattle rustling, and in *The Spinners* — so called because it was long thought to be simply a representation of the royal tapestry workshop — Velázquez uses an appropriate realistic setting to present the story of Arachne's doomed attempt to best Minerva at weaving.

The literal framework and the realistic manner in which Velázquez depicts king, general, or ancient god should not be mistaken for disparagement of these figures. The subtlety of the balance that he achieves between real appearances and the ideal stature of these actions and figures has been illustrated for us in the attempts of another great artist, court painter to a later Spanish king, to imitate Velázquez's success. For in Goya's portraits, the realistic depiction of the stances and Hapsburg features of Spanish royalty makes them seem moronic, destroying any notion of nobility and leaving viewers uncertain to this day whether the responsibility for this impression lies with the artist or the sitter.

It was paradoxically the nineteenth-century artist whose name was most often linked to Velázquez as a realist who understood most fully the essentially ideal and aristocratic nature of his art. Manet thought that Velázquez was the greatest painter who ever lived, and the often puzzling and incommunicative figures in his paintings owe much to Velázquez portraits. But the distance and isolation of Velázquez's figures was continuous with their position in a society which still retained notions of individual heroism. For Manet, living in a century of political and artistic revolution, the distance and isolation of the individual could only be achieved by aesthetic means in the increasingly artificial world of art. The difference between their works strikingly illustrates how different a relationship the artist had to society in their respective centuries. While Velázquez depicted the actual court of Philip IV and its ideals, Manet was forced to create his own court of characters in a purely painted world.

VELDE, Adriaen van de (c. Nov. 10, 1630 – Jan. 21, 1672), and Willem van de (the Younger) (c. Dec. 18, 1633 – Apr. 8, 1707). Dutch painters. Sons of Willem van de Velde the Elder (c.1611 – Dec. 13, 1693), Dutch painter of marine scenes. ADRIAEN (born and died in Amsterdam) studied under his father, then in Haarlem under Jan Wynants and Philips Wouwerman. Married Maria Oudekerk (1657). Best known for his landscapes and keen sense of changing light during the day and the seasons, and for his animals (he was influenced by the great animal painter Paulus Potter). Also painted religious and mythological subjects, and portraits of such well-known contemporaries as Meindert Hobbema and Jan van der Heyden. A characteristic landscape with figures and animals is *Jacob and Laban* (1663, Wallace Collection, London). His brother WILLEM was a leading Dutch marine painter who studied with his father and Simon de Vlieger. Little is known of his life except that he probably visited England with his father and entered service of Charles II of England (1677), and later the service of James II for rest of his life, dying in Greenwich, London. Painted warships and sea fights, storms and sea coasts, including such works as *The Cannon Shot* (Rijksmuseum, Amsterdam) and *Coast Scene, Calm* (1661, National Gallery, London).

REFERENCE: Émile Michel *Les Van de Velde* (Paris 1892).

VENEZIANO, Domenico (c.1405 – May 15, 1461). Italian painter. His name suggests Venetian origin; nothing is known of his early years. By 1439 he was in Florence working on frescoes, now lost, in the Capella Maggiore of S. Egidio. Fra Angelico is thought to be a major influence. Vasari mentions the

Carnesecchi Tabernacle (c.1438, National Gallery, London) as his first work in Florence. The *Adoration of the Magi* tondo (1442–45, Staatliche Museen, Berlin) shows a Flemish flair for detail and the pure colors of Fra Angelico, which also characterize his masterpiece, the famous *St. Lucy Altarpiece* (c.1445) from the church of S. Lucia dei Magnoli, now dispersed. The main panel (Uffizi, Florence), revealing new use of light and shadow, represents — for the first time on same scale — the Madonna and Saints. The panels of the predella are in Staatliche Museen, Berlin; National Gallery, Washington, D.C.; and Fitzwilliam Museum, Cambridge, England. Two attributed portraits survive, of Matteo and Michele Olivieri (National Gallery, Washington, D.C., and Rockefeller Collection, New York), the attributed fresco of John the Baptist and St. Francis (c.1455, S. Croce, Florence), and several Madonnas. One of the earliest and most gifted Florentine Renaissance painters, he exerted great influence on succeeding artists, especially on and through Piero della Francesca.

VERDI, Giuseppe (Fortunino Francesco) (Oct. 10, 1813 – Jan. 27, 1901). Italian composer. Born Le Roncole, near Parma, son of a tavern keeper. Became protégé of Antonio Barezzi, a merchant from neighboring town of Busseto, who sent him to Milan (1831), where he studied for three years under Vincenzo Lavigna. Returned to Busseto (1834) and married his patron's daughter, Margherita (1836; she died 1840). First opera was *Oberto* (produced 1839); reputation in Italy was established with *Nabucco* (1842). Lived in Paris (1847–49), and on return to Busseto brought his mistress, Giuseppina Strepponi, whom he married (1859). After successes of *Rigoletto* (1851), *Il Trovatore* (1853), and *La Traviata* (1853), he produced a number of spectacular works for the Paris Opera (1855–70), including *Don Carlos* (1867). Staged *Un Ballo in maschera* in Rome (1859), and *La Forza del destino* in St. Petersburg (1862). An ardent patriot, Verdi had frequent encounters with Austrian censorship until unification of Italy

(1861); he was then elected to Parliament, but took no active role and resigned (1865). Major works of his late years are *Aïda* (1871), the *Requiem* (1873), honoring Manzoni, *Otello* (1887), and *Falstaff* (1893). Died in Milan and was accorded a state funeral.

REFERENCES: Carlo Gatti *Verdi: The Man and His Music* (tr. New York and London 1955). Spike Hughes *Famous Verdi Operas* (London and Philadelphia 1968). Dyneley Hussey *Verdi* (London and New York 1940, also PB). George Martin *Verdi: His Music, Life and Times* (New York 1963). Charles Osborne *The Complete Operas of Verdi* (London and New York 1970). Francis Toye *Giuseppe Verdi: His Life and Works* (London and New York 1931, PB 1959). Frank Walker *The Man Verdi* (London and New York 1962).

↬

GIUSEPPE VERDI
BY JOSEPH KERMAN

Composers are generally townspeople, most often sons of musicians. Giuseppe Verdi was the son of an impoverished, illiterate peasant innkeeper. Le Roncole in the duchy of Parma, his birthplace, is more a crossroads than a village, and Busseto, three miles away, was a little town of two thousand inhabitants. Even after Verdi had begun a musical career at Milan — which, by the way, had only about 150,000 inhabitants in those days — he allowed himself to be persuaded to return to Busseto as director of the town band. As soon as he made money, he bought property nearby and retired there as a country squire. For all his contact with the wide world, there was always a peasant streak in his personality: conservative, pessimistic and distrustful, tough-minded and hardworking, rigidly devoted to all the old-fashioned values, whether moral, musical, or monetary. The characteristic Verdi anecdote concerns a man who had heard so much talk about him that he journeyed twice to Parma to hear *Aïda,* and then was so disappointed that he applied to the composer for his money back. He was reimbursed for the tickets and the trip, but not for two "detestable suppers at the station," Verdi pointing out rather sharply that these could just as well have been eaten at home.

Coming to opera composition rather late, by the standards of those days, Verdi scored an enormous success with his third, fourth, and fifth operas, *Nabucco, I Lombardi,* and *Ernani* (1842–4). In a space of two years, he became the most talked about composer in Italy. Methodically Verdi set out to make as much money as possible, producing nine operas in the next half dozen years — "years in the galleys," he called them, *anni di galera.* Some of these works were potboilers, some were better received than others, and none is well known or highly regarded today with the exception of *Macbeth* — the only one, apparently, that continued to interest the composer, who rewrote it twenty years later. Much was improved, but the striking thing is how much could be left intact, including the magnificent sleepwalking scene for Lady Macbeth. *Rigoletto, Il Trovatore,* and *La Traviata* (1851–3) mark the climax of Verdi's early career. These three famous operas have many musical parallels despite vast differences in dramatic style, differences that show how extremely wide Verdi's scope was as a dramatist. At the age of forty Verdi was a made man; henceforth he composed slowly and with great deliberation.

A steady advance in musical and psychological subtlety and in momentary dramatic power can be traced in Verdi's next operas, during the 1850's and 1860's. That these find a regular place in the current repertory speaks well for the development of operatic taste. Yet in terms of total musico-dramatic consistency, none of these operas can match *Rigoletto* or *Traviata,* even though many individual elements in them are far superior. At this period, in spite of his dogged search for dramatic subjects and his dictatorial methods with the poets working for him, Verdi was somehow unable to spirit out a satisfactory libretto.

A freethinker, a strong democrat, and a patriot in both political and musical matters: his gods were Palestrina and Rossini rather than Mozart or Beethoven, and Wagner brought out all his Italian peasant hostility. Most of the early operas contain passages that could be, and certainly were, taken as expressions of a passion for Italian liberation; "Viva Verdi" actually became a rallying cry in the Risorgimento. On the death of Rossini in 1868, it was Verdi's idea to have a memorial Mass composed by the leading musicians of Italy, number by number; this scheme fell through, but ultimately Verdi bodied out his own contribution to create the famous Requiem Mass for the patriot-novelist Alessandro Manzoni, his one important nonoperatic composition. Its operatic overtones gave offense for a long time in Germany and England.

After the great success of *Aïda* (1871) Verdi's career was assumed to be easing toward an end. *Simon Boccanegra* and *Don Carlos* were revised and improved (though not improved enough). Then a completely new phase of creative activity was initiated by the intervention of Arrigo Boito, a distinguished literary man as well as a good composer in his own right. Boito is the last of the series of wonderfully devoted human beings who brightened Verdi's dour existence: Antonio Barezzi, the Busseto merchant who practically adopted him and gave him his start; the lovable Giuseppina Strepponi, a fine singer who helped his early career, later his mistress and second wife; Angelo Mariani, a brilliant, erratic conductor who was in fact treated pretty badly by the composer. With infinite patience, Boito fashioned two superb Shakespeare librettos for Verdi, *Otello* (1887) and — a comedy! — *Falstaff* (1893). How much Boito contributed to the radically developed musical style of these works we shall never know. Certain it is that although this style can in retrospect be traced back to *Aïda* and beyond, it represents an extraordinary change for a composer in his seventies.

Otello and *Falstaff* are two of the greatest operas ever written, if not *the* two greatest, and the charge of "Wagnerism" that so irritated Verdi is irrelevant to their actual qualities. If the texture is "continuous" rather than broken up into separate arias and other "numbers," and if the orchestra plays a very large role, all of this simply reaps a harvest which was sown in early nineteenth-century opera by Weber, Meyerbeer, and late Donizetti, and which would have flowered late in the century whether or not Wagner had ever existed. Verdi writes a human drama peopled with characters of astonishing emotional integrity. Wagner writes a drama of ideas in which people's emotions, however skillfully portrayed, often seem calculated on ideological grounds.

As for Verdi's early operas, even the best of these used to be dismissed by advanced critics as simpleminded, vulgar, and reactionary. They have their regrettable moments. But as Isaiah Berlin has remarked, Verdi is the last "naïve" artist in Schiller's sense — an artist working unselfconsciously within a received tradition, accepting its conventions as a basis for slow bending rather than breaking. The numerous recent revivals of Rossini, Bellini, Donizetti, and early Verdi make it very clear why everyone at the time was so impressed by Verdi's robust imagination and dramatic flair. By the early 1850's, Verdi was coaxing convention with consummate power. The last act of *Rigoletto,* for instance, features two of his most notorious "vulgar" tunes; but in the theatre, the much-parodied quartet gains dimension as a musical (and visual) embodiment of a major turning point in the drama, and *La donna è mobile* makes its real point by projecting in musical terms the important news that the corpse in Rigoletto's sack is not the Duke. The cheap frivolity of this tune stresses the contrast between the Duke and the actual victim, Gilda. As for the other conventional numbers in this act, such as they are, the swift trio makes a vivid storm in advance, and the final duet is cut to the bone. If Gilda's *Lassù in cielo* reminds us of the more tedious lachrymosity of early Italian opera, the way Rigoletto keeps breaking into her song reminds us that a vital new dramatic potential has been discovered in the old tradition.

Perhaps the quality of Verdi's "naïveté" could make little headway in those parts of nineteenth-century Europe that were deeply "sentimental" in Schiller's sense — sophisticated, we might say. But this quality has strongly recommended itself where sophistication has run into a blank wall — in Germany since the 1920's, in America since the 1950's.

VERGA, Giovanni (Sept. 2, 1840 – Jan. 27, 1922). Sicilian novelist. Born and died in Catania. From a family of landowners, he was educated privately. His first book was the four-volume *Carbonari della montagna* (1861–62), a historical novel about his grandfather, a Sicilian politician. Moved north to Florence (1865), where he wrote his romances *Una Peccatrice* (1866) and *Storia di una capinera* (1870); then, moving to Milan, he published a number of popular novels, melodramatic works of intrigue and passion such as *Eva* (1873), *Tigre Reale* (1873), *Eros* (1874), and one book of considerable quality, *Nedda* (1874), the story of a Sicilian peasant girl. Returned to Sicily (1880) and wrote the novels which mark Verga as a master of realism (*verismo*): *Vita dei campi* (1880), the tragic *I Malavoglia* (1881), and *Novelle rusticana* (1883). *Vita dei campi* contains the story *Cavalleria rusticana,* on which Mascagni's opera is based. *Mastro-Don Gesualdo* (1888) was his last work of any importance. Verga portrayed the wretched lives of poor Sicilian peasants and fishermen. His dramatic, terse, and sober style is suffused with a lyricism that adds a wealth of compassion to the harshness of his subject matter.

TRANSLATIONS: *Mastro-Don Gesualdo* (1923, new ed. New York 1955), *Little Novels of Sicily* (1925, new ed. New York 1953), and *Cavalleria Rusticana and Other Tales* (London and New York 1928), all translated by D. H. Lawrence. *The House by the Medlar Tree* tr. Eric Mosbacher (New York and London 1953).

REFERENCE: T. G. Bergin *Giovanni Verga* (New Haven, Conn. and London 1931).

VERLAINE, Paul (Mar. 30, 1844 – Jan. 8, 1896). French poet. Born Metz. Raised in Paris, where he attended Lycée Bonaparte and began law studies, abandoned (1864) for clerk's post at Hôtel de Ville. His first book of poems, *Poèmes saturniens* (1866), followed by *Fêtes galantes* (1869), quickly attracted attention, and he became a member of the literary salons. His marriage to Mathilde Mauté de Fleurville (1870) — the inspiration for *La Bonne Chanson* — was soon strained by his bohemian habits and strong, presumably homosexual friendship with the young poet Rimbaud. It ended in legal separation (1872) when the two poets went to England together and finally in divorce (1885). When Rimbaud threatened to leave him during the famous Brussels quarrel (1873), Verlaine wounded him with a revolver and was sentenced to two years in prison. There he underwent a spiritual crisis, resulting in a brief conversion to Catholicism, and wrote, among others, the poem *Art poètique*, later to become a symbolist text. After his release he made several trips, including one to England again, then returned to Paris (1885). Here, despite growing literary fame and adulation, he indulged in alcoholism and debauchery which led to his death. His major books of poetry include *Romances sans paroles* (1874), which contains some of his most haunting verses, such as *Il pleure dans mon coeur* and *Green, Sagesse* (1881), *Jadis et naguère* (1884), and the prose sketches *Les Poètes maudits* on his fellow symbolists.

TRANSLATION: *Selected Poems* tr. C. F. MacIntyre (Berkeley, Calif. 1948 and Cambridge, England, 1949, also PB).

REFERENCES: Antoine Adam *The Art of Paul Verlaine* (tr. New York 1963, also PB). André Benéteau *Étude sur l'inspiration et l'influence de Paul Verlaine* (Washington, D.C. 1930, reprinted New York 1969). Jacques-Henry Bornecque *Verlaine par lui-même* (Paris 1966). A. E. Carter *Verlaine: A Study in Parallels* (Toronto 1969). Claude Cuénot *Le Style de Paul Verlaine* (Paris 1963). Harold Nicolson *Paul Verlaine* (London and New York 1921). C. E. B. Roberts *Paul Verlaine* (London 1937).

VERMEER, Jan (c.Oct. 30, 1632 – Dec. 15, 1675). Dutch painter. Born Delft, where he spent all his life. Probably studied with Carel Fabritius, who evidently influenced him. Married (1653) and that year was admitted to the painters' guild, of which he was twice dean (1662–63, 1670–71). Supported by his trade as art dealer, he received almost no attention during his lifetime for his own work. Not until 1866 was his greatness recognized through French critic William Bürger (real name E. J. T. Thoré, 1807–1869) in articles later collected in his book *Notice sur Van der Meer de Delft*. About forty paintings, many undated, are of certain attribution to Vermeer, whose subjects are chiefly landscapes and interiors with the figure of a woman. He is remarkable for his use of color to create perspective in his landscapes, for the luminous effect of light striking various shapes and surfaces in his interiors, and for the abstract geometry of his compositions. Among his most famous works are *View of Delft* (1660, Mauritshuis, The Hague), *The Letter* and *Maidservant Pouring Milk* (both c.1660, Rijksmuseum, Amsterdam), *Young Woman with a Water Jug* (1663, Metropolitan Museum, New York), *Artist and Model* (1663, Kunsthistorisches Museum, Vienna), *Girl with a Red Hat* (1667, National Gallery, Washington, D.C.), *The Lacemaker* (Louvre, Paris), *The Concert* (Gardner Museum, Boston).

REFERENCES: Pierre Descargues *Vermeer* (Geneva 1966). A. B. de Vries *Jan Vermeer van Delft* (tr. London and New York 1948). Ludwig Goldscheider *Jan Vermeer: The Paintings* (2nd ed. London and Greenwich, Conn. 1967). Lawrence Gowing *Vermeer* (London 1952 and New York 1953). John Jacob *Complete Paintings of Jan Vermeer* (New York 1969).

VERNE, Jules (Feb. 8, 1828 – Mar. 24, 1905). French novelist. Born Nantes, son of a magistrate. Educated at lycée there. Went to Paris to take law degree, but soon became interested in the theatre and began writing plays. Married Honorine Morel (1857). Despite moderate success with plays, Verne did not achieve fame until publication of his novella *Cinq Semaines en ballon* (1863, *Five Weeks in a Balloon*). Coupling a gift for adventure writing with the public interest in new technological discoveries, he continued with a series of highly successful, prophetic science fiction adventure stories: *Voyage au centre de la terre* (1864, *A Journey to the Center of the Earth*), *De la Terre à la lune* (1865, *A Trip to the Moon*), and the even more famous *Vingt Lieues sous les mers* (1870, *Twenty Thousand Leagues Under the Sea*), concerning the adventures of Captain Nemo and his submarine *Nautilus*. During the Franco-Prussian War he went into retirement, but later returned to Paris with several manuscripts, including *L'Ile mystérieuse* (1874, *The Mysterious*

Island) and the perennially popular *Le Tour du monde en quatre-vingt jours* (1873, *Around the World in Eighty Days*), which tells of the amazing feat of the Englishman Philéas Fogg and his valet Passepartout. His books have been translated into many languages, and plays and films have been made from a number of them. Verne was made an officer of the Legion of Honor (1892), and served on the municipal council in Amiens. His last years were marked by enormous popularity and numerous honors. By the time of his death in Amiens, he had written fifty books.

REFERENCES: Kenneth Allott *Jules Verne* (London 1940 and New York 1941). Marguerite Allotte de la Fuÿe *Jules Verne* (tr. London 1954 and New York 1956). Marcel Moré *Le Très Curieux Jules Verne* (Paris 1960) and *Nouvelles Explorations de Jules Verne* (Paris 1963). George H. Waltz *Jules Verne: The Biography of an Imagination* (New York 1943).

VERONESE, Paolo (real name Paolo Caliari) (1528 – Apr. 19, 1588). Italian painter. Born Verona, son of a stonecutter, and had early training there; hence his name. First known work is the *Bevilacqua-Lazise Altarpiece* (1548, Museo di Castelvecchio, Verona). From 1553 he was in Venice, painting such commissioned works in mannerist style as the ceilings of S. Sebastiano, (1555–58) and the tondos in library of S. Marco. At this time also painted such elegant portraits as the voluptuous blond *Bella Nani* (Louvre, Paris) and *Conte Giuseppe da Porto* (Contini Bonacossi Collection, Florence). Developed his rich decorative style in such works as *Supper at Emmaus* (c.1558, Louvre) and *Feast in the House of the Pharisee* (Galleria Sabauda, Turin). The allegorical fresco cycle for the Villa Barbaro at Maser (c.1560) shows his brilliant handling of illusionism and space. With the sumptuous *Marriage at Cana* (1562, Louvre) his style became increasingly daring in displaying the luxury of contemporary life in lavish detail, costumes, opulent use of color, leading to such splendors as *The Family of Darius Before Alexander* (c.1565, National Gallery, London)

and the banquet scenes, including *Feast in the House of Levi* (1573, Accademia, Venice), for which he was censored by the Inquisition. Other works include four allegories of love (c.1575, National Gallery), the famous *Rape of Europa* (1580) and *Triumph of Venice* (1578–85) for Palazzo Ducale, Venice, *Mars and Venus* (Metropolitan Museum, New York). With Tintoretto, Veronese ranks as one of the greatest Venetian decorative painters.

REFERENCES: Nancy R. Bell *Paolo Veronese* (London and New York 1904). A. Orliac *Veronese* (tr. London 1948). P. H. Osmond *Paolo Veronese: His Career and Work* (London and New York 1927).

VERROCCHIO, Andrea del (real name Andrea di Michele di Francesco Cione) (1435 – Oct. 7, 1488). Italian sculptor, painter, and goldsmith. Born Florence, trained as a goldsmith, taking name from his teacher Verrocchi. Little is known of his early years. First important commission: the bronze group *Christ with Doubting Thomas* (1463–83, Or San Michele, Florence). Other commissions followed and overlapped, so his works are hard to date. Completed (1472) tomb of Giovanni and Piero de' Medici (S. Lorenzo, Florence), and produced the elegant bronze *David* (1476, Museo Nazionale, Florence) and bronze *Boy with a Dolphin*. Was commissioned (1481) to execute the great equestrian statue of Bartolommeo Colleoni for Campo San Zanipolo, Venice, where he died before it was completed. (Venetian sculptor Alessandro Leopardi finished it and made the base; it was unveiled in 1496.) His best-known painting is the unfinished *Baptism of Christ* (c.1470, Uffizi, Florence), in which the angel on the left may have been painted by his pupil Leonardo. There are several paintings of *Madonna and Child* (two are in Staatliche Museen, Berlin, and National Gallery, Washington, D.C.). Best known as a sculptor, Verrocchio was a leading figure in the early Renaissance.

REFERENCES: Maud Cruttwell *Verrocchio* (London and New York 1904). John Pope-Hennessy *Italian Renaissance Sculpture* (London 1958). Gunter Passavant *Verrocchio: Complete*

Edition of Sculpture, Paintings and Drawings (London 1969).

VERY, Jones (Aug. 28, 1813 – May 8, 1880). American poet and essayist. Born and died in Salem, Mass. Early education sporadic, but he became a prize student at Harvard (1834–36) and was a tutor in Greek while studying at Harvard Divinity School (1836–38). Believed he was divinely inspired, and produced numerous intensely religious and mystical sonnets, published in the *Western Messenger* and the *Dial*. Declared unfit to be a minister (1838) by Harvard faculty, he allowed himself to be briefly committed to an insane asylum. However, Emerson staunchly supported him and helped him select *Essays and Poems* (1839), the only book he published in his lifetime. A minor transcendental poet, he was admired by William Cullen Bryant and other contemporaries besides Emerson, but his work was too otherworldly to be popular. His belief in complete surrender to the will of God aligned him more to early Puritans and Quakers than to the Unitarianism he was finally licensed to preach (1843), holding temporary pastorates in Eastport, Me. and North Beverley, Mass. Wrote little during last forty years, but two posthumous editions of his work appeared (1883 and 1886).

REFERENCES: William I. Bartlett *Jones Very: Emerson's Brave Saint* (1942, reprinted New York 1968). Edwin Gittleman *Jones Very: The Effective Years, 1833–40* (New York 1967).

VICTORIA, Tomás Luis de (c.1548 – Aug. 27, 1611). Spanish composer. Born Ávila. Little is known of his early life, until he went to Rome (1565) to study for priesthood. But his musical gifts were such that he succeeded Palestrina as *maestro di cappella* at the Collegium Germanicum (1571), and published thirty-three motets (1572), including the notable *O quam gloriosum* and *O vos omnes*, strongly influenced by Palestrina. He was chaplain at S. Girolamo della Carità (1578–83), where St. Philip Neri had established his famous Oratory. His *Passions in the Office for Holy Week* (1585), works

of dramatic intensity and mystical passion, were followed by two volumes of Masses (1586/92). He returned to Madrid (1594), published a variety of church music (1600). His masterpiece, a Requiem (1603) for the Empress Maria, whose chaplain and choirmaster he had been, was his last composition. He died in Madrid. Victoria wrote about twenty Masses, eighteen Magnificates, and forty-four motets, as well as other religious settings. Though he was trained in the Roman polyphonic style, his religious fervor and ecstatic mysticism lend a Spanish quality to his audacious work.

EDITION: *Complete Works* ed. Felipe Pedrell (8 vols. Leipzig 1902–13).
REFERENCES: Gilbert Chase *The Music of Spain* (1941, rev. ed. New York 1960, also PB). Felipe Pedrell *Tomás Luis de Victoria* (Valencia 1918). Gustave Reese *Music in the Renaissance* (1954, rev. ed. New York 1959).

VIGNOLA, Giacomo da (real name Giacomo Barozzi or Barocchio) (Oct. 1, 1507 – July 7, 1573). Italian architect. Born Vignola, near Modena. Studied painting in Bologna with Sebastiano Serlio, moving to Rome (1530). There, as assistant in construction of Vatican (1534–36), came under influence of architects Baldassare Peruzzi and Antonio da Sangallo. After working as sculptor at Fontainebleau (1541–43) and as architect in Bologna (1543–50), settled in Rome (1550). Appointed papal architect to Pope Julius III, and in collaboration with Giorgio Vasari and Bartolommeo Ammanati built for him the beautiful summer villa, Villa Giulia (1551–55), now the Etruscan Museum. Long associated with the Farnese family, he worked with Michelangelo on the Palazzo Farnese, Rome (c.1550–55) and completed (1558) the plan for the huge Palazzo Farnese, Caprarola, begun (c.1520) by Baldassare Peruzzi and/or Giuliano da Sangallo. Succeeded Michelangelo as architect in charge of works at St. Peter's (1564), contributing the idea of two cupolas adjoining the central dome. His brilliant design for the interior of the church of the Gesù, Rome (1568), mother church of the Jesuit order, greatly influenced ecclesiastical architecture throughout Europe. Vignola's use of classical motifs distinguished him from the mannerist architects following Michelangelo and initiated the baroque, as did his treatises *Regola delli cinque ordine d'architettura* (1562, Rules of the Five Orders of Architecture) and *Due Regole della prospettiva pratica* (1583, Two Rules of Practical Perspective). He died in Rome.

VIGNY, Comte Alfred Victor de (Mar. 27, 1797 – Sept. 17, 1863). French poet, playwright, and novelist. Born at Loches, Indre-et-Loire; of aristocratic military family. Raised in Paris, where he attended Lycée Bonaparte and prepared for the École Polytechnique, but instead he became an army officer (1814). Had written two minor tragedies (1817) when he met Victor Hugo, joined the romantic cenacle, and published *Poèmes* (1822). His literary career was further established when Hugo praised his 1824 epic *Eloa*, later included with the famous *Moïse* in *Poèmes antiques et modernes* (1826). Having married a wealthy English girl, Lydia Bunbury (1825), and written a successful historical novel, *Cinq-Mars* (1826), he resigned his commission (1827) and devoted his life to literary pursuits. Success in the theatre came with a translation of *Othello* (1829), *La Marcéchale d'Ancre* (1831), and especially with *Chatterton* (1835), based on an episode from his novel *Stello* (1832). Association with the theatre led to a celebrated liaison with actress Marie Dorval, with whom he broke, however, after her performance in *Chatterton*. *Servitude et grandeur militaire* (1835), stories, discussed the disillusionment of the soldier's life. Retired to his property in Charente, wrote only occasional poems for *La Revue des Deux Mondes*. Elected to French Academy (1845), became director (1849). Not long after his wife's death (1863), he died of cancer, was buried in Montmartre cemetery. Vigny was one of the leaders with Hugo in the romantic movement. His best poems, *Les Destinées*, which include *La Mort du loup* and *La Maison du berger*, appeared posthumously (1864) as did his *Journal d'un poète* (1867).

TRANSLATIONS: *Cinq-Mars* tr. William Hazlitt (London 1847). *The Military Condition* tr. Marguerite Barnett (London and New York 1964).

REFERENCES: Pierre Georges Castex *Vigny* (1952, latest ed. Paris 1967). James Doolittle *Alfred de Vigny* (New York 1967). Edmond Estève *Alfred de Vigny, sa pensée et son art* (Paris 1923). Pierre Flottes *La Pensée politique et sociale d'Alfred de Vigny* (London and New York 1927). Henri Guillemin *M. de Vigny, homme d'ordre et poète* (Paris 1955). Bertrand de La Salle *Alfred de Vigny* (1939, rev. ed. Paris 1963). Paul Viallaneix *Vigny par lui-même* (Paris 1964). Arnold Whitridge *Alfred de Vigny* (London and New York 1933).

VILLA-LOBOS, Heitor (Mar. 5, 1887 – Nov. 17, 1959). Brazilian composer. Born and died in Rio de Janeiro. The precocious son of a well-known writer, his interest in music led him to tour northern Brazil at eighteen, studying regional folk music and composing. He became a cellist and made other journeys in Brazil, writing a variety of works: church music, *Violin Sonata-Fantasia No. 1* (1912), four string quartets (1915–17), two symphonies (1916–17), and symphonic poems, including the remarkable *Amazonas* (1917). In the 1920's he toured Europe as a conductor; in Paris he came under Ravel's influence. His works of this decade include the *Fifth Symphony* (1920), *Wind Quintet* (1928), opera *Malazarte* (1921), and much piano music written for Rubinstein. Began (1930's) his celebrated series of suites *Bachianas Brasileiras* (1930–44), combining elements of Bach's music with Brazilian folk music. A great proponent of Brazilian national music, he was a force in musical education and founded the Conservatorio de Canto Orfeonico (1942). Among his two thousand works are the opera *Jésus* (1918); eighteen ballets; the oratorio *Vidapura* (1918); the twelve *Chôros* (1920–29) for differing combinations of instruments; *Momoprecoce* for piano and orchestra (1929); sixteen string quartets; and many choral arrangements. Villa-Lobos explored the world of special effects, employing new scales, harmonics, and Brazilian percussion instruments and folk music. Use of varied themes, rich color, and vigorous rhythms characterize his music.

REFERENCE: Herbert Weinstock *Heitor Villa-Lobos* (in *The Book of Modern Composers*) (New York 1942).

VILLEHARDOUIN, Geoffroy de (c.1150– c.1213). French chronicler and a leader of the Fourth Crusade. Born Villehardouin, near Troyes (Champagne), France, he was marshal of Champagne from c.1185. Most of our knowledge of him derives from his *Conquête de Constantinople* (written probably c.1212, first published 1585), one of the first important French historical works written in the vernacular rather than Latin. Covering the period 1199– 1207, it vividly describes the crusade in which Villehardouin played a leading part. In an unadorned and restrained style, he uses the third person narrative to describe the crusaders' departure from Venice, the fall of Constantinople, and the establishment of the Latin empire of Constantinople. For his services in the conquest he received a fief in Thrace (1205) and the title of marshal of Rumania. Sometime after 1212 he apparently returned to France, though the date and place of his death are unknown. Villehardouin's chronicle is a masterpiece of early French prose, as well as an important historical document of the Middle Ages.

TRANSLATION: *Joinville and Villehardouin: Chronicles of the Crusades* tr. M. R. B. Shaw (Harmondsworth, England, and Baltimore PB 1963).

REFERENCES: Louis Burgener *L'Art militaire chez Villehardouin et chez Froissart* (Bienne, Switzerland, 1943). J. Longnon *Recherches sur la vie de Geoffroy de Villehardouin* (Paris 1939).

VILLIERS, George. See BUCKINGHAM.

VILLIERS DE L'ISLE-ADAM, Comte Philippe Auguste Mathias de (Nov. 7, 1838 – Aug. 18, 1889). French writer. Born Saint-Brieuc, Brittany, son of impoverished noble family supported by an aunt. Educated at Saint-Brieuc and Laval. Family moved to Paris (1857), where he became acquainted with Parnassians, knew Baudelaire and Wagner, became interested in Poe. Published pamphlet *Deux Essais de poésie* (1858) and book of verse *Premières Poésies* (1859), both at his own expense. After the aunt died (1864), Villiers, poverty-stricken, began series of minor editorial jobs with *Revue des Lettres et des Arts* (1867–68) and other publications. His first story, *Azrael*, and a play, *La Révolte* (1870), were both unsuccessful. Joined National Guard during Franco-Prussian War, and wrote another play, *Le Nouveau Monde* (1875). Still poor and unsuccessful but proud, he became the lover of Marie Élisabeth Dantine, who bore him a son (1881), and whom he married just before he died, in Paris. His finest works appeared in the 1880's: three collections of short stories, *Contes cruels* (1883, tr. *Sardonic Tales* 1927), the satirical *Tribulat Bonhomet* (1887), and *Nouveaux Contes cruels* (1888), also the novel *L'Ève future* (1886). His most famous work appeared posthumously: *Axel* (written 1872, published 1890, tr. 1925), a poetic drama of visionary Wagnerian descriptions of medieval Germany and romantic ideas of death, admired by Edmund Wilson, who used *Axel's Castle* as the title for his study of imaginative literature, and by W. B. Yeats.

TRANSLATIONS: *Cruel Tales* tr. Robert Baldick (London and New York 1963). *Axel* tr. June Guicharnaud (Englewood Cliffs, N.J. 1970).

REFERENCES: Max Daireaux *Villiers de L'Isle-Adam, l'homme et l'oeuvre* (Paris 1936). André Lebois *Villiers de L'Isle-Adam* (Neuchâtel, Switzerland, 1952). A. W. Raitt *Villiers de L'Isle-Adam et le mouvement symboliste* (Paris 1965). Arthur Symons *The Symbolist Movement in Literature* (1899, rev. ed. New York 1919, PB 1958). Edmund Wilson *Axel's Castle: A Study in the Imaginative Literature of 1870– 1930* (New York and London 1931, also PB).

VILLON, François (real name François de Montaubier or François de Loges) (1431–?). French poet. Born Paris.

Took his name from Guillaume de Villon, chaplain of church of St.-Benoît-le-Bétourne, Paris, who befriended him at an early age, housed him, and sent him through school. All that is known of his parents comes from the poet's own verses, as from *Le Testament:*

> *Poor have I been from childhood,*
> *born of a poor and humble tribe;*
> *my father never had a sou,*
> *nor did his father, named Horace.*

Received bachelor's degree (1449) and master of arts (1452) from University of Paris. Three years later occurred the first of his many skirmishes with the law: he fatally wounded a priest in a brawl (1455) and fled Paris. Pardoned (1456), he again fled the city, after a burglary. Imprisoned in Meung-sur-Loire (1461) for another offense, then released, he returned to Paris (1462). Was arrested for petty theft and recognized as the man sought for the 1456 burglary; only the intervention of friends and payment of a fine saved him. Soon again imprisoned because of a brawl, he was tortured and sentenced to be hanged. Awaiting execution, he wrote some of his most moving and memorable verses, including *Ballade des pendus:*

> *Brother men who after us live on,*
> *harden not your hearts against us,*
> *for if you spare some pity for such*
>   *poor creatures,*
> *God will surely grant you his great*
>   *mercy.*

Again saved (1463), he was banished from Paris for ten years "in view of his bad character." On leaving Paris he disappears; no traces exist of his later life or death. The little more than three thousand lines of verse Villon left rank him as pre-eminent among French poets of his time, with his bold directness of speech and poignant personal revelations, his vigorous celebration of life and profound awareness of human mortality. The refrain *"Mais où sont les neiges d'antans"* (But where are the snows of yesteryear) from his *Ballade des dames du temps jadis*) has become part of the French language. Other famous poems: *Ballade pour prier Notre Dame, Ballade de la belle heaulmière, Le Lais* or *Le Petit Testament.*

TRANSLATIONS: *Complete Works* tr. Anthony Bonner (New York 1960 and London 1961). *Complete Poems* tr. Beram Saklatvala (London and New York 1968). *Poems* tr. Norman Cameron (London 1952 and New York 1966, also PB). *Poems* tr. Galway Kinnell (New York PB 1965).

REFERENCES: Robert Anacker *François Villon* (New York 1968). Pierre Champion *François Villon, sa vie et son temps* (1913, latest ed. 2 vols. Paris 1967). E. F. Chaney *François Villon in His Environment* (Oxford 1946). John Fox *The Poetry of Villon* (London and New York 1962). D. B. Wyndham Lewis *François Villon: A Documented Survey* (1928, reprinted Garden City, N.Y. PB 1958). Italo Siciliano *François Villon et les thèmes poétiques du moyen âge* (1934, reprinted Paris 1967).

✍

FRANÇOIS VILLON
BY W. S. MERWIN

Villon's poetry invites us, with an insolence entirely its own, to reconsider several notions that are frequently referred to in discussing poetry. Purity, for one. I mean poetic purity, of course. The term was adopted by the symbolists and made into an idol whose proper devotion they alone knew how to practice. But in poetry, whether it is the imperfectly attainable ideal of certain symbolists of a quality that occurs in some poems almost, it would seem, by accident, purity appears generally as a function of the commitment of imaginative truth to language in a way so absolute and individual that it is impossible to conceive of the result existing in any other terms. Viewed in this way, Villon's poetry is certainly as pure as Mallarmé's, which it resembles as little as he probably resembled the author of *L'Après-midi d'un faune;* it is, in fact, some of the purest poetry in French.

The quality is not convenient for some of the requisites of survival, such as translation. Villon's poetry is so profoundly and bodily embedded in his idiom that very little of what has made it survive until now in his own language, and makes its existence in others desirable, comes across in translations. It is not that the "content" is negligible. (Villon's poems are exceptions, at least, to Goethe's opinion that, with great poetry, some essential part of the greatness could be translated.) It is simply that the real and invaluable content of his poetry is to a very uncommon degree an emotional presence in his words, something that is not paraphrasable, and cannot be conjured up, apparently, in any other terms. To add to the difficulty, the poetic convention in which he worked was a formal and often intricately allusive one, which he managed to treat as his own. He invented none of the conventions he used, from the ballade and rondeau to the ironic versified last will and testament. He used them as he did the language, which he had not invented either, but which would not be mistaken, in his work, for the utterance of any of his contemporaries. And besides, his bent, the tradition he inherited, and his gift, impelled him to an expression that is unfailingly lyrical.

Oddly enough it is Villon's lyricism that has proved particularly vexing to several detractors who have found his personality, as revealed in his poetry, inadmissible. More than one of them has maintained, with a zeal for impoverishment that seems to be reserved for Villon alone, that he should have been one thing or the other: repeatedly able and willing to move his helpless readers with the emotion and sound of his words, or a cruel and bitter wit, a satirist, a thug with a vein of self-pity. He should have been rueful or a mocker but not both. For some reason that would require considerable space even to speculate about, at least one level of irony, if these critics are to be held with, is obtrusive in Villon. Their assumption, evidently, is that the lyric mode of poetry, if it is effective, should speak only for certain familiar, recognizable, and consistent conventions and complexes of soul, whereas the force of Villon, or part of it, stems from the fact that his lyricism gives tongue to the contradictions and bad taste of experience at first hand. Only one critic that I know of, Harold Nicolson, has gone so far as to declare that Villon's lyricism was not there at all. It is perhaps as honest a way as any of denying the stuff of poetry in favor of something fancier, gentler, or nicer. But it bespeaks a deafness that must be indispensable if one wishes to dismiss Villon. For the lyricism is present even where the purport of the writing seems not to call for it, or to be positively at odds with it. In the barbed jokes of *Le Lais*, for instance — a poem which is sometimes treated as a minor, immature, and relatively unserious work, as compared with the *Testament* itself with its obvious tragic and elegiac power. In the passage in *Le Lais* about the "three little naked children . . . all bare as the worm," whom Villon evokes when he is in fact referring to three notorious speculators, even when we are fully aware of the irony of Villon's intention, his pretended compassion for the "orphans" manages to imitate the voice of true feeling so convincingly that the savagery of his attack is at once intensified, made more complex and real, and at the end of it Villon's frustration and bitterness are ours: their complexity turns out to be something we know. This is part of

Villon's real content, and the sound, the motion, the beauty of his language are inseparable from it. Conversely, the irony underlies many of the most overtly plangent passages, even the ballade to the Virgin in the name of his mother: it is hard not to ask at some point, "How much of him is serious?", but throughout the poem something reaches us that is unresolvable and painful. In most of his poetry, whatever note is uppermost and whatever he intends at a particular moment, the rest of Villon is always present and speaking too. It helps to keep everything that survives of him both real and legendary.

VILLON, Jacques (Gaston Duchamp) (July 31, 1875 – June 9, 1963). French painter, half brother of Marcel Duchamp. Born Damville in the Eure, son of a notary and grandson of Rouen painter and engraver. Entered notary's office, Rouen, as a clerk, but became more interested in his course at school of Fine Arts. Published satirical drawings in such Paris papers at Le Rire, and made posters for Parisian cabarets. Also continued engraving. Exhibited at Salon d'Automne from 1904. Influenced at first by Degas and Toulouse-Lautrec, he became a Fauvist, then a Cubist (1911). Mobilized in World War I, he was with camouflage service until 1919. Returned to painting, but made living from engraving (1922–30). After successful exhibitions in New York and Chicago, returned to France, began painting landscapes, considered with his portraits among his finest works. He is noted for vivid luminosity of color, controlled by his drawing and composition. He died at Puteaux.

VINCI, Leonardo da. *See* **LEONARDO DA VINCI.**

VIOLLET-LE-DUC, Eugène Emmanuel (Jan. 27, 1814 – Sept. 17, 1879). French architect, restorer, and writer. Born Paris. Began architectural studies at sixteen, working under Leclère; be-

came interested in Gothic art after seventeen-month visit to Italy. Studied medieval buildings throughout France; began restoration work as restorer of La Madeleine at Vézelay (1839). With J. B. Lassus restored Sainte-Chapelle, Paris (1840) and won competition for restoration of Notre Dame, Paris (1843). Viollet-le-Duc also restored cathedrals of Chartres, Rheims, Amiens (1849), and Sens (1849), and rebuilt fortifications at Carcassonne. He expounded his theory of Gothic in the colossal *Dictionnaire raisonné de l'architecture française du XIe au XVIe siècle* (10 vols. 1854–68) and *Dictionnaire raisonné du mobilier français de l'époque carlovingienne à la Renaissance* (6 vols. 1858–75). There were no superfluous elements in Gothic, he believed; everything, including ornament, served the structure. In *Entretiens sur l'architecture* (1862–72) he claimed that his analysis of Gothic architecture could also be applied to classical styles. Although a mediocre architect himself, his theories influenced the great architects of this century. Considered by some overzealous as a restorer, he nonetheless undoubtedly saved many buildings from ruin. Died in Lausanne, Switzerland.

REFERENCES: P. Abraham *Viollet-le-Duc et le rationalisme médiéval* (Paris 1934). P. Gout *Viollet-le-Duc, sa vie, son oeuvre, sa doctrine* (Paris 1914). J. N. Summerson "Viollet-le-Duc and the Rational Point of View" in *Heavenly Mansions* (London 1949 and New York 1963).

VIRGIL (or VERGIL; full name Publius Vergilius Maro) (Oct. 15, 70 – Sept. 21, 19 B.C.). Roman poet. Born near Mantua in Cisalpine Gaul; of yeoman stock. Educated in Cremona, Milan, and Rome; studied philosophy under Siro, an Epicurean, at Naples. First started writing under patronage of Asinius Pollio. Later, in Rome, joined literary circle of Maecenas (which included Gallus, Varius, Horace, and Propertius), and met Octavian, later Caesar Augustus. Published the *Eclogues* (bucolic poems after the manner of Theocritus) in Rome (37 B.C.); read the *Georgics* (a treatise on farming like Hesiod's *Works and Days*) to Augustus in 29.

Died at Brundisium, buried in Naples. He asked that the *Aeneid,* his great epic on the founding of Rome, be destroyed after his death because it was unfinished, but Augustus preserved it. Though Virgil's models were Greek, he was also influenced by Lucretius and Ennius. The greatest poet of Rome's Golden Age, he brought a new sophistication of technique and style, as well as a loftiness of purpose, to Roman poetry. Scholars disagree as to how much of the *Appendix Virgiliana,* a collection of minor poems attributed to his early years, was written by him.

TRANSLATIONS: *Works* tr. John Dryden (1697, latest ed. London and New York 1961). *Aeneid* tr. C. Day Lewis (London and New York 1952). *Aeneid* tr. W. F. Jackson Knight (Harmondsworth, England, and Baltimore PB 1956). *Eclogues* tr. C. S. Calverley (New York 1962). *Georgics* tr. C. Day Lewis (London 1940 and New York 1947, PB 1964).

REFERENCES: Tenney Frank *Vergil: A Biography* (1922, reprinted New York 1965). T. R. Glover *Virgil* (7th ed. 1942, reprinted New York 1969). W. F. Jackson Knight *Roman Vergil* (1944, reprinted New York 1969) and *Vergil: Epic and Anthropology* (London and New York 1967). Brooks Otis *Virgil: A Study in Civilized Poetry* (Oxford 1964). Viktor Pöschl *The Art of Vergil* (tr. Ann Arbor, Mich. 1962). Kenneth Quinn *Virgil's Aeneid: A Critical Description* (London and Ann Arbor, Mich. 1968). Edward K. Rand *The Magical Art of Virgil* (1931, reprinted Hamden, Conn. 1966). Herbert J. Rose *The Eclogues of Vergil* (Berkeley, Calif. 1942). William Y. Sellar *The Roman Poets of the Augustan Age: Virgil* (3rd ed. 1908, reprinted New York 1965). L. P. Wilkinson *The Georgics of Virgil* (London 1969).

VIRGIL

BY PAUL J. ALPERS

For centuries the name of Virgil was the most august in Western literature. He was the greatest poet produced by, and the greatest poetic interpreter of, the Roman civilization to which all Europe traced its polity and culture. In strictly literary terms, he was the fountainhead and patron of pastoral poetry, and he, rather than Homer, was the exemplary epic poet during the centuries in which heroic poetry was regarded as didactic and allegorical and was assumed to be the highest form of literature.

The *Eclogues,* though his first work, are a major poetic accomplishment, and our awareness of their historical importance may actually impede our recognition of their intrinsic worth. For the nature of Virgil's transformation of his model Theocritus — making the Greek's realistic, humorous, down-to-earth pastorals more ideal, conventional, and spiritualized — not only explains the immense influence of the *Eclogues,* but also encourages us to regard them as frigid and artificial, like most later imitations of them. Quite the contrary, the eclogues have all the life and interest that one would expect from poems that opened up new aesthetic and spiritual territory. Virgil "discovered" Arcadia as we know it: that is, it was in his pastorals that this notably barren and rugged province of Greece was first represented as an ideal landscape, populated by shepherds whose chief occupations were singing and loving. But the *Eclogues* are neither literary in the bad sense nor escapist. Virgil is continually interested in the way pastoral conventions reveal truths about such varied matters as the force of passion, the ideals of civilization, Roman politics, and the powers of poetry.

Turning Greek masterpieces into an authentically Roman poem, as the *Eclogues* do, is pre-eminently the effort and achievement of the *Aeneid.* Here again our recognition of the poem's importance may go along with a feeling of aesthetic distaste. Our strong sympathy for Homer, especially for the bitterly realistic and tragic *Iliad,* may make us less than happy with a poet who turns the Homeric hero into a moral paragon and makes the epic poem as a whole celebrate the destiny of a nation and the establishment of a particular political and social order. But Virgil endows Homeric epic with unwonted moral and historical dimensions not by simplifying, but by a steady contemplation of the realities it presents. For example, Virgil presents Aeneas's Italian enemies as, among other things, dignified, glamorous, pathetic, and powerful. This is of course due to his sense of justice and humanity, but the point to observe is that these do not counteract or complicate his moral purpose, but directly result from and serve it. For his purpose is not to exalt the triumph of the approved side, but to register the process, often tragic and wasteful, by which two sides in conflict become a single people.

Virgil, then, does not palliate the realities of Homer's world, but he does evaluate them differently. To Homer the dangers, hardships, and disasters of war and of a long voyage home are the normal condition of life; there is therefore no irony in a hero's finding fulfillment in battle, no larger moral perspective by which we evaluate the wiles and self-concern of an Odysseus. To Virgil the ordinary events of Homeric epic are in one sense normal — they occur repeatedly, are characteristic of human life, and must be endured — but in another sense not. They hardly ever provide human fulfillment, and they characteristically thwart and destroy what is humanly valuable — a young man and the hopes placed in him, familial and social bonds, the integrity of a personality. Far from giving a triumphant sense of the hero's fulfillment of destiny, the

Aeneid is pervaded by a sense of inevitable costs and conflicts and of the arbitrary and natural losses that haunt human life. Nowhere is the sense of the costs of destiny more powerful than in the most famous episode of the poem — Aeneas's love affair with Dido and his abandoning her when the gods order him to proceed to Italy. Most readers feel that Aeneas's departure does not cost him enough, by way of suffering and moral conflict, but no one could accuse the poet himself of failing to recognize and honor Dido's passionate grandeur and the awesome tragedy of her both abandoning and remaining true to herself, as her ruinous love runs its course to suicide.

Virgil's conduct of his poem itself exemplifies one of the two virtues the poem most celebrates — *humanitas,* the solicitude and feeling for other men simply because they are human beings like ourselves. The other great virtue in the poem is *pietas,* fidelity to one's own family, people, gods, religious rites, social and moral obligations. It is a measure of Virgil's genius that his attention to this virtue (which gives to Aeneas his stock epithet *pius*) does not make the poem Roman in a narrow or limiting sense. Virgil recognizes the dangers of a narrow clannishness precisely because he values *pietas* for the fundamental values it embodies. Hence in the numerous encounters between Aeneas and strangers, the claims of *pietas* and *humanitas* overlap and merge, and the heroic narrative adumbrates the Roman imperial ideal of all mankind united as citizens of one society. It is entirely characteristic that the sixth book, which recounts Aeneas's journey to the underworld, should be motivated by Aeneas's *pietas* towards his father and the new Troy he is destined to establish, and is framed by the loving funeral rites that are so distinctive a feature of the poem. At the same time, this book presents the grandest vision of Rome's history and distinctive greatness, and the loftiest, most mysterious, and most intensely touching visions of human destiny in the poem.

Virgil's other major work is the *Georgics*, which is superficially a treatise on farming. But it includes some of Virgil's most famous passages — the vision of the evil that afflicts Italy torn by civil wars, the grateful celebration of Italy's bountiful soil, the praise of a farmer's life, the comparison of the beehive and human society. Such passages are not digressions but are directly produced by Virgil's concern with a life lived on the soil and with the implications for all men of the conditions of such a life: helplessness in the face of the hardships nature imposes and the disasters she sends; grateful dependence on her bounty and on her lovely and calm aspects; a corresponding awe of and reverence for the gods who are individually identified with separate aspects of nature and of man's yearly round of activities; an awareness of the human truths contained in the social behavior of bees or the madness of horses stung by lust. Even more than the *Aeneid,* the *Georgics* are distinguished by density and rightness of language and versification. (Virgil's death prevented him from giving the *Aeneid* the final verbal polishing he planned.) The interweaving of meanings within lines, the resonance given to individual words and phrases, the connections established between parts of the poem — all delight and astonish, and all bear witness to the poise and profundity of Virgil's meditation on man and his fate.

VITRUVIUS (full name Marcus Vitruvius Pollio) (fl. 25 B.C.). Roman architect. Author of the unique treatise *De*

Architectura (c.27–23 B.C.), the only written source on classical Greek and Roman architecture as well as on Vitruvius's life. According to his prefaces to its ten books, he was a self-made man from a humble background; counted Julius Caesar as a friend; served as superintendent of military machines under Augustus (to whom he dedicated the treatise), an appointment obtained through the good offices of the emperor's sister Octavia; knew Greek and Latin literature; served as a military engineer in north Africa; built a basilica at Fano; was of short height, and at the time of the writing of *De Architectura* was also old, ill, far from wealthy. The work itself, based on his own practical experience as well as on the theories of earlier Greek architects, deals with general architectural subjects (such as city planning, and design of public building) and the most specific details (such as floors, clocks, and stucco decorations). It was incorporated in part, unacknowledged, in the writings of Pliny the Elder, but the whole was preserved through the centuries in the monasteries, where it was well known in the Middle Ages. It emerged in the sixteenth century as the sourcebook for the classical revival of the Italian Renaissance. Alberti first, then Bramante, Michelangelo, Palladio, Raphael, and Vignola turned to Vitruvius for information and inspiration.

TRANSLATION: *Vitruvius: On Architecture* tr. Frank Granger (2 vols. London and New York 1931–34, new ed. Cambridge, Mass. 1955–56).

VIVALDI, Antonio (c.1675 – July 1741). Italian violinist and composer. Born Venice, son of a violinist at St. Mark's, who taught him music. Ordained a priest (1703). He taught the violin intermittently (1704–40) at the Conservatorio dell'Ospedale della Pietà, also traveling in Europe. He composed prolifically, as he was required to supply two concertos each month to the Conservatory. Vivaldi is celebrated for his hundreds of concertos, chiefly for violin. Other instruments for which he composed concertos were the organ, cello, flute, piccolo, oboe, bassoon, viola d'amore, mandolin, and combinations of these. The set of concertos *Il Cimento dell'armonia* contains the famous pieces known as *The Four Seasons*. He also wrote church music and cantatas, the oratorio *Juditha* (1716), forty-six *concerti grossi,* over seventy violin sonatas, and thirty-nine operas. The music published in his lifetime is typical of the best Italian baroque. Vivaldi's influence was widespread, and J. S. Bach arranged many of his works for clavier and organ. Vivaldi developed the ritornello-rondo form for concerto movements, which became the basis for most concertos by later classical composers. He died in Vienna.

REFERENCE: Marc Pincherle *Vivaldi: Genius of the Baroque* (tr. New York and London 1957, also PB).

VLAMINCK, Maurice de (Apr. 4, 1876 – Oct. 11, 1958). French painter. Born Paris, son of musician who taught him to play the violin. Shared studio with André Derain (c.1900) at Chatou. Was overwhelmingly impressed by Van Gogh exhibit (1901), then met Matisse and joined the Fauves group, exhibiting at famous Salon d'Automne show (1905). A protean figure, Vlaminck was a keen bicycle racer, violinist, wrote novels, and painted as he lived, with tremendous gusto, using slashing brushstrokes and loading his canvases with paint squeezed straight from the tube. He rejected (1905) Fauvism, then cubism; became influenced by Cézanne. Began (1915) to turn towards expressionism, finally settled on a sinister realist style with a somber palette. Wrote his memoirs, *Souvenirs de ma vie* (1926, tr. *Dangerous Corner* 1961). Died at Rueil-la-Gadelière, near Paris. A famous Fauve painting of his is *Red Trees* (1906, Musée d'Art Moderne, Paris), while his later style, which resembles Courbet's, is represented by *The Painter's House at Valmondois* (1920, Musée d'Art Moderne).

REFERENCES: George Duthuit *The Fauvist Painters* (tr. New York 1950). Maurice Genevoix *Vlaminck* (Paris 1954). Marcel Sauvage *Vlaminck* (Geneva 1956).

VOLTAIRE (real name François-Marie Arouet) (Nov. 21, 1694 – May 30, 1778).

French writer and philosopher. Born and died in Paris, son of a lawyer. Educated at Jesuit Collège Louis-le-Grand, making lifelong friends of young dukes and marquises there. Studied classics, and leaned early towards literary career rather than law. Took cognomen Voltaire after success of first tragedy *Oedipe* (1718). Was unjustly imprisoned twice in the Bastille, and forced by Chevalier de Rohan into exile to England (1726–28), episodes that fired him for life with an unquenchable sense of justice. In England, came under influence of Newton and Locke, and published early examples of Enlightenment literature. *Lettres philosophiques* (1734) (publicly burned in France), preceded his *Letters Concerning the English Nation* (London, 1733). Retired with his mistress Émilie, marquise du Châtelet, to her husband's estate at Cirey, until her death (1749). There, wrote study of Newton, plays, and began correspondence with future Frederick the Great of Prussia. Through intervention of Madame de Pompadour, Voltaire enjoyed period of favor at Versailles, was appointed royal historiographer, gentleman of the bedchamber to Louis XV, and made member of French Academy. From June 1750 to May 1753 stayed at court of Frederick the Great, but left after a quarrel (later they were reconciled and resumed their correspondence). Meanwhile, Voltaire amassed a fortune by shrewd investment and moneylending to the rich. Bought Les Délices near Geneva, then the estate of Ferney across Swiss border in France (1758). Here he lived luxuriously, visited by all the eminent men and women in Europe, wrote articles for the *Encyclopédie*, novels including *Candide* (1759) and plays, and edited Corneille's works. Through his often anonymous writings became an activist on the part of the underprivileged. Left Ferney (February 1778) for Paris, where he died. Other major works are tragedies *Brutus* (1730), *Zaire* (1732), *Merope* (1743), *Irène* (1778); novel *Zadig* (1747); poems *La Henriade* (1724); philosophical works *Dictionnaire philosophe* (1764) and *Droits des hommes* (1768).

TRANSLATIONS: *Candide* tr. Richard Aldington (1939, new ed. Garden City,

N.Y. 1959). *Candide, Zadig, and Selected Stories* tr. Donald M. Frame (Bloomington, Ind. 1961 and London 1962, also PB). *Notebooks* ed. Theodore Besterman (2nd ed. 2 vols. Toronto 1969). *Selected Letters* ed. and tr. Theodore Besterman (London 1963 and New York 1964). *Selections from Voltaire* tr. G. R. Havens (2nd ed. New York 1940). *Philosophical Dictionary* tr. Peter Gay (2 vols. New York 1962). *The Portable Voltaire* tr. Ben Ray Redman (1949, latest ed. New York PB 1968).

REFERENCES: Theodore Besterman *Voltaire* (New York 1969). Henry N. Brailsford *Voltaire* (1935, latest ed. London and New York PB 1963). J. H. Brumfitt *Voltaire, Historian* (London and New York 1958). Cleveland B. Chase *The Young Voltaire* (New York 1926). Samuel Edwards *The Divine Mistress: A Biography of Émilie du Châtelet, The Beloved of Voltaire* (New York 1970). Peter Gay *Voltaire's Politics* (Oxford and Princeton, N.J. 1959, also PB). Nancy Mitford *Voltaire in Love* (London and New York 1957). Norman L. Torrey *The Spirit of Voltaire* (1938, reprinted New York 1968). Ira O. Wade *Voltaire and Madame du Châtelet* (1941, reprinted New York 1967) and *The Intellectual Development of Voltaire* (Princeton, N.J. 1969).

☞

VOLTAIRE
BY LEWIS GALANTIÈRE

Voltaire said of Louis XIV that he was "not one of the greatest of men but he was one of the greatest of kings." We cannot dispose so neatly of Voltaire himself. He was unquestionably a great man, for the immense influence he came to wield was the product of forces drawn from himself alone: persevering courage, a rapid and imaginative intelligence, an inconceivable capacity for work, and a surpassing literary art of persuasion. But he was not one of your Olympians; there was no serenity in him.

In his eighty-third year he was still able to say, "I write in order to act."

This frail, impetuous man, dogged by ill health and preserved by a sound constitution (whatever that may mean), fought all his life long and fought his bitterest battles after he was sixty. He had only two weapons: for offense, his pen; for defense, a rare ability to make himself a rich man while still in his forties and thus assure himself freedom of movement — he spent most of forty years in exile from Paris — and freedom to write and to publish. He published under 150 pseudonyms, was cunning and devious, acted often on impulse or quick-lit anger and was often panicky, for he had the heart of a lion in the skin of a rabbit.

It was as a poet and by his tragedies in verse that Voltaire first won a European reputation. The Age of Reason had no ear for poetry: Voltaire's verse was conventional, didactic, and moralizing. The plays have long since gone unperformed and the poems are now read in anthologies. Both were for their time only.

A good part of his middle years was devoted to historiography. Two of the histories survive — as literature. *The Age of Louis XIV* was founded on original research and is remarkably objective. The two-thousand page *Essay on the Manners and Mind of the Nations,* for which he read innumerable books, is no longer "scientific" history, but it contains endless penetrating observations and still affords considerable intellectual pleasure.

Obviously, Voltaire's immortality does not rest upon his poetry and histories. The writings we continue to read are the product of his career as the most vigorous critic of the institutions of his age, his career as *philosophe.* In the vocabulary of his time this word was not narrowly applied; it referred to men and women who were skeptical of revealed religion, disturbed by the French monarchy's role as the secular arm of a privileged and fanatical clergy, and repelled by a criminal procedure which still punished persons accused of impiety with torture, strangulation, decapitation, and incineration. The *philosophes* were a circle rather than a "movement"; by no means revolutionary, but open-minded on the article of reforms which did not threaten their rank or property. Voltaire himself had no quarrel with monarchy as an institution, and while profoundly humanitarian, he had no faith in the judgment of the common people in great affairs.

He was, with the English deists, a believer in "natural religion." He believed that organized churches and priesthoods should be done away with; that men were equal in the sight of God and ought to be equal under law. Man's only recourse lay in a stoic courage to "drag our chains to the last" and meanwhile to be compassionate, magnanimous, tolerant, and to advance civilization with the aid of reason and science. Clearly, he was not an atheist. He argued against his materialist-atheist allies, but he did not denounce them, for they had a right to their views. Voltaire saw in religious intolerance — the imposition of a single faith, the denial of freedom of thought and publication — the evil that lay at the root of all other social ills.

"Truth," William Blake wrote, "can never be told so as to be understood, and not be believed." Voltaire wrote to be understood. Limpid, sparkling, ironic with an insidiousness that made the reader think himself a wit, he makes his points in a dialogue between a Jesuit and a Brahmin, opens an article on Job with the words, "Good morning, friend Job," sketches droll characters in didactic pieces as tellingly as a great cartoonist, invents charming parables

and, in his philosophical tales — *Candide, Zadig, The Ingenu, Micromegas,* and the rest — plants seeds of thought while we are dazzled and enchanted. As in the great fairy tales, nothing resembles life, yet all is credible. Ignorance being the primary cause of prejudice and supersition, he enlightens in the moderate and engaging *Letters on the English,* fuses instruction with emotion in the moving *Treatise on Toleration,* with indignation in the daring *Sermon of the Fifty,* with irony in *The Ignorant Philosopher* and the few pages *On the Horrible Danger of Reading;* and, in verse, in the *Discourse on Man,* the poem that gripped all Europe on the Lisbon earthquake of 1755, and other poems.

In 1759, when he was sixty-five, he established himself at Ferney, on the Swiss border, and began to sound the celebrated war cry, *Écrasez l'infâme,* "Stamp out infamy." But though this was a fresh call to arms against the church (Calvinist as well as Catholic), he intervened again and again against civil abuses: serfdom, oppressive taxation of the humble, the law of mortmain, restrictive trade practices. He built a village and erected factories on his estate for Genevan watchmakers and stocking weavers who had been driven out by their employers. This lifelong despiser of *la canaille,* "the rabble," suddenly turned democrat: in *Republican Ideas* (1765) he advocated the town meeting form of self-government and went so far as to seek seats for workers on the Grand Council of the Republic of Geneva.

Meanwhile, there was no abatement of his war against religion. The Jesuit power in France had been broken in 1761 by their lay rivals of the Catholic faith, the Jansenists. The "pitiless" Jansenists, however, still filled the benches of the magistracy in the twelve *parlements* of the realm. Persecution and even execution on religious grounds continued. Everybody knows the story of Jean Calas, the Calvinist condemned at Toulouse to be broken on the wheel and strangled on the charge of murdering his son, who was said (falsely) to have turned Catholic in order to be eligible for admission to the bar. After three years of tireless effort Voltaire obtained a royal ordinance annulling the decision and clearing Calas's name.

With the Calas affair, Voltaire the poet raised himself to the rank of "King Voltaire . . . one of the European powers." Throughout the last quarter century of his life sovereign princes (most notably Frederick II of Prussia) had declared themselves his pupils; the *philosophes* of the entire continent saw in him their leader; certain reforms for which he had clamored were instituted in his lifetime. When, in February 1778, "wrapped in eighty-four years and eighty-four maladies," as he wrote characteristically, the dying man returned to Paris for the first time in twenty-eight years, his journey was a triumphal procession and his four months in the capital were an apotheosis. Crowds never left his door; he and Benjamin Franklin embraced in public; he was able to totter to a gala performance, before a delirious audience, of *Irène*, a feeble tragedy dictated with his last breath. Though not quite the last. That was saved for a mumbled confession which would permit him (though not without trouble) to be buried in consecrated ground — and, probably, in the mind of the ever alert millionaire, to ensure a minimum of difficulty for the heirs of the fortune he bequeathed them.

His immortality presents curious aspects. It is not that of a man of letters. Nor of a sage, for he was not one. Nor of a revolutionary in the political sense of that term. He was a liberator, but without a formal doctrine; the greatest of all guerrilla fighters for man's freedom, precisely against doctrine, whether Platonic, Christian, atheist, by anticipation Marxist, or any other.

VUILLARD, Jean Édouard (Nov. 11, 1868 – June 21, 1940). French painter and graphic artist. Born Cuiseaux, son of army officer. Attended École des Beaux Arts (1886–88), then Académie Julian, where he joined the Nabis group of artists influenced by Gauguin. But the influence of Degas, Monet, and Japanese prints proved stronger than Gauguin's. Vuillard had his first one-man show (1892). He and Pierre Bonnard selected commonplace subject matter, chiefly domestic interiors, which led critics to call them "intimists." Painted nine small panels of Paris park scenes (1894–1914, Musée d'Art Moderne, Paris; Museum of Art, Cleveland) and four panels of women in domestic settings (1896, Musée du Petit Palais, Paris). *Woman Sweeping* (c.1892, Phillips Collection, Washington, D.C.) and *The Vuillard Family at Lunch* (1896) also date from this time. From 1901 he exhibited regularly at the Paris salons. Casual portraits and intimate interiors and their decor are the subjects of his best work as well as scenes of homely domestic pursuits, often featuring his mother and sister, painted in quiet tones. He executed many lithographs; the best-known series is *Paysages et intérieurs* (1899). He died at La Baule.

REFERENCES: André Chastel *Vuillard* (Paris 1946). Claude Roger Marx *Vuillard: His Life and Work* (London and New York 1946). Andrew C. Ritchie *Édouard Vuillard* (New York 1954).

WAGNER (Wilhelm) Richard (May 22, 1813 – Feb. 13, 1883). German composer. Born Leipzig. Largely self-educated. Became music director at theatres in Magdeburg (1834–36), Königsberg (1836), Riga (1837–42). Married Minna Planer (1836; separated 1861). Unfruitful period in Paris (1839–42) was followed by successful years in Dresden, where his operas *Rienzi* (1842), *Der fliegender Holländer* (1843), and *Tannhäuser* (1845) were produced. Participation in 1849 revolution forced Wagner into exile in Switzerland, during which he developed a new concept of opera as "music-drama," exemplified in *Der Ring des Nibelungen*, the first two parts of which (*Das Rheingold* and *Die Walküre*) he wrote in the 1850's. The patronage of Ludwig II of Bavaria brought about performances of *Tristan und Isolde* (1865), *Die Meistersinger von Nürnberg* (1868), and at last the *Ring* cycle (1876). Following a series of love affairs, the most famous of which was with Mathilde Wesendonck, Wagner married Cosima, daughter of Franz Liszt (1870), who bore him three children. They settled in Bayreuth, where together they developed the Bayreuth Festival. It opened (1876) with the four-part *Ring* cycle (*Rheingold, Walküre, Siegfried, Götterdämmerung*), and after their deaths was carried on by their son Siegfried (1869–1930). Wagner's other operas include *Lohengrin* (1850) and *Parsifal* (1882). Other compositions: *Faust Overture* (performed 1844), *Siegfried Idyll* (1870). Wagner wrote the librettos for all his operas in a highly personal poetic style. He also wrote copiously and polemically on the theory of opera, music history, aesthetics, criticism, and on more general topics.

TRANSLATIONS: *Prose Works* (1893–99, reprinted 8 vols. New York 1966) and *Wagner on Music and Drama* (New York 1964, also PB), both translated by W. Ashton Ellis.
REFERENCES: Jacques Barzun *Darwin, Marx, Wagner: Critique of a Heritage* (2nd ed. Garden City, N.Y. PB 1958). Robert Donington *Wagner's Ring and Its Symbols* (1963, rev. ed. New York and London 1969, also PB). Robert Gutman *Richard Wagner: The Man, His Mind, and His Music* (New York and London 1968). Thomas Mann *Essays of Three Decades: Freud, Goethe, Wagner* (tr. London and New York 1947). Ernest Newman *The Life of Richard Wagner* (4 vols. New York and London 1933–46) and *Wagner Nights* (New York 1949 and London 1950). Jack M. Stein *Richard Wagner and the Synthesis of the Arts* (Detroit 1960).

◄≈

RICHARD WAGNER
BY JOSEPH KERMAN

Wagner was the major force in music between the Beethoven-Weber period and that of Debussy and Schoenberg. Outside music, his impact was so great that he actually gave his name to a cultural movement, Wagnerism; no other composer has ever had anything like such an impact.

His boyhood in the 1820's was marked less by strict teaching than by feverish literary and musical enthusiasms, notably for the German romantic opera then emerging under Weber. For the first sixteen years of his professional life Wagner was an opera conductor in various cities. This period was broken by an inactive, miserable period in Paris, and it was crowned by an effective tenure at Dresden from 1843 to 1849. Here he produced *Rienzi, Der fliegender Holländer,* and *Tannhäuser,* and would also have produced *Lohengrin,* if he had not participated (with Bakunin) in the revolution of 1849 and got himself exiled from Germany for over a decade. In exile Wagner wrote theoretical tracts promulgating a revolutionary concept of opera, or "music-drama," as he preferred to call it, a *Gesamtkunstwerk* synthesizing music, poetry, gesture, scene, and myth. The librettos and scores of the 1850's — *Das Rheingold* and *Die Walküre* (part of a projected four-evening cyclic opera, *Der Ring des Nibelungen*) and *Tristan und Isolde* — were, accordingly, so revolutionary that they had no hope of performance. His music, poetry, and doctrine alike were strongly attacked by traditionalists; Wagner replied in kind; he became the most controversial figure in European cultural life. A man of incredible personal fascination, egotism, energy, and ruthlessness, he lived on loans in astonishing number, and contracted several well- or less well-publicized liaisons with married women.

The second turning point in Wagner's career came in 1864 with the accession of Ludwig II of Bavaria. Later to be declared insane, the eighteen-year-old king was already overwhelmed by *Lohengrin* and by Wagner's vision of German art. He took Wagner up, listened to him on matters where he had no business meddling, and instigated belated premieres of *Rheingold, Walküre, Tristan,* and *Die Meistersinger* at Munich. Wagner next conceived the extraordinary idea of a specially designed theatre for periodic Wagner festivals, in the little town of Bayreuth in nothern Bavaria. With the help of Wagner Societies forming all over the world, the money was raised. He wrote the remaining *Ring* operas, *Siegfried* and *Götterdämmerung,* for the opening festival in 1876, and the *Bühnenweihfestspiel, Parsifal,* for that of 1882, less than a year before his death.

It has been said that *Tristan* is the favorite Wagner opera of the Wagnerians, while *Meistersinger* is the favorite of the anti-Wagnerians. The latter (and they are many) can forget all about "godsh and goddeshes" in *Meistersinger;* they can enjoy the ingenious plot, the real-life intrigue and characterization, the local color, the comedy, and so on. Yet Wagner's underlying purpose was serious and allegorical: the drama projects a powerful dialectic about artistic creation and its destiny. Walther von Stolzing — impetuous, noble of birth, untaught save by nature and chivalresque lore — confronts the Mastersingers of Nuremberg, a bourgeois craft guild which jealously cultivates a fossilized musical tradition and rejects anything fresh and new. It is only when the wisest Mastersinger, Hans Sachs, teaches Walther the rules of art (suitably updated) that Walther can fashion the modern "mastersong" that wins the enthusiasm of the assembled townspeople and the hand of Eva. By such a dialectic German art is renewed; the piece ends with an optimistic hymn to German art and a warning against foreign contamination. Wagner, who let it be known that the villian of the opera was modeled on his main journalistic enemy, obviously saw himself as a synthesis of Sachs and Walther.

But cannot we see an analogous myth of the German artist in Wagner's own actual life? We can and we must, if we are to understand how the nineteenth century viewed Wagner, and how Wagnerism played into the greater myth that gripped Germany in the 1930's. In the phenomenon of Wagnerism, Wagner's life, art, and ideas about art are inextricably mixed. By means of revolution and exile, the artist tears himself free of bourgeois society and reviles it ceaselessly in books, pamphlets, and allegorical music-dramas (notably *Tristan* and the *Ring*). He demands that society support him in luxury; he captures a king and plays at running Europe. He captures women, and above all he *builds,* or, rather, he gets society to build a shrine to German art, to which the faithful will make pilgrimage, and for which the artist creates rites that renew the spirit of the *Volk* by dramatizing their racial myths. He endows his own future: a hundred years have passed, and Bayreuth is still going strong. Symbolically opposed to Bayreuth in the German heartland stands the Venusberg, whose vulgar, trivial, commercial art accurately reflects the decadence of life in general. In Paris young Wagner had suffered and failed — and learned a great deal. Then later *Tannhäuser* was whistled off the stage at the Opéra, at a time when Wagner had not seen a new work of his produced for sixteen years. Still smarting from this international incident, Wagner in 1870 offered his services to Bismarck, and when these were rejected, published a wretched dramatic parody on the fall of Paris.

Myths have a way of transforming themselves. What Paris represented for Wagner — everything vile in nineteenth-century culture — Wagner himself came to represent for his sometime admirer Nietzsche. The Bayreuth camp followers turned into proto-Nazis, and the Nazis, after the Nuremberg putsch, took up *Meistersinger* as a party ceremonial.

What fascinated the Bayreuth pilgrims — among whom Paris intellectuals figured prominently — was first of all the grandiosity and high-mindedness of it all. They saw in Wagner not so much the reform of opera as a renewal of drama through the art of music, which Schopenhauer had recently celebrated as the true expression of the Will. Wagner's insistence on feeling rather than reason as the channel of apprehension; his pre-Freudian vision of myth as an essential source of insight; his astonishing realization of the perennial ideal of a combination of the arts — all this found a deep response in the late nineteenth-century mind.

And all this was held together by music. To consider Wagner in purely musical terms would be to minimize him severely, yet he would be able to survive the handicap: simply as music, his great passages hold up as well as any other music of the time, or better. Some of the revolutionary features of his mature style, after *Lohengrin,* are the greatly dilated time-scale — which can be exasperating, but which can also be hypnotic; the new vocal idiom of continuous declamation in place of the set songs and ensemble numbers of older opera; the extended use of the orchestra; the celebrated leitmotif technique, which serves both as a commentary on or carrier of the action and also as the basis for continuous musical development (Nietzsche's "endless melody"); and especially the erosion of classical tonality by means of chromaticism. In this respect the key works are *Tristan* and *Parsifal,* whose famous third-act prelude is a remarkable anticipation of atonality.

The most awesome and ironic tribute to Wagner's lasting impact is Arnold

Schoenberg's *Moses und Aron,* an opera conceived in exile during the 1930's, unfinished, unperformed until the 1950's, and still largely unknown and unappreciated. Written in the twelve-tone technique which Wagner's chromaticism, more than any other single factor, helped to prepare, *Moses und Aron* is at once a grandiose racial epic and an oblique allegory about art and the role of the artist: a sort of Judaic *Meistersinger.* But as Nietzsche could have foretold, there is none of Wagner's optimism here. In the twentieth century, neither art nor nation triumphs.

WALLER, Edmund (Mar. 9, 1606 – Oct. 21, 1687). English poet. Born Coleshill, near Amersham, but moved soon to Beaconsfield in Buckinghamshire. Educated at Eton and King's College, Cambridge. Entered Parliament at sixteen; married London heiress Anne Bankes (1631; she died 1634). Unsuccessfully wooed Lady Dorothea Sidney, whom he commemorated as Sacharissa in his poetry. A royalist, he was fined and banished for being a leader of a plot to seize London for Charles I (1643). Married Mary Bracey (1644). Made amends with Cromwell and returned to England from France (1651); one of his best-known poems is to Cromwell, *A Panegyric to My Lord Protector* (1655). Upon the Restoration, Waller was well received by Charles II and returned to Parliament, where he served for rest of his life, noted for his wit and oratory. His first book, *Poems* (1645), contained many lyrics already set to music by Henry Lawes. It was extremely popular, included the famous *Go, lovely Rose* and *On a Girdle.* One of the first to revive the heroic couplet, he is traditionally considered the first Augustan poet. Other works are *Instructions to a Painter* (1666) and *Of Divine Love* (1685). Died at Beaconsfield.

EDITION: *Poems* ed. George Thorn-Drury (1893, new ed. 2 vols. London and New York 1901).
REFERENCES: Alexander W. Allison ed. *Toward an Augustan Poetic* (Lexington, Ky. 1962). Douglas Bush *Eng-*lish *Literature in the Earlier Seventeenth Century* (2nd ed. Oxford 1962). Warren L. Chernaik *The Poetry of Limitation: A Study of Edmund Waller* (New Haven, Conn. 1968). Samuel Johnson *Lives of the Poets* (London 1779–81).

WALPOLE, Horace (or Horatio), 4th earl of Orford (Sept. 24, 1717 – Mar. 2, 1797). English writer. Born and died in London, youngest son of Sir Robert Walpole. Educated at Eton (1727–34) and King's College, Cambridge (1735–38). Toured Continent with poet Thomas Gray (1739–41), then entered Parliament, serving until 1767. He took no active part in debate, but remained an interested observer. Acquired (1747) the villa Strawberry Hill near Twickenham, and soon began reconstructing it in the Gothic style, thus initiating an important trend in English architecture. Here he amassed a valuable library and art collection, and established a private printing press, publishing his own works and those of friends, notably Gray's *Odes* of 1757. Became earl of Orford (1791). Walpole wrote the first Gothic novel, *The Castle of Otranto* (1765), and the first art history of England, *Anecdotes of Painting* (4 vols. 1762–71); his political diaries were later edited and published as memoirs of the reigns of George II (1822) and George III (1845/59); but his literary talents are best realized in the enormous body of his private correspondence. A bachelor with limitless wealth and leisure, he had a great gift for friendship; his letters combine spontaneity with an innate polish, and present an invaluable picture of Georgian England. Among his most famous correspondents are Gray and Sir Horace Mann.

EDITION: *Letters* ed. W. S. Lewis and others (New Haven, Conn. and Oxford 1937–1961).
REFERENCES: Isabel W. U. Chase *Horace Walpole, Gardenist* (Princeton, N.J. and Oxford 1943). Robert W. Ketton-Cremer *Horace Walpole* (3rd ed. London 1964 and Ithaca, N.Y. 1966). W. S. Lewis *Horace Walpole* (New York and London 1961). Warren H. Smith ed. *Horace Walpole: Writer, Poli-*

tician, and Connoisseur (New Haven, Conn. 1967).

WALTON, Izaak (Aug. 9, 1593 – Dec. 15, 1683). English writer and biographer. Born St. Mary, near Stafford; of yeoman stock. Little is known of his early life. By 1614 he was an ironmonger in London; became a freeman in the company (1618), and was a dealer until his retirement (c.1644). Married Rachel Floud (or Floyd) (1626); she died (1640) and (c.1646) Anne Ken (died 1662). Spent his long retirement traveling about England, visiting his many friends in the clergy, fishing and writing, first at Stafford (1644), then Clerkenwell (1650); after 1662 he lived mainly with George Morley, bishop of Winchester, at Farnham castle. Died at Winchester in home of his daughter, Anne. Buried in the cathedral there. Largely self-educated, he began his literary career in his late forties. Known today principally for the charming and authoritative *The Compleat Angler* (1653; revised for editions in 1655, 1661, and 1668; 5th edition, 1676, had second section by fellow angler and friend Charles Cotton). Also author of biographies of John Donne (first published as preface to volume of Donne's poems, 1640; enlarged and published separately, 1658), Sir Henry Wotton (1651), George Herbert (1670), and Bishop Robert Sanderson (1678). Richard Hooker, whose life he wrote (1665), was the only one of his subjects he did not know personally.

EDITIONS: *The Compleat Walton* ed. Geoffrey Keynes (London 1929). *The Compleat Angler* (London and New York 1935, also PB). REFERENCES: Margaret Bottrall *Izaak Walton* (London and New York 1955, also PB). John R. Cooper *Art of the Compleat Angler* (Durham, N.C. 1968). Edgar Johnson *One Mighty Torrent* (1937, new ed. New York 1955). R. B. Marston *Walton and Some Earlier Writers on Fish and Fishing* (London 1894). Stapleton Martin *Izaak Walton and His Friends* (2nd ed. London and New York 1904). David Novarr *The Making of Walton's Lives* (Ithaca, N.Y. and Oxford 1958). D. A. Stauffer *Eng-*

lish Biography Before 1700 (1930, reprinted New York 1964).

WATTEAU, Jean Antoine (Oct. 10, 1684 – July 18, 1721). French painter. Born Valenciennes of Flemish parents. After studying under obscure local painter, went to Paris (1702) and worked in shop which turned out cheap devotional pictures. Entered studio of Claude Gillot (1704), painter of theatrical scenes and clowns. Four years later began work for Claude Audran, a fashionable decorative artist and keeper of the Luxembourg Palace, where Watteau was able to study the great Rubens cycle of paintings. Returned to Valenciennes (1709) and painted some military scenes. Back in Paris, he was exposed to Flemish and Venetian masters in collection of his friend Pierre Crozat the financier. At last won official recognition with admission to French Academy (1717) upon presentation of *The Embarkation for Cytherea* (Louvre, Paris), and thenceforth became known as a painter of *fêtes galantes*. After a winter in London (1719–20), during which he painted *Halt in the Chase* (Wallace Collection, London), he retired, suffering from tuberculosis, to Nogent-sur-Marne, where he died. One of the leading French rococo painters, Watteau is known for the subtle melancholy and sense of fleeting time suffusing his theatrical scenes and figures of the world of stage and fashion. One of his last works, the *Signboard of Gersaint* (1720–21, Staatliche Schlosser, Berlin) indicates a change in style, back to Flemish naturalism.

REFERENCES: Hélène Adhémar *Watteau, sa vie, son oeuvre* (Paris 1950). Gilbert W. Barker *Antoine Watteau* (London 1939). M. Gauthier *Watteau* (London and New York 1960). Stephen Longstreet *Watteau: Drawings* (Alhambra, Calif. 1966, also PB). K. T. Parker *The Drawings of Watteau* (London 1931). K. T. Parker and Jacques Mathey *Antoine Watteau: Catalogue complet de son oeuvre dessiné* (2 vols. Paris 1957–58). Pierre Schneider *The World of Watteau* (New York 1967).

ANTOINE WATTEAU
BY JOHN WALKER

Born in Valenciennes, a part of Flanders newly acquired by France, Watteau in his work epitomizes the style of the French rococo: first, in its essential derivation from the Low Countries; second, in its slighter rhythms and more delicate phrasing; and finally, in its somewhat enervated sensuality. In Watteau, however, the characteristic gaiety and animation of the rococo is kept from its too frequent monotony by an overtone of pathos, autumnal and pensive.

Coming to Paris at the age of eighteen, Watteau, after a period of drudgery spent in reproducing religious and popular pictures, gained access to the Luxembourg Palace, where he studied the cycle of paintings executed by Rubens for Marie de'Medici, and later to the Crozat collection, in which were drawings and paintings by Teniers, Rubens, Giorgione, Titian, and Paolo Veronese. Although it was in these collections that he formed his style, teaching himself what he could never have learned from his immediate masters, his apprenticeship to two minor artists no doubt affected somewhat his manner of painting: Gillot, a painter of clowns, influencing him in his fondness for the theatre, and Audran, the ornamentalist, in his decorative work done for the Château de la Muette, which has now disappeared. For the prototype, however, of the *fête galante*, Watteau's especial contribution to the subject matter of art, it is usual to turn to two earlier paintings, the *Concert champêtre* by Giorgione, now in the Louvre, and the *Garden of Love* by Rubens, in the Prado. Yet Watteau's style differs essentially from both. It has neither the Arcadian poetry of the one, nor the concrete actuality of the other. It has instead a factitious quality suggestive of the theatre and to be explained only by that passion for playacting characteristic of the eighteenth century. In paintings as poignant and delicate as Mozart's music, Watteau has fixed on canvas the exaggerated gallantry, the graceful pantomime, sometimes in motley, sometimes in everyday dress, of Harlequin, Clown, Columbine; and his compositions, looser than Giorgione or Rubens, suggest the casual groupings, planned yet seemingly contingent, that continually occur behind the footlights. Moreover, the subject of his reception piece for the Academy, *The Embarkation for Cytherea*, was actually suggested by a song in a contemporary play, and his numerous portraits of actors and actresses indicate the close connection between artists and people of the theatre, which was to become a characteristic of French painting, continuing to the drawings and paintings of Degas and Toulouse-Lautrec and down to the present day.

Watteau not only seems to give definite form to the rococo style, but in several ways he is indicative of that change in the tradition of painting which begins in the eighteenth century. He was one of the earliest artists to disregard craftsmanship. His dirty palette, his oil pot in which various colors had mixed together, his badly prepared canvases — all are mentioned by contemporaries and are evidence of the unconcern with technical procedure which in the nineteenth and twentieth centuries is to become common, carrying with it its own punishment of darkened colors and blurred forms. Like the modern painter, also, Watteau was especially dependent on drawings done directly from the model. The Count de Caylus tells how Watteau's friends were dressed in costume and made to pose wherever possible. Later, from books filled with such sketches, Watteau culled the separate figures needed for each painting, one selected here, another there, and the whole concocted into a pictorial design, which was then fitted into a landscape, very often already painted or imagined.

Studies for complete pictures Watteau seems to have prepared only rarely, and as a result formal design is less evident in the composition as a whole than in separate passages, in the phrasing of folds of drapery, the grouping of two or three figures, or the sequence of accents across the foreground. In preferring his drawings to his paintings, Watteau showed himself aware of the fragmentary character of his rhythms, for in the drawings not only is his inability to sustain a rhythmic feeling through a whole picture concealed, but his genius for noting the precise accent, the most delicate contour, the subtlest modeling is miraculously apparent in every stroke of his favorite red, white, and black chalks. As a colorist, however, Watteau was able to orchestrate sustained and delicate harmonies, and in these his use of broken tone anticipates certain developments of nineteenth-century impressionism.

After Watteau's death his entire work was engraved and published at the expense of his friend the manufacturer Jean de Jullienne, and this *Recueil Jullienne* proved to be a mine readily pillaged by imitators, not only for paintings but for the applied arts. As the de Goncourts wrote: "Watteau is the great poet of the eighteenth century. A universe, an entire creation of poetry and dreams, springs from his mind and pervades his work with the elegance of a life of fantasy. A fairyland, a thousand fairylands, have taken wing from the fancy of his brain, the caprice of his art, and the freshness of his genius."

WAUGH, Evelyn (Arthur St. John) (Oct. 28, 1903 – Apr. 10, 1966). English novelist. Born Hampstead, London; son of Arthur Waugh (1866–1946), critic, editor, and publisher. Educated at Lancing School and Hertford College, Oxford, he spent brief periods as an art student and schoolteacher, publishing a critical biography of D. G. Rossetti (1928). Married to Evelyn Gardner (1928, divorced 1930), he was received into Catholic Church (1930). Married Laura Herbert (1937) and joined Royal Marines (1939), serving during World War II as commando officer in West Africa and Crete, and British liaison officer in Yugoslavia. Retired to west of England after war, devoting himself to writing. His major works, brilliantly written and full of mordant satire on twentieth-century life, include *Decline and Fall* (1928), *Vile Bodies* (1930), *Black Mischief* (1932), *Scoop* (1938), *Put Out More Flags* (1942), *Brideshead Revisited* (1945, revised 1960), *The Loved One* (1948), and *Love Among the Ruins* (1953). Waugh also wrote travel books (*Labels*, 1930; *Remote People*, 1932; *Ninety-two Days*, 1934; *A Tourist in Africa*, 1960), serious works of religious intent (*Edmund Campion, Jesuit and Martyr*, 1935; *Helena*, 1950; *The Life of Ronald Knox*, 1959), a trilogy of novels about army life (*Men at Arms*, 1952; *Officers and Gentlemen*, 1955; *Unconditional Surrender*, 1961), and one volume of a projected three-volume autobiography (*A Little Learning*, 1964). He died at his home, Combe Florey, near Taunton, Somerset.

REFERENCES: Malcolm Bradbury *Evelyn Waugh* (Edinburgh 1964). James F. Carens *The Satiric Art of Evelyn Waugh* (Seattle, Wash. 1966, also PB). A. A. De Vitis *Roman Holiday: The Catholic Novels of Evelyn Waugh* (New York 1956 and London 1958). Frances Donaldson *Evelyn Waugh: Portrait of a Country Neighbor* (London 1967 and Philadelphia 1968). Paul A. Doyle *Evelyn Waugh: A Critical Essay* (Grand Rapids, Mich. PB 1969). Stephen J. Greenblatt *Three Modern Satirists:*

Waugh, Orwell, and Huxley (New Haven, Conn. 1965). Frederick J. Stopp *Evelyn Waugh: Portrait of an Artist* (London and Boston 1958).

WEBER, Carl Maria (Friedrich Ernst) von (Nov. 18, 1786 – June 5, 1826). German composer. Born Eutin, near Lübeck, son of Franz Anton von Weber, musical director of Lübeck theatre. Traveled widely when young; then studied (1798) under Michael Haydn, and wrote his first opera, *Die Macht der Liebe und des Weins* (1799), at thirteen. Became conductor at Breslau (1804), first of many such appointments, culminating in directorship of German Opera at Dresden. Composed the operas *Silvana* (1810) and *Abu Hassan* (1811). Married the soubrette Caroline Brandt (1817). His masterpiece, the opera *Der Freischütz* (1820), was immensely popular, but his subsequent operas, *Euryanthe* (1823) and *Oberon* (1826), were less successful. His instrumental compositions include pieces for piano, such as the popular *Invitation to the Dance* (1819), songs, overtures, two piano concertos, chamber music, cantatas, and two Masses. Weber was the first national German romantic composer, and as such freed German opera from the Italianate style and exerted strong influence on not only Wagner but also Schumann and Mendelssohn. He died in London.

REFERENCES: J. Benedict *Weber* (2nd ed. London 1926). Max Maria von Weber *Life of Carl Maria von Weber* (tr. London and New York 1865). William Saunders *Carl Maria von Weber* (1940, reprinted New York 1969). John Warrack *Carl Maria von Weber* (London and New York 1968).

WEBER, Max (Apr. 18, 1881 – Oct. 4, 1961). American painter. Born Bialystok, Russia (now Poland), son of a tailor, and raised in a tradition of Russian Judaism. Emigrated to U.S. with his parents (1891). After public school, studied at Pratt Institute, Brooklyn, N.Y. (1898–1901), under Arthur W. Dow and then taught four years before going abroad (1905). In Paris studied with J. P. Laurens at Académie Julian, made friends with Henri Rousseau,

and enrolled in class with Matisse (1908). Returning to New York (1909), he made extensive study of American Indian art and became a pioneer in modernism, painting under Fauvist, cubist, and futurist influences. First important one-man show, at Alfred Stieglitz's famous 291 Gallery (1911), provoked violent reactions from critics. Married Frances Abrams (1916). His cubist style, as in *Chinese Restaurant* (1915, Whitney Museum, New York) soon gave way (c.1917) to a semi-abstract expressionism; his subjects became more poetic and religious, expressive of his Jewish heritage, as in *The Worshipper* and *The Rabbi* (both 1918, both in collection of Mrs. Nathan J. Miller, New Rochelle, N.Y.). During the late 1930's more contemporary and social themes came into his work, as in *At the Mill* (1939, Newark Museum, Newark, N.J.) and *The Toilers* (1942, collection of Mrs. Max Weber). His late work shows increasing freedom and an energetic use of the line. Throughout his life, Weber combined teaching with painting. He also wrote several books on art theory, among them *Camera Work* (1910), *Cubist Poems* (1914), *Essays on Art* (1916), *Primitives* (1926), and *Woodcuts* (1957). Aside from oils, he produced numerous pastels, gouaches, drawings, and sculptures. Died at Great Neck, New York.

REFERENCES: Museum of Modern Art *Max Weber: Retrospective Exhibition, 1907–1930* (New York 1930). *Max Weber: First Comprehensive Retrospective Exhibition in the West* (University of California, Santa Barbara, Calif. 1968). Lloyd Goodrich *Max Weber* (New York 1949).

WEBERN, Anton von (Dec. 3, 1883 – Sept. 15, 1945). Austrian composer. Born Vienna. Studied musicology at Vienna University (Ph.D. 1906), then composition with Arnold Schoenberg and became his disciple. Held conductorships in Austria and Germany (1908–14). After World War I settled in Mödling; taught composition until the Nazis banned his music and forbade him to teach (1938). His first work was the relatively conventional *Passacaglia* for orchestra (1908). But by 1913, in his *Five Pieces for Orches-*

tra, he had adopted Schoenberg's severe atonality, and his twelve-tone technique by 1924 in *Three Sacred Songs.* Webern's output was small — thirty-one works — and his pieces, for small ensembles, extremely short. They include *Six Orchestral Pieces* (1913), *Symphony* for chamber orchestra (1928), *Variations* for piano (1936), *Das Augenlicht* for chorus and orchestra, and among his last works, three cantatas. Webern reduced music to the barest essentials, fragmenting melody, and carrying precision, brevity, and delicacy to an extreme. The resultant concentration and purity of his music has powerfully influenced such contemporary composers as Igor Stravinsky, Karlheinz Stockhausen, and Pierre Boulez. Webern died at Mittersill, near Salzburg, accidentally shot by an overvigilant American M.P.

REFERENCES: Walter Kolneder *Anton Webern: An Introduction to His Works* (tr. Berkeley, Calif. and London 1968). Hans Moldenhauer and D. Irvine *Anton von Webern: Perspectives* (Seattle, Wash. 1966). Friedrich Wildgans *Anton Webern* (New York 1967).

WEBSTER, John (c.1575–c.1634). English dramatist. Born in London. Hardly anything is known of his life, but after 1600 he was collaborating with Thomas Dekker and other playwrights. Only three plays remain which are undoubtedly by Webster alone: *The White Devil* (c.1608), *The Duchess of Malfi* (c.1614), and the inferior tragicomedy *The Devil's Law-Case* (1623). In none of his plays did he succeed in devising a good plot, and his two masterpieces are sustained by his brooding poetry, his ability to convey the horror of death, a profound tragic sense, and his gift for brilliant phrases which illuminate his dense poetry ("I saw him now going the way of all flesh"; "Cover her face; mine eyes dazzle; she died young"). Adultery, murder, and inevitably revenge are the subject matter of *The White Devil;* here and in *The Duchess of Malfi* he shirks nothing in his portrayal of evil, and only the vitality of his more innocent figures saves the plays from complete nihilism. *The White Devil* is the more vigorous play, in which even the victims of the tragedy are guilty of wrongdoing;

The Duchess of Malfi is more concerned with human suffering and the tragic effects of evil and cruelty. Satire is also a strong element in his tragedies.

EDITION: *Complete Works* ed. F. L. Lucas (4 vols. London and New York 1927).

REFERENCES: Travis Bogard *The Tragic Satire of John Webster* (Berkeley, Calif. and Cambridge, England, 1955). Rupert Brooke *John Webster and the Elizabethan Drama* (1916, reprinted New York 1967). R. W. Dent *John Webster's Borrowing* (Berkeley, Calif. and Cambridge, England, 1960). Clifford Leech *John Webster: A Critical Study* (1951, reprinted New York 1966). Elmer E. Stoll *John Webster* (1905, reprinted New York 1967).

WEDEKIND, Frank (July 24, 1864 – Mar. 9, 1918). German dramatist. Born Hanover, son of a physician. Raised in Switzerland, where he attended Aarau gymnasium (1879–83). Worked successively as publicity manager, journalist, secretary to a circus, and helped found periodical *Simplicissimus.* Established himself as a playwright; his first successful play, *Frühlings Erwachen* (1891, tr. *Spring's Awakening* 1909), dealt with smoldering adolescent sexuality, repressed and corrupted by social convention. It was followed by *Der Erdgeist* (1895, tr. *Earth Spirit* 1914) and *Die Büsche der Pandora* (1904, tr. *Pandora's Box* 1918), two plays about the elemental and destructive female sexual force, personified through the character of Lulu. From these plays Alban Berg wrote the libretto for his opera *Lulu* (1934). Married to an actress (1908), he worked as a cabaret singer, actor, and journalist to support himself. Died in Munich. Other plays include: *Der Marquis von Keith* (1901), *König Nicolo oder So ist das Leben* (1902, tr. *Such Is Life* 1916) and *Hidalla* (1904). A forerunner of expressionism and a savage social critic, Wedekind greatly influenced Bertolt Brecht.

TRANSLATIONS: *Five Tragedies of Sex* (*Spring's Awakening, Earth Spirit, Pandora's Box, Death and the Devil, Castle Wetterstein*) tr. Frances Fawcett and Stephen Spender (London and New

York 1952). *The Lulu Plays* tr. Carl R. Mueller (Greenwich, Conn. PB 1967).
REFERENCE: Sol Gittleman *Frank Wedekind* (New York 1969).

WEILL, Kurt (Mar. 2, 1900 – Apr. 3, 1950). German-American composer. Born in Dessau. Studied under Albert Bing, Humperdinck, and Busoni, settling in Berlin (1921). Produced first opera, *Der Protagonist* (1926). Bertolt Brecht wrote the lyrics for Weill's *Die Dreigroschenoper* (1928, tr. *The Threepenny Opera*), a brilliant adaptation of Gay's *The Beggar's Opera* as a satire of the Berlin underworld. They also collaborated on *Happy End* (1929), distinguished by Weill's haunting songs rather than by the crude plot of gangsters and the Salvation Army; and on the fiercely antimaterialist *Aufstieg und Fall der Stadt Mahagonny* (1930, *The Rise and Fall of the City of Mahagonny*), satirizing life in a boom town, where the only crime is to be broke. After the production of *Die Bürgschaft* (1932), Weill left Nazi Germany, settling in U.S. (1935). There he wrote Broadway hits such as *Knickerbocker Holiday* (1938, with Maxwell Anderson), *Lady in the Dark* (1941, with Moss Hart), *Street Scene* (1947, with Elmer Rice), and *Lost in the Stars* (1949, with Maxwell Anderson, based on Alan Paton's novel *Cry, the Beloved Country*). His folk opera *Down in the Valley* (1948) was also extremely popular. Weill created a popular yet serious musical style, inspired by jazz; though much of his music is savage and harsh, a haunting, nostalgic streak pervades his scores, as in the ballet (for dancers and voice) *Die Sieben Todsünden* (1933, *The Seven Deadly Sins*). Weill married (1926) the actress Lotte Lenya, who has sung and recorded his music. He died in New York.

WELLS, H(erbert) G(eorge) (Sept. 21, 1866 – Aug. 13, 1946). English writer. Born Bromley, Kent, of lower middle-class family. After a sketchy education, was apprenticed (1880) to a draper; then won scholarship to Normal School of Science, London (1884), where he studied with Thomas Henry Huxley. After graduating from London University (B.S. 1888), taught biology, wrote educational articles, and married his first cousin Isabel Mary Wells (1891). They were divorced (1894), and he married his student Amy Catherine Robbins (1895). His pioneering career as a science fiction writer began with publication of his novel *The Time Machine* (1895) and continued with (among others) *The Wonderful Visit* (1895), *The Invisible Man* (1897), *The War of the Worlds* (1898; its radio dramatization by Orson Welles caused the famous Mars invasion panic of 1938), and *The First Men in the Moon* (1901). Abandoning fantasy for realistic social comedy, he reached his highest literary achievement with novels of his middle period. They include *Kipps* (1905), *Tono-Bungay* (1909), *The History of Mr. Polly* (1910), and *Mr. Britling Sees It Through* (1916). A member of the Fabian Society (1903–1908), he gradually evolved his own Utopian philosophy, presented in *Anticipations* (1901), *Mankind in the Making* (1903), and *A Modern Utopia* (1905). His later books, novels of ideas, mostly expound his current preoccupations. Among his other works: the immensely popular *Outline of History* (1920, revised 1931), *The Science of Life* (1931, in collaboration with Julian Huxley and his son G. P. Wells), the reminiscences of *Experiment in Autobiography* (1934); and his last work, the bleak *Mind at the End of Its Tether* (1945). Died in London. An enormously prolific and popular writer, Wells captured the early twentieth century's need to rebel and overthrow oppressive Victorian conventions.

EDITIONS: *Works* (28 vols. London 1924–27). *Complete Short Stories* (London 1966).
REFERENCES: Bernard Bergonzi *The Early H. G. Wells: A Study of the Scientific Romances* (Manchester, England 1961). Vincent Brome *H. G. Wells: A Biography* (London 1951). Lovat Dickson *H. G. Wells: His Turbulent Life and Times* (New York 1969). Mark R. Hillegas *The Future as Nightmare: H. G. Wells and the Anti-Utopians* (New York 1967). Norman Nicholson *H. G. Wells* (London 1950 and Denver, Colo.

1951). W. Warren Wagar *H. G. Wells and the World State* (New Haven, Conn. 1961).

WESLEY, John (June 17, 1703 – Mar. 2, 1791). English clergyman, theologian, and writer, founder of Methodism. Born Epworth, Lincolnshire, son of Rev. Samuel Wesley; elder brother of Charles Wesley, clergyman and hymn writer. Educated at Charterhouse School, London (1714–20) and Christ Church, Oxford (B.A. 1724, M.A. 1727), he was ordained Anglican deacon (1725) and priest (1728). While serving as fellow of Lincoln College, Oxford (1726–35), formed religious study group with his brother Charles, derisively called the Holy Club and the Methodists by university wits. The two brothers went (1735) as missionaries to Savannah, Ga., where John met and was influenced by Moravian missionaries. After his return (1737), he experienced a profound religious conversion (1738), finding spiritual grace through faith in Christ alone. After visiting Moravian leaders in Germany and Holland, he began evangelical work. Although working within the Church of England, he was rejected from many churches and reluctantly began preaching outdoors, traveling thousands of miles a year and preaching constantly. The Methodist Society was officially launched (1739), and Methodist societies sprang up throughout England and (in 1760's) America. Movement finally separated from Established Church when Wesley issued a legal constitution and ordained his own bishops for Methodist societies in America (1784). Though he always considered himself a loyal Anglican priest, his break with the Church of England was complete, if unacknowledged. After two unsuccessful courtships, Wesley made an unfortunate marriage to widow Mary Vazeille (1751); she deserted him (1776). He died in London. Wesley wrote over forty thousand sermons, but is best known for his journal (1735–90), a remarkable human document. Also wrote numerous prose tracts on a wide variety of subjects, and with Charles published a collection of psalms and hymns (1737).

EDITIONS: *The Works of John Wesley* ed. Thomas Jackson (11th ed. 15 vols. London 1856–62). *The Journal* ed. Nehemiah Curnock (8 vols. London 1909–16). *Standard Sermons* ed. Edward H. Sugden (2 vols. London 1921). *Letters* ed. John Telford (8 vols. London and New York 1931).

REFERENCES: W. R. Cannon *The Theology of John Wesley* (New York 1946). V. H. H. Green *The Young Mr. Wesley: A Study of John Wesley and Oxford* (London and New York 1961). T. R. Jeffery *John Wesley's Religious Quest* (New York 1960). Umphrey Lee *The Lord's Horseman* (1928, new ed. New York 1954 and London 1956). F. J. McConnell *John Wesley* (New York and London 1939, also PB). Dorothy Marshall *John Wesley* (London and New York 1965). Robert Southey *Life of John Wesley* (London 1820). Colin Williams *John Wesley's Theology Today* (London and New York 1960).

WEST, Benjamin (Oct. 10, 1738 – Mar. 11, 1820). American painter. Born Springfield, Pa., to Quaker parents. After studying painting with an artist in Philadelphia (1756–59), he sought commissions there and in New York. With the help of Philadelphia merchants he sailed for Europe (1760), remaining there for the rest of his life. After three years in Italy, where he came under influence of J. J. Winckelmann and A. R. Mengs, settled in London (1763), where his Roman paintings enjoyed immediate success. Married Elizabeth Shewell (1764). Soon a leader in the neoclassical movement, he received numerous commissions through patronage of George III and became historical painter to the king (1772–1801). A founder of the Royal Academy of Arts (1768), he succeeded Sir Joshua Reynolds as its president (1792–1820). Many young American painters came to him for advice, among them Charles Willson Peale, Gilbert Stuart, John Singleton Copley, John Trumbull, and Matthew Pratt. Most of his canvases, executed on a heroic scale, are on historical, mythological, or religious subjects. His *Death of General Wolfe* (c.1771, Grosvenor Gallery, London, and other versions) was the first historical work to use contemporary, instead of classical, dress. His *Death on a Pale Horse* (1802, Pennsylvania Academy of the Fine Arts, Philadelphia) anticipates French romantic painting. Among other notable works: *Agrippina with the Ashes of Germanicus* (1767, Yale University Art Gallery, New Haven, Conn.), *Christ Rejected* (1814, Pennsylvania Academy of the Fine Arts), and *Woodcutters in Windsor Great Park* (1795, John Herrick Art Museum, Indianapolis). He died in London.

REFERENCES: Grose Evans *Benjamin West and the Taste of His Times* (Carbondale, Ill. 1959). James T. Flexner *American Painting: The Light of Distant Skies, 1760–1835* (1954, reprinted New York PB 1969). John Galt *The Life of Benjamin West* (1816, reprinted Gainesville, Fla. 1960).

WEST, Nathanael (real name Nathan Wallenstein Weinstein) (Oct. 17, 1904 – Dec. 22, 1940). Born New York City, son of a prosperous building contractor. Attended De Witt Clinton High School and Tufts University; transferred (1922) to Brown University, where he met Quentin Reynolds and S. J. Perelman, later West's brother-in-law (graduated 1924). In Paris (1925–26) he finished his first novel, *The Dream Life of Balso Snell* (published 1931). On return to New York became assistant manager of Kenmore Hotel, then Sutton Hotel, where he wrote second novel, *Miss Lonelyhearts;* parts of it appeared in *Contact* (1932) which West edited with William Carlos Williams. After its publication as a book (1933), with largely unfavorable reviews, West moved to Erwinna, Pa., began *A Cool Million* (published 1934). Went briefly to Hollywood to work on *Miss Lonelyhearts* screenplay; returned there (1935) and worked five years as fairly successful screenwriter. His last novel was a mordant picture of people on the fringes of Hollywood, *The Day of the Locust* (1939). Married Eileen McKinney (April 1940), sister of Ruth McKinney, author of *My Sister Eileen.* That December, West and his wife were both killed in an automobile accident near El Centro, Calif. West's reputation has grown steadily since

his death; his novels are appreciated for their surrealistic dark comedy, satire, and striking use of language. West's credo, stated in his first novel, expresses the black humor of all his work: "I must laugh at myself, and if the laugh is 'bitter,' I must laugh at the laugh. I always find it necessary to burlesque the mystery of feeling at its source."

EDITION: *Complete Works* (1957, latest ed. New York 1966 and London 1968).

REFERENCES: Victor Comerchero *Nathanael West: The Ironic Prophet* (Syracuse, N.Y. 1964, also PB). Stanley E. Hyman *Nathanael West* (Minneapolis PB 1962). James F. Light *Nathanael West: An Interpretative Study* (Evanston, Ill. 1961). Jay Martin *Nathanael West: The Art of His Life* (New York 1970). Randall Reid *The Fiction of Nathanael West* (Chicago 1968).

WEYDEN, Roger van der (or Roger de la Pasture) (c.1400 – June 16, 1464). Flemish painter. Born Tournai. Apprenticed to Robert Campin, the Tournai painter who is thought to be the Master of Flémalle. Roger entered painters' guild of Tournai (1432). Appointed city painter at Brussels (1435), he retained that office until his death. Also received patronage of the Burgundian court, the Ferrarese court and probably the Medici; visited Italy (1450). He died in Brussels. Among his most famous religious works are the *Descent from the Cross* commissioned by the Louvain archers' guild (c.1435, Escorial, exhibited in the Prado, Madrid), the *Columba Altarpiece* (Alte Pinakothek, Munich), the *Last Judgement* (1443–51/2, Hôtel de Dieu, Beaune), the *Seven Sacraments Altarpiece* (1453–60, Musée Royale, Antwerp), the *Bladelin Altarpiece* (Staatliche Museen, Berlin), the *Braque Triptych* (c.1450–52, Louvre, Paris) and *St. Luke Drawing the Virgin* (Museum of Fine Arts, Boston). He was also active as a portrait painter: *Francesco d'Este* is in Metropolitan Museum, New York, and *Young Lady* in National Gallery, Washington, D.C.

REFERENCES: Erwin Panofsky *Early Netherlandish Painting* (2 vols. Cambridge, Mass. and Oxford 1954). Max J. Friedländer *Early Netherlandish Painting* (London 1967).

~

ROGER VAN DER WEYDEN
BY ANNE MARKHAM

The history of early Netherlandish painting can be described in terms of a gradual conquest of the means of reproducing the appearance of reality. By 1410 the delineation of settings had become so accurate that, for the first time, particular places could be identified in paintings. Vast panoramas were conveyed on a tiny scale by means of overlapping, diminution in scale, and aerial perspective. The effects of weather, of different times of day, of different times of year, were thoroughly investigated. Light was apprehended as obeying its own laws. Thus the direction of cast shadows was dependent on the source of light, and the strength of shadows upon the clarity of the atmosphere. Figures were made uniform in scale, more accurate in anatomical construction, and the human tegument was rendered with such precision and detail that a magnifying glass might reveal veins, wrinkles, hair, invisible to the naked eye. The newly developed technique of oil painting permitted a slow consideration and care in execution appropriate to the precise and detailed nature of Flemish painting. Finally, the desire to imitate the appearance of the natural world led painters to eliminate the supernatural — halos, angels, golden streams of light — from their work and to locate sacred scenes in bourgeois settings. Religious symbols no longer appeared as such: they were almost invariably disguised as objects of customary use.

While Roger benefited from the discoveries and advances in technique of his predecessors, he also attempted to redress what he must have felt as an imbalance in favor of the real world at the expense of transcendental religious meanings. Into many of his most realistically executed paintings, Roger introduced devices so patently artificial that we are constantly reminded of the nonnarrative function of the work. In his early *Descent from the Cross* (Prado, Madrid), for instance, Roger sets a group of ten figures within a setting that closely resembles the niche customarily employed for carved wooden statuettes in the compartments of High Gothic retables. The friezelike composition is appropriate to a carved relief. Yet it was not Roger's intention to imitate in paint the appearance of a wooden reredos. The textures he describes are those of cloth, grass, flesh, hair. His figures look and move like real people, not wooden figures. His purpose here was evidently to draw our attention to the respective roles in the redemption of mankind of Christ and the Madonna. Christ, through his sacrifice on the cross, is the primary agent in the salvation of mankind, but the Madonna, too, participated in man's redemption through the suffering she vicariously felt at her Son's crucifixion. In visual terms this is conveyed through the identity of pose and view and the swooning of both figures. Thus the artist equates the Passion of Christ with the compassion of the Virgin.

In the *Granada-Miraflores Altarpiece* (Granada, New York, and Berlin) and the *St. John Triptych* (Berlin) Roger inserts into the foremost plane of the picture space arches embellished with carved statuettes, very much like the archivolt of a Gothic portal. Thus a barrier between the illusionistic space of the painting and the real space of the observer is erected. The arch also serves to define the picture space behind it as unreal, for the arch and setting have no logical or spatial connection with one another. Finally, the arch with its numerous religious scenes or statuettes functions like a prolegomenon to the symbolic meaning of the scene itself.

Other devices besides the limitation of the setting are utilized to counterbalance the naturalism of the scene and suggest a transcendental meaning. In the *Seven Sacraments Altarpiece* (Antwerp) there is a descending hierarchy of scale through the holy witnesses of the Crucifixion, to the crucified Christ, and lastly, the mortals who perform the sacred rites. Here, in the *Last Judgment* of Beaune, and in the *Braque Triptych* (Louvre), explicative titles are inscribed on the surface of the panel according to the medieval fashion. The golden background of the Beaune *Last Judgment* also represents a reversion to the archaistic supernaturalism of earlier painting.

The evolution of a lucid picture of Roger's stylistic development suffers from the absence of any precisely dated extant work. Nevertheless, Roger's oeuvre can be analyzed into two stylistic poles which most likely characterize early and late works. One pole, exemplified by the *Descent from the Cross*, consists of figures robust in proportion, rendered in foreshortened views, whose volume is suggested by modeling in light and shade and by the encircling folds of garments. Torsos and limbs are bent and turned to such an extent that distortions of the anatomy frequently occur. Settings are constructed according to the modern, rational techniques and the figures are made to inhabit space. Light penetrates a dense atmosphere as in the work of Jan van Eyck. Thus colors are subdued and outlines blurred. Through the richness of color and the wealth of detail the early paintings make a sensuous impression. Yet one's feelings are af-

fected too: profound emotion is externalized in Roger's early figures through strongly individualized poses, gestures, and expressions.

The dependence of many of these works on those of Robert Campin suggests that they are early works. Roger van der Weyden was an apprentice of Campin's from 1427 to 1432. From his master he borrowed facial types, a jigsaw puzzle kind of composition, and the linking of figures on the surface through continuous curves to which the poses contribute. The poses and design of *St. Luke Drawing the Virgin* (Boston) manifestly derive from Robert Campin's *Merode Annunciation* (New York).

The other stylistic pole is characterized by elongated and attenuated figures whose diminished plasticity is reflected in profile views, an almost total disappearance of shading, and straight, continuous contours. Figures stand rigidly erect as in the Frankfurt *Madonna and Saints,* so that each figure is isolated from the other. This compositional isolation is paralleled by emotional isolation: figures do not communicate with one another, nor even seem aware of one another's existence. Indeed, figures do not seem to feel at all, and like medieval saints function above all as bearers of symbolic attributes. Forms are represented with crystalline clarity: edges are extremely hard and drapery folds have the brittleness of stone. Compositions now are excessively tectonic and rigidly symmetrical. The construction of space no longer makes empirical use of linear perspective, and often, as in the *St. John Triptych,* figures are squashed up against the picture plane while a tunnel-like space, with which they have no connection, recedes behind them. Here, one senses the culmination of the tendency to combat the progressive naturalism of early Netherlandish painting by a militant assertion of the dogma of the church.

Between these two poles stands Roger's most famous altarpiece, the *Columba Altarpiece* in the Munich Alte Pinakothek. While the figures have become elongated, they have not altogether lost their plasticity. While figures are less mobile than those of Roger's early works, their poses introduce curves which serve to link disparate figures on the surface of the painting. While emotion is subdued, it is nonetheless apparent. Although figures are pushed as far forward as the picture space will allow, they nevertheless inhabit more than one plane. The particularly sumptuous, glittering, fractured style of this work, as well as numerous motifs, reflects the influence of the *Adoration of the Magi* by the Cologne painter Stefan Lochner, which Roger could have seen on his way to Rome for the jubilee of 1450. That Roger did make such a trip is witnessed by Bartolommeo Fazio, who wrote that Roger admired the frescoes of Gentile da Fabriano in St. John's in the Lateran. Several compositions, such as the *Lamentation Over the Dead Christ* (Uffizi, Florence), derive from Italian pictures; several paintings were actually executed for Italian patrons; and Italian critics were well informed of Roger's work. What the Italians admired, above all, in the art of Roger van der Weyden, according to Michelangelo, was its piety, which could "bring tears to the eyes of the devout." and even today it is for that that Roger's art stands out among all Netherlandish paintings.

WHARTON, Edith (Newbold Jones) (Jan. 24, 1862 – Aug. 12, 1937). American writer. Born New York City; of wealthy old New York family, with whom she traveled extensively in Europe (1867–73). Privately educated. Published *Verses* (1878), and stories collected as *The Greater Inclination* (1899). Married Edward Wharton of Boston (1885), but the marriage was difficult, and after she had settled permanently in Paris (1907) she divorced him (1913). Her first three novels, *The Touchstone* (1900), *The Valley of Decision* (1902), and *Sanctuary* (1903), were poorly received. Began lasting friendship with Henry James (1902), who had great influence on her writing. *The House of Mirth* (1905), a novel of manners exposing the hollowness of New York society and the cruelty of convention, brought wide recognition at home and abroad. The short novel *Ethan Frome* (1911), a tale of frustrated love with a tragically ironic denouement, was highly successful and followed by another major work, *The Age of Innocence* (1920), which won the Pulitzer prize. Other novels of manners on the theme of the stifling effect of social convention on people of integrity and innocence are *The Reef* (1921), *Summer* (1917), *Old New York* (1924), *Hudson River Bracketed* (1929), *The Gods Arrive* (1932), *The Buccaneers* (1938; unfinished). Another Wharton theme, scorn for social climbers and nouveaux riches, is developed in *The Custom of the Country* (1913). Other collections of short stories include *Xingu and Other Stories* (1916), *Certain People* (1930), *Ghosts* (1937). Wharton also wrote literary criticism, poetry, travel books, and a work on interior decorating. She received the Cross of the Legion of Honor from the French government (1916) for work during World War I. She died at St. Brice-sous-Foret, France.

EDITION: *Collected Short Stories* ed. R. W. B. Lewis (2 vols. New York 1968).
REFERENCES: Millicent Bell *Edith Wharton and Henry James* (New York 1965 and London 1966). Irving Howe ed. *Edith Wharton: A Collection of Critical Essays* (Englewood Cliffs, N.J. 1962, also PB). Grace Kellogg *The Two Lives of Edith Wharton: The Woman and Her Work* (New York 1965). Percy Lubbock *Portrait of Edith Wharton* (1947, reprinted New York 1969). Jay Martin *Harvests of Change: Ameri-*

can Literature, 1865–1914 (Englewood
Cliffs, N.J. 1967, also PB). Blake Nevius
Edith Wharton: A Study of Her Fiction
(Berkeley, Calif. and Cambridge, Eng-
land, 1953, also PB).

WHISTLER, James Abbott McNeill (July
10, 1834 – July 17, 1903). American
etcher, painter, and lithographer. Born
Lowell, Mass. Accompanied family to
Russia (1843–49), where his father, a
military engineer, was building railroad from St. Petersburg to Moscow.
Attended West Point (1851–54), then
worked briefly as map draftsman for
U.S. coast survey; began etching in
spare time. Went to Paris (1855) to
study painting under Charles Gleyre;
published first set of etchings there
(1858). Moved to London (1859),
where he developed reputation as a
dandy and wit, and knew Swinburne
and later Wilde. Also became interested in and influenced by Japanese
art. Produced Thames series of etchings (1860), praised by Baudelaire,
and the important early paintings At
the Piano (1859, private collection,
Cincinnati), Blue Wave (1860, Hill-
Stead Museum, Farmington, Conn.),
and The White Girl (1862, National
Gallery, Washington, D.C.) which after
rejection caused a sensation when exhibited at Salon des Refusés, Paris
(1863). Painted famous portraits, including the immensely popular painting of his mother (1872, Louvre, Paris)
and portraits of Thomas Carlyle (1873,
Glasgow Art Gallery), Rose Whistler
(Museum of Fine Arts, Boston), Miss
Cicely Alexander (1873, National Gallery, London), and others; also painted
his Nocturne series. Sued Ruskin
(1878) for writing of Nocturne in
Black and Gold: The Falling Rocket
(1874, Institute of Arts, Detroit) as
"flinging a pot of paint in the public's
face." Won case, but received only one
farthing in damages. Bankrupt, he
went to Venice (1879–80) and re-
couped his finances and reputation
with two series of etchings. Returned
to London to find his portraits and
etchings the rage. Began to lecture and
write. Ten O'Clock (1885) expressed
his views regarding musical analogies
in pictorial art, and promulgated the
doctrine of art for art's sake. Elected

to Royal Society of British Artists
(1884); president (1886–88). Married
Beatrix Godwin (1888). Wrote The
Gentle Art of Making Enemies (1890).
After producing Dutch series of etchings and many lithographs during
1890's, returned to Paris (1892), where
he taught at Académie Carmen (1898–
1901). Died in London.

REFERENCES: Albert Eugene Gallatin
Portraits of Whistler: A Critical Study
and an Iconography (New York and
London 1918). Horace Gregory The
World of James McNeill Whistler (New
York 1959). James Laver Whistler (2nd
ed. London 1951). Mortimer Menpes
Whistler As I Knew Him (New York
and London 1904). Hesketh Pearson
The Man Whistler (London and New
York 1952). Elizabeth R. Pennell The
Art of Whistler (New York 1928).
Elizabeth R. and Joseph Pennell The
Life of James McNeill Whistler (5th
ed. Philadelphia and London 1911).
Denys Sutton Nocturne: The Art of
James McNeill Whistler (London 1963
and Philadelphia 1964) and James
McNeill Whistler: Paintings, Etchings,
Pastels, and Watercolors (London and
Greenwich, Conn. 1966).

✍

WHISTLER

BY JOHN GOLDING

Despite the vividness of the impact left
by Whistler's personality upon his age,
his position in the history of nineteenth-
century art is hard to define. He was
an artist of exquisite taste and sensibility, which he put at the service of a
genuinely independent vision. Yet he
produced a mere handful of works
which could be described as universally
significant, and even these can hardly
support a confrontation with comparable canvases by the greatest of his contemporaries. He was a celebrated wit
and an inspired conversationalist, but
in retrospect his mind appears to have
been inferior to its own intellectual
pretensions. His famous Ten O'Clock
lecture is today more interesting as an
apologia for the doctrine of art for art's

sake at its most extreme than for any intrinsic originality. Perhaps the key to his art and his influence is to be seen in the restlessness and diversity of his background and personality. Throughout his life he was acutely aware of himself as an outsider. He was a Yankee who saw himself as a Southerner and who once claimed to have been born in Russia. In Paris he was an arrogant "original" who ultimately refused to face the challenge of competing with his peers. In London he was a worldly aesthete out to scandalize and undermine the values of a philistine establishment. His importance lay not least in the fact that he managed to bridge such a remarkable number of worlds.

Whistler's apprenticeship in Paris lasted a relatively short time, but the impact of French art, both visual and literary, was to have a decisive influence upon his entire career. Later in life he denounced Courbet and the whole doctrine of realism, but from Courbet and from Fantin Latour's reinterpretation of Courbet's style, he acquired a feeling for the sensuous properties of paint and a respect for the painting as an object in its own right, having a material existence independent of any narrative content, that was to work as a healthy antidote to the literary and anecdotic quality of so much contemporary English art. His art was touched by that of the Pre-Raphaelites, but the French experience enabled him to avoid their self-consciousness and occasional preciosity. From French painting he learnt, too, an approach to formal problems that was, in his early work at least, genuinely experimental. The spatial and compositional devices in his first mature works of the late 1850's and early 1860's anticipate developments in the art of both Degas and Manet, although their achievements were soon to eclipse his own.

But if the works of his first period show him at his most progressively original, it was through his encounter with Oriental art that he was to discover himself as an artist and to make his first significant contribution to the history of art. For while Oriental art was seized upon simultaneously by several Western artists, Whistler was the first to manifest its influence overtly in his paintings and to popularize it, particularly in England, as a symbol of refined and emancipated aesthetic sensibility. Artists such as Degas, Manet, Van Gogh, and Gauguin explored the linear, spatial, and compositional properties of Japanese art, but for Whistler its decorative qualities were uppermost. In a letter to a friend he wrote, "It seems to me that colour ought to appear in a picture continually here and there, in the same way that a thread appears in an embroidery. In this way the whole will form a harmony. Look how well the Japanese understood this. They never look for contrast, on the contrary, they're after repetition." In a sense the decorative solutions suggested by his study of Japanese prints drained his art of its earlier pioneering vitality, but at the same time he was becoming aware of the limitations of his talents and of his true artistic bent. The *Nocturnes* of the 1870's and the portraits painted early in the decade, in which the compositional refinement and the decorative sophistication of Japanese art have been completely assimilated, mark the summit of his career as a painter. If they stand slightly to one side of the major developments taking place in European art, they are deservedly amongst the most popular and best loved works of the period.

Simultaneously, by his emphasis on musical titles or subtitles for his works,

Whistler was underlining an important current in contemporary aesthetics. By the mid-nineteenth century ideas about the interrelations or correspondences between the arts had become common currency in French literary circles, and Whistler must have been made very aware of them through his enthusiasm for the works of Baudelaire and his knowledge of Gautier's poetry. But it was only during the second half of the century that music became firmly established as queen of the arts because of its nonimitative qualities, and Whistler was the painter who took the first conscious step towards the musicalization of painting that was to reach a climax in the first coloristic abstractions executed by Kupka and Kandinsky soon after 1910. The ideas that Whistler was expressing may have come to him from others, but this did not lessen their impact upon his public; and if his *japonisme* had a profound influence on the visual taste of his time, his insistence, during the 1870's and 1880's, on the necessity of divorcing form from content was to have an equally strong influence on many subsequent aesthetic theories of visual perception.

Whistler's late years became increasingly absorbed in controversy and in the mechanics of cementing his reputation as an eccentric public figure. In fact, from the '80's onward he was producing relatively little painting and his style was becoming increasingly mannered and thin in quality, although he brought off a number of striking portraits, which in their dash and worldliness anticipate the Edwardian society portraits of Sargent. And if he had not succeeded in rescuing English art from the doldrums into which it was subsiding, he had at least become a cult figure for the young men of the pre-Edwardian age who were out to reverse

Victorian moral and aesthetic standards. But it was his contact with some of the most brilliant figures in the French literary world that provided his life with a satisfactory and moving final chapter. Despite the many visual influences his art had undergone, it was perhaps the aesthetic of the French literary tradition exemplified by Baudelaire that had ultimately the deepest effect upon his art. And the fascination which the aging Whistler had for such men as Mallarmé, Huysmans, and the young Proust, surely lay in the fact that in his eccentric clothes, his affectations of speech and gesture, and in his painted face, they must have seen the last tangible vestiges of the nineteenth-century dandy as he had been invented by Baudelaire some fifty years before.

———

WHITE, Stanford (Nov. 9, 1853 – June 25, 1906). American architect. Born New York City, son of literary critic Richard Grant White. Entered office of Gambrill and Richardson (1872), where he was trained as a draftsman (1872–78) by H. H. Richardson, whom he assisted in construction of Trinity Church, Boston (1872–77). In 1879 joined Charles F. McKim and William R. Mead to found McKim, Mead, and White, one of the most prominent and influential architectural firms in American history. Married Bessie Springs Smith (1884). Although initially influenced by "Richardsonian Romanesque," later he preferred to work in the classical or Renaissance styles. His talent was for decorative ornamentation, and his interest in interior design led to a wide knowledge of antiques. Aside from his collaborative efforts with his partners, White's individual works include the following New York landmarks: Washington Arch, at the foot of Fifth Avenue (1889); the Century Club (1891); the first Madison Square Garden (1891); the Metropolitan Club (1894); the Herald Building (1894); the Madison Square Presbyterian Church (1906); the old Tiffany and Company building (1906); the Gorham

Building (1906). Only the first two still stand. White was murdered at the Madison Square Garden Roof by Harry K. Thaw, who was apparently motivated by jealousy over his wife, Evelyn Nesbit Thaw, a former chorus girl.

REFERENCES: Wayne Andrews *Architecture, Ambition, and Americans* (New York 1955, PB 1964). Charles C. Baldwin *Stanford White* (New York 1931). Gerald Langford *The Murder of Stanford White* (Indianapolis 1962 and London 1963).

WHITMAN, Walter (May 31, 1819 – Mar. 26, 1892). American poet. Born West Hills, Long Island; of Quaker parentage. The family moved to Brooklyn, where Whitman received an elementary education and began omnivorous reading, including the Bible and great Greek, Oriental and other translated classics. Worked as a printer, journalist, and schoolteacher (1832–45). Published a temperance novelette, *Franklin Evans, or The Inebriate* (1842). Became editor of the *Brooklyn Eagle* (1846) but his views supporting abolitionism and free soil resulted in his discharge (1848). Traveling to New Orleans for another newspaper job enabled him to see a good deal of the country. Brought out first edition (1855) of *Leaves of Grass*, which contained twelve poems, including *Song of Myself*, and was enthusiastically hailed by Emerson. Constantly revising and adding new poems, he published nine editions of *Leaves of Grass* in his lifetime. Went to Virginia (1862) to nurse his brother wounded in Civil War, then volunteered as a nurse in Washington. Two books came from the war: poetry, *Drum-Taps* (1865), and prose, *Specimen Days and Collect* (1882). Obtained government clerkship after the war but was dismissed for his "immoral" book, *Leaves of Grass*. A second appointment in the attorney general's office lasted until 1873, when he was stricken with paralysis and forced to retire. He settled in Camden, N.J., where he died. Two late works: prose, *Democratic Vistas* (1871), and poems, *November Boughs* (1888). Whitman's flowing free-verse rhythms and joyous celebration of self-awareness and the union of the body and nature influenced twentieth-century poetry; his visionary concept of the poet's role was in part a development of Emerson's notion of the poet.

EDITION: *Complete Writings* ed. R. M. Bucke and others (1902, reprinted 10 vols. Grosse Pointe, Mich. 1968). *Leaves of Grass: A Facsimile of the First Edition* ed. Richard Bridgman (San Francisco 1968).

REFERENCES: Gay Wilson Allen *The Solitary Singer: A Critical Biography of Walt Whitman* (1955, rev. ed. New York 1967). Newton Arvin *Whitman* (1938, reprinted New York 1969). Roger Asselineau *The Evolution of Walt Whitman* (tr. 2 vols. Cambridge, Mass. and Oxford 1960/62). Henry S. Canby *Walt Whitman, an American* (Boston 1943). F. O. Malthiessen *American Renaissance* (New York 1941, also PB). Edwin H. Miller *Walt Whitman's Poetry: A Psychological Journey* (New York 1969, also PB). Roy H. Pearce ed. *Whitman: A Collection of Critical Essays* (Englewood Cliffs, N.J. 1962, also PB). Bliss Perry *Walt Whitman: His Life and Work* (New York 1906). Horace Traubel *With Walt Whitman in Camden* (5 vols. Philadelphia and Urbana, Ill. 1906–63). Howard J. Waskow *Whitman: Explorations in Form* (Chicago 1966).

✍

WALT WHITMAN
BY JAMES D. HART

None of the activities or writings of Whitman's first thirty-six years (equal to the span of Byron's whole life) suggested that his publication of *Leaves of Grass* at that age would suddenly begin a career as a major poet. Yet, like the transcendental persona in his poem — the "child who went forth" — all of Whitman's experiences, early and late, contributed to the greatness of his one ever-changing, ever-increasing volume.

Born in a farming village on Long Island, which he more poetically and primitivistically called "fish-shaped Paumanok," he was one of nine children of a house builder and of "a perfect mother," from whom the poet got some of his Quaker views and diction. On the island he heard "the soothing rustle of the waves," speared eels, moved among longshoremen, fishermen, "strange, unkempt, half-barbarous herdsmen," and half-breed Indians, and, after swimming off the "bare unfrequented shore," he would "race up and down the hard sand, and declaim Homer or Shakespeare to the surf and sea-gulls." In the port city of Brooklyn, where his schooling lasted about six years, he enjoyed "the blab of the pave," and from its waterfront he watched "the run of the flood-tide" and delighted in crossing by ferry to New York. First in the smaller city, later in the large one, he learned to set type for newspapers; still later he wrote his own journalism as well as conventionally sentimental stories and verses.

Settling in "mast-hemm'd Manhattan," he luxuriated in the life of the metropolis, riding its omnibuses and becoming friendly with the drivers, sauntering the streets, listening to Emerson lecture, talking himself at a Tammany meeting, enjoying the theatre, and reveling in the opera's "vocalism of sun-bright Italy." He left this surging city only when offered a job on a newspaper in the more exotic New Orleans. His two-week trip by train and stagecoach across the Alleghenies and by steamboat down the Ohio and Mississippi took him through a larger America than he had known and into the wider world of a lush Latin life with a French and Spanish heritage — a world that he enjoyed for three months. Usually associated with this experience is his poem *Once I Pass'd Through a Populous City*, in which he declared, "yet now of all that city I remember only a woman . . . who passionately clung to me," and although Whitman said the poem was not autobiographical

it has sometimes been considered evidence to support his later statement that he was the father of six illegitimate children, one born to a Southern woman. The discovery that in an early draft the lover was a man has been thought to prove the poet's homosexuality, in keeping with the partly amorous, partly paternal affection he showed for rough, robust men and the philosophic faith of his poems celebrating an ideal democracy compounded of "the manly love of comrades." But whatever the erotic effect of the trip, the voyage itself and his return by Chicago, the Great Lakes, and Niagara Falls helped prepare him to be a poet of all the people, "a Southerner soon as a Northerner," who could declare "of every hue and caste am I, of every rank and religion."

For several years after his return while he continued as a journalist Whitman experimented with a free poetic style suited to new encompassing ideas, as different from his earlier, conventional writing as was the style of dress that now transformed him from a dandy to the open-shirted "Walt Whitman, an American, one of the roughs." Out of these views and these ways in 1855 came a book with the cryptic title *Leaves of Grass*, symbolizing "a uniform hieroglyphic . . . sprouting alike in broad zones and narrow zones, growing among black folks as among white." Its twelve untitled poems were preceded by a preface declaring that the ideal poet, loving the universe, must draw his materials from nature and reveal the cosmic plan which unites past, present, and future. His mission is to represent the common people, differing from them only in superior vision, conveying his themes in simple, natural ways that are possessed of an organic growth, in which each part is harmonious with the whole.

Only three or four hundred copies of Whitman's work were sold but Emerson was delighted by what he called "the most extraordinary piece of wit and wisdom that America has yet contributed."

With Emerson's letter as blurb, an enlarged book of thirty-three poems was issued the next year, and slowly it was altered and augmented for the third edition of 1860, a volume of 456 pages, containing 122 new poems, including the section *Calamus,* on the spiritual love of man for man, complementing *Children of Adam,* poems on physical love, identifying the sexual impulse with spiritual force.

The Civil War took Whitman from New York journalism and bohemian literature to the Southern battlefronts, where a brother was injured in service and where the poet saw the horrors that led him to devote himself to volunteer work for wounded soldiers, Northern and Southern, bringing them food and cheer, changing their dressings, and copying their dictated letters in the hospitals of Washington, D.C. The city became his home for eleven years as he got jobs with the army paymaster and the Department of the Interior. From the latter he was discharged when the secretary was shocked by a copy of *Leaves of Grass* upon which he chanced, but a friend came to Whitman's defense with a pamphlet, *The Good Gray Poet,* whose title gave him his sobriquet. Out of wartime and Washington experiences also came Whitman's own book, *Drum-Taps,* descriptive poems of battles and hospitals, whose sequel contained his elegies to Lincoln, *When Lilacs Last in the Dooryard Bloom'd,* one of his greatest works, and *Oh Captain! My Captain!,* popular because of its regularity of rhyme, rhythm, and refrain. For eight years after the war Whitman

worked in the attorney general's office, publishing two new editions of *Leaves of Grass* and a prose pamphlet, *Democratic Vistas,* on the ideals of democracy and individualism.

A stroke of paralysis finally forced him to leave job and capital for Camden, N.J., to live with a brother and in the summers on a nearby farm, where he wrote *Specimen Days and Collect,* reminiscences of his life in New York and Washington, concluding with quiet observations of nature. Although he grew feebler he continued to write brief poems. He also made trips to Colorado and to Canada and received many visitors from this country and from foreign lands where his reputation was great. Before his death, aged almost seventy-three, he wrote *A Backward Glance O'er Travel'd Roads,* showing that his life experience and poetic expression were in keeping with the spirit of his times but disclosing too that he was far more than a poet of his period.

WHITTIER, John Greenleaf (Dec. 17, 1807 – Sept. 7, 1892). American poet and abolitionist. Born of Quaker stock on a farm in Haverhill, Mass., where he attended winter terms at the district school. A few poems published in regional newspapers attracted attention of William Lloyd Garrison, who became his lifelong friend. Through him Whittier became editor of a Boston paper (1829), which involved him actively in the abolitionist movement; he wrote a fiery pamphlet for the cause, *Justice and Expediency* (1833), attended a rally in Philadelphia that year, and thenceforth devoted all his energies to antislavery. Became member of Massachusetts legislature (1834–35), founded the Liberal Party, served as editor of *Pennsylvania Freeman* (1838–40) and the Washington *National Era* (1847–60). The poems he wrote were on behalf of the cause, collected in *Voices of Freedom* (1846). His earlier interest in regional history, revealed in his first book, *Legends of New England in Prose and Verse* (1831) was revived in *Leaves from Margaret Smith's Journal in the Province of Massachusetts Bay 1678–1679* (1849). After the Civil War he produced the work that made him famous, *Snow-bound* (1866), a long winter idyll of life on the family farm. He is also remembered for numerous ballads such as *Barbara Frietchie, Barefoot Boy,* and *Skipper Ireson's Ride,* which made him the voice of rural New England. A widely popular figure in his later years, he also wrote over a hundred hymns. He died in Hampton Falls, N.H.

REFERENCES: Lewis Leary *John Greenleaf Whittier* (New York 1962, also PB). Albert Mordell *Quaker Militant: John Greenleaf Whittier* (1933, reprinted Port Washington, N.Y. 1969). John B. Pickard *John Greenleaf Whittier: An Introduction and Interpretation* (New York 1961, also PB). Samuel T. Pickard *Life and Letters of John Greenleaf Whittier* (1894, reprinted 2 vols. New York 1969). John A. Pollard *John Greenleaf Whittier: Friend of Man* (Boston 1949, reprinted Hamden, Conn. 1969). Edward C. Wagenknecht *John Greenleaf Whittier: A Portrait in Paradox* (New York 1967).

WILDE, Oscar (Fingal O'Flahertie Wills) (Oct. 16, 1854 – Nov. 30, 1900). British writer. Born Dublin; his father was an eminent surgeon and his mother a minor Irish poet. Attended Trinity College, Dublin, won scholarship at Magdalen College, Oxford (1874), where he early gained a reputation for the brilliant wit and studied aestheticism which were to dominate his later work. Won Newdigate poetry prize with *Ravenna* (1878). Already a minor celebrity when he settled in London (1879), he was famous enough to be satirized by Gilbert and Sullivan in *Patience* (1881), the year of his first book, *Poems.* A lecture tour in America (1882) added to his renown, while his financial position was made secure when he married the wealthy Constance Lloyd (1884); they had two sons. He produced little during his editorship of *Women's World* (1887–89), but *The Happy Prince and Other Tales* (1888) was followed by *Intentions*

(1891) and that same year the famous novel *The Picture of Dorian Gray.* Immense theatrical success came with *Lady Windermere's Fan* (1892), *Salomé* (1893), *A Woman of No Importance* (1893), *An Ideal Husband* (1895), and his masterpiece, *The Importance of Being Earnest* (1895). At the height of his career, he took proceedings against the marquis of Queensberry, father of his friend Lord Alfred Douglas, for libel, lost the suit, and was then convicted on charges of homosexuality. Sentenced to two years' hard labor at Reading Gaol, he there wrote the confessional letter-essay *De Profundis* (not published until 1905, and not in its entirety until 1950). Upon his release went to live at Berneval, in France, where he wrote his best poem, *The Ballad of Reading Gaol* (1898). A broken man, he led a pathetic and dissipated life until his death in Paris.

EDITIONS: *Complete Works* ed. Robert Ross (1908, reprinted 15 vols. New York 1969). *Works* ed. G. F. Maine (London 1952 and New York 1954). *Letters* ed. Rupert Hart-Davis (London and New York 1962).

REFERENCES: Lord Alfred Douglas *Oscar Wilde: A Summing-Up* (2nd ed. London 1950 and New York 1965). Frank Harris *Oscar Wilde* (1916, new ed. East Lansing, Mich. 1959). Vyvyan B. Holland *Son of Oscar Wilde* (London and New York 1954) and *Oscar Wilde: A Pictorial Biography* (London and New York 1960). H. Montgomery Hyde *Oscar Wilde: The Aftermath* (London and New York 1963). Phillipe Jullian *Oscar Wilde* (tr. London and New York 1969). Vincent O'Sullivan *Aspects of Wilde* (London and New York 1936). Hesketh Pearson *The Life of Oscar Wilde* (1946, latest ed. London 1966). Edouard Roditi *Oscar Wilde* (Norfolk, Conn. 1947).

WILLIAM IX of Aquitaine. *See* GUILLAUME.

WILLIAMS, William Carlos (Sept. 17, 1883 – Mar. 4, 1963). American writer and physician. Born and died in Rutherford, N.J. Educated at Horace Mann School, New York, the Château de Lancy, Geneva, and briefly, the Lycée Condorcet, Paris. Received degree in medicine (1906) from University of Pennsylvania; there he became a close friend of Ezra Pound, who influenced his early poetry. After New York internship and postgraduate study in pediatrics at University of Leipzig, Williams returned (1910) to Rutherford to practice medicine until 1951 and, beginning with *Poems* (1909), to turn out poetry, fiction, and essays. Married Florence Herman (1912). His most ambitious and characteristic poem was the five-volume *Paterson* (1946–58). Other volumes of poetry: *Al Que Quiere!* (1917), *Sour Grapes* (1921), *Collected Poems* (1921–34), *An Early Martyr* (1935), *Adam and Eve and the City* (1936), *The Complete Collected Poems of William Carlos Williams* (1938), *The Wedge* (1944), *The Clouds* (1948), *The Collected Later Poems* (1950), *The Collected Earlier Poems* (1951), *Desert Music* (1954), *Journey to Love* (1955), and *Pictures from Brueghel* (1962). Major prose works include the essays *In the American Grain* (1925), *Selected Essays* (1954); the novels *A Voyage to Pagany* (1928), *White Mule* (1937), *In the Money* (1940), and *The Build-Up* (1952); his *Autobiography* (1951); *Selected Letters* (1957); and the collected short stories *The Farmer's Daughters* (1961). Among many honors was the Pulitzer prize for poetry, awarded posthumously (1963), as was the Gold Medal for Poetry by the National Institute of Arts and Letters.

REFERENCES: *Selected Poems* with an introduction by Randall Jarrell (Norfolk, Conn. 1963, revised and enlarged 1969; also PB). Vivienne Koch *William Carlos Williams* (Norfolk, Conn. 1950). *The William Carlos Williams Reader* ed. with introduction by M. L. Rosenthal (Norfolk, Conn. 1969, also PB). *Imaginations* ed. Webster Schott (Norfolk, Conn. 1970).

≈

WILLIAM CARLOS WILLIAMS
BY BABETTE DEUTSCH

The child who thrust into life in a New Jersey suburb on September 17, 1883, and, seventy-nine years later, then a retired family doctor and a world-acknowledged poet, died in the same suburb, had in his veins the mingled blood of English, Basque, French, and Dutch-Jewish forebears. Yet (or therefore?) he was as American as the sparrow, the skyscraper, the tough fragrant locust tree, all of which he celebrated.

William Carlos Williams was first of all a poet. He often expressed resentment at having to practice medicine to pay the way for his writing. But that he enjoyed his practice, which was largely among the poorer working people in and near his native town, is evident in the references to it in his poems and his fiction. His life had the character of a music, not without dissonances, in which two themes or two voices — two necessities — are constantly counterposed. Similarly contrapuntal is the poetry and the prose in his writing.

Again, there is the counterpointing of concrete details — "(Make a song out of that: concretely)" — and abstract themes. Prominent among these is the necessity for using what he called "the American idiom," in contradistinction to English literariousness.

In Williams's major work, *Paterson*, prose and poetry flank each other in more ways than one. It illustrates his contention that the local is the matrix of the universal. His concern with the local is of course found equally in his prose, which includes short stories, novels, essays, plays, his autobiography, and that inimitable picture of the country Pound claimed he could not know: *In the American Grain*. This is a kind of composite portrait, based on original documents, starting with Red Eric of Norway, ending with Lincoln. The plays deal with various aspects and forms of love. The novels are quasi-autobiographical. Several have to do with the childhood of his wife, and are notable for their sharp character delineation.

From first to last Williams harps on the power of the imagination. He speaks of it early as the single force able "to refine, to clarify, to intensify the eternal moment in which alone we live." His shorter poems are in effect remarkable small epiphanies. Whether the moment is delightful or sordid, rare or ordinary, a moment of fulfilled love or of deprivation and despair, the poet's ability to refine, to clarify, to intensify it, makes for its enhancement. Partly this is because he sees things with the eye of a painter. "Eyes," he once wrote to a friend, "stand first in the poet's equipment." This belief is natural to a man who had once thought to make painting his profession. For him, art is a revelation of the artist's mind. But it is as obviously a revelation of the world around him as of that within. And always Williams observes with gusto. He never flinches from the ugly and the mean, but more often than not his subject matter is a flower, a tree, a bird.

During his schooldays in Switzerland, by his own account, "the green-flowered asphodel made a tremendous impression" on him. One of his last poems is the long love song to his wife: *Of Asphodel That Greeny Flower.* In *Paterson* he speaks of the world that spreads for him ". . . like a flower opening," and will close for him "as might a rose." Elsewhere he dwells delightedly on a particular daisy, primrose, petunia, stalk of Queen Anne's lace. Similarly, the common sparrow on page after page in the liveliest manner hops, chirps, pecks, takes his dust bath, fights, mates. Williams speaks somewhere of Chaucer and Whitman as "contemporaries of mind." Of course he felt akin to both.

Paterson was vaguely foreshadowed in his first "long" poem, *The Wanderer.* Over the years he wrote several passages that, sometimes in altered shape,

he was to incorporate in the finished work. The fact that he felt the need to go on with it when it had seemed complete is indicative of its character: like Wordsworth's *Prelude,* it embodies the "Growth of a Poet's Mind." Book I opens with a Joycean picture of Paterson, for this city on the eastern seaboard is also a man, as the "low mountain" with the park for her head is the woman, his mate. The first theme is stated at the start: "No ideas but in things." Another is the need for a language which will be both expressive and intelligible. And there is the question, with its implied affirmation, in book III, which, like the others, acknowledges our weakness, stupidity, brutality, filth — "What end but love, that stares death in the eye?"

Paterson is inclusive and complex. Like every long poem, it has faults, but its scope is great enough, its detail work fine enough, to make it one of the most notable American poems, possibly *the* most notable. Naturally it touches on Williams's conviction that American poets should use "the American idiom." He kept returning also to the subject of measure, although he never formulated his theories about it adequately. His preference was for a loosely cadenced line, almost conversational in tone. Towards the last he developed a triadic, laddered line, with one stress to each section:

> *Of asphodel, that greeny flower,*
> > *like a buttercup*
> > > *upon its branching stem —*
>
> *save that it's green and wooden —*
> > *I come, my sweet,*
> > > *to sing to you.*

Whatever he sang of, it was with an indomitable zest that provides what his friend Stevens demanded of a poem: an enhancement of reality.

WILMOT John. *See* **ROCHESTER.**

WILSON, Richard (Aug. 1, 1714 – May 12, 1782). Welsh painter. Born Penegoes, Montgomeryshire, son of a country clergyman. Went to London to study under Thomas Wright, a portrait painter (1729–35). First known work is portrait of *Captain Smith* (1744, Hagley Hall, Staffordshire). In the 1740's he became established as a portraitist and topographical painter. Spent most of 1750's in Italy, concentrating on landscape. His Italian pictures, strongly influenced by Claude Lorrain, include *Lago di Agnano* (Ashmolean Museum, Oxford), *Lake Nemi* (1768, Metropolitan Museum, New York), and *Ponte Molle, Monte Mario* (1754, National Museum, Cardiff). Back in England (1757), he continued to paint Italian landscapes based on sketches, as well as English and Welsh scenes, such as *Okehampton Castle, Devon* (City Museum, Birmingham), *Cader Idris* (National Gallery, London), and *Snowdon* (Walker Art Gallery, Liverpool). He was a founder of the Royal Academy (1768) and its librarian from 1776, a post he accepted to offset his poverty. He died in Llanberis, Caernarvonshire. Although inspired by such seventeenth-century painters as Claude, Nicolas Poussin, and Albert Cuyp, his poetic landscapes, full of clear air and subtle light, were admired by John Constable and J. M. W. Turner.

REFERENCES: A. Bury *Richard Wilson, R.A.: The Grand Classic* (Leighon-Sea, England, 1947). W. G. Constable *Richard Wilson* (London and Cambridge, Mass. 1953). Brinsley Ford *The Drawings of Richard Wilson* (London 1951). Ellis K. Waterhouse *Painting in Britain, 1530–1790* (3rd ed. Harmondsworth, England, 1969).

WINTERS, Yvor (Oct. 17, 1900 – Jan. 25, 1968). American poet and critic. Born Chicago. Attended University of Chicago, but contracted tuberculosis and spent three years bedridden in Santa Fe, N.M. After two years' teaching, went to University of Colorado (M.A. 1925) and later studied for Ph.D. at Stanford (1934), where he remained as professor of English. Married Janet Lewis, author of *The Invasion* (1920). Was an editor of *Gyroscope* (1928–29), and advisory editor for *Hound and Horn* (1932–34). His early poetry, *The Immobile Wind* (1921), *The Magpie's Shadow* (1922), and *The Bare Hills* (1927), was influenced by Ezra Pound, William Carlos Williams, and Marianne Moore. Poetry of later collections — *The Proof* (1930), *The Journey* (1931), and *Before Disaster* (1934) — is written in more traditional forms, with strict rhymes and meters. *Collected Poems* appeared in 1952 (revised 1960). Winters's often dogmatic literary criticism appears in *Maule's Curse: Seven Studies in the History of American Obscurantism* (1938) and *The Anatomy of Nonsense* (1943), published together under the title *In Defense of Reason* (1947), and in collection *The Function of Criticism* (1957). His criticism is based on belief in the moral function of poetry. He died in Palo Alto.

REFERENCES: Babette Deutsch *Poetry in Our Time* 2nd ed. Garden City, N.Y. PB 1963). Stanley Edgar Hyman *The Armed Vision* (New York 1948, also PB). Keith F. McKean *The Moral Measure of Literature* (Denver, Colo. 1961). John Paul Pritchard *Criticism in America* (Norman, Okla. 1956).

WITZ, Konrad (c.1400–c.1445). Swiss painter. Born Rottweil, Württemberg. Nothing is known of his early life and training, but his work shows strong Flemish influence. Moved to Basel (c.1430), became a citizen (1435), and married Ursula Treyger. Commissioned (1435) to paint the *Heilsspiegelaltar* (Mirror of Salvation altar; panels in Basel, Geneva, Dijon, Berlin, Strasbourg, Nuremberg); the extant panels depict heavy thickset figures, painted with stern realism. Completed the *St. Peter Altarpiece* (1444) for St. Peter's cathedral, Geneva (Musée d'Art et d'Histoire); only the wings survive. These panels dramatically depict *Christ Walking on the Water,* set against a panoramic landscape of Lake Geneva; the *Liberation of St. Peter;* the *Adoration of the Magi;* and *St. Peter Recom-*

mending Cardinal de Mies to the Virgin. Other panels, an *Annunciation* (Germanisches National Museum, Nuremberg), *St. Catherine and Mary Magdalene* (Musée des Beaux Arts, Strasbourg), and *Joachim and Anna at the Golden Gate* (Kunstmuseum, Basel), probably came from an altarpiece for a Dominican convent in Basel. Simplicity and power, rather than grace or subtlety, characterize Witz's art, in which he used landscape and architecture to heighten his pictures' monumentality. Died in Basel.

WOLF, Hugo (Philipp Jakob) (Mar. 13, 1860 – Feb. 22, 1903). Austrian composer. Born Windischgraz. Received rudimentary musical training from his father, a leather dealer. Attended Vienna Conservatory (1875), where his outspoken and independent ways resulted in expulsion. A convinced Wagnerian, he became the virulent music critic of the *Wiener Salonblatt,* a weekly journal (1883–87), directing attacks against Brahms. He was composing all this time, but had difficulty getting performed his larger-scale works such as the *String Quartet* (1878–84) and symphonic poem *Penthesilea* (1883–85). But his songs brought him success: his fifty-three *Mörike Lieder* (1888) and twenty *Eichendorff Lieder* (1880–88), the fifty-one *Goethe Lieder* (1888–89) and the forty-four songs of the *Spanisches Liederbuch* (1891) secured his reputation. Composed two parts of his forty-six-song cycle, the *Italienisches Liederbuch* (1890/96), and *Drei Gedichte von Michelangelo* (1877). Wrote the orchestral *Italienische Serenade* (1893); his opera *Der Corregidor* was staged (1896). His last years were spent in an asylum for the insane; he died in Vienna. Wagner was Wolf's inspiration, reflected in the rich chromatic harmony and dense contrapuntal texture. His settings, invariably sensitive to the text, range from brooding intensity to lighthearted charm, but whatever the mood, voice and piano are inseparably and subtly linked.

REFERENCES: Ernest Newman *Hugo Wolf* (2nd ed. New York 1966, also PB). Eric Sams *The Songs of Hugo Wolf* (London 1961). Frank Walker *Hugo Wolf: A Biography* (1951, rev. ed. London and New York 1968).

WOLFE, Thomas (Clayton) (Oct. 3, 1900 – Sept. 15, 1938). American novelist. Born Asheville, N.C., son of a stonecutter. Attended University of North Carolina (B.A. 1920) and Harvard (M.A. 1922); specialized in playwriting. Wolfe's early and frustrated ambition was to become a successful playwright, and his first published work was a drama written at college, *The Return of Buck Gavin: The Tragedy of a Mountain Outlaw* (published in *Carolina Folk Plays: 2nd Series,* 1924). Taught English at New York University (1924–30), with intervals of travel abroad; thereafter, he wrote fulltime in New York and Europe. First novel, *Look Homeward, Angel* (1929), edited by Maxwell Perkins, was a spectacular success. Three others, also edited by Perkins, followed: *Of Time and the River* (1935) and, posthumously, *The Web and the Rock* (1939) and *You Can't Go Home Again* (1940). Fell ill of pneumonia. This produced a recurrence of tuberculosis of the lungs, which led to fatal tuberculosis of the brain (1938). He died in Johns Hopkins Hospital, Baltimore, following an operation. Other works include *From Death to Morning* (1935), a collection of short stories; *The Story of a Novel* (1936), a record of how he wrote his second book; and *The Hills Beyond* (1941), a collection of hitherto unprinted stories, studies, and fragments.

REFERENCES: Pamela Hansford Johnson *The Art of Thomas Wolfe* (New York PB 1963). Herbert J. Muller *Thomas Wolfe* (Norfolk, Conn. 1947). Elizabeth Nowell *Thomas Wolfe: A Biography* (New York 1960 and London 1961). Robert Raynolds *Thomas Wolfe: Memoir of a Friendship* (Austin, Tex. 1966). Louis D. Rubin, Jr. *Thomas Wolfe: The Weather of His Youth* (Baton Rouge, La. 1955). Andrew Turnbull *Thomas Wolfe* (New York and London 1968, also PB). Floyd C. Watkins *Thomas Wolfe's Characters: Portraits from Life* (Norman, Okla. 1957).

THOMAS WOLFE
BY ANDREW TURNBULL

"Someday I'm going to write a play with fifty, eighty, a hundred people — a whole town, a whole race, a whole epoch — for my soul's ease and comfort," Thomas Wolfe foretold in 1923. At his death fifteen years later he left behind him, instead of the play, a multi-volumed autobiographical novel of epic intent. His singularity was the giant reach he manifested from the start. At an age when Fitzgerald was writing *This Side of Paradise* and Hemingway the stories of his Michigan boyhood, Wolfe was a would-be dramatist grappling with intangibles like the race question and the decay of the Old South. Yet he did not achieve real scope and universality (qualities he admired in the Greeks and the Elizabethans) till he dropped through the trapdoor of his own most private past and began unburdening his memories in a novel, his eight-year apprenticeship in the theatre having come to naught.

Wolfe was scored by a bizarre, painful upbringing. His father, a Pennsylvania Dutchman and a tombstone cutter, had been born near Gettysburg twelve years before the battle, which he vividly recalled. Like the country he came from he was lavish, sensuous, and grandiose, while Wolfe's mother, whose family had scratched their living from the mountains around Asheville during Reconstruction, was flinty, parsimonious, and repressed. Her acquisitiveness and unrelenting practicality irked her husband, who avenged himself by periodic drunkenness. Thomas Wolfe, the youngest of the seven children of this precarious union, accompanied his mother when she opened a boardinghouse during one of her husband's bad spells, and much as he hated "the great, chill tomb" of the Old Kentucky Home, the artist in him profited from the assortment of types that came under his observation there. His nature was centrifugal and expansive. Chafing at his imprisonment in the mountain-ringed town of Asheville, he dreamed of the country at large, which took on the wondrous, fabulous quality he would give it in his books.

Reading them, one gets the impression that Wolfe was a Titan battling against odds, but that was the stance from which it pleased him to write; actually, he was more fortunate than many an artist in the people who helped him and the opportunities afforded him. Desperate to achieve, he would have starved if necessary, but the need did not arise. His mother believed in him without understanding what he was trying to do, and when hard pressed he had her pocketbook to fall back on. As a schoolboy he caught the eye of a gifted teacher who encouraged his love of books and poetry, and his hopes of becoming an author. At the University of North Carolina he was successful and admired, and at Harvard Graduate School, Professor George Pierce Baker did everything in his power to launch him as a playwright. Failing in that, he became an English instructor at New York University under sympathetic and indulgent superiors. Wolfe had a contagious sense of his destiny — of the mighty contribution he felt he could make. A chance meeting with the stage designer Aline Bernstein, on a ship returning from Europe, opened the gates. Her love alleviated the tortures of his misguided ambition, she helped him to realize that the theatre wasn't his medium, and she presided over his life while he wrote his first book. Through her good offices he came to the attention of editor Maxwell Perkins, who proved the indispensable midwife in putting his work before the public.

Appearing on the eve of the Wall Street crash, *Look Homeward, Angel* was both a *succès d'estime* and a *succès de scandale*. It established Wolfe as a voice in the land, as someone to watch, while cutting him off from his home town, where his tale was reviled as malicious gossip. He now began to think of himself as an American spokesman in the Whitman tradition, and his early gropings towards a second novel included prose-poetic chants evoking the nation. The five-year struggle to produce a worthy successor to *Look Homeward, Angel* was the central episode of his headlong career. Working in seclusion in Brooklyn, he seemed unable to master his proliferating material, and the magnitude of his effort brought him to the edge of madness. Perkins, urging him on, likened his role during this period to that of a man trying to hang on to the fin of a plunging whale. At last a manuscript was turned in, whereupon Perkins repeated his procedure with *Look Homeward, Angel*, only now the task was far greater. He did not tamper with Wolfe's style; his editing was a matter of architecture, of persuading Wolfe to cut here and add there, in order to give harmony and proportion to the whole. Even so, *Of Time and the River* was criticized for its formlessness, but it swept its author to fame with big sales and excited reviews. At thirty-five Wolfe found himself in the forefront of American novelists.

Lionized and made a cult of, he let nothing come for long between him and the grueling satisfaction of his work. "I've got to hurry to get it all down," he would reflect. "They say I'll write myself out, but I won't live that long." Six and a half feet tall, long-limbed, broad-shouldered and beefy, with a head that seemed too small, this derrick of a man had the strangeness of some visitor from Mars. Part of him was a bon vivant seizing and draining the moment, exulting in simple pleasures, though underlying everything one felt his restless discomfort. "Tom was always," a friend observed, "held down by some kind of bonds, wasn't he? The shortness of a path, the smallness of a room, or the lack of space in people's motives." His family loyalty was intense, but he lived in tumult and his friendships were troubled. After *Look Homeward, Angel* he had broken with Mrs. Bernstein, eighteen years his senior, and after *Of Time and the River* he broke with Perkins to gainsay rumors that he couldn't write his books without Perkins at his elbow. He took criticism badly, sensing perhaps that his writing like his whole being was out of scale, and had to be done the way he did it. The summer of 1938, after completing the manuscript from which two posthumous novels would be carved, he went on a holiday to the Pacific Northwest, where he contracted a fatal tuberculosis of the brain.

A wit has said that reading Wolfe is like driving up the Storm King Highway and seeing a sign LOOK OUT FOR FALLING ROCKS. Fragmentary, sprawling, garrulous, and undisciplined, his work is easy to criticize but redeemed by perdurable virtues. Wolfe was a belated nineteenth-century romantic who wrote, as he talked, from the fire, from the thing welling up inside him. His big scenes have an unforgettable richness, fullness, and aliveness, and the best of his prose combines splendor and eloquence with an all-embracing humanity and a conquering, affirmative vision of man's earthly struggles.

WOLLSTONECRAFT, Mary. *See* Godwin.

WOOD, Grant (Devolson) (Feb. 13, 1892 – Feb. 12, 1942). American painter. Born Anamosa, Iowa. Studied at the Minneapolis Handicraft Guild (1910–12), Art Institute of Chicago (1912–14), and Académie Julian in Paris (1923), then settled in Cedar Rapids, Iowa. Commissioned to design a stained-glass window for the Cedar Rapids Memorial Building, he went to Munich (1928), where the best stained-glass workers were to be found. Here the works of fifteenth- and sixteenth-century Flemish and German painters and of contemporary German realists inspired the creation of the genre for which he is famous, a stark portrayal of the sober people of rural America. First paintings in this style were *John B. Turner — Pioneer* (1929) and a portrait of Wood's mother, *Woman with Plants* (1929, Cedar Rapids Art Association). The exhibition in Chicago of his masterpiece, *American Gothic* (1930, Art Institute of Chicago), established both his reputation and the regionalist trend in American painting. From 1934, he taught fine arts at the University of Iowa in Iowa City, where he died. Married Sara Maxon (1935). Other well-known works are the satirical *Daughters of Revolution* (1932) and *Parson Weems' Fable* (1939).

REFERENCE: Garwood Darrell *Artist in Iowa: A Life of Grant Wood* (New York 1944).

WOOLF, (Adeline) **Virginia** (Stephen) (Jan. 25, 1882 – Mar. 28, 1941). English writer. Born London, daughter of Sir Leslie Stephen, editor of the *Dictionary of National Biography* and eminent man of letters. Youngest of four children by his second marriage; her mother died when she was thirteen. Educated at home, she had the run of her father's magnificent library. After his death (1904), she and her sister Vanessa, and their brothers Thoby and Adrian, moved to Gordon Square, Bloomsbury. From 1905 she wrote reviews for the *Times Literary Supplement*. After Thoby's death and Vanessa's marriage to Clive Bell, she and Adrian settled in a house in Fitzroy Square (1907); it became the center for the so-called Bloomsbury Group, which included John Maynard Keynes, Lytton Strachey, and Roger Fry. Mar-

ried (1912) Leonard Woolf, writer and political thinker. Together they founded the Hogarth Press (1917). Her first novels, *The Voyage Out* (1915) and *Night and Day* (1919), were traditional in form. The sketches *Monday or Tuesday* (1921) sounded the beginnings of her experimental, impressionistic style in which the individual consciousness becomes one with the life around it. A succession of extraordinary novels followed: *Jacob's Room* (1922), *Mrs. Dalloway* (1925), *To the Lighthouse* (1927), *The Waves* (1931), *The Years* (1937), *Between the Acts* (1941). In addition there was the fantasy *Orlando: A Biography* (1928), a feminist essay, *A Room of One's Own* (1929), volumes of short stories and literary criticism, *Flush: A Biography* (1933) and *Roger Fry: A Biography* (1940). *A Writer's Diary* (1953) and *Letters* (1956) were published posthumously. Virginia Woolf had suffered from a mental breakdown during World War I; threatened by its return in 1941, she drowned herself in the River Ouse, near her home in Rodmell, near Lewes, Sussex.

REFERENCES: Joan Bennett *Virginia Woolf: Her Art as a Novelist* (2nd ed. Cambridge, England, and New York 1964, also PB). Bernard Blackstone *Virginia Woolf: A Commentary* (London and New York 1949). R. L. Chambers *The Novels of Virginia Woolf* (Edinburgh 1947). David Daiches *Virginia Woolf* (1942, rev. ed. New York PB 1963). E. M. Forster *Virginia Woolf* (Cambridge, England, and New York 1942). Jean Guiget *Virginia Woolf and Her Works* (tr. London 1965 and New York 1966). John K. Johnstone *The Bloomsbury Group* (New York and London 1954). Brownlee J. Kirkpatrick ed. *A Bibliography of Virginia Woolf* (1957, rev. ed. London 1967). Harvena Richter *Virginia Woolf: The Inward Voyage* (Princeton, N.J. 1970). Leonard Woolf *Beginning Again: An Autobiography of the Years 1911–1918* (London and New York 1964) and *Downhill All the Way: An Autobiography of the Years 1919–1939* (London and New York 1967). A full biography is now (1971) being prepared by her nephew Quentin Bell.

VIRGINIA WOOLF

BY WILLIAM ABRAHAMS

That Virginia Woolf was a writer of genius and a great artist can be now taken as axiomatic. Even so, some thirty years after her death her achievement remains as difficult to "place" as it is to define. A great artist, yes; but a great novelist, as we speak of George Eliot or Henry James, or Stendhal or Tolstoy? Here one must pause. The formulation commonly resorted to is to describe her as a great woman of letters, which indeed she was, with her novels, short stories, literary studies and reviews, essays, polemical volumes, fantastical entertainments (as in *Orlando*), her biography of Roger Fry, her letters, her diaries — the sheer amount of writing, for a woman plagued by periodic mental illness and its attendant anxieties, is extraordinary. But however convenient the formulation, it glides over an essential point: that — to adapt an epigram of Wilde's — Mrs. Woolf put her talent in her nonfiction, her genius in her novels, the six extraordinary novels that begin with *Jacob's Room* in 1922 and end with *Between the Acts* in 1941, which was published unrevised a few months after she drowned herself in the River Ouse, across the fields from her home in Rodmell, Sussex. There is genius in each of the six, but not, it needs to be said, equally so, and of them all it is *To the Lighthouse* that seems the most sure, unassailable, enduring achievement, a landmark alike in Mrs. Woolf's work and in the history of the modern English novel.

Her first novel, *The Voyage Out*, appeared in 1915 when she was thirty-three — a late starter herself, she converted the circumstance to a *post facto* principle that writers oughtn't to publish in their twenties — and her second, *Night and Day*, four years later.

Conventional in subject matter and style, they are talented, intelligent, and not very interesting, novels that float deftly enough in the shallow mainstream of late Edwardian fiction, and suggest that if Mrs. Woolf had wanted, she might well have made a career for herself as a kind of lady Galsworthy. But this was precisely what she did not want. It is a complex question as to how much it was dissatisfaction with the novel as she herself was writing it, or how much with the contemporary novel in general, that prompted her to abandon the career she had begun as a traditionalist, and to go on thereafter, ever more adventurously, as a modernist, experimenting and inventing within a wholly new genre: what we think of now as the novel by Virginia Woolf.

In her essay *Modern Fiction* (1919) she remarked, "For us at this moment the form of fiction most in vogue" — and she is thinking particularly of the novels of Bennett, Wells, and Galsworthy — "more often misses than secures the thing we seek. Whether we call it life or spirit, truth or reality, this, the essential thing, has moved off, or on, and refuses to be contained any longer in such ill-fitting vestments as we provide. Nevertheless, we go on perseveringly, conscientiously, constructing our two and thirty chapters" — in *Night and Day* there are four and thirty — "after a design which more and more ceases to resemble the vision in our minds. So much of the enormous labour of proving the solidity, the likeness to life, of the story is not merely labour thrown away but labour misplaced . . . to provide a plot, to provide comedy, tragedy, love, interest, and an air of probability embalming the whole. . . . Is life like this? Must novels be like this?" Mrs. Woolf's answer to both questions is no; and to recapture "the essential thing," the essence of "life" as she felt it to be, she was prepared to jettison a great deal.

The novels that she wrote thereafter are remarkably, almost perilously free of "vestments," as she records, recaptures, or responds to, not so much events as impressions of events, "trivial, fantastic, evanescent or engraved with the sharpness of steel," the life of Monday or Tuesday as it comes to us in "a myriad impressions." Very little happens in these novels: it is sensibility, not action, that determines their form. The moment, or group of moments — and ideally, she writes somewhere in her diary, a single moment in all its ramifications would make an entire novel — is heightened, brought into a new existence, by being looked at, felt, responded to, with a vision wholly personal and freed from the demands of conventional fiction. Essentially, her characters, one and all, are seeing eternity in a grain of sand; the effect is to charge the novel with something of the intensity one ordinarily associates with poetry. It is not a question of language so much as of vision: a use of sensibility. Surely Mrs. Woolf, as a novelist, is in closer relation to T. S. Eliot's *Portrait of a Lady* than to *The Portrait of a Lady* by Henry James.

The risk can't be minimized. To jettison so much of the traditional "stuff of fiction" is to impose a fearful, at times excessive, weight upon sensibility, and often in these very beautiful explorations of Mrs. Woolf's, one has a sense of disembodiment: sensibility, yes, but curiously remote and attenuated, as though not quite attached to an identifiable character. It is a risk that was triumphantly surmounted in *To the Lighthouse,* for there, in Mr. and Mrs. Ramsay — drawn, as we know, from her own parents — the novelist of sensibility proved herself a novelist of character, at no cost to vision or design.

Mrs. Woolf remains an exemplary figure. One thinks of Emily Brontë, another writer of genius outside the great tradition of the English novel, writing as she must. Such artists transcend categories. Mrs. Woolf, too, wrote as she must and because she must: the act of writing was central to her life. In the final entry in *A Writer's Diary* — itself a volume of enduring interest — she observed, "And now with some pleasure I find that it's seven; and must cook dinner. Haddock and sausage meat. I think it is true that one gains a certain hold on sausage and haddock by writing them down." Four days later she was dead.

WORDSWORTH, William (Apr. 7, 1770 – Apr. 23, 1850). English poet. Born Cockermouth, near the Lake District. Attended school at Hawkshead and St. John's College, Cambridge. A summer walking tour through France and Switzerland (commemorated in *The Prelude,* 1804–1805) inspired him to return to France (1791), after taking his B.A. There he fell in love with Annette Vallon, by whom he had a daughter, and was aroused by the democratic spirit of the French revolution. For financial reasons, however, he returned to England, finally settling with his sister Dorothy in a cottage at Racedown, Dorset, to devote himself to poetry. Developed a close friendship with Coleridge; together they issued *Lyrical Ballads, With a Few Other Poems* (1798), containing Coleridge's *The Ancient Mariner* and Wordsworth's *Tintern Abbey.* The second edition (1800) contains Wordsworth's famous *Preface* in which he set forth the credo of the romantic movement. Returning to the Lake District, at Grasmere (1799), he finally came into his father's inheritance, and married (1802) Mary Hutchinson. Though marked by numerous personal tragedies, these were the years of his greatest works (his *Poems in Two Volumes* was published in 1807) and growing reputation. Appointed

(1813) as revenue collector for Westmorland. Became poet laureate (1843), long after his productive period had passed. He died at Rydal Mount and was buried at Grasmere. Among his most famous poems are *Ode: Intimations of Immortality, Tintern Abbey, The Solitary Reaper, Resolution and Independence,* the "Lucy" poems, and many sonnets.

EDITIONS: *Poetical Works* ed. Ernest de Selincourt and Helen Darbishire (5 vols. Oxford 1940–49). *The Letters of William and Dorothy Wordsworth* (2nd ed. 6 vols. Oxford 1967–   ).
REFERENCES: F. W. Bateson *Wordsworth: A Re-Interpretation* (2nd ed. London and New York 1956, also PB). Edith C. Batho *The Later Wordsworth* (1933, reprinted New York 1963). Arthur Beatty *William Wordsworth: His Doctrine and Art in Their Historical Relations* (3rd ed. Madison, Wis. 1961, also PB). John F. Danby *The Simple Wordsworth: Studies in the Poems* (London 1960 and New York 1961). Helen Darbishire *The Poet Wordsworth* (Oxford 1950, PB 1966). H. W. Garrod *Wordsworth: Lectures and Essays* (2nd ed. 1927, reissued Oxford 1954). George M. Harper *William Wordsworth: His Life, Works, and Influence* (1916, latest ed. 2 vols. New York 1960). Geoffrey H. Hartman *Wordsworth's Poetry, 1787–1814* (New Haven, Conn. 1964, also PB). John Jones *The Egotistical Sublime: A History of Wordsworth's Imagination* (London 1954 and New York 1964). Émile Legouis *The Early Life of William Wordsworth* (tr. 2nd ed. 1921, reprinted New York 1965). George W. Meyer *Wordsworth's Formative Years* (Ann Arbor, Mich. and London 1943). Mary Moorman *William Wordsworth: A Biography* (2 vols. Oxford 1957/65, also PB).

✍

WILLIAM WORDSWORTH
BY LIONEL TRILLING

Probably no great poet is held in such equivocal regard as Wordsworth. That he is properly to be called great is seldom denied — since there are two manifestly pre-eminent English poets, the triadic nature of the human mind proposes that there must be a third, and it is Wordsworth who is most often nominated to stand beside Shakespeare and Milton. Yet many who acknowledge his stature will not admit his charm. They see him as an obligatory poet whose interest and importance consist chiefly in his commanding place in literary history, in his decisive influence upon the generation of romantic poets that followed his. And there are those to whom he speaks in the voice both of magic and truth, who give him a passionate admiration which is felt as a personal devotion.

Those who love him have much to contend with. He is the most uneven of great poets. Part of his legend is the "marvelous decade" of his twenty-seventh to his thirty-seventh year, which was followed by more than four decades of work in which the genius of the earlier time shows itself but in flashes. It is not only that the later work is of inferior inspiration — its informing intention is exactly the one most likely to alienate the modern reader, that of defining the moral law and showing the way to the observance of it which will lead to happiness of a sort. Even in the work of the great decade there are moments of sententiousness, dullness, and bathos that must take aback even his most committed admirers.

To see a poet over the whole extent of his career is inevitably to see a person too, and those who love Wordsworth must grant that as a person he is not easily lovable. He has nothing of the engagingness of Keats or Shelley or Byron. Their youth is ever before us, it speaks from their portraits and their letters as well as from their verse, and it is irresistible. But although Wordsworth's youth is one of his great themes, he writes of it as a thing that is past, and although we cannot fail to know how passionate it was, its passions were of an austere kind. Wordsworth lived to be eighty and De Quincey records it of him that he presented the appearance of age even before he reached his prime, an impression that is confirmed by his portraits; they show a face in which sadness and kindness may be found, but chiefly sternness and reserve. His letters, interesting in their substance, are never spontaneous, gay, or intimate; his social demeanor could be forbidding. This greatest of the romantic poets has none of the endearing traits we associate with a "romantic" personality, and one can understand the feelings of the learned critic who remarked on the good that had been done to Wordsworth's reputation by the discovery that in his youth he had fathered an illegitimate daughter — Wordsworth, the critic said, "is now one of us."

Yet for those who do love Wordsworth, the presumable barriers to their devotion serve only to intensify it. To them the great poems show forth the more wonderfully and mysteriously because the mass of the lesser work suggests that they might not have shown forth at all: the condition of any epiphany or miracle is the prepotency of unilluminated commonplace. And since the essence of many of the great poems is the emotion of fellow feeling, a *caritas* of unique strength and tenderness, this seems the more momentous because it issues from a temperament capable of sternness, even of censoriousness.

The magic and the truth of Wordsworth's poetry may be said to derive from its preoccupation with the concept, and even more with the sensation, of *being*. The word itself made a large claim upon the poet's imagination. In traditional grammar, *be* is called a "copulative," that is, a word whose function is merely that of joining other elements of speech. Teachers of composition commonly say that it is a "weak" word and therefore to be avoided, if possible, in favor of stronger verbs. To Wordsworth it was the strongest word in the language. Something of his feeling about it is made explicit in a letter to his wife's sister, Sara Hutchinson, who had expressed disappointment with *Resolution and Independence,* now generally thought to be one of his greatest poems; he undertakes to explain what he has done in the poem, speaks of the "expectation" he believes he has aroused that "something spiritual or supernatural" is to appear, and goes on to say, "What is brought forward? 'A lonely place, a Pond' 'by which an old man *was*, far from all house or home' — not stood, not sat, but *'was'* — the figure presented in the most naked simplicity possible." In the exquisite *She Dwelt Among the Untrodden Ways,* it is said of Lucy not that she died but that she "ceased to be": the statement, when contemplated, is awesome. One phrase in *The Prelude,* "the sentiment of being," suggests the whole purport of the poem, which might be described as an epic of selfhood, its narrative consisting of episodes in which the awareness of particular existence, the sensation of I, is variously but always intensely experienced. The sensation does not give rise to what Carlyle called "that unanswerable question: Who am I; the thing that can say 'I'?" — William Wordsworth knew very well who "I" was: a dedicated spirit singled out by destiny, "fostered" and "ministered" to by the "Powers" of Nature, himself a power, and, in some sense that he did not wholly understand and did not need to understand, the creator of the universe whose creature and favorite child he was. The sentiment of being was for Wordsworth the ground of the "pleasure" and the "joy" that he believed to be the true end of human life, and the more because it evokes the certitude that the universe is charged with energy and intention — with love, or something like it.

The great transaction with Nature, conducted in the poetic mode that Keats called the "egotistical sublime," whereby Wordsworth redeemed the universe from the mechanism of the eighteenth century and restored to it its ancient soul, was, as Whitehead judged, one of the most notable intellectual acts of the epoch. As a form of actual belief it did not establish itself. The growing authority of science has not, of course, sustained the mechanistic view, but neither has it given ground for credence of the animate universe of Wordsworth's imagination. But this, if it can command no literal assent, exists as a great "myth," comparable in power to that of Milton's epic, and likely to come closer to the hearts of contemporary readers.

The sentiment of being that gave rise to Wordsworth's cosmological vision was also the source of his great ethical perception. Out of his own intense consciousness of his selfhood and of its transcendent value, he saw and celebrated the selfhood of others. As he grew older and rejoiced less in himself than formerly, he became more committed to the morality of precept; and even in his great period his sense of the fellow creature is touched by the conventional philanthropy of his day, but characteristically it arises not from any idea but from a direct, unmediated perception: he sees other human beings in the light that is cast upon them by his own sensation of I. He knows them to be, as he himself is, of transcendent value. It persists, this human preciousness, even if most of the human qualities have been eroded away by the years almost to the point of inanimateness — he who saw in the very rocks a "moral life" finds an ultimate grace and mystery in the pertinacious endurance of the aged persons of *Old Man Travelling, The Old Cumberland Beggar,* and *Resolution and Independence.* The idiot boy, in the poem of that name, is no less wonderful in his being than the poet himself, or than the wind, and the silent girl of the Lucy poems, impalpable and evanescent as the mist or a moment of sunlight on grass, is as transcendently significant.

WREN, Sir Christopher (Oct. 20, 1632 – Feb. 25, 1723). English architect. Born East Knoyle, Wiltshire, son of a clergyman. Educated at Wadham College, Oxford (M.A. 1653), he achieved early fame as a mathematician and astronomer; was professor of astronomy at Gresham College, London (1657–61) and at Oxford (1661–73). Designed his first building, the chapel of Pembroke College, Cambridge (1663). Spent nine months in France (1665–66) studying architecture; was particularly impressed by buildings in progress for Louis XIV in and around Paris. After the Great Fire (1666), he prepared a plan for reconstruction of London, designed the new St. Paul's Cathedral (built 1675–1710) and fifty-two London churches (1670–1711), notably St. Stephen Walbrook, St. Bride, Fleet Street, and St. Mary-le-Bow, also Greenwich Hospital (1696–1735). As surveyor general of works (1669–1718) was in charge of all royal and government building in Great Britain. Knighted (1673). Married Faith Coghill (1669), and after her death, Jane Fitzwilliam (1676). Died in London; buried in St. Paul's. Outstanding among his many secular works are the library of Trinity College, Cambridge (1676–84), Chelsea Hospital (1682–91), Hampton Court (1689–94), Kensington palace (1689–1702).

REFERENCES: Nikolaus Pevsner *Christopher Wren, 1632–1723* (New York PB 1960). Eduard F. Sekler *Wren and*

His Place in European Architecture (tr. New York and London 1956). Sir John Summerson *Sir Christopher Wren* (1953, reprinted Hamden, Conn. and London 1965) and *Architecture in Britain, 1530–1830* (5th ed. Harmondsworth, England, 1969). M. D. Whinney and O. Millar *English Art, 1625–1714* (Oxford 1957). Christopher Wren (his son) *Parentalia, or Memoirs of the Family of the Wrens* (London 1750, reprinted Farnborough, England, 1965).

✍

SIR CHRISTOPHER WREN
BY MARGARET WHINNEY

Sir Christopher Wren dominates English architecture in the second half of the seventeenth century as Inigo Jones does in the first half. Both were surveyors to the Crown, and therefore in charge of all state building; both were learned men, though both lacked formal architectural training; and both turned to architecture after they were thirty. There the resemblance ends. Jones visited Italy more than once and was deeply influenced by antique and Italian Renaissance architecture. Wren never went further than Paris, but he studied architectural books and engravings, and borrowed freely from many sources. Wren was given better opportunities and was to show himself a competent administrator, able to organize large schemes of work, much of which still survives.

He came of a distinguished family, his father being dean of Windsor and his uncle bishop of Ely. From boyhood he showed great aptitude for mathematics and scientific invention, and before he was thirty he held chairs of astronomy in London and Oxford. He was one of the foundation members of the Royal Society in 1661, and in 1680, though he had by then abandoned science for architecture, he became its president. This background of science is crucial for his architecture.

It gave him an interest in experiment and a flexibility of mind which enabled him to adjust himself to new solutions of any given problem, and his mastery of mathematics helped him to solve the considerable structural problems he was to face during his career.

His earliest important building, the Sheldonian Theatre in Oxford (begun 1664), is immature externally, but very remarkable internally, for the roof has a span of seventy feet supported by trusses above the ceiling, and so the floor was unencumbered by columns. After nine important months in Paris, he returned in the spring of 1666, and was soon to be presented with great opportunities.

The Great Fire of London in September 1666 destroyed many acres of buildings, including many churches, and left the cathedral in ruins. Several plans, Wren's among them, for a new, regular city were produced, but the citizens could not wait for a decision and rebuilt houses and shops on the old sites. Wren, however, was put in charge of a commission for the rebuilding of churches. More than fifty were rebuilt, the work going on in some places till after 1700. Since they were for Protestant worship the plans are simple and the designs plain; but even so they show great variety in interior arrangement and above all in their steeples. Unfortunately many were destroyed in the bombing of London in 1940–41, but some, such as St. Stephen Walbrook, St. Bride, Fleet Street, and St. Mary-le-Bow have been restored, and in other cases the steeple still stands.

The churches were more urgent than St. Paul's Cathedral, where services could still be held in the ruined nave, but by 1668 this was found to be unsafe, and Wren was commissioned to design a new building. Work on it was to occupy him continuously till 1711. Two designs were made and rejected, the second being a fine domed building on a Greek cross plan, unlike anything yet existing in England, which is preserved in a splendid wooden model still in the cathedral library. In 1675 work was begun on a Latin cross plan from which, after many changes during execution, the present cathedral was evolved. In it, Wren achieved a compromise between his wish for a great central space and the clergy's desire for the traditional long nave. And his invention is seen at its greatest in the magnificent dome which covers the central space, for it is built in three layers, a low dome which is agreeable inside, a tall hidden cone which carries the lantern, and the beautiful lead-covered dome seen from without. The recent cleaning of the entire cathedral has revealed the beauty of the surface ornament, but the devices Wren used to support the dome and the vaults of nave and choir remain, as he intended, hidden, mainly behind the upper part of the outer walls. The two west towers, built between 1704 and 1708, show Wren's interest, late in life, in a more baroque style of architecture; and their changing silhouettes and strong variations of light and shade are, without question, planned as a contrast to the simple serenity of the dome. To some who admire the richly decorated baroque churches of the Continent, St. Paul's may seem a little austere, but Wren had to suit the needs of his patrons, and his achievement has immeasurable dignity.

Although he was ceaselessly occupied for more than forty years with work in the City of London, he fulfilled other important commissions. In 1676 he began the library of Trinity College, Cambridge. This, with its superimposed columns and its open arcade, is one of his most elegant buildings, but once again the interior effect is obtained by a hidden device. In the next decade he had two commissions from the crown, both of which entailed the arrangement of a complex of buildings. The palace for Charles II at Winchester was never finished, but Chelsea Hospital (for old soldiers) remains much as he left it. It achieves its effect by the contrast of long, simple wings of brick, and a central block partly of stone surmounted by a small cupola.

Planning on a grand scale was to occupy much of his time, and though little was carried out as he wished, the abortive plans have great interest, for they show how he was moving towards the baroque. The first scheme for Hampton Court palace, and the unrealized plan for rebuilding Whitehall palace in 1698, carry on the conception of the linked blocks seen at Chelsea, but on a much grander scale. Hampton Court, as built, is a skillful adaptation of new work to an old site, and the long garden façade with its balance of horizontals and verticals is agreeable rather than grand.

Kensington palace, since much altered, was again a compromise between new work and an older building; but though the Hospital for Seamen at Greenwich, begun in 1696, entailed the absorption of part of the old palace, here at least Wren was able to plan on a grand scale. The twin domes of hall and chapel and the long colonnades beyond them make this one of his most impressive works. Here and at St. Paul's he takes his place among the great architects of the seventeenth century.

WRIGHT, Frank Lloyd (June 8, 1869 – Apr. 9, 1959). American architect. Born Richland Center, Wis. Attended University of Wisconsin (1884–87), then worked for seven years with architects Denkmar Adler and Louis H. Sullivan. First independent commission was the Winslow house, Chicago (1893), followed by series of "Prairie houses" which, with the Robie house, Chicago (1909), and Wright's home Taliesin, Spring Green, Wis. (1911), became the basis of twentieth-century residential design. During a second period of his work (1912–36) he developed such structural innovations as the "slab" skyscraper and the glass and metal wall for office buildings. Not yet fully recognized in America, Wright was acclaimed in Europe, received his largest commission from Japan to build the famous Imperial Hotel, Tokyo (1916–22). His best-known house is probably Falling Water, Bear Run, Pa. (1936–37), now on display, no longer a private dwelling. Recognition of his aesthetic and functional ideas at last led to the third period of monumental commissions such as the administration buildings (1939) and laboratory tower (1950) of the Johnson Wax Company, Racine, Wis., and the Solomon R. Guggenheim Museum (1959), New York City, his last creation. Taliesin West, in the desert outside Phoenix, Ariz. (begun 1938), became his winter home, studio, and school for followers. He was married three times. Died in Phoenix. His *Autobiography* (1932, revised 1943) and numerous writings express his architectural philosophy, which with his buildings has had widespread influence on contemporary architecture.

REFERENCES: Peter Blake *Frank Lloyd Wright* (Harmondsworth, England, and Baltimore PB 1964). Henry R. Hitchcock *In the Nature of Materials: The Buildings of Frank Lloyd Wright, 1887–1941* (2nd ed. New York 1969). Herbert Jacobs *Frank Lloyd Wright* (New York 1965). Grant C. Manson *Frank Lloyd Wright: The First Golden Age* (New York and London 1958). Vincent Scully *Frank Lloyd Wright* (New York and London 1960, also PB). Norris K. Smith *Frank Lloyd Wright: A Study in Architectural Content* (Englewood Cliffs, N.J. 1966, also PB). Olgivanna Lloyd Wright *Frank Lloyd Wright: His Life, His Work, His Words* (New York 1966).

☞

FRANK LLOYD WRIGHT
BY ALBERT BUSH-BROWN

Frank Lloyd Wright, the most celebrated American architect, attempted, as no architect had, to create distinctive architecture for the diverse landscapes of an entire continent. Champion of the idea that architecture should reflect its site, Wright argued that America, as a new nation with a new society, should express its special aspirations in an architecture wholly its own. His art was so original that even the recent generation of students, although nurtured in urban premises and technical resources alien to his, find in his drawings and buildings that virtuosity in shaping space which has been the talent of only the greatest masters of architecture.

The brilliance Wright displayed in composing the houses he built in Buffalo and Chicago before World War I, indeed before he was forty years old, won international fame, especially in Germany and Holland and, later, in Japan, where Wright designed the Imperial Hotel in Tokyo in 1916–22. In the United States, Wright's infrequent clients were a few small, progressive, private institutions, an occasional commercial firm, and, chiefly, Midwestern businessmen for whom Wright designed houses. Commissions for banks, office buildings, and factories were rare, and large corporate or governmental commissions went to classicists or Gothicists, leaving Wright for nearly seventy years to exercise his art, always brilliantly and often resentfully, chiefly in domestic architecture.

Wright's early and bold insistence upon stating cubic mass, the nature of stone and brick and copper, and the unornamented puncturing of sheer walls by windows and doors, making of the house a compact block sheltered by a dominant hipped roof, soon was subsumed within a passion for achieving passages of open, articulated, continuous spaces. By connecting spaces, Wright achieved an extensive, interweaving, horizontal composition of roofs and masses which he balanced asymmetrically, vertical elements penetrating horizontal planes, with interior spaces flaring from a central chimney mass, rising into a high space carved into a second story, unexpectedly capturing light from a clerestory or room beyond, and flowing in vistas past structure reduced to intermittent brick piers, beneath roofs and cantilevered eaves, over terraces and courts, and into the landscape beyond. All of his genius with space, with compact scale dramatically released to generous vista, with variegated light, with occult balances of intermittent masses, with cantilevers that soared, while piers and chimneys anchored, came to unrivaled harmony in the Robie house of 1909.

The Robie house has little precedent. It owes something to the nineteenth-century architects of rambling, picturesque houses, something to Japanese architecture, and something, too, to the master of dynamic composition, Henry Hobson Richardson, but the Robie house is Wright's own, an original, autochthonous creation, achieved fully within the principles of Chicago's revolutionary theory of architecture, as stated by Wright's teacher, Louis Sullivan. That it also joins a larger discourse, the cubism of artists in Europe, shows that Wright braided many strands. There was first the romantic idea of honest expression: that a building should faithfully express its materials and structure, as Viollet-le-Duc had argued, without any classic ornament, which John Ruskin abhorred; there was, second, the idea that a building's form should evolve from its disposition of interior spaces

in accordance with function, as Henry Latrobe and Horatio Greenough had proposed; there was, third, the conviction that there should be expression of something new in the times (Georg Wilhelm Friedrich Hegal, Gottfried Semper) and specifically of the new technical resources, such as steel skeletons and electric light and elevators (John Wellborn Root); there was, fourth, the enthusiasm for declaring a distinctively American art (Emerson, Hawthorne, Whitman); and finally, there was the complex theory derived by Sullivan from Darwin and Spencer that insisted that a building should be a form evolved as an organism evolves, fitted to survive in its landscape, adapted to its environment, and expressive of its purpose.

Most of those currents of thought Wright grasped early in the progressive air of Chicago. His family's Unitarianism prepared him to design the Unity Church in Oak Park (1906). His childhood instruction by Froebel's system of education through construction with blocks prepared him to design the playhouse and school of his beautiful Avery Coonley house, Riverside, Illinois (1908), where John Dewey and his students were educational advisers. All of those currents, amounting to form-breaking and function-making, were not readily united. Wright's essay *The Art and Craft of the Machine* announced his revolt in 1901; and he developed his theory of an "organic architecture: the architecture of democracy" in his Princeton lectures of 1930 and London lectures of 1939, as well as in his *Autobiography* (1932, 1943) which offers insight into the life his family and apprentices led at Taliesin East, the house Wright built over many years at Spring Green, Wisconsin.

Were Wright's talents circumscribed

by Taliesin East and the houses he built before 1930, he would be remembered as the finest architect of the nineteenth-century romantic tradition. But four facets of Wright's talent early won him a place in modern design. In 1904 Wright achieved in the Larkin Building at Buffalo (destroyed 1950) an unprecedented integration of circulation, structure, ventilation, plumbing, furniture, office equipment, and lighting. Second, his plans for Midway Gardens in Chicago (1914) and the Imperial Hotel in Tokyo (1916–22) organized complex modern institutions and, third, showed inventiveness in structural technique, such as the Imperial Hotel's earthquake construction. Fourth, Wright dealt with urban problems, beginning with row apartments in 1895 and culminating in his drawing for a high-rise tower cantilevered from a central shaft, the St. Mark's Tower project for New York (1929). Like many of his projects, the Tower appears in Broadacre City, the coherent, self-sufficient community Wright designed in 1931–35.

However, his interest in twentieth-century problems did not lead Wright to the mechanistic style of Gropius or the sculptural purism of Le Corbusier. For about ten years after 1915, Wright drew upon Mayan massing and ornament (Barnsdall house, Hollywood, 1920), casting the ornament in concrete blocks (Millard house, Pasadena, 1923), and Wright did not achieve a decisively modern style until Le Corbusier and others, including Richard Neutra, had dramatized a sheer, stripped geometry. Even then Wright's style was eminently personal, insisting upon having buildings reflect unique sites: the Kaufmann house, Falling Water, Bear Run, near Connellsville, Pennsylvania (1936–37), with its cantilevered, interlocked, reinforced concrete terraces poised over the waterfall and subtly paraphrased in stone; the Pauson house at Phoenix, Arizona (1940), with its battered ashlar and shiplapped wooden walls reflecting the mountains and desert — a theme of organic adaptation that was never better than in Wright's Taliesin West, his home on Maricopa Mesa, near Phoenix, built 1938–59.

From those fantastic rural houses little could be learned about how Wright would respond to an urban setting or to the rigorous program of a corporate client. His first major opportunity after the Imperial Hotel came with the commission for the administration building of the Johnson Wax Company. That building, erected at Racine, Wisconsin (1936–39), with a tower for research added in 1950, astonished the architectural world not for its structural innovation of dendriform columns, with their vaguely Minoan reference, but for the nobility of exterior mass and the serenity of graceful interior spaces. Thereafter a college, Florida Southern at Lakeland, Florida, was encouraged to retain Wright to design its campus (1938–59), which suffers from an obsession with multifaceted form. But Wright was to succeed with complex pyramids, as suggested by his Lake Tahoe project of the Twenties, when he built the Beth Sholom Synagogue at Elkins Park, Pennsylvania (1959), a Mycenaean sacred mountain. Such a temple, housing a sanctuary of light and approached by a continuous spiral, fascinated the elderly Wright. He juxtaposed circle and fragmented rhombus at Florida Southern College, recalling Hadrian's Villa at Tivoli; then he set a helix inside the Morris Gift Shop at San Francisco (1948–49), preparatory to the six-story helix for the Guggenheim Museum at New York (1946–59).

Of Wright's operatic proposal for the Golden Triangle in Pittsburgh (1947), nothing is visible save his masterful drawings; what was built by other hands is expedient and vulgar. Wright countered the commonplace with unbridled, ecstatic, even febrile imagination: the hyperbole of the Grand Opera and Civic Auditorium at Baghdad, Iraq (1957), which suggest how far Wright's imagination had transcended any client's capacity to realize his dream of sanctuaries and gardens, land and machines, water and air, future and history.

WRIGHT, Joseph (known as Wright of Derby) (Sept. 3, 1734 – Aug. 29, 1797). English painter. Born and died in Derby. Trained as a portrait painter by Thomas Hudson, he lived in Derby, a cradle of the then burgeoning industrial revolution. After his marriage (1773), Wright visited Italy, where he studied works of antiquity in Rome. In England again (1775), he spent two years in Bath before settling in Derby. Elected associate of Royal Academy (1781), but refused (1784) to become a member. Painted a great variety of pictures: realistic portraits of local dignitaries, such as Sir Richard Arkwright and Erasmus Darwin (National Portrait Gallery, London), landscapes of the Lake District (*Ullswater*) and the mountainous areas of Derbyshire, views of Vesuvius erupting, illustrations for the works of Shakespeare and Milton, and scientific pictures in artificial light. The latter, including *The Orrery* (1766, Art Gallery, Derby) and *Experiment with the Air Pump* (1768, Tate Gallery, London), all date from 1763 to 1773. Wright painted many other moonlight and candlelight pictures, such as *The Gladiator* (1765) and *The Alchymist* (1771), in which his fascination with the new machinery is blended with a spirit of romance. His historical pictures include *The Destruction of the Floating Batteries at Gibraltar* and *Belshazzar's Feast*.

REFERENCES: William Bemrose *The Life and Works of Joseph Wright* (London 1885). F. D. Klingender *Art and the Industrial Revolution* (1947, rev. ed. London and New York 1968). Benedict Nicolson *Joseph Wright of Derby* (2 vols. London and New York 1968). S. C. K. Smith and H. C. Bemrose *Wright of Derby* (London and New York 1922).

WYATT, James (Aug. 3, 1746 – Sept. 4, 1813). English architect. Born Burton Constable, Staffordshire, the son of Benjamin Wyatt, a builder. Studied architecture in Italy (1762–68). Back in England, he modeled his designs on those of the Adam brothers. Became suddenly fashionable after opening (1772) of the Pantheon, London (destroyed 1792); the plan was based on Hagia Sophia, Constantinople, though the dome was derived from the Pantheon, Rome. He then designed Heaton Hall, Manchester (1772), and the interior of Heveningham Hall, Suffolk (1778). Appointed (1796) surveyor general and executed much work for George III, but he is remembered as a domestic architect. A versatile designer, he employed the Greek revival style in such houses as Castle Coole and Dodington House, Gloucestershire (1798–1808); and the Gothic and rococo style for Lee Priory, Kent, and Ashridge, Hertfordshire (1808–13). For the eccentric William Beckford he designed the colossal Gothic Fonthill Abbey, Wiltshire (1795–1807, now demolished), with its stupendous tower. Wyatt also restored sections of Durham, Salisbury, and Hereford cathedrals and Westminster Abbey. This firsthand experience of Gothic and his training as a classical architect led to the impressive variety of his designs. Became president of Royal Academy (1806). Died at Marlborough in a carriage accident; buried in Westminster Abbey.

REFERENCE: Antony Dale *James Wyatt* (1936, rev. ed. Oxford 1956).

WYATT, Sir Thomas (1503 – Oct. 11, 1542). English poet. Born at Allington castle, Kent, son of Sir Henry Wyatt. Educated at St. John's College, Cambridge. A courtier to Henry VIII, he was made clerk of the king's jewels (1524) and in following year began his long diplomatic career with a mission to France. On a visit to Italy (1526), he became acquainted with the work of Italian poets, especially Petrarch. A friend (probably lover) of Anne Boleyn, he was implicated in her condemnation and imprisoned in the Tower (1536), but was soon released and the following year was knighted. Served as ambassador to Spain, but was again sent to the Tower (1540) as a result of charges by a rival ambassador; this time was saved through intervention of Catherine Howard. Thereafter he retired to Allington, writing his epigrams, poems, and paraphrases of psalms (published as *Certayne Psalmes,* 1549). Knight of the shire for Kent (1542), he sat in Parliament and was asked to conduct the Spanish ambassador to London. En route he was stricken with fever and died at Sherborne, Dorset. Though a few of Wyatt's verses had been published in an early miscellany, *The Court of Venus,* his work was little known outside court circles until after his death, when he was included in the famous *Tottel's Miscellany* (1557) with Henry Howard, earl of Surrey. Known today for introducing (along with Surrey) the Petrarchan sonnet to English literature, Wyatt also made translations and wrote rondeaux, satires, and lyrics, including some of his finest poems, such as *Forget Not Yet, My Lute, Awake!,* and *They Flee From Me That Something Did Me Seek.* The poet's son, Thomas (c.1521–1554) was famous for Wyatt's Rebellion, his part in the insurrection to prevent the marriage of Mary I with the future Philip II of Spain. The queen's forces quelled the rebellion as Wyatt marched with his men into London, and he was beheaded as a traitor.

EDITION: *Collected Poems* ed. Kenneth Muir (1949, latest ed. London and Cambridge, Mass. 1963, also PB).
REFERENCES: Edmund K. Chambers *Sir Thomas Wyatt and Some Collected Studies* (London 1933, reprinted New York 1965). A. K. Foxwell *A Study of Sir Thomas Wyatt's Poems* (London 1911, reprinted New York 1964). Kenneth Muir *Life and Letters of Sir Thomas Wyatt* (Liverpool, England, 1963). Raymond Southall *The Courtly Maker* (Oxford and New York 1964).

Patricia Thomson *Sir Thomas Wyatt and His Background* (London 1964 and Stanford, Calif. 1965). E. M. W. Tillyard *The Poetry of Sir Thomas Wyatt: A Selection and a Study* (London 1929).

———

WYCHERLEY, William (c.1640 – Jan. 1, 1716). British dramatist. Born Clive, near Shrewsbury, son of the marquis of Winchester's chief steward. Educated in France and at Queen's College, Oxford. Entered Inner Temple, London, but preferred court society to the study of law: he became a protégé of Charles II's mistress the duchess of Cleveland, to whom he dedicated his first play, *Love in a Wood* (1671). His three other plays were written shortly after: *The Gentleman Dancing-Master* (1673), the coarse and satirical *The Country Wife* (1675), a masterpiece of moral realism, and *The Plain Dealer* (1677), in which the Puritan Manly is based on Alceste in Molière's *Le Misanthrope.* Married the countess of Drogheda (c.1680), but upon her death (1681) the will was contested, and the litigation costs resulted in Wycherley's spending seven years in debtors' prison. He wrote no more plays, only mediocre verse, much of it polished up by the young Alexander Pope: *Poetical Epistles to the King and Duke* (1683) and *Miscellany Poems* (1704). His plays, with their brilliance, wit, inventiveness, and penetrating depiction of the vices of the age, rank with the best Restoration drama. He died in London.

EDITION: *Complete Works* ed. Montague Summers (London 1924 and New York 1964).
REFERENCES: Willard Connely *Brawny Wycherley: First Master in English Modern Comedy* (1930, reprinted Port Washington, N.Y. 1969). Bonamy Dobrée *Restoration Comedy* (Oxford 1924). Norman N. Holland *The First Modern Comedies: The Significance of Etherege, Wycherley and Congreve* (Cambridge, Mass. and Oxford 1959, also PB). Henry Ten Eyck Perry *The Comic Spirit in Restoration Drama* (1925, reprinted New York 1962). Rose A. Zimbardo *Wycherley's Drama* (New Haven, Conn. 1965).

———

WYLIE, Elinor (Hoyt) (Sept. 7, 1885 – Dec. 16, 1928). American poet and novelist. Born in Somerville, N.J.; of prominent Pennsylvania family. Educated privately. Moved to Washington, D.C., with family (1897), where her father later became solicitor general of U.S. Married Philip Hichborn (1905) and had a son. Eloped with Horace Wylie of Washington (1910). Wylie's wife refused to divorce him, so the couple went to England (1911) to escape growing scandal. Published her first work of poetry, *Incidental Numbers,* anonymously in England (1912). Returned to Boston (1916) and married Wylie the next year. Lived in Maine, Georgia, and Washington, then moved to New York City (1921), where she was quickly accepted by literary society. *Nets to Catch the Wind* (1921), her first important work, containing *Velvet Shoes, Spring Pastoral,* and other poems, received immediate acclaim. It was followed by *Jennifer Lorn: A Sedate Extravaganza,* her first novel (1923). Divorced (1923), she married William Rose Benét the same year. *The Venetian Glass Nephew,* a novel, was serialized in *Century Magazine* (1925). Her best-known novel, *The Orphan Angel* (1926; *Mortal Image* in England), was a fantasy about Shelley visiting America. Shelley's poems served as chief model for much of her own poetry, the most notable volume of which is *Angels and Earthly Creatures* (1929). It includes the sonnet cycle *One Person* (privately published in England, 1928). Other works: *Black Armour* (1923) and *Trivial Breath* (1928), poetry; and *Mr. Hodge and Mr. Hazard* (1928), a novel. Died in New York of a stroke. Although her novels — mannered, satirical fantasies — were well received during her lifetime, she is known today chiefly for her distinctive lyric poetry, which is a polished blend of romantic impulse and metaphysical technique.

EDITIONS: *Collected Poems of Elinor Wylie* (New York 1932). *Collected Prose of Elinor Wylie* (New York 1933).

REFERENCES: William Rose Benét *The Prose and Poetry of Elinor Wylie* (Norton, Mass. 1934). Emily Clark *Innocence Abroad* (New York and London 1931). Nancy Hoyt *Elinor Wylie: The Portrait of an Unknown Lady* (Indianapolis, 1935). Elizabeth S. Sergeant *Fire Under the Andes* (1927, reprinted Port Washington, N.Y. 1966). Rebecca West *Ending in Earnest* (1931, reprinted Freeport, N.Y. 1967).

XENOPHON (c.430–354 B.C.). Greek historian. Born Athens, son of Gryllus. Was a pupil of Socrates as a young man. Joined (401 B.C.) the mercenary army recruited by Cyrus of Persia, who hoped to seize the Persian throne from his elder brother Artaxerxes. In the battle of Cunaxa in the interior of Persia, Cyrus was victorious but he himself was killed, and Xenophon played a major role in leading the Greek contingent back to safety. On his return to Greece he joined various Spartan military expeditions; for this he was exiled from Athens. Lived in Sparta for a time, then removed to Corinth, where he died. Fourteen works of Xenophon survive, of varied subjects and interest. Perhaps most famous is the *Anabasis,* an account of the Persian expedition. The *Hellenica* is an account of Greek history from the point at which Thucydides left off. The *Memorabilia* contains reminiscences of Socrates; Xenophon's Socrates, however — a down-to-earth, practical moralist — is strikingly different from Plato's unworldly philosopher. The *Oeconomicus* is a treatise on estate management, and gives a vivid glimpse of domestic life in fourth-century Greece. The *Cyropaedia* is a laudatory biography of Cyrus. Xenophon's morality is simple and rigorous; Athenian though he was, his temperamental affinity was for the severe Spartan way of life. There is little that is original in Xenophon, but he is generally clear and well informed, and writes with a sense for the dramatic.

TRANSLATIONS: *Cyropaedia* tr. Walter Miller (1914–25, latest ed. 2 vols. Cambridge, Mass and London 1960–61). *Memorabilia and Oeconomicus* tr. E. C. Marchant (1938, latest ed. Cambridge, Mass. and London 1959). *The March Up-Country: Xenophon's Anabasis* tr. W. H. D. Rouse (London 1948 and Ann Arbor, Mich. 1958, also PB). *The Persian Expedition* tr. Rex Warner (1949, latest ed. Harmondsworth, England, and Baltimore PB 1967). *Recollections of Socrates, and Socrates' Defense Before the Jury* tr. Anna S. Benjamin (Indianapolis 1965, also PB). *History of My Times* tr. Rex Warner (Harmondsworth, England, and Baltimore PB 1966).

REFERENCES: Edouard Delebecque *Essai sur la vie de Xénophon* (Paris 1957). Jean Luccioni *Les Idées politiques et sociales de Xénophon* (Paris 1947) and *Xénophon et le socratisme* (Paris 1953).

YEATS, Jack (Aug. 29, 1871 – Mar. 28, 1957). Irish painter. Born London, where his father, portrait painter John Butler Yeats, was then living. Spent eighth to sixteenth years in Sligo, on northwest coast of Ireland, where he acquired his first impetus as an artist and an imaginative attachment to Irish landscape and rural life that provided the settings and subject matter for many of his later works. First painted in oils in 1897. Visited Venice (1898), and in same year married Mary Cottenham White. His first exhibition was in Dublin (1899). During first two decades of the century his reputation was enhanced, especially in literary circles, by his illustrations for several works by J. M. Synge (including *The Aran Isles,* 1907) and for a series of poetry broadsheets published in Dublin by the Cuala Press and edited by his brother, poet William Butler Yeats. The selection of five of his works for the legendary Armory Show in New York (1913) brought him his first international recognition. During 1930's he came to be acknowledged as the foremost Irish painter of modern times; important retrospective exhibitions of his work were held in London (National Gallery, 1942; Tate Gallery, 1948). Yeats's work has often been compared, in style and temperament, to that of the modern Czech painter Oscar Kokoschka, though the figures and lighting in his paintings belong distinctly to the Irish countryside. He once stated that the most stirring sights in the world were a man plowing and a ship at sea, and his fondness for horses and for sporting events — with the tumult and joyful confusion of an Irish crowd — is frequently evident in his paintings. Yeats had a lively interest in literature and wrote several plays on Irish rural life that were produced in Dublin and London, and which earned him a small but permanent place in the history of the Irish literary "renaissance." He died in Dublin.

REFERENCE: T. G. Rosenthal *Jack Yeats* (Bristol, England, 1966).

YEATS, William Butler (June 13, 1865 – Jan. 28, 1939). Irish poet, dramatist, critic. Born near Dublin, in Sandymount, into Anglo-Irish Protestant family. His father, John Butler Yeats, was a distinguished painter whose friendship with later Pre-Raphaelites influenced son's early poetry. Studied painting in Dublin (1884–6), but abandoned art for writing. First achieved success with *The Wanderings of Oisin* (1889). Early poetry of such volumes as *The Secret Rose* (1897) and *The Wind Among the Reeds* (1899) was influenced by interest in the occult, Irish nationalism, and love for the Irish patriot Maud Gonne. Joined Theosophical Society, London (1887), and edited poems of William Blake with E. J. Ellis (1893). An advocate of national art, he founded Irish literary societies in London and Dublin (1891–92); became president of the Irish National Theatre Society (1902) and director, along with Synge and Lady Gregory, of the Abbey Theatre (1904). Many of his own plays incorporate Irish tradition, such as *The Countess Kathleen* (1892), *Deirdre* (1904), and *The Death of Cuchulain* (1939). His interest in Japanese Noh plays, stimulated by Ezra Pound, led to the experimental techniques of *At the Hawk's Well* (1915) and *Purgatory* (1938). His poetry gradually grew less esoteric, as manifest in *Poems Written* *in Discouragement* (1913), *Responsibilities* (1914), and *The Wild Swans at Coole* (1917). Married Georgie Hyde-Lees (1917), whose automatic writing aided him in compiling *A Vision* (1925, rev. ed. 1937), the summary of his symbolic system. They had two children, Anne Butler (1919) and William Michael (1921). Moved into Thoor Ballylee (1919), the restored Norman tower in Galway that became a major symbol in his work. Served as senator in the Irish Free State (1922–28). Received Nobel prize for literature (1923), and honorary degrees from Trinity College, Dublin (1922), and Oxford (1933). His late poems, among his finest, appear in *The Tower* (1928), *The Winding Stair* (1933), and *Last Poems* (1940). He died at Roquebrunne (Alpes-Maritimes), France, and is buried at Drumcliffe, Sligo, as he had requested in *Under Ben Bulben.*

EDITIONS: *Collected Poems* (2nd ed. London 1950 and New York 1951). *Collected Plays* (2nd ed. London 1952 and New York 1953). *Autobiography* (rev. ed. New York 1953 and London 1955, also PB). *A Vision* (2nd ed. New York 1961 and London 1962, also PB). *Essays and Introductions* (London and New York 1961, also PB). *Eleven Plays* ed. A. Norman Jeffares (New York PB 1968).

REFERENCES: Richard Ellman *Yeats: The Man and the Masks* (New York 1948 and London 1949, also PB) and *The Identity of Yeats* (New York and London 1954, also PB). T. R. Henn *The Lonely Tower* (2nd ed. London and New York 1965, also PB). Joseph Hone *W. B. Yeats, 1865–1939* (2nd ed. London and New York 1962, also PB). A. Norman Jeffares *W. B. Yeats: Man and Poet* (1949, new ed. New York 1966, also PB). Louis MacNeice *The Poetry of W. B. Yeats* (London and New York 1941, PB 1967). John Unterecker *A Reader's Guide to William Butler Yeats* (New York and London 1959, also PB).

☙

WILLIAM BUTLER YEATS
BY HOWARD NEMEROV

W. B. Yeats, widely agreed to be the greatest poet of the modern age, was not in any obvious way a *modern* poet at all; those who like their histories consistent may profitably consider his example. For if the identifying traits of "the modern" are what they are so often said to be, liberalism, secularism, rationalism or scientism, appearing in poetry as tending to freedom of form, nervousness, the dominance of image over discursive thought, and a certain metropolitan concession to chaos, Yeats is at almost all points opposed: conservative, aristocratic, religious — though with neither god nor creed save what he made for himself — and minded to magic, which he thought of not as domination over nature but as the evocation by symbols of the prophetic soul of the wide world dreaming on things to come. His universality, far from being cosmopolitan and direct, as in Eliot, for instance, or Pound, is frequently mediated through the local and parochial materials of Irish myth, Irish history; and his poetry for the most part, from first to last, holding out against "free verse," comes locked in rhyming stanzas, because, he says, "all that is personal soon rots; it must be packed in ice or salt."

In one essential respect, however, his work is in agreement with that of such contemporaries as Eliot, Pound, and Joyce: its theme is the confrontation with the wonder and terror of history, and his attempt, like theirs, is to find a form for this immense force with the aid of mythological figures, stories, symbols that might exalt, dignify, and direct the chaos of the personal and contemporary. With this object, it may be said, he was able to view even the politics of the struggle for Irish independence as Athenian, and he drew up into the ambit of timeless traditions his own life and the lives of those around him, becoming in a sense at last the archetype of himself; for "on the throne and on the cross alike," he wrote, "the myth becomes a biography."

This remarkable attempt at remaking the self required of the poet an austerity and energy no less remarkable, a conscious turning away, in middle life, from a style already formed, and the conscious rejection of a character already formed. He writes of an early poem, "dissatisfied with its yellow and its dull green, with all that overcharged colour inherited from the romantic movement, I deliberately reshaped my style, deliberately sought out an impression as of cold light and tumbling clouds. I cast off traditional metaphors and loosened my rhythm, and recognising that all the criticism of life known to me was alien and English, became as emotional as possible but with an emotion I described to myself as cold." At the same time he gives up all thought of finding the self —

> *That is our modern hope, and by*
> *its light*
> *We have lit upon the gentle,*
> *sensitive mind*
> *And lost the old nonchalance of*
> *the hand*

— in favor of seeking definition in all that is most opposite to self, "the mysterious one," summoned by symbol, who will look

> . . . *most like me, being indeed*
> *my double,*
> *And prove of all imaginable*
> *things*
> *The most unlike, being my*
> *anti-self* . . .

Rejecting the moods of distance and nostalgia for lost fairylands that characterize his early work, the qualities he seeks henceforth are hardness and coldness; like Dante, he will "set his chisel to the hardest stone," and find "the unpersuadable justice." Instead of forlorn lament, the poetic posture will be one of pride, recklessness, fury, and tragic gaiety. And although remaining unalterably opposed to science, technology, commerce, and other characteristics of a leveling age, he makes, with magical and occult help as well as the help of tradition, a system of his own which is oddly scientific-looking in its appeal to strange geometries and arrangements of numbers, as well as in its capacity for generating incredible complexities from apparently simple principles. This system, described in several versions of the book called *A Vision*, formulates recipes for describing psychology, history, and metaphysics in their largely deterministic relations, and Yeats told several contradictory accounts of its provenance, the most famous being that it was dictated to his wife by unknown instructors who said at the outset, "We have come to give you metaphors for poetry." To the question whether he "actually believes" in the literal truth of his visionary designs, however, he replies: "I can but answer that if sometimes, overwhelmed by miracle as all men must be when in the midst of it, I have taken such periods literally, my reason has soon recovered; and now that the system stands out clearly in my imagination I regard them as stylistic arrangements of experience, comparable to the cubes in the drawing of Wyndham Lewis and to the ovoids in the sculpture of Brancusi. They have helped me to hold in a single thought reality and justice."

It is commonly thought nowadays that no man can make himself into a great poet by consciously willing to be so, or by the construction of systems however ingeniously elaborated, and what we have said of *A Vision* might make it appear merely a curiosity of literature, save for one thing, that Yeats did become a great poet, and by all the signs he managed to do so in a remarkable degree by the force of his will and the energy of his intelligence applied to the systematic exfoliation of a whole world from a few themes and relations, based chiefly on the thought of the relation of opposites deriving in the first place from the images of sun and moon. It remains to say briefly in what consists the greatness of the work, and that is not easy. But something like this.

Order and force are the limiting terms of art, the opposites that together compose the world. To these forms of art correspond two limiting desires of the spirit, for death and for life. It is as though for Yeats the contemplation of these polar opposites released immense energies in the form as it were of an alternating current of desire; to stand at one pole was at once to wish passionately for the other. As Yeats put this movement between extreme terms, "I am always, in all I do, driven to a moment which is the realisation of myself as unique and free, or to a moment which is the surrender to God of all that I am."

This is a simple-appearing idea, perhaps, but it puts one at the center of his poetic creation. In the timeless golden stasis of his Byzantium, his "artifice of eternity," his clockwork golden bird can find but one subject for his song: history, or what is past, or passing, or to come. Any retirement from the brute violence of life into the heaven of pure idea induces a brutal and violent return. The key poems that stand as emblems of this mental fight are *Sailing to Byzantium* and *Byzantium*, but the agon itself is given full expository form in *A Dialogue of Self*

and Soul, where after all the Soul's eloquent persuasion to death and the dark of the absolute the Self looks steadily at the filth and horror of life and affirms its will to live it all again. As Yeats put it aphoristically, in a late poem looking back over his career,

> *Players and painted stage took*
> *all my love,*
> *And not those things that they*
> *were emblems of.*

By some such magic of the opposites the poet many times in a long life renewed himself into a tragic joy transcending the stoicism and pessimism at its natural base. To see and hear this happening in the poetry is for the rest of us a source of life.

YOUNG, Edward (June 1683 – Apr. 5, 1765). English poet and dramatist. Born Upham, son of a country clergyman. Educated at Winchester and Oxford. His first works were two bombastic tragedies: *Busiris* (1719) and *The Revenge* (1721). He also wrote satires, collected as *The Love of Fame, the Universal Passion* (1725–28). Took orders (1727) and the following year became chaplain to George II. Then, disappointed with his failure to achieve worldly success, he became rector of Welwyn, Hertfordshire (1730), where he remained the rest of his life. Married Lady Elizabeth Lee, the earl of Lichfield's widowed daughter (1731). After her death (1741) he published the nine parts of his famous *Night Thoughts* (1742–45), a melancholic, pious, blank verse meditation on "life, death, and immortality." This long contemplation became the rage of Europe, and Young won the fame he craved. Dr. Johnson called it "a wilderness of thought." Published a third tragedy, *The Brothers* (1753). Young's poetry is best known today for such pungent epigrammatic lines as "Procrastination is the thief of time" and "Death loves a shining mark." Although a poet of the Augustan age, his pensive gloom makes him a precursor of romanticism.

EDITION: *Poetical Works* ed. J. Mitford (1844, reprinted 2 vols. Westport, Conn. 1970).

REFERENCES: Isabel S. Bliss *Edward Young* (New York 1969). Henry C. Shelley *The Life and Letters of Edward Young* (London and New York 1914). Cecil V. Wicker *Edward Young and the Fear of Death: A Study in Romantic Melancholy* (Albuquerque, N. Mex. 1952).

ZOFFANY, Johann (or **John**) (1733 – Nov. 11, 1810). Anglo-German painter. Born Frankfurt-am-Main. Studied in Italy before going to England (1761) after an unhappy marriage (in Germany). Discovered by David Garrick and the earl of Bute, he first won recognition with an example of his favorite genre, a theatrical scene: *Garrick in "The Farmer's Return"* (1762). Began to exhibit his paintings regularly, and became a founder member of the Royal Academy (1768). Visited Italy (1772–79), equipped with money from George III; among other commissions he painted the Tuscan royal family for Maria Theresa of Austria. He enjoyed royal patronage, and many of his best-known paintings are in the Royal Collection, Windsor Castle: *Queen Charlotte and the Two Eldest Princes* (c.1766), *The Members of the Royal Academy* (1772), and *The Tribuna of the Uffizi Gallery, Florence* (1772–76), a spectacular conversation piece depicting English gentlemen admiring works of Raphael and Titian. Lived in India (1783–89), where he painted *Colonel Mordaunt's Cock-Match* (1786) and *Tiger Hunt in the East Indies* (1788). His many portraits include studies of Garrick, *Mrs. Oswald* (c.1770, National Gallery, London), and *Self-Portrait* (1761, National Portrait Gallery, London). Zoffany's skill lay in ingenious conversation pieces and lively dramatic scenes. He died at Kew, Surrey.

REFERENCES: Lady Victoria Manners and G. C. Williamson *John Zoffany* (London and New York 1920). Oliver Millar *Zoffany and His Tribuna* (London and New York 1967). Ellis K. Waterhouse *Painting in Britain, 1530–* 1790 (3rd ed. Harmondsworth, England, 1969).

ZOLA, Émile (Édouard Charles Antoine) (Apr. 2, 1840 – Sept. 29, 1902). French novelist. Born and died in Paris. The son of a civil engineer from Italy, he spent his childhood in Aix. Moved to Paris (1858), twice failed his baccalaureate. Lived in great poverty, then found jobs and eventually became a journalist. By 1866 he devoted himself entirely to writing. His first book, *Contes à Ninon* (1864) was followed by his first novel, *La Confession de Claude* (1866), a grim autobiographical story of an attempt to reform a prostitute. Married Alexandrine Meley (1870). His realism was developed in *Thérèse Raquin* (1867) and *Madeleine Férat* (1868), and his fatalistic philosophy formed the basis of his series of twenty novels, *Les Rougon-Macquart* (1871–93), the story of one family and its fortunes. These ferocious, often sordid works include *L'Assommoir* (1877), about alcoholism; *Nana* (1880), a study of debased aristocracy; *Germinal* (1885), a novel of class warfare; and *La Débâcle* (1892), a bloodcurdling novel of the Franco-Prussian War. Established (1888) a permanent liaison with laundress Jeanne Rozerot; they had two children. His later series of novels, *Les Trois Villes* (1894–98) and *Les Quatre Évangiles* (1899–1902), tend to be sentimental and tractlike. Zola boldly intervened in support of Alfred Dreyfus in his open letter *J'accuse* (1898); during ensuing lengthy legal proceedings for libel he fled to England, where he lived almost a year. Despite his unorthodoxy he was at his death accorded a state funeral, and is interred in the Pantheon. Zola's passion for detail, his insight into environmental factors, and his visionary exploration of human animality more than offset his occasional crudity.

REFERENCES: Marc Bernard *Zola* (tr. New York 1960, also PB). Elliott M. Grant *Émile Zola* (New York 1966). F. W. J. Hemmings *Émile Zola* (2nd ed. Oxford 1966). Matthew Josephson *Zola and His Time* (1928, reprinted New York 1969). Angus Wilson *Émile Zola: An Introductory Study of His Novels* (1952, rev. ed. London and New York 1965, also PB).

ZURBARÁN, Francisco de (Nov. 7, 1598 – Aug. 27, 1664). Spanish painter. Born Fuentes de Cantos, Estremadura. Married three times. By 1614 he was an apprentice at Seville, and settled in Llarena as a painter (1617). The surviving works of this period display the sobriety and schematic quality of his style: *Crucifixion* (1627, Art Institute of Chicago), *St. Serapion* (1628, Wadsworth Atheneum, Hartford, Conn.), and the *St. Bonaventura* cycle (1629). Moved to Seville (1629), where he produced an altarpiece of St. Joseph (1629, St. Médard, Paris; Musée des Beaux Arts, Besançon). He also painted the *Vision of Blessed Alonso Rodriguez* (1630, Academia de S. Fernando, Madrid) and the celebrated *Apotheosis of St. Thomas Aquinas* (1631, Museo Provincial, Seville) — both employing horizontally divided compositions. In 1636 Zurbarán began the cycle of ecstatic saints for the charterhouse of Jerez (Museo Provincial, Cadiz). Painted the richly colored *Annunciation, Adoration of the Magi, Adoration of the Shepherds,* and *Circumcision* (1638–39, Musée de Peinture, Grenoble). Other major works include the cycle of St. Jerome's life for Guadalupe monastery (1638–39) and two *St. Francis* paintings (1639, National Gallery, London). In his late years his work declined as he strove to emulate Murillo's suavity. His distinctive pictures of saints are filled with Caravaggesque darkness rather than light, but he could use a Venetian range of color when he chose. Died in Madrid.

REFERENCES: José Cascales y Muñoz *Francisco de Zurbarán* (tr. New York 1918). Philip Hendy *Spanish Painting* (London 1946). M. S. Soria *The Paintings of Zurbarán* (London 1953).